T0211750

# Lecture Notes in Computer Science 11814

More information about this series at http://www.springer.com/series/7409

Tran Khanh Dang · Josef Küng ·
Makoto Takizawa · Son Ha Bui (Eds.)

# Future Data and Security Engineering

6th International Conference, FDSE 2019
Nha Trang City, Vietnam, November 27–29, 2019
Proceedings

Springer

*Editors*
Tran Khanh Dang
Ho Chi Minh City University of Technology
Ho Chi Minh City, Vietnam

Josef Küng
Johannes Kepler Universität Linz
Linz, Austria

Makoto Takizawa
Hosei University
Tokyo, Japan

Son Ha Bui
Telecommunications University
Nha Trang City, Vietnam

ISSN 0302-9743 ISSN 1611-3349 (electronic)
Lecture Notes in Computer Science
ISBN 978-3-030-35652-1 ISBN 978-3-030-35653-8 (eBook)
https://doi.org/10.1007/978-3-030-35653-8

LNCS Sublibrary: SL3 – Information Systems and Applications, incl. Internet/Web, and HCI

This Springer imprint is published by the registered company Springer Nature Switzerland AG
The registered company address is: Gewerbestrasse 11, 6330 Cham, Switzerland

# Preface

In this volume we present the accepted contributions for the 6th International Conference on Future Data and Security Engineering (FDSE 2019). The conference took place during November 27–29, 2019, at the Telecommunications University in Nha Trang City, Vietnam. The proceedings of FDSE are published in the LNCS series by Springer. Besides DBLP and other major indexing systems, FDSE proceedings have also been indexed by Scopus and listed in Conference Proceeding Citation Index (CPCI) of Thomson Reuters.

The annual FDSE conference is a premier forum designed for researchers, scientists, and practitioners interested in state-of-the-art and state-of-the-practice activities in data, information, knowledge, and security engineering to explore cutting-edge ideas, to present and exchange their research results, and advanced data-intensive applications, as well as to discuss emerging issues on data, information, knowledge, and security engineering. At the annual FDSE, the researchers and practitioners are not only able to share research solutions to problems of today's data and security engineering themes, but are also able to identify new issues and directions for future related research and development work.

The "two-stage" call for papers resulted in the submission of 159 papers. A rigorous and peer-review process was applied to all of them. This resulted in 52 accepted papers (including 14 short papers, acceptance rate: 32.7%) and 2 keynote speeches, which were presented at the conference. Every paper was reviewed by at least three members of the international Program Committee, who were carefully chosen based on their knowledge and competence. This careful process resulted in the high quality of the contributions published in this volume. The accepted papers were grouped into the following sessions:

- Advanced Studies in Machine Learning
- Advances in Query Processing and Optimization
- Big Data Analytics and Distributed Systems
- Deep learning and Applications
- Cloud Data Management and Infrastructure
- Security and Privacy Engineering
- Authentication and Access Control
- Blockchain and Cyber Security
- Emerging Data Management Systems and Applications

In addition to the papers selected by the Program Committee, internationally recognized scholars delivered keynote speeches: "Big Data Analytics: Opportunities in Business and Service Revolution," presented by Prof. Jian Yang from Macquarie University, Australia; "Group security and Individual Privacy," presented by Prof. Vitalian Danciu from Ludwig-Maximilians-Universität München, Germany; "Optimization Methods for Computational Geometry," presented by Prof. Phan Thanh An from Institute of Mathematics, Vietnam Academy of Science and Technology, Vietnam; "Current Severe Internet Attacks and Protecting Technology," presented by Prof. Tai Myoung Chung from Sungkyunkwan University, South Korea; "On Generalizing Association Rule Mining: Grand Pivot Reports and Genuine Impact," presented by Prof. Dirk Draheim from Tallinn University of Technology, Estonia; "A New Test Suite Reduction Approach Based on Hypergraph Minimal Transversal Mining," presented by Prof. Sadok Ben Yahia from Tallinn University of Technology, Estonia; "Network Security," presented by Prof. Fukuda Kensuke from National Institute of Informatics, Japan; and Prof. Josef Küng from Johannes Kepler Universität Linz, Austria, presented his work on "Applied Knowledge Processing."

The success of FDSE 2019 was the result of the efforts of many people, to whom we would like to express our gratitude. First, we would like to thank all authors who submitted papers to FDSE 2019, especially the invited speakers for the keynotes. We would also like to thank the members of the committees and external reviewers for their timely reviewing and lively participation in the subsequent discussion in order to select such high-quality papers published in this volume. Last but not least, we thank Prof. Bui Son Ha and the Organizing Committee members from Telecommunications University in Nha Trang City for their great hospitality and support of FDSE 2019.

November 2019

Tran Khanh Dang
Josef Küng
Makoto Takizawa
Son Ha Bui

# Organization

## Honorary Chair

Roland Wagner        Johannes Kepler Universität Linz, Austria

## Program Committee Chairs

Tran Khanh Dang      Ho Chi Minh City University of Technology, Vietnam
Makoto Takizawa      Hosei University, Japan
Josef Küng      Johannes Kepler Universität Linz, Austria

## Steering Committee

Elisa Bertino      Purdue University, USA
Tai M. Chung      Sungkyunkwan University, South Korea
Dirk Draheim      Tallinn University of Technology, Estonia
Kazuhiko Hamamoto      Tokai University, Japan
Dinh Nho Hao      Institute of Mathematics, Vietnam Academy of Science
     and Technology, Vietnam
Koichiro Ishibashi      The University of Electro-Communications, Japan
M - Tahar Kechadi      University College Dublin, Ireland
Dieter Kranzlmüller      Ludwig-Maximilians-Universität München, Germany
Fabio Massacci      University of Trento, Italy
Atsuko Miyaji      Osaka University and Japan Advanced Institute
     of Science and Technology, Japan
Erich Neuhold      University of Vienna, Austria
Cong Duc Pham      Université de Pau et des Pays de l'Adour, France
Silvio Ranise      Fondazione Bruno Kessler, Italy
A Min Tjoa      Technische Universität Wien, Austria
Xiaofang Zhou      The University of Queensland, Australia

## Local Organizing Committee

Bui Son Ha (Co-chair)      Telecommunications University, Nha Trang City,
     Vietnam
Tran Khanh Dang (Chair)      Ho Chi Minh City University of Technology, Vietnam
La Hue Anh      Ho Chi Minh City University of Technology, Vietnam
Truong Quynh Chi      Ho Chi Minh City University of Technology, Vietnam
Josef Küng      Johannes Kepler Universität Linz, Austria

| Nguyen Thanh Tung | Ho Chi Minh City University of Technology, Vietnam |
| Que Nguyet Tran Thi | Ho Chi Minh City University of Technology, Vietnam |
| Nguyen Mau Uyen | Telecommunications University, Nha Trang City, Vietnam |
| Nguyen Dinh Thanh | Ho Chi Minh City University of Technology, Vietnam |
| Mai Duc Trung | Ho Chi Minh City University of Technology, Vietnam |

## Publicity Chairs

| Nguyen Quoc Viet Hung | Griffith University, Australia |
| Phan Trong Nhan | Ho Chi Minh City University of Technology, Vietnam |
| Tran Minh Quang | Ho Chi Minh City University of Technology, Vietnam |
| Le Hong Trang | Ho Chi Minh City University of Technology, Vietnam |
| Nam Ngo-Chan | University of Trento, Italy |

## Program Committee

| Artur Andrzejak | Heidelberg University, Germany |
| Stephane Bressan | National University of Singapore, Singapore |
| Hyunseung Choo | Sungkyunkwan University, South Korea |
| Vitalian Danciu | Ludwig-Maximilians-Universität München, Germany |
| Nguyen Tuan Dang | Saigon University, Vietnam |
| Tran Cao De | Can Tho University, Vietnam |
| Thanh-Nghi Do | Can Tho University, Vietnam |
| Nguyen Van Doan | Japan Advanced Institute of Science and Technology, Japan |
| Le Dinh Duy | University of Information Technology, Vietnam National University, Ho Chi Minh City, Vietnam, and National Institute of Informatics, Japan |
| Johann Eder | Alpen-Adria-Universität Klagenfurt, Austria |
| Jungho Eom | Daejeon University, South Korea |
| Fukuda Kensuke | National Institute of Informatics, Japan |
| Alban Gabillon | Université de la Polynésie française, France |
| Verena Geist | Software Competence Center Hagenberg, Austria |
| Clavel Manuel | Vietnamese-German University, Vietnam |
| Tran Van Hoai | Ho Chi Minh City University of Technology, Vietnam |
| Nguyen Viet Hung | University of Trento, Italy |
| Trung-Hieu Huynh | Industrial University of Ho Chi Minh City, Vietnam |
| Tomohiko Igasaki | Kumamoto University, Japan |
| Michael Felderer | University of Innsbruck, Austria |
| Eiji Kamioka | Shibaura Institute of Technology, Japan |
| Surin Kittitornkun | King Mongkut's Institute of Technology Ladkrabang, Thailand |
| Andrea Ko | Corvinus University of Budapest, Hungary |
| Duc Anh Le | Center for Open Data in the Humanities, Japan |
| Faizal Mahananto | Sepuluh Nopember Institute of Technology, Indonesia |

# Contents

**Invited Keynotes**

Individual Privacy Supporting Organisational Security . . . . . . . . . . . . . . . . . 3
  *Vitalian Danciu*

A New Test Suite Reduction Approach Based on Hypergraph Minimal
Transversal Mining . . . . . . . . . . . . . . . . . . . . . . . . . . . . . . . . . . . . 15
  *Shaima Trabelsi, Mohamed Taha Bennani, and Sadok Ben Yahia*

**Advanced Studies in Machine Learning**

Machine Learning Based Monitoring of the Pneumatic Actuators'
Behavior Through Signal Processing Using Real-World Data Set . . . . . . . . . 33
  *Tibor Kovács and Andrea Kő*

A Comparative Study of the Use of Coresets for Clustering
Large Datasets . . . . . . . . . . . . . . . . . . . . . . . . . . . . . . . . . . . . . . . . 45
  *Nguyen Le Hoang, Tran Khanh Dang, and Le Hong Trang*

Leakage Classification Based on Improved Kullback-Leibler Separation
in Water Pipelines. . . . . . . . . . . . . . . . . . . . . . . . . . . . . . . . . . . . . . . 56
  *Thi Ngoc Tu Luong and Jong-Myon Kim*

Mining Incrementally Closed Itemsets over Data Stream
with the Technique of Batch-Update . . . . . . . . . . . . . . . . . . . . . . . . . . . 68
  *Thanh-Trung Nguyen, Quang Nguyen, and Ngo Thanh Hung*

A Combination Solution for Sleep Apnea and Heart Rate Detection
Based on Accelerometer Tracking. . . . . . . . . . . . . . . . . . . . . . . . . . . . . 85
  *Thuong Le-Tien, Phuc Nguyen, Thien Luong-Hoai, Minh Nguyen-Binh,
  Tuan Vu-Minh, Hoang Pham-Thai, and Duc Nguyen-Huynh*

A Model for Real-Time Traffic Signs Recognition Based on the YOLO
Algorithm – A Case Study Using Vietnamese Traffic Signs . . . . . . . . . . . . 104
  *An Cong Tran, Duong Lu Dien, Hiep Xuan Huynh,
  Nguyen Huu Van Long, and Nghi Cong Tran*

Disease Prediction Using Metagenomic Data Visualizations Based
on Manifold Learning and Convolutional Neural Network . . . . . . . . . . . . . 117
  *Thanh Hai Nguyen and Thai-Nghe Nguyen*

An Efficient Model for Sentiment Analysis of Electronic Product
Reviews in Vietnamese . . . . . . . . . . . . . . . . . . . . . . . . . . . . . . . . . . . 132
  Suong N. Hoang, Linh V. Nguyen, Tai Huynh, and Vuong T. Pham

**Advances in Query Processing and Optimization**

Computing History-Dependent Schedules for Processes
with Temporal Constraints . . . . . . . . . . . . . . . . . . . . . . . . . . . . . . . . . 145
  Johann Eder

Finding All Minimal Maximum Subsequences in Parallel. . . . . . . . . . . . . . 165
  H. K. Dai

OCL2PSQL: An OCL-to-SQL Code-Generator
for Model-Driven Engineering . . . . . . . . . . . . . . . . . . . . . . . . . . . . . . . 185
  Hoang Nguyen Phuoc Bao and Manuel Clavel

**Big Data Analytics and Distributed Systems**

Framework for Peer-to-Peer Data Sharing over Web Browsers . . . . . . . . . . . 207
  Vishwajeet Pattanaik, Ioane Sharvadze, and Dirk Draheim

Efficiently Semantic-Aware Pairwise Similarity: an Applicable Use-Case . . . . 226
  Trong Nhan Phan

Lower Bound on Network Diameter for Distributed
Function Computation . . . . . . . . . . . . . . . . . . . . . . . . . . . . . . . . . . . . . 239
  H. K. Dai and M. Toulouse

**Deep Learning and Applications**

A Combined Enhancing and Feature Extraction Algorithm to Improve
Learning Accuracy for Gene Expression Classification. . . . . . . . . . . . . . . . 255
  Phuoc-Hai Huynh, Van-Hoa Nguyen, and Thanh-Nghi Do

Age and Gender Estimation of Asian Faces Using Deep
Residual Network . . . . . . . . . . . . . . . . . . . . . . . . . . . . . . . . . . . . . . . . 274
  Hoang Nguyen and Hieu Trung Huynh

Light-Weight Deep Convolutional Network-Based Approach
for Recognizing Emotion on FPGA Platform . . . . . . . . . . . . . . . . . . . . . . 287
  Thuong Le-Tien, Hanh Phan-Xuan, and Sy Nguyen-Tan

Metagenome-Based Disease Classification with Deep Learning
and Visualizations Based on Self-organizing Maps . . . . . . . . . . . . . . . . . . 307
  Thanh Hai Nguyen

## Cloud Data Management and Infrastructure

On Analyzing the Trade-Off Between Over-Commitment Ratio
and Quality of Service in NFV Datacenter . . . . . . . . . . . . . . . . . . . . . . .        323
   Manh-Hung Tran, Thien-Binh Dang, Vi Van Vo, Duc-Tai Le,
   Moonseong Kim, and Hyunseung Choo

Dynamic Data Management Strategy on Cloud Network
by Fog Computing Model . . . . . . . . . . . . . . . . . . . . . . . . . . . . . . . .        332
   Takeshi Tsuchiya, Ryuichi Mochizuki, Hiroo Hirose, Tetsuyasu Yamada,
   Keiichi Koyanagi, Quang Tran Minh, and Tran Khanh Dang

Openness in Fog Computing for the Internet of Things . . . . . . . . . . . . . . .        343
   Quang Tran Minh, Phat Nguyen Huu, Takeshi Tsuchiya,
   and Michel Toulouse

A Top-Down Scheduling for Time Efficient Data Aggregation in WSNs . . . .        358
   Vi Van Vo, Dung T. Nguyen, Duc-Tai Le, Manh-Hung Tran,
   Moonseong Kim, and Hyunseung Choo

## Security and Privacy Engineering

A New Technique to Improve the Security of Elliptic Curve Encryption
and Signature Schemes . . . . . . . . . . . . . . . . . . . . . . . . . . . . . . . . . .        371
   Tun Myat Aung and Ni Ni Hla

A Visual Model for Privacy Awareness and Understanding
in Online Social Networks . . . . . . . . . . . . . . . . . . . . . . . . . . . . . . . .        383
   Tran Tri Dang and Josef Küng

A Method to Enhance the Security Capability of Python IDE . . . . . . . . . . . .        399
   Vinh Pham, Namuk Kim, Eunil Seo, Jun Suk Ha,
   and Tai-Myoung Chung

Studying Machine Learning Techniques for Intrusion Detection Systems . . . .        411
   Quang-Vinh Dang

## Authentication and Access Control

Enforcing Access Controls in IoT Networks . . . . . . . . . . . . . . . . . . . . . .        429
   Emmanuel Bruno, Romane Gallier, and Alban Gabillon

Resource-Constrained IoT Authentication Protocol: An ECC-Based Hybrid
Scheme for Device-to-Server and Device-to-Device Communications . . . . . .        446
   Chau D. M. Pham, Thao L. P. Nguyen, and Tran Khanh Dang

Adventures in the Analysis of Access Control Policies. . . . . . . . . . . . . . . .    467
  Anh Truong

**Blockchain and Cybersecurity**

Detect Abnormal Behaviours in Ethereum Smart Contracts Using
Attack Vectors . . . . . . . . . . . . . . . . . . . . . . . . . . . . . . . . . . . . . . . .    485
  Quoc-Bao Nguyen, Anh-Quynh Nguyen, Van-Hoa Nguyen,
  Thanh Nguyen-Le, and Khuong Nguyen-An

MyWebGuard: Toward a User-Oriented Tool for Security and Privacy
Protection on the Web. . . . . . . . . . . . . . . . . . . . . . . . . . . . . . . . . . . .    506
  Panchakshari N. Hiremath, Jack Armentrout, Son Vu, Tu N. Nguyen,
  Quang Tran Minh, and Phu H. Phung

Blockchain-Based Open Data: An Approach for Resolving Data Integrity
and Transparency . . . . . . . . . . . . . . . . . . . . . . . . . . . . . . . . . . . . . . .    526
  Dinh-Duc Truong, Thanh Nguyen-Van, Quoc-Bao Nguyen,
  Nguyen Huynh Huy, Tuan-Anh Tran, Nhat-Quang Le,
  and Khuong Nguyen-An

**Emerging Data Management Systems and Applications**

GMeta: A Novel Algorithm to Utilize Highly Connected Components
for Metagenomic Binning. . . . . . . . . . . . . . . . . . . . . . . . . . . . . . . . . .    545
  Hong Thanh Pham, Le Van Vinh, Tran Van Lang, and Van Hoai Tran

Visualization of Medical Images Data Based on Geometric Modeling . . . . . .    560
  Van Sinh Nguyen, Manh Ha Tran, and Son Truong Le

Evaluating Session-Based Recommendation Approaches on Datasets
from Different Domains. . . . . . . . . . . . . . . . . . . . . . . . . . . . . . . . . . . .    577
  Tran Khanh Dang, Quang Phu Nguyen, and Van Sinh Nguyen

Exploiting Social Data to Enhance Web Search . . . . . . . . . . . . . . . . . . . . .    593
  Vo Hoang Phuc, Vu Thanh Nguyen, and Le Dinh Tuan

Retinal Vessels Segmentation by Improving Salient Region Combined
with Sobel Operator Condition . . . . . . . . . . . . . . . . . . . . . . . . . . . . . . .    608
  Nguyen Thanh Binh, Vo Thi Hong Tuyet, Nguyen Mong Hien,
  and Nguyen Thanh Thuy

Energy Saving Solution for Air Conditioning Systems. . . . . . . . . . . . . . . . .    618
  Vu Thu Diep, Phan Duy Hung, and Ta Duc Tung

## Short Papers: Security and Data Engineering

Identifying Minimum Set of Persons that Influenced
by a Promotion Campaign . . . . . . . . . . . . . . . . . . . . . . . . . . . . . . . . . .   631
   Ngo Thanh Hung, Huynh Thanh Viet, Le Nhut Truong,
   and Musab Bassam Yousef Zghoul

Facial Expression Recognition on Static Images . . . . . . . . . . . . . . . . . . . .   640
   Tan Quan Ngo and Seokhoon Yoon

Cryptocurrencies Price Index Prediction Using Neural Networks
on Bittrex Exchange . . . . . . . . . . . . . . . . . . . . . . . . . . . . . . . . . . . . .   648
   Phan Duy Hung and Tran Quang Thinh

Application of Fuzzy Logic in University Suggestion System
for Vietnamese High School Students . . . . . . . . . . . . . . . . . . . . . . . . . .   656
   Phan Duy Hung and Nguyen Cong Minh

Towards an Improvement of Complex Answer Retrieval System . . . . . . . . . .   665
   Lam Ha and Dang Tuan Nguyen

Keyword-Search Interval-Query Dynamic Symmetric
Searchable Encryption . . . . . . . . . . . . . . . . . . . . . . . . . . . . . . . . . . . .   673
   Huy-Hoang Chung-Nguyen, Viet-An Pham, Dinh-Hieu Hoang,
   and Minh-Triet Tran

The Implicit Effect of Items Rating on Recommendation System . . . . . . . . .   681
   Thi Dieu Anh Nguyen, Thanh Nguyen Vu, and Tuan Dinh Le

Counting People Using Images from Two Low Cost Webcams . . . . . . . . . . .   688
   Phan Duy Hung

Predicting the Price of Bitcoin Using Hybrid ARIMA
and Machine Learning . . . . . . . . . . . . . . . . . . . . . . . . . . . . . . . . . . . .   696
   Dinh-Thuan Nguyen and Huu-Vinh Le

Deep Learning Approach for Receipt Recognition . . . . . . . . . . . . . . . . . . .   705
   Anh Duc Le, Dung Van Pham, and Tuan Anh Nguyen

Efficient CNN Models for Beer Bottle Cap Classification Problem . . . . . . . .   713
   Quan M. Tran, Linh V. Nguyen, Tai Huynh, Hai H. Vo,
   and Vuong T. Pham

An Approach for Plagiarism Detection in Learning Resources . . . . . . . . . . .   722
   Tran Thanh Dien, Huynh Ngoc Han, and Nguyen Thai-Nghe

Detecting Kuzushiji Characters from Historical Documents
by Two-Dimensional Context Box Proposal Network . . . . . . . . . . . . . . . . .   731
   Anh Duc Le

An Empirical Study on Fabric Defect Classification Using
Deep Network Models.................................... 739
  Nguyen Thi Hong Anh and Bui Cong Giao

**Author Index** ........................................... 747

# Invited Keynotes

# Individual Privacy Supporting Organisational Security

Vitalian Danciu[✉]

Institut für Informatik, Ludwig-Maximilians-Universität München,
Oettingenstraße 67, 80538 München, Germany
danciu@nm.ifi.lmu.de
http://www.mnm-team.org/~danciu

**Abstract.** The large-scale change emergent from the global proliferation of cloud computing, smart homes, the internet of things and machine
learning requires a novel view on the flow of confidential information and
its classification. The security of an organisation is affected by the privacy enjoyed by its members. Sufficient data on those members can be
leveraged in a so-called abduction attack aiming to extract confidential
information from the organisation. The intention of this paper is to foster awareness of this effect. To illustrate it we develop a model of actors
and data flows and discuss three scenarios in which he confidentiality
achievable by an organisation is limited by the privacy of its members.

**Keywords:** Security · Privacy · De-anonymisation

## 1 Introduction

The last decades have seen the proliferation of ubiquitous information services
provided to the general public without direct financial cost to the individual
user. The operators of these services routinely collect data about their users,
with the intent to generate revenue, e.g., by serving targeted advertisements. The
landscape of IT services is growing and includes services increasingly critical to
the general public. This development has been accompanied by diverse malicious
activities, including bulk unsolicited email (spam), theft of information, theft of
identity, denial of service, defacing of web property and fraud. Such incursions
are met with stepped-up security devices and policies.

Such instances of the *innovation–exploitation–reaction* process show that,
as an information society, we are still in an exploratory "shake-down" phase,
despite what the disruptive effect of the intensive introduction of information
processing and digital communication on public and private life might suggest.
In many countries, the reactions have been underpinned by laws, in an attempt
to suppress attacks or privacy breaches originating in their legal domain. They
include the prohibition to tamper, remotely, with others' IT infrastructure as well
as rules and obligations with respect to the handling of personal data. However,

© Springer Nature Switzerland AG 2019
T. K. Dang et al. (Eds.): FDSE 2019, LNCS 11814, pp. 3–14, 2019.
https://doi.org/10.1007/978-3-030-35653-8_1

there are also indications [20] for privacy regulations remaining unenforced for the benefit of data analysis revenue.

The meaning of the terms "security" and "privacy" have been consolidated during this period, driven by events as those described.

*Information security* concerns itself with the protection of stored data and communication processes. It's scope is the *"preservation of confidentiality, integrity and availability of information"* [4][1], as well as authenticity, accountability, non-repudiation and reliability.

*Privacy* is a multi-faceted term [16]. It has been discussed long before the advent of computers in law research [21] as the rights of a person with respect to normally confidential information obtained without the person's consent. Modern interpretations of the term include rights even after consent has been given, in the sense of *data protection*, concerning itself also with the collection, processing and exchange of data pertaining to a (natural) person. In public discourse, the terms "security" and "privacy" are often found as contrary weights of the balance between the security of a country (claimed to require information about its citizens) and the privacy of the individual. Such arguments typically discuss the amount of privacy that is sacrificed with the aim of improving security. Privacy has been argued to be important to society for reasons of the self-development of its individual members [7]. This reason is valid in the context of the formulation of law and the shepherding of culture. It does not seem compelling in a setting where benefit is a function of revenue or of services consumed. Therefore, in this paper, we explore a reason that might have more appeal in that setting, by illustrating how organisational security can be undermined by the choice to waive privacy.

## 1.1  Hypothesis

To control access to undisclosed, i.e., private information, information security techniques (specifically cryptography) are commonly used to protect data locally or during transmission. Therefore, privacy is often perceived by computer scientists as an application of information security to the personal sphere.

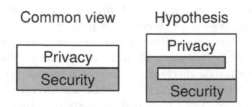

**Fig. 1.** Inter-reliant disciplines.

---

[1] Numeric references to sections of the original text removed from quotation.

In this paper, I argue that the reverse holds true also: that privacy of personal data is a prerequisite of effective information security.

In particular, we explore how the security of an organisation is limited by the privacy of its members, hence: the security of the organisation as an application of the privacy of the individual. Figure 1 offers an illustration of these two views.

## 1.2   Synopsis

The intention of this paper is to raise awareness for attacks on the confidentiality of the information held by an organisation by means of indirectly observing the behaviour of its members.

The hypothesis is discussed within the framework of the model detailed in Sect. 2. The model reduces real-world complexity to a small set of actors, their inter-relationships and the constraints under which they act. We introduce in Sect. 3 three simple scenarios in which an organisation wishes to retain secrecy of some internal information while an adversary would try to acquire this information. For each, we outline how the desired information can be inferred from legally available data. We discuss the implication of this ability and a selection of countermeasures in Sect. 4 before summarising our observations in Sect. 5.

## 2   Model

We develop a model consisting of definitions of roles, their relationships, as well as the domains of data relevant to individuals. Within the model, we formulate a number of plausible assumptions as to the behaviour of the different roles. The purpose of the model is on the one hand to constrain the complexity of the real world to a manageable level (while retaining plausibility) and on the other hand to establish a terminology for use in the remainder of the paper.

### 2.1   Actors

We identify the following six roles, sketched in Fig. 2 as relevant to our analysis.

*The Organisation* is a company or other organisation that wishes to keep its internal information a secret.

*The Adversary* wishes to acquire some secret information of the organisation. The adversary cannot be a member of the organisation, nor the organisation itself. The adversary may be an organisation in the general sense, a group of people or a single individual.

*A Person* is a member of the organisation (e.g., an employee of a company) that works on site but does not reside on site. The person uses common information services to reduce chores, make payments, participate in social life, for entertainment and so on. Persons are the sources of personal data.

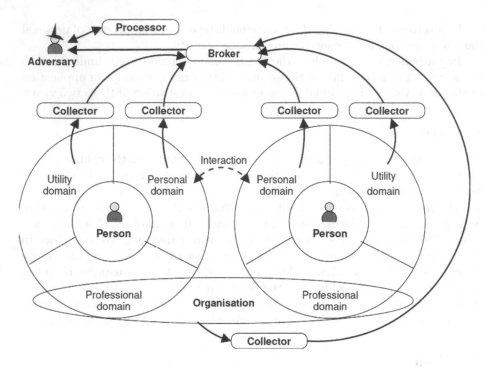

**Fig. 2.** Actors, domains and data flow

*A Collector* directly collects data from persons. Collectors include providers of pure information services (electronic content providers, search engines, communication applications), network service providers, utility providers (electricity, heating, gas), vendors of IoT-based devices but also vendors of enhanced traditional products (cars, domestic appliances) and financial companies.

*A Processor* processes data for further use. Processing includes aggregation, profiling, indexing, tracking of use and analysis for a specific purpose (e.g., the assessment of usage of a service over time).

*A Trader* facilitates the exchange of data sets and the sale of data sets for profit.

### 2.2 Domains

We differentiate between three disjunct domains, that denote authority over their own set of functions and the data they process: the professional, personal and utility domain. The domains structure the devices employed by persons, allowing them to generate data within the professional and personal domains and to trigger data generation within the utility domain.

*The professional domain* is that in which the person acts on behalf of the organisation. It encompasses a person's interaction with communication and information systems provided by the organisation and using utilities at the organisation's site (e.g., network connectivity).

*The personal domain* encompasses the functions that pertain to the private sphere of the person. That includes private communication, entertainment, private transport, home automation.

*The utility domain* encompasses the person's use of devices whose function requires information services outside the personal domain and utility services (network connectivity, electricity, gas, public transportation, home delivery services etc.), that may generate data collectable by the respective utility provider.

## 2.3 Behaviour

*Times and Places.* We assume that the organisation operates a single site and a single network. Constraining the model simplifies the demonstration of the analysis without invalidating its approach in principle. At any given point in time, a person is located:

- at work, at the organisation site
- at their home
- en-route
- at a third location from a (small) set (e.g., store, gym, restaurant), that are visited regularly

We differentiate between working hours, spent at the organisation's site and leisure time, spent at home or at a third location.

*Fair Play.* We assume, that laws and policies are respected by all roles. While this may not always be the case in reality, the purpose of our analysis is to show how confidentiality may be broken without resorting to illegal means. Thus, we assume that:

- Data is being collected, processed and traded with consent.
- Collectors perform (pseudo-)anonymisation if required by law.
- Organisation policy prohibits their members to disseminate information pertaining directly to the organisation's concerns.
- The adversary refrains from any direct attack on the organisation, including direct social engineering targeting single persons.

*Data Proliferation.* We assume a rich, growing and free data market. Despite the public outrage following some of the leaks of personal data in the last years, the privacy policies of many corporations offering "free" services assert that collected data may be passed on to third parties. Thus, the public outcries appear to be more motivated by the use that data has been put to, such as in the Cambridge Analytica affair [6], than the fact that it has been processed by third parties. In accordance with these observations, we assume, that:

– Consent is given freely, as a matter of course, due to the rather low valuation of private data. While in a 2005 experiment [8], the median bid for providing location information was £10, research from 2018 [19] shows even lower bids for private data. Solove [17] discusses the reasons for why consent is currently ineffective as an instrument for privacy. Even people knowledgeable of computer security and data privacy appear to choose to exchange data for services rendered, or to simply fail to exercise their opt-out rights.

Hence, exchange of data and remuneration is not technically limited, i.e., if a data point is collectable, then it is available for analysis.

– Proliferation of data sources in the personal and utility domains of a person is ubiquitous, due to the pervasive use of personal network devices (phones, tablets, wearables, etc.) and the proliferation of "smart" appliances connected by the Internet of Things. The privacy implications of this emerging network have been discussed [1–3,5] but mostly in the sense of requiring consent from the users whose privacy may be implicated by the dissemination of the data.

## 3    Abductive Attack Outline

The adversary uses the data available to infer the confidential information of the organisation. We call this an *abductive attack*, since the adversary's result is acquired by the abductive inference and constitutes a best interpretation that cannot be verified without knowledge of ground truth.

### 3.1    Example Scenarios

Consider the following three scenarios in which the adversary attempts to acquire knowledge about undisclosed, internal aspects of an organisation. For each scenario we develop a procedure usable by the adversary to acquire the desired information starting only with the information presented in the respective scenario in addition organisation's physical location and its network address range. All scenarios are framed within the bounds of the model described in Sect. 2 and constitute cases in which the adversary is apt to break the confidentiality of the organisation.

*Current Production Load. A production site, a factory, wants to keep confidential the production load from their (overseas) customers. During times of high production load, the factory employs additional workers in order to fill three shifts. The impact on the organisation, if the production load is disclosed, may include the loss of potential contracts, if the apparent situation contradicts the available capacity advertised to customers.*

Persons who travel to the organisation's site and arrive there within a time interval, then leave the organisation's site approximately eight hours later, may be workers. The number of time intervals for arrival should indicate to the adversary the number of shifts currently employed by the organisation.

Data items, that can indicate arrivals, include

- Location data from phones in proximity of the site
- The amount of traffic issued from the organisation's network to sign-in services
- The number of passengers on collective transport, that serves a station near the site
- The number of vehicles in the site's parking
- The number of transactions at nearby shops, that may be visited by employees before or after work
- The number of transactions at vending machines at the site

We note that the extraction of single identities is not strictly necessary for the task. The adversary may conclude the desired information by studying the variance of one of the data items and increase the certainty of the result by studying two or more.

It is also important to note that, in this special case, the adversary can attain his goal without resorting to the use of personal data. This suggests, that the privacy of utilities and devices may be of importance to security considerations, even when a direct connection to single persons' behaviour can be excluded.

*Time of Deployment. A military unit in peacetime wants to keep confidential their schedule of deployment to maneuvers or exercises. Between exercises, personnel are authorized to leave the unit's site during leisure and during the night. The impact on the organisation, if the schedule is disclosed, includes a bad performance in the exercise or disturbance by observers from the general public.*

The adversary can predict deployments in the short term by inferring them from a change in the behaviour of the members of the unit. For example, an exercise starting in the early morning would prompt members of the unit to either stay on-site over the night or to rise extra early. Both behaviour patterns are indirectly observable but require the creation of unique identities of the organisation's members in order to distinguish instances of one pattern from the other. Thus, the adversary acquires the unique digital identity of a set of people within the organisation and for each the

- *home location*, which can be acquired from location data or address data or utility providers
- duration of the person's *time en-route* between *home* and the organisation's site, which can be approximated by plotting the route between the two locations
- *regular home departure time*, i.e., the regular time of the day when the person prepares to travel from home, that may be mapped by an interval of activity followed by the cessation of events at the home location by observing utility use, network traffic. It can be determined more directly, from sensor data (e.g., increased use of appliances) or, if available, from location updates.
- *home arrival time*, i.e., the point in time when a person arrives at the home location. That point in time can be determined by the same means as the home departure time.

In an instance where the regular time for travel changes for one person, we can infer, that the person is due to arrive at the organisation's site after the person's typical *en-route time*. An accumulation of instances of this kind would predict an imminent deployment to the adversary. This pattern may be preceded by the observation that some of the organisation's members failed to arrive at home the day before, in contrast to their regular behaviour. If timely prediction is important to the adversary, these latter instances may be exploited as first signs of an imminent event. Prediction accuracy might be improved by accounting for regular visits to *away* locations, regular variations in the persons' respective schedules

We note that in isolation, the data items correlated by the adversary are innocuous but become instrumental when combined with a correct assumption about a mechanism (in this case: commuting between home and the organisation's site).

*Identities of Research Personnel. A research company wishes to keep confidential the exact identity of its research employees, in order to avoid their recruiting by competitors. The company files applications for public research grants when offers of grants are published. Before application deadlines, research personnel works longer hours in order to complete the proposal documents.*

The adversary formulates the conjecture that those persons whose working hours change in proximity of a deadline are the targets of recruiting by competitors. Their identification makes use of data items and correlations already described in the previous two scenario examples. The difference in this scenario is the need for the extraction of actual identities.

Using the publicly available time-frames of grant applications, the adversary can select a set of candidates, as in the "Time of deployment" scenario, e.g., by observing commute times. The adversary needs to attempt to de-anonymise each of the persons in the candidate set.

## 3.2   Assets

Beside deduction from facts, the examples employ analysis of behaviour and, in one case, de-anonymisation.

*Behaviour Interpretation.* The behaviour of people can be observed indirectly by evaluating effects in their environment. Data from utility sensors as well as communication meta-data represent such effects. It can be procured *passively*, by trading for data already in the market or *actively*, by stimulation. Active acquisition entails pro-active requests for consent to a candidate group of individuals, observation of the reaction of users to time- or place-constrained prompts/offers, etc.

*De-anonymisation.* There is a plethora of statistical and other data analysis techniques. We will not review them in this text, with the exception of *de-anonymisation*, to counter the notion that once personal data has been de-identified it cannot be linked to its source. Collectors and brokers of data may be required to anonymise the data they collect, thus disconnecting it from the known identity of the user. However, de-anonymisation has been shown to be effective with only few data points, e.g., for credit card data [9], for web browsing data [18], and for video-on-demand ratings [15]. Zhou et al. conclude [22] that anonymisation techniques for social network data should be developed reactively in order to be effective. Such findings suggest that mandatory anonymisation may increase the effort of the adversary but not obviate the achievement of his goal.

## 4 Discussion

The scenarios described in Sect. 3.1 have sketched the use of seemingly harmless personal and non-personal data produced by persons within the organisation to deduct confidential information items of the organisation.

### 4.1 Properties

The *abductive attack* described in Sect. 3 has a number of interesting properties. It is:

1. performed within the boundaries of the law. The data exchange and processing employed are legal, and the methods for inferring the desired information points are similar or identical to those used in academic research, or in the prosaic activity of a private detective.
2. indirect, as the organisation itself is never targeted directly.
3. undetectable during initiation and execution and virtually untraceable post mortem. Even knowledge of the adversary's actions does not immediately enable the organisation to conclude that it is being targeted.
4. executable by the adversary remotely, from another legal domain, provided data trading and processing by third parties is legal and available at the adversary's location.
5. executable without special authority or knowledge by using the *broker* and *processor* roles. The adversary needs neither authority for collecting data nor expertise in finding and correlating it.

### 4.2 Limitations

Not every kind of secret can be acquired by the means illustrated in the scenarios. To be effective, the approach must tie in to the behaviour of persons observable in their personal and utility domains.

The method relies on the correct formulation of a theory by the adversary, that allows interpretation of the available data by abduction. Even the theories in the examples in Sect. 3.1, simple and plausible as they seem, may not hold for every production site, military unit or research lab. Therefore, a targeted attack seems difficult to automate fully, as it requires the judgement of a human mind.

It might be possible, however, to increase the level of automation by recording patterns of judgement.

Finally, the accuracy of the information gained cannot be ascertained without at least verifying several instances of the same case. Obviously, this property originates in the abductive nature of the process.

## 4.3 Countermeasures

The abductive attack seems impossible if the data produced by all persons associated with an organisation is insufficient to derive with any useful probability a given confidential item of information that the organisation wishes to safeguard. Since an assurance of this state is implausible, the organisation and its members should aim to limit the data that is useful to the adversary.

Similar problems have been studied in the context of statistical databases, to address combinations of queries that, while harmless alone, would allow the inference of priviledged information if their results were combined. Dwork introduces the concept of *differential privacy* to address this issue in [10, 12]. This line of study is valuable and is being applied in privacy audit systems (e.g., [13]). The introduction of noise in the data has been shown [11] to suppress the exposure of private information.

The structural dissimilarity of databases with the global data market seems to obviate the introduction of such measures in the cases described in this paper. While privacy is being pursued by the operator of the database for the benefit of the persons registered therein, there is neither a single operator for the data market, nor is there an incentive for the operators that do exist, to act.

Organisations may wish to guard themselves against instances of abductive attacks that may constitute industrial espionage. However, interfering with the lives of their members beyond the professional domain of our model may prove difficult for all but very few organisations. Incentives for the protection of personal data could be given by

- subsidising paid, anonymous services for the benefit of its members – to avoid them using the "free" ones,
- guiding in the choice of devices and services and
- raising awareness for the security risk to the organisation.

Suppressing abductive attacks by policy seems difficult: policy makers would have to differentiate between inference as used in any research and that performed with a malicious intent. Scholars have proposed granting rights to the so-called *ad-hoc groups* [14] that are assembled through analysis and classification of individuals' behaviour. The members of an ad-hoc group may correspond to the members of an organisation.

# 5   Conclusion

Analysis of personal data, as any conceptual tool, may be used for society's benefit, for example in medical and pharmaceutical research or reputation systems. However, a rich data market paired with automated data analysis render possible the inference of confidential information of an organisation from the personal and utility data produced by its members.

Corporations, i.e., commercial organisations may wish to guard confidential information. Especially during strategic restructuring (merger, acquisition) even small items of information being disclosed may have a large impact. The protections afforded individual persons by law do not extend to organisations. Hence, the victim organisations are third parties to an exchange between their members and the data industry.

It is important to note that today the process of acquisition of confidential data can be automated to a high degree thus lowering both the financial and the time cost for the procedure. If the "reward" for the adversary justifies the cost of obtaining and processing the necessary data, the subversion of an organisation's confidentiality becomes possible without substantial legal risk or risk of detection.

# References

1. Comments of the Electronic Privacy Information Center to the Federal Trade Commission on privacy and security implications of the Internet of Things. Published comments, Federal Trade Commission (FTC) (2013)
2. Internet of Things - privacy & security in a connected world. FTC Staff Report. Federal Trade Commission, January 2015
3. Internet of Things - status and implications of an increasingly connected world. Report to congressional requesters, United States Government Accountability Office Center for Science, Technology, and Engineering, May 2017
4. Information technology - security techniques - information security management systems - overview and vocabulary. International Standard ISO/IEC 27000:2018. International Organization for Standardization (2018)
5. Boeckl, K., et al.: Considerations for managing Internet of Things (IoT) cybersecurity and privacy risks. Draft NISTIR 8228. National Institute of Standards and Technology (NIST) (2018)
6. Cadwalladr, C., Graham-Harrison, E.: Revealed: 50 million Facebook profiles harvested for Cambridge Analytica in major data breach. The Guardian, March 2018
7. Cohen, J.E.: Configuring the networked self: law, code, and the play of everyday practice. Yale University Press (2012)
8. Danezis, G., Lewis, S., Anderson, R.: How much is location privacy worth? In: Proceedings of the Workshop on the Economics of Information Security Series (WEIS) (2005)
9. de Montjoye, Y.-A., Hidalgo, C.A., Verleysen, M., Blondel, V.D.: Unique in the crowd: the privacy bounds of human mobility. Sci. Reports 3(1376) (2013)
10. Dwork, C.: Differential privacy. In: Bugliesi, M., Preneel, B., Sassone, V., Wegener, I. (eds.) ICALP 2006. LNCS, vol. 4052, pp. 1–12. Springer, Heidelberg (2006). https://doi.org/10.1007/11787006_1

11. Dwork, C., McSherry, F., Nissim, K., Smith, A.: Calibrating noise to sensitivity in private data analysis. J. Privacy Confidentiality **7**(3), 17–51 (2017)
12. Dwork, C., Naor, M.: On the difficulties of disclosure prevention in statistical databases or the case for differential privacy. J. Privacy Confidentiality **2**(1) (2010)
13. Lu, H., Li, Y., Vaidya, J., Atluri, V.: An efficient online auditing approach to limit private data disclosure. In: 12th International Conference on Extending Database Technology (EDBT). Research Collection School Of Information Systems (2009)
14. Mittelstadt, B.: From individual to group privacy in big data analytics. Philos. Technol. **30**, 475–494 (2017)
15. Narayanan, A., Shmatikov, V.: Robust de-anonymization of large sparse datasets. In: Proceedings of the 2008 IEEE Symposium on Security and Privacy, Washington, DC, pp. 111–125. IEEE Computer Society (2008)
16. Renaud, K., Galvez-Cruz, D.: Privacy: aspects, definitions and a multi-faceted privacy preservation approach. In: Proceedings of the 2010 Information Security for South Africa Conference, ISSA 2010, pp. 1–8, September 2010
17. Solove, D.J.: Privacy self-management and the consent dilemma. Harvard Law Rev. **126**(7) (2013)
18. Su, J., Shukla, A., Goel, S., Narayanan, A.: De-anonymizing web browsing data with social networks. In: Proceedings of the 26th International Conference on World Wide Web, WWW 2017, pp. 1261–1269. Republic and Canton of Geneva, Switzerland. International World Wide Web Conferences Steering Committee (2017)
19. Tan, J., Sharif, M., Bhagavatula, S., Beckerle, M., Mazurek, M., Bauer, L.: Comparing hypothetical and realistic privacy valuations, pp. 168–182, October 2018
20. Vinocur, N.: How one country blocks the world on data privacy. Politico, 24 April 2019
21. Warren, S.D., Brandeis, L.D.: The right to privacy. Harvard Law Rev. **4**(5), 193–220 (1890)
22. Zhou, B., Pei, J., Luk, W.S.: A brief survey on anonymization techniques for privacy preserving publishing of social network data. SIGKDD Explor. Newsl. **10**(2), 12–22 (2008)

# A New Test Suite Reduction Approach Based on Hypergraph Minimal Transversal Mining

Shaima Trabelsi[1], Mohamed Taha Bennani[1], and Sadok Ben Yahia[1,2(✉)]

[1] Faculty of Sciences of Tunis, University of Tunis El Manar,
LIPAH-LR11ES14, 2092 Tunis, Tunisia
`shaima.9777@gmail.com`, `{taha.bennani,sadok.benyahia}@fst.utm.tn`
[2] Tallinn University of Technology, Akadeemia tee 15a, 12618 Tallinn, Estonia
`sadok.ben@taltech.ee`

**Abstract.** Test Suite Reduction (TSR) approaches aim at selecting only those test cases of a test suite to reduce the execution time or decrease the cost of regression testing. They extract the tests that cover test requirements without redundancy, or exercise changed parts of the System Under Test (SUT) or parts affected by changes, respectively. We introduce DTSR (Deterministic Test Suite Reduction), that relies on the hypergraph structural information to select the candidate test cases. Requirement data, which are associated with the test cases, optimize the selection by retaining a deterministic set. To do so, DTSR considers a test suite as a hypergraph, where its nodes are equivalent to tests, and its hyperedges are similar to requirements. The algorithm extracts a subset of the minimal transversals of a hypergraph by selecting the minimum number of test cases satisfying the requirements. We compare our new algorithm versus search based ones, and we show that we outperform the pioneering approaches of the literature. The reduction rate varies from 50% up to 65% of the initial set size.

**Keywords:** Test-suite reduction · Hypergraphs · Minimal transversal

## 1 Introduction

A test requirement or objective is an artifact of a software program that a test case has to satisfy or cover. For example, the "edge-pair" requirement consists of a sequence of two successive edges of the program. Besides, a coverage criterion is a rule or collection of rules that yield test requirements. Hence, if the coverage criterion is to cover every edge-pair, then it will produce one test requirement for every two successive edges. To fulfill a coverage criterion, software testers should provide a set of tests, that performs all requirements.

A collection of tests, which jointly satisfy coverage criteria, is also called a *test suite*. Nevertheless, sometimes testers may find that certain tests may fulfill two different requirements. Therefore, they may generate test suite holding

© Springer Nature Switzerland AG 2019
T. K. Dang et al. (Eds.): FDSE 2019, LNCS 11814, pp. 15–30, 2019.
https://doi.org/10.1007/978-3-030-35653-8_2

redundant tests as some of its proper subsets may still be satisfy the set of requirements. A test case, in a suite, is said to be *redundant*, if the same testing objectives would still be satisfied after its removal from the set. Inversely, when an essential test is removed from a suite, then one or more test objectives would never more be fulfilled. For example, suppose that a program has six edge-pairs, namely $R_1$, $R_2$, $R_3$, $R_4$, $R_5$, and $R_6$. Let T be a test suite, which contains four tests $t_1$, $t_2$, $t_3$, and $t_4$. Let us suppose that $t_1$ and $t_2$ satisfy $R_1$ and $R_2$, respectively. So, if even though $t_3$ and $t_4$ respectively cover $R_3$, $R_4$ and $R_6$ and $t_4$ also covers $r_5$, then $t_3$ is found to be redundant and $t_1$ and $t_2$ are essential ones.

Selecting a representative subset from large-size suites consists of retaining only essential tests. It not only reduces the execution time but also, decreases the cost of regression testing. Nevertheless, software practitioners are uncertain about its efficiency on unveiling faults [8,22,25]. They claim that even though removing redundant tests from the initial suite may decrease the fault detection capability.

The problem of finding an optimal representative set, which has the least number of elements, is called *Test suite Reduction* (TSR) and has been shown to be NP-complete. Commonly, finding the optimal representative set is equivalent to solving the set covering problem. Earlier researches have been introduced to tackle the set covering problems such as Greedy, heuristic GE, GRE, and HGS. According the recent surveys [18–20], which provide a broad overview of minimization and selection techniques, these approaches use exclusively the coverage of the requirement as a base to determine the reduced set. However, other researches have employed a search techniques to find the diverse subsets of a test suite. They employ different types of search algorithms, such as Genetic Algorithm [2,11,27] and dynamic programming [1,4,23,24], to find the optimal solution based on a given fitness function. They are prompt to compute the solution set unless they rely on a dynamic fitness function. Other studies have dealt with similarity [10,14] and integer linear programming to investigate test suite reduction problem [3]. The former finds the most different test cases from a test suite, while the latter determines the global optimal solution for the reduction problem.

This paper introduces a new algorithm to, called DTSR[1], to tackle the TSR issue. The main originality of DTSR stands in the modeling of TSR as the mining of minimal transversals of a hypergraph. Indeed, we handle the test cases as nodes and the requirements as hyper-edges. Our exact computing method generates a subset of minimal transversals that "exactly" contains the tests of need to cover the predefined requirements. We have applied our algorithm to a data set from the literature and have shown that it outperforms the pioneering approaches of the literature.

The remainder of this paper is organised as follows. Section 2 discusses the classical approaches reducing test suites. Section 3 introduces some of the basic concepts related to hypergraphs and data mining. It also defines our new

---

[1] DTSR stands for deterministic TSR.

algorithm, computing a representative subset, and describes an illustrative execution trace. Section 4 compares our algorithm with classical approaches. Moreover, we suggest a further possible extension of the work in Sect. 5.

## 2   Scrutiny of the Related Work

As introduced in the previous Sect. 1, select a minimal subset of test cases, such that all feasible required elements of a program are covered, can be modeled by Minimum Cover. Binary ILP not only models this type of problems but also applies mathematical programming techniques to compute the optimal cover sizes. For small to mid-sized problems, ILP can compute exact solutions to Minimum Cover. By developing binary ILP models of the test suite minimization problem, authors had established that the obtained solutions are better than those based on heuristics. Previous work with ILP for software testing includes the automatic test data generation, optimal path selection, and selective retesting.

Although the optimization using ILP is a relevant and exact process, several authors believe its benefit is impacted by fault detection capability. The set of test cases, which is computed, does not often unveil the same faults as the initial set. Zhang et al. have proposed an approach to time-aware test-case prioritization using ILP, which reorder test cases to increase their rate of fault detection. To reduce a test suite using multi-objectives, Baller et al. have applied ILP to approach optimal solutions. Further, they have developed an incremental heuristic for deriving a sequence of representative. It approaches the optimal solution involving other objectives such as fault detection capability. Chen et al. have noticed that ILP approach can generate minimum test suites but it may cost exponential time. They have introduced a degraded ILP (DILP) approach to bridge the gap between the ILP method and heuristic ones. The DILP indentifies a lower bound of minimum test suite and then searches a small test suite close to this bound. Steinmann and Frenkel have shown that ILP helps to locate several faults, which riddle the software, by breaking down the localization problem into several smaller ones that can be dealt with independently.

Black et al. [6] had defined a binary integer linear programming model for test suite minimization that pursues two objectives. The first reduces tests regarding the all-uses inter-procedural data flow testing criterion while, simultaneously, a weighting second criterion maximizes the error detection rate. They had shown that test suites minimized are effective at revealing subsequent program faults. Hsu and Orso [15] had proposed MINTS, which is a framework handling problems that involve any number of criteria. It leverages several state-of-the-art ILP solvers to compute the optimal solution. Lin et al. [21] have claimed that multi-criteria test-suite minimization problem is inherently nonlinear since test cases are often dependent on each other. As a result, they have implemented the framework called Nemo, which formulates the multi-criteria test-suite minimization problem as an integer nonlinear programming problem. Thus, they programmatically transform this nonlinear problem into a linear one and then solve the latter using modern linear solvers. Gotlieb et Marijan [13] have proposed an app- roach based on search among network maximum flows, called FLOWER. It takes as input a test suite and the requirements they cover and generates flow net- work which is transversed to find its maximum flows. It uses the Ford-Fulkerson method to compute maximum flows and Constraint Programming techniques to search among optimal flows. This approach has outperformed a non-optimized implementation of the Integer Linear Programming approaches.

In an early study, evaluating the impact of test suite reduction of real appli- cations on the fault detection capability, Zhang et al. [28] have found that tra- ditional test-suite reduction techniques have reduced JUnit test suites with- out substantially reducing their fault-detection capability. Conversely, in recent research, Shi et al. [26] performed an extensive study of test suite reduction using real failures in (failed) builds. After running the tests on Travis, they found that Failed Build Detection Loss can be up to 52.2%, which is higher than suggested by traditional TSR metrics.

Based on its mathematical foundations, the hypergraph theory has a wide range of applications such as machine learning, bioinformatics, and spectral graph theory, etc. Thus, our approach will rely on the concept of minimal transversal to Tackle the TSR issue.

## 3   The DTSR Algorithm for Rest Suite Reduction

Graph theory is a useful tool to solve some problems in data management, such as storing, processing, and analyzing large volumes of graph data. However, the concept of the edge in graph theory can only show a pairwise relation, which might not be sufficient to model associations between specific values of categor- ical variables in large data sets. To model the relationship between a test and the set of requirement it covers, we introduce the hypergraph theory. It allows any subsets of the vertices set to be a hyperedge, instead of exactly two vertices defined in the traditional graph.

We start by defining the concept of a hypergraph and its various represen- tations, particularly the incidence matrix. Then, we characterize two types of sub-hypergraphs, obtained by removing some vertices, which are the transversal and its minimization [5]. In the remainder, we start by sketching some prelimi- naries from the hypergraph theory that will be used in the sequel. Then, we thoroughly describe the DTSR algorithm for test suite reduction. This section comes to an end by the presentation of an illustrative example glancing how the DTSR algorithm works on a toy example.

### 3.1   Basic Concepts of Hypergraphs

**Definition 1.** *Hypergraph*
*Let the couple $\mathcal{H} = (\chi, \xi)$ where $\chi = \{x_1, x_2, x_3, \ldots, x_n\}$ is finite set and $\xi = \{e_1, e_2, \ldots, e_m\}$ is finite family of $\chi$. H is a hypergraph such that:*

$$\bigcup_{i=1}^{m} e_i = \chi \mid \forall i \in \{1, \ldots, m\}, e_i \neq \emptyset \qquad (1)$$

The elements $x_1, x_2, \ldots, x_n$ are called *vertices* or *nodes*, whereas the sets $e_1, e_2, \ldots, e_m$ are the hyperedges of the hypergraph.

Figure 1 illustrates a hypergraph $\mathcal{H} = (\chi, \xi)$ of order 8 and size 15 such that $\chi = \{1, 2, 3, 4, 5, 6, 7, 8\}$ and $\xi = \{\{1, 2\}, \{2, 3, 7\}, \{3, 4, 5\}, \{4, 6\}, \{6, 7, 8\}, \{7\}\}$

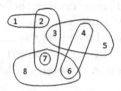

**Fig. 1.** Example of a hypergraph

A hypergraph $\mathcal{H} = (\chi, \xi)$ can be represented by an incidence matrix which rows represent the vertices and columns represent the hyperedges of $\mathcal{H}$ in order that:

$$\mathcal{IM}_{\mathcal{H}}[e_i, x_j] = \begin{cases} = 1 \text{ if } x_j \in e_i \\ = 0 \text{ otherwise.} \end{cases} \qquad (2)$$

Fig. 2 depicts the matrix incidence of the hypergraph given by Fig. 1.

|       | $x_1$ | $x_2$ | $x_3$ | $x_4$ | $x_5$ | $x_6$ | $x_7$ | $x_8$ |
|-------|-------|-------|-------|-------|-------|-------|-------|-------|
| $e_1$ | 1     | 1     | 0     | 0     | 0     | 0     | 0     | 0     |
| $e_2$ | 0     | 1     | 1     | 0     | 0     | 0     | 1     | 0     |
| $e_3$ | 0     | 0     | 1     | 1     | 1     | 0     | 0     | 0     |
| $e_4$ | 0     | 0     | 0     | 1     | 0     | 1     | 0     | 0     |
| $e_5$ | 0     | 0     | 0     | 0     | 0     | 1     | 1     | 1     |
| $e_6$ | 0     | 0     | 0     | 0     | 0     | 0     | 1     | 0     |

**Fig. 2.** Incidence matrix of the hypergraph given by Fig. 1

**Definition 2.** *Transversal*
*Let $\mathcal{H} = (\chi, \xi)$ be a hypergraph. A set $\mathcal{T} \subset \chi$ is a transversal of $\mathcal{H}$ if it meets every hyperedge, which is described by the following expression:*

$$\forall i \in \{1, 2, \ldots, m\}, \mathcal{T} \cap e_i \neq \emptyset \qquad (3)$$

Extracting hypergraph minimal transversals has been shown to have myriad of applications in computer science, e.g., database theory, logic, and AI, to cite but a few [17].

**Definition 3.** *Minimal transversal*
*A transversal $\mathcal{T}$ is minimal if it doesn't exist $\mathcal{T}'$ a subset of $\mathcal{T}$ where $\mathcal{T}'$ is a transversal.*

$\mathcal{M_H}$ denotes in the sequel the set of minimal transversals defined on $\mathcal{H}$. From the hypergraph, given in Fig. 1, the following set of minimal transversals is drawn: $\mathcal{M_H} = \{\{1,4,7\}, \{7,4,2\}, \{7,6,3,1\}, \{7,6,3,2\}, \{7,6,5,1\}, \{7,6,5,2\}\}$. The minimal cardinality of transversal is denoted by $\tau(\mathcal{H})$ of the hypergraph $\mathcal{H}$:

$$\tau(\mathcal{H}) = \{min|T|, \forall T \in \mathcal{M_H}\} \qquad (4)$$

Therefore, the smallest minimal transversal of the hypergraph $\mathcal{H}$ shown in Fig. 1 includes, in terms of cardinality, three vertices, i.e. $\tau(\mathcal{H}) = 3$.

The minimal traversal can be defined by the concept of an *essential itemset* that could be extracted from an extraction context. In the following, let us start by highlighting the close connection between the latter and a hypergraph.

**Definition 4.** *Extraction context We can formally represent a database as an extraction context $\mathcal{K} = (\mathcal{O}, \mathcal{I}, \mathcal{R})$. It is a triplet where $\mathcal{O}$ and $\mathcal{O}$ are respectively finite sets of objects(transactions) and attributes(items) and $\mathcal{R}$ is a binary(incidence) relation between $\mathcal{O}$ and $\mathcal{I}$ (i.e $\mathcal{R} \subseteq \mathcal{O} \times \mathcal{I}$). Taking as an example the hypergraph of Fig. 1, the corresponding extraction context is shown in Table 1.*

Table 1. Extraction context of the hypergraph depicted in Fig. 1

| | $x_1$ | $x_2$ | $x_3$ | $x_4$ | $x_5$ | $x_6$ | $x_7$ | $x_8$ |
|---|---|---|---|---|---|---|---|---|
| $e_1$ | × | × | | | | | | |
| $e_2$ | | × | × | | | | | |
| $e_3$ | | | × | × | × | | | |
| $e_4$ | | | | × | | × | | |
| $e_5$ | | | | | | × | × | × |
| $e_6$ | | | | | | | × | |

**Definition 5.** *Disjunctive support of an itemset.*
*The disjunctive support of an itemset $X$ is the number of transactions that contain at least one of the items of $X$.*

$$Supp(\vee X) = |\{o \in \mathcal{O}|(\exists i \in \mathcal{I}, (o, i) \in \mathcal{R})\}| \qquad (5)$$

An essential itemsets is characterized by a disjunctive support and is defined as follows.

**Definition 6.** *Essential itemset [7]*
*Let $\mathcal{H} = (\chi, \xi)$ be a hypergraph and $I \subseteq \chi$. $\mathcal{I}$ is said to be an essential set of vertices if and only if:*

$$Supp(\vee I) > max\{Supp(\vee I \smallsetminus \{x\})|x \in I\} \qquad (6)$$

It is important to remind that the essential itemsets extracted from a hypergraph satisfy the order property of essential itemsets. If $I$ is an essential itemset, then $\forall\ I_1 \subset \mathcal{I}$, $I_1$ is also an essential itemset. Thus, the notion of minimal transversal can be redefined through the support of a set of vertices and the notion of the essential itemset [12, 16], according to Proposition 1.

**Proposition 1.** *Minimal Transversal*
*A subset of vertices $\mathcal{X} \subseteq \chi$ is a minimal transversal of the hypergraph $\mathcal{H}$, if $\mathcal{X}$ is essential and if its disjunctive support is equal to the number of hyperedges of $\mathcal{H}$, i.e., $X$ is an essential set such that $Supp(\vee X) = |\xi|$.*

### 3.2   Description of the DTSR Algorithm

This section presents the main idea of the TSR algorithm based on minimal transversal computation. The goal is to determine the smallest set of tests that are likely to best represent the original test suite. Hence, we propose to conceptualize the test suite following the form of a hypergraph, in which the vertices stand for the tests and hyperedges are the requirements. According to this projection, the minimized test suite is equivalent to the minimal transversal of the hypergraph. Our proposed DTSR algorithm computes the set of all possible minimized test suites. To the best of our knowledge, no prior algorithm has addressed the TSR issue through the determination of the minimal transversals of a hypergraph. The first originality of DTSR stands in the efficient pruning of worthless space to explore since it excludes those, which are unable to contain a minimal transversal. Moreover, this algorithm gathers deterministic minimized sets, which is crucial while reducing a set of tests. The DTSR algorithm, whose pseudo-code is given by Algorithm 1, starts by computing the support of each node and sorts them in increasing order (line 5). Thus, it rapidly creates the maximal clique of non-transversals, i.e., the largest space in which is not possible to find minimal transversals. The lager this maximal clique, the higher the pruning of the search space is. After initializing the list *toExploreList*, DTSR generates one by one the set of k-candidates. For each k-candidate, i.e, set of size $k$, DTSR computes its disjunctive support. If the latter is strictly greater than the maximum of its direct subsets and its support is equal to the number of hyperedges then this candidate is marked as a minimal transversal and added to the set $\mathcal{M_H}$. DTSR repeats this step until the *toExploreList* list is empty.

By obtaining the set of all possible minimized test suites, we can choose the minimized test suite, which minimizes (or maximizes) a criterion. For example, w e would look to minimize the percentage of the covered tests or alternatively look for maximizing the necessary fault detection capability.

### 3.3   Illustrative Example

In the following, we present an illustrative example glancing how the DTSR algorithm works on a toy extraction context given by Table 2. Table 2 shows the satisfiability relationship between the test cases $t_1, \ldots, t_8$ in and the requirements $R_1, \ldots, R_6$.

---

**Algorithm 1:** DTSR Algorithm

---

**Require:** $\mathcal{H} = (\mathcal{T}, \mathcal{R})$: hypergraph
**Ensure:** $\mathcal{M_H}$: set of possible minimized test suites
1: **global variables**
2:     $MaxClique \leftarrow \emptyset, toExploreList \leftarrow \emptyset,$
3:     $\mathcal{M_H} \leftarrow \emptyset$, itemset $\leftarrow \chi$
4: **end global variables**
5: sort(itemset)
6: **foreach** $i \in itemset$ **do**
7: Transversal $\leftarrow$ Transversal $\cup$ i
8: **if** $support(Transeversal) = |\xi|$ **then**
9: insertFirst(i,ToExploreList)

      **else**
10: $MaxClique \leftarrow MaxClique \cup i$

      **while** $ToExploreList \neq \emptyset$ **do**
11: $Transversal \leftarrow \emptyset$
12: $Current \leftarrow ToExploreList[0]$
13: $ToExploreList \leftarrow ToExploreList \backslash ToExploreList[0]$
14: $itemset \leftarrow GenerateItemsets(Current)$
15: $sort(itemset)$
16: **foreach** $i \in itemset$ **do**
        **if** $support(i) = |\xi|$ **then**
17: $\mathcal{M_H} \leftarrow \mathcal{M_H} \cup i$
      **else**
        **if** $support(i) > support(Current)$ **then**
18: $Transversal \leftarrow Transversal \cup i$
19: **if** $support(Transeversal)=|\xi|$ **then**
20: insertFirst(i,ToExploreList)
        **else**
21: $MaxClique \leftarrow MaxClique \cup i$

      **return** $(\mathcal{M_H})$

---

In what follows, we present the iterations produced by DTSR on the test suite presented in Table 2:

**Table 2.** Satisfiability matrix between requirements and test cases

|       | $t_1$ | $t_2$ | $t_3$ | $t_4$ | $t_5$ | $t_6$ | $t_7$ | $t_8$ |
|-------|-------|-------|-------|-------|-------|-------|-------|-------|
| $R_1$ | 1 | 1 | 0 | 0 | 0 | 0 | 0 | 0 |
| $R_2$ | 0 | 1 | 1 | 0 | 0 | 0 | 1 | 0 |
| $R_3$ | 0 | 0 | 1 | 1 | 1 | 0 | 0 | 0 |
| $R_4$ | 0 | 0 | 0 | 1 | 0 | 1 | 0 | 0 |
| $R_5$ | 0 | 0 | 0 | 0 | 0 | 1 | 1 | 1 |
| $R_6$ | 0 | 0 | 0 | 0 | 0 | 0 | 1 | 0 |

**Iteration 1:**

In the beginning, we calculate the disjunctive support of items. The nodes that were produced during this iteration are shown below:

| Item | 1 | 2 | 3 | 4 | 5 | 6 | 7 | 8 |
|---|---|---|---|---|---|---|---|---|
| Disjunctive support | 1 | 2 | 2 | 2 | 1 | 2 | 3 | 1 |

Secondly, we order ascendingly items according to their disjunctive supports:

| Item | 1 | 5 | 8 | 2 | 3 | 4 | 6 | 7 |
|---|---|---|---|---|---|---|---|---|
| Disjunctive support | 1 | 1 | 1 | 2 | 2 | 2 | 2 | 3 |

After that, we have to stick element by element and check whether if the disjunctive support of the obtained element is equal to the cardinality of the requirement set, to wit 6. If it is the case, then the last topped-up element can lead to a transversal and it is stored in *ToExploreList*. Otherwise, the last topped-up item is added to the *MaxClique* list.

$$\left\{ \begin{array}{l} Transversal = \{1\} | support(\{1\}) = 1 < 6 \\ \Rightarrow \left\{ \begin{array}{l} ToExploreList = \emptyset \\ Maxclique = \{1\} \end{array} \right. \end{array} \right.$$

$$\left\{ \begin{array}{l} Transversal = \{1,5\} | support(\{1,5\}) = 2 < 6 \\ \Rightarrow \left\{ \begin{array}{l} ToExploreList = \emptyset \\ Maxclique = \{\{1\}, \{5\}\} \end{array} \right. \end{array} \right.$$

$$\left\{ \begin{array}{l} Transversal = \{1,5,8\} | support(\{1,2,3\}) = 3 < 6 \\ \Rightarrow \left\{ \begin{array}{l} ToExploreList = \emptyset \\ Maxclique = \{\{1\}, \{5\}, \{8\}\} \end{array} \right. \end{array} \right.$$

$$\left\{ \begin{array}{l} Transversal = \{1,5,8,2\} | support(\{1,5,8,2\}) = 4 < 6 \\ \Rightarrow \left\{ \begin{array}{l} ToExploreList = \emptyset \\ Maxclique = \{\{1\}, \{5\}, \{8\}, \{2\}\} \end{array} \right. \end{array} \right.$$

$$\left\{ \begin{array}{l} Transversal = \{1,5,8,2,3\} | support(\{1,5,8,2,3\}) = 2 < 6 \\ \Rightarrow \left\{ \begin{array}{l} ToExploreList = \emptyset \\ Maxclique = \{\{1\}, \{2\}, \{3\}\} \end{array} \right. \end{array} \right.$$

$$\left\{ \begin{array}{l} Transversal = \{1,5,8,2,3,4\} | support(\{1,5,8,2,3,4\}) = 5 < 6 \\ \Rightarrow \left\{ \begin{array}{l} ToExploreList = \emptyset \\ Maxclique = \{\{1\}, \{5\}, \{8\}, \{2\}\{3\}, \{4\}\} \end{array} \right. \end{array} \right.$$

$$\left\{ \begin{array}{l} Transversal = \{1,5,8,2,3,4,6\} | support(\{1,5,8,2,3,4,6\}) = 5 < 6 \\ \Rightarrow \left\{ \begin{array}{l} ToExploreList = \emptyset \\ Maxclique = \{\{1\}, \{5\}, \{8\}, \{2\}, \{3\}, \{4\}, \{6\}\} \end{array} \right. \end{array} \right.$$

$$\left\{ \begin{array}{l} Transversal = \{1,5,8,2,3,4,6,7\} | support(\{1,5,8,2,3,4,6,7\}) = 6 = 6 \\ \Rightarrow \left\{ \begin{array}{l} ToExploreList = \{\{7\}\} \\ Maxclique = \{\{1\}, \{5\}, \{8\}, \{2\}, \{3\}, \{4\}, \{6\}\} \end{array} \right. \end{array} \right.$$

As we can note, none of the subsets of $\{1, 5, 8, 2, 3, 4, 6\}$ is a minimal transversal. Therefore, we can skip exploring a tremendous part of the search space.

**Iteration 2:**
We will go through the elements of the list and treat them one by one. In this iteration, the element to be treated is the singleton $\{7\}$. Now, we will generate 2-items:

| Item | $\{7,1\}$ | $\{7,5\}$ | $\{7,8\}$ | $\{7,2\}$ | $\{7,3\}$ | $\{7,4\}$ | $\{7,6\}$ |
|---|---|---|---|---|---|---|---|
| Disjunctive support | 4 | 4 | 3 | 4 | 4 | 5 | 4 |

As we observe the results, none of the itemsets is a minimal transversal because all itemsets have a disjunctive support value less than 6.

Note that the itemset $\{7, 5\}$ will not be processed because it does not fulfill the first condition of a minimal transversal which called essentiality condition, i.e. Support($\{7, 5\}$) = Support ($\{7\}$).

Thus, we start by sorting the elements:

| Item | $\{7,1\}$ | $\{7,2\}$ | $\{7,3\}$ | $\{7,5\}$ | $\{7,6\}$ | $\{7,4\}$ |
|---|---|---|---|---|---|---|
| Disjunctive support | 4 | 4 | 4 | 4 | 4 | 5 |

After sorting the itemsets we start to produce the elements of the two lists *MaxClique* and *toExploreList*.

$$
\begin{cases}
Transversal = \{7,1\}|support(\{1\}) = 4 < 6 \\
\Rightarrow \begin{cases} ToExploreList = \emptyset \\ Maxclique = \{\{7,1\}\} \end{cases}
\end{cases}
$$

$$
\begin{cases}
Transversal = \{7,1,2\}|support(\{7,1,2\}) = 4 < 6 \\
\Rightarrow \begin{cases} ToExploreList = \emptyset \\ Maxclique = \{\{7,1\},\{7,2\},\} \end{cases}
\end{cases}
$$

$$
\begin{cases}
Transversal = \{7,1,2,3\}|support(\{7,1,2,3\}) = 5 < 6 \\
\Rightarrow \begin{cases} ToExploreList = \emptyset \\ Maxclique = \{\{7,1\},\{7,2\},\{7,3\}\} \end{cases}
\end{cases}
$$

$$
\begin{cases}
Transversal = \{7,1,2,3,5\}|support(\{7,1,2,3,5\}) = 5 < 6 \\
\Rightarrow \begin{cases} ToExploreList = \emptyset \\ Maxclique = \{\{7,1\},\{7,2\},\{7,3\},\{7,5\}\} \end{cases}
\end{cases}
$$

$$
\begin{cases}
Transversal = \{7,1,2,3,5,6\}|support(\{7,1,2,3,5,6\}) = 6 = 6 \\
\Rightarrow \begin{cases} ToExploreList = \{\{7,6\}\} \\ Maxclique = \{\{7,1\},\{7,2\},\{7,3\},\{7,5\}\} \end{cases}
\end{cases}
$$

$$
\begin{cases}
Transversal = \{7,1,2,3,5,4\}|support(\{7,1,2,3,5,4\}) = 6 = 6 \\
\Rightarrow \begin{cases} ToExploreList = \{\{7,4\},\{7,6\}\} \\ Maxclique = \{\{7,1\},\{7,2\},\{7,3\},\{7,5\}\} \end{cases}
\end{cases}
$$

We can check that it does exist a minimal transversal such that it is a subset of $\{7, 1, 2, 3, 5\}$.

**Iteration 3:**
We will explore the first element in toExploreList which is $\{7, 4\}$ and generate the 3-items:

| Item | $\{7,4,6\}$ | $\{7,4,1\}$ | $\{7,4,2\}$ | $\{7,4,3\}$ | $\{7,4,5\}$ |
|---|---|---|---|---|---|
| Disjunctive support | 5 | 6 | 6 | 5 | 5 |

As we can see, we have 2 minimal transversals so $\mathcal{M}_{\mathcal{H}} = \{\{7, 4, 1\}, \{7, 4, 2\}\}$. To note that the itemset will be ignored since it does not fulfill the essentiality condition of a minimal transversal (its disjunctive support is equal to that of its subset $\{7, 4\}$).

We sort the remaining elements:

| Item | $\{7,4,6\}$ | $\{7,4,3\}$ |
|---|---|---|
| Disjunctive support | 5 | 5 |

$$\begin{cases} Transversal = \{7,4,6,3\} | support(\{7,4,6,3\}) = 5 < 6 \\ \Rightarrow \begin{cases} ToExploreList = \{\{7,6\}\} \\ Maxclique = \{\{7,4,6,3\}\} \end{cases} \end{cases}$$

In this case, the exploration of this branch comes to the end. We backtrack to explore the remaining element of the ToExploreList.

**Iteration 4:**
In this iteration, we will treat the itemset $\{7, 6\}$ and generate the 3-items:

| Item | $\{7,6,1\}$ | $\{7,6,2\}$ | $\{7,6,3\}$ | $\{7,6,5\}$ |
|---|---|---|---|---|
| Disjunctive support | 5 | 5 | 5 | 5 |

None of them is a minimal transversal. So we have to build our lists:

$$\begin{cases} Transversal = \{7,6,1\} | support(\{7,6,1\}) = 5 < 6 \\ \Rightarrow \begin{cases} ToExploreList = \emptyset \\ Maxclique = \{\{7,6,1\}\} \end{cases} \end{cases}$$

$$\begin{cases} Transversal = \{7,6,1,2\} | support(\{7,6,1,2\}) = 5 < 6 \\ \Rightarrow \begin{cases} ToExploreList = \emptyset \\ Maxclique = \{\{7,6,1\}, \{7,6,2\}\} \end{cases} \end{cases}$$

$$\begin{cases} Transversal = \{7,6,1,2,3\} | support(\{7,6,1,2,3\}) = 6 = 6 \\ \Rightarrow \begin{cases} ToExploreList = \{\{7,6,3\}\} \\ Maxclique = \{\{7,6,1\}, \{7,6,2\}\} \end{cases} \end{cases}$$

$$\begin{cases} Transversal = \{7,6,1,2,5\} | support(\{7,6,1,2,5\}) = 5 < 6 \\ \Rightarrow \begin{cases} ToExploreList = \{\{7,6,3\},\{7,6,5\}\} \\ Maxclique = \{\{7,6,1\},\{7,6,2\}\} \end{cases} \end{cases}$$

**Iteration 5:**
we start by exploring the fist element in *ToExploreList* which is $\{7,6,3\}$.

| Item | $\{7,6,3,5\}$ | $\{7,6,3,1\}$ | $\{7,6,3,2\}$ |
|---|---|---|---|
| Disjunctive support | 5 | 6 | 6 |

We have 2 minimal transversals, then we update $\mathcal{M_H}=\{\{7,4,1\},$ $\{7,4,2\},\{7,6,3,1\},\{7,6,3,2\}\}$.

**Iteration 6:**
Now, we have to explore the 3-itemset: $\{7,6,5\}$

| Item | $\{7,6,5,1\}$ | $\{7,6,5,2\}$ |
|---|---|---|
| Disjunctive support | 6 | 6 |

We have 2 minimal transversals, then $\mathcal{M_H} = \{\{7,4,1\},\{4,4,2\},\{7,6,3,1\},$ $\{7,6,3,2\},\{7,6,5,1\},\{7,6,5,2\}\}$.
We stop exploring this branch and the overall execution comes to the end.
Finally, the output is:
$\mathcal{M_H} = \{\{7,4,1\},\{7,4,2\},\{7,6,3,1\},\{7,6,3,2\},\{7,6,5,1\},\{7,6,5,2\}\}$.

Table 3 summarizes the values of the global variables obtained in each iteration.

**Table 3.** Execution trace of the DTSR algorithm on the test suite given by Table 2

| Iteration 1 | Iteration 2 |
|---|---|
| $ToExploreList = \{\{t_7\}\}$ | $ToExploreList = \{\{t_7,t_4\},\{t_7,t_6\}\}$ |
| $MaxClique = \{\{t_1\},\{t_2\},\{t_3\},\{t_4\},\{t_5\},\{t_6\}\}$ | $MaxClique = \{\{t_7,t_1\},\{7,2\},\{t_7,t_3\},\{t_7,t_5\}\}$ |
| $\mathcal{M_H} = \emptyset$ | $\mathcal{M_H} = \emptyset$ |
| Iteration 3 | Iteration 4 |
| $ToExploreList = \{\{t_7,t_6\}\}$ | $ToExploreList = \{\{t_7,t_6,t_3\},\{t_7,t_6,t_5\}\}$ |
| $MaxClique = \{\{t_7,t_4,t_6,t_3\}\}$ | $MaxClique = \{\{t_7,t_6,t_1\},\{t_7,t_6,t_2\}\}$ |
| $\mathcal{M_H} = \{\{t_7,t_4,t_1\},\{t_7,t_4,t_2\}\}$ | $\mathcal{M_H} = \{\{t_7,t_4,t_1\},\{t_7,t_4,t_2\}\}$ |
| Iteration 5 | Iteration 6 |
| $ToExploreList = \{\{t_7,t_6,t_5\}\}$ | $ToExploreList = \emptyset$ |
| $MaxClique = \{\{t_7,t_6,t_1\},\{t_7,t_6,t_2\}\}$ | $MaxClique = \emptyset$ |
| $\mathcal{M_H} = \{\{t_7,t_4,t_1\},\{t_7,t_4,t_2\},$ | $\mathcal{M_H} = \{\{t_7,t_4,t_1\},\{t_7,t_4,t_2\},$ |
| $\{t_7,t_6,t_3,t_1\},\{t_7,t_6,t_3,t_2\}\}$ | $\{t_7,t_6,t_3,t_1\},\{t_7,t_6,t_3,t_2\},$ |
|  | $\{t_7,t_6,t_5,t_1\},\{t_7,t_6,t_5,t_2\}\}$ |

# 4 Preliminary Evaluations

In this section, we first present the data set as well as the evaluation metrics of use in our experimental study. Then, we present the results obtained by DTSR versus the pioneering ones dedicated to the TSR task.

## 4.1 Data Set and Measures

This evaluation consists of setting up a performance analysis of the minimized test suite obtained by DTSR compared to the minimized test suites obtained by the other algorithms according to the Test minimization percentage (TMP) criterion. The latter is used to assess the amount of reduction in the number of test cases [27]. Formally, TMP is computed as follows:

$$TMP = (1 - |MTS| \div |OTS|) \times 100\% \tag{7}$$

where:

- $|OTS|$: cardinality of the original test suite;
- $|MTS|$: cardinality of the minimized test suite.

*Notice that* TMP value ranges from 0% to 100% and a higher value of TMP shows that more test cases are reduced in the minimized test suite.

## 4.2 Evaluation of the TMP Criterion

In the following, we will evaluate the reduction rate of the number of tests by calculating the TMP value of the minimized test suite obtained. We are considering that all the test cases have the same weight in terms of cost. So our evaluation consists of evaluating the number of remaining test cases in the new generated test suite. To perform the experimental study, we tested the DTSR algorithm using the benchmark data set, already used by Chen and Lau [9]. The latter used this dataset to assess the performances of their proposed meta-heuristics algorithms as a TSR solution. The results of the DTSR algorithm are illustrated in Table 4 as well as those of its competitors, as given by Chen and Lau [9].

As shown in by the statistics given in Table 4, none of the greedy, H, GE, GRE reaches the optimized solution for all of the seven considered instances. Contrariwise, DTSR always succeeded to locate the minimized test, to wit the best value of TMP.

We are pretty sure that the result of the DTSR algorithm is the most minimized, since we have generated all possible minimized test suites and the choice was confirmed after this generation.

The other algorithms have witnessed the difficulty of indeterminacy since the arbitrary choice in case of equivalence of test cases in terms of requirements coverage. Consequently, neither of H, GE nor GRE is always the best choice to opt for [9].

**Table 4.** Performance analysis of minimized test suites obtained in terms of TMP

| Algorithm | 1 | 2 | 3 | 4 | 5 | 6 | 7 |
|-----------|-------|-------|-------|-------|-------|-------|-------|
| Greedy | 42.86 | 33.33 | **66.66** | **66.66** | 54.54 | 37.50 | **55.55** |
| H | 42.86 | **50.00** | 55.55 | 55.55 | 63.63 | 37.50 | **55.55** |
| GE | 42.86 | 33.33 | **66.66** | **66.66** | 54.54 | 37.50 | **55.55** |
| GRE | **57.14** | 33.33 | 55.55 | **66.66** | 54.54 | **50.00** | 44.44 |
| DTSR | **57.14** | **50.00** | **66.66** | **66.66** | **63.63** | **50.00** | **55.55** |

## 4.3   Number of Reduced Test Suite

Most of the algorithms, previously proposed in the literature as a solution to the TSR problem, produce a single minimized set of tests. In contrast, DTSR extracts all the minimized test suites possible from the original test suite. Table 5 shows the number of minimized test suites obtained for each test suite.

**Table 5.** Number of minimized test suites obtained for each test suite.

| Test suite number | 1 | 2 | 3 | 4 | 5 | 6 | 7 |
|-------------------|----|----|----|----|----|----|----|
| Number of test cases | 7 | 6 | 9 | 9 | 11 | 8 | 9 |
| Number of requirements | 19 | 19 | 19 | 11 | 12 | 11 | 11 |
| Number of minimized test suites obtained by DTSR | 8 | 5 | 21 | 8 | 21 | 10 | 12 |

The results, shown in Table 5, highlight that DTSR sharply outperforms its competitors, which are Greedy, GE, and GRE. Indeed the latter provides a single test suite minimized. Fortunately, DTSR provides more than one, which helps the tester to choose a test suite according to the criterion to optimize such as, FDC the fault detection capability or the overall performance time).

## 5   Conclusion

In this paper, we associate the concepts of vertices and hyperedges to the tests and the hyperedges, respectively. We have introduced the DTSR algorithm and an example of its execution footprint. The preliminary results show that it outperforms the classical algorithms such as Greedy, GE, and GRE. The reduction rate varies from 50% up to 65% of the initial set size according the data set already used in the literature. Moreover, our algorithm is deterministic and computes all the optimal solutions. Those results inspire us to endeavor other mappings of the vertices and hyperedges to compute reduced test suites, which would optimize arbitrary objective functions. We may, for example, maximize the fault detection capability belonging to real software solutions.

# References

1. Anderson, J., Azizi, M., Salem, S., Do, H.: On the use of usage patterns from telemetry data for test case prioritization. Inf. Softw. Technol. **113**, 110–130 (2019). https://doi.org/10.1016/j.infsof.2019.05.008
2. Arrieta, A., Wang, S., Markiegi, U., Arruabarrena, A., Etxeberria, L., Sagardui, G.: Pareto efficient multi-objective black-box test case selection for simulation-based testing. Inf. Softw. Technol. **114**, 137–154 (2019)
3. Baller, H., Lity, S., Lochau, M., Schaefer, I.: Multi-objective test suite optimization for incremental product family testing. In: Proceedings of 2014 IEEE Seventh International Conference on Software Testing, Verification and Validation. IEEE (2014)
4. Banias, O.: Test case selection-prioritization approach based on memorization dynamic programming algorithm. Inf. Softw. Technol. **115**, 119–130 (2019)
5. Berge, C.: Hypergraphs: Combinatorics of Finite Sets, vol. 45. Elsevier, Amsterdam (1984)
6. Black, J., Melachrinoudis, E., Kaeli, D.: Bi-criteria models for all-uses test suite reduction. In: Proceedings of the 26th International Conference on Software Engineering (2004)
7. Casali, A., Cicchetti, R., Lakhal, L.: Essential patterns: a perfect cover of frequent patterns. In: Proceedings of the 7th International Conference on DaWaK, pp. 428–437. Copenhagen, Denmark (2005)
8. Chen, J., et al.: Test case prioritization for object-oriented software: an adaptive random sequence approach based on clustering. J. Syst. Softw. **135**, 107–125 (2018)
9. Chen, T., Lau, M.: Heuristics towards the optimization of the size of a test suite. WIT Trans. Inf. Commun. Technol. **14**, 415–424 (1970)
10. Cruciani, E., Miranda, B., Verdecchia, R., Bertolino, A.: Scalable approaches for test suite reduction. In: Proceedings of the 41st International Conference on Software Engineering, pp. 419–429 (2019)
11. Garousi, V., Oezkan, R., Betin-Can, A.: Multi-objective regression test selection in practice: an empirical study in the defense software industry. Inf. Softw. Technol. **103**, 40–54 (2018)
12. Ghabry, I., Yahia, S.B., Jelassi, M.N.: Selection of bitmap join index: approach based on minimal transversals. In: Ordonez, C., Bellatreche, L. (eds.) DaWaK 2018. LNCS, vol. 11031, pp. 302–316. Springer, Cham (2018). https://doi.org/10.1007/978-3-319-98539-8_23
13. Gotlieb, A., Marijan, D.: Flower: optimal test suite reduction as a network maximum flow. In: Proceedings of the 2014 International Symposium on Software Testing and Analysis, pp. 171–180 (2014). https://doi.org/10.1145/2610384.2610416
14. Hierons, R.M.: FSM quasi-equivalence testing via reduction and observing absences. Sci. Comput. Program. **177**, 1–18 (2019)
15. Hsu, H.Y., Orso, A.: Mints: a general framework and tool for supporting test-suite minimization. In: Proceedings of IEEE 31st International Conference on Software Engineering, pp. 419–429 (2009)
16. Jelassi, M.N., Largeron, C., Ben Yahia, S.: Efficient unveiling of multi-members in a social network. J. Syst. Softw. **94**, 30–38 (2014)
17. Jelassi, M.N., Largeron, C., Ben Yahia, S.: Concise representation of hypergraph minimal transversals: approach and application on the dependency inference problem. In: 9th IEEE International Conference on Research Challenges in Information Science, RCIS 2015, Athens, Greece, 13–15 May 2015, pp. 434–444 (2015)

18. Khan, S.U., Lee, S.P., Ahmad, R.W., Akhunzada, A., Chang, V.: A survey on test suite reduction frameworks and tools. Int. J. Inf. Manage. **36**(6), 963–975 (2016)
19. Khan, S.R., Lee, S., Javaid, N., Abdul, W.: A systematic review on test suite reduction: approaches, experiment's quality evaluation, and guidelines. IEEE Access **6**, 11816–11841 (2018)
20. Kiran, A., Butt, W.H., Anwar, M.W., Azam, F., Maqbool, B.: A comprehensive investigation of modern test suite optimization trends, tools and techniques. IEEE Access **7**, 89093–89117 (2019)
21. Lin, J.W., Jabbarvand, R., Garcia, J., Malek, S.: Nemo: multi-criteria test-suite minimization with integer nonlinear programming. In: Proceedings IEEE/ACM 40th International Conference on Software Engineering (ICSE), pp. 1039–1049 (2018)
22. Liu, Y., Li, M., Wu, Y., Li, Z.: A weighted fuzzy classification approach to identify and manipulate coincidental correct test cases for fault localization. J. Syst. Softw. **151**, 20–37 (2019)
23. Pradhan, D., Wang, S., Yue, T., Ali, S., Liaaen, M.: Search-based test case implantation for testing untested configurations. Inf. Softw. Technol. **111**, 22–36 (2019)
24. Romano, S., Scanniello, G., Antoniol, G., Marchetto, A.: Spiritus: a simple information retrieval regression test selection approach. Inf. Softw. Technol. **99**, 62–80 (2018)
25. Schwartz, A., Puckett, D., Meng, Y., Gay, G.: Investigating faults missed by test suites achieving high code coverage. J. Syst. Softw. **144**, 106–120 (2018)
26. Shi, A., Gyori, A., Mahmood, S., Zhao, P., Marinov, D.: Evaluating test-suite reduction in real software evolution. In: Proceedings of the 27th ACM SIGSOFT International Symposium on Software Testing and Analysis, pp. 84–94 (2018)
27. Wang, S., Ali, S., Gotlieb, A.: Cost-effective test suite minimization in product lines using search techniques. J. Syst. Softw. **103**, 370–391 (2015)
28. Zhang, L., Marinov, D., Zhang, L., Khurshid, S.: An empirical study of JUnit test-suite reduction. In: Proceedings of the IEEE 22nd International Symposium on Software Reliability Engineering (2011)

# Advanced Studies in Machine Learning

# Machine Learning Based Monitoring of the Pneumatic Actuators' Behavior Through Signal Processing Using Real-World Data Set

Tibor Kovács(✉) and Andrea Kő

Corvinus University of Budapest, Fővám Tér 8, Budapest, Hungary
{tibor.kovacs,andrea.ko}@uni-corvinus.hu

**Abstract.** Application of machine learning in smart manufacturing could enrich condition-based maintenance, enabling to monitor more complex signals describing the behavior of an equipment. Predicting equipment malfunction or failure could not only reduce manufacturing cost but could also improve product quality and supply reliability, aspects equally important these days. This research describes a machine learning based method to diagnose the condition of pneumatic actuators by processing complex signals from this type of equipment. It is using real-world data from a Hungarian multinational manufacturer of electrical components. The "Manufacturing Data Life Cycle" conceptual framework by Tao et al. [1] was followed for data processing, including data cleaning, pre-processing and classification by hierarchical clustering. The method was able to identify those signal patterns that indicate abnormal behavior of the equipment. Data volume was a challenge for this work, overcome by using parallel and GPU execution of computations.

**Keywords:** Machine learning · Big data processing · Clustering · Condition-based maintenance · Fault detection · Signal pattern identification

## 1 Introduction

Data is a key enabler for smart manufacturing, coming from various sources and in different forms. Signals from equipment carry valuable information about its health, how well it functions and if its condition deviates from past states. It is also used to predict its future behavior. Textual information in the forms of log files and error messages are also available nowadays to describe machine status and to help understanding and interpreting the signals. The amount of data could however be overwhelming and remain useless if not processed and mapped into information that is understood by users. Because of the data volume, velocity, variety and veracity, it is not feasible to expect humans to analyze signal data using traditional manufacturing tools. There are more efficient techniques than inspecting data visually, especially when the patterns that describe certain machine behavior are complex and rare.

Condition based maintenance is a well-established technique in manufacturing. Monitoring equipment parameters like the temperature and vibration of bearings, or the electric current of motors are used in many operations. When applying these

© Springer Nature Switzerland AG 2019
T. K. Dang et al. (Eds.): FDSE 2019, LNCS 11814, pp. 33–44, 2019.
https://doi.org/10.1007/978-3-030-35653-8_3

techniques, normally a control limit is set for the monitored parameter, often established empirically, to alert the risk of failure when the parameter is outside of the set limit. Preventing machine failure not only reduces the cost of maintenance by avoiding consequential damage that often follows break-downs but could also eliminate producing defective products with hidden faults that are difficult to detect [2, 3]. Using smart manufacturing broadens the application of condition-based maintenance, enabling to monitor those types of equipment, where setting a single control limit is not sufficient, that would require the identification of a particular signal pattern [1]. Searching for patterns is a well-known method in machine learning (ML), it is used e.g. in monitoring network activities to identify intrusions.

The aim of this work is to (1) present an approach and the challenges of data preprocessing of signals from real-world data and (2) to identify and classify the signals from this data set that belong to different machine states, including the ones that indicate abnormal behavior by analyzing signal patterns of pneumatic actuators using machine learning techniques. The classified signal patterns are envisaged to be used for developing a predictive analytics application, that helps identifying those machine states that exhibit equipment malfunctions. Being able to raise early warnings for equipment malfunctions would help improving overall manufacturing performance by improving product quality, boosting efficiency, reducing scrap rates and maintenance costs.

Research questions discussed in this paper are the following:

- How big data time-series from sensors could be analyzed with machine learning techniques to identify the irregular behavior of an equipment and to classify different types of malfunction?
- What is the appropriate unsupervised learning model in data pre-processing and what are the challenges to overcome?

## 2   Related Works

Data produced by the modern manufacturing industry shows explosive growth reaching more than 1000 EB annually [4]. Manufacturers started to recognize the strategic importance of data; it became a key enabler for manufacturing competitiveness [1]. Smart manufacturing aims to exploit the data collected via manufacturing intelligence throughout the product lifecycle in order to make a positive impact on all aspects of manufacturing [5]. Compared with traditional manufacturing, smart manufacturing has an extreme focus on real-time data collection and conversion through physical and computational processes. Data describing the manufacturing process could usually be obtained from: (a) manufacturing information systems (e.g., ERP, CRM or SCM), (b) industrial IoT technologies (e.g. operating conditions of a production equipment measured by sensors, (c) smart products and product-service systems by IoT technologies (e.g. recording product performance in the context of usage conditions), (d) social networking and e-commerce platforms (e.g. user data, users profiles and preferences) and (e) open databases provided by governments (e.g. civic infrastructure) [1]. Types of manufacturing data can be structured (e.g. databases), semi-structured (e.g. XML documents), or unstructured (e.g., equipment and error logs)

[6]. Emerging technologies, like artificial intelligence (AI), the Internet of Things (IoT), cloud computing, mobile Internet play a strategic role in supporting data-driven manufacturing. Tao et al. [1] proposed the following steps of translating data to useful information, referring as the "manufacturing data life cycle (MDLF)": collection, transmission, storage, processing, visualization, and application.

Data in a manufacturing environment is collected from numerous sources in a variety of ways. Equipment and product data are usually collected through smart sensors, RFID tags or other sensing devices aiming to monitor equipment and product behavior in real-time. The vast amount of data collected from manufacturing processes must be transmitted and integrated efficiently and stored securely. Traditionally, manufacturing companies stored mainly structured data, however recently unstructured data (especially log files) became also valuable sources of information. Data storage in the cloud could be a cost-effective and flexible option, however because of security restrictions it may not be feasible for many companies. Data processing deals with discovering knowledge from large volumes of manufacturing data. It starts with the pre-processing steps of data cleaning and data reduction. Data pre-processing has a crucial impact on the final results; it is usually a complex and non-trivial operation. Data cleaning typically includes removing redundant, misleading, duplicated, inconsistent information. In the manufacturing environment, missing values are common, and they pose a challenge to the application of machine learning algorithms [7]. There are various approaches for replacing missing values, however they influence the original data set. This is a common problem and widely discussed from theoretical and practical aspects in the literature [8, 9]. The following step of the data processing is data reduction, which transforms the massive volume of data into ordered, meaningful, and simplified forms. Data analysis is the next data processing phase, covering a wide variety of techniques, including machine learning, data mining, time-series analysis, large-scale computing, and the use of forecasting models. Clustering, classification, prediction, and deviation analysis from the data mining methods are used extensively in this field. Visual analytics and visualization support the communication with end users, it helps having a clear, user-friendly view of the data and a ore easy understanding the data processing results. Tao et al. [1] recognized three phases of data applications. The first phase (design) helps in demand analysis, smart design and market forecasting through better understanding of customers, competitors and markets. The second phase (manufacturing) supports decision making, product quality control and equipment supervision. The third phase (MRO - maintenance, repair and operations) enriches monitoring operations, fault predictions and smart maintenance.

Machine learning became popular in manufacturing over the past 20 years. It got the first significant attention in the 1980s, but because of the immaturity of the available technology at the time and the subsequent difficulties of implementation, adaption was insignificant [10]. With the increased spreading of the Industrial Internet of Things (IoT), Industry 4.0, and smart manufacturing more data is being generated than ever and ML has a new opportunity in manufacturing applications. Machine learning is a subset of artificial intelligence covering diverse areas. ML has several definitions, one of them that is widely used is the following: ML allows computers to solve problems without being specifically programmed to do so [11]. ML techniques can be structured in various ways. Supervised, unsupervised, and reinforcement learning are widely used categories [12], but other taxonomies are available as well. Some researchers divide ML to active and passive learning, where 'active learning is generally used to refer to a learning problem or a system where the learner has some role in determining on what data it will be trained [13], while passive learning describes a situation where the learner has no control over the training set.

ML techniques can be classified according to their role in manufacturing too. Schwabacher and Goebel [14] provided a taxonomy of the Integrated Systems Health Management (ISHM) system, where they distinguished between model-based and data-driven ISHM algorithms. The model-based category had two sub-classes: physics-based (systems of differential equations) and classical AI categories (e.g. expert systems, and qualitative reasoning). The data-driven category includes conventional numerical methods, like linear regression and machine learning. They mapped ISHM problems (fault detection, diagnostics and prognostics) for algorithm types (physics-based, classical AI, conventional numerical methods and machine learning). According to this matrix, clustering as a machine learning method is common in fault detection underpinning our case. Supervised learning methods fit well for challenges and problems faced in manufacturing applications as manufacturing data is often labeled and expert feedback is available. Unsupervised learning methods are becoming increasingly important, providing an extensive field for research. One typical goal in unsupervised learning is to discover unknown classes of items by clustering, which is a relevant approach in fault detection [15]. Common examples of unsupervised learning are clustering, association rules, and self-organizing maps [13]. Unsupervised learning is beneficial in manufacturing application in outliers' identification in manufacturing data [16] or when no expert feedback available. Due to the fast increase of unlabeled data in manufacturing, hybrid methods that combine the machine learning approaches with one or more other approaches are becoming more common [14]. An example for these hybrid methods could be the application of unsupervised learning as data pre-processing for supervised learning [17]. As class distribution imbalance of a training data set for supervised machine learning application poses a performance problem, balancing the training data set by under-sampling the majority class could mitigate this problem. Lin et al. [17] used k-nearest neighbor (kNN) clustering method in their research to create a balanced training data set. In our research kNN clustering could not be used as no a priori knowledge was available about the number of different machine states, hence the use of hierarchical clustering.

Compared with the traditional methods, intelligent fault diagnosis is able to rapidly and efficiently processing massive amounts of collected signals, and it could provide accurate fault diagnostic results [18]. Intelligent fault diagnosis includes the following main steps: signal acquisition, feature extraction and selection, and fault classification [19, 20]. The feature extraction phase aims to extract representative features from the collected signals based on signal processing techniques, like time-domain statistical analysis, Fourier spectral analysis and wavelet transformation [21]. These features may contain useless or insensitive information, which could negatively affect the diagnosis results. Feature selection is applied to select sensitive features through dimension reduction strategies, like principal component analysis (PCA), or distance evaluation technique [22]. In the fault classification step, because of the unlabelled data, unsupervised learning techniques like clustering, k-nearest neighbor (kNN), and support vector machine (SVM) [23] are used.

Several papers analyzed the role of big data in smart maintenance. Fassois and Sakellariou [24] gave an overview of the principles and techniques of time series methods for fault detection, identification and estimation in vibrating structures. They presented two case studies about (1) fault detection in an aircraft stiffened panel and (2) fault detection and estimation in an aircraft skeleton structure. Helwig et al. [2] and Sharma et al. [3] discussed sensor fault detection, while Munirathinam et al. [25] and Al Tobi et al. [26] dealt with fault prediction. Al Tobi et al. aimed at the automatic fault diagnosis of centrifugal pumps based on artificial intelligence methods [26]. Their data collection was performed in an experimental setup environment, and their suggested data analysis framework included the combination of wavelet transformation, feature extraction and classification with MLP-ANN (Multilayer Perceptron Artificial Neural Network) and SVM (Support Vector Machine).

## 3   Case Study – the Proposed Approach

This case study is using real world data and it is part of a smart manufacturing - predictive analytics R&D project of a Hungarian multinational manufacturer of electrical components. The company, a global leader in connectivity solutions manufactures a vast range of industrial connectors, cables and electronics components such as sensors, relays and switches. Their products are used in a wide range of applications, including factory machinery, rail and transit vehicles, HVAC systems, medical instrumentation, as well as communication, computers and power supply components. The company places great importance on research and development; the aim of this work is to monitor the behavior of pneumatic actuators through signal processing, with the longer-term goal of developing condition-based maintenance tools. The data was collected during 2018–2019.

Condition monitoring of rotary machines like bearings or gearboxes is well established. Measuring the temperature or analyzing the vibration spectrum of the equipment could provide valuable information about its behavior. Monitoring reciprocating parts could be more difficult as the signals are non-stationary and the Fourier spectrum calculations may introduce false alarms or missed detections [27]. Pattern recognition, a technique that is frequently used in big data applications could improve the reliability of failure prediction compared with methods developed for rotary parts. This case study aims at analyzing signals from a common, inexpensive reciprocating part: a pneumatic actuator that is widely used in machines of mass manufacturing. The signal is related to the movement generated by the device; the shape of the signal is related to the wear and tear of its parts. No feature extraction has been applied as a single signal was used to describe the behavior of the component. The anticipated benefit from being able to predict the failure of the component is not as much of reducing manufacturing or maintenance cost but rather preventing to produce defective products, ones that are difficult to detect.

A signal of 0–20 mV was collected at $7.8 \times 10^{-5}$ s frequency from the actuator and recorded as .csv files. As the recording was automatic, signals were collected both for operating and idling machine states. Under normal operating conditions, the actuator runs in a sequence of 6–8 cycles followed by a set waiting time. External conditions: mainly differences in compressed air pressure may affect the cycle time and the signal amplitude. The cycle time was set to 1.56 s; however, it was not stable, it could vary as much as 1%. Disturbances like jamming could also influence the cycle time or could even cause the sequence of cycles prematurely aborted. Figure 1. shows a sequence of 7 cycles, the fourth being different, indicating defective operation.

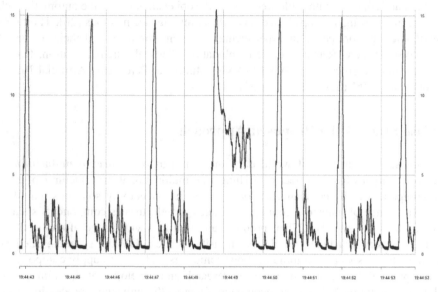

**Fig. 1.** Signal of a sequence of 7 cycles from a pneumatic actuator

The data was processed following the steps that Tao et al. [1] suggested as the "manufacturing data life cycle": collection, transmission, storage, processing, visualization, and application. The data processing was carried out in R environment [28]. Approximately 20 GB of data was collected per month, recording more than 100 000 cycles of operation.

Tao et al. [1] points out that data must be preprocessed to remove redundant, misleading and inconsistent information. Data cleaning therefore should take care of missing values, format conversions, duplicates and garbage cleaning. Our data processing started with *format conversion* transforming the .csv data into xts time series objects [29]. The format conversion step involved removing redundant data from the files (the redundant information was the summary statistics that was calculated and recorded at regular intervals in the .csv files), assigning timestamps to each data points and splitting them to contiguous sequences. *Duplicates removal* was not necessary in our case, however there were data of useless information: recordings of idle machine states, empty signals, noise or erratic signals. The *garbage cleaning* step therefore required to identify these sequences of empty or erratic signals. To identify these signals, an indicator was calculated for each sequence and used to decide if the data should be further analyzed or be discarded. The indicator was defined as the average of the rolling standard deviation through a set window. If the indicator was greater than a pre-defined value, then sequence had sufficient information and was processed further. Other methods, like STL (Seasonal time series decomposition utilizing local regression) [30] were also tested, but discarded due to increased computational intensity.

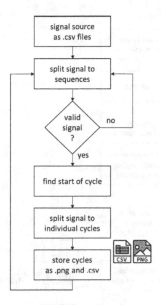

**Fig. 2.** Process flow of signal pre-processing

The next step of data processing was splitting the sequences to individual signals of reciprocating cycles. Each cycle started with a peak while the shape of the signal was different carrying information about the conditions of the pneumatic actuator. The height of the signal varied, even for consecutive cycles of similar machine conditions, influenced by external factors like, differences in air pressure or electric current of the plant. The operation of the actuator was not encoded, the cycle time was somewhat instable, and the sequences may be aborted due to jamming, therefore the start of each cycle had to be identified individually. The start of the cycle was identified as the earliest local maximum above a threshold. The algorithm should be able to handle those recordings too, that started in the middle of a reciprocating cycle, hence setting the threshold. Due to the nature of the data, subsequent to application of a noise filter using a rolling average function, a simple hill-climbing algorithm was used to find the local maximum indicating the start of the cycle. The end of the cycle was determined as a constant cut-off time, set as less than the average cycle time. It was defined as such due to the instability of cycle time. The signal data was then split between these start and end times and stored as both.csv files for further processing and .png pictures for the quick observation of a cycle pattern (Fig. 2). The visualization of the cycle patterns, in line with the MDLF model of Tao et al. [1] was found particularly useful when identifying and comparing patterns belonging to different clusters and machine conditions. The performance of processing the data, including the garbage cleaning and splitting to individual cycles was 0.21 s per cycle or 1.05 s per MB using parallel execution of 12 cores of an AMD Ryzen 2920X processor at 3.5 GHz. Although this performance is faster than the generation of data, data processing should be optimized in the future to improve its efficiency and reduce its resource intensity.

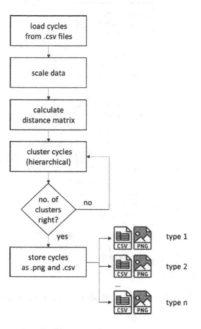

**Fig. 3.** Process flow of clustering

According to the research goal, we aimed to identify the irregular behavior of an equipment and classify different types of malfunction. Due to the unlabeled data source we had, and the need of discovering unknown classes of items, unsupervised machine learning method is relevant to apply. Therefore, the data pre-processing was followed by using an unsupervised learning method, *agglomerative hierarchical clustering* to classify and group the signals that display similar patterns (Fig. 3). Euclidean distance was used to calculate the dissimilarity matrix as the input for the clustering. This method of distance calculation was chosen as Ward's agglomerative clustering method [32] was used, and its input required to be a dissimilarity matrix that is based on Euclidean distances. Ward's method minimizes the total within-cluster variance, at each step the pair of clusters with minimum between-cluster distance are merged. Setting the appropriate number of clusters was done as an iterative process, with manual interaction, reviewing the pictures of the signals belonging to different clusters. This process was also used to overcome the potential problem of non-convex clusters, starting with larger number of clusters and merging them to the optimal numbers using human intervention. The clustering was performed using the fastcluster [31] R package. Due to the data volume (the data set that was used to calculate the dissimilarity matrix of 5842 signals comprised more than 100 million items), computations were accelerated by parallelizing the data loading process and calculating the dissimilarity matrix in GPU (Graphical Processing Unit), using the R packages of doParallel [33], foreach [34] for parallel execution and the rpud [35] package for the dissimilarity matrix calculation. Data loading was found to be limiting, taking 157 s. for 5842 signals, suggesting that data size reduction may need to be added to the pre-processing phase. Data processing was completed by copying the .csv and .png files belonging to different clusters into separate folders for further use.

As a result of the process described above, it was possible to identify and cluster those distinct signal patterns that deviate from the normal behavior of the equipment (Fig. 4). Approximately 10% of the data fell into this category of abnormal behavior, that is typical for many machine learning problems [36]. Patterns displaying abnormal behavior were further analyzed using equipment log files, trying to determine the possible reasons for the differences. The output of the data processing: different signal patterns stored in separate folders will be used in the following phase of the research to build a sample dataset (training and test) for a predictive analytical model.

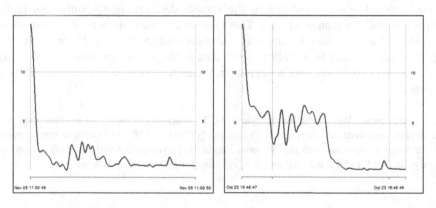

**Fig. 4.** Signal pattern of a reciprocating cycle indicating normal and defective behavior

# 4 Conclusion

Smart manufacturing pays a particular attention to real-time data collection and conversion through physical and computational processes; data became a key enabler for supporting manufacturing competitiveness, it has a strategic importance. Data driven applications could serve different purposes; among others, they could help monitoring operations, predicting malfunctions or supporting smart maintenance. This paper presented an approach of monitoring the behavior of pneumatic actuators through signal processing using a real-world data set. This approach could be applied to monitoring other types of equipment, where the shape and the pattern of a signal collected from the equipment carries valuable information about its status and condition. Data was collected from a Hungarian multinational manufacturer of electrical components during 2018–2019. The presented signal pre-processing steps enabled to scan through large amounts of data to identify, classify and group signals displaying different (normal or faulty) behavior of the equipment. The signal patterns were stored as .png and .csv files, to be used in the next phase of the research building a predictive analytical model. Being able to visually examine the data storing as it was also stored as .png picture files were found particularly useful to quickly analyze different patterns. In addition, equipment log files were used to determine the potential reasons of signal patterns deviating from normal behavior. Our research used real-world data unlike the test bench environment for sensor fault detection in hydraulic systems of Helwig et al. [2] or the experimental environment-based fault diagnosis approach of Al Tobi et al. [26].

The next phase of the research will focus on the preparation of a predictive analytical model of equipment failure aiming at identifying the malfunctions of the pneumatic actuator in advance and developing an early warning system. Data volume remains a challenge, therefore optimizing data processing and reducing data size may be required. Machine learning, artificial neural networks or deep learning methods are considered for developing this predictive analytical model, all require sufficient amount of training and test data sets. Clustering helps preparing the training and test data sets for the next phase of the research. One of the key challenges related to the predictive analytical model is the imbalance in the sample data set: significantly less faulty patterns are available than good ones. There are several methods in the literature about managing imbalanced sample data sets, amongst other SMOTE [37], or ADASYN [38], however our aim is to collect more data belonging to the minority of faulty patterns through additional data collection and scanning using the process described in this paper.

**Acknowledgement.** We would like to thank TE Connectivity Hungary to provide data and being able to participate in their research. Project no. NKFIH-869-10/2019 has been implemented with the support provided from the National Research, Development and Innovation Fund of Hungary, financed under the Tématerületi Kiválósági Program funding scheme.

# References

1. Tao, F., Qi, Q., Liu, A., Kusiak, A.: Data-driven smart manufacturing. J. Manuf. Syst. **48**, 157–169 (2018). https://doi.org/10.1016/j.jmsy.2018.01.006
2. Helwig, N., Pignanelli, E., Schütze, A.: Detecting and compensating sensor faults in a hydraulic condition monitoring system. In: Proceedings Sensor, pp. 641–646 (2015). https://doi.org/10.5162/sensor2015/D8.1
3. Sharma, A.B., Golubchik, L., Govindan, R.: Sensor faults: detection methods and prevalence in real-world datasets. ACM Trans. Sens. Netw. **6**, 1–39 (2010). https://doi.org/10.1145/1754414.1754419
4. Yin, S., Kaynak, O.: Big data for modern industry: challenges and trends. Proc. IEEE **103**, 143–146 (2015). https://doi.org/10.1109/JPROC.2015.2388958
5. O'Donovan, P., Leahy, K., Bruton, K., O'Sullivan, D.T.J.: An industrial big data pipeline for data-driven analytics maintenance applications in large-scale smart manufacturing facilities. J. Big Data **2**, 1–26 (2015). https://doi.org/10.1186/s40537-015-0034-z
6. Gandomi, A., Haider, M.: Beyond the hype: big data concepts, methods, and analytics. Int. J. Inf. Manage. **35**, 137–144 (2015). https://doi.org/10.1016/j.ijinfomgt.2014.10.007

7. Pham, D.T., Afify, A.A.: Machine-learning techniques and their applications in manufacturing. Proc. Inst. Mech. Eng. Part B J. Eng. Manuf. **219**, 395–412 (2005). https://doi.org/10.1243/095440505X32274

8. Graham, J.W.: Missing Data. Springer, New York (2012). https://doi.org/10.1007/978-1-4614-4018-5

9. Kabacoff, R.I.: Advanced methods for missing data. In: R in Action Data Analysis and Graphics with R. Manning Publications Co., p. 472 (2011)

10. Piddington, C., Pegram, M.: An IMS test case - global manufacturing. In: Proceedings of the IFIP TC5/WG5.7 Fifth International Conference on Advances in Production Management Systems. North-Holland Publishing Co., Amsterdam, The Netherlands, pp. 11–20 (1993)

11. Samuel, A.L.: Some studies in machine learning using the game of checkers. II—recent progress. IBM J. Res. Dev. **11**, 601–617 (1967). https://doi.org/10.1147/rd.116.0601

12. Wuest, T., Weimer, D., Irgens, C., Thoben, K.-D.: Machine learning in manufacturing: advantages, challenges, and applications. Prod. Manuf. Res. **4**, 23–45 (2016). https://doi.org/10.1080/21693277.2016.1192517

13. Sammut, C., Webb, G.I.: Encyclopedia of Machine Learning. Springer, Boston (2010). https://doi.org/10.1007/978-0-387-30164-8

14. Schwabacher, M., Goebel, K.: A survey of artificial intelligence for prognostics. In: AAAI Fall Symposium, pp. 107–114 (2007)

15. Byington, C.S., Watson, M., Edwards, D., Dunkin, B.: In-line health monitoring system for hydraulic pumps and motors. In: 2003 IEEE Aerospace Conference Proceedings (Cat. No. 03TH8652). IEEE, pp. 3279–3287 (2003)

16. Hansson, K., Yella, S., Dougherty, M., Fleyeh, H.: Machine learning algorithms in heavy process manufacturing. Am. J. Intell. Syst. **6**, 1–13 (2016). https://doi.org/10.5923/j.ajis.20160601.01

17. Lin, W.-C., Tsai, C.-F., Hu, Y.-H., Jhang, J.-S.: Clustering-based undersampling in class-imbalanced data. Inf. Sci. **409–410**, 17–26 (2017). https://doi.org/10.1016/j.ins.2017.05.008

18. Lei, Y., Jia, F., Lin, J., et al.: An intelligent fault diagnosis method using unsupervised feature learning towards mechanical big data. IEEE Trans. Industr. Electron. **63**, 3137–3147 (2016)

19. Worden, K., Staszewski, W.J., Hensman, J.J.: Natural computing for mechanical systems research: a tutorial overview. Mech. Syst. Signal Process. **25**, 4–111 (2011)

20. Shatnawi, Y., Al-Khassaweneh, M.: Fault diagnosis in internal combustion engines using extension neural network. IEEE Trans. Industr. Electron. **61**, 1434–1443 (2013)

21. You, D., Gao, X., Katayama, S.: WPD-PCA-based laser welding process monitoring and defects diagnosis by using FNN and SVM. IEEE Trans. Industr. Electron. **62**, 628–636 (2014)

22. Lei, Y., He, Z., Zi, Y., Chen, X.: New clustering algorithm-based fault diagnosis using compensation distance evaluation technique. Mech. Syst. Signal Process. **22**, 419–435 (2008)

23. Yin, S., Ding, S.X., Xie, X., Luo, H.: A review on basic data-driven approaches for industrial process monitoring. IEEE Trans. Industr. Electron. **61**, 6418–6428 (2014)

24. Fassois, S.D., Sakellariou, J.S.: Time-series methods for fault detection and identification in vibrating structures. Philos. Trans. R. Soc. Lond. Ser. A. Math. Phys. Eng. Sciences **365**, 411–448 (2007). https://doi.org/10.1098/rsta.2006.1929

25. Munirathinam, S., Ramadoss, B.: Big data predictive analtyics for proactive semiconductor equipment maintenance. In: 2014 IEEE International Conference on Big Data (Big Data), pp. 893–902 (2014)

26. Al Tobi, M.A.S., Bevan, G., Ramachandran, K.P., et al.: Experimental set-up for investigation of fault diagnosis of a centrifugal pump. World Acad. Sci. Eng. Technol. Int. J. Mech. Aerosp. Ind. Mechatron. Manuf. Eng. **11**, 470–474 (2017)
27. Bardou, O., Sidahmed, M.: Early detection of leakages in the exhaust and discharge systems of reciprocating machines by vibration analysis. Mech. Syst. Signal Process. **8**, 551–570 (1994). https://doi.org/10.1006/mssp.1994.1039
28. R Development Core Team R: A Language and Environment for Statistical Computing (2008)
29. Ulrich, J.M., Ryan, J.A., Bennett, R., Joy, C.: R package 'xts' (2018)
30. Cleveland, R.B., Cleveland, W.S., McRae, J.E., Terpenning, I.: STL: a seasonal-trend decomposition procedure based on loess. J. Official Stat. **6**, 3–73 (1990)
31. Müllner, D.: Fastcluster: fast hierarchical, agglomerative clustering routines for R and Python. J. Stat. Softw. **53** (2015). https://doi.org/10.18637/jss.v053.i09
32. Ward, J.H.J.: Hierarchical grouping to optimize an objective function. J. Am. Stat. Assoc. **58**, 236–244 (1963). https://doi.org/10.1080/01621459.1963.10500845
33. Calaway, R., Tenenbaum, D., Microsoft, Weston S.: R package: doParallel (2018). https://cran.r-project.org/package=doParallel
34. Calaway, R., Microsoft, Weston S.: R package: foreach (2017). https://cran.r-project.org/package=foreach
35. Yau, C.: R package: rpud GPU computation in R (2018)
36. Weiss, G.M.: Imbalanced Learning: Foundations, Algorithms, and Applications: Foundations of Imbalanced Learning, pp. 13–41 (2012)
37. Chawla, N.V., Bowyer, K.W., Hall, L.O., Kegelmeyer, W.P.: SMOTE: synthetic minority over-sampling technique nitesh. J. Artif. Intell. Res. **16**, 321–357 (2002). https://doi.org/10.1613/jair.953
38. He, H., Bai, Y., Garcia, E.A., Li, S. ADASYN: adaptive synthetic sampling approach for imbalanced learning. In: 2008 IEEE International Joint Conference on Neural Networks (IEEE World Congress on Computational Intelligence), pp. 1322–1328 (2008)

# A Comparative Study of the Use of Coresets for Clustering Large Datasets

Nguyen Le Hoang, Tran Khanh Dang$^{(\boxtimes)}$, and Le Hong Trang

Faculty of Computer Sicence and Engineering,
Ho Chi Minh City University of Technology, VNU-HCM, 268 Ly Thuong Kiet,
District 10, Ho Chi Minh City, Vietnam
nlhoang1203@gmail.com, {khanh,lhtrang}@hcmut.edu.vn

**Abstract.** Coresets can be described as a compact subset such that models trained on coresets will also provide a good fit with models trained on full data set. By using coresets, we can scale down a big data to a tiny one in order to reduce the computational cost of a machine learning problem. In recent years, data scientists have investigated various methods to create coresets. The two state-of-the-art algorithms have been proposed in 2018 are ProTraS by Ros & Guillaume and Lightweight Coreset by Bachem et al. In this paper, we briefly introduce these two algorithms and make a comparison between them to find out the benefits and drawbacks of each one.

**Keywords:** Big data · Coresets · Clustering · $k$-mcans · $k$-median

## 1 Introduction

Dealing with big data problems need to overcome challenges such as big amount in volume, variety, and velocity. Many methods have been proposed for several years to deal with big data. A common approach is based on high performance computing models. This, however, is not always available. Another option is finding suitable algorithms to reduce the computational complexity from large size datasets that may contain billions of data points. The idea of finding a relevant subset from original data to decrease the computational cost brings scientists to the concept of coreset, which was first applied in geometric approximation by Agarwal et al. in 2004 [1,2]. The problem of coreset constructions for $k$-median and $k$-means clustering was then stated and investigated by Har-Peled et al. in [3,4].

In recent years, many coreset construction algorithms have been proposed for a wide variety of clustering problems. These research always try to find good algorithms that create samples that are more correct or being faster. Even though there are many investigations about this, the two most current state-of-the-art that fascinates us are the lightweight coreset by Bachem et al. [5,6] and ProTraS algorithm by Ros and Guillaume [11]. The lightweight coreset concept defines a new type of coreset in which generated samples provide a good fit with full data

© Springer Nature Switzerland AG 2019
T. K. Dang et al. (Eds.): FDSE 2019, LNCS 11814, pp. 45–55, 2019.
https://doi.org/10.1007/978-3-030-35653-8_4

set for $k$-means clustering. The ProTraS, in the other hand, is a algorithm based on the farthes-first-traversal algorithm that also creates coresets of a data. In this paper, we make a comparison between these two algorithms and discuss the advantages as well as the disadvantages of each method.

The rest of this paper is organized as follows. In Sect. 2, we discuss some related works and background used in this paper, we also introduce briefly about Lightweight Coreset and ProTraS algorithm with improved process by Trang et al. [13] in this section. We do experiments, comparisons and discussions by using relative error in Sect. 3. We end this paper by the conclusion in Sect. 4 of this paper.

## 2    Background and Related Works

### 2.1    $k$-clustering

$k$-means clustering is a popular method, originally from signal processing, for cluster analysis in data mining. The standard algorithm was first proposed by S. Lloyd of Bell Labs in 1957, and was published later in 1982 [14]. The algorithm was then developed by Inaba et al. [15], Vega et al. [16], Matousek [17], or the $k$-Means++ by Arthur and Vassilvitskii in [20]. $k$-median clustering is a variation of $k$-means where instead of calculating the mean for each cluster to determine its centroid, one instead calculates the median. There are also plenty research about this algorithm such as Arora [18], Charikar et al. [19], etc. In this paper, we refer $k$-clustering for both $k$-median and $k$-means. The $k$-clustering problems can be stated as follows. Let $X \subset \mathbb{R}^d$, the $k$-clustering problems are to find $Q \subset \mathbb{R}^d$ with $|Q| = k$ such that these functions are minimized

$$\phi_X(Q) = \sum_{x \in X} d(x, Q) = \sum_{x \in X} \min_{q \in Q} ||x - q|| \text{ and} \tag{1}$$

$$\phi_X(Q) = \sum_{x \in X} d(x, Q)^2 = \sum_{x \in X} \min_{q \in Q} ||x - q||^2, \tag{2}$$

where (1) and (2) are for $k$-median and $k$-means, respectively.

### 2.2    Coresets for $k$-clustering and ProTraS Algorithm

**Coresets for $k$-Clustering.** If the data set $X$ mentioned above is big enough, it is hard and expensive to solve these $k$-median and $k$-means problems properly. Therefore, instead of solving on $X$, one of the classical techniques is the extraction of small amount information from the given data, and performing the computation on this extracted subset. However, in many circumstances, it is not easy to find this most relevant subset. Consequently, attention has shifted to developing approximation algorithms. The goal now is to compute an $(1+\varepsilon)$-approximation subset, for some $0 < \varepsilon < 1$. The framework of coresets has recently emerged as a general approach to achieve this goal [2]. The definition of coresets for $k$-clustering can be stated as follows.

---

**Algorithm 1.** ProTraS [11]

---

**Require:** $P = \{x_i\}$, for $i = 1, 2, \ldots, n$, a tolerance $\epsilon > 0$.
**Ensure:** A sample $S = \{y_j\}$ and $P(y_j)$, for $j = 1, 2, \ldots, s$.
1: Initialize a pattern $x_{init} \in P$.
2: $y_1 = x_{init}, P(y_1) = \{y_1\}, S = \{y_1\}$, and $s = 1$.
3: **repeat**
4:    **for all** $x_i \in P \setminus S$ **do**
5:       $y_k = \arg\min_{y_j \in S} d(x_l, y_j)$.
6:       $P(y_k) = P(y_k) \cup \{x_l\}$.
7:    **end for**
8:    $maxWD = cost = 0$.
9:    **for all** $y_k \in S$ **do**
10:       $x_{max}(y_k) = \arg\max_{x_i \in P(y_k)} d(x_i, y_k)$.
11:       $d_{max}(y_k) = d(x_{max}(y_k), y_k)$.
12:       $p_k = |P(y_k)| d_{max}(y_k)$.
13:       **if** $p_k > maxWD$ **then**
14:          $maxWD = p_k$.
15:          $y^* = y_k$.
16:       **end if**
17:       $cost = cost + p_k/n$.
18:    **end for**
19:    $x^* = x_{max}(y^*)$.
20:    $S = S \cup \{x^*\}$ and $s = s + 1$.
21:    $P(y^*) = \{x^*\}$.
22: **until** $cost < \epsilon$
23: **return** $S$ and $P(y_j)$, for $j = 1, 2, \ldots, s$.

---

**Definition 1.** *Let $\varepsilon > 0$, the weighted set $C$ is a $(k, \varepsilon)$- coreset of $X$ if for any $Q \subset \mathbb{R}^d$ of cardinality at most $k$,*

$$|\phi_X(Q) - \phi_C(Q)| \le \varepsilon\phi_X(Q). \tag{3}$$

We also note that (3) can be rewritten as

$$(1 - \varepsilon)\phi_X(Q) \le \phi_C(Q) \le (1 + \varepsilon)\phi_X(Q).$$

**ProTraS Algorithm.** Some coreset construction algorithms have been proposed in recent years for clustering problems. Most of existing methods are based on sampling or exponential grids. In 2017, Ros and Guillaume proposed DENDIS [9] and DIDES [10] which are based on the farthest-first-traversal (*fft*) principle. These are iterative algorithms based on the hybridization of distance and density concepts. They differ in the priority given to distance or density, and in the stopping criterion defined accordingly. Later, the authors proposed a better algorithm called ProTraS [11] which is both easy to tune and scalable. ProTraS is given in Algorithm 1 Later, Trang et al. in [12,13] introduced an improvement for ProTraS. The idea of this improvement is the post-processing task of ProTraS by replacing a representative in the sample obtained by Pro-TraS by the center of the group represented by it. Thereby, objects located at the boundary side of clusters will be replaced by interior ones of those. The new obtained sample thus has separated clusters. This helps to improve the quality of clustering process. The detail of this improvement algorithm is given in Algorithm 2.

---

**Algorithm 2.** Coreset-based algorithm for sampling [13]

---

**Require:** $P = \{x_i\}$, for $i = 1, 2, \ldots, n$, a tolerance $\epsilon > 0$.
**Ensure:** A sample $S = \{y_j\}$ and $P(y_j)$, for $j = 1, 2, \ldots, s$.
1:
2: Call ProTraS for $P$ and $\epsilon$ to obtain $S = \{y_j\}$ and $P(y_j)$.
3: $S' = \emptyset$.
4: **for all** $y_j \in S$ **do**
5:     **if** $|P(y_j)|$ is greater than a threshold **then**
6:         $y_k^* = \arg\min_{y_k \in P(y_j)} \sum_{y_l \in P(y_j)} d(y_k, y_l)$.
7:         $S' = S' \cup \{y_k^*\}$.
8:     **end if**
9: **end for**
10: $S = S'$.
11: **return** $S$ and $P(y_j^*)$, for $j = 1, 2, \ldots, s'$, where $s' \leq s$.

---

### 2.3   Lightweight Coresets

**Lightweight Coresets for $k$-Clustering.** In inequality 3 of Coresets, the right term $\varepsilon\phi_X(Q)$ allows the approximation error to scale with the quantization error as well as to include both the additive and multiplicative errors. Bachem et at in [5] interpret and split these errors that lead to the definition of Lightweight Coresets as follows.

**Definition 2.** *Let $\varepsilon > 0$ and $k \in \mathbb{N}$. Let $X \subset \mathbb{R}^d$ be a set of points with mean $\mu(X)$. The weighted set $C$ is an $(\varepsilon, k)$-lightweight coreset of $X$ if for any set $Q \subset \mathbb{R}^d$ of cardinality at most $k$,*

$$|\phi_X(Q) - \phi_C(Q)| \leq \frac{\varepsilon}{2}\phi_X(Q) + \frac{\varepsilon}{2}\phi_X(\{\mu(X)\}) \tag{4}$$

In (4), the $\frac{\varepsilon}{2}\phi_X(Q)$ term allows the approximation error to scale with the quantization error and constitutes the multiplicative part; while the $\frac{\varepsilon}{2}\phi_X(\{\mu(X)\})$ term scales with the variance of the data and corresponds to the additive approximation error term that is invariant of the scale of the data.

Even though there are differences in definitions between Coresets and Lightweight Coresets, Bachem et al. in [5] have shown that as we decrease $\varepsilon$, the true cost of the optimal solution obtained on the lightweight coreset approaches the true cost of the optimal solution on the full data set in an additive manner.

**Construction of Lightweight Coresets.** The construction is based on importance sampling. Let $q(x)$ be any probability distribution on $X$ and $Q$ any set of $k$ centers in $\mathbb{R}^d$. The quantization error can be approximated by sampling $m$ points from $X$ using $q(x)$ and assigning them weights inversely proportional to $q(x)$. The $q(x)$ is defined as follows:

$$q(x) = \frac{1}{2} \frac{1}{|X|} + \frac{1}{2} \frac{d(x, \mu(X))^2}{\sum_{x' \in X} d(x', \mu(X))^2}.$$

The construction for lightweight coreset is described as in Algorithm 3.

---

**Algorithm 3.** Lightweight Coreset [5]

---

**Require:** Set of data points $X$, coreset size $m$
**Ensure:** Lightweight Coreset $C$
1: $\mu \leftarrow$ mean of X
2: **for all** $x \in X$ **do**
3:     $q(x) \leftarrow \frac{1}{2} \frac{1}{|X|} + \frac{1}{2} \frac{d(x, \mu)^2}{\sum_{x' \in X} d(x', \mu)^2}$
4: **end for**
5: $C \leftarrow$ sample points from where each point is sampled with probability and has weight $w_x = \frac{1}{m \cdot q(x)}$
6: **return** lightweight coreset $C$

---

# 3 Comparative Results

## 3.1 Experiment Setup

In this section, we compare the samples obtained from lightweight coreset in Algorithm 3 and from the improvement of ProTraS in Algorithm 2. We use 15 datasets from data clustering repository of the computing school of Eastern Finland University[1], and from GitHub clustering benchmark[2]. These datasets are described in Table 1. We display some data examples in Fig. 1. We compare three different subsampling methods:

- Uniform Sampling: a naive approach to coreset constructions which is based on uniform sub-sampling of the data. This may be regarded as the baseline since it is commonly used in practice.
- Lightweight Coreset: the method mentioned in Algorithm 3. The idea is to perform importance sampling where data point is sampled with probability $\frac{1}{2}$ uniformly at random or with probability $\frac{1}{2}$ proportional to its squared distance to the mean of the data.
- Improved ProTraS: this is described in Algorithm 2. The idea is based on ProTraS with the post-processing to improve the correctness.

**Table 1.** Datasets for experiments

| Data ID | Name | Size | No. of clusters |
|---------|------|------|-----------------|
| D1 | Flame | 240 | 2 |
| D2 | Jain | 373 | 2 |
| D3 | Aggregation | 788 | 7 |
| D4 | R15 | 600 | 15 |
| D5 | D31 | 3,100 | 31 |
| D6 | Unbalance | 6,500 | 8 |
| D7 | A1 | 3,000 | 20 |
| D8 | A2 | 5,250 | 35 |
| D9 | A3 | 7,500 | 50 |
| D10 | S1 | 5,000 | 15 |
| D11 | S2 | 5,000 | 15 |
| D12 | S3 | 5,000 | 15 |
| D13 | S4 | 5,000 | 15 |
| D14 | t4.8k | 8,000 | 6 |
| D15 | Birch3 | 100,000 | 100 |

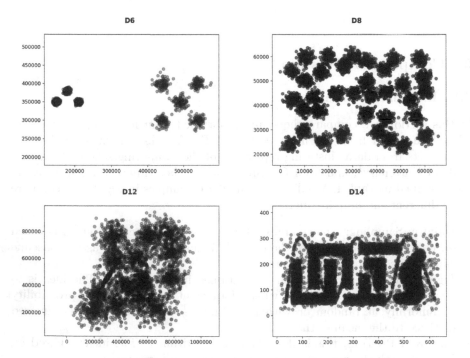

**Fig. 1.** Some datasets for experiments

These three algorithms need different input parameters, Algorithms 1 and 2 need the value of $\varepsilon$ while Algorithm 3 and the uniform sampling need sample size as input. Therefore, we first run Algorithm 1 and postprocessing in Algorithm 2 with $\varepsilon = 0.1$ and $\varepsilon = 0.2$, then we use the sample size of this first step results as the input parameter for lightweight coreset and uniform sampling. The experiment for each data set is described as follows:

1. Step 1. Use kmeans++ [20] to cluster the full data set
2. Step 2. Generate coreset by improved ProTraS in [12]
   (a) Step 2.1. Apply Algorithm 1 to full data set
   (b) Step 2.2. Apply Algorithm 2 to the sample from step 2.1
3. Step 3. With the coreset size from step 2, we generate sample by uniform sampling
4. Step 4. With the coreset size from step 2, we generate sample for lightweight coreset by Algorithm 3
5. Step 5. Use kmeans++ to solve the $k$-means clustering problem on each subsample.
6. Step 6. We measure the elapsed time and compute the relative error for each method and subsample size compared to the full solution from step 1.

Since the experiments of uniform sampling and lightweight coresets are randomized, we run them 20 times with different random seeds and compute sample averages. All experiments were implemented in Python and run on an Intel Core i7 machine with $8 \times 2.8$ GHz processors and 16 GB memory.

**Table 2.** Experiment Results - Relative Error Values

| DataID | $\varepsilon = 0.1$ | | | | $\varepsilon = 0.2$ | | | |
|--------|------|---------|-------------|-------------|------|---------|-------------|-------------|
|        | Size | Uniform | Algorithm 2 | Algorithm 3 | Size | Uniform | Algorithm 2 | Algorithm 3 |
| D1  | 166  | 0.0021 | 0.0007 | 0.0128 | 90   | 0.0509 | 0.0246 | 0.0852 |
| D2  | 108  | 0.0265 | 0.0272 | 0.0852 | 56   | 0.0662 | 0.0136 | 0.1696 |
| D3  | 202  | 0.0524 | 0.0256 | 0.2205 | 130  | 0.2217 | 0.0030 | 0.1396 |
| D4  | 184  | 0.0681 | 0.5659 | 0.1080 | 97   | 0.4483 | 0.5308 | 0.5478 |
| D5  | 851  | 0.0337 | 0.0247 | 0.0261 | 329  | 0.2440 | 0.2821 | 0.0173 |
| D6  | 176  | 0.1815 | 0.0369 | 0.0711 | 89   | 0.3412 | 0.1132 | 0.6877 |
| D7  | 261  | 0.1180 | 0.2564 | 0.1704 | 97   | 0.7396 | 0.7936 | 0.7588 |
| D8  | 315  | 0.0754 | 0.3161 | 0.1063 | 116  | 0.5928 | 0.4947 | 0.3260 |
| D9  | 341  | 0.3194 | 0.4441 | 0.3290 | 119  | 1.4656 | 1.5380 | 1.2776 |
| D10 | 237  | 0.5862 | 0.0241 | 0.6890 | 96   | 0.7154 | 1.5268 | 1.5437 |
| D11 | 327  | 0.1780 | 0.1596 | 0.1513 | 120  | 0.6766 | 0.2340 | 0.6150 |
| D12 | 422  | 0.0466 | 0.1804 | 0.0581 | 155  | 0.4842 | 0.2953 | 0.3965 |
| D13 | 448  | 0.1020 | 0.3030 | 0.1967 | 166  | 0.2308 | 0.2725 | 0.1273 |
| D14 | 1532 | 0.0084 | 0.0153 | 0.0552 | 1126 | 0.0562 | 0.0300 | 0.0341 |
| D15 | 424  | 0.4662 | 0.5454 | 0.4869 | 153  | 0.1144 | 0.8543 | 0.8621 |

---

[1] https://cs.joensuu.fi/sipu/datasets.
[2] https://github.com/deric/clustering-benchmark.

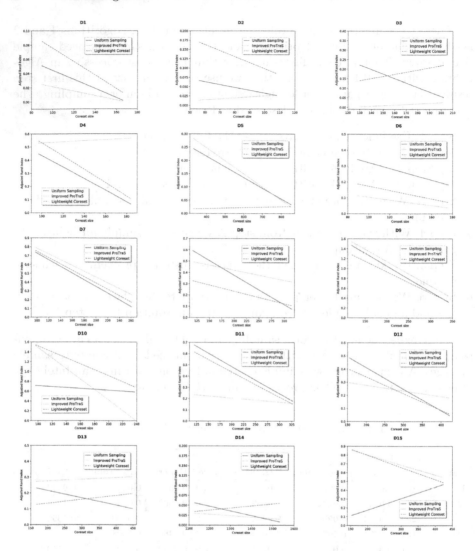

**Fig. 2.** Relative error in relation to subsample size

## 3.2 Results and Discussion

In the experiments, we compare three coreset construction methods: uniform sampling as the baseline, lightweight coreset and ProTraS with the post-processing improvements. We use relative error as the measurement for correctness and the run-time comparison. The results are expressed as follows.

– The relative errors are shown in Table 2. For each $\varepsilon = 0.1$ and $\varepsilon = 0.2$ of ProTraS, we have the relative errors for Uniform sampling (denoted as $Uniform$), the improved ProTraS (denoted as $Algorithm2$) and lightweight coreset (denoted as $Algorithm3$). For this type of measurement, method with

**Table 3.** Experiment Results - Runtime (in second(s)) of each sample

| DataID | $\varepsilon = 0.1$ | | | | $\varepsilon = 0.2$ | | | |
| | Size | Uniform | Algorithm 2 | Algorithm 3 | Size | Uniform | Algorithm 2 | Algorithm 3 |
|---|---|---|---|---|---|---|---|---|
| D1 | 166 | 0.0004 | 88 | 0.0006 | 90 | 0.0003 | 18 | 0.0004 |
| D2 | 108 | 0.0003 | 50 | 0.0007 | 56 | 0.0002 | 10 | 0.0003 |
| D3 | 202 | 0.0004 | 533 | 0.0006 | 130 | 0.0003 | 164 | 0.0004 |
| D4 | 184 | 0.0003 | 319 | 0.0006 | 97 | 0.0003 | 59 | 0.0004 |
| D5 | 851 | 0.0005 | 129040 | 0.0009 | 329 | 0.0003 | 8300 | 0.0006 |
| D6 | 176 | 0.0003 | 3091 | 0.0010 | 89 | 0.0004 | 500 | 0.0009 |
| D7 | 261 | 0.0003 | 4290 | 0.0008 | 97 | 0.0002 | 294 | 0.0006 |
| D8 | 315 | 0.0003 | 12776 | 0.0009 | 116 | 0.0003 | 806 | 0.0007 |
| D9 | 341 | 0.0004 | 23068 | 0.0012 | 119 | 0.0002 | 1234 | 0.0010 |
| D10 | 237 | 0.0004 | 5804 | 0.0009 | 96 | 0.0003 | 501 | 0.0008 |
| D11 | 327 | 0.0003 | 14343 | 0.0010 | 120 | 0.0003 | 895 | 0.0007 |
| D12 | 422 | 0.0003 | 29844 | 0.0009 | 155 | 0.0003 | 1789 | 0.0007 |
| D13 | 448 | 0.0004 | 32860 | 0.0009 | 166 | 0.0003 | 1983 | 0.0009 |
| D14 | 1532 | 0.0007 | 1928116 | 0.0015 | 1126 | 0.0006 | 775071 | 0.0012 |
| D15 | 424 | 0.0028 | 559332 | 0.0116 | 153 | 0.0011 | 32183 | 0.0095 |

smaller value is a better method. To make this comparison visually appealing and easier to read, we use graphs shown in Fig. 2.

Figure 2 shows that the approximation error decreases for all methods as the sample size is decreased. In most cases, these three methods seem to have similar relative errors. In fact, the improved ProTraS has smaller values than others, hence, this method can be considered to create a better coreset. The uniform sampling, surprisingly, has relative errors smaller than the lightweight coreset in most cases. However, this is understandable since the coreset size in these experiments is too small compared to the quantity of full data.

- The time comparison is shown in Table 3. This measurement is estimated in second (s) unit. It is obviously that the improved ProTraS is much more slower than the other. ProTraS is built based on the farther-first-traversal algorithm in which the points are selected sequently and need executing points by points while the uniform sampling and lightweight coreset both are based on sampling method which is extremely fast.

## 4 Conclusions

In this paper, we introduce the two state-of-the-art coreset constructions, the lightweight coreset [5] and the ProTraS algorithm [11] with post-processing improvement [12]. We use relative error to compare these two methods along with uniform sampling as the baseline.

Even though ProTraS and its improvement defeat other methods in the experiments, the speed of ProTraS is a big concern when comparing to other sampling-based methods. This method needs a lot of computation to create coreset, that's why it is very slow.

In the other hand, the lightweight coreset completed all experiment at a glance, however, the correctness of the created-sample is still a big problem. Since this is sampling-based method, we need to check the probability that the result is good enough or not.

Finally, each method mentioned in this paper has its own advantages and disadvantages. The options 'Slow but more accuracy' or 'Fast but less correct' will be weighed before applying any of these algorithms in practice.

**Acknowledgment.** This work is supported by a project with the Department of Science and Technology, Ho Chi Minh City, Vietnam (contract with HCMUT No. 42/2019/HD-QPTKHCN, dated 11/7/2019).

# References

1. Agarwal, P.K., Procopiuc, C.M., Varadarajan, K.R.: Approximating extent measures of points. J. ACM (JACM) **51**(4), 606–635 (2004)
2. Agarwal, P.K., Procopiuc, C.M., Varadarajan, K.R.: Geometric approximation via coresets. Comb. Comput. Geom. **52**, 1–30 (2005)
3. Har-Peled, S., Kushal, A.: Smaller coresets for $k$-median and $k$-means clustering. In: Symposium on Computational Geometry (SoCG), pp. 126–134. ACM (2005)
4. Har-Peled, S., Mazumdar, S.: On coresets for $k$-means and $k$-median clustering. In: Symposium on Theory of Computing (STOC), pp. 291–300. ACM (2004)
5. Bachem, O., Lucic, M., Krause, A.: Scalable and distributed clustering via lightweight Coresets. In: International Conference on Knowledge Discovery and Data Mining (KDD) (2018)
6. Bachem, O., Lucic, M., Krause, A.: Practical Coreset constructions for machine learning. arXiv preprint (2017)
7. Phan, T.N., Dang, T.K.: A lightweight indexing approach for efficient batch similarity processing with MapReduce. SN Comput. Sci. **1**(1) (2020)
8. Dang, T.K., Tran, K.T.K.: The meeting of acquaintances: a cost-efficient authentication scheme for light-weight objects with transient trust level and plurality approach. Secur. Commun. Netw. (2019)
9. Ros, F., Guillaume, S.: DENDIS: a new density-based sampling for clustering algorithm. In: Expert Systems with Applications, vol. 56, pp. 349–359 (2016)
10. Ros, F., Guillaume, S.: DIDES: a fast and effective sampling for clustering algorithm. In: Knowledge and Information Systems, vol. 50, pp. 543–568 (2017)
11. Ros, F., Guillaume, S.: ProTraS: a probabilistic traversing sampling algorithm. In: Expert Systems with Applications, vol. 105, pp. 65–76 (2018)
12. Trang, L.H., Van Ngoan, P., Van Duc, N.: A sample-based algorithm for visual assessment of cluster tendency (VAT) with large datasets. In: Dang, T.K., Küng, J., Wagner, R., Thoai, N., Takizawa, M. (eds.) FDSE 2018. LNCS, vol. 11251, pp. 145–157. Springer, Cham (2018). https://doi.org/10.1007/978-3-030-03192-3_11
13. Trang, L.H., Bangui, H., Ge, M., Buhnova, B.: Scaling big data applications in smart city with Coresets. In: Proceedings of the 8th International Conference on Data Science, Technology and Applications (DATA 2019), pp. 357–363 (2019)
14. Lloyd, S.P.: Least squares quantization in PCM. IEEE Trans. Inf. Theor. **28**, 129–137 (1982)

15. Inaba, M., Katoh, N., Imai, H.: Applications of weighted Voronoi diagrams and randomization to variance-based $k$-clustering. In: Proceeding of 10th Annual Symposium on Computational Geometry, pp. 332–339 (1994)
16. de la Vega, W.F., Karpinski, M., Kenyon, C., Rabani, Y.: Approximation schemes for clustering problems. In: Proceedings of the 35th Annual ACM Symposium on Theory of Computing, pp. 50–58 (2003)
17. Matousek, J.: On approximate geometric $k$-clustering. Discrete Comput. Geom. **24**, 61–84 (2000)
18. Arora, S.: Polynomial time approximation schemes for Euclidean traveling salesman and other geometric problems. J. Assoc. Comput. Mach. **45**(5), 753–782 (1998)
19. Charikar, M., O'Callaghan, L., Panigrahy, R.: Better streaming algorithms for clustering problems. In: Proceedings of the 35th Annual ACM Symposium on Theory of Computing, pp. 30–39 (2003)
20. Arthur, D., Vassilvitskii, S.: $k$-means++: the advantages of careful seeding. In: Proceedings of the Eighteenth Annual ACM-SIAM Symposium on Discrete Algorithms, pp. 1027–1035 (2007)

# Leakage Classification Based on Improved Kullback-Leibler Separation in Water Pipelines

Thi Ngoc Tu Luong and Jong-Myon Kim[✉]

Department of Computer Engineering, University of Ulsan, Ulsan, Korea
ngtu.mta@gmail.com, jmkim07@ulsan.ac.kr

**Abstract.** One of the least difficult, quickest, and most useful strategies for the characteristic selection of real applications such as leak detection systems is the selection method based on Kullback-Leibler divergence. Nevertheless, this technique has issues when the preparation dataset is not sufficiently expansive. This paper proposes an improvement on this method to overcome its limitations. The assessment results show that the proposed strategy is steadier, more dependable, and has higher precision than the original technique.

**Keywords:** Acoustic emissions · Leakage classification · Kullback-Leibler divergence

## 1 Introduction

Regularly, 20–30% of the water in a water circulation framework is lost, and some frameworks may lose as much as 50% [1]. Therefore, leakage in water supply pipelines is an issue of increasing interest because of its related budgetary expense from wasting resources as well as its capacity to act as an entrance for contaminants into the treated water system.

Numerous strategies have been proposed for leak identification in water pipelines, including visual examination, electromagnetic techniques, acoustic techniques, ultrasound techniques, radiographic techniques, and thermography techniques [2]. Recently, acoustic emission (AE) methods have been shown to be an amazing instrument for on-line leak discovery given the way that the leakage can discharge elastic energy as a type of transient pressure waves and produce signs representative of irregular AE occurrences [3]. Numerous endeavors have been made to examine the acoustic characteristics of a leakage source, spreading attributes of acoustic waves along pipelines, and the connection of AE signals with various parameters like leakage rate, material and geometric properties of pipelines, propagating distance, working conditions, and so forth [4–10]. Compared with leak identification strategies utilizing hydrophones or accelerometers for estimating liquid-borne waves or vibrations [11, 12], AE methods utilize signals that are extremely sensitive to leakage [13]. Some effective identifications have been published with noticeable distinguishing distances [14, 15] and flexibility with respect to different pipe materials [16, 17].

© Springer Nature Switzerland AG 2019
T. K. Dang et al. (Eds.): FDSE 2019, LNCS 11814, pp. 56–67, 2019.
https://doi.org/10.1007/978-3-030-35653-8_5

Leakage detection utilizing AE signals has experienced various periods of advancement. Parameter examination based on AE signals is a typical technique utilized for early leak detection. To separate leakage signals from ecological commotion, a few qualities are built from the crude AE information, incorporating factual parameters in the time area [18] as well as in recurrence space [19]. The general programmed leak recognition process incorporates the following steps: gathering crude signs, preprocessing signals, distinguishing signal characteristics, and arranging signals dependent on those characteristics [20].

While extraction of characteristics fundamentally improves the exactness and reliable quality of a break detecting framework, characteristic selection (CS) likewise assumes a basic job in pattern recognition. CS means to dispense with unimportant or superfluous characteristics, allowing for less complex and quicker AI models. Since leak discovery is a common application, CS strategies for it should be basic, quick, and productive.

One helpful CS method, which has the least complex and lightest computational requirements, utilizes the Kullback-Leibler (KL) separation, which is also known as Cross Entropy or KL divergence, to rank characteristics depending on their discrimination in [21]. KL separation is obtained by ascertaining the discrepancy between conditional probability distributions of two classes, $p(x_k|w_1)$ and $p(x_k|w_2)$, as shown in Eq. 1.

$$d = \sum_{k=1}^{n} p(x_k|w_1) \log_2 \frac{p(x_k|w_1)}{p(x_k|w_2)} + \sum_{k=1}^{n} p(x_k|w_2) \log_2 \frac{p(x_k|w_2)}{p(x_k|w_1)} \qquad (1)$$

Here, $w_1, w_2$ symbolize class 1 and class 2, respectively, and $x_k$ is a type of characteristic for the $k$th specimen. It should be noted that $p(x_k|w_1)$ and $p(x_k|w_2)$ are required to be completely continuous with respect to each other [22]. On the off chance that $p(x_k|w_1) = 0$, it is suggested that $p(x_k|w_2) = 0$ and vice versa; this situation can be ignored if the training dataset is sufficiently large and covers a large portion of the likelihood space of characteristics. Nonetheless, leak signals are affected by different conditions, including physical force, stream rate, encompassing media, pipe material, and pipe size [23, 24]. In this manner, training data in real conditions may not depict the entire space. For this situation, characteristic assessment as in [21] may not be precise, thus, the quality of leak categorization may be diminished.

To address this issue, this study proposes an improved method based on combining KL separation and a comparative distance coefficient of two conditional probability distributions. In the proposed method, computed values are used to rank characteristics from strongest to weakest, and consequently, the leading characteristics are chosen to categorize the leak.

The rest of this paper is organized as follows. Section 2 clarifies the proposed method. Section 3 depicts the experimental setup and results. The final section presents the conclusions.

# 2 Proposed Algorithm

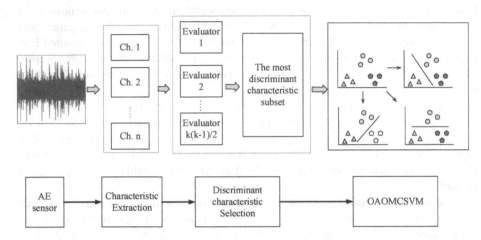

**Fig. 1.** Leak classification scheme

A regular method for leak classification is given in Fig. 1. This strategy incorporates three primary stages: characteristic extraction, characteristic selection, and leak classification. Each stage is presented in detail as follows.

## 2.1 Characteristic Extraction

To recognize different leakage marks, the most broadly utilized acoustic characteristics are separated from the AE signals, as presented in Tables 1 and 2.

**Table 1.** Common characteristics in time-space of the AE signals

| No. | Characteristics | Expressions |
|---|---|---|
| 1 | Peak ($peak(\mathbf{x})$) | $\max\{|\mathbf{x}|\}$ |
| 2 | Root-mean-square ($rms(\mathbf{x})$) | $\sqrt{\frac{1}{N}\sum_{i=1}^{N} x_i^2}$ |
| 3 | Kurtosis | $\frac{1}{N}\sum_{i=1}^{N}\left(\frac{x_i - mean(\mathbf{x})}{std(\mathbf{x})}\right)^4$ |
| 4 | Crest factor | $\frac{\max\{|\mathbf{x}|\}}{rms(\mathbf{x})}$ |
| 5 | Impulse factor | $\frac{peak(\mathbf{x})}{\frac{1}{N}\sum_{i=1}^{N}|x_i|}$ |
| 6 | Shape factor 1 | $\frac{rms(\mathbf{x})}{\frac{1}{N}\sum_{i=1}^{N}|x_i|}$ |
| 7 | Skewness | $\frac{1}{N}\sum_{i=1}^{N}\left(\frac{x_i - mean(\mathbf{x})}{std(\mathbf{x})}\right)^3$ |
| 8 | Square-mean-root ($smr(\mathbf{x})$) | $\left(\frac{1}{N}\sum_{i=1}^{N}\sqrt{|x_i|}\right)^2$ |

*(continued)*

**Table 1.** (*continued*)

| No. | Characteristics | Expressions |
|---|---|---|
| 9 | Margin factor | $\frac{peak(\mathbf{x})}{smr(\mathbf{x})}$ |
| 10 | Peak-to-peak ($pp(\mathbf{x})$) | $\max\{|\mathbf{x}|\} - \min\{|\mathbf{x}|\}$ |
| 11 | Kurtosis factor | $\frac{1}{rms(\mathbf{x})^3}$ |
| 12 | Energy | $\sum_{i=1}^{N} x_i^2$ |
| 13 | Clearance factor | $\frac{peak(\mathbf{x})}{smr(\mathbf{x})}$ |
| 14 | Shape factor 2 | $\frac{pp(\mathbf{x})}{\frac{1}{N}\sum_{i=1}^{N}|x_i|}$ |
| 15 | 5$^{\text{th}}$ normalized moment | $\frac{1}{N}\sum_{i=1}^{N}\left(\frac{x_i - mean(\mathbf{x})}{std(\mathbf{x})}\right)^5$ |
| 16 | 6$^{\text{th}}$ normalized moment | $\frac{1}{N}\sum_{i=1}^{N}\left(\frac{x_i - mean(\mathbf{x})}{std(\mathbf{x})}\right)^6$ |
| 17 | Entropy | $-\sum_{i=1}^{N} p_i \log_2 p_i$ |

Here, $\mathbf{x} = [x_1, x_2, \ldots, x_N]$ denotes a signal in time-space,

$$mean(\mathbf{x}) = \frac{1}{N}\sum_{i=1}^{N} x_i, \quad std(\mathbf{x}) = \sqrt{\frac{1}{N}\sum_{i=1}^{N}(x_i - mean(\mathbf{x}))^2}, \text{ and}$$

$$p_i = \frac{x_i^2}{\sum_{i=1}^{N} x_i^2}.$$

**Table 2.** Common characteristics in frequency-space of the AE signals

| No. | Characteristics | Expressions |
|---|---|---|
| 18 | Spectral centroid | $\frac{\mathbf{X} \times \mathbf{f}^T}{\sum_{i=1}^{N} X_i}$ |
| 19 | Root-mean-square of frequency | $\sqrt{\frac{1}{N}\sum_{i=1}^{N} X_i^2}$ |
| 20 | Root variance of frequency | $\sqrt{\frac{1}{N}\sum_{i=1}^{N}(X_i - mean(\mathbf{X}))^2}$ |
| 21 | Frequency spectrum energy | $\sum_{i=1}^{N} X_i^2$ |

Here, $\mathbf{X} = [X_1, X_2, \ldots, X_N]$ denotes a signal in frequency-space associated with the frequency vector $\mathbf{f} = [f_1, f_2, \ldots, f_N]$.

## 2.2  Characteristic Selection Based on Improved KL Separation

It is assumed that characteristic values $\{x_k|w_c\}$ are Gaussian random variables, where $w_c$ denotes a type of class. Measurably, the conditional probability that each of those values lies in the range $[\mu - 3\sigma, \mu + 3\sigma]$ is equivalent to 99.73% [25], where $\mu$ and $\sigma$ are the mean and standard deviation, respectively. Thus, when evaluating a characteristic, its conditional probability space corresponding to each class can be treated as $[\mu - 3\sigma, \mu + 3\sigma]$. To avoid intermittent errors when estimating KL separation, instead of computing $p(x_k|w_c)$ over the entire set of $\{x_k|w_c\}$, only values that lie in the intersection of the probability spaces of the two considered classes are computed. If the training set is not large enough, it is possible that one of the two $p(x_k|w_c)$ is zero, but this does not mean that the other is also zero. In this case, the KL separation can be considered as infinite. With the same pair of classes, if there is more than one characteristic having infinite separation, their discriminability cannot be compared properly. Therefore, in such cases, a comparative distance coefficient (see Eq. 2) is used instead of KL separation in evaluating such characteristics.

$$d_c = 1000 - \frac{\sigma_1 + \sigma_2}{|\mu_1 - \mu_2|} \qquad (2)$$

In the event that the $d_c$ estimate is higher, this implies that the standard deviation of each class is smaller, and/or the mean estimations of the two classes contrast more between one another. At that point, the separation is better. The number 1000 ensures that $d_c$ is always greater than any real finite KL separation.

Specifically, the proposed CS process occurs as follows. First, extracted characteristics are normalized by rescaling to "[0 1]", before applying the separation calculations corresponding to each pair of classes. These calculations quantify the improved KL separations. If any characteristic has an infinite KL separation, then it has the replacement $d_c$. Afterward, these separation values are used to rank the characteristics from strongest to weakest. Finally, leading characteristics are picked to categorize the leak.

## 2.3   Leak Classification

This investigation utilizes a One-Against-One Multiclass Support Vector Machine (OAOMCSVM) to group leaks. OAOMCSVM is a state-of-the-art strategy that is applicable to real classification [26]. This strategy sets up $k(k - 1)/2$ classifiers that are trained independently on data from two different classes. When considering the $k(k - 1)/2$ classifiers, the balloting technique is max-vote. On the off chance that more than one class has similar ballots, the smaller index will be chosen.

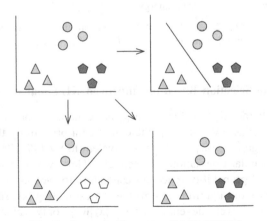

**Fig. 2.** Example illustrating OAOMCSVM

# 3    Experiments and Results

A pressurized water pipeline system that imitates field transmission pipelines, shown in Fig. 2, is utilized to gather AE signals. The stream rate of water in the pipeline is kept constant by a pump. AE sensors are set on the two sides of the test pipe segment to receive AE signals. These sensors are fastened on the external surface of the pipe. An interconnect-information securing (PCI-DAQ) board is utilized to obtain AE signals at a sampling rate of 1 MHz. The duration time of each signal is one second. In this work, there are five leak circumstances with the following pinhole sizes: 0 mm (normal), 0.3 mm, 0.5 mm, 1 mm, and 2 mm (see Figs. 3 and 4). This valve is utilized to mimic the leaks. The separation between the sensors and valve is 1 m. Table 3 describes the acquired AE signals of five circumstances, and the dataset used to evaluate the proposed method. Figures 5 and 6 illustrate AE signals in different circumstances in time-domain and frequency-domain.

**Table 3.** The AE dataset used to evaluate the proposed method

| Sampling rate = 1 MHz Length of signals = 1 s | No. of signals for each leak condition | | | | |
|---|---|---|---|---|---|
| | Normal | 0.3 mm | 0.5 mm | 1.0 mm | 2.0 mm |
| Training subset | 56 | 56 | 56 | 56 | 56 |
| Test subset | 14 | 14 | 14 | 14 | 14 |
| Total dataset | 70 | 70 | 70 | 70 | 70 |

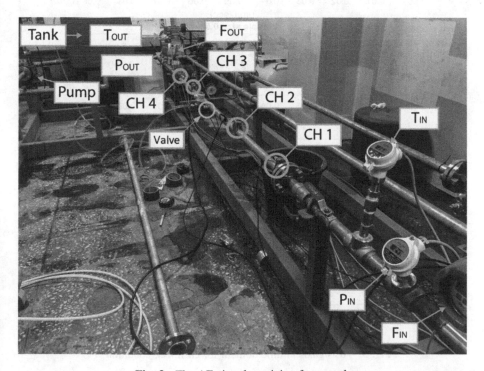

**Fig. 3.** The AE signal receiving framework

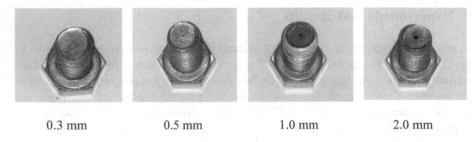

0.3 mm            0.5 mm            1.0 mm            2.0 mm

**Fig. 4.** Pinholes with diverse diameters

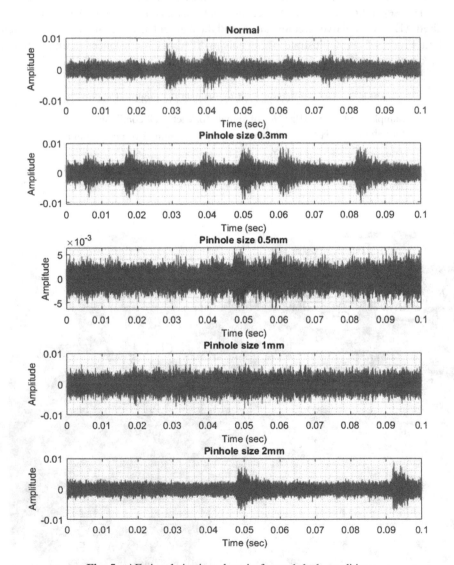

**Fig. 5.** AE signals in time-domain for each leak condition

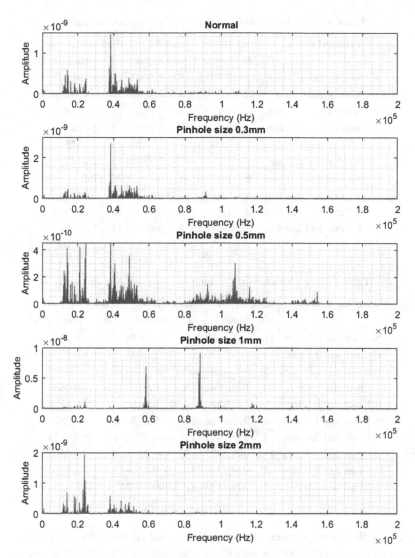

**Fig. 6.** Frequency spectra of AE signals for each leak condition

From the acquired AE signals, 21 popular characteristics are extracted. To obtain the most discriminative characteristics, these characteristics are assessed by characteristic evaluators. Tables 4 and 5 list the three best characteristics relating to each pair of classes according to the original and improved KL methods, respectively.

**Table 4.** Top characteristics ranking by original KL separation

| Validated classes | Rank #1 | | Rank #2 | | Rank #3 | |
|---|---|---|---|---|---|---|
| | No. | Value | No. | Value | No. | Value |
| Normal and 0.3 mm | 2 | 2.5082 | 19 | 2.5082 | 20 | 1.7912 |
| Normal and 0.5 mm | 18 | Inf | 6 | 4.3839 | 20 | 1.4559 |
| Normal and 1.0 mm | 8 | Inf | 6 | 2.7202 | 14 | 2.3378 |
| Normal and 2.0 mm | 6 | 1.5199 | 14 | 1.1084 | 2 | 1.0949 |
| 0.3 mm and 0.5 mm | 2 | 3.0420 | 19 | 3.0420 | 7 | 1.7875 |
| 0.3 mm and 1.0 mm | 8 | Inf | 17 | 2.0793 | 5 | 2.0141 |
| 0.3 mm and 2.0 mm | 8 | Inf | 11 | Inf | 20 | Inf |
| 0.5 mm and 1.0 mm | 8 | Inf | 11 | Inf | 6 | 3.2437 |
| 0.5 mm and 2.0 mm | 8 | Inf | 18 | Inf | 20 | 4.0039 |
| 1.0 mm and 2.0 mm | 2 | Inf | 8 | Inf | 11 | Inf |

**Table 5.** Top characteristics ranking by improved KL separation

| Validated classes | Rank #1 | | Rank #2 | | Rank #3 | |
|---|---|---|---|---|---|---|
| | No. | Value | No. | Value | No. | Value |
| Normal and 0.3 mm | 11 | 1.6110 | 8 | 0.1698 | 20 | 0.0071 |
| Normal and 0.5 mm | 18 | 3.2239 | 8 | 1.0743 | 11 | 0.7175 |
| Normal and 1.0 mm | 8 | 999.4294 | 20 | 998.6929 | 11 | 2.6222 |
| Normal and 2.0 mm | 8 | 0.1682 | 20 | 0.0584 | 13 | 0.0488 |
| 0.3 mm and 0.5 mm | 18 | 0.8550 | 20 | 0.6567 | 11 | 0.1158 |
| 0.3 mm and 1.0 mm | 8 | 999.2568 | 11 | 0.2834 | 18 | 0.2834 |
| 0.3 mm and 2.0 mm | 8 | 999.7882 | 11 | 999.6716 | 18 | 999.4724 |
| 0.5 mm and 1.0 mm | 11 | 999.5377 | 8 | 999.3543 | 20 | 998.6693 |
| 0.5 mm and 2.0 mm | 8 | 999.7544 | 18 | 999.7209 | 13 | 3.2239 |
| 1.0 mm and 2.0 mm | 11 | 999.7123 | 18 | 999.5533 | 8 | 999.5106 |

It is clear that in some cases, the original KL method has difficulty ranking characteristics (since separation values are assigned as infinite), while the proposed method does not experience any similar problems.

In addition, Table 6 demonstrates that the improved method provides better outcomes compared with the original method. The 10-fold cross-validation results show that the proposed method surpasses the original by five times, implying that the quality of the improved KL method is steadier. The improved method, which has an average arrangement exactness of 96.00%, beats the original method, which has an average precision of 92.29%.

**Table 6.** 10-fold cross-validation results

| Subsets | KL separation (%) | Improved KL separation (%) |
|---|---|---|
| 1 | 85.71 | 97.14 |
| 2 | 94.29 | 100.00 |
| 3 | 80.00 | 91.43 |
| 4 | 100.00 | 100.00 |
| 5 | 85.71 | 91.43 |
| 6 | 97.14 | 97.14 |
| 7 | 97.14 | 97.14 |
| 8 | 94.29 | 94.29 |
| 9 | 100.00 | 100.00 |
| 10 | 88.57 | 91.43 |
| **Average** | **92.29** | **96.00** |

Furthermore, the classification results represented by confusion matrices in Tables 7 and 8 demonstrate that the proposed method is more reliable. In particular, as opposed to the proposed strategy, the original technique misclassifies between the normal and the largest pinhole size classes more than between different classes, and the classification precision of the original KL technique for the biggest pinhole size of 2.0 mm is worse than for 0.5 mm and 1.0 mm.

**Table 7.** Classification results of the original KL method

| Actual | Predicted | | | | |
|---|---|---|---|---|---|
| | Normal | 0.3 mm | 0.5 mm | 1.0 mm | 2.0 mm |
| Normal | 8 | 0 | 1 | 0 | 5 |
| 0.3 mm | 0 | 13 | 1 | 0 | 0 |
| 0.5 mm | 0 | 0 | 14 | 0 | 0 |
| 1.0 mm | 0 | 0 | 0 | 14 | 0 |
| 2.0 mm | 2 | 0 | 0 | 0 | 12 |

**Table 8.** Classification results of the improved KL method

| Actual | Predicted | | | | |
|---|---|---|---|---|---|
| | Normal | 0.3 mm | 0.5 mm | 1.0 mm | 2.0 mm |
| Normal | 14 | 0 | 0 | 0 | 0 |
| 0.3 mm | 1 | 13 | 0 | 0 | 0 |
| 0.5 mm | 0 | 0 | 14 | 0 | 0 |
| 1.0 mm | 0 | 0 | 0 | 14 | 0 |
| 2.0 mm | 2 | 0 | 0 | 0 | 12 |

# 4 Conclusions

The selection technique using the KL separation is among the least troublesome, fastest, and most powerful CS techniques, and is appropriate for real-world applications. That said, this procedure has issues when the training dataset is not extensive enough. To address this issue, this paper proposes an improved method based on combining KL separation and a comparative distance coefficient of two conditional probability distributions. The evaluation results showed that, as opposed to the original KL strategy, the proposed technique is more stable, dependable, and precise.

**Acknowledgement.** This work was supported by the Korea Institute of Energy Technology Evaluation and Planning (KETEP) and the Ministry of Trade, Industry & Energy (MOTIE) of the Republic of Korea (No. 20172510102130, No. 20192510102510).

# References

1. Frauendorfer, R., Liemberger, R.: The Issues and Challenges of Reducing Non-Revenue Water. Asian Development Bank (2010)
2. Liu, Z., Kleiner, Y.: State of the art review of inspection technologies for condition assessment of water pipes. Measurement **46**, 1–15 (2013)
3. Sinha, D.N.: Acoustic sensor for pipeline monitoring. Gas Technology Management Division Strategic Center for Natural Gas and Oil National Energy Technology Laboratory, p. 2 (2005)
4. Gao, Y., Brennan, M., Joseph, P., Muggleton, J., Hunaidi, O.: A model of the correlation function of leak noise in buried plastic pipes. J. Sound Vibr. **277**, 133–148 (2004)
5. Gao, Y., Brennan, M., Joseph, P.: A comparison of time delay estimators for the detection of leak noise signals in plastic water distribution pipes. J. Sound Vibr. **292**, 552–570 (2006)
6. Brunner, A.J., Barbezat, M.: Acoustic emission monitoring of leaks in pipes for transport of liquid and gaseous media: a model experiment. In: Advanced Materials Research, pp. 351–356. Trans Tech Publications (2006)
7. Yang, J., Wen, Y., Li, P.: Leak location using blind system identification in water distribution pipelines. J. Sound Vibr. **310**, 134–148 (2008)
8. Tang, X., Liu, Y., Zheng, L., Ma, C., Wang, H.: Leak detection of water pipeline using wavelet transform method. In: 2009 International Conference on Environmental Science and Information Application Technology, pp. 217–220. IEEE, (2009)
9. Khulief, Y., Khalifa, A., Mansour, R.B., Habib, M.: Acoustic detection of leaks in water pipelines using measurements inside pipe. J. Pipeline Syst. Eng. Pract. **3**, 47–54 (2011)
10. Juliano, T.M., Meegoda, J.N., Watts, D.J.: Acoustic emission leak detection on a metal pipeline buried in sandy soil. J. Pipeline Syst. Eng. Pract. **4**, 149–155 (2012)
11. Puust, R., Kapelan, Z., Savic, D., Koppel, T.: A review of methods for leakage management in pipe networks. Urban Water J. **7**, 25–45 (2010)
12. Yazdekhasti, S., Piratla, K.R., Atamturktur, S., Khan, A.A.: Novel vibration-based technique for detecting water pipeline leakage. Struct. Infrastruct. Eng. **13**, 731–742 (2017)
13. Gao, Y., Brennan, M.J., Joseph, P., Muggleton, J., Hunaidi, O.: On the selection of acoustic/vibration sensors for leak detection in plastic water pipes. J. Sound Vibr. **283**, 927–941 (2005)

14. Anastasopoulos, A., Kourousis, D., Bollas, K.: Acoustic emission leak detection of liquid filled buried pipeline. J. Acoust. Emission **27**, 27–39 (2009)
15. Lim, J.: Underground pipeline leak detection using acoustic emission and crest factor technique. In: Shen, G., Wu, Z., Zhang, J. (eds.) Advances in Acoustic Emission Technology. SPP, vol. 158, pp. 445–450. Springer, New York (2015). https://doi.org/10.1007/978-1-4939-1239-1_41
16. Hunaidi, O., Chu, W., Wang, A., Guan, W.: Detecting leaks in plastic pipes. J. Am. Water Works Assoc. **92**, 82–94 (2000)
17. Martini, A., Troncossi, M., Rivola, A.: Leak detection in water-filled small-diameter polyethylene pipes by means of acoustic emission measurements. Appl. Sci. **7**, 2 (2017)
18. Grosse, C.U., Ohtsu, M.: Acoustic Emission Testing. Springer, Heidelberg (2008). https://doi.org/10.1007/978-3-540-69972-9
19. Meng, L., Yuxing, L., Wuchang, W., Juntao, F.: Experimental study on leak detection and location for gas pipeline based on acoustic method. J. Loss Prev. Process Ind. **25**, 90–102 (2012)
20. Kang, J., Park, Y.-J., Lee, J., Wang, S.-H., Eom, D.-S.: Novel leakage detection by ensemble CNN-SVM and graph-based localization in water distribution systems. IEEE Trans. Ind. Electron. **65**, 4279–4289 (2018)
21. Li, S., Song, Y., Zhou, G.: Leak detection of water distribution pipeline subject to failure of socket joint based on acoustic emission and pattern recognition. Measurement **115**, 39–44 (2018)
22. Lin, J.: Divergence measures based on the Shannon entropy. IEEE Trans. Inf. Theory **37**, 145–151 (1991)
23. Hunaidi, O., Chu, W.T.: Acoustical characteristics of leak signals in plastic water distribution pipes. Appl. Acoust. **58**, 235–254 (1999)
24. Moore, S.: A review of noise and vibration in fluid-filled pipe systems. Acoustics, Brisbane, Australia (2016)
25. Ribeiro, M.I.: Gaussian probability density functions: properties and error characterization. Institute for Systems and Robotics, Lisboa, Portugal (2004)
26. Santosa, B.: Multiclass classification with cross entropy-support vector machines. Procedia Comput. Sci. **72**, 345–352 (2015)

# Mining Incrementally Closed Itemsets over Data Stream with the Technique of Batch-Update

Thanh-Trung Nguyen[1], Quang Nguyen[1(⊠)],
and Ngo Thanh Hung[2(⊠)]

[1] Department of Information Technology, Hong Bang International University,
Ho Chi Minh City, Vietnam
{trungnt,quangn}@hiu.vn
[2] Faculty of Information Technology, Ho Chi Minh City University
of Technology, Ho Chi Minh City, Vietnam
nt.hung@hutech.edu.vn

**Abstract.** Currently incremental mining techniques can be divided into two groups: direct-update technique and batch-update technique. Mining closed item sets is one of the core tasks of data mining. In addition, advances in hardware technology and information technology have created huge data streams in recent years. Therefore, mining incrementally closed item sets over data streams with the batch-update technique is necessary. Incremental algorithms are always associated with an intermediate structure such as tree, lattice, table... In the previous study, the author proposed an intermediate structure which is a linear list called constructive set. In this paper, an incremental mining algorithm based on the constructive with the batch-update technique is proposed in order to mine data streams.

**Keywords:** Batch-update · Constructive set · Data mining · Data stream · Incremental mining

## 1 Introduction

Frequent itemsets mining is a core operation of data mining. Therefore, frequent itemsets mining over data streams has attracted a lot of research interest. Compared to other operations over data streams, frequent itemsets mining poses major challenges due to the computational cost and the large memory need, as well as the requirement for accuracy of mining results. In the case of data streams, one might want to find frequent itemsets on sliding windows or entire data streams [3, 6].

A data stream is defined as a sequence of transactions. To handle and mine data streams, there are three commonly used window models: landmark window, sliding window, damped window. A window is a sequence of transactions occurring from a specific starting point of time to a specific ending point of time.

A data stream $D$ is defined as a sequence of transactions, $D = (t_1, t_2, ..., t_i, ...)$ where $t_i$ is the transaction occurs at the $i^{th}$ point of time. To handle and mine data

© Springer Nature Switzerland AG 2019
T. K. Dang et al. (Eds.): FDSE 2019, LNCS 11814, pp. 68–84, 2019.
https://doi.org/10.1007/978-3-030-35653-8_6

streams, there are three commonly used window models. A window is a sequence of transactions occurring from the $i^{th}$ to the $j^{th}$, denoted $W[i,j] = (t_i, t_{i+1}, \ldots, t_j)$.

Landmark window: In this model, frequent itemsets are found from a starting point of time i until the present time t. In other words, frequent itemsets are found over the window W [i, t]. A special case of the Landmark window is i = 1. In this case, frequent itemsets are mined over the entire data stream. One note in this model is that each time after the start of time is equally important. However, in many cases, recent times are of great interest. The next two models focus on this case.

Sliding window: Given the length of the sliding window is w and the current time is t. The frequent itemsets are mined in the window W [t − w + 1, t]. When the time changes, this window will remain the same size and move along with the current time. This model does not care about data that appears before t − w + 1.

Damped window: This model assigns a large weight to transactions that occur near the current time. To do this, the decay rate is defined and used to update (by multiplication) transactions that appear before a new transaction occurs. Correspondingly, the frequency of an itemset is also determined based on the weight of each transaction.

Mining closed itemsets is a general case of frequent itemsets mining. Besides, one of important features of data streams is that they are often mined in a distributed environment. So, with the requirement of mining closed itemsets over many data streams, it needs incremental mining algorithms with the batch-update technique and an effective intermediate structure.

The constructive set along with the algorithm of batch-update technique introduced in the Sect. 3 can be applied for mining closed itemsets over many data streams.

In the recent period, the trend of using concept lattice for the purpose of mining incrementally closed sets has been focused. Concept lattices [2] are hierarchical structures between concepts. One concept consists of three components: an object set, an attribute set, and a relation between the two sets. Correspondingly, one concept can include closed item set, transaction set and the relation between the two sets [11]. There are two groups for the methods for maintaining the concept lattice: direct-update, a new transaction is added individually to the lattice, and merge-lattice, new lattice of newly added transactions is integrated with the original lattice.

The direct-update group consists of the algorithms proposed in [4, 5, 7, 9, 10, 13, 14].

The methods of [1, 12] belong to the merge-lattice group.

More specifically, merge-lattice is a batch-update technique of incremental mining with the concept lattice as the intermediate structure.

Most recently, [15] proposed two batch-update incremental algorithms with the intermediate structure FP-tree in 2010 and 2012. The BIT (Batch Incremental Tree) algorithm in [15] merges two FP-trees to obtain a new FP-tree.

In [16], the authors proposed to apply the same principle they used in [15] but with the FP-Growth algorithm, i.e., they have used batch-update incremental mining to build the FP-tree by using the FP-Growth algorithm, and named BIT_FPGrowth.

In the next section, the concepts, definitions, algorithms and propositions in [8] are outlined as the background knowledge in this paper.

## 2 Background Knowledge

Transaction database is $T = (O, I, \mathcal{R})$ – a trio, with a set $O \neq \emptyset$ consisting of transaction objects $o_1, o_2, \ldots, o_n$, $|O| = n$; a set $I \neq \emptyset$ of transaction items $i_1, i_2, \ldots, i_m$, $|I| = m$ and $\mathcal{R}$ is a binary relation on $O \times I$.

The transaction set of $T$ has a representation of $n \times m$ bit matrix $R = (\rho_{pq})$, $\rho_{pq} = \mathcal{R}$ $(o_p, i_q) \in \{0, 1\}$, $o_p \in O$, $i_q \in I$, $p = 1, 2, \ldots, n$, $q = 1, 2, \ldots, m$, and $\rho_{pq} = 1$ if $o_p$ deals with $i_q$, $\rho_{pq} = 0$ otherwise.

For a transaction set $T = (O, I, \mathcal{R})$, each row of transaction matrix $R$ is described by a m bit-chain, called *bit pattern*, namely bit pattern with size m or m-bit pattern: $b = b_1 b_2 b_3 \ldots b_{m-1} b_m$, $b_k \in \{0, 1\}$, $k = 1, 2, \ldots, m$

Given two m-bit patterns $a = a_1 a_2 a_3 \ldots a_{m-1} a_m$ and $b = b_1 b_2 b_3 \ldots b_{m-1} b_m$, then: $a = b \Leftrightarrow a_k = b_k$, $\forall k \in \{1, \ldots, m\}$

*Composition* pattern of a, b is established by the & (AND) operation on bits of a, b: $a \& b = c = c_1 c_2 c_3 \ldots c_{m-1} c_m \Leftrightarrow c_k = a_k \times b_k$, $\forall k \in \{1, \ldots, m\}$

When a & b = b, pattern a has more bits 1 than that of pattern b, in other words b *covers* a or a *is covered by* b, denoted $a \propto b$, thus: $a \propto b \Leftrightarrow a \& b = b$. The negation operator is a $!\propto b$.

The number of appearances of a bit pattern a in $T$ is the *frequency* of a, denoted $f_a$. To describe a bit pattern with its frequency, we may use a dot as a delimitation.

If there are some bits whose values are not specified, the character * is used to indicate the 'aggregation' of these possible values. Since then, the *group patterns* should be identified. A bit pattern is a specific case of a group pattern when its all bits have a definite value of 0 or 1.

If u, v are group patterns with size m, the composition of u and v, also denoted u & v, is a pattern: $w = w_1 w_2 w_3 \ldots w_{m-1} w_m = u \& v$ with $w_k = 1$ if $u_k \times v_k = 1$ and $w_k = *$ otherwise, for k = 1, .., m.

If u & v = v, the group pattern u is called '*is covered by* v', also denoted $u \propto v$.

The number of appearances of a group pattern u in the transaction set O is *frequency* of u corresponding with O, also denoted $f_u$.

*Composition* group pattern of group patterns $u.f_u$ and $v.f_v$ is a group pattern $w.f_w$, denoted $w.f_w = u.f_u \& v.f_v$ with: $w = u \& v$ and $f_w = f_u + f_v$.

A group pattern $u.f_u$ is called *private* group pattern of a group pattern $v.f_v$, denoted $u.f_u \lll v.f_v$, if it happens u = v and $f_u \leq f_v$.

On the other hand, with two group patterns u, v, if $u \neq v$, $u \propto v$ and $f_u \leq f_v$ then v is *wide* group pattern of u, denoted $u.f_u \ll v.f_v$. The relation $\lll$ is considered to be a specific case of $\ll$.

Let $T = (O, I, \mathcal{R})$, $O \subseteq O$, $I \subseteq I$, *rectangle* (rct) $R = \langle O, I \rangle$ in $\mathcal{R}$ is the set of elements of $O \times I \subseteq \mathcal{R}$. In order, $|O|$, $|I|$ are the vertical dimension, the horizontal dimension of R, the size of R is $|O| \times |I|$. With rct $R = \langle O, I \rangle$, the projections R on the set of objects, the set of items are defined by $Pr_o(R) = O$, $Pr_i(R) = I$.

Rct $\langle O', I' \rangle$ is called *be contained* by rct $\langle O, I \rangle$, denoted $\langle O', I' \rangle \subseteq \langle O, I \rangle$, if $O' \subseteq O$, $I' \subseteq I$. When O', I' are strictly contained by O, I, it is denoted $\langle O', I' \rangle \in \langle O, I \rangle$.

A rct is *maximal* if it is not contained by any other rct of $\mathcal{R}$.

Let the transaction database $T = (O, I, \mathcal{R})$, the set of maximal group patterns is defined as the *constructive set* P of $T$, each maximal group pattern is called a *constructive pattern*. So: $\forall p.f_p \in P$, $\nexists u.f_u \in P, u \neq p : u \propto p$ and $f_u \geq f_p$.

```
ALGORITHM ConPatSet(O,P)
// Procedure for Creating a Constructive Pattern Set P
// in:   Set of objects: O = {o₁,o₂,.. , oₙ}
// out:  P constructive set on O, nP=|P|.
1. Begin
2.     for i:= 1 to n do
3.        replace all 0-bits in oᵢ with *;
4.     P = { o₁ }; nP:=1;
5.     for i:= 2 to n do P := IncPatSet(oᵢ,P,nP);
6. end.
```

```
ALGORITHM IncPatSet(o,P,nP)
// Function for updating constructive pattern set when increasing a new object
// in:   new object o, current constructive set P
// out:  P new constructive set
 1. if all bits in o equal * then return P;    // o∉P
 2. if all bits in o equal 1 then {
 3.     for p∈P do f_p := f_p+1;        // statements in A-block
 4.     if o∉P then append o to P; return P; }
 5. Q := {o};                          // statements in B-block
 6. for p∈P do {
 7.   q := o&p;
 8.   if all bits in q equal * then continue  // q∉P
 9.   else Q:=Q∪{q}; }
10. S := Q; R := ∅;        // statements in C-block: Filtered-PatSet(Q)
11. for q∈Q do {
12.   s := q;
13.   for r∈S do if q≪r then s := r;
14.   R := R∪{s}; nP:=nP+1; }     // set of new creative patterns
15. Q := ∅;                // statements in D-block: Filtered-PatSet(P)
16. for p∈P do {
17.   q := p;
18.   for r∈R do if p≪r then q := r;
19.   Q := Q ∪ {q}; nP:=nP+1;} // updated old creative patterns
20. Return P := Q ∪ R;  // creative pattern set with incremental object
```

```
ALGORITHM DesPatSet(o,P)
// Updating a Constructive Pattern Set P when descending an object
//  in:   Descended object o, Current set P
// out:   Updated constructive set P
1. Q := ∅;
2. for p∈P do
3.    if o ∝ p then {
4.       f_p := f_p-1; Q := Q∪{p}; }
5. for q∈Q do {
6.    for p∈P do {
7.       if p«q then {
8.          P := P\{q}; break; } } }
9. Return P.
```

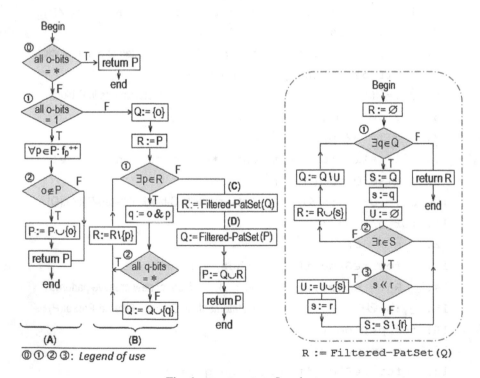

**Fig. 1.** IncPatSet flowchart

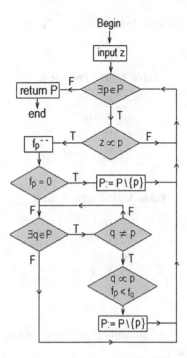

**Fig. 2.** DesPatSet flowchart

The Figs. 1 and 2 show the flowcharts of the algorithms IncPatSet and DesPatSet.

## 3  The Proposed Algorithm for the Batch-Update Technique

This section builds the algorithm to consolidate two constructive sets obtained from any two batches into a constructive set for both batches.

The following is an illustration of the idea for the algorithm (Table 1).

**Table 1.** The transaction set $T_4$

|       | $i_1$ | $i_2$ | $i_3$ |
|-------|-------|-------|-------|
| $o_1$ | 0     | 0     | 1     |
| $o_2$ | 0     | 1     | 0     |
| $o_3$ | 0     | 1     | 1     |
| $o_4$ | 1     | 0     | 0     |
| $o_5$ | 1     | 0     | 1     |
| $o_6$ | 1     | 1     | 0     |
| $o_7$ | 1     | 1     | 1     |

Dividing the transactions into two batches: $\{o_1, o_2, o_3\}$ and $\{o_4, o_5, o_6, o_7\}$ (Tables 2 and 3).

**Table 2.** The first batch

|       | $i_1$ | $i_2$ | $i_3$ |
|-------|-------|-------|-------|
| $o_1$ | 0     | 0     | 1     |
| $o_2$ | 0     | 1     | 0     |
| $o_3$ | 0     | 1     | 1     |

**Table 3.** The second batch

|       | $i_1$ | $i_2$ | $i_3$ |
|-------|-------|-------|-------|
| $o_4$ | 1     | 0     | 0     |
| $o_5$ | 1     | 0     | 1     |
| $o_6$ | 1     | 1     | 0     |
| $o_7$ | 1     | 1     | 1     |

Executing the `ConPatSet` algorithm on these batches. The constructive set received from the two batches:

The batch $\{o_1, o_2, o_3\}$ : $P_1 = \{^{**}1.2(1), ^*1^*.2(2), ^*11.1(3)\}$

The batch $\{o_4, o_5, o_6, o_7\}$ : $P_2 = \{1^*1.2(1), 1^{**}.4(2), 11^*.2(3), 111.1(4)\}$

Consolidating $P_1$ and $P_2$:

- In turn performing the operator & between the elements of $P_1$ with the elements of $P_2$ to obtain the set M of new elements.
- Removing the new elements that are contained mutually in M.
- Removing the elements of $P_1$ which are contained by the elements in M.
- Removing the elements of $P_2$ which are contained by the elements in M.
- Combining the remaining elements of $P_1$, $P_2$ and M to obtain the complete constructive set P.

$$P_1(1)\& P_2(1) : \underline{^{**}1.2} \& 1^*1.2 = \text{}^{**}\,\mathbf{1.4}$$
$$\& P_2(2) : ^{**}\,1.2 \& 1^{**}.4 = \underline{^{***}}$$
$$\& P_2(3) : ^{**}\,1.2 \& 11^*.2 = \underline{^{***}}$$
$$\& P_2(4) : ^{**}\,1.2 \& 111.1 = \underline{^{**}1.3}$$

$$P_1(2)\& P_2(1) : ^*\,1^*.2 \& 1^*1.2 = \underline{^{***}}$$
$$\& P_2(2) : ^*\,1^*.2 \& 1^{**}.4 = \underline{^{***}}$$
$$\& P_2(3) : \underline{^*1^*.2} \& 11^*.2 = ^*\,\mathbf{1^*.4}$$
$$\& P_2(4) : ^*\,1^*.2 \& 111.1 = \underline{^*1^*.3}$$

$$P_1(3) \& P_2(1) : {}^* 11.1 \& 1^* 1.2 = \underline{{}^{**} 1.3}$$
$$\& P_2(2) : {}^* 11.1 \& 1^{**}.4 = \underline{{}^{***}}$$
$$\& P_2(3) : {}^* 11.1 \& 11^*.2 = \underline{{}^* 1^*.3}$$
$$\& P_2(4) : \underline{{}^* 11.1} \& 111.1 = {}^* \mathbf{11.2}$$

After removing (underline) the new elements (results) that contain mutually, the set M remains 3 elements (bold).

After removing (underline) the elements of $P_1$ which are contained by the elements in M, $P_1$ remains 0 element.

After removing (underline) the elements of $P_2$ which are contained by the elements in M, $P_2$ remains 4 elements.

So the set $P$ of the union of 2 batches has 7 elements. The full constructive set $P$ is:

$$P = \{{}^{**}1.4, {}^*1^*.4, {}^*11.2, 1^*1.2, 1^{**}.4, 11^*.2, 111.1\}$$

Another detailed illustration is distribution processing on two data streams at two different locations with sliding window having the length of 6 (Tables 4 and 5).

The constructive set of the location 1 consists of 10 elements:

**Table 4.** Location 1

|       | $o_1$ | $o_2$ | $o_3$ | $o_4$ | $o_5$ | $o_6$ |
|-------|-------|-------|-------|-------|-------|-------|
| $i_1$ | 1     | 0     | 1     | 1     | 1     | 0     |
| $i_2$ | 1     | 1     | 1     | 1     | 1     | 1     |
| $i_3$ | 0     | 1     | 0     | 1     | 1     | 1     |
| $i_4$ | 1     | 0     | 1     | 0     | 1     | 1     |
| $i_5$ | 1     | 1     | 1     | 1     | 1     | 0     |

**Table 5.** Location 2

|       | $o_1$ | $o_2$ | $o_3$ | $o_4$ | $o_5$ |
|-------|-------|-------|-------|-------|-------|
| $i_1$ | 1     | 0     | 1     | 1     | 0     |
| $i_2$ | 0     | 1     | 1     | 0     | 1     |
| $i_3$ | 0     | 1     | 0     | 1     | 0     |
| $i_4$ | 1     | 0     | 1     | 0     | 1     |
| $i_5$ | 1     | 0     | 1     | 1     | 1     |

$$P_1 = \{11^*11.3(1), {}^*11^*1.3(2), 11^{**}1.4(3), {}^*1^{**}1.5(4), 111^*1.2(5), 11111.1(6),$$
$${}^*1^*1^*.4(7), {}^*11^{**}.4(8), {}^*1^{***}.6(9), {}^*111^*.2(10)\}$$

The constructive set of the location 2 consists of 10 elements:

$$P_2 = \{{}^*11^{**}.1(1), 1^{**}11.2(2), 11^*11.1(3), {}^{**}\,1^{**}.2(4), 1^{***}1.3(5), 1^*1^*1.1(6),$$
$${}^{***}11.3(7), {}^*\,1^{***}.3(8), {}^*\,1^*11.2(9), {}^{****}\,1.4(10)\}$$

Need to find the constructive set at the present time for the union of both locations:

- In turn performing the operator & between the elements of $P_1$ with the elements of $P_2$ to obtain the set M of new elements.
- Removing the new elements that are contained mutually in M.
- Removing the elements of $P_1$ which are contained by the elements in M.
- Removing the elements of $P_2$ which are contained by the elements in M.
- Combining the remaining elements of $P_1$, $P_2$ and M to obtain the result constructive set P.

$$
\begin{aligned}
P_1(1) \& \, P_2(1) &: 11^*11.3 \,\& \,{}^*11^{**}.1 = \underline{{}^*1^{***}.4} \\
\& \, P_2(2) &: 11^*11.3 \,\& \,\underline{1^{**}11.2} = \mathbf{1^{**}11.5} \\
\& \, P_2(3) &: \underline{11^*11.3} \,\& \,\underline{11^*11.1} = \mathbf{11^*11.4} \\
\& \, P_2(4) &: 11^*11.3 \,\& \,{}^{**}1^{**}.2 = \underline{{}^{*****}} \\
\& \, P_2(5) &: 11^*11.3 \,\& \,\underline{1^{***}1.3} = \underline{1^{***}1.6} \\
\& \, P_2(6) &: 11^*11.3 \,\& \,1^*1^*1.1 = \underline{1^{***}1.4} \\
\& \, P_2(7) &: 11^*11.3 \,\& \,{*}{*}{*}\underline{11.3} = {}^{***}\ \mathbf{11.6} \\
\& \, P_2(8) &: 11^*11.3 \,\& \,\underline{{}^*1{*}{*}{*}.3} = \underline{{}^*1^{***}.6} \\
\& \, P_2(9) &: 11^*11.3 \,\& \,\underline{{}^*1^*11.2} = {}^*\ \mathbf{1^*11.5} \\
\& \, P_2(10) &: 11^*11.3 \,\& \,\underline{{}^{****}1.4} = \underline{{}^{****}1.7}
\end{aligned}
$$

$$
\begin{aligned}
P_1(2) \& \, P_2(1) &: {}^*11^*1.3 \,\& \,\underline{{}^*11^{**}.1} = \underline{{}^*11^{**}.4} \\
\& \, P_2(2) &: {}^*11^*1.3 \,\& \,1^{**}11.2 = \underline{{}^{****}1.5} \\
\& \, P_2(3) &: {}^*11^*1.3 \,\& \,11^*11.1 = \underline{{}^*1^{**}1.4} \\
\& \, P_2(4) &: {}^*11^*1.3 \,\& \,\underline{{}^{**}1^{**}.2} = \underline{{}^{**}1^{**}.5} \\
\& \, P_2(5) &: {}^*11^*1.3 \,\& \,1^{***}1.3 = \underline{{}^{****}1.6} \\
\& \, P_2(6) &: {}^*11^*1.3 \,\& \,1^*1^*1.1 = {}^{**}\ \mathbf{1^*1.4} \\
\& \, P_2(7) &: {}^*11^*1.3 \,\& \,{}^{***}11.3 = \underline{{}^{****}1.6} \\
\& \, P_2(8) &: {}^*11^*1.3 \,\& \,\underline{{}^*1^{***}.3} = \underline{{}^*1^{***}.6} \\
\& \, P_2(9) &: {}^*11^*1.3 \,\& \,{}^*1^*11.2 = \underline{{}^*1^{**}1.5} \\
\& \, P_2(10) &: {}^*11^*1.3 \,\& \,\underline{{}^{****}1.4} = \underline{{}^{****}1.7}
\end{aligned}
$$

$P_1(3) \& P_2(1) :\ 11^{**}1.4 \& {}^*11^{**}.1 = \underline{{}^*1^{***}.5}$

$\& P_2(2) :\ 11^{**}1.4 \& 1^{**}11.2 = \underline{1^{***}1.6}$

$\& P_2(3) :\ \underline{11^{**}1.4} \& 11^*11.1 = \mathbf{11^{**}1.5}$

$\& P_2(4) :\ 11^{**}1.4 \& {}^{**}1^{**}.2 = \underline{{}^{****}}$

$\& P_2(5) :\ 11^{**}1.4 \& 1^{***}1.3 = \mathbf{1^{***}1.7}$

$\& P_2(6) :\ 11^{**}1.4 \& 1^*1^*1.1 = \underline{1^{***}1.5}$

$\& P_2(7) :\ 11^{**}1.4 \& {}^{***}11.3 = \underline{{}^{****}1.7}$

$\& P_2(8) :\ 11^{**}1.4 \& \underline{{}^*1^{***}.3} = \underline{{}^*1^{***}.7}$

$\& P_2(9) :\ 11^{**}1.4 \& {}^*1^*11.2 = \underline{{}^*1^{**}1.6}$

$\& P_2(10) :\ 11^{**}1.4 \& \underline{{}^{****}1.4} = \underline{{}^{****}1.8}$

$P_1(4) \& P_2(1) :\ {}^*1^{**}1.5 \& {}^*11^{**}.1 = \underline{{}^*1^{***}.6}$

$\& P_2(2) :\ {}^*1^{**}1.5 \& 1^{**}11.2 = \underline{{}^{****}1.7}$

$\& P_2(3) :\ \underline{{}^*1^{***}1.5} \& 11^*11.1 = \underline{{}^*1^{**}1.6}$

$\& P_2(4) :\ {}^* 1^{**}1.5 \& {}^{**}1^{**}.2 = \underline{{}^{****}}$

$\& P_2(5) :\ {}^*1^{**}1.5 \& 1^{***}1.3 = \underline{{}^{****}1.8}$

$\& P_2(6) :\ {}^*1^{**}1.5 \& 1^*1^*1.1 = \underline{{}^{****}1.6}$

$\& P_2(7) :\ {}^*1^{**}1.5 \& {}^{***}11.3 = \underline{{}^{****}1.8}$

$\& P_2(8) :\ {}^*1^{**}1.5 \& \underline{{}^*1^{***}.3} = {}^*1^{***}.8$

$\& P_2(9) :\ {}^*1^{**}1.5 \& {}^*1^*11.2 = {}^*\ \mathbf{1^{**}1.7}$

$\& P_2(10) :\ {}^*1^{**}1.5 \& \underline{{}^{****}1.4} = {}^{****}\ \mathbf{1.9}$

$P_1(5) \& P_2(1) :\ 111^*1.2 \& \underline{{}^*11^{**}.1} = \underline{{}^*11^{**}.3}$

$\& P_2(2) :\ 111^*1.2 \& 1^{**}11.2 = \underline{1^{***}1.4}$

$\& P_2(3) :\ 111^*1.2 \& 11^*11.1 = \underline{11^{**}1.3}$

$\& P_2(4) :\ 111^*1.2 \& \underline{{}^{**}1^{**}.2} = \underline{{}^{**}1^{**}.4}$

$\& P_2(5) :\ 111^*1.2 \& \underline{1^{***}1.3} = \underline{1^{***}1.5}$

$\& P_2(6) :\ 111^*1.2 \& \underline{1^*1^*1.1} = \mathbf{1^*1^*1.3}$

$\& P_2(7) :\ 111^*1.2 \& {}^{***}11.3 = \underline{{}^{****}1.5}$

$\& P_2(8) :\ 111^*1.2 \& \underline{{}^*1^{***}.3} = \underline{{}^*1^{***}.5}$

$\& P_2(9) :\ 111^*1.2 \& {}^*1^*11.2 = \underline{{}^*1^{**}1.4}$

$\& P_2(10) :\ 111^*1.2 \& \underline{{}^{****}1.4} = \underline{{}^{****}1.6}$

$$P_1(6)\,\&\,P_2(1): 11111.1\,\&\,\underline{^*11^{**}.1} = \underline{^*11^{**}.2}$$
$$\&\,P_2(2): 11111.1\,\&\,\underline{1^{**}11.2} = \underline{1^{**}11.3}$$
$$\&\,P_2(3): 11111.1\,\&\,\underline{11^*11.1} = \underline{11^*11.2}$$
$$V P_2(4): 11111.1\,\&\,\underline{^{**}1^{**}.2} = \underline{^{**}1^{**}.3}$$
$$\&\,P_2(5): 11111.1\,\&\,\underline{1^{***}1.3} = \underline{1^{***}1.4}$$
$$\&\,P_2(6): 11111.1\,\&\,\underline{1^*1^*1.1} = \underline{1^*1^*1.2}$$
$$\&\,P_2(7): 11111.1\,\&\,\underline{^{***}11.3} = \underline{^{***}11.4}$$
$$\&\,P_2(8): 11111.1\,\&\,\underline{^*1^{***}.3} = \underline{^*1^{***}.4}$$
$$\&\,P_2(9): 11111.1\,\&\,\underline{^*1^*11.2} = \underline{^*1^*11.3}$$
$$\&\,P_2(10): 11111.1\,\&\,\underline{^{****}1.4} = \underline{^{****}1.5}$$

$$P_1(7)\,\&\,P_2(1): {}^*1^*1^*.4\,\&\,{}^*11^{**}.1 = \underline{^*1^{***}.5}$$
$$\&\,P_2(2): {}^*1^*1^*.4\,\&\,1^{**}11.2 = \underline{^{***}1^*.6}$$
$$\&\,P_2(3): \underline{^*1^*1^*.4}\,\&\,11^*11.1 = \underline{^*1^*1^*.5}$$
$$\&\,P_2(4): {}^*1^*1^*.4\,\&\,{}^{**}1^{**}.2 = \underline{^{*****}}$$
$$\&\,P_2(5): {}^*1^*1^*.4\,\&\,1^{***}1.3 = \underline{^{*****}}$$
$$\&\,P_2(6): {}^*1^*1^*.4\,\&\,1^*1^*1.1 = \underline{^{*****}}$$
$$\&\,P_2(7): {}^*1^*1^*.4\,\&\,{}^{***}11.3 = {}^{***}\,\mathbf{1^*.7}$$
$$\&\,\mathbf{P_2}(8): {}^*1^*1^*.4\,\&\,\underline{^*1^{***}.3} = \underline{^*1^{***}.7}$$
$$\&\,P_2(9): {}^*1^*1^*.4\,\&\,{}^*1^*11.2 = {}^*\,\mathbf{1^*1^*.6}$$
$$\&\,P_2(10): {}^*1^*1^*.4\,\&\,{}^{****}1.4 = \underline{^{*****}}$$

$$P_1(8)\,\&\,P_2(1): \underline{^*11^{**}.4}\,\&\,\underline{^*11*{*}.1} = {}^*\,\mathbf{11^{**}.5}$$
$$\&\,P_2(2): {}^*11^{**}.4\,\&\,1^{**}11.2 = \underline{^{*****}}$$
$$\&\,P_2(3): {}^*11^{**}.4\,\&\,11^*11.1 = \underline{^*1^{***}.5}$$
$$\&\,P_2(4): {}^*11^{**}.4\,\&\,\underline{^{**}1^{**}.2} = {}^{**}\,\mathbf{1^{**}.6}$$
$$\&\,P_2(5): {}^*11^{**}.4\,\&\,1^{***}1.3 = \underline{^{*****}}$$
$$\&\,P_2(6): {}^*11^{**}.4\,\&\,1^*1^*1.1 = \underline{^{**}1^{**}.5}$$
$$\&\,P_2(7): {}^*11^{**}.4\,\&\,{}^{***}11.3 = \underline{^{*****}}$$
$$\&\,P_2(8): {}^*11^{**}.4\,\&\,\underline{^*1^{***}.3} = \underline{^*1^{***}.7}$$
$$\&\,P_2(9): {}^*11^{**}.4\,\&\,{}^*1^*11.2 = \underline{^*1^{***}.6}$$
$$\&\,P_2(10): {}^*11^{**}.4\,\&\,{}^{****}1.4 = \underline{^{*****}}$$

$P_1(9) \& P_2(1) : \underline{*1^{***}.6} \& *11^{**}.1 = \underline{*1^{***}.7}$

$\& P_2(2) : *1^{***}.6 \& 1^{**}11.2 = \underline{*****}$

$\& P_2(3) : *1^{***}.6 \& 11^*11.1 = \underline{*1^{***}.7}$

$\& P_2(4) : *1^{***}.6 \& **1^{**}.2 = \underline{*****}$

$\& P_2(5) : *1^{***}.6 \& 1^{***}1.3 = \underline{*****}$

$\& P_2(6) : *1^{***}.6 \& 1^*1^*1.1 = \underline{*****}$

$\& P_2(7) : *1^{***}.6 \& ***11.3 = \underline{*****}$

$\& P_2(8) : *1^{***}.6 \& \underline{*1^{***}.3} = * \mathbf{1^{***}.9}$

$\& P_2(9) : *1^{***}.6 \& *1^*11.2 = \underline{*1^{***}.8}$

$\& P_2(10) : *1^{***}.6 \& ****1.4 = \underline{*****}$

$P_1(10) \& P_2(1) : *111^*.2 \& \underline{*11^{**}.1} = \underline{*11^{**}.3}$

$\& P_2(2) : *111^*.2 \& 1^{**}11.2 = \underline{***1^*.4}$

$\& P_2(3) : *111^*.2 \& 11^*11.1 = \underline{*1^*1^*.3}$

$\& P_2(4) : *111^*.2 \& \underline{**1^{**}.2} = \underline{**1^{**}.4}$

$\& P_2(5) : *111^*.2 \& 1***1.3 = \underline{*****}$

$\& P_2(6) : *111^*.2 \& 1^*1^*1.1 = \underline{**1^{**}.3}$

$\& P_2(7) : *111^*.2 \& ***11.3 = \underline{***1^*.5}$

$\& P_2(8) : *111^*.2 \& \underline{*1^{***}.3} = \underline{*1^{***}.5}$

$\& P_2(9) : *111^*.2 \& *1^*11.2 = \underline{*1^*1^*.4}$

$\& P_2(10) : *111^*.2 \& ****1.4 = \underline{*****}$

After removing (underline) the new elements (results) that contain mutually, the set M remains 15 elements (bold).

After removing (underline) the elements of $P_1$ which are contained by the elements in M, $P_1$ remains 4 elements: (2), (5), (6), (10).

After removing (underline) the elements of $P_2$ which are contained by the elements in M, $P_2$ remains 0 element.

So the set P of the union of the 2 locations has 19 elements.

$P = \{1^{**}11.5, 11^*11.4, ***11.6, *1^*11.5, **1^*1.4, 11^{**}1.5, 1^{***}1.7, *1^{**}1.7, ****1.9, 1^*1^*1.3, ***1^*.7, *1^*1^*.6, *11^{**}.5, **1^{**}.6, *1^{***}.9, *11^*1.3, 111^*1.2, 11111.1, *111^*.2\}$

The following is the algorithm for consolidating two constructive sets:

```
ALGORITHM BatchMerge(PM, PS)
//Input: PM, PS: 2 constructive sets of any 2 batches.
//Output: The new constructive set PM consolidate from PM and PS.
1.   M = Ø  // M: the set of new elements
2.   for each x₁ ∈ PM do
3.     flag = 0
4.     for each x₂ ∈ PS do
5.       q = x₁ o x₂
6.       if q ≠ *  // q differs from the bitchain whose all bits are *
7.         if x₁ ⊆ q then x₁.sign = -1 //mark x₁
8.         if x₂ ⊆ q then x₂.sign = -1 //mark x₂
9.         for each y ∈ M do
10.          if y ⊆ q then
11.            M = M \ {y}
12.            break for
13.          endif
14.          if q ⊆ y then
15.            flag = 1
16.            break for
17.          endif
18.        endfor
19.       else
20.         flag = 1
21.       endif
22.       if flag = 0 then M = M ∪ {q}
23.     endfor
24. endfor
25. for each x₁ ∈ PM do
26.   if x₁.sign ≠ -1 then M = M ∪ {x₁}
27. for each x₂ ∈ PS do
28.   if x₂.sign ≠ -1 then M = M ∪ {x₂}
29. return PM = M // the new PM is now M
```

**Proposition 1:** *Suppose the transaction set $O = \bigcup_{i=1}^{k} O_i$. Corresponding to each batch $O_i$, it has the constructive set $P_i$ obtained from the algorithm* ConPatSet*. The constructive set $P$ of $O$ is determined by applying the algorithm* BatchMerge *in turn with* $k$ $P_i$.

*Proof:* The proposition is proved by the inductive method upon $k$ batches $O_i$.

If $k = 1$ then the algorithm ConPatSet returns the constructive set $P$ for $O = O_1$.

If $k = 2$, it names the two batches $O_1$ and $O_2$, names $m$ elements of the constructive set of $O_1$ $u_1.p_1$, ..., $u_m.p_m$, and names $n$ elements of the constructive set of $O_2$

$v_1.q_1, \ldots, v_n.q_n$. It needs to show that the algorithm BatchMerge will provide the constructive set of the union of $O_1$ and $O_2$ ($O_1 \cup O_2$). It calls w.r an element of the constructive set of $O_1 \cup O_2$. It calls $w_1.r_1$ the part of w.r in $O_1$, i.e. $w_1 = w$ and $r_1$ is the number of times w appears in $O_1$. It defines $w_2.r_2$ in the similar way. From there, it must have $r_1 + r_2 = r$. In addition, there must be one of elements in the constructive set of $O_1$, called $u_1.p_1$, so that $u_1 \propto w$ and $p_1 = r_1$. Indeed, according to the definition of elements in a constructive set, there must be one $u_1.p_1$ such that $u_1 \propto w$ and $p_1 \geq r_1$. There is also one $v_1.q_1$ in $O_2$ such that $v_1 \propto w$ and $q_1 \geq r_2$. Then, there must be $p_1 = r_1$ and $q_1 = r_2$ because otherwise w will appear $p_1 + q_1 > r_1 + r_2 = r$ times in $O_1 \cup O_2$. Now, when applying the algorithm BatchMerge, there is at least one element w'.r with $w' = u_1$ & $v_1$, and specifically w' must cover w. Then, in fact, w' must be w, otherwise, there will be one element w'.r with $w' \propto w$ but the frequency of w' is greater than the frequency of w, and so w.r cannot be an element in the constructive set. So, w.r is created when using the algorithm BatchMerge as desired.

Suppose it has proved the correctness of the proposition for k batches. Now it needs to prove the accuracy of the proposition for k + 1 batches. Symbols of these batches are $O_1, O_2, \ldots, O_k, O_{k+1}$. According to the inductive hypothesis, it is possible to find the constructive set for k batches $O_1, O_2, \ldots, O_k$ by using the algorithm BatchMerge.

Set $S = \bigcup_{i=1}^{k} O_i$, now applying the two batches case proven above to S and $O_{k+1}$, the algorithm BatchMerge will create the constructive set of $S \cup O_{k+1}$, this means that the constructive set for the union of k + 1 batches $O_1, \ldots, O_k, O_{k+1}$ is formed $\square$.

## 4 Experiment

Experiments are conducted on computers with similar configurations: Intel(R) Core (TM) i3-2100 CPU @ 3.10 GHz (4 CPUs), $\sim$3.1 GHz and 4096 MB main memory. Operating System: Windows 7 Ultimate 64-bit (6.1, Build 7601) Service Pack 1. Programming language: C#.NET.

The proposed methods below tested on the *T10I4D100K* dataset available on the website http://fimi.ua.ac.be/data/. The first 10,000 transactions of *T10I4D100K* are run sequentially with the algorithm ConPatSet and recorded results in Table 6.

The Fig. 3 depicts a parallel solution for the algorithm BatchMerge between the server $\mathcal{M}$ and s workstations $\mathcal{S}\alpha$.

Specifically, the computer network used to experiment the solution including one server $\mathcal{M}$ connected to s workstations $\mathcal{S}\alpha$, $\alpha = 1,..,s$; The database at each workstation is $\mathcal{T}_\alpha = (O_\alpha, I, \mathcal{R}_\alpha)$.

The experiment for the parallel solution has 4 phases. The tasks ①, ④, ⑥ belong to the server. The tasks ②, ③, ⑤ belong to the workstations. The arrows indicate the order between the tasks.

With the first 10,000 transactions of *T10I4D100K*, the computer network consists of 1 server and 17 computers with the same configuration as above. The computers are located in separate locations. The server will divide 10,000 transactions into 17 batches corresponding to 17 data streams (16 batches: 590 transactions and 1 batch: 560 transactions) (Table 7).

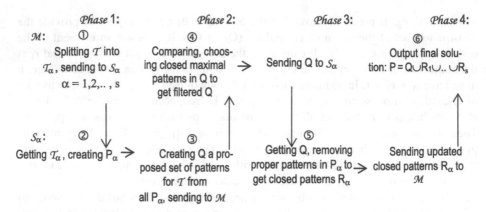

**Fig. 3.** Parallel solution for the algorithm BatchMerge

**Table 6.** Results when running sequentially the algorithm ConPatSet on a single computer.

| Data set | Number of transactions | The maximum number of items in a transaction | The maximum number of items in the data set | Running time (seconds) | Number of closed sets |
|---|---|---|---|---|---|
| T10I4D100K | 10,000 | 26 | 1,000 | 702.14 | 139,491 |

**Table 7.** Results of running the algorithm ConPatSet at locations

| Location | No. of transactions | Running time (second) | No. of closed sets |
|---|---|---|---|
| 1 | 590 | 0.47 | 3,613 |
| 2 | 590 | 0.43 | 3,750 |
| 3 | 590 | 0.45 | 3,811 |
| 4 | 590 | 0.39 | 3,571 |
| 5 | 590 | 0.44 | 3,849 |
| 6 | 590 | 0.42 | 3,685 |
| 7 | 590 | 0.38 | 3,440 |
| 8 | 590 | 0.44 | 3,913 |
| 9 | 590 | 0.37 | 3,392 |
| 10 | 590 | 0.37 | 3,513 |
| 11 | 590 | 0.40 | 3,679 |
| 12 | 590 | 0.39 | 3,543 |
| 13 | 590 | 0.37 | 3,375 |
| 14 | 590 | 0.39 | 3,483 |
| 15 | 590 | 0.38 | 3,311 |
| 16 | 590 | 0.41 | 3,817 |
| 17 | 560 | 0.38 | 3,606 |

After running the algorithm `ConPatSet` at locations, the constructive sets are sent back to the server to consolidate by the algorithm `BatchMerge`. The consolidation time is 154.79 s and the number of last closed sets is 139,491. Therefore, the total execution time is:

Time to distribute and collect data + Maximum running time at locations + Consolidation time = 17.64 s + 0.47 s + 154.79 s = 172.90 s.

## 5  Conclusion

This paper proposes the algorithm with batch-update technique for incremental mining using the constructive set as the intermediate structure.

In the future, a parallelization solution for the algorithm will be proposed. The next step is to test the parallelization solution with large volume data on Hadoop-Spark environment and MapReduce technique.

**Acknowledgement.** This work is funded by Hong Bang International University under grant code GV1907.

## References

1. Ceglar, A., Roddick, J.F.: Incremental association mining using a closed-set lattice. J. Res. Pract. Inf. Technol. **39**(1), 35–45 (2007)
2. Ganter, B., Wille, R.: Formal Concept Analysis: Mathematical Foundations. Springer, Heidelberg (1999)
3. Giannella, C., Han, J., Pei, J., Yan, X., Yu, P.S.: Mining frequent patterns in data streams at multiple time granularities. In: Kargupta, H., Joshi, A., Sivakumar, K., Yesha, Y. (eds.) Data Mining: Next Generation Challenges and Future Directions. AAAI/MIT (2003)
4. Gupta, A., Bhatnagar, V., Kumar, N.: Mining closed itemsets in data stream using formal concept analysis. In: Bach Pedersen, T., Mohania, M.K., Tjoa, A.M. (eds.) DaWaK 2010. LNCS, vol. 6263, pp. 285–296. Springer, Heidelberg (2010). https://doi.org/10.1007/978-3-642-15105-7_23
5. Hu, K., Lu, Y., Shi, C.: Incremental discovering association rules: a concept lattice approach. In: Proceeding of PAKDD99, Beijing, pp. 109–113 (1999)
6. Jin, R., Agrawal, G.: An algorithm for in-core frequent itemset mining on streaming data. In: ICDM 2005 Proceedings of the Fifth IEEE International Conference on Data Mining, pp. 210–217, 27–30 November 2005
7. La, P.-T., Le, B., Vo, B.: Incrementally building frequent closed itemset lattice. Expert Syst. Appl. **41**(6), 2703–2712 (2014)
8. Nguyen, T.-T.: Mining incrementally closed item sets with constructive pattern set. Expert Syst. Appl. **100**, 41–67 (2018)
9. Rouane-Hacene, M., Huchard, M., Napoli, A., Valtchev, P.: Relational concept analysis: mining concept lattices from multi-relational data. Ann. Math. Artif. Intell. **67**(1), 81–108 (2013)
10. Szathmary, L., Valtchev, P., Napoli, A., Godin, R., Boc, A., Makarenkov, V.: Fast mining of iceberg lattices: a modular approach using generators. In: CLA, volume 959 of CEUR Workshop Proceedings, pp. 191–206 (2011)

11. Szathmary, L., Valtchev, P., Napoli, A., Godin, R., Boc, A., Makarenkov, V.: A fast compound algorithm for mining generators, closed itemsets, and computing links between equivalence classes. Ann. Math. Artif. Intell. **70**, 81–105 (2013)
12. Valtchev, P., Missaoui, R.: Building concept (galois) lattices from parts: generalizing the incremental methods. In: Delugach, H.S., Stumme, G. (eds.) ICCS-ConceptStruct 2001. LNCS (LNAI), vol. 2120, pp. 290–303. Springer, Heidelberg (2001). https://doi.org/10. 1007/3-540-44583-8_21
13. Valtchev, P., Missaoui, R., Godin, R.: A framework for incremental generation of closed itemsets. Discrete Appl. Math. **156**(6), 924–949 (2008)
14. Vo, B., Hong, T.P., Le, B.: A lattice-based approach for mining most generalization association rules. Knowl.-Based Syst. **45**, 20–30 (2013)
15. Totad, S.G., Geeta, R.B., Prasad Reddy, P.V.G.D.: Batch processing for incremental FP-tree construction. Int. J. Comput. Appl. IJCA **5**(5), 28–32 (2010)
16. Totad, S.G., Geeta, R.B., Prasad Reddy, P.V.G.D.: Batch incremental processing for FP-tree construction using FP-Growth algorithm. Knowl. Inf. Syst. **33**, 475–490 (2012)

# A Combination Solution for Sleep Apnea and Heart Rate Detection Based on Accelerometer Tracking

Thuong Le-Tien[1(✉)], Phuc Nguyen[2(✉)], Thien Luong-Hoai[1],
Minh Nguyen-Binh[1], Tuan Vu-Minh[1], Hoang Pham-Thai[1],
and Duc Nguyen-Huynh[1]

[1] Department of Electrical and Electronics Engineering,
University of Technology, VNU-HCM, Ho Chi Minh City, Vietnam
thuongle@hcmut.edu.vn
[2] Institute for Biomedical Technology, University of Applied Science,
Mannheim, Germany
p.nguyen@hs-mannheim.de

**Abstract.** In this paper, we propose a combined solution to collect and detect both the heart rate and the obstruction sleep apnea using only vibration signals measured at the patient's neck. Our proposed wearable device can capture vibration signals caused by the respiratory activities and the blood flows in the common carotid artery (CCA) and the internal jugular vein (IJV) on the patient's neck area during sleeping. The data are sent to a server via WIFI connection and stored in a database for further analysis. Our system is accurate and low-cost for capturing the signals and monitoring many patients simultaneously. Moreover, the paper approach also goes deeper into signal processing by using a combination of the Savitzky-Golay filter, a lowpass filter, peak detecting and clustering techniques to extract the heart rate from the vibration of the carotid artery and the jugular. We also propose an algorithm for detecting the apnea state of a monitored patient using the bispectral analysis. In our initial experiments, the proposed algorithms obtain positive achievements.

**Keywords:** Obstructive sleep apnea · Heart rate extraction · Bispectral analysis · Accelerometer tracking

## 1 Introduction

### 1.1 The Obstructive Sleep Apnea (OSA)

**OSA Overview.** The Obstructive Sleep Apnea (OSA) is one of the most common respiratory disorders related to sleep. It is characterized by pauses of breathing caused by a complete or partial closure of the upper airway during sleep [1]. Sleep apnea are divided into three types: central sleep apnea (CSA) which happens because of the missing signal between the brain and the group of muscles whose function is to control the respiratory activity, obstructive sleep apnea (OSA) whose reason is the obstruction of the airway, and mixed sleep apnea (MSA) which is the combination of both CSA

© Springer Nature Switzerland AG 2019
T. K. Dang et al. (Eds.): FDSE 2019, LNCS 11814, pp. 85–103, 2019.
https://doi.org/10.1007/978-3-030-35653-8_7

and OSA [2]. Among three types, OSA is the major sleep disorder. The cause of this sleep disorder shown in Fig. 1 is the relaxation of muscles in the back of the throat supporting the soft palate, the triangular piece of tissue hanging from the soft palate, the tonsils, the sidewalls of the throat and the tongue [3]. As a result, the throat then becomes narrow or even completely get blocked, which leads to loud snoring noises when the patient breathes in and out. That is considered as a common symptom of patients suffering from OSA.

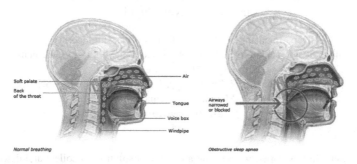

**Fig. 1.** The cause to OSA [4]

According to Javaheri et al. [5], OSA occurs when the respiratory activity is paused for at least 10 s or even longer leading to interrupt individual natural sleep pattern; this accounts for the decline of blood oxygen level and heart rate [4]. The people suffering from OSA have multiple health problems such as cardiovascular disease, stress, dementia, etc., as shown by Surrel et al. [6]. In addition, if the patient cannot breathe because the apnea lasts too long, it will lead to sudden death. Therefore, a device that indicates detection and diagnoses sleep apnea is necessary.

**Relation Between Heart Rate, Respiratory Rate and OSA.** In literature, a variety of parameters are used to detect sleep apnea syndromes. Nam et al. [7] monitored a diversity of parameters such as respiratory rate, heart rate, body temperature, body movements, and blood pressure and concluded that respiratory rate was considered to be one of the most crucial parameters, since it obviously shows the process of inhalation and exhalation as well as indicates sleep apnea. Based on the respiratory rate, some sorts of cardio-respiratory signals such as breathing signal, heart signal and snore signal can be extracted. As reported by Penzel et al., in a comparison of diverse algorithms for apnea detection from ECG recording, most common features are generated from the time series of heartbeats, the ECG morphology, and from the ECG derived respiratory (EDR) signal [8]. Apparently, heart rate is actually associated with breathing in a phenomenon known as respiratory sinus arrhythmia (RSA). When we breathe in, our heart rate rises slightly and then declines as we breathe out [9].

In terms of the relationship between heart rate and OSA, according to G. Surrel et al., the signal's energy shifted towards low frequencies for two different time-series: the series of time intervals between two heartbeats (RR-interval) and the series of R-peak amplitudes with respect to S-amplitudes (RS-amplitude). Additionally, by using spectrogram of RR-interval series, they shown that the signal's energy of OSA events are higher than normal breathing [7]; in other words, there is a clear correlation between the OSA events and the signal's energy in low frequencies.

## 1.2 Related Works

**The OSA Detection Algorithms.** To determine which methods are suitable for OSA detection, many researchers have carefully analyzed the ECG data and then created the needed and relevant features such as RR intervals, RS amplitudes for the next stage. In next stage – the classification stage, different machine learning algorithms have been implemented to detect the OSA occurrences from the chosen features. Those algorithms include the support vector machines (SVM) [10, 11], naïve Bayes classifiers (NB) [11, 12], k-nearest neighbors (KNN) [10, 11], etc. The classification accuracy exceeds 75% in almost all cases.

In another research in 2018, Surrel et al. [6] proposed a wearable system for monitoring the OSA using a single-channel electrocardiogram signal. Then, they developed a low-complexity time-domain analysis to compute the OSA score based on the patient's RR intervals and RS amplitudes of the ECG signal. They also optimized the algorithm to run on a constrained embedded device. Therefore, their system has a classification accuracy of 88.2% and a battery lifetime of up to 46.8 days. However, the classification using hand-crafted features from the raw data is a labor-intensive process. The researchers have to continually come up with new features and evaluate the performances of them on the available datasets using different traditional classification methods.

Recently, the rapid development of the deep learning methods provides a new and different approach to avoid manual feature engineering process. In 2014, Antony et al. [13] implemented a deep neural network with a stacked auto-encoder to classify the ECG signal. Their techniques give the average accuracy of 88%, and they outperform the KNN method and are comparable to other methods such as the SVM, NB classifiers from the literature. In another research in 2018, Li et al. [14] proposed a deep neural network with a sparse auto-encoder and a discriminative Hidden Markov Model. About 84.7% classification accuracy and 88.9% classification sensitivity is achieved in their OSA detection method.

All the mentioned researches above were based on the public Apnea-ECG database available from PhysioNet. The database contains 70 nighttime ECG records from sleep apnea patients [15]. Because of its annotation quality and the amount of data, this database provides an excellent starting point and encourages the competitions between OSA detection methodologies. However, in 2018, Papini et al. [16] shows that the apnea classification algorithms, which are trained on this database, perform poorly in other databases with a broader and more complex spectrum of the apneic events and sleep disorders. This reduction can be explained by the relation between the complexity of breathing events, the ambient noise from the power line and the muscle movements, the non-breathing sleep events and the non-OSA sleep pathologies.

**The Sleep Monitoring Devices.** Numerous methods have been proposed to acquire respiratory signals to detect sleep apnea, yet they mainly focus on developing algorithms and designing complex devices. A standard method is Polysomnography (PSG) [17] which requires multiple electrodes and a respiration mask to monitor necessary features such as an electrocardiogram (ECG), electroencephalogram (EMG), electromyogram (EEG) and electrooculogram (EOG). Admittedly, this approach has high accuracy, but this technique cannot be done at home. The reason is that the recorded data must be analyzed by specialists and required a special room with high-quality devices. Another method which uses a microphone is proposed by Avalur [18]. The sound data during sleep of patients was recorded using a microphone to extract the inhalation and exhalation from the raw data, yet this method is usually affected by ambient noise from the environment and the device needs to be placed near the patient's mouth to obtain a good result. In another research of Surrel et al. [6], they proposed a wearable, accurate, and energy-efficient system for monitoring obstructive sleep apnea on a long-term basis. This approach used a single-channel electrocardiogram signal to compute the sleep apnea score with a classification accuracy up to 88,2%. Although this research reduces the gap between home healthcare and professional supervision, its cost is still high to implement, and difficult to widely deployed for diagnosing and treatment purpose.

**The Respiratory Rate and Heart Rate Extractions from Biosignals.** The respiratory rate has been focused to be estimated from Photoplethysmography (PPG) and ECG signals in numerous researches, yet RR-interval estimation from the accelerometer as a motion-based sensor has been limited in research studies. In the research of Jarchi et al. [19], they proposed a method to extract respiratory rate from an accelerometer sensor and compared the results with normal method PPG. The result is that two types of signal modalities (PPG and accelerations) have shown to be in close agreement for many segments across patients.

In the research of Ruangsuwana et al. [20], this study explored methods to derive respiratory rate from ECG data, and they have divided the methods into two groups: amplitude and interval methods, yet the interval methods are more accurate than the amplitude methods. Additionally, they used the correlation coefficients and the root means square error (RMSE) to compare the ECG breathing extraction methods to the breathing sensor signal. The performance of the ECG Mean method exhibited robustness to noise and was similar to the performance of the interval methods with a 0.830 correlation coefficient to the measured breathing rate and an RMSE of 1.41 bpm.

The Heart Rate (HR) is determined by finding the inverse of RR-interval which is the time difference between two consecutive R-peaks present in every QRS complex [21]. HR is expressed in beats per minute (BPM). The normal range of HR is 60–100 BPM [22]. The formula used to calculate heart rate (HR) is Heart Rate = [360/ (RR-interval in samples)] * 60 beats/min [23]. In the research of Sahoo et al. [24], they put the raw ECG to pre-processing to eliminate noises and passed through bandpass filter are shown. As a result, they could identify the RR interval to calculate a heart rate.

Based on what we have mentioned above, the second purpose of this paper is proposing a method to acquire vibration signals from an accelerometer, and then extract these data to heart rate for OSA detection.

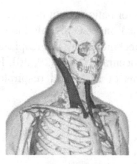

**Fig. 2.** The location of sternocleidomastoid (the red area) (Color figure online).

In this paper, we propose a low-power and compact size device with low cost using an accelerometer to capture the vibration signals from the sternocleidomastoid area, near the CA and IJV (Fig. 2) of patients. The data is sent to a server via WIFI connection; simultaneously, we develop some signal processing algorithms to extract heartrate from snore signals and to detect OSA periods.

The rest of this paper is organized as follows. In Sect. 2, we present the propose materials and methods to generate a device and system propose. Next, in Sect. 3 the experimental setup is illustrated, followed by the corresponding results. Finally, we evaluate the device's performance and discuss the advantages and disadvantages of our proposed method in the future, in Sect. 4.

## 2   Our Proposed Materials and Methods

### 2.1   An Overview of Our System

While there are many progresses of OSA detection algorithms and hardware in the world, to our knowledge, no previous similar work on Vietnamese patient has been done due to the lack of a publicly available Vietnamese sleep and OSA data. In this paper, we introduce a system as shown in Fig. 3. Our long-term goal is a commercial system can be deployed in a hospital and monitor many patients simultaneously. Our prototype system consists of a small wearable device, a server and MySQL database. A medical pad with an accelerometer sensor is placed above the windpipe, near the carotid artery and the jugular of the patient's neck to get the neck's vibration data. During sleep, the recorded signals from the sensor are sent to an embedded device, which has a NodeMCU ESP8266 module as the microcontroller. Those data are then streamed to the server via WIFI connection. The flowchart of the system is shown in Fig. 4.

Palpation of an arterial pulse can be used to assess the cardiac performance, determine cardiac rate and rhythm, or localizing the peripheral lesions. Examination of the carotid pulse is generally directed toward evaluating the status of the heart [25]. In terms of sleep apnea detection, our wearable device captures vibration signals on the patient's neck, when patients perform the respiratory process (inhaling and exhaling activities) the dimension of the neck is changed; this accounts for why accelerometer sensor can acquire respiratory information. Simultaneously, the electrode pad set up on carotid artery also collects the information about the electrocardiogram. In recent years, methods for OSA detection based on ECG signals have been investigated intensively [26–28]. Additionally, several techniques by the respiratory approach to classification sleep apnea events have a high accuracy result [29, 30]. Based on these researches, our study will combine the analysis of ECG and respiratory signal for observing and detecting OSA.

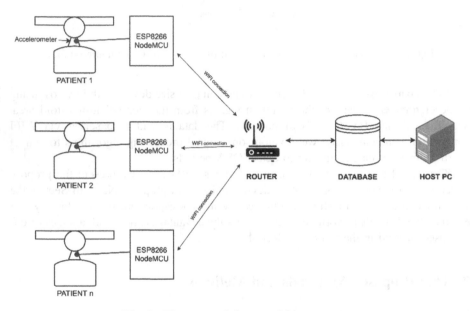

**Fig. 3.** The proposed data acquisition system.

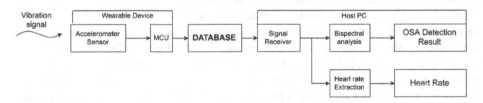

**Fig. 4.** Flow chart of the system.

In this research, we propose a Heartrate Detection Algorithm to capture heart rate signal from the breathing signal obtained by the sensor. According to Roche et al. [31], analyzing Heart Rate Variability is an accurate and inexpensive way in clinically suspected OSA patients and they found that the sensitive percentage was 90%. The algorithm will be explained later in next sections. Besides, to monitor OSA events, we also use bispectral analysis, calculating the bicoherence of the breathing signal to extract the information about the phases and magnitudes of OSA and non-OSA signals.

## 2.2 The Detailed Hardware

We use NodeMCU ESP8266 which is a self-contained WIFI networking solution. It supports Tensilica L106 32-bit processor which achieves extra low power consumption and reaches a maximum clock speed of 160 MHz, maximum 16 MB Flash memory, 50 kB RAM and the wireless protocol is 802.11b/g/n. We also consider MPU6050 sensor module that combines a 3-axis gyroscope, 3-axis accelerometer and a Digital Motion Processor. It is attached to a medical pad, which will be placed on the sternocleidomastoid of patients to capture respiratory signals and heartbeat signals. The NodeMCU ESP8266 can communicate with this module by using I2C communication protocol. In terms of bispectral analysis and other uses, we also use a Dell Inspiron 3558 with 4 GB RAM and i5-5200U CPU 2.20 GHz. The laptop can be replaced by other laptops in which MATLAB can be properly run. The overall device is presented in Fig. 5.

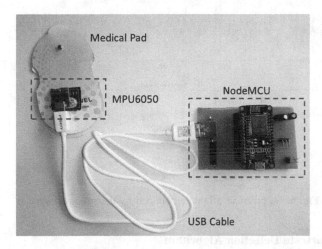

**Fig. 5.** The proposed prototype including a NodeMCU, an MPU6050 and a medical pad

For the simplicity, a laptop simultaneously acts as a localhost server where the signals are sent to and as a client that requests data from the server for signal analysis. The ESP8266 is used as another client that sends data from the accelerometer to the server. We use XAMPP software to create the localhost server as well as the MySQL Database for data storage.

This process involves three steps. The first step is database preparation which involves creating a user account, a database and a table on phpMyAdmin. The table consists of 4 columns, the first of which is the timestamp in which the server receives data sent from ESP8266 and the three next columns are three signals in x, y and z axis. In the second step, the server is programmed to insert data and the corresponding timestamp into a new row of the table if they are sent from the ESP8266 to the server. In the third step, a MATLAB program with the support of Database Toolbox is executed to get all the data in the database for data illustration and further analysis. Finally, the data are saved into *.csv files for further analysis.

The waveform of signals of a recorded sample obtained by the proposed system is illustrated in Fig. 6. It can be seen that the signals have some specific properties such as a signal of an axis can clearly represent the respiratory activity and the amplitude of snoring periods are significantly higher than that of OSA periods, which are considered as important factors to design the OSA detection algorithm.

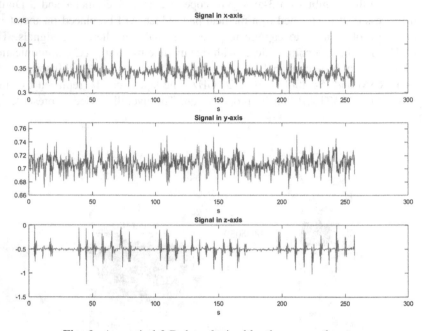

**Fig. 6.** A practical 3-D data obtained by the proposed system

## 2.3    The Heartrate Detection Algorithm

After being measured using our proposed hardware, the vibration data, which includes the respiratory signal and heart rate signal, are stored and analyzed in the PC client using MATLAB. The heart rate is determined by the proposed algorithms as described in the Fig. 7.

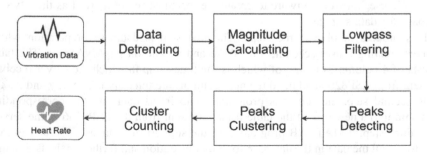

**Fig. 7.** Our proposed heart rate extractor algorithm flowchart

First, the trend in the collected data is estimated using the lowpass Savitzky-Golay filter (polynomial order = 4, frame length = 21) [32]. The Savitzky-Golay filters tend to preserve features – like the local minima and maxima – through a least-square polynomial fit around each point [33]. Therefore, using the Savitzky-Golay filters, the baseline of the noisy data due to the slow body motion and breath of human can be estimated, while the vibration peaks caused by the faster blood flow in the common carotid artery (CCA) and the internal jugular vein (IJV) is maximally removed in the baseline. Using the data subtraction between the original data and the estimated baseline, the trends of value slowly changing are removed, and the peaks are retained in the result data.

**Algorithm 1**: The peaks and valleys clustering algorithm

| | |
|---|---|
| **Input:** | The "peaks" and "valleys" data points $x$ |
| | A time vector *time* that associates with $x$ |
| | A time difference threshold *minDistance* |
| **Output:** | An $m{\times}3$ matrix *foundClusters* with: |
| | $m$ is number of clusters; $i$ is the index of a found cluster, $i = \overline{1, m}$ |
| | *foundClusters*$(i, 1)$ is the start time of cluster $i$ |
| | *foundClusters*$(i, 2)$ is the end time of cluster $i$ |
| | *foundClusters*$(i, 3)$ is the timepoint of the largest peak in cluster $i$ |

```
1:   Initiate timeDifference and localMaximaValues vectors
2:   For 2≤ i ≤ length(x):
3:       timeDifference(i-1) ← time(i) – time(i-1)
4:   End for
5:   localMaximaValues ← Find all the local maxima in the timeDifference
     vector with the minimum peak separation minDistance
6:   m ← length(localMaximaValues)
7:   Initiate the mx3 foundClusters matrix
8:   endIdx ← 0
9:   For 1 ≤ i ≤ m:
10:      startIdx ← endIdx + 1
11:      endIdx ← Find the corresponding index in the vector time of the
         localMaximaValues(i)
12:      maxIdx ← index of the largest value in cluster x(startIdx:endIdx)
13:      foundClusters(i, 1) ← time(startIdx)
14:      foundClusters(i, 2) ← time(endIdx)
15:      foundClusters(i, 3) ← time(maxIdx)
16:  End for
17:  Return foundClusters
```

Second, the magnitude of the acceleration at each data point $a(i)$ is calculated using 3-axis acceleration values $a_x(i), a_y(i), a_z(i)$ as:

$$a(i) = \sqrt{a_x^2(i) + a_y^2(i) + a_z^2(i)} \tag{1}$$

Then, the resulting magnitudes are digitally low-pass filtered at 8 Hz. The American Heart Association states the normal resting adult human heart rate is 60–100 bpm or 1–2 beats per second [28]. Therefore, the passband edge frequency is chosen at 8 Hz for safely capturing those heart pulse signals and leaving out the higher frequency signals.

After the low-pass filter, we find all the local maxima and minima in the data using the built-in function *findpeaks()* of MATLAB. All the local maxima ("peaks") and local minima ("valleys") are then clustered to classify each found data point into a specific heart pulse using the algorithm as described in the Algorithm 1. Finally, we count the number of clusters during a specific period and convert to the heartbeats per minute (BPM) using the following equation:

$$BPM = \frac{number\ of\ clusters}{time\ duration\ of\ the\ current\ signal} * 60 \tag{2}$$

The idea behind the peaks detecting and clustering steps is that in the collected data, we observed that when the ventricle contracts and blood is pumping through the CCA and IJV, the heart pulses cause large fluctuations in the data. Thus, they create a lot of "peaks" and "valleys" in this signal region. Between the pulses, the signal remains steady and doesn't have many "peaks" and "valleys". Therefore, the number of peaks and valleys and the time duration between them is used to identify clusters in the signal.

## 2.4    The Bispectral Analysis and Bicoherence Calculation

There are various methods in processing the collected signals. The most general approach is utilizing Power Spectral Density (PSD) to identify abnormal frequencies. However, this method can only detect linear mechanisms in the signal since the information about the coupling between frequencies and phase relations are not included [28]. To overcome this problem, in this paper we use the high order spectra analysis, specifically bispectral analysis.

Given a real stationary random signal with zero mean $\{x(k)\}$, the third-order cumulant is

$$c(m, n) = E\{x(k)x(k + n)x(k + m)\} \tag{3}$$

where $E\{\cdot\}$ denotes the expectation operation. The bispectrum of a signal is defined as the Fourier transform of its third-order cumulant

$$B(\omega_1, \omega_2) = \sum_{m=-\infty}^{\infty} \sum_{n=-\infty}^{\infty} c(m, n)\exp\{-j(\omega_1 m + \omega_2 n)\} \tag{4}$$

or in terms of expectation operation,

$$B(\omega_1, \omega_2) = E\{X(\omega_1)X(\omega_2)X^*(\omega_1 + \omega_2)\} \tag{5}$$

Where $X(\omega)$ is the Fourier transform of $x(n)$ and $*$ denotes complex conjugate of X.

Bispectrum of a signal is symmetrical. A complete understanding of the bispectrum can be inferred from the knowledge of the region $\omega_1 \geq 0, \omega_1 \geq \omega_2, \omega_1 + \omega_2 \leq \pi$. Equation (5) indicates that the bispectrum contains information regarding the interactions between two harmonic components of the signal. This makes bispectral analysis a more powerful tool than power spectrum in processing nonlinear processes, such as the activities of the upper airway, where phase coupling between harmonies can also contain useful information [35]. The nonlinear characteristics of snore signals can be better examined exploiting this property. By observing peaks in bispectrum of the signal, where the degree of phase coupling between two frequencies $(\omega_1, \omega_2)$ is high, we can hope to detect when patients are suffering from sleep apnea.

To achieve such result, we will employ bicoherence, a normalized bispectrum, as a feature of high-order spectral analysis. The bicoherence is defined as:

$$b(\omega_1, \omega_2) = \frac{B(\omega_1, \omega_2)}{P(\omega_1)P(\omega_2)P(\omega_1 + \omega_2)} \qquad (6)$$

As can be seen from its definition, bicoherence is a quantity combination of two different spectral order entities, namely power spectrum and bispectrum. The correlation between two simultaneously measured signal can also be examined using bicoherence [36].

**Algorithm 2**: OSA Detection using Bispectral Analysis

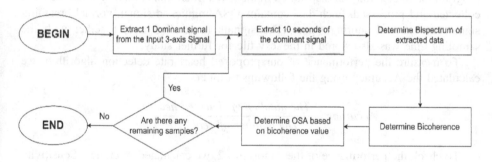

In order to find the dominant signal from 3-axis-data, each signal is divided into frames and the highest variance among all the variances of all frames is considered as the variance of the corresponding signal. Then, the signal with the highest variance value will be chosen as the dominant signal. The reason is that when the patient snores, the vibration will cause the strong fluctuations of the signal and thus, a larger value of variance. Due to the sleeping posture, the dominant signal can be any of the x-axis, y-axis or z-axis and will vary from patients to patients. Because of that reason, the first step in our algorithm after collecting data is to calculate the variances to find the dominant signal which will be the input to the next steps in the process.

After the dominant signal is selected, the analysis algorithm will be executed with the input is the data from the chosen signal. The number of the samples input will be chosen such that the corresponding time will be approximately 10 s, which is the minimum time required to determine whether or not a patient is suffering from OSA symptoms. Next, the bicoherence and its energy will be calculated. Compare with the previous results the algorithm, the system will be able to detect an event of OSA by means of a sudden fall in the energy of bicoherence below the threshold which is determined empirically.

## 3 Experiments

### 3.1 Data Preparations

The data was collected from 5 male participants. First, an access point was set up, and a connection was established between the laptop and the device through that access point. The laptop in this setup acted as a localhost and got data from the device through a WIFI connection. The connecting procedure was defined in the program which is pre-load into the device. The volunteers first attached a medical pad with the accelerometer to the sternocleidomastoid and laid down on the bed comfortably. The volunteer then breath following instructions given by the research team member. Next, the device was powered by the 3.7 DC Battery and executed the pre-load procedure to connect to the access point. The MATLAB program which performed the analysis algorithm was triggered after 1 s of the start of data collection session to ensure that there were enough samples in the collected data. The data was then forwarded to the MATLAB program for calculation and then stored in the .csv format file. A total of 9 samples was collected and processed. Each data contains OSA-mimicked signal, normal breathing signal, and normal snoring signal. The signals from all 3 axes together with the sampling time was also stored in the .csv file for further study.

To measure the performance of our proposed heart rate detection algorithm, we calculated the Accuracy using the following formula:

$$Accuracy = \frac{The\ number\ of\ detected\ heart\ rate}{The\ number\ of\ real\ heart\ rate} \tag{7}$$

To check the performance of the Algorithm 2, we calculated Accuracy, Sensitivity and Specificity formulas as follows:

$$Accuracy = \frac{TP + TN}{TP + TN + FP + FN} \tag{8}$$

$$Sensitivity = \frac{TP}{TP + FN} \tag{9}$$

$$Specificity = \frac{TN}{TN + FP} \tag{10}$$

where TP is the number of cases correctly identified as OSA, FP is the number of cases incorrectly identified as OSA, TN is the number of cases correctly identified as non-OSA and FN is the number of cases incorrectly identified as non-OSA.

## 3.2    Experiment Descriptions and Results

**The Proposed Heartrate Detection Algorithm.** After applying the Heartrate Detection Algorithm, we obtain the results as shown in Fig. 8. In that figure, we can see from in the raw data, the bias of each axis changes due to the movement of human's body. After detrending, the bias and trends are eliminated, and the signal fluctuates around the zero value (y = 0).

With the obtained detrended signal, we calculate the magnitudes of each point and plot them in Fig. 9a. To remove high-frequency noise, we apply a low pass filter and obtained the graph as shown in Fig. 9b. In Fig. 9c, the blue stars represent all the detected local extremes. After clustering and wrapping them in rectangles, the maxima of each cluster is indicated by the red point. Counting the number of red points will give us the heart rate information.

The average accuracy is 83.78%. Because of the weak vibration of the carotid artery and the jugular in some samples, our algorithm cannot detect exactly the heart rate information, thus the accuracy is degraded. However, despite the difficulty of getting dataset, out proposed algorithm brings a positive result.

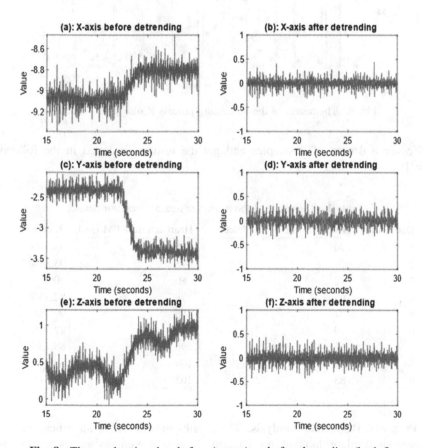

**Fig. 8.** The acceleration data before (a, c, e) and after detrending (b, d, f)

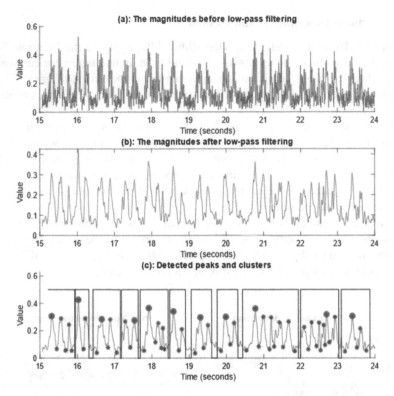

**Fig. 9.** The results of the processing process (Color figure online)

We use a dataset of 9 samples and get the results illustrated in the following Table 1:

**Table 1.** The result of the heart rate detection on our dataset

| Data number | Heart rate in BPM (detection) | Heart rate in BPM (real) | Accuracy |
|---|---|---|---|
| 1 | 70 | 75 | 93.33% |
| 2 | 70 | 75 | 93.33% |
| 3 | 72 | 80 | 90% |
| 4 | 65 | 78 | 82.35% |
| 5 | 77 | 86 | 90% |
| 6 | 70 | 90 | 77.78% |
| 7 | 66 | 96 | 68.75% |
| 8 | 80 | 100 | 80% |
| 9 | 83 | 105 | 78.51% |

**The Proposed Bispectral Analysis.** The lengths of window in identification of the dominant signal algorithm and in calculating bicoherence energy values process were

200 and 20, respectively, the scale factor was chosen as 0.5. The estimated bicoherence of a normal snoring data and that of an OSA-mimicked data are shown in Fig. 10. It is noticeable that the sharpest peak of the normal signal is located near the origin, meanwhile that of the OSA signal is placed far away from the origin. The energy of each window of the former and latter signal are also illustrated in Figs. 11 and 12.

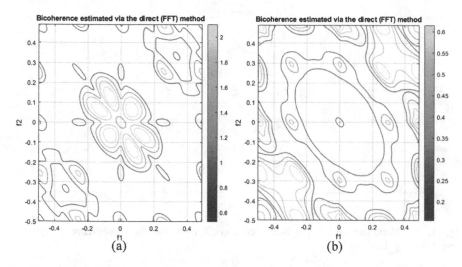

**Fig. 10.** Estimated bicoherence of a normal snoring signal (a) and OSA-mimicked signal (b)

In case of normal snoring signal, there are some short periods in which the signal had minor amplitude values. These periods are normal signal from exhalation activity and have short duration (about 2–3 s), therefore, they were not considered as OSA events. As a result, the energy values were higher than the threshold value (the orange cline) and the value of the OSA detecting line (the red line) was zero. Furthermore, the value of the first 49 samples in Bicoherence graph was zero because the number of samples per window is 50 when calculating bicoherence coefficients. Therefore, the first 49 samples did not satisfy the requirement of length. This zone was ignored in OSA detection process.

In terms of snoring signal with OSA, it is clear that the bicoherence coefficients significantly decrease in OSA periods. The bicoherence energy was lower than the threshold, as a consequence, the OSA detecting line had high value in the OSA zones. In addition, the first indexes of the detected OSA zones were 49 samples later than those of the OSA zones in the dominant signal. It is because when the OSA first occurs in the i-th sample in the dominant signal, the indexes of the first and the last sample of the window used for bicoherence calculation are (i − 49) and i, which is still in the normal snoring period. After 49 samples, the window starts at the i-th sample and ends at (i + 49)-th sample, which is a complete OSA zone. This delay ensures that the OSA zone is recognized only when its duration is at least 10 s.

Testing the proposed algorithms on all 9 recorded data, we obtained the Table 2. The data no.4 was purely normal snoring signal, therefore, the algorithm detected no

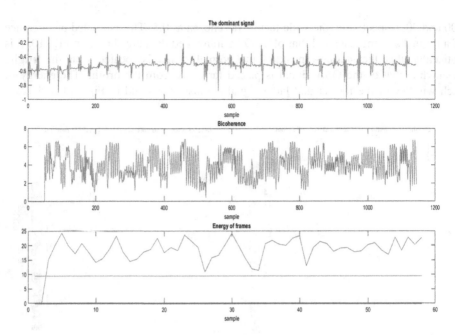

**Fig. 11.** The dominant signal, the bicoherence coefficients and the bicoherence energy in a normal snoring data

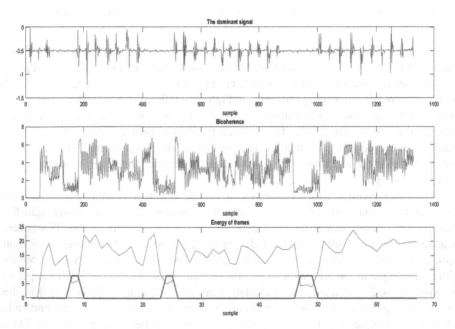

**Fig. 12.** The dominant signal, the bicoherence coefficients and the bicoherence energy in an OSA-mimicked data

**Table 2.** OSA detection results in 9 testing data

| Data no. | No. of OSA periods | | No. of non-OSA periods | |
|---|---|---|---|---|
| | Detection | Reality | Detection | Reality |
| 1 | 2 | 2 | 3 | 3 |
| 2 | 2 | 2 | 2 | 2 |
| 3 | 2 | 2 | 2 | 2 |
| 4 | 0 | 0 | 1 | 1 |
| 5 | 1 | 1 | 1 | 1 |
| 6 | 2 | 3 | 3 | 3 |
| 7 | 2 | 2 | 3 | 3 |
| 8 | 1 | 5 | 5 | 5 |
| 9 | 1 | 2 | 3 | 3 |

OSA period during the record. However, the algorithm failed to detect all OSA events in data no.8. It is because the duration of some mimicked-OSA periods in that data is nearly 10 s, which means that they do not satisfy the required number of samples to be considered as OSA events. It can be derived from the Table 2 that the accuracy of this approach is 90.42%, sensitivity is 79.58% and specificity is 100%.

## 4 Conclusion and Future Works

In this paper, we propose a monitoring system and a combined solution of detecting the occurrence of OSA using the heart rate and bispectral analysis. Our embedded device is small, low-cost while still maintains the accurate capture both of the breath/ snore and heartbeat vibration. In our experiments, the heart rate detection algorithm is able to extract the heart rate from the noisy vibration signal with the accuracy of 83.78%. And with our proposed OSA detection based on the bispectral analysis, the accuracy is 89,89%, sensitivity is 78.14% and specificity is 100%.

However, there are still some drawbacks in our progress so far. First, the bispectral approach requires a good hardware configuration leading to a high computational cost. Second, the strong vibration from the human voice and snore can interfere with the heart pulses, therefore the heart pulses are masked by the noises and cause some difficulty in heart rate detection.

In future, we will address those issues and work towards the goal of making a wearable device, which can extract the heart rate and use these features with the bispectral analysis for detecting the Obstructive Sleep Apnea in real-time. Furthermore, an alert mechanism to wake up patients whenever the OSA occurs will be investigated and implemented to prevent sudden death while sleeping.

**Acknowledgment.** This research is partly funded by Ho Chi Minh City University of Technology under student research grants for the French-Vietnamese program.

# References

1. Caylak, E.: The genetics of sleep disorders in humans: narcolepsy, restless legs syndrome, and obstructive sleep apnea syndrome. Am. J. Med. Genet. Part A **149A**, 2612–2626 (2009)
2. Thuong, L., Phuc, N., Hoang, P., Tuan, V., Thien, L., Duc, N.: Accelerometer Sensor Model for Sleep Apnea Detection with Bispectral Signal Analysis. University of Technology Ho Chi Minh City, Vietnam, Dept. of Elec. and Electronics Eng (2019)
3. Sleep apnea - Symptoms and causes. https://www.mayoclinic.org/diseases-conditions/sleep-apnea/symptoms-causes/syc-20377631. Accessed 8 Jul 2019
4. Institute for Quality and Efficiency in Health Care (IQWiG), Obstructive sleep apnea: Overview. https://www.ncbi.nlm.nih.gov/books/NBK279274/
5. Javaheri, S., et al.: Sleep Apnea. J. Am. Coll. Cardiol. **69**, 841–858 (2017)
6. Surrel, G., Aminifar, A., Rincon, F., Murali, S., Atienza, D.: Online obstructive sleep apnea detection on medical wearable sensors. IEEE Trans. Biomed. Circuits Syst. **12**, 762–773 (2018)
7. Nam, Y., Kim, Y., Lee, J.: Sleep monitoring based on a tri-axial accelerometer and a pressure sensor. Sensors **16**, 750 (2016)
8. Penzel, T., McNames, J., de Chazal, P., Raymond, B., Murray, A., Moody, G.: Systematic comparison of different algorithms for apnoea detection based on electrocardiogram recordings. Med. Biol. Eng. Comput. **40**, 402–407 (2002)
9. CurioCity – CurioCité, Why does your heart rate decrease when you take a deep breath? http://explorecuriocity.org/Explore/ArticleId/705/why-does-your-heart-rate-decrease-when-you-take-a-deep-breath-705.aspx
10. Yılmaz, B., Asyalı, M., Arıkan, E., Yetkin, S., Özgen, F.: Sleep stage and obstructive apneaic epoch classification using single-lead ECG. BioMedical Eng. OnLine **9**, 39 (2010)
11. Isa, S.M., Ivan Fanany, M., Jatmiko, W., Murni Arymurthy, A.: Sleep apnea detection from ECG signal: analysis on optimal features, principal components, and nonlinearity. In: 5th International Conference on Bioinformatics and Biomedical Engineering. IEEE (2011)
12. Chazal, P., Penzel, T., Heneghan, C.: Automated detection of obstructive sleep apnoea at different time scales using the electrocardiogram. Physiol. Meas. **25**, 967–983 (2004)
13. Kaguara, A., Nam, K.M., Reddy, S.: A deep neural network classifier for diagnosing sleep apnea from ECG data on smartphones and small embedded systems (2014)
14. Li, K., Pan, W., Li, Y., Jiang, Q., Liu, G.: A method to detect sleep apnea based on deep neural network and hidden Markov model using single-lead ECG signal. Neurocomputing **294**, 94–101 (2018)
15. Penzel, T., Moody, G., Mark, R., Goldberger, A., Peter, J.: The apnea-ECG database. Comput. Cardiol. **27**, 255–258 (2000)
16. Papini, G., et al.: On the generalizability of ECG-based obstructive sleep apnea monitoring: merits and limitations of the Apnea-ECG database. In: 2018 40th Annual International Conference of the IEEE Engineering in Medicine and Biology Society (EMBC) (2018)
17. Bucklin, C., Das, M., Luo, S.: An inexpensive accelerometer based sleep-apnea screening technique. In: IEEE 2010 National Aerospace & Electronics Conference, USA, pp 396–399 (2010)
18. Avalur, D.S.: Human Breath Detection using a Microphone. University of Groningen, Groningen (2013)
19. Jarchi, D., Rodgers, S., Tarassenko, L., Clifton, D.: Accelerometry-based estimation of respiratory rate for post-intensive care patient monitoring. IEEE Sens. J. **18**, 4981–4989 (2018)

20. Ruangsuwana, R., Velikic, G., Bocko, M.: Methods to extract respiration information from ECG Signals. In: IEEE International Conference on Acoustics, Speech and Signal Processing (2010)
21. Pang, L., Tchoudovski, I., Braecklein, M., Egorouchkina, K., Kellermann, W., Bolz, A.: Real time heart ischemia detection in the smart home care system. In: Proceedings of IEEE on Engineering in Medicine and Biology Society (EMBS), vol. 886, pp. 3703–3706 (2005)
22. All About Heart Rate (Pulse). https://www.heart.org/en/health-topics/high-blood-pressure/the-facts-about-high-blood-pressure/all-about-heart-rate-pulse
23. Acharya, U., Suri, J., Spaan, J.: Advances in Cardiac Signal Processing. Springer (2007)
24. Sahoo, G., Ari, S., Patra, S.: ECG signal analysis for detection of Heart Rate and Ischemic Episodes. ISSN **3**, 2249–7277 (2013)
25. Walker, H., Hall, W., Hurst, J.: Clinical methods. Butterworths, Boston (1990)
26. Sharma, M., Agarwal, S., Acharya, U.: Application of an optimal class of antisymmetric wavelet filter banks for obstructive sleep apnea diagnosis using ECG signals. Comput. Biol. Med. **100**, 100–113 (2018)
27. Atri, R., Mohebbi, M.: Obstructive sleep apnea detection using spectrum and bispectrum analysis of single-lead ECG signal. Physiol. Meas. **36**, 1963–1980 (2015)
28. Janbakhshi, P., Shamsollahi, M.: Sleep apnea detection from single-lead ECG using features based on ECG-derived respiration (EDR) signals. IRBM **39**, 206–218 (2018)
29. Avcı, C., Akbaş, A.: Sleep apnea classification based on respiration signals by using ensemble methods. Bio-Med. Mater. Eng. **26**, S1703–S1710 (2015)
30. Aydoğan, O., Öter, A., Güney, K., Kıymık, M., Tuncel, D.: Automatic diagnosis of obstructive sleep apnea/hypopnea events using respiratory signals. J. Med. Syst. **40**, 274 (2016)
31. Roche, F.: Screening of obstructive sleep apnea syndrome by heart rate variability analysis. Circulation AHA J. **100**(13), 1411–1415 (1999)
32. Savitzky, A., Golay, M.: Smoothing and differentiation of data by simplified least squares procedures. Anal. Chem. **36**, 1627–1639 (1964)
33. Pandia, K., Ravindran, S., Cole, R., Kovacs, G., Giovangrandi, L.: Motion artifact cancellation to obtain heart sounds from a single chest-worn accelerometer. In: IEEE International Conference on Acoustics, Speech and Signal Processing. IEEE (2010)
34. Mendel, J.: Tutorial on higher-order statistics (spectra) in signal processing and system theory: theoretical results and some applications. Proc. IEEE **79**, 278–305 (1991)
35. Nikias, C., Raghuveer, M.: Bispectrum estimation: a digital signal processing framework. Proc. IEEE **75**, 869–891 (1987)
36. Emin Tagluk, M., Sezgin, N.: A new approach for estimation of obstructive sleep apnea syndrome. Expert Syst. Appl. **38**, 5346–5351 (2011)

# A Model for Real-Time Traffic Signs Recognition Based on the YOLO Algorithm – A Case Study Using Vietnamese Traffic Signs

An Cong Tran[✉], Duong Lu Dien, Hiep Xuan Huynh, Nguyen Huu Van Long, and Nghi Cong Tran

Can Tho University, Can Tho, Vietnam
{tcan,hxhiep,nhvlong}@ctu.edu.vn

**Abstract.** The rapid development of the automobile resulted in the traffic infrastructure becomes more and more complicated. Both type and the number of traffic signs on the streets are increasing. Therefore, there is a need for applications to support drivers to recognize the traffic signs on the streets to help them avoid missing traffic signs. This paper proposes an approach to detecting and classifying Vietnamese traffic signs based on the YOLO algorithm, a unified deep learning architecture for real-time recognition applications. An anchor boxes size calculation component based on the k-means clustering algorithm is added to identify the anchor boxes size for the YOLO algorithm. A Vietnamese traffic sign dataset including 5000 images containing 5704 traffic signs of types was collected and used for evaluation. The F1 score of the tiny model (the fastest but the most inaccurate model) achieved is about more than 92% and the detection time is approximately 0.17 s (in our testing environment: laptop CPU Intel 3520M, 8 GB RAM, no GPU). In comparison with similar research in Vietnamese traffic sign recognition, the proposed approach in this paper shows a potential result that provides a good trade-off between the recognition accuracy and recognition time as well as the feasibility for real applications.

**Keywords:** Vietnamese traffic signs · Detection · YOLO Algorithm · Deep learning · K-means clustering

## 1 Introduction

The growth of automobiles results in the changes of traffic infrastructure. The number and types of road signs have been increased to respond to the development of the new infrastructure. As a result, the drivers have to remember more and more road signs as well as pay more attention to traffic signs when they are driving, i.e. more observation is needed. Therefore, it is necessary to have real-time traffic sign detection and classification systems to support drivers, to help

© Springer Nature Switzerland AG 2019
T. K. Dang et al. (Eds.): FDSE 2019, LNCS 11814, pp. 104–116, 2019.
https://doi.org/10.1007/978-3-030-35653-8_8

them in avoiding missing traffic signs, which may lead to dangerous situations or event accidents. Besides, traffic sign detection and classification can also be applied in many other potential applications such as in developing smart cars or self-driving cars, etc.

Due to the important applications of traffic sign recognition, i.e. including detection and classification, many studies on this problem have been pursued since the 90s. In Arturo de la Escalera et al. research conducted in 1997, the authors proposed a method for traffic sign recognition, which uses the color threshold to segment the image and shape analysis to detect the road signs. Then, the neural network is used to classify the detected signs. The proposed method had been evaluated using a small dataset, including 9 images for training the neural network and 10 images for testing. However, the images in this dataset are taken in the natural scenes and in ideal conditions, i.e. without noise. Such selection was affected by the disadvantage of the proposed method, that is, this method is sensitive to the noise. It is easy to mis-classify the objects that have similar shape or color to the road signs such as advertisement panels, which is very popular in the urban environment.

Similar to the above, some other studies on traffic sign recognition around that time were also based on image processing techniques combined with similarity measurement algorithm or on the combination of image processing techniques and machine learning algorithm using popular feature descriptors such as in [2,3,5,6,9,11]. Gavrila [6] uses a template-based correlation method and distance transforms to identify potential traffic signs in images. Then, a radial basis function network is used for classifying the recognized traffic signs. The template-based correlation method has a high computational cost and thus it is not suited to real-time recognition systems. Barnes and Zelinsky [2] use the fast radial symmetry detector to the image stream from a camera mounted in a car eliminate almost all non-sign pixels from the image stream. Then, they apply normalized cross-correlation to classify the signs. This method is suitable for circular signs only and thus they evaluate the method on the Australian road signs only. In order to detect triangular, square and octagonal signs, Loy Gareth and Barnes Nick use a similar technique in [9]. The symmetric nature of these shapes, together with the pattern of edge orientations exhibited by equiangular polygons with a known number of sides is used to establish possible shape centroid locations in the image. This approach is invariant to in-plane rotation and returns the location and size of the shape detected. However, this increases the computational cost so it cannot work in real-time. Unfortunately, the color-based methods are sensitive to strong light, poor light and other bad weather condition.

In recent years, with the increase in the amount of data and the computational power of computers, deep learning has become a new trend in both research and application areas. Many new neural network models have been introduced to solve the traditional problems by using the data-oriented approach, i.e. the huge amount of data is used with deep neural networks, and this method produces promising results. Therefore, recent research in traffic sign recognition also apply deep learning methods and they archived outstanding performance [4,7,12,15,17]. Cireşan et al. [4] proposed a multi-column deep neural network for classification running on a graphical processing unit and obtained a better-than-human recognition rate. Jin et al. [7] used a convolution neural network (CNN) with a hinge loss stochastic gradient descent method, which achieved a high detection rate. Quian et al. [12] used CNN as a classifier to learn the discriminative feature of max pooling position to classify traffic signs and obtained a good performance in comparison with the state-of-the-art method. Youssef et al. [17] used a procedure based on color segmentation, histogram of oriented gradient, and a CNN for traffic sign detection. This research achieves better recognition accuracy and computational speed. However, in this research line, it is important for the real-time recognition and thus it is necessary to find more network structures to improve the recognition accuracy and processing time.

There are also some studies on Vietnamese traffic sign recognition, which are more closely related to our work in this paper [1,10]. Mai et al. [10] combined the color-based and shape-based method for image segmentation and localization. Then, the SIFT matching is applied to match the keypoints of the extracted pictogram with the keypoints of template images in the database to detect the sign. The recognition accuracy is approximately 95%. However, the dataset is rather small with 600 images that belong to six types of dangerous signs. Also, this method is rather slow with the detection time is more than 2 s, in which the segmentation and localization take about 0.34 s and classification takes more than 1.8 s. In Truong et al. research [1], the authors used the HOG feature and neural network for traffic sign detection. A color-based segmentation is used beforehand to segment the red and blue traffic signs. Then, a shape-based method is used to identify the boundary of the potential candidates. Finally, the HOG feature of detected candidates are fed into a 3-layer neural network for training. The reported accuracy is about 95% and the detection time is approximately 0.12 s. This is a good performance in terms of both accuracy and recognition time. However, in general, the color-based is sensitive to lighting changes while the shape-based cue is insensitive to lighting changes but could be distracted by cluttered background [16].

With the prominent representation capacity and outstanding performance of deep learning methods in traffic sign recognition, in this study, we propose to use YOLO, a state-of-the-art deep learning model to recognize Vietnamese traffic signs. This learning model introduces several architectures that provide different levels of the trade-off between recognition accuracy and recognition time. Therefore, it is very flexible and can be adjusted to adapt to a particular circumstance, such as the hardware limitation, constraint on the accuracy, and the like. We used the k-means clustering algorithm [8] to cluster the bounding boxes of the traffic signs to identify the anchors' size for the YOLO algorithm. This study also introduces a new Vietnamese traffic sign dataset including 5704 images of 22 types of the traffic signs. These images are extracted from the videos recorded by a phone camera that was attached to the front of a motorcycle. The videos were mainly recorded in the urban areas, there exist many noises and distractions.

The paper is structured as follows: the proposed model for Vietnamese traffic sign recognition is presented in Sect. 2, including the description of the Vietnamese traffic sign system, the overall model of the proposed method and the structure of the YOLO algorithm. Then, the evaluation dataset and evaluation result are reported in Sect. 3. Finally, the conclusion and future work of this research are discussed in Sect. 4.

## 2    Traffic Sign Detection Using YOLO Algorithm

### 2.1    Vietnamese Traffic Signs

There are 144 traffic signs in the Vietnamese traffic sign system. They are grouped into 4 groups: prohibitory or restrictive signs (40 signs), warning signs (47 signs), mandatory signs (10 signs) and indication signs (47 signs). Some Vietnamese traffic signs are shown in Fig. 1 and an image in which there exists a traffic sign is demonstrated in Fig. 2.

**Fig. 1.** Example of Vietnamese traffic signs

**Fig. 2.** Traffic sign in a dashcam image

## 2.2 Vietnamese Traffic Sign Recognition Model Based on YOLO Algorithm

Traffic sign recognition includes two main tasks: (i) detect the traffic signs within the images, and (ii) classify the detected signs. In this research, we propose a model for recognizing the Vietnamese traffic signs based on the YOLO algorithm. We also employ the k-means clustering algorithm for identifying the anchors' size, one of the important hyper-parameters of the YOLO algorithm. Our proposed approach is presented in Fig. 3.

First, the training data is labeled including the bounding box for traffic signs within the images and the label of the traffic signs. Then, we use the k-means clustering algorithm to cluster the bounding boxes to calculate the anchors' size. The labeled data together with the calculated anchors' size are put into the YOLO algorithm to build the traffic sign recognition model. This model then will be use to recognize the traffic signs inside images. Detail of the basic steps are described below.

## 2.3 The YOLO Network Architecture

YOLO (You Only Look Once) is an object detection approach which was first introduced in 2015 by Redmon and his colleagues [13]. This is a unified for real-time object detection in which a single neural network is used to predict bounding boxes and class probabilistic directly from full image in one inference. Therefore, it is known as an extremely fast deep learning model.

The features from the entire image are used to predict each bounding box. All bounding boxes across all classes are also predicted simultaneously. This enables end-to-end training and real-time speed while maintaining high average precision [13]. To do so, YOLO divides the input image into S × S grids. Each cell in the grid predicts $B$ bounding boxes and confidence score of bounding boxes. Each

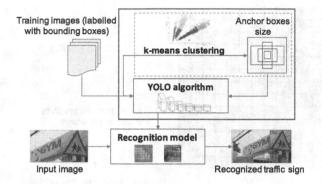

**Fig. 3.** Architecture of the Vietnamese traffic sign recognition system

bounding box consists of five prediction $(b_x, b_y, b_w, b_h, p)$. The $(b_x, b_y)$ coordinates are the center of the box relative to the bound of the grid cell. The $b_w$ and $b_h$ are the width and height of the bounding box which are predicted relative to the whole image. Finally, the predicted confidence $p$ is calculated as follow:

$$p = Pr(Object) \times IOU_{pred}^{truth}$$

$Pr(Object) = 1$ if the grid cell contains a part of a ground truth box, otherwise it is zero. The $IOU_{pred}^{truth}$ is the intersection over union between the predicted bounding box and the ground truth box.

Each grid cell also has conditional class probabilities $C = Pr(Class_i| Object)$, which represent the conditioned probabilities on the grid cell containing an object. Details of the calculation of $C$ can be found in [13]. Figure 4 demonstrates the above process of YOLO.

At the detection time, the multiplication of $C$ and $p$: $Pr(Class_i \mid Object) \times Pr(Object) \times IOU_{pred}^{truth}$ gives us the class-specific confidence scores for each box. These scores represent both the probability of that class appearing in the box and how well the predicted box fits the object.

The above model is implemented as a convolutional neural network (CNN). The initial convolution layers extract features from the images while the fully connected layers predict the output probabilities and coordinates. The YOLO algorithm has several versions and each of them has different numbers of convolutional layers and fully connected layers. The first version of YOLO has 24 convolutional layers followed by 2 fully connected layers as shown in Fig. 5.

An incremental version of YOLO, named YOLOv3, is introduced in [14] with faster detection time and better detection accuracy. In our study, we focus on the real-time detection with limited hardware condition, that is suited to the embedded systems. Therefore, so we use the tiny version of the YOLO v3 algorithm. This version has 13 convolutional layers followed by multiple subsampling layers to extract the image features. The YOLOv3 has an important improvement to the previous versions that is the capability to make detection at three different

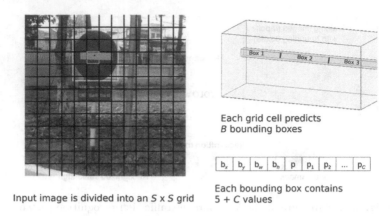

Input image is divided into an S x S grid

Each grid cell predicts
B bounding boxes

| $b_x$ | $b_y$ | $b_w$ | $b_h$ | p | $p_1$ | $p_2$ | ... | $p_c$ |

Each bounding box contains
5 + C values

**Fig. 4.** Basic calculations in the YOLO Algorithm

scale. It can also predict more bounding boxes than the previous ones. So, this algorithm is better than the previous version at detecting small objects.

### 2.4 Identify the Anchor Boxes Size

To identify the appropriate sizes of anchor boxes for the YOLO algorithm, we use the k-means clustering algorithm [8] as described in Fig. 3. The YOLOv3 tiny version detect boxes at 2 different scales: $13 \times 13$ and $26 \times 26$. For each scale, YOLOv3 tiny uses three anchor boxes. Therefore, the number of anchor box sizes needed by the YOLOv3 tiny is 6. To calculate these required values, the size of all bounding boxes in the training data are clustered by the k-means algorithm into 6 clusters, i.e. the number of anchor boxes' size needed by YOLO. The centroids of 6 clusters are the six anchor sizes to be provided to the YOLOv3 tiny algorithm.

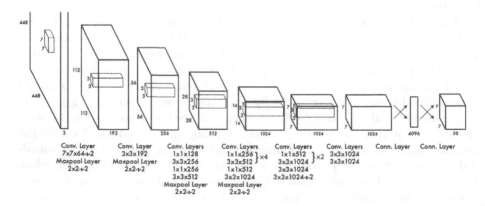

**Fig. 5.** The YOLO architecture [13]

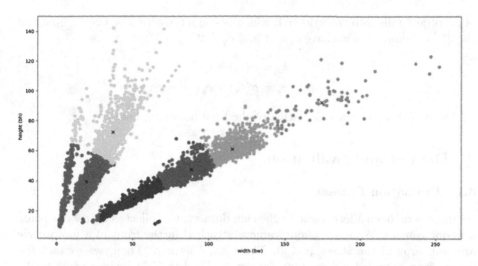

**Fig. 6.** The bounding box sizes clustering by k-means algorithm

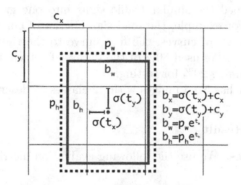

**Fig. 7.** Calculate the final bounding boxes [14]

In this study, the k-means clustering on our training data set returns six anchor boxes size, those are (20, 39), (51, 28), (37, 72), (89, 48), (116, 61), and (180, 95). This calculation is described in Fig. 6.

The anchor box sizes are also used in the detection step. In the detection layer of each scale, the size of bounding boxes $(b_x, b_y, b_w, b_h)$ are computed based on the values of the feature map $(t_x, t_y, t_w, t_h)$. The object width and height are calculated by the linear function:

$$b_w = p_w + e^{t_w}$$
$$b_h = p_h + e^{t_h}$$

$p_w$ and $p_h$ are the width and height of the anchor box respectively. The object center $(b_x, b_y)$ is the sum of the sigmoid of $(t_x, t_y)$ and an offset $(c_x, c_y)$, which is the coordinator of gird cell containing the object. For example, if the center of an object falls into the grid cell, which is the intersection of the $1^{st}$ row and the $2^{nd}$ column, then we have $c_x = 1$ and $c_y = 2$,

$$b_x = \sigma(t_x) + c_x$$
$$b_y = \sigma(t_y) + c_y$$

Figure 7 describe the calculation of the final bounding boxes.

# 3    Dataset and Evaluation

## 3.1    Evaluation Dataset

As there is no open Vietnamese traffic sign dataset, we collected a new one using a phone camera. We use a phone camera attached in the front of a motorcycle and run around the street in Can Tho City, Vietnam. Then, we extract the image from recorded videos. Our dataset finally has 5704 images of 33 traffic sign categories. Then, we labeled the image using the image labeling software labelImg[1] and grouped the similar traffic signs into one group to reduce the number of classes. For example, the road sign "Series of curves, the first curve to the left" and "Series of curves, the first curve to the right" are group into the "Series of curves". We used 80% of the dataset for training the recognition model and the remaining 20% for testing.

The final dataset has 5704 images with 22 classes as described in Table 1.

## 3.2    Evaluation Result

**Evaluation Metrics.** We use the following evaluation metrics to evaluate the proposed model:

- True positive (TP): model recognizes the object correctly, i.e. the model predict the class name correctly and the IoU value between predicted bounding box and ground truth box must be greater than or equal to 0.5.
- False Negative (FN): the traffic sign exists in the image but the model cannot recognize it.
- False Positive (FP): the model recognizes wrong object or correct object class but the IoU value between predicted bounding box and ground truth box is less than 0.5.
- Precision $= \dfrac{\text{TP}}{\text{TP} + \text{FP}}$
- Recall $= \dfrac{\text{TP}}{\text{TP} + \text{FN}}$
- F1 score: $F1 = 2 \times \dfrac{\text{Precision} \times \text{Recall}}{\text{Precision} + \text{Recall}}$

**Table 1.** Description of evaluation dataset

| No | Label | Description | Train | Test |
|----|-------|-------------|-------|------|
| 1 | 102 | No entry | 204 | 22 |
| 2 | 130 | No stopping or parking or waiting | 268 | 66 |
| 3 | 131 | No parking or waiting | 180 | 54 |
| 4 | 201a | Curve to the left | 100 | 36 |
| 5 | 201b | Curve to the right | 130 | 45 |
| 6 | 202 | Series of curves | 180 | 41 |
| 7 | 203 | Road narrows | 54 | 35 |
| 8 | 205 | Road junction | 307 | 79 |
| 9 | 207 | Road junction with priority | 773 | 182 |
| 10 | 208 | Road junction with priority | 145 | 29 |
| 11 | 209 | Traffic signals ahead | 125 | 25 |
| 12 | 221 | Rough road surface | 110 | 16 |
| 13 | 224 | Pedestrian crossing ahead | 428 | 100 |
| 14 | 225 | Children | 425 | 116 |
| 15 | 233 | Other danger | 111 | 24 |
| 16 | 245 | Slow | 62 | 12 |
| 17 | 302 | Keep right | 136 | 54 |
| 18 | 303 | Roundabout | 108 | 23 |
| 19 | 423 | Pedestrian crossing | 310 | 90 |
| 20 | Crowded | Start of a crowded area | 50 | 11 |
| 21 | end_crowded | End of a crowded area | 29 | 10 |
| 22 | traffic_light | Traffic light | 304 | 95 |
| | | **Total** | **4539** | **1165** |

**Evaluation Result.** After using 80% of the dataset to train the recognition model using the proposed approach, we used the remaining 20% to evaluate the model. The evaluation result is given in Table 2.

$$- \text{ Precision} = \frac{\text{TP}}{\text{TP} + \text{FP}} = \frac{1005}{1005 + 58} \approx 0.95$$

$$- \text{ Recall} = \frac{\text{TP}}{\text{TP} + \text{FN}} = \frac{1005}{1005 + 118} \approx 0.89$$

$$- \text{ F1} = 2 \times \frac{\text{Precision} \times \text{Recall}}{\text{Precision} + \text{Recall}} = 2 \times \frac{0.95 \times 0.89}{0.95 + 0.89} \approx 0.92$$

The recognition time on a laptop CPU Intel 3520M, 8 GB RAM (no GPU) is about 0.17 s per image. This result provides a good trade-off between detection

[1] https://github.com/tzutalin/labelImg.

**Table 2.** Evaluation result

| No | Traffic sign | True positive | False negative | False positive |
|----|--------------|---------------|----------------|----------------|
| 1 | 102 | 22 | 0 | 0 |
| 2 | 130 | 61 | 4 | 1 |
| 3 | 131 | 54 | 0 | 0 |
| 4 | 201a | 21 | 0 | 15 |
| 5 | 201b | 36 | 0 | 9 |
| 6 | 202 | 41 | 0 | 0 |
| 7 | 203 | 12 | 1 | 22 |
| 8 | 205 | 78 | 0 | 1 |
| 9 | 207 | 180 | 1 | 1 |
| 10 | 208 | 29 | 0 | 0 |
| 11 | 209 | 25 | 0 | 0 |
| 12 | 221 | 16 | 0 | 0 |
| 13 | 224 | 99 | 1 | 0 |
| 14 | 225 | 115 | 0 | 1 |
| 15 | 233 | 23 | 0 | 1 |
| 16 | 245 | 12 | 0 | 0 |
| 17 | 302 | 40 | 14 | 0 |
| 18 | 303 | 20 | 2 | 1 |
| 19 | 423 | 90 | 0 | 0 |
| 20 | Crowded | 9 | 0 | 2 |
| 21 | end_crowded | 5 | 1 | 4 |
| 22 | traffic_light | 1 | 94 | 0 |
| **Total** | | **989** | **118** | **58** |

time and detection accuracy and the detection time is suited to the real-time applications. It should be noted that the YOLO algorithm used in this evaluation is the tiny version, which is optimized to detection time. Therefore, if we need a better detection accuracy, we may use the full model of the YOLO algorithm.

In compare with former research on Vietnamese traffic sign recognition system, our system produces a good balance between performance and detection accuracy. Our system is better than the model proposed in [10] in both detection accuracy and detection time. However, we achieved a lower accuracy than [1]. This can be explained by two reasons. First, our dataset was collected in the city roads and thus it has more noise (i.e. the objects that are similar to traffic signs within the images) than the dataset used in [1]. Second, we are using the tiny version, which is mainly optimized for detection time by using a shallow network architecture. Therefore, if we have strong hardware, we can use deeper network architecture to improve the detection accuracy.

# 4 Conclusion and Future Work

In this study, we proposed a model for the Vietnamese recognition system. This model bases on the YOLOv3 algorithm, particularly the tiny version for real-time applications. We use the k-means clustering algorithm to compute the anchor box sizes for the YOLO algorithm. The evaluation result shows that our model gives a good trade-off between detection accuracy and detection time and can be used for real-time applications.

However, the detection accuracy is still lower than some of the state-of-the-art studies in traffic size recognition. As explained above, this may be caused by the shallow network architecture used or some other potential reasons such as the difference of the evaluation dataset, etc. This, together with investigations on the network parameters, will require further research.

# References

1. Bao, T.Q., Chen, T.H., Dinh, T.Q.: Road traffic sign detection and recognition using hog feature and artificial neural network. Can Tho University J. Sci. **15**, 47–54 (2015)
2. Barnes, N., Zelinsky, A.: Real-time radial symmetry for speed sign detection. In: IEEE Intelligent Vehicles Symposium, pp. 566–571. IEEE (2004)
3. Besserer, B., Estable, S., Ulmer, B., Reichardt, D.: Shape classification for traffic sign recognition. IFAC Proc. Vol. **26**(1), 487–492 (1993)
4. Cireşan, D., Meier, U., Masci, J., Schmidhuber, J.: Multi-column deep neural network for traffic sign classification. Neural Netw. **32**, 333–338 (2012)
5. Garcia-Garrido, M.A., Sotelo, M.A., Martin-Gorostiza, E.: Fast traffic sign detection and recognition under changing lighting conditions. In: 2006 IEEE Intelligent Transportation Systems Conference, pp. 811–816. IEEE (2006)
6. Gavrila, D.M.: Traffic sign recognition revisited. In: Förstner, W., Buhmann, J.M., Faber, A., Faber, P. (eds.) Mustererkennung 1999, pp. 86–93. Springer, Heidelberg (1999). https://doi.org/10.1007/978-3-642-60243-6_10
7. Jin, J., Fu, K., Zhang, C.: Traffic sign recognition with hinge loss trained convolutional neural networks. IEEE Trans. Intell. Transp. Syst. **15**(5), 1991–2000 (2014)
8. Lloyd, S.: Least squares quantization in PCM. IEEE Trans. Inf. Theory **28**(2), 129–137 (1982)
9. Loy, G., Barnes, N.: Fast shape-based road sign detection for a driver assistance system. In: 2004 IEEE/RSJ International Conference on Intelligent Robots and Systems (IROS) (IEEE Cat. No. 04CH37566), vol. 1, pp. 70–75. IEEE (2004)
10. Mai, B.Q.L., Dao, P.T., Huynh, H.T., Doan, D.A.: Recognition of Vietnamese warning traffic signs using scale invariant feature transform. In: International Conference on Communications and Electronics (2014)
11. Piccioli, G., De Micheli, E., Parodi, P., Campani, M.: Robust method for road sign detection and recognition. Image Vis. Comput. **14**(3), 209–223 (1996)
12. Qian, R., Yue, Y., Coenen, F., Zhang, B.: Traffic sign recognition with convolutional neural network based on max pooling positions. In: 2016 12th International Conference on Natural Computation, Fuzzy Systems and Knowledge Discovery (ICNC-FSKD), pp. 578–582. IEEE (2016)

13. Redmon, J., Divvala, S., Girshick, R., Farhadi, A.: You only look once: unified, real-time object detection. In: Proceedings of the IEEE Conference on Computer Vision and Pattern Recognition, pp. 779–788 (2016)
14. Redmon, J., Farhadi, A.: Yolov3: an incremental improvement. arXiv preprint arXiv:1804.02767 (2018)
15. Shao, F., Wang, X., Meng, F., Rui, T., Wang, D., Tang, J.: Real-time traffic sign detection and recognition method based on simplified gabor wavelets and CNNs. Sensors 18(10), 3192 (2018)
16. Yang, M., Lv, F., Xu, W., Gong, Y., et al.: Detection driven adaptive multi-cue integration for multiple human tracking. In: 2009 IEEE 12th International Conference on Computer Vision (ICCV), pp. 1554–1561. IEEE (2009)
17. Youssef, A., Albani, D., Nardi, D., Bloisi, D.D.: Fast traffic sign recognition using color segmentation and deep convolutional networks. In: Blanc-Talon, J., Distante, C., Philips, W., Popescu, D., Scheunders, P. (eds.) ACIVS 2016. LNCS, vol. 10016, pp. 205–216. Springer, Cham (2016). https://doi.org/10.1007/978-3-319-48680-2_19

# Disease Prediction Using Metagenomic Data Visualizations Based on Manifold Learning and Convolutional Neural Network

Thanh Hai Nguyen[✉] and Thai-Nghe Nguyen

Can Tho University, Can Tho, Vietnam
{nthai,ntnghe}@cit.ctu.edu.vn

**Abstract.** Deep learning algorithms have obtained numerous achievements in image classification, speed recognition, video processing. Visualizing metagenomic data is a challenge because of its complexity and high-dimensional. In this paper, we introduce several approaches based on dimensionality reduction algorithms and data density to visualize features which reflect the species abundance. The sophisticated methods used in this study, that are unsupervised approaches, carry out dimensionality reduction and map the data into a 2-dimensional space. From the visualizations obtained, deep learning techniques are leveraged to enhance the prediction performance for colorectal cancer. We show by experiments on five Metagenome-based colorectal cancer datasets from different regions such as Chinese, Austrian, American, German and French cohorts that the proposed visualizations allow to visualize biomedical signatures and improve the prediction performance compared to classical machine learning.

**Keywords:** Dimensionality reduction algorithms · Manifold learning · Metagenomics · Visualization · Disease prediction · Convolutional neural network

## 1 Introduction

Metagenomic data is a novel source to improve the human disease prediction. However, leveraging this data source for enhancing the efficiency in prognosis and diagnosis is still facing numerous challenges. Metagenomic data is usually characterized by so many features, even up to millions of features while the link among features to the diseases are not explored completely. Moreover, people face difficulties to interpret high-dimensional data. Therefore, numerous studies have attempted to propose a vast of methods to visualize metagenomic data. The authors have presented approaches to try to explore and discovery new knowledge from metagenomic to protect and improve human health.

As shown in numerous research in data visualization, visualizing features in 2D where people are easy to interpret is crucial to find patterns in data. This

© Springer Nature Switzerland AG 2019
T. K. Dang et al. (Eds.): FDSE 2019, LNCS 11814, pp. 117–131, 2019.
https://doi.org/10.1007/978-3-030-35653-8_9

technique is an indispensable method for exploring data and a key for discoveries. The tools for visualizing data by charts using Office software have been using by many non-programmers. Pie chart as described in [2] is considered as the best-known chart to exhibit data composition. Bar chart is also a useful tool to exhibit a data distribution, shaped as rectangular colorful bars for each group of data. The height of the bars indicates the values of corresponding groups. These chart types are also provided widely from numerous sources such as Microsoft Office, Python, R [4], *Amphora Vizu* [6], package of *metricsgraphics* [7] and *gplots* in R [8], and so on.

Some authors have proposed tools to reveal metagenomic data composition. One of such popular tools is Krona. This software illustrate a metagenome as nested concentric rings shaping a circle together. Each ring represents a taxonomic rank. The tool exhibits a multi-level view of the structures of metagenome data. Another good tool is designed to use on web interface is MG-RAST [13]. This tool illustrates metagenomics in the hierarchy regardless of magnitude. MEGAN is also a useful software that enables us to analyze and explore the taxonomic content of large metagenomic data. A comparison among 3 these common methods are presented in [5] and shown in Fig. 1.

Besides diagram and schemes for visualizing metagenomic data, many researchers have proposed robust algorithms to visualize features in 2D where we apply deep learning techniques to do prediction tasks. PCA, Isomap, t-SNE have been leveraged in numerous studies. These algorithms enable scientists to find interesting structures in data. From these structures, new knowledge may be discovered easier. In [26], authors presented some ways to present metagenomic features in images where Convolutional neural networks applied to improve the prediction performance compared to classical machine learning.

In this paper, we explore and investigate different approaches based on manifold learnings for visualizing features of metagenomic datasets reflecting species abundance in samples of colorectal cancer. Our objective is to propose efficient data representations based on data density which produce compact and informative images, which not only present data distributions visually but also can be used for the classification, e.g., Convolutional Networks, to the proposed visualizations for the prediction tasks. Our work's contribution is multi-fold:

- This study has investigated a vast of visualization approaches based on manifold learning algorithms to reflect bacterial abundance at genus level of colorectal cancer. Some of them such as Spectral Embedding reveal promising results even comparing to Fill-up where all points are visible.
- We introduce a method with 'transparent trick' which can improve the performance where the visualizations based on the dimensionality reduction algorithms suffer the issue of numerous overlapped points. Visualizations with Manifold learning also are conducted from data density, so this method is a robust baseline to compare the efficient of visualizations based on manifold learning.
- An extended version of the Fill-up approach also is developed based on the density of data.

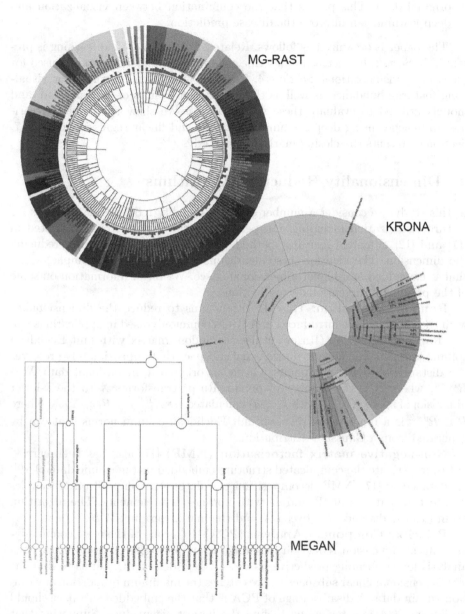

**Fig. 1.** Visualization Comparison of The acid drainage metagenome [3] using MG-RAST [13], MEGAN [18], and Krona [5]. The figure is provided from [5].

– The generated Visualizations classified by shallow deep learning architectures exhibit encouraging results compared to classical machine learning on the original data. This proves that the combination between visualization and deep learning can improve the disease prediction.

The paper is organized as follows. Related work on manifold learning is presented in Sect. 2. In Sect. 3, we describe six species abundance datasets used for performing visualizations. Sections 4, 5, and 6 present the methods for visualizing feature abundance as well as the comparison results of each method, and models utilized to evaluate these visualizations. We show the results of various approaches using deep learning techniques and linear regression in Sect. 7. Section 8 presents the closing marks of the study.

## 2    Dimensionality Reduction Algorithms

In this study, we consider a number of dimensionality reduction approaches for feature visualization including unsupervised learning algorithms. As stated in [11] and [12], manifold learning methods are a robust framework for reducing the dimension. The idea for these algorithms is to find a more compact space that is embedded in a higher dimensional space. We recall information on some of the prominent dimensionality reductions.

**Random Projection**: This algorithm aims to reduce the dimensionality with the core idea was introduced in [14] and commonly-used in applications [15, 16]. Random Projection (Rn_pr) utilizes a random matrix with unit Euclidean column norms to find a lower-dimensional subspace that approximately preserves the distances between the points. Given an original $d$-dimensional data $X \in R^{N \times d}$, where N is the number of points. Rn_pr transforms X to the $k$-lower dimensional space $X^{RP}_{k \times N}$ (with $k \ll d$) calculated by $X^{RP}_{k \times N} = R_{k \times d} X_{d \times N}$ where $R \in R^{d \times k}$ is a random matrix with unit Euclidean column norms that can be generated from a Gaussian distribution.

**Non-negative matrix factorization (NMF)** [17] also has been carried out to investigate the complicated structure embedded metagenomic data [9,19]. As detailed in [17], NMF decomposition calculates a decomposition of samples A into two matrices of $W$ and $H$ with non-negative elements. The algorithm optimizes the distance $d$ between $X$ and the matrix product $WH$.

**Principal Component Analysis** (PCA) [10] is one of the most commonly-used linear dimension reduction for numerous applications in exploratory data analysis for performing predictive models. A key idea of PCA aims to find the low-dimensional linear subspace where catches the maximum proportion of variation within data. A disadvantage of PCA is that the embedded subspace should be linear. PCA is a technique to find the largest eigenvalues. Supposing that the data $x_1, x_2, ..., x_n$, PCA calculates the eigenvalues and corresponding eigenvectors of the (r×r) sample covariance matrix. In order to embed to $k$-lower-dimensional space, PCA preserves only those eigenvalue-eigenvector combinations for which the $k$ largest eigenvalues interpret a high proportion of the total variation in the data.

**Multidimensional scaling** (MDS) is a form of non-linear dimensionality reduction presented in [20]. The technique aims to place each point in $N$-dimensional space where distances between points are preserved as well as possible. Classical MDS uses Euclidean distances.

**Isomap** was presented in [21] as an extended version of MDS by changing the Euclidean distances with another type of distance (geodesic distances). This method aims to solve high dimensional data using the measured local metric information to learn the structure of data with numerous applications. As in [22], authors applied Isomap to predict key clinical variables. The author in [12] stated that there are two various types of manifold learning including local and global methods. Isomap is a global manifold learning approach with the embeddings based on geodesic distances between all pairs of points.

**Locally Linear Embedding (LLE)** is a type of local manifold learning method introduced in [23]. As in [12] stated that LLE looks a manifold as a collection of potentially overlapping areas. In the case where the manifold is smooth and the number of points in a neighborhood is minor, the regions look like as locally linear. LLE and Isomap have the main difference that is the way LLE performs in the second step. LLE supposes that every manifold as locally linear. Therefore, each point can be approximated by linear function of its K nearest neighbors. The details of the algorithm can be found in [11,12,23].

**Laplacian Eigenmaps- (or called as Spectral Embedding (SE))**: applies spectral decomposition to the corresponding graph Laplacian. Similar to LLE, SE focus only o retaining local neighborhood relationships in the input space [24]. In some cases, SE is equivalent to LLE. Details of the algorithms are presented in [12,24]

**t-SNE** [25] is one of the best techniques for dimensionality reduction used more and more recently [27]. t-SNE performs well and seems to like to an appropriate method for visualizing data in 2–3D compared to other manifold methods. Additionally, t-SNE does not only illustrates the local structure of data but also preserves the global structures of the data like clusters.

## 3   Benchmark Datasets

In this study, we illustrate the visualization algorithms on five metagenomic datasets (Table 1) consisting of 526 metagenomic samples of colorectal cancer (COL) disease from American (C1 dataset), Austrian (C2), Chinese (C3), German and French cohorts (C4). These cohorts were analyzed in [1]. Additional dataset (C5) was created by merging C1, C2, C3 and C4. These datasets include shotgun metagenomic sequencing sequences (using Illumina Hiseq 2000/2500271 sequencing platform with similar sequencing depths (read length 100 bp, and target sequencing depth 5 GB)) with 271 controls and 255 COL cases. Low quality sequences were eliminated using Trimmomatic v_0.36 [1,30]. For each sample, the value of each feature reflects species abundance, and is represented as a real number - the total abundance of all species in each sample sums to 1.

**Table 1.** Information on five metagenomic datasets of colorectal cancer

|  | C1 | C2 | C3 | C4 | C5 |
|---|---|---|---|---|---|
| #features | 1976 | 1981 | 1932 | 1980 | 1985 |
| #samples | 100 | 109 | 165 | 152 | 526 |
| #patients | 48 | 46 | 73 | 88 | 255 |
| #controls | 52 | 63 | 92 | 64 | 271 |
| Ratio of patients | 0.48 | 0.42 | 0.44 | 0.58 | 0.49 |
| Ratio of controls | 0.52 | 0.58 | 0.56 | 0.42 | 0.52 |

# 4    Image Generation and Models for the Evaluation

Two methods of binnings including SPecies Bins (SPB) and binning based on Quantile Transformation Bins (QTF) [26] are utilized to generate images. We create $48 \times 48$ gray images for SPB and QTF. Jet colormap is utilized to visualize features clearly in the figures in Sects. 5, and 6.

Similar to [26], We use a convolutional neural network (CNN) architecture with one convolutional layer including 64 filters of $3 \times 3$ followed by a max pooling of $2 \times 2$ to evaluate the considered visualizations and a model with only one fully-connected layer (FC). All networks use Adam [29] optimization, a batch size of 16, learning rate $= 0.001$, loss function: binary cross entropy, run through 500 epochs using Early Stopping with epoch patience of 5. Classification performances are assessed by an average Area Under the Curve (AUC) on 10-fold stratified cross validation. The same folds are used for all classifiers.

# 5    Visualizations Based on Dimensionality Reduction Algorithms

Data visualization is a good way to see the structures of data so that with the visualized shape of data probably enhances the learning to get a better performance. High dimensional data are usually very difficult to explore and to interpret corresponding machine learning models. However, we can try to investigate data while plotting them in two or three dimensional space. A key idea of this approach is that we can find the structures of high-dimensional data shaped in 2D images where deep learning techniques for images can be applied to improve prediction results.

Figures 2 and 3 visualize average species abundance of samples in training set of C5 dataset with different methods such as t-SNE, PCA, Rd_pr, SE, Isomap, LLE, MDS, NMF. We observe that the t-SNE performs well in both SPB (using original abundance) and QTF (transformed data). For original abundance in Fig. 2, t-SNE reveals the best among considered algorithms. SE seems to take the second place, while the others exhibit poor visualization with numerous overlapped points. Figure 3 shows the visualizations with data scaled with QTF.

t-SNE and MDS present similar visualizations that formed as a ball while NMF apparently extends points to corners.

We suppose that the newly created images illustrated on Figs. 2 and 3 can be of a help to improve the classification. We hope that arranging together species that have the similar magnitude of abundance is informative, and the produced synthetic images are reasonable input for a deep learning algorithm.

In order to apply dimensionality reduction methods to visualize high-dimensional data, first, the features of all samples in training set from raw data are transformed by a dimensionality reduction algorithm such as PCA, NMF, Random Projection, t-SNE, MDS, Isomap, LLE, SE into a global map. This map is then used to generate images for training and testing data. Each species is represented as a point on the map and only species that are present are shown either in abundance or presence using the same color schemes as above. All of nonlinear manifold learning approaches such as Isomap, LLE, and etc. depend on the size of neighborhoods around each point [12] with parameters of K and $\epsilon$ and finding an optimal value for numerous situations have been still investigating. The global maps are built based on training sets with the number of neighbors to consider for each point of 5 (this equivalents to the parameter of perplexity for t-SNE), learning rate = 100, and the number of iterations set to 300. The packages for manifold learning approaches are available in scikit-learn (Python library) [28].

As seen from our experiments with the dimensionality reduction on the C5 dataset with different manifold learning algorithms at Figs. 2 and 3, for SPB on original data, t-SNE gives the best visualization with less overlapped points while there are numerous hidden points in the others. In the case, the most critical features are overlapped by the ones which are less important, the performance in prediction might be decreased because of losing information. In order to reduce the effects of overlapping problem, we use the "transparency trick" that suffers from a large amount of overlapped points. The transparency parameter can be fixed in the interval between 0 and 1, and it indicates the transparency of the markers plotted. A value of 0 determines all points are opaque while 1 means that transparency is not applied. In our experiments, for visualizations by manifold learning methods, we set the transparent value to 0.5. As shown in Table 2 with the performance of CNN model on t-SNE representation with QTF, "transparency trick" really help to improve the performance for most cases.

**Table 2.** Performance Comparison between use of transparency (with the transparent value of 0.5 and non-use of transparency (the transparent value of 1.0)

| Transparent value | C1 | C2 | C3 | C4 | C5 | AVG |
|---|---|---|---|---|---|---|
| 0.5 | 0.705 | 0.776 | 0.769 | 0.802 | 0.761 | 0.763 |
| 1 | 0.711 | 0.768 | 0.746 | 0.774 | 0.725 | 0.745 |

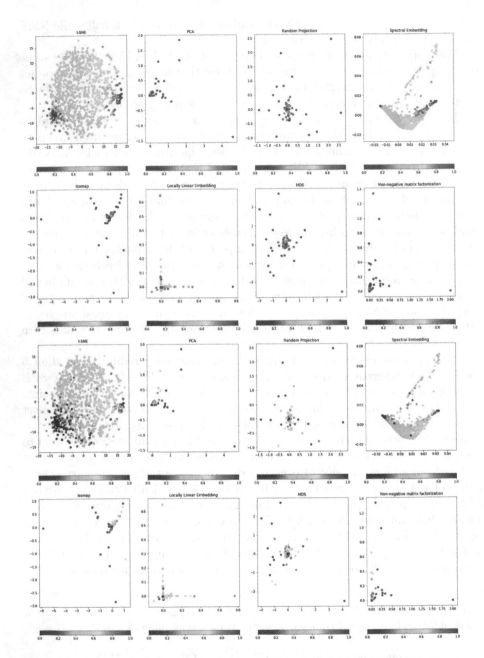

**Fig. 2.** Examples of Global maps (the first row (From left-right: t-SNE, PCA, Random Projection, Spectral Embedding) and the second row (From left-right: Isomap, LLE, MDS, NMF) and samples created from the global maps above (the third and fourth rows with the same order as the first and second rows) with SPB bins using CRC dataset. Top: Global maps. Down: images of samples

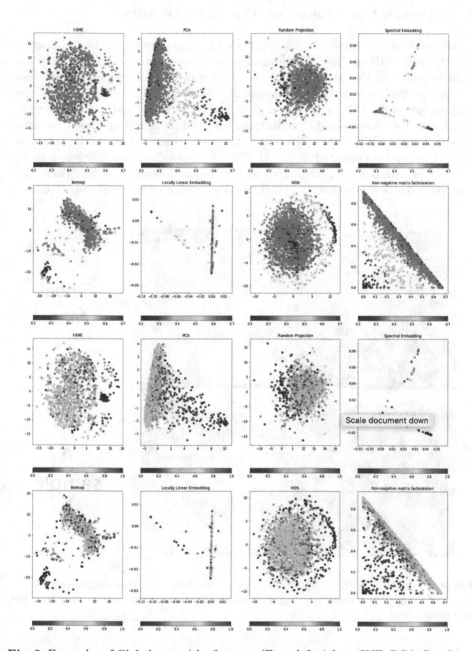

**Fig. 3.** Examples of Global maps (the first row (From left-right: t-SNE, PCA, Random Projection, Spectral Embedding) and the second row (From left-right: Isomap, LLE, MDS, NMF) and samples created from the global maps above (the third and fourth rows with the same order as the first and second rows) with QTF bins using CRC dataset. Top: Global maps. Down: images of samples

# 6    Visualizations Based on the Data Density

In this section, we introduce an approach for illustrating data based on data density using *Fill-up* [26]. Fill-up arranges values of features into a matrix in a right-to-left order by row top-to-bottom. This approach solves the overlap issues of the approaches based on dimensionality reduction algorithms. In [26], the authors presented Fill-up using the phylogenetic ordering and random sorting. Similar to the dimensionality reduction, we conduct a Fill-up based on data density (namely **Fill_den**) where the features own high values will be arranged close together (as exhibited in Fig. 4). The average value of each features in all samples in training set is computed and sorted in ascending order. Then, the ordered features are organized in a right-to-left order by row top-to-bottom.

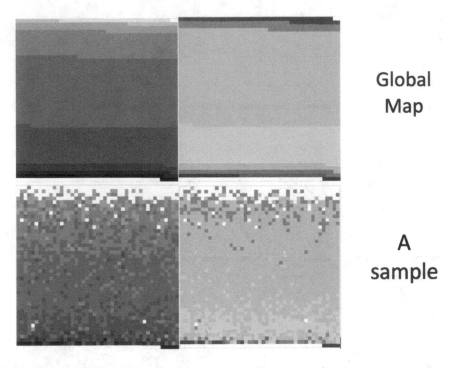

**Fig. 4.** Examples of *Fill_den* with Global maps (the first row) reflecting average abundance of samples in a training set and a sample (the second row) illustrating by gray and color scales.

# 7    The Results

We show results in the average AUC on 10-cross validation of the considered visualizations using various binning (SPB, QTF) in Tables 3 and 4 respectively

and different learning algorithms including CNN (1) and FC (2) installed to
do prediction tasks. The average performance of five datasets is computed and
shown in the last column (AVG) of tables. The results which are higher than RF's
performance are formatted bold text. We also include Fill-up with phylogenetic
ordering [26] (**Fill_phy**) for the comparison. In order to evaluate the efficiency
of the proposed visualizations, we also run some classic machine learning such
as Support Vector Machine (SVM) and Random Forests (RF) on raw data. We
use Linear kernel for SVM while the number of trees is up to 500 for RF, these
parameters provided the best results in [26]. Moreover, the architecture of CNN
and FC models are the same as in [26]. As observed from tables, RF outperforms
SVM in all datasets. In addition, SVM is the worst algorithm comparing to the
others.

**Table 3.** Performance comparison (in AUC) of manifold methods using gray images
and SPB.

| Model | | C1 | C2 | C3 | C4 | C5 | AVG |
|---|---|---|---|---|---|---|---|
| CNN | Fill_den | 0.707 | **0.744** | **0.755** | **0.800** | 0.756 | **0.753** |
| CNN | Fill_phy | 0.647 | 0.725 | **0.825** | **0.802** | 0.752 | **0.750** |
| CNN | isomap | **0.717** | **0.803** | 0.648 | 0.672 | 0.731 | 0.714 |
| CNN | LLE | 0.557 | **0.744** | 0.688 | 0.696 | 0.729 | 0.683 |
| CNN | MDS | 0.675 | **0.820** | 0.665 | **0.802** | 0.722 | 0.737 |
| CNN | NMF | 0.681 | **0.795** | 0.651 | 0.658 | 0.678 | 0.692 |
| CNN | PCA | **0.718** | **0.758** | 0.652 | 0.636 | 0.668 | 0.686 |
| CNN | Rd_pro | 0.669 | **0.792** | 0.674 | 0.734 | 0.760 | 0.726 |
| CNN | SE | 0.610 | **0.749** | **0.772** | **0.838** | **0.796** | **0.753** |
| CNN | t-SNE | 0.623 | **0.758** | **0.764** | **0.805** | 0.751 | 0.740 |
| FC | Fill_den | 0.648 | **0.778** | **0.756** | **0.846** | 0.755 | **0.757** |
| FC | Fill_phy | 0.680 | **0.748** | **0.759** | **0.830** | 0.753 | **0.754** |
| FC | isomap | 0.558 | **0.765** | 0.451 | 0.692 | 0.557 | 0.605 |
| FC | LLE | 0.469 | 0.725 | 0.598 | 0.615 | 0.614 | 0.604 |
| FC | MDS | 0.569 | **0.790** | 0.577 | 0.641 | 0.539 | 0.623 |
| FC | NMF | 0.592 | **0.804** | 0.594 | 0.573 | 0.450 | 0.602 |
| FC | PCA | 0.675 | 0.712 | 0.536 | 0.591 | 0.505 | 0.604 |
| FC | Rd_pro | 0.626 | **0.780** | 0.560 | 0.627 | 0.570 | 0.633 |
| FC | SE | 0.626 | 0.714 | 0.673 | 0.771 | 0.708 | 0.699 |
| FC | t-SNE | 0.610 | 0.729 | 0.700 | 0.772 | 0.721 | 0.706 |
| RF | | 0.715 | 0.742 | 0.702 | 0.787 | 0.761 | 0.741 |
| SVM | | 0.488 | 0.698 | 0.476 | 0.744 | 0.644 | 0.610 |

Similar to observations from visualizations, the performances in classification
also reveal the same results. For data without transformation, Fill-up achieves

the best average AUC on all considered datasets while LLE reveals the worst one for all considered visualizations. It is noteworthy that SE obtains very promising performances with 4 out of 5 higher results compared to RF. It also exhibits a better result than RF and outperforms the average AUC of 0.750 of the study in [1] in the merged dataset (C5). Although visualizations based on manifold learning suffer the overlapped problem, some of them demonstrate promising results. SE exhibits a slight increase in the average AUC compared to Fill-up where all of features is visible. As we expected, deep learning with CNN model outperforms the shallow FC model in most cases. The overall performance of models on visualizations using QTF is greater than SPB as well as the quality of the visualizations is also better. The performance in most cases is improved comparing to SPB for the merged dataset (C5). Visualizations based on data scaled with QTF produce the better prediction results for datasets of C1, C3 while SPB exhibits greater performance for C2, C4.

The samples who came from Germany and France (C4) can get benefits from the proposed methods combined with the CNN model with the maximum AUC up to 0.848 while many of other results with SPB reach to over 0.8. The proposed methods exhibit the efficiency on samples from European countries (C2, C4) while it is a challenge to predict colorectal cancer from American samples (C1). Although there are still numerous overlapped points comparing to Fill-up, some of manifold learning algorithms (such as SE, Rd_pro)) still outperform Fill-up for the merged dataset. This proves that the performance in visualization with manifold learning approaches increase when we have more data.

## 8    Conclusion

We introduced approaches based on visualizations and deep learning algorithms for Metagenome-based Disease Prediction. Although the study is only investigated for predicting colorectal cancer, the method can be applied directly to any other diseases based on metagenome, in order to perform a more advanced function-based analysis. Our results reveal the proposed method is a promising tool which can help not only visualize biomarkers but also enhance the disease prediction performance through using deep learning.

Data visualization is a challenge, especially in metagenomic data where data are very complex and high-dimensional, and where the number of samples is rather small. We have investigated several dimensionality reduction and projection into 2D, and compared to the fill-up based on data density. These algorithms are promising tools for visualizing metegenomic data.

Deep learning techniques are leveraged to classify patients based on the proposed visualizations. As exhibited from the result, CNN outperform FC in almost all cases for SPB. SE, MDS are promising algorithms for visualizing metagenomic features as well as can combine deep learning to improve the classification performances.

Our numerical results show that the Fill-up outperforms the approaches based on dimensionality reduction because all points using Fill-up are visible

**Table 4.** Performance comparison (in AUC) of manifold methods using gray images and QTF.

| Model | | C1 | C2 | C3 | C4 | C5 | AVG |
|---|---|---|---|---|---|---|---|
| CNN | Fill_den | 0.692 | 0.742 | **0.769** | **0.796** | 0.758 | **0.751** |
| CNN | Fill_phy | 0.763 | **0.791** | **0.788** | **0.803** | 0.754 | **0.780** |
| CNN | isomap | 0.701 | 0.730 | 0.693 | 0.718 | 0.756 | 0.719 |
| CNN | LLE | 0.658 | 0.627 | 0.663 | 0.655 | **0.769** | 0.674 |
| CNN | MDS | **0.723** | **0.751** | 0.697 | 0.699 | 0.749 | 0.724 |
| CNN | NMF | 0.708 | **0.791** | **0.734** | 0.703 | 0.736 | 0.734 |
| CNN | PCA | **0.728** | 0.796 | **0.719** | 0.691 | 0.733 | 0.733 |
| CNN | Rd_pro | 0.714 | **0.756** | **0.768** | 0.719 | **0.795** | **0.751** |
| CNN | SE | 0.660 | 0.652 | **0.723** | 0.623 | **0.816** | 0.695 |
| CNN | t-SNE | **0.761** | **0.776** | **0.705** | 0.769 | **0.802** | **0.763** |
| FC | Fill_den | **0.721** | **0.771** | **0.775** | 0.783 | 0.747 | **0.759** |
| FC | Fill_phy | 0.686 | **0.789** | **0.749** | **0.804** | 0.746 | **0.755** |
| FC | isomap | **0.718** | 0.708 | 0.676 | 0.727 | **0.786** | 0.723 |
| FC | LLE | 0.624 | 0.690 | 0.656 | 0.641 | 0.750 | 0.672 |
| FC | MDS | **0.718** | **0.759** | **0.744** | 0.753 | **0.782** | **0.751** |
| FC | NMF | **0.717** | **0.749** | **0.727** | 0.711 | **0.801** | 0.741 |
| FC | PCA | **0.720** | **0.758** | 0.688 | 0.703 | **0.791** | 0.732 |
| FC | Rd_pro | **0.719** | 0.742 | 0.688 | 0.742 | **0.806** | 0.739 |
| FC | SE | 0.563 | 0.701 | 0.691 | 0.655 | 0.761 | 0.674 |
| FC | t-SNE | **0.718** | 0.760 | 0.631 | 0.763 | **0.779** | 0.730 |
| RF | | 0.715 | 0.742 | 0.702 | 0.787 | 0.761 | 0.741 |
| SVM | | 0.488 | 0.698 | 0.476 | 0.744 | 0.644 | 0.610 |

while other techniques suffer from the fact that some points are overlapping in 2D. However, we notice that QTF can improve the visualizations based manifold learning algorithms. Data scaled by QTF has been increased the quality of visualization and the performance in the prediction. From the results, we see that visualizations based on some of the considered manifold learning algorithms also present encouraging results comparing to Fill-up when we apply to the merged data. This shows that if we have more data, we can improve the visualization based on manifold learning methods. We provided "transparency trick" applying to the visualizations with more overlapped points. Although "transparency trick" produced the efficient in the prediction, further research should take into account in deep on the overlapped issues to provide better results.

Due to some limitation of computation resources, we only use shallow CNN architecture, further studies should investigate deeper CNN architecture to improve the performance. We expect that our method can help to better stratify patients and develop approaches of personalized medicine.

# References

1. Dai, Z., et al.: Multi-cohort analysis of colorectal cancer metagenome identified altered bacteria across populations and universal bacterial markers. Microbiome **6**, 70 (2018). https://doi.org/10.1186/s40168-018-0451-2. ISSN 2049-2618
2. Sudarikov, K., et al.: Methods for the metagenomic data visualization and analysis. Curr. Issues Mol. Biol. **24**, 37–58 (2017). ISSN: 14673037
3. Oh, J., et al.: Biogeography and individuality shape function in the human skin metagenome. Nature **514**, 59–64 (2014). https://www.nature.com/articles/nature13786. ISSN 1476-4687
4. R Development Core Team: A Language and Environment for Statistical Computing (2008). ISBN: 3-900051-07-0
5. Ondov, B.D., et al.: Interactive metagenomic visualization in a web browser. BMC Bioinform. **12**, 385 (2011)
6. Kerepesi, C., et al.: AmphoraNet: the webserver implementation of the AMPHORA2 metagenomic workflow suite. Gene, 538–540 (2013). https://doi.org/10.1016/j.gene.2013.10.015
7. Rudis, B., Almossawi, A., Ulmer, H.: 'metricsgraphics', CRAN repository (2015). https://CRAN.R-project.org/package=metricsgraphics
8. Warnes, G.R., et al.: Package 'gplots', CRAN repository (2016). https://CRAN.R-project.org/package=gplots
9. Jiang, X., et al.: Manifold learning reveals nonlinear structure in metagenomic profiles. In: 2012 IEEE International Conference on Bioinformatics and Biomedicine (2012)
10. Alshawaqfeh, M., et al.: Consistent metagenomic biomarker detection via robust PCA. Biol. Direct **12**(1), 4 (2016)
11. Huo, X., et al.: A survey of manifold-based learning methods. In: Recent Advances in Data Mining of Enterprise Data: Algorithms and Applications, pp. 691–745 (2007). https://doi.org/10.1142/9789812779861_0015
12. Izenman, A.J.: Introduction to manifold learning. Wiley Interdisc. Rev.: Comput. Stat. **5**, 439–446 (2012)
13. Meyer, F., et al.: The metagenomics RAST server - a public resource for the automatic phylogenetic and functional analysis of metagenomes. BMC Bioinform. **9**(1), 386 (2011)
14. Johnson, W.B., Lindenstrauss, J.: Extensions of Lipschitz mappings into a Hilbert space. In: Conference in Modern Analysis and Probability. New Haven, Conn. (1982)
15. Grellmann, C., et al.: Random projection for fast and efficient multivariate correlation analysis of high-dimensional data: a new approach. Front. Genet. **7**, 102 (2016)
16. Lahiri, S., et al.: Random projections of random manifolds; arXiv:1607.04331 [cs, q-bio, stat] (2016)
17. Févotte, C., Idier, J.: Algorithms for nonnegative matrix factorization with the beta-divergence; arXiv:1010.1763 [cs] (2010)
18. Huson, D.H., Auch, A.F., Qi, J., Schuster, S.C.: MEGAN analysis of metagenomic data **17**, 377–386. https://www.ncbi.nlm.nih.gov/pmc/articles/PMC1800929/. ISSN 1088-9051
19. Gillis, N.: The Why and How of Nonnegative Matrix Factorization; arXiv:1401.5226 [cs, math, stat] (2010)

20. Borg, I., Groenen, P.J.F.: Modern Multidimensional Scaling. SSS. Springer, New York (2005). https://doi.org/10.1007/0-387-28981-X
21. McQueen, J., Meila, M., VanderPlas, J., Zhang, Z.: Manifold Learning with Millions of points; arxiv (2005)
22. Park, H.: ISOMAP induced manifold embedding and its application to Alzheimer's disease and mild cognitive impairment. Neurosci. Lett. **513**, 141–145 (2012)
23. Roweis, S.T., Saul, L.K.: Nonlinear dimensionality reduction by locally linear embedding. Science **290**(5500), 2323–2326 (2012)
24. Talwalkar, A., Kumar, S., Rowley, H.: Large-scale manifold learning. In: 2008 IEEE Conference on Computer Vision and Pattern Recognition (2008)
25. Maaten, L.V.D., Hinton, G.: Visualizing data using t-SNE. J. Mach. Learn. Res. **9**, 2579–2605 (2008)
26. Nguyen, T.H., et al.: Disease classification in metagenomics with 2D embeddings and deep learning. In: The Annual French Conference in Machine Learning (CAP 2018) (2018)
27. Hamel, P., Eck, D.: Learning features from music audio with deep belief networks (2010)
28. Garreta, R., Moncecchi, G.: Learning Scikit-Learn: Machine Learning in Python. Packt Publishing Ltd (2013)
29. Kingma, D.P., et al.: Adam: A Method for Stochastic Optimization; CoRR abs/1412.6980 (2014)
30. Bolger, A.M., Lohse, M., Usadel, B.: Trimmomatic: a flexible trimmer for illumina sequence data. Bioinformatics **30**, 2114–2120 (2014). ISSN 1367–4811

# An Efficient Model for Sentiment Analysis of Electronic Product Reviews in Vietnamese

Suong N. Hoang[1,2(✉)] ⬨, Linh V. Nguyen[1] ⬨, Tai Huynh[1,2], and Vuong T. Pham[1,3]

[1] Kyanon Digital, Ho Chi Minh City, Vietnam
{suong.hoang,linh.nguyenviet,tai.huynh,vuong.pham}@kyanon.digital
[2] Advosights, Ho Chi Minh City, Vietnam
{suong.hoang,tai.huynh}@advosights.com
[3] Saigon University, Ho Chi Minh City, Vietnam
vuong.pham@sgu.edu.vn
https://kyanon.digital, https://advosights.com

**Abstract.** In the past few years, the growth of e-commerce and digital marketing in Vietnam has generated a huge volume of opinionated data. Analyzing those data would provide enterprises with insight for better business decisions. In this work, as part of the Advosights project, we study sentiment analysis of product reviews in Vietnamese. The final solution is based on Self-attention neural networks, a flexible architecture for text classification task with about 90.16% of accuracy in 0.0124 second, a very fast inference time.

**Keywords:** Vietnamese · Sentiment analysis · Electronics product review

## 1 Introduction

Sentiment analysis aims to analyze human opinions, attitudes, and emotions. It has been applied in various fields of business. For instance, in our current project, Advosights, it is used to measure the impact of new products and ads campaigns through consumer's responses.

In the past few years, together with the rapid growth of e-commerce and digital marketing in Vietnam, a huge volume of written opinionated data in digital form has been created. As the result, sentiment analysis plays a more critical role in social listening than ever before. So far, human effort is the most common solution for sentiment analysis problems. However, this approach generally does not result in the desired outcomes and speed. Human check and labeling are time consuming and error-prone. Therefore, developing a system that automatically classifies human sentiment is highly essential.

Supported by Kyanon Digital.

While we can easily find a lot of sentiment analysis researches for English, there are only a few works for Vietnamese. Vietnamese is a unique language and it differs from English in a number of ways. To apply the same techniques that work for English to Vietnamese would yield inaccurate results. This has motivated our systematic study in sentiment analysis for Vietnamese. Since our project, Advosights, initially served a well-known electronics brand, we decided to focus our study on electronic product reviews. Broader scopes will be studied in future works.

Our initial approach was to build a sentiment lexicon dictionary. Its first version was based on some statistical methods [4–6] to estimate the sentiment score for each word from a list, collected manually based on Vietnamese dictionaries. This approach did not work well because the dataset came from casual reviews, that were practically spoken language with a lot of slang words and acronyms. This fact made it almost impossible to build a dictionary that cover all of those words. We then tried to use a simple neural network to learn sentiment lexicons from corpus automatically [12]. This also did not work well because some words in Vietnamese have same morphology, but they have different meanings in different contexts. For example, the words "*đã*" in two sentences "nhìn *đã* quá" and "*đã* quá cũ" have different meanings. But by using the dictionary, they have the same sentiment score.

Some machine learning-based approaches have been studied. For examples, CountVectorizer and Term Frequency–Inverse Document Frequency (Tf-idf) were used for word representations. Support Vector Machine (SVM) and Naive Bayes were used as classifiers. However, the results were not very encouraging.

We also investigated various types of recurrent neural networks (RNNs) such as long short-term memory (LSTM) [1], Bi-Directional LSTM (biLSTM) [2] or gated recurrent unit (GRU) [9], etc. Although some of them achieved pretty good accuracy, the models were heavy and had very long inference time. Our final model is based on the Self-attention neural network architecture Transformer [16], a well known state of the art technique in machine translation. It provided top accuracy and has very fast inference time when running on real data.

The paper is organized as follows. In Sect. 2, some description of self-attention is provided for motivation. In Sect. 3, our architecture is presented. The experiments are described in Sect. 4. Finally, conclusions and remarks are included in Sect. 5.

## 2   Background

Inspired by human sight mechanism, Attention was used in the field of visual imaging about 20 years ago [3]. In 2014, a group from Google DeepMind applied Attentions to the RNN for image classification tasks [7]. After that, Bahdanau et al. [8] applied this mechanism to encoder-decoder architectures in machine translation task. It became the first work to apply Attention mechanism to the field of Natural Language Processing (NLP). Since then, Attention became more and more common for the improvement in various NLP tasks based on neural networks such as RNN/CNN [10,11,14,15,17,19].

In 2017, Vaswani et al. first introduced Self-attention Neural Network [16]. The proposed architecture, Transformer, did not follow the well-known idea of recurrent network. This paper paved the way and Self-attention have become a hot topic in the field of NLP in the last few years. In this section, we describe their approach in detail.

## 2.1   Attention

The first description of Attention Mechanism in Machine Neural Translation [8] was well known as a process to compute weighted average context vectors for each state of the decoder $s_i$ by incorporating the relevant information from all of the encoder states $h_j$ with the previous decoder hidden state $s_{i-1}$, which is determined by a alignment weights $\alpha_{ij}$ between each encoder state and previous hidden state of the decoder, to predict next state of the decoder. It can be summarized by the following equations:

$$c_i = \sum_{j=1}^{n} \alpha_{ij} h_j \tag{1}$$

$$\alpha_{ij} = \frac{exp(e_{ij})}{\sum_{k=1}^{n} exp(e_{jk})} \tag{2}$$

$e_{ij} = a(s_{i-1}, h_j)$, where $a(s_{i-1}, h_j)$ is a function to compute the compatibility score between $s_{i-1}$ and $h_j$.

**Scaled Dot-Product Attention:** Let us consider $s_{i-1}$ as a query vector $q$. And $h_j$ now duplicated, one is key vector $k_j$ and the other is value vector $v_j$ (in current NLP work, the key and value vector are frequently the same, there for $h_j$ can be considered as $k_j$ or $v_j$). The equations outlined above generally look like:

$$c = \sum_{j=1}^{n} \alpha_j v_j \tag{3}$$

$$\alpha_j = \frac{exp(e_j)}{\sum_{k=1}^{n} exp(e_k)} \tag{4}$$

In [16] paper, Vaswani et al. using the scaled dot-product function for the compatibility score function

$$e_j = a(q, k_j) = \frac{qk_j^T}{\sqrt{d_{model}}} \tag{5}$$

where $d_{model}$ is dimension of input vectors or $k$ vector ($q$, $k$, $v$ have the same dimension as input embedding vector).

**Self-attention:** Self-attention is a mechanism to apply Scaled Dot-Product Attention to every token of the sentence for all others. It means for each token, this process will compute a context output that incorporates informations of itself and information about how it relates to others tokens in the sentence.

By using a linear feed-forward layer as a transformation to create three vectors (query, key, value) for every token in sentence, then apply the attention mechanism outlined above to get the context matrix. But it seems very slow and takes a bunch of time for whole process. So, instead of creating them individually, we consider $Q$ is a matrix containing all the query vectors $Q = [q_1, q_2, ..., q_n]$, $K$ contains all keys $K = [k_1, k_2, ..., k_n]$, and $V$ contains all values $V = [v_1, v_2, ..., v_n]$. As the result, this process can be done in parallel [16].

$$Attention(Q, K, V) = softmax(\frac{QK^T}{\sqrt{d_{model}}})V \qquad (6)$$

**Multi-head Attention:** Instead of performing Self-attention a single time with $(Q, K, V)$ of dimensions $d_{model}$. Multi-head Attention performs attention $h$ times with $(Q, K, V)$ matrices of dimensions $d_{model}/h$, each time for applying Attention, it is called a head. For each head, the (Q,K,V) matrices are uniquely projected with different dimensions $d_q$, $d_k$ and $d_v$ (equal to $d_{model}/h$), then self-attention mechanism is performed to yield an output of the same dimension $d_{model}/h$ [16]. After all, outputs of $h$ heads are concatenated, and apply a linear projection layer once again. This process can be summarized by the following equations:

$$MultiHead(Q, K, V) = Concat(head_1, head_2, ..., head_h)W^O$$
$$\text{where } head_i = Attention(QW_i^Q, KW_i^K, VW_i^V) \qquad (7)$$

Where the projections are parameter matrices $W_i^Q \in R^{d_{model} \times d_k}, W_i^K \in R^{d_{model} \times d_k}, W_i^V \in R^{d_{model} \times d_v}, W^O \in R^{hd_v \times d_{model}}$.

## 2.2    Positional Information Embedding Representation

Self-attention can provide context matrix containing information about how a token relates with the others. However, this attention mechanism still has limit, losing positional information problem. It does not care about the order of tokens. That means outputs of this process is invariant with the same set of tokens with order permutations. So, to make it work, neural networks need to incorporate positional information to the inputs. Sinusoidal Positional Encoding technique is commonly used to solve this problem.

**Sinusoidal Position Encoding:** This technique was proposed by Vaswani et al. [16]. The main point of this technique is to create Position Encoding

$(PE)$ using sinusoidal and cosinusoidal functions to encode the position. The $PE$ function can be write by following equation:

$$PE(position, 2i) = Sin(\frac{position}{10000^{2i/d_{model}}})$$ (8)

$$PE(position, 2i+1) = Cos(\frac{position}{10000^{2i/d_{model}}})$$ (9)

where $position$ starts from 1 and $i$ is $i_{th}$ dimension of $d_{model}$ dimensions. It means that for each dimension of the positional encoding corresponds to a different sinusoids.

The advantages of this technique is it can add positional information for sentences longer than those in training dataset.

## 3   Our Approach

### 3.1   Model Architecture

We proposed a simple model using a single modified 12 heads Self-attention block (See Fig. 2), described below.

Original Sinusoidal Position Encoding [16] used "adding" operation to incorporate positional informations as a input. That means while performing Self-attention, representation informations(Word Embeddings) and positional informations(Positional Embeddings) have the same weights (these two information are equal).

$$z = Embedding + PE$$ (10)

In Vietnamese, we assumed that the positional information has more contributions to create contextual semantics than representation informations. Therefore, we used "concatenate" operation to incorporate positional informations. That made representation informations may have a different weights with positional informations during the transformation process.

$$z = Concat(Embedding, PE)$$ (11)

We added a block inspired by paper "Squeeze-and-Excitation Networks", Hu et al. [18] for the average attention mechanism and the gating mechanism by stacking a GobalAveragePooling1D layer then forming a bottleneck with two fully-connected layers (see Fig. 1). The first layer is dimensionality-reduction layer with reduction ratio $r$ (in our experiment default is 4) with a non-linear activation and then the second layer is dimensionality-increasing layer to return the result to $d_{model}$ dimension also with a sigmoid activation function, which scale the feature value into range $[0, 1]$. It means this layer computes how much a feature incorporates information to contextual semantics. We call this technique Embedding Feature Attention.

$$y = \sigma(W_{fc_2}\delta(W_{fc_1}x))$$ (12)

Where $x$ is input of block. $y$ is output of block. $\sigma$ is a non-linear activation function. $\delta$ is a non-linear activation function. $W_{fc_1}, W_{fc_2}$ are trainable matrices.

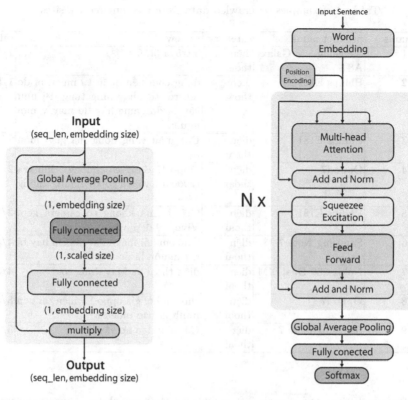

**Fig. 1.** Squeeze-Excitation architecture.

**Fig. 2.** Self-attention Neural Networks architecture for sentiments classification task.

## 4 Experiments

We implemented from scratch some layers that are needed for this work, such as: Scaled-dot product Attention, Multihead Attention, Feed-Forward Network and re-trained word embeddings for Vietnamese spoken language.

All experiments were deployed on 26 GB RAM, CPU Intel Xeon Processor E31220L v2, GPU Tesla K80 for 20 epochs, 64 of batch size for comparison and all neural network models used focal-crossentropy as the training loss.

### 4.1 Datasets

There is no public dataset for electronics product reviews in Vietnamese. We had to crawl user reviews from several e-commerce websites, such as Tiki, Lazada, shopee, Sendo, Adayroi, Dienmayxanh, Thegioididong, fptshop, vatgia. Based on our purposes, we chose some data fields to collect and store. Some data samples are presented in Table 1 below.

**Table 1.** Examples for crawled data from e-commerce websites.

| username | product name | category | review | rating |
|---|---|---|---|---|
| user 1 | Samsung Galaxy A8+ | điện thoại | Ytt5ya 5t55 | 1/5 |
| user 2 | Philips E181 | điện thoại | đang chơi liên quân tự nhiên bị đơ đơ. rồi tự nhảy lung tung. Bị như vậy là do game hay do máy v mọi người. | 1/5 |
| user 3 | Philips E181 | điện thoại | Đặt màu vàng đồng mà giao màu bạc | 2/5 |
| user 4 | Oppo f7 | điện thoại | Oppo f7 đang có chương trình trả trước 0% và trả góp 0% đúng không ạ? | 2/5 |
| user 5 | Philips E181 | điện thoại | Giá đó mà không có camera kép, Vivo V9 đẹp hơn. | 2/5 |
| user 6 | Samsung Note 7 | điện thoại | Cho em hỏi máy m5c của em hay bị tắt nguồn là do sao ạ? | 4/5 |
| user 7 | Nokia 230 Dual SIM | điện thoại | điện thoại vs Máy dùng tốt | 4/5 |
| user 8 | Oppo f7 | điện thoại | cho em hỏi giá oppo F7 hiện tại bên mình là bao nhiêu ạ? | 5/5 |
| user 9 | Samsung Note 7 | điện thoại | Có màu đen ko vậy? | 5/5 |

After analyzing and visualizing, we found that the dataset was very imbalanced (see the description below) and noisy. There were some meaningless reviews (*user1* in Table 1). Some of them did not have sentiments (*user4*, *user8* and *user9* in Table 1). Sometimes, the ratings do not reflect the sentiment of reviews, (see *user6* in Table 1). Therefore, a manual inspection step was applied to clean and label the data. We also built a tool for labeling process to made it smoothly and faster (see Fig. 3).

- Corpus have only 2 labels (positive and negative).
- Total 32,953 documents in labeled corpus:
  - Positives: 22,335 documents.
  - Negatives: 10,618 documents.

Next, to make the dataset balanced, we duplicated some short negative documents and segmented the longer ones. In final result we have over $43,500$ documents in corpus with $22,335$ positives and $21,236$ negatives.

Using for training models, we splitted corpus into 3 sets as following: training set: $27,489$, validation set: $6,873$, test set: $8,591$.

**Fig. 3.** Sentiment checking tool interface.

### 4.2 Preprocessing

For automatic preprocessing, we mainly used available researches. We applied a sentence tokenizer [21] for each documents. All links, phone numbers and email addresses were replaced by *"urlObj"*, *"phonenumObj"* and *"mailObj"*, respectively. Words tokenizer from Underthesea [20] for Vietnamese was also applied.

### 4.3 Embeddings

We used fastText [13] model for word embeddings. In many cases, users may type a wrong word accidentally or intentionally. fastText deals with this problem very well by encoding at the characters level. When users type wrong or very rare words or out-of-vocabulary words, fastText still can represent those words with an embedding vector that most similar to word met in trained sentences. This has made fastText become the best candidate to represent user inputs.

There had been no fastText pre-trained model for Vietnamese spoken language. Therefore, we trained fastText model for Vietnamese vocabulary as embedding pre-trained weights from a corpus over 70,000 documents of multi-products reviews crawled from ecomerce sites mentioned in Subsect. 4.1 with no label. Rare words that occur less than 5 times in the vocabulary were removed. Embedding size was 384. After training, we had 5,534 vocabularies in total.

### 4.4 Evaluation Results

We used the same word embeddings as mentioned above for all models and evaluated all models on test set which has 8591 documents. To demonstrate the significance of our model, we compare our model with 6 base line RNNs models such as Long-Short Term Memory (LSTM), Gated Recurrent Units (GRU), bidirectional LSTM, bidirectional GRU, stacked bidirectional LSTM and stacked bidirectional GRU with the following configurations.

- Vanilla LSTM and GRU: 1 layer with 1,024 units.
- Bidirectional model of LSTM and GRU: 1 layer with 1,024 units in forward and 1,024 units in backward.

– Stacked bidirectional model of LSTM and GRU: 2 stacked layers with 1,024 units in forward and 1,024 units in backward for each layer.

Table 2 shows that our model gave the best inference time with top accuracy in test set. Also, in fact, this model ran in production have shown good prediction than the top of baseline models, stacked Bidirectional Long-short Term Memory, especially with complex sentences such as "giá cao như này thì t mua con ss gala S7 cho r" "quảng cáo lm lố vl", "với tôi thì trong tầm giá nv vẫn có thể chấp nhận đk" or "Nhưng vì đây là dòng điện thoại giá rẻ, nên cũng k thể kì vọng hơn đc" (See Figs. 4 and 5).

**Table 2.** Inference times and macro-f1 scores

| Methods | Avg. inference time (s) | Macro-f1 (%) |
|---|---|---|
| LSTM | 0.4748 | 48.9(23) |
| bi-LSTM | 0.9373 | 90.0(05) |
| stacked bi-LSTM | 1.7967 | 90.1(32) |
| GRU | 0.3738 | 48.9(23) |
| bi-GRU | 0.5863 | 88.9(25) |
| stacked bi-GRU | 1.4830 | 89.9(72) |
| **Self-attention** | **0.0124** | **90.1(64)** |

```
marketing thì trông rất tuyệt. nhưng khi cầm trên tay thì trời ơi, quá tệ.
nhìn chung thật sự đây là dòng của hãng.
nói chung là k thể'nào chấp nhận được như vậy với hãng dt lớn nv
-------------------------------------------------
[ANALYZING...]
 + marketing thì trông rất tuyệt . => [POSITIVE]
 + nhưng khi cầm trên tay thì trời_ơi , quá tệ . => [NEGATIVE]
 + nhìn_chung thật_sự đây là dòng đt cùi nhất từng xuất_hiện của hãng . => [NEGATIVE]
 + nói_chung là k thể'nào chấp_nhận được như_vậy với hãng dt lớn nv => [NEGATIVE]
{'NEGATIVE': 3, 'POSITIVE': 1}
=================================================================================
chơi game cực kì khó chịu, khó chịu kinh khủng. màn hình thì bị giật lag.
nhưng nếu chỉ xài đề'lướt web hay facebook thì rất ok.
Nhưng vì đây là dòng điện thoại giá rẻ, nên cũng k thể'kì vọng hơn đc.
tóm lại thì nói chung vẫn ổn trong tầm giá. với tôi thì trong tầm giá nv vẫn có thể'chấp nhận đk
-------------------------------------------------
[ANALYZING...]
 + chơi game cực_kì khó_chịu , khó_chịu kinh_khủng . => [NEGATIVE]
 + màn_hình thì bị giật lag . => [NEGATIVE]
 + nhưng nếu chỉ xài đề'lướt web hay facebook thì rất ok . => [POSITIVE]
 + Nhưng vì đây là dòng điện_thoại giá rẻ , nên cũng k thể'kì vọng hơn đc . => [NEGATIVE]
 + tóm_lại thì nói_chung vẫn ổn trong tầm giá . => [POSITIVE]
 + với tôi thì trong tầm giá nv vẫn có thể'chấp_nhận đk => [NEGATIVE]
{'NEGATIVE': 4, 'POSITIVE': 2}
=================================================================================
giá cao như này thì t mua con ss gala S7 cho r. quảng cáo lm lố'vl. siêu tệ
-------------------------------------------------
[ANALYZING...]
 + giá cao như này thì t mua con ss gala S7 cho r . => [NEGATIVE]
 + quảng_cáo lm lố'vl . => [POSITIVE]
 + siêu tệ => [NEGATIVE]
{'NEGATIVE': 2, 'POSITIVE': 1}
=================================================================================
mean inference times: 1.7967446978935828
```

**Fig. 4.** Stacked bidirectional long-short term memory for sentiments analysis in Vietnamese examples

```
marketing thì trông rất tuyệt. nhưng khi cầm trên tay thì trời ơi, quá tệ.
nhìn chung thật sự đây là dòng đt cùi nhất từng xuất hiện của hãng.
nói chung là k thể'nào chấp nhận được như vậy với hãng đt lớn nv
--------------------------------------------------
[ANALYZING...]
 + marketing thì trông rất tuyệt . => [POSITIVE]
 + nhưng khi cầm trên tay thì trời_ơi , quá tệ . => [NEGATIVE]
 + nhìn_chung thật_sự đây là dòng đt cùi nhất từng xuất_hiện của hãng . => [NEGATIVE]
 + nói_chung là k thể'nào chấp_nhận được như_vậy với hãng đt lớn nv => [NEGATIVE]
{'NEGATIVE': 3, 'POSITIVE': 1}
======================================================================================
chơi game cực kì khó chịu, khó chịu kinh khủng. màn hình thì bị giật lag.
nhưng nếu chỉ xài đề'lướt web hay facebook thì rất ok.
Nhưng vì đây là dòng điện thoại giá rẻ, nên cũng k thể'kì vọng hơn đc.
tóm lại thì nói chung vẫn ổn trong tầm giá. với tôi thì trong tầm giá nv vẫn có thể'chấp nhận đk
--------------------------------------------------
[ANALYZING...]
 + chơi game cực_kì khó_chịu , khó_chịu kinh_khủng . => [NEGATIVE]
 + màn_hình thì bị giật lag . => [NEGATIVE]
 + nhưng nếu chỉ xài đề'lướt web hay facebook thì rất ok . => [POSITIVE]
 + Nhưng vì đây là dòng điện_thoại giá rẻ , nên cũng k thể'kì_vọng hơn đc . => [POSITIVE]
 + tóm_lại thì nói_chung vẫn ổn trong tầm giá . => [POSITIVE]
 + với tôi thì trong tầm giá nv vẫn có_thể'chấp_nhận đk => [POSITIVE]
{'NEGATIVE': 2, 'POSITIVE': 4}
======================================================================================
giá cao như này thì t mua con ss gala S7 cho r. quảng cáo lm lô'vl. siêu tệ
--------------------------------------------------
[ANALYZING...]
 + giá cao như này thì t mua con ss gala S7 cho r . => [NEGATIVE]
 + quảng_cáo lm lô'vl . => [NEGATIVE]
 + siêu tệ => [NEGATIVE]
{'NEGATIVE': 3, 'POSITIVE': 0}
======================================================================================
mean inference times: 0.012444697893582858
```

**Fig. 5.** Self-attention neural network for sentiments analysis in Vietnamese examples

## 5  Conclusion

In this paper we demonstrated that using Self-attention Neural Network is faster than previous state of the art techniques with the best result in test set and achieved exceptionally good results when ran in prodution (Predictions make sense to human in unlabeled data with very fast inference time).

For future work, we plan to extend stacked multi-head self-attention architectures. We are also interested in seeing the behaviour of the models explored in this work on much larger datasets (beyond the electronics product reviews) and more classes.

**Acknowledgment.** We thank our teammates, Tran A. Sang, Cao T. Thanh, and Ha H. Huy for helpful discussions and supports.

## References

1. Hochreiter, S., Schmidhuber, J.: Long short-term memory. Neural Comput. **9**(8), 1735–1780 (1997)
2. Schuster, M., Paliwal, K.K.: Bidirectional recurrent neural networks. IEEE Trans. Sig. Process. **45**(11), 2673–2681 (1997)
3. Schneider, W.X.: An Introduction to "Mechanisms of Visual Attention: A Cognitive Neuroscience Perspective" (1998) https://pdfs.semanticscholar.org/b719/918bdf2e71571a3cbb2a6aaaec3f1b6af9e6.pdf

4. Esuli, A., Sebastiani, F.: Senti-wordnet: a publicly available lexical resource for opinion mining. In: Proceedings of LREC, vol. 6, pp. 417–422 (2006)
5. Baccianella, S., Esuli, A., Sebastiani, F.: Sentiwordnet 3.0: an enhanced lexical resource for sentiment analysis and opinion mining. In: Proceedings of LREC, vol. 10, pp. 2200–2204 (2010)
6. Mohammad, S.M., Kiritchenko, S., Zhu, X.: NRC-canada: building the state-of-the-art in sentiment analysis of tweets. In: Proceedings of SemEval-2013 (2013)
7. Mnih, V., et al.: Recurrent models of visual attention. In: Neural Information Processing Systems Conference (NIPS) (2014). arXiv preprint arXiv:1406.6247
8. Bahdanau, D., Cho, K., Bengio, Y.: Neural machine translation by jointly learning to align and translate. accepted in International Conference on Learning Representations (ICLR) (2015). arXiv preprint arXiv:1409.0473, 2014
9. Chung, J., Gulcehre, C., Cho, K., Bengio, Y.: Empirical Evaluation of Gated Recurrent Neural Networks on Sequence Modeling. arXiv preprint arXiv:1412.3555 (2014)
10. Cheng, J., Dong, L., Lapata, M.: Long short-term memory-networks for machine reading. Computing Research Repository (CoRR) (2016). arXiv preprint arXiv:1601.06733
11. Lu, J., Yang, J., Batra, D., Parikh, D.: Hierarchical question-image co-attention for visual question answering. In: Advances in Neural Information Processing Systems 29, pp. 289–297. Curran Associates Inc. (2016)
12. Vo, D.T., Zhang, Y.: Don' t Count, Predict! An Automatic Approach to Learning Sentiment Lexicons for Short Text (2016). https://www.aclweb.org/anthology/P16-2036
13. Bojanowski, P., Grave, E., Joulin, A., Mikolov, T.: Enriching Word Vectors with Subword Information. arXiv preprint arXiv:1607.04606 (2016)
14. Kokkinos, F., Potamianos, A.: Structural attention neural networks for improved sentiment analysis. arXiv preprint arXiv:1701.01811 (2017)
15. Daniluk, M., Rocktaschel, T., Welbl, J., Riedel, S.: Frustratingly short attention spans in neural language modeling. arXiv preprint arXiv:1702.04521 (2017)
16. Vaswani, A., et al.: Attention is all you need. In: Guyon, I., et al. (eds.) Advances in Neural Information Processing Systems 30, pp. 5998–6008. Curran Associates Inc. (2017). arXiv preprint arXiv:1706.03762 (2017). http://papers.nips.cc/paper/7181-attention-is-all-you-need.pdf
17. Gehring, J., Auli, M., Grangier, D., Yarats, D., Dauphin, Y.N.: Convolutional sequence to sequence learning. arXiv preprint arXiv:1705.03122 (2017)
18. Hu, J., Shen, L., Albanie, S., Sun, G., Wu, E.: Squeeze-and-Excitation Networks. arXiv preprint arXiv:1709.01507 (2017)
19. Zhou, Y., Zhou, J., Liu, L., Feng, J., Peng, H., Zheng, X.: RNN-based sequence-preserved attention for dependency parsing (2018). https://www.aaai.org/ocs/index.php/AAAI/AAAI18/paper/view/17176
20. Anh, V., et al.: Underthesea. https://github.com/undertheseanlp/underthesea
21. Natural Language Toolkit. https://www.nltk.org/

# Advances in Query Processing and Optimization

# Computing History-Dependent Schedules for Processes with Temporal Constraints

Johann Eder[✉]

Department of Informatics-Systems, Alpen-Adria Universität Klagenfurt,
Klagenfurt, Austria
johann.eder@aau.at

**Abstract.** The importance of adequate management of temporal aspects of process aware information systems is beyond dispute. A particular problem for the management of temporal constraints is to check whether a process definition is correct, where correctness is defined by history-dependent controllability. This means to check whether a history-dependent schedule exists, which obeys all temporal constraints. A schedule defines temporal execution intervals for process steps, in a history-dependent schedule a step might have several execution intervals depending on the control decisions made before this process step is activated. We present a procedure for checking the history-dependent controllability of processes with temporal constraints which is both sound and complete and effectively computes history-dependent schedules for temporally constrained business processes.

**Keywords:** Business process management · Workflow · Temporal constraints · Controllability

## 1 Introduction

Processes have been successfully introduced for modeling dynamic phenomena in many areas like business, production, health care, etc. in various forms like workflows [19], extended transactions [25], business processes [11], web-service orchestrations [9], etc. As many of these applications require to adequately deal with temporal aspects a substantial body of research addresses to master the plentitude of temporal aspects of process engineering: from the modeling of temporal aspects, to the formulation of different notions of correctness of process models with temporal constraints, to check the temporal correctness of process definitions, to compute execution schedules for processes and to support adherence to temporal constraints at runtime with proactive time management (see [4,17,21] for an overview).

One of the most elaborated notions of correctness of a process model with temporal constraints is the *controllability* of process definitions [7,30]. In a nutshell: the concept of controllability regards a process definition as correct, if it is possible to state a schedule such that all temporal constraints are obeyed, if

© Springer Nature Switzerland AG 2019
T. K. Dang et al. (Eds.): FDSE 2019, LNCS 11814, pp. 145–164, 2019.
https://doi.org/10.1007/978-3-030-35653-8_11

all process steps are executed within the intervals defined in the schedule [8]. Satisfiability, or conformance [7, 14] is not sufficient or strong enough, as satisfiability only checks whether there exists an execution of the process without time failures. However, in contrast to controllability it does not guarantee that in all circumstances, i.e. for all flow decisions and for all durations of activities within their minimum and maximum duration interval, all temporal constraints can be obeyed.

Controllability, nevertheless, was soon found to be too strict [7, 14]. This lead to the development of more relaxed notions of controllability. *History-dependent controllability* allows that the execution interval for a step in a history-dependent schedule depends on the observations of flow decisions before the activation of this step. *Dynamic controllability* relaxes this notion even further and requires that there is a strategy for a process controller to make decisions based on all temporally prior observations (flow decisions and observed duration of activities) such that no temporal constraints is violated. Similar problems where studied in the area of AI and in the area of constraint satisfaction in form of temporal constraint networks of different flavors as described in [7].

Several algorithms for checking controllability resp. dynamic controllability of process definitions with several sets of temporal constraints have been proposed for different flavors of process models, e.g. [2, 5, 7, 12, 22, 23, 26, 33]. Nevertheless, an algorithm which is computationally feasible, both sound and complete and effectively computes a history-dependent schedule is still missing. It is the ambition of this paper to contribute to closing this gap. We build on our earlier approaches for checking the correctness of temporal process specification and the computation of execution plans (schedules) [14–16, 18].

In the following we use a seemingly rather simple model for defining processes with temporal constraints, we only consider contingent nodes and upper-bound constraints on end-events of activities. This is, however, no restriction of the expressiveness, as we can show, that our lean process model is expressive enough to also express non-contingency of activities, lower-bound constraints, constraints on the start-events of activities, and contingent and non-contingent constraints on links [13].

The particular contributions of this paper are: (1) We provide a formalization of history-dependent controllability. (2) We propose a procedure for checking the history-dependent controllability of temporally constrained process definitions and proof that it is both sound and complete. (3) This algorithm also computes a history-dependent schedule. (4) We proof that the problem of computing a history-dependent schedule for a time constrained process has exponential complexity in the worst case.

The rest of this paper is organized as follows: In Sect. 2 we define our process modelling notation and introduce history dependent schedules and history dependent controllability. In Sect. 3 we present an algorithm for computing history-dependent schedules with the help of a timed graph. In Sect. 4 we study the complexity of the problem of computing a history-dependent schedule.

In Sect. 5 we contrast your approach to related work and in Sect. 6 we draw some conclusions.

# 2    Process Model, Temporal Constraints, and History-Dependent Schedules

## 2.1    Process Model

We consider here a minimal but quite expressive process model: We focus on the standard minimum workflow control patterns [32]: acyclic workflow nets composed of nodes and edges. Some of the nodes are XOR-splits and -joins. All other nodes contain implicitly AND-splits and -joins. Xor splits have exactly 2 outgoing and Xor-joins 1 or 2 incoming nodes. This definition of a process graph is a relaxation of the usual workflow net definitions. Xor-joins have the semantics of simple merge, i.e. it is not possible that more than predecessors of an Xor-join-node will be executed in a single process instance. For all nodes with the exception of XOR-splits: if there are several successor nodes, then the semantics is that of an (implicit) AND-split. For all nodes with the exception of XOR-joins: if there are several predecessors the semantics is that of an AND-join.

In addition, we consider the following temporal information and constraints: minimum and maximum duration of nodes, and upper-bound constraints. See Fig. 1 as an example for such a process with labels, discussed below. Xor-split nodes are represented as diamonds, xor-join nodes as shaded diamonds. Upper-bound constraints are represented as dashed arrows from destination to source.

Temporal aspects are represented by durations and time points in form of real numbers, where all durations have to be greater or equal 0. Time points are represented as distance to a time origin (here usually the time-point of the start of a process). Activity instances start at a certain time point (time point for the start event of an activity instance) and end at a certain time point (end event); their distance is the duration of an activity instance. In the following we only consider *contingent* activities whose duration between their minimum and maximum duration which can only be observed but not controlled.

In analogy to [7] we use propositional labels for nodes to indicate through which path(s) a node can be reached, i.e. which decisions were taken to reach a node. In contrast to [7] we define a label as a set of different possible decisions which can lead to the considered node.

**Definition 1 (propositional terms).** *Let $L$ be a set of propositional letters. Let $p \in L$ then $p$ and $\neg p$ are literals, $\mathcal{L}$ is the set of all literals over $l$. Let $l_1, \ldots l_n$ be literals, then $l_1 \wedge \ldots \wedge l_n$ are conjunctive terms. We call $t$ a minterm over a set of letters $L$, if $t$ is a conjunctive term and for each $p \in L$ either $p$ or $\neg p$ appears in $t$. $\mathcal{M}(\mathcal{L})$ is the set of all minterms over $\mathcal{L}$. Two terms $t_1, t_2$ are compatible $(t_1 \simeq t_2)$, if there exist a minterm $t \in \mathcal{M}(\mathcal{L})$ such that $t \rightarrow t_1 \wedge t \rightarrow t_2$.*

*Let $L = L_1, \ldots L_n$ be sets of conjunctive terms over $\mathcal{L}$. We define the cross conjunction of $L$ as $\bigotimes L = \{l_1 \wedge \ldots \wedge l_n | l_i \in L_i, 1 \leq i \leq n\}$.*

We assign a unique propositional letter $p$ to each xor-split and adorn one outgoing edge of the split node with $p$, the other with $\neg p$. The labels we assign to the nodes are sets of conjunctive terms over the propositional letters of predecessors of these nodes. Each term in the label of a nodes represents a different path to reach this node. In the following we define the representation of the model in form of a process graph formally.

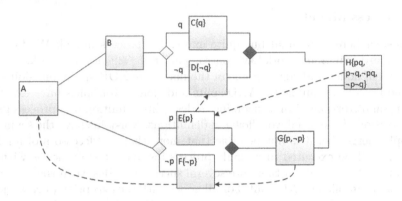

**Fig. 1.** Process graph with labels

**Definition 2 (Process Graph).** $P(N, E, B, L)$ *is a temporally constrained process graph, iff* $(N, E)$ *forms a connected direct acyclic graph with a set of nodes* $N$ *and a set of edges* $E$. *A node* $n$ *has the following properties:* $n.l \in L$, $n.L \in \mathcal{P}(\mathcal{L})$ *and* $n.type \in \{node, xs, xj\}$, $n.d$ *(minimum duration) and* $n.x$ *(maximum duration). An edge* $e \in E$ *has the property* $e.l \in \{True\} \cup L \cup \{\neg l | l \in L\}$. $B$ *consist of upper-bound constraints* $(s, d, \delta)$ *where* $s \in N$ *is the source and* $d \in N$ *is the destination node, and* $\delta \geq 0$ *is some real.*

*The function* $n.l$ *assigns a unique propositional letter* $p \in L$ *to each xor-split node* $n \in N$.

*For each Xor-split node* $x$ *there are two outgoing edges* $e_1$ *and* $e_2$ *in* $E$ *with* $e_1.l = x.l$ *and* $e_2.l = \neg x.l$. *All other edges have the label TRUE.*

*A process graph has at least 1* start *node, which has no predecessor and at least 1* stop *node which has no successor. There is a path from every start node to every stop node. Every node is on a path from a start node to a stop node. A node of type* $xs$ *has exactly 2 successor nodes, a node of type* $xj$ *can have one or two predecessor nodes.*

$E^+$ *denotes the transitive closure of* $E$. *For a node* $n$, $n.Pred$ *denotes the set of all direct predecessors of* $n$: $n.Pred := \{m | \exists (m, n) \in E\}$, *and* $n.Succ$ *the set of all direct successors of* $n$: $n.Succ := \{m | \exists (n, m) \in E\}$. $n.Pred^+$ *denotes the set of all (direct or indirect) predecessors of* $n$: $n.Pred^+ := \{m | \exists (m, n) \in E^+\}$, *and* $n.Succ^+$ *is the set of all successor of* $n$: $n.Succ^+ := \{m | \exists (n, m) \in E^+\}$.

*The label of a node* $n$ *is defined as (1.)* $n.L = \{True\}$, *if* $n$ *is a start node; (2.)* $n.L = \bigcup_{m \in n.Pred} m.L$, *if* $n.type = xj$; *(3.)* $n.L = \bigotimes \{m.L | m \in n.Pred\}$ *for any other node.*

It is easy to see that every well formed workflow net [31] can be represented as process graph according to the definition above. Figure 1 shows an example for a process graph with labels.

To avoid questionable process definitions with impossible paths, ill defined joins and void constraints we define requirements for well-formed process graphs: For simple-merge Xor-joins it must not happen that both of its predecessor are executed in a single instance, i.e. the predecessors of an Xor-join node must have disjoint labels. For all nodes except (except Xor-join nodes) we require that their predecessors are not mutually exclusive, i.e. *False* must not appear in labels of nodes. And finally, for source and destination nodes of an upper bound constraint there has to be the possibility for an instance of the process in which both are activated - requiring that their labels are compatible.

**Definition 3 (Well formed).** *A process graph $P(N, E, B, L)$ is well formed, iff*
*(1.) $\forall n, n_1, n_2 \in N : n.type = xj, n_1 \neq n_2, (n_1, n), (n_2, n) \in E \Rightarrow n_1.L \wedge n_2.L \rightarrow False$, and*
*(2.) $\forall n \in N \; \forall p \in n.L : p \neq False$, and*
*(3.) $\forall (s, d, \delta) \in B : \exists t \in \mathcal{M}(\mathcal{L}) : t \rightarrow s.L, t \rightarrow d.L$*

In the following we assume that all process graphs are well-formed which has the consequence that the terms in a label are pairwise disjoint.

**Lemma 1.** *For a well formed process graph $P(N, E, B, L)$, $\forall n \in N, \forall t_1 \neq t_2 \in n.L : t_1 \rightarrow \neg t_2$).*

*Proof.* Follows from Definitions 2 and 3.

**Lemma 2.** *For a well formed process graph $P(N, E, B, L)$, $\forall n \in N, n.type \neq xj, \exists t \in \mathcal{M} : \forall m \in n.Pred : t \rightarrow m.L$.*

*Proof.* Follows from Definition 3(2.): if the labels of the predecessor of a node are incompatible, then the cross product of their labels would contain False.

## 2.2 History-Dependent Schedules and History-Dependent Controllability

A schedule assigns execution intervals to each node in a process graph. A process is *controllable* if it admits a schedule. This notion is known to be too restrictive [14, 23] and therefore, the notion of a history-dependent schedule was introduced which offers the possibility to define the execution intervals for a node depending on past decisions or observations. In the definition of history-dependent controllability we use here, the execution interval of a node might depend the observed outcomes of Xor-splits preceding this node in the process definition. There are other more general definitions of dynamic controllability [7, 23] where all information (in particular start and end time of activities) which temporally precede a node can be used.

Now can define the semantics of the temporal constraints by defining which possible execution scenarios (traces with time stamps) are considered as correct. A *history-dependent* scenario takes into account that not every node of the process appears in every process instance due to Xor-splits. The possible combinations of nodes are determined by any possible combination of decisions which are in turn represented by all minterms over the propositional letters of the process definition. In such a history-dependent scenario a node $n$ can have different time-points for different minterms. A history-dependent scenario is valid, if each of its scenario projections (defined by a particular minterm) is a valid scenario.

**Definition 4 (History-dependent scenario).** *A history-dependent scenario $\bar{S}$ for $P(N, E, L, B)$ associates for each $t \in \mathcal{M}(\mathcal{L})$ each $n \in N$ with $t \rightarrow n.L$ with 2 timestamps $t_s$ and $t_e$, the timepoints of the start and end events of a process instance. We call $(t, n, t_s, t_e) \in \bar{S}$ a scenario entry.*

*$\bar{S}$ is valid, iff $\forall t \in \mathcal{M}(\mathcal{L}) \vee (l, n, nl_s, nl_e), (l, m, ml_s, ml_e) \in \bar{S}$*

*(1.) $nt_s + n.d \leq nt_e \leq nt_s + n.x$,*

*(2.) $n < m \Rightarrow nt_e \leq mt_s$, and*

*(3.) $\forall (n, m, \delta) \in B : mt_e \leq nt_e + \delta$.*

In a *history-dependent* schedule the execution interval for a node $n$ in the process graph may depend only on the decisions taken before the execution of $n$. The decisions are observed by monitoring which outgoing edge of XOR split nodes preceding $n$ were taken, resp. which successors of an Xor-split were enabled. So different paths to a node $n$ might lead to different execution intervals for $n$. The label of a node $n$ in a process graph $P$ exactly contains the different possibilities for reaching this node. So in a history-dependent schedule we assign (possibly different) execution intervals to each node for each of the terms in its label.

**Definition 5 (History-dependent schedule).** *A history-dependent schedule $S$ for a process graph $P(N, E, L, B)$ associates each $n \in N$ and each $p \in n.L$ with intervals for the start and end events of $n$. We write $(n, p, (F_s, T_s), (F_e, T_e)) \in S$ for a schedule entry.*

$F_s$ (say *From start*) represents the earliest time point for starting node $n$ , $T_s$ (*To start*) the latest time point for finishing $n$, and $F_e$ (*From end*) the earliest time point for finishing $n$, and finally $T_e$ (*To end*) the latest time point for finishing $n$. In the following we sometimes abbreviate $(F_s, T_s)$ with $V_s$, $(F_e, T_e)$ with $V_e$, or $V_s, V_e$ with $V$. The definition of history-dependent controllability requires that a history-dependent schedule exists such that each scenario is valid, if its timepoints are within the limits of the execution intervals defined in the history-dependent schedule.

**Definition 6 (History-dependent controllability).** *A process graph $P(N, E, L, B)$ is history-dependent controllable, iff it has a history-dependent schedule $S$ such that each history-dependent scenario $\bar{S}$ is valid, if for each minterm $t$ for each scenario entry $(t, n, t_s, t_e) \in \bar{S}$ for $(n, p, (F_s, T_s), (F_e, T_e)) \in S$ with $t \rightarrow p$: $F_s \leq t_s \leq T_s$ and $F_e \leq t_e \leq T_e$.*

This definition is well formed since each minterm $t$ implies at most one term in the label of a node, as all terms in a label are pairwise disjoint (Lemma 1).

**Definition 7 (Correct history-dependent schedule).** *A history-dependent schedule $S$ of a process $P(N, E, L, B)$ is correct, iff $\forall n, m \in N$, $\forall (n, p, (F_s, T_s), (F_e, T_e)) \in S$, $\forall (m, q, (F'_s, T'_s), (F'_e, T'_e)) \in S$ with $p \simeq q$*
*(1.) $F_e = T_s + n.d$,*
*(2.) $T_e = F_s + n.x$*
*(3.) $F_e + n.x - n.d \leq T_e$,*
*(4.) $n < m \Rightarrow T_e \leq F'_s$,*
*(5.) $(n, m, \delta) \in B, p \simeq q \Rightarrow T'_e \leq F_e + \delta$.*

**Lemma 3.** *A process is history-dependent controllable, iff it has a correct history-dependent schedule.*

If a process admits a correct schedule, then for all nodes $n$ it also admits a correct schedule where the node $n$ starts at time point 0.

**Lemma 4 (0-schedule).** *If there is a correct history-dependent schedule $S$ for $P(N, E, L, B)$, then for each $n \in N$ there is a correct schedule $S_n^0$ with $n.F_s = n.T_s = 0$.*

*Proof.* Let $S$ be a correct schedule, let $n \in N$, let $(n, p, (\tau_s, \tau_s), (\tau', \tau'')) \in S$. Then $S_n^0$ is derived from $S$ by adding $-\tau$ to all From and To values in $S$. $S_n^0$ is a correct schedule since addition of scalars is an equivalence transformation for the inequalities of Definition 7 and $n.Fs = n.Ts = 0$.

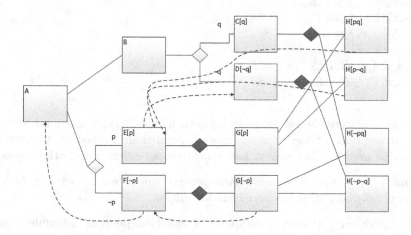

**Fig. 2.** Timed graph

# 3    Computation of History-Dependent Schedules

## 3.1    Schedule and Timed Graph

For computing a history-dependent schedule for a temporally constrained process we use an intermediary structure called (unfolded) timed graph [15, 16]. Let $P(N, E, L, B)$ be a process graph. The timed graph of $P$ consists of a node for each label of each node in $N$. Figure 2 shows the timed graph for the process of Fig. 1. The upperbound constraints are shown as dashed arrows from destination to source.

In a timed graph we consider intervals for the end event of each node $x$ for each term in $x.L$. We will show later that all entries of a 0-schedule have to be within these intervals. A node $n$ of the timed graph cannot finish before $n.E_b$ (Earliest time point best case) all contingent activities up to $n$ finish at their minimum duration and not before $n.E_w$ (Earliest time point worst case), if they take their maximum duration. The L-values represent time points when a node has to finish at the latest to satisfy all temporal constraints: if $n$ finishes before $n.L_b$ all constraints are satisfied, if all succeeding contingent activities only take their minimum duration; if $n$ finishes before $n.L_w$ if all succeeding activities use their maximum duration.

**Definition 8 (Timed Graph).** $U(N, E, L, B)$ *is a timed graph for a process* $P(N', E', L, B')$, *iff* $N = \{(n, l) | n \in N', l \in n.L\}$, $E = \{((n, l), (m, k)) | (n, m) \in E', l \simeq k\}$, $B = \{((n, l), (m, k), \delta) | (n, m, \delta) \in B', l \simeq k\}$.

*Each* $n \in N$ *is associated with intervals for end events of activities:* $E_b, E_w,$ $L_w, L_b$. *A timed graph is correct, iff* $\forall n \in N, \forall m \in n.Pred$:
*(1.)* $n.E_w \leq n.L_w$,
*(2.)* $m.E_w + n.x \leq n.E_w$,
*(3.)* $m.E_b + n.d \leq n.E_b$,
*(4.)* $m.L_w + n.x \leq n.L_w$,
*(5.)* $m.L_b + n.d \leq n.L_b$,
*(6.)* $\forall(s, d, \delta) \in B, s.E_b + \delta \leq d.E_w$,
*(7.)* $\forall(s, d, \delta) \in B, s.L_w + d \leq d.L_b$.

We now analyze the relationship between a timed graph and a schedule. It is easy to see that a timed graph is more general than a schedule. However, as we describe precisely in the next Lemma, processes either have both or none.

**Lemma 5.** *A temporally constrained process graph has a correct history-dependent schedule, iff it has correct timed graph.*

*Proof.* Algorithm 1 (CompS) computes a history-dependent schedule from a correct timed graph. We can be shown that this tomed graph is correct by checking all conditions of Definition 7 assuming the conditions of Definition 8 to hold. On the other hand, the values of a correct history-dependent schedule can be immediately used for a correct timed graph by setting $n.E_b = n.E_w = n.F_e$ and $n.L_b = n.L_w = n.F_s$ for each $n$.

**Algorithm 1.** CompS(U,C) Compute history-dependent schedule for correct timed graph

```
1: {Input: U(N, E, L, B) timed graph, C nodes of a clique}
2: {Output: correct history-dependent schedule S}
3: front := {n ∈ C with m ∈ C with (m, n) ∈ E}
4: for all n ∈ front do
5:     {Schedule entries for start nodes}
6:     n.F_s := n.E_b − n.d; n.T_s := n.F_s
7:     n.F_e := n.E_b; n.T_e := n.F_e + n.x − n.d
8: end for
9: for all n ∈ C − front in a topological order do
10:     n.F_s := max({n.E_b − n.d} ∪ {m.T_e|m ∈ n.Pred})
11:     n.T_s := n.F_s
12:     n.F_e := n.F_s + n.d
13:     n.T_e := n.T_s + n.x
14: end for
15: return
```

Since there is exactly one entry in a history-dependent schedule of a process $P$ for each node of its timed graph and vice versa, we will denote the execution intervals of the schedule entries as attributes of the nodes of the timed graph.

## 3.2 Partitioning of a Timed Graph

There is a dependency between the values in the timed graph through the predecessor/successor relations of the nodes. If the E-value of a node $n$ is increased the E-values of all direct and indirect successors have to be increased (in general), and vice versa for a decrease of the L-value of a node $n$ the L-values of the predecessor nodes have to be decreased. Upper-bound constraints form another kind of dependency. If the E-value of a destination node is increased then the E-value of *preceding* source node has to be increased and vice versa if an L-value of a source node is reduced, so are the L-Values of the *succeeding* destination nodes. So for a source node and a succeeding destination node, an increase or reduction of E and L values of one of the nodes influences the E and L values of the other nodes. This also holds for all the nodes between source and destination. Furthermore, if source nodes of other constraints are dependent, so are their destination nodes, and so forth. We call such a set of mutually dependent nodes a *clique*. We represent this dependency with the relations $F$ and $G$.

The timed graph in Fig. 2 has 6 cliques: $C_1 = \{A, F[\neg p], G[\neg p]\}, C_2 = \{B\}, C_3 = \{C[q]\}, C_4 = D[\neg q], E[p], H[p, q], H[p \neg q]\}, C_5 = \{H[\neg pq]\}, C_6 = \{H[\neg p \neg q]\}$. Figure 3 shows the cliques and their partial order.

**Definition 9 (dependency relation).** *For a timed graph $U(N, E, L, B)$ we define the dependency relations $F = E \cup \{(n, n)|n \in N\} \cup \{(d, s)|\exists \delta\ (s, d, \delta) \in B\}$. $F^+$ is the transitive closure of $F$, $G = \{(n, m)|(n.m) \in F^+, (m, n) \in F^+\}$.*

**Lemma 6.** *The dependency relation $G$ of a timed graph $U$ is reflexive, transitive and symmetric, and thus defines an equivalence relation.*

Since $G$ is an equivalence relation we can use it to partition the set of nodes of the timed graph. We call an equivalence class a clique.

**Definition 10 (Clique).** *For a timed graph $U(N, E, L, B)$ with dependency relation $G$ we define a subset $C$ of $N$ as a clique, iff there is a node $n \in N$ and $C = \{m | (n, m) \in G\}$. A clique which consists of one node is called* trivial *clique.*

Nodes which are not constrained by any upper-bound constraint form a clique of size 1, a trivial clique. Nodes of a clique need not be connected in $E$. Cliques form an acyclic graph with respect to edges of $E$. This property is represented in the following lemma and then used for defining a partial order on cliques.

**Lemma 7 (Clique order).** *Let $C_1, C_2$ be cliques with $C_1 \neq C_2$. $\forall n \in C_1, \forall m \in C_2, (n, m) \in F^+ \Rightarrow (m, n) \notin F^+$.*

Now we can define a partial order on cliques.

**Definition 11 (Partial order on cliques).** *Let $C_1, C_2$ be cliques. $C_1 < C_2$, iff $C_1 \neq C_2, \exists n \in C_1, m \in C_2, (n, m) \in F^+$.*

A clique $C$ has some nodes which have no predecessors wrt. $E$ within $C$. We call these the *front* nodes of C. Furthermore, there are some *rear* nodes which have no successors according to $E$ within the clique $C$.

**Definition 12 (Front and rear nodes).** *For a clique $C$ of a timed graph $U(N, E, L, B)$ we define the front nodes of $C$ as $C^f = \{n \in C | m \in C, (m, n) \in E\}$, and the rear nodes of $C$ as $C^r = \{n \in C | m \in C, (n, m) \in E\}$.*

Front nodes in non-trivial cliques are sources of upper-bound constraints and rear nodes are destinations of upper-bound constraints.

**Lemma 8.** $|C| > 1 \Rightarrow \forall s \in C^f \exists d, \delta : (s, d, \delta) \in B$.

### 3.3   Combining Schedules

Let $C_1$ and $C_2$ be cliques with $C_2$ immediately following $C_1$ (i.e. there is an edge in $F$ from a node of $C_1$ to a node in $C_2$). Let $S_1$ be a correct schedule for $C_1$ and $S_2$ a correct schedule for $C_2$. We construct a joint schedule for $C_1$ and $C_2$ by first computing an offset for clique $C_2$ and then we build the union of two schedules after adding the offset to all execution intervals of $S_2$:

Since a clique can have several predecessor cliques, we generalize this computation. We combine the schedule of a clique with a schedule of a (sub)process (defined by a subset of nodes, where no node in the clique depends on a node of the subprocess. In the following $S + c$ stands for adding the scalar $c$ to each of the values $F_s, T_s, F_e$, and $T_e$ of each entry in the schedule $S$.

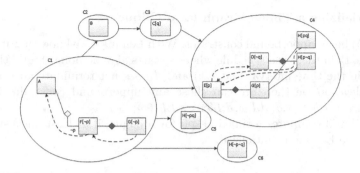

**Fig. 3.** Clusters and their dependencies

**Lemma 9 (Combine schedules).** *Let $U(N, E, L, B)$ be a timed graph. Let $C_1$ be a union of (some) cliques, let $F$ be the dependency relation in $U$. Let $C_2$ be a clique in $U$ with $\forall c_1 \in C_1, \forall c_2 \in C_2$ with $(c_2, c1) \notin F^+$.*

*Let $S_1$ resp. $S_2$ be correct schedules for $C_1$ resp. $C_2$. Then $S = S_1 \cup (S_2 + \Delta)$ where $\Delta = max(\{0\} \cup \{c_1.T_e - c2.F_s | c_1 \in C_1, c_2 \in C_2, (c_1, c_2) \in E\} \cup \{c_1.T - \delta | c_1 \in C_1, \exists c2 \in C_2 : (c_2, c_1, \delta) \in B\})$ is a correct schedule.*

*Proof.* With the proof of Lemma 4 we know that a schedule derived by adding a scalar to a correct schedule is correct. Since each of the schedules $S_1$ and $S_2 + \Delta$ is correct, we have to check the inequalities between values from S1 and S2. If there is no dependency between $C_1$ and $C_2$ then the union of $S_1$ and $S_2$ with an offset of 0 is a correct schedule for the union of $C_1$ and $C_2$. Since there is no upper bound constraint with a source in $C_1$ and destination in $C_2$ (according to the preconditions), it is sufficient to check whether (1) for all edges in $E$ from a node $c_1$ in $C_1$ to a node $c_2$ in $C_2$: $c_1.T \leq c_2.F_s + \Delta$ and (2) wether all upper bound constraints with a source in $C_2$ and a destination in $C_1$ are satisfied. (1) holds since $c_1.T \leq c_2.Fs + (c_1.T - c2.F_s) \leq c_2.F_s + \Delta$. (2) holds since for all $(s, d, \delta) \in B$ with $s \in C_2$, and $d \in C_2$ the offset requires that $d.T - \delta \leq \Delta \leq s.F$.

Based on this lemma we can now compute a history-dependent schedule for a process graph by iteratively combining the history-dependent schedules of its cliques in some topological order. This leads to the following theorem:

**Lemma 10 (Partition schedules).** *A process graph has a correct schedule, iff each of the cliques of its timed graph is correct.*

*Proof.* If a process has a correct history-dependent schedule then these values constitute also a correct timed graph which implies that each its cliques is correct. In the other direction: If each clique has a correct timed graph we can stitch together a correct history-dependent schedule for the whole process according to Lemma 9.

## 3.4   Initializing a Timed Graph for a Clique

Let $(s, d, \delta)$ be an upperbound constraint. With Lemma 4 we know that if there is a schedule, then there is a schedule where $s$ starts at time point 0 (and therefore the ends in the time interval $(s.d, s.x)$ and $d$ does not terminate after $s.x + \delta$. For initialization we therefore can chose any upperbound constraint and set $s.Ew := s.x; n.Eb := s.d; d.Lw, d.Lb := s.Eb + \delta;$

Algorithm 3 computes a timed graph for a clique, if at least one E-value at and least one L-value is initialized.

---

**Algorithm 2.** CTGC(U,C) Compute correct timed graph for a clique

---
```
 1: {U(N,E,L,B) is a timed graph}
 2: {C is a clique in U}
 3: if |C| := 1 then
 4:    {trivial clique}
 5:    for all n ∈ C do
 6:       n.Ew := n.x; n.Eb := n.d;
 7:       n.Lw, n.Lb := n.Ew
 8:    end for
 9: else
10:    F := front(C) {the front nodes of the clique}
11:    (s, d, δ) := pick({(s, d, δ) ∈ B|s ∈ F})
12:    for all n ∈ C do
13:       n.Ew := −∞; n.Eb := −∞;
14:       n.Lw, n.Lb := ∞
15:    end for
16:    s.Ew := s.x; s.Eb := s.d;
17:    d.Lw, d.Lb := s.Eb + δ;
18:    ok := CompTG(C)
19: end if
20: return ok
```
---

## 3.5   Computing a Correct Timed Graph

The procedure of computing a timed graph consists of the following steps. First, we initialize the temporal values of the timed graph. Then we compute the timed graph according to the structural constraints defined by the topology of the graph by forward calculation of E-values and backward calculation of L Values. Then we check all upper-bound constraints and if they are violated incorporate them by increasing the E-values of the source node and/or the L-values of the destination node. This procedure is repeated until all constraints are satisfied or there is a node $n$ for which the invariant $n.E < n.L$ is violated and hence no solution exists. This algorithm is an adaption of the algorithms presented in [16].

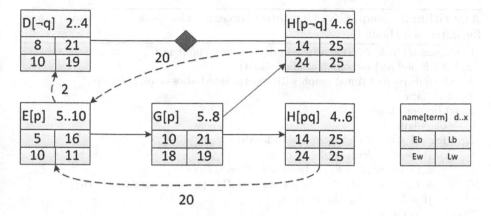

**Fig. 4.** Correct timed graph for cluster C4

Figure 4 shows the timed graph for the clique $C_4$ of our example. $E$ was selected as seed node. $C$ as seed node would not lead to a correct timed graph. The values are the E-and L-values after CompTG finished successfully.

The next theorem states that the CompTG procedure is a sound and complete, which means that if there is a correct schedule for a temporally constrained process then the procedure will compute a correct schedule and return TRUE and if there is no correct schedule for the process it will return FALSE.

**Lemma 11.** *CompTG (Algorithm 3) and CGTC (Algorithm 2) are sound and complete in the sense that (a) if they return TRUE then the computed timed graph is correct, and (b) if it returns FALSE then there is no correct timed graph for the initialized clique.*

*Proof.* For trivial cliques soundness and completeness are trivially true. For non-trivial cliques soundness of be easily shown as in CompTG all conditions for a correct timed graph are either checked explicitly in the algorithm or are ensured by the assignments in the forward and backward calculations.

For showing completeness we assume that a correct 0-schedule exists with seed-node $s$. For any destination node $d$ with $(s, d, \delta) \in B$ Definition 7 requires that $d.T_e \leq \delta$ which is the value with which $d.L_b$ is initialized. So since CTGC tries all front nodes as seed nodes for the initialization, if a correct history-dependent schedule exists then the timed graph is correctly initialized. Further we observe that for every node every execution interval of a correct history-dependent o-schedule has to be within the interval of E- and L- values with which the timed graph is initialized. Additionally, it is easy to show that the requirements of correctness for a history-dependent schedule are more strict than for a correct timed graph. The forward resp. backward calculations set the E-values to the lowest resp. greatest values that satisfy the conditions (1) to (5) of Definition 8. The algorithm iteratively checks all temporal constraints. If an inequality in the definition of a constraint is violated the algorithm sets

---

**Algorithm 3.** CompTG(U, C) returns: boolean – Compute correct timed graph for initialized clique U

---

1: {Input: $U(N, E, L, B)$ is a timed graph, $C$ is a clique in $U$}
2: { All E and at least one L are initialized}
3: {Output: correct timed graph with incorporated ubcs or ok is false}
4: ok := false
5: **while** not ok **do**
6:    ok:= true
7:    **for all** $n \in C$ in a topological order **do**
8:        {forward calculation}
9:        $n.E_b := max(\{n.E_b\} \cup \{p.E_b + n.d | p \in n.Pred\})$
10:       $n.E_w := max(\{n.E_w, n.E_b + n.x - n.d\} \cup \{p.E_w + n.x | p \in n.Pred\})$
11:       **if** $n.L_w < n.E_w$ **then**
12:          **return** false
13:       **end if**
14:    **end for**
15:    **for all** $n \in C$ in a reverse topological order **do**
16:       {backward calculation}
17:       $n.L_w := min(\{n.L_w\} \cup \{s.L_w - s.x | s \in n.Succ\})$
18:       $n.L_b := min(\{n.L_b\} \cup \{s.L_b - s.d | s \in n.Succ\})$
19:       **if** $n.L_w < n.E_w$ **then**
20:          **return** false
21:       **end if**
22:    **end for**
23:    **for all** $(s, d, \delta) \in B, (s, d \in C)$ **do**
24:       {incorporation of upper-bound constraints}
25:       **if** $\delta < (d.E_w - s.E_b)$ **then**
26:          ok:= false
27:          $s.E_b := max(s.E_b, d.E_w - \delta)$
28:          $s.E_w := max(s.E_w, s.E_b)$
29:       **end if**
30:       **if** $\delta < (d.L_b - s.L_w)$ **then**
31:          ok:= false
32:          $d.L_b := min(d.L_b, s.L_w + \delta)$
33:          $d.L_w := min(d.L_w, d.L_b)$
34:       **end if**
35:    **end for**
36: **end while**
37: **return** true

---

the E-values to the smallest and L-values to the greatest values such that this inequality is satisfied and thus computes the largest interval which avoids this violation. So if the algorithm cannot compute a correct timed graph, there is no correct timed graph (and hence also no correct history-dependent schedule).

With this theorem we can conclude that applying the CompS procedure to an unfolded version of a temporally constrained process with a deadline is a sound and complete algorithm for checking its history-dependent controllability.

**Algorithm 4.** checkCG() Check Controllability

---

{U(N,E,L,B) is a timed graph for process P(N',E',L,B')}
$S := \emptyset$
**for all** cliques $C$ in $U$ in a topological order **do**
  $ok := CTGC(C)$
  **if** $ok$ **then**
    CompS(C)
  **else**
    **return** FALSE
  **end if**
  $\Delta := max(\{0\} \cup \{s.T_e - s_2.F_s | s \in S, s_2 \in C, (s_1, s_2) \in E\} \cup \{d.T_e - \delta | d \in S, \exists s \in C : (s, d, \delta) \in B\})$
  **for all** $s \in C$ **do**
    $s.F_s := s.F_s + \Delta; \ s.T_s := s.T_s + \Delta$
    $s.F_e := s.F_e + \Delta; \ s.T_e := s.T_e + \Delta$
  **end for**
  $S := S \cup C$
**end for**
**return** TRUE

---

### 3.6   Check History-Dependent Controllability

The algorithms checkCG, CTGC, CompS, compTG implement the insights into the controllability problem formalized in the definitions and lemmas above. With these algorithms we can check the history-dependent controllability of any process definition with contingent durations and upper-bound constraints.

**Lemma 12 (Effectiveness).** *The procedures checkCG, CTGC, CompTG and CompS will always terminate.*

From the considerations above we see that these algorithms are a sound and complete checking procedure which we summarize in the following theorem.

**Theorem 1.** *Algorithm 4 is a sound and complete procedure to check the history-dependent controllability of processes with contingent nodes and upper-bound constraints.*

*Proof.* The Theorem follows from the Lemmas 4, 5, 9, 10 and 11.

## 4   Problem Complexity

In this section we study the complexity of the problem of computing history dependent schedules. We do that by analyzing the possible size of a history dependent schedule for a given process model. We formalize and show below that in the worst case the size of a schedule is exponential in the number of XOR-splits.

**Theorem 2 (problem complexity).** *The problem of a generating a schedule for a process with temporal constraints is of exponential complexity in the number of XOR-splits.*

*Proof.* We proof this theorem by constructing a process (*proof-process*) for $n$ XOR-splits with a set of temporal constraints and show that in its only schedule there is an activity which has $2^n$ different disjoint scheduling intervals. Figure 5 shows the pattern for this process. It consist of an activity $A$ followed by $n$ Xor-blocks numbered from $n$ to 1 followed by activity $D$. Each Xor block $X_i, 1 \leq i \leq n$ consists of two alternate activities $B_i$ and $C_i$. The min- and max-durations of the nodes are as follows: $B_i.d = B_i.x = 1$ and $C_i.d = C_i.x = 2^{i-1} + 1$ for all $i$ from 1 to $n$, $D.d = D.x = 1$. All other nodes have duration 0. We define the following upper-bound constraints: $\{(B_{i+1}, B_i, C_i.d), (C_{i+1}, B_i, 1), (Bi + 1, Ci, 1), (C_{i+1}, C_i, C_{i+1}.d)|1 \leq n - 1\}$, $(A, B_n, 1), (A, C_n, C_n.d), (B_1, D, 1), (C_1, D, 1)$. After some calculations it is easy to see that there is only 1 schedule and in this schedule there are $2^n$ non-overlapping intervals for activity D: $[n + 1, n + 1] \ldots [2^n + n]$. Figure 6 shows the schedule for $n = 3$.

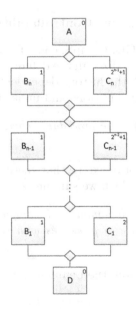

**Fig. 5.** Pattern for the proof-process

# 5    Related Work

There is already quite some body of research results in the area of temporal aspects of workflows and business processes. We refer to [4, 17, 21] for an overview.

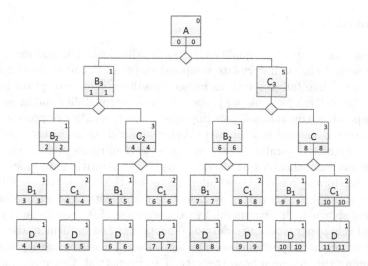

**Fig. 6.** Computed Schedule for the proof-process with the problem size $n = 3$

Recently the work of Lanz et al. [27,28] contributed to the consolidation of expressing temporal constraints and defining the semantics of temporal constraints. The upper-bound constraints used here are correspond to TP 3 "maximum time lag between events". Early approaches checking temporal qualities of process definitions are [1,16,29] with techniques rooted in network analysis, scheduling, or constraint networks. These techniques stimulated the development of more advanced networks, the consideration of interorganizational processes and for supporting temporal service level agreements for service compositions [3,20].

Our approach is based on the algorithms for computing schedules for time constrained workflows presented in [14], but is extended to capture the uncertainty of the duration of contingent activities. In another stream of research studying temporal constraint networks [10] which were applied for workflows in [1] and now reached the necessary expressiveness for analyzing business process models: checking the controllability [6] and dynamic controllability of temporal networks, as discussed in [7]. In particular, [5,22,24] present algorithms for checking the controllability of conditional simple temporal networks with a sound-and-complete for conditional simple temporal networks with uncertainty, the type of network corresponding to the process models discussed here. Our approach tries to contribute to the integration of time management in workflows, temporal consistency in service composition [20] and temporal constraint networks. Algorithms for other types of temporal constraint networks have been proposed in [2,33].

# 6   Conclusions

Among the most important quality criteria for the definition and execution of processes is that the do not violate temporal constraints and to meet temporal requirements. Time failures such as missed deadlines cause exception handling and might be costly. Therefore, we propose to use controllability and in particular history-dependent controllability as important characteristics of processes.

We presented a sound and complete algorithm for checking history-dependent controllability of temporally constrained process definitions and for computing history-dependent schedules at design time. This algorithm provides a good basis for developing more efficient algorithms for the computation of history-dependent schedules with better average case complexity. The worst case complexity was shown to be exponential in the number of Xor-splits in a process. The aim of this paper was not to develop a particular fast implementation but to study the principal properties of such an algorithm. There are many possibilities for continuing this research both theoretical and practical. Our major aim is to compute schedules, and to support the time aware execution of processes with the aim to reduce temporal failures. To improve the qualities of schedules (e.g. a good distribution of slack time) and efficient algorithms for computing "good schedules" remain on our agenda.

# References

1. Bettini, C., Wang, X.S., Jajodia, S.: Temporal reasoning in workflow systems. Distrib. Parallel Databases **11**(3), 269–306 (2002)
2. Cairo, M., Rizzi, R.: Dynamic controllability made simple. In: LIPIcs-Leibniz International Proceedings in Informatics, vol. 90. Schloss Dagstuhl-Leibniz-Zentrum fuer Informatik (2017)
3. Cardoso, J., Sheth, A., Miller, J., Arnold, J., Kochut, K.: Quality of service for workflows and web service processes. J. Web Semant. **1**(3), 281–308 (2004)
4. Cheikhrouhou, S., Kallel, S., Guermouche, N., Jmaiel, M.: The temporal perspective in business process modeling: a survey and research challenges. Serv. Oriented Comput. Appl. **9**(1), 75–85 (2015)
5. Cimatti, A., Hunsberger, L., Micheli, A., Posenato, R., Roveri, M.: Dynamic controllability via timed game automata. Acta Informatica 1–42 (2016)
6. Combi, C., Gozzi, M., Posenato, R., Pozzi, G.: Conceptual modeling of flexible temporal workflows. ACM Trans. Auton. Adapt. Syst. (TAAS) **7**(2), 19 (2012)
7. Combi, C., Hunsberger, L., Posenato, R.: An algorithm for checking the dynamic controllability of a conditional simple temporal network with uncertainty - revisited. In: Filipe, J., Fred, A. (eds.) ICAART 2013. CCIS, vol. 449, pp. 314–331. Springer, Heidelberg (2014). https://doi.org/10.1007/978-3-662-44440-5_19
8. Combi, C., Posenato, R.: Controllability in temporal conceptual workflow schemata. In: Dayal, U., Eder, J., Koehler, J., Reijers, H.A. (eds.) BPM 2009. LNCS, vol. 5701, pp. 64–79. Springer, Heidelberg (2009). https://doi.org/10.1007/978-3-642-03848-8_6
9. Daniel, F., Pernici, B.: Insights into web service orchestration and choreography. Int. J. E-Bus. Res. (IJEBR) **2**(1), 58–77 (2006)

10. Dechter, R., Meiri, I., Pearl, J.: Temporal constraint networks. Artif. Intell. **49**(1–3), 61–95 (1991)
11. Dumas, M., La Rosa, M., Mendling, J., Reijers, H.A., et al.: Fundamentals of Business Process Management, vol. 1. Springer, Heidelberg (2013). https://doi.org/10.1007/978-3-642-33143-5
12. Eder, J., Franceschetti, M., Köpke, J.: Controllability of business processes with temporal variables. In: Proceedings of the 34th ACM/SIGAPP Symposium on Applied Computing, pp. 40–47. ACM (2019)
13. Eder, J., Franceschetti, M., Köpke, J., Oberrauner, A.: Expressiveness of temporal constraints for process models. In: Woo, C., Lu, J., Li, Z., Ling, T.W., Li, G., Lee, M.L. (eds.) ER 2018. LNCS, vol. 11158, pp. 119–133. Springer, Cham (2018). https://doi.org/10.1007/978-3-030-01391-2_19
14. Eder, J., Gruber, W., Panagos, E.: Temporal modeling of workflows with conditional execution paths. In: Ibrahim, M., Küng, J., Revell, N. (eds.) DEXA 2000. LNCS, vol. 1873, pp. 243–253. Springer, Heidelberg (2000). https://doi.org/10.1007/3-540-44469-6_23
15. Eder, J., Gruber, W., Pichler, H.: Transforming workflow graphs. In: Konstantas, D., Bourrières, J.P., Léonard, M., Boudjlida, N. (eds.) Interoperability of Enterprise Software and Applications, pp. 203–214. Springer, London (2006). https://doi.org/10.1007/1-84628-152-0_19
16. Eder, J., Panagos, E., Rabinovich, M.: Time constraints in workflow systems. In: Jarke, M., Oberweis, A. (eds.) CAiSE 1999. LNCS, vol. 1626, pp. 286–300. Springer, Heidelberg (1999). https://doi.org/10.1007/3-540-48738-7_22
17. Eder, J., Panagos, E., Rabinovich, M.: Workflow time management revisited. Seminal Contributions to Information Systems Engineering, pp. 207–213. Springer, Heidelberg (2013). https://doi.org/10.1007/978-3-642-36926-1_16
18. Eder, J., Pichler, H.: Response time histograms for composite web services. In: Proceedings. IEEE International Conference on Web Services, 2004, pp. 832–833. IEEE (2004)
19. Georgakopoulos, D., Hornick, M., Sheth, A.: An overview of workflow management: from process modeling to workflow automation infrastructure. Distrib. Parallel Databases **3**(2), 119–153 (1995)
20. Guermouche, N., Godart, C.: Timed model checking based approach for web services analysis. In: ICWS, pp. 213–221. IEEE (2009)
21. Hashmi, M., Governatori, G., Lam, H.P., Wynn, M.T.: Are we done with business process compliance: state of the art and challenges ahead. Knowl. Inf. Syst. **57**(1), 79–133 (2018)
22. Hunsberger, L., Posenato, R.: Simpler and faster algorithm for checking the dynamic consistency of conditional simple temporal networks. In: IJCAI, pp. 1324–1330 (2018)
23. Hunsberger, L., Posenato, R., Combi, C.: The dynamic controllability of conditional STNs with uncertainty. arXiv preprint arXiv:1212.2005 (2012)
24. Hunsberger, L., Posenato, R., Combi, C.: A sound-and-complete propagation-based algorithm for checking the dynamic consistency of conditional simple temporal networks. In: Temporal Representation and Reasoning (TIME), IEEE (2015)
25. Jajodia, S., Kerschberg, L.: Advanced Transaction Models and Architectures. Springer, Boston (2012). https://doi.org/10.1007/978-1-4615-6217-7
26. Lanz, A., Posenato, R., Combi, C., Reichert, M.: Controllability of time-aware processes at run time. In: Meersman, R., et al. (eds.) OTM 2013. LNCS, vol. 8185, pp. 39–56. Springer, Heidelberg (2013). https://doi.org/10.1007/978-3-642-41030-7_4

27. Lanz, A., Reichert, M., Weber, B.: Process time patterns: a formal foundation. Inf. Syst. **57**, 38–68 (2016)
28. Lanz, A., Weber, B., Reichert, M.: Workflow time patterns for process-aware information systems. In: Bider, I., et al. (eds.) BPMDS/EMMSAD -2010. LNBIP, vol. 50, pp. 94–107. Springer, Heidelberg (2010). https://doi.org/10.1007/978-3-642-13051-9_9
29. Marjanovic, O., Orlowska, M.E.: On modeling and verification of temporal constraints in production workflows. Knowl. Inf. Syst. **1**(2), 157–192 (1999)
30. Morris, P.H., Muscettola, N.: Temporal dynamic controllability revisited. In: AAAI, pp. 1193–1198 (2005)
31. Aalst, W.M.P.: Workflow verification: finding control-flow errors using petri-net-based techniques. In: van der Aalst, W., Desel, J., Oberweis, A. (eds.) Business Process Management. LNCS, vol. 1806, pp. 161–183. Springer, Heidelberg (2000). https://doi.org/10.1007/3-540-45594-9_11
32. Van der Aalst, W., ter Hofstede, A., Kiepuszewski, B., Barros, A.B.: Workflow patterns. Distrib. Parallel Databases **14**(1), 5–51 (2003)
33. Zavatteri, M., Viganò, L.: Conditional simple temporal networks with uncertainty and decisions. Theor. Comput. Sci. **797**, 77–101 (2019)

# Finding All Minimal Maximum Subsequences in Parallel

H. K. Dai$^{(\boxtimes)}$

Computer Science Department, Oklahoma State University,
Stillwater, OK 74078, USA
dai@cs.okstate.edu

**Abstract.** A maximum contiguous subsequence of a real-valued sequence is a contiguous subsequence with the maximum cumulative sum. A minimal maximum contiguous subsequence is a minimal contiguous subsequence among all maximum ones of the sequence. We have previously designed and implemented a domain-decomposed parallel algorithm on cluster systems with Message Passing Interface that finds all successive minimal maximum subsequences of a random sample sequence from a normal distribution with negative mean. The parallel cluster algorithm employs the theory of random walk to derive an approximate probabilistic length upper bound for overlapping subsequences in an appropriate probabilistic setting, which is incorporated in the algorithm to facilitate the concurrent computation of all minimal maximum subsequences in hosting processors. We present in this article: (1) a generalization of the parallel cluster algorithm with improvements for input of arbitrary real-valued sequence, and (2) an empirical study of the speedup and efficiency achieved by the parallel algorithm with synthetic normally-distributed random sequences.

**Keywords:** All maximum subsequences · Theory of random walk · Message passing interface · Parallel algorithm

## 1 Preliminaries

Algorithmic and optimization problems in sequences and trees arise in widely varying applications such as in bioinformatics and information retrieval. Large-scale (sub)sequence comparison, alignment, and analysis are important research areas in computational biology. Time- and space-efficient algorithms for finding multiple contiguous subsequences of a real-valued sequence with large cumulative sums help identify statistically significant subsequences in biological sequence analysis with respect to an underlying scoring scheme. Such algorithms provide an effective filtering pre-process even with simplistic random-sequence models of independent residues.

© Springer Nature Switzerland AG 2019
T. K. Dang et al. (Eds.): FDSE 2019, LNCS 11814, pp. 165–184, 2019.
https://doi.org/10.1007/978-3-030-35653-8_12

For a real-valued sequence $X = (x_\eta)_{\eta=1}^n$, the cumulative sum of a non-empty contiguous subsequence $(x_\eta)_{\eta=i}^j$, where $i$ and $j$ are in the index range $[1, n]$ with $i \leq j$, is $\sum_{\eta=i}^j x_\eta$ (and that of the empty sequence is 0). All subsequences addressed in our study are contiguous in real-valued sequences; the terms "subsequence" and "supersequence" will hereinafter abbreviate "contiguous subsequence" and "contiguous supersequence", respectively.

For a subsequence $Y$ of $X$, denote by $\sigma(Y)$ the cumulative sum of $Y$; $\sigma(Y) = 0$ if $Y$ is empty. A maximum subsequence of $X$ is one with the maximum cumulative sum. A minimal maximum subsequence of $X$ is a minimal subsequence, with respect to (contiguous) subsequence-containment, among all maximum subsequences of $X$. Note that: (1) $X$ is non-positively valued if and only if the empty subsequence is the unique minimal maximum subsequence of $X$, and (2) the minimality constraint on the maximum cumulative sum translates into that all non-empty prefixes and suffixes of a minimal maximum subsequence of $X$ have positive cumulative sums.

Very often in practical applications it is not sufficient to find just a single or even all maximum subsequences of a sequence $X$. What is rather required is to find many or all pairwise disjoint subsequences having cumulative sums above a prescribed threshold. Observe that subsequences having major overlap with a maximum subsequence tend to have good cumulative sums. We define the sequence of all successive non-empty minimal maximum subsequences $(S_1, S_2, \ldots)$ of $X$ inductively as follows:

1. [Basis] The subsequence $S_1$ is a non-empty minimal maximum subsequence of $X$, provided such a subsequence exists; that is, with $\sigma_0$ denoting the set $\{\sigma(S) \mid S \text{ is a subsequence of } X\}$:

    if    $\max \sigma_0 = 0$, then the basis is complete,
    else  select a (non-empty) minimal subsequence $S_1 \in \arg\max \sigma_0$
          (breaking ties arbitrarily).

2. [Induction] Assume that the sequence $(S_1, S_2, \ldots, S_i)$ of non-empty subsequences of $X$, where $i \geq 1$, has been constructed, the subsequence $S_{i+1}$ is a non-empty minimal subsequence (with respect to subsequence-containment) among all non-empty maximum subsequences (with respect to cumulative sum) that are disjoint from each of $\{S_1, S_2, \ldots, S_i\}$, provided such a subsequence exists; that is, with $\sigma_i$ denoting the set:

    $\{\sigma(S) \mid S \text{ is a subsequence of } X \text{ disjoint from each of } \{S_1, S_2, \ldots, S_i\}\}$ :

    if    $\max \sigma_i = 0$, then the induction is complete,
    else  select a (non-empty) minimal subsequence $S_{i+1} \in \arg\max \sigma_i$
          (breaking ties arbitrarily).

Denote by $\mathrm{Max}(X)$ the set of all successive non-empty minimal maximum subsequences or their corresponding index subranges (when the context is clear) of a real-valued sequence $X$.

Efficient algorithms for computing the sequence of all successive minimal maximum subsequences of a given sequence are essential for statistical inference in large-scale biological sequence analysis and information retrieval process. In biomolecular sequences, high (sub)sequence similarity usually implies significant structural or functional similarity. When incorporating good scoring schemes, this provides a powerful statistical paradigm for identifying biologically significant functional regions in biomolecular sequences (see [8,12,13,15,16,18]), such as transmembrane regions [5] and deoxyribonucleic acid-binding domains [14] in protein analyses. A common approach is to employ an application-dependent scoring scheme that assigns a score to each single constituent of an examined biomolecular sequence, and then find all successive minimal maximum subsequences of the underlying score sequence having large cumulative sums above a prescribed threshold. A theory of logarithmic odds ratios, developed in [12] and [2], yields an effective logarithmic likelihood-ratio scoring function in this context. The non-positivity of the expected score of a random single constituent tends to delimit unrealistic long runs of contiguous positive scores.

We designed/implemented in [6,7] two parallel algorithms that find all successive non-empty minimal maximum subsequences of a real-valued sequence; our studies were motivated by the linear-time sequential algorithm for this computation problem [18] and major applications such as in bioinformatics and textual information retrieval. Our main results in these two studies are summarized as follows:

1. Developed a parallel algorithm on the theoretical parallel random-access model (PRAM) in the work-time framework that solves the problem: For a real-valued sequence of length $n$, the parallel algorithm runs in logarithmic parallel time ($O(\log n)$ steps) and optimal linear work (total of $O(n)$ operations), and
2. Designed and implemented a parallel algorithm on cluster systems (with Message Passing Interface) that solves the problem via a domain decomposition of an input sequence into overlapping subsequences in subsequence-hosting processors: The efficacy of the practical parallel algorithm with random sample sequences critically depends on an application of the theory of random walk, which develops an approximate probabilistic length upper bound for the common intersection of overlapping subsequences in an appropriate probabilistic setting for the random sample sequences from normal distributions with negative mean. The length bound is incorporated in the algorithm to facilitate concurrent and independent computations of all non-empty minimal maximum subsequences in hosting processors.

In our presented study, the parallel cluster algorithm is generalized with improvements for arbitrary input of real-valued sequence, and its performance in speedup and efficiency is assessed in an empirical study with synthetic normally-distributed random sample sequences.

For computing a single (minimal) maximum subsequence of a length-$n$ real-valued sequence $X$, a simple sequential algorithm solves this problem in $O(n)$

optimal time. A parallel algorithm [1] on the PRAM model solves the single maximum subsequence problem in $O(\log n)$ parallel time using a total of $O(n)$ operations (work-optimal).

A generalization of the single maximum subsequence problem and the selection problem is the sum-selection that, for given input length-$n$ sequence $X$, range-bound $[l, u]$, and rank $k$, finds a subsequence of $X$ such that the rank of its cumulative sum is $k$ among all subsequences with cumulative sum in $[l, u]$. A randomized algorithm [17] solves the sum-selection problem in expected $O(n \log(u - l))$ time.

For the problem of finding the sequence of all successive minimal maximum subsequences of a length-$n$ real-valued sequence $X$, a recursive divide-and-conquer strategy can apply the linear-time sequential algorithm above to compute a minimal maximum subsequence of $X$ whose deletion results in a prefix and a suffix for recursion. The algorithm has a (worst-case) time-complexity of $\Theta(n^2)$. Empirical analyses of the algorithm [18] on synthetic data sets (sequences of independent and identically distributed uniform random terms with negative mean) and score sequences of genomic data indicate that for these types of input the expected running time grows at $\Theta(n \log n)$.

In order to circumvent the iterative dependency in computing the sequence of all successive non-empty minimal maximum subsequences, Ruzzo and Tompa [18] prove a structural characterization of the sequence as follows.

**Theorem 1** [18]. *For a non-empty real-valued sequence $X$, a non-empty subsequence $S$ of $X$ is in $\mathrm{Max}(X)$ if and only if:*

1. *[Monotonicity] The subsequence $S$ is monotone: every proper subsequence of $S$ has its cumulative sum less than that of $S$, and*
2. *[Maximality of Monotonicity] The subsequence $S$ is maximal in $X$ with respect to monotonicity, that is, every proper supersequence of $S$ contained in $X$ is not monotone.*

Note that the notion of monotonicity introduced in Theorem 1 differs from the monotonicity of (sub)sequences as functions over their index (sub)ranges. Due to Theorem 1, we also term $\mathrm{Max}(X)$ as the set of all maximal monotone subsequences of $X$. This gives a structural decomposition of $X$ into $\mathrm{Max}(X)$ in the following remark.

**Remark 2.** *Let $X$ be a non-empty real-valued sequence. Then:*

1. *Every non-empty monotone subsequence of $X$ is contained in a maximal monotone subsequence in $\mathrm{Max}(X)$; in particular, every positive term of $X$ is contained in a maximal monotone subsequence in $\mathrm{Max}(X)$, and*
2. *The set $\mathrm{Max}(X)$ is a pairwise disjoint collection of all maximal monotone subsequences of $X$.*

Based on the structural characterization of $\mathrm{Max}(X)$, Ruzzo and Tompa [18] present a sequential algorithm that computes $\mathrm{Max}(X)$ in $O(n)$ optimal sequential time and $O(n)$ space (worst case). Alves, Cáceres, and Song [3] develop a parallel algorithm for computing $\text{Max}(X)$ of a length-$n$ sequence $X$ on the bulk synchronous parallel/coarse grained multicomputer model of $p$ processors in $O(\frac{n}{p})$ computation time and $O(1)$ communication rounds. Each processor computes the local Max-set of its hosting subsequence and its two subsets of (local) minimal maximum subsequences that are mergeable as prefixes and suffixes with members of non-local neighboring Max-sets, and resolves the mergeability via the underlying monotonicity/maximality.

In the following section, we introduce successive structural decompositions of a sequence $X$ that lead to computing $\text{Max}(X)$ with a domain-decomposed parallel algorithm implemented on cluster systems with Message Passing Interface. The structural decomposition of an input sequence and its characterization developed for the parallel cluster algorithm are responsible for facilitating the application of random walk for an overlapping domain decomposition in a practical probabilistic setting. Note that we present the skeletons for the main results without lengthy derivations and proofs, which are detailed in [7] and the full version of this article.

## 2 Structural Decompositions of $X$ for Computing $\text{Max}(X)$

For a real-valued sequence $X = (x_\eta)_{\eta=1}^n$, denote by $s_i(X)$ the $i$-th prefix sum $\sum_{\eta=1}^i x_\eta$ of $X$ for $i \in [1, n]$, and $s_0(X) = 0$. We abbreviate the prefix sums $s_i(X)$ to $s_i$ for all $i \in [0, n]$ when the context is clear.

For a subsequence $Y$ of $X$, we introduce the following denotations for commonly-used statistics of $Y$:

$\sigma(Y)$:        introduced in Section 1; cumulative sum of $Y$ ($\sigma(Y) = 0$ if $Y$ is empty);

$\alpha(Y; X)$, $\beta(Y; X)$:   starting and ending indices of $Y$ in $X$, respectively;

$\gamma(Y; X)$:        index subrange $[\alpha(Y; X), \beta(Y; X)]$ of $Y$ in $X$ ($\gamma(Y; X) = \emptyset$ if $Y$ is empty);

$\gamma_+(Y; X)$:      set of all indices in $\gamma(Y; X)$ yielding positive terms of $Y$.

When considering the subsequence $Y$ as a sequence in its own context we abbreviate $\alpha(Y; Y)$, $\beta(Y; Y)$, $\gamma(Y; Y)$, and $\gamma_+(Y; Y)$ to $\alpha(Y)$, $\beta(Y)$, $\gamma(Y)$, and $\gamma_+(Y)$, respectively.

The notion of maximal monotonicity leads to progressive structural decompositions of $X$ as follows:

1. A sufficient condition for partitioning $X$ into subsequences whose Max-sets can be computed independently and concurrently with an improved linear-time sequential algorithm in local subsequence-hosting processors, and
2. The adoption of a domain decomposition of $X$ into overlapping subsequences with which the above sufficient condition (for independence of Max-computations) can be satisfied and analyzed in an appropriate probabilistic setting.

An ideal domain decomposition of a sequence $X$ is a partition of $X$ into a family $\mathcal{X}$ of pairwise disjoint non-empty subsequences of $X$ that are length-balanced and Max-independent: $\text{Max}(X) = \cup_{Y \in \mathcal{X}} \text{Max}(Y)$ ($Y$ as a sequence in its own right). We first find a sufficient condition for the Max-independence that can be computed locally in subsequence-hosting processors.

The characterization of monotonicity suggests to consider the following two functions on indices of positive terms of $X$ with index range $\gamma(X)$ ($= [1, n]$). Let $\epsilon'_X : \gamma_+(X) \to [\alpha(X) + 1, \beta(X) + 1]$ ($= [2, n+1]$) denote the nearest-smaller-or-equal right-match of the prefix sum $s_{i-1}$ of $X$:

$$\epsilon'_X(i) = \begin{cases} \min\{\eta \in [i+1, \beta(X)] \mid s_{i-1} \geq s_\eta\} & \text{if the minimum exists,} \\ \beta(X) + 1 \, (= n+1) & \text{otherwise.} \end{cases}$$

A symmetric analogue of $\epsilon'_X$ is the nearest-smaller left-match function $\overline{\epsilon}'_X : \gamma_+(X) \to [\alpha(X) - 1, \beta(X) - 1]$ ($= [0, n-1]$):

$$\overline{\epsilon}'_X(i) = \begin{cases} \max\{\eta \in [\alpha(X), i-1] \mid s_{\eta-1} < s_{i-1}\} & \text{if the maximum exists,} \\ \alpha(X) - 1 \, (= 0) & \text{otherwise.} \end{cases}$$

Figure 1 illustrates the computation of the two functions $\overline{\epsilon}'$ and $\epsilon'$. From the definitions of $\overline{\epsilon}'_X$ and $\epsilon'_X$, we note that the families $\{[\overline{\epsilon}'_X(i), i] \mid i \in \gamma_+(X)\}$ and $\{[i, \epsilon'_X(i)] \mid i \in \gamma_+(X)\}$ satisfy the parenthesis structure similar to that of Mon—but permitting abutting index subranges (at subrange ends) in the $\overline{\epsilon}'_X$-family. Both $\overline{\epsilon}'_X$ and $\epsilon'_X$ help locate the (minimum) starting and (maximum) ending indices, respectively, of a maximal monotone subsequence of $X$ containing the positive term $x_i$: determine if a merge of multiple maximal monotone subsequences covering the index subrange $[\overline{\epsilon}'_X(i), i]$ may occur.

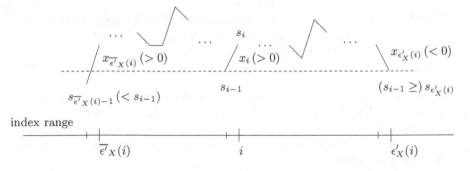

**Fig. 1.** For index $i \in \gamma_+(X)$, $\overline{\epsilon}'_X(i) = \max\{\eta \in [\alpha(X), i-1] \mid s_{\eta-1} < s_{i-1}\}$ (if the maximum exists) and $\epsilon'_X(i) = \min\{\eta \in [i+1, \beta(X)] \mid s_{i-1} \geq s_\eta\}$ (if the minimum exists).

Consider a sequential partition of a sequence $X$ into $m$ consecutive subsequences $X_1, X_2, \ldots, X_m$ with which $\alpha_i^+ \in \gamma(X_i)$ denotes the index of the first positive term of $X_i$ (if exists) for $i = 1, 2, \ldots, m$. We establish a sufficiency condition for the $\mathrm{Max}(X)$-independence of the partition of $X$ incrementally in the following two lemmas via the left-match function $\overline{\epsilon}'_X$ and (local) right-match function $\epsilon'_{X_i}$ for each $i \in \{1, 2, \ldots, m-1\}$.

**Lemma 3.** *If a sequential partition $(X_\eta)_{\eta=1}^m$ of a real-valued sequence $X$ satisfies that $\overline{\epsilon}'_X(\alpha_\eta^+) = \alpha(X) - 1$ (when such $\alpha_\eta^+$ exists) for $\eta = 1, 2, \ldots, m$, then the partition is $\mathrm{Max}$-independent, that is, $\mathrm{Max}(X) = \cup_{\eta=1}^m \mathrm{Max}(X_\eta)$.*

Lemma 3 gives a sufficient condition via the left-match function $\overline{\epsilon}'_X$ for the Max-independence of a partition of $X$, but the computation of $\overline{\epsilon}'_X$ on $\alpha_i^+$ (if exists) for $i = 1, 2, \ldots, m$ requires some global knowledge of $X$ for subsequence-hosting processors. We consider viable alternatives based on a local computation of the right-match function $\epsilon'_{X_i}$ in Lemma 4 and its intuitive equivalence in terms of prefix sums by the $X_i$-hosting processor for each $i \in \{1, 2, \ldots, m\}$ in Lemma 5.

**Lemma 4.** *Let $(X_\eta)_{\eta=1}^m$ be a sequential partition of a real-valued sequence $X$ with $X_\eta$, for $\eta = 1, 2 \ldots, m$, represented as a sequence in its own right over its index range $\gamma(X_\eta)$. If the partition satisfies the following $\epsilon'$-closure condition: for all $i \in \{1, 2, \ldots, m-1\}$ and all $j \in \gamma_+(X_i)$, $\epsilon'_{X_i}(j) \in [j+1, \beta(X_i)]$, then the partition is $\mathrm{Max}$-independent: $\mathrm{Max}(X) = \cup_{\eta=1}^m \mathrm{Max}(X_\eta)$.*

**Lemma 5.** *For a non-empty real-valued sequence $Y$, the right-match function $\epsilon'_Y : \gamma_+(Y) \to [\alpha(Y) + 1, \beta(Y) + 1]$ satisfies the $\epsilon'$-closure condition stated in Lemma 4 (for all $j \in \gamma_+(Y), \epsilon'_Y(j) \in [j+1, \beta(Y)]$) if and only if the sequence $Y$ satisfies the following minimum prefix-sum condition: the ending prefix sum of $Y$, $s_{\beta(Y)}(Y)$, is a global minimum of $s_i(Y)$ for all $i \in [\alpha(Y) - 1, \beta(Y)]$.*

The minimum prefix-sum condition, equivalent to the $\epsilon'$-closure condition as shown in Lemma 5, exposes a stringent sufficiency for Max-independence of a priori sequential partition of a sequence $X$: for all $i \in \{1, 2, \ldots, m-1\}$, the ending prefix sum is a global minimum of all prefix sums of $X_i$. We incorporate the minimum prefix-sum condition into constructing a posteriori sequential partition of $X$ as follows that forms the basis in designing a domain-decomposed parallel algorithm in computing $\mathrm{Max}(X)$.

For two sequences $X$ and $Y$, denote the concatenation of $X$ and $Y$ by the juxtaposition $XY$. Let $X$ be a non-empty real-valued sequence with a sequential partition $\mathcal{P}(X) = (X_1, X_{1,2}, X_2, X_{2,3}, X_3, \ldots, X_{m-1}, X_{m-1,m}, X_m)$. For notational simplicity, let $X_{0,1} = \emptyset$ and $X_{m,m+1} = \emptyset$.

For every $i \in \{1, 2, \ldots, m-1\}$, denote by $\beta_i^*$ the maximum/right-most index $\eta \in \gamma_+(X_{i-1,i}X_i)$, if non-empty, such that $s_{\eta-1}(X_{i-1,i}X_i)$ is the minimum prefix sum of those of $X_{i-1,i}X_i$ over $\gamma_+(X_{i-1,i}X_i)$; that is,

$$\beta_i^* = \max \arg \min\{s_{\eta-1}(X_{i-1,i}X_i) \mid \eta \in \gamma_+(X_{i-1,i}X_i) \ (\neq \emptyset)\}.$$

We say that the sequential partition $\mathcal{P}(X)$ satisfies the $\epsilon'$-locality condition if, for every $i \in \{1, 2, \ldots, m-1\}$ with non-empty $\gamma_+(X_{i-1,i}X_i)$, $\epsilon'_{X_{i-1,i}X_iX_{i,i+1}}(\beta_i^*) \in [\beta_i^* + 1, \beta(X_{i-1,i}X_iX_{i,i+1})]$.

From the $\epsilon'$-localized sequential partition $\mathcal{P}(X)$, we derive a Max-independent sequential partition $\widetilde{\mathcal{P}}(X) = (X''_{i-1,i}X_iX'_{i,i+1})^m_{i=1}$ where $X''_{i-1,i}$ and $X'_{i,i+1}$ are respectively the suffix of $X_{i-1,i}$ and prefix of $X_{i,i+1}$ that are determined by $\epsilon'$-computation as follows. Recall that $X_{0,1} = \emptyset$ and $X_{m,m+1} = \emptyset$ for notational simplicity, let $X''_{0,1} = \emptyset$ and $X'_{m,m+1} = \emptyset$ accordingly. For every $i \in \{1, 2, \ldots, m-1\}$, define $X'_{i,i+1}$ as:

$$\begin{cases} \emptyset & \text{if } \gamma_+(X_{i-1,i}X_i) = \emptyset, \\ \emptyset & \text{if } \gamma_+(X_{i-1,i}X_i) \neq \emptyset \text{ and } \epsilon'_{X_{i-1,i}X_iX_{i,i+1}}(\beta^*_i) \in [\beta^*_i + 1, \beta(X_{i-1,i}X_i; X_{i-1,i}X_iX_{i,i+1})], \\ \text{the prefix of } X_{i,i+1} \text{ with index subrange } [\alpha(X_{i,i+1}; X_{i-1,i}X_iX_{i,i+1}), \epsilon'_{X_{i-1,i}X_iX_{i,i+1}}(\beta^*_i)] \\ \quad \text{otherwise (i.e., } \gamma_+(X_{i-1,i}X_i) \neq \emptyset \text{ and } \epsilon'_{X_{i-1,i}X_iX_{i,i+1}}(\beta^*_i) \in \gamma(X_{i,i+1}; X_{i-1,i}X_iX_{i,i+1}) \\ \quad (= [\alpha(X_{i,i+1}; X_{i-1,i}X_iX_{i,i+1}), \beta(X_{i,i+1}; X_{i-1,i}X_iX_{i,i+1})])), \end{cases}$$

and $X''_{i,i+1}$ to be the (remaining) suffix of $X_{i,i+1}$ such that $X'_{i,i+1}X''_{i,i+1} = X_{i,i+1}$. Observe that the first two cases in defining $X'_{i,i+1}$ may be absorbed into the third case.

The following theorem summarizes our efforts in establishing a sufficient condition for a structural decomposition of an input sequence that permits concurrent computations of local Max-sets.

**Theorem 6.** *Assume that $X$ is a non-empty real-valued sequence with an $\epsilon'$-localized sequential partition $\mathcal{P}(X) = (X_1, X_{1,2}, X_2, X_{2,3}, X_3, \ldots, X_{m-1}, X_{m-1,m}, X_m)$ and its derived sequential partition $\widetilde{\mathcal{P}}(X) = (X''_{\eta-1,\eta}X_\eta X'_{\eta,\eta+1})^m_{\eta=1}$. Then:*

*1. The partition $\widetilde{\mathcal{P}}(X)$ is Max-independent:* $\text{Max}(X) = \cup^m_{\eta=1} \text{Max}(X''_{\eta-1,\eta}X_\eta X'_{\eta,\eta+1})$, *and*
*2. For all $i \in \{1, 2, \ldots, m\}$,*

$$\text{Max}(X_{i-1,i}X_iX'_{i,i+1}) - \{Y \in \text{Max}(X_{i-1,i}X_iX'_{i,i+1}) \mid \alpha(Y; X_{i-1,i}X_iX'_{i,i+1})$$
$$\in \gamma(X'_{i-1,i}; X_{i-1,i}X_iX'_{i,i+1})\}$$
$$= \text{Max}(X''_{i-1,i}X_iX'_{i,i+1}).$$

*Hence,*

$$\text{Max}(X) = \cup^m_{\eta=1} \text{Max}(X''_{\eta-1,\eta}X_\eta X'_{\eta,\eta+1})$$
$$= \cup^m_{\eta=1}(\text{Max}(X_{\eta-1,\eta}X_\eta X'_{\eta,\eta+1})$$
$$- \{Y \in \text{Max}(X_{\eta-1,\eta}X_\eta X'_{\eta,\eta+1}) \mid \alpha(Y; X_{\eta-1,\eta}X_\eta X'_{\eta,\eta+1}) \in \gamma(X'_{\eta-1,\eta}; X_{\eta-1,\eta}X_\eta X'_{\eta,\eta+1})\}).$$

# 3    Probabilistic Analysis of the Locality Condition

The structural decomposition of a non-empty real-valued sequence $X$ in Theorem 6 suggests a basis for an ideal decomposition of $X$ with length-balance and Max-independence—provided the decomposition satisfies the $\epsilon'$-locality condition. While the $\epsilon'$-localized decomposition $\widetilde{\mathcal{P}}(X)$ is the (derived) sequential partition $(X''_{\eta-1,\eta}X_\eta X'_{\eta,\eta+1})^m_{\eta=1}$ in $m$ pairwise disjoint subsequences, our domain-decomposed parallel algorithm computing $\text{Max}(X)$ will employ $m$ processors with the $i$-th processor hosting the subsequence $X_{i-1,i}X_iX_{i,i+1}$ for $i \in \{1, 2, \ldots, m\}$. The subsequences $X_{i-1,i}X_iX_{i,i+1}$ and $X_{i,i+1}X_{i+1}X_{i+1,i+2}$

hosted in successive $i$-th and $(i+1)$-th processors have the common subsequence $X_{i,i+1}$ that serves as a buffer to capture the $\epsilon'$-locality originated from $X_{i-1,i}X_i$ and a floating separation between successive Max-sets: $\text{Max}(X''_{i-1,i}X_iX'_{i,i+1})$ and $\text{Max}(X''_{i,i+1}X_{i+1}X'_{i+1,i+2})$. A longer common subsequence facilitates the satisfiability of the $\epsilon'$-locality of the preceding subsequence while a shorter one avoids redundant computation among successive processors.

Denote by $\mathbb{R}$ the set of all reals. We analyze the length bound of the common subsequences probabilistically for random sequences of independent and identically distributed terms, via the theory of random walk in $\mathbb{R}^1$, in this section. For basic definitions and results in random walks, see [9]; for convenience some are stated as follows.

Let $x_1, x_2, \ldots$ be a sequence of pairwise independent and identically distributed random variables. Denote by $(S_\eta)_{\eta=0}^\infty$ the sequence of prefix-sum random variables with $S_0 = 0$ and $S_i = \sum_{\eta=1}^i x_\eta$ for $i \geq 1$, which corresponds to a general random walk in $\mathbb{R}^1$ for which $S_i$ gives the position at epoch/index $i$. A record value occurs at (random) epoch $i \geq 1$ corresponds to the probabilistic event "$S_i > S_\eta$ for each $\eta \in [0, i-1]$". For every positive integer $j$, the $j$-th strict ascending ladder epoch random variable is the index of the $j$-th occurrence of the probabilistic event above. We define analogously the notions of: (1) strict descending ladder epochs by reversing the defining inequality from ">" to "<", and (2) weak ascending and weak descending ladder epochs by replacing the defining inequalities by "$\geq$" and "$\leq$", respectively.

The first strict ascending ladder epoch is the random index of the first entry into $(0, +\infty)$, and the continuation of the random walk beyond this epoch is a probabilistic replica of the entire random walk. Other variants of (strict/weak, ascending/descending) ladder epoch yield similar behavior.

Viewing the sequence $X$ in the Max-computation in a probabilistic context and following the above-stated denotations and construction of the Max-independent sequential partition $\widetilde{\mathcal{P}}(X)$ from an $\epsilon'$-localized sequential partition $\mathcal{P}(X)$, we produce a probabilistic upper bound on the length of the common subsequences in $\widetilde{\mathcal{P}}(X)$ via the mean and variance of a variant of the first ladder epoch.

For a sequence of pairwise independent and identically distributed random variables $x_1, x_2, \ldots$ and its associated random-walk sequence $(S_\eta)_{\eta=0}^\infty$ of prefix-sum random variables, denote by $T_1$ its first weak descending ladder epoch. Hereinafter, we assume the following probability notations and condition:

1. The sequence $(x_\eta)_{\eta=1}^\infty$ follows a common random variable $x_1$ with $\text{prob}(x_1 > 0) > 0$. For notational simplicity, denote by $p$ and $\bar{p}\,(= 1-p)$ the probabilities $\text{prob}(x_1 > 0)$ and $\text{prob}(x_1 \leq 0)$, respectively, and
2. For our Max-computing problem, the sequence $X = (x_\eta)_{\eta=1}^n$ with sufficiently large $n$ is a size-$n$ random sample from the common probability distribution of $x_1$ in $(x_\eta)_{\eta=1}^\infty$.

Denote by $T$ the conditional weak descending ladder epoch $T_1 \mid x_1 > 0$.

**Remark 7.** *Ideally in* $\widetilde{\mathcal{P}}(X)$, *we desire that:*

$$|X'_{i,i+1}| \left(= \|[\alpha(X_{i,i+1}; X_{i-1,i}X_iX_{i,i+1}), \epsilon'_{X_{i-1,i}X_iX_{i,i+1}}(\beta^*_i)]\|\right)$$
$$\leq \|[\beta^*_i, \epsilon'_{X_{i-1,i}X_iX_{i,i+1}}(\beta^*_i)]\| = \epsilon'_{X_{i-1,i}X_iX_{i,i+1}}(\beta^*_i) - \beta^*_i + 1.$$

*Thus, if we select the common subsequence* $X_{i,i+1}$ *such that* $|X_{i,i+1}| \geq \lceil E(T) + \delta\sqrt{\mathrm{Var}(T)} \rceil$ *for some positive real* $\delta$, *then we have the following chain of probabilistic events:*

$$\text{“}\epsilon'_{X_{i-1,i}X_iX_{i,i+1}}(\beta^*_i) - \beta^*_i + 1 \geq |X_{i,i+1}|\text{”}$$
$$= \text{“}j = \beta^{*"}_i \cap \text{“}\epsilon'_X(j) - j + 1 \geq |X_{i,i+1}|\text{”}$$
$$\text{(where } j \text{ is a random index in } \gamma_+(X))$$
$$\subseteq \text{“}\epsilon'_X(j) - j + 1 \geq |X_{i,i+1}|\text{”} \subseteq \text{“}(\epsilon'_X(j) - j + 1) - E(T) \geq \delta\sqrt{\mathrm{Var}(T)}\text{”},$$

*and, in accordance with Chebyshev's inequality,*

$$\text{prob}\left(\text{random index-difference } \epsilon'_{X_{i-1,i}X_iX_{i,i+1}}(\beta^*_i) - \beta^*_i + 1 \geq |X_{i,i+1}|\right)$$
$$\leq \text{prob}\left(T - E(T) \geq \delta\sqrt{\mathrm{Var}(T)}\right) \leq \text{prob}\left(|T - E(T)| \geq \delta\sqrt{\mathrm{Var}(T)}\right) \leq \frac{1}{\delta^2},$$

*or, equivalently,*

$$\text{prob}\left(\text{index-difference } \epsilon'_{X_{i-1,i}X_iX_{i,i+1}}(\beta^*_i) - \beta^*_i + 1 < |X_{i,i+1}|\right)$$
$$\geq \text{prob}\left(|T - E(T)| < \delta\sqrt{\mathrm{Var}(T)}\right) \geq 1 - \frac{1}{\delta^2}.$$

*These will be applied to bound the likelihood of* (*non-*)*satisfiability of the* $\epsilon'$-*locality condition for* $\mathcal{P}(X)$.

We now relate the conditional weak descending ladder epoch to the unconditional one and then, in an appropriate probabilistic setting, the means and variances of the two random variables. The unconditional and conditional ladder epochs $T_1$ and $T$ ($= T_1 \mid X_1 > 0$) have sample spaces of $\{1, 2, \ldots\}$ and $\{2, 3, \ldots\}$, respectively, and for every $t \in \{2, 3, \ldots\}$,

$$\text{prob}(T = t) = \text{prob}(T_1 = t \mid X_1 > 0)$$
$$= \frac{\text{prob}(T_1 = t \cap X_1 > 0)}{\text{prob}(X_1 > 0)} = \frac{1}{p}\text{prob}(T_1 = t)$$

due to the subset-containment of the probabilistic events: "$T_1 = t(\geq 2)$" $\subseteq$ "$X_1 > 0$".

**Lemma 8.** *Assume that the variance, hence the mean, of the unconditional weak descending ladder epoch* $T_1$ *exist. The means and variances of the unconditional and conditional ladder epochs* $T_1$ *and* $T = T_1 \mid X_1 > 0$ *are related as follows:*

1. $E(T) = \frac{1}{p} E(T_1) - \frac{\bar{p}}{p}$ *and*
2. $\mathrm{Var}(T) = \frac{1}{p} \mathrm{Var}(T_1) - \bar{p}(\frac{1}{p}(E(T_1) - 1))^2$.

**Remark 9.** *Remark 7 and Lemma 8 suggest to seek lower and upper bounds on* $E(T_1)$ *and an upper bound on* $\mathrm{Var}(T_1)$ *for their use with the mean- and variance-relationships—which translate to non-trivial bounds on* $E(T)$ *and* $\mathrm{Var}(T)$. *Note that, by the assumption of positive* $\mathrm{prob}\,(\mathrm{x}_1 > 0)$, *we have* $E(T_1) > 1$.

For our Max-computing problem, we consider and assume hereinafter (unless explicitly stated otherwise) that the sequence $X = (x_\eta)_{\eta=1}^n$ is a random sample from a normal distribution with mean $-a$ and variance $b^2$ for some positive reals $a$ and $b$. That is, a sequence of pairwise independent and identically distributed random variables $\mathrm{x}_1, \mathrm{x}_2, \ldots$ with a common normal distribution with mean $-a$ and variance $b^2$ gives rise to the observed values $x_1, x_2, \ldots$. In applications, the knowledge of the mean and variance of the common random variable is known or can be approximated.

The negativity of the mean $(-a)$ of the underlying normal distribution is desired in order to avoid yielding unrealistically long minimal maximum subsequences for viable applications. Formally for the induced random-walk sequence $(S_\eta)_{\eta=0}^\infty$ of $(\mathrm{x}_\eta)_{\eta=1}^\infty$, since $E(\mathrm{x}_1)$ is finite and negative, the first (weak descending) ladder epoch $T_1$ has a proper probability distribution with finite mean and the random walk drifts to $-\infty$ ([9] Section XII.2).

For notational simplicity, denote by $\lambda$ the "mean to standard deviation" ratio $\frac{E(\mathrm{x}_1)}{\sqrt{\mathrm{Var}(\mathrm{x}_1)}}$; $\lambda = \frac{-a}{b}$ for a common normal distribution $\mathrm{x}_1$ with mean $-a$ and standard deviation $b$.

**Theorem 10.** *For a sequence of pairwise independent and identically distributed random variables* $(\mathrm{x}_\eta)_{\eta=1}^\infty$ *with a negative (common) finite mean* $E(\mathrm{x}_1)$ *and a positive probability* $p\,(= \mathrm{prob}\,(\mathrm{x}_1 > 0))$, *the unconditional and conditional first weak descending ladder epochs,* $T_1$ *and* $T\,(= T_1 \mid \mathrm{x}_1 > 0)$ *respectively, satisfy the followings:*

1. *[General Case]* $E(T_1) = \exp(\sum_{\eta=1}^\infty \frac{\mathrm{prob}\,(S_\eta > 0)}{\eta})$ *and* $E(T) = \frac{1}{p} \exp(\sum_{\eta=1}^\infty \frac{\mathrm{prob}\,(S_\eta > 0)}{\eta}) - \frac{\bar{p}}{p}$, *and*
2. *[Normally-Distributed Case] For a common normal distribution of* $(\mathrm{x}_\eta)_{\eta=1}^\infty$ *with mean* $-a$ *and variance* $b^2$ *for some positive reals* $a$ *and* $b$ *and for every positive integer* $l$:

$$1 < (\prod_{\eta=1}^{l-1}(1 - \exp(-\frac{\lambda^2}{2\sin^2(\eta\pi/(2l))})))^{-\frac{1}{2l}} \leq E(T_1)$$

$$\leq (\prod_{\eta=1}^{l}(1 - \exp(-\frac{\lambda^2}{2\sin^2(\eta\pi/(2l))})))^{-\frac{1}{2l}}$$

*and*

$$\frac{1}{p}(\prod_{\eta=1}^{l-1}(1 - \exp(-\frac{\lambda^2}{2\sin^2(\eta\pi/(2l))})))^{-\frac{1}{2l}} - \frac{\bar{p}}{p} \leq \mathrm{E}(T)$$

$$\leq \frac{1}{p}(\prod_{\eta=1}^{l}(1 - \exp(-\frac{\lambda^2}{2\sin^2(\eta\pi/(2l))})))^{-\frac{1}{2l}} - \frac{\bar{p}}{p}.$$

Denote by $\mu'$ and $\mu''$ for a fixed $l$-value the lower and upper bounds, respectively, on the mean $\mathrm{E}(T_1)$ obtained in Theorem 10:

$$\mu' = (\prod_{\eta=1}^{l-1}(1 - \exp(-\frac{\lambda^2}{2\sin^2(\eta\pi/(2l))})))^{-\frac{1}{2l}} \text{ and } \mu'' = (\prod_{\eta=1}^{l}(1 - \exp(-\frac{\lambda^2}{2\sin^2(\eta\pi/(2l))})))^{-\frac{1}{2l}}.$$

In our implementation for the empirical study detailed in Sect. 5, we use $l = 6$.

**Remark 11.** *The range-constraint on* $\mathrm{E}(T_1)$*:* $\mathrm{E}(T_1) \in [\mu', \mu'']$ *induces an upper bound on* $\mathrm{Var}(T_1)$ *via some stochastic relationships of the first- and second-order moments of the first weak descending ladder epoch* $T_1$*, its associate (first weak descending) ladder height* $S_{T_1}$*, and the common distribution* $\mathrm{X}_1$ *of the underlying random walk.*

*The following scenario will appear in upper-bounding* $\mathrm{Var}(T_1)$ *and* $\mathrm{Var}(T)$*: a quadratic polynomial* $Q$ *with negative leading coefficient and two distinct real roots* $R'$ *and* $R''$ *($R' < R''$) serves as an upper bound on a nonnegative quantity* $v$ *(such as a variance):* $0 \leq v \leq Q(s)$ *where* $s$ *is a real-valued statistics, and possibly, additional knowledge on* $s$ *provides a range-constraint:* $s \in [c', c'']$ *with* $[c', c''] \cap [R', R''] \neq \emptyset$*:*

1. *Without any range-constraint on* $s$*, the nonnegativity of* $v$*, which is upper-bounded by* $Q(s)$*, gives the range-constraint for admissible values of* $s$*:* $s \in [R', R'']$*, and* $v \leq Q(s) \leq \max\{Q(s) \mid s \in \mathbb{R}\} = \max\{Q(s) \mid s \in [R', R'']\} = Q(\frac{1}{2}(R' + R''))$*.*
2. *The additional range-constraint on* $s$*:* $s \in [c', c'']$ *yields a tighter range-constraint:* $s \in [c', c''] \cap [R', R''] (\neq \emptyset)$*, i.e.,* $s \in [\max\{c', R'\}, \min\{c'', R''\}]$*, and*

$$v \leq Q(s) \leq \max\{Q(s) \mid s \in \mathbb{R}\} \leq \begin{cases} Q(c'') & \text{if } c'' \leq \frac{1}{2}(R' + R''), \\ Q(\frac{1}{2}(R' + R'')) & \text{if } c' \leq \frac{1}{2}(R' + R'') \leq c'', \\ Q(c') & \text{if } \frac{1}{2}(R' + R'') \leq c'. \end{cases}$$

Denote by $q_1$ and $q$ the two quadratic polynomial forms that represent upper bounds on $\mathrm{Var}(T_1)$ and $\mathrm{Var}(T)$, respectively, in Theorem 12 below:

1. $q_1(t) = 2(-t^2 + (1 + \frac{2}{\lambda^2})t)$ with two distinct real roots $r_1'$ and $r_1''$ ($r_1' < r_1''$): $r_1' = 0$ and $r_1'' = 1 + \frac{2}{\lambda^2}$, and

2. $q(t) = -\frac{1}{p}(2 + \frac{\bar{p}}{p})t^2 + \frac{2}{p}(1 + \frac{2}{\lambda^2} + \frac{\bar{p}}{p})t - \frac{\bar{p}}{p^2}$ with its discriminant:

$$\Delta = (\frac{2}{p}(1 + \frac{2}{\lambda^2} + \frac{\bar{p}}{p}))^2 - 4(-\frac{1}{p}(2 + \frac{\bar{p}}{p}))(-\frac{\bar{p}}{p^2}) = \frac{4}{p^2}(1 + \frac{4}{\lambda^2} + \frac{4}{\lambda^4} + \frac{4\bar{p}}{\lambda^2 p}) > 0,$$

and two distinct real roots $r'$ and $r''$ ($r' < r''$):

$$r' = \frac{\frac{2}{p}(1 + \frac{2}{\lambda^2} + \frac{\bar{p}}{p}) - \sqrt{\Delta}}{2\frac{1}{p}(2 + \frac{\bar{p}}{p})} \quad \text{and} \quad r'' = \frac{\frac{2}{p}(1 + \frac{2}{\lambda^2} + \frac{\bar{p}}{p}) + \sqrt{\Delta}}{2\frac{1}{p}(2 + \frac{\bar{p}}{p})}.$$

**Theorem 12.** *For a sequence of pairwise independent and identically distributed random variables $(\mathrm{x}_\eta)_{\eta=1}^\infty$ with a negative (common) finite mean $\mathrm{E}(\mathrm{X}_1)$, a finite (common) third-order absolute moment $\mathrm{E}(|\mathrm{X}_1|^3)$, and a positive probability $p$ ($= \mathrm{prob}\,(\mathrm{X}_1 > 0)$), the unconditional and conditional first weak descending ladder epochs $T_1$ and $T$ ($= T_1 \mid \mathrm{X}_1 > 0$) respectively, satisfy the followings:*

1. *[General Case] For $T_1$: $r' \leq \mathrm{E}(T_1) \leq r''$ and*

$$\mathrm{Var}(T_1) < q_1(\mathrm{E}(T_1)) \leq \begin{cases} q_1(r'') & \text{if } r'' \leq \frac{1}{2}(r_1' + r_1''), \\ q_1(\frac{1}{2}(r_1' + r_1'')) & \text{if } r' \leq \frac{1}{2}(r_1' + r_1'') \leq r'', \\ q_1(r') & \text{if } \frac{1}{2}(r_1' + r_1'') \leq r'; \end{cases}$$

*and for $T$: $\frac{1}{p}r' - \frac{\bar{p}}{p} \leq \mathrm{E}(T) \leq \frac{1}{p}r'' - \frac{\bar{p}}{p}$ and $\mathrm{Var}(T) < q(\mathrm{E}(T_1)) \leq q(\frac{1}{2}(r' + r''))$.*

2. *[Normally-Distributed Case] With a common normal distribution of $(\mathrm{x}_\eta)_{\eta=1}^\infty$ with mean $-a$ and variance $b^2$ for some positive reals $a$ and $b$: For $T_1$: $\mu' \leq \mathrm{E}(T_1) \leq \mu''$ and*

$$\mathrm{Var}(T_1) < q_1(\mathrm{E}(T_1)) \leq \begin{cases} q_1(\mu'') & \text{if } \mu'' \leq \frac{1}{2}(r_1' + r_1''), \\ q_1(\frac{1}{2}(r_1' + r_1'')) & \text{if } \mu' \leq \frac{1}{2}(r_1' + r_1'') \leq \mu'', \\ q_1(\mu') & \text{if } \frac{1}{2}(r_1' + r_1'') \leq \mu'; \end{cases}$$

*and for $T$: $\frac{1}{p}\mu' - \frac{\bar{p}}{p} \leq \mathrm{E}(T) \leq \frac{1}{p}\mu'' - \frac{\bar{p}}{p}$ and*

$$\mathrm{Var}(T) < q(\mathrm{E}(T_1)) \leq \begin{cases} q(\mu'') & \text{if } \mu'' \leq \frac{1}{2}(r' + r''), \\ q(\frac{1}{2}(r' + r'')) & \text{if } \mu' \leq \frac{1}{2}(r' + r'') \leq \mu'', \\ q(\mu') & \text{if } \frac{1}{2}(r' + r'') \leq \mu'. \end{cases}$$

## 4    Domain-Decomposed Parallel Algorithm for Max-Computation

We present the overall algorithms, Max_Sequential and Max_Parallel, implemented on cluster systems with Message Passing Interface (MPI) in which subsequence-hosting processors employ Max_Sequential, which is a linear-time sequential algorithm computing Max improved from Ruzzo-Tompa algorithm in [18]. Two improvements are included in Max_Sequential: (1) having computed the Max-set of the consumed prefix of an input sequence incrementally, the longest contiguous subsequence of all positive (unconsumed) terms succeeding the (consumed) prefix is formed as a maximal subsequence to seed possible backward merges in updating the Max-set of the consumed input, and (2) in order to avoid unnecessary comparisons of prefix sums, a stack is used to store the index-subrange information of all maximal monotone subsequences comprising the Max-set of the consumed prefix/input. Improvements to the algorithm and work in progress will be addressed in the conclusion.

The algorithms Max_Sequential and Max_Parallel are implemented on the supercomputer cluster of High-Performance Computing Center at Oklahoma State University. The hardware configuration of the cluster consists of 252 standard compute nodes, each with dual Intel Xeon E5-2620 (hex-core) 2.0 GHz CPUs, with 32 GB of 1333 MHz RAM. Its network configuration comprises an InfiniBand interconnect network, Gigabit Ethernet for I/O, and an ethernet management network. The implementation is in C language with OpenMPI 1.4. Up to 128 cores are used in the implementation for our empirical study.

algorithm Max_Sequential
input:              A length-$n$ real-valued sequence $X$.
output:             The sequence of all successive non-empty minimal maximum (that is, maximal monotone) subsequences of $X$ occupying low-order subarray of an array $M[1..\lceil\frac{n}{2}\rceil]$ ($|\operatorname{Max}(X)| \leq \lceil\frac{n}{2}\rceil$).
data structures: On consumed input $X'$ (prefix of $X$):
                    1. (sub)array $M[1..(i-1)]$: the canonical list $(Y_1, Y_2, \ldots, Y_{i-1})$ of $\operatorname{Max}(X')$;
                    2. stack $St$: the longest sublist of $\operatorname{Max}(X')$, $(Y_{(1)}, Y_{(2)}, \ldots)$ (which is not necessarily contiguous):

$$\min\{s_{\eta-1}(X') \mid \eta \in \gamma_+(X')\}$$
$$= s_{\alpha(Y_{(1)};X')-1} < s_{\alpha(Y_{(2)};X')-1} < \cdots, \text{ and}$$
$$\max\{s_\eta(X') \mid \eta \in \gamma_+(X')\} = s_{\beta(Y_{(1)};X')} \geq s_{\beta(Y_{(2)};X')} \geq \cdots;$$

                    3. subsequence $Y_i$: the incremental input of the longest (contiguous) subsequence of positive terms of $X$ immediately succeeding $X'$.
begin
1. Initialize: $M[0] := \emptyset$;  $\alpha(Y_0; X) := 0$;  $\beta(Y_0; X) := 0$;  $St := \emptyset$;  $i := 1$;
2. Compute $\gamma(Y_i; X)$, if non-empty:
    $\alpha(Y_i; X) := \min\{\eta \in \gamma_+(X) \mid \eta > \beta(Y_{i-1}; X)\}$;
    $\beta(Y_i; X) := \min\{\eta \in \gamma_+(X) \mid \eta > \beta(Y_{i-1}; X) \text{ and } \eta + 1 \notin \gamma_+(X)\}$;

    if $\alpha(Y_i; X)$ does not exist, then output $M[1..(i-1)]$;    halt; end if;
3. Absorb $Y_i$, and, if necessary, update $i$, $M[1..(i-1)]$, and $St$:
    3.1.   while $i > 1$ and $St \neq \emptyset$ loop

$j := \text{Top}(St)$;
if $s_{\alpha(Y_j;X)-1}(X) \geq s_{\alpha(Y_i;X)-1}(X)$ then $\text{Pop}(St)$;
else if $s_{\beta(Y_j;X)}(X) < s_{\beta(Y_i;X)}(X)$
      then $\{$ $\text{Pop}(St)$; $\beta(Y_j;X) := \beta(Y_i;X)$; $i := j$; $\}$
  else goto step 3.2;
  end if;
  end loop;
  3.2.  $\text{Push}(St,i)$; $M[i] := Y_i$; $i := i+1$;   goto step 2;
end Max_Sequential;

algorithm Max_Parallel
input:  A length-$n$ real-valued sequence $X$; distribution of overlapping length-balanced subsequences in $m$ subsequence-hosting processors; length $\rho$ for the common intersection of overlapping successive subsequences.
output: The sequence of all successive non-empty minimal maximum (that is, maximal monotone) subsequences of $X$.
begin
1. Construct, for input sequence $X$, the above-stated partition (in Section 3) $\mathcal{P}(X) = (X_1, X_{1,2}, X_2, X_{2,3}, X_3, \ldots, X_{m-1}, X_{m-1,m}, X_m)$ (with $X_{0,1} = \emptyset$ and $X_{m,m+1} = \emptyset$) such that: (1) for all $i \in \{1, 2, \ldots, m\}$, processor $P_i$ hosts the subsequence $X_{i-1,i}X_iX_{i,i+1}$ in a length-balanced manner except possibly for the last processor $P_m$, and (2) for all $i \in \{1, 2, \ldots, m-1\}$, length of common intersection of overlapping successive subsequences: $|X_{i,i+1}| = \rho$; hence, for all $i \in \{1, 2, \ldots, m-1\}$, $|X_{i-1,i}X_i| = \lfloor \frac{n-\rho}{m-1} \rfloor$ and $|X_{i,i+1}| = \rho$, and $|X_{m-1,m}X_mX_{m,m+1}| = n - (m-1)\lfloor \frac{n-\rho}{m-1} \rfloor$;
2. Decide if $\mathcal{P}(X)$ is an $\epsilon'$-localized partition:
  2.1.  for all $i \in \{1, 2, \ldots, m\}$
      $\{1 \leq i \leq m-1$: processor $P_i$ computes: $\mathit{is\_\epsilon'\text{-}localized}_i :=$
          $(\gamma_+(X_{i-1,i}X_i) = \emptyset) \vee (\epsilon'_{X_{i-1,i}X_iX_{i,i+1}}(\beta_i^*)$
                      $\in [\beta_i^* + 1, \beta(X_{i-1,i}X_iX_{i,i+1})]$);
      $i = m$:      processor $P_m$ computes: $\mathit{is\_\epsilon'\text{-}localized}_m := \text{true}$;$\}$
    end for;
  2.2.  Compute $\mathit{is\_\epsilon'\text{-}localized} := \wedge_{\eta=1}^{m-1} \mathit{is\_\epsilon'\text{-}localized}_\eta$
      using prefix-sum (Allreduce) function;
  2.3.  for all $i \in \{1, 2, \ldots, m\}$
      processor $P_i$ updates: $\mathit{is\_\epsilon'\text{-}localized}_i := \mathit{is\_\epsilon'\text{-}localized}$;
    end for;
3. If $\mathcal{P}(X)$ is $\epsilon'$-localized, then compute $\text{Max}(X)$ via Theorem 6: determine $X'_{i,i+1}$ for all $i \in \{1, 2, \ldots, m-1\}$ and compute $\text{Max}(X''_{i-1,i}X_iX'_{i,i+1})$ for all $i \in \{1, 2, \ldots, m\}$:
for all $i \in \{1, 2, \ldots, m\}$ processor $P_i$ decides:
  if $\mathit{is\_\epsilon'\text{-}localized}_i$ then
    $\{1 \leq i \leq m-1$: processor $P_i$ sends $\epsilon'_{X_{i-1,i}X_iX_{i,i+1}}(\beta_i^*)$ to processor $P_{i+1}$;
             processor $P_{i+1}$ receives $\epsilon'_{X_{i-1,i}X_iX_{i,i+1}}(\beta_i^*)$;
    $i = m$:      null;$\}$

Invokes Max_Sequential to compute $\mathrm{Max}(X''_{i-1,i}X_iX'_{i,i+1})$;
   else
    goto step 4;
   end if;
  end for;
  halt;
4. Invoke a parallel algorithm adapted from the Max-computing PRAM-algorithm presented in [6] in which two embedded problems are solved by parallel algorithms implemented with MPI: "all nearest smaller values" [10] and "range-minima" [11];
end Max_Parallel;

**Remark 13.** *Theorems 10 and 12 provide a framework for deriving bound-constraints on the means and variances of the unconditional and conditional first weak descending ladder epochs, in order to support applications of the parallel algorithm Max_Parallel with random sample sequences. For random sample sequences from normal distributions with negative mean, the algorithm Max_Parallel applies Theorem 12: part 2 to translate the bound-constraints to explicit bounds that are integrated in the algorithm with minimal modifications in its input and pre-processing computation as stated below:*

1. *The input to Max_Parallel consists of: a length-n real-valued sequence $X$ (a random sample satisfying the assumptions in Theorem 12: part 2) and a prescribed probability threshold $\delta$ (Remark 7: Chebyshev's inequality); distribution of overlapping length-balanced subsequences in $m$ subsequence-hosting processors; and*
2. *For step 1, the pre-processing computation in item 2: for all $i \in \{1, 2, \ldots, m-1\}$, $|X_{i,i+1}|$ is the least upper bound of $\lceil \mathrm{E}(T) + \delta\sqrt{\mathrm{Var}(T)} \rceil$ computed via Theorem 12: part 2.*

## 5    Empirical Study of Speedup and Efficiency

We have assessed the performance of the parallel algorithm Max_Parallel in accordance with Remark 13 in a small-scale empirical study on a 252-node cluster with synthetic random data. The random input sequences in prescribed parametric conditions and the pre-processing computation are described below, together with the performance statistics to be collected.

1. $N = 100$ trial-sequences: each is a random sample/sequence of length $n = 20 \cdot 10^6$ from a normal distribution with mean $-0.25$ and variance $1.0$,
2. Computed upper bounds for the mean and standard deviation of the conditional first weak descending ladder epoch $T$ are: $\mathrm{E}(T) \leq 7.982$ and $\sqrt{\mathrm{Var}(T)} \leq 22.892$ (Theorem 12: part 2), respectively.
   In accordance with Remark 7, Chebyshev's inequality is applied with the parameter $\delta = 3$, and $\mathrm{E}(T) + \delta\sqrt{\mathrm{Var}(T)} \leq 76.658$. This results in an approximate length upper bound of 76 for the common intersection of overlapping subsequences in the cluster-based algorithm Max_Parallel, and

3. Performance measures in (absolute) speedup and efficiency of Max_Parallel are collected in two sets of mean-statistics: (3.1) the set of conditional mean-statistics on "success" scenario (satisfiability of the $\epsilon'$-locality condition for the first $(m-1)$ processors) from $N$ trial-sequences and the Max-computing by (local) Max_Sequential in Max_Parallel: steps 1–3, and (3.2) the set of unconditional ones for Max_Parallel: all steps.

Based on the optimal sequential-time algorithm [18], the (mean) optimal sequential time for the Max-computation of a length-$n$ sequence, $T^*(n)$, is approximately 0.661 s for the synthetic random data prepared above (when averaged over $N = 100$ sequences).

We tabulate below the above-stated two sets of mean-statistics of the running time, speedup, and efficiency of Max_Parallel for $\delta = 3$ (in Remark 7 and Max_Parallel: step 1) and $m$ processors with $m \in \{1, 2, 4, 8, 16, 32, 64, 128\}$:

$$T_m(n) \text{ (in seconds)}, \quad S_m(n) = \frac{T^*(n)}{T_m(n)}, \quad \text{and} \quad E_m(n) = \frac{T_1(n)}{mT_m(n)}, \quad \text{respectively.}$$

Note that, since $\text{prob}(\text{satisfiability of } \epsilon'\text{-locality for single processor}) \geq 1 - \frac{1}{\delta^2}$ $(= \frac{8}{9})$, the expected number $N_{\text{succ}}$ of "successes" from $N$ trial-sequences is lower-bounded as follows:

$$N_{\text{succ}} = N \, \text{prob}(\text{satisfiability of } \epsilon'\text{-locality for single processor})^{m-1}$$

$$\geq N(1 - \frac{1}{\delta^2})^{m-1} \, (= N(\frac{8}{9})^{m-1}).$$

| | mean-statistics over $N$ lower bound on empirical-(expected) | | conditional on "success" scenario: mean-statistics over empirical-$N_{\text{succ}}$ | | | unconditional: mean-statistics over $N$ | | |
|---|---|---|---|---|---|---|---|---|
| $m$ | $N_{\text{succ}}$ | $N_{\text{succ}}$ | $T_m(n)$ | $S_m(n)$ | $E_m(n)$ | $T_m(n)$ | $S_m(n)$ | $E_m(n)$ |
| 1 | 100.00 | 100 | 0.671831 | 0.9839 | 1.0000 | 0.671833 | 0.9839 | 1.0000 |
| 2 | 88.89 | 100 | 0.350113 | 1.8880 | 0.9594 | 0.350118 | 1.8879 | 0.9594 |
| 4 | 70.23 | 97 | 0.182331 | 3.6253 | 0.9212 | 0.183179 | 3.6085 | 0.9169 |
| 8 | 43.85 | 93 | 0.088841 | 7.4402 | 0.9453 | 0.090174 | 7.3303 | 0.9313 |
| 16 | 17.09 | 91 | 0.044414 | 14.8826 | 0.9454 | 0.045837 | 14.4206 | 0.9161 |
| 32 | 2.60 | 83 | 0.022588 | 29.2632 | 0.9295 | 0.024112 | 27.4137 | 0.8707 |
| 64 | 0.06 | 65 | 0.010881 | 60.7479 | 0.9647 | 0.012910 | 51.2005 | 0.8131 |
| 128 | 3.19E–05 | 44 | 0.005552 | 119.0558 | 0.9454 | 0.009221 | 71.6840 | 0.5692 |

The statistical and empirical results tabulated in the two columns: the above-stated lower bound on (expected) $N_{\text{succ}}$ and empirical-$N_{\text{succ}}$ show that the constraints on $E(T)$ and $\text{Var}(T)$ (Theorem 12: part 2) in bounding $E(T) + \delta\sqrt{\text{Var}(T)}$ (Max_Parallel: step 1) serve as a good predictor for $N_{\text{succ}}$. For the conditional statistics on "success" scenario, the speedup and efficiency are close to their theoretical bounds of $m$ and 1, respectively, for all $m \in \{1, 2, 4, 8, 16, 32, 64, 128\}$. For the unconditional ones, the case for each $m \in \{1, 2, 4, 8, 16, 32\}$ achieves the same performance in speedup and efficiency that are close to the theoretical limits. When $m$ is 64 and 128, even for a small $\delta$ ($= 3$), the speedup and efficiency are about $\frac{4}{5}$ and $\frac{3}{5}$, respectively, of their theoretical bounds.

The empirical results shown above meet the theoretical expectations. We have also performed similar empirical studies as mentioned above for random sequences of comparable lengths from various normal distributions on up to 128 processors. The results show good mean-statistics of time-complexity, speedup, and efficiency of Max_Parallel. We expect that the algorithm can scale up with good performance measures for larger-size problems on cluster systems with more processors. The speedup and efficiency performance of an improved Max_Parallel depends on the extent of resolving violations of $\epsilon'$-locality among neighbor processors and tradeoffs involving $\delta$ and $m$.

## 6  Conclusion

The problem of computing the set of all successive non-empty minimal maximum subsequences of a real-valued sequence has linear sequential complexity, and it is solved very efficiently by an optimal linear-time sequential algorithm, hence achieving good speed-ups on a practical parallel system is a challenge. The underlying support for the overlapping domain-decomposed parallel algorithm (on cluster systems with Message passing Interface) for random sample sequences is an application of the theory of random walk in $\mathbb{R}^1$, which derives an approximate probabilistic length upper bound for the common intersection of overlapping subsequences in an appropriate probabilistic setting for the random sequences. The length bound is incorporated in the algorithm to ensure the probabilistic satisfiability of the $\epsilon'$-locality/Max-independence, which admits concurrent and independent computations of all non-empty minimal maximum subsequences in hosting processors. We confirm the efficacy and efficiency of the practical parallel algorithm with a small-scale empirical study with synthetic random sample sequences from normal distributions with negative mean.

Our work in progress includes: (1) a comparative empirical/probabilistic study based on current implementation and refining the algorithm to detect and resolve violations of $\epsilon'$-locality among near-neighbor processors, and (2) derivations of upper bounds for the variances of the unconditional and hence conditional ladder epochs $T_1$ and $T$ ($= T_1 \mid x_1 > 0$) in Sect. 3 based on other different approaches.

There are three directions for general theoretical developments. First, the length bound of the common subsequences (to capture the $\epsilon'$-locality) is achieved via explicit bounds on the mean/variance of the first ladder epoch in the underlying random walk with normal distribution. This leads to a deserving study for general probability distribution. Second, for biomolecular sequence analysis, there are more complex scoring schemes and other notions of (minimal) maximality for ranking subsequences of a real-valued sequence in the literature (see, for example, [4]), developing efficient parallel algorithms for their computation is interesting. Finally, a length upper bound for minimal maximum subsequences can be used as a parameter in studying the parameterized complexity of the Max-computation on practical models of parallel computation.

# References

1. Akl, S.G., Guenther, G.R.: Applications of broadcasting with selective reduction to the maximal sum subsegment problem. Int. J. High Speed Comput. **3**(2), 107–119 (1991)
2. Altschul, S.F.: Amino acid substitution matrices from an information theoretic perspective. J. Mol. Biol. **219**(3), 555–565 (1991)
3. Alves, C.E.R., Cáceres, E.N., Song, S.W.: Finding all maximal contiguous subsequences of a sequence of numbers in $O(1)$ communication rounds. IEEE Trans. Parallel Distrib. Syst. **24**(3), 724–733 (2013)
4. Bernholt, T., Hofmeister, T.: An algorithm for a generalized maximum subsequence problem. In: Correa, J.R., Hevia, A., Kiwi, M. (eds.) LATIN 2006. LNCS, vol. 3887, pp. 178–189. Springer, Heidelberg (2006). https://doi.org/10.1007/11682462_20
5. Brendel, V., Bucher, P., Nourbakhsh, I.R., Blaisdell, B.E., Karlin, S.: Methods and algorithms for statistical analysis of protein sequences. Proc. Nat. Acad. Sc. U.S.A. **89**(6), 2002–2006 (1992)
6. Dai, H.-K., Su, H.-C.: A parallel algorithm for finding all successive minimal maximum subsequences. In: Correa, J.R., Hevia, A., Kiwi, M. (eds.) LATIN 2006. LNCS, vol. 3887, pp. 337–348. Springer, Heidelberg (2006). https://doi.org/10.1007/11682462_33
7. Dai, H.K., Wang, Z.: A parallel algorithm for finding all minimal maximum subsequences via random walk. In: Dediu, A.-H., Formenti, E., Martín-Vide, C., Truthe, B. (eds.) LATA 2015. LNCS, vol. 8977, pp. 133–144. Springer, Cham (2015). https://doi.org/10.1007/978-3-319-15579-1_10
8. Dembo, A., Karlin, S.: Strong limit theorems of empirical functionals for large exceedances of partial sums of I.I.D. variables. Ann. Probab. **19**(4), 1737–1755 (1991)
9. Feller, W.: An Introduction to Probability Theory and Its Applications. Wiley Series in Probability and Mathematical Statistics, 2nd Edn., vol. 2. Wiley, New York (1971)
10. He, X., Huang, C.-H.: Communication efficient BSP algorithm for all nearest smaller values problem. J. Parallel Distrib. Comput. **61**(10), 1425–1438 (2001)
11. JáJá, J.: An Introduction to Parallel Algorithms. Addison-Wesley, Boston (1992)
12. Karlin, S., Altschul, S.F.: Methods for assessing the statistical significance of molecular sequence features by using general scoring schemes. Proc. Nat. Acad. Sci. U.S.A. **87**(6), 2264–2268 (1990)
13. Karlin, S., Altschul, S.F.: Applications and statistics for multiple high-scoring segments in molecular sequences. Proc. Nat. Acad. Sci. U.S.A. **90**(12), 5873–5877 (1993)
14. Karlin, S., Brendel, V.: Chance and statistical significance in protein and DNA sequence analysis. Science **257**(5066), 39–49 (1992)
15. Karlin, S., Dembo, A.: Limit distributions of maximal segmental score among Markov-dependent partial sums. Adv. Appl. Probab. **24**, 113–140 (1992)
16. Karlin, S., Dembo, A., Kawabata, T.: Statistical composition of high-scoring segments from molecular sequences. Ann. Stat. **18**(2), 571–581 (1990)

17. Lin, T.-C., Lee, D.T.: Randomized algorithm for the sum selection problem. Theoret. Comput. Sci. **377**(1–3), 151–156 (2007)
18. Ruzzo, W.L., Tompa, M.: A linear time algorithm for finding all maximal scoring subsequences. In: Proceedings of the Seventh International Conference on Intelligent Systems for Molecular Biology, pp. 234–241. International Society for Computational Biology (1999)

# OCL2PSQL: An OCL-to-SQL Code-Generator for Model-Driven Engineering

Hoang Nguyen Phuoc Bao$^{(\boxtimes)}$ and Manuel Clavel

Faculty of Engineering, Vietnamese-German University, Thu Dau Mot City, Vietnam
ngpbhoang1406@gmail.com, manuel.clavel@vgu.edu.vn

**Abstract.** The Object Constraint Language (OCL) is a textual, declarative language typically used as part of the UML standard for specifying constraints and queries on models. Several attempts have been proposed in the past for translating OCL expressions into SQL queries in the context of Model Driven Engineering (MDE). To cope with OCL expressions that include iterators, previous attempts resorted to imperative features (loops, cursors) of SQL, with the consequent loss of efficiency. In this paper, we define (and implement) a novel mapping from OCL to SQL that covers (possibly nested) iterators, without resorting to imperative, non-declarative features of SQL. We show with a preliminary benchmark that our mapping generates SQL queries that can be efficiently executed on mid- and large-size SQL databases.

**Keywords:** OCL · SQL · Model-driven engineering · Code-generation

## 1 Introduction

In the context of software development, model-driven engineering (MDE) aspires to develop software systems by using *models* as the driving-force. Models are artifacts defining the different aspects and views of the intended software system. Ideally, the *gap* between the models and the real software systems would be covered by appropriate *code-generators*.

The Unified Modeling Language [12] is the facto standard modeling language for MDE. Originally, it was conceived as a graphical language: models were defined using diagrammatic notation. However, it promptly became clear that UML diagrams were not expressive enough to define certain aspects of the intended software systems, and the Object Constraint Language (OCL) [11] was added to the UML standard. OCL is a textual language, with a formal semantics. It can be used to specify in a precise, unambiguous way complex *constraints* and *queries* over models. For example, to define *integrity constraints* and *authorization constraints* in the context of secure database-centric application model-driven development [5].

© Springer Nature Switzerland AG 2019
T. K. Dang et al. (Eds.): FDSE 2019, LNCS 11814, pp. 185–203, 2019.
https://doi.org/10.1007/978-3-030-35653-8_13

In the past a number of mappings from OCL to other languages have been proposed, each with its own goals and limitations. In particular, [7,8,10,13] introduce different mappings from OCL to SQL. The limitations of these mappings, when used as OCL-to-SQL code-generators in a software development process driven by UML/OCL models, can be organized into two groups. The first group contains the limitations related to *language coverage*, i.e., how much part of the OCL language a mapping can cover. The second group contains the limitations related to *execution-time efficiency*, i.e., how much time it takes to execute a query generated by a mapping.

In this paper we provide a novel solution to the question of whether OCL queries can be *transformed* into executable software. Our solution covers a significant subset of the OCL language, including (possibly) nested iterators as well as undefined values. It also reduces significantly the limitation of previous mappings regarding execution-time efficiency.

*Organization.* The rest of the paper is organized as follows. In Sect. 2 we introduce background material about SQL and OCL. Next, in Sect. 3 we define the sub-language of OCL that our OCL-to-SQL mapping currently covers. Then, in Sect. 4 we introduce our mapping, which is defined recursively over the sub-language presented in Sect. 3. Next, in Sect. 5 we discuss some preliminary benchmarks. Finally, in Sect. 6 we review previously proposed OCL-to-SQL, and we conclude, in Sect. 7, with some closing remarks and future work.

## 2    Background

SQL [14] is a special-purpose programming language designed for managing data in relational database management systems (RDBMS). Originally based upon relational algebra and tuple relational calculus, its scope includes data insert, query, update and delete, schema creation and modification, and data access control. Although SQL is to a great extent a declarative language, it also includes procedural elements. In particular, the procedural extensions to SQL support stored procedures which are routines (like a subprogram in a regular computing language, possibly with loops) that are stored in the database.

*Notation.* Let $tb$ be a table. Let $r$ and $col$ be, respectively, a row and a column of $tb$. In what follows, we denote by $col(r)$ the value stored in the column $col$ in the row $r$. Let $qry$ be an SQL-query. Let $db$ be an SQL-database. We denote by $\text{Exec}(qry, db)$ the result of executing $qry$ on $db$.

OCL [11] is a language for specifying constraints and queries using a textual notation. Every OCL expression is written in the context of a model (called the contextual model). OCL is strongly typed. Expressions either have a primitive type, a class type, a tuple type, or a collection type. OCL provides standard operators on primitive data, tuples, and collections. For example, the operator **includes** checks whether an element is inside a collection. OCL also provides a dot-operator to access the values of class instances' attributes and association-ends in the given data model instance. For example, suppose that the contextual model includes a class $c$ with an attribute $at$ and an association-end $as$. Then, if $o$ is an object of class $c$ in the given data model instance, the expression $o.at$ refers to the value of the attribute $at$ for the object $o$ in this data model instance, and $o.as$ refers to the objects linked to the object $o$ through the association-end $as$. OCL provides operators to iterate over collections, such as `forAll`, `exists`, `select`, `reject`, and `collect`. Collections can be *sets*, *bags*, *ordered sets* and *sequences*, and can be parametrized by any type, including other collection types. Finally, to represent *undefinedness*, OCL provides two constants, namely, null and invalid, of a special type. Intuitively, null represents an unknown or undefined value, whereas invalid represents an error or exception. OCL is a pure specification language: when an expression is evaluated, it simply returns a value without changing anything in the model.

*Notation.* Let $e$ be an OCL expression. In what follows, we denote by FVars($e$) the set of variables that occur *free* in $e$, i.e., that are not *bound* by any iterator. Let $e$ be an OCL expression, and let $v$ be a variable introduced in $e$ by an iterator expression $s ->iter (v \mid b )$. In what follows, $\text{src}_e(v)$ denotes the *source* $s$ of $v$ in $e$. Let $e$ be an OCL expression and let $e'$ be a subexpression of $e$. Then, we denote by $\text{SVars}_e(e')$ the set of variables which (the value of) $e'$ depends on, and is defined as follows:

$$\text{SVars}_e(e') = \bigcup_{v \in \text{FVars}(e')} \{v\} \cup \text{SVars}_e(\text{src}_e(v)).$$

Let $e$ be an OCL expression, such that $\text{FVars}(e) = \emptyset$. Let $\mathcal{O}$ be an OCL Scenario. In what follows, we denote by $\text{Eval}(e, \mathcal{O})$ the result of *evaluating* $e$ in $\mathcal{O}$, according to the semantics of the language.

In what follows, without loss of generality, we assume that the names of the iterator variables within an OCL expression are unique.

## 3   The OCL2PSQL Language

The OCL2PSQL-language is currently defined by the following inductive rules:[1]

- true and  false are OCL2PSQL-expression of type Bool.
- $i$ is an OCL2PSQL-expression, for $i$ an integer number. The type of $i$ is Integer.
- $w$ is an OCL2PSQL-expression, for $w$ a string. The type of $w$ is  String.
- $c$ .allInstances() is an OCL2PSQL-expression, for $c$ a class-type. The type of $c$ .allInstances() is Set($c$).

---

[1] Notice that we do not include in our language operations on collections of collections, nor we support the invalid value. Since SQL does not *natively* support (parametrized) structured collections, mappings from OCL to SQL would need to explicitly *encode* this "structure" in the generated queries, as proposed in [8]. Similarly, since SQL does not *natively* support the *invalid* value, mappings from OCL to SQL would have to handle this value in "ad hoc" ways. Currently, none of the other mappings is able to support (parametrized) structured collections or the  invalid value.

- $v$ .at is an OCL2PSQL-expression, for $v$ a variable of a class-type $t$, and $at$ an attribute of the class-type $t$. The type of $v$ .at is the type of $at$.
- $v$ .ase is an OCL2PSQL-expression, for $v$ a variable of a class-type $t$, and $ase$ an association-end of the class-type $t$. The type of $v$ .ase is Set($c'$), where $c'$ is the class at the other end of $ase$.
- $l = r$ is an OCL2PSQL-expression, for $l$ and $r$ OCL2PSQL-expressions of the same predefined type or class-type. The type of $l = r$ is Bool.
- $s \rightarrow$size() is an OCL2PSQL-expression, for $s$ an OCL2PSQL-expression of type Col($t$), where Col is either Set or Bag and $t$ is a predefined type or a class-type. The type of $s \rightarrow$size() is Integer.
- $s \rightarrow$forAll($v \mid b$ ) is an OCL2PSQL-expression, for $s$ an OCL2PSQL-expression of type Col($t$), where Col is either Set or Bag, with $t$ a class type or a predefined type, and where $v$ is a variable of the type $t$, and $b$ is an OCL2PSQL-expression of type Bool. The type of $s \rightarrow$forAll($v \mid b$ ) is Bool.
- $s \rightarrow$exists($v \mid b$ ) is an OCL2PSQL-expression, for $s$ an OCL2PSQL-expression of type Col($t$), where Col is either Set or Bag, with $t$ a class type or a predefined type, and where $v$ is a variable of the type $t$, and $b$ is an OCL2PSQL-expression of type Bool. The type of $s \rightarrow$exists($v \mid b$ ) is Bool.
- $s \rightarrow$select($v \mid b$ ) is an OCL2PSQL-expression, for $s$ an OCL2PSQL-expression of type Col($t$), where Col is either Set or Bag, with $t$ a class type or a predefined type, and where $v$ is a variable of the type $t$, and $b$ is an OCL2PSQL-expression of type Bool. The type of $s \rightarrow$select($v \mid b$ ) is Set($t$).
- $s \rightarrow$collect($v \mid b$ ) is an OCL2PSQL-expression, for $s$ an OCL2PSQL-expression of type Col($t$), where Col is either Set or Bag, with $t$ a class type or a predefined type, and where $v$ is a variable of the type $t$, and $b$ is an OCL2PSQL-expression of type $u$, where $u$ either a class-type or a predefined type or a type Col($u'$), where $u'$ either a class-type or a predefined type. The type of $s \rightarrow$collect($v \mid b$ ) is Bag($u$).
- $s \rightarrow$flatten() is an OCL2PSQL-expression, for $s$ an OCL2PSQL-expression of type Bag(Col($t$)), where Col is either Set or Bag, with $t$ a predefined type or a class-type. The type of $s \rightarrow$flatten() is Bag($t$).
- $l$ .oclIsUndefined() is an OCL2PSQL-expression, for $l$ an OCL2PSQL-expression of type $t$, with $t$ a predefined type or a class-type. The type of $l$ .oclIsUndefined() is Bool.

## 4   The OCL2PSQL Mapping

To illustrate the definition of our mapping, we will use the following example throughout this section. Consider the diagram CarOwnership shown in Fig. 1. It models a simple domain, where there are only *cars* and *persons*. The persons can own cars (they are their *owners*), and, logically, the cars can be owned by persons (they are their *ownedCars*). No restriction is imposed regarding *ownership*: a person can own many different cars (or none), and a car can be owned by many different persons (or by none). Finally, each car can have a *color*, and each person can have a *name*.

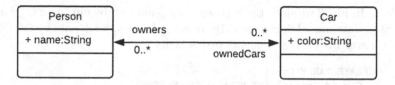

**Fig. 1.** The `CarOwnership` model

## 4.1 Data Models

Firstly, we formally define the valid *context* for OCL2PSQL expressions. An OCL2PSQL-*data model* is a tuple $\langle C, AT, AS \rangle$ where:

- $C$ is a set of *classes* c.
- $AT$ is a set of *attribute* declarations. An attribute declaration $\langle at, c, t \rangle$ denotes that $at$ is an attribute, of type $t$, of the class $c$.
- $AS$ is a set of *association* declarations. An association declaration $\langle as, ase_l, c_l, ase_r, c_r \rangle$ denotes that $as$ is an association between two classes, $c_l$ and $c_r$, where $ase_l$ is the association-end whose *source* is $c_l$ and *target* is $c_r$, and, vice versa, $ase_r$ is the association-end whose *source* is $c_r$ and *target* is $c_l$.

Next, we define a mapping map() from OCL2PSQL-data models to SQL-schemata.

Let $\mathcal{D} = \langle C, AT, AS \rangle$, be a data model. Then map($\mathcal{D}$) is defined as follows:

- For every $c \in C$,

```
CREATE TABLE c (
    c_id int NOT NULL
      AUTO_INCREMENT PRIMARY KEY);
```

- For every attribute $\langle at, c, t \rangle \in AT$

```
ALTER TABLE c ADD COLUMN at SqlType(t);
```

where:
- if $t = $ Integer, then SqlType($t$) = int;
- if $t = $ String, then SqlType($t$) = varchar;
- if $t \in C$, then SqlType($t$) = int.

Moreover, if $t \in C$, then

```
ALTER TABLE c ADD FOREIGN KEY fk_c_iat(at)
    REFERENCES t(t_id);
```

- For every association $\langle as, ase_l, c_l, ase_r, c_r \rangle \in AS$,

```
CREATE TABLE as (
    ase_l int,
    ase_r int,
    FOREIGN KEY fk_c_l_ase_l(ase_l)
      REFERENCES c_l(c_l_id),
    FOREIGN KEY fk_c_r_ase_r(ase_r)
      REFERENCES c_r(c_r_id));
```

*Example 1.* In Fig. 2 we show the SQL-schema generated by our mapping for the OCL2PSQL-data model `CarOwnership`. In what follows, we denote by `CarDB` the database create with the aforementioned schema.

```
CREATE TABLE Car (
   Car_id int(11) NOT NULL AUTO_INCREMENT,
   color varchar(255) DEFAULT NULL,
   PRIMARY KEY (Car_id)
) ENGINE=InnoDB

CREATE TABLE Person (
   Person_id int(11) NOT NULL AUTO_INCREMENT,
   name varchar(255) DEFAULT NULL,
   PRIMARY KEY (Person_id)
) ENGINE=InnoDB

CREATE TABLE Ownership (
   ownedCars int(11) DEFAULT NULL,
   owners int(11) DEFAULT NULL,
   KEY fk_ownership_ownedCars (ownedCars),
   KEY fk_ownership_owners (owners),
   CONSTRAINT ownership_ibfk_1
      FOREIGN KEY (ownedCars) REFERENCES Car (Car_id),
   CONSTRAINT ownership_ibfk_2
      FOREIGN KEY (owners) REFERENCES Person (Person_id)
) ENGINE=InnoDB
```

**Fig. 2.** Example: map(`CarOwnership`)

## 4.2   Data Model Instances

Firstly, we formally define the instances of OCL2PSQL-data models, i.e., the valid *scenarios* for evaluating OCL2PSQL-expressions. Let $\mathcal{D} = \langle C, AT, AS \rangle$ be a data model. A $\mathcal{D}$-*instance* is a tuple $\langle OC, OAT, OAS \rangle$ where:

- $OC$ is a set of objects declarations. An object declaration $(oc, c)$ denotes that $oc$ is an object of the class $c$.
- $OAT$ is a set of attribute value declarations. An attribute value declaration $\langle \langle at, c', t \rangle, (oc, c), vl \rangle$ denotes that the value of the attribute $at$ in the object $oc$ is $vl$.
- $OAS$ is a set of association link declarations. Each association link declaration $\langle \langle as, ase_l, c_l, ase_r, c_r \rangle, (oc_l, c_l), (oc_r, c_r) \rangle$ denotes that the objects $oc_l$ and $oc_r$ are linked through the association $as$, in such a way that $oc_r$ is among the objects linked to $oc_l$ through the association-end $ase_l$, and, vice versa, $oc_l$ is among the objects linked to $oc_r$ through the association-end $ase_r$.

Next, we define a mapping map() from instances of OCL2PSQL-data models to SQL-databases.

Let $\mathcal{D} = \langle C, AT, AS \rangle$ be an OCL2PSQL-data model. Let $\mathcal{OD} = \langle OC, OAT, OAS \rangle$ be a $\mathcal{D}$-*instance*. Then map($\mathcal{O}$) is defined as follows:

- For every $oc \in OC$,

  `INSERT INTO` $c$ `VALUES ()` `;`

  For our reference, let id($oc$) denote the integer-value automatically generated for the column $c\_$`id`.

- For every $\langle\langle at, c', t\rangle, (oc, c), vl\rangle \in OAT$

  `UPDATE` $c$ `SET` $at$ `=` $vl$ `WHERE` $c\_$`id` `=` id($oc$)`;`

- For every $\langle as, ase_l, c_l, ase_r, c_r\rangle \in OAS$,

  `INSERT INTO` $as$ `(`$ase_l$`,` $ase_r$`) VALUES (`$oc_l$`,` $oc_r$`)` `;`

## 4.3 Expressions

Finally, in this section we recursively define our mapping map() from OCL2PSQL-expressions to SQL-queries. The correctness of our mapping could be formalized as follows: Let $e$ be an OCL2PSQL-expression, such that FVars($e$) = $\emptyset$, and let $\mathcal{O}$ be an OCL2PSQL-*scenario*. Then,

$$\text{Exec}(\text{map}_e(e), \text{map}(\mathcal{O})) \equiv_{\text{OCL2PSQL}} \text{Eval}(e, \mathcal{O}).$$

The different cases in our recursive definition below follow the same key idea underlying our mapping: namely, let $e$ be an OCL2PSQL-expression, let $e'$ be a subexpression of $e$, and let $\mathcal{O}$ be an OCL2PSQL-scenario. Then, Exec(map$_e$($e'$), map($\mathcal{O}$)) returns a table, with a column `res`, a column `val`, and, for each $v \in \text{SVars}_e(e')$, a column `ref`$\_v$. Informally, for each row in this table: (i) the columns `ref`$\_v$ contain a valid "instantiation" for the iterator variables of which the evaluation of $e'$ depends on (if any); (ii) the column `val` contains 0 when evaluating the expression $e'$, with the "instantiation" represented by the columns `ref`$\_v$, evaluates to the *empty set*; otherwise, the column `val` contains 1; (iii) when the column `val` contains 1, the column `res` contains the result of evaluating the expression $e'$ with the "instantiation" represented by the columns `ref`$\_v$; when the column `val` contains 0, the value contained in the column `res` is not meaningful. More concretely,

*Remark 1.* Let $e$ be an OCL2PSQL-expression. Let $e'$ be a subexpression of $e$, such that FVars($e'$) = $\emptyset$. Let $\mathcal{O}$ be an OCL2PSQL-scenario. Then, Exec(map$_e$($e'$), map($\mathcal{O}$)) returns a table, with a column `res` and column `val`, such that, for each row $r$, `val`($r$) = 1. Intuitively, each row in the table returned by Exec(map$_e$($e'$), $\mathcal{O}$) represents an element in Eval($e'$, $\mathcal{O}$), and vice versa.

*Remark 2.* Let $e$ be an OCL2PSQL-expression. Let $e'$ be a subexpression of $e$, such that FVars($e'$) is not empty. Let $\mathcal{O}$ be an OCL2PSQL-scenario. Then, Exec(map$_e$($e'$), $\mathcal{O}$) returns a table, with a column `res`, a column `val`, and, for each $v \in \text{SVars}_e(e')$, a column `ref`$\_v$, and such that, for each row $r$, `val`($r$) is either 1 or 0. Intuitively, for each row $r$ in the table returned by Exec(map$_e$($e'$), $\mathcal{O}$)

- if $\mathtt{val}(r)$ is 1, then $\mathtt{res}(r)$ is an element in $\mathrm{Eval}(\theta(e'), \mathcal{O})$, and vice versa, where $\theta$ is the substitution $\{v \mapsto \mathtt{ref\_}v(r) \mid v \in \mathrm{SVars}(e')\}$.
- if $\mathtt{val}(r)$ is 0, then $\mathrm{Eval}(\theta(e'), \mathcal{O}) = \emptyset$, where, as before, $\theta$ is the substitution $\{v \mapsto \mathtt{ref\_}v(r) \mid v \in \mathrm{SVars}(e')\}$.

## Variables

Let $e$ be an OCL2PSQL-expression. Let $e'$ be a subexpression of $e$. Let $e' = v$, where $v$ is a variable. Then,

$\mathrm{map}_e(v) =$
```
SELECT
  TEMP_dmn.res as res,
  TEMP_dmn.res as ref_v,
  TEMP_dmn.val as val,
  TEMP_dmn.ref_v' as ref_v', for each v' ∈ SVars_e(src(v))
FROM (map_e(src(v))) as TEMP_dmn.
```

## Attributes

Let $e$ be an OCL2PSQL-expression. Let $e'$ be a subexpression of $e$. Let $e' = v$ $.att$, where $v$ is a variable of class-type $c$ and $att$ is an attribute of the class $c$. Then,

$\mathrm{map}_e(v\ .att) =$
```
SELECT
  c.att as res,
  TEMP_obj.val as val,
  TEMP_obj.ref_v' as ref_v', for each v' ∈ SVars_e(v)
FROM (map_e(v)) as TEMP_obj
LEFT JOIN c
ON TEMP_obj.ref_v = c.c_id AND TEMP_obj.val = 1.
```

## Association-ends

Let $e$ be an OCL2PSQL-expression. Let $e'$ be a subexpression of $e$. Let $e' = v$ $.ase$, where $v$ is a variable of class-type $c$, and $ase$ is an association-end of the class $c$. Let $\mathrm{Assoc}(ase)$ be the association to which $ase$ belongs, and let $\mathrm{Oppos}(ase)$ be the association-end at the opposite end of $ase$ in $\mathrm{Assoc}(ase)$. Then,

$\mathrm{map}_e(v\ .ase) =$
```
SELECT
  Assoc(ase).ase as res,
  CASE Assoc(ase).Oppos(ase) IS NULL
    WHEN 1 THEN 0
    ELSE 1 END as val,
```

```
TEMP_obj.ref_v' as ref_v', for each v' ∈ SVars_e(v)
FROM (map_e(v)) as TEMP_obj
LEFT JOIN Assoc(ase)
ON TEMP_obj.ref_v = Assoc(ase) .Oppos(ase) AND TEMP_obj.val = 1.
```

## AllInstances

Let $e$ be an OCL2PSQL-expression. Let $e'$ be a subexpression of $e$. Let $e' = c$ .allInstances(), where $c$ is a class type. Then,

$\mathrm{map}_e(c$ .allInstances()$)=$
```
SELECT c_id as res, 1 as val FROM c.
```

## Equality

Let $e$ be an OCL2PSQL-expression. Let $e'$ be a subexpression of $e$. Let $e' = (l =r)$. We need to consider the following cases:

- $\mathrm{FVars}(l) = \mathrm{FVars}(r) = \emptyset$. Then,

  $\mathrm{map}_e(l =r) =$
  ```
  SELECT
    TEMP_left.res = TEMP_right.res as res,
    1 as val
  FROM (map_e(l)) AS TEMP_left, (map_e(r)) AS TEMP_right
  ```

- $\mathrm{FVars}(l) \neq \emptyset$, $\mathrm{SVars}(r) \subseteq \mathrm{SVars}(l)$. Then,

  $\mathrm{map}_e(l =r) =$
  ```
  SELECT
    TEMP_left.res = TEMP_right.res as res,
    CASE TEMP_left.val = 0 OR TEMP_right.val = 0
      WHEN 1 THEN 0
      ELSE 1 END as val,
    TEMP_left.ref_v as ref_v, for each v ∈ SVars_e(l)
  FROM (map_e(l)) AS TEMP_left
  [LEFT] JOIN (map_e(r)) AS TEMP_right
  [ON] TEMP_left.ref_v = TEMP_right.ref_v, for each v ∈ SVars_e(l) ∩ SVars_e(r).
  ```

- $\mathrm{FVars}(r) \neq \emptyset$, $\mathrm{SVars}(l) \subseteq \mathrm{SVars}(r)$. As before, but swapping the order of the elements in the left-join.
- $\mathrm{FVars}(l) \neq \emptyset$, $\mathrm{FVars}(r) \neq \emptyset$, $\mathrm{SVars}(l) \not\subseteq \mathrm{SVars}(r)$, and $\mathrm{SVars}(r) \not\subseteq \mathrm{SVars}(l)$. Then,

  $\mathrm{map}_e(l =r) =$
  ```
  SELECT
    TEMP_left.res = TEMP_right.res as res,
    CASE TEMP_left.val = 0 OR TEMP_right.val = 0
      WHEN 1 THEN 0
  ```

```
    ELSE 1 END as val,
  TEMP_left.ref_v, for each v ∈ SVars_e(l),
  TEMP_right.ref_v, for each v ∈ SVars_e(r)
FROM (map_e(l)) AS TEMP_left, (map_e(r)) AS TEMP_right
```

## Size

Let $e$ be an OCL2PSQL-expression. Let $e'$ be a subexpression of $e$. Let $e' = s$ $->$size(). We need to consider the following cases:

– $\text{FVars}(s) = \emptyset$. Then,

```
map_e(s ->size()) =
SELECT
  COUNT(*) as res,
  1 as val
FROM (map_e(s)) AS TEMP_src.
```

– $\text{FVars}(l) \neq \emptyset$, Then,

```
map_e(s ->size()) =
SELECT
  CASE TEMP_src.val = 0
    WHEN 1 THEN 0
    ELSE COUNT(*) END as res,
  TEMP_src.ref_v as ref_v, for each v ∈ SVars_e(s)
  1 as val
FROM (map_e(s)) AS TEMP_src
GROUP BY TEMP_src.ref_v, for each v ∈ SVars_e(s), TEMP_src.val.
```

## Collect

Let $e$ be an OCL2PSQL-expression. Let $e'$ be a subexpression of $e$. Let $e' = s$ $->$collect($v \mid b$). We need to consider the following cases:

– $v \in \text{FVars}(b)$ and $\text{FVars}(e') = \emptyset$.

```
SELECT TEMP_body.res as res,
  TEMP_body.val as val,
FROM (map_e(b)) as TEMP_body
```

– $v \in \text{FVars}(b)$ and $\text{FVars}(e') \neq \emptyset$.

```
SELECT TEMP_body.res as res,
  TEMP_body.val as val,
  TEMP_body.ref_v' as ref_v', for each v' ∈ SVars(s),
  TEMP_body.ref_v' as ref_v', for each v' ∈ SVars(b) \ SVars(s) \ {v}
FROM (map_e(b)) as TEMP_body
```

– $v \notin \text{FVars}(b)$. Similarly, but the source and the body would need to be *joined* using a JOIN-clause.

## Exists

Let $e$ be an OCL2PSQL-expression. Let $e'$ be a subexpression of $e$. Let $e' = s$ $\rightarrow$exists$(v \mid b)$. We need to consider the following cases:

- $v \in \mathrm{FVars}(b)$ and $\mathrm{FVars}(e') = \emptyset$. Then

```
SELECT
  COUNT(*) > 0 as res,
  1 as val
FROM (map_e(b)) as TEMP_body
WHERE TEMP_body.res = 1
```

- $v \in \mathrm{FVars}(b)$ and $\mathrm{FVars}(e') \neq \emptyset$. Then

```
SELECT
  CASE TEMP_src.ref_v IS NULL
    WHEN 1 THEN 0
    ELSE TEMP.res END as res,
  1 as val,
  TEMP_src.ref_v' as ref_v', for each v' ∈ SVars(s),
  TEMP_body.ref_v' as ref_v', for each v' ∈ SVars(b) \ SVars(s) \ {v}
FROM (map_e(s)) as TEMP_src
LEFT JOIN (
  SELECT COUNT(*) > 0 as res,
    TEMP_body.ref_v' as ref_v', for each v' ∈ SVars(b) \ {v}
  FROM (map_e(b)) as TEMP_body
  WHERE TEMP_body.res = 1
  GROUP BY TEMP_body.ref_v', for each v' ∈ SVars(b) \ {v}
) as TEMP_body
ON TEMP_src.ref_v' = TEMP_body.ref_v', for each v' ∈ SVars(s)
```

- $v \notin \mathrm{FVars}(b)$. Similarly, but the source and the body would need to be *joined* using a JOIN-clause.

## ForAll

Let $e$ be an OCL2PSQL-expression. Let $e'$ be a subexpression of $e$. Let $e' = s$ $\rightarrow$forAll$(v \mid b)$. We need to consider the following cases:

- $v \in \mathrm{FVars}(b)$ and $\mathrm{FVars}(e') = \emptyset$. Then

```
SELECT
  COUNT(*) = 0 as res,
  1 as val
FROM (map_e(b)) as TEMP_body
WHERE TEMP_body.res = 0
```

– $v \in \text{FVars}(b)$ and $\text{FVars}(e') \neq \emptyset$.

```
SELECT
  CASE TEMP_src.ref_v IS NULL
    WHEN 1 THEN 1
    ELSE TEMP.res END as res,
  1 as val,
  TEMP_src.ref_v' as ref_v', for each v' ∈ SVars(s),
  TEMP_body.ref_v' as ref_v', for each v' ∈ SVars(b) \ SVars(s) \ {v}
FROM (map_e(s)) as TEMP_src
LEFT JOIN (
  SELECT COUNT(*) = 0 as res,
    TEMP_body.ref_v' as ref_v', for each v' ∈ SVars(b) \ {v}
  FROM (map_e(b)) as TEMP_body
  WHERE IFNULL(TEMP_body.res, 0) = 0 AND TEMP_body.val = 1
  GROUP BY TEMP_body.ref_v', for each v' ∈ SVars(b) \ {v}
) as TEMP_body
ON TEMP_src.ref_v' = TEMP_body.ref_v', for each v' ∈ SVars(s)
```

– $v \notin \text{FVars}(b)$. Similarly, but the source and the body would need to be *joined* using a JOIN-clause.

## Select

Let $e$ be an OCL2PSQL-expression. Let $e'$ be a subexpression of $e$. Let $e' = s$ –>select$(v \mid b)$. We need to consider the following cases:

– $v \in \text{FVars}(b)$ and $\text{FVars}(e') = \emptyset$.

```
SELECT
  TEMP_body.ref_v as res,
  TEMP_body.val as val
FROM (map_e(b)) as TEMP_body
  WHERE TEMP_body.res = 1
```

– $v \in \text{FVars}(b)$ and $\text{FVars}(e') \neq \emptyset$.

```
SELECT
  CASE TEMP_src.val = 0 OR TEMP_body.ref_v IS NULL
    WHEN 1 THEN NULL
    ELSE TEMP_src.res END as res,
  CASE TEMP_src.val = 0 OR TEMP_body.ref_v IS NULL
    WHEN 1 THEN 0
    ELSE 1 END as val,
  TEMP_src.ref_v' as ref_v', for each v' ∈ SVars(s),
  TEMP_body.ref_v' as ref_v', for each v' ∈ SVars(b) \ SVars(s) \ {v}
FROM (map_e(s)) as TEMP_src
LEFT JOIN (
```

```
         SELECT * FROM (map_e(b)) as TEMP
         WHERE TEMP.res = 1) AS TEMP_body
  ON TEMP_src.res = TEMP_body.ref_v,
     TEMP_src.ref_v' = TEMP_body.ref_v', for each v' ∈ SVars(s).
```

– $v \notin$ FVars($b$). Similarly, but the source and the body would need to be *joined* using a JOIN-clause.

## OclIsUndefined

Let $e$ be an OCL2PSQL-expression. Let $e'$ be a subexpression of $e$. Let $e' = s$. oclIsUndefined(). Then,

```
map_e(s. oclIsUndefined()) =
SELECT
  CASE TEMP_src.val = 0
    WHEN 1 THEN NULL
    ELSE TEMP_src.res IS NULL as res END as res,
  TEMP_src.val as val,
    TEMP_ref.v' as ref_v', for each v' ∈ SVars_e(s)
FROM map(s) as TEMP_src.
```

## Flatten

Let $e$ be an OCL2PSQL-expression. Let $e'$ be a subexpression of $e$. Let $e' = e''$ ->flatten(). Currently, $e''$ must be a collect-expression, $e'' = s$ ->collect($v \mid b$), where $b$ is of type Col($t$), where Col is either Set or Bag, and where $t$ is a predefined type or a class-type.

We need to consider the following cases:

– FVars($e'$) = ∅.

```
  SELECT
    TEMP_src.res as res,
    1 as val
  FROM (map_e(e'')) as TEMP_src
    WHERE TEMP_src.val = 1
```

– FVars($e'$) ≠ ∅. Let assume that $v \in$ FVars($b$).

```
  SELECT
    CASE TEMP_flat.val IS NULL
      WHEN 1 THEN NULL
      ELSE TEMP_flat.res END as res,
    CASE TEMP_flat.val IS NULL
      WHEN 1 THEN 0
```

```
     ELSE TEMP_flat.val END as val,
   TEMP_flat.ref_v' as ref_v', for each v' ∈ SVars(s)
FROM (map_e(s)) as TEMP_src
LEFT JOIN (
   SELECT * FROM (map_e(e'')) as TEMP
   WHERE TEMP.val = 1) as TEMP_flat
ON TEMP_src.ref_v' = TEMP_flat.ref_v', for each v' ∈ SVars(s)
```

## 5    Preliminary Benchmarks

As part of the work presented here, we have implemented in Java the OCL2PSQL mapping. The interested reader can experiment with the latest version of our tool at:[2]

http://cs.vgu.edu.vn/se/tools/ocl2psql/.

In this section we provide some experiments to evaluate our mapping with respect to execution-time efficiency of the generated queries.[3] To this end, we will consider different *scenarios* of the database CarDB, introduced in Example 1. In particular, CarDB($n$) will denote an instance of the database CarDB containing $10^n$ cars and $10^{(n-1)}$ persons, where each car is owned by one person and each person owns 10 different cars, and each car has a color different from 'no-color', and each person has a name different from 'no-name'. We use a server machine, with Intel(R) Xeon(R) CPU E5-2620 v3 at 2.40 GHz with 16 GB RAM, using MySQL 5.7.25.[4] The execution-times reported here correspond to the arithmetic mean of 50 executions. The figures reported are given in seconds, unless otherwise stated.

First, suppose that we want to know the number of cars whose color is 'no-color'. In SQL we can use the following query:

```
SELECT COUNT(*) FROM (SELECT * FROM Car WHERE color = 'no-color') AS TEMP;
```

In OCL we can specify the same query using the following expression:

Car.allInstances()−>select(c|c.color ='no−color')−>size()

If we execute the above queries on CarDB(6) and CarDB(7), (without indexing the column color) in the table Car, we obtain the following results. The figures shown in the row "OCL2PSQL" correspond to the execution-time of the SQL-query generated, for the above OCL expression, by the OCL2PSQL mapping.

---

[2] At the time of writing, our tool temporarily uses an OCL parser that requires adding contextual information to the OCL expressions to be input. Please, check the latest information about this issue in our tool's web site.

[3] SQL engines have highly optimized strategies for executing queries over large databases. Our OCL2PSQL mapping follows some of the well-known optimization "tips" for SQL engines. Nevertheless, we should be aware that "development [for SQL engines] is ongoing, so no optimization tip is reliable for the long term." (MySQL 8.0 Reference Manual, (13.2.11.11 Optimizing Subqueries).

[4] Although we have used MySQL for running our examples, we believe that our overall results should apply likewise to the other SQL engines.

|          | CarDB(6) | CarDB(7) |
|----------|----------|----------|
| SQL      | 0.22     | 2.28     |
| OCL2PSQL | 0.26     | 3.30     |

Next, suppose that we want to know if there is at least one car whose color is different from 'no-color'. In SQL we can use the following query,

```
SELECT COUNT(*) > 0
FROM (SELECT * FROM Car WHERE color <> 'no-color') AS TEMP;
```

We can specify in OCL the original query using the following expression:

Car.allInstances()->exists(c|c.color <>'no-color')

If we execute the above queries on CarDB(6) and CarDB(7), without indexing the column color in the table Car, we obtain the following results.

|          | CarDB(6) | CarDB(7) |
|----------|----------|----------|
| SQL      | 0.22     | 2.72     |
| OCL2PSQL | 0.28     | 3.28     |

Finally, suppose that we want to know the number of cars that has at least one owner whose name is 'no-name'. In SQL we can also use the following query, which uses joins (instead of correlated subqueries):

```
SELECT COUNT(*)
FROM (SELECT COUNT(*) > 0 FROM Car
      JOIN Ownership
      on Car_id = ownedCars
      JOIN Person
      ON Person.Person_id = owners
      WHERE Person.name = 'no-name'
      GROUP BY Car_id) AS TEMP;
```

We can specify in OCL the original query using the following expression:

Car.allInstances()->select(c|c.owners->exists(p|p.name ='no-name'))->size()

If we execute the above queries on CarDB(6) and CarDB(7), without indexing the column name in the table Person, we obtain the following results.

|          | CarDB(6) | CarDB(7) |
|----------|----------|----------|
| SQL      | 0.04     | 0.28     |
| OCL2PSQL | 0.36     | 4.24     |

# 6    Related Work

To the best of our knowledge, OCL2SQL [6, 10] was the first attempt of mapping OCL into SQL. Based on a set of transformation *templates*, OCL2SQL automatically generates SQL queries from OCL expressions. OCL2SQL only covers (a subset of) OCL boolean expressions. Moreover, the high execution-time for the queries generated by OCL2SQL makes it impractical, as an OCL-to-SQL code-generator, for large scenarios. For example, [4] reported that the query generated by OCL2SQL for the expression:

Writer.allInstances()−>forAll(a|a.books−>forAll(b|b.page >300))

takes more than 45 min to execute on a scenario consisting of $10^2$ writers and $10^5$ books, each writer being the author of $10^3$ books and each book having exactly 150 pages.[5]

MySQL4OCL [8] is defined recursively over the structure of OCL expressions. For each OCL expression, MySQL4OCL generates a *stored procedure* that, when called, creates a *temporary table* containing the values corresponding to the evaluation of the given expression. More concretely, for the case of iterator expressions, the stored procedure generated by MySQL4OCL repeats, using a *loop*, the following process: (i) it *fetches* from the iterator's source collection a new element, using a *cursor*; (ii) it calls the stored procedure corresponding to the iterator's body with the newly fetched element as a *parameter*; (iii) it processes the resulting temporary table according to the semantics of the iterator's operator. Although cursors and loops (inside stored procedures) allow MySQL4OCL to cover a large subclass of the OCL language (including nested iterators), they also bring about a fundamental limitation to the use of MySQL4OCL as an OCL-to-SQL code-generator: they often impede the highly-optimized execution strategies implemented by SQL engines.

An interesting method for efficiently checking OCL constraints by means of SQL queries is proposed in [13]. According to this method, an OCL constraint is satisfied if its corresponding SQL query returns the empty set. As in the case of OCL2SQL, this method is limited to (a subset of) OCL boolean expressions. With regards to execution-time efficiency, the figures provided in [13] are not easily comparable with *normal* execution times, since the generated SQL queries are computed in an *incremental* way. More specifically, "whenever a change in the data occurs, only the constraints that may be violated because of such change are checked and only the relevant values given by the change are taken into account."

SQL-PL4OCL [7] closely follows the design of MySQL4OCL and, consequently, bears the same fundamental limitation regarding execution-time efficiency, as we illustrate with an example below. Still, with respect to its predecessor, SQL-PL4OCL simplifies the definition of the mapping, improves the execution-time of the generated queries (by reducing the number of temporary

---

[5] The experiment was carried out on a machine with Intel Pentium M 2.00 GHz 600 MHz, and 1 GB of RAM.

tables), and implements some of the features that were left in [8] as future work: namely, handling the *null* value and supporting (unparameterized) sequences.

To illustrate the *costly* consequences, in terms of execution-time efficiency, of using cursors and loops to implement OCL iterator expressions, consider the following OCL query:

Car.allInstances()−>select(c|c.owners−>exists(p|p.name ='no−name'))−>size().

The stored procedure generated by SQL-PL4OCL for this query is given in [7] (Example 11). Now, if we call this stored procedure on the scenarios CarDB(3), CarDB(4), CarDB(5), CarDB(6), and CarDB(7), we obtain the following execution-times:

|  | CarDB(3) | CarDB(4) | CarDB(5) | CarDB(6) | CarDB(7) |
|---|---|---|---|---|---|
| SQL-PL4OCL | 0.76 | 6.17 | 1 min 3.02 | 10 min 24.00 | > 90min |

Note that the above query, when implemented in SQL in the *expected* way (without cursors and loops), takes less than 1 second to execute on the scenario CarDB(7), while the stored procedure generated by SQL-PL4OCL (using cursors and loops) did not finish its execution after 90 min. As reported in Sect. 5, the SQL-query generated by OCL2PSQL takes less than 10 seconds to execute on the scenario CarDB(7). OCL2PSQL diverts completely from MySQL4OCL/SQL-PL4OCL in that it does not rely on the use of cursors and loops for implementing iterator expressions, neither does it create temporary tables for storing interme-diate results. Instead, (i) for intermediate results, it uses standard *subqueries* and (ii) for iterator expressions, it adds to the subquery corresponding to the itera-tor's body an extra column corresponding to the iterator's variable. Intuitively, this column stores the element in the iterator's source that is "responsible" for the result that is stored in the corresponding row.

Finally, there have been also different proposals [1,3,4,9] in the past for what we may call OCL *evaluators*. These are tools that *load* first the scenario on which an OCL expression is to be evaluated, and then *evaluate* this expression using an OCL interpreter. As reported in [4], the (insurmountable) problem with OCL evaluators is the time required for *loading* a large scenario: none of the existing tools were able to finish loading a scenario with $10^6$ objects after 20 min.

# 7   Concluding Remarks and Future Work

The Object Constraint Language (OCL) plays a key role in adding precision to UML models, and therefore it is called to be a main actor in model-driven engineering (MDE). However, to fulfill this role, smart/advanced *code-generators* must bridge the gap between UML/OCL models and executable code. This is certainly the case for secure database-centric applications [2].

In this paper, we have defined (and implemented) a novel mapping, called OCL2PSQL, from a significant subset of OCL to SQL. Our mapping generates queries that can perform *on par with* queries manually implemented in SQL for non-trivial examples, overcoming the main limitations of previously proposed mappings.

Looking ahead, we recognize that manually implementing in SQL *complex* queries is not an easy task; in fact, we can argue that it is a more difficult task than specifying them in OCL. Suppose, for example, that we are interested in querying our database CarDB (without assuming that every car has at least one owner) about: (i) if it *exists a car whose owners all have the name 'no-name'*, and (ii) *how many cars have at least one owner with no name declared yet*. We can specify (i) in OCL as follows:

Car.allInstances()−>exists(c|c.owners−>forAll(p|p.name='no−name'))

Similarly, we can specify ii) in OCL as follows:

Car.allInstances()−>select(c|c.owners−>exists(p|p.name.oclIsUndefined()))−>size()

We invite the reader to implement (i) and (ii) in SQL, and draw his/her own conclusions. In our opinion, this state of affairs offers exciting opportunities for smart/advanced OCL-to-SQL code-generators.

Our challenge now is two-fold. On the one hand, we want to extend our mapping to cover the part of the OCL language that is not covered yet. In particular, (i) collection of collections (e.g., OCL expressions that represent set of sets, or sequences, or ordered sets); (ii) operations on collections of collections (e.g., union, intersection); (iii) type operations (e.g., oclIsTypeOf or oclAsType, which are particularly relevant when dealing with UML models that include *generalizations*); and (iv) invalid values. On the other hand, we want to formally prove the *correctness* of our mapping, based on the semantics of SQL and OCL, using an interactive theorem prover (proof assistant) like Isabelle/HOL or Coq.

Finally, we plan to use our mapping to generate appropriate executable code from UML/OCL models containing OCL invariants, and pre and post conditions. Notice that these are ultimately OCL queries of type Boolean, and therefore are covered by our mapping.

**Acknowledgments.** This work has been supported by the Vietnamese-German University (VGU-PSSG grant 14/01 - 11/06/2019).

# References

1. Baar, T., Markovic, S.: The RoclET tool (2007). http://www.roclet.org/index.php
2. Basin, D.A., Clavel, M., Egea, M., de Dios, M.A.G., Dania, C.: A model-driven methodology for developing secure data-management applications. IEEE Trans. Softw. Eng. **40**(4), 324–337 (2014)
3. Chiorean, D., Bortes, M., Corutiu, D., Botiza, C., Carcu, A.: An OCL environment (OCLE) 2.0.4 (2005). Laboratorul de Cercetare in Informatica, University of BABES-BOLYAI. http://lci.cs.ubbcluj.ro/ocle/

4. Clavel, M., Egea, M., de Dios, M.A.G.: Building an efficient component for OCL evaluation. ECEASST **15** (2008)
5. de Dios, M.A.G., Dania, C., Basin, D., Clavel, M.: Model-driven development of a secure eHealth application. In: Heisel, M., Joosen, W., Lopez, J., Martinelli, F. (eds.) Engineering Secure Future Internet Services and Systems. LNCS, vol. 8431, pp. 97–118. Springer, Cham (2014). https://doi.org/10.1007/978-3-319-07452-8_4
6. Demuth, B., Hussmann, H.: Using UML/OCL constraints for relational database design. In: France, R., Rumpe, B. (eds.) UML 1999. LNCS, vol. 1723, pp. 598–613. Springer, Heidelberg (1999). https://doi.org/10.1007/3-540-46852-8_42
7. Egea, M., Dania, C.: SQL-PL4OCL: an automatic code generator from OCL to SQL procedural language. Softw. Syst. Model. **18**, 769–791 (2017)
8. Egea, M., Dania, C., Clavel, M.: MySQL4OCL: a stored procedure-based MySQL code generator for OCL. ECEASST **36** (2010)
9. Gogolla, M., Büttner, F., Richters, M.: USE: A UML-based specification environment for validating UML and OCL. Sci. Comput. Program. **69**, 27–34 (2007)
10. Heidenreich, F., Wende, C., Demuth, B.: A framework for generating query language code from OCL invariants. ECEASST **9** (2008)
11. Object Management Group. Object constraint language specification version 2.4. Technical report, OMG, February 2014. https://www.omg.org/spec/OCL/About-OCL/
12. Object Management Group. Unified Modeling Language. Technical report, OMG, December 2017. https://www.omg.org/spec/UML/About-UML/
13. Oriol, X., Teniente, E.: Incremental checking of OCL constraints through SQL queries. In: Brucker, A.D., Dania, C., Georg, G., Gogolla, M., (eds.) OCL@MoDELS, volume 1285 of CEUR Workshop Proceedings, pp. 23–32. CEUR-WS.org (2014)
14. ISO/IEC 9075-(1–10) Information technology - Database languages - SQL. Technical report, International Organization for Standardization (2011). http://www.iso.org/iso

# Big Data Analytics and Distributed Systems

# Framework for Peer-to-Peer Data Sharing over Web Browsers

Vishwajeet Pattanaik[2]($\boxtimes$) (iD), Ioane Sharvadze[1]($\boxtimes$), and Dirk Draheim[2] (iD)

[1] Microsoft, Tallinn, Estonia
ioane.sharvadze@gmail.com

[2] Information Systems Group, Tallinn University of Technology, Tallinn, Estonia
{vishwajeet.pattanaik,dirk.draheim}@taltech.ee

**Abstract.** The Web was originally designed to be a decentralized environment where everybody could share a common information space to communicate and share information. However, over the last decade, the Web has become increasingly centralized. This has led to serious concerns about data ownership and misuse of personal data. While there are several approaches to solve these problems, none of them provides a simple and extendable solution. To this end, in this paper, we present an application-independent, browser-based framework for sharing data between applications over peer-to-peer networks. The framework aims to empower end-users with complete data ownership, by allowing them to store shareable web content locally, and by enabling content sharing without the risk of data theft or monitoring. We present the functional requirements, implementation details, security aspects, and limitations of the proposed framework. And finally, discuss the challenges that we encountered while designing the framework; especially, why it is difficult to create a server-less application for the Web.

**Keywords:** Data ownership · Decentralization · Human-computer interaction · Peer-to-peer · Social web · Security · Web apps · WebRTC

## 1 Introduction

The World Wide Web was originally designed to be a decentralized network and 'a common information space' where users could 'communicate by sharing information'[1]. However, as pointed out by numerous researchers, over the last decade the Web has become increasingly centralized [13,17,20]. Furthermore, the rising interest in social web platforms like Facebook, Twitter, and Google [9] is making the situation worse; as more and more users are drawn towards such closed platforms. Such platforms that have already opted to centralize user resources into closed data silos [17], each controlling their silos using proprietary authentications and access control mechanisms.

---

[1] W3C—The World Wide Web: A very short personal history.

© Springer Nature Switzerland AG 2019
T. K. Dang et al. (Eds.): FDSE 2019, LNCS 11814, pp. 207–225, 2019.
https://doi.org/10.1007/978-3-030-35653-8_14

Due to this nature of web applications, users typically end up creating dedicated accounts on multiple platforms; thereby bounding themselves to particular services and resources [17]. Furthermore, users trust such web applications and service providers to store and manage their personal data with the intention to receive personalized services. However, as recent incidents [2] indicate such centralized data silos could also be utilized to harvest user data [8], manipulate user mindset [1], and to spread fake news and propaganda [12].

Events like these have given rise to some serious concerns, not only about data ownership and misuse of personal data; but also about the inability of such applications to allow for secure data exchange between different platforms. While researchers have developed several remarkable artifacts [3,4,16–18] that attempt to resolve these challenges, however, most of these platforms are still not being utilized by end-users as much. A possible reason for this lack of acceptance might simply be the lack of technical know-how and coding skills required to fully utilize such artifacts. It's difficult to determine precisely 'why end-users might decide to adopt a technology and not the others'; as this (i.e., Acceptability Engineering) is still a rather new field of research, which needs to be developed further [10]. We argue that in case of general internet users, the reasons might simply be the lack of familiarity [11], and the heterogeneity of platforms and tools available online. We are convinced that by providing end-users with a secure platform that can be integrated into any browser, we should be able to provide end-users with a more fluid experience when sharing data/information online.

To this end, we set out to provide a solution that attempts to reduce dependency on centralized servers (i.e., data silos) and empowers end-users with true data ownership. We present a platform-independent, browser-based framework for sharing data between applications over peer-to-peer (P2P) networks. The framework aims to empower end-users with complete data ownership, by allowing them to locally store shareable data and then share it directly with other users; without the risk of data theft or monitoring.

Ultimately, we would like to integrate the said framework into our ongoing research [5,14] on 're-decentralizing the Web'; by eliminating the need for servers and allowing users to communicate with each other without any middleware. The proposed framework is designed to enable P2P communication for a crowdsourcing information system (CIS) called Tippanee [14]. The Tippanee CIS is currently being developed as Google Chrome browser extension that allows end-users to weave, critique and share web page elements, independent of content ownership on the Web. However, as mentioned earlier, due to the recent increase of interest in user privacy and data-ownership, it has become imperative that such a P2P framework must be designed as a 'generic system'. Developing such a generic framework should empower both web-developers and end-users, by providing Application Programming Interface (API) based server-free communication between applications and by preventing misuse of user data, respectively.

In this paper, we present the client library and web services, that allow applications to store data on user devices and share them over a P2P network.

We explain the functional requirements, implementation details, security aspects, and limitations of the framework. And finally, we discuss the challenges that we encountered while designing the framework; and especially, why it is difficult to create a server-less application for the Web.

## 2  Related Work

In this section, we briefly summarize recent scientific contributions that attempt to tackle the issues of data ownership and privacy. Each of these platforms allows users to create and share data via decentralized networks. Analyzing these platforms and understanding their approaches, contributions and limitations helped us identify the gaps; and thus, derive a clear problem definition.

### 2.1  Musubi

Musubi [4] is a mobile social application platform that enables users to share data in real-time feeds. The platform ensures data safety and privacy by supporting end-to-end public key encryption and allows users to interact with their friends directly through their address books. Additionally, the platform provides end-users with complete data ownership by allowing them to store all their data on their phones. The framework is limited to mobile app communications; however, since establishing direct P2P connections over mobile networks (3G) is not possible, data transfer is completely dependent on a centralized service Trusted Group Communication Protocol [4].

While Musubi's goals might seem similar to ours, there are some subtle differences in both. For instance, unlike the proposed system, Musubi only supports group sharing and does not support public data sharing. Also, Musubi always requires a server for data transfer, i.e. every single message sent between users must be routed through a server. Contrary to this, the proposed system does not require a server to store or relay data (in case both sender and receiver are online).

### 2.2  CIMBA

CIMBA or Client-Integrated Micro-Blogging Architecture [17] is a decentralized social web application that enables data ownership by allowing users to choose where their data is stored. The architecture uses WebID[2] [7,19] and WebID-TLS[3] to identify users at the Web scale and to authenticate requests.

The platform fully decouples the application web server from the user's database. And thus, allows users to have full control of their databases. The platform allows its users to decide which data they would like to share, with which web application, and which data they would like to keep private. As an added advantage, the platform also supports data reuse by allowing web apps to reuse the user's social graph; thus further unlocking the silos [17].

---

[2] W3C—WebIDs and the WebID Protocol.

[3] W3C—WebID Authentication over TLS (editor's draft).

## 2.3  Solid

Solid [13, 18] is a decentralized platform for social web applications, that allows users to manage their data independent of web applications. Unlike in conventional web applications where user data is stored and managed by the web application provider, Solid users are required to store their data in a personal online data stores (called pods). Web applications are allowed to access users' data, based on the permissions provided by the users. The users are identified using WebID [7, 19] and have full control over how their data is accessed. Users can also switch between applications and pods at any time. The platform uses Resource Description Framework (RDF) based resources to exchange data between applications and pods [13, 18].

We argue that although Solid supports data ownership, however, it still stores data on non-user devices. Also, for an average non-technical users tasks like setting up servers or finding free hosting services might seem really tedious. We are of the opinion that, removing the need for any configuration and storing users' data onto their personal computers should improve the users' experience. Also, since linked-data does not provide solutions for real-time P2P data sharing, it would be challenging to develop real-time social applications such as chats on such a platform.

## 2.4  Dokieli

Dokieli [3] is a decentralized browser-based authoring and annotation platform. Similar to CIMBA and Solid, the platform supports social interactions and allows users to retain the ownership of their data. Documents created in dokieli are both independent and interoperable, as they follow the standards and best practices of HTML, RDF, and Linked Data [3]. Like CIMBA and Solid, dokieli too enhances user's data ownership experience. Unfortunately, all of these platforms are bound by their technologies; which can discourage developers from adopting these recommendations. Finally, as mentioned earlier, none of these platforms allow storage on personal computers and end-to-end communication.

## 3  Challenges

Given this lack of a generic, application-independent data-sharing platform for P2P networks over the Web; in this paper, we attempt to provide answers to the following questions:

– **How to establish P2P network between web browsers?**
  The aim of this research question is to understand how P2P networks could be established over web browsers; and to examine how Socket.IO and WebRTC could be used to establish communication in such a scenario? This is also important as answering this question would help solve the NAT traversal [6] problem using JavaScript.

– **How to create a server-less P2P network?**
  This question is critical, as the answer would help us establish whether P2P
  networks can be initiated in truly server-less conditions. And, if that's not
  possible; what other alternate approaches could be used to reduce dependency
  on servers?
– **How to forward messages to a user who is currently offline?**
  Since the proposed framework has to be deployed over P2P networks, it is
  vital to understand how the system would behave if the message receiver is
  not online. By brief analysis, it would mean that one would not be able to
  establish a P2P connection in such scenario. However, would it be possible to
  devise a fallback solution that could still deliver messages? If so, how would
  the system function?

## 3.1   Functional Requirements

As stated previously, since the proposed framework was initially designed to be
a part of the Tippanee platform; to model adequate solutions, we decided to first
examine the requirements from our previous work in data management [5,14]
and then generalize these requirements for other applications. Since Tippanee
is a social application, it needs the ability to share and control data visibility.
Having such restrictions on data access means that proposed framework should
be built with security and privacy in mind. Also, from a developer's perspective,
it should be easy to integrate this functionality, and so the framework should be
simple enough to hide data management complexity from application developers.
  Keeping these factors in mind, we laid out the following functional requirements for the proposed P2P framework:

– **Private Share** means that the web content stored by a user (hereby referred
  to as *sender*) should be viewed/modified only by the same user and the data
  should only be available on the user's local computer.
– **Public Share** means that all members of *sender*'s community (or, network)
  should be able to search and download the stored web content.
– **Private Share Between Friends** is a mix of *Private Share* and *Public
  Share*, such that in this case the *sender* can share the stored web content
  with a selected set of members within the network. So, while for the selected
  members of the network, the content (or, message) would seem public; for the
  other members, the content would seem private. This means the framework
  should handle the delivery of the data to the peers from the *sender*'s device.
– **Offline Peer.** This requirement is crucial in the P2P framework as members
  of the network might not always be online to receive messages. Hence, the
  framework should be able to securely hold the message until the *receiver*
  comes online.
– **Saving the Data.** The framework should allow local storage, so users can
  view stored content even when they are not connected to the network; or
  in-case the shared content is lost or deleted by the *sender*.

– **Security & Integrity.** While the proposed network would be distributed, the framework should pay key attention to data authenticity. This is imperative as malicious users should not be allowed to tamper with the content shared by the *senders*. And the *receivers* should be able to verify if a message was sent by an authentic user. To enhance data ownership further, the servers in between should not be able to extract or read the shared data; i.e., the stored data should be encrypted.

– **Technical Requirements.** Finally, the framework should work with browser-based web applications and browser extensions. Since web applications and extensions may present different technical requirements for framework, the framework should be completely generic. Also, the framework should be able to run as background page (within the browser), so that the application can receive connections and share/receive data even when the extension is closed.

## 3.2 Limitations

During the initial literature review, we found that it is not possible to establish a P2P communication between users without a third party server [6]. The reason for this is that, in the real world environment, most devices on the Web are hidden behind Network Address Translators (NAT). This means that not all the users on the Web have a unique Internet Protocol (IP) address. NATs provide devices with a local address, which is only unique within the local network and not within the Wide Web. It is the NAT's job to translate local IPs into unique public IP and port configurations for communication with outside systems. This means that if a device is connected to a network with NAT, multiple devices within the network will receive same public IP, but with different ports configurations. Once a device is momentarily disconnected from the network, it might receive a different IP and port configuration; thereby forbidding incoming connection requests to the device.

To overcome this problem, peers should start requesting connections to each other simultaneously. In such a case, the NAT will most likely (in 64% cases for TCP connections) enable Peer-to-Peer connection. This technique is referred to as Hole Punching [6]. Unfortunately, this also means that in some 36% cases, it would not be even possible to send data to a peer without a middleware server. Keeping this issue in mind, one must provide a fallback mechanism in the form of a relay service; which we describe further, in the following sections.

## 4  Proposed Framework

Building on the requirements and limitations described in the previous sections; in this section, we present the different design choices we had to keep in mind while designing the proposed framework.

## 4.1   Why Server?

**P2P Connection Establishment.** In order to establish a P2P connection, it is necessary for both peers to share their IP addresses with one another. When both peers have each other's IP addresses, they will need to request connections simultaneously. However, as mentioned earlier, since most devices exist behind NATs, establishing a connection when either peer is behind a NAT would require NAT hole punching. For symmetric NAT traversal, the devices would have to start sending data to peer public IP & port; for this reason alone it is imperative to have a server, that allows two peers to share their public IP addresses and thus assist in establishing the P2P connection.

This challenge was resolved by the advent of Google's WebRTC (web real-time communications) protocol. WebRTC is a set of APIs that is implemented by most contemporary browsers. It was first implemented in Google Chrome browser and thus it fulfills the browser supporting requirements of our framework. Since WebRTC is only an API, to provide a complete solution, we had to develop a signaling implementation that could be used to establish WebRTC connection. To this end, we decided to use Socket.IO [10], since the library is well documented and widely popular.

With the WebRTC approach, before establishing the connection, both peers would have to first connect to the signaling server. Once both peers have exchanged their IPs, they can connect with each other and start sharing data directly (without the server).

**Public Data Holding.** In order to forward publicly shared data (or, messages), the data would have to be stored on a public server. Also, since members of the network might not be familiar with one another, it would not be possible to establish a P2P connection. And sending a request (to store the shared public message) to all members of the network would be extremely inefficient. Hence for the proposed network, we decided that all publicly shared data would be stored and indexed in the server. Peers who might choose to access the public data would be allowed to request for the same.

**Sharing Data When Peer Is Offline.** Another reason for using a server within the framework is that a peer might not be online when some data is being shared. Imagine a scenario where the *sender* shares a message with the *receiver*, but the *receiver* is not online. In this case when the *receiver* comes online, the *sender* may or may not be online. Without a server in place, it would not be possible for them to share the data unless both peers are online simultaneously. Hence, by simply using a server to hold undelivered messages temporarily, the issue of sharing messages with offline peers could be resolved.

Keeping these factors in mind we decided to include a server (as a fallback mechanism) in the proposed P2P framework.

## 4.2 Server Architecture

Taking into account the challenges we described in Sect. 3; in order to empower users with privacy and data ownership, the said server must achieve the following goals: the server should not be application-specific, the server's APIs should be implemented separately, and the server's role in the message exchange process should be kept to a bare minimum. Ultimately, the said server should be application-independent and should have negligible access to the hosted data.

Decoupling the applications from the server implementation in this manner would allow the use of different servers with different implementations that support the same APIs. This will provide server maintainers the freedom to choose how much (undelivered) data to hold, which applications to communicate with and to add additional security checks to secure the server. By nature of this solution, since the server would have no direct access to the stored data, it would not be able to check data integrity; and hence, users would be in charge of validating sender identity and data integrity.

Interestingly, the Musubi platform [4] also uses a similar methodology to secure user data. The platform allows developers to use common servers to share data between users. However, the data is encrypted such that only the users themselves can verify the sender's identity and data integrity. However, unlike the proposed solution, Musubi is designed for mobile phones and lacks peer-to-peer data sharing support.

**Solution.** To accomplish the requirements of P2P data sharing, we designed two different services. The first service allows peers to establish a connection (which we refer to as "Live-Rooms"). And, the second service supports message exchange and peer communication with offline users. We refer to this service as the "Message Box". As illustrated in Fig. 1, the first service is for establishing P2P connections, while, the second is just temporary data storage space, similar to a real-world post office. Both services are designed to be independent, and thus applications can choose different service providers, or opt to support only one of them.

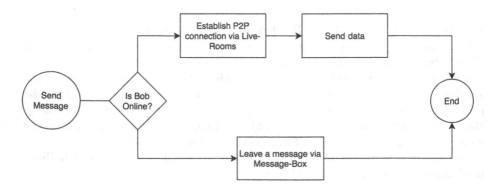

**Fig. 1.** Illustration of the message sending process

## 4.3   Live-Rooms

The 'Live-Rooms' service is designed to enable fast (real-time) data sharing between users with P2P traffic. The service is designed as a common space where online users gather and wait for incoming connections. Each user can connect to the 'Room' associated with their user ID. Whenever a user wants to connect to other users, they can connect to the Live-Room and ask for connection to specified users' ID. Once the request is complete, users can then decide whether they want to accept an incoming connection or not. Once two users are connected, they can send/receive data and messages, verify delivery and finally close connections when needed.

## 4.4   Message Box

The 'Message Box' service has a more extensive role within the framework. In order to achieve the required goals, the service must fulfill several functionalities: (1) list message-ID's for user; (2) download messages by message-IDs; (3) save shared messages; (4) list public messages by keys; (5) download public messages by keys; and (6) save public messages with keys.

Among these, the first three functionalities are required for message relay (when the *receiver* is not online). Whereas, the last three functions are required for storing/querying public data shared by users. Based on these requirements and functionalities, for our current implementation, we used a popular client-server architecture called REST [15].

## 4.5   Client-Side

To facilitate the development of various applications based on the proposed framework, the complexity of data handling is hidden from the application developers. The library is compiled into a single JavaScript file so that it can be added to HTML as a single script. Doing so allows the developers to use the framework's functionalities with a simple API. Also, this prevents the client library from exposing the inner implementation to the users, while providing an abstraction to manage (save, delete, receive, query) public, private and shared data.

**Configurations.** For the initial version of the client library we provide five configurable (optional) parameters including: 'Live-Rooms' URL, 'Message-Box' URL, 'Message-Box' synchronization interval, Local Database Name, and 'Live-Rooms' WebRTC configuration' (that contains STUN server URLs). For 'Live-Rooms' and 'Message Box' URLs, the default public service URLs are used. In our current implementation, these default services are maintained on the Heroku Cloud Application platform. In our implementation, the local database names are generated with default names, which are generated based on user IDs. This feature is important as, the database name can be changed based on changes in user ID; hence preventing users from reading other users' data. In case of automatic database names, the application uses the corresponding user's database.

Also, to further assist in establishing a P2P connection, 'Live-Rooms' WebRTC configuration is designed to allow changes to the default STUN server URLs. This provides developers with some flexibility as they can decide whether they would like to use the default STUN server (maintained by Google) or their own STUN servers (for more control over performance and security).

**API Usage.** To use the proposed library in a web application, developers simply have to import a single JavaScript library file. The library includes the following Javascript methods:

- **sync()** The Sync method provides a way to force synchronization between 'Message Box' and application. This is especially useful if the application needs to get fresh data and cannot wait for the scheduled update interval. In applications, such a scenario might occur when the user forces synchronization by clicking the refresh button.
- **fetchPublicDataByKey()** method comes into play when a user sends a request to read the public data. The client library fetches the 'Message Box' for all available public data and returns it to the user. It is important to note that, the returned public data is not saved onto the user's device unless the user requests for the same. Users are allowed to view the data available on the public channel, and they may then decide whether they would like to store a copy of the public data on their local device.
- **publish(key, callback)** The Publish method simply makes the shared data publicly available. This requires a key to make the data identifiable by other users. Once a piece of data is published, a copy of the same is then stored onto the server (by the 'Message-Box' service).
- **getByKey(key, callback)** This method is used to retrieve data with an application-defined key. Note that the key is not required to be unique, so users would either receive a list of results in the callback or, null if nothing is found.
- **getByAuthor(key, callback)** This method, works similar to the **get-ByKey** method, however the results are queried by author ID (i.e., the author's public key).
- **saveData(data, sharedWith, callback)** This method stores the shared data onto to server, but only until the recipient of the message comes online.
- Finally, the **listenDataChanges(callback)** method is a convenience method that synchronizes the application with the storage. If a user sends a message via 'Live-Rooms' or, retrieves a message through the 'Message-Box', the user gets new data objects in the callback. The method also allows for local database querying and displays fresh results if needed.

**Background Synchronization.** The proposed library is designed to work with both web applications and with browser extensions (only Google Chrome for now). The difference being that extensions can store unlimited data (within browser storage) and have the ability to synchronize data even if the user has not opened the application.

In the Google Chrome browser, extensions have a notion of background pages; that allow application developers to run scripts even when the HTML page is not open (or selected) by the user. The library uses the background page to establish and maintain 'Live-Rooms' connections, and to share/receive data by fetching new messages from the 'Message Box' at scheduled times. Unlike browser extensions, regular web applications can only support background synchronization when the application is open in a browser tab.

## 5   Implementations

As mentioned in Sect. 4.2 we designed the 'Live-Rooms', 'Message Box' and 'Client Library' modules as distinct entities. This helped us reduce coupling and allowed us to extend the functionalities without modifying other modules. The implementation code of the modules is available as a repository on GitHub.

### 5.1   Live-Rooms

The 'Live-Rooms' is designed using the Socket.IO library. The module is divided into two separate parts: the Web-Client and the Server-Client. The server-client is written in JavaScript Node.js framework. While the module could be designed using other JavaScript web frameworks, we choose Node.js as it is the most popular choice among developers[4].

The server is implemented using the Socket.IO library, as, for the proposed framework both server and client need to send bidirectional events. Consider the scenario, where a client might need to send several messages and then wait for an event from a server. For this reason, the client needs to have a consistent connection with the server, so that the server can notify the client when other peers request connection. Other solutions like pooling could be applied in this scenario, but since clients will have to send several signaling messages through the server, managing several signaling messages with pooling approach would be less efficient and complex. The socket implementation, on the other hand, can tackle multiple bidirectional messages, due to its notion of events. The first ("connect") event occurs when the user connects to the server. At this point, the user has a ready socket that can be used to send and receive a message to and from the server.

---

[4] Stack Overflow—Developer Survey Results 2017.

**Message Contract and Events.** Once a user is connected to the server, the server expects several types of events from the user. Every message sent by the user must be a JavaScript object with *fromPublicKey*, *toPublicKey* and *data* attributes. The 'fromPublicKey' holds the public key of the message sender, the 'toPublicKey' holds the public key of the receiver, and other attributes are shared as 'data'.

In our implementation, the first event expected by the server is called 'enter_my_room'. The event fires when a user is ready to provide his/her public key. The server then adds the user to a 'room' named with same public key. In Socket.IO, this notation of 'room' enables us to label sockets. This also helps to check if a peer is online and if the peer has received redirect messages from other peers; thereby enabling multiple parallel signaling between peers. If an event fails, the server usually sends an "error" event to notify the client about the failed action. The server also sends a failed message so that the client can reset their state and try again if needed.

Once a user joins the said room, the server is ready to notify all peers of the connection requests. The user can also initiate a peer connection at this stage. To initiate connection requests, the event 'connection_request' is called. Note that this event also requires peer public key, so that peers can receive an event. At this stage a peer can either accept or ignore 'connection_request'. By accepting the request client starts sending events named 'signalling_message'; which are redirected from one peer to another. The process of sending WebRTC signaling messages leads to establishment of P2P connections (as illustrated in Fig. 2).

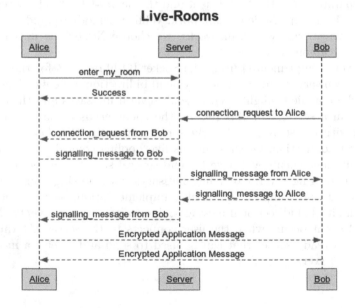

**Fig. 2.** Illustration of the P2P network establishment process

## 5.2    Message-Box and Storage

The Message-Box is designed using the JavaScript framework called Express.js. The Message-Box is designed as a REST API and includes methods to – (1) list all messages for user, (2) get messages by message IDs, (3) save messages, (4) list all public messages by keys, (5) get public messages by IDs, and (6) publish messages. Message-Box documentation is deployed on online API documentation tool (see Fig. 3), that provides the possibility to describe API easily, add sample responses, and mock the functionalities. For storing messages, we used the NoSQL database Mongo DB (please see Fig. 4 for the message schema.) in our implementation.

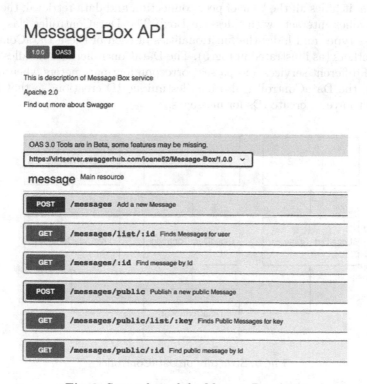

**Fig. 3.** Screenshot of the Message-Box API

**Deployment and Evaluation.** To evaluate the proposed framework and the implemented artifact, we deployed a web application on Heroku with the database established in mLab. The mLab database platform was then connected to the 'Message-Box' service and the Heroku server.

**DataController.** The DataController is the main class that handles all data within the system. It holds the system state and delegates functionalities to

```
var messageSchema = mongoose.Schema({
    message: String,
    sharedWith: [String],
    key: String,
    public: Boolean,
    author: String
});
```

**Fig. 4.** Message database schema

the different data controllers, namely: Local, Live and Cloud. The Local DataController's task is to save/query data in local storage. While the Live Data-Controller interacts with 'Live-Rooms' service and saves/receives data via P2P connection, it hides all the logic of peer connection and data retrieval; the Cloud DataController interacts with 'Message Box'. The DataController class unites all of these types and hides the functionalities of each of these DataControllers from the others (as illustrated in Fig. 5). The DataController also handles configuration of different services and passes corresponding parameters when needed. Internally, the DataController also handles unique ID creation, so that library users don't have to create IDs for messages.

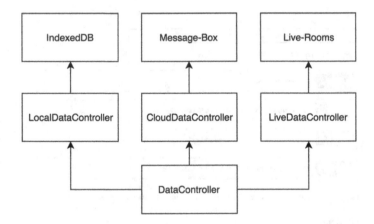

**Fig. 5.** Structure of DataController

The different stages of the DataController are as flows:

- When initialized, it creates all the controllers.
- During synchronization it tries to fetch data from Cloud DataController.
- The 'getByKey' and 'getByAuthor' function delegates to Local DataController, if the user is searching current data.
- The 'saveData' first saves data with Local DataController, then tries Live DataController, if a peer is not online, the message is saved to the Cloud DataController.
- The 'listenDataChanges' waits for data updates from Live and Cloud Data-Controllers.

**Live DataController.** The Live DataController as described above, is responsible for using 'Live-Rooms' service. Upon creation, it connects users to their rooms and listens to 'connection_request' and 'signaling_message' events. When a 'connection_request' is received, it starts the P2P connection establishment process. The connection establishment process starts with the gathering of ICE (Interactive Connectivity Establishment) candidates. The ICE candidates are then sent to the remote peer using 'signaling_message'. The ICE candidates are needed to perform NAT traversal. By default, ICE candidates are configured to be free STUN services provided by Google. When remote peers receive a signaling message, they also start to gather ICE candidates and send them to their peer using 'Live-Rooms'. After the ICE candidates are shared, data channels are opened and users can start sending data using the P2P connection. The Live DataController also holds the opened data channels so that it doesn't have to create new connections every time user sends a piece of information. When the data channel is broken, new connection establishment process is started; if multiple errors occur, a return null callback is sent to the sender, so that other service can try sending information.

**Cloud DataController.** Cloud DataController handles 'Message-Box' service interaction. It has several public functions: 'sync', 'save', 'publish', and 'fetch public by key'. When a 'sync message is fired', it connects to the message box listing endpoint, gets a list of messages and downloads them one by one. 'Save' and 'publish' functions on the other hand, only send a message to the server. 'Save' requires a list of public keys, that have access to the message. Whereas, 'publish' makes the message publicly available and associates them with the key. Finally, the 'fetch public by key' searches for public messages associated with key and downloads them.

**Local DataController.** For implementing Local DataController IndexedDB is used. We choose to use IndexedDB due to its good browser compatibility and flexible API, which helps to store information on local disk and its ability to query using different attributes. As name suggests, IndexedDB can index data using keys to provide fast retrieval of the information. Because the framework requirement is to provide two queries, by key and by author, two indexes are created. Both keys are not unique, so the API returns a list of results sorted by creation date or null in case of errors. Before saving the data, the controller checks if both key and ID are present. Note that, as mentioned previously, the ID is generated by DataController.

**Background Page.** When running in the Chrome app, the client has to manage its state in the background page. In this case the application is able to synchronize messages even when the program is not running in the foreground. This is an important part of the requirements, as clients might not always run the application. Initially we tried to construct the 'DataController' instance in background page and then attempted to access it directly from the foreground application for querying and saving. Unfortunately, this approach did not work, since the foreground and background pages run in different contexts, and while it is possible to access primitive variables using 'getBackgroundPage' method, Chrome browser can only send JSON-serializable types between pages. Since we are using socket objects in 'DataController', it cannot be JSON-serialized properly; hence, it is not possible to have the 'DataController' in the foreground page. To overcome this challenge the 'DataControllerClient' and the 'DataController-Receiver' were created. These two classes reside within different pages/contexts of the application. Because it's impossible to directly interact with objects that are in the background page, JSON messages (that contain action information) are sent to the background page, which it receives and then executes the actions with DataController.

To pass information from the foreground page to the background page, we used 'Chrome Message Passing', where 'DataControllerClient' can send a JSON object with 'action' and 'params' attributes. The 'action' attribute points to the DataController method that should be called, whereas, the 'params' are parameters that need to be pass to the method. 'DataControllerReceiver' listens to the message in the background page, reads 'action' and executes method in same context with provided 'params'.

Since the 'DataControllerClient' is for application use, that is why it is created on the front page. It has the very same API as 'DataController', with a difference that it delegates functionality to 'DataController' that resides in 'DataControllerReceiver'. Figure 6 shows this behavior in case 'DataControllerClient' is instantiated in Chrome Application. If the 'DataControllerClient' is created in regular web applications, then there is no need for a background page; this is why the client creates a 'DataController' inside class and executes actions locally. For this reason, application can use 'DataControllerClient' and run the same code as a Chrome Extension or a Web application, and the 'DataControllerClient' can handle both cases without changing the code.

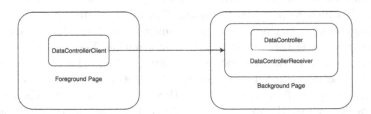

**Fig. 6.** Illustration of 'DataController' in Chrome Extension

## 6   Conclusion

To summarize, in this paper we set out to design and develop a P2P data-sharing framework that enables developers to create applications with powerful data ownership and privacy features. The proposed framework is motivated by the rising issue of data ownership and privacy in the World Wide Web. To this end, we first provided a brief description of the state-of-art in data ownership and privacy. Drawing from the insights and solutions provided by these artifacts, we identified several requirements that when implemented as a framework could support users by providing them more data ownership and by reducing the role of servers in data exchange over the Web. The proposed framework is a simple tool that can be integrated into various kinds of applications. Our trials show that such a framework is undoubtedly useful for chat applications, where real-time data sending via peer-to-peer networks is critical. The framework is explicitly designed to secure user data and hence makes tampering with data extremely difficult. Applications based on the framework can create public channels where any user can query using application-defined keys and can share data both within closed groups and in public. Our implementation demonstrates data synchronization even when peers are offline. Additionally, the framework is built with multiple parts and services; and hence can be easily extended with custom functionalities. Developers are allowed to make changes to multiple parts of the framework and can, therefore, extend the functionalities of the system according to their requirements. Independent developers are also allowed to implement custom policies for data handling; whereas organizational implementations of the framework allows enforcement of user authentication on data sharing services, such as 'Message Box' and 'Live-Rooms', so that only people with specific access can use a service. As part of our future work, we plan to improve the framework further, based on support from the community. We would like to better understand developers' needs for data management and evolve the proposed framework into a more useful tool, for both developers and end-users.

# References

1. Bakir, V., McStay, A.: Fake news and the economy of emotions. Digit. J. **6**(2), 154–175 (2018). https://doi.org/10.1080/21670811.2017.1345645
2. Cadwalladr, C., Graham-Harrison, E.: Revealed: 50 million Facebook profiles harvested for Cambridge analytica in major data breach, March 2018. https://www.theguardian.com/news/2018/mar/17/cambridge-analytica-facebook-influence-us-election. The Guardian. Accessed 13 Aug 2019
3. Capadisli, S., Guy, A., Verborgh, R., Lange, C., Auer, S., Berners-Lee, T.: Decentralised authoring, annotations and notifications for a read-write web with dokieli. In: Cabot, J., De Virgilio, R., Torlone, R. (eds.) ICWE 2017. LNCS, vol. 10360, pp. 469–481. Springer, Cham (2017). https://doi.org/10.1007/978-3-319-60131-1_33
4. Dodson, B., Vo, I., Purtell, T., Cannon, A., Lam, M.: Musubi: disintermediated interactive social feeds for mobile devices. In: Proceedings of the 21st International Conference on World Wide Web, WWW 2012, pp. 211–220. ACM, New York (2012). https://doi.org/10.1145/2187836.2187866
5. Draheim, D., Felderer, M., Pekar, V.: Weaving social software features into enterprise resource planning systems. In: Piazolo, F., Felderer, M. (eds.) Novel Methods and Technologies for Enterprise Information Systems. LNISO, vol. 8, pp. 223–237. Springer, Cham (2014). https://doi.org/10.1007/978-3-319-07055-1_18

6. Ford, B., Srisuresh, P., Kegel, D.: Peer-to-peer communication across network address translators. In: Proceedings of the Annual Conference on USENIX Annual Technical Conference, ATEC 2005, pp. 13–13. USENIX Association, Berkeley (2005). http://dl.acm.org/citation.cfm?id=1247360.1247373

7. Heitmann, B., Kim, J.G., Passant, A., Hayes, C., Kim, H.G.: An architecture for privacy-enabled user profile portability on the web of data. In: Proceedings of the 1st International Workshop on Information Heterogeneity and Fusion in Recommender Systems, HetRec 2010, pp. 16–23. ACM, New York (2010). https://doi.org/10.1145/1869446.1869449

8. Isaak, J., Hanna, M.J.: User data privacy: Facebook, Cambridge analytica, and privacy protection. Computer **51**(8), 56–59 (2018). https://doi.org/10.1109/MC.2018.3191268

9. Kaplan, A.M., Haenlein, M.: Users of the world, unite! The challenges and opportunities of social media. Bus. Horiz. **53**(1), 59–68 (2010). https://doi.org/10.1016/j.bushor.2009.09.003

10. Kim, H.C.: Acceptability engineering: the study of user acceptance of innovative technologies. J. Appl. Res. Technol. **13**(2), 230–237 (2015). https://doi.org/10.1016/j.jart.2015.06.001

11. Knight, R.: Convincing skeptical employees to adopt new technology, August 2015. https://hbr.org/2015/03/convincing-skeptical-employees-to-adopt-new-technology. Harvard Business Review. Accessed 13 Aug 2019

12. Lazer, D.M.J., et al.: The science of fake news. Science **359**(6380), 1094–1096 (2018). https://doi.org/10.1126/science.aao2998

13. Mansour, E., et al.: A demonstration of the solid platform for social web applications. In: Proceedings of the 25th International Conference Companion on World Wide Web, WWW 2016 Companion, pp. 223–226. International World Wide Web Conferences Steering Committee, Republic and Canton of Geneva (2016). https://doi.org/10.1145/2872518.2890529

14. Pattanaik, V., Norta, A., Felderer, M., Draheim, D.: Systematic support for full knowledge management lifecycle by advanced semantic annotation across information system boundaries. In: Mendling, J., Mouratidis, H. (eds.) CAiSE 2018. LNBIP, vol. 317, pp. 66–73. Springer, Cham (2018). https://doi.org/10.1007/978-3-319-92901-9_7

15. Richards, R.: Representational state transfer (REST), pp. 633–672. Apress, Berkeley (2006). https://doi.org/10.1007/978-1-4302-0139-7_17

16. Sambra, A., Guy, A., Capadisli, S., Greco, N.: Building decentralized applications for the social web. In: Proceedings of the 25th International Conference Companion on World Wide Web, WWW 2016 Companion, pp. 1033–1034. International World Wide Web Conferences Steering Committee, Republic and Canton of Geneva (2016). https://doi.org/10.1145/2872518.2891060

17. Sambra, A., Hawke, S., Berners-Lee, T., Kagal, L., Aboulnaga, A.: CIMBA: client-integrated microblogging architecture. In: Proceedings of the 2014 International Conference on Posters & Demonstrations Track, ISWC-PD 2014, vol. 1272, pp. 57–60. CEUR-WS.org, Aachen (2014). http://dl.acm.org/citation.cfm?id=2878453.2878468

18. Sambra, A.V., et al.: Solid: a platform for decentralized social applications based on linked data. Technical report, MIT CSAIL & Qatar Computing Research Institute (2016). https://www.semanticscholar.org/paper/Solid-%3A-A-Platform-for-Decentralized-Social-Based-Sambra-Mansour/5ac93548fd0628f7ff8ff65b5878d04c79c513c4

19. Story, H., Harbulot, B., Jacobi, I., Jones, M.: FOAF+SSL: RESTful authentication for the social web. In: CEUR Workshop Proceedings (2009)
20. Van Kleek, M., et al.: Social personal data stores: the nuclei of decentralised social machines. In: Proceedings of the 24th International Conference on World Wide Web, WWW 2015 Companion, pp. 1155–1160. ACM, New York (2015). https://doi.org/10.1145/2740908.2743975

# Efficiently Semantic-Aware Pairwise Similarity: an Applicable Use-Case

Trong Nhan Phan[✉]

Faculty of Computer Science and Engineering, HCMC University of Technology,
VNU-HCM, Ho Chi Minh City, Vietnam
nhanpt@hcmut.edu.vn

**Abstract.** Pairwise similarity is an essential operation in multidisciplinary fields of study. However, its operation is expensive due to its complexity as well as the evolution of big data. Besides, similarity scores without semantics leads to neither accurate nor practical results. In this paper, we study the problem of pairwise similarity in terms of semantics, efficiency, and increment. More concretely, we build our own synonym database and organize it in a reflexive synonym index to support us in semantic-aware pairwise similarity. In addition, we employ cache to perform incremental similarity computing in the process of pair-by-pair similarity search. Moreover, we design our feature-based hierarchy to eliminate irrelevant candidate objects before doing pairwise similarity. Furthermore, we analyze a practical case and apply our method into such social network-based applications in order to demonstrate its feasibility and efficiency in reality.

**Keywords:** Pairwise similarity · Indexing · Semantics · Increment · Multi-feature

## 1 Introduction

Pairwise similarity is a popular operation aiming at similarity between all pairs in a database. Also, this operation is well-known in different fields of study such as machine learning and data mining [12,13], similarity search [16], and protein-protein interaction [15]. In fact, pairwise similarity is not a new problem, but it has to face big challenges due to its operation complexity. For instance, if we have n objects in our database, the complexity is $O(n^2)$. Besides, big data still enhances the complexity of pairwise similarity. With the rapid development of technology as well as application, both generated, collected, and processed data become larger than ever [3]. Thus, it poses a new challenge on traditional processing. Moreover, similarity search in general and pairwise similarity in particular need to consider semantics. Without it, the similarity result would be neither accurate nor practical in reality.

On the other hand, social network-based applications provide strong interactions and links among their users, including matching and recommendation.

© Springer Nature Switzerland AG 2019
T. K. Dang et al. (Eds.): FDSE 2019, LNCS 11814, pp. 226–238, 2019.
https://doi.org/10.1007/978-3-030-35653-8_15

For example, some would like to search for those who have similar gender, age, location, interest, relationship, hobby, education, and so on. To get these functionalities more interesting, the similarity concept can be used as their core. With a very large amount of social networking users, it is important to have a fast similarity computing over its complexity.

In this paper, we propose an efficiently semantic-aware pairwise similarity method while considering additional emerging data. Our method may be applied into various application domains such as social network-based applications. Specifically, our main contributions are as follows:

– We add semantic feature in the process of pairwise similarity and build a reflexive synonym index to improve its search performance.
– We present our way for incremental similarity computing by using cached data.
– We show our strategy to eliminate redundant candidates for multi-feature pairwise similarity.
– We analyze a practical use-case that shows how our proposed method is applied into a social network-based application.

The rest of paper is organized as follows. Section 2 presents our related work. Additionally, Sect. 3 introduces our background related to similarity search and pairwise similarity. In Sect. 4, we propose our method for efficient pairwise similarity. After that, we analyze a practical use-case in Sect. 5 before making our remarks in Sect. 6.

## 2    Related Work

Xie et al. [11] introduce a profile matching algorithm based on bloom filter for proximity-based mobile social networking. In addition, the authors present a novel similarity-measuring method by considering time-based features and user interests in mobile social networking. Having a different approach, Gautam et al. [4] propose a profile matching architecture in online social network with unique identification number. Meanwhile, Phan and Dang [8] propose a lightweight indexing approach for efficient batch similarity processing with MapReduce. Their main idea is to build lightweight indexes that speed up the performance of similarity search in terms of single and query batch processing. Moreover, they employ MapReduce to deal with large amounts of data. Nevertheless, semantics is not counted in these studies.

In another work, Gray et al. [5] show a random forest-based similarity measure for multi-model classification, which is based on pairwise similarity. The method is applied into medical images to classify Alzheimer. Besides, Xia et al. [10] use pairwise similarity matrix to train image data for image retrieval in large data sets while Yi et al. [14] address semi-supervised clustering algorithms exploring pairwise similarity to improve clustering accuracy. In parallel, Kang et al. [6] applies pairwise similarity into clustering relevant factors in natural images to detect text lines. With the approach that is aware of semantics,

Amiri et al. [1] research on context-sensitive auto-encoders for text pair similarity. Nevertheless, those literature focuses on applying similarity computing for classification based on machine learning while leaves the complexity solving in the process of pairwise similarity behind.

## 3 Preliminaries

### 3.1 Similarity Queries

Given a corpus, denoted as $\Omega$, consisting of a set of objects $Obj_n$, which is formally represented as $\Omega = \{Obj_1, Obj_2, Obj_3, \ldots, Obj_n\}$, similarity search [17] is the principle operation that retrieves all objects that satisfy required constraints in the corpus $\Omega$. These kinds of constraints may be different from query to query. Depending on a particular constraint, we have the variety of typical types of similarity queries as follows.

- **Pairwise Similarity Query.** For each document object in the corpus $\Omega$, the similarity search computes the similarity score of one object with every (n-1) other objects in $\Omega$.
- **Pivot Query.** When given a query object called a pivot $Q_i$, the similarity search computes how much similar the pair $(Q_i, Obj_j)$ is for every objects $Obj_j$ in $\Omega$.
- **Range Query.** When given a pre-defined similarity threshold $\epsilon$, the similarity search gets all objects in the corpus $\Omega$, whose similarity scores are greater or equal to $\epsilon$.
- **K-Nearest Neighbor Query.** When given a query object $Q_i$ and a pre-defined k parameter, the similarity search retrieves k objects that are the most similar to the query object $Q_i$.

### 3.2 Similarity Measures

A similarity measure is a method to evaluate how similar a pair is. There are many popular similarity measures such as Euclidean distance, Cosine similarity, Hamming distance, or Jaccard coefficient [17] to produce similarity scores. Normally, the similarity score is usually standardized into the interval [0, 1]. If the similarity value of a pair is close to 1, it means that the pair is more similar. In contrast, if the similarity value of a pair is near to 0, it means that the pair is less similar.

Sometimes, a similarity distance concept is used rather than similarity measure. It is derived by (1 - similarity score). In this paper, we use Jaccard coefficient, a well-known metric for fast set-based similarity [8], to illustrate our method as follow.

$$SIM(Q_j, D_p) = \frac{\parallel Q_j \cap D_p \parallel}{\parallel Q_j \cup D_p \parallel} \tag{1}$$

In that, $\parallel Q_j \cap D_p \parallel$ is the intersection cardinality between $Q_j$ and $D_p$ while $\parallel Q_j \cup D_p \parallel$ is the union cardinality between $Q_j$ and $D_p$.

# 4   Our Proposed Solution

## 4.1   Semantic-Aware Similarity

Most of the time, doing similarity search is not aware of semantics, which leads to inaccurate non-exact matching results. For example, consider a simple case with two sentences as follows:

Sentence 1 ($S_1$): "Dad brings me to the Disney World today."
Sentence 2 ($S_2$): "My father takes me to the Disney land."

If we lexically compute the similarity score between the two sentences $S_1$ and $S_2$, we see that $S_1$ and $S_2$ share 4 italics words as { *"me"*, *"to"*, *"the"*, *"Disney"*}. With Jaccard coefficient for instance, we have the result as follow:

$S_1$: "Dad brings *me to the Disney* World today."
$S_2$: "My father takes *me to the Disney* land."

$$SIM(S_1, S_2) = \frac{4}{(16 - 4)} = \frac{1}{3} = 0.33 \tag{2}$$

However, our brains say that two sentences should be the same. It is because they consider semantics of the whole sentences rather than lexical words. Let us consider the two sentences $S_1$ and $S_2$ in another more semantic way such as synonyms. In this example, we employ WordNet [2,7,9] to look for synonym words. An example of synonym word list is illustrated in Table 1. As a result, if we re-compute the similarity score between the two sentences, where $S_1$ and $S_2$ share 6 italics words as { *"dad"*/*"father"*, *"bring"*/*"take"*, *"me"*, *"to"*, *"the"*, *"Disney"*}, with Jaccard coefficient for instance, we have the result as follow:

$S_1$: *"Dad brings me to the Disney* World today."
$S_2$: "My *father takes me to the Disney* land."

$$SIM(S_1, S_2) = \frac{6}{(16 - 6)} = \frac{3}{5} = 0.6 \tag{3}$$

As we observe that there are synonyms from the two sentences. Specifically, we have two synonym pairs as "dad" similar to "father" and "bring" similar to "take." Consequently, the intersection between the two sentences has two more common elements, and we get the final similarity score as 0.6, which is higher than the previous similarity score 0.33. The new score, therefore, reflects better similarity in terms of semantics than the old score.

## 4.2   Reflexive Synonym Index

In this section, we propose to build our own synonym database so that we can achieve the two-folds:

**Table 1.** An example of synonym word list.

| No. | Word | Synonym |
|---|---|---|
| ... | ... | ... |
| 200 | dad | dada, daddy, pa, papa, pappa, pop |
| 300 | bring | convey, take, work, play, wreak, make for, get, fetch |
| 400 | world | universe, existence, creation, cosmos, macrocosm, domain, reality, earth, globe, populace, public, human race, humanity, humankind, human beings, humans, mankind, man |
| 500 | land | ground, soil, domain, demesne, dry land, earth, solid ground, terra firma, country, state, kingdom, realm, estate, landed estate, acres, demesne, nation, commonwealth, res publica, body politic |
| ... | ... | ... |

- Our synonym database is independent of that of third party;
- We can speed up the synonym search by re-organizing synonym words in an indexing structure;

The former means that we have our synonym database ownership for our application while the latter means that we can have our synonyms as indexes to faster find them in the database. If we have a synonym database as in Table 1, the complexity, on the average, for linearly searching a synonym is $O(n)$. In order to reduce the searching cost, we re-organize our database in an indexing structure as shown in Fig. 1. In that, we organize each word in the form of key $K_i$, and its synonyms in the form of value $V_j$. It is worth noting that those $K_i$ and $V_j$ are organized in an order fashion. When there is a search for synonym, we can perform binary search rather than linear search on those $K_i$ and $V_j$. As a result, the complexity, on the average, for searching a synonym is $O(\log_2 n)$.

Another problem is to ensure the availability of searching synonyms in our dictionary. For instance, if we look for the synonyms of "dad," we can obtain them from the synonym list in the row number 200 as illustrated in Table 1. However, what if we want to search for the synonyms of "daddy," it is unavailable in the Word column, but in the Synonym column (i.e., the synonym list). In this situation, we need to look for the synonym lists that contain the word "daddy," which is inefficient in terms of performance. Other than avoiding linear search, we build our synonym database in a reflexive way to enhance the synonym search as follows:

- Firstly, we need to build a basic synonym database. We obtain the word list form the English dictionary, then we search each word for its synonym list from a reliable source like WordNet [2,7,9]. Our initial result looks like those in Table 1;
- Secondly, we re-organize our synonym database according to our indexing scheme as shown in Fig. 1;
- Thirdly, for each key $K_i$, we scan the value $V_j$, and for each value $V_j$, we check whether the value $V_j$ exists in the key $K_i$ with its synonym list or not. If not,

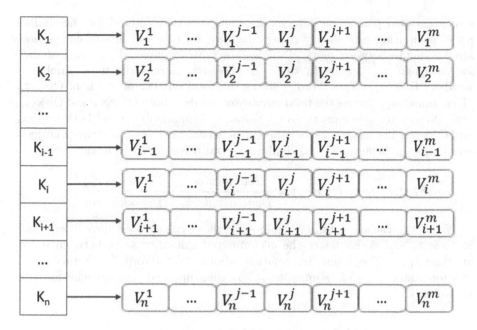

**Fig. 1.** Synonym indexing.

we create a new one with full list of synonyms. If existing, we complement the full list of synonyms when necessary. For example, we scan the value $V_j$ of the key "dad," correspondingly with {"dada", "daddy", "pa", "papa", "pappa", "pop"}. For the word "dada," we check whether it exists in the key. If no, we create a new key "dada" with full list of synonyms {"dad", "daddy", "pa", "papa", "pappa", "pop"}. If yes, we ensure that the key "dada" has that full list of synonyms. The checking process is repeated for the remaining words of the value $V_j$ of the key "dad." Doing by this way, we already build our reflexive synonym index.

## 4.3 Incremental Computing

There would be no problem if the similarity score between a pair is static. Unfortunately, the score usually changes when there are new data updated between a pair. It may happen in many typical scenarios like social network-based applications. As a consequence, when there is any change between a pair, we have to re-compute their similarity score. On the one hand, calculating pairwise similarity is costly due to a large amount of pairs. On the other hand, the similarity re-computing process includes operations we have already computed before hand. Therefore, it would be inefficient to do pairwise similarity whenever there are new data that emerge in such applications.

In our method, we would like to do pairwise similarity in an incremental manner. In order to do that, we build our cache to store computed similarity scores between pairs. The data in the cache are then re-used for the similarity re-computing process. By doing this way, we can save lots of calculations already made between pairs. Table 2 shows an example of our cached data for each pair at time $t_k$. In that, "TotalWord$_x$" stores the total number of words of Object$_x$, "TotalWord$_y$" stores the total number of words of Object$_y$, "Denominator$_{xy}$" stores the total number of words of both Object$_x$ and Object$_y$, and "Numerator$_{xy}$" stores the total number of common words of both Object$_x$ and Object$_y$. Let us assume that there is new data at time $t_{k+1}$ between Object$_x$ and Object$_y$, the accumulated similarity score is computed as follow:

$$SIM(Object_x, Object_y) = \frac{Numerator_{xy}^{t_k} + Numerator_{xy}^{t_{k+1}}}{Denominator_{xy}^{t_k} + Denominator_{xy}^{t_{k+1}}} \quad (4)$$

With the cached data, we can re-use those calculations have been made at time $t_k$ and derive faster the accumulated similarity score between a pair at time $t_{k+1}$. The latest information about "TotalWord$_x$", "TotalWord$_y$", "Denominator$_{xy}$", and "Numerator$_{xy}$" is then updated in the cache for later re-usability.

Table 2. An example of cached data at time $t_k$.

| Object$_1$-Object$_2$ | $TotalWord_1 = \sum_{i=1}^{n} W_1^i$ |
|---|---|
| | $TotalWord_2 = \sum_{j=1}^{m} W_2^j$ |
| | $Denominator_{12} = \sum_{i,j=1}^{n,m} (W_1^i \cup W_2^j)$ |
| | $Numerator_{12} = \sum_{i,j=1}^{n,m} (W_1^i \cap W_2^j)$ |
| Object$_1$-Object$_3$ | $TotalWord_1 = \sum_{i=1}^{n} W_1^i$ |
| | $TotalWord_3 = \sum_{j=1}^{m} W_3^j$ |
| | $Denominator_{13} = \sum_{i,j=1}^{n,m} (W_1^i \cup W_3^j)$ |
| | $Numerator_{13} = \sum_{i,j=1}^{n,m} (W_1^i \cap W_3^j)$ |
| ... | ... |
| Object$_x$-Object$_y$ | $TotalWord_x = \sum_{i=1}^{n} W_x^i$ |
| | $TotalWord_y = \sum_{j=1}^{m} W_y^j$ |
| | $Denominator_{xy} = \sum_{i,j=1}^{n,m} (W_x^i \cup W_y^j)$ |
| | $Numerator_{xy} = \sum_{i,j=1}^{n,m} (W_x^i \cap W_y^j)$ |

## 4.4  Multi-feature Pairwise Similarity

In many application scenario, we may need to compute pairwise similarity between two objects, which is based on multiple features. For instance, two users in social network-based application may want to look for their similarity about gender, age, location, interest, relationship, hobby, education, and so on. It would be a big cost when we do pairwise similarity for each required feature. To speed up the performance of similarity search, we build a feature hierarchy to filter those not relevant to our need. In other words, we may choose some features as pivots to obtain a subset of candidates on the remaining features. This subset is expected to be much smaller than the universal candidate set.

As illustrated in Fig. 2, there are two features in the feature hierarchy. We can follow the branch from the root to obtain the subset of candidates such as those have the "Value 1" from "Feature 1" and "Value 12" from "Feature 2." For other example, if a user wants to look for those who are similar to her or him on gender, age, and hobby, we only compute similarity for those who have the same gender and age as the user's.

Once we obtain the candidate set, we can derive pairwise similarity between A and B by the following equation:

$$SIM(A, B) = \frac{C_1}{F_1} * W_1 + \frac{C_2}{F_2} * W_2 + ... + \frac{C_n}{F_n} * W_n$$

$$where \sum_{i=1}^{n} W_i = 1 \tag{5}$$

In that, $C_i$ is the common part of the whole set of feature $F_i$, and $W_i$ is the weight for each corresponding feature $F_i$ in the feature set.

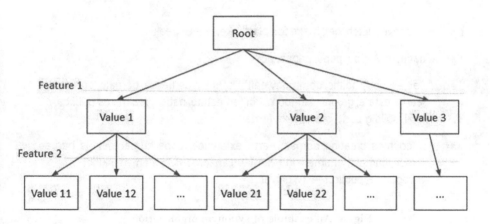

**Fig. 2.** An example of feature hierarchy.

## 5   An Applicable Use-Case

### 5.1   Application Scenario

To better illustrate our method for efficiently semantic-aware pairwise similarity, we apply it into a social network-based application like Friendster[1] or

---

[1] http://www.friendster.com.

Friendfinder[2]. In this application, there is a need for a user to search others for similarity about gender, age, location, interest, relationship, hobby, education, and so on. In addition, users can look for similar timelines so that they can share their emotions or activities within a day. If they have common sympathy, they may be friend candidates.

In order to support these functionalities, we firstly organize our dictionary, where we can search for synonyms, and then perform pairwise similarity search as described in the following sub-sections.

## 5.2   Synonym Organization

With regard to our synonym indexing method in Sect. 4.2, we organize synonym words in a form of key-value. Figure 3 shows our example of synonym organization. In that, we organize the key values in an alphabet manner, and it happens the same with the value list corresponding to the key. It is worth noting that words are fulfilled to have reflexive synonym index.

In our application, we employ Google Firebase[3], which is well-known for its real-time database with efficiency and low latency, for our dictionary indexing.

```
[.]: "..."

bring: "convey, fetch, get, make for, play, take, work, wreak"

dad: "dada, daddy, pa, papa, pappa, pop"

land: "acres, body politic, commonwealth, country, demesne, domain, dry land,
        earth, estate, ground, kingdom, landed estate, nation, realm, res publica,
        soil, solid ground, state, terra firma"

world: "cosmos, creation, domain, earth, existence, globe, human beings, human
        race, humanity, humankind, humans, macrocosm, man, mankind,
        populace, public, reality, universe"
```

**Fig. 3.** An example of synonym organization.

## 5.3   Cache Management

In order to implement our incremental computing as discussed in Sect. 4.3, we build our cached data as illustrated in Fig. 4. In our cache, we keep the data in the form of key-value pair per day. The key is the ID pair of two users, and the value is the cached information of that two users at the latest time.

---

[2] https://getfriendfinder.com.

[3] https://firebase.google.com/.

**Fig. 4.** An example of cached data from our application.

### 5.4   Friend Recommendation

In our application, friend recommendation is an interesting feature that recommends friends to users based on their profiles. More specifically, our challenge is to find those that are the most similar to a particular user with regard to his or her gender, age, location, interest, and characteristic. Due to the fact that pairwise similarity in this case is more expensive, we need to build a profile hierarchy to support us filtering redundant pairs in advance.

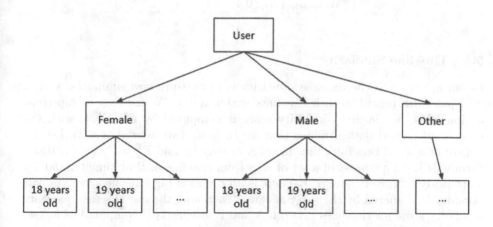

**Fig. 5.** An example of profile hierarchy from our application.

As discussed in Sect. 4.4, Fig. 5 visualizes an example of profile hierarchy on gender and age from our application. With the profile hierarchy, we can examine those who belong to a branch of the hierarchy. For instance, a user A would like to look for a female friend, 19 years old. We can follow the path "User" - "Female" - "19 years old" from the profile hierarchy to obtain the candidates. Given the profiles of user A and B in the Table 3, we have the similarity between A and B, according to the Eq. 5 as follows:

$$SIM(A, B) = \frac{1}{5} * 0.7 + \frac{2}{5} * 0.3 = 0.26 \tag{6}$$

$$SIM(B, A) = \frac{1}{5} * 0.4 + \frac{2}{5} * 0.6 = 0.32 \tag{7}$$

**Table 3.** An example of user profile.

| | |
|---|---|
| A's profile | Gender: Male |
| | Age: 19 |
| | Characteristics: friendly, sociable, romantic |
| | Hobby: music, movie, football |
| | $W_{hobby}$: 0.3 |
| | $W_{characteristics}$: 0.7 |
| B's profile | Gender: Female |
| | Age: 19 |
| | Characteristics: friendly, outgoing, laborious |
| | Hobby: book, travel, movie, music |
| | $W_{hobby}$: 0.6 |
| | $W_{characteristics}$: 0.4 |

### 5.5 Timeline Similarity

In our application, the timeline similarity is to measure how similar between a user pair with regard to their timelines within a day. We use tags to represent a timeline. The timeline similarity score is computed by the Eq. 4, with the support of cached data. Assume that we consider two users A and B. Let $T_A^1$ consist of a set of tags from timeline of A at time $t_1$, and $T_A^1 = \{$"mom", "dad", "study"$\}$. Let $T_B^1$ consist of a set of tags from timeline of B at time $t_1$, and $T_B^1 = \{$"daddy", "travel", "relax"$\}$. There is no common tag but one synonym pair "daddy/dad" shared by the two timelines. Therefore, the initial semantic-aware similarity score for timelines between A and B at time $t_1$ is computed as follow:

$$SIM(A, B) = \frac{1}{(6-1)} = \frac{1}{5} = 0.2 \tag{8}$$

That similarity calculation between user A and user B at time $t_1$ is then stored in our cache for later re-usability, which is illustrated in Fig. 6.

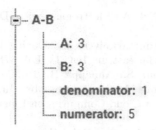

**Fig. 6.** The latest similarity calculation between user A and user B is stored in our cache for later re-usability.

Later on, assume that user A posts a new timeline with new tags at time $t_2$. Let $T_A^2$ consist of a set of tags from timeline of A at time $t_2$, and $T_A^2 = \{$"cafe", "rested"$\}$. There is now one synonym pair "rested/relax" between A and B. According to the Eq. 4, the accumulated similarity score between A and B at time $t_2$ is quickly derived as follow:

$$SIM(A,B) = \frac{1+1}{(5+2)} = \frac{2}{7} \approx 0.29 \qquad (9)$$

## 6  Conclusion and Future Work

In this paper, we propose a method for efficiently computing pairwise similarity in the context of big data as well as semantics point of view. More specifically, we build a reflexive synonym index to effectively look up synonyms during the process of pairwise similarity. Additionally, we show that our method can perform pair-by-pair computing in an incremental manner whenever there are additional emerging data. Moreover, we design our feature-based hierarchy to reduce the number of irrelevant objects before actually doing similarity search. Furthermore, we apply our method into a practical use-case of social network-based application to show the efficiency and feasibility of our proposed method.

For our future work, we would need to build a prototype for its application. Besides, we also would like to do more empirical experiments with real data to examine how efficient our method is in practice.

**Acknowledgment.** This research is funded by Ho Chi Minh City University of Technology-VNU-HCM, under the grant number T-KHMT-2018-26. We also give our thanks to Vu Tuan Minh and Tran Ngoc Thai Minh, HCMC University of Technology, for their support in our work.

## References

1. Amiri, H., Resnik, P., Boyd-Graber, J., Daume III, H.: Learning text pair similarity with context-sensitive autoencoders. In: Proceedings of the 54th Annual Meeting of the Association for Computational Linguistics, Berlin, Germany, pp. 1882–1892 (2016)

2. Fellbaum, C. (ed.): WordNet: An Electronic Lexical Database. MIT Press, Cambridge (1998)
3. Gantz, J., Reinsel, D.: The digital universe in 2020: big data, bigger digital shadows, and biggest growth in the far east. In: IDC IVIEW White Paper (2012)
4. Gautam, B., Jain, V., Jain, S., Annappa B.: Profile matching of online social network with aadhaar unique identification number. In: Proceedings of 2016 IEEE International Conference on Cloud Computing in Emerging Markets, pp. 168–169 (2016)
5. Gray, K.R., Aljabar, P., Heckemann, R.A., Hammers, A., Rueckert, D.: Random forest-based similarity measures for multi-modal classification of Alzheimer-s disease. Neuro Image **65**, 167–175 (2013)
6. Kang, L., Li, Y., Doermann, D.: Orientation robust text line detection in natural images. In: Proceedings of the IEEE Conference on Computer Vision and Pattern Recognition, pp. 4034–4041 (2014)
7. Miller, G.A.: WordNet: a lexical database for English. Commun. ACM **38**(11), 39–41 (1995)
8. Phan, T.N., Dang, T.K.: A lightweight indexing approach for efficient batch similarity processing with MapReduce. SN Comput. Sci. **1**(1), 1–16 (2019)
9. Princeton University: About WordNet. WordNet, Princeton University (2010)
10. Xia, R., Pan, Y., Lai, H., Liu, C., Yan, S.: Supervised hashing for image retrieval via image representation learning. In: Proceedings of the AAAI Conference on Artificial Intellignece, pp. 2156–2162 (2014)
11. Xie, K., Wang, X., Li, W., Zhe, Z.: Bloom-filter-based profile matching for proximity-based mobile social networking. In: Proceedings of the 13th Annual IEEE International Conference on Sensing, Communication, and Networking (2016)
12. Yang, T., Jin, R.: Extracting certainty from uncertainty: transductive pairwise classification from pairwise similarities. Adv. Neural Inf. Process. Syst. **27**, 262–270 (2014)
13. Yang, Y., Wang, Z., Yang, J., Wang, J., Chang, S., Huang, T.S.: Data clustering by laplacian regularized L1-graph. In: Proceedings of the Twenty-Eighth AAAI Conference on Artificial Intelligence (2014)
14. Yi, J., Zhang, L., Jin, R., Qian, Q., Jain, A.: Semi-supervised clustering by input pattern assisted pairwise similarity matrix completion. In: Proceedings of the 30th International Conference on Machine Learning (2013)
15. Zaki, N., Lazarova-Molnar, S., El-Hajj, W., Campbell, P.: Protein-protein interaction based on pairwise similarity. BMC Bioinform. **10**(150), 12 (2009)
16. Zezula, P.: Future trends in similarity searching. In: Navarro, G., Pestov, V. (eds.) SISAP 2012. LNCS, vol. 7404, pp. 8–24. Springer, Heidelberg (2012). https://doi.org/10.1007/978-3-642-32153-5_2
17. Zezula, P., Amato, G., Dohnal, V., Batko, M.: Similarity search - the metric space approach. In: Series: Advances in Database Systems, vol. 32, XVIII, 220 p. (2006). ISBN: 0-387-29146-6

# Lower Bound on Network Diameter
# for Distributed Function Computation

H. K. Dai[1]([✉]) and M. Toulouse[2]

[1] Computer Science Department, Oklahoma State University,
Stillwater, OK 74078, USA
dai@cs.okstate.edu
[2] Computer Science Department, Vietnamese-German University,
Binh Duong New City, Vietnam
michel.toulouse@vgu.edu.vn

**Abstract.** Parallel and distributed computing network-systems are modeled as graphs with vertices representing compute elements and adjacency-edges capturing their uni- or bi-directional communication. Distributed function computation covers a wide spectrum of major applications, such as quantized consensus and collaborative hypothesis testing, in distributed systems. Distributed computation over a network-system proceeds in a sequence of time-steps in which vertices update and/or exchange their values based on the underlying algorithm constrained by the time-(in)variant network-topology. For finite convergence of distributed information dissemination and function computation in the model, we study lower bounds on the number of time-steps for vertices to receive (initial) vertex-values of all vertices regardless of underlying protocol or algorithmics in time-invariant networks via the notion of vertex-eccentricity in a graph-theoretic framework. We prove a lower bound on the maximum vertex-eccentricity in terms of graph-order and -size in a strongly connected directed graph, and demonstrate its optimality via an explicitly constructed family of strongly connected directed graphs.

**Keywords:** Distributed function computation · Linear iterative schemes · Information dissemination · Finite convergence · Vertex-eccentricity

## 1 Introduction

Parallel and distributed computation algorithms, decentralized data-fusion architectures, and multi-agent systems are modeled as networks of interconnected vertices that compute common value(s) based on initial values or observations at the vertices. Key computation and communication requirements for these network/system paradigms include that their vertices perform local/internal computations and regularly communicate with each other via an underlying protocol. Fundamental limitations and capabilities of these algorithms and systems

© Springer Nature Switzerland AG 2019
T. K. Dang et al. (Eds.): FDSE 2019, LNCS 11814, pp. 239–251, 2019.
https://doi.org/10.1007/978-3-030-35653-8_16

are studied in the literature with wide scopes of viable applications in computer science, communication, and control and optimization (see, for examples, [1,5,6,12,13]). Brief and informal descriptions of some example studies are as follows:

1. Quantized consensus [7]: Consider an order-$n$ network with an initial network-state in which each vertex assumes an initial (integer) value $x_i[0]$ for $i = 1, 2, \ldots, n$. The network achieves a quantized consensus when, at some later time, all the $n$ vertices simultaneously arrive with almost equal values $y_i$ for $i = 1, 2, \ldots, n$ (that is, $|y_i - y_j| \leq 1$ for all $i, j \in \{1, 2, \ldots, n\}$) while preserving the sum of all initial values (that is, $\sum_{i=1}^{n} x_i[0] = \sum_{i=1}^{n} y_i$).
2. Collaborative distributed hypothesis testing [8]: Consider a network-system of $n$ vertices (sensors/agents) that collaboratively determine the probability measure of a random variable based on a number of available observations/measurements. For the binary setting in deciding two hypotheses, each vertex collects measurement(s) and makes a preliminary (local) decision $d_i \in \{0, 1\}$ in favor of the two hypotheses for $i = 1, 2, \ldots, n$. The $n$ vertices are allowed to communicate, and the network-system resolves with a final decision by, for example, the majority rule (that is, computes the indicator function of the event $\sum_{i=1}^{n} d_i > \frac{n}{2}$) in distributed fashion.
3. Solitude verification [5]: Consider an unlabeled network of $n$ vertices (processes) in which each vertex is in one of a finite number of states: $s_i$ for $i = 1, 2, \ldots, n$. Solitude verification on the network checks if a unique vertex with a given state $s$ exists in the network, that is, computes the Boolean function for the equality $|\{i \in \{1, 2, \ldots, n\} \mid s_i = s\}| = 1$.
4. Fundamental iterative limits of distributed function computation [12,19]: Consider a generic distributed information processing system to attain collective goals via iterative or non-iterative inter-vertex communication. Lower and upper bounds on numbers of iterations for achieving finite convergence of distributed information dissemination and function computation are studied via: structural-controllability and -observability theories [12] and information-theoretic techniques [19] in deterministic and probabilistic settings that capture initial-value/input distribution, network-topological and communication constraints, and/or estimation/output performance.

While there is a wide spectrum of algorithms in the literature that solve distributed computation problems such as the above, there are also studies that deal with algorithmic and complexity issues constrained by underlying time-(in)variant network-topology, resource-limitations associated with vertices, time/space and communication tradeoffs, convergence criteria and requirements, etc. We present in the following sections a model of distributed computing systems and some previous related works.

## 1.1  Model of Distributed Computing Systems

Most graph-theoretic definitions in this article are given in [2]. We will abbreviate "directed graph" and "directed path" to digraph and dipath, respectively.

We consider the topological model and algorithmics detailed in [12] for distributed function computation, and provide its abstraction components as follows:

1. Network-topology: A distributed computing system is modeled as a digraph $G$ with $V(G)$ and $E(G)$ denoting its sets of vertices and directed edges, respectively. Uni-directional communication on $V(G)$ is captured by the adjacency relation represented by $E(G)$: for all distinct vertices, $u, v \in V(G)$, $(u, v) \in E(G)$ if and only if vertex $u$ can send information to vertex $v$ (and $v$ can receive information from $u$). Note that bi-directional communication between $u$ and $v$ is viewed as the co-existence of the two directed edge $(u, v)$ and $(v, u)$ in $E(G)$.

   Distributed computation over the network proceeds in a sequence of time-steps. At each time-step, all vertices update and/or exchange their values based on the underlying algorithm constrained by the network-topology, which is assumed to be time-invariant.

2. Resource capabilities in vertices: The digraph $G$ of the network-topology is vertex-labeled such that messages are identified with senders and receivers. The vertices of $V(G)$ are assumed to have sufficient computational capabilities and local storage. Generally we assume that: (1) all communications/transmissions between vertices are reliable and in correct sequence, and (2) each vertex may, in the current time-step, receive the prior-step transmission(s) from its in-neighbor(s), update, and send transmission(s) to its out-neighbor(s) in accordance to the underlying algorithm.

   The domain of all initial/input and observed/output values of the vertices of $G$ is assumed to be an algebraic field $\mathbb{F}$.

3. Linear iterative scheme (for algorithmic lower- and upper-bound results): For a vertex $v \in V(G)$, denote by $x_v[k] \in \mathbb{F}$ the vertex-value of $v$ at time-step $k = 0, 1, \ldots$. A function with domain $\mathbb{F}^{|V(G)|}$ and codomain $\mathbb{F}$ is computed in accordance to a linear iterative scheme. Given initial vertex-values $x_v[0] \in \mathbb{F}$ for all vertices $v \in V(G)$ as arguments to the function, at each time-step $k = 0, 1, \ldots$, each vertex $v \in V(G)$ updates (and transmits) its vertex-value via a weighted linear combination of the prior-step vertex-values constrained by neighbor-structures: for all $v \in V(G)$ and $k = 0, 1, \ldots$,

$$x_v[k + 1] = \sum_{u \in V(G)} w_{vu} x_u[k],$$

where the prescribed weights $w_{vu} \in \mathbb{F}$ for all $v, u \in V(G)$ that are subject to the adjacency-constraints $w_{vu} = 0$ (the zero-element of $\mathbb{F}$) if $u$ is not adjacent to $v$ (that is, $(u, v) \notin E(G)$); equivalently,

transpose of $(x_v[k + 1] \mid v \in V(G)) = W \cdot$ transpose of $(x_v[k] \mid v \in V(G))$

where the two vectors of vertex-values and $W$ are indexed by a common discrete ordering of $V(G)$ with $W = [w_{vu}]_{(v,u) \in V(G) \times V(G)}$.

## 1.2  Related Work

Based on the framework and its variants for distributed function computation, researches and studies are focused on mathematical interplays among:

- time-(in)variance of network-topology
- granularity of time-step: discrete versus continuous
- choice of base field: special (real or complexes) versus arbitrary (finite or infinite)
- characterization of calculable functions
- convergence criteria and rates (finite, asymptotic, and/or probabilistic)
- adoption and algebraic properties of weight-matrix for linear interactive schemes: random weight-matrix, spectrum of eigenvalues, base field, etc.
- resilience and robustness of computation algorithmics for network-topology in the presence/absence of malicious vertices
- lower and upper bounds on (linear) iteration required for the convergence of calculable functions

Summarized results, research studies, and references are available in, for examples, [12–15, 17, 18].

Sundaram and Hadjicostis [12, 13] present their research findings in the finite convergence of distributed information dissemination and function computation in the model with linear iterative algorithmics stated above, among other contributions in distributed function computation and data-stream transmission in the presences of noise and malicious vertices. More specifically, (1) they employ structural theories in observability and invertibility of linear systems over arbitrary finite fields to obtain lower and upper bounds on the number of linear iterations for achieving network-consensus for finite convergence of arbitrary functions, and (2) the bounds are valid for all initial vertex-values of arbitrary finite fields as arguments to the functions in connected time-invariant topologies with almost all random weight-matrices.

For a time-invariant topology with underlying digraph $G$ and a vertex $u \in V(G)$, denote by $\deg_{G,\text{in}}(u)$ the in-degree of $u$ in $G$, and by $\Gamma_{G,\text{in}}(u)$ the in-neighbor of $u$ in $G$; hence $\Gamma^*_{G,\text{in}}(u)$ denotes the in-closure of $u$ in $G$, that is,

$$\Gamma^*_{G,\text{in}}(u) = \cup_{\eta \geq 0} \Gamma^\eta_{G,\text{in}}(u)$$
$$= \{v \in V(G) \mid \text{there exists a dipath in } G \text{ from } v \text{ to } u\}.$$

Consider all possible families of directed trees that are: (1) a vertex-decomposition of $\Gamma^*_{G,\text{in}}(u) - \{u\}$, and (2) rooted in (as subset of) $\Gamma_{G,\text{in}}(u)$. Denote by:

$$\alpha_{G,u} = \min\{\max\{\text{order}(T_i) \mid 1 \leq i \leq n\} \mid$$
$$\{T_i\}_{i=1}^n \text{ is a family of directed trees that are: (1) a vertex-}$$
$$\text{decomposition of } \Gamma^*_{G,\text{in}}(u) - \{u\}, \text{ and (2) rooted in (as sub-}$$
$$\text{set of) } \Gamma_{G,\text{in}}(u)\}.$$

Their upper-bound result for a vertex $u \in V(G)$ is stated as follows: for every linear iterative scheme with random weight-matrix over a finite base field $\mathbb{F}$ of cardinality:

$$|\mathbb{F}| \geq (\alpha_{G,u} - 1)(|\Gamma^*_{G,\text{in}}(u)| - \deg_{G,\text{in}}(u) - \frac{1}{2}\alpha_{G,u}),$$

then, with probability of at least:

$$1 - \frac{1}{|\mathbb{F}|}(\alpha_{G,u} - 1)(|\Gamma^*_{G,\text{in}}(u)| - \deg_{G,\text{in}}(u) - \frac{1}{2}\alpha_{G,u}),$$

the vertex $u$ can calculate arbitrary functions of arbitrary initial vertex-values $x_v[0] \in \mathbb{F}$ for all $v \in \Gamma^*_{G,\text{in}}(u)$ via the linear iterative scheme within at most $\alpha_{G,u}$ time-steps.

In addition to the probabilistic upper-bound result on the number of time-steps for (general) distributed function computation via linear iterative schemes with random weight-matrix, Sundaram and Hadjicostis [12,13] employ observability theory of linear systems to study the linear-functional case for distributed computation (of linear functions), and achieve an upper bound via the minimal polynomial of the underlying weight-matrix.

Toulouse and Minh [16] study the linear functional case with prescribed time-invariant network-topology over random weight-matrices, and obtain various empirical upper-bound results.

In accordance with an information-theoretic framework, Xu and Raginsky [19,20] study the fundamental time-step limits of distributed function computation in a constrained probabilistic setting. The lower- and upper-bound results are based on tradeoffs between: (1) the minimal amount of information necessarily extracted about the function value by any accuracy- and confidence-constrained algorithm, and (2) the maximal amount of information about the function value obtained by any algorithm within specified time-step and communication bounds. The lower-bound analysis indicates the dependence of computation time-steps on the diameter of the underlying network-graph, while the upper-bound one relies on cutset-capacity arguments.

Furthermore, there have been several other recent theoretical developments in distributed computation and optimization. Olshevsky and Tsitsiklis [11] prove lower bounds on the worst-case convergence time for various classes of linear, time-invariant (in network-topology), distributed consensus methods. Kuhn, Moscibroda, and Wattenhofer [9] study lower and upper bounds on local/distributed computability and approximability (amount of local information, approximation ratio, communication round) for a large class of optimization problems: minimum vertex cover, minimum (connected) dominating set, maximum matching, maximal independent set, and maximal matching.

Note that we present the skeletons for proving the main results without lengthy details in the abstract. Complete results, proofs, and derivations of claims/theorems are provided in the full version of this article.

## 2  Recent Studies on Distributed Function Computation

Sundaram conjectures in [12] that $\alpha_{G,u}$ may also serve as a lower bound on the number of time-steps for a vertex $u \in V(G)$ to receive the initial vertex-values of all $v \in \Gamma^*_{G,\text{in}}(u)$ regardless of underlying protocol or algorithmics. Hence, linear iterative schemes are time-optimal in disseminating information over arbitrary time-invariant connected networks.

Toulouse and Minh [16] refute the conjecture via the notion of rank-step sequences for linear iterative schemes over a small-scale (explicit) connected network. We extend the explicit counter-example in Fig. 1 with a simple direct combinatorial argument in Theorem 1.

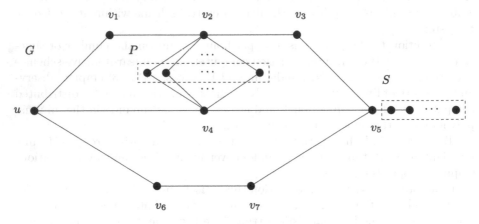

**Fig. 1.** A counter-example graph $G$, in which the embedded parallel component $P$ and serial component $S$ satisfying order$(P) =$ order$(S)$, to the lower-bound conjecture in terms of $\alpha_{G,u}$ in [12].

**Theorem 1.** *For the annotated graph $G$ in Fig. 1, $\alpha_{G,u}$, the minimum of the maximum tree-order of a directed forest among all possible directed forests that are vertex-decomposition of $\Gamma^*_{G,\text{in}}(u) - \{u\}$ and rooted in (as subset of) $\Gamma_{G,\text{in}}(u)$, satisfies that:*

$$\alpha_{G,u} = \text{order}(S) + 3.$$

**Proof-Sketch.** In accordance with the min-max formulation of $\alpha_{G,u}$, a direct justification for the counter-example is proceeded as follows:

1. We view the annotated graph $G$ in Fig. 1 in which each edge represents the co-existence of its two directed versions. For the vertex $u \in V(G)$, the number of time-steps to receive the initial vertex-values of all $v \in \Gamma^*_{G,\text{in}}(u) \, (= V(G))$, regardless of underlying protocol or algorithmics, is order$(S) + 2$—which is realized by the dipath composed of the serial component $S$ and vertices $v_5$, $v_4$, and $u$.

2. We show that $\alpha_{G,u} = \text{order}(S)+3$, hence $\alpha_{G,u}$ can not serve as a lower bound on the number of time-steps mentioned in item 1 above—as suggested in the conjecture [12].

To show the upper-bound inequality: $\alpha_{G,u} \leq \text{order}(S) + 3$, we consider the following family of directed trees, $\{\hat{T}_i\}_{i=1}^3$, which are a vertex-decomposition of $\Gamma_{G,\text{in}}^*(u) - \{u\}$ and are rooted in (as subset of) $\Gamma_{G,\text{in}}(u)$: $\hat{T}_1$ is composed of the serial component $S$ and vertices $v_5$, $v_7$, and $v_6$ with $\text{order}(\hat{T}_1) = \text{order}(S) + 3$, and $\hat{T}_2$ and $\hat{T}_3$ saturate the remaining vertices in the parallel component $P$ and vertices $v_3$, $v_2$, $v_1$, and $v_4$ in an almost equipotent manner with $\text{order}(\hat{T}_2) = \lfloor \frac{\text{order}(P)+4}{2} \rfloor$ and $\text{order}(\hat{T}_3) = \lceil \frac{\text{order}(P)+4}{2} \rceil$. Since the two components $P$ and $S$ are equipotent, we can establish that:

$$\alpha_{G,u} \leq \max\{\text{order}(\hat{T}_i) \mid 1 \leq i \leq 3\}$$
$$= \text{order}(\hat{T}_1) = \text{order}(S) + 3.$$

To show the reverse inequality that $\alpha_{G,u} \geq \text{order}(S)+3$, consider an arbitrary family of $n$ (where $n \leq 3$) ordered trees that are a vertex-decomposition of $\Gamma_{G,\text{in}}^*(u) - \{u\}$ and are rooted in (as subset of) $\Gamma_{G,\text{in}}(u)$. A case-analysis on the possible values of $n$ yields the desired lower-bound inequality. ∎

In order to complement the explicitly constructed counter-example to the lower-bound conjecture on the number of time-steps for distributed function computation and information dissemination with respect to a given vertex, we follow with a lower-bound study on the number of time-steps for a vertex $u \in V(G)$ to receive the initial vertex-values of all $v \in \Gamma_{G,\text{in}}^*(u)$ regardless of underlying protocol or algorithmics in a time-invariant network via the notion of vertex-eccentricity.

Consider an arbitrary vertex $u \in V(G)$, and assume a non-trivial $\Gamma_{G,\text{in}}^*(u)$ $(|\Gamma_{G,\text{in}}^*(u)| > 1)$ hereinafter. We develop a lower bound on the number of time-steps required for the vertex $u$ to receive the (initial) vertex-values of all vertices of $\Gamma_{G,\text{in}}^*(u)$ (regardless of underlying protocol, including linear iterative schemes).

For two vertices $u$ and $v$ of $G$, $\overrightarrow{d}_G(u,v)$ denotes the directed distance from $u$ to $v$ in $G$, that is,

$$\overrightarrow{d}_G(u,v) = \begin{cases} \text{length of a shortest dipath from } u \text{ to } v \text{ in } G & \text{if exists,} \\ \infty & \text{otherwise.} \end{cases}$$

For a vertex $u$ of $G$, $e_{G,\text{in}}(u)$ denotes the in-eccentricity of $u$ in $G$, which is the maximum directed distance from a vertex to $u$ in $G$, that is,

$$e_{G,\text{in}}(u) = \max\{\underbrace{\overrightarrow{d}_G(v,u)}_{\text{minimum length of a dipath from } v \text{ to } u \text{ in } G} \mid v \in V(G)\}.$$

Following the above-stated distributed computation framework as in [13] and for their conjecture, we develop in [4] a lower-bound result based on the notion of eccentricity (instead of "order" or "size" as in the conjecture).

**Theorem 2.** [4] *For a digraph $G$ and a vertex $u \in V(G)$, $e_{G,\mathrm{in}}(u)$, the maximum directed distance from a vertex to $u$ in $G$, satisfies that:*

$$e_{G,\mathrm{in}}(u) = 1 + \min\{\max\{\underbrace{e_{T_i,\mathrm{in}}(\mathrm{root}(T_i))}_{=\,\mathrm{depth}(T_i)} \mid 1 \le i \le n\} \mid$$

$\{T_i\}_{i=1}^n$ *is a family of directed trees that are:*
*(1) a vertex-decomposition of $\Gamma^*_{G,\mathrm{in}}(u) - \{u\}$, and*
*(2) rooted in (as subset of) $\Gamma_{G,\mathrm{in}}(u)\}$.*

The min-max formulation of $e_{G,\mathrm{in}}(u)$, which was developed above in Theorem 2 for lower-bounding the number of time-steps for function computation by vertex $u$ in $\Gamma^*_{G,\mathrm{in}}(u)$, motivates us to study lower bounds for (maximum) vertex-eccentricity in terms of common graph-parameters of the underlying graph $G$: (1) maximum in-degree (in [4]), and (2) order and size (main results of this abstract).

We give in Theorem 3 a lower bound on $e_{G,\mathrm{in}}(u)$ from the knowledge of the maximum in-degree of $G$ (vertex-spanned by $\Gamma^*_{G,\mathrm{in}}(u)$), which yields a (possibly weaker) lower bound on the number of time-steps for vertex $u$ to access values/information of all the vertices in $\Gamma^*_{G,\mathrm{in}}(u)$.

Denote by $\Delta_{G,\mathrm{in}}(u)$ $(\ge 1)$ the maximum in-degree of the subdigraph of $G$ vertex-spanned by $\Gamma^*_{G,\mathrm{in}}(u)$.

**Theorem 3.** [4] *For a digraph $G$ and a vertex $u \in V(G)$,*

$$e_{G,\mathrm{in}}(u) \ge \begin{cases} |\Gamma^*_{G,\mathrm{in}}(u)| - 1 & \text{if } \Delta_{G,\mathrm{in}}(u) = 1, \\ \log_{\Delta_{G,\mathrm{in}}(u)}((\Delta_{G,\mathrm{in}}(u) - 1)|\Gamma^*_{G,\mathrm{in}}(u)| + 1) - 1 & \text{otherwise} \\ & (\Delta_{G,\mathrm{in}}(u) \ge 2). \end{cases}$$

We can obtain desired lower bounds in analogous fashion with similar graph-parameters such a regularity in-degree, and maximum and regularity degrees.

## 3   Maximum Vertex-Eccentricity and Graph-Order and -Size

The diameter of a digraph $G$, denoted by $\mathrm{dia}(G)$, is the maximum in-eccentricity of all the vertices of $G$; that is,

$$\mathrm{dia}(G) = \max\{e_{G,\mathrm{in}}(u) \mid u \in V(G)\}$$
$$= \max\{\overrightarrow{d}_G(u,v) \mid u, v \in V(G)\}.$$

A digraph $G$ is strongly connected if for every pair of vertices $u, v \in V(G)$, there exists a dipath from $u$ to $v$ (and vice-versa) in $G$.

For a strongly connected digraph, we study a lower bound on its diameter in terms of its order and size, and show the optimality of the diameter-bound with a family of explicitly constructed strongly connected digraphs.

**Theorem 4.** *For a strongly connected digraph $G$,*

$$|E(G)| \geq \begin{cases} |V(G)| & \text{if } \mathrm{dia}(G) = |V(G)| - 1, \\ |V(G)| - 1 + \frac{2(|V(G)|-1)}{\mathrm{dia}(G)} & \text{otherwise} \\ \text{equivalently, } \mathrm{dia}(G) \geq \frac{2(|V(G)|-1)}{|E(G)|-|V(G)|+1} & (\mathrm{dia}(G) \leq |V(G)| - 2). \end{cases}$$

**Proof-Sketch.** For the case of full diameter: $\mathrm{dia}(G) = |V(G)| - 1$, the extremity of $\mathrm{dia}(G)$ gives that $|E(G)| \geq |V(G)| - 1$, and the strong connectedness of $G$ increases the lower bound by 1: $|E(G)| \geq |V(G)|$. A size-optimal strongly connected digraph of full diameter is shown in Fig. 2(a).

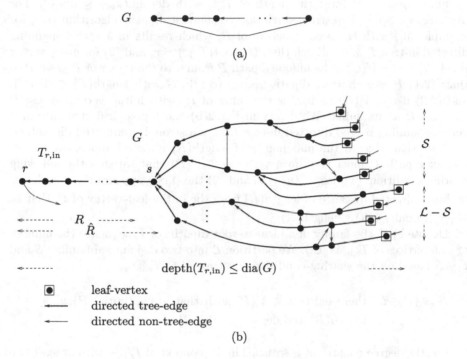

(a)

(b)

●     leaf-vertex
——    directed tree-edge
—     directed non-tree-edge

**Fig. 2.** For a strongly connected digraph $G$: (a) when $\mathrm{dia}(G) = |V(G)| - 1$ (full diameter): $|E(G)| \geq |V(G)|$; (b) when $\mathrm{dia}(G) \leq |V(G)| - 2$: $\mathrm{dia}(G) \geq \frac{2(|V(G)|-1)}{|E(G)|-|V(G)|+1}$.

We study the general case, henceforth, $\mathrm{dia}(G) \leq |V(G)| - 2$. Our approach in deriving a desired lower bound on $|E(G)|$, hence on $\mathrm{dia}(G)$, relies on: (1) embedding in $G$ a vertex-spanning rooted directed tree with depth of $\mathrm{dia}(G)$, and (2) then relating the order $|V(G)|$, size $|E(G)|$, and diameter $\mathrm{dia}(G)$ of $G$ via a classification/enumeration of all leaf-to-root dipaths into families of dipaths with shared versus non-shared suffixes (towards the root).

In order to have a refined derivation, the rooted directed tree is seeded with a maximum-length stemming dipath to ensure the consideration of near-leaf proximity of the first/lowest common descendants of shared suffixes of the leaf-to-root dipaths.

Denote by $R$ a longest dipath of vertices with in-degree of 1 in $G$, that is, (1) for every vertex $u \in V(R)$, $\deg_{G,\text{in}}(u) = 1$, and (2) length$(R)$ is the maximum among those of dipaths satisfying item (1). Note that $0 \leq$ length$(R) \leq$ dia$(G) - 1$. Denote by $r$ the terminal vertex of $R$, and by $\hat{R}$ the dipath that concatenates the unique vertex $s$ (and its directed edge) adjacent to the initial vertex of $R$ together with the dipath $R$.

Employing $\hat{R}$ as a seed-structure, we grow a vertex-spanning rooted (at the terminal vertex $r$ of $R$) directed in-tree $T_{r,\text{in}}$ of $G$ [10] in which for every vertex $u \in T_{r,\text{in}}$ $(= V(G))$, there exists a unique dipath from $u$ to $r$ in $T_{r,\text{in}}$.

Furthermore, we limit the depth of $T_{r,\text{in}}$ with depth$(T_{r,\text{in}}) \leq$ dia$(G)$. For instance, we apply Dijkstra's single-source shortest-dipaths algorithm (see, for example, [3]) with the seed-structure of $\hat{R}$, which results in a vertex-spanning directed in-tree $T_{r,\text{in}}$ of $G$ such that: (1) root$(T_{r,\text{in}}) = r$, and (2) for every vertex $u \in V(T_{r,\text{in}})$ $(= V(G))$, the unique dipath $P$ from $u$ to the root $r$ of $T_{r,\text{in}}$ satisfies that: (2.1) $P$ is a shortest dipath from $u$ to $r$ in $G$ with length$(P) \leq$ dia$(G)$, and (2.2) if $u \in V(\hat{R})$ then $P$ is the suffix of $\hat{R}$ (with initial vertex $u$) else $P$ contains $\hat{R}$ as its suffix. We depict in Fig. 2(b) the topological structure of a vertex-spanning rooted directed in-tree $T_{r,\text{in}}$ of a strongly connected digraph $G$.

Note that, due to the maximality of length$(R)$ imposed above, every leaf-to-root dipath $P$ must contain a vertex $u \in V(P)$ that satisfies the following sharing-condition: (1) $\deg_{G,\text{in}}(u) \geq 2$, and (2) the (first) appearance of such $u$ is within a directed distance of length$(\hat{R})$ from the initial leaf-vertex of $P$, that is, $\overrightarrow{d}_{T_{r,\text{in}}}(\text{initial}(P), u) \leq$ length$(\hat{R})$.

Denote by $\mathcal{L}$ the family of all leaf-to-root dipaths of $T_{r,\text{in}}$ (hence the number of leaf-vertices of $T_{r,\text{in}}$ is $|\mathcal{L}|$). We partition $\mathcal{L}$ into two disjoint subfamilies $\mathcal{S}$ and $\mathcal{L} - \mathcal{S}$ based on the sharing-condition constrained to $T_{r,\text{in}}$:

$$\mathcal{S} = \{P \in \mathcal{L} \mid \text{there exists } u \in V(P) \text{ such that } \overrightarrow{d}_{T_{r,\text{in}}}(\text{initial}(P), u) \leq \text{length}(\hat{R}) \text{ and } \deg_{T_{r,\text{in}},\text{in}}(u) \geq 2\};$$

that is, the degree-constraint is satisfied in the context of $T_{r,\text{in}}$—with at least two tree-edges of $E(T_{r,\text{in}})$ incident/convergent to the first/lowest common descendant $u$ shared with other dipath(s) of $\mathcal{L}$. An annotated configuration of leaf-to-root dipaths of $\mathcal{S}$ versus $\mathcal{L} - \mathcal{S}$ is illustrated in Fig. 2(b).

After embedding $T_{r,\text{in}}$ in $G$, we enumerate $V(G)$ and $E(G)$ with respect to the partition $\{\mathcal{S}, \mathcal{L} - \mathcal{S}\}$ and establish an upper and lower bounds on $|V(G)|$ and $|E(G)|$, respectively as follows.

1. Upper-bounding $|V(G)|$:

$$|V(G)| \leq \frac{|\mathcal{S}|}{2}\text{dia}(G) + |\mathcal{L} - \mathcal{S}|(\text{dia}(G) - \text{length}(R) - 1) + \text{length}(R) + 2.$$

2. Lower-bounding $|E(G)|$:

$$|E(G)| \geq \begin{cases} |V(G)| - 1 + |\mathcal{L} - \mathcal{S}| + |\mathcal{L}| & \text{if } \mathcal{S} \subsetneq \mathcal{L}, \\ |V(G)| - 1 + |\mathcal{L} - \mathcal{S}| + |\mathcal{L}| + 1 & \text{otherwise } (\mathcal{S} = \mathcal{L}). \end{cases}$$

We combine the above upper bound on $|V(G)|$ and lower bound on $|E(G)|$ to achieve the desired lower bound on $\operatorname{dia}(G)$ in terms of $|V(G)|$ and $|E(G)|$:

$$|E(G)| \geq |V(G)| - 1 + \frac{2(|V(G)| - 1)}{\operatorname{dia}(G)};$$

equivalently,

$$\operatorname{dia}(G) \geq \frac{2(|V(G)| - 1)}{|E(G)| - |V(G)| + 1}. \qquad \blacksquare$$

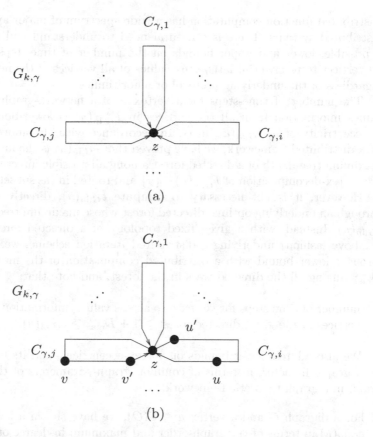

**Fig. 3.** For each positive integers $k$ and $\gamma$: (a) the strongly connected digraph $G_{k,\gamma}$ is an amalgamation of $k$ (mutually edge-disjoint) copies of a directed cycle of $\gamma + 1$ vertices: $C_{\gamma,1}, C_{\gamma,2}, \ldots, C_{\gamma,k}$ that share a common vertex; (b) when $\gamma \geq 2$ and $i, j \in \{1, 2, \ldots, k\}$ with $i \neq j$, $(u', v')$ is a diametrical pair of vertices in $C_{\gamma,i}$ and $C_{\gamma,j}$, respectively, with $\vec{d}_{G_{k,\gamma}}(u', v') = 2\gamma$.

We construct a family of strongly connected digraphs that achieve the optimality of the above-derived diameter-bound. For each positive integer $\gamma$, denote by $C_\gamma$ a directed cycle of $\gamma + 1$ vertices, and for each positive integer $k$, define a strongly connected digraph $G_{k,\gamma}$ to be an amalgamation of $k$ (mutually edge-disjoint) copies of $C_\gamma$: $C_{\gamma,1}, C_{\gamma,2}, \ldots, C_{\gamma,k}$ that share a common vertex $z$. Figure 3(a) show the topological structure of $G_{k,\gamma}$.

**Corollary 5.** *The family of strongly connected digraphs $G_{k,\gamma}$ for all positive integers $k$ and $\gamma$ is optimal for the relationship of the graph-parameters: order, size, and diameter established in Theorem 4—as illustrated with the annotated digraph $G_{k,\gamma}$ in Fig. 3(b).*

# 4   Conclusion

Distributed function computation has a wide spectrum of major applications in distributed systems. There is a natural need to understand and approximate, if possible, lower and upper bounds on the number of time-steps for some or all vertices to receive (initial) vertex-values of all vertices of the network-graph, regardless of the underlying protocol or algorithmics.

The number of time-steps for a vertex $u$ of a network-graph $G$ to collect values/information from all the vertices in $\Gamma_{G,\text{in}}^*(u)$ is lower-bounded by the in-eccentricity of $u$, $e_{G,\text{in}}(u)$, in $G$. In accordance with the above-stated min-max distributed framework, we have proved that $e_{G,\text{in}}(u)$ is the minimum of the maximum tree-depth of a directed forest among all possible directed forests that are vertex-decomposition of $\Gamma_{G,\text{in}}^*(u) - \{u\}$ and rooted in (as subset of) $\Gamma_{G,\text{in}}(u)$.

However, it is not necessary to compute $e_{G,\text{in}}(u)$, directly or indirectly, through an underlying optimal directed forest whose maximum tree-depth yields $e_{G,\text{in}}(u)$. Instead, with a given/fixed topology of a directed forest (described in above fashion) underlying a distributed iteration scheme, we can obtain a stronger lower bound with a distributed computation of the maximum depth $D_{\max}$ among all the directed trees in the forest, and note that:

> number of time-steps for vertex $u$ to access values/information from all vertices in the given directed forest $\geq 1 + D_{\max} \geq e_{G,\text{in}}(u)$.

We also address lower bounds on vertex-eccentricity and its maximum version, graph-diameter, in terms of common graph-parameters of the underlying graph in a graph-theoretic framework:

1. For a digraph $G$ and a vertex $u \in V(G)$, we have shown a lower bound on $e_{G,\text{in}}(u)$ in terms of the graph-order and maximum in-degree of $G$, and
2. For a strongly connected digraph $G$, we have proved a lower bound on $\text{dia}(G)$ in terms of the graph-order and -size of $G$, and have demonstrated the optimality of the diameter-bound for a family of (explicitly constructed) strongly connected digraphs.

# References

1. Ayaso, O., Shah, D., Dahleh, M.A.: Information theoretic bounds for distributed computation over networks of point-to-point channels. IEEE Trans. Inf. Theory **56**(12), 6020–6039 (2010)
2. Bondy, J.A., Murty, U.S.R.: Graph Theory. Graduate Texts in Mathematics, vol. 244. Springer, London (2008)
3. Cormen, T.H., Leiserson, C.E., Rivest, R.L., Stein, C.: Introduction to Algorithms, 3rd edn. MIT Press, Cambridge (2009)
4. Dai, H.K., Toulouse, M.: Lower bound for function computation in distributed networks. In: Dang, T.K., Küng, J., Wagner, R., Thoai, N., Takizawa, M. (eds.) FDSE 2018. LNCS, vol. 11251, pp. 371–384. Springer, Cham (2018). https://doi.org/10.1007/978-3-030-03192-3_28
5. Fich, F.E., Ruppert, E.: Hundreds of impossibility results for distributed computing. Distrib. Comput. **16**(2–3), 121–163 (2003)
6. Hendrickx, J.M., Olshevsky, A., Tsitsiklis, J.N.: Distributed anonymous discrete function computation. IEEE Trans. Autom. Control **56**(10), 2276–2289 (2011)
7. Kashyap, A., Basar, T., Srikant, R.: Quantized consensus. Automatica **43**(7), 1192–1203 (2007)
8. Katz, G., Piantanida, P., Debbah, M.: Collaborative distributed hypothesis testing. Computing Research Repository, abs/1604.01292 (2016)
9. Kuhn, F., Moscibroda, T., Wattenhofer, R.: Local computation: lower and upper bounds. J. ACM **63**(2), 17:1–17:44 (2016)
10. Mehlhorn, K., Sanders, P.: Algorithms and Data Structures: The Basic Toolbox. Springer, Heidelberg (2008). https://doi.org/10.1007/978-3-540-77978-0
11. Olshevsky, A., Tsitsiklis, J.N.: Convergence speed in distributed consensus and averaging. SIAM J. Control Optim. **48**(1), 33–55 (2009)
12. Sundaram, S.: Linear iterative strategies for information dissemination and processing in distributed systems. Ph.D. thesis, University of Illinois at Urbana-Champaign (2009)
13. Sundaram, S., Hadjicostis, C.N.: Distributed function calculation and consensus using linear iterative strategies. IEEE J. Sel. Areas Commun. **26**(4), 650–660 (2008)
14. Sundaram, S., Hadjicostis, C.N.: Distributed function calculation via linear iterative strategies in the presence of malicious agents. IEEE Trans. Autom. Control **56**(7), 1495–1508 (2011)
15. Toulouse, M., Minh, B.Q.: Applicability and resilience of a linear encoding scheme for computing consensus. In: Muñoz, V.M., Wills, G., Walters, R.J., Firouzi, F., Chang, V. (eds.) Proceedings of the Third International Conference on Internet of Things, Big Data and Security, IoTBDS 2018, Funchal, Madeira, Portugal, 19–21 March 2018, pp. 173–184. SciTePress (2018)
16. Toulouse, M., Minh, B.Q., Minh, Q.T.: Invariant properties and bounds on a finite time consensus algorithm. Trans. Large-Scale Data- Knowl.-Centered Syst. **41**, 32–58 (2019)
17. Wang, L., Xiao, F.: Finite-time consensus problems for networks of dynamic agents. IEEE Trans. Autom. Control **55**(4), 950–955 (2010)
18. Xiao, L., Boyd, S.P., Kim, S.-J.: Distributed average consensus with least-mean-square deviation. J. Parallel Distrib. Comput. **67**(1), 33–46 (2007)
19. Xu, A.: Information-theoretic limitations of distributed information processing. Ph.D. thesis, University of Illinois at Urbana-Champaign (2016)
20. Xu, A., Raginsky, M.: Information-theoretic lower bounds for distributed function computation. IEEE Trans. Inf. Theory **63**(4), 2314–2337 (2017)

# Deep Learning and Applications

# A Combined Enhancing and Feature Extraction Algorithm to Improve Learning Accuracy for Gene Expression Classification

Phuoc-Hai Huynh[1]([✉]), Van-Hoa Nguyen[1], and Thanh-Nghi Do[2,3]

[1] Information Technology Faculty, An Giang University, Angiang, Viet Nam
hphai@agu.edu.vn
[2] College of Information Technology, Can Tho University, Cantho, Vietnam
[3] UMI UMMISCO 209 (IRD/UPMC), Sorbonne University,
Pierre and Marie Curie University, Paris 6, France

**Abstract.** In recent years, gene expression data combined with machine learning methods revolutionized cancer classification which had been based solely on morphological appearance. However, the characteristics of gene expression data have very-high-dimensional and small-sample-size which lead to over-fitting of classification algorithms. We propose a novel gene expression classification model of multiple classifying algorithms with synthetic minority oversampling technique (SMOTE) using features extracted by deep convolutional neural network (DCNN). In our approach, the DCNN extracts latent features of gene expression data, then the SMOTE algorithm generates new data from the features of DCNN was implemented. These models are used in conjunction with classifiers that efficiently classify gene expression data. Numerical test results on fifty very-high-dimensional and small-sample-size gene expression datasets from the Kent Ridge Biomedical and Array Expression repositories illustrate that the proposed algorithm is more accurate than state-of-the-art classifying models and improve the accuracy of classifiers including non-linear support vector machines (SVM), linear SVM, $k$ nearest neighbors and random forests.

**Keywords:** Synthetic over sampling · Enhancing data · Deep convolutional neural network · Support vector machines · Classification · Gene expression data

## 1 Introduction

In recent decades, cancer has become a major public health issue in the world. According to the World Health Organization (WHO), the cancer patient rises to 18.1 million new cases and 9.6 million cancer deaths in 2018. Therefore, more and more studies have been done finding effective solutions to diagnose and treat this disease in recent years. However, there are still many challenges in cancer

© Springer Nature Switzerland AG 2019
T. K. Dang et al. (Eds.): FDSE 2019, LNCS 11814, pp. 255–273, 2019.
https://doi.org/10.1007/978-3-030-35653-8_17

treatment because possible causes of cancer are genetic disorders or epigenetic alterations in the somatic cells [1]. Moreover, cancer could be known as a disease of altered gene expression. There are many proteins are turned on or off and they dramatically change the basic activity of the cell. Microarray technology enables researchers to investigate and address issues which is once thought to be impractical for the simultaneous measurement of the expression levels of thousands of genes in a single experiment [2]. Information of gene expression profile may be used to find and diagnose diseases or to see how well the body responds to treatment, so many algorithms have been done to analyse gene expression data. During the past decade, many classification algorithms have been used to classify gene expression data, which include support vector machines (SVM) used by [3], neural network in [4], $k$ nearest neighbors ($k$NN) in [5], C4.5 decision trees (C4.5) in [6], random forests (RF) in [7], decision trees based bagging and boosting style algorithm in [8], bagging of oblique decision stumps (Bag-RODS) and boosting of oblique decision stumps (Boost-RODS) in [9].

In spite of many classification algorithms for gene expression data have risen during recent years but these algorithms remain a critical need to improve classifying accuracy. There are two main research challenges that most state-of-the-art classification algorithms are facing when dealing with gene expression data including very-high-dimensional and small-samples-size. These challenges mean that a characteristic of microarray gene expression data is that the number of variables (genes) $n$ far exceeds the number of samples $m$, commonly known as "curse of dimensionality" problem. These issues lead to statistical and analytical challenges and conventional statistical methods give improper result due to the high dimension of gene expression data with a limited number of patterns [10]. In practice, it isn't feasible when to build machine learning model due to the extremely large feature sets with millions of features and high computing cost. In addition, another challenge of gene expression classification model is that training data sample size is relatively small compared to features vector size, therefore the classification models may give poor classification performance due to over-fitting.

In order to solve the issues of classifying gene expression, people often use dimension reduction and enhancing data methods. In recent, the problem very-high-dimensional data can be solve by feature extraction with DCNN [11–14]. The main advantage of this network is the ability to extract new latent features from the gene expression data, then send them to the classifiers. To tackle the small-sample-size task, many studies have used enhancing methods to improve classification accuracy. SMOTE [15] is a very popular over-sampling method that generates new samples in by interpolation from the minority class. A benefit of using SMOTE is that this algorithm can generate new data from original data and it can use to enhance training sample size. However, this algorithm often use on low-dimensional data [16] because it seems beneficial but less effective for very-high-dimensional data. The cause of this problem is that the interpolation process using $k$ nearest neighbors algorithm. For this reason, it could suffer over-fitting problem for very-high-dimensional data. In practical, this over-sampling algorithm for $k$NN without variable selection shouldn't be used because it strongly biases the classification towards the minority class [17]. Therefore, it often is combined with data preprocessing methods including feature selection or feature extraction.

In this paper, we proposed a new learning algorithms for the precise classification of gene expression data of non-linear support vector machine (SVM), linear SVM (LSVM), $k$NN, RF with SMOTE using features extracted by DCNN (call DCNN-SMOTE-[SVM, LSVM, $k$NN, RF]). The algorithms perform the training task with three main steps. First of all, we use new DCNN model to extract new features from gene expression data. The new features can improve the dissimilarity power of gene expression representations and thus obtain a higher accuracy rate than original features. Secondly, we propose SMOTE algorithm to enhance gene expression data using new features extracted by extraction model. Two new algorithms are used in conjunction with the classifiers learn to classify gene expression data efficiently. Results of 50 low-sample-size and very-high-dimensional microarray gene expression datasets from Kent Ridge Biomedical [18] and Array Expression repositories [19] illustrate that the proposed DCNN-SMOTE-SVM are more accurate the state-of-the-art classifying models including: SVM [20], LSVM [21], $k$NN [22], RF [23], C4.5 [24,25]. In addition, DCNN and SMOTE also improve accurate of classifiers including linear SVM, RF and $k$NN.

The paper is organized as follows. Section refrela gives a brief overview of DCNN, SMOTE, and our proposed. Section 4 discusses about related works. Section 3 shows the experimental results, and the conclusions are presented in the final section.

## 2    Related Works

Our proposal is in some aspects related to classification approaches for gene expression data. The first approach is the popular frameworks for gene expression classification involve the main steps as follows: the feature extraction or the feature selection of gene expression, and learning classifiers. [26] applied GA/$K$NN method to generate the subset of the features and then use $k$NN algorithm to classify. In recent years, deep convolutional neural network has achieved remarkable results in computer vision [27], text classification [28]. In addition, DCNN is also used for omics, biomedical imaging and biomedical signal processing [29]. The paper of [30] proposed to use deep learning algorithm based on the deep convolutional neural network, for classification of gene expression data. Lyu et al. use DCNN [31] to predict over 11,000 tumors from 33 most prevalent forms of cancer. These algorithms aim reduce dimension of data. More recent DCNN-SVM [13] propose to classify gene expression data. In addition, many other methods have been implemented for extracting only the important information from the gene expression data thus reducing their size [32–35]. Feature extraction creates new variables as combinations of others to reduce the dimensionality of the selected features.

The second approach use enhancing data methods, then use in conjunction with SVM that efficiently classify small-sample-size data. The paper [36] propose enhancing the gene expression classification of support vector machines with generative adversarial networks. SynTReN algorithm generate gene expression data using network topology method [37]. Moreover, there have been several applications of the enhancing data in bioinformatics, such as [38,39]. SMOTE is a enhancing data method to generate new data with equal probabilities [15]. In spire of, its behaviour on high-dimensional data has not been thoroughly investigated [40]. The paper [41] is shown in the high-dimensional setting only $k$NN algorithm based on the Euclidean distance seem to benefit substantially from the use of SMOTE, provided that feature selection is performed before using SMOTE.

In our algorithm, we take advantages of both approaches DCNN and SMOTE to solve two main issues of classifying gene expression data. Firstly, we use the benefits of DCNN to extract new latent features from gene expression data. This measure is proposed in previous our paper [13] that can address issue very-high-dimension of gene expression. However, we upgrade new architecture of DCNN for gene expression data classification in our approach. The new feature vector size is only approximately 10% compare with origin size. Secondly, we propose SMOTE algorithms to generate new samples from new features extracted by DCNN. The advantages of DCNN for classifying gene expression data are taken advantage when using SMOTE algorithm to generate new data as well as to tackle limit of this algorithm for gene expression data. In addition, in this paper we also apply our model for other algorithms including support vector machine [42], linear SVM [21], $k$ nearest neighbors [22], random forests [23] and decision trees C4.5 [24,25].

## 3 Methods

In our study, we use multiple classifying algorithms, SMOTE and DCNN for the precise classification of gene expression data. Our learning approach is composed of three phases that is illustrated in Fig. 1. Firstly, the new DCNN is used to extract new features from gene expression data. Secondly, we use SMOTE algorithm to enhance gene expression data using new features extracted by DCNN. Finally, these algorithms are used in conjunction with the various classifiers learn to classify gene expression data efficiently.

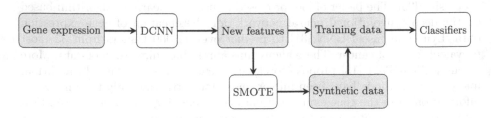

**Fig. 1.** The workflow of our method

## 3.1 Feature Extraction Gene Expression Data by DCNN

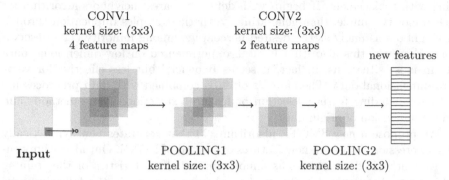

**Fig. 2.** A new DCNN architecture for feature extraction in processing gene expression data.

DCNN plays a dominant role in the community of deep learning models [43]. It is a multi-layer neural network architecture that is directly inspired by the visual cortex of the human brain [44]. In network structure, the successive layers are designed to learn progressively higher-level features, until the last layer which produces categories. Once training processing is completed, the last layer, which is a linear classified operating on the features extracted by the previous layers. Although DCNN is the most widely used method in the field of image processing. However, it is a algorithms that is rarely used in gene expression classification.

In order to develop a powerful classifier which can implicitly extract sparse feature relations from an extremely large feature space, we propose to a extraction model based on DCNN, which is one of the state-of-the-art learning techniques. The architecture of this model consists of two convolutional layers, two pooling layers, and a fully connected layer which is shown in Fig. 2. The layers are respectively named CONV1, POOLING1, CONV2, POOLING2, and output (numbers indicate the sequential position of the layers). The input layer receives the gene expression in the 2-D matrix format. We embedded each high-dimensional vector expression data into a 2-D image by adding some zeros at the last line of the image. The first CONV1 layer contains 4 feature maps and kernel size $(3 \times 3)$. The second layer, POOLING1 layer, is taken as input of the average pooling output of the first layer and filter with $(2 \times 2)$ sub-sampling layer. CONV2 uses convolution kernel size $(3 \times 3)$ to output 2 feature maps POOLING2 is a $(2 \times 2)$ sub-sampling layer. We propose to use the Tanh activation function as neurons. The final layer has a variable number of maps that combine inputs from all map in POOLING2. The feature maps of the final sub sampling layer are then fed into the actual classifier consisting of an arbitrary number of fully connected layers. The output layer uses to extract new features from original gene expression data.

## 3.2 Enhancing Gene Expression Data by SMOTE

Synthetic Minority Over-sampling Technique was first introduced by [15] that is an over-sampling approach. The main idea of this algorithm is that the minority class is over-sampled by creating synthetic examples rather than by oversampling with replacement. It begins with define $k$ nearest neighbors algorithm for each minority sample, than generating synthetic examples duplication through its neighbors as many as the desired percentage among minority class observations. However, this algorithm is often experimented on low-dimensional data [16] in most situations. In fact, it seems beneficial but less effective for very-high-dimensional data. Therefore, it often is combined with data preprocessing methods including feature selection or feature extraction. These methods aim reduce dimension of origin data.

We propose a new SMOTE algorithm (1) that generates new synthetically gene expression data from new features extracted of DCNN. Our algorithm generates synthetic data which has almost similar characteristics of the training data points. Synthetic data points ($x_{new}$) are generated in the following way. Firstly, the algorithm takes the feature vectors and its nearest neighbors, computes the distance between these vectors. Secondly, the difference is multiplied by a random number ($\lambda$) between 0 and 1, and it is added back to feature vector. This causes the selection of a random point along the line segment between two specific features. Then, linear support vector machine is used to set label for generating samples with constant $C = 10^3$. An amount of new samples ($p\%$) and $k$ nearest neighbors are hyper parameters of the algorithm.

---

**Algorithm 1:** SMOTE(S, p, k)

---

**Data**: number of samples S; amount of SMOTE p%; number of nearest
         neighbors $k$
**Result**: : $(p/100) * S$ synthetic samples
initialization;
$p = (int)(p/100)$;
$nf$ = number of attributes;
$data$: array for original data;
$count$: number of synthetic data generated;
$synthetic$: array for synthetic data;
(*Compute k nearest neighbors for each sample*);
**for** $i \leftarrow 1$ **to** S **do**
    Compute k nearest neighbors for i, save the indices $\rightarrow$ nnarray;
    *Generate data from original data*;
    **while** $p \neq 0$ **do**
        Choose a random number between 1 and $k$ call it $nn$.;
        In this step chooses one of the $k$ nearest neighbors of $i$;
        **for** $f \leftarrow 1$ **to** $nf$ **do**
            $dif = data[nnarray[nn]][f] - data[i][f]$ ;
            $synthetic[k][f] = data[i][f] + random(0,1) * dif$;
        $count++$ ;
        $p = p - 1$ ;

---

### 3.3 Gene Expression Classification of SVM with SMOTE Using Features Extracted from DCNN

The original SVM algorithm was invented by Vapnik [42]. SVM algorithm is systematic and properly motivated by the statistical learning theory. This algorithm is a supervised learning model that is widely applied for classifications and regressions [45].

The SVM algorithm find the best separating plane furthest from the different classes. To achieve this purpose, the SVM tries to maximize the distance between two boundary hyperplanes to reduce the probability of misclassification. The optimal hyperplane found by SVM is maximally distant from the two classes of labeled points located on each side (Fig. 3). In practice, the SVM algorithm gives good accuracy in classifying very-high-dimensional data. Although the SVM is well-known as an efficient model for classifying gene expression data, the small-sample-size training datasets degrade the classification performance of any model [46]. In addition to performing linear classification, the algorithm has been very successful in building highly non-linear classifiers by means of kernel-based learning methods [47]. Kernel-based learning methods aim to transform the input space into higher dimensions, such as a radial basis function (RBF), sigmoid function, and polynomial function. In the proposed approach, a non-linear SVM with an RBF kernel is used for classifying gene expression after extraction feature and enhancing data.

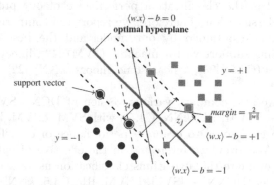

**Fig. 3.** SVM for binary classification

The proposed algorithm is effective combination of three algorithms DCNN, SMOTE and SVM. The algorithm performs the training task with three main phases (Fig. 1).

First of all, we implement a new DCNN that extract new features from origin gene expression data. Our model has take advantage of DCNN is that this model can learn latent features from very-high-dimensional input spaces. This process can be viewed as projection of data from higher dimensional space to a lower dimensional space. Moreover, these new features we can improve the dissimilarity power of gene expression representations and thus obtain higher accuracy rate than original features.

Although the data dimension has reduced but training data sample size is relatively diminutive compared to feature vector size, so that classifiers may give poor classification performance due to over-fitting. In a second order phase training, our model use SMOTE generates new sample from features extracted by DCNN model. In our approach, in the very-high-dimensional data setting only $k$NN classifiers based on the Euclidean distance seem to benefit substantially from the use of over-sampling, provided that feature extraction by extraction model is performed before using this algorithm. For traditional over-sampling algorithm, it is not effective for very-high-dimensional data and this problem has tackled by DCNN model in our approach.

Last but not least, our model generates new training data following which the classifiers learns to classify gene expression data efficiently in this phase. The classifiers consist non-linear SVM, linear SVM, $k$NN, RF and C4.5 that are used to classify new data. In our approach, we propose to use RBF kernel type in SVM model because it is general and efficient [45]. Moreover, the combination of DCNN and SMOTE can improve accuracy classification of linear SVM, RF and $k$NN.

## 4   Evaluation

We are interested in the classification performance of our proposal for gene expression data classification. Therefore, we report the comparison of the classification performance obtained by our model and the best state-of-the-art algorithms including support vector machine (SVM) [42], linear SVM (LSVM) [21], decision trees (C4.5) [25], $k$ nearest neighbors ($k$NN) [22], random forests (RF) [23].

In addition, we also compare various version of DCNN-SMOTE (DCNN-SMOTE $\rightarrow$ [SVM, LSVM, RF, $k$NN, C4.5]) with SVM, LSVM, RF, $k$NN, C4.5. These results are used so as to evaluate performance of classifiers after using DCNN-SMOTE. Moreover, we interested in the effective of enhancing model, therefore we also evaluate the algorithms classification using features extracted by extraction model (DCNN $\rightarrow$ [SVM, LSVM, RF, C4.5, $k$NN]), then they are compared to our proposed.

In order to evaluate the effectiveness in classification tasks, we have implemented DCNN-SMOTE-SVM and its version in Python using Scikit [48] and TensorFlow [49] libraries. Other algorithms like RF, C4.5 in Scikit library. We use the highly efficient standard SVM algorithm LibSVM [21] with one-versus-one strategy for multi-class. We used the Student's test to assess classification results of learning algorithms.

All tests were run under Linux Mint on a 3.07 GHz Intel(R) Xeon(R) CPU PC with 8 GB RAM.

**Table 1.** Description of microarray gene expression datasets

| ID | Name | ♯Samples | Dim | Classes | Protocols | ID | Name | ♯ Samples | Dim | Classes | Protocol |
|----|------|---------|-----|---------|-----------|----|------|----------|-----|---------|----------|
| 1 | Leukemia Golub | 72 | 7129 | 2 | trn-tst | 26 | E-GEOD-62452 | 130 | 33297 | 2 | loo |
| 2 | Breast Veer | 97 | 24481 | 2 | trn-tst | 27 | E-GEOD-51981 | 148 | 54675 | 2 | loo |
| 3 | Colon | 62 | 2000 | 2 | loo | 28 | E-GEOD-21122 | 158 | 22283 | 7 | loo |
| 4 | Breast Chowdaly | 104 | 22283 | 2 | loo | 29 | E-GEOD-73685 | 183 | 33297 | 8 | loo |
| 5 | Leukemia Armstrong | 72 | 12582 | 2 | trn-tst | 30 | E-GEOD-32537 | 217 | 22283 | 7 | loo |
| 6 | Lung Bhattacharjee | 181 | 12533 | 2 | trn-tst | 31 | E-GEOD-44077 | 226 | 33252 | 4 | loo |
| 7 | Lung Gordon | 180 | 12533 | 2 | loo | 32 | E-GEOD-30784 | 229 | 54675 | 3 | loo |
| 8 | Dlbcl Shipp | 58 | 7129 | 2 | loo | 33 | E-GEOD-29272 | 268 | 22283 | 2 | loo |
| 9 | Breast Gravier | 168 | 2905 | 2 | loo | 34 | E-GEOD-22470 | 271 | 22283 | 2 | loo |
| 10 | Leukemia Chiaretti | 128 | 22283 | 6 | loo | 35 | E-GEOD-68606 | 274 | 22283 | 16 | loo |
| 11 | E-GEOD-30540 | 35 | 54675 | 2 | loo | 36 | E-GEOD-2034 | 286 | 22283 | 2 | loo |
| 12 | E-GEOD-14858 | 40 | 54675 | 2 | loo | 37 | E-GEOD-21050 | 310 | 54613 | 4 | 10-fold |
| 13 | E-GEOD-29354 | 52 | 22283 | 2 | loo | 38 | E-GEOD-16134 | 310 | 54613 | 4 | 10-fold |
| 14 | E-GEOD-39716 | 53 | 22215 | 3 | loo | 39 | E-GEOD-20685 | 327 | 54627 | 6 | 10-fold |
| 15 | E-GEOD-66533 | 53 | 33297 | 3 | loo | 40 | E-GEOD-13070 | 364 | 54675 | 2 | 10-fold |
| 16 | E-GEOD-65106 | 58 | 54675 | 3 | loo | 41 | E-GEOD-68468 | 390 | 22283 | 6 | 10-fold |
| 17 | E-GEOD-31189 | 59 | 33297 | 3 | loo | 42 | E-GEOD-50409 | 428 | 54613 | 2 | 10-fold |
| 18 | E-GEOD-37364 | 92 | 54675 | 2 | loo | 43 | E-GEOD-26253 | 432 | 17419 | 2 | 10-fold |
| 19 | E-GEOD-51024 | 94 | 54675 | 4 | loo | 44 | E-GEOD-6532 | 327 | 22645 | 3 | 10-fold |
| 20 | E-GEOD-3726 | 96 | 54675 | 2 | loo | 45 | E-GEOD-31312 | 498 | 54630 | 3 | 10-fold |
| 21 | E-GEOD-36771 | 107 | 54675 | 2 | loo | 46 | E-GEOD-39582 | 566 | 54755 | 6 | 10-fold |
| 22 | E-GEOD-37751 | 107 | 54675 | 2 | loo | 47 | E-GEOD-33315 | 575 | 22283 | 10 | 10-fold |
| 23 | E-GEOD-43458 | 110 | 33252 | 2 | loo | 48 | E-GEOD-47460 | 582 | 15261 | 10 | 10-fold |
| 24 | E-GEOD-31552 | 111 | 33297 | 3 | loo | 49 | E-GEOD-36376 | 433 | 22283 | 2 | 10-fold |
| 25 | E-GEOD-19804 | 120 | 54675 | 2 | loo | 50 | E-GEOD-7307 | 677 | 54675 | 12 | 10-fold |

## 4.1   Experiments Setup

Experiments are conducted with fifty very-high-dimensional datasets from the Biomedical [18] and Array Express repositories [19]. The characteristics of datasets are summarized in Table 1.

The evaluation protocols are illustrated in the last column of Table 1. With datasets having training set (trn) and testing set (tst) available, we use the training data to tune the parameters of the algorithms for obtaining a good accuracy in the learning phase. Then the obtained model is evaluated on the test set. With a datasets having less than 300 data points, the test protocol is leave-one-out cross-validation (loo). For the others, we use 10-fold cross-validation protocols remains the most widely to evaluate the performance [50]. The total classification accuracy measure is used to evaluate the classification models.

As for training model, we tune the parameters for three algorithms including DCNN, SMOTE and the parameters of classifiers.

In order to train network, we use Adam for optimization [51] with batch size is 8 to 32. We start to train with a learning rate of 0.00002 for all layers, and then rise it manually every time when the validation error rate stopped improving. Cross entropy is used to define a loss function in DCNN. The number of epochs is 200.

In our algorithm, the number of neighbors ($k$) is chosen in 1, 3, 5, 7, 9. The samples were over-sampled (p) at 100%, 200% and 300% of its original samples size. We tune the hyper-parameter $\gamma$ of RBF kernel and the cost $C$ (a trade-off between the margin size and the errors) to obtain the best correctness.

**Table 2.** Hyper-parameters of DCNN-SMOTE-SVM

| ID | k | p(%) | C | $\gamma$ | ID | k | p(%) | C | $\gamma$ |
|---|---|---|---|---|---|---|---|---|---|
| 1 | 3 | 300 | 1E+05 | 1E-05 | 26 | 9 | 200 | 1E+01 | 1E-03 |
| 2 | 9 | 300 | 1E+03 | 1E-04 | 27 | 3 | 100 | 1E+04 | 1E-05 |
| 3 | 9 | 200 | 1E+05 | 1E-05 | 28 | 9 | 400 | 1E+01 | 1E-02 |
| 4 | 3 | 100 | 1E+01 | 1E-02 | 29 | 3 | 100 | 1E+02 | 1E-04 |
| 5 | 3 | 100 | 1E+05 | 1E-05 | 30 | 3 | 150 | 1E+05 | 1E-02 |
| 6 | 11 | 200 | 1E+02 | 1E-04 | 31 | 9 | 200 | 1E+04 | 1E-05 |
| 7 | 3 | 100 | 1E+01 | 1E-02 | 32 | 3 | 100 | 1E+03 | 1E-05 |
| 8 | 11 | 200 | 1E+05 | 1E-04 | 33 | 9 | 100 | 1E+05 | 1E-05 |
| 9 | 3 | 100 | 1E+05 | 1E-05 | 34 | 11 | 150 | 1E+05 | 1E-03 |
| 10 | 3 | 100 | 1E+05 | 1E-04 | 35 | 3 | 100 | 1E+05 | 1E-05 |
| 11 | 3 | 100 | 1E+05 | 1E-05 | 36 | 5 | 400 | 1E+04 | 1E-04 |
| 12 | 9 | 200 | 1E+03 | 1E-05 | 37 | 9 | 100 | 1E+01 | 1E-03 |
| 13 | 3 | 100 | 1E+05 | 1E-02 | 38 | 3 | 100 | 1E+03 | 1E-05 |
| 14 | 3 | 100 | 1E+05 | 1E-05 | 39 | 3 | 100 | 1E+05 | 1E-04 |
| 15 | 3 | 100 | 1E+05 | 1E-05 | 40 | 9 | 100 | 1E+03 | 1E-05 |
| 16 | 5 | 300 | 1E+02 | 1E-03 | 41 | 9 | 150 | 1E+02 | 1E-03 |
| 17 | 3 | 100 | 1E+05 | 1E-05 | 42 | 3 | 100 | 1E+05 | 1E-05 |
| 18 | 11 | 200 | 1E+05 | 1E-05 | 43 | 9 | 100 | 1E+01 | 1E-04 |
| 19 | 9 | 100 | 1E+05 | 1E-05 | 44 | 9 | 200 | 1E+02 | 1E-04 |
| 20 | 9 | 100 | 1E+05 | 1E-04 | 45 | 9 | 100 | 1E+03 | 1E-05 |
| 21 | 3 | 100 | 1E+05 | 1E-05 | 46 | 9 | 200 | 1E+03 | 1E-05 |
| 22 | 9 | 100 | 1E+01 | 1E-03 | 47 | 3 | 100 | 1E+01 | 1E-03 |
| 23 | 9 | 100 | 1E+05 | 1E-05 | 48 | 3 | 100 | 1E+01 | 1E-04 |
| 24 | 3 | 100 | 1E+04 | 1E-05 | 49 | 9 | 200 | 1E+05 | 1E-05 |
| 25 | 9 | 100 | 1E+01 | 1E-04 | 50 | 9 | 100 | 1E+01 | 1E-05 |

The cost $C$ is chosen in $1, 10, 10^2, 10^3, 10^4, 10^5$, and the hyper-parameter $\gamma$ of RBF kernel is tried among $1.E-1, 1.E-2, 1.E-3, 1.E-4, 1.E-5$. All the optimal parameters is show in Table 2.

With other algorithms, the cost constant $C$ of linear SVM is set to $10^3$. In non-linear SVM, we adjust the hyper-parameter $\gamma$ and the cost $C$ to get the best result. RF learns 200 decision trees to classify all datasets. $k$NN tries to use $k$ among $\{1, 3, 5, 7\}$.

## 4.2 Classification Results

Table 3 gives results of classifying algorithms on 50 gene expression datasets. The best results are bold faces and the second ones are italic. The plot charts in Figs. 4, 5 and 6 also visualise classification results. Table 4 summarizes results of these statistical tests with paired Student ratio test present the mean accuracy of these models.

**Table 3.** Classification results of 15 models on 50 datasets (%)

| ID | SVM | LSVM | kNN | RF | C 4.5 | DCNN→ | | | | | DCNN-SMOTE→ | | | | |
|----|-----|------|-----|-----|-------|------|------|-----|-----|------|------|------|-----|-----|------|
| | | | | | | SVM | LSVM | kNN | RF | C4.5 | SVM | LSVM | kNN | RF | C4.5 |
| 1 | 97.06 | 97.06 | 88.24 | 82.36 | 91.18 | 97.06 | 97.01 | 91.18 | 67.65 | 85.29 | 97.06 | 97.06 | 97.06 | 85.29 | 85.29 |
| 2 | 63.16 | 63.16 | 47.37 | 73.68 | 63.16 | 73.68 | 63.16 | 52.63 | 73.68 | 63.16 | 89.47 | 89.47 | 57.89 | 78.95 | 78.95 |
| 3 | 85.48 | 80.65 | 85.48 | 79.52 | 74.19 | 87.10 | 82.26 | 80.64 | 80.65 | 66.13 | 88.71 | 88.71 | 85.48 | 80.65 | 77.41 |
| 4 | 90.08 | 97.12 | 90.38 | 92.17 | 92.31 | 98.08 | 98.08 | 98.08 | 94.23 | 85.58 | 98.08 | 98.08 | 93.27 | 96.15 | 86.54 |
| 5 | 86.67 | 86.67 | 99.33 | 86.67 | 86.67 | 100 | 100 | 100 | 100 | 100 | 100 | 100 | 99.33 | 100 | 100 |
| 6 | 98.66 | 98.66 | 96.64 | 100 | 90.60 | 98.66 | 98.66 | 100 | 97.32 | 70.47 | 99.33 | 99.33 | 99.33 | 99.33 | 91.94 |
| 7 | 82.87 | 100 | 99.45 | 97.78 | 93.37 | 100 | 98.90 | 92.82 | 93.92 | 87.85 | 98.9 | 98.90 | 93.92 | 95.58 | 91.71 |
| 8 | 55.17 | 56.90 | 58.62 | 59.62 | 56.90 | 58.62 | 55.17 | 55.17 | 51.72 | 62.07 | 63.79 | 62.07 | 50 | 51.72 | 55.17 |
| 9 | 78.98 | 76.19 | 67.86 | 69.13 | 80.95 | 84.52 | 77.38 | 70.24 | 70.83 | 63.10 | 78.57 | 76.79 | 71.43 | 70.24 | 74.4 |
| 10 | 83.59 | 84.38 | 73.44 | 76.56 | 68.75 | 85.16 | 84.38 | 64.84 | 75.00 | 71.88 | 85.94 | 85.94 | 72.65 | 75 | 65.63 |
| 11 | 74.29 | 74.29 | 60.00 | 71.43 | 51.43 | 74.29 | 74.29 | 68.57 | 71.43 | 60.00 | 80.00 | 80.00 | 71.43 | 74.29 | 68.57 |
| 12 | 87.50 | 74.29 | 85.00 | 71.43 | 51.43 | 87.50 | 85.00 | 85.00 | 85.00 | 80.00 | 87.5 | 85.00 | 85.00 | 88.00 | 85.00 |
| 13 | 79.25 | 71.70 | 69.81 | 71.70 | 58.49 | 79.25 | 77.36 | 77.36 | 77.36 | 71.70 | 79.25 | 79.25 | 79.25 | 79.24 | 73.58 |
| 14 | 86.79 | 90.57 | 84.91 | 79.25 | 84.91 | 90.57 | 90.57 | 90.57 | 86.79 | 67.92 | 90.57 | 90.57 | 90.57 | 90.57 | 79.25 |
| 15 | 96.55 | 96.55 | 93.10 | 89.66 | 77.59 | 96.55 | 96.55 | 93.10 | 93.10 | 79.31 | 96.55 | 96.55 | 93.10 | 91.38 | 75.86 |
| 16 | 74.58 | 74.58 | 55.93 | 61.02 | 64.41 | 71.19 | 71.19 | 54.24 | 59.32 | 55.93 | 71.19 | 59.53 | 61.02 | 67.8 | 66.1 |
| 17 | 56.52 | 69.57 | 57.61 | 59.78 | 45.65 | 72.83 | 71.74 | 55.43 | 56.52 | 55.43 | 73.91 | 72.83 | 63.04 | 58.69 | 63.04 |
| 18 | 80.85 | 73.40 | 76.60 | 76.60 | 87.23 | 79.79 | 78.72 | 76.60 | 75.53 | 65.96 | 79.11 | 78.72 | 76.6 | 75.83 | 75 |
| 19 | 95.83 | 95.83 | 93.75 | 95.83 | 91.67 | 96.88 | 96.88 | 93.75 | 96.88 | 92.71 | 98.96 | 97.92 | 92.7 | 96.88 | 89.58 |
| 20 | 96.15 | 90.38 | 94.23 | 96.15 | 87.50 | 94.23 | 92.31 | 92.31 | 92.31 | 82.69 | 96.15 | 96.15 | 96.15 | 92.3 | 82.69 |
| 21 | 93.46 | 92.52 | 85.98 | 92.52 | 85.98 | 91.59 | 91.59 | 81.31 | 86.92 | 86.91 | 92.52 | 92.52 | 85.05 | 87.85 | 85.98 |
| 22 | 87.96 | 84.26 | 80.56 | 89.81 | 79.63 | 89.81 | 84.23 | 83.33 | 87.96 | 82.41 | 87.96 | 83.33 | 85.19 | 88.89 | 81.3 |
| 23 | 98.18 | 98.18 | 96.36 | 94.55 | 91.82 | 98.18 | 98.18 | 93.63 | 95.45 | 94.55 | 99.09 | 99.09 | 95.45 | 96.36 | 93.64 |
| 24 | 88.29 | 87.39 | 79.28 | 86.49 | 77.48 | 89.19 | 87.39 | 77.48 | 87.39 | 72.07 | 89.19 | 88.29 | 77.48 | 87.39 | 74.77 |
| 25 | 94.17 | 94.17 | 88.33 | 95.83 | 85.00 | 95.83 | 95.00 | 85.00 | 95.83 | 90.00 | 95.83 | 95.00 | 87.5 | 95.83 | 90 |
| 26 | 80.00 | 80.00 | 71.54 | 82.31 | 62.31 | 80.77 | 80.77 | 77.69 | 81.54 | 70.00 | 81.54 | 80.77 | 77.69 | 81.54 | 73.08 |
| 27 | 77.03 | 79.05 | 59.46 | 66.89 | 71.62 | 79.73 | 79.73 | 66.22 | 68.24 | 62.84 | 80.41 | 79.73 | 69.59 | 68.24 | 64.86 |
| 28 | 86.71 | 87.34 | 82.91 | 85.44 | 70.89 | 87.34 | 87.34 | 85.44 | 84.81 | 68.99 | 87.34 | 85.44 | 81.01 | 84.81 | 61.39 |
| 29 | 80.87 | 80.33 | 78.69 | 77.60 | 75.96 | 80.33 | 80.87 | 74.32 | 79.23 | 64.48 | 80.33 | 78.69 | 75.96 | 79.23 | 63.93 |
| 30 | 77.88 | 77.97 | 75.58 | 77.46 | 62.74 | 79.72 | 78.80 | 78.80 | 79.72 | 74.65 | 79.72 | 80.18 | 80.18 | 80.18 | 76.04 |
| 31 | 99.56 | 99.56 | 98.23 | 98.32 | 94.32 | 99.12 | 99.12 | 97.34 | 97.79 | 94.25 | 99.56 | 99.12 | 97.79 | 98.23 | 94.25 |
| 32 | 91.70 | 92.14 | 88.21 | 88.21 | 83.41 | 90.83 | 90.39 | 85.15 | 88.65 | 85.59 | 92.14 | 92.14 | 89.51 | 90.39 | 86.03 |
| 33 | 99.25 | 99.25 | 99.25 | 99.25 | 97.01 | 99.25 | 99.25 | 99.25 | 99.25 | 97.76 | 99.25 | 99.25 | 99.25 | 99.25 | 98.5 |
| 34 | 91.51 | 90.45 | 88.19 | 85.63 | 78.87 | 91.14 | 90.77 | 85.98 | 85.24 | 80.07 | 91.88 | 91.51 | 87.45 | 84.5 | 83.39 |
| 35 | 100 | 100 | 77.37 | 100 | 100 | 100 | 100 | 88.32 | 100 | 100 | 100 | 100 | 100 | 100 | 100 |
| 36 | 73.08 | 87.41 | 82.87 | 86.71 | 83.94 | 89.51 | 87.76 | 79.37 | 80.07 | 78.32 | 88.11 | 87.76 | 81.81 | 82.86 | 73.78 |
| 37 | 43.91 | 62.38 | 54.75 | 72.44 | 59.85 | 95.08 | 94.02 | 93.40 | 95.05 | 90.87 | 95.09 | 94.08 | 92.7 | 94.44 | 86.91 |
| 38 | 95.49 | 93.55 | 88.99 | 92.27 | 85.84 | 96.14 | 96.14 | 88.36 | 92.56 | 88.71 | 96.46 | 94.86 | 88.42 | 92.29 | 88.41 |
| 39 | 88.01 | 84.43 | 74.40 | 85.79 | 68.89 | 89.93 | 89.93 | 69.63 | 76.76 | 53.46 | 89.35 | 87.74 | 71.75 | 77.72 | 51.75 |
| 40 | 50.54 | 76.31 | 56.62 | 68.13 | 59.88 | 71.42 | 69.79 | 55.47 | 62.33 | 59.33 | 69.77 | 65.13 | 61.02 | 68.34 | 59.34 |
| 41 | 63.38 | 97.20 | 89.78 | 94.16 | 95.44 | 94.37 | 94.37 | 88.32 | 100 | 100 | 95.93 | 96.17 | 84.13 | 84.38 | 78.03 |
| 42 | 76.21 | 72.90 | 57.70 | 65.19 | 60.12 | 74.11 | 72.18 | 61.45 | 66.60 | 61.22 | 75.54 | 74.10 | 61.21 | 65.4 | 60.92 |
| 43 | 65.94 | 66.38 | 58.13 | 60.25 | 51.25 | 66.66 | 63.46 | 57.20 | 62.48 | 52.07 | 64.57 | 84.51 | 58.5 | 61.52 | 57.08 |
| 44 | 91.45 | 89.53 | 88.99 | 91.06 | 83.39 | 91.45 | 90.54 | 89.93 | 91.14 | 85.29 | 91.45 | 89.66 | 90.84 | 91.45 | 91.45 |
| 45 | 86.41 | 86.14 | 71.87 | 84.75 | 64.64 | 97.99 | 97.98 | 96.80 | 97.19 | 94.21 | 97.99 | 97.79 | 98.39 | 98.19 | 96.79 |
| 46 | 84.73 | 83.10 | 68.01 | 78.52 | 60.03 | 83.69 | 83.68 | 98.76 | 98.41 | 92.17 | 83.86 | 83.32 | 83.52 | 98.24 | 89.41 |
| 47 | 87.46 | 83.51 | 62.99 | 80.33 | 69.33 | 88.01 | 87.84 | 73.70 | 75.80 | 56.30 | 88.00 | 85.25 | 75.66 | 76.18 | 50.91 |
| 48 | 81.01 | 80.68 | 77.15 | 78.52 | 65.29 | 80.44 | 80.27 | 75.66 | 76.17 | 65.97 | 79.81 | 77.16 | 76.16 | 78.38 | 70.96 |
| 49 | 100 | 100 | 96.53 | 99.30 | 97.68 | 79.60 | 100 | 100 | 99.77 | 97.23 | 100 | 100 | 100 | 100 | 99.77 |
| 50 | 82.90 | 74.01 | 82.27 | 82.93 | 63.81 | 82.31 | 81.27 | 92.46 | 93.20 | 84.93 | 82.89 | 81.42 | 82.88 | 94.99 | 75.03 |

First and foremost, we evaluate feature extraction and enhancing data algorithms. We compare the accuracy of classifying algorithms (SVM, LSVM, $k$NN and RF) and various versions of DCNN-SMOTE including (DCNN-SMOTE-SVM, DCNN-SMOTE-LSVM, DCNN-SMOTE-$k$NN and DCNN-SMOTE-RF).

At first sight, Tables 3, 4 and Fig. 6 show that DCNN-SMOTE-SVM, DCNN-SMOTE-LSVM, DCNN-SMOTE-$k$NN, DCNN-SMOTE-RF significantly increases the mean accuracy of 4.83, 3.37, 2.9, 2.08% points compared to SVM, LSVM, $k$NN and RF respectively. All p-values are less than 0.05. In detail, DCNN-SMOTE-SVM has good performances compared to SVM with 29 wins, 11 ties, 10 defeats, p-value = 1.33E-03 as well as DCNN-SMOTE-LSVM has 34 wins, 7 ties, 9 defeats (p-value = 8.72E-03) compared to LSVM. In the comparison to $k$NN, DCNN-SMOTE-$k$NN outperforms 29 out of 50 datasets (29 wins, 4 ties, 17 defeats, p-value = 2.26E-03). Besides, DCNN-SMOTE-RF has 29 wins, 12 ties, 9 defeats (p-value = 2.78E-02) compared to RF. These results show effective of DCNN and SMOTE that improve accuracy of SVM, LSVM, RF and $k$NN classifiers. In the comparison between DCNN-SMOTE-C4.5 with C4.5, DCNN-SMOTE-C4.5 slightly superior to decision tree of C4.5 with 27 wins, 2 tie, 21 defeat, p-value = 1.06E-01 (not significant different).

In addition, it is clear that DCNN-SMOTE-SVM shows the best performance. Tables 3 and 4 show that it significantly improves the mean accuracy of 4.82, 3.53, 9.40, 5.55, 12.48% points compared to SVM, LSVM, $k$NN, RF and C4.5 respectively. All p-values are less than 0.05. In detail, it has 29 wins, 10 ties, 11 defeats (p-value = 1.33E-03) against SVM and 33 wins, 11 ties, 6 defeats (p-value = 4.68E-04) compared to LSVM. This model has also 48 wins, 1 tie, 1 defeat (p-value = 5.57E-09) compared to $k$NN and 41 wins, 5 ties, 4 defeats (p-value = 6.01E-09) compared to RF. In the comparison to C4.5, our model outperforms 46 out of 50 datasets (46 wins, 1 ties, 3 defeat, p-value = 3.12E-12).

Moreover, DCNN-SMOTE-SVM model efficiently classify more than various versions including DCNN-SMOTE→[LSVM, $k$NN, RF and C4.5]. In detail, this model gives good performances compared to DCNN-SMOTE→[LSVM, $k$NN, RF and C4.5] which improves the mean accuracy of 0.63, 5.67, 3.47, 9.7 respectively.

Furthermore, DCNN, SMOTE models enhance the accuracy of classifiers compared to the algorithms classifications using the features extraction from DCNN. It is clear that DCNN-SMOTE→[SVM, LSVM, $k$NN, RF, C4.5] increase the mean accuracy of 0.98, 1.09, 3.15, 1.06, 1.00% points compared to DCNN →[SVM, LSVM, $k$NN, RF, C4.5]. These results show using DCNN and SMOTE is effectively more than our paper previous [13].

The running time of a our model includes three parts: the time to train the deep convolutional networks for extracting the features, the time to generate new samples and the training time for the classifier on the new data. The average time of the first part on 50 datasets is 48.26 s. The average time of the second part is 29.37 s. Finally, the average time of the second part for SVM, $k$NN, LSVM, RF and C4.5 in the our model are, respectively, 0.91, 0.08, 1.83, 2.75 and 1.37 s. While the running time of SVM, $k$NN, LSVM, RF and C4.5 are 8.48, 0.31, 54.85, 10.76 and 6.3 s.

**Table 4.** Summary of the accuracy comparison

| Accuracy | Means | Win | Tie | Lose | p-value |
|---|---|---|---|---|---|
| SVM | 83.34 | | | | |
| DCNN-SVM | 87.19 | | | | |
| DCNN-SMOTE-SVM | **88.17** | | | | |
| LSVM | 84.64 | | | | |
| DCNN-LSVM | 86.45 | | | | |
| DCNN-SMOTE-LSVM | 87.54 | | | | |
| $k$NN | 78.77 | | | | |
| DCNN-$k$NN | 81.45 | | | | |
| DCNN-SMOTE-$k$NN | 82.51 | | | | |
| RF | 82.62 | | | | |
| DCNN-RF | 83.31 | | | | |
| DCNN-SMOTE-RF | 84.70 | | | | |
| DCNN-SMOTE-SVM & SVM | | 29 | 11 | 10 | 1.33E-03 |
| DCNN-SMOTE-LSVM & LSVM | | 34 | 7 | 9 | 8.72E-03 |
| DCNN-SMOTE-$k$NN & $k$NN | | 29 | 4 | 17 | 2.26E-03 |
| DCNN-SMOTE-RF & RF | | 29 | 12 | 9 | 2.78E-02 |
| DCNN-SMOTE-C4.5 & C4.5 | | 27 | 2 | 29 | *1.06E-01* |
| DCNN-SMOTE-SVM & DCNN-SVM | | 23 | 17 | 10 | *8.20E-02* |
| DCNN-SMOTE-LSVM & DCNN-LSVM | | 25 | 11 | 14 | *1.59E-01* |
| DCNN-SMOTE-$k$NN & DCNN-$k$NN | | 31 | 8 | 11 | *8.45E-02* |
| DCNN-SMOTE-RF & DCNN-RF | | 28 | 12 | 10 | *7.06E-02* |
| DCNN-SMOTE-C4.5 & DCNN-C4.5 | | 30 | 5 | 15 | *1.47E-01* |
| DCNN-SMOTE-SVM & SVM | | 29 | 11 | 10 | 1.33E-03 |
| DCNN-SMOTE-SVM & LSVM | | 33 | 11 | 6 | 4.68E-04 |
| DCNN-SMOTE-SVM & $k$NN | | 48 | 1 | 1 | 5.57E-09 |
| DCNN-SMOTE-SVM & RF | | 41 | 5 | 4 | 6.01E-09 |
| DCNN-SMOTE-SVM & C4.5 | | 46 | 1 | 3 | 2.91E-12 |
| DCNN-SMOTE-SVM & DCNN-SMOTE-LSVM | | 29 | 17 | 4 | *2.09E-01* |
| DCNN-SMOTE-SVM & DCNN-SMOTE-$k$NN | | 40 | 8 | 2 | 2.27E-08 |
| DCNN-SMOTE-SVM & DCNN-SMOTE-RF | | 35 | 8 | 7 | 6.99E-05 |
| DCNN-SMOTE-SVM & DCNN-SMOTE-C4.5 | | 46 | 3 | 1 | 6.17E-11 |

These experiments allow us to believe that our approach efficiently handle gene expression data with the small sample size in very-high-dimensional input. Moreover, the combination of DCNN and SMOTE is not only improve performance of non-linear SVM and but also linear SVM, $k$NN and random forests.

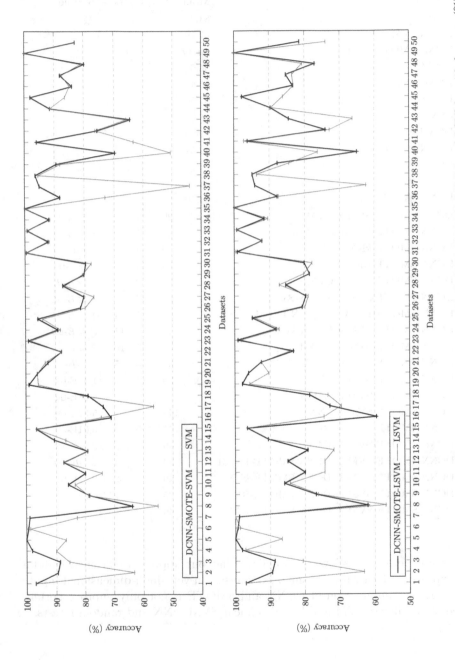

**Fig. 4.** Comparison the accuracy of DCNN-SMOTE-SVM and SVM, DCNN-SMOTE-LSVM and LSVM on 50 datasets (%).

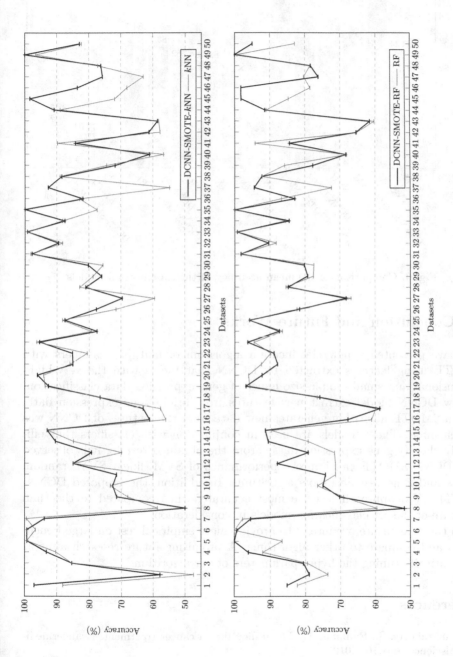

**Fig. 5.** Comparison the accuracy of DCNN-SMOTE-RF and RF, DCNN-SMOTE-*k*NN and *k*NN on 50 datasets (%).

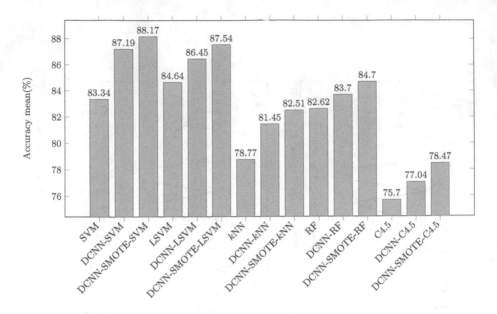

**Fig. 6.** Comparison of the mean accuracy of the classification models

## 5    Conclusion and Future Works

We have presented a new classification algorithm of multiple classifiers with SMOTE using features extracted by DCNN that tackle with the very-high-dimensional and small-sample-size issues of gene expression data classification. A new DCNN model extract new features from origin gene expression data, then a SMOTE algorithm generates new data from the features of DCNN was implemented. These models are used in conjunction with classifiers that efficiently classify gene expression data. From the obtained results, it is observed that DCNN-SMOTE can improve performance of SVM, linear SVM, random forests and $k$ nearest neighbors algorithms. In addition, the proposed DCNN-SMOTE-SVM approach has the most accurate, when compared to the than the-state-of-the-art classification models in consideration.

In the near future, we intend to provide more empirical test on large benchmarks and compare to other algorithms. A promising future research aims at automatically tuning the hyper-parameters of our algorithms.

## References

1. Chakraborty, S., Rahman, T.: The difficulties in cancer treatment. Ecancermedicalscience **6**, ed16 (2012)
2. Schena, M., Shalon, D., Davis, R.W., Brown, P.O.: Quantitative monitoring of gene expression patterns with a complementary DNA microarray. Science **270**(5235), 467–470 (1995)

3. Furey, T.S., Cristianini, N., Duffy, N., Bednarski, D.W., Schummer, M., Haussler, D.: Support vector machine classification and validation of cancer tissue samples using microarray expression data. Bioinformatics **16**(10), 906–914 (2000)
4. Khan, J., et al.: Classification and diagnostic prediction of cancers using gene expression profiling and artificial neural networks. Nat. Med. **7**(6), 673 (2001)
5. Li, L., Weinberg, C.R., Darden, T.A., Pedersen, L.G.: Gene selection for sample classification based on gene expression data: study of sensitivity to choice of parameters of the GA/KNN method. Bioinformatics **17**(12), 1131–1142 (2001)
6. Netto, O. P., Nozawa, S. R., Mitrowsky, R. A. R., Macedo, A. A., Baranauskas, J. A., Lins, C.: Applying decision trees to gene expression data from DNA microarrays: a leukemia case study. In: XXX Congress of the Brazilian Computer Society, X Workshop on Medical Informatics, p. 10 (2010)
7. Díaz-Uriarte, R., De Andres, S.A.: Gene selection and classification of microarray data using random forest. BMC Bioinform. **7**(1), 3 (2006)
8. Tan, A.C., Gilbert, D.: Ensemble machine learning on gene expression data for cancer classification. Appl. Bioinform. **2**(3 Suppl.), S75–S83 (2003)
9. Huynh, P.H., Nguyen, V.H., Do, T.N.: Random ensemble oblique decision stumps for classifying gene expression data. In: Proceedings of the Ninth International Symposium on Information and Communication Technology, SoICT 2018, pp. 137–144. ACM, New York (2018)
10. Pinkel, D., et al.: High resolution analysis of DNA copy number variation using comparative genomic hybridization to microarrays. Nat. Genet. **20**(2), 207 (1998)
11. Singh, R., Lanchantin, J., Robins, G., Qi, Y.: Deepchrome: deep-learning for predicting gene expression from histone modifications. Bioinformatics **32**(17), i639–i648 (2016)
12. Liu, J., Wang, X., Cheng, Y., Zhang, L.: Tumor gene expression data classification via sample expansion-based deep learning. Oncotarget **8**(65), 109646 (2017)
13. Huynh, P.-H., Nguyen, V.-H., Do, T.-N.: A coupling support vector machines with the feature learning of deep convolutional neural networks for classifying microarray gene expression data. In: Sieminski, A., Kozierkiewicz, A., Nunez, M., Ha, Q.T. (eds.) Modern Approaches for Intelligent Information and Database Systems. SCI, vol. 769, pp. 233–243. Springer, Cham (2018). https://doi.org/10.1007/978-3-319-76081-0_20
14. Huynh, P.H., Nguyen, V.H., Do, T.N.: Novel hybrid DCNN-SVM model for classifying RNA-sequencing gene expression data. J. Inf. Telecommun. **3**(4), 533–547 (2019). https://doi.org/10.1080/24751839.2019.1660845
15. Chawla, N.V., Bowyer, K.W., Hall, L.O., Kegelmeyer, W.P.: Smote: synthetic minority over-sampling technique. J. Artif. Intell. Res. **16**, 321–357 (2002)
16. Van Hulse, J., Khoshgoftaar, T.M., Napolitano, A.: Experimental perspectives on learning from imbalanced data. In: Proceedings of the 24th International Conference on Machine Learning, pp. 935–942. ACM (2007)
17. Blagus, R., Lusa, L.: Smote for high-dimensional class-imbalanced data. BMC Bioinform. **14**(1), 106 (2013)
18. Jinyan, L., Huiqing, L.: Kent ridge bio-medical data set repository. Technical report (2002)
19. Brazma, A., et al.: ArrayExpress a public repository for microarray gene expression data at the EBI. Nucleic Acids Res. **31**(1), 68–71 (2003)
20. Vapnik, V.N.: The Nature of Statistical Learning Theory. Springer, New York (1995)
21. Chang, C.C., Lin, C.J.: LIBSVM: a library for support vector machines. ACM Trans. Intell. Syst. Technol. (TIST) **2**(3), 27 (2011)

22. Fix, E., Hodges, J.: Discriminatory analysis-nonparametric discrimination: small sample performance. Technical report, California University, Berkeley (1952)
23. Breiman, L.: Random forests. Mach. Learn. **45**(1), 5–32 (2001)
24. Breiman, L., Friedman, J. H., Olshen, R., Stone, C. J.: Classification and Regression Trees, vol. 8, pp. 452–456. Wadsworth International Group (1984)
25. Quinlan, J.R.: C4.5: Programs for Machine Learning. Morgan Kaufmann Publishers Inc., San Francisco (1993)
26. Li, Y., et al.: A comprehensive genomic pan-cancer classification using the cancer genome atlas gene expression data. BMC Genom. **18**(1), 508 (2017)
27. Krizhevsky, A., et al.: Imagenet classification with deep convolutional neural networks. In: Advances in Neural Information Processing Systems, pp. 1097–1105 (2012)
28. Kim, Y.: Convolutional neural networks for sentence classification. arXiv preprint arXiv:1408.5882 (2014)
29. Min, S., Lee, B., Yoon, S.: Deep learning in bioinformatics. Briefings. Bioinformatics **18**, bbw068 (2016)
30. Zeebaree, D.Q., Haron, H., Abdulazeez, A.M.: Gene selection and classification of microarray data using convolutional neural network. In: 2018 International Conference on Advanced Science and Engineering (ICOASE), pp. 145–150. IEEE (2018)
31. Lyu, B., Haque, A.: Deep learning based tumor type classification using gene expression data. In: Proceedings of the 2018 ACM International Conference on Bioinformatics, Computational Biology, and Health Informatics, BCB 2018, pp. 89–96. ACM, New York (2018)
32. Ambroise, C., McLachlan, G.J.: Selection bias in gene extraction on the basis of microarray gene-expression data. Proc. Nat. Acad. Sci. **99**(10), 6562–6566 (2002)
33. Vert, J.P., Kanehisa, M.: Graph-driven feature extraction from microarray data using diffusion kernels and kernel CCA. In: Advances in Neural Information Processing Systems, pp. 1449–1405 (2003)
34. Wang, A., Gehan, E.A.: Gene selection for microarray data analysis using principal component analysis. Stat. Med. **24**(13), 2069–2087 (2005)
35. Sun, G., Dong, X., Xu, G.: Tumor tissue identification based on gene expression data using DWT feature extraction and PNN classifier. Neurocomputing **69**(4–6), 387–402 (2006)
36. Huynh, P.H., Nguyen, V., Do, T.N.: Enhancing gene expression classification of support vector machines with generative adversarial networks. J. Inf. Commun. Converg. Eng. **17**, 14–20 (2019)
37. Van den Bulcke, T., et al.: SynTReN: a generator of synthetic gene expression data for design and analysis of structure learning algorithms. BMC Bioinform. **7**, 43 (2006)
38. Costa, P., et al.: End-to-end adversarial retinal image synthesis. IEEE Trans. Med. Imaging **37**(3), 781–791 (2018)
39. Moeskops, P., Veta, M., Lafarge, M.W., Eppenhof, K.A.J., Pluim, J.P.W.: Adversarial training and dilated convolutions for brain MRI segmentation. In: Cardoso, M.J., et al. (eds.) DLMIA/ML-CDS -2017. LNCS, vol. 10553, pp. 56–64. Springer, Cham (2017). https://doi.org/10.1007/978-3-319-67558-9_7
40. Lusa, L., et al.: Class prediction for high-dimensional class-imbalanced data. BMC Bioinform. **11**(1), 523 (2010)
41. Fernández, A., García, S., Herrera, F., Chawla, N.V.: Smote for learning from imbalanced data: progress and challenges, marking the 15-year anniversary. J. Artif. Int. Res. **61**(1), 863–905 (2018)

42. Vapnik, V.N.: An overview of statistical learning theory. IEEE Trans. Neural Netw. 10(5), 988–999 (1998)
43. Hinton, G.E., Salakhutdinov, R.R.: Reducing the dimensionality of data with neural networks. Science 313(5786), 504–507 (2006)
44. Hubel, D.H., Wiesel, T.: Shape and arrangement of columns in cat's striate cortex. J. Physiol. 165(3), 559–568 (1963)
45. Burges, C.J.: A tutorial on support vector machines for pattern recognition. Data Min. Knowl. Disc. 2(2), 121–167 (1998)
46. Popovici, V., et al.: Effect of training-sample size and classification difficulty on the accuracy of genomic predictors. Breast Cancer Res. 12(1), R5 (2010)
47. Cristianini, N., Shawe-Taylor, J.: An Introduction to Support Vector Machines and Other Kernel-Based Learning Methods. Cambridge University Press, Cambridge (2000)
48. Pedregosa, F., et al.: Scikit-learn: machine learning in python. J. Mach. Learn. Res. 12, 2825–2830 (2011)
49. Abadi, M., Agarwal, A., Barham, P., Brevdo, E., Chen, Z.: TensorFlow: Large-Scale Machine Learning on Heterogeneous Systems (2015)
50. Wong, T.T.: Performance evaluation of classification algorithms by k-fold and leave-one-out cross validation. Pattern Recogn. 48(9), 2839–2846 (2015)
51. Kingma, D.P., Ba, J.: Adam: a method for stochastic optimization. In: Proceedings of the 3rd International Conference on Learning Representations (ICLR) (2014)

# Age and Gender Estimation of Asian Faces Using Deep Residual Network

Hoang Nguyen[1] and Hieu Trung Huynh[1,2(✉)]

[1] Vietnamese-German University, Thu Dau Mot, Binh Duong, Vietnam
cs2014_hoang.ng@student.vgu.edu.vn, hthieu@ieee.org
[2] Industrial University of Ho Chi Minh City, Ho Chi Minh City, Vietnam

**Abstract.** In recent years, with the rise of deep learning and computer vision, researchers have been looking deeply into the age and gender estimation problem due to its practical influences. A lot of fields, from insurance, retails to marketing, could benefit tremendously from the presence of a reliable estimator, as it would allow companies to easily identify their customer demographics. A great number of models have been proposed, and they have achieved remarkable results. However, because of the lack of open-source, multiethnic dataset, most modern Age and Gender estimating model are trained solely based on white people with Western facial features, and thus fall short with non-Caucasian people. Therefore, in this paper, using a newly-improved Asian face database, we developed an applicable Wide ResNet model to predict the age and the gender of a person using just one image, assuming he/she comes from an Asian background. The model has shown some promising results, as it can match the performance of Microsoft's how-old API estimator in a specific dataset.

**Keywords:** Deep Learning · Convolutional Neural Network · ResNet · Wide ResNet · Age and Gender estimation

## 1 Introduction

It is evident that industrial corporations are always actively searching for ways to utilize the power deep learning to get an insight of their customer segments since any firm that come into possession of such tool can harvest a massive amount of data, smoothly increase their revenues and benefits, surpass their competitors and dominate their corresponding market. Nonetheless, personal information such as gender and age can be difficult to collect on a large scale, since they are relatively sensitive, and not all customers have the spare time to fill out multiple surveys at once. However, there are a fair number of surveillance cameras installed around the facilities and it should be rather easy for companies to extract facial pictures of their visitors for security and research purpose. Therefore, many companies are in an urgent need of a trust-worthy tool that can reasonably predict their customers' identity features, using just the faces.

© Springer Nature Switzerland AG 2019
T. K. Dang et al. (Eds.): FDSE 2019, LNCS 11814, pp. 274–286, 2019.
https://doi.org/10.1007/978-3-030-35653-8_18

In this paper, we dedicate the time and effort to collect and improve upon a mutlti-purpose Asian face dataset with the intention of partially addressing the problem of Age and Gender estimation of Asian people. Ultimately, the final aim of my paper is to make the best use of the data, as well as the existing Deep Learning techniques to put together a well-rounded implementation of Wide ResNet in order to create a reliable program that can be able to extract the age and gender of a certain Asian person with reasonable accuracy on both aspects.

## 2    Related Work

The Age and Gender estimation problem is certainly not a brand-new issue. It has long been studied and researched by many teams, a handful of which proposed several different architectures, including state-of-the-art ones. In [4], Ku et al. proposes examining several pictorial frames of a same person in order to make a more robust and stable prediction. Whereas in [2], Hayashi suggests that instead of completely leaving the feature-extraction step to the convolutional neural network(CNN) model as a black-box, it is advisable to manually extract facial identification landmarks such as wrinkles and use that to enhance the model performance, as they are indications of age. Those are all plausible approaches to such problem.

Eventually, in [5] and [6], Rothe et al. came up with a revolutionary method called Deep EXpectation (DEX) to address the situation. Their method is strikingly simple. In the beginning, they crop and align the face using available toolkits, have them flow through a regular VGG-16 network and treat the age detection task as a classification problem with 101 classes (representing the age from 0 to 100). Finally, after receiving the Softmax distribution for the 101-dimension vector, they perform a dot product operation between that vector and with another vector containing discrete value from 0 to 100 to receive the expected Value. It is argued that this process is more robust and stable than the both the logistic regression as well as the linear regression approach, while yielding a better result at the same time. As presented in [6], they claimed that their implementation is the current state-of-the-art in predicting the subject's apparent age, as tested on the IMDB-WIKI dataset. These two papers are the main academic resources whose concept we will utilize into the model with to achieve desirable result.

## 3    Proposed Method

This section presents in-depth the CNN model architecture design as well as other implementation details, including weight initialization, weight decay, regularization and validation split. Our work improves the existing structures and algorithms with further development using methods proposed by recent creditable publications and research papers.

## 3.1  Wide ResNet Architecture

Regarding the model architecture for our Age and Gender estimator, we used a variation of the popular ImageNet-champion Residual Network, called Wide Residual Network, or Wide ResNet, introduced by Zagoruyko and Komodakis in [7]. The fundamental concept lies behind this network is that in addition to making use of the skip-connection like the regular ResNet, this variation enhances its features extraction capability by rearranging the order of layers in a block, from conv-BN-ReLU to BN-ReLU-conv and also expand in terms of the feature channels by a widening factor $k$. As for the rearrangement of the layers order, [7] showed through experimental results that the new order indeed executes faster than the original one, while at the same time achieving a better accuracy level.

In terms of the feature channel extension, there is an ongoing debate on whether the width or the depth of the network contributes more to the overall success of the model. Conventionally, the original ResNet model suggests that in order to achieve higher accuracy, researchers could just simply increase the deepening factor $N$, also referred to as the number of blocks in a certain stage, or the number of stages in general without having worry about gradient vanishing/exploding like older architecture due to the powerful skip-connection. In other words, keep on stacking more layers until reaching a desirable results was the most straight-forward method. However, deeper network also subsequently increases the number of parameters in linear time and make it longer and harder to converge. Furthermore, there is also the problem of diminishing feature reuse (few residual blocks learning useful representations or many blocks sharing very little information with small contribution to the final goal) in very deep and thin residual networks.

Thus, instead of senselessly stacking more layers and waste computational resources, Wide ResNet suggests addressing the above problems by increasing the number of channels by a factor of $k$, allowing each block to learn a more meaningful feature representation of the data. Although this makes the total number of parameters grows in quadratic time, most modern GPU are programmed to make parallel computation on large tensors for efficient, hence reducing the total amount of time needed for training a model [1]. Furthermore, adding a simple dropout layer between two BN-ReLU-conv sequences also gives more room for model generalization. The specific architecture is described in Table 1.

Similar to the original Wide ResNet, our implementation begins with a 2D convolutional layer to extract the early features, with a $3 \times 3$ convolution block and a 16 feature channels. The main difference with our model is that instead of taking the input shape $32 \times 32 \times 3$, we decided to double it to $64 \times 64 \times 3$, since the Megaage_Asian dataset [9] contains picture with higher resolution, which gives clearer edge and facial feature to detect. Following that, there are 3 main groups, each group all consists of 2 convolutional blocks (here, $N = 2$) and an additional dropout layer with the dropout probability of 0.2 between those blocks to prevent overfitting. Each block contains one BN layer, one ReLU layer and one convolutional layer. During the transition between two groups, the size

**Table 1.** Structure of wide residual networks. Network width is determined by factor k, here k = 8. Groups of convolutions are shown in brackets where N is a number of blocks in group, here N = 2. Downsampling is performed by the first layers in groups conv3 and conv4. The Final 2 fully-connected layers perform prediction based on the flatten layer

| Group name | Output size | Block type = B(3,3) |
|---|---|---|
| conv1 | [ 64 × 64, 16 ] | [ 3 × 3, 16 ] |
| conv2 | [ 64 × 64, 16 × k ] | $\begin{bmatrix} 3 \times 3, 16 \times k \\ 3 \times 3, 16 \times k \end{bmatrix} \times N$ |
| conv3 | [ 32 × 32, 32 × k ] | $\begin{bmatrix} 3 \times 3, 32 \times k \\ 3 \times 3, 32 \times k \end{bmatrix} \times N$ |
| conv4 | [ 16 × 16, 64 × k ] | $\begin{bmatrix} 3 \times 3, 64 \times k \\ 3 \times 3, 64 \times k \end{bmatrix} \times N$ |
| avg-pool | [ 16 × 16, 64 × k ] | [ 8 × 8 ] |
| flatten | [ 1 × 16 × 16 × 64 × k ] | N/A |
| fc-gender | [ 1 × 2 ] | N/A |
| fc-age | [ 1 × 101 ] | N/A |

of features is halved, while the channel planes are doubled. In case the input and output size do not share the same dimension, a 1D convolutional layer is applied in order to resize the layer to a matching dimensionality. Finally, after all the convolutional groups have been performed, the data then flow through one average pooling layer (with block size of 8 × 8) and flattened out. Two final fully-connected layers are then applied simultaneously to the flatten feature vector to perform both the Age and Gender classification. The Gender classification layer is a 2-dimensional Softmax vector, representing the distribution probability that the person is either a male or a female. Similarly, the Age classification vector is 101-dimensional, relative to the possible human age between 0 and 100 (here we presume that people only live up to 100 year for simplicity).

## 4    Training

This section continues to elaborate in details of the training process workflow of our Wide ResNet, from pre-process steps to validation measurements.

### 4.1    Dataset Analysis

Conventionally, most research teams refer to the IMDB - WIKI dataset when they tackle the Age and Gender detection problem, since it is among the most popular public datasets, with 523,051 images of celebrities along with their age and gender. However, it only contains an extremely small portion of people with Asian background. Therefore, models trained on that dataset unsurprisingly underperformed when presented with Asian descendants. Considering that Asian people makes up to approximately 60% of the world population, that is indeed a serious downfall for such models. Consequently, I did a handful of research and finally came across the Megaage_Asian dataset collected by MMLAB, the Chinese University of Hong Kong or SenseTime [9]. The dataset consists of 40,000 up-close, frontal and non-blurry Asian facial images, along with the subject's age and gender, stored in a separate .txt file. The images in the dataset mostly belong to people from different Asian ethnicity such as Thailand, Vietnam or Japan, cropped and aligned centering around their faces, varying from different angles and light direction. The age of the subjects range between 1 and 70 which is truly diversified. Some samples from the dataset are shown in Fig. 1.

**Fig. 1.** Samples from the Megaage_Asian dataset. The dataset is truly diversified, as it contains people with different age, gender & ethnicity

For clearance, identifying one's gender is not as challenging as figuring out one's age, as a normal human can execute the former task almost flawlessly. Thus, although our gender labels are not professionally verified, it still holds certain merits. The dataset consists of 40,000 thousands pictures for training, and 3,945 other pictures for testing, which is a reasonable amount for the task at hands. The female:male ratio is 20684:23261, or roughly 9:10. The distribution of the age range can be interpreted from the Histogram as shown in Fig. 2.

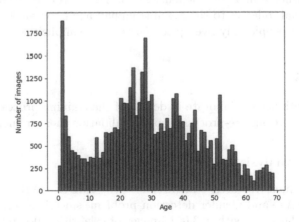

**Fig. 2.** Age distribution of the dataset. Although it is not exactly Uniform, the dataset still offers people with a variety of age range

## 4.2  Regularization and Image Augmentation

Initially, we implemented conventional regularization and image augmentation such as L1, L2 regularization, batch normalization, dropout, image shifting, rotating and flipping to prevent the model from overfitting. However, after the first couple of training processes, it came to our attention that the model still heavily suffer from the state of overfitting. We eventually tackle the troublesome problem by re-implementing two plausible and highly cited papers: Random Erasing [10] and Mixup [8].

**Random Erasing.** The idea behind this method is truly intuitive. As human, we can still perceive the information conveyed by the image even if there are some slight distortion, as long as the distorted portion is not too big that it covers important structure parts. A powerful model should be able to perform at the same level, grasp the context of an image from structure of the overall object architecture, rather than each individual pixels block. Thus, Random Erasing was introduced to assist model in reaching that intelligent stage. In brief, the algorithm performs as follow. During the training phase of the model, any image will either be kept unchanged or randomly have a rectangle region of an arbitrary size assigned with arbitrary pixel values. By simply introducing a reasonable noise to the training sample, this method enhances the model to become less prone to overfitting. We enforced the algorithm with similar set of hyper-parameters as concluded in [10]. To further elaborate, the process can be described as a sequence of mathematical operations. Before putting into training, each image $I$ has a probability of $p$ of activating Random Eraser, and inherently, a probability of $1 - p$ to remain unchanged. The original size of the image is:

$$S = W \times H \tag{1}$$

A randomly selected rectangle region $I_e$ with area ratio $s_a$ is chosen between $s_l$ and $s_h$. An aspect ratio $r_e$ is also uniformly randomly initialized between $r_1$ and $r_2$. The program then calculates the area of $I_e$ as:

$$S_e = s_a \times S \tag{2}$$

which is then used to calculate:

$$H_e = \sqrt{S_e \times r_e} \tag{3}$$

$$W_e = \sqrt{\frac{S_e}{r_e}} \tag{4}$$

Afterwards, another point $P = (x_e, y_e)$ is arbitrarily chosen within $I$, and the region $I_e = (x_e, y_e, x_e + W_e, y_e + H_e)$ is then set to a certain value in the range $[0, 255]$. If $I_e$ falls outside $I$, $P$ is re-selected until the requirement is satisfied. In our implementation, we set $p = 0.5, s_l = 0.02, s_h = 0.4, r_1 = 0.3, r_2 = \frac{1}{0.3}$, similar to the original paper. The resulting images are forwarded to the next stage (Fig. 3).

**Fig. 3.** Example of Random Erasing on face dataset. Here, the random erased portion affects very little on our perception of the subject's age and gender, which is 26, Male

**Mixup.** After the training samples is pre-processed with Random Erasing, an extra measurement is taken to further guarantee the generalization of the same model. In essence, rather than handling each images independently, Mixup groups pairs of samples and their labels together before training the CNN on a convex combination of such pairs. A weakly-trained model will design an overly-complex mapping between an image and its label, then fail to recognize very similar images with slight modification or adversarial generation. To tackle such problem, the Mixup helps regularizing the neural network to favor simple linear behavior in-between training sample instead of complex correlations. The method is proven to enhance robustness, stability and accuracy of models on popular dataset like ImageNet, CIFAR-10 and CIFAF-100 dataset, resulting in state-of-the-art architecture. Despite its powerful capability, Mixup can be easily implemented within a few lines of code with minimal overhead. To put it briefly, Mixup creates virtual training samples through the formula:

$$\tilde{x} = \lambda x_i + (1 - \lambda)x_j \tag{5}$$

$$\tilde{y} = \lambda y_i + (1 - \lambda)y_j \tag{6}$$

where $x_i$ and $x_j$ are raw input vectors; $y_i$ and $y_j$ are one-hot encoding labels; $(x_i, y_i)$ and $(x_j, y_j)$ are two randomly drawn examples from the mini training batch, and $\lambda \in [0, 1]$. In the proposed model, for simplicity purposes, we draw $\lambda$ from a Beta distribution with $\alpha = \beta = 0.2$, i.e $\lambda \sim Beta(0.2, 0.2)$ [8]. The output is now ready to be fed into the CNN for training (Fig. 4).

**Fig. 4.** Example of Random Erasing + Mixup. After being randomly erased, the two images on the left and right are mixed up with $\lambda = 0.5$ to create the middle image. Note that their one-hot labels are also combined

### 4.3    Implementation Details

The entire code and our implementations can be found at: https://github.com/amidadragon/asian-age-gender-estimation.

To put it all together, the complete workflow of our methods is described as following. To start, all images are rescaled to the size of $64 \times 64$. Afterwards, the dataset is separated into training set and testing set with the ratio of $9 : 1$, which has 36,000 and 4,000 images relatively. Each mini-batch of 32 training samples consecutively undergo a pre-processing series of Random Erasing and Mixup before feeding onto the network. Regarding the Wide ResNet, the parameters are randomly initialized using the He random formula [3]:

$$w^{[l]} = X \times \sqrt{\frac{2}{n^{l-1}}} \tag{7}$$

where $w^{[l]}$ is the parameters of layer $l$, $X \sim \mathcal{N}(0,1)$ and $n^{l-1}$ is the number of neurons in the previous layer (layer $l - 1$). This initialization method allows models to converge to a global minimum faster and more efficient. The weights are optimized by the mini-batch gradient descent with the initialized learning rate $\alpha$ set as 0.1, it is decayed overtime through the formula:

$$\alpha = \frac{\alpha_{prev}}{1 + decay\_rate \times epoch\_nums} \tag{8}$$

where $\alpha$ is new learning rate, $\alpha_{prev}$ is the previous learning rate and decay\_rate is set as $1e - 6$. After each epoch, the model is freshly tested on a new validation set that it has never observed before in order to evaluate its generalization power and make necessary adjustments. Only the model which has the best scores on the validation dataset is saved and used for further inspections.

## 5    Experimental Results

This section discusses about our evaluation of the model with the proposed metrics, while also compares it to other existing implementations of age and gender detection module.

### 5.1    Model Evaluation

The entire Wide ResNet is implemented using Python programming language along with its libraries such as OpenCV, NumPy and Keras deep learning framework, trained on Amazon Web Service (AWS), with 8 GB of GPU and 60 GB of Memory. After 48 h of intensive training, Fig. 5 depicts the training history of the Wide ResNet model. It can be interpreted from the figure that the gender validation accuracy peaked at 92%, which is a rather reasonable result compares to other proposed methods. However, the fascinating discovery lies within the age classification. The age accuracy peaks at 15% around epoch 80, but that is not the metrics we intent to examine for the age classification problem, since

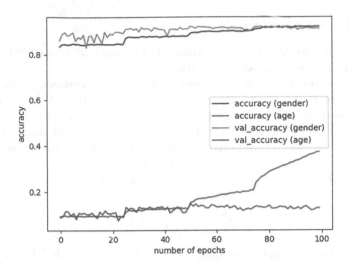

**Fig. 5.** Training process of Wide ResNet. Keep in mind that the validation accuracy (the green and red line) are the metrics that ultimately matters (Color figure online)

precisely predicting a person age is a challenging task for any person, or even professional anthropologists. Hence, we utilize the DEX method mentioned in [5,6] to calculate the predicted age value. In terms of the DEX method, the Softmax distribution only serves as an intermediate means to determine the final age prediction, unlike regular classification model. The expected value for the subject's age is calculated by the formula:

$$E(O) = \sum_{i=0}^{100} y_i o_i \tag{9}$$

where $O = \{o_0, o_1, ..., o_{100}\}$ is the Softmax output probabilities and $y_i$ are the discrete years, ranging from 0 to 100, corresponding to each class $i$. $E(O)$ is the final prediction for a person's age. With $E(O)$ at our disposal, we compute the MAE over the 4,000 testing images by:

$$MAE = \frac{\sum_{i=1}^{n} |\hat{y}_i - E_i(O)|}{n} \tag{10}$$

where $n$ is the number of images, $\hat{y}_i$ and $E_i(O)$ are the actual and predicted age of the person in image $i$, respectively. For the validation set, $MAE \approx 4.2$. To avoid bias in the model selection step, we also perform the exact measurement with the 3,945 testing images, which yields $MAE \approx 4.05$. The result indicates that, on average, the model miss a person's age by a margin of roughly 4 years. Bare in mind that, excluding the young childhood phase when the face might alter dramatically, an average person face does not change too much in a four-year period.

**Fig. 6.** Same person, four years apart (20 & 24)

Figure 6 shows an example predicted by our model (the prediction is placed in the blue rectangle). The two images are from the same person, with similar lighting and face angle. The only difference is that they are taken four years apart. The model is actually 20 and 24 respectively when these two images were taken. Hardly any difference can be detected just from a hasty observation.

It may state that the gender aspect is easier to predict, because there exists only two options to choose, either male or female, and it is also an effortless task for human to perform with very high accuracy. However, the age feature is definitely significantly harder to recognize, because there are more than 100 possible cases. Each individual person has different facial features, depending on their living conditions and ethnicity. In addition the light direction and facial angle could also affect how old a certain people may look.

**Fig. 7.** Some accurately predicted images. The number on the left is the subject actual age, and the right is my prediction

Figure 7 shows some images where our model makes the most plausible guesses. It can be observed that they have natural filter and light, as well as neutral emotion.

There are some images which result in low accuracy by our model as shown in Fig. 8. Some faces emerging such images make up unnaturally, or have a big smile. They result in more wrinkles and eventually give out a feeling that the individuals in the image appear different from they actually are. It could also be that they just possess different facial features in general. On the other hand, there are also images with heavy photoshop resulting in noticeably and undeniably younger.

**Fig. 8.** Inaccurately predicted images

Since an MAE score can be difficult to fully interpret, we also trained the same model, with similar hyper-parameters on the same data with age mapped to a certain age range, based on different phases of a human life circle as shown in Table 2, it includes Toddlers, Teenagers, Young Adults, Adults, Midlife and Seniors.

**Table 2.** Age group

| Group 0 | Group 1 | Group 2 | Group 3 | Group 4 | Group 5 |
|---------|---------|---------|---------|---------|---------|
| 0–11 | 12–18 | 19–25 | 26–32 | 33–39 | 40–100 |

The new model achieved an accuracy level of 67,66% and a 96,3% 1-off accuracy, the confusion matrix is illustrated in Fig. 9.

| y_truely_pred | 0 | 1 | 2 | 3 | 4 | 5 |
|---------------|------|-----|-----|-----|-----|-----|
| 0 | 1133 | 95 | 18 | 5 | 2 | 0 |
| 1 | 69 | 286 | 158 | 15 | 3 | 0 |
| 2 | 2 | 79 | 431 | 219 | 15 | 3 |
| 3 | 1 | 8 | 159 | 368 | 95 | 14 |
| 4 | 2 | 1 | 31 | 129 | 181 | 61 |
| 5 | 0 | 1 | 2 | 23 | 66 | 270 |

**Fig. 9.** Confusion matrix

From the confusion matrix in Fig. 9, we can infer that most of the mistakes are between Group 2 (19–25) and Group 3 (26–32). A reasonable explanation would be that, at these phases, they reach a certain maturity and stable facial feature, and do not change as drastically as other phases, hence the confusion of the model, similar to human. Toddlers and teenagers, on the other hands, go through dramatic changes with their hormones level, resulting in distinct facial features.

## 5.2    Discussion

With our best knowledge, it is difficult to find previous researches which have run on experiment with the same testing dataset. [5] and [6] provide that they achieved the MAE score of 5.0 on the IMDB-WIKI dataset, but that is not to be compared to ours, since their data is much larger, also the distribution differ greatly. However, Microsoft actually published a similar API to predict age and gender of a certain person through just one submitted image. We requested the API to check out its accuracy on the same testing dataset. The result is quite surprising as it turned out. Our model got 1% better than the Microsoft in terms of gender accuracy, and 0.2 worse off in term of MAE score. This is not in anyway a statements that our model outperforms that of Microsoft. Microsoft Deep Leaning model presumably generalizes better to non-Asian individuals, while our model would not make such rivalry prediction. However, with a limited amount of only 40,000 images, and 48 h of GPU training, we were able to partially match the performance of Microsoft, who has in their possession billions of images and GPU computational power. This could place a foundation for future development using similar network architecture (Fig. 10).

**Fig. 10.** Our model (left) vs Microsoft's model (right). My model matched that of Microsoft in some instances. She subject is actually 38 years old

## 6   Conclusion

The Age and Gender estimation is the puzzle that many researchers are looking for a solution, due to its extremely rewarding applications in the real-world applications. With our work, we have introduced a method to partially addressing that problem, by focusing only on the Asian population and using state-of-the-art Deep Learning and Computer Vision algorithms to achieve high accuracy. The proposed approach is based on a well-rounded Wide ResNet and evaluated on an Asian-only face dataset. The experimental results shown that the proposed method has promising outcomes including a small error rate and a reasonable accuracy level. We believe that it has a lot of potential to be further improved in the future. The Wide ResNet has demonstrated its powerful capability. With some engineering effort, more data and computational power, we are certain that we could bring the accuracy to a higher level. Also, besides Dropout, Random Erasing and Mixup, more pre-processing and data augmentation techniques could be applied to the model to bring it out of the current slightly overfitting state. Above all, such model could easily be scaled-up to work for other non-Asian individuals as well through Transfer Learning, with only a small amount of new data needed.

**Acknowledgement.** This work was supported by the Ho Chi Minh city Department of Science and Technology [grant numbers 1131/QD-SKHCN, 06/2018/HD-QKHCN].

# References

1. Dietz, M.: Understand deep residual networks-a simple, modular learning framework that has redefined state-of-the-art (2017). https://blog.waya.ai/deep-residual-learning-9610bb62c355

2. Hayashi, J., Koshimizu, H., Hata, S.: Age and gender estimation based on facial image analysis. In: Palade, V., Howlett, R.J., Jain, L. (eds.) KES 2003. LNCS (LNAI), vol. 2774, pp. 863–869. Springer, Heidelberg (2003). https://doi.org/10.1007/978-3-540-45226-3_118

3. He, K., Zhang, X., Ren, S., Sun, J.: Delving deep into rectifiers: Surpassing human-level performance on imagenet classification. CoRR abs/1502.01852 (2015). http://arxiv.org/abs/1502.01852

4. Ku, C.-L., Chiou, C.-H., Gao, Z.-Y., Tsai, Y.-J., Fuh, C.-S.: Age and gender estimation using multiple-image features. In: Sun, Z., Shan, S., Yang, G., Zhou, J., Wang, Y., Yin, Y.L. (eds.) CCBR 2013. LNCS, vol. 8232, pp. 441–448. Springer, Cham (2013). https://doi.org/10.1007/978-3-319-02961-0_55

5. Rothe, R., Timofte, R., Gool, L.V.: DEX: deep expectation of apparent age from a single image. In: EEE International Conference on Computer Vision Workshops (ICCVW), December 2015

6. Rothe, R., Timofte, R., Gool, L.V.: Deep expectation of real and apparent age from a single image without facial landmarks. Int. J. Comput. Vis. (IJCV) **126**, 144–157 (2018)

7. Zagoruyko, S., Komodakis, N.: Wide residual networks. CoRR abs/1605.07146 (2016). http://arxiv.org/abs/1605.07146

8. Zhang, H., Cissé, M., Dauphin, Y.N., Lopez-Paz, D.: mixup: beyond empirical risk minimization. CoRR abs/1710.09412 (2017). http://arxiv.org/abs/1710.09412

9. Zhang, Y., Liu, L., Li, C., Loy, C.C.: Quantifying facial age by posterior of age comparisons (2017)

10. Zhong, Z., Zheng, L., Kang, G., Li, S., Yang, Y.: Random erasing data augmentation. CoRR abs/1708.04896 (2017). http://arxiv.org/abs/1708.04896

# Light-Weight Deep Convolutional Network-Based Approach for Recognizing Emotion on FPGA Platform

Thuong Le-Tien[1(✉)], Hanh Phan-Xuan[2], and Sy Nguyen-Tan[2]

[1] Department of Electrical and Electronics Engineering,
Ho Chi Minh City University of Technology, Ho Chi Minh City, Vietnam
thuongle@hcmut.edu.vn
[2] Ho Chi Minh City University of Technology, Ho Chi Minh City, Vietnam
phantyp@gmail.com, tansyab1@gmail.com

**Abstract.** Emotion being a subjective thing, leveraging knowledge and science behind labeled data and extracting the components that constitute it. With the development of deep learning in computer vision, emotion recognition has become a widely-tackled research problem. For mobility and privacy reasons, the required image processing should be local on embedded computer platforms with performance requirements and energy constraints. For this purpose, in this work, we propose a Field Programmable Gate Array (FPGA) architecture applied for this task using independent method called convolutional neural network (CNN [1]). The design flow is evaluated by implementing the previously trained CNN to recognize facial emotions from face image implemented in python on a PC. The project explains the process of porting the CNN algorithm from python to C/C++ and then executing it on a ZYNQ FPGA board. Once we have trained a network, weights from the Tensorflow model will be convert as C-arrays. After having the weights as C arrays, they can be implemented to FPGA system. This method was trained on the posed-emotion dataset (FER2013). The results show that with more fine-tuning and depth, the CNN model can outperform the state-of-the-art methods for emotion recognition. The bottleneck of the CNN [2] is the convolutional layers and that is why different solutions for that accelerator are analyzed and the performance of each solution is tested.

**Keywords:** Convolutional neural network · Tensorflow model · Vivado · FPGA · FER2013

## 1 Introduction

The exponential growth of data science during the recent decade motivates for innovative methods to extract high semantic information from raw sensor data such as videos, images and human speech sequences [3,4]. Among the proposed methods, Convolutional Neural Networks (CNNs) [5,6] have become the real

© Springer Nature Switzerland AG 2019
T. K. Dang et al. (Eds.): FDSE 2019, LNCS 11814, pp. 287–306, 2019.
https://doi.org/10.1007/978-3-030-35653-8_19

standard by delivering good accuracy in many applications related to machine vision supported by machine learning or deep learning (e.g. classification [7], detection [8], segmentation [9]) and speech recognition [10]. Although these models are limited in the ability to only identify some basic emotions in millions of combinations daily complex emotions of people, discrete emotions models are still preferred and most common. In this paper, we use a model of Deep Learning to be able to identify the emotions simultaneously deployed on an FPGA platform. CNN [6] is one of the popular methods to best serve the field of image processing and biometric identification. Use of the CNN in facial recognition opens up opportunities for deep learning development. Model implemented on FPGA system will reduce the cost of computation to meet real-time processing needs.

Field-Programmable Gate Arrays (FPGA) are applied to reduce computational cost with hardware parallelism, therefore a deep learning model can be implemented. The majority of the traditional methods have used hand-crafted features or shallow learning. However, the natural emotion contests in the world are organized. These competitions have collected a wealth of diverse and comprehensive data on human emotions that promote the introduction of new effective methods of identifying emotions such as CNN. In the meanwhile, due to the dramatically increased chip processing abilities (e.g., GPU units) and well-designed network architecture, studies in various fields have begun to transfer to deep learning methods, which have achieved the state-of-the-art recognition accuracy and exceeded previous results by a large margin. Likewise, given with more effective training data of facial expression, deep learning techniques have increasingly been implemented to handle the challenging factors for emotion recognition in the wild. This growth comes at the price of a large computational cost as CNNs [6]. As a result, dedicated hardware is required to accelerate their execution. Graphics Processing Units (GPUs), are the global used platform to implement CNNs [6] as they offer the best performance in terms of pure computational throughput. Nevertheless, in terms of energy consumption, Field-Programmable Gate Array (FPGA) solutions are known to be more power efficient (vs GPUs). As a result, numerous FPGA-Based CNN [6] accelerators have been proposed, targeting embedded systems. While GPU implementations have demonstrated state-of-the-art computational performance, CNN acceleration is incontinently moving towards FPGAs for two reasons. Firstly, recent motivation in FPGA technology put FPGA performance within striking distance to GPUs with a reported equivalent performance. Second, recent trends in CNN [6] development increase the performance of CNNs and use energy efficient model. As a result, next generation CNN [6] accelerators are expected to have better computational throughput. To achieve both goals of recognizing facial expression from candid images and setting a FPGA Based neural network, we propose to use deep learning methods. In our learning based approach, we propose to use convolutional neural networks (CNNs) without extra features such as histogram of oriented gradients (HOG), which in the past have been proved to be effective in image classification. Compared with the feature based approach, since the features are automatically learned from images, we expect that the CNN-based approach would be able to keep performance in recognition. It uses only the raw pixels of images for training, or if it's better to feed some extra information to the CNN (such as face landmarks or HOG features). The results show that the CNN can perform well in FPGA. The algorithm was implemented on a Zynq-XC7Z045 FPGA, and this architecture can recognize 500 faces in a frame, which make it possible for a real time system. As a summary, this paper has the following contributions: A FPGA platform for facial expression recognition using convolutional neural networks. The results have been shown the effective approach in recognizing facial expression of candid images.

### 1.1   Hardware Description Language and Register Transfer Level

These processes describe combinational logic, basic arithmetic operations as well as registers, and are driven by the rising and falling edges of a clock signal. RTL descriptions are very close to the logic gates and wires that are actually available in the underlying FPGA or ASIC technology, and therefore the hardware that results from RTL synthesis can be closely controlled.

### 1.2   Vivado

Vivado enables developers to synthesize their designs, perform timing analysis, examine RTL diagrams, simulate a design's reaction to different stimuli, and configure the target device with the programmer. Vivado is a design environment for FPGA products from Xilinx, and is tightly-coupled to the architecture of such chips, and cannot be used with FPGA products from other vendors.

## 2   Proposed System

### 2.1   Dataset

For emotion recognition, several datasets are available for research, varying from a few hundred high resolution photos to tens of thousands smaller images. The main we will discuss is the FERC-2013 [11,12]. The data of FER consists of $48 \times 48$ pixel grayscale images of faces. The faces have been automatically registered so that the face is more or less centered and occupies about the same amount of space in each image. The task is to categorize each face based on the emotion shown in the facial expression in to one of seven categories (see Fig. 1) (0 = Angry, 1 = Disgust, 2 = Fear, 3 = Happy, 4 = Sad, 5 = Surprise, 6 = Neutral). The training set consists of 28,709 examples. The public test set used for the leader board consists of 3,589 examples. The final test set, which was used to determine the winner of the competition, consists of another 3,589 examples.

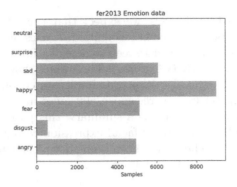

**Fig. 1.** The dataset structure [11]

**Data Cleaning.** In the database there are some images that are not good (e.g. some images are pixelated, irrelevant, from animations). If using these images for identification, the accuracy will decrease and the model will not be optimized. If the image is very homogenous, the maximum value of the histogram will be very high (that is to say above a certain threshold) then this image is filtered out. Therefore, It has been tried to filter them by looking at the maximum of the histogram. The removal of these images has a very positive effect on the final result (see Fig. 2).

**Fig. 2.** The removed irrelevant data [11]

**Data Merger.** After this step, We realized that the difference between emotions 0 and 1 is very small and the number of photos in the 2 training and test sets is not too much. If we keep the model, it will decrease accuracy because these emotions are not recognized correctly due to data imbalance. Therefore, the recognized emotions and labels are reduced to 6: 0-(Angry + Disgust), 1-Fear, 2-Happy, 3-Sad, 4-Surprise, 5-Neutral (see Fig. 3).

**Data Preparation for CNN.** For the initial database, the amount of "happy" images was even bigger (8k), it was decided to be skip 3k random "happy" class images. This also helps with the speed of execution, since our database it's a bit smaller. Finally, data is modified a little bit to be correctly fed into the CNN. What has been done is convert, normalize and subtract the mean value from the data images. The label values of the classes are converted to a binary one_hot vector.

**Fig. 3.** The structure of FER training set after applying merger [11]

This two subsets have both an associated label to train the neural network and to test its accuracy with the test data. The number of images used for each category of emotions is shown both for the train as for the test data. The size of each batch it has been chosen to 64 because, after analyzing the performances, we discovered that decreasing the batch size actually improved the accuracy.

## 2.2 CNN Architecture

The implementation of the model starts with simple models then develops based on the results of that image after the evaluation process is completed. The first model will be initialized with simple parameters and common calculation functions. After receiving unintended results as well as having this phenomenon of over-fitting in the training process, the model was further developed by applying multiple methods simultaneously.

One of the most challenging to be done while constructing a convolutional neural network is the choice of the number and dimension of the filter to be used as well as the number of layers to employ.

Of course there is not a standard design, because it depends on the dataset and the features of the different images and on the complexity of the task. For our purpose the filter size is initialized with a high value and then reduced slowly.

Besides, the activation layer that has been employed is the ReLU one (Rectified Linear Units) which is the most used and most efficient since it helps to alleviate the vanishing gradient problem. The ReLU layer applies the non-linear function $f(x) = \max(0, x)$ to the input basically just eliminating all the negative activations, the bias vector b was initialized to a small positive value that is to prevent killing of gradient when input is negative. Finally, dropout layers can be used to deactivate with a defined probability a random set of activations in that specific layer which in the forward pass is then considered as set to zero. Also this technique can help to prevent the overfitting problem.

Comparison between each structure as well as the characteristics of each model described in the following table (see Table 1). The results are markedly improved. After the trained model on the computer model is used to deploy to embedded systems. In the used CNN there are 6 convolutional layers using $8 \times 8$ or $4 \times 4$ feature maps, each followed by a ReLU and sometimes by max-pooling. Each layer recognizes 22 feature maps. The last seventh layer is a fully connected

**Table 1.** Two architectures of the CNN used for comparison.

| | Comparison table | |
|---|---|---|
| | Model 1 | Model 2 (proposed model) |
| The equation of the classifier | y = softmax (ReLU (x * W1 + b1)W2 + b2) | x = maxpool2x2 [13] (ReLU (ReLU(x * W1 + b1) * W2 + b2)) 3 times for W3, b3, W4, b4, W5, b5, W6, b6 y = softmax [14, 15] (xWnorm6+bnorm6) |
| Hyperparameter | Filters with size $8 \times 8$ | 1, 2, 3 layers the filter used are 22 with a dimension of $8 \times 8$, 4, 5, 6 a dimension of $4 \times 4$ |
| | AdamOptimizer with a learning rate of 0.004 s | AdamOptimizer with a learning rate of 0.001 s. The dropout probability has been set to 0.5 |

layer which transforms 22 $6 \times 6$ images into the classification constants. The detailed overview of the algorithm is shown below (see Table 2). To train all the feature maps automatically, a labeled dataset of more than 35 000 images set was used. One can observe, that some of the features have a real physical meaning and could represent part of a human face. Both feature maps and the resulting images can be positive or negative, floating point. After performing a set of convolutions (22 * 22 in that case) on the corresponding input images (22 in that case, by row) with different kernels, columns of the resulting images (22 in that case) are added (pixel by pixel) to obtain again the number of resulting images after the layer (22 in that case). After the convolution, some the constant values are added to the (22 in that case) images and ReLU operation is performed on each pixel. The algorithm performed by a tensorflow library, a python and then C/C++ implementation has been written. To allow the reader to understand the algorithm structure and operations performed (Table 3). The execution in python/tensorflow on a PC is very fast as for the high-level language, since

**Table 2.** The overview of the used CNN architectures.

| | L1 | L2 | L3 | L4 | L5 | L6 | L7 |
|---|---|---|---|---|---|---|---|
| N Kernel | 22 | 484 | 484 | 484 | 484 | 484 | $6 \times 6 \times 22$ to 6 (matrix multiplication) |
| Kernel length | 8 | 8 | 8 | 4 | 4 | 4 | |
| N_img (in) | 1 | 22 | 22 | 22 | 22 | 22 | |
| N_img (out) | 22 | 22 | 22 | 22 | 22 | 22 | |
| Img_length | 48 | 48 | 24 | 24 | 6 | 6 | |

**Table 3.** Timing result per single 48 × 48 grey-scale face image.

| | | | |
|---|---|---|---|
| -1 | PC (3.4 GHz Intel) in Python | Tensorflow | 3.55 s |
| -2 | PC (3.4 GHz Intel) in Python | Loops (single thr) | 125 s |
| -3 | PC (3.4 GHz Intel) in C/C++ | Loops (single thr) | 0.6 s |
| -4 | Zynq PetaLinux (900 MHz) in C/C++ | Loops (single thr) | 11.5 s |

the library is well optimized. Hence, even the python code (-1) is high-level, it's very close to the C++. Execution (-3) Is the fastest, because it's executed on the fastest machine and the code is most low-level (C++). To identify the bottlenecks of the algorithm, the profiling was executed on the C-code. The results for each layer are shown below (see Figs. 4 and 5).

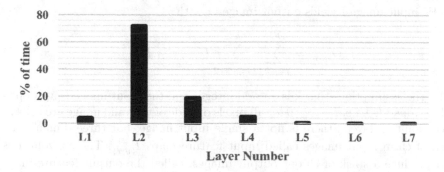

**Fig. 4.** CNN algorithm timing distribution - Layer.

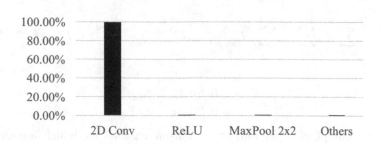

**Fig. 5.** CNN algorithm timing distribution - Function.

The most computationally expensive is Layer 2, since it has 22 48 × 48 input images because it has the highest parameters from each of the layers. Acceleration of the functions of 2D image convolution, because it's the most computationally heavy task executed with the most of time, should visibly shorten the classification time. Due to the acceleration, there will be some delays to exchange information between the processor and the accelerator, it'd be valuable to design a solution that would also minimize this communication time.

## 3  FPGA Implementation

### 3.1  Convolutional Layers and Matrix Multiplication

The central operation to be accelerated is the 2D convolution [16] of multiple input feature maps with a number of small filter kernels. The two-dimensional convolution of an input image and a filter can be intuitively understood as the result from sliding the filter over the input image, and taking the dot product between the filter and the pixels underneath at each possible filter position. For a filter of

$$< A, B > = \sum_{i=0}^{n-1} A_i . B_i \tag{1}$$

has size $k * k$, each dot product $A_0.B_0 + A_1.B_1 + ... + A_{n-1}.B_{n-1}$ requires $k^2$ multiplications and additions. The 2D convolution between $k * k$ filter F and $H * W$ input image I yields output image O with

$$O_{(y,x)} = \sum_{j=-k/2}^{k/2} \sum_{i=-k/2}^{k/2} I_{(y-j,x-i)} . F_{(j,i)} \tag{2}$$

under the assumptions that k is an odd integer and the input image is appropriately zeropadded, i.e. $I_{(y,x)} = 0$ for all pixels outside of the valid image area $W * H$ In convolution layers, there is not a single input image, but three dimensional stack of ch_in input images called input feature maps $I_{(y,x)}^{(ci)}$. The convolutions then produce a stack of ch_out output images, called the output feature maps $O_{(y,x)}^{(co)}$ by applying a bank of filters $F^{(ci,co)}$. Under the above assumptions, a convolution layer computes

$$O_{(y,x)}^{(co)} = \sum_{ci=0}^{ch_{in}-1} \left( \sum_{j=-k/2}^{k/2} \sum_{i=-k/2}^{k/2} I_{(y-j,x-i)}^{(ci)} . F_{(j,i)}^{(ci,co)} \right) = \sum_{ci=0}^{ch_{in}-1} < I_{(M)}^{ci}, F^{(ci,co)} > \tag{3}$$

with

$$M = \begin{pmatrix} y + [k/2]...y - [k/2] \\ x + [k/2]...x - [k/2] \end{pmatrix} \tag{4}$$

for every output pixel $(y, x)$ and every output channel $co$, which amounts to a total of $n_{MACC} = H * W * ch_{in} * ch_{out}k^2$ multiplications and accumulations. Despite requiring a high computational effort, the mathematical operations behind convolution layers are not complex at all, and offer a lot of opportunities for data reuse and parallelization.

This approach transforms the 2D convolution into one large matrix multiplication. For this, each local input region (the image region underneath each possible filter location) is stretched out into a column vector, and all the column vectors are concatenated to form a matrix C. Since the filter's receptive fields usually overlap, every image pixel is replicated into multiple columns of C. The filter weights are similarly unrolled into rows, forming the matrix R. The 2D convolution is then equivalent to a matrix product RC, which can be calculated very efficiently using highly optimized linear algebra (BLAS) routines which are available for CPUs, GPUs and DSPs. For a small 33 filter, matrix C is already blown up by a factor of 9 compared to the original input image. This makes it necessary to split the problem into a number of overlapping tiles, and later stitch the results back together, which artificially increases the complexity of the problem. On FPGAs and in ASICs, matrix multiplications can be efficiently implemented with a systolic architecture. A suitable systolic array consists of a regular grid of simple, locallyconnected processing units. Each of them performs one multiplication and one addition, before pushing the operands on to their neighbors. Thanks to the locality of computation, communication and memory, these architectures are very hardware-friendly.

The Matrix Multiplication is well suited for general-purpose architectures such as GPUs. They are especially efficient for large problem sizes and batched computation. However, their additional memory consumption and the resulting need for tiling and re-stitching introduce artificial memory and computation requirements, which reduce the resource efficiency of the architecture. Our focus on the regular, well-optimized CNN further eliminates the need to support all kinds of different parameter combinations. Therefore, we believe the direct 2D convolution approach as formulated in Eqs. 2 and 3 to be the most efficient way to implement an FPGA-based accelerator, regarding both memory and computational requirements.

## 3.2   Quantization

The usual requirement for signal processing using FPGA is quantization, since they cannot easily handle the floating-point operations. For the purpose of the CNN acceleration, all of the operations to be accelerated have to be performed in the fixed-point domain. To clarify the needs for the CNN, the summary of the filter coefficients is shown below (see Table 4). The maximum value of the coefficients is usually very close to 1 and none of the values are bigger than 2.0 (2 bits for integer value). However, especially for the layers 3, 5, the maximum values are quite high and exceed 2.0 value. That is why, the fixed point value used in the computation should include some more bits for the high integer values. Another consideration is using different fixed point scheme for filter coefficients and the result calculation.

The quantization sweep was performed for the following fixed-point schemes:

- 2.5 to 2.10 - max value: $(-2, 2)$
- 3.5 to 3.10 - max value: $(-4, 4)$
- 4.5 to 4.10 - max value: $(-8, 8)$
- 5.5 to 5.10 - max value: $(-16, 16)$

**Table 4.** The filter coefficients (constant)

| Max W1: 0.5815 | Avg W1: 0.0004 | Min W1: $-0.9423$ |
|---|---|---|
| Max W2: 0.9198 | Avg W1: $-0.0357$ | Min W2: $-1.3937$ |
| Max W3: 0.8179 | Avg W2: $-0.0141$ | Min W3: $-1.0259$ |
| Max W4: 0.6043 | Avg W3: $-0.0392$ | Min W4: $-0.9901$ |
| Max W5: 0.6264 | Avg W4: $-0.0127$ | Min W5: $-1.1540$ |
| Max W6: 0.6241 | Avg W5: $-0.0219$ | Min W6: $-0.8395$ |
| Max Wn6: 0.6827 | Avg Wn6: $-0.0214$ | Min Wn6: $-1.1442$ |

## 3.3   Resource Available on the Xilinx SoC Platform

To accelerate the algorithm, Xilinx ZC7006 platform has been chosen. It has multiple available resources, including a ZynQ processor – to run the algorithm in software – and FPGA which could accelerate it. The summary of its properties is shown below (see Table 5). The most important property of the platform is the number of DSPs, since for convolution a lot of multiplications-addition operations are done. The availability of internal BRAMs is also important, since they can be used to store parts of image data for faster access.

**Table 5.** The resource of zc706 Evaluation Kit

| Name | Number | Comments |
|---|---|---|
| DSPs | 900 | |
| BRAMs | 545 | Each BRAM at least 8 kB |
| FFs | 437200 | |
| LUTs | 218600 | |

## 3.4   Image Convolution Acceleration

The main purpose in accelerating is to operate in parallel. Most of the data processed does not depend on each other, so it can be easily paralleled. The activities used here are multiplied - accumulated. That's why perhaps the best solution would be to use DSP present on the FPGA platform. Because the same image pixel and the same kernel pixels are used a lot.

The idea of this solution is inspired from the paper "Optimizing Loop Operation and Dataflow in FPGA Acceleration of Deep Convolutional Neural Networks [17]. Unlike the previous solution, the registers here do not take a lot of FPGA resources and it's using a different approach to the parallelization. The solution is using an additional level of image storage: internal FPGA BRAMs, which have 2 ports and are accessible both from the processor (by some automated interface)

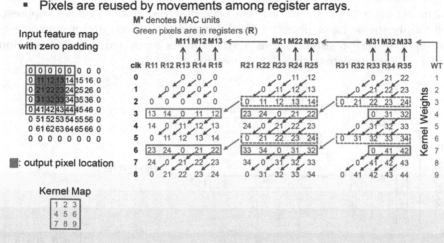

**Fig. 6.** The way of pixel re-utilization and parallelization. This example is based on 9-pixel kernel (3 × 3) and 9-pixel block (3 × 3) [17].

and from the accelerator. The paper presents very efficient pixel management technique and different level of parallelization (see Fig. 6).

After 9 clock cycles, the convolution result of the 3 × 3 pixel block is available in DSP. Furthermore, the same pixel shifter can be used to use it with another set of DSPs and another set of Kernels to calculate parallel block results.

The decision on the exact level of parallelism is determined based on the number of DSPs. In particular, 900 DSPs are available. The CNN algorithm has an image size of 48 × 48, 24 × 24, 6 × 6, so it is reasonable to create a single block size (calculated as the result of single convolution after N clock cycles) as 6 × 6 and because CNN has 22 images image as input/output, so it is reasonable to use 6 * 6 * 22 = 792 DSP. This means, the 88% DSP available is used.

**Pixel Shifting Logic.** At first clock cycle, the initial pixels are loaded (either from the previous blocks or from the img_BRAM) and the pixels start to shift, shifting in the NEXT_PIX which also comes from BRAM or previous block. At the end, all the loaded pixels appear in the output registers INIT-SAVE-REG (6 pixels to initialize the next block) an SAVE-REG (7 pixels saved and then multiplexed as NEXT_PIX for the next block) to be utilized (see Fig. 7).

Each pixel shifter is responsible for 6 pixels and therefore we need 6 of them to shift 6 × 6 block image. The pixels are loaded from BRAM at the first cycle, and then only last pixel shifter takes the image from different image BRAMs and all others are taking the values from the previous block.

**Pixel Multiplication/Addition.** For the purpose of parallel addition and multiplication, a block of 792 DSP has been designed. Each cycle it's supposed to multiply the 36 input pixels by 22 different kernel pixels and accumulate it into separate DSP registers. It has a synchronous zero (zero the accumulation result) and accumulate enable signals (see Fig. 8).

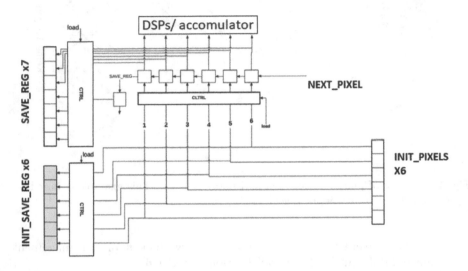

**Fig. 7.** Block diagram of the single block pixel shifter.

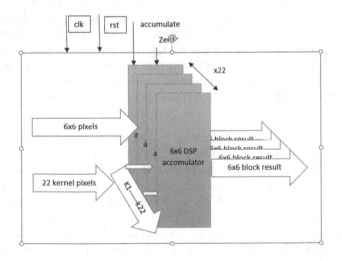

**Fig. 8.** Block diagram of the pixel accumulator block (792 DSPs).

**ReLU Rectifier in Hardware.** Each kernel is $8 \times 8 = 64$ pixels and 22 kernel results are parallelized. Hence, for each kernel single pixel needs to be accessible in parallel. For instance, 1st pixel of all 22 kernels for L1 needs to be available in parallel.

The kernel pixels are also 12 bits, and it's need 22 of them in one cell to be read in parallel. Therefore, $22 * 22 = 264$. The BRAM cell size needs to be the power of 2, so the BRAM cell size has been chosen as 512 bits. The kernel values are aligned to LSB and all the MSB are padded with 0's.

1st layer uses only 22 kernels but L2-L6 uses 484 kernels each. That is why, the number of BRAM kernel cells is $64 * 1 + 5 * 64 * 22 = 7104$. The 6 b constants for each layer, are stored at the end of the BRAM size. That is why, the final number of cells is $7104 + 6 = 7110$.

**State Machine.** The main purpose of the state machine is to manage the addresses of the BRAMs, based on layer number (which determines image size, sector to R/W, number of input images etc.) and control the pixel shifting logic, DSPs and writing the result. The simplified state machine diagram is shown below (see Fig. 9).

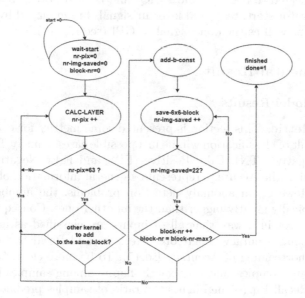

**Fig. 9.** Simplified state machine diagram.

- Nr-pix - counts from 0 to 63, when the DSPs are accumulating the kernel result.
- Nr-img-saved - from 0 to 21, when saving the images needed to iterate through the DSP results.

- Block-nr (block_row and block_col) - the results are computed in $6 \times 6$ blocks and each image has $8 \times 8$ blocks (for $48 \times 48$ image), $4 \times 4$ blocks (for $24 \times 24$ image) or $1 \times 1$ block (for $6 \times 6$ image).

State:

- Wait-start - waiting for start signal. Connected to GPIO. CALC_LAYER - wait for the result, change the kernel pixels and shift the pixel values.
- Add-b-const - puts the kernel address to point to the b constant for the current layer and make them accumulate it in the DSP (the pixels at this point are multiplexed to be 1.0, and therefore the DSP-value += pixel-value * b-const (from kernel BRAM), pixel value = 1.0 so DSP-value += b-const.
- Save-$6 \times 6$_block - reads what in the current cell, writes the partial value from the DSPs, reads another cell and writes another partial result from the DSPs.
- Finished – when all the image blocks ($8 \times 8$ for L1–L2, $4 \times 4$ for L3–L4, $1 \times 1$ for L5–L6) are saved, the done flag is put to 1.

**Block Design with ZynQ Processor.** To be able to load the kernel coefficients and images, each BRAM ports 1 has been connected to the BRAM controller (connected to AXI bus and ZynQ) and BRAM port 2 to the accelerator. The accelerator start, reset and layer_nr signals are managed by connecting it into a GPO, as well as the done signal to GPI (see Fig. 10).

## 4    Experimental Result

### 4.1    CNN Model Results

**Evaluation Metric.** This section is presented some metrics for evaluating the model. The result of classification will be in 4 possible cases, namely True Positive (TP), True Negative (TN), False Positive (FP), and False Negative (FN). In these four metrics, the Accuracy represents a general information of the models performance. However, in anomaly detection problems, the number of happy samples are typically greatly bigger than the all other ones. Consequently, if the model is simply set in a way that all of inputs are classified as happy, it can reach a spectacular accuracy. Therefore, Precision and Recall are exploited to overcome the shortcoming of Accuracy Eq. (5). To be more clear, the Precision reflects how many samples that are exactly happy among samples indicated as happy, whilst Recall Eq. (6) highlights the ratio of samples predicted as happy inside definite happy samples. Besides, we hope that there is a unique metric, representing ability of a model in the problem of skewed distribution detection, instead of two these metrics of Precision and Recall (Table 6).

$$Accuracy = \frac{(TP + TN)}{TP + TN + FP + FN} \tag{5}$$

$$Recall = \frac{(TP)}{TP + FN} \tag{6}$$

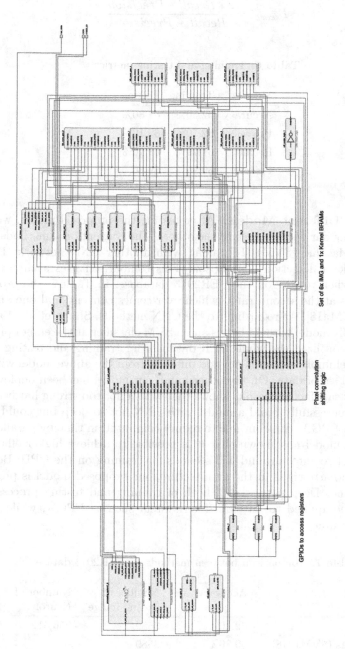

**Fig. 10.** System block diagram with BRAMs and ZynQ processor.

$$Precision = \frac{(TP)}{TP + FP} \tag{7}$$

$$F_{score} = \frac{2 * Recall * Precision}{Recall + Precision} \tag{8}$$

**Table 6.** Training and testing metrics

| Metrics | Training | Testing |
|---------|----------|---------|
| Accuracy | 62.50% | 61.80% |
| Precision | 62.70% | 62.10% |
| Recall | 61.20% | 61.10% |
| F-score | 59.90% | 59.80% |

**Compare to Different Models.** After testing the proposed model, we continue comparing our performance to the others. The conventional methods, Support Vector Machine (SVM) [18], along with another CNN network [19] are chosen to make a detection comparison. This comparison uses accuracy metric obtained when testing on the FER2013 database. In Table 7, the proposed method stands at the second rank, which over-comes conventional one and left behind the SVM [18]. As regarding to the CNN methods, Shima et al. [19] used a powerful CNN model with 14 layers and a SVM classifier at the end of pipeline as well as they utilized the whole FER database for training and testing. However, our model implemented is not too different from the above model with the same standard set of data. On the other hand, our model has been deployed on FPGA and for satisfactory results shows that with a not too strong hardware we were able to successfully build a model with CNN not so deep but could reach high precision. FPGAs can continue to reduce computation time by parallel processing so the model has shown that it is possible to achieve higher efficiency. Our model just requires around 400 seconds for training on the CPU. Besides, because of the narrowness in the architecture, our proposed model is probably faster than other Deep networks in both of training and testing process, this network can be applied to an embedded system such as FPGA, while it can keep a high accuracy.

**Table 7.** Comparison between methods on FER2013 dataset

| Method | Accuracy | Number of testing image | Number of Neurons |
|--------|----------|-------------------------|-------------------|
| Shima [19] | 62.40% | 3589 | 256,512 |
| Anonymous (SVM) [18] | 59.80% | 3589 | – |
| Proposed | 61.80% | 3000 | 1568 |
| F-score | 59.90% | 59.80% | |

## 4.2   FPGA Implementation Results

**Quantization Results.** To analyze the effect of each quantization case on the classification result, the CNN algorithm was performed on the same 128 test images, with the coefficients being quantized from 3. Results are taken after each class, according to the maximum value of the signed points can be stored. The probability of class 64 * 6 is compared with the result from 2 and the average and maximum errors were calculated to show the best diagram. Quantization scanning is performed for a range of 2 to 5 integer value bits and 5 to 10 bits for fractional values (see Table 8). The quantization error drops dramatically when increasing the number of bits. The best trade-off between the number of bits and reasonable error is fixed point 4.8 meaning 4 bits for Integer part and 8 bits for Fractional part.

**Table 8.** CNN quantisation - mean error/max error

| Fractional bits | Integer bits | | | |
|---|---|---|---|---|
| | 2 | 3 | 4 | 5 |
| 5 | 0.18/0.99 | 0.17/0.99 | 0.18/0.99 | 0.16/0.99 |
| 6 | 0.15/0.99 | 0.15/0.99 | 0.13/0.99 | 0.11/0.99 |
| 7 | 0.14/0.99 | 0.11/0.99 | 0.07/0.96 | 0.07/0.95 |
| 8 | 0.13/0.99 | 0.1/0.99 | **0.03/0.52** | 0.02/0.49 |
| 9 | 0.12/0.98 | 0.09/0.98 | 0.02/0.31 | 0.01/0.31 |
| 10 | 0.12/0.98 | 0.09/0.93 | 0.01/0.19 | 0.01/0.02 |

**Pixel Shifting Logic Results.** Each image shifter is taking its data from its own BRAM (first 8 cycles) or the previous pixel shifter (other cycles). The last (right) pixel shifter takes its data from different image BRAMs every clock cycle (it's a data source for the system). The test bench for pixel shifter is shown below (see Fig. 11).

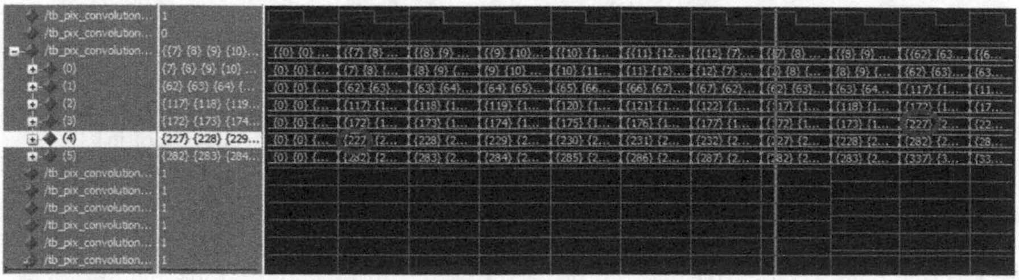

**Fig. 11.** Test bench of the pixel shifter.

**FPGA Resource.** The aforementioned solution had been synthesized in Vivado suite with standard implementation parameters. There are four kinds of hardware resources on FPGA: Look-up Tables Unit (LUT), Flip-Flop Unit (FF), BRAM Unit (BRAM) and Digital Signal Processing Unit (DSP). The system works with a very heavy and deep model to detect emotion, but a system like the XC7Z045 can still be found to show that the system has the cost advantage in computing. In addition, the system achieves the desired accuracy when compared to other methods that have been processed on a computer that is not an embedded system, which shows that the system has the structural advantage. The details of the implementation are shown below (see Fig. 12).

| Resource | Utilization | Available | Utilization % |
|----------|-------------|-----------|---------------|
| LUT | 26081 | 218600 | 11.93 |
| LUTRAM | 1533 | 70400 | 2.18 |
| FF | 35694 | 437200 | 8.16 |
| BRAM | 309.50 | 545 | 56.79 |
| DSP | 792 | 900 | 88.00 |
| IO | 4 | 362 | 1.10 |
| BUFG | 2 | 32 | 6.25 |

**Fig. 12.** The detail summary of used resources.

**Time Consumption.** The current acceleration results the 2D convolution is not a bottleneck any more (Table 9). Thanks to multiple DSP utilization and smart pixel shifting logic the amount of time to compute convolutions and image accumulations results was reduced massively. Unfortunately, there is a max-pooling algorithm to be performed between L2 and L3 and between L4 and L5. This algorithm is not implemented in hardware, therefore all the images need to be transferred from BRAM to the operational memory, the algorithm is executed and the results is transferred back to BRAMs. The transfer between L2 and L3 is much bigger (and therefore much longer) because the image size there is $48 \times 48$ – after max-pooling $24 \times 24$, transfer of 22 images. The transfer between L4 and

**Table 9.** Timing results after acceleration

|  | Software timings [s] | Accelerated timings [s] | FPGA accel. (xNR) | Possibility when maxpool is implemented on FPGA (xNR) |
|--|----------------------|-------------------------|-------------------|------------------------------------------------------|
| Python/tensorflow | 3 |  | 149 | 48051 |
| PC C/C++ | 0.6 |  | 30 | 1508 |
| ZynQ Petalinux | 11.5 | 0.02 | 571 | 28212 |
|  | Before |  | Now | Future |
| Classification/second | 0.1–2 |  | 50 | ∼500 |

L5 is much smaller – BRAM to mem: 22 images, $24 \times 24$, mem to BRAM 22 image $6 \times 6$ each.

If we reduce the bottleneck of Max-Pooling (implement it in hardware), the acceleration results can be obtained much faster, i.e. at least every 3 ms. After finishing the acceleration, a netlist file was export for future chip implementation (see Fig. 13).

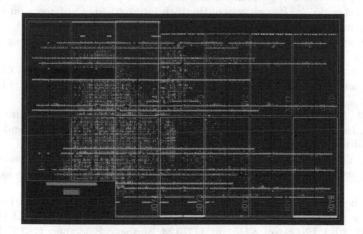

**Fig. 13.** The netlist file exported from accelerator.

## 5    Conclusion

In this work, the proposed method provides a solution to identify human emotions through the face. The implementation process compares the evaluation between multiple methods. The given method shows the accuracy is not too inferior to traditional methods. We then implemented a model that trained down a specific hardware system as an FPGA system, which proved that not only our neural networks achieved very high accuracy as complex networks (Alex Net [20], Google Net [21], etc). It is also very light to deploy for hardware systems weaker than our computers. The results are relatively good, the model has minimized the calculation time as well as energy saving. This research opens up the future we can reduce to the smallest time thanks to deploying network layers to hardware.

## References

1. Brandon Rohrer. http://brohrer.github.io/how_convolutional_neural_networks_work.html
2. https://www.kernix.com/blog/a-toy-convolutional-neural-network-for-image-classification-with-keras_p14

3. Ververidis, D., Kotropoulos, C.: Automatic speech classification to five emotional states based on gender information. In: Proceedings of the EUSIPCO2004 Conference, Austria, pp. 341–344 (2004)
4. Cowie, R., et al.: Emotion recognition in human computer interaction. IEEE Signal Process. Mag. 18(1), 32–80 (2001)
5. LeCun, Y., Bengio, Y., Hinton, G.: Deep Learning. Nature 521 (2015). https://doi.org/10.1038/nature14539
6. Glorot, X., Bengio, Y.: Understanding the difficulty of training deep feedforward neural networks. In: Proceedings of the 13th International Conference on Artificial Intelligence and Statistics, Sardinia, Italy, PMLR9, pp. 249–256 (2010)
7. Russakovsky, O., et al.: Imagenet large scale visual recognition challenge. Int. J. Comput. Vis., 211–252 (2012)
8. Girshick, R.: Fast R-CNN. In: Proceedings of the IEEE Conference on Computer Vision and Pattern Recognition, CVPR 2015, Boston, MA, USA, pp. 1440–1448 (2015)
9. Long, J., Shelhamer, E., Darrell, T.: Fully convolutional networks for semantic segmenta. In: Proceedings of the IEEE Conference on Computer Vision and Pattern Recognition, CVPR 2015. Boston, MA, USA, pp. 3431–3440 (2015)
10. Zhang, Y., et al.: Towards end-to-end speech recognition with deep convolutional neural networks. In: Proceedings of Interspeech Conference, San Francisco, USA (2016)
11. Goodfellow, I.J., et al.: Challenges in representation learning: a report on three machine learning contests. In: Lee, M., Hirose, A., Hou, Z.-G., Kil, R.M. (eds.) ICONIP 2013. LNCS, vol. 8228, pp. 117–124. Springer, Heidelberg (2013). https://doi.org/10.1007/978-3-642-42051-1_16
12. Martinez, B., Valstar, M.F.: Advances, challenges, and opportunities in automatic facial expression recognition. In: Kawulok, M., Celebi, M.E., Smolka, B. (eds.) Advances in Face Detection and Facial Image Analysis, pp. 63–100. Springer, Cham (2016). https://doi.org/10.1007/978-3-319-25958-1_4
13. Britz, D.: http://www.wildml.com/2015/11/understanding-convolutional-neural-networks-for-nlp/
14. Anh Tran-The. http://labs.septeni-technology.jp/technote/ml-20-convolution-neural-network-part-3/
15. Phan-Van, H.: Neural Network Lecture, Danang University of Science and Technology (2013)
16. http://developer.apple.com/../ConvolutionOperations.html
17. Ma, Y., et al.: Optimizing loop operation and dataflow in FPGA acceleration of deep convolutional neural networks. Arizona University (2017)
18. Horseman, A.: SVM for Facial Expression Recognition. A demonstrate project using SVM (2007). https://github.com/amineHorseman/facial-expression-recognition-svm/commit/aecd525367f6d77e5d274de7c6f0166d5bfa4bb9
19. Shima, A., Azar, F.: Convolutional neural networks for facial expression recognition. In: Proceedings of the Stanford University report (2016). http://cs231n.stanford.edu/reports/2016/pdfs/005_Report.pdf
20. Jain, A.: (2016). https://www.analyticsvidhya.com/blog/2016/04/deep-learning-computer-vision-introduction-convolution-neural-networks/
21. Szegedy, C., et al.: Going deeper with convolutions

# Metagenome-Based Disease Classification with Deep Learning and Visualizations Based on Self-organizing Maps

Thanh Hai Nguyen[✉]

Can Tho University, Can Tho, Vietnam
nthai@cit.ctu.edu.vn

**Abstract.** Machine learning algorithms have recently revealed impressive results across a variety of biology and medicine domains. The applications of machine learning in bioinformatics include predicting of biological processes (for example, prediction tasks on gene function), prevention of diseases and personalized treatment. In the last decade, deep learning has gained an impressive success on a variety of problems such as speech recognition, image classification, and natural language processing. Among various methodological variants of deep learning networks, the Convolutional Neural Networks (CNN) have been extensively studied, especially in the field of image processing. Moreover, Data visualization is considered as an indispensable technique for the exploratory data analysis and becomes a key for discoveries. In this paper, a novel approach based on visualization capabilities of Self-Organizing Maps and deep learning is proposed to not only visualize metagenomic data but also leverage advances in deep learning to improve the disease prediction. Several solutions are also introduced to reduce negative affects of overlapped points to enhance the performance. The proposed approach is evaluated on six metagenomic datasets using species abundance. The results reveal that the proposed visualization not only shows improvements in the performance but also allows to visualize biomedical signatures.

**Keywords:** Visualization for metagenomics · Convolutional Neural Network · Deep learning · Self-organizing maps · Overlapped issue

## 1 Introduction

The visualization of metagenomic data is still a challenging issue in computational biology due to its very large dimensionality, as well as complex interactions among microbes. In addition, metagenomic data also shows complicated correlations with confounding environmental factors [2] (for example, total organic carbon, total nitrogen and pH [3]). As illustrated in numerous studies, data visualization is considered as an indispensable technique for the exploratory data analysis and becomes a key for discoveries [1]. A good visualization should discriminate between specific groups to extract the characteristics of these groups.

© Springer Nature Switzerland AG 2019
T. K. Dang et al. (Eds.): FDSE 2019, LNCS 11814, pp. 307–319, 2019.
https://doi.org/10.1007/978-3-030-35653-8_20

In addition, an ideal visualization method enables us to analyze such large-scale data efficiently.

In [1], the authors stated that Metagenomics visualization has become an attractive domain with a vast of publications introducing numerous novel approaches every year, and presenting new techniques based on the visualization for generating and verifying novel biological hypotheses. They presented an overview of the existing approaches to visualize metagenomic data. Furthermore, the study also pointed out the best-known visualization of compositional data is a pie chart which shaped like a circular graphic separated into pieces. Each such piece represents a group of corresponding data in percent. Pie chart is available, implemented popularly to a variety of softwares and platforms such as Python, R [4], Excel, and so on. Krona [5] is one of such popular tools commonly-used in the research community. The software presents a metagenome as nested concentric rings shaping a circle together. Each ring matches to a taxonomic rank. This visualization reveals a multi-level view of the structures of metagenome data. MG-RAST [14] is a type of the web-based display, represents metagenomics in the hierarchy regardless of magnitude. MEGAN is a software that enables us to analyze and explore the taxonomic content of large metagenomic data. A comparison among 3 these common methods are presented in [5].

A bar chart that is also a useful tool to represent a data distribution, forms as rectangular colorful bars for each group of data. The height of these bars reflects the values of corresponding groups. A vast of tools provided include *AmphoraV-izu* [6], package of *metricsgraphics* [7] and *gplots* in R [9]. *Phinch* [10] is also a helpful software to show taxonomic composition of microbial communities.

As [1] presented, an abundance table, where the rows representing the samples and columns corresponding to features, is considered as a standard method to represent the community structure inferred from metagenomic datasets. In this table, each cell contains the value of the relative abundance corresponding taxa in the sample. A heat map table is an extended version of abundance table. Each cell in this table is filled by a color. The different abundance between 2 cells is identified by distinct colors. The R package *d3heatmap* [11] provides a variety of options to build a vast of kinds of heatmaps. In addition, *Anvi'o* is also able to figure a heat map of nucleotide positions.

Finding the global structure of microbial community using metagenomic data is really a substantial challenge. Besides charts and tables, due to very large dimensionality of data, researchers also have attempted recently dimension reduction algorithms such as Isomap, Principle component analysis (PCA), t-SNE in numerous metagenomic studies [12,13]. Each sample is characterized by hundreds or thousands of features (relative abundance of individual species or genus), and a dimensionality reduction method can be applied. A new reduced data can be presented as a point (or dot, pixel) on the scatter plot of two (2D) or three (3D) principal components.

As stated in [1], recent discoveries in microbial data using metagenomic data have substantially increased our understanding on the structure and possible functions of bacterial in the human body. These discoveries are incredibly difficult to complete without a good visual tool to go deeply into the analysis. RF is state-of-the-art method for Clinical predictive modeling in applications [17–19] while deep learning has also obtained achievements in numerous applications such as image recognition. This leads to motivation in the transformation from numerical data to images. Although the benefits of visualization on metagenomic data was demonstrated by a vast of studies, applying these visualizations for prediction tasks using deep learning techniques are not taken into account completely. In [15], some approaches using visualizations were presented but the results for colorectal cancer was still lower than the classic machine learning such as Random Forests (RF). Further research on prediction for this disease is needed for finding methods to improve the classification performance.

In this paper, Self Organizing Maps (SOM) are considered and evaluated the efficiency on visualizing features of metagenomic data. The contribution of this work is multi-fold:

- The visualization capability of SOM is leveraged to illustrate metagenomic features in 2D maps. It is also combined with deep learning to improve the performance in prediction tasks. The experiments have shown encouraging results compared to classical machine learning and other state-of-the-arts in data visualizations such as Fill-up [15].
- Various methods to reduce the affects of the overlapped points are also investigated including representative selection and combination among the overlapped points. In addition, the proposed method is a potential approach for feature selection for high-dimensional data.

The paper is organized as follows. Six species abundance datasets used for performing visualizations are described in Sect. 2. In Sect. 3, the visualization methods and models utilized to evaluate these visualizations are introduced. The results of various approaches using deep learning techniques on the generated images are presented in Sect. 4. Section 5 presents the closing marks of the study.

## 2  Metagenomic Data Benchmarks

The proposed approach runs on six metagenomic datasets (Table 1) including species abundance i.e. data indicating how present (or absent) is an OTU (Operational taxonomic unit) in human gut. The set of datasets consists of six datasets including bacterial species related to various diseases, namely: liver cirrhosis (CIR), colorectal cancer (COL), obesity (OBE), inflammatory bowel disease (IBD) and Type 2 Diabetes (T2D) [21–25,27,28], with CIR (n = 232 samples with 118 patients), COL (n = 48 patients and n = 73 healthy individuals), OBE (n = 89 non-obese and n = 164 obese individuals), IBD (n = 110 samples of which 25 were affected by the disease) and T2D (n = 344 individuals of which n = 170 are T2D patients). In addition, one dataset, namely WT2, that includes 96 European women with n = 53 T2D patients and n = 43 healthy individuals is also considered. These data were obtained using the default parameters of MetaPhlAn2 [26] as detailed in Pasolli et al.

**Table 1.** Information on six considered datasets.

| Group A | CIR | COL | IBD | OBE | T2D | WT2 |
|---|---|---|---|---|---|---|
| #features | 542 | 503 | 443 | 465 | 572 | 381 |
| #samples | 232 | 121 | 110 | 253 | 344 | 96 |
| #patients | 118 | 48 | 25 | 164 | 170 | 53 |
| #controls | 114 | 73 | 85 | 89 | 174 | 43 |
| Ratio of patients | 0.51 | 0.40 | 0.23 | 0.65 | 0.49 | 0.552 |
| Ratio of controls | 0.49 | 0.60 | 0.77 | 0.35 | 0.51 | 0.448 |

# 3 Self Organizing Maps for Metagenomic Images Generation

The Self-Organizing Map (SOM) [20] is considered as a famous artificial network associated with the unsupervised learning manner. It is an efficient method to map from a high dimensional input space into a more compact space, usually to a two-dimensional (2D) output space. The two-dimensional representation is practical for a visualization, since the mapping conserves topological relations between features. In addition, the continuous input space can be plotted into a discrete output space. The SOM belongs to competitive learning methods. Neurons compete to be activated and only one is activated at a time. The winning neuron is called the winner. When the winner is set, all the other neurons have to re-organize themselves.

Given high-dimensional data $x \in R^d$, the connection weights between observations i and the neurons of the grid $j$ can be presented as:

$$wj = w_{ij} : j = 1, ..., K; i = 1; ..., n \tag{1}$$

where $K$ is the number of neurons on the grid. A discriminate function (Eq. 2) which is widely used, and which we also use in our experiments, is the squared Euclidean distance between an observation $x$ and the weight vector $w_j$, for all $j$

$$D_j(x) = \sum_{i=1}^{n}(x_i - w_{ji})^2 \tag{2}$$

Fill-up is described in [15] as followings. Images are created by arranging abundance values into a matrix in a right-to- left order by row top-to-bottom. Fill-up revealed promising results using Convolutional Neural Networks (CNN). A strong point of Fill-up is that all features are visible, so it usually exhibits better performance than other visualization approaches based on manifold learning.

In this study, the package of minisom[1] is installed to visualize features of metagenomic datasets. The coordinates of all features are obtained from minisom and plotted on 2D space. The map has the size of 48 × 48 with an example

---

[1] https://github.com/JustGlowing/minisom.

illustrated in Fig. 1. At the beginning, training set is used to learn and build coordinates in 2D of all features (we called as "global map"). Each pair of coordinates of (x, y) exhibits the position of a feature which is visualized as a point in the image. The color for each feature depends on the magnitude of the feature. In this study, gray scale/colormap and Species Bin (SPB) [15] are employed to generate the images of $48 \times 48$ pixels. All the features in each sample in both training and test sets are visualized based on these coordinates of the global map. Figure 1A illustrates features in WT2 dataset visualized by SOM with the map of $48 \times 48$ while the number of points in each coordinate is plotted in Fig. 1B. As shown in the graph 1B, we can see numerous point in the map are overlapped by the others. Especially, there is only one feature shown at coordinates (40, 20) while more than 30 points are overlapped by that point. SOM generates clusters which groups similar features together. Therefore, similar features can be visualized with the same coordinates. As a result, numerous points may be overlapped by the others as the graph shown in Fig. 1B.

In order to reduce the negative affects of the issue of the overlapped points, several methods have been attempted in this study with semitransparent color, calculating the average value of each group of the overlapped points, and selecting representative feature based on the important scores computed by Random Forests or selecting the maximum value among overlapped features. For an image suffering overlapped points, we cannot see the points hidden by the others. When we use semitransparent color for gray images, the coordinates with numerous overlapped points will get darker. The transparency parameter can be fixed in the interval between 0 and 1, and it indicates the transparency of the markers plotted. A value of 0 determines all points are transparent while 1 means that transparency is not applied. The transparency rate (the parameter of alpha in the plot function of python) used in this study is set to 0.5. Another solution is that we can calculate an average value for all overlapped points at that coordinate ("Avg"). Other approaches use a representation for each group of the overlapped points. The representation can be obtained by selecting the feature which owns the highest ("Max") value among features in the group. Besides, we can run Random Forests to calculate the important score of each feature and, then, choose the best one in the group ("RF"). For example, the features of $x1$, $x2$, $x3$ have values of 0.0005, 0.002, 0.000001, respectively. If we use "Max", then $x2$ is chosen. In the case, Random Forests algorithm is used to select the representation, the important score of each feature is computed and ranked to arrange the feature. We note that the representation selection stage is done in training set to avoid the overfitting issue. RF is used in this research with 500 trees. In Figs. 2 and 3, we can see the global maps which show average abundance of each feature in training set of WT2 dataset (Fig. 2) and a sample Fig. 3 visualized with coordinates from the global maps with various approaches using SOM. Features are visualized by SOM with a learning rate (for SOM) of 0.5, an iteration of 100, and the map size of $48 \times 48$. In order to observe easily, jet colormap is used for Figs. 2 and 3, only gray images are used in the experiments.

Similar to [15], a shallow Convolutional Neural Network (CNN) including one convolutional layer with 64 filters followed by a max pooling of $2 \times 2$ (stride of 2) and one fully connected layer is employed to do the prediction tasks on the generated images. All networks utilize Adam optimization [16], a learning rate of 0.001 with the loss function of binary cross-entropy and a batch size of 16. The maximum epoch which is applied can reach to 500 with an epoch patience (Early Stopping) of 5 to reducing the overfitting problem. The performance is assessed by an average accuracy on 10 stratified cross validation. The same folds are used for all classifiers.

## 4   The Results

**Table 2.** Performance (in ACC) comparison of SOM with different approaches to reduce affects of overlapped points and state-of-the-art including MetAML and Fill-up. The results that are better than MetAML, Fill-up are reported in **bold**, *Italic*, respectively.

| Approaches | Solutions for overlapping issue | CIR | COL | IBD | OBE | T2D | WT2 | AVG |
|---|---|---|---|---|---|---|---|---|
| SOM | Semitransparent color | **0.888** | *0.852* | **0.848** | **0.664** | *0.675* | *0.781* | 0.785 |
| SOM | Avg | 0.867 | *0.820* | **0.837** | **0.661** | **0.666** | *0.729* | 0.763 |
| SOM | RF | 0.854 | *0.803* | **0.865** | **0.665** | **0.648** | *0.738* | 0.762 |
| SOM | Max | 0.858 | *0.820* | **0.847** | **0.649** | 0.657 | *0.729* | 0.760 |
| Fill-up | | 0.905 | 0.793 | 0.868 | 0.680 | 0.651 | 0.705 | 0.767 |
| RF | | 0.877 | 0.805 | 0.809 | 0.644 | 0.664 | 0.703 | 0.750 |

The results of the experiments are illustrated in Table 2 which includes prediction performance in Accuracy (ACC) of various approaches. Overall, the proposed method is the one that obtains the most robust results. Here the results are compared to MetAML [8] and Fill-up [15]. MetAML is a metagenomic computation framework using classical machine learning as Support vector Machine and Random Forest while Fill-up was introduced in [15] aiming to present all features in images. All features visualized by Fill-up are visible in the images. We report the performance of MetAML using Random Forest and Fill-up with the same CNN configuration.

As observed from Table 2, the performances almost improve the previous reports. The results show that SOM is promising algorithm for predicting disease based on metagenomic data. SOM with semitransparent color gives better results for all six considered datasets compared to MetAML. Moreover, it outperforms Fill-up 3 out 6 datasets although the method still suffers the issue of the overlapped points.

By comparing the results among methods for the issue of overlapped points in Fig. 4, we can see that using semitransparent color outperforms the others. In addition, this method shows less overfitting with a shorter distance

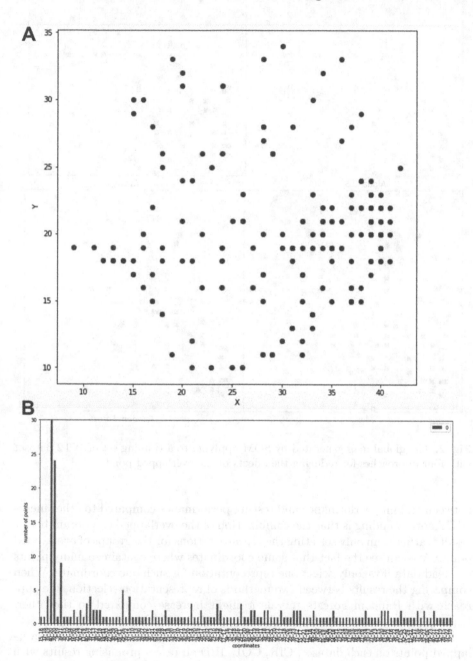

**Fig. 1.** A: The features in WT2 dataset are arranged by SOM. B: the graph shows the number of points on each coordinate shown in Figure A

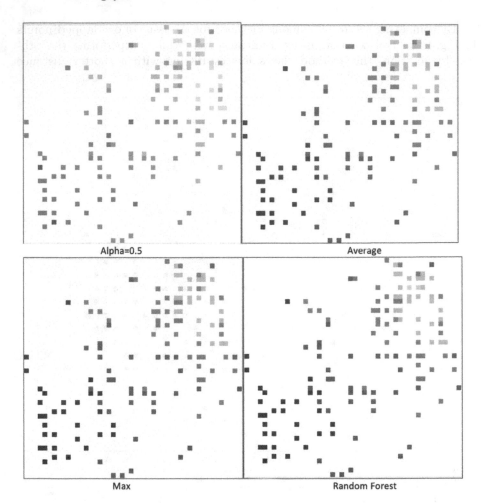

**Fig. 2.** The global map generated by SOM applying to a training set of WT2 dataset with four approaches for reducing the affects of the overlapped points

between training performance and testing performance compared to other methods. Another finding is that the combination of the overlapped can obtain better results rather than only selecting the representations for the groups of overlapped points. We can see the fact that some coordinates where contain so many points can lead data if we only select one representation for such one coordinate. When comparing the results between two methods of representation selection, the approach with Random Forests reveals a slight increase compared to the other. Especially, this approach obtains the best ACC for IBD dataset.

Figures 5, 6, 7 illustrate the results comparison of four solutions for the overlapped points on each dataset. CIR, COL, IBD all reveal promising results with all performance being greater than 0.8, while T2D and OBE exhibit the worst.

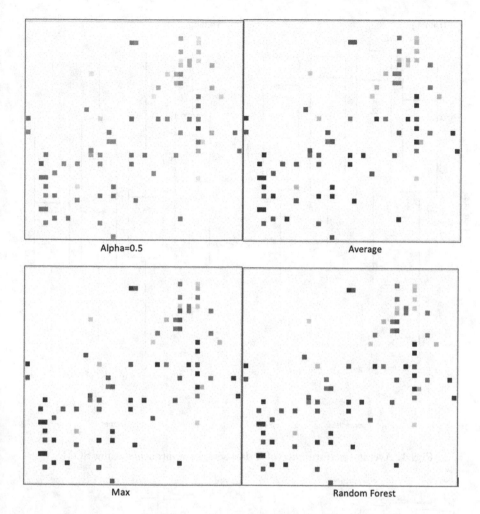

**Fig. 3.** A sample of WT2 dataset visualized by the coordinates from the global map in Fig. 2 with various approaches.

Fill-up failed to obtain a good performance compared to MetAML for predicting colorectal cancer. However, in this study, the performance is improved with SOM. Moreover, the results on WT2 also reveal encouraging results compared to the-state-of-the-art.

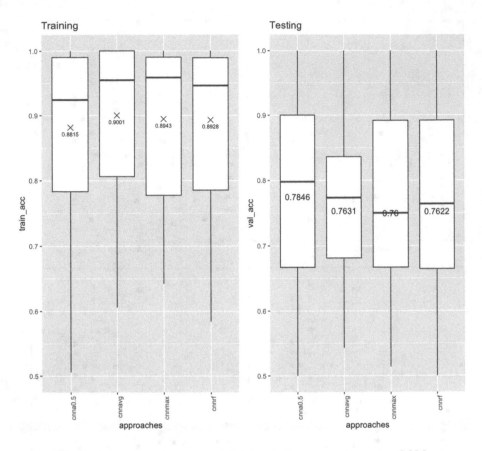

**Fig. 4.** Average performance of 6 datasets for approaches using SOM.

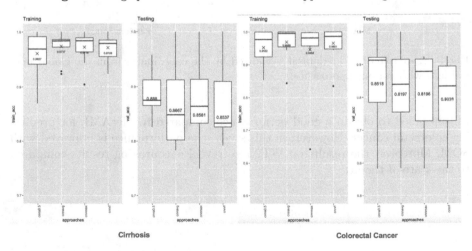

**Fig. 5.** Performance of CIR and COL datasets with SOM using different solution for reducing affects of the overlapped points.

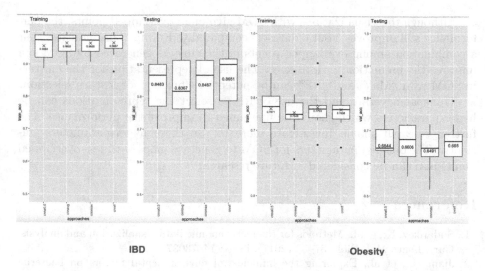

**IBD**                                    **Obesity**

**Fig. 6.** Performance of IBD and OBE datasets with SOM using different solution for reducing affects of the overlapped points

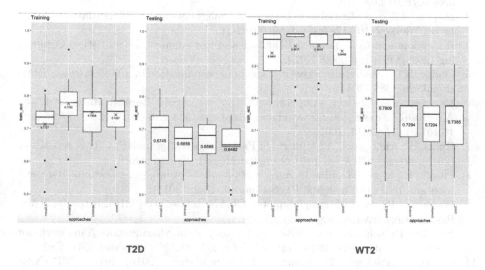

**T2D**                                    **WT2**

**Fig. 7.** Performance of T2D and WT2 datasets with SOM using different solution for reducing affects of the overlapped points

## 5    Conclusion

In this study, a visualization method using SOM with various solutions for the overlapped points is investigated and illustrates encouraging results on six metagenomic datasets. This may be considered as a promising aspect of using SOM for metagenomic data.

Although the visualizations with SOM give more overlapped points, the performance still improves 3 out 6 datasets compared to Fill-up. This indicates that a combination among overlapped points in the clusters generated by SOM can improve the prediction performance. The use of representation for the clusters in SOM with "Max" and "RF" can be potential efficiency for feature selection.

Transparency rate and the use of RF to select the representations can be hyper-parameters which should be fine-tuned to improve the performance. The further research should investigate more to use these hyper-parameters efficiently. The optimal parameters for SOM to generate maps with less overlapped points also can be considered in future research.

# References

1. Sudarikov, K., et al.: Methods for the metagenomic data visualization and analysis. Curr. Issues Mol. Biol., 37–58 (2017). ISSN: 14673037
2. Jiang, L., et al.: Exploring the influence of environmental factors on bacterial communities within the rhizosphere of the cu-tolerant plant, Elsholtzia splendens. Scientific Report (2016). ISSN: 2045–2322. https://www.ncbi.nlm.nih.gov/pmc/articles/PMC5080579/
3. Morton, J.T., et al.: Balance trees reveal microbial niche differentiation (2017). https://doi.org/10.1128/mSystems.00162-16
4. R Development Core Team: A Language and Environment for Statistical Computing (2008). ISBN: 3-900051-07-0
5. Ondov, B.D., et al.: Interactive metagenomic visualization in a Web browser. BMC Bioinform., 385 (2011)
6. Kerepesi, C., et al.: AmphoraNet: the webserver implementation of the AMPHORA2 metagenomic workflow suite. Gene, 538–540 (2013). https://doi.org/10.1016/j.gene.2013.10.015
7. Rudis, B., Almossawi, A., Ulmer, H.: Package 'metricsgraphics', CRAN repository (2015). https://CRAN.R-project.org/package=metricsgraphics
8. Pasolli, E., et al.: Machine learning meta-analysis of large metagenomic datasets: tools and biological insights. PLoS Comput. Biol. (2016)
9. Warnes, G.R., et al.: Package 'gplots', CRAN Repository (2016). https://CRAN.R-project.org/package=gplots
10. Bik, H.: Phinch: an interactive, exploratory data visualization framework for metagenomic datasets (2014). https://doi.org/10.6084/m9.figshare.951915.v1
11. Cheng, J.: Package 'd3heatmap', CRAN repository (2016). https://CRAN.R-project.org/package=d3heatmap
12. Jiang, X., et al.: Manifold learning reveals nonlinear structure in metagenomic profiles. In: 2012 IEEE International Conference on Bioinformatics and Biomedicine (2012)
13. Alshawaqfeh, M., et al.: Consistent metagenomic biomarker detection via robust PCA. Biology Direct (2016)
14. Meyer, F., et al.: The metagenomics RAST server - a public resource for the automatic phylogenetic and functional analysis of metagenomes. BMC Bioinform. (2011)
15. Nguyen, T.H., et al.: Disease classification in metagenomics with 2D embeddings and deep learning. In: The Annual French Conference in Machine Learning (CAP 2018) (2018)

16. Kingma, D.P., et al.: Adam: a method for stochastic optimization, CoRR abs/1412.6980 (2014)
17. Sarica, A., Cerasa, A., Quattrone, A.: Random forest algorithm for the classification of neuroimaging data in Alzheimer's disease: a systematic review. PMC (2017). https://doi.org/10.3389/fnagi.2017.00329
18. Ma, H., Xu, C.-F., Shen, Z., Yu, C.-H., Li, Y.-M.: Application of machine learning techniques for clinical predictive modeling: a cross-sectional study on nonalcoholic fatty liver disease in China. BioMed Res. Int. (2018). https://doi.org/10.1155/2018/4304376
19. LaPierre, N., Ju, C.J., Zhou, G., Wang, W.: MetaPheno: a critical evaluation of deep learning and machine learning in metagenome-based disease prediction. PubMed (2019). https://doi.org/10.1016/j.ymeth.2019.03.003
20. Kohonen, T.: The self-organising map. In: Proceedings of the IEEE (1990)
21. Karlsson, F.H., et al.: Gut metagenome in European women with normal, impaired and diabetic glucose control. Nature **498**, 99–103 (2013)
22. Qin, N., et al.: Alterations of the human gut microbiome in liver cirrhosis. Nature **513**, 59–64 (2014)
23. Pasolli, E., Truong, D.T., Malik, F., Waldron, L., Segata, N.: Machine learning meta-analysis of large metagenomic datasets: tools and biological insights. PLoS Comput. Biol. **12**, e1004977 (2016)
24. Le Chatelier, E., et al.: Richness of human gut mi- crobiome correlates with metabolic markers. Nature **500**, 541–546 (2013)
25. Qin, J., et al.: A human gut microbial gene catalogue established by metagenomic sequencing. Nature **464**, 59–65 (2010)
26. Truong, D.T., et al.: MetaPhlAn2 for enhanced metagenomic taxonomic profiling. Nat. Methods **12**, 902–903 (2015)
27. Zeller, G., et al.: Potential of fecal microbiota for early-stage detection of colorectal cancer. Mol. Syst. Biol. **10**, 766 (2014)
28. Qin, J., et al.: A metagenome-wide association study of gut microbiota in type 2 diabetes. Nature **490**, 55–60 (2012)

# Cloud Data Management and Infrastructure

# On Analyzing the Trade-Off Between Over-Commitment Ratio and Quality of Service in NFV Datacenter

Manh-Hung Tran[1], Thien-Binh Dang[1], Vi Van Vo[1], Duc-Tai Le[1],
Moonseong Kim[2(✉)], and Hyunseung Choo[1(✉)]

[1] Department of Electrical and Computer Engineering, Sungkyungkwan University,
Seoul, South Korea
{hungtm,dtbinh,vovanvi,ldtai,choo}@skku.edu
[2] Department of Liberal Arts, Seoul Theological University, Bucheon-si, South Korea
moonseong@stu.ac.kr

**Abstract.** Network Function Virtualization (NFV) is one of the key technologies in 5G. It inherits virtualization technology in cloud computing and promises to bring many benefits for industry such as saving energy and reducing capital expenditure. Resource over-commitment is a significant technique of virtualization to fully utilize the resources of a cloud datacenter. Deploying VNFs with difference over-commitment ratios in an NFV datacenter leads to different results of the number of servers used and the order of VNFs placed in each physical server. This also affects Quality of Service (QoS) and energy consumption in the NFV datacenter. However, to the best of our knowledge, there has been no study to find exactly how much resource over-commitment is sufficient to meet the QoS while reducing the energy used in an NFV datacenter. In this paper, we analyze and evaluate the effect of CPU over-commitment ratio in VNF placement problem while considering the QoS and energy efficiency for NFV datacenters. After exhausting simulations, we have found out a proper value for CPU over-commitment ratio for NFV datacenters. By employing that ratio, an NFV datacenter could reduce up to 16.8% total power consumption compared with the others not using the over-provisioning technique.

**Keywords:** VNF placement · Over-commitment ratio · Saving energy · OpenStack · Network function virtualization

## 1 Introduction

Network functions virtualization (NFV) defines standards for computing, storage, and networking resources that can be used to build virtualized network functions (VNF). It promises to bring many benefits [1] to a datacenter and is the core technology for the 5G network. Applying this technology help to reduce capital expenses, fast services deployment and to cut down the energy used in

© Springer Nature Switzerland AG 2019
T. K. Dang et al. (Eds.): FDSE 2019, LNCS 11814, pp. 323–331, 2019.
https://doi.org/10.1007/978-3-030-35653-8_21

a datacenter. By switching middle-boxes (e.g. Load-balancer, Firewalls, Mobility Management) from dedicated hardware to software as VNFs and deploy on a virtual machine (VM) or a container in NFV infrastructure (NFVI), it can take advantages of the virtualization technology. NFVI is a key component of the NFV architecture [2] that describes the hardware and software components where VNFs are deployed. One of the most prominent NFVI's open source is OpenStack [3,4].

In the NFVI, the virtualization layer maps the virtual resources to the physical server according to a specific ratio in the NFVI configuration. This ratio is called the over-commitment ratio in the virtualization technology. The main aspects of virtualization technology not only are resource isolated but also resource consolidation, since more VMs may reside on the same physical server. The over-commitment ratio will effect the numbers of VNFs could be hosted in the physical server. For instance, the higher ratio value the more VNFs could be placed in the same host. By allowing to provision more virtual resources than physical resources, this technique aims to fully utilize the resources and to reduce the number of active servers. However, the more VNFs are placed in the same physical machine the higher possibility of SLA violations.

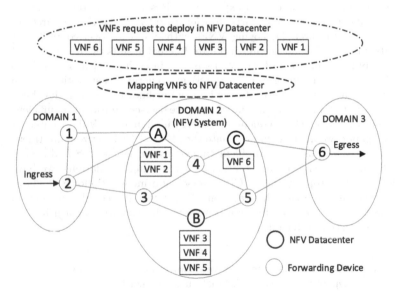

**Fig. 1.** VNF placement in NFV datacenter scenario

Along with an exponential increase of network services (NS) and the benefits of NFV, having a separate NFV datacenter is really necessary. An NFV datacenter is a cloud datacenter used for deploying NS and running VNFs. It could be placed in DOMAIN 2 depicted in Fig. 1 inside a cloud datacenter. It also could be separate and independent with cloud datacenter. In NFV datacenter point of view, saving as much energy as possible in order to reduce the electricity cost, is a top concerned. In order to maximize the energy efficiency, one approach is placing as many VNFs as possible on the smallest set of physical servers while trying to guarantee the expected quality of service (QoS) to the end-users.

It is extremely important to get an accurate over-commitment ratio value for NFV datacenter configuration. In the literature, there is a guideline [5] for setting values for over-commitment ratio in a general cloud datacenters. However, these setting cannot be applied directly on NFV datacenter in which VNFs usually require a stringent delay to guarantee QoS. Although, the value of the over-commitment ratio has a significant effect on energy efficiency and QoS in the NFV datacenter. So far, there is a lack of papers studying the right over-commitment ratio value for an NFV datacenter. In this paper, we study the effect of over-commitment ratio through simulation for VNF placement like OpenStack VMs schedule. We analyze the trade-off between power consumption and QoS in NFV datacenter to find out a proper ratio value. In the simulation, we use an online algorithm for solving VNF placement and assume the number of physical servers is easily extendable. We also assume the server has no VNF running will power down and not consume energy. The main contributions of this paper are as follow:

- We develop a simulation for VNF placement in an NFV datacenter.
- We evaluate and analyze the value of the over-commitment ratio in NFV datacenter and suggest a proper value for NFVI setting.

The remainder of the paper is organized as follows: In Sect. 2, the preliminary is presented. The simulation setting and performance analysis are discussed in Sect. 3. Finally, Sect. 4 we conclude the paper with final remarks and provide our perspectives for future work.

## 2  Preliminary

### 2.1  OpenStack

OpenStack is an open source cloud computing platform for public and private clouds [6] and could be used as an NFVI in NFV architecture. It includes nine key components (e.g. Nova, Swift, Cinder, Neutron) which are distributed as parts of an OpenStack system and is officially maintained by the OpenStack community. Nova is one of the nine key components which is used for deploying and managing large numbers of VMs to handle computing tasks. It means that the VM is managed and scheduled to deploy in a physical server by nova-scheduler service. The algorithm that the nova-scheduler used in VM placement is WORST-FIT algorithm [7] with three steps. Firstly, the algorithm applies filters to determine which hosts are eligible for consideration, i.e. finding a list of hosts has enough resource for a VM resource request when dispatching a resource as an accepted hosts list. Secondly, it weights the resource in the accepted hosts' list follows a normalized function. Finally, it chooses the most weighted hosts for deploying the VM, i.e. choosing the least resource utilization hosts. OpenStack supports over-commitment resource (CPU, RAM, HDD) for VM placement. It has three variable over-commitment ratios for CPU, RAM and HDD in the setting file, e.g. cpu_allocation_ratio, ram_allocation_ratio, disk_allocation_ratio. The default values for those variables are 16, 1.5, 1 respectively for CPU, RAM, and HDD.

## 2.2 Resource Over-Commitment Ratio

A resource over-committing is a process of allocating more virtualized resource (e.g. CPUs, memory) than physical resources of the system. In our work, we only consider CPU as the main resource which is a bottleneck resource of the physical server and only analyze VNF placement with CPU over-commitment ratios in our simulation. CPU over-commitment ratio (in short, we could name it as $CPU_{ratio}$) is a ratio between the number of virtual CPUs (vCPUs) and the number of physical CPUs (pCPUs) in the host (e.g. 1:1, 1.5:1, 2:1). For example, $CPU_{ratio}$ of 1.5:1 means the number of vCPUs can be provisioned up to 1.5 times the number of pCPUs. If the number of pCPUs is 24 then the number of vCPUs equal to $24 \times 1.5 = 32$ vCPUs. CPU over-commitment means running more vCPUs on a host than the total number of pCPU in that host without impacting VM performance and allows under-utilized VMs to run on fewer servers which saves power and money. The number of vCPUs could calculate by the following formulation:

$$vCPU = CPU_{ratio} \times pCPU \qquad (1)$$

Various forums are filled with questions from users requesting insight into acceptable CPU over-commitment ratios in a real-world environment. The Dell white paper [5] establishes the following CPU over-commitment ratios (vCPU:pCPU) guidelines for a general cloud datacenter after extensive testing:

- 1:1 to 3:1 is no problem.
- 3:1 to 5:1 may cause performance degradation (e.g. delay increasing).
- 6:1 or greater often causes problem (e.g. system crashing).

However, the right $CPU_{ratio}$ value depends on many factors including workload type, physical CPUs and how complementary the workloads of the VMs are. While some responses continue to advocate for a 1:1 ratio, from a pure density standpoint for guaranteeing QoS to business-critical applications like SQL, Exchange, Oracle, SAP, etc. [8]. But guidance from industry experts suggests that no more than a 1.5:1 $CPU_{ratio}$ [9]. And, Ankita Rani et al. [10] have used 1.5:1 as the $CPU_{ratio}$ value through resulting of their experiment with VM placement in an OpenStack testbed. The VNFs also is considered as a critical application software so in this work, we look for a proper value of the $CPU_{ratio}$ from 1:1 to 1.5:1.

## 2.3   VNF Placement Problem and QoS

VNF placement is important to ensure effective resource and power management in an NFV datacenter. It involves selecting a suitable host for a VNF such that resource requirements of VNFs are fulfilled. A good VNF placement scheme will ensure that servers overload do not arise and yet consolidation can be done effectively. The basic scenario for VNF placement in NFV datacenter is shown in Fig. 1. The VNF placement problem is an NP-hard problem [11,12] and could be mapped to the bin-packing problem. The bin-packing problem could be solved by an online algorithm (e.g FIST-FIT, BEST-FIT, WORST-FIT) or offline algorithm (e.g FIRST-FIT Decreasing, Dynamic Programming, ILP).

The VNF placement problem can be solved in two stages. The first stage is called initialization stage or initial VNF placement, in which VNFs are instantiated and hosted on to the appropriate servers as per their resource capabilities and service level agreement (SLA) between customers and a service provider. In this stage, the problem could be solved by an online algorithm of bin packing problem. The second stage is called optimization stage or VNF dynamic placement. After initial placement of VNFs is completed, the running VNF is migrated from the present servers to other prospective servers based on optimization constraints. The VNFs migration is manually done by a system administrator or is automatically done by system mechanisms. The system mechanisms could be the local optimization by using static thresh-hold based policy or the global optimization by using an offline algorithm to find an optimal solution for an NFV datacenter. In this paper, we only work with the first stage of the VNF placement problem.

One of the constraints in VNF placement problem is to satisfy the QoS of NS. In our work, to measure the QoS, we calculate the percentage of overloaded servers in an NFV datacenter after all VNFs are deployed. An overloaded server is a server that has more than 100% expected workload, for example, the number of requested jobs coming at the same time larger than the CPU capability processing of a server. Expected workload of a server is a value of total expected workload of all VNFs which locate in that server. In the industrial, a server load near 100% may cause dropped requests or unusable response times, leading to services performance significant degradation. Hence, the overloaded server could affect to service processing time so it could violate the QoS.

## 3   Performance Analysis

### 3.1   Simulation Environment

To evaluate and analyze the VNF placement with difference CPU over-commitment ratios, we have developed a simulator tool using C++ programing language. This section presents a settings and performance metrics of conducted simulations.

**Physical Infrastructure:** In our simulation, we use the specification of a Dell power edge R620 v4 with two six core processors with Hyper-threading enabled [13] as a compute node in the NFV datacenter. It means that each physical server has 24 pCPUs ($6 \times 2 \times 2$). We assume all servers have the same specification as above.

**VNF:** As a practical use case, we use the VNF types from papers [14,15]. The number of vCPUs required for each VNF is randomly selected in set {2, 4, 6, 8}. For example, the vCPU of VNF Firewall is 4 and NAT function is 2. The number of VNFs request to deploy in the NFV datacenter is varied from 100 to 1000 with an increment of 100.

**Workload:** In this paper, we apply CPU utilization of a server as a server workload. The expected workload of each VNF is randomly fixed between 1% and its maximum workload ($WL_{max}$) value. The $WL_{max}$ is the CPU utilization in the physical server when the VNF run in full load, and can be computed as follows:

$$WL_{max} = (\frac{vCPU_{req}}{pCPU}) \times 100\% \tag{2}$$

where $vCPU_{req}$ is the number vCPU required of a VNF, pCPU is the physical CPU of a server and $WL_{max}$ is the maximum expected workload of a VNF in the physical server.

**Server Power Model:** The power consumption of the servers depends on several factors (e.g CPU load, memory, HDD, network load). In the literature, many papers [16–18] have used a linear power model. In which, the power consumption can be simplified as:

$$P = P_{idle} + (P_{peak} - P_{idle}) \times U \tag{3}$$

where $P_{idle}$ is the power consumption of a server in idle state, i.e. a server is power on but not experiencing any load, $P_{peak}$ is the power consumption when a server has 100% load, and $U$ is the CPU utilization of a server (value between 0 and 1). With a Dell power edge R620 server in our simulation, $P_{idle}$ equals to 125.8 W and $P_{peak}$ is 242.9 W [19].

**CPU Over-Commitment Ratio:** The ratio values using in the simulation are varied from 1:1 to 1.5:1 and step by 0.1.

**Algorithm:** We modify the WORST-FIT algorithm in bin-packing problem for fitting with the Openstack in terms of saving energy. Instead of fixing the number of servers as traditional WORST-FIT, we assume that the number of servers is easily extendable. Firstly, the NFV datacenter only powers on a limited number of compute nodes (at least one compute node should be activated), if remaining resource is not enough for deploying VNF then it will power on another node

---

**Algorithm 1:** MOD-WORST-FIT

---

    **Input**   : VNF request to deploy $v$,
                   Set of active servers $S$
    **Output**: Updated set of active servers $S$
1  $req \leftarrow$ resource-requirement $(v)$; /*vCPU requirement of VNF $v$*/
2  $i \leftarrow argmax_j$ free-resource$(S[j])$; /*get index of an active server j having the highest free resource*/
3  $res \leftarrow$ free-resource $(S[i])$;
4  **if** $req \leq res$ **then**
5    |  Deploy VNF $v$ into server $S[i]$;
6  **else**
7    |  $s \leftarrow$ power on a new server;
8    |  $S \leftarrow S \cup \{s\}$;
9    |  Deploy VNF $v$ into server $s$;
10 **end**
11 **return** $S$ ;

---

in order to minimize the power consumption of an idle server. The detail of the algorithm is presented in Algorithm 1 with two inputs and output is an updated set of active servers.

**Performance Metric:** The main performance metrics employed in our work are the percentage of overloaded servers and total power consumption. The percentage of overloaded servers can be calculated by the expression below.

$$OS_{percent} = \frac{OS_{num}}{TS_{num}} \times 100\% \tag{4}$$

where $OS_{percent}$ represents for the percentage of overloaded servers, $OS_{num}$ is a value of the number of overloaded servers and $TS_{num}$ is the total number of servers used in the NFV datacenter. While total power consumption represents the total power consumption of all servers used in NFV datacenter after all VNFs are deployed. The power consumption of each server is calculated by using formulation (3).

## 3.2 Performance Results

The results are obtained from 100 times simulation for each scenario setting and are calculated by using average value from the results of the simulation. In our experiments, we run the simulation for two different combinations of the number of VNFs and the $CPU_{ratio}$ value. Figure 2 illustrates the percentage of number of overloaded servers in an NFV datacenter. The increasing of the number of overloaded servers leading to the increasing of probability of violated QoS. With ratio 1.5, the percentage of overloaded servers dramatically increase from 3% to over 30%, while others have a slight increase with maximum value below 10%. In general, the lower ratio is better to guarantee the QoS. The total power

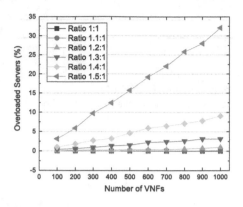 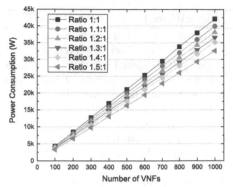

**Fig. 2.** Percentage of the overloaded servers

**Fig. 3.** Power consumption of the NFV datacenter

consumption of the NFV datacenter is shown in Fig. 3. The power consumption of datacenter is increased when the number of VNFs increase. It is clearly shown that the higher ratio is better in term of saving energy and 1:1 is the worst case for power consumption with total power is over 42 KW while the ratio 1.5:1 is the best among all ratios with maximum power consumption is around 32.5 KW. However, in order to trade-off the power consumption and guarantee QoS (e.g. guarantee the number of overloaded servers smaller than 10%) the ratio 1.4:1 should be chosen. Comparing ratio 1.4:1 and ratio 1:1, it could save up to 16.8% total power consumption of the NFV data center. In conclusion, ratio 1.4:1 is the best value of CPU over-commitment to trade-off the power consumption and QoS of the NFV data center.

## 4    Conclusion

In this paper, we evaluate and analyze the value of the over-commitment ratio in NFV datacenter. By developing a simulation for VNF placement in an NFV datacenter we found that the best CPU over-commitment value is 1.4:1 to deal with the trade-off between the power consumption and QoS. By using this ratio, we reduced up to 16.8% power consumption of the NFV datacenter compared with ratio 1:1.

As future work, we will mathematically formulate the problem and then solve it in a general case. We also will examine the effect of CPU over-commitment ratios to the optimization stage of the VNF placement process in NFV datacenter.

**Acknowledgment.** This research was supported in part by Korean government, under by AI Graduate School Support Program (No. 2019-0-00421) supervised by the Ministry of Science and ICT (MSIT) and ICT Consilience Creative program (IITP-2019-2015-0-00742) supervised by the Institute of Information & Communications Technology Planning & Evaluation (IITP), respectively.

# References

1. Hawilo, H., Shami, A., Mirahmadi, M., Asal, R.: NFV: state of the art, challenges, and implementation in next generation mobile networks (vEPC). IEEE Network **28**, 18–26 (2014)
2. ETSI white paper, Network Function Virtualization: Architectural Framework (2013). http://www.etsi.org/deliver/etsi_gs/nfv/001_099/002/01.01.01_60/gs_nfv002v010101p.pdf
3. Beloglazov, A., Buyya, R.: OpenStack neat: a framework for dynamic consolidation of virtual machines in OpenStack clouds - a blueprint. Cloud Computing and Distributed Systems (CLOUDS) Laboratory (2012)
4. Al-Shabibi, A: CORD: Central Office Re-architected as a Datacenter, A Whitepaper by ON.LAB, AT&T, ONOS and PMC, OpenStack Summit (2015)
5. Davis, D.M.: Demystifying CPU Ready (% RDY) as a Performance Metric, Dell white paper (2012)
6. https://opensource.com/resources/what-is-openstack
7. https://docs.openstack.org/nova/queens/admin/configuration/schedulers.html
8. http://www.joshodgers.com/tag/cpu-overcommitment, (2018)
9. https://www.linkedin.com/pulse/cpu-overcommitment-vmware-ronny-berntzen (2016)
10. Rani, A., Peddoju, S.K.: A workload-aware VM placement algorithm for performance improvement and energy efficiency in OpenStack Cloud, In: ICCCA (2017)
11. Panigrahy, R., Talwar, K., Uyeda, L., Wieder, U.: Heuristics for vector bin packing (2011). http://research.microsoft.com
12. Ochoa-Aday, L., Cervelló-Pastor, C., Fernández-Fernández, A., Grosso, P.: An online algorithm for dynamic NFV placement in cloud-based autonomous response networks. Symmetry **10**, 163 (2018)
13. ur Rahman, H., Wang, G., Chen, J., Jiang, H.: Performance evaluation of hypervisors and the effect of virtual CPU on performance. In: IEEE SmartWorld (2018)
14. Pham, C., Tran, N.H., Ren, S., Saad, W., Hong, C.S.: Traffic-aware and energy-efficient vNF placement for service chaining: joint sampling and matching approach. IEEE Trans. Serv. Comput. (2018)
15. Zhang, X., Wu, C., Li, Z., Lau, F.C.: Proactive VNF provisioning with multi-timescale cloud resources: fusing online learning and online optimization. In: IEEE INFOCOM (2017)
16. Marotta, A., Kassler, A.: A power efficient and robust virtual network functions placement problem. In: 28th International Teletraffic Congress (2016)
17. Khosravi, A., Andrew, L.L.H., Buyya, R.: Dynamic VM placement method for minimizing energy and carbon cost in geographically distributed cloud data centers. IEEE Trans. Sustain. Comput. **2**(2), 183–196 (2017)
18. Ranjana, R., Radha, S., Raja. J.: Performance study of resource aware energy efficient VM placement algorithm. In: IEEE WiSPNET (2016)
19. ENERGY STAR Power and Performance Data Sheet. http://www.dell.com/downloads/global/products/pedge/en/Dell-PowerEdge-R620-750W-E5-2620-40-Family-Data-Sheet.pdf

# Dynamic Data Management Strategy on Cloud Network by Fog Computing Model

Takeshi Tsuchiya[1]([✉]), Ryuichi Mochizuki[1], Hiroo Hirose[1], Tetsuyasu Yamada[1], Keiichi Koyanagi[2], Quang Tran Minh[3], and Tran Khanh Dang[3]

[1] Suwa University of Science, Nagano, Japan
{tsuchiya,hirose,yamada}@rs.sus.ac.jp
[2] Waseda University, Tokyo, Japan
keiichi.koyanagi@waseda.jp
[3] Ho Chi Minh City University of Technology, VNU-HCM,
Ho Chi Minh City, Vietnam
{quangtran,khanh}@hcmut.edu.vn

**Abstract.** This paper proposes a data management platform using a fog computing model. It enables to construct of dynamic user data plane adapted to diverse range and several kinds of functions for these users. In particular, this paper implements a sample recommendation application of movie information being able to control the data on fog nodes. However, this paper does not include the quantitative evaluation applying to application services.

**Keywords:** Fog computing model · Dynamic user group · Cloud computing

## 1 Introduction

Web services have become an essential part of infrastructure in our everyday lives. Most Web services currently provided are constructed on the Cloud computing environment in the viewpoints of the service scaling and stability, and these are flexible services that can adapt to the usage situation and network environment. In this, situation, almost of SNS (Social Network Services) requires registration of static personal information; residence, academic and work history to users for receiving the benefits of services. And it also requires dynamic personal information; the location of smartphone, and the session information for various services stored in cookies. These users' personal information are sent to above web services. The web services receiving such information will manage and use by their own manner. However, problems such as information leakage by Web service providers [1] and the malicious collection of personal information [2] occur at a high rate of frequency, and this is causing many users to feel anxious about distributing personal information on the cloud computing environment.

© Springer Nature Switzerland AG 2019
T. K. Dang et al. (Eds.): FDSE 2019, LNCS 11814, pp. 332–342, 2019.
https://doi.org/10.1007/978-3-030-35653-8_22

A system known as a distributed PDS (Personal Data Store) [3] has been proposed, in which each user manages each personal information without accumulating them. In this proposal, encrypted personal information is managed on the cloud by the person themselves, and a decryption key is only provided for the web services allowed to use by each user. In other words, it enables to control personal information provided to web services by users. However, the permission or prohibition of personal information managed by actual users cannot be clearly controlled. For example, there are following type of confidentially; personal information with high level confidentiality that cannot be published under any circumstances, such as credit card information or bank account information, the information with medium-level confidentiality such as names, addresses, or telephone numbers that can be used to identify individuals, and the information with low-level confidentiality, such as birth years, school names, areas of residence, and positional information history, which on their own cannot identify an individual, but can do so when used in combination. These cannot be treated in the same way. At the same time, there are required to protect personal information with a diverse range of granularity, such as the cases where the publication of personal information is determined based on individual personalities and thoughts and beliefs, and cases where the range of publication is determined based on the publication targets, such as reliability of the web service, internal groupware, and hobby circles. In particular, recommendations for information and web personalization based on such personal information have recently become mainstream, and the problem of trade-off between the publication of personal information and the convenience of services has become more complex.

In this paper, we propose a data management platform which controls the shared personal and group information based on the status of the situations with applying diverse levels of granularity. More specifically, it will be possible to perform on the user side of dynamically constructed users and groups both privacy protection by the controlling managed data and the data analysis previously performed within the cloud.

## 2    Related Works

In recent years, a large number of devices are being connected to the Internet caused by the progress of the computer network environment and IoT technology. So the fog computing model is proposed which enables to distribute cloud functions to edge nodes in the network for increasing cloud throughput [4]. In the model shown in Fig. 1, fog node providing server functions is allocated between the cloud network and the users. More specifically, fog node is a computing resource, and enables to provide several kinds of services like data processing and storage services with transparently as middleware for users. For this reason, the function provided by the fog nodes is depended on the application. Therefore, we adopt this fog model in this paper, and propose service framework for adapting usage methods and environment of user.

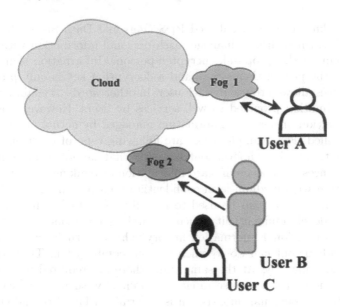

**Fig. 1.** Outline of fog computing model

In [5], proposal model is similar to fog computing model used for personal data management. This proposal model is targeted for analysis of audio data that diagnosed the medical condition on the fog node realizes. It includes personal information of patients which required with high confidentiality. Proposal system only send diagnostic data to cloud, and do not send unrelated to the diagnosis data such as conversation. At this time, the fog node controls the information to be sent to the cloud network as diagnosis data or not caused by the personal privacy by the content of conversation dynamically. In this case,

As the information acquired on the cloud network is not all, it would be worth performance of services than expected use of all information for the processing of statistical and machine learning. In this research, the problem can be solved by the considering that the cloud networks is reliable, and all information is accumulating and analyzing them of all users [3].

## 3    Proposed Method

In this section, we clarify the proposed method using fog nodes.

### 3.1    Approach

In the proposal method, the fog node is intended for processing the information sent to the cloud network. The conventional fog node concept is fixed between the user and the cloud network. In the proposal, the fog nodes are allocated dynamically where in the nearest computer to user from the computer resources

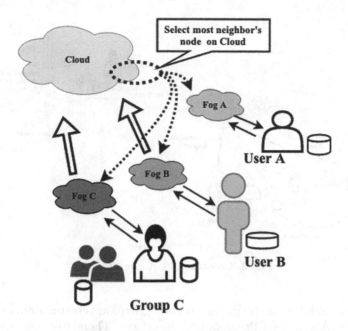

**Fig. 2.** Outline of proposal method

composing the cloud network as shown in Fig. 2. In order to process and control information according to the user group scale, a fog node and user data processing policy notification method and a protocol for dynamically setting up a network between users are required. In order to process and control information on the fog node for individual users and group granularity, It is necessary the method to notify for data processing policy and protocol for setting up the network among fog nodes and users.

## 3.2  Allocation and Construction

The allocation of fog nodes is determined adaptively by determination of targeted group members. Specifically, the root user constructing user group selects the users applied to same policy of information management. For example, it assumes to construct the group of users with diverse ranges of scale and flexibility such as groups linked in actual society which are families, group members in departments of company, and who have never met actually like fan clubs of an artist. Besides, there enables to transmit and share any information among members of the group applied same policy of information management without restriction as same way as to the cloud network, there enables to transmit them with restrictions among non-members. At this time, the judgements and processing of communications is done on the fog node.

Constructing a user group is assumed to be done by the one of user node composed group or the provider of application service. Though this proposal is

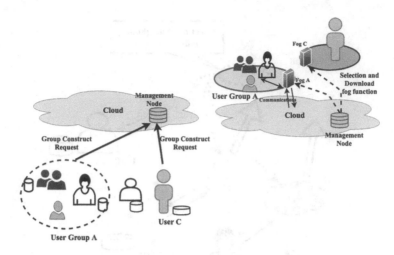

**Fig. 3.** Construction of user group

assumed as a middleware service, in any case, groups are created from application via the API (Application Programming Interface). Thereafter, the closest node to the member of user group composing cloud network is selected as fog nodes. Therefore, it means constructing a logical network layer with the fog nodes as gateway upper current cloud network. It also means constructing independent user groups. At this time, management nodes are allocated on the cloud network, which manages user group and fog node information. It also manages all related information of recent nodes show in Fig. 3.

In the case of selecting the fog node, it is necessary to select the optimal node from many candidates from composing cloud network. If only the distance from the group member of nodes is a condition, there will be problems in the view of service operation such as stability and processing capability. Thus far, the authors of this paper have proposed a node selection method based on multiple metrics in [6], and adopt it for composing distributed storage service in [7]. This paper examines same approach for selecting fog node with extending the method.

The construction of the user group begins with notification of the constituent members of the group to above mentioned management node shown in Fig. 3. The management node registers the group and its members, and notifies the construction of group to this members. Then the selection method for fog node is examined, and chosen the top node satisfying the best conditions from candidates. As previously described, these conditions will become a topic for future study. The nodes received this notification from the management node register to the group, and reflects in the application.

### 3.3 Functions of Fog Node

The communication of constructed user group can be classified into two types; one is communication among the nodes belonging to constructed user group (i.e., communication on the logical network). Another is communication among the nodes including outside nodes of the logical network. Basically, fog nodes do not substitute in communication among the nodes within the user group, and can behave freely as same as communication on current network. But the case for communing including outside nodes of the user group is intervened by the fog node. The fog node enables to hide all communications from outside of logical network to logical network by substituting communication. In addition, it is possible to substitute flexible on only fog node except for communication to a specific node or specific communication protocol, and not limit other communication. This can be done by defining the policy setting to the initializing user group. It has the flexibility for various application services. The changes of the policy to the user group enables to be changed directly on the fog node via the API. It is expected that several kinds of extensions for developers such as provision of specific services use of fog model, provision of fog functions to external users via API and so on.

Data processing on the fog node is arbitrarily determined by the application and service. Currently, it is assumed to provide some basic functions for deriving the privacy of user group, statistical processing of the data, and processing for machine learning. The fog nodes exist as micro services of cloud network providing computational resources, storage, and databases.

Depending on usage of fog node by the application, It has the possibility to generate large processing load for single fog node. At this time, The fog node addition is triggered by a certain condition, for example average of CPU load or throughput of management data there are conditions for fog node selection, we are looking at triggers to add fog nodes under certain conditions, such as threshold for average CPU load being set, or management data throughput as same manner as the its selection. When adding the fog node, it is necessary to request to the management node as same as shown in Sect. 3.2, there will be notification of member of group nodes and their applications. Thereafter, the fog nodes may be reduced in the same way.

Adding or Separation of member of group nodes are done by notifying to the management node. Unexpected separation from the user group caused by disconnections from the network, etc., are detected by the periodical checking the members of group nodes from the fog node when the user group is created. If the case of detected the separation of member nodes, the fog node notifies the management node, and it updates the information of member of group nodes and notifies them.

## 3.4  Link Up with the Application Service

Applications using the cloud network enables to conceal the communications and data among group node from outside of the logical network by substituting the fog node for all access to members of user group from external users. Additionally, the fog node enables to restrict part of commutations like specific external nodes and some protocols. Other communications can be unrestricted. This is defined based on the group policy set when initializing the user group. It enables to apply

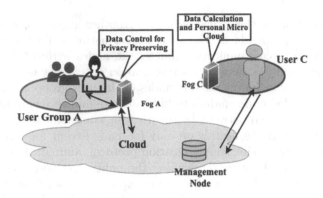

**Fig. 4.** Exp. usage of fog node

the diverse range of applications flexibly. The policy of user group can be changed directly in the fog node via the API adapted to the situations. Furthermore, it is necessary to consider a variety of developments for the future, such as the provision of specific services to members of user group by the fog node and to external users via the API (Fig. 4).

In the case of requiring the node information composing user group and fog node in the application, it can be acquired by inquiring to the management node.

As the proposed method of this research is supposed to be provided as middleware, there are no restrictions on the applications, and it is possible to configure services flexibly using fog nodes.

## 4    Implementation

In this section, we will describe the implementation of the method proposed in the previous chapters. In this paper, the implementation of the sequence up until the user group is constructed has been completed, and we will describe the process from that point hereafter.

### 4.1    Implementation Environment

In the current implementation, the proposed method, shown in Fig. 2, is implemented as a platform. At this time, each node, which is assumed to be a user using the application service, management node managing the user information on the nodes in the Cloud, and the Cloud nodes, use this platform. Furthermore, the functions provided by the fog node are implemented as a virtualized container, and the nodes implementing the platform can be executed anywhere (Table 1).

### 4.2    Implementation of the User Group

When constructing the user group, the member users comprising the group are specified from the Web interface providing the management nodes shown in

**Table 1.** Implementation Environment

| Environment | Specification |
|---|---|
| Proposal Platform | Node.js (v10.15.0) [8] |
| Fog Node functions | Docker Desktop (2.0.0.3) [9] |

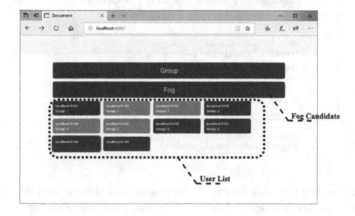

**Fig. 5.** Web IF on management node

Fig. 5. In the current documentation, notification of the User ID of each constituent member is sent to the management server.

Participation in or withdrawal from the user group is done by the user in question or by the nodes comprising the group notifying their User ID to the management node. This User ID is also used to identify management nodes and nodes using the top-tier application services.

### 4.3   Implementation of Fog Nodes

As, at the current time, an algorithm for selecting the fog nodes has not been implemented on the management server, nodes constituting the Cloud in the vicinity are fog node candidates, and the nodes constituting the user groups are selected from these nodes.

As the fog nodes implement functions as a virtualized container (the Docker [9] container in the current implementation), all of the nodes using the platform implementing the proposed nodes can be implemented as fog node functions. In other words, all the nodes in the Cloud closest to the sub-group exist in the sub-group and can provide services, such as processing the data for the user group as fog nodes. At this time, the fog node may physically exist with the user in the same node, but operates as one container in the virtual environment, so the users act independently. Therefore, as long as there is not much load on the fog node, this is not considered to greatly impact the user.

The operation of the fog node is described in the group policy created in the management node API when constructing the sub-group. This policy is sent

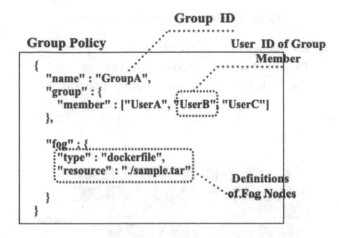

**Fig. 6.** Exp. configuration of group policy

when allocating the fog node function. An example of this group policy is shown in Fig. 6. This policy is described in JSON format, and includes the name of the constituted user group (Group ID) and the User ID of the constituent members. Functions provided by the fog nodes often have complex behavior and cannot be simply described in the policy, and in the current implementation, they operate with fog node functions as executable virtual environment containers. At this time, the parameters for execution and startup information are described in the policy.

## 4.4  Example Application

An example application using proposed method is below. This application is assumed that it is used as for recommendation service based on the big data. The animation movie viewing data set [10] is used as learning data and user usage data. This data set consists of 300,000 user histories data, and 140,000 user reviews. In this implementation, the user histories are used as for learning, and the proposed method is applied to one user's history.

The user group shown in Fig. 7 consists of one user. The user enables to acquire recommended movies based on others viewing history using the Item2Vec [11] model learned by the viewing histories of other users. The fog node detects the viewing history which can identify the individual from the recommendation information based on the user's inputted, and inquires the user whether it can be disclosed or node. For example, movies which do not have viewing histories of other users, cases where the combination of viewing histories has features, etc. if the user permits, this data is provided to other users and external services, but not if it is denied. That is, the viewing history including the privacy of the user is not transmitted.

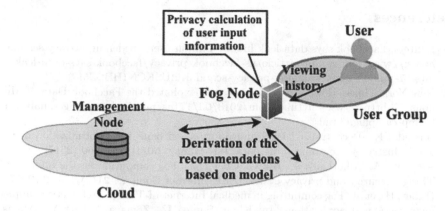

**Fig. 7.** Privacy preserving for recommendation services

# 5  Considerations and Issues

Here, we shall describe some observations and issues regarding the current state of the method proposed in this paper.

The proposal method use of fog computing model in this paper enables to realize the constructing user group dynamically and providing some kinds of data processing service on the fog node adapted to the requirements from applications and users. However, since the current implementation uses the node selection method on Peer-to-Peer network by the authors for fog node selection, it is necessary to clearly the characteristics of fog node selection, and its evaluation in the assumed services. Additionally, although this paper discusses the creation of user groups and allocation of fog nodes, it is necessary to clarify and evaluate what kind of applications suited for the proposed method and what kind of API functions provided by the managed node and fog nodes.

As an issue related for the development of the proposed method, it is necessary to examine the method of cooperation among the fog nodes such as collaborations among multiple user groups and scaling of fog node. There are many other issues to be resolved when implementing actual services.

# 6  Conclusion

In this paper, we proposed a data management platform using a fog computing model. The proposed method enabled to construct dynamic user data plane adapted to diverse range and several kinds of functions for users. In particular, this paper implements a sample recommendation application of movie information being able to control the data on fog nodes. However, this paper does not include the quantitative evaluation applying to application services.

**Acknowledgement.** This work was partly supported by MEXT KAKENHI Grant Number 17K01149.

# References

1. Reuters: Facebook says data leak hits 87 million users, widening privacy scandal. https://www.reuters.com/article/us-facebook-privacy/facebook-says-data-leak-hits-87-million-users-widening-privacy-scandal-idUSKCN1HB2CM
2. New York Times: How Trump Consultants Exploited the Facebook Data of Millions. https://www.nytimes.com/2018/03/17/us/politics/cambridge-analytica-trump-campaign.html
3. Hashida, K.: Decentralized PDS and information bank total optimization of life and industry by ecentralized big data. Inf. Manag. **60**(4), 251–260 (2017)
4. Alrawais, A., Alhothaily, A., Hu, C., Cheng, X.: Fog computing for the Internet of Things: security and privacy issues. IEEE Internet Comput. **21**(2), 34–42 (2017)
5. Dubey, H., et al.: Fog computing in medical Internet-of-Things: architecture, implementation, and applications. In: Khan, Samee U., Zomaya, Albert Y., Abbas, Assad (eds.) Handbook of Large-Scale Distributed Computing in Smart Healthcare. SCC, pp. 281–321. Springer, Cham (2017). https://doi.org/10.1007/978-3-319-58280-1_11
6. Tsuchiya, T., Miyosawa, T., Hirose, H., Koyanagi, K.: Virtualization model of a large logical database for diffused data by peer-to-peer cloud computing technology. In: Proceeding of the Thirteenth International Conference on Networks, February 2014
7. Yoshinaga, H., Tsuchiya, T., Koyanagi, K.: Scalable and persistent multimedia data management system using the distributed interval trees, In: Proceedings of Euro IMSA, pp. 86–92, July 2009
8. Node.js. https://nodejs.org/
9. Docker. https://www.docker.com/
10. MyAnimeListDataset. https://www.kaggle.com/azathoth42/myanimelist
11. Barkan, O., Koenigstein, N.: Item2Vec: neural item embedding for collaborative filtering. In: IEEE 26th International Workshop on Machine Learning for Signal Processing (2016)

# Openness in Fog Computing for the Internet of Things

Quang Tran Minh[1(✉)], Phat Nguyen Huu[2], Takeshi Tsuchiya[3], and Michel Toulouse[4]

[1] Ho Chi Minh City University of Technology, VNU-HCM, Ho Chi Minh City, Vietnam
quangtran@hcmut.edu.vn
[2] Hanoi University of Science and Technology, Hanoi, Vietnam
phat.nguyenhuu@hust.edu.vn
[3] Suwa University of Science, Chino, Japan
tsuchiya@rs.sus.ac.jp
[4] Vietnamese German University, Thu Dau Mot City, Vietnam
michel.toulouse@vgu.edu.vn

**Abstract.** Fog computing is a promising technology for global-scale Internet of Things (IoT) applications as it allows moving resources (computing, storage, networking) close to IoT devices, thus helping to reduce communication latency, network load, energy consumption and operational cost. In order to realize these advantages, application and management services provided by fog landscape should be flexibly implemented. This paper investigates the "Openness" in fog computing and proposes a suitable scheme where the "Openness" can be conveniently implemented in fog nodes. We applied the proposed mechanism to a real-world application, namely the traffic light optimization (TLO) problem, to validate its effectiveness and feasibility. The evaluation results reveal the effectiveness of the proposed approach.

**Keywords:** Edge/Fog computing · IoTs · Openness · Flexibility · Programmability

## 1 Introduction

The Internet of Things (IoT) has emerged as a revolutionary technology to offer a large-scale connected "smart" world where billions of things in the physical world are connected with each other to share data and services. This technology enables the acceleration of the $4^{th}$ industrial revolution and realization of smart city or smart community eco-systems.

In order to realize large-scale IoT services and applications, a suitable computing is necessary. IoT devices (embedded in everyday objects) are limited in terms of computing resources, memory capacity, energy and bandwidth. Cloud-assisted Internet of Things or Cloud-of-Things (CoT) are suitable technologies as

© Springer Nature Switzerland AG 2019
T. K. Dang et al. (Eds.): FDSE 2019, LNCS 11814, pp. 343–357, 2019.
https://doi.org/10.1007/978-3-030-35653-8_23

they offer large-scaled and on-demand networked computing resources to manage, store, process and share IoT data and services [1].

However, the CoT paradigm is facing increasing difficulties to handle Big data generated by IoT services associated with billions of connected devices. If every device-captured data is transferred to data centers (DCs) on the cloud for processing and storage, and a large amount of information is disseminated back to users or actuators on the physical world. This huge traffic volume is likely to generate network congestion, even network malfunction.

In order to deal with the aforementioned issues, *Edge-of-Things (EoT)*, and *Edge/Fog computing* [2] have been introduced. Fog computing allows moving compute and storage resources closer to IoT devices where data is generated and consumed. Fog computing devices could be smart gateways or routers deployed at the network edge, local PCs and even mobile devices such as smartphones or tablets carried by users offering computing and storage capabilities. These devices play their own roles of determining what data should be stored or processed locally (for low latency and saving network bandwidth) and what needs to be sent to the Cloud for further analysis. It is clear that EoT complements the CoT paradigm in terms of providing high scalability, low delay, location awareness, and leveraging local resources which are available at the network edges.

Although the benefit of Fog computing in the IoTs is clear [3,4], this technology is still in its infancy, and therefore needs to be thoroughly investigated. As discussed in the OpenFog Reference Architecture (OpenFog RA) - a set of core principles ('pillars') for building a sustainable Fog-based computing system [5] - there are eight main pillars presenting key attributes of the system that needs to be implemented. Our work focuses on the "Openness" including "Scalability" and "Programmability", as these are essential pillars for the flexibility and robustness of the fog computing based IoT systems. The main contributions of this work is summarized as follows:

(i) We analyze the openness in fog computing and propose an appropriate mechanism to implement this pillar supporting the ease in IoT service deployment.

(ii) We validate the appropriateness of the proposed model in a real-world ITS application, namely on Adaptive Traffic Signal Control (ATSC) model [6].

The rest of the paper is organized as follows: Sect. 2 reviews related work. The proposed approach on openness design features is presented in Sect. 3. Section 4 describes a prototyping system of the proposed method while the evaluation results are presented in Sect. 5. Section 6 concludes the paper.

## 2   Related Work

Fog/edge computing brings compute, storage and networking resources closer to the data generators and the consumers [2]. This computing approach is a highly virtualized platform that provides compute, storage, and networking services between end devices and traditional Cloud's DCs, typically but not exclusively located at the network edge. Fog/edge computing addresses essential issues on the Cloud-centric approach, hence helps to reduce communication costs for carrying a large amount of data and information from real-world environment to DCs for computation and storage. Therefore, response time, energy consumption, and operation costs can be drastically reduced, which are essential requirements for realizing large-scale IoT applications [5].

Essential challenges, potential applications, and benefits of fog computing have been investigated in various studies [3,4,7,8]. Studies in [9] analyze the essential roles of fog computing for extending continuous links of IoT data and services from the Cloud to the network edges, while studies in [10] propose architectural imperatives for fog computing and analyze use cases, requirements, and architectural techniques for Fog-enabled IoT networks. However, fog computing is still in its infancy, with inherent difficulties that need to be thoroughly investigated such as resource provisioning in distributed environments of fog computing [11,12], or the openness in fog computing which we will investigate in this paper.

Among the eight main pillars representing key attributes of fog computing as discussed in OpenFog RA [5], "Openness" is one of the crucial criteria which helps to implement fog-computing based service easily, flexibly and for scalable systems. This work focuses on investigating the "Openness" which includes "Scalability" and "Programmability" in the proposed fog computing model which can be applied to real-world applications such as Intelligent Transportation Systems (ITS) services.

ITS has been growing as one important technology in developing sustainable society and economics [13]. Among many services, ITS provides traffic state estimation as well as traffic light optimization (TLO) which are helpful in alleviating traffic congestion [14]. Adaptive Traffic Signal Control (ATSC) [6] is a popular method of TLO that has widely been applied around the world. By collecting traffic data which represent current traffic state, traffic light signal cycles of each intersection can be calculated and updated continuously. This way, the system can predict traffic congestion or detect unusual incidents in order to control traffic flows by changing traffic light cycles. Collecting traffic data from mobile phones or IoT devices carried by vehicles and then flexibly processing such data at the network edges is a new paradigm for pervasive urban traffic management.

There have been various mechanisms to calculate traffic light signal cycles using specific information of roads, traffic flows and turning rates. According to [15], every intersection has to find its saturation flow and turning rate in order to calculate traffic light cycles. By applying Webster formulas, the study in [16] has modeled traffic optimization in an area by optimizing traffic light cycles in each intersection, while [17] utilizes the Extension Neural Network to search for the best light cycles using the historical data about traffic conditions.

In the aforementioned studies, systems need to collect a huge amount of traffic data. Centralized computing methods such as Cloud Computing have been used extensively to support and deliver transportation applications in general where traffic data is gathered and processed at DCs on the cloud. Although this scheme is robust for applications requiring large computational resources and historical data, it is inefficient for delay-sensitive ATSC services since data need to be quickly processed for issuing almost real-time traffic light control instructions [18,19].

Fortunately, fog computing [20] proposes solutions to those shortcomings of Cloud Computing in ITS. Fog computing utilizes computing, storage and network resources within and at the network edges. For example, processing is performed closer to the data sources. This way, computing tasks can be distributed closer to users and things, which greatly reduce the burden of the cloud while still satisfying the latency-sensitivity requirements. Studies in [18,19] also support the idea of applying fog computing for solving traffic problems, thanks to its mobility, location awareness and its ability to lower service's latency.

Studies in [21,22] present a visionary concept of fog vehicle computing where vehicles are utilized to augment the computing and storage power of fogs, providing on-demand ITS services. They also discuss about the remaining challenges such as service provision, privacy, security, and task scheduling on the fogs. Study in [23] proposes a fog-based privacy-preserved pseudonym scheme where the pseudonym management is shifted to the fogs to utilize contextual information such as location, number of vehicles at hotspots for making decisions.

Our work is different from the existing works discussed above as it focuses on traffic management service, namely traffic light optimization leveraging the potential of fog computing. The proposed model uses traffic signals to control the flow of traffic on streets. The service utilizes the familiar red, amber and green traffic signal aspect to provide time-sharing for traffic at road intersections [13]. The traffic conditions of entries (road segments) at each intersection is updated timely by fog nodes deployed at corresponding intersections, hence significantly mitigate latency and deployment cost compared to those in the cloud-based approaches.

# 3   Openness Design Features on Fog Computing

This section presents our proposed framework satisfying openness in fog computing in order to flexibly deploy new IoT services.

## 3.1   Overall Architecture

The overall architecture of the proposed model is depicted in Fig. 1. It consists of three tiers, namely the *IoT service* tier, the *Fog landscape*, and the *Cloud service* tier. As described in Fig. 1a, the fog service landscape is composed of fog computing nodes which are already available at network edges such as access points (AP), routers, local servers and so on. These nodes are clustered into colonies to process IoT services requested by local or regional users (i.e., close to or covered by the colony). Each fog colony consists of a fog orchestration node (denoted as $F_1, F_2$ in the figure) serving as a service fog endpoint (SFE) and several fog cells/nodes (denoted as $f_{1.x}, f_{2.y}$ in the figure). SFEs provide services/contents

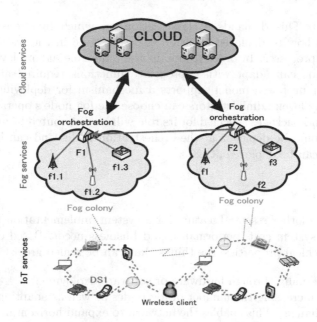

**Fig. 1.** Overall architecture of the proposed fog computing framework with the openness.

that could not be provided from the IoT service tier. SFEs also serve as intermediate processing nodes used for data pre-processing or data integration before being forwarded to DCs on the cloud for further computation. This scheme helps mitigating communication and computation costs, hence reduces latency of local-based services for local users which are essential for delay-sensitive IoT applications. Further details of this architecture can be found in [24]. This paper focuses on the openness of IoT service deployment on the fog landscape (i.e., the *Fog service* tier).

## 3.2 Openness

Openness has a great impact on a fog computing ecosystem and IoT platforms. This is apparent in the diversity of the vendor solutions to system cost, quality and innovation. In this sense, openness is regarded as a principle supporting fog nodes in addressing business needs. Our proposed model aims at creating an open standardization which supports multiple operating system distributions: Red-Hat Enterprise Linux, Ubuntu, Debian, and OpenSUSE. The goal is that hardware failures can be flexibly substituted by off-the-shelf devices supplied by any vendor. This design also simplifies the installation process to help administrators in easily using and managing IoT services on the fog landscape.

Another target of the proposed approach is to focus on fog computing multi-level hierarchy characteristic. Each level has many fog nodes with different roles like fog cells and orchestration nodes described in the overall architecture (see Sect. 3.1). This demands a classification on which functions should be deployed and how to deployed them on each fog node in the installation and management processes. In order to obtain the "any role at any level" feature, i.e., a fog node can adapt with appropriate functions required at each level efficiently, our proposed model supports a mechanism for deploying fog nodes to work at any level: administrators can choose the fog node's operating role at installation and packages specified for its role will be distributed from the server. This server could be deployed at the orchestration nodes and can be remotely accessible or can be deployed at DCs.

## 3.3   Scalability

Scalability is another essential feature for a system implementation that adapts to workload, system cost, performance and business needs. Based on fog computing hierarchical properties, the things that can be scaled are:

- Nodes: internally through hardware or software deployment.
- Networks: increasing the number of fog nodes as well as adapting with environment changes. This enables the network to expand horizontally and vertically which helps to ease the burden on fog nodes with the same level in the hierarchy.
- Infrastructure: storage, network connectivity, analytic services can be scaled.

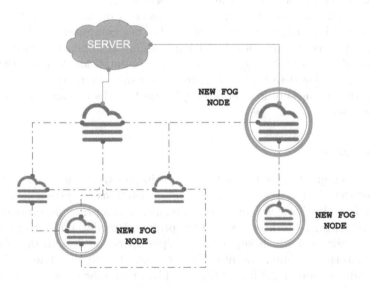

**Fig. 2.** Scaling Fog network.

The proposed model enables network scalability by allowing addition of fog nodes into an existing topology conveniently. Concretely, newly added fog nodes are able to detect its geographical position (via its GPS model) in order to identify the most suitable zone (managed by a corresponding orchestration node) to connect with as described in Fig. 2.

## 3.4  Programmability

Programmability makes the deployment more adaptive to changes in the system requirements, allowing users to add new functions to the framework efficiently via programming at the software and hardware layers. Our proposed framework implements this pillar by allowing user to create new programs running on the cloud or orchestration nodes which are controlled by user remotely. These programs are then deployed on the requiring nodes by sending Javascript utilities via POST requests as depicted in Fig. 3. As discussed before, the security pillar is not required in the current design, hence this implementation approach is acceptable. Openness combining with security constraints are deferred to a future work.

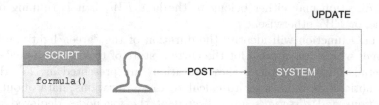

**Fig. 3.** User can interact with server via POST request.

# 4  Prototyping

This section describes the implementation of a prototype for the proposed framework which can be deployed in real-world applications for traffic light optimization (TLO) services.

## 4.1  Traffic Light Optimization

TLO service which is adaptive with current traffic states at intersections could help to optimize the road utilization and avoid traffic congestion. This part describes a model that optimizes traffic the light cycle for an intersection. This work considers TLO problems for typical intersections in urban traffic networks as depicted in Fig. 4.

As shown, vehicles enter an intersection from four directions, namely from the West ($FW$ - as illustrated in the Fig. 4), from the East ($FE$), from the South ($FS$), and from the North ($FN$). Each entry consists of two lanes denoted as the *inner-lane* ($a$) and the *outer-lane* ($b$). For example, a vehicle traveling in

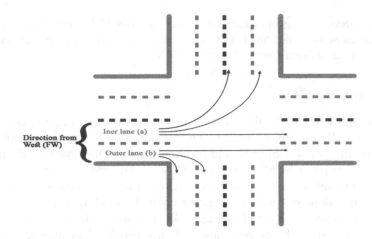

**Fig. 4.** An intersection with 4 entry directions, two lanes for each.

the *FW* direction may either belong to the lane $FW_a$ if it is running on the inner-lane, or $FW_b$ otherwise.

The TLO function will identify the duration of the "green light" and "red light" times which are suitable for the current state of traffic in different directions. Details on calculation of these durations are presented in [25]. Here it is worth noticing that in order to calculate these durations, data about vehicles' *locations* and *directions* are collected at the fog nodes deployed at the corresponding traffic lights. In addition, fog nodes should predict the number of vehicles which will enter the corresponding intersection in the upcoming phase. Therefore, fog nodes at different intersections (but in the same region) communicate with each other to share the traffic related data. On the other hand, the orchestration node collects data reported from fog nodes to analyze and then appropriately control traffic lights on its region based on the analyzed information.

### 4.2    System Components

As presented in Sect. 3.1, the prototype system consists of orchestration nodes, fog cells, and traffic light units (actuators). This section describes the implementation details of these components.

> **Orchestration node:** each orchestration node contains 4 modules: a *view module*, a *computing module*, a *database module*, and a *timing module*.

– **View module:** displays statistical data collected from nodes in its region.
– **Computing module:** carries out calculations based on statistical data.
– **Database module:** stores traffic related data collected from vehicles and statistical data generated by fog nodes.

- **Timing module:** triggers the updating of the database after a certain period of time.

  **Fog cell/node:** each fog cell contains 4 modules: a *Restful API*, a *computing module*, a *database module*, and a *timing module*.

- **Restful API:** defines communication routes between fog nodes, between a fog node and vehicles, and between a fog node and traffic lights.
- **Computing module:** carries out necessary calculations to optimize traffic light cycles.
- **Database module:** stores traffic related data collected from vehicles and statistical data generated by fog nodes.
- **Timing module:** keeps time to trigger a fog node when a certain amount of time has passed.

  **Traffic light unit:** each traffic light unit contains *actuators* and a *timing module*.

- **Actuators:** control traffic signals in an intersection in accordance with instructions from the corresponding fog node.
- **Timing module:** triggers the traffic light to send requests for new traffic signal data from the corresponding fog node.

## 5    Evaluation

This section evaluates the effectiveness of the proposed framework in terms of mitigating latency, energy consumption and operational cost when deploying ATSC services.

### 5.1    Evaluation Environment

To evaluate the effectiveness of the proposed approach compared to Cloud-based approach for ATSC services, we use iFogSim [26] - a toolkit for modeling and simulating Fog/Cloud services developed by the CLOUDS Lab (University of Melbourne). This tool allows us to describe the network topology, specify system instances describing the links between them and simulate tasks that run throughout the system. We have run the prototype described in Sect. 4 in the context of the above simulation tool in order to mimic real-world traffic optimization applications. We evaluated the *latency, energy consumption* and *cost of operations* in the proposed approach compared to the cloud-based counterpart.

In the simulation, we assume that there are $A$ intersections, each of which has 1 fog node collecting information from $B$ cars (e.g., 4 fog nodes at 4 intersections, each of which processes data from 30 cars at the consideration time). The simulation is conducted in two modes, namely the Fog mode and the Cloud mode as illustrated in Fig. 5 and is described as follows:

- **Fog mode:** In this mode, traffic related data is gathered and processed at fog nodes placed at intersections, utilizing the proposed framework. These fog nodes also control their traffic lights.
- **Cloud mode:** In this mode, data gathering, processing and traffic lights controlling are processed at the cloud.

Specification of the devices used at each layer in the above topology are shown in Table 1.

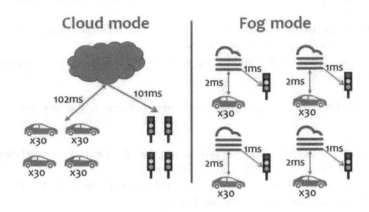

**Fig. 5.** Simulation topology: Cloud mode (left), Fog mode (right).

**Table 1.** Devices' specification

| Device | Cloud | Fog node | Vehicle |
|---|---|---|---|
| CPU (MIPS) | 684,000 | 2,200 | 1,000 |
| RAM (MB) | 128,000 | 1,000 | 500 |
| Bandwidth (Mbps) | 150 | 50 | 10 |
| Power (W) | 120–50 | 5.1–1.9 | 1.5–0.5 |
| Cost per MIPS ($/MIPS/s) | 0.0003 | 0.0003 | 0.0003 |

Task description for the TLO services is presented in Table 2. Here, clients/vehicles periodically collect GPS data received from their own GPS modules and then send the PGS data (via SEND_THE_DATA task) to the corresponding Fog nodes or to the Cloud according to different deployment modes. Fog nodes or the Cloud must respond with a packet containing the node Id (UPDATE_NODE_ID) and periodically update the new traffic light cycles to the traffic lights (TRAFFIC_LIGHTS_CTRL).

**Table 2.** Task specification

| Task | CPU length (MIP) | Netw length (Bytes) |
|------|------------------|---------------------|
| GPS | 2 | 0 |
| SEND_DATA | 3 | 500 |
| UPDATE_NODE_ID | 2 | 500 |
| TRAFFIC_LIGHTS_CTRL | 2 | 500 |

## 5.2 Evaluation Results

According to the evaluation results shown in Fig. 6, the proposed approach obtains significantly lower latency compared to its cloud-based counterpart. The results only consist of transmission delay and queuing delay as the execution delay in this case is too small to be counted since the complexity is not high. With other use cases that require more complex computational works, tasks are distributed to both the Cloud and Fog layers, which results in more distinct latency.

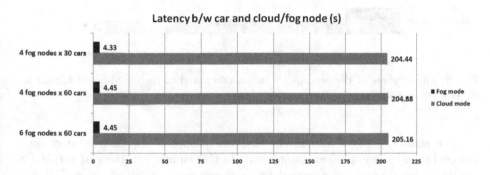

**Fig. 6.** Effectiveness of the proposed method compared to the cloud-based one, in terms of latency.

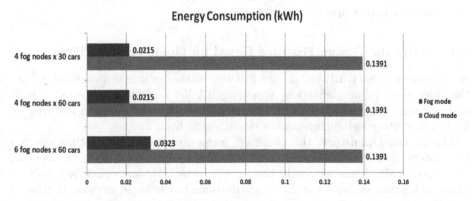

**Fig. 7.** Effectiveness of the proposed approach compared to the cloud-based method, in terms of energy consumption.

The evaluation results in Fig. 7 show that the centralized data processing at the cloud is more power-consuming than using a set of multiple lightweight nodes in the proposed approach. The energy consumes in the Fog mode is the sum of all fog nodes' energy consumption as cloud was not used in this mode. The results also reveal that the more fog nodes being deployed, the more energy the system consumes. This is considered a trade-off for improving latency performance. However, with the development of low-power micro-computers and other technologies such as FPGA, it is believed that more hardware solutions with better energy consumption performance than the one being used in this simulation will be introduced.

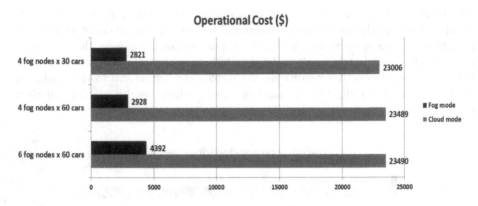

**Fig. 8.** Effectiveness of the proposed solution compared to the cloud-based approach, in terms of cost saving.

The results in Fig. 8 also reveal that the proposed approach is more economical than its cloud-based counterpart. In this simulation, the *cost per MIPS* metric in fog devices are assumed to be the same as in cloud. In reality, fog devices are believed to be remarkably low-cost which will result in lower cost of operations. Also, relatively to energy consumption, deploying more fog nodes will results in higher operational cost.

### 5.3   Verify the Design Features Based on OpenFog RA Pillars

As presented in Sect. 3.1, the design features of the proposed framework follow the three main pillars defined by OpenFog RA [5], namely "Openness", "Scalability", and "Programmability". This section verifies these design features by using our prototype implementation described in Sect. 4.

As for the *Openness*, the proposed framework supports multiple operating system distributions, namely Red-Hat Enterprise Linux, Ubuntu, Debian, and OpenSUSE. A survey conducted by W3Techs [27] shows that over 86% of Linux web server systems use these distributions to run their services. Hardware suppliers will target these types of operating system in manufacturing in order to match the market needs. This means the proposed approach can be flexibly installed on most of hardware products in the market.

As for the *Scalability*, the proposed approach can be scaled via "Fog network". In addition, it can be scaled via:

- Fog Node: by replacing hardware with better specifications and performance.
- Fog Infrastructure: services can be replaced depending on hardware replacement. Communication means (e.g., WiFi, LoRa, mobile networks) can also be replaced or upgraded in different scenarios.

As for *Programmability*, the proposed framework allows administrators to modify and interact with its system by sending JavaScript functions via POST requests. As the security pillar is not the main consideration in this design state, this implementation is acceptable.

## 6    Conclusion

This paper proposed a novel approach to traffic light optimization using fog computing. Applying fog architecture to the ATSC solution, the proposed approach enables traffic system to automatically and efficiently adapt to the current traffic conditions. Simulation results conducted by iFogSim show that the proposed fog computing model can provide remarkably better performances than the traditional cloud computing approach in terms of latency, energy consumption and operation cost saving.

Despite showing basic properties of a fog based solution, the current version of the proposed framework does not support features relating to resource provisioning between fog nodes and verification of connected devices. Therefore, more research on remaining pillars should be thoroughly conducted to improve the robustness of the proposed framework.

**Acknowledgement.** This research is funded by Vietnam National University Ho Chi Minh City (VNU-HCM) under grant **number C2019-20-18**.

## References

1. Nan, Y., Li, W., Bao, W., Delicato, F.C., Pires, P.F., Zomaya, A.Y.: Cost-effective processing for delay-sensitive applications in cloud of things systems. In: IEEE 15th International Symposium on Network Computing and Applications (NCA), Cambridge, MA, pp. 162–169 (2016)
2. Bonomi, F., Milito, R., Zhu, J., Addepall, S.: Fog computing and its role in the internet of things. In: Proceedings of MCC12, Helsinki, Finland, pp. 14–15 (2012)
3. Dastjerdi, A., Gupta, H., Calheiros, R.N., Ghosh, S.K., Buyya, R.: Fog computing: principles, architectures, and applications. In: Internet of Things: Principles and Paradigms, Chap. 4. Morgan Kaufmann (2016)
4. Sarkar, S., Chatterjee, S., Misra, S.: Assessment of the suitability of fog computing in the context of internet of things. IEEE Trans. Cloud Comput. **PP**(99), 1–14 (2015)

5. OpenFog Consortium Architecture Working Group: Openfog reference architecture for fog computing [opfra001.020817], Technical report, pp. 1–162 (2017)

6. Adaptive signal control technology, August 2019. https://www.fhwa.dot.gov/innovation/everydaycounts/edc-1/asct.cfm

7. Vaquero, L., Merino, L.: Finding your way in the fog: towards a comprehensive definition of fog computing. ACM SIGCOMM Comput. Commun. Rev. **44**(5), 27–32 (2014)

8. Yi, S., Hao, Z., Qin, Z., Li, Q.: Fog computing: platform and applications. In: Third IEEE Workshop on Hot Topics in Web Systems and Technologies (HotWeb), Cambridge, Washington, DC, pp. 73–78 (2015)

9. Montero, R.S., Rojas, E., Carrillo, A.A., Llorente, I.M.: Extending the cloud to the network edge. Computer **50**(4), 91–95 (2017)

10. Byers, C.C.: Architectural imperatives for fog computing: use cases, requirements, and architectural techniques for fog-enabled iot networks. IEEE Commun. Mag. **55**(8), 14–20 (2017)

11. Yu, Y.-J., Chiu, T.-C., Pang, A.-C., Chen, M.-F., Liu, J.: Virtual machine placement for backhaul traffic minimization in fog radio access networks. In: IEEE International Conference on Communications (ICC), pp. 1–7 (2017)

12. Gu, L., Zeng, D., Guo, S., Barnawi, A., Xiang, Y.: Cost efficient resource management in fog computing supported medical cyber-physical system. IEEE Trans. Emerg. Topics Comput. **5**(1), 108–119 (2017)

13. McQueen, B., McQueen, J.: Intelligent Transportation Systems Architectures. Artech House Publishers, Boston (1999)

14. Quang, T.M., Eiji, K.: Traffic state estimation with mobile phones based on the "3R" philosophy. IEICE Trans. Commun. **E94-B**(12), 3447–3458 (2011)

15. Webster, F.V.: Traffic Signal Settings (1958)

16. Kesur, K.B.: Optimization of mixed cycle length traffic signals. J. Adv. Transp., 432–437 (2012)

17. Chao, K.-H., Lee, R.-H., Wang, M.-H.: An intelligent traffic light control based on extension neural network, department of electrical engineering, pp. 22–24. National Chin-Yi University of Technology, Taichung (2008)

18. Giang, N., Leung, V.C.M., Lea, R.: On developing smart transportation applications in fog computing paradigm. In: Proceedings of the 6th ACM Symposium on Development and Analysis of Intelligent Vehicular Networks and Applications, pp. 91–97 (2016)

19. Darwish, T.S.J., Bakar, K.A.: Fog based intelligent transportation big data analytics in the internet of vehicles environment: motivations, architecture, challenges, and critical issues. IEEE Access **6**, 15 679–15 701 (2018)

20. Bonomi, F., Milito, R., Zhu, J., Addepalli, S.: Fog computing and its role in the internet of things. In: Proceedings of the First Edition of the MCC Workshop on Mobile Cloud Computing, pp. 14–15 (2012)

21. Sookhak, M., et al.: Fog vehicular computing: augmentation of fog computing using vehicular cloud computing. IEEE Veh. Technol. Mag. **12**(3), 55–64 (2017)

22. Xiao, Y., Zhu, C.: Vehicular fog computing: vision and challenges. In: 2017 IEEE International Conference on Pervasive Computing and Communications Workshops (PerCom Workshops), pp. 6–9, March 2017

23. Kang, J., Yu, R., Huang, X., Zhang, Y.: Privacy-preserved pseudonym scheme for fog computing supported internet of vehicles. IEEE Trans. Intell. Transp. Syst., 1–11 (2017)

24. Quang, T., Nguyen, D., Le, V., Nguyen, D., Pham, T.: Task placement on fog computing made efficient for IoT application provision. Wireless Commun. Mob. Comput. **2019**(12), 1–17 (2019)
25. Quang, T.M., Chanh, T.M., Tuan, L.A., Binh, N.T., Triet, T.M., Balan, R.K.: Fogfly: a traffic light optimization solution based on fog computing. In: Proceedings of the 2018 ACM International Joint Conference and 2018 International Symposium on Pervasive and Ubiquitous Computing and Wearable Computers (UbiComp 2018), pp. 1130–1139. ACM, New York (2018)
26. Gupta, H., Dastjerdi, A., Ghosh, S.K., Buyya, R.: iFogSim: a toolkit for modeling and simulation of resource management techniques in internet of things, edge and fog computing environments. Technical report, CLOUDS-TR-2016-2, Cloud Computing and Distributed Systems Laboratory, The University of Melbourne (2016)
27. Usage statistics and market share of Linux for websites. https://w3techs.com/technologies/details/os-linux/all/all

# A Top-Down Scheduling for Time Efficient Data Aggregation in WSNs

Vi Van Vo[1], Dung T. Nguyen[1], Duc-Tai Le[1], Manh-Hung Tran[1], Moonseong Kim[2(✉)], and Hyunseung Choo[1(✉)]

[1] Sungkyungkwan University, Seoul, South Korea
{vovanvi,nguyentiendzung,ldtai,hungtm,choo}@skku.edu
[2] Seoul Theological University, Bucheon, South Korea
moonseong@stu.ac.kr

**Abstract.** Time efficient data aggregation is a crucial problem in wireless sensor networks where computational and battery power are limited. In a data aggregation process, intermediate nodes combine all received data and then forward to the next node. Current researches concern energy or time efficient of sensors in wireless sensor networks. The paper proposes a top-down scheduling scheme to minimize the aggregation time. The proposed scheme reduces the possibility of collision when transmitting on a link by considering its adjacent links and neighbors of the receiver. The collision prevention leads to an aggregation time reduction. Simulation results show that the proposed scheme reduces up to 18% compared with the state-of-the-art top-down approach on data aggregation.

**Keywords:** Wireless sensor networks · Data aggregation · Top-down approach

## 1 Introduction

The data aggregation is very important in wireless sensor networks applications, such as environmental monitoring, battlefield surveillance, spatial exploration, where the sink nodes aggregate and receive the sensed data for analysis [1]. Because the sensor nodes are deployed in such dangerous areas that are difficult to approach; moreover, the sensor nodes are deployed in huge numbers so they are mostly non-rechargeable or irreplaceable. Thus, sensor nodes have limited energy resources, the primary problem is to improve the lifetime of the network in wireless sensor network [2]. It is advised to turn the sensor nodes off when they are idle to save the energy. When aggregating the data from all nodes, collisions, in which data is from the different nodes transmitted to the same node at the same time, may happen. The time schedule is proposed to avoid the collisions.

Convergecast is a communication pattern to aggregate data in Wireless Sensor Networks [3]. Convergecast is defined as a many-to-one pattern where the sink node collects data from sensor nodes in the network using wireless communication links. There are two types of data aggregation convergecast: (1) Data

T. K. Dang et al. (Eds.): FDSE 2019, LNCS 11814, pp. 358–368, 2019.
https://doi.org/10.1007/978-3-030-35653-8_24

aggregation, in which, the intermediate nodes will process the data (get the maximum or average data between sensed data from previous nodes) before sending to the next hop (2) Raw data convergecast in which intermediate nodes forward the sensed data directly to the sink node without modification [4]. It is advised to use the raw data aggregation in some wireless sensor networks application due to the fact that intermediate nodes use low performance and low power processors which are not good to process the data packets.

In this work, we focus on data aggregation in the network. Assume that a wireless sensor network is given, Time Division Multiple Access (TDMA), which divides the time into time slot and each sensor node transmits data only in its assigned time slot to avoid the collisions, is used as the medium access protocol [5]. The data from sensor nodes is transmitted to the sink node form as Tree-based. The tree-based approach defines aggregation from constructing an aggregation tree, sink node consider as a root and source node consider as a leaves. Information flowing of data start from leaves node up to root means sink [6]. The proposed method solves a bottom-up problem by using a top-down approach. At the end of the schedule, all the time slot will be reversed the order to abide by the dependencies the aggregation tree. The result shows that the proposed idea can improve the schedule length compared to the Minimum Interference Network Topology (MINT) heuristic which is proposed in [7]. The outlined algorithm is present in Sect. 2 to explain how the proposed idea improves the schedule length.

The rest of this paper is organized as follows: We present the proposed scheme in Sect. 2. In the Sect. 3, we evaluate the proposed scheme by simulations. Finally, we summarize our scheme and outline some future research directions.

## 2 Proposed Scheme

Given a communication graph and a sink node, the proposed scheme can generate an aggregation tree while assembling the aggregation schedule. This is a top-down approach solving the bottom-up problem which is data aggregation.

### 2.1 Overall Idea

The algorithm builds the aggregation scheduling by gradually grow the aggregation tree. It starts with a designated sink node, $s$, which is added to the growing tree. Nodes in the growing tree are scheduled ones. The $s$ is in the set $V'$ in which $V'$ is a set of nodes in the growing tree. We define $E'$ is a set of links in the growing tree. Initially, $E'$ is the empty set because there is only the sink node in the growing tree. At the beginning, the *timeslot* is set to 1.

While the number of nodes in $V'$ is not equal to the number of nodes in $V$, a candidate set, $C$, is selected. The $C$, is a set of links in which their sources are nodes in $V$ and their destinations are nodes in $V'$. One or more links from the candidate set, are added to the growing tree. They are greedily added by using the function *select_candidate*() which is illustrated in next Subsect. 2.2.

---

**Algorithm 1:** Proposed Idea Algorithm

---

   **Input** : Communication graph $G(V, E)$, sink node $s$
   **Output:** A schedule for data aggregation,
            An aggregation tree
1  $V' \leftarrow \{s\}$
2  $E' \leftarrow \emptyset$
3  $t \leftarrow 1$
4  **while** $V \neq V'$ **do**
5      $C \leftarrow \{(u, v) \in E \mid u \in V \setminus V' \wedge v \in V'\}$
6      **while** $C \neq \emptyset$ **do**
7           $(u_c, v_c) = \text{select\_candidate}(C)$
8           $E' \leftarrow E' \cup (u_c, v_c)$
9           $C \leftarrow C \setminus \{(u_c, v_c) \cup \text{conflict}(C, (u_c, v_c))\}$
10         $V' \leftarrow V' \cup u_c$
11     **end**
12     $t \leftarrow t + 1$
13 **end**

---

After selecting one or more links from the candidate set, the links will greedily fill in the current time slot. These links are scheduled in the same time slot as long as they do not conflict with their destination who are already added in the growing tree. There are two kinds of conflicts which are outlined in the Subsect. 2.3. The link are chosen from the $C$ determined by a function $conflict()$ which is also outlined in the Subsect. 2.3.

When there is no more links in the $C$ can be added to the growing tree, the *timeslot* counter increases, then a new $C$ is determined, one or more links in that $C$ continue being added to the growing tree greedily in that time slot. So on and so forth, the algorithm continues until all nodes in the network are scheduled, it means the number of nodes in $V'$ is equal to the number of nodes in $V$.

In final, we will obtain a connected network without conflicting, the final time slot counter is a schedule length. The actual time slots assigned for the links in the schedule are generated by reversing the time slot counter used in the algorithm. So that, the order of assigned links is reversed, the first link added to the growing tree is scheduled last and the last link added to the growing tree is scheduled in the first time slot.

## 2.2 Scheduling Metrics

The collision in Wireless Sensor Networks happens when two different nodes send data to a same node at the same time. Two kind of collisions can happen, one case is primary collision and another case is secondary collision. In the primary collision, one node cannot receive data from two different nodes at the same time. As demonstrated in Fig. 1(a) at the same time, node A cannot receive the data from node B and node C; otherwise a conflict can happen at node A if node B and node C keep transmit the data to node A, then node A cannot receive any data from other nodes. In the secondary collision as showed in the

Fig. 4(b), when a node transmits the data, it transmits omnidirectional way; It means when node B transmits data to node A; at the same time, node C in the neighbor set of the node A sends data to node D, but node A also receives data from node C because a node transmit data in onmidirectional way, then a conflict happens at the node A. So that, to avoid the secondary collision, when one node transmit data to a receiving node; at that time, the neighbor nodes of the receiving nodes must not transmit data.

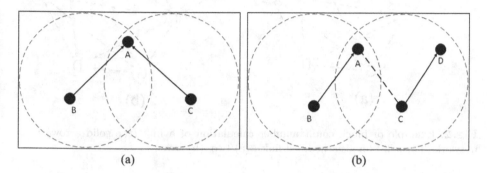

(a)                                                    (b)

**Fig. 1.** Collisions in Wireless Sensor Networks: (a) Primary collision, (b) Secondary collision

In our algorithm, the links are selected to schedule in one time slot based on a strategy, named Block Count strategy. Block Count of a link is number of remaining links in Candidate Set that would be blocked because of a collision with the link in the current time slot. This strategy is a dynamic one, so the block count of a link can be different in different time slot. A link sometimes has many Block Count numbers, sometimes it has zero Block Count number. An example of block count number of a link is given as illustrated in the Fig. 2.

The selected candidates are picked up greedily from the candidate set to schedule in the same time slot as long as they do not conflict to each other. A link which has smallest number of Block Count is selected to add to the growing tree in the current time slot. However, in many cases there are many links having same smallest Block Count, then the candidate selection strategy is to choose a link whose has the least neighbors in the receiver side (The receiver side is the set of nodes which are already added to the growing tree) as showed in an example of picking a link between links having same smallest Block Count in the Fig. 3. If in a same time slot there are some links both having same smallest Block Count numbers and having same smallest neighbors in the receiver side, then a link is selected randomly between those links to add to the growing tree.

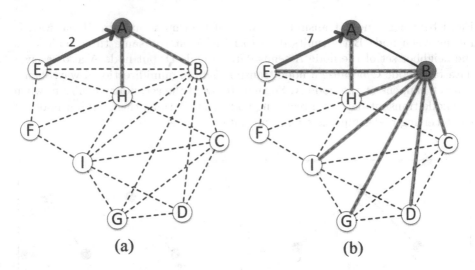

**Fig. 2.** Example of block count number calculation of a link (the solid arrow) in a network (The solid line is scheduled link): (a) two, (b) seven

## 2.3 Conflicted Links Removal

The conflict() function returns the set of links in Candidate set, $C$, in which u $\in V\backslash V'$ has an edge $(u, v_c)$ (it means that u is in the neighbor set of $v_c$). If node u is a neighbor of node $v_c$, the link $(u, v_c)$ is a candidate in the Candidate Set, $C$, so link $(u, v_c)$ must not be removed to avoid a primary collision with link $(u_c, v_c)$; or $v \in V\backslash V'$ has an edge $(u_c, v)$ (it means that $v$ is in a neighbor set of $u_c$). If node $v$ is a neighbor of node $u_c$, the link $(u_c, v)$ should be removed to make sure that one node only transmit data to another node in a time slot.

## 2.4 Example

An example is given to illustrate our proposed idea against the reference scheme (MINT: Minimum Interference Network Topology) as shown in Fig. 3. We present nine nodes example topology and a sample execution of the algorithm. In the initialization, A is the sink node adding to the growing tree (Fig. 3a), V' = A. A set of candidate links (BA, EA, HA) is selected in the first time slot (Fig. 3b), since they have same block count number and same neighbor in the growing tree, a link, which is BA from the candidate set is randomly picked up to schedule in this time slot (Fig. 3c), V' = A, D. Because there is no more link can be scheduled in this time slot, the time slot counter increases to two. A new candidate set is determined (Fig. 3d). All of the links in candidate set have same block count numbers, while MINT scheme randomly select one link to, which is EA, to schedule among the links in the candidate set (Fig. 3e1), our proposed scheme considers the neighbor nodes in the growing tree. The nodes C, D, G, I have one neighbor in the growing tree, so that we randomly select one link in the set of link

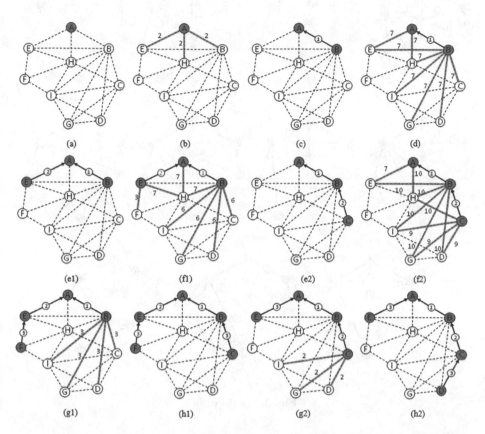

**Fig. 3.** Example run on a nine-node network: (a) communication graph, (b) Candidate set in time slot 1, (c) scheduled link in time slot 1, (d) Candidate set in time slot 2, (e1) scheduled links of MINT scheme in time slot 2, (f1) Candidate set of MINT scheme in time slot 3, (e2) scheduled links of proposed scheme in time slot 2, (f2) Candidate set of proposed scheme in time slot 3, (g1) Candidate set and scheduled links of MINT scheme in time slot 3, (h1) scheduled links of MINT scheme in time slot 3, (g2) Candidate set and scheduled links of proposed scheme in time slot 3, (h2) scheduled links of proposed scheme in time slot 3, (i1) Candidate set of MINT scheme in time slot 4, (j1) scheduled links of MINT scheme in time slot 4, (i2) Candidate set of proposed scheme in time slot 4, (j2-1) candidate set and scheduled links of proposed scheme in time slot 4, (i2) Candidate set of proposed scheme in time slot 4, (j2-1) candidate set and scheduled links of proposed scheme in time slot 4, (j2-2) scheduled links of proposed scheme in time slot 4, (k1) Candidate set of MINT scheme in time slot 5, (l1) scheduled links of MINT scheme in time slot 5, (k2) Candidate set of proposed scheme in time slot 5, (l1) candidate set and scheduled links of proposed scheme in time slot 5, (m) scheduled links of proposed scheme in time slot 5, (n) Reverse time slots order

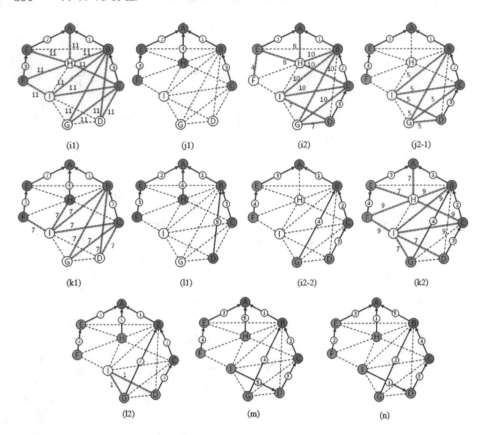

(i1)    (j1)    (i2)    (j2-1)

(k1)    (l1)    (i2-2)    (k2)

(l2)    (m)    (n)

**Fig. 3.** (*continued*)

CB, DB, GB, IB to schedule. In this case, the link CB is selected (Fig. 3e2). Due to the fact that there is no more link can be scheduled in this time slot, time slot now is increment. A new candidate set is calculated in the time slot 3 for MINT and our proposed scheme (Fig. 3f1 and f2, respectively). FE is selected to add to the growing tree since it has smallest block count number (Fig. 3g1). There are 4 more links, which are CB, DB, GB, IB, they do not conflict with the FE, and they have same block count number, then a link, which is CB, among them is randomly selected to add to the growing tree (Fig. 3h1). For our proposed scheme, the link EA has smallest block count number, then it is picked up to add to the growing tree. After that, also in time slot 3, there are 3 candidate links left, which are DC, GI and IC. They have same block count number as well as same neighbor in the growing tree, one link is picked up among them randomly which is DC (Fig. 3h2). The time slot counter is increment due to the fact that there are no candidate link remaining. In the time slot 4, the candidate set is determined as shown in Fig. 3i1 and i2 for MINT and proposed scheme, respectively. For MINT, since all candidate links have same block count number, one link is randomly picked up to add to the growing tree, that is HA (Fig. 3j1).

For our proposed scheme, FE is picked up to add to the growing tree since it has smallest block count number. In the current time slot, there are some links remaining in the candidate set, they have same block count number. However, DC has only one neighbor in the growing tree, then it is added to schedule in this time slot. The time slot counter increases, so on and so forth all the links are schedule in the time slot 5 in our proposed scheme (Fig. 3m), but there are 2 more links are not scheduling yet in MINT scheme (Fig. 3l1). When all nodes in the network are scheduled the time slot numbers are reversed to satisfy the bottom-up flow of the aggregation (Fig. 3n).

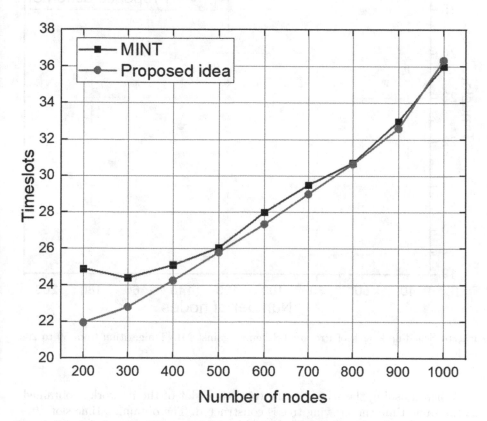

**Fig. 4.** Schedule length of Proposed Scheme against MINT algorithm from 200 to 1000 nodes

## 3   Performance Evaluation

In our simulation, we randomly deployed nodes on a rectangular area of $200 \times 200$ unit$^2$. All the nodes have a transmission range of 25 units. The distance of the nodes is calculated by Euclidean distance, the nodes consider as neighbors of a node if their distances are less than or equal to the transmission range of that node. The sink node is always generated randomly in each network topology. We simulate the random network by varying the number of nodes between 200 to 1000. Due to fact that the network size and the transmission range are constants, the higher number of nodes increases the higher network density is.

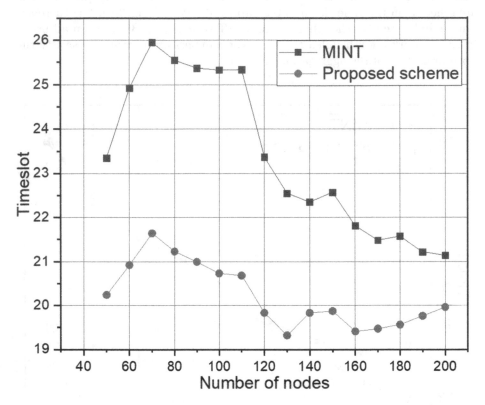

**Fig. 5.** Schedule length of Proposed Scheme against MINT algorithm from 50 to 200 nodes

When finishing the schedule, the total time slot of the network is obtained, at the same time the growing tree is constructed. The obtaining time slot after finishing the schedule means the latency of data aggregation of the network. Thus, the lower obtained time slot is, the better scheme are using. Every certain number of nodes, we run on 20 different random topologies, the present results are average time slots.

In [7] the MINT scheme is also presented top-down approach. The MINT algorithm is similar to our proposed idea, the different point is when selecting a link among the candidate set to schedule, in MINT scheme, after some scheduled links are picked up from the candidate set by using metric block count which is defined in the section II.B, if those links have same smallest block count number, the scheme will randomly pick up one link among them to schedule in that time slot. In our proposed scheme, whereas, a link will be picked up to add to growing tree if one end of that link has least neighbors in the growing tree. If there are two or more links in which one end has same least neighbors in the growing tree, our proposed scheme randomly pick up a link among them to add to the growing tree in that time slot.

Results showed in Fig. 4 demonstrates the improvement of the proposed idea compare with MINT algorithm. The proposed scheme can improve up to 12% of schedule length compare with MINT algorithm. Since a link in which when one end has least neighbors in receiver side is chosen, that link affects less nodes then more links can be selected in the same time slot. The reason is when that link is chosen, the affected neighbors is minimized and the number of links can be selected to schedule in one time slot is maximized. When the network is more condensed, the improvement of the schedule length is less. The network from 500 up to 1000 nodes, the schedule length of two schemes look similar. If the number of nodes is higher than 1000 nodes in $200 \times 200$ unit$^2$, the neighbors of a node will be very high, this is not reasonable in practical. So that we do not consider the case larger number of nodes.

We also simulate the proposed scheme with low density (from 50 to 200 nodes in $200 \times 200$ unit$^2$ with the transmission range is set 30) against MINT scheme, the results are shown in Fig. 5. Our proposed scheme can improve up to 18% comparing with MINT scheme. From 50 to 70 nodes, the density is small in $200 \times 200$ unit$^2$ area, then the nodes are not distributed equally in the area, some regions have high density, others have low density, that is the reason why it takes more time to schedule the nodes in these networks. When the number of nodes increase (from 80 nodes), the number of nodes is high enough to spread all the area, then the aggregation time for the nodes decreases gradually.

## 4  Conclusion

In this paper we present the proposed idea based on MINT algorithm. This is a top-down approach solving bottom-up problem that is data aggregation in wireless sensor networks. MINT algorithm is one of the best top-down approach for aggregating the sensed data, but our proposed idea can improve the aggregation time comparing to the MINT from 5 to 10% when the number of scheduling nodes is small (the density is about 10 to 20 nodes in the transmission area). We use link as a metric to select a best link to schedule in each iteration in the proposed idea's algorithm. The best link helps to reduce the aggregation time when the scheduling is finished.

Our proposed scheme works very well with small number of nodes, so that it is suitable apply it into delay-constraint problem in the future work. We believe that our future work will significantly improve the aggregation time when combining the data in wireless sensor networks.

**Acknowledgments.** This work was supported by Institute of Information & communications Technology Planning & Evaluation (IITP) grant funded by the Korea government (MSIT) (No.2019-0-00421, AI Graduate School Support Program).

# References

1. Akyildiz, I.F., Vuran, M.C.: Wireless Sensor Networks, vol. 4. Wiley, Hoboken (2010). https://doi.org/10.1002/9780470515181
2. Yu, B., Choi, W., Lee, T., Kim, H.: Clustering algorithm considering sensor node distribution in wireless sensor networks. J. Inf. Process. Syst. **14**, 926–940 (2018)
3. Gandham, S., et al.: Distributed time-optimal scheduling for convergecast in wireless sensor networks. Comput. Netw. **52**, 610–629 (2008)
4. Incel, O.D., Ghosh, A., Krishnamachari, B., Chintalapudi, K.: Fast data collection in tree-based wireless sensor networks. IEEE Trans. Mob. Comput. **11**(1), 86–99 (2012)
5. Park, J., Lee, S., Yoo, S.: Time slot assignment for convergecast in wireless sensor networks. J. Parallel Distrib. Comput. **83**, 70–82 (2015)
6. Maraiya, K., Kant, K., Gupta, N.: Wireless sensor network: a review on data aggregation. Int. J. Sci. Eng. Res. **2**, 1–6 (2011)
7. Jakob, M., Nikolaidis, I.: A top-down aggregation convergecast schedule construction. In: 2016 9th IFIP Wireless and Mobile Networking Conference (WMNC), Colmar, pp. 17–24 (2016)

# Security and Privacy Engineering

# A New Technique to Improve
# the Security of Elliptic Curve Encryption
# and Signature Schemes

Tun Myat Aung[✉] and Ni Ni Hla[✉]

University of Computer Studies, Yangon 11411, Myanmar
{tunmyataung, ni2hla}@ucsy.edu.mm

**Abstract.** Elliptic curve encryption and signature schemes are nowadys widely used in public communication channels for network security services. Their security depends on the complexity of solving the Elliptic Curve Discrete Logarithm Problem. But, there are several general attacks that are vulnerable to them. The paper includes how to put into practice of complex number arithmetic in prime field and binary field. Elliptic curve arithmetic is implemented over complex fields to improve the security level of elliptic curve cryptosystems. The paper proposes a new technique to implement elliptic curve encryption and signature schemes by using elliptic curves over complex field. The security of elliptic curve cryptosystems is greatly improved on implementing an elliptic curve over complex field. The proposed technique requires double the memory space to store keys but the security level is roughly squared.

**Keywords:** Complex field · Elliptic curve · Encryption · Implementation · Signature · Security

## 1 Introduction

Elliptic Curve Cryptosystem (ECC) is a public key cryptosystem based on elliptic curves. In ECC every entity connecting in the public communication channel generally has a pair of keys, a public key and a private key to perform cryptographic transformations such as encryption, decryption, signing, verification and authentication. The private key must be kept secret but the corresponding public key is distributed to all entities connecting in the public communication channel. ECC provides the security services such as data confidentiality, data integrity, message authentication, entity authentication, non-repudiation, and public key distribution. Nowadays, ECC becomes a major role in the industry of information and network security technology. It becomes the industrial standard as a consequence of an increase in speed and a decrease in power consumption during implementation as a result of less memory usage and smaller key sizes.

The elliptic curve over finite field $E(GF)$ is a cubic curve defined by the general Weierstrass Eq. (1) [2] over $GF$ where $a_i \in GF$ and $GF$ is a finite field.

$$y^2 + a_1xy + a_3y = x^3 + a_2x^2 + a_4x + a_6. \tag{1}$$

© Springer Nature Switzerland AG 2019
T. K. Dang et al. (Eds.): FDSE 2019, LNCS 11814, pp. 371–382, 2019.
https://doi.org/10.1007/978-3-030-35653-8_25

Elliptic curves are driven from the general Weierstrass Eq. (1). The elliptic curve $E(GF(p))$ is determined by the Eq. (2) [2]:

$$y^2 = x^3 + ax + b \tag{2}$$

where $p > 3$ is a prime and $a, b \in GF(p)$ satisfy that $4a^3 + 27b^2 \neq 0$. ($a_1 = a_2 = a_3 = 0$; $a_4 = a$ and $a_6 = b$ corresponding to the general Weierstrass equation)

Elements over $GF(2^m)$ must be firstly generated by using a reduction polynomial $f(x)$. These elements are applied to construct an elliptic curve $E(GF(2^m))$ over $GF(2^m)$. The elliptic curve $E(GF(2^m))$ is determined by the Eq. (3) [2]:

$$y^2 + xy = x^3 + ax^2 + b \tag{3}$$

where $a, b \in GF(2^m)$ and $b \neq 0$.

Nowadays, ECC becomes a major role in the industry of information and network security technology. It becomes the industrial standard as a consequence of an increase in speed and a decrease in power consumption during implementation as a result of less memory usage and smaller key sizes. Its security depends on the complexity of solving the Elliptic Curve Discrete Logarithm Problem (ECDLP). Although the ECDLP is thought to be a difficult problem, it has not stopped attackers attempting to attack on ECC. Several attacks have been created, experienced and analyzed by mathematicians over the years, to discover defects in ECC. Some attacks have done partially well, but others have not.

The paper proposes a new technique to implement elliptic curve encryption and signature schemes by using elliptic curves over complex field. The structure of the paper is as follows. The Sect. 2 includes finite field arithmetic- prime field arithmetic and binary field arithmetic, and elliptic curve arithmetic over prime field and binary field. In Sect. 3, we discuss complex field arithmetic. The Sect. 4 presents implementation scheme and how to implement elliptic curve ElGamal encryption and signature schemes by using elliptic curves over complex field. The Sect. 5 discusses reasonably the security of original ECC and the security improvement of ECC implemented by using elliptic curves over complex field. Finally, the Sect. 6 includes our conclusion and suggestions.

## 2   Background Methodology

### 2.1   Finite Field Arithmetic

A finite field, generally denoted by $F$, is a field that consists of a finite number of elements. It can be applied to the rational number system, the real number system and the complex number system. It includes a set of elements together with two arithmetic operations: addition denoted by the symbol $+$ and multiplication denoted by the symbol . that satisfy the following arithmetic properties [3, 10]:

- The Law of Commutativity: $x + y = y + x$; $x.y = y.x$, for all $x, y \in F$.
- The Law of Associativity: $(x + y) + z = x + (y + z)$; $(x.y)z = x(y.z)$, for all $x, y, z \in F$

- The Law of Distributivity: $(x+y)z = x.z + y.z$, for all $x, y, z \in F$.
- The Law of Identity: Zero, denoted by 0, is the additive identity so that $z + 0 = z$ for all $z \in F$. Besides, one, denoted by 1, is the multiplicative identity so that $z.1 = z$ for all $z \in F$.
- The Law of Additive Inverse. For any $z \in F$, there exists a unique additive inverse $-z \in F$ so that $z + (-z) = 0$.
- The Law of Multiplicative Inverse. For any $z \in F$ where $z \neq 0$, there exists a unique multiplicative inverse $z^{-1} \in F$ so that $z.z^{-1} = 1$.

Galois open that the elements in the field to be finite and the number of elements should be $p^m$, where $p$ is a prime number called the characteristic of the field and $m$ is a positive integer. The finite fields are generally called Galois fields and also signified by $GF(p^m)$. When m = 1, then the field $GF(p)$ is called a prime field. When m $\geq$ 2, then the field $GF(p^m)$ is called an extension field. The number of elements in a finite field is called the order of the field. Any two fields are isomorphic when their orders are the same [3].

Finite field $F$ has additive group that performs on the arithmetic addition operation as well as multiplicative group that performs on the arithmetic multiplication operation. However, the subtraction of field elements is defined in the expressions of addition operation. For instance, let $x, y \in F$, $x - y$ is defined as $x + (-y)$, where $-y$ is the additive inverse of $y$. Correspondingly, the division of field elements is defined in the expression of multiplication operation. For instance, let $x, y \in F$ with $y \neq 0$, $x/y$ is defined as $x.y^{-1}$, where $y^{-1}$ is the multiplicative inverse of $y$ [10].

**Prime Field.** A finite field of prime order $p$ is called prime field denoted by $GF(p)$. It contains a set of integer elements modulo $p$, $\{0, 1, 2, \ldots, p-1\}$ with additive and multiplicative groups that performed modulo $p$. For any integer $x$, $x \bmod p$ refers to the integer remainder $r$ that obtained upon dividing $x$ by $p$. This operation is called reduction modulo $p$. In this case, the remainder $r$ is the unique integer element between 0 and $p - 1$, i.e. $0 \leq r \leq p - 1$ [3].

**Binary Field.** A finite field of order $2^m$ is called binary field denoted by $GF(2^m)$. It also refers to the finite field with characteristic-two. The elements of $GF(2^m)$ can be constructed by applying a polynomial basis representation defined by the Eq. (4). In this case, the elements of $GF(2^m)$ are the binary polynomials with degree at most $m - 1$ [3]

$$GF(2^m) = a_{m-1}x^{m-1} + a_{m-2}x^{m-2} + \ldots + a_2 x^2 + a_1 x + a_0, a_i \in \{0, 1\} \qquad (4)$$

$f(x)$ is defined as an irreducible binary polynomial with degree $m$ if $f(x)$ cannot be factored as a product of binary polynomials with degree less than $m$. Let $a(x)$ and $b(x)$ be the elements of $GF(2^m)$. They are the binary polynomials with degree at most $m - 1$. The addition of elements in $GF(2^m)$ refers to the addition of binary polynomials, that is, $a(x) \oplus b(x)$. The multiplication of elements in $GF(2^m)$ refers to the expression $a(x) \times b(x) \bmod f(x)$. Let $c(x) = a(x) \times b(x)$ and $c(x)$ be a binary polynomial with degree more than $m$. The result of the expression $c(x) \bmod f(x)$ refers to the unique remainder polynomial $r(x)$ with degree less than $m$ that obtained upon the division of $c(x)$ by $f(x)$; this operation is called *reduction modulo f(x)*. The division of elements in $GF(2^m)$ refers to the expression $a(x)/b(x) \bmod f(x)$. The division of elements in $GF(2^m)$ is calculated as the expression $a(x) \times b(x)^{-1} \bmod f(x)$.

## 2.2 Elliptic Curve Arithmetic

The addition of two points on an elliptic curve uses the chord-and-tangent rule that results a third point on the curve. The addition operations with the points on an elliptic curve generate a group with point at infinity $O$ serving as its identity. It is the group of points on an elliptic curve that is used in the construction of elliptic curve cryptosystems. The geometric explanation of the point addition rule supports easy understanding. Let $P = (x_1, y_1)$ and $Q = (x_2, y_2)$ be two distinct points on an elliptic curve. Assume that the point $R = (x_3, y_3)$ is obtained by addition of $P$ and $Q$. This point addition is illustrated in Fig. (1). The line connecting through $P$ and $Q$ intersects the elliptic curve at the point called $-R$. $R$ is the reflection of $-R$ with respect to the x-axis. Assume that doubling of $P$ is $R = (x_3, y_3)$ in the case of $P = (x_1, y_1)$. This point doubling is illustrated in Fig. (2). The tangent line drawing from point $P$ intersects the elliptic curve at the point called $-R$. $R$ is the reflection of $-R$ with respect to the x-axis as in the case of addition.

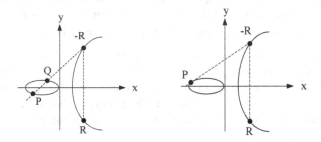

**Fig. 1.** Addition $(R = P + Q)$     **Fig. 2.** Doubling $(R = P + P)$

**Elliptic Curve Arithmetic Over $GF(p)$.** The followings are algebraic methods for the addition of two points on $E(GF(p))$ and the doubling of a point on $E(GF(p))$ [2].

- $P + O = O + P = P$ and $P + (-P) = O$ for all $P \in E(GF(p))$. If $P = (x, y) \in E(GF(p))$, the point $(x, -y)$ is signified by $(-P)$ that is called the inverse of P. $O$ is the point at infinity serving as additive identity.
- (Point Addition). Let $P, Q \in E(GF(p))$, $P = (x_1, y_1)$ and $Q = (x_2, y_2)$ where $P \neq \pm Q$. Then $P + Q = (x_3, y_3)$. In this case, $x_3 = \lambda^2 - x_1 - x_2$ and $y_3 = \lambda(x_1 - x_3) - y_1$. where $\lambda = (y_2 - y_1)/(x_2 - x_1)$.
- (Point Doubling). Let $P = (x_1, y_1) \in E(GF(p))$ where $P \neq -P$. Then $2P = (x_3, y_3)$. In this case, $x_3 = \lambda^2 - 2x_1$ and $y_3 = \lambda(x_1 - x_3) - y_1$ where $\lambda = (3x_1^2 + a)/2y_1$.

**Elliptic Curve Arithmetic Over** $GF(2^m)$**.** The followings are algebraic methods for the addition of two distinct points on $E(GF(2^m))$ and the doubling of a point on $E(GF(2^m))$.

- $P + O = O + P = P$ and $P + (-P) = O$ for all $P \in E(GF(2^m))$. If $P = (x, y) \in E(GF(2^m))$, the point $(x, x + y)$ is signified by $(-P)$ that is called the inverse of $P$. $O$ is the point at infinity serving as additive identity.
- (Point Addition). Let $P, Q \in E(GF(2^m))$, $P = (x_1, y_1)$ and $Q = (x_2, y_2)$ where $P \neq \pm Q$. Then $P + Q = (x_3, y_3)$. In this case, $x_3 = \lambda^2 + \lambda - x_1 + x_2 + a$, $y_3 = \lambda(x_1 + x_3) + x_3 + y_1$ where $\lambda = (y_2 + y_1)/(x_2 + x_1)$.
- (Point Doubling). Let $P = (x_1, y_1) \in E(GF(2^m))$ where $P \neq -P$. Then $2P = (x_3, y_3)$. In this case, $x_3 = \lambda^2 + \lambda + a$ and $y_3 = x_1^2 + \lambda x_3 + x_3$ where $\lambda = x_1 + (y_1/x_1)$.

## 3 Proposed Technique

The attacks on ECC depend on the reduction of the elliptic curve discrete logarithm problem (ECDLP) to a discrete logarithm problem (DLP). Generally, the resulting DLP requires exponential time algorithms to solve, which makes it infeasible. However, the resulting DLP can be solved in sub–exponential time (or faster) if the original elliptic curve field satisfies certain conditions. ECC security mostly depends on the complexity of solving the Elliptic Curve Discrete Logarithm Problem (ECDLP). It can attack on ECDLP if the cyclic group order of the points is not sufficiently large. We propose to develop elliptic curve cryptosystems using elliptic curves over complex field in order that the cyclic group order becomes more larger.

### 3.1 Complex Field Arithmetic

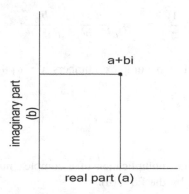

**Fig. 3.** Complex plane

A finite field with complex numbers is called complex field denoted by $Z(n)$. The complex field over $GF(p)$ is denoted by $Z(GF(p))$. Similarly, the complex field over $GF(2^m)$ is denoted by $Z(GF(2^m))$. A complex field contains a finite number of complex numbers. A complex number is a number that can be expressed in the form $a + bi$, where $a$ and $b$ are integer numbers under one of finite fields, in which $a$ is called the real part, and $b$ is called the imaginary part. In geometry, a complex number, $a + bi$, can be represented by a point $(a, b)$ in two-dimensional complex plane using the horizontal axis for the real part and the vertical axis for the imaginary part [8]. It is demonstrated in Fig. (3).

The following rules [8] are applied for addition, subtraction, multiplication, division, reciprocal and scalar multiplication that are the arithmetic operations of complex numbers over finite field.

**Addition.** The addition of two complex numbers $x = a_1 + b_1 i$ and $y = a_2 + b_2 i$ is defined by the Eq. (5).

$$x + y = (a_1 + a_2) + (b_1 + b_2)i. \tag{5}$$

**Subtraction.** The subtraction of two complex numbers $x = a_1 + b_1 i$ and $y = a_2 + b_2 i$ is defined by the Eq. (6).

$$x - y = (a_1 - a_2) + (b_1 - b_2)i \tag{6}$$

**Multiplication.** The multiplication of two complex numbers $x = a_1 + b_1 i$ and $y = a_2 + b_2 i$ is defined by the Eq. (7).

$$x.y = (a_1 a_2 - b_1 b_2) + (a_1 b_2 + a_2 b_1)i. \tag{7}$$

**Reciprocal.** The reciprocal of a nonzero complex number $z = a + bi$ is defined by the Eq. (8).

$$\frac{1}{z} = z^{-1} = \frac{a}{a^2 + b^2} - \frac{b}{a^2 + b^2}i. \tag{8}$$

**Division.** The division of two complex numbers $x = a_1 + b_1 i$ and $y = a_2 + b_2 i$ is defined by the Eq. (9).

$$\frac{x}{y} = x.y^{-1}. \tag{9}$$

**Scalar Multiplication.** The multiplication of a complex number $z = a + bi$ and the scalar integer $k$ is defined by the Eq. (10).

$$k.z = k.a + k.bi. \tag{10}$$

# 4 Implementation Scheme

At first level, the PrimeField class including methods for addition, subtraction, multiplication, division, additive inverse and multiplicative inverse, finite field arithmetic operations of $GF(p)$ is implemented by using methods of java BigInteger class. Similarly, the BinaryField class including methods for addition, subtraction, multiplication, division, additive inverse and multiplicative inverse, finite field arithmetic operations of $GF(2^m)$ is implemented by using java BigInteger class. The details of the implementation and mathematical proofs at the first level were presented in the reference [5]. At second level, the ComplexFp class including methods for addition, subtraction, multiplication, division, additive inverse and multiplicative inverse, complex arithmetic operations of $Z(GF(p))$, complex field based on $GF(p)$, is implemented by using methods of PrimeField class. Similarly, the ComplexF2m class including methods for addition, subtraction, multiplication, division, additive inverse and multiplicative inverse, complex arithmetic operations of $Z(GF(2^m))$, complex field based on $GF(2^m)$, is implemented by using methods of BinaryField class. The details of the implementation and mathematical proofs at the second level were presented in the reference [7]. At third level, the ECCFpCx class including methods for point addition, point doubling and point multiplication, elliptic curve arithmetic operations of $E(Z(GF(p)))$, the elliptic curve based on complex field $Z(GF(p))$, is implemented by using methods of ComplexFp class. Similarly, the ECCF2mCx class including methods for point addition, point doubling and point multiplication, elliptic curve arithmetic operations of $E(Z(GF(2^m)))$, the elliptic curve based on complex field $Z(GF(2^m))$, is implemented by using methods of ComplexF2m. The details of the implementation and mathematical proofs at the third level were also presented in the reference [7]. At fourth level, elliptic curve cryptosystems, ElGamal encryption and signature schemes, are implemented by using corresponding methods of ECCFpCx class and ECCF2mCx class. The details of the implementation and mathematical proofs at the fourth level were also presented in this paper. For the implementation logic design of elliptic curve cryptosystems over complex fields, the general hierarchy is shown in Fig. 4.

## 4.1 Implementation of Elliptic Curve ElGamal Encryption Scheme Using $E(Z(GF(p)))$

Let's consider to encrypt and decrypt the message using the elliptic curve $E : y^2 = x^3 + x + (1 + 5i)$ over $Z(GF(7))$ where $a = 1$ and $b = 1 + 5i$. The followings are the results of elliptic curve ElGamal encryption scheme [11] implemented on the given curve using the methods of our system ECCFpCx class.

**Key Generation.** Entity A and Entity B agree to choose the point $P = (5, 3 + 2i)$ with prime order n = 47 as a base point. Entity B compute a private key and a public key as followings.

- Entity B chooses an integer $d = 13$ as a private key.
- Entity B computes $Q = d \times P = 13 \times (5, 3 + 2i) = (1 + 5i, 4 + 5i)$ as a public key.

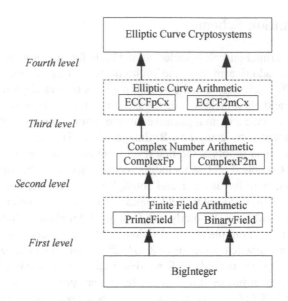

**Fig. 4.** Implementation logic Design

**Encryption Scheme.** Entity A chooses the point $M = (2 + 5i, 3 + 6i)$ as a message to encrypt with the public key $Q = (1 + 5i, 4 + 5i)$. The cipher text is computed as followings.

- Entity A chooses an integer $r = 3$ as a random number.
- Entity A computes: $C_1 = r \times P = 3 \times (5, 3 + 2i) = (5 + 6i, 5)$.
- Entity A computes: $C_2 = M + (r \times Q) = (2 + 5i, 3 + 6i) + 3.(1 + 5i, 4 + 5i) = (1 + 1i, 2 + 2i)$.
- Entity A sends the points $C_1$ and $C_2$ to Entity B as cipher texts.

**Decryption Scheme.** Entity B receives the points $C_1 = (5 + 6i, 5)$ and $C_2 = (1 + 1i, 2 + 2i)$ as cipher texts to decrypt with the private key $d = 13$. The message plain text is computed as following.

- Entity B computes the message $M = C_2 - (d \times C_1) = (1 + 1i, 2 + 2i) - 13.(5 + 6i, 5) = (2 + 5i, 3 + 6i)$.

### 4.2    Implementation of Elliptic Curve ElGamal Signature Scheme Using $E(Z(GF(p)))$

Let's consider to sign the message and verify the signature using the elliptic curve $E : y^2 = x^3 + x + (1 + 5i)$ over $Z(GF(7))$ where $a = 1$ and $b = 1 + 5i$. The followings are the results of elliptic curve ElGamal signature scheme [11] implemented on the given curve using the methods of our system ECCFpCx class.

**Key Generation.** Entity A and Entity B agree to choose the point $P = (5, 3 + 2i)$ with prime order n = 47 as a base point. Entity A computes a private key and a public key as followings.

- Entity A chooses an integer $d = 13$ as a private key.
- Entity A computes $Q = d \times P = 13 \times (5, 3 + 2i) = (1 + 5i, 4 + 5i)$ as a public key.

**Signing Scheme.** Entity A computes the signature as the followings to sign the message with the private key $d = 13$.

- Entity A chooses an integer $k = 3$ as a random number.
- Entity A computes: $R = k \times P = 3 \times (5, 3 + 2i) = (5 + 6i, 5)$.
- Entity A computes: $r = R.x.real \bmod n = 5 \bmod 47 = 5$.
- Entity A computes: $h = h(m) = 4$ as the hash value of the signing message.
- Entity A computes: $s = k^{-1}(h + rd) \bmod n = 16 \times (4 + 5 \times 13) \bmod 47 = 42$.
- Entity A sends $(R, s)$ to Entity B as the signature of the signing message.

**Verifying Scheme.** Entity B receives $(R, s)$ as the signature of the signing message and computes the followings to verify the signature with the public key $Q = (1 + 5i, 4 + 5i)$.

- Entity B computes: $V_1 = s \times R = 42 \times (5 + 6i, 5) = (6 + 6i, 5 + 3i)$.
- Entity B computes: $r = R.x.real \bmod n = 5 \bmod 47 = 5$.
- Entity B computes: $h = h(m) = 4$ as the hash value of the same signing message.
- Entity B computes: $U_1 = h \times P = 4 \times (5, 3 + 2i) = (4 + 2i, 3 + 3i)$.
- Entity B computes: $U_2 = r \times Q = 5 \times (1 + 5i, 4 + 5i) = (2i, 4 + 6i)$.
- Entity B computes: $V_2 = U_1 + U_2 = (6 + 6i, 5 + 3i)$.
- Entity B accepts the signature, since $V_1 = V_2$.

## 5  Security Issue

The complexity of solving ECDLP determines the security of ECC. Let $P$ and $Q$ be the points on an elliptic curve such that $Q = kP$, where $k$ is an integer number. $k$ is called the discrete logarithm of $Q$ to the base $P$. Known two points, $P$ and $Q$, it is unable to compute $k$, when the cyclic group order of the points is enough large. It was studied in the reference [6] that Baby-Step, Giant-Step method, Pollard's Rho method and Pohlig-Hellman method could attack on ECDLP if the cyclic group orders of the points on the elliptic curves were not sufficiently large.

The cyclic group orders of points on the elliptic curves over $GF(p)$ and $GF(2^m)$ are computed by using our systems, ECCFp and ECCF2m, implemented in the reference [1] and shown in Appendixes 1 and 2 respectively. The cyclic group orders of points on the elliptic curves over $Z(GF(p))$ and $Z(GF(2^m))$ are also computed by using our systems, ECCFpCx and ECCF2mCx, implemented in the reference [7] and shown in Appendixes 3 and 4 correspondingly. Among them, the cyclic group order of points on the elliptic curves over $Z(GF(p))$, which is shown in Appendix 3, becomes quadratic under the finite field of the same size. According to Hasses's theorem [4], the cyclic group order on the elliptic curves over $Z(GF(p))$ may be between $q+1-2\sqrt{q}$ and $q+1+2\sqrt{q}$, where $q=p^2$ as Gaussian integers [9]. The cyclic group order of the points on the elliptic curves over $Z(GF(p))$ shown in Appendix 3 is 47 which is between $49+1-2\sqrt{49}=36$ and $49+1+2\sqrt{49}=64$. Thus, the security level, in terms of the cyclic group order, is roughly squared. The problem solving of ECDLP is computationally harder and more time–consuming in complex field. Therefore, the security of ECC is greatly improved on implementing an elliptic curve over complex field-$Z(GF(p))$. The proposed technique enables system developers to achieve a higher level of security with a small increase in storage.

# 6   Conclusion

The paper presented a new technique to implement elliptic curve encryption and signature schemes by using elliptic curves over complex field. The proposed technique applies the finite fields of complex numbers instead of rational integers. The proposed technique requires double the space to store keys. The security of the new implementation system is higher than the original curve over the same prime due to the quadratic increase in the cyclic group order of the points on the curve over the prime field of complex numbers. In each arithmetic operation the underlying hardware or software is required to handle smaller integers at the scale of the real or imaginary part, which enables the system designer to use two small size units working in parallel to twofold the processing speed at the same level of security. The proposed technique makes elliptic curve attacks more difficult and time consuming. The high level security can be achieved with low storage requirements for the systems with limited capacity like smart cards.

# Appendix 1. Cyclic Group Orders of the Points on the Curve $E$ : $y^2 = x^3 + x + 1$ Over $GF(7)$.

| Points | | Group orders |
|---|---|---|
| P | (0, 1) | 5 |
| 2P | (2, 5) | 5 |
| 3P | (2, 2) | 5 |
| 4P | (0, 6) | 5 |
| 5P | $O$ | |

## Appendix 2. Cyclic Group Orders of the Points on the Curve $E$: $y^2 + xy = x^3 + x^2 + 1$ Over $GF(f(x))$ Where $f(x) = x^3 + x + 1$.

| Points | | Group orders | Points | | Group orders |
|---|---|---|---|---|---|
| P | (4, 3) | 14 | 8P | (7, 0) | 7 |
| 2P | (5, 0) | 7 | 9P | (2, 7) | 14 |
| 3P | (6, 3) | 14 | 10P | (3, 3) | 7 |
| 4P | (3, 0) | 7 | 11P | (6, 5) | 14 |
| 5P | (2, 5) | 14 | 12P | (5, 5) | 7 |
| 6P | (7, 7) | 7 | 13P | (4, 7) | 14 |
| 7P | (0, 1) | 2 | 14P | O | |

## Appendix 3. Cyclic Group Orders of the Points on the Curve $E$: $y^2 = x^3 + x + (1 + 5i)$ Over $Z(GF(7))$.

| Points | | Group orders | Points | | Group orders |
|---|---|---|---|---|---|
| P | $(5, 3 + 2i)$ | 47 | 25P | $(2 + 4i, 1i)$ | 47 |
| 2P | $(4i, 4 + 1i)$ | 47 | 26P | $(5 + 1i, 6 + 2i)$ | 47 |
| 3P | $(5 + 6i, 5)$ | 47 | 27P | $(2 + 6i, 3i)$ | 47 |
| 4P | $(4 + 2i, 3 + 3i)$ | 47 | 28P | $(2i, 4 + 6i)$ | 47 |
| 5P | $(4 + 4i, 5 + 6i)$ | 47 | 29P | $(3 + 6i, 4 + 6i)$ | 47 |
| 6P | $(3 + 3i, 6 + 4i)$ | 47 | 30P | $(1 + 1i, 2 + 2i)$ | 47 |
| 7P | $(5 + 4i, 5i)$ | 47 | 31P | $(5 + 3i, 5 + 1i)$ | 47 |
| 8P | $(4 + 5i, 5 + 2i)$ | 47 | 32P | $(6 + 6i, 5 + 3i)$ | 47 |
| 9P | $(2 + 5i, 4 + 1i)$ | 47 | 33P | $(1 + 6i, 1 + 1i)$ | 47 |
| 10P | $(4 + 6i, 3 + 1i)$ | 47 | 34P | $(1 + 5i, 3 + 2i)$ | 47 |
| 11P | $(5 + 5i, 3 + 6i)$ | 47 | 35P | $(1 + 2i, 4 + 5i)$ | 47 |
| 12P | $(1 + 2i, 3 + 2i)$ | 47 | 36P | $(5 + 5i, 4 + 1i)$ | 47 |
| 13P | $(1 + 5i, 4 + 5i)$ | 47 | 37P | $(4 + 6i, 4 + 6i)$ | 47 |
| 14P | $(1 + 6i, 6 + 6i)$ | 47 | 38P | $(2 + 5i, 3 + 6i)$ | 47 |
| 15P | $(6 + 6i, 2 + 4i)$ | 47 | 39P | $(4 + 5i, 2 + 5i)$ | 47 |
| 16P | $(5 + 3i, 2 + 6i)$ | 47 | 40P | $(5 + 4i, 2i)$ | 47 |
| 17P | $(1 + 1i, 5 + 5i)$ | 47 | 41P | $(3 + 3i, 1 + 3i)$ | 47 |
| 18P | $(3 + 6i, 3 + 1i)$ | 47 | 42P | $(4 + 4i, 2 + 1i)$ | 47 |
| 19P | $(2i, 3 + 1i)$ | 47 | 43P | $(4 + 2i, 4 + 4i)$ | 47 |
| 20P | $(2 + 6i, 4i)$ | 47 | 44P | $(5 + 6i, 2)$ | 47 |
| 21P | $(5 + 1i, 1 + 5i)$ | 47 | 45P | $(4i, 3 + 6i)$ | 47 |
| 22P | $(2 + 4i, 6i)$ | 47 | 46P | $(5, 4 + 5i)$ | 47 |
| 23P | $(1 + 3i, 1 + 2i)$ | 47 | 47P | O | |
| 24P | $(1 + 3i, 6 + 5i)$ | 47 | | | |

# Appendix 4. Cyclic Group Orders of the Points on the Curve $E$: $y^2 + xy = x^3 + x^2 + (1 + 5i)$ Over $Z(GF(f(x)))$ Where $f(x) = x^3 + x + 1$.

| | Points | Group orders |
|---|---|---|
| P | $(1, 2 + 5i)$ | 5 |
| 2P | $(5i, 6 + 1i)$ | 5 |
| 3P | $(1 + 4i, 7 + 5i)$ | 5 |
| 4P | $(3 + 2i, 6)$ | 5 |
| 5P | $O$ | |

# References

1. Aung, T.M., Hla, N.N.: Implementation of elliptic curve arithmetic operations for prime field and binary field using java BigInteger class. Int. J. Eng. Res. Technol. (IJERT) **6**(08), 454–459 (2017). https://doi.org/10.17577/ijertv6is080211
2. Forouzan, B.A.: Elliptic curve cryptosystems. In: Cryptography and Network Security, International Edition, pp. 321–330. McGraw-Hill Press, Singapore (2008)
3. Forouzan, B.A.: Mathematics of cryptography. In: Cryptography and Network Security, International Edition, pp. 98–117. McGraw-Hill Press, Singapore (2008)
4. Hankerson, D., Menezes, A., Vanstone, S.: Elliptic curve arithmetic. In: Guide to Elliptic Curve Cryptography, pp. 75–152. Springer, New York (2004). https://doi.org/10.1007/0-387-21846-7_3
5. Hla, N.N., Aung, T.M.: Implementation of finite field arithmetic operations for large prime and binary fields using java BigInteger class. Int. J. Eng. Res. Technol. (IJERT) **6**(08), 450–453 (2017). https://doi.org/10.17577/ijertv6is080209
6. Hla, N.N., Aung, T.M.: Attack experiments on elliptic curves of prime and binary fields. In: Abraham, A., Dutta, P., Mandal, J.K., Bhattacharya, A., Dutta, S. (eds.) Emerging Technologies in Data Mining and Information Security. AISC, vol. 755, pp. 667–683. Springer, Singapore (2019). https://doi.org/10.1007/978-981-13-1951-8_60
7. Hla, N.N., Aung, T.M.: Experiments on implementation of elliptic curve arithmetic over complex fields using java BigInteger Class. J. Commun. (JCM) **14**(4), 293–300 (2019). https://doi.org/10.12720/jcm.14.4.293-300
8. Kreyszig, E.: Complex numbers and their geometric representation. In: Advanced Engineering Mathematics, 10th edn, pp. 608–612. Wiley, New York (2011)
9. Mohamed, E., Elkamchouchi, H.: Elliptic curve cryptography over Gaussian integers. Int. J. Comput. Sci. Netw. Secur. **4**(1), 413–416 (2009)
10. Rosen, K.H.: Number theory and cryptography. In: Discrete Mathematics and its Applications, 7th edn., pp. 237–294. McGraw-Hill Press, New York (2011)
11. Rabah, K.: Elliptic Curve ElGamal Encryption and Signature Schemes. Inf. Technol. J. **4**(3), 299–306 (2005)

# A Visual Model for Privacy Awareness and Understanding in Online Social Networks

Tran Tri Dang[1]([⊠]) and Josef Küng[2]

[1] Ho Chi Minh City University of Technology,
VNU-HCM, Ho Chi Minh City, Vietnam
tridang@hcmut.edu.vn
[2] University of Linz, Linz, Austria

**Abstract.** The number of users participating in online social networks is increasing significantly recently. As a result, the amount of information created and shared by them is exploding. On one hand, sharing information online helps people stay in touch with each other, although virtually. But on the other hand, sharing too much information may lead to sensitive personal data being leaked unexpectedly. To protect their users' private information, online social network providers often employ technical methods like access control and cryptography among others. Although these approaches are good enough for their designated purposes, they provide little to no protection when are used wrongly. To reduce the number of mistakes users may make, online social network providers also offers them visual interfaces, instead of lengthy and boring texts, for privacy settings selection and configuration. Unfortunately, private information is stilled shared publicly, with or without its owners' awareness. In this paper, we attempt to mitigate the privacy leakage problem by proposing a novel visual model for measuring and representing users' privacy in online social network environment and associated privacy controller for protecting it. A concrete instance of the model has been designed and implemented. A demonstration of the model instance has been executed for one of the biggest social networks, Facebook. Initial results indicate the effectiveness of the proposed model and its concrete instance. However, a more important and difficult problem is whether online social network providers are willing to apply these results, which may affect sharing activities and go against their business objectives.

**Keywords:** Visual model · User interface design · Information visualization · Privacy awareness · Privacy policy understanding · Online social network

## 1 Introduction

According to "The global state of digital in 2019 report"[1], the number of internet users is nearly 4.4 billion, while the number of active social media users is reaching 3.5 billion. Some of the biggest online social networks, such as Facebook, YouTube, WhatsApp, etc. each has more than one billion active user accounts. Online social

---

[1] Hootsuite: The global state of digital in 2019 report, https://hootsuite.com/pages/digital-in-2019.

© Springer Nature Switzerland AG 2019
T. K. Dang et al. (Eds.): FDSE 2019, LNCS 11814, pp. 383–398, 2019.
https://doi.org/10.1007/978-3-030-35653-8_26

media is not only used as a platform for building personal relationships and sharing individual life events, but also as a new tool for pursuing business advantages [1] and even influencing political election outcomes [2].

Definitely, there are certain benefits of having online connections [3], but the problems caused by it are not less important. Because online interaction and information sharing are perceived as enjoyable [4] and trustworthy [5], it is natural to see social network participants creating and consuming a lot of information. However, sharing too much, especially private and personal, data may cause privacy issues for data owners. When an online social network user's personally identifiable information (a.k.a. PII), such as email address, phone number, and social security number, is known, it can be used to recognize his/her actions within the original network, and even on other sites as well [6]. To reduce the risks of personal information leakage, privacy protection techniques has been proposed and implemented.

From the technical perspective, traditional data management techniques like access control [7] and encryption [8] can be used to provide some kinds of privacy protection. As an example, online social networks usually imitate real-life social networks by offering their users different levels of connection with each other. These connections may be named similarly to their real-life counterparts, such as family, relative, friend, public, etc. Based on these connection levels, access control techniques can be implemented to let data owners select appropriate groups to share data with. Likewise, data encryption can be used to protect private information, so that only intended audience can see it. Although technical techniques are good enough for their designated purposes, they provide little to no protection when are used wrongly. For example, a sensitive piece of information should only be shared with some selected close friends, but the data owner may mistakenly share it with every friends. Furthermore, because online social network providers often define their own terms and conditions, data owners may understand them incorrectly without recognizing that issue.

As is demonstrated by the above example, keeping online social network users' privacy under their control requires more than just technical solutions. Users must be equipped with appropriate tools to accomplish their intended purposes without mistakes. This is not an easy task for UI/UX designers though [9–11]. We argue that, at least, designed interfaces need to achieve the following two objectives: awareness and understanding. Awareness means data owners are aware of different choices and appropriate consequences, while understanding means they are able to make right decisions according to their intended objectives. Awareness and understanding are interrelated to each other. Without awareness, users can make mistakes without realizing it. Similarly, without understanding, users cannot evaluate choices to make the right decision. This paper presents our work and its initial results in increasing awareness and understanding of online social network users by improving current interfaces. In particular, we proposed a visual model for privacy representation and associated privacy controller. Based on the model, a concrete construction has been implemented and then evaluated using the Facebook social network. The rest of the paper is structured as follows: in Sect. 2, we review the related works; Sect. 3 presents our visual model; Sect. 4 describes our experiments with the model using Facebook; and finally, Sect. 5 concludes the paper with plans for future works.

# 2 Related Works

## 2.1 Privacy Awareness

Security and privacy notices have been used in consumer applications to grab end users' attention when the users have to make important decisions for their next possible actions. These notices have been used extensively in web browser applications. In a survey paper, security and privacy notices in web browsers are classified into proactive and reactive display modes, depending on how much effort is required from users to be aware of them [12]. In the proactive approach, end users proactively recognize legitimate and fraudulent websites themselves with the helps of visual components situated in browsers' chrome and content area [13, 14]. On the other hand, in the reactive approach, web browsers detect possible problems and present them to end users, waiting for their decisions [15, 16]. Although security and privacy notices are essential elements of most internet applications, the effectiveness of them is questionable. Some research results indicated that typical privacy notices do not help users make informed decisions and sometimes are ignored by them completely [17, 18]. The work of Schaub et al. pointed out several reasons to explain the ineffectiveness of privacy notices such as conflation of requirements, lack of choice, low utility, high burden, and decoupled notices [19]. Wagner et al. proposed a cycle called I-AM, which stands for Inform Alert Mitigate, to assess and improve the way eHealth apps communicate privacy aspects and mitigation options to end users [20]. The authors of I-AM argued that current privacy best practices and frameworks only focus on the Inform stage, thus they proposed an analytical cycle which also deals with issues raised in the Alert and Mitigation stages. More general works, such as guidelines [19] and design spaces [21] have been suggested for privacy notice designers, expecting users' awareness can be increased by applying them to existing interfaces.

## 2.2 Privacy Understanding

Besides making end users aware of privacy choices, another important objective of well designed privacy – oriented interfaces is to provide adequate support for understanding complicated privacy configurations. In a report, Madejski and Bellovin showed that the privacy setting on the popular online social network Facebook is not clear enough for end users to configure their sharing preferences correctly [22]. In domains other than online social network, there are similar issues with privacy understanding for end users. P3P (Platform for Privacy Preferences) is a formal, machine-readable language for expressing privacy policies that is standardized across websites. However, P3P is not a user friendly language. To make P3P more comprehensible to end users, Reader et al. proposed P3P Expandable Grid, an information visualization technique for privacy policy presentation using interactive matrices [23]. Although the original technique, Expandable Grid, was shown very effective for files' permission policy authoring [24], P3P Expandable Grid provided no better result than using natural language to express privacy policy. In another work, Ghazinour et al. developed a visualization model and graphical tool to depict, display, and understand privacy policy [25].

Visual interfaces for online social networks' privacy configuration have been proposed. Lipford et al. developed Audience View to Facebook users, offering more supports in configuring privacy settings [26]. With that interface, Facebook users can see how their profiles look like under different audiences, such as friends or search results. Experiment results showed the new interface helps users configure privacy more accurately. In another work, Lipford et al. compared the Audience View interface with the Expandable Grid interface for privacy setting. Although there are significant differences in form and style, the performance achieved between two interfaces is not much [27]. Each one has its own advantages and disadvantages. As such, a reasonable combination may provide a better alternative [27]. An interesting approach, in which automatic privacy configuration is coupled with visual interface design, was proposed in VeilMe [28]. VeilMe learns the privacy personality of end users based on their social activities. From there, it offers initial privacy preferences which users can adjust by visual interactive means.

# 3 The Visual Model

There are two main elements of our visual model: the privacy object and the privacy controller. While the privacy object presents the privacy – related characteristics of data sharing actions on online social networks, the privacy controller defines how end users interact with the privacy object in a safe way. These two elements work together to provide end users with awareness and understanding. The relationship between the privacy object, the privacy controller, and the end user is depicted in Fig. 1.

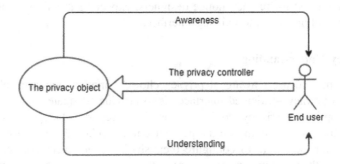

**Fig. 1.** The main elements of the proposed model.

## 3.1 The Privacy Object

A data sharing action on online social networks is associated with a privacy object. This privacy object describes how much exposure the action generates across different dimensions. In the current version of our model, the privacy object contains five independent dimensions: Who, What, When, Where, and Whom.

- Who dimension: this is the source of the sharing action. This dimension defines how many people are affected in a privacy object. Note that the affected people are not necessarily the person creates the share. For example, someone posts a status and tags her friends in that status. Although her friends are not the creators of the status, they are affected by it.
- What dimension: this is the content of the sharing action. This dimension defines how much sensitivity of information is exposed in a privacy object. If the content of a share is neutral or just public information, there is no much sensitivity exposed. However, if the content includes private details of the source, a big amount of sensitivity is leaked.
- When dimension: this is the posted time of the sharing action. This dimension defines how much time accuracy is exposed in a privacy object. For some sharing actions, such as posting funny images, the posted time are not important. But for other actions, like sharing a journey schedule while it is still in progress, the posted time may reveal unexpectedly private information.
- Where dimension: this is the location marked in the sharing action. This dimension defines how much location accuracy is exposed in a privacy object. Shares may contain no information about their locations. Locations are also varied significantly in detailed levels: some locations expose shares' countries or cities; while others expose specific addresses or offices.
- Whom dimension: this is the target audience of the sharing action. This dimension defines how many people can access a privacy object. It's value can be the same as the Who dimension's in the same privacy object (i.e. only affected people can access the shares). But usually, its value is bigger than the Who dimension's because of the nature of sharing actions.

Using the privacy object with these five dimensions to represent sharing actions, the information exposure in each share can be measured quantitatively. In the next section, we will present a sample metric which is suitable for privacy objects on the Facebook online social network.

### 3.2   A Sample Metric for Facebook's Privacy Objects

For any sharing action on Facebook, the following choices will be made, either explicitly or implicitly, by the share creator:

- Who: how many people are involved in the share?
- What: what should I write or quote in the share?
- When: do I share it now or later?
- Where: should a location is marked in the share?
- Whom: who can view the share?

For each of the choices, the share creator can select a value that is extremely low exposure, extremely high exposure, or another value in between. We assign the lowest and highest exposed values in each dimension as in Table 1. It should be noted that this metric is not finished yet and still under development.

**Table 1.** A sample metric for privacy objects on the Facebook platform

| Dimension | Least exposed value | Most exposed value |
|---|---|---|
| Who | Only the creator | Maximum tagged people |
| What | Public information | Personal information |
| When | Long after the event | At the same time of event |
| Where | No location | Exact address |
| Whom | Only the creator | The public |

Explanation of the sample metric:

- Who: if the share creator does not tag anyone in his/her share, the Who dimension's value of the privacy object is lowest; on the other hand, if the share creator tags the maximum number of people (at the time of this writing, this number is $50^2$), the Who dimension's value is highest. Note that this metric does not consider the different levels of influence of each tagged person.
- What: if the share creator shares a public information (i.e. just hyperlinks), the What dimension's value of the privacy object is lowest; on the other hand, if the share creator shares a combination of many types of content such as text, image, hyperlink, etc. about himself/herself, the What dimension's value is highest. Note that this metric does not consider the actual content of the share.
- When: if the share creator creates a posts long after the described event, the When dimension's value of the privacy object is lowest; on the other hand, if the share creator posts a share immediately when the described event happens, the When dimension's value is highest.
- Where: if the share creator marks no location, the Where dimension's value of the privacy object is lowest; on the other hand, if the share creator marks an exact location address, the Where dimension's value is highest. Note that this metric does not consider if the marked locations are real or fake, not does it consider the different sensitivities (e.g. a public library vs. a casino) of the locations neither.
- Whom: if the share creator selects the audience as "Only me", the Whom dimension's value of the privacy object is lowest; on the other hand, if the share creator selects the audience as Public, the Whom dimension's value is highest. Note that this metric only considers the size of the audience, not the nature of the audience.

The privacy object with its five dimensions can be constructed visually. In this version, the privacy object is displayed as a radar chart with five axes. Each axis corresponds to one dimension. A sample visual privacy object is depicted in Fig. 2. The data point on each axis represents the value on that dimension of the privacy object. It is easy to see that the larger the area of the chart, the more exposure the sharing action creates.

---

[2] Facebook Help Center, https://www.facebook.com/help/227499947267037.

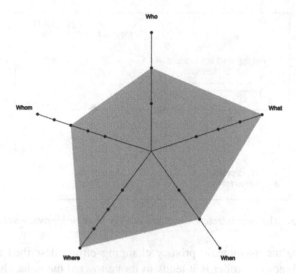

**Fig. 2.** The privacy object is presented as a filled radar chart.

### 3.3  The Privacy Controller

When end users change options of their shares, the corresponding privacy objects' values and shapes change accordingly. In our model, the changes to privacy options are accomplished via the privacy controller. The main objective of the privacy controller is to allow end users to change privacy options in a safe way.

Using the radar chart visual presentation of the privacy object described above, end users move data points along axes to change related dimensions' values accordingly. On each axis, moving a data point toward the center of the chart decreases the privacy exposure of the corresponding dimension. Similarly, moving the data point in the opposite direction increases the privacy exposure of the dimension. As an example, using the sample metric in Table 1, the farthest point from the center on the Where axis represents a location with an exact address. As a user moves that point toward the chart's center, the accuracy of the marked location decreases gradually, such as from an exact address to a city name, from a city name to a country name, etc. and eventually to no location marked.

We apply the soft paternalistic approach [29] to encourage end users to move data points toward the privacy object chart's center to keep the information exposure as low as possible. To move data points toward the edge of the chart, more effort is required. This is to make sure that in case end users are not aware of their privacy choices, it is easier for them to set the exposure level less than expected, but harder to make the exposure level more than expected. In particular, we use the mouse pointer to select and move data points. When a data point is selected, by clicking on it, it can only be moved toward the chart center. At the same time, a small suggestion will be displayed near the mouse pointer, letting the users know that they can move the selected data point in both directions by holding the Shift key down. This interaction is depicted visually in Fig. 3.

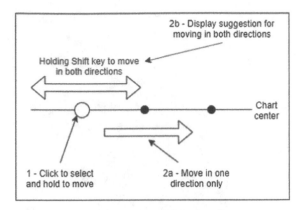

**Fig. 3.** The user interaction mechanism for changing privacy values.

In addition to the asymmetric privacy changing efforts described above, another feature of the privacy controller is it tends to move toward the radar chart's center. In other words, the privacy controller tends to set the initial values for the five dimensions of the privacy object as least exposed as possible. So, if there is a share being created, and the creator has no privacy preferences, all dimensions' initial values are set to the values in the "Least exposed value" column of Table 1.

## 4    Experiments

### 4.1    Experiment Setup

We want to test whether the proposed model can increase the awareness and understanding of users when they use it for sharing activities. A concrete instance of the model has been developed as a web application. We also invited several volunteer senior students of an undergraduate class at Ho Chi Minh City University of Technology to join the experiments. The total number of students for the experiments is 15. They were first told that their choices are recorded, analyzed, and published later, but no individual choice and associated personal information are revealed to the public. They were also told that the time it takes for them to accomplish any task is somewhat important in this research, so they should do things and make decisions according to their personal preferences and do not think too much about what are the right choices. After agreeing to the above conditions, they are presented with a web interface in which we use the Facebook Login SDK[3] (see Fig. 4) to request access permissions to their public profile information such as their full name and profile picture. Although the web application we've developed doesn't interact with their real Facebook accounts in anyway, we use the Facebook Login SDK to be able to show their full name and profile picture, with the main purpose is to make the participants perceive as their selections affect their real Facebook accounts.

---

[3] Facebook Login for developers, https://developers.facebook.com/docs/facebook-login.

**Fig. 4.** The Facebook Login SDK is used to get and show users' full name and picture.

## 4.2 The Affect on User Awareness

The experiment we describe in this section is used to measure the affect of our visual model on users' awareness. In particular, we want to measure the performance of end users in recognizing the differences in privacy settings between two shares, using either a simple interface similar to the Facebook's, or our proposed visual model interface. For each of the five privacy dimensions, we create two predefined values: one with less exposure and one with more exposure. The predefined values are listed in Table 2.

**Table 2.** There are two predefined values for each privacy dimension.

| Dimension | Less exposure | More exposure |
| --- | --- | --- |
| Who | Only the user | All 15 users |
| What | A general URL | A text about the experiment |
| When | Share tomorrow | Share now |
| Where | Ho Chi Minh City | The address of HCMUT |
| Whom | Friend of the user | The public |

We divide the volunteer users into three groups. The first group has 5 people and they are presented with the simple interface only. The second group has 5 people and they are presented with the proposed model interface only. The third group also has 5 people, but they are presented with both interfaces. In each step, a pair of share (displayed in either the simple interface or our novel interface) is presented to the volunteer users. Only one dimension's value is changed between each pair, to make the differences between two shares are not too many. To illustrate, Fig. 5 displays how a change in the Who dimension looks like using the simple interface (top row) and our proposed visual model (bottom row). On each row, the privacy is exposed less in the left part and more in the right part.

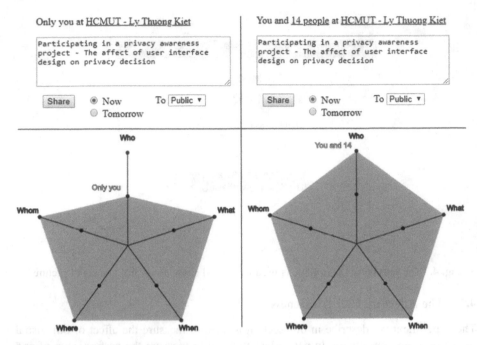

**Fig. 5.** A change in the Who dimension's value is displayed using the simple interface (top row) and our visual model (bottom row). In both cases, the privacy is exposed less on the left, and more on the right.

Each user in the first and second group is presented with 5 pairs of shares. On each pair, there is only one difference in one dimension of the two presented privacy objects. On the other hand, each user in the third group is presented with 10 pairs of shares, 5 of which using the simple interface, and another 5 using our model interface.

After the experiment, each user in the first and second groups is asked what is changed in each pair, and what does the change mean. The number of users can recognize the change on each dimension for each interface is summarized in Table 3. For a user who can recognize changes, one additional question for that user is then asked: what does that change mean to a user's privacy?

**Table 3.** The number of users can recognize the change on each dimension.

| Dimension | Simple interface | Our visual model |
|-----------|------------------|------------------|
| Who       | 4                | 5                |
| What      | 5                | 5                |
| When      | 2                | 5                |
| Where     | 3                | 5                |
| Whom      | 4                | 5                |

Because this experiment is set up with only two values for each dimension, the radar chart' shape changes noticeably (see the bottom row of Fig. 5) when one dimension's value changes. As a result, all changes on five dimensions of the privacy objects arc recognized by all people in the second group (using our visual model). On the other hand, only the change on the What dimension is recognized by all people in the first group (using the simple interface). One possible explanation for this is because the What dimension corresponds to the content, and it is the element occupies the largest space in the simple interface. The changes on the Who and Whom dimensions are also recognized by most people. We think the reason for this is because all of the participants possess online social accounts, so they are familiar with concepts like tagging (Who dimension) and "Who should see this" (Whom dimension) already. The same reason can be used to explain the low number of participants who are able to recognize the changes in the When and Where dimensions. When we ask people who can recognize changes the second question, all of them know that the change is related to the degree of shared information exposure. This result is as expected, because we personally think that recognizing a small change is more difficult than understanding the meaning of that change.

For the users of the third group, after using both interfaces, all of them can recognize the changes on all dimensions. So, we ask the users in this group an additional question: which interface let you see the changes easier? One user chooses the simple interface, three users choose the proposed visual model, and the remaining one chooses "both are equals".

## 4.3  Using the Privacy Controller

The privacy controller is used to change the five dimensions' values of the privacy object. In this experiment, we want to evaluate the effectiveness of the privacy controller for protecting privacy. The value of the What dimension is fixed in this experiment because changing it involves typing some texts, but we are only interested in seeing how the users use the mouse to change privacy options (due to the fact that it is the only supported interaction mechanism of the privacy controller). For other dimensions, we assign 3 predefined values for each, with different degree of exposure. The predefined values are listed in Table 4.

**Table 4.** Except the What, there are 3 predefined values for each privacy dimension.

| Dimension | Least exposed | Medium exposed | Most exposed |
|---|---|---|---|
| Who | Only you | You and 1 | You and 14 |
| When | Share tomorrow | Share 6 h later | Share now |
| Where | Ho Chi Minh City | District 10 | The address of HCMUT |
| Whom | Only you | Friend | The public |

At first, each dimension's value is set at the medium exposed value. We divide the students into two groups: the first group consists of 10 people, and the second group consists of 5. We then ask the users of the first group to change the privacy settings in either direction. The users in the second group are asked to change privacy settings in both directions.

For the users in the first group, there are 33 changes which decrease privacy exposure, and only 7 changes which increase privacy exposure. There are 3 users who increase privacy exposure. For the users in the second group, we see the time it takes them to increase privacy exposure is longer than the time it takes to decrease privacy exposure. But this result is only valid for one or two first dimensions. After making some changes, they are familiar with changing privacy in both directions and the time difference now is almost not noticeable. We then ask them for their personal opinion about the effort to change privacy settings. As expected from the asymmetric inter-action mechanism of the privacy controller, all of them say increasing privacy exposure is more difficult than decreasing it.

### 4.4   Supporting Privacy Policy Understanding

In this experiment, we want to learn about the visual model's support to end users in privacy policy understanding. In particular, we want to compare the effectiveness of our visual model with the textual display of policy settings in Facebook. From Face-book privacy page, we select one option under the "Your Activity" category and two options under the category "How People Find and Contact You" for the experiment. The details of the options and their available choices are listed in Table 5.

**Table 5.**  Selected privacy options and their available choices.

| Privacy option | Choices (from least exposed to most exposed) |
|---|---|
| Who can see your future posts? | Only me, Specific friends, Friends, Public |
| Who can send you friend requests? | Friends of friends, Everyone |
| Who can see your friend list? | Only me, Specific friends, Friends, Public |

For each privacy option, all users are presented first with the question text. Then, all available choices are displayed in the visual model's radar chart for the users to choose. As clearly stated in the questions and available choices, these policy options affect only the Whom dimension of the privacy object. As a result, only the axis corresponds to the Whom dimension is changeable. Initially, for each option's question, the least exposed value is selected ("Only me" for the first and third options, and "Friends of friends" for the second option). As users use the mouse to change the data point's location, appropriate text value is displayed. A sample screenshot is depicted in Fig. 6.

After using the radar chart to adjust privacy options, the users are asked whether the visual presentation add more insights into privacy choices. 12 out of 15 people answer yes. They say using the area of the radar chart to represent the degree of privacy exposure make it easier and faster for them to know the result than reading descriptive text. But when we ask them if it is possible to remove the choices' text from the chart, they all say no. They think the text is essential. Without it, they only know the relative levels of exposure for the choices but not the exact exposure details. As a result, they are not confident enough to use only the chart to configure privacy options.

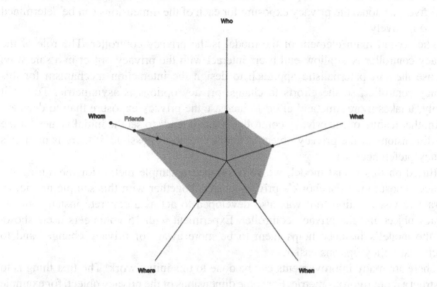

**Fig. 6.** Users use the visual model's radar chat to change privacy options.

### 4.5   Discussion

The results of the above experiments show that our proposed visual model and its concrete implementation do support users in protecting their privacy in online social network environment. The supports to privacy protection are accomplished by three features of the model: the first one is privacy changes are easier to detect, which will increase users' awareness; the second one is the asymmetric effort in changing privacy options, which makes unexpected changes to increase privacy exposure is harder to happen; and the last one is the visual display of privacy option choices together with standard text make privacy policy easier to understand. Due to the small number of volunteer users, there is no statistically significant conclusion can be stated from the experiments. But this initial results show the potential bright future of this model.

# 5  Conclusions

In this paper, we have proposed a visual model for representing and protecting privacy of online social network users. The model consists of two main elements: a privacy object and a privacy controller. The privacy object's role is to capture the privacy characteristics of actions happen on online social networks. The details of the privacy object are included in its five dimensions: Who (Who are included in the share?), What (What the share is about?), When (When the share is created?), Where (Where the share is created?) and Whom (Who is the target audience of the share?). By answering these five questions, the privacy exposure for each of the dimensions can be determined more objectively.

The second main element of the model is the privacy controller. The role of the privacy controller is to allow end users interact with the privacy object in a safe way. We use the soft paternalistic approach to design the interaction mechanism for this privacy controller, so the efforts to change privacy options is asymmetric. To put it simply, it takes more time and effort to increase the privacy exposure than to decrease it. Another feature of the privacy controller is that it tends to set the initial values for the five dimensions of the privacy object as least exposed as possible, if there is no user's privacy preferences set.

Based on this visual model, we've developed a sample metric for measuring the privacy exposure the Facebook's privacy object. Together with this sample metric, an interactive visualization tool was also developed to act as a concrete instance of the privacy object and the privacy controller. Experiment with 15 volunteers users shows that the model's instance helps them to be more aware of privacy changes and to understand policy options easier.

There are many improvements can be done to this initial work. The first thing is to construct a more rigorous metric. For some dimensions of the privacy object, for example the What dimension, it is not easy to define exposure level. Our plan for this issue is to define a categorical structure on these dimensions, and then define a linear order under each category. Another possible approach is to use a user-defined metric, in which the users will input their own opinion on what is important for them, and what is not.

Although the privacy controller is effective for setting privacy options on online social networks, its usability has not been evaluated yet. In our experiments, the proposed model interface is designed with just enough components to accomplish sharing tasks. This is certainly not true for real applications, which besides essential components, there are many other components showing relevant and irrelevant information together. When the visual model's interface is put into real applications, the use of it maybe affected greatly. This is another question we want to answer in future works.

**Acknowledgment.** This research is funded by Vietnam National University HoChiMinh City (VNU-HCM) under grant number C2018-20-12. We would like to thank D-STAR lab members from HCMUT who proofread and provided constructive feedback. We also would like to thank volunteer students from my teaching classes who devoted their time and effort in the experiment of this research.

# References

1. Huang, Z., Benyoucef, M.: From e-commerce to social commerce: a close look at design features. Electron. Commer. Res. Appl. **12**, 246–259 (2013). https://doi.org/10.1016/j.elerap.2012.12.003
2. Safiullah, M., Pathak, P., Singh, S., Anshul, A.: Social media as an upcoming tool for political marketing effectiveness. Asia Pacific Manag. Rev. **22**, 10–15 (2017). https://doi.org/10.1016/j.apmrv.2016.10.007
3. Lampe, C., Ellison, N., Steinfield, C.: The benefits of facebook "friends:" Social capital and college students' use of online social network sites. J. Comput. Commun. **12**, 1143–1168 (2007). https://doi.org/10.1111/j.1083-6101.2007.00367.x
4. Bayer, J.B., Ellison, N.B., Schoenebeck, S.Y., Falk, E.B.: Sharing the small moments: ephemeral social interaction on Snapchat. Inf. Commun. Soc. **19**, 956–977 (2016). https://doi.org/10.1080/1369118X.2015.1084349
5. Bilgihan, A., Barreda, A., Okumus, F., Nusair, K.: Consumer perception of knowledge-sharing in travel-related onlinesocial networks. Tour. Manage. **52**, 287–296 (2016). https://doi.org/10.1016/j.tourman.2015.07.002
6. Krishnamurthy, B., Wills, C.E.: On the leakage of personally identifiable information via online social networks. In: ACM SIGCOMM Computer Communication Review, p. 112 (2012). https://doi.org/10.1145/1672308.1672328
7. Sandhu, R., Samarati, P.: Access control: principle and practice. IEEE Commun. Mag. **32**, 40–48 (1994)
8. Menezes, A.J., Van Oorschot, P.C., Vanstone, S.A.: Handbook of applied cryptography (1996)
9. Whitten, A., Tygar, J.D.: Why Johnny can't encrypt: a usability evaluation of PGP 5.0. In: Proceedings of the 8th USENIX Security Symposium, pp. 169–184 (1999)
10. Sheng, S., Broderick, L., Hyland, J.J., Koranda, C.A.: Why Johnny still can't encrypt: evaluating the usability of email encryption software. In: Symposium on Usable Privacy and Security, pp. 3–4 (2006)
11. Herzberg, A.: Why Johnny can't surf (safely)? attacks and defenses for web users. Comput. Secur. **28**, 63–71 (2009). https://doi.org/10.1016/j.cose.2008.09.007
12. Dang, T.K., Dang, T.T.: A survey on security visualization techniques for web information systems. Int. J. Web Inf. Syst. **9**, 6–31 (2013). https://doi.org/10.1108/17440081311316361
13. Adelsbach, A., Gajek, S., Schwenk, J.: Visual spoofing of SSL protected web sites and effective countermeasures. In: Deng, R.H., Bao, F., Pang, H., Zhou, J. (eds.) ISPEC 2005. LNCS, vol. 3439, pp. 204–216. Springer, Heidelberg (2005). https://doi.org/10.1007/978-3-540-31979-5_18
14. Dhamija, R., Tygar, J.D.: The battle against phishing: dynamic security skins. In: Symposium on Usable Privacy and Security (SOUPS), pp. 77–88 (2005). https://doi.org/10.1145/1073001.1073009
15. Herzberg, A., Jbara, A.: Security and identification indicators for browsers against spoofing and phishing attacks. ACM Trans. Internet Technol. **8**, 1–36 (2008). https://doi.org/10.1145/1391949.1391950
16. Sunshine, J., Egelman, S., Almuhimedi, H., Atri, N., Cranor, L.F.: Crying wolf: an empirical study of SSL warning effectivenes. In: 18th USENIX Security Symposium, pp. 399–432 (2009). https://doi.org/10.1016/S1353-4858(01)00916-3
17. Cate, F.H.: The limits of notice and choice. IEEE Secur. Priv. **8**, 59–62 (2010). https://doi.org/10.1109/MSP.2010.84

18. Cranor, L.F.: Necessary but not sufficient: standardized mechanisms for privacy notice and choice. J. Telecommun. High Technol. Law. **10**, 273–308 (2012)
19. Schaub, F., Balebako, R., Cranor, L.F.: Designing effective privacy notices and controls. IEEE Internet Comput. **21**, 70–77 (2017). https://doi.org/10.1109/MIC.2017.75
20. Wagner, I., He, Y., Rosenberg, D., Janicke, H.: User interface design for privacy awareness in eHealth technologies. In: 2016 13th IEEE Annual Consumer Communications & Networking Conference (CCNC), pp. 38–43. IEEE (2016)
21. Schaub, F., Balebako, R., Durity, A.L., Cranor, L.F.: A design space for effective privacy notices. In: The Cambridge Handbook of Consumer Privacy, pp. 365–393 (2018). https://doi.org/10.1017/9781316831960.021
22. Madejski, M., Bellovin, S.M.: The failure of online social network privacy settings. (2011)
23. Reeder, R.W., Kelley, P.G., McDonald, A.M., Cranor, L.F.: A user study of the expandable grid applied to P3P privacy policy visualization. In: Proceedings of the ACM Conference on Computer and Communications Security, pp. 45–54 (2008). https://doi.org/10.1145/1456403.1456413
24. Reeder, R.W., et al.: Expandable grids for visualizing and authoring computer security policies. In: Conference on Human Factors in Computing Systems – Proceedings, pp. 1473–1482 (2008). https://doi.org/10.1145/1357054.1357285
25. Ghazinour, K., Majedi, M., Barker, K.: A model for privacy policy visualization. In: Proceedings - International Computer Software and Applications Conference, pp. 335–340 (2009). https://doi.org/10.1109/COMPSAC.2009.156
26. Lipford, H.R., Besmer, A., Watson, J.: Understanding privacy settings in facebook with an audience view. In: Proceedings of the 1st Conference on Usability, Psychology, and Security, pp. 1–8 (2008). https://doi.org/10.1.1.140.7904
27. Lipford, H.R., Watson, J., Whitney, M., Froiland, K., Reeder, R.W.: Visual vs. compact: a comparison of privacy policy interfaces. In: Conference on Human Factors in Computing Systems – Proceedings, pp. 1111–1114 (2010). https://doi.org/10.1145/1753326.1753492
28. Wang, Y., Gou, L., Xu, A., Zhou, M.X., Yang, H., Badenes, H.: VeilMe: an interactive visualization tool for privacy configuration of using personality traits. In: Conference on Human Factors in Computing Systems – Proceedings, pp. 817–826 (2015). https://doi.org/10.1145/2702123.2702293
29. Acquisti, A., et al.: Nudges for privacy and security: Understanding and assisting users' choices online. ACM Comput. Surv. **50** (2017). https://doi.org/10.1145/3054926

# A Method to Enhance the Security Capability of Python IDE

Vinh Pham[1], Namuk Kim[2], Eunil Seo[2], Jun Suk Ha[3],
and Tai-Myoung Chung[1(✉)]

[1] Department of Computer Science and Engineering,
Sungkyunkwan University, Suwon, Korea
vinhpham@g.skku.edu, tmchung@skku.edu
[2] Department of Electrical and Computer Engineering,
Sungkyunkwan University, Suwon, Korea
{nukim8275,seoei2}@g.skku.edu
[3] Department of Mathematics and Computer Science,
University of Illinois at Urbana-Champaign, Urbana, USA
junsukh2@illinois.edu

**Abstract.** The majority of applications running on the Internet are web applications; however, these applications are vulnerable to arbitrary code execution and database manipulation by Cross-Site Scripting or SQL injection attacks. The fundamental reason of these vulnerabilities is that web applications use a string type for assembling heterogeneous computer languages' syntax for a particular language. To cope with these vulnerabilities, we propose a language-based scheme, in which the programming language itself provides security capabilities by a method of the syntax embedded in Python. Furthermore, the proposed solution supports backward compatibility and higher portability to other languages as well as Python. To improve the debugging difficulty caused by a language-based scheme, we propose a trace-processor that has post-mortem debug ability. We implement the proposed solution as a development environment, named Python-S, based on CPython's source code. Python-S successfully displays the protection capabilities for the SQL injection attack.

**Keywords:** Code injection · Python · Web application · Programming language

## 1 Introduction

Web applications are frequently targeted by attackers due to their ease of use, omnipresence, demand, and growing number of users. Consequently, the number of security vulnerabilities reported in connection with web applications has been steadily increasing, in parallel to the growing significance of a web application paradigm. According to OWASP [1], SANS Institute [2], and Trustwave [3], code injection vulnerabilities are the most potent vulnerabilities that threaten

© Springer Nature Switzerland AG 2019
T. K. Dang et al. (Eds.): FDSE 2019, LNCS 11814, pp. 399–410, 2019.
https://doi.org/10.1007/978-3-030-35653-8_27

the security of web applications. As a result, web application security has started to attract more attention than ever before from both academia and industry.

OWASP Top 10 Most Critical Web Application Security Risks [1] ranks two code injection vulnerabilities second and seventh:

- **SQL Injection (SQLi):** is a web security vulnerability in which SQL commands are injected into data-plane input in order to affect the execution of predefined SQL commands. A successful SQL injection exploit can read sensitive data, modify data (Insert/Update/Delete) or execute administrative operations on the database [1].
- **Cross-site Scripting (XSS):** is a web security vulnerability in which malicious scripts are injected into otherwise benign and trusted websites. XSS occurs when an attacker uses a web application to send malicious code, generally in the form of a browser side script, to a different end user [1].

This paper will examines the most basic web application model, "One Web Server, One Database", as well as a web application in the form of CGI (Common Gateway Interface) Scripts. An HTTP server can be setup in a way that whenever a file from a certain directory is requested, that file is not sent back. Instead, it is executed as a program. The program's outputs are sent back to the user's browser to be displayed. This configuration of HTTP server is called the Common Gateway Interface and the programs (more specifically, the requested file) are called the CGI scripts [4].

Web applications usually employ different heterogeneous computer languages. In the rest of this paper, we will use the following naming conventions:

- **Hosting Language:** The language that was used to program the actual application. In our paper, we define Python as a hosting language.

- **Foreign Language:** All other computer languages that are used within the application. (e.g., SQL, HTML, and JavaScript)

According to Stack Overflow's annual Developer Survey 2019 [5] and JetBrains Python Developers Survey 2018 [6], Python is the fastest-growing programming language today, with 52% of respondents stating that they use Python for web development. It is necessary to have a solution for the injection problems of web applications that is written in Python language.

Based on the above observation, we design and implement a development environment, the so-called Python-S. Python-S has language-based security features, that prohibit developers from writing source code involuntarily and implicitly assembling foreign language code from attacker-provided malicious string values. In this paper, our contributions are as follows:

- We present an additional security syntax that helps protect Python web application against SQLi and XSS attacks.
- We implement Python-S compiler and interpreter based on CPython.
- We verify the protection capabilities of Python-S to prevent the SQL injection attack.

– We propose the trace-processor obtaining post-mortem debugging ability, which becomes a component of an enhanced IDE of Python language.

The remainder of this paper is organized as follows. Section 2 discusses related work. Section 3 explains the design principle of our proposed solution. Section 4 describes how we implemented Python-S based on the original CPython's source code and components. Section 5 justifies Python-S against a concrete SQLi attack scenario. Section 6 provides the Discussion while Sect. 7 concludes the paper.

## 2  Related Work

Although extensive research has been conducted and a large amount of effort has been spent over the decades, code injection attacks against web applications are still prevalent. Some notable academic work has been published in the field of security of web applications as follows. Our approach can be categorized into *Secure programming* category.

– *Secure programming:* Juillerat [7] designed a Java library (Stone) that can enforce security to create robust, secure web applications and manage the vulnerabilities of SQLi and XSS. Grabowski et al. [8] developed a type system for Java language to enforce secure programming guidelines to the prevention of XSS attacks.
– *Vulnerability detection (or prediction) & prevention:* Kals et al. [9] developed a black-box vulnerability scanner (named Secubat) with the ability to identify SQL and XSS. Shar and Tan [10] developed a prototype PHPMinerI that predicts SQLI and XSS by employing machine-learning techniques on input sanitization patterns.
– *Attack detection (or prediction) & prevention:* Su and Wassermann [11] proposed SQLCHECK that prevents SQLi attacks by context-free grammar and parsing techniques. XSSDS [12] is a proxy-based system, which intercepts and compares the HTTP requests and responses to detect XSS attacks.

Up until the time writing this paper, to the best of our knowledge, Python-S is the first security-oriented initial IDE for Python. In term of Python's security capability, more specifically, the programming language extensibility approach for enhancing it's security capability, there are some latest research that we consider as closely related to our work and will be mentioned here as follow.

Fulton et al. introduced *regular string types* [13] which employed *regular expression* to statically verify that sanitization for user input has been performed correctly. This is equivalent to our work in the way that authors also objected using string type in web application programming because it's risk of vulnerabilities. However, they just implemented their work as a Python library in order to prove their hypothesis but not an complete solution for Python.

PyT [14] and Pythia [15] are two tools that detecting web application vulnerabilities for Flask and Django web programming framework, respectively. They might be equivalent with our proposed solution in the way that they also

employed Python's primitive components (package) or modified Python's interpreter in order to achieve their target. But our Python-S is different from them
in term that not only Python-S isn't binded to any specific web framework but
also Python-S is a code injection vulnerability mitigation solution, not vulnerabilities detecting solution. More over, by implementing as an IDE, Python-S can
be integrated more techniques into and evolved in the future in order to solve
other security problems.

# 3   Design Principle

## 3.1   The String Type's Defect

Usually, while programming in Python, a foreign language code (e.g., a SQL
command) was assembled by concatenating the *data* (provided by the user, but
it could be by an attacker as well) as a variable, at the end of a pre-defined
string, which represents a portion of SQL *code*.

```
1    sql = "SELECT * FROM customer WHERE userid = '%s'"%uid
```

In most cases, this method works well. However, when the *data* is malformed
and combined with the *code*, the final results end up having a completely different
meaning or expression from what the programmer intended.

The programmer's intent is that the *data* must not carry any code meaning,
just simply the value. But an external entity's (such as a database management
system or web browser) interpreter (parser) can't distinguish between the *code*
and the *data*, because they are serialized as a whole single string.

The fault is in our string-based method of assembling foreign language code,
because it doesn't provide any capability for strictly separating *code* and *data*.
Hence, an attacker can exploit this discord in the respective view of the programmer and application to conduct a code injection attack, as in Fig. 1. Because
external interpreters have no knowledge of the programmer's intent, they just
simply parse the dispatched foreign language code according to their language
grammar. By providing malformed data, the attacker can cause the external
interpreter viewing dispatched code with different code's meaning from the programmer's intent, as in Fig. 2.

$$\underbrace{SELECT \ * \ FROM \ customer \ WHERE \ userid \ =}_{Code} \ \underbrace{uid}_{Data}$$

$$\underbrace{SELECT \ * \ FROM \ customer \ WHERE \ userid \ = uid}_{String}$$

**Fig. 1.** The discord in the respective view of programmer and application

$$SELECT \underbrace{\phantom{SELECT}}_{Code} * \underbrace{\phantom{xx}}_{Data} FROM \underbrace{\phantom{FROM}}_{Code} customer \underbrace{\phantom{customer}}_{Data} WHERE \underbrace{\phantom{WHERE}}_{Code} userid \underbrace{\phantom{userid}}_{Data} = \underbrace{\phantom{=}}_{Code} X \underbrace{\phantom{X}}_{Data} OR \underbrace{\phantom{OR}}_{Code} '1' \underbrace{\phantom{'1'}}_{Data} = \underbrace{\phantom{=}}_{Code} '1' \underbrace{\phantom{'1'}}_{Data}$$

SELECT * FROM customer WHERE userid = X OR '1' = '1'

Code   Data   Code   Data   Code   Data   Code Data Code Data Code Data

*Malformed Data*

**Fig. 2.** SQLi attack by providing malformed data

### 3.2 Language-Base Scheme Concept

We employ the approach introduced in the research by Jonh et al. [16] to secure Python as a hosting language. This research proposes a language-based concept of assembly foreign language syntax that provides a robust security guarantee. The concept is constructed on three key elements: **Datatype**, **Language integration**, and **External interface**.

By employing a new **datatype** (replacement of string type) to encapsulate foreign language code, we can tokenize the code. This helps enforce explicit code creation and strict separation of *code* and *data* (enforcement that all creation of foreign language code must be explicit by the hosting language's capabilities - **language integration**).

For example, when encapsulated in the new **datatype**, the SQL command at Sect. 3.1 can be represented as follows:

```
1  sql = { select-token, meta-char(*), from-token,
2          tablename-token(customer), where-token,
3          fieldname-token(userid), metachar(=), metachar('),
4          stringliteral(uid's value), metachar(') }
```

In order to execute a successful code injection attack, the attacker must cause the hosting language application to dynamically includes parts of his malicious values into a new datatype, explicitly in a syntactical code context, such as tokens of code, or literal data. At this point, only data (raw string or number without syntactic meaning) are allowed to be added to the new datatype. Consequently, the developer is not able to write source code that involuntarily and implicitly creates embedded code from the attacker-provided string value. Hence, string-based code injection is impossible [17].

The **External interface** plays a role as a mediate abstract layer between the hosting language application and other external entity interpreters. This layer provides secured code serialization operation that will translate foreign language codes encapsulated in the above specific-purpose **datatype** into a character-based representation, because most of external entities, such as SQL DBMS or web browser's accepted HTTP responding, still prefer string-based type as their communication tool.

### 3.3 Backward-Compatible

In order to get the old Python source code backward-compatible with our solution, we employed the "Mark-up Signifier" programming procedure of

Johns et al. [18], which is described in Sect. 4.1. With just a few syntax modifications to the source code, previously written Python web applications can obtain code injection resistance provided by our solution. This also helps the programmer to easily and comfortably adapt to our solution while assembling foreign language code within Python source code.

### 3.4    Trace-Processor

Johns et al. [18] has the drawback that the code written by the programmer is different from the pre-processed code that is actually interpreted. There is a chance that error occurs within the code region that was processed by the pre-processor (which is explained in Sect. 4.1). When debugging these errors, the debugger will refer to lines of code that are unknown to the programmer.

Taking into consideration the fact that most contemporary web applications were developed in the Event-driven design paradigm, traditional debug techniques (e.g. trial and error, setting break-point or print-out of the variable's value) can't cover all execution paths, which may lead to errors within the pre-processed code region. Moreover, by the web application's nature, it will be an advantage if web application can be fault-tolerant. That means that rather than stopping when error occurs, the web application should continue running and handling errors by an exception handler (such as Python "*try - except*" procedure), as well as allow the programmer to debug after an error has occurred.

For this reason, we propose additionally using a trace-processor that runs alongside the hosting language application. We constructed the trace-processor based on the Python's Debugger (*pdb*), which has already obtained post-mortem debugging ability. When an error occurs (an exception is raised), the hosting language application will use the Python sys.exc_info() function to catch the Python interpreter's system specific parameters (e.g., *sys.last_traceback*, *sys.last_value*, *sys.last_type*), and will then continue running or handling the exception. Later, the trace-processor can use these system specific parameters in order to reconstruct the Python interpreter's call stack, up until the point where the exception was raised. The call stack contains frames that are essentially a snapshot of the execution of hosting language web application at the moment that an error occurs. Hence, the programmer can inspect all necessary information (e.g. line of error code, local variables in each function up until the exception), to locate the error.

Suppose a Python program is written using a markup signifier as shown in Fig. 3(a). After this source code is pre-processed, the code will be formed as shown in Fig. 3(b). As mentioned in Sect. 4.1, pre-processed code is different from the original code. To deal with the difference between the original and pre-processed code during debugging, a line number table is generated that stores the line numbers of modified code, which correspond to each line number of the original code being stored.

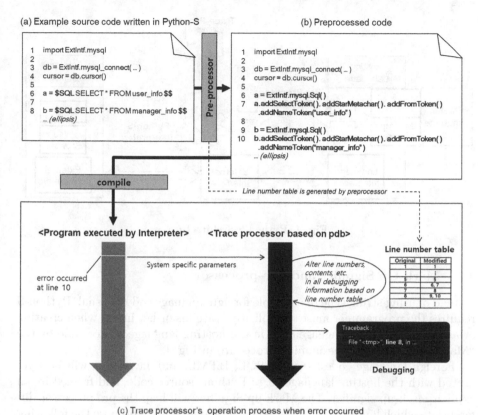

**Fig. 3.** Trace processor's operation process

While pre-processed code is executed by the interpreter, suppose an error occurs at line 10. Then system specific parameters are delivered to the trace-processor, and it reconstructs the call stack to trace the source of the problem. When printing debugging information, line numbers, and contents are altered by referencing the line number table, so that the programmer can understand the information (see Fig. 3(c)).

# 4  Implementation

According to our design principle, we implemented three components and a trace-processor into Python; furthermore, we modified CPython to operate with the secured Python source code that has new syntax. Figure 4 describes the overall architecture of Python-S with the following components.

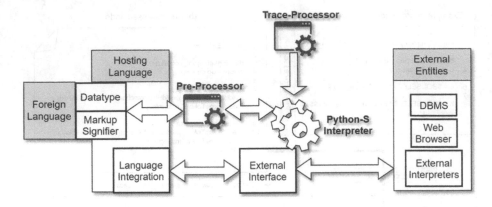

**Fig. 4.** Python-S architecture

## 4.1  Mark-Up Signifier and Pre-processor

Instead of using string type to assemble foreign language code as usual, Python-S requires the programmer must to explicitly state his or her intent when creating or assembling foreign language code in the hosting language source code by the "Mark-up Signifier" programming procedure in Fig. 4.

Foreign language codes, such as SQL, HTML, and JavaScript will be integrated with the hosting language (e.g., Python) source code, and framed by an explicit mark-up signifier. The Mark-up Signifier will help the pre-processor differentiate which language the followed code belongs to. We propose the following mark-up signifier for each foreign language, as follows:

```
1   \\ Mark-up Signifier for SQL language
2   s = $SQL SELECT * FROM $$
3   \\ Mark-up Signifier for HTML language
4   h = $HTML <p> This is a paragraph.</p> $$
5   \\ Mark-up Signifier for JavaScript language
6   j = $JS var d = new Date(); $$
```

A source-to-source pre-processor completely scans Python source code, before it is compiled by the Python's compiler. The pre-processor identifies the mark-up signifiers, and automatically adds API-calls that corresponds to the foreign language that the mark-up signifier represents.

```
1   \\ s = $SQL SELECT * FROM $$
2   s.addSelectToken().addStarMetachar().addFromToken()
```

## 4.2  Language Integration Through API

Python language must be upgraded in order to co-operate with the pre-processor. To obtain this target, we design the new datatype in the form of a Python programming library (API). This API will provide an interface that will be used by a pre-processor. The API contains methods that are called by the pre-processor to tokenize foreign language code into three token classes (code-token, identifier-token, and data-token) depending on their language syntactic characteristics. When those API's methods are called, they create a token, and add it to the new datatype variable.

### 4.3   External Interface as Abstract Layer

We design the External Interface, which is a centralized instance that contains the domain-specific knowledge about the respective foreign languages, in the form of a Python module, as in Fig. 4. In order to prevent potential code injection risks, programmers are forced to communicate with external entities, such as querying to a database, or responding to an HTTP request, only via this specific module. We present the usage of the External Interface in the case of HTML responding and SQL querying, as follows:

```
1    import ExtIntf \\ Import External Interface module
2    ExtIntf.secure_htmlrespond(h) \\ Respond to and HTML request
3    \\ Query SQL database
4    ExtIntf.secure_connect("localhost","testuser","test123","TESTDB")
5    ExtIntf.secure_execute(s)
```

## 5   Evaluation

In this section, we describe how Python-S works through a simple example of a log-in web page, which receives a username and password from a user, and passes a query to the MySQL database to verify the user information. The procedures of Python pre-processing are as follows: Fig. 5(a) shows how the log-in page is configured. Figure 5(b) shows that the Python source code for handling the log-in procedure can be written using markup signifiers. Figure 5(c) shows that after the source code is pre-processed, the code contains script-specific object generation script and API calls for each SQL command token.

The defense procedures for SQL injection attacks are as follows: Fig. 6(a) shows that a malicious user enters the code for SQL injection attack. Figure 6(b) shows that through the pre-processed code, an SQL object is generated, and APIs or methods are called sequentially according to the SQL command token. Each call appends the query string to S.Sql_String, and inqueue according to the type value to S.TokenType_Queue. When the successive 'addX' API calls are completed, S.Sql_String and S.TokenType_Queue contains data as shown in Fig. 6(c).

Finally, log-in handling code calls secure_execute method with argument S, and in the method, checkSqlDeformation method checks if there is potential SQL injection attack code in S in Fig. 7. In this example, due to malicious code injection, the contents of ActualTokenType_Queue are different from S.TokenType_Queue. Therefore, checkSqlDeformation method returns FALSE, and the SQL command is not executed.

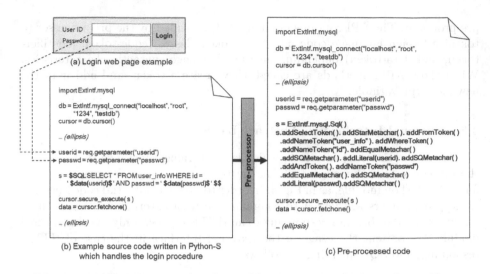

**Fig. 5.** SQL injection attack prevention example - 1) Python source code pre-processing

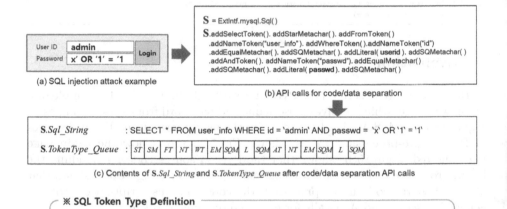

(c) Contents of S.*Sql_String* and S.*TokenType_Queue* after code/data separation API calls

**※ SQL Token Type Definition**

- *ST*  : **SELECT** Token
- *FT*  : **FROM** Token
- *NT*  : Name Token
- *WT*  : **WHERE** Token
- *AT*  : **AND** Token
- *OT*  : **OR** Token
- *SM*  : ' * ' Meta Character
- *EM*  : ' = ' Meta Character
- *SQM* : " ' " Meta Character
- *L*  : Literal

**Fig. 6.** SQL injection attack prevention example - 2) SQL injection attack attempt

*in* cursor.secure_execute( **S** ) → checkSqlDeformation( )

**Fig. 7.** SQL injection attack prevention example - 3) Detection and Prevention

# 6   Discussion

Usually, Python web application development employs not only Python's primitive component, but also it's abundant extensions in terms of library. Most Python extensions that require heavy calculation or raw performance (e.g., image processing) are still based on C language, because of it's effectiveness by nature as a low-level language. Although an application written in Python is already a memory safe program, there is still a possibility that a running Python program catches a memory error when it employs such C extension. In the future, we plan to extend Python-S to mitigate memory error (e.g., buffer overflow) for Python-S applications.

# 7   Conclusion

In this paper, we propose and implement Python-S, which is a security enhanced IDE of Python. Web applications developed by Python-S have security capabilities to prevent code injection attacks, such as SQLi and XSS. Python-S supports backward-compatibility for Python source code. We demonstrate that Python-S web application successfully defends against an SQL injection attack; furthermore, Python-S will foster secure web applications.

# References

1. OWASP Homepage. https://www.owasp.org
2. Cwe/sans top 25 most dangerous software errors (2011). http://www.sans.org/top25-software-errors/
3. 2011 Trustwave Global Security Report. https://www.trustwave.com
4. Python 3 - CGI Programming. https://www.tutorialspoint.com
5. Stack Overflow's annual Developer Survey (2019). https://insights.stackoverflow.com/survey/2019#most-popular-technologies
6. JetBrains Python Developers Survey (2018). https://www.jetbrains.com/research/python-developers-survey-2018/
7. Juillerat, N.: Enforcing code security in database web applications using libraries and object models. In: Proceedings of the 2007 Symposium on Library-Centric Software Design, pp. 31–41. ACM (2007)
8. Grabowski, R., Hofmann, M., Li, K.: Type-based enforcement of secure programming guidelines — code injection prevention at SAP. In: Barthe, G., Datta, A., Etalle, S. (eds.) FAST 2011. LNCS, vol. 7140, pp. 182–197. Springer, Heidelberg (2012). https://doi.org/10.1007/978-3-642-29420-4_12
9. Kals, S., Kirda, E., Kruegel, C., Jovanovic, N.: SecuBat: a web vulnerability scanner. In: Proceedings of the 15th International Conference on World Wide Web, pp. 247–256. ACM (2006)
10. Shar, L.K., Tan, H.B.K.: Predicting SQL injection and cross site scripting vulnerabilities through mining input sanitization patterns. Inf. Softw. Technol. **55**(10), 1767–1780 (2013)
11. Su, Z., Wassermann, G.: The essence of command injection attacks in web applications. ACM SIGPLAN Not. **41**(1), 372–382 (2006)

12. Johns, M., Engelmann, B., Posegga, J.: XSSDS: server-side detection of cross-site scripting attacks. In: 2008 Annual Computer Security Applications Conference (ACSAC), pp. 335–344. IEEE (2008)
13. Fulton, N., Omar, C., Aldrich, J.: Statically typed string sanitation inside a Python. In: Proceedings of the 2014 International Workshop on Privacy & Security in Programming. ACM (2014)
14. Micheelsen, S., Thalmann, B.: A static analysis tool for detecting security vulnerabilities in python web applications (2016)
15. Giannopoulos, L., et al.: Pythia: identifying dangerous data-flows in Django-based applications. EuroSec@ EuroSys (2019)
16. Johns, M.: Towards practical prevention of code injection vulnerabilities on the programming language level (2007)
17. Johns, M., Beyerlein, C., Giesecke, R., Posegga, J.: Secure code generation for web applications. In: Massacci, F., Wallach, D., Zannone, N. (eds.) ESSoS 2010. LNCS, vol. 5965, pp. 96–113. Springer, Heidelberg (2010). https://doi.org/10.1007/978-3-642-11747-3_8
18. Johns, M.: Code-injection vulnerabilities in web applications — exemplified at cross-site scripting. IT Inf. Technol. Methoden Innov. Anwend. Inform. Inf. **53**(5), 256–260 (2011)

# Studying Machine Learning Techniques for Intrusion Detection Systems

Quang-Vinh Dang(⊠)

Data Innovation Lab, Industrial University of Ho Chi Minh City,
Ho Chi Minh City, Vietnam
dangquangvinh@iuh.edu.vn

**Abstract.** Intrusion detection systems (IDSs) have been studied widely in the computer security community for a long time. The recent development of machine learning techniques has boosted the performance of the intrusion detection systems significantly. However, most modern machine learning and deep learning algorithms are exhaustive of labeled data that requires a lot of time and effort to collect. Furthermore, it might be late until all the data is collected to train the model.

In this study, we first perform a comprehensive survey of existing studies on using machine learning for IDSs. Hence we present two approaches to detect the network attacks. We present that by using a tree-based ensemble learning with feature engineering we can outperform state-of-the-art results in the field. We also present a new approach in selecting training data for IDSs hence by using a small subset of training data combined with some weak classification algorithms we can improve the performance of the detector while maintaining the low running cost.

**Keywords:** Intrusion Detection System · Machine learning · Classification

## 1 Introduction

Intrusion Detection System (IDS) is an important component in a computer security system [33]. The task of a IDS is to detect malicious activities in the computer system, hence enable quick reaction to the attacks. The task of IDSs can be traced back to 1980 in the work of Anderson [4] where the author proposed a "computer security threat monitoring and surveillance system" that can detect the following behaviors: "Use outside of normal time," "Abnormal frequency of use," "Abnormal volume of data reference," and "Abnormal patterns of reference to programs or data."

Given the vital role of computer systems in our daily life today, the IDS attracts more and more attention from both academia and industry in recent years. According to IDC Cybersecurity Spending Guide 2019, worldwide spending on security might exceeds 100 billions of US Dollar in 2019 [13]. According to

© Springer Nature Switzerland AG 2019
T. K. Dang et al. (Eds.): FDSE 2019, LNCS 11814, pp. 411–426, 2019.
https://doi.org/10.1007/978-3-030-35653-8_28

Kaspersky Security Lab, while the number of denial services which keeps growing since 2013 [43], the attackers now also focus on more advanced attacks [25].

On the other hand, more and more advanced attack techniques have been invented over time, started with lone-wolf attacks in the early of 1990s to corporate- and government-supported today. As the consequence, the traditional methods based on signature and experts rule are no longer sufficient [34].

Over years, IDSs that based on machine learning techniques have been developed [33]. These techniques utilize the cutting-edge development in machine learning research community in addition to the huge dataset gathered in cyber-security research. We review state-of-the-art results in Sect. 2.

The main problem of the existing methods based on machine learning techniques is that they are trained on one single huge dataset, hence prone to be over-fitting when new types of attack are presented. These techniques usually required a huge data that might not be always ready but might take time to be collected. On the other hand, many widely used machine learning algorithms in IDSs do not support online-learning, i.e. they need to be trained from beginning if new data arrives. These techniques usually require a high computational power. Moreover, even the researchers have designed comprehensive machine learning systems for IDSs, the predictive performance is not yet to be perfect, hence there exists a room for the improvement.

In this paper, we survey the existing machine learning techniques for IDSs and perform a details benchmark on the real dataset collected by [41] in Sect. 2. Then we present our two approaches in using machine learning for IDSs: either we use a complicated machine learning algorithm with a *blind* attack, or use a light and fast algorithm with some training sampling techniques. We show that the supervised-based approaches on IDSs are mostly solved by heavy machine learning algorithms such as *xgboost* [12]. We propose a technique to sub-sampling the training data set hence we can improve the predictive performance of *weak* algorithms such as Naive Bayes classifier.

## 2    Literature Review

In general, there are two main approaches in using machine learning for IDSs: supervised learning approaches in which a model tries to distinguish between benign and malicious traffic flow, and unsupervised learning approaches, mostly anomaly-detection based methods, in which a model tries to distinguish between benign and other traffic flow. We do not discuss in this paper the traditional signature-based intrusion detection approach [24] such as the well-known system Snort [37].

### 2.1    Supervised Learning Approaches

Most of off-the-shelf supervised learning approaches have been used in IDS studies [22]. In short, the main task of a supervised classifier is to predict a network flow is a benign or malicious attack, given a set of network flows with labels (benign/attack) before for training.

**Traditional Machine Learning Approaches.** Traditional machine learning approaches such as SVM, logistic regression or decision tree have been used for a long time in IDSs.

The authors in [3,26,28,42] proposed to use decision-tree for the classification problem. A decision-tree is a classification algorithm that aiming to build a sequential rules in term of *if-else* by minimizing the loss function in separating the groups. The most common loss function using in building a decision tree is Gini [3]. While the authors of [3,26,28] simply build a decision tree on a given dataset, [42] combined the decision-tree technique with Genetic Algorithm [30] for feature generation to achieve a better predictive performance (Fig. 1).

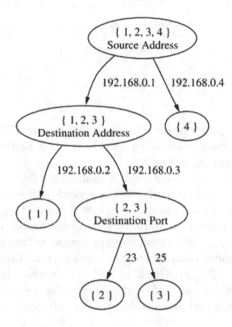

**Fig. 1.** A decision tree built by Kruegel et al. [26]

Another popular traditional classification algorithm is used widely in IDS is Support Vector Machine (SVM) [5,35]. The core principle of SVM is to find an optimized hyper-plane that can classify between two classes. In practice, the most difficult task in building SVM models is to find a good kernel.

Combination of several techniques has been proposed in early of 2000s [42]. By the development of ensemble learning techniques, random forest has been chosen as the most widely used technique [36]. The idea of random-forest is to build multiple decision trees then combine the individual prediction of each tree. Random forest has been proven to outperform other classification techniques in well-defined dataset [16]. The random forest algorithm is visualized in Fig. 2.

**Deep Learning Based Approaches.** In recent years, deep learning research achieves several important breakthrough results [15–18]. It is no surprise that

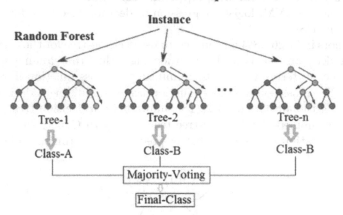

**Fig. 2.** Random forest

researchers utilize the power of deep learning methods in IDS. However, mostly feed-forward neural networks are being used in IDSs. A multi-layer feed-forward neural network is visualized in Fig. 3.

The authors in [19] proposed to use a multi-layer feed-forward neural networks instead of traditional methods such as logistic regression or SVM in IDSs. The authors of [45] considered not only features generated by the system log but also using word embedding techniques to learn from system calls.

Besides a simple multi-layer feed-forward neural networks, several research studies have utilized more complicated networks such as ConvNet or Recurrent Neural Networks [46]. The approach of [46] is presented in Fig. 4. The main problem of that approach and other similar approaches based on spatial and temporal relations of network flows is that these information must be kept within the system.

## 2.2 Anomaly-Detection Approaches

Different from supervised-based approaches, anomaly-detection approaches do not assume a labeled dataset but try to learn what is *benign* flow and detect any un-normal network flows [14]. Hence, the main assumption of an anomaly-detection algorithm is that the *benign* flows is the majority class in the data.

Anomaly-detection algorithms can be divided into two sub-groups: statistical-based algorithms and machine-learning based algorithms. Statistical algorithms rely on statistical attributes of the data such as Z-score or Mahalanobis distance to detect anomaly. We summary several popular distance functions in Table 1 based on the survey of [9] and in Table 2 based on the study of [8].

On the other hand, machine-learning anomaly-detection algorithms rely on machine learning techniques to learn the pattern of the normal data, then detect if a new instance belongs to the class of normal data or not. Eskin et al. [20]

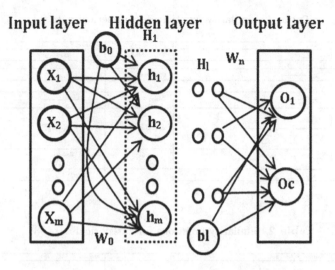

**Fig. 3.** The structure of a deep neural network.

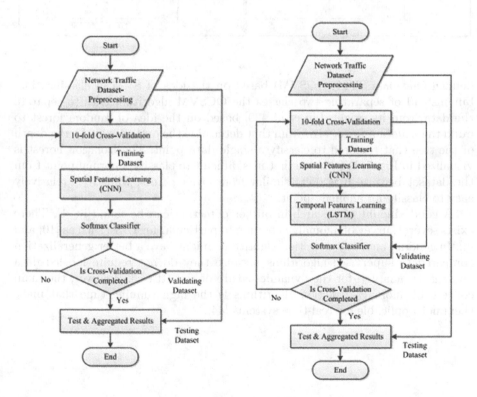

**Fig. 4.** HAST-IDS system [46]

**Table 1.** Similarity functions for numerical data [9]

| Name | Measure, $S_i(x_i, y_i)$ | Name | Measure, $S_i(x_i, y_i)$ |
|---|---|---|---|
| Euclidean | $\sqrt{\sum_{i=1}^{d}|x_i - y_i|^2}$ | Weighted Euclidean | $\sqrt{\sum_{i=1}^{d}\alpha_i|x_i - y_i|^2}$ |
| Squared Euclidean | $\sum_{i=1}^{d}|x_i - y_i|^2$ | Squared-chord | $\sum_{i=1}^{d}(\sqrt{x_i} - \sqrt{y_i})^2$ |
| Squared $X^2$ | $\sum_{i=1}^{d}\frac{(x_i-y_i)^2}{x_i+y_i}$ | City block | $\sum_{i=1}^{d}|x_i - y_i|$ |
| Minkowski | $\sqrt[p]{\sum_{i=1}^{d}|x_i - y_i|^p}$ | Chebyshev | $\max_{i}|x_i - y_i|$ |
| Canberra | $\frac{\sum_{i=1}^{d}|x_i-y_i|}{x_i+y_i}$ | Cosine | $\frac{\sum_{i=1}^{d}x_iy_i}{\sqrt{\sum_{i=1}^{d}x_i^2}\sqrt{\sum_{i=1}^{d}y_i^2}}$ |
| Jaccard | $\frac{\sum_{i=1}^{d}x_iy_i}{\sum_{i=1}^{d}x_i^2+\sum_{i=1}^{d}y_i^2-\sum_{i=1}^{d}x_iy_i}$ | Bhattacharyya | $-\ln\sum_{i=1}^{d}\sqrt{(x_iy_i)}$ |
| Pearson | $\sum_{i=1}^{d}(x_i - y_i)^2$ | Divergence | $2\sum_{i=1}^{d}\frac{(x_i-y_i)^2}{(x_i+y_i)^2}$ |
| Mahalanobis | $\sqrt{(x-y)^t\sum^{-1}(x-y)}$ | - | - |

**Table 2.** Similarity functions for categorical data [8]

| $w_k, k=1...d$ | Measure, $S_k(x_k, y_k)$ | $w_k, k=1...d$ | Measure $S_k(x_k, y_k)$ |
|---|---|---|---|
| $\frac{1}{2}$ | $Overlap = \begin{cases} 1 & \text{if } x_k = y_k \\ 0 & \text{otherwise} \end{cases}$ | $\frac{1}{d}$ | $Eskin = \begin{cases} 1 & \text{if } x_k = y_k \\ \frac{n_k^2}{n_k^2+2} & \text{otherwise} \end{cases}$ |
| $\frac{1}{d}$ | $IOF = \begin{cases} 1 & \text{if } x_k = y_k \\ \frac{1}{1+\log f_k(x_k)\times \log f_k(y_k)} & \text{otherwise} \end{cases}$ | $\frac{1}{d}$ | $OF = \begin{cases} 1 & \text{if } x_k = y_k \\ \frac{1}{1+\log \frac{N}{f_k(x_k)}\times\log\frac{N}{f_k(y_k)}} & \text{otherwise} \end{cases}$ |

defined One-class SVM (OCSVM) based on the idea of SVM in classification, but instead of separating two classes the OCSVM algorithm tries to separate the data from its origin. Liu et al. [29] based on the idea of random forest to build the *isolation forest* algorithm that determine the outlier score by the depth of the tree that required to classify a single data point. The Isolation Forest is visualized in Fig. 5. We can see that it is difficult to classify a normal point from the dataset because it is quite similar from other points, while it is relatively easy to classify an anomaly point.

A good amount of research in outlier detection can be found in [1]. There exists several survey of anomaly detection in particular for IDSs, such as [10] and [6]. In general, anomaly-detection algorithms might have a better generalization compared to supervised algorithms because they do not require labeled data and can be adapted for the dynamic nature of the attacks. However, the main concern of anomaly-detection algorithms is the high running time that make them not applicable for real-time systems [44].

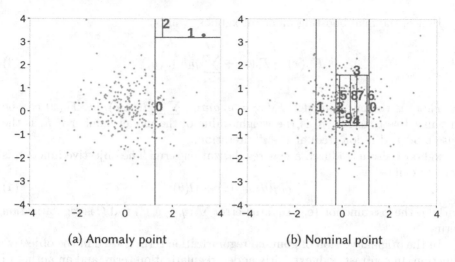

(a) Anomaly point                    (b) Nominal point

**Fig. 5.** Isolation Forest tries to isolate an instance from others. Harder an instance to be isolated, more *normal* it is.

## 3   Our Approaches

In this study we mainly rely on two learning approaches: Naive Bayes for a lightweight solution and xgboost for heavy computational power resource.

### 3.1   Naive Bayes Learning

Naive Bayes is probably one of the most simple learning algorithm we might have today. Naive Bayes relies on Bayes's theorem as

$$P(A|B) = \frac{P(B|A)P(A)}{P(B)} \tag{1}$$

Naive Bayes assume the independence between features, hence it can be learnt very fast as:

$$P(f_1, f_2, ..f_n|BENIGN) = \prod_1^n P(f_i|BENIGN) \tag{2}$$

then assign the prediction as the highest probability class.

### 3.2   xgboost

*xgboost* stands for eXtreme Gradient Boosting [12] is a recent ensemble technique that has been introduced as one member of gradient boosting family [21]. The main idea of gradient boosting techniques is to build multiple sequential learners (will be referred as *weak learners*) where the next learner tries to correct the error made by the previous one.

Hence, the final boosting model of xgboost will be:

$$F_m(x) = F_0(x) + \sum_{i=1}^{M} \rho_i h_i(x, a_i) \tag{3}$$

$F_0(x)$ is the initial model: $F_0(x) = argmin_\rho \sum_{i=1}^{N} l(y_i, \rho)$, i.e. $F_0(x)$ can be initialized as constant. $\rho_i$ is the weight value of the model number $i$, $h_i$ is the base model (decision tree) at the $i^{th}$ iteration.

xgboost also introduced a new regularization term. The objective function is usually defined as:

$$obj(\theta) = l(\theta) + \Omega(\theta) \tag{4}$$

with $l$ is the loss function (e.g. squared-error $\sum (y_i - \hat{y}_i)^2$) and $\Omega$ is regularization term.

In the original version of gbm, no regularization term is used in the objective function. In contrast, xgb explicitly added regularization term, and an author of xgb in fact called their model as "regularized gradient boosting"[1].

On the other hand, gbm introduced *shrinkage* as regularization techniques that are being used also by xgb. To use shrinkage, while updating the model in each iteration:

$$F_m(X) = F_{m-1}(X) + \nu.\rho_m h(x; a_m), 0 < \nu \leq 1 \tag{5}$$

The idea is, instead of taking the *full* step toward the steepest-descent direction, we take only a *part* of the step determining by the value of $\nu$.

xgboost is fully integrated to distributed data management systems such as Apache Spark that allows us to perform xgboost in very huge dataset. To the best of our knowledge there is not yet any attempt to use xgboost in IDSs.

## 4   Experimental Results

### 4.1   Datasets

Probably the KDD'99 dataset is the most popular dataset has been used for evaluation of the IDSs[2] [2,23,38]. However, the dataset has been criticized by several research studies, such as the details analysis done by [31,32]. Mainly, the dataset is questioned for the generation process and the inconsistency in the data description [40]. Furthermore, the dataset is created on a Solaris-based system that has very little in common with popular operating systems today (Mac OS, MS Windows, Ubuntu) [2].

In this study, we decided to use the attacking datasets gathered by [41] and made public by Canadian Institute for Cybersecurity[3]. We will refer to the

---

[1]  https://www.quora.com/What-is-the-difference-between-the-R-gbm-gradient-boosting-machine-and-xgboost-extreme-gradient-boosting/answer/Tianqi-Chen-1.

[2]  http://kdd.ics.uci.edu/databases/kddcup99/kddcup99.html.

[3]  https://www.unb.ca/cic/datasets/ids.html.

dataset as ISCXIDS2012 dataset as suggested by the creators. The dataset is collected in total seven days in 2010 with different types of attacks.

We describe the details number of each type of network flows in following:

- Monday
  - 529918 BENIGN flows.
- Tuesday
  - 432074 BENIGN flows.
  - 7938 FTP-Patator[4].
  - 5897 SSH-Patator.
- Wednesday
  - 440031 BENIGN.
  - 231073 DoS Hulk.
  - 10293 DoS GoldenEye.
  - 5796 DoS slowloris.
  - 5499 DoS Slowhttptest.
  - 11 Heartbleed.
- Thursday morning
  - 168186 BENIGN.
  - 1507 Web Attack Brute Force.
  - 652 Web Attack XSS.
  - 21 Web Attack SQL Injection.
- Thursday afternoon
  - 288566 BENIGN.
  - 36 Infiltration.
- Friday morning
  - 189067 BENIGN.
  - 1966 Bot.
- Friday afternoon 1
  - 97718 BENIGN.
  - 128027 DDos.
- Friday afternoon 2
  - 127537 BENIGN.
  - 158930 PortScan.

Each network flow is provided with a list of 78 features. A snapshot of the dataset is presented in Fig. 6. We might notice that the distribution of the classes is extremely imbalanced: while the majority of the network flows are BENIGN, the DDos flows occupied a huge share of the network but there is very few Heartbleed flows for instance.

---

[4] https://tools.kali.org/password-attacks/patator.

| | Destination Port | Flow Duration | Total Fwd Packets | Total Backward Packets | Total Length of Fwd Packets | Total Length of Bwd Packets | Fwd Packet Length Max | Fwd Packet Length Min | Fwd Packet Length Mean | Fwd Packet Length Std | ... | min_seg_size_forward | Active Mean | Active Std | Active Max | Active Min | Idle Mean | Idle Std | Idle Max | Idle Min | Label |
|---|---|---|---|---|---|---|---|---|---|---|---|---|---|---|---|---|---|---|---|---|---|
| 0 | 49188 | 4 | 2 | 0 | 12 | 0 | 6 | 6 | 6.0 | 0.0 | _ | 20 | 0.0 | 0.0 | 0 | 0 | 0.0 | 0.0 | 0 | 0 | BENIGN |
| 1 | 49188 | 1 | 2 | 0 | 12 | 0 | 6 | 6 | 6.0 | 0.0 | _ | 20 | 0.0 | 0.0 | 0 | 0 | 0.0 | 0.0 | 0 | 0 | BENIGN |
| 2 | 49188 | 1 | 2 | 0 | 12 | 0 | 6 | 6 | 6.0 | 0.0 | _ | 20 | 0.0 | 0.0 | 0 | 0 | 0.0 | 0.0 | 0 | 0 | BENIGN |
| 3 | 49188 | 1 | 2 | 0 | 12 | 0 | 6 | 6 | 6.0 | 0.0 | _ | 20 | 0.0 | 0.0 | 0 | 0 | 0.0 | 0.0 | 0 | 0 | BENIGN |
| 4 | 49486 | 3 | 2 | 0 | 12 | 0 | 6 | 6 | 6.0 | 0.0 | _ | 20 | 0.0 | 0.0 | 0 | 0 | 0.0 | 0.0 | 0 | 0 | BENIGN |

**Fig. 6.** A snapshot of the dataset.

## 4.2   Metrics

As the dataset is extremely imbalanced, the common used metrics such as accuracy do not necessarily reflect the true performance of an algorithm [11]. We will use ROC AUC (Receiver Operating Characteristic - Area Under the Curve) or AUC for short to evaluate our algorithm. The ROC is plotted against True Positive Rate and False Positive Rate as visualized in Fig. 7. The AUC will be calculated as the area of the grey area and will take the value between 0 and 1, higher is better.

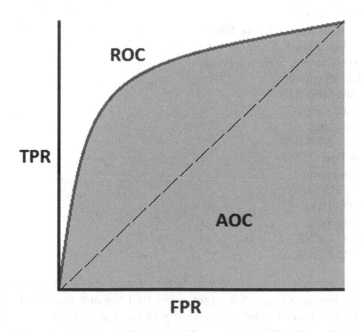

**Fig. 7.** ROC AUC measures the Area Under the Curve between the plot line created by True Positive Rate and False Positive Rate of a model on a dataset.

AUC can penalize the *majority* prediction, i.e. to predict everything as the major class. In this case the accuracy will be very high, but the AUC will be 0. We note that AUC is available for binary classification only.

## 4.3  Data Division

We divide the original dataset into three parts: training set, validation set and test set by the ratio 60%, 20% and 20% respectively. We keep the validation set and test set as fixed set and perform sampling on training set only in case.

## 4.4  Results

## 4.5  Full Training Data

**Binary Classification.** In binary settings, we convert all attacks into one single class "ATTACK" in comparison to "BENIGN". The focus here is to detect network attack without detecting the exact attack type. We display the predictive performance of the model in Table 3. We notice the significant out-performance of ensembles learning (random forest, xgboost) against other models.

**Table 3.** AUC of different classifier in binary setting.

| Algorithm | AUC |
|---|---|
| Naive Bayes | 0.5 |
| Logistic Regression | 0.55 |
| SVM (linear kernel) | 0.62 |
| OCSVM (RBF kernel) | 0.57 |
| Random Forest | 0.92 |
| xgboost | 0.9992 |

We display the feature importance of the xgboost model in Fig. 8. We notice that the most importance feature in term of *gain*, i.e. "the relative contribution of the corresponding feature to the model calculated by taking each feature's contribution for each tree in the model" is *Destination Port*. It might be surprised at the first sight, but in fact most of network attacking flow (68.6%) has the destination port of 80 but the ratio in normal flow is only 10.4%.

**Multi-class Classification.** In multi-class settings, we treat each attack type as different. The confusion matrix of the xgboost model is displayed in Fig. 9. The accuracy of the model is 99.8%.

## 4.6  Sub-training Data

As the predictive performance of xgboost is almost perfect if we use the entire training dataset, we suspect that we do not need all the training data for the model. We analyze how much data we actually need for xgboost to perform well.

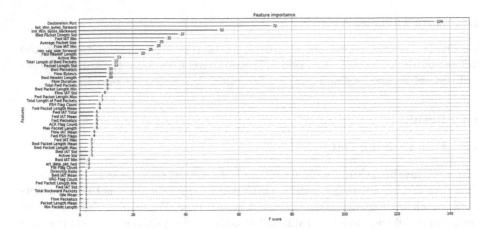

**Fig. 8.** Feature Importance in binary classification settings

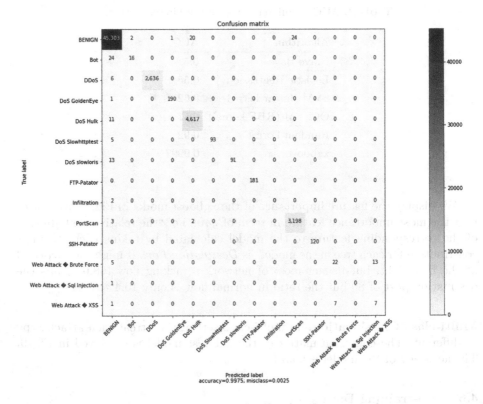

**Fig. 9.** Confusion matrix of multi-classification result

We realize that the xgboost can perform very well in CICIDS'12 dataset with a little training data. In fact, starting from 1% of training data the xgboost model can achieve the $AUC$ of 98.7% already.

**Sample Selection.** As the xgboost model can perform well with quite little of training data, our next question is can we find a way to select this set of data for other *weaker* algorithms, such as Naive Bayse. We recall that, by using the entire training dataset the Naive Bayes achieved the *AUC* of approximate 0.5, i.e. the Naive Bayes does not learn anything and in fact has the same performance with random guessing.

The core reason for Naive Bayes to not perform well is that the distribution of training data is far from the distribution of testing data, while the Naive Bayes model lacks the flexibility to learn that [47]. Our plan is to find the most close sub-set of training data compared to the testing set. However, the distance metrics in high-dimension data might become unstable [7]. Due to that reason, we first apply dimension reduction by Principal Component Analysis (PCA) before calculating the distance.

By selecting top 10% of training data in term of the distance to the testing set we can improve the *AUC* of Naive Bayes to 0.86 which is significant higher than the *naive* usage on the entire dataset.

### 4.7   Discussion

CICIDS'2012 is a comprehensive dataset to evaluate the performance of IDSs in an effort to replace the outdated KDD'99 dataset. CICIDS'12 has attracted a lot of attention from the research community. The predictive performance has been increased over years. In this study we showed that the problem defined in CICIDS'2012 is almost solved by using gradient boosting technique, implies that we need a new and more complicated dataset as the ground for evaluation of IDSs.

On the other hand, there is not much effort in studying and using simple techniques like Naive Bayes recently due to the attention in deep learning techniques. Nevertheless we show that Naive Bayes still can achieve quite a high predictive performance given a proper training dataset, meaning that there is still a room for improvement of these algorithms.

## 5   Conclusions and Future Works

In this study, we showed that the problem of intrusion detection with CICIDS'2012 can be solved mostly perfect with recent ensemble machine learning technique like xgboost, even with a small training dataset. We also show that by using sample selection method based on PCA algorithm we can improve the predictive performance of a simple learning algorithm like Naive Bayes.

In the future research we will study different methods for sample selections, particularly using uncertainty estimation techniques [27, 39].

# References

1. Aggarwal, C.C.: Outlier Analysis, 2nd edn. Springer, New York (2017). https://doi.org/10.1007/978-1-4614-6396-2
2. Ahmed, M., Mahmood, A.N., Hu, J.: A survey of network anomaly detection techniques. J. Netw. Comput. Appl. **60**, 19–31 (2016)
3. Amor, N.B., Benferhat, S., Elouedi, Z.: Naive bayes vs decision trees in intrusion detection systems. In: SAC, pp. 420–424. ACM (2004)
4. Anderson, J.P.: Computer Security Threat Monitoring and Surveillance. James p. Anderson Co., Fort Washington (1980)
5. Bhamare, D., Salman, T., Samaka, M., Erbad, A., Jain, R.: Feasibility of supervised machine learning for cloud security. CoRR abs/1810.09878 (2018)
6. Bhuyan, M.H., Bhattacharyya, D.K., Kalita, J.K.: Network anomaly detection: methods, systems and tools. IEEE Commun. Surv. Tutorials **16**(1), 303–336 (2014)
7. Blum, A., Hopcroft, J., Kannan, R.: Foundations of data science. Vorabversion eines Lehrbuchs (2016)
8. Boriah, S., Chandola, V., Kumar, V.: Similarity measures for categorical data: a comparative evaluation. In: SDM, pp. 243–254. SIAM (2008)
9. Cha, S.H.: Comprehensive survey on distance/similarity measures between probability density functions. Int. J. Math. Models Meth. Appl. Sci. **1**(2), 1 (2007)
10. Chandola, V., Banerjee, A., Kumar, V.: Anomaly detection: a survey. ACM Comput. Surv. **41**(3), 15:1–15:58 (2009)
11. Chawla, N.V.: Data mining for imbalanced datasets: an overview. In: Maimon, O., Rokach, L. (eds.) Data Mining and Knowledge Discovery Handbook, pp. 875–886. Springer, Heidelberg (2009). https://doi.org/10.1007/978-0-387-09823-4_45
12. Chen, T., Guestrin, C.: Xgboost: a scalable tree boosting system. In: KDD, pp. 785–794. ACM (2016)
13. Corporation ID: Worldwide semiannual security spending guide, March 2019
14. Dang, Q.: Outlier detection on network flow analysis. CoRR abs/1808.02024 (2018)
15. Dang, Q.: Trust assessment in large-scale collaborative systems. (Évaluation de la confiance dans la collaboration à large échelle). Ph.D. thesis, University of Lorraine, Nancy, France (2018)
16. Dang, Q., Ignat, C.: Measuring quality of collaboratively edited documents: the case of wikipedia. In: CIC, pp. 266–275. IEEE Computer Society (2016)
17. Dang, Q., Ignat, C.: An end-to-end learning solution for assessing the quality of wikipedia articles. In: OpenSym, pp. 4:1–4:10. ACM (2017)
18. Dang, Q., Ignat, C.: Link-sign prediction in dynamic signed directed networks. In: CIC, pp. 36–45. IEEE Computer Society (2018)
19. Diro, A.A., Chilamkurti, N.: Distributed attack detection scheme using deep learning approach for internet of things. Future Gener. Comput. Syst. **82**, 761–768 (2018)
20. Eskin, E.: Anomaly detection over noisy data using learned probability distributions. In: ICML, pp. 255–262. Morgan Kaufmann (2000)
21. Friedman, J.H.: Greedy function approximation: a gradient boosting machine. Ann. Stat. **29**, 1189–1232 (2001)
22. He, Z., Zhang, T., Lee, R.B.: Machine learning based ddos attack detection from source side in cloud. In: CSCloud, pp. 114–120. IEEE Computer Society (2017)
23. Horng, S., et al.: A novel intrusion detection system based on hierarchical clustering and support vector machines. Expert Syst. Appl. **38**(1), 306–313 (2011)

24. Jyothsna, V., Prasad, V.R., Prasad, K.M.: A review of anomaly based intrusion detection systems. Int. J. Comput. Appl. **28**(7), 26–35 (2011)
25. Kaspersky: The Kaspersky Lab DDoS Q4 Report (2019)
26. Kruegel, C., Toth, T.: Using decision trees to improve signature-based intrusion detection. In: Vigna, G., Kruegel, C., Jonsson, E. (eds.) RAID 2003. LNCS, vol. 2820, pp. 173–191. Springer, Heidelberg (2003). https://doi.org/10.1007/978-3-540-45248-5_10
27. Lakshminarayanan, B., Pritzel, A., Blundell, C.: Simple and scalable predictive uncertainty estimation using deep ensembles. In: NIPS, pp. 6402–6413 (2017)
28. Li, X., Ye, N.: Decision tree classifiers for computer intrusion detection. J. Parallel Distrib. Comput. Pract. **4**(2), 179–190 (2001)
29. Liu, F.T., Ting, K.M., Zhou, Z.: Isolation forest. In: ICDM, pp. 413–422. IEEE Computer Society (2008)
30. Lu, W., Traore, I.: Detecting new forms of network intrusion using genetic programming. Comput. Intell. **20**(3), 475–494 (2004)
31. Mahoney, M.V., Chan, P.K.: An analysis of the 1999 DARPA/Lincoln laboratory evaluation data for network anomaly detection. In: Vigna, G., Kruegel, C., Jonsson, E. (eds.) RAID 2003. LNCS, vol. 2820, pp. 220–237. Springer, Heidelberg (2003). https://doi.org/10.1007/978-3-540-45248-5_13
32. McHugh, J.: Testing intrusion detection systems: a critique of the 1998 and 1999 darpa intrusion detection system evaluations as performed by lincoln laboratory. ACM Trans. Inf. Syst. Secur. (TISSEC) **3**(4), 262–294 (2000)
33. Milenkoski, A., Vieira, M., Kounev, S., Avritzer, A., Payne, B.D.: Evaluating computer intrusion detection systems: a survey of common practices. ACM Comput. Surv. **48**(1), 12:1–12:41 (2015)
34. Radford, B.J., Apolonio, L.M., Trias, A.J., Simpson, J.A.: Network traffic anomaly detection using recurrent neural networks. CoRR abs/1803.10769 (2018)
35. Reddy, R.R., Ramadevi, Y., Sunitha, K.V.N.: Effective discriminant function for intrusion detection using SVM. In: ICACCI, pp. 1148–1153. IEEE (2016)
36. Resende, P.A.A., Drummond, A.C.: A survey of random forest based methods for intrusion detection systems. ACM Comput. Surv. **51**(3), 48:1–48:36 (2018)
37. Roesch, M., et al.: Snort: lightweight intrusion detection for networks. In: LISA, vol. 99, pp. 229–238 (1999)
38. Sallay, H., Bourouis, S.: Intrusion detection alert management for high-speed networks: current researches and applications. Secur. Commun. Netw. **8**(18), 4362–4372 (2015)
39. Segù, M., Loquercio, A., Scaramuzza, D.: A general framework for uncertainty estimation in deep learning. CoRR abs/1907.06890 (2019)
40. Shafi, K., Abbass, H.A.: Evaluation of an adaptive genetic-based signature extraction system for network intrusion detection. Pattern Anal. Appl. **16**(4), 549–566 (2013)
41. Shiravi, A., Shiravi, H., Tavallaee, M., Ghorbani, A.A.: Toward developing a systematic approach to generate benchmark datasets for intrusion detection. Comput. Secur. **31**(3), 357–374 (2012)
42. Stein, G., Chen, B., Wu, A.S., Hua, K.A.: Decision tree classifier for network intrusion detection with GA-based feature selection. In: ACM Southeast Regional Conference, vol. 2, pp. 136–141. ACM (2005)
43. Symantec: Internet security threat report (2014)

44. Tiwari, A.: Real-time intrusion detection system using computational intelligence and neural network: review, analysis and anticipated solution of machine learning. In: Chandra, P., Giri, D., Li, F., Kar, S., Jana, D.K. (eds.) Information Technology and Applied Mathematics. AISC, vol. 699, pp. 153–161. Springer, Singapore (2019). https://doi.org/10.1007/978-981-10-7590-2_11

45. Vinayakumar, R., Alazab, M., Soman, K.P., Poornachandran, P., Al-Nemrat, A., Venkatraman, S.: Deep learning approach for intelligent intrusion detection system. IEEE Access **7**, 41525–41550 (2019)

46. Wang, W., et al.: HAST-IDS: learning hierarchical spatial-temporal features using deep neural networks to improve intrusion detection. IEEE Access **6**, 1792–1806 (2018)

47. Widmer, G., Kubat, M.: Learning in the presence of concept drift and hidden contexts. Mach. Learn. **23**(1), 69–101 (1996)

# Authentication and Access Control

# Enforcing Access Controls in IoT Networks

Emmanuel Bruno[2] , Romane Gallier[1] , and Alban Gabillon[1(✉)]

[1] Université de la Polynésie Française, Punaauia, BP 6570,
98702 Faa'a, French Polynesia
`alban.gabillon@upf.pf`
[2] Université de Toulon, CNRS, LIS, UMR 7020, 83957 La Garde, France
`emmanuel.bruno@univ-tln.fr`

**Abstract.** The MQTT (Message Queuing Telemetry Transport) protocol has become the main protocol for managing messages on Internet of Things (IoT). In earlier papers, we defined a highly expressive ABAC (Attribute-Based Access Control) model for regulating MQTT-based IoT communications. Our model allows us to express various types of contextual security rules, (temporal security rules, content-based security rules, rules based on the frequency of events etc.). These rules regulate not only publications and subscriptions but also distribution of messages to subscribers. In this paper we present an access control enforcement system based on our model. Our system is built according to the XACML architecture standard. The Policy Enforcement Point (PEP) is written in Python and acts as a proxy between the nodes and the MQTT broker. It intercepts MQTT requests and transfer them to the Policy Decision Point (PDP). RDF and SHACL are used to represent security rules and more generally any knowledge contained in the Policy Information System (PIP). We conduct some experiments that show that our solution is viable in terms of performances.

**Keywords:** Security policy · MQTT · ABAC · Policy enforcement

## 1 Introduction

The MQTT (Message Queuing Telemetry Transport) protocol has become the main protocol for managing messages on Internet of Things (IoT). It is an ISO standard (ISO/IEC PRF 20922) [1] and the 3.1 version became an OASIS specification in 2013 [2]. The MQTT protocol is a messaging protocol that supports asynchronous communication between parties. It is based on the publication-subscription paradigm where,

- clients communicate with a broker,
- clients are publishers and/or subscribers,
- the broker maintains a hierarchy of topics
- a publisher posts a message into a topic,
- the broker forwards the published message to the subscribers of the topic.

In [3, 4], we defined a highly expressive ABAC (Attribute-Based Access Control) model for regulating MQTT-based IoT communications. Our model is based on first-order logic and allows us to specify contextual security rules regulating not only

© Springer Nature Switzerland AG 2019
T. K. Dang et al. (Eds.): FDSE 2019, LNCS 11814, pp. 429–445, 2019.
https://doi.org/10.1007/978-3-030-35653-8_29

publications and subscriptions to topics but also *distribution*[1] of messages to subscribers. The security rules can be based on various conditions (temporal, content-based etc.) including the frequency of some events. Our model includes an administration model which is topic-based i.e. each topic has at least one administrator who updates the security policy which is referring to the topic. Rights delegation is also supported.

In this paper we present an access control enforcement system based on our model. Our system is built according to the XACML architecture standard [5]. The Policy Enforcement Point (PEP) is written in Python and acts as a proxy between the nodes and the MQTT broker. It intercepts MQTT requests and transfer them to the Policy Decision Point (PDP). Security rules written in RDF are translated into SHACL shapes/rules [6]. We use TopBraid [7] (a plugin for Jena an open source framework for RDF and the semantic web) to process these SHACL rules. Any event occurring within the system (security decision, error, request etc.) is saved into the Policy Information Point (PIP) for traceability purpose and can be referred to in any contextual security rule.

The remainder of this paper is organized as follows: In Sect. 2, we recall the main characteristics of the MQTT protocol. In Sect. 3 we recall the main features of our ABAC model for IoT networks. In Sect. 4 we give an extensive presentation of our access control enforcement system. We describe the components (PEP, PDP, PIP etc.) of our system and how they interact with each other. We also conduct some experiments which show that our solution is viable in terms of performances. In Sect. 5, we review existing related works. In Sect. 6, we conclude this paper.

## 2   MQTT Overview

The MQTT protocol is a messaging protocol that supports asynchronous communication between parties. It is based on the publication-subscription paradigm where,

- clients communicate with a broker,
- clients are publishers and/or subscribers,
- the broker maintains a hierarchy of topics,
- a publisher posts a message into a topic,
- the broker forwards the published message to the subscribers of the topic.

In Fig. 1, sensors (*S1* and *S2*) sends messages to *Analytics* through *topic A*. *Monitor* sends commands to sensors through *topic B*. the various *subscribe* and *publish* messages are represented on the figure. A topic is identified by a path in a topic tree. For example: *apartment1/room2/CeilingLight*. A Topic filter is a string containing wildcards allowing to address a branch of the topic tree +, #. For examples, *temperatures/#* addresses any topic having temperature as path root and *home/+/temperatures* addresses topics such as *home/room1/temperature*, *home/room2/temperature* etc. See [2] for more details about the use of wildcards in MQTT topics.

---

[1] Note that in the MQTT protocol the distribution of messages is implemented by means of *publish* messages. From a security point of view, we prefer to make a clear distinction between the privilege to publish in a given topic (this privilege can be held by any node) and the privilege to deliver messages to subscribers (this privilege can only be held by the broker).

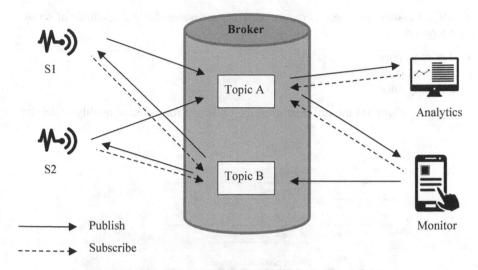

**Fig. 1.** Pub-Sub architecture

The types of messages generated by the MQTT protocol are as follows:

- CONNECT: *Client requested to connect to server*
- CONNACK: *Connect acknowledgement*
- PUBLISH: *Publish message*
- PUBACK: *Publish acknowledgement*
- PUBREC: *Publish received*
- PUREL: *Publish released*
- PUBCOMP: *Publish complete*
- SUBSCRIBE: *Client subscribe request*
- SUBACK: *Subscribe acknowledgement*
- UNSUBSCRIBE: *Unsubscribe request*
- UNSUBACK: *Unsubscribe acknowledgement*
- PINGREQ: *PING request*
- PINGRESP: *PING response*
- DISCONNECT: *Client is disconnecting*

The client initiates communication with the server by sending a CONNECT message containing its identifiers. The server responds with a CONNACK message that validates or not the establishment of the connection.

Once the client has established the connection, he can:

- Post a message in a topic via a PUBLISH message
- Subscribe to a topic or a set of topics (SUBSCRIBE)
- Unregister at a previous subscription (UNSUBSCRIBE)
- Disconnect from the server (DISCONNECT)

When a message is published, the server distributes the responses by sending a PUBLISH message to each subscriber.

MQTT allows customers to request delivery guarantee. Several qualities of service are proposed:

- 0 at most once
- 1 at least once
- 2 exactly once

Figure 2 illustrates the different message exchange for different quality of service.

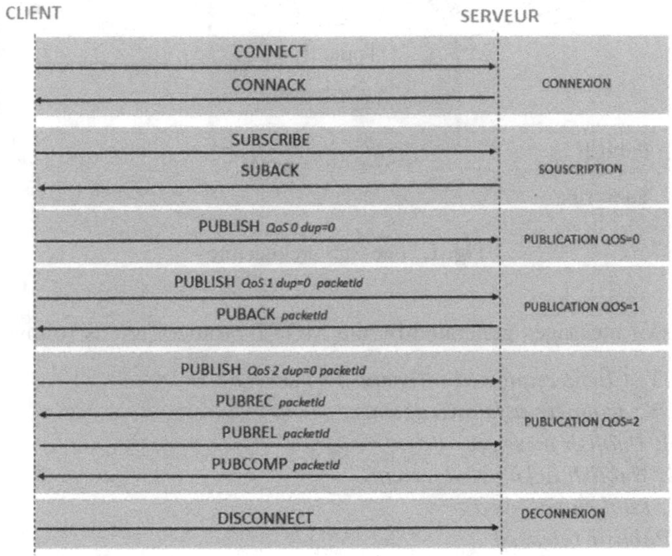

**Fig. 2.** MQTT messages

## 3   Overview of the ABAC Model

Our model is fully detailed in [3, 4]. In this section we only recall its basic principles without entering into the formal aspects.

- Our model offers the possibility to regulate not only publications into topics made by clients, subscriptions but also *distribution* of messages by the broker to subscribers (implemented by means of PUBLISH messages in the MQTT protocol). Controlling distribution of messages is essential to regulate the various flows of messages coming from the broker. Solely controlling subscriptions is too coarse grained to achieve that task.
- Our model allows for various types of dynamic and contextual authorization rules i.e. authorization rules whose outcome (permit or deny) depends on some contextual conditions applying to the nodes, the messages (including the content of the messages) or the environment. In particular, *authorization rules based on the frequency of events* are supported since controlling the rate at which a node may send or receive messages is important in many IoT applications.

We defined our model using mathematical logics allowing us to express contextual rules like the followings:

- *sensor1* is denied publishing messages in topic *alarms/sensor1* during daytime
- guest nodes are permitted to subscribe to the alarm's hierarchy of topics
- *sensor1* is permitted to publish messages in topic *alarms/sensor1* as long as it does not post more than 5 alert messages per 24 h.
- The broker is denied delivering to guest nodes more than one alert message per 24 h from topic *alarms/sensor1*.
- etc.

Potential conflicts between permit rules and deny rules are solved by a conflict resolution policy chosen among the standard XACML resolution policies [5]. Security administration of our model is topic based i.e. we assume there is at least one security administrator defining the security policy for each topic. Rights delegation is supported i.e. a security administrator for a given topic may grant to another user the right to define the security policy regarding that topic. We suggest the reader to refer to [3, 4] to learn more about our model.

## 4 Access Control Enforcement System

In [3, 4], we describe a first proof-of-concept prototype. This first prototype is based on (i) OWL2 [8] ontologies for representing nodes, topics and events, (ii) SWRL rules [9] for representing the security policy and (iii) an OWL2 inference engine [10] for computing a security decision (*permit*/*deny*). However, this approach has proved to be inefficient in terms of performance. In this section we present a new prototype based on RDF [11] and SHACL [6] and we evaluate its performance.

### 4.1 Architecture

The implantation of our security model relies on the W3C Resource Description Framework (RDF 1.1) Model [12]. We use RDF as a logical model to formally represent the security policy. We also use RDF as a physical model since each identifiable object (node, topic, event, security rule, etc.) is represented as a resource. In other words, RDF statements describe resources, contextual information, events occurring in the system and the security policy. We use an inference engine to compute security decisions. Each security decision and the proof graph which has led to the decision are automatically added to our contextual database for further processing. As a general principle, any event occurring within our access control enforcement system is monitored and saved into the contextual database. Recording events like publication/subscription requests, security decisions, processing errors etc. is not only important for traceability purpose but also allows us to refer to these events in dynamic contextual access control rules.

Recently, the W3C has proposed the Shapes Constraint Language (SHACL) recommendation [6] as a solution to define and validate constraints on RDF graphs by means of SHACL *shapes*. SHACL has also been extended with a rule mechanism [13] where conditions can even include SPARQL queries [14]. Therefore, we can translate any security rule defined with our model into an SHACL shape/rule. Instead of processing security rules with a generic rule reasoner as we did in our first prototype, we now translate our security rules into SHACL shapes/rules. We apply these SHACL shapes/rules to RDF publication/subscription requests to produce security decisions. Processing SHACL shapes/rules has proved to be much more efficient than processing SWRL rules and ontologies with a generic rule reasoner.

Our access control enforcement system is built according to the XACML architecture, that is, it has a Policy Enforcement Point (PEP), a Policy Decision Point, a Policy Information Point (PIP – contextual database) and a Policy Administration Point (PAP). Figure 3 depicts the general workflow of our prototype. RDF Security rules are first translated into SHACL shapes/rules. Any MQTT request is intercepted by the PEP, which has been implemented as a proxy between end points and the MQTT broker. The PEP submits to the PDP the RDF request. The PDP uses knowledge from the PIP and applies the SHACL rules on the request to compute a decision together with the RDF proof graph which has led to the decision. Decision and proof graph are returned to the PEP and saved into the PIP.

Our prototype is written in Java 9 and Python. It is based on the Apache Jena Framework to store and manipulate RDF data. SHACL validation is done using TopBraid [7] which is an open source plugin for Jena. The PEP is written in Python. Our prototype provides the user with a REST API to manage the PIP, the policies and the request/response workflow.

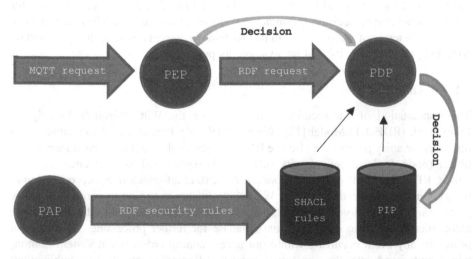

**Fig. 3.** Access control engine workflow

The remainder of Sect. 4 gives more information about each component (PEP, PDP, PIP, Policy database). The last subsection evaluates the performance of our prototype.

## 4.2    Policy Enforcement Point (PEP)

The PEP is located between the nodes and the MQTT broker (See Fig. 4). It acts as a proxy. In order to control the access rights, the PEP intercepts all the messages circulating on the network i.e. the messages sent by the clients, but also the messages sent by the broker. Publication, subscription and distribution messages are forwarded to the Policy Decision Point (PDP). Then depending on the PDP answer they are forwarded to their intended recipient or blocked by the PEP.

The proxy and the broker are on the same local area network. We assume that direct connections to the MQTT broker circumventing the proxy are impossible. Such assumption can be implemented by means of a firewall blocking external connections to the broker. The PEP does not rely on any broker so any MQTT broker can be used. Nodes need to be set to interact with the proxy and not with the broker. For the sake of simplicity, we assume there is only one broker.

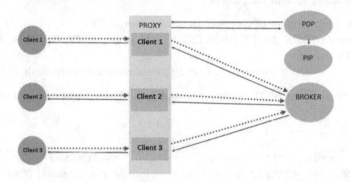

**Fig. 4.**  A high-level view of the system architecture

The purpose of our Access Control Enforcement System is to control the messages published on the server, the subscriptions as well as the distribution of messages by the server. All messages go through the proxy. The PEP manages a connection handler. This routine listens for connection requests. Upon receipt of a connection request (CONNECT message), two connections are set up, one with the server, one with the client. Respectively two threads are launched to listen on these two connections (Fig. 5). The connection handler forwards to the threads the client credentials, client address and the received data. The server responds with a CONNACK message that is directly forwarded to the client. CONNACK messages indicate whether the server has accepted the connection or not. If the connection is accepted, then it is kept open until a DISCONNECT packet is sent or until it is accidentally broken. If the client sends a PUBLISH message, a *pepEvent* with a publish action is created and sent to the PDP. If the request matches the security policy, then the PDP returns a *permit* decision event and the PEP forwards the message to the server. If the PDP returns a *deny* decision event, then the PUBLISH message is blocked. The same logics applies for both SUBSCRIBE messages and distributed messages (PUBLISH messages sent by the broker to the subscribers). Other MQTT packets are forwarded directly to the client or servers through the proxy.

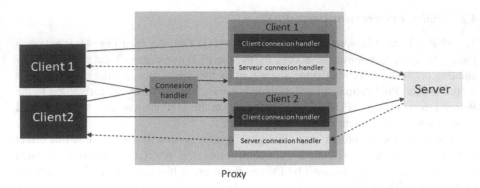

**Fig. 5.** PEP connection listener

The PEP takes several parameters:

- The maximum number of connections (*max_conn*)
- The address (*ADDR_MQTT_BROKER*) and the port (*MQTT_BROKER_PORT*) of the MQTT server.
- The port on which it listens for incoming client connections (default 1883)

The PEP transforms MQTT publication and subscription requests into a set of RDF statements.

```
prefix  xsd:  <http://www.w3.org/2001/XMLSchema#> .
@prefix smd: <http://bruno.univ-tln.fr/smartdemo/1.0#> .
@prefix mqsec:   <http://bruno.univ-tln.fr/mqsec/1.0#> .
@prefix broker1: <urn:broker1:> .

1 smd:e1
2   a mqsec:pepEvent ;
3   mqsec:timestamp "2019-05-02T09:00:00Z"^^xsd:dateTime ;
4   mqsec:action        mqsec:subscribe ;
5   mqsec:source        smd:u1 ;
6   mqsec:target        broker1:topic1:subtopic1 .
```

**Fig. 6.** Publish request event

Figure 6 represents a MQTT publish request event. For easy reading, the Turtle RDF syntax is used. Our engine supports multiple RDF syntaxes (mainly Turtle for easy human reading/writing and JSON-LD for machine to machine exchanges). Resources and predicates in the namespace *mqsec*: belong to our model and resources in the *smd*: namespace are specific to this running example. *smb:e1* (line 1) defines the event as a resource. Five statements apply to the event (line 2–6):

- the class of the event *mqsec:pepEvent* (line2). Main concepts of our model are defined with RDFS a standard RDF vocabulary for data modelling.
- the timestamp (line 3) which is a typed literal
- the action (line 4). The action object is a resource defined in the *mqsec* model (either *mqsec:subscribe* or *mqsec:publish*).
- the source (origin of the action - line 5) defined as a resource
- the target (a MQTT topic on a broker - line 6) defined as a resource

### 4.3  Policy Decision Point

The decision made by the Policy Decision Point (PDP) about requests (instances of *mqsec:pepEvent*) consists of one or more predicates defining the decision and optionally the explanation of the decision.

```
1  smd:e2   a  mqsec:pepEvent ;
2   mqsec:action "subscribe" ;
3   mqsec:applicable-rule[mqsec:decision  mqsec:allow ;
4    mqsec:rule   smd:rule2-application ;
5    mqsec:conflict-resolution-policy
         <xacml:rule-combining-algorithm:ordered-deny-overrides> .
6   ] ;
7   mqsec:source  smd:u1 ;
8   mqsec:target   broker1:topic1/subtopic2 ;
9   mqsec:timestamp "2019-05-02T09:05:00"^^xsd:dateTime .
10  smd:rule1-application
12       a  mqsec:RuleApplication ;
13         mqsec:order  1 ;
14         mqsec:says    [ a  rdf:Statement ;
15                         rdf:object     mqsec:deny ;
16                         rdf:predicate mqsec:decision ;
17                         rdf:subject    smd:e2
18                      ] .
19  smd:rule2-application
20       a  mqsec:RuleApplication ;
21         mqsec:order  2 ;
22         mqsec:says   [ a rdf:Statement ;
23                         rdf:object    mqsec:allow ;
24                         rdf:predicate  mqsec:decision ;
25                         rdf:subject     smd:e2
26                      ] .
```

**Fig. 7.** A PDP decision

Figure 7 represents the response of the PDP to a new event *mqsec:e2* (lines 1–9). Lines 3 states that the decision is *mqsec:allow*, line 4 states that the explanation is *smd: rule2-application* (optional) and line 5 the conflict resolution policy used (optional). If the explanation mode is activated an *mqsec:RuleApplication* resource is created for each security rule applying to the request (line 12–18 for rule 1 and lines 19–26 for rule 2). The first rule with order 1 (line 13) says that event *e2* is denied, the second rule with order 2 (line 21) says that it is permitted. The final decision (lines 1–9) states that the request is allowed according to the conflict resolution policy (order/deny - line 5).

Such a decision is returned to the PEP for enforcement and saved into the PIP for traceability purpose. Moreover, saving security decisions into the PIP allows us to write events based security rules, like security rules based on the frequency of some events (e.g. *sensor1* is permitted to publish messages in topic *alarms/sensor1* as long as it does not post more than 5 alert messages per 24 h).

The PDP uses TopBraid to process the security rules written in SHACL (see next subsection) and issue security decisions.

## 4.4    Policy Database

Security rules are first written in RDF either by hand or by using a dedicated graphical user interface. Then, they are automatically translated into SHACL shapes/rules.

Figure 8 shows a simple security policy composed of three rules and a conflict resolution policy. The first rule defines the default policy (deny). The second rule grants to everybody the right to subscribe to any subtopic belonging to the *topic/subtopic3* hierarchy hosted by *broker1*. According to the conflict resolution policy, this rule takes precedence over the first rule. The third rule grants the publish right to the user <*urn: mqsec:subject:jh1234*> (see PIP for details) on the same topics.

Figure 9 shows the translation of rule 2 (from Fig. 8) in a SHACL rule. Without giving too much details, let us highlight the two following features:

- In bold, the conditions of the rule are translated in SHACL conditions.
- In italic, a SPARQL query produces the partial decision if the rule holds.

Note that the conflict resolution policy is translated as a SHACL rule in the same way but with a lower priority and so applies after all the partial decisions have already been inferred to produce the final decision. As we mentioned earlier, processing SHACL rules with TopBraid has proved to be more efficient than processing SWRL rules with a generic inference engine.

For computing security decisions, the PDP uses dynamic knowledge represented as RDF statements in the Policy Information Point (PIP). The PIP is automatically and constantly expanded with any kind of events occurring within the system (requests, security decision etc.). Recorded events are useful for traceability purpose and the accumulated knowledge can possibly be used in contextual conditions of security rules (for example to limit the number of grants to a resource by day).

The PIP holds also a full representation of the system in terms of RDF resources (users, broker, nodes, topics etc.). Finally, it also includes a representation of the concepts related to various security models (roles hierarchy for RBAC, attributes for ABAC, security levels for MAC etc.)

```
smd:rule1
    a mqsec:pepEventRule ;
    rdfs:label "Rule 1" ;
    rdfs:comment "Default rule, deny all.
                 No condition so applies to all events."@en ;
    mqsec:order 1 ;
    mqsec:decision mqsec:deny .

 smd:rule2
    a mqsec:pepEventRule ;
    rdfs:label "Rule 2" ;
    mqsec:order 2 ;
    mqsec:condition-action "subscribe" ;
    mqsec:condition-target "broker1:topic1/subtopic3/*" ;
    mqsec:decision mqsec:allow .

 smd:rule3
    a mqsec:pepEventRule ;
    rdfs:label "Rule 3" ;
    mqsec:order 3 ;
    mqsec:condition-action "publish" ;
    mqsec:condition-target-pattern
                "broker1:topic1/subtopic3/*" ;
    mqsec:condition-user <urn:mqsec:subject:jh1234> ;
    mqsec:decision mqsec:allow .

smd:conflict-resolution-policy
   a mqsec:pepEventRule ;
   rdfs:label "Conflict resolution policy" ;
   rdfs:comment "highest order applies, deny overrides."@en ;
   mqsec:conflict-resolution-policy
     <xacml:rule-combining-algorithm:ordered-deny-overrides> .
```

**Fig. 8.** A simple security policy defined in our high-level vocabulary

Figure 10 shows some RDF some statements representing the broker, a topic and a user. Note that we use XACML attributes whenever possible (*xacml1:* and *xacml3:* prefixes). The fact that we fully describe the IoT network and all kind of events means that we can reason about any aspect of the IoT network in the evaluation of our security rules.

```
md:rule2 a sh:NodeShape , mqsec:pepEventRule ;
          rdfs:label               "Rule 2" ;
          mqsec:condition-action   "subscribe" ;
          mqsec:condition-target   "broker1:topic1/subtopic3/*";
          mqsec:decision           mqsec:allow ;
          mqsec:order              2 ;
          sh:rule                  [
            a sh:SPARQLRule ;
            mqsec:order    2 ;
            sh:condition [
             sh:property [
                     sh:path mqsec:target ;
                     sh:pattern  "^broker1:topic1/subtopic3/*$"
            ] ] ;
            sh:condition [
             sh:property [
                     sh:path mqsec:action ;
                     sh:pattern  "^subscribe$"
            ] ] ;
            sh:construct     "PREFIX
           rdf:<http://www.w3.org/1999/02/22-rdf-syntax-ns#>
           PREFIX mqsec: <http://bruno.univ-tln.fr/mqsec/1.0#>
           CONSTRUCT {<http://bruno.univ-
           tln.fr/smartdemo/1.0#rule2-application>
           a mqsec:RuleApplication ;
             mqsec:says [
               a rdf:Statement ;
               rdf:subject $this ;
               rdf:predicate mqsec:decision ;
               rdf:object <http://bruno.univ-tln.fr/mqsec/1.0#al
           low>; ];
            mqsec:order 2 .} WHERE {optional
           {<http://bruno.univ-tln.fr/smartdemo/1.0#rule2>
           mqsec:decision ?decision  }}" ;
            sh:order        1 ;
            sh:prefixes     mqsec: , rdf: ;
            sh:targetClass  mqsec:pepEvent
          ] ;
          sh:targetClass           mqsec:pepEvent .
```

**Fig. 9.** Translation of a rule of the security policy in SHACL

```
@prefix xacml1: <urn:oasis:names:tc:xacml:1.0:> .
@prefix xacml3: <urn:oasis:names:tc:xacml:3.0:> .
<urn:mqsec:broker:broker1>
a mqsec:Broker ;
    mqsec:name "broker1" .
<urn:mqsec:topic:broker1:topic1:subtopic1>
  a mqsec:topic ;
  a xacml3:attribute-category:resource ;
      smd:topic "broker1:topic1:subtopic1" .
<urn:mqsec:subject:jh1234>
a xacml1:subject-category:access-subject ;
    xacml1:subject:subject-id "jh1234" ;
    smd:role smd:physician .
```

**Fig. 10.** RDF resources

## 4.5   Performance Analysis

We analyze the transmission time of messages, i.e. the time taken by a published message to reach a subscriber. We compare the transmission time in a configuration where the security policy is enabled and the requests intercepted by the PEP with a configuration where the clients are directly connected to the server with no security enforcement. We conduct our tests on a desktop PC equipped with an i764bit Quad Core CPU and 16Gbit of RAM. The broker is Mosquitto 1.6.0 [15] which is an MQTT v3.1.1 broker. The clients (publishers and subscribers) are implemented in python and rely on the Paho-mqtt1.4.0 libraries. Paho-mqtt implements versions 3.1 and 3.1.1 of the MQTT protocol.

Our experiment configuration is inspired from a similar work presented in [16]. It is the following:

- The subject tree is generated randomly so that each node has between 0 and 5 children. The maximum height of the tree is 5. From the topic tree a list of possible topics for subscription and publication is generated. Similarly, a list of possible topic-filters is created.
- Each subscriber issues a single subscription on a topic generated randomly in the subject tree, with a random quality of service between 0 and 2.
- Each publisher posts one message on a randomly generated topic. The payload of the message contains the identifier of the publisher, the topic, a timestamp corresponding to the time of emission, and a random quality of service.
- The security policy is randomly generated. It contains 100 rules. Each rule contains:
  - A priority between 0 and 5
  - An action: (publish or subscribe)
  - A target: (a random topic or a set of topics)
  - A decision: (allow or deny)

- Clients are all generated at the same time. Upon receipt of a message by a subscriber, the timestamp corresponding to the time of emission is retrieved from the payload and subtracted to the reception time to compute the transmission time.
- We consider a set of experiments for scenarios composed of 50, 100, 250, 500, 750 and 1000 subscribers each including 1000 publishers (see Table 1).

**Table 1.** Configuration scenarios

|                       | C1   | C2   | C3   | C4   | C5   | C6   |
|-----------------------|------|------|------|------|------|------|
| Number of Subscribers | 50   | 100  | 250  | 500  | 750  | 1000 |
| Number of Publishers  | 1000 | 1000 | 1000 | 1000 | 1000 | 1000 |

Results of our measurements are shown in Fig. 11. Figure 11 shows that the difference between the average transmission time of one request with the PEP and the average transmission time of one request without the PEP is constant and approximately equal to 100 ms, regardless of the scenario. This shows that our prototype is scalable and that our approach is very promising. In a similar work presented in [16], the authors developed a prototype where the average transmission time increased linearly with the number of subscribers.

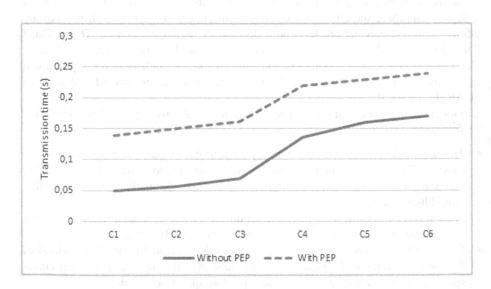

**Fig. 11.** Average transmission time per scenario.

The difference of 100 ms mainly consists of,

- the time required to process the event by the PEP,
- the time required to process the request by the PDP,
- the transmission times between the PDP and the PEP.

We separately measured the average time to process the request by the PDP and we found out that it is constant and approximately equal to 55 ms.

Our prototype can still be optimized. For instance, we are planning to use web sockets instead of the REST API. This should improve transmission times between the PEP and the PDP.

## 5   Related Works

The paper which resembles the most to our approach is [16]. Like us, the authors consider that the protection object is the message. Therefore, they also regulate the distribution of messages by the broker. They use the ABAC model although they do not define, as we do, an ABAC profile for IoT applications. They consider two type of security policies: the security policy expressed by administrators regulating the right to publish/receive messages and the security policy expressed by users in terms of preferences. They do not mention rights delegation. Their Policy Enforcement Point (PEP) is implemented as a proxy between the MQTT broker and the nodes. Having in mind the performances, they manage the security policy within a key value datastore (Redis[2]). However, they do not say much on the Policy Decision Point (PDP) and on analyzing the security policy using a reasoning engine. Moreover, Redis does not allow for complex queries and does not seem to be the right choice for storing highly expressive contextual policies. Finally, our prototype has shown better performance than their prototype (see Sect. 4.5).

In [17], the authors define the secKit tool integrated in the IOT network simulator developed as part of the FP7 iCore project [18]. This tool is used to define security policies protecting the data exchanged between the different components (virtual objects, composite virtual objects) which abstract the IoT network. secKit is based on a collection of models for modeling objects, data, time, roles, activities, interactions, risk, contexts, trust management and so on. It was implemented as a Mosquitto plugin [15]. Authorizations rules can be positive or negative and include obligations. Authorization rules are Event Condition Action (ECA) rules. This formalism makes it possible to express contextual and dynamic authorizations but requires the implementation of an event manager capable of intercepting all events. Many aspects related to this tool are not clearly defined. Authors claim that the tool supports many features, but they do not elaborate on the features (expressive power, risks, trust management, obligations, conflicts resolution etc.). Therefore, it is very difficult to have a clear view of the model supported by secKit. Note also that the tool secKit seems to be abandoned. The source code of an alpha version can be downloaded from gitHub (https://github.com/iot-icore/iCore-security-toolkit) but has not been modified for 5 years.

In [19], the authors describe a NOS (NetwOrked Smart object) middleware, located between the objects and the MQTT client. NOS intercepts the messages intended to be published, normalizes them (i.e. extracts metadata) and according to a security policy implementing the ABAC model decides whether to grant the publication of the

---

[2] https://redis.io/.

message. If the message is authorized, it is encrypted by means of a temporary key corresponding to the subject (topic) where the message is to be published. Once encrypted the message is published by the MQTT client. Customers wishing to subscribe to a topic, contact the NOS which according to the security policy will issue them or not the key to decipher the messages of the subject. This approach frees the MQTT broker from the evaluation and enforcement of the authorization policy. It requires, however, to set up a key management mechanism and offers a rather coarse level of granularity since the object of protection is not the message but the subject (thus including all the messages published in the subject). NOS has been implemented using the node.js platform and the objects transmit their messages via the http protocol. Currently NOS is not available for download. In [20], the same authors improve their architecture by proposing a solution to distribute and synchronize the security policies hosted by the NOS of several IoT networks. Their synchronization protocol uses the MQTT protocol.

# 6  Conclusion

In this paper, we have developed a prototype of a secure MQTT broker based on our ABAC security model. This prototype is built according to the XACML architecture and uses RDF and SHACL languages. We have conducted some experiments showing that our prototype is viable in terms of performance.

Regarding future works, we are planning to investigate the following issues:

- We will extend our prototype to the case of a pub-sub architecture consisting of several *bridged* brokers. In such a scenario, we might need to apply the solution presented in [20] to synchronize the security policy at every node of the pub-sub architecture.
- We will also consider an IoT network consisting of a TCP/IP network hosting the pub-sub architecture coupled with a Low Power Wide Area Network (LPWAN) hosting the sensors. In such a scenario, we might also need to implement solutions proposed by others [21, 22] to move, for scaling purposes, the security controls at the various gateways between the TCP/IP network and the LPWAN network.

# References

1. ISO/IEC 20922:2016 - Information technology – Message Queuing Telemetry Transport (MQTT) v3.1.1. https://www.iso.org/standard/69466.html. Accessed 11 Jan 2018
2. Banks, A., Gupta, R.: MQTT Version 3.1.1, vol. 29. OASIS Standard (2014)
3. Gabillon, A., Bruno, E.: Regulating IoT messages. In: Su, C., Kikuchi, H. (eds.) ISPEC 2018. LNCS, vol. 11125, pp. 468–480. Springer, Cham (2018). https://doi.org/10.1007/978-3-319-99807-7_29
4. Gabillon, A., Bruno, E.: A security model for IoT networks. In: Dang, T.K., Küng, J., Wagner, R., Thoai, N., Takizawa, M. (eds.) FDSE 2018. LNCS, vol. 11251, pp. 39–56. Springer, Cham (2018). https://doi.org/10.1007/978-3-030-03192-3_4

5. Moses, T., et al.: Extensible access control markup language (XACML) version 2.0. Oasis Standard, vol. 200502 (2005)
6. Knublauch, H., Kontokostas, D.: Shapes Constraint Language (SHACL). W3C Candidate Recommendation, vol. 11, no. 8 (2017)
7. SHACL API in Java based on Apache Jena. Contribute to TopQuadrant/shacl development by creating an account on GitHub. TopQuadrant, Inc. (2019)
8. W.O.W. Group, et al.: OWL 2 Web Ontology Language Document Overview (2009)
9. Horrocks, I., et al.: SWRL: a semantic web rule language combining OWL and RuleML. W3C Member Submission, vol. 21, p. 79 (2004)
10. Carroll, J.J., Dickinson, I., Dollin, C., Reynolds, D., Seaborne, A., Wilkinson, K.: Jena: implementing the semantic web recommendations. In: Proceedings of the 13th International World Wide Web Conference on Alternate Track Papers & Posters, pp. 74–83 (2004)
11. McBride, B.: The resource description framework (RDF) and its vocabulary description language RDFS. In: Staab, S., Studer, R. (eds.) Handbook on Ontologies, pp. 51–65. Springer, Heidelberg (2004). https://doi.org/10.1007/978-3-540-24750-0_3
12. Status for resource description framework (RDF) model and syntax specification. https://www.w3.org/1999/.status/PR-rdf-syntax-19990105/status. Accessed 25 May 2019
13. SHACL advanced features. https://w3c.github.io/data-shapes/shacl-af/#rules. Accessed 23 Jun 2019
14. Pérez, J., Arenas, M., Gutierrez, C.: Semantics and complexity of SPARQL. ACM Trans. Database Syst. TODS **34**(3), 16 (2009)
15. Light, R.: Mosquitto-an open source MQTT v3.1 broker (2013). http://mosquitto.org
16. Colombo P., Ferrari, E.: Access control enforcement within MQTT-based Internet of Things ecosystems. In: Proceedings of the 23rd ACM on Symposium on Access Control Models and Technologies, pp. 223–234 (2018)
17. Neisse, R., Steri, G., Fovino, I.N., Baldini, G.: SecKit: a model-based security toolkit for the Internet of Things. Comput. Secur. **54**, 60–76 (2015)
18. Giaffreda, R.: iCore: a cognitive management framework for the Internet of Things. In: Galis, A., Gavras, A. (eds.) FIA 2013. LNCS, vol. 7858, pp. 350–352. Springer, Heidelberg (2013). https://doi.org/10.1007/978-3-642-38082-2_31
19. Rizzardi, A., Sicari, S., Miorandi, D., Coen-Porisini, A.: AUPS: an open source AUthenticated publish/subscribe system for the Internet of Things. Inf. Syst. **62**, 29–41 (2016)
20. Sicari, S., Rizzardi, A., Miorandi, D., Coen-Porisini, A.: Dynamic policies in Internet of Things: enforcement and synchronization. IEEE Internet Things J. **4**(6), 2228–2238 (2017)
21. Sicari, S., Rizzardi, A., Miorandi, D., Coen-Porisini, A.: Security towards the edge: sticky policy enforcement for networked smart objects. Inf. Syst. **71**, 78–89 (2017)
22. Phung, P.H., Truong, H.-L., Yasoju, D.T.: P4SINC-an execution policy framework for IoT services in the edge. In: IEEE International Congress on Internet of Things (ICIOT), pp. 137–142 (2017)

# Resource-Constrained IoT Authentication Protocol: An ECC-Based Hybrid Scheme for Device-to-Server and Device-to-Device Communications

Chau D. M. Pham, Thao L. P. Nguyen, and Tran Khanh Dang[✉]

Ho Chi Minh City University of Technology, VNU-HCM,
Ho Chi Minh City, Vietnam
phamducminhchau@gmail.com, phuongthao.nguyenle@gmail.com,
khanh@hcmut.edu.vn

**Abstract.** Recently, the Internet of Things (IoT) has emerged as one of the building blocks of future digital industrial technologies. Along with its huge open opportunities, it is also coming with different challenges, in which security issues are especially getting more and more attention. The resource constraints of IoT devices makes them even more difficult for us to develop secure authentication protocols that can be actually applied in practice. In this paper, we propose an extended authentication scheme which not only provides a centralized management from powerful servers to lower the burden on the device ends, but also allows direct connections between devices in the same networks. Computations in the proposed protocol are designed to use Elliptic Curve Cryptography (ECC) and only low-cost operations such as exclusive-or, concatenation, and hash function to provide efficient resource consumption. This study includes our security analysis which proves the proposed scheme is resilient to common attacks to IoT systems. The performance analysis is also given to show that it is applicable for practical applications as the process only consumes at most 38.2 mJ on each device in addition to the amount required by the original protocol.

**Keywords:** Internet of Things · Elliptic Curve Cryptography · Authentication protocol · Device-to-device

## 1 Introduction

The Internet of Things (IoT), firstly introduced by Ashton [1] in 1999, has opened new opportunities for the research community to study its wide variety of aspects. Single-function embedded devices have been developed into smart things with impressive abilities to handle more complex tasks as well as to connect with each other. Things in IoT can be anything with embedded processors that can connect to their networks and exchange their data. These "things" are becoming

© Springer Nature Switzerland AG 2019
T. K. Dang et al. (Eds.): FDSE 2019, LNCS 11814, pp. 446–466, 2019.
https://doi.org/10.1007/978-3-030-35653-8_30

more and more familiar with our daily activities. New IoT products are introduced for all the aspects of our modern life. The number of IoT devices has now reached more than one billion [2]. IHS has forecast that the IoT market would reach 75.4 billion of devices by 2025 [3]. In 2012, Gartner, a market research company, affirmed in [4]: "The Internet of Things concept will take more than 10 years to reach the Plateau of Productivity - mainly due to security challenges, privacy policies, data and wireless standards, and the realization that the Internet of Things requires the build-out of a topology of services, applications and a connecting infrastructure". IoT devices are small but very powerful. They are equipped with sensors and/or actuators, so they can recognize changes in their surroundings for corresponding activities [5,6]. However, there are cases that researchers are successful in attacking IoT systems and taking over the control of smart things or making those systems unusable [7–10]. As we can see, security is one of the most important factors of an IoT system. How these devices can interact and authenticate with each other is still a difficult question, which has been attracting many researchers. Authentication in IoT is different from the other systems because of its specific properties: the uncontrolled environment, the heterogeneity, the requirement of scalability, and the limited resources [11].

The most popular model of an IoT eco-system is all machines directly connected and controlled by centralized servers in their local networks. These servers are often deployed with powerful storage and computing resources so that they can handle complicated processes and computations for their client nodes. In other words, in this model client nodes completely depend on their servers for any tasks such as computing, storing, accessing resources and applications, guaranteeing security and so on. Any action of nodes in the same networks is involved with the administration of their servers. This model is widely applied in practice, especially in IoT systems due to the fact that such systems have considerable diversity in their devices with very different resource capabilities. Thus, focusing on servers as the centralized management systems without the need of paying too much attention on the details of devices makes this model easier to be employed and justified. On the other hand, it nevertheless puts too much workload on the servers as well as possibly breaks down the whole system when these servers become out of usage. This model can severely suffer when attackers flood a huge number of physical objects into the network at an unexpected scale.

To restrain the dependence on servers, the Device-to-Device (D2D) communication is taken into consideration [12]. Unlike Human-to-Human (H2H) communication, there is no human interaction in D2D communication. Hence, devices have to be designed for connection self-establishment and authentication with others. There are two kinds of D2D: Standalone D2D and Network-Assisted D2D. These two structures differ by the existence of a helping infrastructure to organize communication and resource utilization. In Network-Assisted D2D, a gateway is required for the operation, and devices are connected by cellular networks. This model requires a high capacity and energy-efficient mobile networks, which is not affordable in some countries and areas. About Standalone D2D, devices initiate requests for communicating with nearby devices by short-range connection mechanisms such as Bluetooth. One device will send signals to express its connection requests with other devices. Consequently, devices will need to authenticate not only with the servers but also among themselves. This will be useful in case there is no connection from devices to servers, e.g. when power blackout occurs and the servers do not have any backup power resource. With Standalone D2D, the IoT systems still work because most of the embedded devices have the battery within and will be unaffected by the local area power outage. So, they can continue their connection with others without interruption. As a result, one device need the capability to verify if it is connecting to legitimate devices without the existence of their servers. As a result, a list of things in the current network has to be stored and well managed by each device, which becomes be a problem for the small ones. Because most of the smart devices are designed for specific tasks, they have very limited resources in the term of memory, energy, and CPU, which means they cannot run too complicated algorithms for registration or authentication, or store too much data.

It is clear that the authentication in both models above has many advantages and also weaknesses, raising the motivation of finding a better way to retain their good characteristics while avoiding their outages. In this paper, we propose an authentication protocol using a hybrid model in which servers still take the responsibility for controlling the access rights and managing the list of the things in the IoT local network, while supporting in device-device authentication before they can start their communications on their owns. The protocol is based on the Elliptic Curve Cryptography (ECC) and low-cost operations such as exclusive-or, concatenation, and hash function to achieve the efficiency in resource consumption. It is then evaluated and validated in terms of the resilience against common attacks as well as energy amount used.

The rest of this paper is organized as follow. Section 2 reviews some related works recently proposed. We then make clear about our motivation for this scheme in Sect. 3. In Sect. 4, we provide a preview of Wang et al.'s authentication scheme. Section 5 is where we thoroughly explain our proposed scheme. In Sect. 6, we demonstrate the resilience of our proposed protocol to different attacks. Performance analyses are carried out and reported in Sect. 7. Finally, concluding remarks and future work are shown in Sect. 8.

## 2 Related Work

Authentication has been known as one of the security aspects to protect any system from possible attacks. This process helps to manage and allow only legitimate entities to access a system as well as its resources. An authentication protocol authentication suggests a way to verify if an object has the right to connect and communicate with one or some other objects in the same systems, and then establish secure communications between them. Different authentication protocols have been proposed for IoT, which can be categorized into two main groups: the ones using asymmetric cryptosystems and the rest using symmetric schemes [13]. In addition, other approaches besides complex cryptographic techniques have also been suggested such as voting protocol employing the blind signature techniques and dynamic ballots for authenticating and guaranteeing users' privacy in electronic voting [14], key-based management and rating-based authentication [15].

In the first group, it is common for proposed schemes to be based on the Public Key Cryptography (PKC) [16]. PKC has been widely used especially in the context of the Internet. The Transport Layer Security (TLS) [17] is a very popular standard protocol in which digital certificates of websites are distributed to their clients as public keys in order to verify identities of the servers and secure the communications followed. However, TLS is not suitable in the practice of IoT because of its strict underlying TCP transport protocol which is not suitable for limited resource devices. To deal with this problem, another transport protocol, Datagram Transport Layer Security (DTLS) [18] is proposed to replace TLS. Although DTLS operates on Unreliable Transport Protocol (UDP), it is still proved to provide the same security level as TCP. In 2012, [19] proposed an implementation for DTLS on sensors with Trusted Platform Module (TPM) installed. Despite its advantages of high security and data integrity with reasonable energy amount consumed, the need of deploying TPM hardware for each sensor is expensive and not scalable. Another direction is using raw public keys to encrypt messages exchanged with the assumption that everyone knows others' public keys. Rabin et al. [20] proposes a protocol with the design quite similar to RSA, a public key cryptosystem widely used for secure data transmission. Although their proposed scheme consumes energy as much as RSA for encryption, decryption using this scheme is much faster because it needs only one squaring for each message. Nonetheless, the requirement of a high cost of computation and energy makes it still unsuitable for IoT devices. Recent works [21,22] try to replace RSA with Elliptic Curve Cryptography (ECC) to achieve less energy in consideration of the same security levels [23]. Overall, solutions in this approach requires public keys to be first distributed and stored in each device of the system. Therefore, the key distribution mechanism is the main challenge of these solutions. Also, the fact that each device has to keep a long list of others' public keys makes them inefficient in the aspects of storage and scalability.

Solutions in the second group are based on symmetric cryptographic schemes in which the protocols aim to securely distribute the symmetric keys, i.e. secret keys, to the whole system. Those keys are used for encrypting and decrypting later communications. The main challenges for such solutions are how these keys can be generated and safely distributed to target objects. [24] proposes a broadcast authentication scheme based on Bloom filter data structure. Using an enhanced version of Bloom filter, i.e. XOR Bloom Filter Authentication, the scheme reduces communications' delay and cost by decreasing the computational overhead as well as their error rates. In [25], the authors propose an ultra-lightweight protocol for heterogeneous wireless sensor network which used nonces, XOR, concatenation operations for mutual authentication between sensors and users in the same network. Recently, Wang et. al in [26] propose an

ECC-based authentication protocol in which devices register with a centralized server to create secret cookie data. The cookie data are then used to later authenticate the device to the server. In this study, the authors point out the security holes in two previous studies on this protocol [27, 28] and propose potential enhancements. Also, the authors analyze and prove their proposed protocol to be resilient to different attacks. In the aspect of resource consumption, this protocol is based on energy-efficient cryptography, ECC, and only uses simple operations like XOR, concatenation and hash function. Furthermore, it requires to store not too much data on devices' ends. However, in Wang et al.'s work, they only propose the authentication for devices and their servers, while communications among devices have been missing throughout the development of this protocol.

## 3   Motivation

How we can reduce the workload of servers but also utilize it to keep the security level of a system is a big challenge and also our main concern. Embedded devices are not designed to handle complex computing tasks, so we need a security solution that is both lightweight and efficient. Applying Standalone D2D in a smart system context, two devices have to first authenticate with each other to prevent any security defect from happening afterwards. A smartphone of your neighbor should not be able to open the doors of your house. As a result, we need to solve a problem: how a "thing" knows the others are "friends" and let them authenticate when the server is unreachable.

We will use smarthome as an example of this problem. As in Fig. 1, there are some entities can be connected to a smart home system. The devices, in this case, can be a smartphone, a smartwatch or even a car with embedded a system on a chip (SoC) allowing it to be "smart". Basically, the main server of the house controls the authentication of devices as well as knows which device can join the system. Nevertheless, when the number of devices becomes big in the future, managing many things can cause a high workload for the server and probably affect the network traffic. Moreover, when the server gets any problem and is out of service, the whole organization will become unusable. Supposing that we have a PC acting as a server in our smart home system. When this

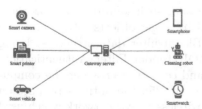
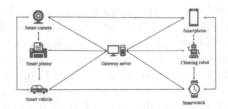

Fig. 1. Smart home network architecture.    Fig. 2. Improved smart home network architecture.

PC is broken, we cannot turn on the lights in the kitchen or open the garage door, since the connections to the controller have been lost. The more we are dependent on the server, the more serious your system gets when the server is attacked. DDoS attacks can make your smart home system come to a standstill.

One of the possible solutions is to connect all the devices, so when the servers are down, one of the remained things can act as a controller for the other devices. Figure 2 expresses our idea about an improved network architecture for Smart Home systems. We will utilize the server for complex algorithms only while restraining the server interference in devices connections. All the devices would have the ability to connect and authenticate with other devices within the smart home network via the help of the server in their initial phase. With our above example, if the PC is out of usage, a smartphone or tablet can act as a controller because it has been registered with the kitchen lights and the garage door. As a result, security in this architecture is a huge problem while we are trying to connect a lot of things together. Many dangerous situations can happen if strangers try to open the garage door with their smartphones. Without security, this architecture cannot be successful in the real world. We need to make sure that illegal things are not able to join the network. In this research, we will propose a protocol that supports D2D authentication with the assistance of the centralized gateway server. Since there are two phases in a security scheme: registration and authentication, in our proposed scheme, after registering with each other via the help from servers, two devices can communicate with each other securely without the existence of server in authentication phase. Via this scheme, we expect to solve the issue about the dependence of IoT devices on their servers to minimize the damage when the servers go down but still maintain the security of the whole smart systems.

## 4   Preview of Wang-Scheme

In our protocol, we extend an existing scheme of Wang et al. [26], hereinafter referred to as Wang-Scheme. Wang-Scheme improves a scheme introduced by Kalra and Sood [27], which aims to authentication for resource-constrained devices in IoT environment along with a better security assurance. Understanding about Wang-Scheme is necessary before getting to our proposed protocol.

Table 1 lists the notations used in Wang-Scheme. In their scheme, Wang et al. assume there are a trusted server and several devices $D_i(D_i \in D)$ wanting to connect to this server. $X$ is the secret value that is only held by the server. There are also other public parameters such as two cryptographic hash functions $H$ and $h$, an elliptic curve $E$ and a generator $G$ on $E$. $H$ maps an arbitrary string to a string $l_H$-bit, while $h$ maps an arbitrary string to a string $l_h$-bit. $\mathcal{G}$ is an additive group on $E$ and $G$ is generator of this group.

In the registration phase, an embedded device $D_i$ chooses a unique identification $ID_i$ and sends it to the server. After receiving the request from $D_i$, the

**Table 1.** Description of the notations used in Wang-Scheme.

| Notation | Description |
|---|---|
| $D_i$ | An embedded device registered in the system |
| $D$ | The set of devices $D = \{D_1, D_2, ..., D_i\}$ |
| $S$ | The server |
| $A$ | The attacker |
| $ID_i$ | The identification of the device $D_i$ |
| $H$ | A cryptographic hash function with an output of $l_H$-bit $H = \{0,1\}^* \to \{0,1\}^{l_H}$ |
| $h$ | A cryptographic hash function with an output of $l_h$-bit $h = \{0,1\}^* \to \{0,1\}^{l_h}$ |
| $\mathcal{G}$ | An additive group implemented by an elliptic curve |
| $G$ | A generator of the group $\mathcal{G}$ - a public parameter |
| $EXP\_Time$ | The expiry time of a particular device |
| $X$ | The server's secret key |
| $SK$ | A session key outputted at the end of a scheme |
| $\|$ | Concatenation operation |
| $\oplus$ | XOR operation |
| $\times$ | Linear multiplication with a point on the elliptic curve |

server generates a random number $R_i$ of length $l_H$-bit then computes $CK$, $CK'$, $T_i$, $A_i$ and $A_i'$ as follow:

$$CK = h(R \parallel X \parallel EXP\_Time \parallel ID_i) \tag{1}$$

$$CK' = CK_i \times G \tag{2}$$

$$T_i = R_i \oplus H(X) \tag{3}$$

$$A_i = h(R_i \oplus H(X) \parallel CK_i') \tag{4}$$

$$A_i' = A_i \times G \tag{5}$$

$CK'$ is then sent back to the device as a response from the server for registration phase. The server stores the values of $\{ID_i, EXP\_Time, T_i, A_i'\}$, whereas the device stores the value of $CK'$. These values will be required in the next phase when the authentication between the device and the server takes place.

In the authentication phase, the embedded device generates a $l_h$-bit long random number $N_1$. From $N_1$, $P_1$ and $P_2$ are calculated by (6) and (7), then sent to the server for authentication.

$$P_1 = N_1 \times G \tag{6}$$

$$P_2 = H(P_1 \parallel N_1 \times CK') \tag{7}$$

Through $EXP\_Time$, $X$ and $T_i$, the server can recompute $CK$ and use it to check if $P_1$ and $P_2$ are valid by computing $P'_2$ as (8) and comparing it to $P_2$.

$$P'_2 = H(P_1 \parallel CK \times P_1) \tag{8}$$

In case $P'_2 = P_2$ showing that they are valid, the server will randomly generate a long number $N_2$, and compute $P_3$ and $P_4$ as (9) and (10).

$$P_3 = N_2 \times G \tag{9}$$

$$P_4 = H(P'_2 \parallel N_2 \times A'_i) \tag{10}$$

With the calculated results, the server returns the value of $\{T_i, P_3, P_4\}$ to $D_i$. Now, it is the turn of device to verify the server by reconstructing $A_i$. $A_i$ is calculated as (11) from $CK'$ and $T_i$. If $A_i$ is correct, then $P'_4$ which is calculated as (12) will equal to $P_4$, and the process is continued. Otherwise, the authentication process fails when $P_4$ and $P'_4$ have different values.

$$A_i = h(T_i \times CK') \tag{11}$$

$$P'_4 = H(P_2 \parallel A_i \times P_3) \tag{12}$$

The device uses $P_3$ and $P'_4$ to compute $V_i$ and $SK_i$ as (13) and (14). $V_i$ is afterwards sent to the server for crosschecking with computed $V'_i$ in (15). $V_i$ is supposed to have the same value as $V_i$. If it does, the authentication process will accomplish. And $SK$ in (14) and $SK'$ in (16) will be equal to each other. $SK$ then becomes the secret key between $D_i$ and the server for their current session.

$$V_i = H(P'_4 \parallel N_1 \times P_3) \tag{13}$$

$$SK = H(P_3 \parallel N_1 \times P_3) \tag{14}$$

$$V'_i = H(P_4 \parallel N_1 \times P_3) \tag{15}$$

$$SK' = H(P_3 \parallel N_2 \times P_1) \tag{16}$$

Figure 3 describes the authentication process in Wang-Schene. This scheme is demonstrated by the authors to be robust against different types of attacks and suitable in the IoT context since it does not require a lot of CPU resource. The ECC-based mutual authentication protocol between devices and server provides a safer authentication environment but also reduces the power intake for computations comparing with RSA. However, in this scheme the server controls everything. Furthermore, all connections between devices must go through it, which is not very efficient as we have stated. Therefore, in the next section, we introduce a new scheme which not only keeps the security but also reduces the dependence on servers in device cooperation of this protocol.

## 5   Proposed Scheme

In this section, we present the complete authentication protocol between devices in the IoT network, which is an extension of Wang-Scheme [26]. As we have stated in Sect. 4, Wang-Scheme is designed to resolve the security holes existing in its previous versions [27,28] and is proved to be safe from various attacks. On considering the idea of this protocol, we have been deeply inspired by its performance since most of the computations use low-cost operations such as exclusive-or (XOR), concatenation, hash function in the combination with ECC. Furthermore, devices using this protocol are also not required to store too much data for authentication. However, only mutual authentications between registration servers and devices have been proposed, while such authentications between end-devices are still missing throughout the studies. In fact, communications between end-devices happen very often especially in the IoT context, thus should be treated as seriously as those between them and servers. Our proposed protocol aims to fill this gap while preserving the advantages of computation and storage efficiency of the original protocols.

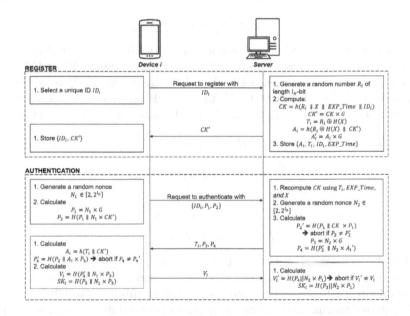

**Fig. 3.** Representations of Wang-Scheme for device-server authentication.

### 5.1   An Overview of Network Entities

IoT systems consist of various kinds of components highly connected to each other in which all components can communicate and interact with each other. These components are very diverse ranging from large devices like servers, household devices, cars, gateways, etc. to small ones such as smartphones or sensors.

Our proposed protocol is partially based on the centralized management model for the connection, authentication and access control among IoT devices. Therefore, despite the fact that they are different in term of functions, resource constraints and sizes, those IoT components are represented by two main types of entities in our protocol:

- *Trusted servers:* The centralized servers which are responsible for storing, managing, authenticating and controlling access of devices within their systems. Our study works with the assumption that those servers are trustful and well protected that it is very hard for attackers to compromise their security or cause any data leakage.
- *Devices:* Other components controlled and managed by the servers are devices. Although these devices may vary in their size and characteristics as mentioned, in this paper, we mainly focus on ones with low computational and storage capabilities, as well as limited energy capacity.

In fact, concentrating the control on just some centralized trusted servers brings many advantages in the context of IoT systems. In fact, servers have great capabilities of computation and storage while not being limited on their power consumption. Therefore, having these servers store most of the data and handle complicated computations will reduce the workload on other devices in the system. The existence of these centralized servers also helps the whole system quickly employ complex management policies such as access control or the privileges provisions for devices and users. Those advantages of the centralized model greatly outweigh other models, which have inspired us to continue developing the protocol based on it.

## 5.2  Protocol Description

The proposed authentication protocol consists of three main phases as represented in Fig. 4:

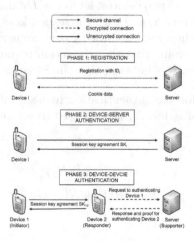

**Fig. 4.** Three phases of the authentication protocol.

– *Phase 1: Registration*
  This is the very first step for every device when joining the system. Its purpose is to register a device's identity with the server. At the end of this phase when the server completes calculating and storing its authentication data, the device will be responded with a secure cookies data used for later authentication phases.

– *Phase 2: Authentication between the servers and device*
  Authentication process happens before devices can start their connections with the rest of the network, which is firstly between them and the servers. In this phase, the device presents its credentials, i.e. its cookies data, to the server. The server then verifies those credentials of the devices to know if it is allowed to connect. Simultaneously, the device also needs to be guaranteed that it is actually connecting to the true server. That is why by the end of this phase valid devices and the server should be mutually authenticated by each other and their common session keys will be created.

– *Phase 3: Authentication between two devices*
  As communications among devices happen more often than between them and the servers in IoT systems, they also need to be mutually authenticated by each other before making communications. The goal of this phase is similar to the second phase, that is, their identities are verified, and common session keys are created for later securing the messages exchanged.

The protocol in *Phase 1* and *Phase 2* is kept the same as the original protocol which we have described in Sect. 5 and Fig. 3. In this paper, we integrate and extend the original protocols with *Phase 3*, when two devices mutually prove their authenticity with each other. This is also the main contribution of this work. In this paper, we keep our notations almost the same as the original protocol shown in Table 1 so that readers can better follow up. The subsequent description of our scheme will be based on the case study, that is, after completing *Phase 1* and *Phase 2*, the two devices, let us say $D_1$ and $D_2$, have successfully authenticated with the server $S$, and with the session keys $SK_1$ and $SK_2$ respectively generated. Next, they want to start a new connection between them to exchange some data. Providing that the connection request is first coming from $D_1$, the authentication process between them in *Phase 3* will be as follows.

– **Step 1:** To prepare for the authentication request with $D_2$, $D_1$ generates a random number $N_1$ of $l_h$-bit. $N_1$ is then used to compute $P_1$ and $P_2$ as (17), (18) and (19).

$$P_1 = N_1 \times G \tag{17}$$

$$N_1' = N_1.h(SK_1) \tag{18}$$

$$P_2 = H(P_1 \parallel N_1' \times G) \tag{19}$$

- **Step 2:** $P_1$, $P_2$ and $ID_1$, are sent from $D_1$ to $D_2$ in a connection request. When $D_2$ receives this request, it generates another random nonce having the same length with $N_1$ ($l_h$-bit). Using this nonce, $D_2$ computes $P_3$ as (20).

$$P_3 = N_2 \times G \tag{20}$$

Next, $D_2$ asks the server to verify the connection request of $D_1$ by forwarding this request plus the value of $P_3$ to the server. As we know, after completing *Phase 2* each device is authenticated by the server and a common session key is generated at the end of that phase. Hence, all later messages between devices and the server will be encrypted with their session keys in order to guarantee their security by preventing overhearing and tampering. Such encrypted communications are denoted by $Enc()$ as shown in Fig. 5.

- **Step 3:** When the server receives the message from $D_2$, it first retrieve the information about $D_1$ and $D_2$ from its database to check whether they are having the permissions for communicating with each other or not. In details, the server needs to check and make sure the following statements are true.

  - $D_1$ and $D_2$ have been successfully authenticated with the server and their sessions have not been expired yet.

  - $D_1$ and $D_2$ are permitted to connect and communicate with each other.

Please note that in this proposed scheme, we only consider the minimum requirements that allowed any two devices to connect. Further constraints can be added depending on the security requirements of particular systems. If both of the above statements are true, the server will use $P_1$ and its stored session key $SK_1$ with $D_1$ to compute $P_2'$ as (21). This value should be equal to the received value of $P_2$ as shown in the proof (22).

$$P_2' = H(P_1 \parallel h(SK_1) \times P_1) \tag{21}$$

*Proof:*

$$\begin{aligned}
P_2' &= H(P_1 \parallel h(SK_1) \times P_1) \\
&= H(P_1 \parallel h(SK_1) \times (N_1 \times G)) \\
&= H(P_1 \parallel (h(SK_1).N_1) \times G) \\
&= H(P_1 \parallel N_1' \times G) \\
&\equiv P_2
\end{aligned} \tag{22}$$

Comparing $P_2$ and $P_2'$, the server will abort the authentication process between the two devices if these values do not equal to each other. Otherwise, it calculates $P_4$ as in (23), then encryptes it with $SK_2$ before sending it back to $D_2$ so that the two devices can continue on generating the common cryptographic key between them.

$$P_4 = H(P_3 \parallel h(SK_1) \times P_1) \tag{23}$$

- **Step 4:** On receiving the value instead of an aborting message from the server, $D_2$ is guaranteed that the connection request is truly generated by $D_1$. Therefore, $D_2$ generates an expiry time $EXP\_Time_{12}$, sends $P_3$ and $P_4$ to $D_1$, then continues to calculate the common session key between them by (24).

$$SK_{12} = H(P_1 \parallel N_2 \times P_1) \tag{24}$$

However, $D_2$ will not store this session key to its database until it receives a final confirmation from $D_1$ when it is sure that the two devices have been able to generate the same session key themselves. The reason for this final confirmation will be explained in the next steps.

- **Step 5:** When receiving the response from $D_2$, $D_1$ needs to verify if it is truly $D_2$ (but not an adversary) it is talking to. In order to do this, $D_1$ re-computes $P_4'$ by (25) and compares the result with the value $P_4$ received from $D_2$. The fact that only the server having the ability to generate $P_4$ (with $SK_1$) then securely sending this value to $D_2$ guarantees that $D_2$ is not impersonated by any adversary. As a result, $D_1$ can now authenticate $D_2$.

$$P_4' = H(P_3 \parallel N_1' \times G) \tag{25}$$

*Proof:*

$$
\begin{aligned}
P_4' &= H(P_3 \parallel N_1' \times G) \\
&= H(P_3 \parallel (N_1 . h(SK_1)) \times G) \\
&= H(P_3 \parallel h(SK_1) \times (N_1 \times G)) \\
&= H(P_3 \parallel h(SK_1) \times P_1) \\
&\equiv P_4
\end{aligned}
\tag{26}
$$

The common session key $SK_{21}$ with $D_2$ is calculated by (27). We can see that $SK_{21}$ should equals $SK_{12}$ as $N_1 \times P_3 \equiv N_2 \times P_1 \equiv (N_1 . N_2) \times G$. After achieving the common session key, $D_1$ sends the encryption of $P_1$ by the key $SK_{21}$ to $D_2$. Similarly, $D_1$ chooses an expiry time $EXP\_Time_{21}$. It completes the authentication process after storing $ID_2$, $EXP\_Time_{21}$ and $SK_{21}$ to its memory.

$$SK_{21} = H(P_1 \parallel N_1 \times P_3) \tag{27}$$

- **Step 6:** $D_2$ receives the confirmation from $D_1$. It then decrypts the confirmation message with the key created in Step 4. If $P_1$ can be achieved from the decrypted message, $D_2$ finally updates $ID_1$, the key $SK_{12}$ and the expiry time $EXP\_Time_{12}$ to its storage. This final step is necessary because any hacker can capture a connection request from $D_1$ and replay it afterwards. If $D_2$ does not wait for this final confirmation, it may mistakenly update an invalid session key and the current secure connection with $D_1$ will be corrupted. Hence, the final confirmation from $D_1$ will help to avoid such replay attack.

We can see that the protocol is designed to achieve an another important property: Only the two devices know the common session key between them. It is true that even the server who supports their mutual authentication cannot compute this session key. In fact, this brings many advantages from the perspective of security and privacy, which will be further discussed and analyzed in Sect. 6. We also note that any message in this phase is associated with a timeout to prevent any long delay. If any message is expired before the authentication process completes, the protocol will be terminated and the process will be then considered as failed. Figure 5 summarizes the whole process of this phase.

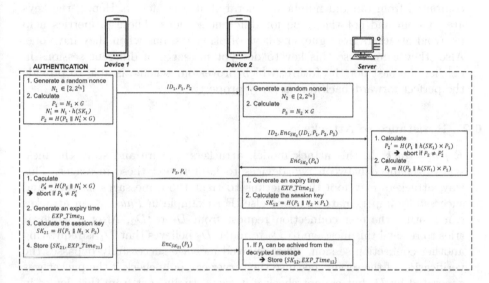

**Fig. 5.** Representations of the authentication protocol between two devices with the support of the centralized server.

# 6   Security Analysis

In this section, we address the security properties as well as the resilience to multiple attacks offered by our proposed model. The analysis mainly focuses on *Phase 3* in which two devices mutually authenticate each other. The security proofs for *Phase 1* and *Phase 2* (Registration and Device-Server Authentication) should be referred to [26].

## 6.1   Security Properties

- *Mutual authentication:* As shown in our proposed protocol, each device is able to authenticate the identity of the other. Therefore, the mutual authentication is achieved with this scheme.

- *Confidentiality:* Confidentiality refers to the cipher algorithm and key agreement, and confidentiality of private device data. These demands are successfully fulfilled in the proposed protocol. At the end of *Phase 3*, two devices agree on a common session key for securing their further conversations. Despite private data of devices being used during the authentication phase, the protocol still guarantees the confidentiality of such data with the use of random nonces for each run and final wrappers with hash functions. This way even if an attacker capture the data $(P_2, P_4)$ while being transmitted, it can neither re-use nor derive the actual secret session keys wrapped inside.
- *Perfect forward/backward secrecy:* In our proposed protocol, each session is computed from random numbers generated at each device. Hence, the keys are random and not the same for different sessions. These properties help us avoid attackers from guessing keys of other sessions when they have one. Also, they cannot use this key to decrypt messages of different sessions in neither the past nor the future, which proves our scheme is able to provide the perfect forward/backward secrecy property.

## 6.2  Resistance to Attacks

- *Replay attack:* In this attack model, attackers capture and store the messages exchanged between two devices to later repeat these messages. This way, attackers may fool their victims to treat those messages as valid and successfully impersonate someone else. For example in *Phase 3*, an attacker can capture the first connection request from $D_1$ to $D_2$. After a while, it tries to re-send this message to $D_2$ to make $D_2$ believes that $D_1$ is requesting another connection session. This replayed message successfully bypasses the verification of the server, because the server can only check if the packet was generated by $D_1$ but cannot check if it was actually sent from this device in the current run. However, such attempts of attack would fail at the next step when $P_3$ and $P_4$ are responded to the attacker. The attacker does not hold the corresponding nonce of the replayed message so it cannot compute the new session key between the two devices. For $D_2$, when receiving the response from the server, it does not immediately update the computed session key but waits for a confirmation from $D_1$. When the timeout for this confirmation is reached, the authentication process at $D_1$ will be aborted.
- *Impersonation attack:* In this case, attackers send connection requests with the identities of other devices to impersonate them. Thank to the support of the server, attackers who do not hold the right session key cannot generate a valid message $(P_2)$. Therefore, they fail to attack $D_2$ by impersonating $D_1$ using its identification.
- *Stolen session key attack (agent compromised):* This attack happens when attackers steal the session key of a device. With the stolen key, the attackers can only read the messages sent in the corresponding session of this device. They cannot deduce or recompute any private information about their victims such as $CK_i'$ or their session keys with other devices or servers.

- *Insider attack:* The proposed protocol is against attacks of internal users in the system. For attackers who are some other devices, they cannot impersonate or access private information of another device as discussed in the previous attacks. In case attackers are some of the administrators who control the server, their administrative privileges may become a serious issue. Indeed, authentication models with centralized servers playing key-distributing roles usually face the same problems of privacy. Since those servers control the session keys of every device, they can access and read all messages transmitted in the system. As a result, those systems failed to guarantee users' privacy. The proposed protocol tries to avoid this issue by only granting the server a support role in the authentication process between devices. In other words, the server cannot compute the final session key between the two devices because it cannot recover the values of $N_1$ and $N_2$. Moreover, because the server does not store any session keys or data which can be used to re-compute them, communications between devices remains safe even when the server database is leaked.
- *Offline dictionary attack:* In this type of attack, the attacker will try to capture the messages between stack holders and try to guess the sensitive information in them. In our model, we use $N_1$ and $N_2$, which are random numbers generated in every authentication session, to generate the session key. We do not use any sensitive information or meaningful phrase such as password, hence, our proposed protocol is safe with this kind of attack.
- *Brute force attack:* In order to make this attack successful, attacker must guess the correct $N_1$ and $N_2$ via $P_1$, $P_2$, $P_3$ and $P_4$. Even when he can get these values, he cannot have the session key $SK_1$ and $SK_2$ between $D_1$ and $D_2$ with the server. Hence, this attack is not applicable in our protocol.
- *Man-in-the-middle attack:* This is an attack where the attacker secretly relays and possibly change the messages in communication between two devices which believe they are directly communicating with each other. The malicious users may be able to capture $P_1$, $P_2$, $P_3$ and $P_4$ by eavesdropping. However, without $N_1$ and $N_2$, there is nothing attacker can do, since in ECC crytography, we can prove that guess $N_1$ from $P_1 = N_1 \times G$ is impossible.

The above analysis proves that the proposed protocol is resistant to different kinds of attacks while providing data integrity as every modification in transferred messages will cause the authentication process to be terminated. The model also provides the final important result that is the mutual authentication between devices. In other words, when this phase completes successfully, every device is guaranteed about the identities of the ones it is talking to.

# 7 Performance Analysis

While making sure the proposed protocol is able to survive different attacks, another important aspect to be analyzed is the performance of its energy consumption. As we have emphasized our point throughout the paper, schemes designed for IoT must be suitable for devices with very constrained power. A protocol will fail in practice if it cannot prove itself to be such designs. Consequently, in this section, we will analyze how much energy needed by each device in *Phase 3*. Although there are three entities enrolling in the phase: $D_1$, $D_2$ and the server, we only take low-powered devices, $D_1$ and $D_2$, under consideration for this analysis.

In our enhanced protocol for mutual authentication between devices, the main operations used by each device are hashing, elliptic curve point multiplication and encryption/decryption using symmetric session keys. The hash function uses SHA-1 with the output length of 128 bits. Encrypting/decrypting messages with session keys is supposed to use AES with key size also of 128-bit. By taking the advantage of the secure channels set up in *Phase 2*, any data transmitted between the server and devices will be encrypted with the symmetric cryptographic scheme AES. The selected Elliptic Curve is the same as [26], which is Curve m-221 for which ECDLP and ECDH are believed to hold, represented by (28). The order of G is 221-bit length ($l_h$).

$$y^2 = x^3 + 117050x^2 + x \ mod \ p = 2^{221} - 3 \qquad (28)$$

To align the performance analysis with [26], we consider the wireless sensor networks with Tmote Sky (also known as TesloB) nodes as our target for future implementations of the protocol. According to the experiment results in [30], SHA-1 consumes 0.057 mJ per its operation. An Elliptic Curve Diffie-Hellman operation takes only 1.76 s, and consumes 9.48 mJ [26]. Meanwhile, encryption and decryption with AES need only 0.009 mJ per operation with 128-bit data [29]. Assumptions on the data length to be encrypted and transmitted is presented in Table 2, later will be used to calculate the number of encryption/decryption operations performed. And Table 3 shows the summary of the energy consumption analysis of the devices using our scheme.

**Table 2.** Data length of variables and messages exchanged.

| Data | Length |
|------|--------|
| $ID_1$, $ID_2$ | < 64-bit |
| $N_1$, $N_2$ | 221-bit |
| $P_1$, $P_3$ | 442-bit |
| $P_2$, $P_4$ | 128-bit |
| $EXP\_Time$ | 64-bit |
| $SK_1$, $SK_2$ | 128-bit |
| Message $\{ID_1, P_1, P_2, P_3\}$ | 9 blocks of 128-bit |
| Message $\{P_4\}$ | 1 block of 128-bit |
| Message $\{P_1\}$ | 4 blocks of 128-bit |

**Table 3.** The energy used by two devices for their mutual authentication with our proposed protocol.

| Device | Operation | Energy cost (mJ) | Times | Total energy consumption (mJ) |
|---|---|---|---|---|
| $D_1$ | Hash (SHA-1) | 0.057 | 4 | $4 \times 0.057 + 4 \times 0.009 +$ $4 \times 9.48 = 38.184$ |
| | Encryption/Decryption (AES) | 0.009 | 4 | |
| | ECC multiplication | 9.48 | 4 | |
| $D_2$ | Hash (SHA-1) | 57 | 1 | $1 \times 0.057 + 10 \times 0.009 +$ $2 \times 9.48 = 19.107$ |
| | Encryption/Decryption (AES) | 9 | 10 | |
| | ECC multiplication | 9.48 | 2 | |

We can see that in this phase, $D_1$ takes only 4 hash and decryption of 4 128-bit data blocks while these numbers are respectively 1 and 10 for $D_2$. From the result, it is clear that only small amounts of energy, respectively 38.2 mJ at $D_1$ and 19.1 mJ at $D_2$, are needed for the authentication process. This result shows that our third phase for authenticating between devices only requires an additional consumption of upto 38.2 mJ as reminded that the original protocol (*Phase 2*) requires devices to spend 47.6 mJ (4 hash and 5 multiplication operations with 0.057 mJ per hash and 9.48 mJ per ECC operation) to authenticate with the server. Regarding the storage needed, each device needs only spaces to store a session key (128-bit length) for each device it communicates with. In addition, an expiry time (64-bit) may also be stored for the session. For those reasons, our enhanced protocol successfully preserves the advantages of the original one as most of the data needed for authentication are stored at the server, which will lower the storage burden at the device end.

## 8    Conclusions and Future Work

In this paper, we introduce a new authentication scheme allowing both device-to-server and device-to-device communications in IoT systems. If a device gets the approval from its control server to be a part of the system, this server will support it in authenticating with other devices. When the authentication process completes, two devices can communicate without the participation of their server. It is essential to not only reduce the workload of the servers but also to restrain server-dependence of embedded devices. This new authentication protocol is proposed in order to achieve such goals. We use ECC and simple operations to provide a authentication protocol not only light-weight but also safe. Security analysis conducted in our work shows the resistance to common cyber attacks in the IoT environment of the proposed scheme. Furthermore, we prove that our scheme only consumes an additional amount of approximately 38.2 mJ for device-device authentication phase and takes just 128-bit for storing its session key and a small space for its expiry time. Through theoretical profound analysis, we demonstrate that the scheme is safe and can be applied with light-weight embedded devices. In the future, we will do further research about the privacy preserving in the protocol to improve the security level of the proposed scheme. Since most of embedded devices nowadays have sensors to detect changes in the real world, the information they contain may accordingly be sensitive and should not be exposed. The association of the authentication process and different kinds of privacy protection [31–33] are possibilities to extend the security capabilities of our protocol, especially with resource-constrained IoT devices. On this account, which data can be shared between two devices after completing authenticating is a huge problem that should be further studied.

**Acknowledgement.** This research is funded by Vietnam National University Ho Chi Minh City (VNU-HCM) under grant number B2018-20-08. We also thank other members of the project, specially PhD candidates: Tran Tri Dang, Ai Thao Nguyen Thi, and Que-Nguyet Tran Thi, for their meaningful help and comments during this paper preparation.

# References

1. Ashton, K.: That "Internet of Things" thing. RFID J. **2**(5), 97–114 (2009)
2. IHS. n.d. Number of Internet of Things (IoT) devices connected worldwide in 2017 and 2018, by selected type (in millions), Statista. https://www.statista.com/statistics/789615/worldwide-connected-iot-devices-by-type/. Accessed 22 Nov 2018
3. IHS. n.d. Internet of Things (IoT) Connected Devices Installed Base Worldwide from 2015 to 2025 (in billions), Statista. https://www.statista.com/statistics/471264/iot-number-of-connected-devices-worldwide/. Accessed 22 Nov 2018
4. LeHong, H., Velosa, A.: Hype cycle for the internet of things. Gartner Group, 21 (2014)
5. Zhou, Q, Zhang, J.: Research prospect of Internet of Things geography. In: 19th International Conference on Geoinformatics 2011, pp. 1–5. IEEE (2011)
6. Yu, Y., Wang, J., Zhou, G.: The exploration in the education of professionals in applied Internet of Things engineering. In: 4th International Conference on Distance Learning and Education, pp. 74–77. IEEE (2010)
7. Desai, P., Sheth, A., Anantharam, P.: Semantic gateway as a service architecture for IoT interoperability. In: International Conference on Mobile Services, pp. 313–319. IEEE (2015)
8. Oren, Y., Keromytis, A.D.: From the aether to the ethernet-attacking the internet using broadcast digital television. In: 23rd USENIX Security Symposium (USENIX Security 14), pp. 353–368 (2014)
9. Cesare, S.: Breaking the security of physical devices. Talk at Blackhat, 14 (2014)
10. Liang, L., Zheng, K., Sheng, Q., Huang, X.: A denial of service attack method for an IoT system. In: 8th International Conference on Information Technology in Medicine and Education, pp. 360–364. IEEE (2016)
11. Vasilomanolakis, E., Daubert, J., Luthra, M., Gazis, V., Wiesmaier, A., Kikiras, P.: On the security and privacy of internet of things architectures and systems. In: 2015 International Workshop on Secure Internet of Things, pp. 49–57. IEEE (2015)

12. Alkurd, R., Shubair, R.M., Abualhaol, I.: Survey on device-to-device communications: challenges and design issues. In: 12th International New Circuits and Systems Conference (NEWCAS), pp. 361–364. IEEE (2014)
13. Nguyen, K.T., Laurent, M., Oualha, N.: Survey on secure communication protocols for the Internet of Things. Ad Hoc Netw. **32**, 17–31 (2015)
14. Nguyen, T.A.T., Dang, T.K.: Enhanced security in internet voting protocol using blind signature and dynamic ballots. Electron. Commer. Res. **13**(3), 257–272 (2013)
15. Tran, K.K., Pham, M.K., Dang, T.K.: A light-weight tightening authentication scheme for the objects' encounters in the meetings. In: Dang, T.K., Küng, J., Wagner, R., Thoai, N., Takizawa, M. (eds.) FDSE 2018. LNCS, vol. 11251, pp. 83–102. Springer, Cham (2018). https://doi.org/10.1007/978-3-030-03192-3_8
16. Nechvatal, J.: Public key cryptography. In: Simmons, G. (ed.) Contemporary Cryptology: The Science of Information Integrity. IEEE (1992)
17. Dierks, T., Allen, C.: The TLS protocol version 1.0 (1999)
18. Rescorla, E., Modadugu, N.: Datagram transport layer security (2006)
19. Kothmayr, T., Schmitt, C., Hu, W., Brünig, M., Carle, G.: A DTLS based end-to-end security architecture for the Internet of Things with two-way authentication. In: 37th Annual IEEE Conference on Local Computer Networks-Workshops, pp. 956–963. IEEE (2012)
20. Rabin, M.O.: Digitalized signatures and public-key functions as intractable as factorization (No. MIT/LCS/TR-212), Massachusetts Instituite of Technology Cambridge Laboratory for Computer Science (1979)
21. He, D., Zeadally, S.: An analysis of RFID authentication schemes for Internet of Things in healthcare environment using elliptic curve cryptography. IEEE IoT J. **2**(1), 72–83 (2014)
22. Chaudhry, S.A., Farash, M.S., Naqvi, H., Sher, M.: A secure and efficient authenticated encryption for electronic payment systems using elliptic curve cryptography. Electron. Commer. Res. **16**(1), 113–139 (2016)
23. Gura, N., Patel, A., Wander, A., Eberle, H., Shantz, S.C.: Comparing elliptic curve cryptography and RSA on 8-bit CPUs. In: Joye, M., Quisquater, J.-J. (eds.) CHES 2004. LNCS, vol. 3156, pp. 119–132. Springer, Heidelberg (2004). https://doi.org/10.1007/978-3-540-28632-5_9
24. Chang, S.M., Shieh, S., Lin, W.W., Hsieh, C.M.: An efficient broadcast authentication scheme in wireless sensor networks. In: Proceedings of the ACM Symposium on Information, Computer and Communications Security, pp. 311–320. ACM (2006)
25. Khemissa, H., Tandjaoui, D., Bouzefrane, S.: An ultra-lightweight authentication scheme for heterogeneous wireless sensor networks in the context of Internet of Things. In: Bouzefrane, S., Banerjee, S., Sailhan, F., Boumerdassi, S., Renault, E. (eds.) MSPN 2017. LNCS, vol. 10566, pp. 49–62. Springer, Cham (2017). https://doi.org/10.1007/978-3-319-67807-8_4
26. Wang, K.H., Chen, C.M., Fang, W., Wu, T.Y.: A secure authentication scheme for Internet of Things. Pervasive Mobile Comput. **42**, 15–26 (2017)
27. Kalra, S., Sood, S.K.: Secure authentication scheme for IoT and cloud servers. Pervasive Mobile Comput. **24**, 210–223 (2015)
28. Chang, C.C., Wu, H.L., Sun, C.Y.: Notes on "Secure authentication scheme for IoT and cloud servers". Pervasive Mobile Comput. **38**, 275–278 (2017)
29. De Meulenaer, G., Gosset, F., Standaert, F.X., Pereira, O.: On the energy cost of communication and cryptography in wireless sensor networks. In: IEEE International Conference on Wireless and Mobile Computing, Networking and Communications, pp. 580–585. IEEE (2008)

30. Kausar, F., Hussain, S., Park, J.H., Masood, A.: Secure group communication with self-healing and rekeying in wireless sensor networks. In: Zhang, H., Olariu, S., Cao, J., Johnson, D.B. (eds.) MSN 2007. LNCS, vol. 4864, pp. 737–748. Springer, Heidelberg (2007). https://doi.org/10.1007/978-3-540-77024-4_67

31. Thi, Q.N.T., Si, T.T., Dang, T.K.: Fine grained attribute based access control model for privacy protection. In: Dang, T.K., Wagner, R., Küng, J., Thoai, N., Takizawa, M., Neuhold, E. (eds.) FDSE 2016. LNCS, vol. 10018, pp. 305–316. Springer, Cham (2016). https://doi.org/10.1007/978-3-319-48057-2_21

32. Nguyen, T.A.T., Dang, T.K.: Privacy preserving biometric-based remote authentication with secure processing unit on untrusted server. IET Biometrics 8(1), 79–91 (2018)

33. Dang, T.K., Tran, K.T.: The meeting of acquaintances: a cost-efficient authentication scheme for light-weight objects with transient trust level and plurality approach. Secur. Commun. Netw. 2019, 18 (2019)

# Adventures in the Analysis of Access Control Policies

Anh Truong[✉]

Ho Chi Minh City University of Technology, VNU-HCM, Ho Chi Minh City, Vietnam
anhtt@hcmut.edu.vn

**Abstract.** Access Control is becoming increasingly important for today's ubiquitous systems which provide mechanism to prevent sensitive resources against unauthorized users. In access control models, the administration of access control policies is an important task that raises a crucial analysis problem: if a set of administrators can give a user an unauthorized access permission. In this paper, we consider the analysis problem in the context of the Administrative Role-Based Access Control (ARBAC), one of the most widespread administrative models. We describe how we design heuristics to enable an analysis tool, called ASASPXL, to scale up to handle large and complex ARBAC policies and a sequence of analysis problems. An extensive experimentation shows that the proposed heuristics play a key role in the success of the analysis tool over the state-of-the-art analysis tools.

**Keywords:** Access control · Security analysis · Automated verification · Model checking · Role-Based Access Control

## 1 Introduction

Modern information systems contain sensitive information and resources that need to be protected against unauthorized users who want to steal it. The most important mechanism to prevent this is Access Control [4] which is thus becoming increasingly important for today's ubiquitous systems. In general, access control systems protect the resources of the systems by controlling who has permission to access what objects/resources.

Today, one of the most widely adopted access control models in the real world is Role-Based Access Control (RBAC) model [12]. In general, RBAC access control policies specify which users can be assigned to roles which, in turn, are granted permissions to perform certain operations in the system. RBAC policies need to be evolved according to the rapidly changing environments and thus, it is demanded to have some mechanisms to control the modification of the policies. Administrative RBAC (ARBAC) [3] is the corresponding widely used administrative model for RBAC policies. In ARBAC, certain specific users, called administrators, are provided some permissions to execute operations, called administrative actions, to modify the RBAC policies. In fact, permissions to perform

© Springer Nature Switzerland AG 2019
T. K. Dang et al. (Eds.): FDSE 2019, LNCS 11814, pp. 467–482, 2019.
https://doi.org/10.1007/978-3-030-35653-8_31

administrative actions must be restricted since administrators can only be partially trusted. For instances, some of them may collude to, inadvertently or maliciously, modify the policies (by sequences of administrative actions) so that untrusted users can get sensitive permissions. Thus, automated analysis techniques taking into consideration the effect of all possible sequences of administrative actions to identify the safety issues, i.e. administrative actions generating policies by which a user can acquire permissions that may compromise some security goals, are needed.

Several automated analysis techniques (see, e.g., [1,5,10,15,16]) have been developed for solving the user-role reachability problem, an instance of the safety issues, in the ARBAC model. Recently, a tool called ASASPXL [11] has been shown to perform better than the state-of-the-art tools on sets of benchmark problems in [9,15]. The main advantage of the analysis technique inside ASASPXL over the state-of-the-art techniques is that the tool can solve the user-role reachability problem with respect to a finite but unknown number of users in the policies manipulated by the administrative actions. However, ASASPXL does not scale to solve problems in some recently proposed benchmarks in [16]. This is because the so-called state explosion problem has not been handled carefully and thus, prevent ASASPXL to tackle such benchmarks. Additionally, ASASPXL does not also scale to solve a sequence of reachability problems. The main reason is that the explored states during the previous analysis processes are not optimized.

In this paper, we study how to design heuristics to enable ASASPXL to analyze large and complex instances of user-role reachability problems and also to analyse the sequence of reachability problems more efficiently. The main idea is to try to alleviate the state explosion problem, which is well-known problem in model checking techniques, and reuse as many as possible the explored states, in the analysis of ARBAC policies. We also perform an exhaustive experiment to conduct the effectiveness of proposed heuristics and compare ASASPXL's performance with the state-of-the-art analysis tools.

The paper is organized as follows. Section 2 introduces the RBAC, ARBAC models, and the related analysis problem. Section 3 briefly introduces the framework to automatically analyse the infinite state transition systems, namely MCMT. The proposed heuristics to enable ASASPXL to scale to solve user-role reachability problem are described in Sect. 4. Section 5 summarizes our experiments and Sect. 6 concludes the paper.

## 2    Administrative Role-Based Access Control

In the *Role-Based Access Control (RBAC)* model [12], access decisions are based on the roles that individual users have as part of an organization. Permissions are grouped by role name and correspond to various uses of a resource. Roles can have overlapping responsibilities and privileges, i.e. users belonging to different roles may have common permissions. Thus, it would be inefficient to repeatedly specify common permissions for a certain set of roles. To overcome this problem, (so-called) role hierarchies reflect the natural structure of an enterprise and make the specification of policies more compact by requiring that one role may implicitly include the permissions that are associated with another role.

Once RBAC policies are determined they need to be maintained according to the evolving needs of the organization. For flexibility and scalability, large systems usually require several administrators, and thus there is a need not only to have a consistent RBAC policy but also to ensure that the policy is only modified by the administrators who are allowed to do so. One of the most popular administrative frameworks is the Administrative RBAC (ARBAC) model [3] whose main insight is to use RBAC to control how RBAC policies may evolve through administrative actions that assign or revoke user memberships into roles. Since administrators can be only partially trusted, administration privileges must be limited to selected parts of the RBAC policies, called *administrative domains*. The ARBAC model defines administrative domains by using roles and RBAC itself to control how security officers can delegate (part of) their administrative permissions to trusted users. In this way, several administrators are able to modify the RBAC policy of a large system by following certain rules.

**Formalization.** Let $U$ be a set of users, $R$ a set of roles, and $P$ a set of permissions. Users are associated to roles by a binary relation $UA \subseteq U \times R$ and roles are associated to permissions by another binary relation $PA \subseteq R \times P$. A role hierarchy is a partial order $\succeq$ on $R$, where $r_1 \succeq r_2$ means that $r_1$ is *more senior than* $r_2$ for $r_1, r_2 \in R$. A user $u$ is a *member* of role $r$ when $(u, r) \in UA$. A user $u$ *has permission* $p$ if there exists a role $r \in R$ such that $(p, r) \in PA$ and $u$ is a member of $r$. A *RBAC policy* is a tuple $(U, R, P, UA, PA, \succeq)$.

Usually (see, e.g., [15]), administrators may only update the relation $UA$ while $PA$ and $\succeq$ are assumed constant. An administrative domain is specified by a *pre-condition*, i.e. a finite set of expressions of the forms $r$ or $\bar{r}$ (for $r \in R$), called *role literals*. A user $u \in U$ *satisfies* a pre-condition $C$ if, for each $\ell \in C$, $u$ is a member of $r$ when $\ell$ is $r$ or $u$ is not a member of $r$ when $\ell$ is $\bar{r}$ for $r \in R$. Permission to assign users to roles is specified by a ternary relation *can_assign* containing tuples of the form $(C_a, C, r)$ where $C_a$ and $C$ are pre-conditions, and $r$ a role. Permission to revoke users from roles is specified by a binary relation *can_revoke* containing tuples of the form $(C_a, r)$ where $C_a$ is a pre-condition and $r$ a role. In both cases, we say that $C_a$ is the *administrative pre-condition*, $C$ is a *(simple) pre-condition*, $r$ is the *target role*, and a user $u_a$ satisfying $C_a$ is the *administrator*. When there exist users satisfying the administrative and the simple (if the case) pre-conditions of an administrative action, the action is *enabled*. The relation *can_revoke* is only binary because simple pre-conditions are useless when revoking roles (see, e.g., [15]).

The semantics of the administrative actions in $\psi := (can\_assign, can\_revoke)$ is given by the binary relation $\rightarrow_\psi$ defined as follows: $UA \rightarrow_\psi UA'$ iff there exist users $u_a$ and $u$ in $U$ such that either $(i)$ there exists $(C_a, C, r) \in can\_assign$, $u_a$ satisfies $C_a$, $u$ satisfies $C$ (i.e. $(C_a, C, r)$ is enabled), and $UA' = UA \cup \{(u, r)\}$ or $(ii)$ there exists $(C_a, r) \in can\_revoke$, $u_a$ satisfies $C_a$ (i.e. $(C_a, r)$ is enabled), and $UA' = UA \setminus \{(u, r)\}$. A *run* of the administrative actions in $\psi :=$

$(can\_assign, can\_revoke)$ is a possibly infinite sequence $UA_0, UA_1, ..., UA_n, ...$ such that $UA_i \rightarrow_\psi UA_{i+1}$ for every $i \geq 0$.

A pair $(u_g, R_g)$ is called a *(RBAC) goal* for $u_g \in U$ and $R_g$ a finite set of roles. The cardinality $|R_g|$ of $R_g$ is the *size* of the goal. Given an initial RBAC policy $UA_0$, a goal $(u_g, R_g)$, and administrative actions $\psi = (can\_assign, can\_revoke)$; (an instance of) the *user-role reachability problem* consists of establishing if there exists a finite sequence $UA_0, UA_1, ..., UA_n$ (for $n \geq 0$) where (i) $UA_i \rightarrow_\psi UA_{i+1}$ for each $i = 0, ..., n - 1$ and (ii) in the policy $UA_n$ we have that $u_g$ is a member (explicit or implicit) of each role in $R_g$.

The definition of the user-role reachability problem considered here is the same of that in [15]. In the rest of the paper, we focus on user-role reachability problems where $U$ and $R$ are finite, $P$ plays no role, and $\succeq$ is ignored because it can be eliminated by a pre-processing [13]. Thus, a RBAC policy is a tuple $(U, R, UA)$ or simply $UA$ when $U$ and $R$ are clear from the context.

# 3    Framework to Analyse Infinite State Transition Systems

MCMT [7] attempts to solve reachability problems for a certain class of infinite state systems whose state variables are arrays, that can be seen as functions mapping indexes to elements. Such transition systems can be used as suitable abstractions of parametrised protocols, sequential programs manipulating arrays, etc. The main idea underlying MCMT is to use a backward reachability procedure that repeatedly computes pre-images of the set of *goal* states, that is usually obtained by complementing a certain safety property that the system should satisfy. The set of backward reachable states of the system is obtained by taking the union of such pre-images. At each iteration of the procedure, it is checked whether the intersection with the initial set of states is non-empty (*safety* test), reporting the *unsafety* of the system, i.e. there exists a (finite) sequence of transitions that leads the system from an initial state to one satisfying the goal. Otherwise, when the intersection is empty, it is checked if the set of backward reachable states is contained in the set computed at the previous iteration (*fix-point* test), reporting the *safety* of the system, i.e. no (finite) sequence of transitions leads the system from an initial state to one satisfying the goal. The peculiarity of MCMT is that sets of states and transitions are represented by first-order formulae so that the computation of pre-images boils down to logical manipulations and the safety and fix-point tests are reduced to satisfiability checks of first-order formulae. The resulting satisfiability problems are efficiently solved by state-of-the-art tools, called Satisfiability Modulo Theories (SMT) solvers.

MCMT was successfully used for the verification of several infinite state systems [6] and features some interesting heuristics to automatically synthesize invariants that can be used to prune the search space of the system that become also available to the user for a deeper understanding of the structure of the system. For more details on MCMT, the interested reader is pointed to [7]. Since model checking techniques have been found quite useful for the analysis of authorization policies, it would be interesting to apply MCMT in this context. Unfortunately, as observed in [1], there some practical problems to do this. Two of the most important ones are the following:

**P1** MCMT permits only mono-dimensional arrays while RBAC policies seem to require at least bi-dimensional arrays to encode the characteristic function of the binary relation $UA$.

**P2** MCMT restricts the number of existentially quantified variables in formulae representing transitions to (at most) two while can_assign and can_revoke actions usually require more of such variables.

These and other problems have lead us to build a new tool, called ASASP [1], based on the same ideas of MCMT but specifically tuned for the symbolic analysis of authorization policies. We were successfull in doing this as ASASP shows a better scalability than RBAC-PAT [8] on a set of synthetic user-role reachability problems introduced in [15]. However, our aim in building ASASP was to reach a good trade-off between efficiency and expressivity. In fact, we were able to extend the classical ARBAC policies with attributes and to efficiently solve the associated user-role reachability problems in [2]. Key to the expressivity of ASASP input language is the capability of handling arbitrary (possibly infinite) set of roles—such as those depending on parameters, see, e.g., [14]—and several existentially quantified variables in formulae representing transitions that are fundamental to express conditions involving role hierarchies and attribute values [2].

Almost at the same time of [1], a new tool, called MOHAWK [9], has been proposed for the analysis of ARBAC policies especially tailored to error-finding rather than verification as it is the case of both RBAC-PAT and ASASP. In [9], it is shown that MOHAWK outperforms RBAC-PAT on the problems in [15] and on a new set of synthetic, much larger problems. Indeed, we tried ASASP on new problems of MOHAWK and, rather disappointingly, it was not able to scale up and handle large problem instances. After a careful analysis of the behavior of ASASP, we made the following crucial observations.

**O1** Since the set $R$ of roles is finite, it is not necessary to use the binary relation $UA$ to record user-role assignments. It is sufficient to replace it with a finite collection of sets, one per role. Formally, let $R = \{r_1, ..., r_n\}$ for $n \geq 1$, define $U_{r_i} = \{u | (u, r_i) \in UA\}$ for $i = 1, ..., n$. Straightforward modifications to the definition of $\rightarrow_\psi$ (for $\psi$ a pair of relations can_assign and can_revoke), given in Sect. 2, allows one to replace $UA$ with the $U_{r_i}$'s.

**O2** Since the role-hierarchy can be pre-processed before attempting to solve a user-role reachability problem (see, e.g., [13]), the definition of $\rightarrow_\psi$, for a given tuple in can_assign or can_revoke, existentially quantifies over two users, the administrator and the user to which the administrative action is going to be applied.

On the one hand, the two observations suggest that ASASP expressivity is too much for modelling large synthetic problems (as those in [9]) that are characterized by simple pre-conditions in which even role hierarchies are not used. Since it is well-known that expressivity and efficiency are opposing forces when developing automated analysis techniques, we believe this to be one of the main reasons for the poor results obtained by ASASP on the problems in [9]. On the other hand, **O1** and **O2** pave the way to the use of MCMT on this kind of synthetic problems as they remove the two problems discussed above. In particular, we can represent the characteristic function of a $U_{r_i}$ by using a mono-dimensional array $a_{r_i}$ mapping users to Booleans; thus overcoming **P1**. Also **P2** is no more a problem as MCMT supports the definition of transitions by formulae containing (at most) two existentially quantified variables.

We illustrate the encoding in MCMT of user-role reachability problem by means of an excerpt of an example from [15].

*Example 1.* Let $U = \{u_1, u_2\}$, $R = \{r_a, r_1, ..., r_8\}$, and $UA := \{(u_1, r_1), (u_1, r_4), (u_1, r_7), (u_2, r_a)\}$ and the tuple $(\{r_a\}, \{r_1\}, r_2)$ is in can_assign whereas the tuple $(\{r_a\}, r_1)$ is in can_revoke. The goal of the user-role reachability problem is $\{(u_1, r_6)\}$.

To formalize this problem in MCMT, we introduce one array per role $u_r$ for $r \in R$ mapping a user in $U$ to a Boolean that encodes the characteristic function of the set $U_r$, as defined above. The initial relation $UA$ can be expressed as follows:

$$\forall x. \left[ \begin{array}{l} u_{r_1}(x) \leftrightarrow x = u_1 \wedge u_{r_4}(x) \leftrightarrow x = u_1 \wedge u_{r_7}(x) \leftrightarrow x = u_1 \wedge u_{r_a}(x) \leftrightarrow u = u_2 \wedge \\ \neg u_{r_2}(x) \wedge \neg u_{r_3}(x) \wedge \neg u_{r_5}(x) \wedge \neg u_{r_6}(x) \end{array} \right]$$

The tuple $(\{r_a\}, \{r_1\}, r_2)$ in can_assign is formalized as

$$\exists x_a, x. \left[ u_{r_a}(x_a) \wedge u_{r_1}(x) \wedge \forall y. (u'_{r_2}(y) \leftrightarrow (y = x \vee u_{r_2}(x))) \right]$$

and $(\{r_a\}, r_1)$ in can_revoke as

$$\exists x_a, x. \left[ u_{r_a}(x_a) \wedge u_{r_1}(x) \wedge \forall y. (u'_{r_1}(y) \leftrightarrow (y \neq x \wedge u_{r_2}(x))) \right]$$

where $u_r$ and $u'_r$ indicates the value of $U_r$ immediately before and after, respectively, of the execution of the administrative action and we have omitted identical updates, i.e. a conjunct $\forall y. (u'_r(y) \leftrightarrow u_r(y))$ for each $r$ not mentioned in the formula. Finally, the goal can be represented as $\exists x. u_{r_6}(x) \wedge x = u_1$.     □

We built a translator to create MCMT reachability problems out of user-role reachability problems and MCMT on the problems resulting from the translations of those in [9]: the results were still disappointing in terms of scalability. After analysing the behavior of MCMT, we identified another important source of complexity: the number of transitions or, equivalently, the number of tuples in can_assign and can_revoke is so large that the heuristics implemented in MCMT to control the state space explosion problem are not enough. This is due to the fact that the problems that MCMT is successful in solving comprise tens of transitions, each one involving complex conditions and updates of data structures and updates. Instead, the transitions obtained from the translation of user-role reachability problems in [9] are hundreds or thousands (up to 80,000) involving, as discussed above and shown in the example, simple conditions and updates. In the following section, we describe how this difficulty can be tamed by designing a suitable wrapper around MCMT in order to generate a sequence of user-role reachability problems with an increasing number of transitions. We will also explain how the solution of the problem $P_i$ (for $i > 0$) in the sequence can be speeded up by caching the invariants synthesized by MCMT in the runs to solve $P_0, ..., P_{i-1}$. The synthesized invariants encode "structural" properties of the user-assignment relation $UA$; e.g., 'a given role can be assigned to no user' or 'if a user is not assigned to a certain set of roles then he/she will not be assigned to the roles in another set.' Clearly, this kind of properties is using when solving problem $P_i$. For example, if we know from a previous run of MCMT that no user can be assigned to role $r_7$ and the goal of the user-role reachability problem is $(u, \{r_1, r_7, r_9\})$, we can immediately conclude that the goal is unreachable.

## 4    asasp 2.1: New Clothes for Analyzing ARBAC Policies

In this section, we describe the architecture of our technique. ASASP 2.1 receives an ARBAC policy and a safety query as its input. In case it finds a sequence of transitions (including can_assign, can_revoke rules) that leads the RBAC system to the query state, the result UNSAFE is reported. Otherwise, ASASP 2.1 reports that the system is SAFE. Figure 1 illustrates the architecture of ASASP 2.1.

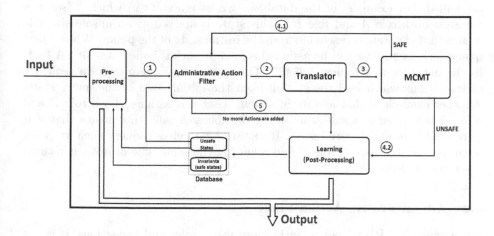

**Fig. 1.** ASASP 2.1 architecture

In general, the policy and the query are verified through the following steps:

**Pre-processing:** The query is analyzed to find the answer in the database. If an answer is found, the result is reported without running the remains of the technique.

**Administrative Action Filter:** The policy and the query are analyzed to filter the related transitions and roles for current verification step.

**Model checking:** The technique verifies the filtered policy. The model checker MCMT [7] is used in the verification.

**Learning:** The learning component analyzes the verification result before outputting them.

We discuss the details of these steps here in the remains of this section. Because of the separate administration restriction [..], we do not care the administrative roles in ASASP 2.1.

### 4.1   Pre-processing

In general, the time spent in running the model checker holds the most important part in the amount of time taken for the verification process of automatic analysis techniques. Therefore, if we reduce the time spent in running the model checker, the total time will also be reduced significantly. With our technique, if the answer is found in this pre-processing step, ASASP 2.1 returns the result without calling other components, including MCMT, and hence the time for verification process is reduced.

In order to speed up the verification processes, the states which have been visited in the previous verifications are saved to a database. When a new query is issued, ASASP 2.1 first checks the database to find the answer for the query. If it finds the answer, the result is reported. Otherwise, the remains of the technique are called. For example: in the database, we have a state in which "User $x$ is assigned both role $A$ and role $B$." This state is marked as an unsafe state. It means that the state is reachable from the initial state of the policy. When a new query such as "User $x$ can be assigned role $A$ or not" is issued, ASASP 2.1 finds in the database and returns UNSAFE. This means that there exists a sequence of transitions which lead the system from the initial state to the query state. Another example is that a state in which "User $y$ is assigned both role $B$ and role $C$" is marked as a safe state in the database. A safe state means that it is unreachable from the initial state. If ASASP 2.1 receives a query such as "User $y$ can be assigned role $A$, role $B$ and role $C$ at the same time or not", it returns the result SAFE quickly.

### 4.2   Administrative Action Filter

For a complex ARBAC policy with many users, roles and transitions, it is not efficient to analyze the entire policy. Many previous techniques fail to verify these policies. The reason is that the model checkers used in these techniques require large resources, including memory and processor, to verify the entire policies, meanwhile, hardware technologies currently can not satisfy these requirements. Therefore, there is a need to filter these policies before sending to the model checkers for verifying. The model checkers then can verify these filtered policies in a reasonable time.

In this analysis step, our technique removes all the redundant transitions, users and roles which do not relate to the current verification process. Moreover, the technique also reuses the states which have been verified in the previous verification processes to speed up the current verification.

The idea to filter the complex policies comes from the one in [9]. In this technique, the authors refine the complex policies according to the related-by-assignment relationship between roles. At each refinement step, the technique selects the users, roles and transitions which relate to the roles in the current priority degree. The refined policy is then verified by a model checker. In our technique, we do not define the priority of each role, we just care which roles is related to the current analysis step. The roles related to the first analysis step are the roles in the safety query. We call the set of the roles related to the current analysis step as a current related role set. In the current analysis step, ASASP 2.1 analysis the policy to extract the transitions related to current analysis step. A transition is related to the current analysis step if its goal contains at least one role in the current related role set. For example, in the first analysis step of the policy in Fig. 2, the current related role set contains role Manager. The set of the transitions related to the first analysis step contains $(Admin, QC \wedge IT, Manager)$, $(Admin, Tester, Manager)$, and $(Admin, Manager)$.

> **Roles:**    Admin, Manager, Developer, QA, QC, Tester, IT
> **UA:**       (Alice, Admin) (Bob, Developer) (Bob, QA)
> **Can_revoke rules:**
>               (Admin, Manager)
>               (Admin, Developer)
>               (Admin, Tester)
> **Can_assign rules:**
>               (Admin, Developer ^ QA, Tester ^ QC)
>               (Admin, QC ^ IT, Manager)
>               (Admin, Tester, Manager)
>               (Admin, True, Developer)
> **Safety query:**
>               Bob, Manager

**Fig. 2.** An example of ARBAC policy

Moreover, ASASP 2.1 also considers removing the transitions which are not able to be executed in the current verification step. The idea comes from the observation that a transition may be executed if the preconditions of the transition are satisfied (e.g., the transition $(Admin, QC \wedge IT, Manager)$ may be executed if there is at least one user who has both roles $QC$ and $IT$). In our technique, we use the idea with less constraint as follows: a transition may be executed (and therefore this transition will be added to the current filtered policy) if each role in its precondition is:

- In the initial state or
- In the current related role set and there is at least a transition in the original policy whose goal contains the role.

For example in Fig. 2; we assume that the current related role set includes Manager and Tester. The transition $(Admin, Developer \wedge QA, Tester \wedge QC)$ is a transition related to the current analysis step because its goal $Tester \wedge QC$ contains the role Tester. Furthermore, all roles in its precondition $Developer \wedge QA$ are in the initial state. This transition therefore is added to the current filtered policy. The transition $(Admin, QC \wedge IT, Manager)$ is also a transition related to the current analysis step. However, it is not added to the current filtered policy because the roles in its precondition are not in the current related role set and there is no transition whose goal contains the role $IT$.

After running the current analysis step, ASASP 2.1 will calculate the set of the roles related to next analysis step. The next related role set will contain all roles in the current related role set. Moreover, for each assignment transition (can_assign rule) in the set of the transitions related to the current analysis step, the roles in its precondition will also be added to the next related role set if: for each role in the precondition, there is at least a transition in the original policy whose goal contains the role. For example in Fig. 2, we assume that the current related role set includes Manager. The set of transitions related to the current analysis step is $\langle (Admin, QC \wedge IT, Manager), (Admin, Tester, Manager), (Admin, Manager) \rangle$. After running the analysis step, the next related role set will be $\langle Manager, Tester \rangle$. The roles $QC$ and $IT$ of the transition $(Admin, QC \wedge IT, Manager)$ are not added to the next related role set because there is no transition in the original policy whose goal contains the role $IT$.

One of the key points in our technique is to reuse the states which have been visited in the previous verifications. Normally, the users tend to query the policy many times with different safety queries, hence the reuse of visited states will reduce the time taken by the model checker significantly. In our technique, the results of the previous verifications were analyzed by the learning component after the model checker found the answer for the previous queries. All states extracted from the results and their statuses (safe or unsafe) were saved to the database. This information is then added to each analysis step of the current verification. Intuitively, each unsafe state can be considered as an initial state of the filtered policy of the current analysis step. If the state in the query can be reachable from one of these initial states, it is also unsafe. However, this implementation requires that the model checker supports the system with multiple initial states. In the current version of ASASP 2.1, we use another way to add the visited states to the current filtered policy. The idea is that:

- For each unsafe state, a new transition which "connects" the initial state to the unsafe state will be added to the filtered policy.
- For each safe state, we remove from the filtered policy the transitions whose preconditions contain the roles in the safe state.

For example in Fig. 3(a), from the previous verifications, state B, C and D are un-safe states while state G is a safe state. At the current verification, two new transitions are added and one transition is removed. The current policy is shown in Fig. 3(b). If we want to check state E, we just go backward to state C and

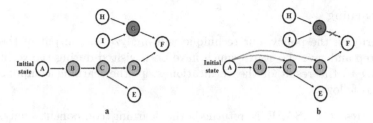

**Fig. 3.** Reusing visited states

then can reach the initial state. If we want to check state F, we do not care the states G, H and I.

After executing the current analysis step, the filtered policy is transfer to the verification step in order to determine whether the query state is safe or not. If the state is unsafe, ASASP 2.1 will call the learning step to analyze the results and then terminate the verification process. Otherwise, ASASP 2.1 will call the next analysis step to refilter the policy. After the next analysis step, if some transitions can be added to the current filtered policy, the verification step then will be called to verify the new filtered policy. If the current filtered policy is not changed, the results of the verification step will be transfer to the learning step and the verification process is terminated after finishing the learning step.

## 4.3 Model Checking

In this step, ASASP 2.1 translates the filtered policy and the query to an infinite state based system in the MCMT code. It then invokes MCMT to verify the system. If MCMT determines that the query is satisfied in the filtered policy, it returns the result UNSAFE as well as a log file. The log file contains a sequence of transitions that leads the system from the initial state to the query state. Similarly, the result SAFE and a log file are also returned if the model checker determines that the query is not satisfied in the filtered policy. In this case, the log file provides a list of invariants which are tracked during the verification. In case MCMT returns the result UNSAFE, the log file and the result are transferred to the learning component. In this component, the log file is analyzed in order to extract the unsafe states. No additional verification step is executed and the result is outputted after being analyzed. Conversely, ASASP 2.1 calls again the analysis step to refilter the policy with the next related role set and an additional verification step may then be executed. After the analysis step, if some additional transitions are added to the previous filtered policy, ASASP 2.1 will call the verification step again. Otherwise, it transfers the result and the log file of the previous verification step to the learning component. In this case, the learning component analyzes the log file to get the safe states and then outputs the result SAFE.

### 4.4 Learning

After verifying the policy, our technique will analyze the output of the verification step and save the states which have been visited during the verification. According to the result of the verification step, the learning component will process as follows:

- If the result UNSAFE is returned, the learning component analyzes the sequence of transitions which leads the RBAC system from the initial state to the query state. The states which are extracted from the analysis of these transitions then will be saved as unsafe states.
- If the result is SAFE, the learning component will extract invariants which have been tracked during the verification step. These invariants then will be saved as safe states.

In the next section, we provide an example to describe ASASP 2.1's operations in detail.

### 4.5 Worked Out Example

We illustrate ASASP 2.1's operations using the example in Fig. 2. The safety query in this example asks whether Bob can be assigned to the role Manager or not. Table 1 describes the status of the analysis component during the verification: (RS: Current related role set; RT: Current set of related transitions; NRS: Next related role set; FT: the set of transitions in the current filtered policy). After the analysis step 1, MCMT returns the result SAFE. Therefore, a new analysis step is executed. When MCMT verifies the filtered policy in the analysis step 2, the result UNSAFE is returned. ASASP 2.1 then calls the learning component to analyze the output of the verification step 2. The query state can be reached by executing the following sequence of transitions:

- *Bob* is assigned to *Tester* and *QC* by the transition (*Admin, Developer* ∧ *QA, Tester* ∧ *QC*).
- *Bob* is then assigned to *Manager* by the transition (*Admin, Tester, Manager*).

**Table 1.** The status of the analysis component during verification

| Step | RS | RT | NRS | FT | Result |
|---|---|---|---|---|---|
| 1 | *Manager* | (*Admin, QC* ∧ *IT, Manager*)<br>(*Admin, Tester, Manager*)<br>(*Admin, Manager*) | *Manager*<br>*Tester* | (*Admin, Manager*) | SAFE |
| 2 | *Manager*<br>*Tester* | (*Admin, Manager*)<br>(*Admin, Tester*)<br>(*Admin, Developer* ∧ *QA,*<br>*Tester* ∧ *QC*)<br>(*Admin, QC* ∧ *IT, Manager*)<br>(*Admin, Tester, Manager*) | *Manager*<br>*Tester* | (*Admin, Manager*)<br>(*Admin, Tester*)<br>(*Admin, Developer* ∧ *QA,*<br>*Tester* ∧ *QC*)<br>(*Admin, Tester, Manager*) | UNSAFE |

The learning component finds and saves the unsafe state (*Bob*, *Developer* $\wedge$ *QA* $\wedge$ *Tester* $\wedge$ *QC* $\wedge$ *Manager*) to the database. The state means that the user *Bob* has roles *Developer*, *QA*, *Tester*, *QC* and *Manager* at the same time. At the next verification, if the query asks whether *Bob* can be assigned to the role *QC* or not, ASASP 2.1 returns the result UNSAFE without running the model checker.

## 5    Experimental Evaluation

In this section, we show the evaluation we conducted in order to evaluate the effectiveness of our technique. In [9], the authors compared MOHAWK to other state-of-the-art verification tools for ARBAC policies such as symbolic model checking, bounded model checking and RBAC-PAT [8]. They also demonstrated that MOHAWK is more efficient than other tools. In this paper, instead of comparing our tool to the symbolic model checking, the bounded model checking or RBAC-PAT, we just compare ASASP to MOHAWK and show that our tool analyzes ARBAC policies better than MOHAWK.

We use the dataset which was used to compare MOHAWK to other verification tools as shown in [9]. The dataset includes three test suites. The first one (called as Test suite 1) contains policies with positive conjunctive can_assign rules and non-empty can_revoke rules. The second one (called as Test suite 2) includes policies with mixed conjunctive can_assign rules and empty can_revoke rules while the last one (Test suite 3) contains policies with mixed conjunctive can_assign rules and non-empty can_revoke rules. For each policy in the test suites, we call ASASP and MOHAWK 5 times with different safety queries and measure the average time taken for the verification process. All experiments were performed on an Intel Core 2 Duo T6600 (2.2 GHz) CPU, 2 GB Ram and Ubuntu 11.10.

Table 2 describes the experimental results.

MOHAWK takes two stages to verify an ARBAC policy. In the first stage, it slices the original policy and then, in the second stage, the sliced policy is verified by the refinement steps. We consider that the time taken for the verification process is the sum of time consumed by these stages. The table shows that our tool answers the safety queries faster than MOHAWK in most cases. In other word, these experimental results demonstrate the effectiveness of our technique.

We also test our technique in verifying a sequence of safety queries. It means that ASASP receives a set of safety queries, it verifies the first query and then the second query, and so on until the last query. We perform the verification of an ARBAC policy with a set of 8 different safety queries. Figure 4 shows that the time which ASASP takes for verifying n-th query is smaller than the one of the previous verifications. The reason is that ASASP reuses the states which have been visited in the previous verifications and hence, the time taken for the current verification may be reduced.

**Table 2.** Experimental results for single queries

| Test suite | Number of roles, rules | Time for verification | | | Variance | |
|---|---|---|---|---|---|---|
| | | Mohawk (Slicing time + Refinement time) | | ASASP 2.1 | Mohawk | ASASP 2.1 |
| Test suite 1 | 3, 15 | **0.42** | (0.17 + 0.25) | 0.12 | 0.00034 | 0.00126 |
| | 5, 25 | **0.50** | (0.20 + 0.30) | 0.22 | 0.00104 | 0.02188 |
| | 20, 100 | **0.60** | (0.28 + 0.32) | 0.11 | 0.00048 | 0.00314 |
| | 40, 200 | **0.94** | (0.39 + 0.55) | 0.10 | 0.19242 | 0.00294 |
| | 200, 1000 | **2.65** | (1.25 + 1.40) | 0.18 | 0.7027 | 0.02758 |
| | 500, 2500 | **4.87** | (2.27 + 2.60) | 0.43 | 7.0337 | 0.29594 |
| | 4000, 20000 | **16.90** | (11.41 + 5.49) | 1.64 | 1.26694 | 0.11166 |
| | 20000, 80000 | **71.56** | (44.70 + 26.86) | 24.17 | 7.56264 | 0.27724 |
| | 30000, 120000 | **195.54** | (119.39 + 76.15) | 59.08 | 66.4833 | 0.38058 |
| | 40000, 200000 | **455.14** | (263.82 + 191.32) | 109.07 | 32.35406 | 2.42496 |
| | 80000, 400000 | **2786.33** | (1600.22 + 1186.11) | 398.63 | 1251.832 | 0.51542 |
| Test suite 2 | 3, 15 | **0.40** | (0.16 + 0.24) | 0.12 | 0.00046 | 0.00204 |
| | 5, 25 | **0.50** | (0.19 + 0.31) | 0.21 | 0.0019 | 0.02012 |
| | 20, 100 | **0.54** | (0.25 + 0.29) | 0.10 | 0.00036 | 0.00242 |
| | 40, 200 | **1.21** | (0.37 + 0.84) | 0.10 | 1.07136 | 0.00108 |
| | 200, 1000 | **2.54** | (1.24 + 1.30) | 0.14 | 0.6452 | 0.01008 |
| | 500, 2500 | **5.02** | (2.29 + 2.73) | 0.43 | 5.91882 | 0.32836 |
| | 4000, 20000 | **14.33** | (9.65 + 4.68) | 1.48 | 0.53058 | 0.06206 |
| | 20000, 80000 | **74.32** | (45.35 + 28.97) | 24.99 | 13.9347 | 0.0716 |
| | 30000, 120000 | **194.85** | (115.58 + 79.27) | 57.09 | 42.39056 | 0.18292 |
| | 40000, 200000 | **470.89** | (262.39 + 208.50) | 98.49 | 585.6608 | 0.26196 |
| | 80000, 400000 | **2753.12** | (1589.97 + 1163.15) | 360.96 | 1493.596 | 3.19596 |
| Test suite 3 | 3, 15 | **0.41** | (0.17 + 0.24) | 0.09 | 0.00012 | 0.00078 |
| | 5, 25 | **0.47** | (0.19 + 0.28) | 0.08 | 0.00164 | 0.0001 |
| | 20, 100 | **0.77** | (0.29 + 0.48) | 0.54 | 0.0771 | 0.08822 |
| | 40, 200 | **0.77** | (0.38 + 0.39) | 0.37 | 0.0012 | 0.00468 |
| | 200, 1000 | **5.93** | (1.53 + 4.4) | 1.51 | 47.2814 | 0.20348 |
| | 500, 2500 | **3.78** | (2.15 + 1.73) | 1.12 | 0.05662 | 0.00298 |
| | 4000, 20000 | **14.05** | (9.96 + 4.09) | 11.13 | 0.09255 | 0.317425 |
| | 20000, 80000 | **80.61** | (48.64 + 31.97) | 27.25 | 23.98093 | 2.974775 |
| | 30000, 120000 | **259.15** | (148.35 + 110.80) | 97.55 | 325.5216 | 6343.912 |
| | 40000, 200000 | **604.17** | (346.10 + 258.07) | 110.65 | 1247.141 | 110.9948 |
| | 80000, 400000 | **3477.19** | (1951.41 + 1525.78) | 402.22 | 2776.703 | 0.50856 |

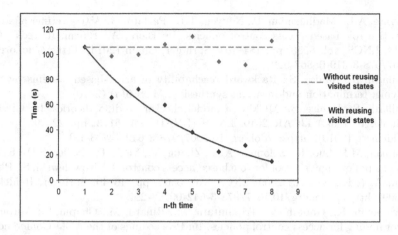

**Fig. 4.** Experimental results for a sequence of queries

# 6 Conclusions, Related and Future Work

We have presented techniques to enable the MCMT framework to solve instances of user-role reachability problem. We have also designed a set of heuristics that help our analysis techniques to be more scalable. The main idea is to reduce as much as possible the number of administrative actions in the original problem and reuse the visited states of previous analysis processes. We have shown that the proposed techniques do not miss errors in buggy policies and performs significantly better than MOHAWK on the larger problem instances in [9]. As future work, we plan to consider the combination of backward and forward reachability procedure to speed up the analysis of the model checker.

**Acknowledgements.** This work was funded by Vietnam National University-Ho Chi Minh City under the research project C2018-20-10.

# References

1. Alberti, F., Armando, A., Ranise, S.: ASASP: automated symbolic analysis of security policies. In: Bjørner, N., Sofronie-Stokkermans, V. (eds.) CADE 2011. LNCS (LNAI), vol. 6803, pp. 26–33. Springer, Heidelberg (2011). https://doi.org/10.1007/978-3-642-22438-6_4
2. Alberti, F., Armando, A., Ranise, S.: Efficient symbolic automated analysis of administrative role based access control policies. In: ASIACCS. ACM Pr. (2011)
3. Crampton, J.: Understanding and developing role-based administrative models. In: Proceedings 12th ACM Conference on Computer and Communication Security (CCS), pp. 158–167. ACM Press (2005)
4. De Capitani di Vimercati, S., Foresti, S., Jajodia, S., Samarati, P.: Access control policies and languages. Int. J. Comput. Sci. Eng. (IJCSE), **3**(2), 94–102 (2007)

5. Ferrara, A.L., Madhusudan, P., Nguyen, T.L., Parlato, G.: VAC - verifier of administrative role-based access control policies. In: Biere, A., Bloem, R. (eds.) CAV 2014. LNCS, vol. 8559, pp. 184–191. Springer, Cham (2014). https://doi.org/10.1007/978-3-319-08867-9_12

6. Ghilardi, S., Ranise, S.: Backward reachability of array-based systems by SMT solving: termination and invariant synthesis. LMCS **6**(4) (2010)

7. Ghilardi, S., Ranise, S.: MCMT: a model checker modulo theories. In: Giesl, J., Hähnle, R. (eds.) IJCAR 2010. LNCS (LNAI), vol. 6173, pp. 22–29. Springer, Heidelberg (2010). https://doi.org/10.1007/978-3-642-14203-1_3

8. Gofman, M.I., Luo, R., Solomon, A.C., Zhang, Y., Yang, P., Stoller, S.D.: RBAC-PAT: a policy analysis tool for role based access control. In: Kowalewski, S., Philippou, A. (eds.) TACAS 2009. LNCS, vol. 5505, pp. 46–49. Springer, Heidelberg (2009). https://doi.org/10.1007/978-3-642-00768-2_4

9. Jayaraman, K., Ganesh, V., Tripunitara, M., Rinard, M., Chapin, S.: Automatic error finding for access-control policies. In: Proceedings of the ACM Conference on Computer and Communications Security (CCS). ACM (2011

10. Li, N., Tripunitara, M.V.: Security analysis in role-based access control. ACM Trans. Inf. Syst. Secur. (TISSEC) **9**(4), 391–420 (2006)

11. Ranise, S., Truong, A., Armando, A.: Boosting model checking to analyse large ARBAC policies. In: Jøsang, A., Samarati, P., Petrocchi, M. (eds.) STM 2012. LNCS, vol. 7783, pp. 273–288. Springer, Heidelberg (2013). https://doi.org/10.1007/978-3-642-38004-4_18

12. Sandhu, R., Coyne, E., Feinstein, H., Youmann, C.: Role-based access control models. IEEE Comput. **2**(29), 38–47 (1996)

13. Sasturkar, A., Yang, P., Stoller, S.D., Ramakrishnan, C.R.: Policy analysis for administrative role based access control. In: Proceedings of the 19th Computer Security Foundations (CSF) Workshop. IEEE Computer Society Press, July 2006

14. Stoller, S.D., Yang, P., Gofman, M.I., Ramakrishnan, C.R.: Symbolic reachability analysis for parameterized administrative role based access control. In: Proceedings of SACMAT 2009, pp. 445–454 (2007)

15. Stoller, S.D., Yang, P., Ramakrishnan, C.R., Gofman, M.I.: Efficient policy analysis for administrative role based access control. In: Proceedings of the 14th Conference on Computer and Communications Security (CCS). ACM Press (2007)

16. Yang, P., Gofman, M.L., Stoller, S., Yang, Z.: Policy analysis for administrative role based access control without separate administration. J. Comput. Secur. (2014)

# Blockchain and Cybersecurity

# Detect Abnormal Behaviours in Ethereum Smart Contracts Using Attack Vectors

Quoc-Bao Nguyen[1], Anh-Quynh Nguyen[2], Van-Hoa Nguyen[3],
Thanh Nguyen-Le[3], and Khuong Nguyen-An[1(✉)]

[1] University of Technology (HCMUT), VNU-HCM, Ho Chi Minh City, Vietnam
{1510180,nakhuong}@hcmut.edu.vn
[2] Nanyang Technological University, Singapore, Singapore
aqnguyen@ntu.edu.sg
[3] Verichains Lab, Ho Chi Minh City, Vietnam
{vanhoa,thanh}@verichains.io

**Abstract.** Blockchain has gradually been popularized by its transparency, fairness, and democracy. This technology has opened the door to the development of Ethereum, a blockchain platform with smart contracts that can hold and automatically transfer tokens. Like a legacy computer program, smart contracts are vulnerable to security bugs. In recent years, many successful attacks on Ethereum network have been recorded, cost victims millions of dollars. In this paper, we classify attack vectors of Ethereum smart contracts, then propose some behaviour-based methods to detect them. To realize the ideas, we implement ABBE, a tool that can not only discover known attacks but also detect zero-day vulnerabilities.

**Keywords:** Smart contract · Security · Ethereum · Blockchain

## 1 Introduction

The term *smart contract* was conceived by Szabo [24] in 1994, which simply describes a computer program facilitating the terms and conditions of a real-world contract. These negotiations are presented as 'if-else' statements. For example, "if A transfers money to B, A may gain access to B's apartment". Different from normal contracts, smart contracts automatically enforce these negotiations once the predefined conditions are satisfied, without the interference of an authorized notary or a trusted third-party. Although this concept has existed since the early of 90s, due to a missing prerequisite, namely, a decentralized platform, smart contracts could not come into use until the birth of blockchain technology.

Since Nakamoto [18] introduced the concept of blockchain in 2008, a large amount of attention has been paid to this prominent technology. At this time, Nakamoto represented his idea through an implementation version named Bitcoin. The blockchain technology is claimed to have many interesting properties,

T. K. Dang et al. (Eds.): FDSE 2019, LNCS 11814, pp. 485–505, 2019.
https://doi.org/10.1007/978-3-030-35653-8_32

including *transparency, fairness*, and *democracy*. These properties are manifested whilst all member nodes in the network hold a replica of the blockchain shared-data. The data is publicly-verifiable, tamper-resistant even in the absence of a trusted party. This is because all nodes have equal rights to commit new updates into the shared-data of blockchain. In order to guarantee the network synchronization, every new update must be processed through a cryptographic scheme which ensures all new records are verified by all nodes and securely appended into the database of these nodes. In 2014, in the a improvement proposal of Bitcoin, a new op-code was added to describe a specific time in the future at which the transaction will be executed. There remains the fact that this enhancement is not enough to make up the features of a smart contract. In 2013, Buterin *et al.* [8] first combined the concept of smart contract and the blockchain technology and successfully implemented into a platform named Ethereum. Among current blockchain platforms, Ethereum, whose capitalization has reached 34 million dollars in June 2019[1], stands out to be the most prominent framework supporting smart contracts.

Due to being developed and running on top of blockchain infrastructure, smart contracts inherit certain interesting properties. The bytecode of smart contracts is immutable i.e., cannot be tampered once deployed. Moreover, the results returned after smart contract execution are irreversible and permanently recorded inside the blockchain database. However, smart contracts basically are computer programs which may contain vulnerabilities due to either mistakes of developers or the instinct of programming language. Recall that the most interesting property of smart contracts is the ability to hold *ether*, which creates economic incentive to be attacked. Many security vulnerabilities have been discovered by systematic exposition [2], practical development experience [10] and analysis of Ethereum smart contracts [14]. Some of these vulnerabilities actually *have been* exploited in real world attacks leading to *hundred millions dollars* drained [1,11,20,23].

To address these issues, many security research teams [14,17,21,26] have conducted solutions for auditing smart contracts' source code before deploying them onto the blockchain. However, this approach only deals with security issues in the development stage, which is before the execution stage in a life-cycle of a product. It is demanding to identify whether the execution of smart contracts contains any security issues. A solution addressing this problem can be helpful for smart contracts' developer team as they can detect abnormal behaviours, or worst, recognize money loss in their contracts and make quick responses to those incidents. Moreover, this solution can be used by blockchain developer to improve their infrastructure regarding to occurred issues. However, up to now, there is no related work tackling the above-mentioned problem.

Indeed, the smart contracts cannot start to execute themselves but have to be triggered by several external entities such as other contracts or, especially, by users. The appearance of security issues is now mostly from the transactions that users send to the smart contracts. This paper proposes several methods

---

[1] https://coinmarketcap.com/currencies/ethereum/.

to discover abnormal behaviours in Ethereum smart contracts of Ethereum by detecting their attack vectors. We built a tool named ABBE to demonstrate the methods.

Our contributions in this paper are threefold:

- Our work collects known vulnerabilities from many scattered sources and systematically classified them.
- We then define an attack vector for each vulnerability. Afterwards, we record all tracks that are left by each attack vectors and classified them according to some properties.
- Since each property in these tracks category requires different preliminaries to be detected, we also implement several modules to handle them. A tool named ABBE, is implemented and can detect abnormal executions in all transactions of Ethereum smart contracts.

## 2    Backgrounds of Ethereum Smart Contracts

Ethereum is a transaction-based state machine in which smart contracts execute as regards the intentions of developers. Ethereum has its own virtual machine, named Ethereum Virtual Machine (EVM), to execute smart contract code.

```
1  contract BobCompany {
2      mapping (address => uint) stock;
3      uint stockPrice;
4      constructor () {
5          stock[0x0000000000000000000000000000000000deadbeef] = 100
6      };
7      function buyStock (address _from, address _to, uint _amount) payable
           {
8          if (stock[_from] == 0 || msg.value == 0) throw;
9          if (stock[_from] > _amount && _amount*stockPrice < msg.value) {
10             stock[_from] -= _amount;
11             stock[_to] += _amount;
12         }
13     }
14     function sellStock(address _from, uint _amount) {
15         if (stock[_from] > _amount) {
16             stock[_from] -= _amount;
17             msg.sender.transfer(_amount*stockPrice);
18         }
19     }
20 }
```

**Listing 1.** An example of smart contract

**Programming.** At first, smart contracts are programmed in high-level programming languages, e.g. **Solidity** (a likewise of C and Javascript), **Vyper** (a contract-oriented language), **LLL** (a low-level language similar to Lisp), etc. A simple smart contract written in Solidity is illustrated in Listing 1 which features buying stock of Bob company. In this contract, Bob owns initially 100 percent of his company stock which defined in **constructor** function (line 5). This constructor executes exactly once during the **deployment** of contract.

**Deployment.** In order to be run on-top of EVM, the source code is compiled into EVM bytecode [27]. Afterwards, an address is determined for this new contract. Information of the address along with its corresponding bytecode is storcd by all nodes in blockchain network assuring these data could not be altered after deploying.

**Execution.** Assume that, Alice—a businesswoman—is willing to buy a couple of stock from Bob's company, she actually sends an appropriate amount of *ethers*[2] via a *transaction* to the contract. Afterwards, the contract verifies some pre-defined conditions to proceed her demand. For example, if Bob held no stock or Alice did not send any *ether* (line 8), the contract could raise an exception to revert all temporary changes, return Alice's ether, etc., but all fees are consumed. Otherwise, if all conditions were satisfied as shown in line 9, the contract would make changes in Alice and Bob's balances, respectively. Moreover, if Alice calls `sellStock` function (line 14) to sell a couple of her stocks, the contract will essentially create a *call*, a.k.a. *internal transaction*, to finish her order (line 19). Note that, a contract is able to send ethers to another normal account or invoke functions of other smart contracts. It is important to be aware that each transaction may interact with contract to invoke a function and requires fees (named *gas*[3] in Ethereum) to be processed by *all* nodes in the blockchain. Due to this reason, smart contracts are only suitable for low computational effort tasks such as signature verification, money transfer. The restriction placed by gas is for preventing the whole Ethereum network from being abused.

# 3   Taxonomy of Vulnerabilities

## 3.1   Reentrancy

In terms of transaction processing, *atomicity* and *sequentiality* are two among four essential properties of a transaction. Those properties are represented as a non-recursive function cannot be invoked until the function execution state ends up in a terminated state. However, *fallback* and *call* functions may break those properties of contracts, since they allow an adversary to continuously recall, or to *re-entrant*, before the termination of the transaction. This vulnerability is illustrated in a simple version contract (see Listing 2) of the historical attack of the Decentralized Autonomous Organization (DAO) [11] in 2016, which caused the loss of $60M dollars in total.

```
contract Alice {                      contract Fraudster {
    bool sent = false;                    function () payable {
    function send(address c){                 Alice(msg.sender).send(this);
        if (!sent) {                      }
            c.call.value(1)();        }
            sent = true;
        }
    }
}
```

**Listing 2.** Contract contains reentrancy

---

[2] Name of the cryptocurrency used in Ethereum blockchain. Ether can be transferred among accounts and exchanged to other currencies. 1 ether will be exchanged for each US$217 (recorded at Aug 18, 2019).

[3] Price per each unit of gas is determined by the sender. The higher the price, the faster the transaction may be processed. All consumed gas must be paid in ether.

In this contract, `Alice` is able to call to an arbitrary contract deployed at address c with an empty signature, which means invoking the fallback of recipient, and unlimited gas. For re-withdrawal prevention, `sent` is meant to be set to `true` after c successfully withdraws 1 ether. However, before switching to the terminated state, the fallback of `Fraudster` re-enters the `send` function of `Alice` and forces her to transfer ether endlessly, since `sent` still has value equal to `false`.

## 3.2  Gasless Send

A `send` function can be used in order to transfer ether among accounts with a gas stipend equals to 2300 units. However, this limited amount of gas is only enough to perform a single instruction (transferring ethers in this case) and cannot used for executing more complicated business logic that may lead to an "*out-of-gas*" exception. Different from `c.call.value(amount)()` at which the callee's signature is empty and all remaining gas is passed, `send` and `call` will return `false` to the caller contract (instead of throwing an exception and terminating transaction execution), and continue to execute the rest of instructions after the call to c with the remaining gas. Note that, the return values of `call` and `send` are often disregarded by developers; therefore, the remnant of code continues to execute at risk without any restriction.

## 3.3  Force-Sending Ether by Suicide

A smart contract is able to self-destruct for cleaning up all related information about itself in the blockchain data, including its bytecode and storage. These pieces of data will no longer exist from this point. And after the moment of self-destruction, this contract will transfer all ether that it is holding to another pre-defined contract.

Unlike a regular call, `selfdestruct` function does not invoke the fallback function of the recipient, but the balance of recipient is altered without any restriction. Assume that, the recipient is not allowed to receive any ether to prevent some adverse functions can occur. For example, a contract may discard all incoming ether transfers to it by reverting the transactions which trigger its fallback function. This is because some negative impacts may happen if the contract balance contains a positive value.

## 3.4  Integer Overflow

In Ethereum smart contract, balance of an arbitrary account is presented by an unsigned 256-bit integer denoted as `uint256`. After transferring, balances of the sender and receiver will be updated respectively. Because operations are being done in the 32-byte integer field, an integer overflow can happen in case there is no verification. Consider a contract (illustrated in Listing 3), where Alice will be able to withdraw some ether if her balance satisfies to some conditions. However, if the conditions are set unrestrictedly, she still can proceed her `transfer` call. In Ethereum, let imagine a 1-byte integer works as an odometer, clocking from 0 to 255 and rollover to 0 afterwards. Hence, in 32-byte field, the operation of 0−1 yields a result of `0xFFFFFFFFFFFFFFFFFFFFFFFFFFFFFFFFFFFFFFFF` $\approx 3.4 \times 10^{38}$, instead of −1. This means that the business logic of smart contract works unintendedly since Alice's withdrawal draft is not rejected. Alice now, therefore, can endlessly withdraw 1 ether from the contract until contract balance runs out at 0.

```
1 function withdraw() {
2     if (balance[alice] > 1) {
3         balance[alice]--;
4         alice.transfer(1);
5     }
6 }
```

**Listing 3.** Contract contains integer overflow

### 3.5 Array Overflow

Recall that contracts in Ethereum hold the root of a Merkle Patricia tree in which all permanent data of the corresponding contract is stored. Each node in the tree is identified by a 256-bit index. Each contract, therefore, has ability to store up to $2^{256}$ 32-byte *virtual* storage slots. It seems that collision cannot happen since variables are stored in distinct slots.

However, Hoyte [12] showed that there may exist unexpected data overridden if a dynamic array is declared in contract. In Listing 4, `isAttacked` and `map` variables are stored at `0x00..00` and `0x00..01` slot (64 hex-character in length), respectively. Since `map` is a dynamically allocated variable, its elements must be stored somewhere else which is nonconsecutive to two mentioned variables. The index of the first element of `map` is `map[0]` $\rightarrow$ `KECCAK256(index_of_map)` = `KECCAK256("00...01")` = `0xd874...2827`, and the rest follows this slot. Because the dynamic array has no upper-bound for its number of elements, the index of element will increase linearly as the array expands. This results in an element will be allocated at index of `0xFF...FF` (64 F's). The next element will be in the `0x00..00` slot (slot indexes are also 256-bit integer) which are collided to value of `isAttacked`.

```
1 contract ArrayOverflowBug {
2     bool public isAttacked;
3     uint256[] map;
4
5     function set(uint256 key, uint256 value) public {
6         // Expand dynamic array as needed
7         if (map.length <= key) {
8             map.length = key + 1;
9         }
10
11         map[key] = value;
12     }
13 }
```

**Listing 4.** Contract contains array overflow

## 3.6 Uninitialized Storage Pointer

In EVM, both memory and storage are used for handling stored value of contract variable. According to Ethereum's specification, a variable declared outside of a function are stored in storage by default. Meanwhile, the position where to store in-function variable is determined by the corresponding variable type. In details, elementary type variables (e.g. `int`, `bytes`, `bool`, etc.) are stored in memory; other complex types such as `array` and `struct`, however, have their value in storage.

```
1  contract StructStorageBug {
2      struct Donation {
3          uint256 timestamp;
4          uint256 etherAmount;
5      }
6      Donation[] public donations;  // slot 0
7      address public owner;          // slot 1
8
9      function donate(uint256 etherAmount) public payable {
10         Donation donation;
11         donation.timestamp = now;
12         donation.etherAmount = etherAmount;
13
14         donations.push(donation);
15     }
16 }
```

**Listing 5.** Contract contains uninitialised storage pointer

Related to this innate of EVM, Beyer [4] explained a complex attack exploiting this dangerous behaviour. Consider a sample contract in Listing 5. If a donor transfers ether to this contract, it will record the amount and time the donation would have been sent. All donations are handled by an array of structures `donations` which is stored at slot 0 of storage. In addition, the fundholder has her address declared at slot 1. This `owner` address is required to perform some severe tasks such as drawing on the fund and must not be amended unless all pre-defined conditions are satisfied. However, notice that a local variable `donation` is declared at Line 10, whose type belongs to complex types. Hence, `donation` is not stored in memory but becomes a pointer to storage. Note that, the `donation` variable is not initialized resulting being allocated at slot 0 of storage by default, instead of at memory. Hence, in the next following line, the assignment to `donation.timestamp` will be essentially overriding over the `donations` variable. Similarly, `owner` will be overridden by the assignment to `etherAmount` property. In order to gain permission to this contract, an adversary could simply make a donation with his account address as parameter.

## 3.7 Overridden by Delegate Call

Since smart contracts have limitation in code size at approximately 24 KB [7], they may need to recycle functions from other contracts as using libraries in program development. Solidity allows contract to invoke functions of other contracts via `delegatecalls` whereas the context of storage, information of `msg.sender` and `msg.value` are preserved [6]. However, this call may be considered as a security risk for the caller contract because it must trust the callee contract which is permitted to commit changes on caller's storage [9].

In many cases, the address of caller is immutably determined in the callee contract source code. Problems will occur if this address can be manipulated by an adversary. Note that, all variables in the caller are treated as pointers to the callee's storage, which means all amendments during callers' execution will affect on callee's storage without any verification. The detailed explanation for a historical attack to "multi-sig" wallet Parity was described in [20].

# 4    Detection Methods for Attack Vectors

In this section, we introduce our detection methods for each type of attack vectors. In simple terms, smart contracts may contain vulnerabilities, which cause contracts to run on an unplanned scenario. However, these vulnerabilities are still harmless until an adversary takes advantage by exploiting them. Generally, he must send transactions, which are termed as attack vectors in security field, to exploit these vulnerabilities. These attack vectors are divided into categories, which will be explained in detail in Subsect. 4.1, according to the tracks that they left during the execution of attacking. The detailed explanation of the methods for detecting these attacks can be found in the subsections following the classification.

## 4.1    Category of Attack Vectors

In order to establish categories for assigning the known attack vectors, we show typical examples to illustrate how vital evidence left whilst attacking. In terms of **transaction result**s, the **final result**, which is comprised of the shift in involved addresses balance, consumed gas amount, etc., can be used to label the category. For example, the average gas amount used to proceed a transaction in Ethereum blockchain is approximately 21,000 units. This common number of gas usage can help detect any transaction consuming a huge amount of gas. Besides, the **intermediate result** calculated during transaction execution, including temporary values of all operations in stack and memory of smart contract, can lead to a successful attack. Consider a step in stack using SUB operator with two corresponding parameters 0 and 1, this operation leads to a result of 0xFFFF..FF (64 F's) since integer overflow happens here. This unusual output can be worse if these numbers, respectively, present for an adversary tried to send 1 unit of token, while her balance was at 0 but the receiver got an unacceptably high amount of value.

In another aspect, each contract is able to store $2^{256}$ 32-bytes-long slots, which form contract **storage**. Any modifications in the storage also help to recognize whether the smart contract has been exploited. Some attacks seemed to alter the storage values to unusual ones. The irregularity is presented in **value of variable**, where i.e., the address of an immutable contract **owner** has been changed to an extraordinary address. For another example, the balance of an account is often declared in **balance** variable. If this variable contains an extremely high value, we may consider it as being modified by an unusual behaviour. Moreover, changes in storage can be counted as abnormal regarding to **type of variable**. In some attack scenarios, the storage slots are overwritten by values whose type mismatches to the declared type of corresponding variables. For instance, assume that `uint256` variable holds the value of `0x54686973497341537472696e6700..00` which infers to a meaningful string—`ThisIsAString`. In such cases, we can imply that there have occurred abnormal transactions.

**Table 1.** Category of attack vectors according to their tracks

| Level | Attack vector | Result | | Storage | |
|-------|---------------|--------|----------|---------|------|
| | | Final | Internal | Value | Type |
| Solidity | Reentrancy | ✓ | ✓ | — | — |
| | Gasless send | — | ✓ | — | — |
| | Force-sending ether by suicide | — | ✓ | — | — |
| EVM | Integer overflow | — | ✓ | — | — |
| | Array overflow | — | ✓ | ✓ | ✓ |
| | Uninitialised storage pointer | — | ✓ | ✓ | ✓ |
| | Overridden by delegate call | — | ✓ | ✓ | ✓ |

To sum up, our category of attack vectors consists of the unusual value in final and intermediate results of the transaction; and the extraordinary modification in type and value in the storage of the involved smart contract. Table 1 represents our classification. Recall that the findings of these attack vectors along with their description are collected from [2] and many security blogs and will be represented in the next following subsections.

Additionally, based on possible methods to detect whether an incoming transaction is an attack vector, detecting each attack vector requires vary inputs. During experiments, we found that there are three valuable factors may be used as input for the detection. For details, we need to perform the detection algorithms on only the newest transaction or all previous transactions. Moreover, only contract bytecode is involved in the detection stage, or we also need the information of corresponding source code. And lastly, the storage is whether used as input data to detect the attack. Table 2 summarizes the necessary inputs for detecting each type of attack vectors.

## 4.2 Reentrancy

During the exploitation of this attack, a chain of nested internal function calls was created, in which internal calls have a same information of sender and recipient. In order to capture the attack, we re-execute the transaction and verify if there exists any nested internal calls with duplicated patterns. Note that, the duplicated calls do not need to be called right after another call, but can be squeezed in by some manipulated calls created by the attacker.

**Table 2.** Inputs for detecting each type of attack vectors

| Attack vector | Transaction | Contract | Storage |
|---|---|---|---|
| Integer overflow | Current | Bytecode | No |
| Reentrancy | Current | Bytecode | No |
| Gasless send | Current | Bytecode | No |
| Force-send ether by suicide | Current | Bytecode and sourcecode | No |
| Array overflow | Current | Bytecode | No |
| Uninitialised storage pointer | All | Bytecode and sourcecode | Yes |
| Overridden by delegate call | All | Bytecode and sourcecode | Yes |

### 4.3   Gasless Send

The detection method for this kind of attack is similar to *reentrancy* case. Note that, in *gasless send* attack vector, there exists at least a failed internal transaction while its parent transaction executes successfully. At EVM bytecode level, an internal transaction is considered as success if its last instruction is either STOP or SSTORE [16]. Meanwhile, an internal transaction fails to execute when reach to these following conditions (see Fig. 1):

- Function call is reverted by assert() function and generates INVALID instruction;
- Function call is reverted by either revert() or throw() and generates REVERT instruction;
- Execution is terminated at an arbitrary step where gas stipend is all consumed, resulting in a field named error = {} generated in debug logs.

To detect this kind of attack vector, we track through nested calls, starting from the deepest transaction in debug logs, and apply these following steps.

**Step 1.** Verify whether current transaction is reverted, according to above-listed conditions;
**Step 2.** Verify whether ancestor transaction is consequently reverted:
  - If ancestor transaction is an internal call, we will apply Step 1 to this transaction;
  - If ancestor transaction is a normal transaction, we will need to make sure that this transaction executes successfully, described by false value in failed field of debug calls.

### 4.4   Force-Sending Ether by Suicide

In this kind of attack vector, we consider the recipient contract as the supervised target (instead of the contract committing suicide). Note that, payable keyword is used to declare that this contract ignores all ether. Therefore, we detect suicide to force-send ether by two steps:

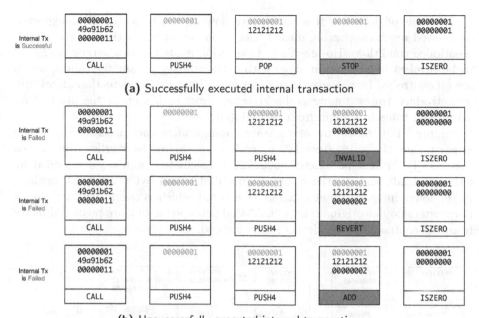

(a) Successfully executed internal transaction

(b) Unsuccessfully executed internal transaction

**Fig. 1.** Stack states of internal transaction

- Generating abstract syntax tree (AST) while compiling sourcecode. Checking value of `payable` field of fallback function.
- Re-executing all transactions in blockchain, and filtering `SELFDESTRUCT` instruction with its corresponding recipient address. Verifying if this address matches address of supervised contract.

## 4.5   Integer Overflow

The root cause of integer overflow vulnerabilities is because all arithmetic operations are not checked for overflow at the EVM level. However, this instinct is not improperly developed due to two important purposes. Firstly, reducing the number of computational steps that allows users to pay a smaller fee of gas. Secondly, EVM needs overflowed results for some specific tasks. For example, to invert `0x00001010` to `0x11110101`, EVM will start at `0xFFFFFFFF = 0 - 1` and calculate `0x00001010 XOR 0xFFFFFFFF` to get the desired result. In an Ethereum improvement proposal, Alex Beregszaszi [3] listed all possible cases lead to integer overflow, including:

- `DIV` and `SDIV` with a zero divisor;
- `ADD`, `MUL`, `EXP` equals to a result whose length is greater than 256 bits;
- `SUB` when the subtrahend exceeds minuend;
- `SDIV` when $-2^{255}$ divided by $-1$;
- `ADDMOD` and `MULMOD` with mod equals 0;
- `SIGNEXTEND` when the parameter of position is greater than 31.

In terms of detecting this integer overflow attack, we catch all unexpected overflowed results appearing during transaction execution satisfying the above-mentioned conditions. However, all exploitation related to this attack are found to be invoked by a function along with extraordinary parameter values, which are all controlled by the adversary. In order to improve the detection algorithm, we introduce tracer aiming at backtracking over each step in the stack if an overflowed value has origin from user's input.

Figure 2 illustrates how stack state changes after each instruction. In the upper image, the result from ADD op-code is considered as overflow due to two reasons, (i) the first parameter 00000022 is calculated from a value loaded by CALLDATALOAD, and (ii) the result is truncated to a 4 bytes value. Meanwhile, in the lower image, although ADD gives a result which is overflowed, two input parameters do not originate in a CALLDATALOAD opcode but are pushed directly from the contract's bytecode via PUSHx instead.

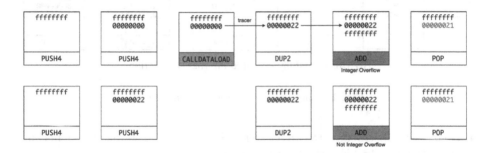

**Fig. 2.** Example of stack trace in integer overflow

### 4.6  Array Overflow

The detection method for this case recycles results from *integer overflow*. Indeed, starting from instructions detected as related to integer overflow attack vector, we track straightforwardly through stack states to capture SSTORE instructions which use overflowed value to determine the index of slot to modify (see Fig. 3).

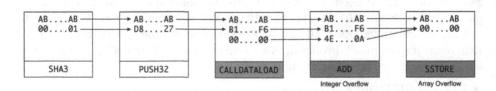

**Fig. 3.** Stack states of array overflow attack vector

## 4.7    Uninitialized Storage Pointer

It is important to note that all data transfers (reading and writing) among stack, memory and storage are done over 32-bit field. However, there is no type checking is done for all operations in EVM, including those transfer operations. Because of that, type-mismatching between variable type and variable usage context can occur. For instance, an arbitrary `address` variable as `owner` in the previous example can easily overridden by a `uint256` value. In fact, according to Solidity documentation[4], each type of variable in EVM has different layout of state variable. Therefore, to detect whether a write-access is trying to override the storage, we propose a heuristic based on involved constructs' type.

On purpose of implementing this heuristic, we need the help of a storage recreator for each contract. From the input of AST and amendments on each transaction, we can recover the information of each byte in storage including its corresponding type, value and to which variable this byte belongs. On each transaction altering contract storage, we will mark it as a suspicious transaction if one of the following condition is violated:

1. Unallocated bytes i.e. bytes that present the value of no variable, are written illegally;
2. A slot belonging to a `mapping` variables is altered;
3. A slot of a non-string variable contains an in-string-format value;
4. A huge value is stored in a slot that represents value of a dynamic array.

Finally, the algorithm to detect this kind of attack is described as follow.

**Step 1.** Filtering all transactions interacting to the supervised contract;
**Step 2.** On each transaction, seeking for `SSTORE`:
- If this operation is performed on an untracked slot, marking its corresponding type;
- Else, verifying this operation according to above-defined conditions.

## 4.8    Overridden by Delegate Call

The detection method for this attack vector is similar to *Uninitialized storage pointer* (see Subsect. 4.7) since it is based on storage overrides. The only difference is we need to verify whether the `SSTORE` is performed in the context of a `DELEGATECALL` whose caller is the supervised contract.

## 5    System Architecture

In order to investigate attack vectors sent to smart contracts in Ethereum blockchain, we introduce ABBE—the abnormal behaviours detecting tool. Our tool takes several information of contracts as input parameters as regards type of

---

[4] https://solidity.readthedocs.io/en/latest/miscellaneous.html#layout-of-state-variables-in-storage.

attack vectors. This section presents our proposed architecture for ABBE, which is comprised of five components as illustrated in Fig. 4.

**Contract Initialization.** At the first step, the Contract Initialiser module gets *address* and *sourcecode* with respect to the supervised contract for initialization purpose. Users must specify the *address* at the beginning. Meanwhile, this module will seek for the *source-code* of contract in Etherscan. Etherscan is the de facto location for exploring and seeking Ethereum transactions, tokens, smart contracts, etc. The source-code that belongs to an arbitrary smart contract is committed by the developers and is double-checked on Etherscan by comparing two versions of bytecode, one is fetched from Ethereum blockchain and the other one is taken after compiling the submitting sourcecode. In case of the source-code is missing in Etherscan, another option is preferred, a local path leading to *sourcecode* must be specified by the users.

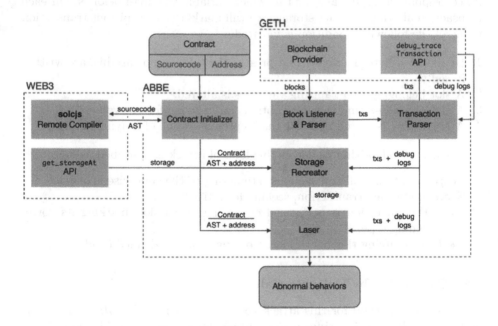

**Fig. 4.** System architecture of ABBE

**Block Parsing and Transaction Parsing.** After loading, this module continues to compile sourcecode of the smart contract into bytecode form. During this step, the compiler generates an abstract syntax tree containing information about type, scope, and other properties of all tokens in contract source. Note that there are nearly 50 versions of Solidity compiler which may be used to compile the contract source code. Because of this massive amount of releases, instead of importing all releases of compiler, the Initialiser finishes this step with the help of a remote compiler solcjs[5], featured by web3 library, for the sake of convenience.

Simultaneously, the Block Listener and Parser module serves as a listener that fetches new blocks from the Blockchain Provider. Blockchain Provider essentially is the main application programming interface (API) of an Ethereum client, which is GETH in this tool. All new blocks are generated, processed by GETH and are emitted to all connections that GETH holds via its main API. On input the new block, this module parses it into block header along with all transactions grouped inside. Each parsed transaction will be processed by the Transaction Parser module in the next step.

**Transaction Parser.** This module takes all information of each transaction as its input, and then filters out the data of hash, sender address, receiver address, consumed gas amount, etc. The use of this information helps call the debug_traceTransaction API to generate corresponding debug logs. This API is provided by the GETH provider mentioned in the previous step.

**Storage Recreation.** Following these steps, the relevant information of smart contracts including the *AST* of contract and *debug logs* of all executed transactions (regardless of whether their transaction type is normal or internal) from genesis block is used as input for the Storage Recreator module. At this time, the Storage Recreator creates a mapping table of variables' name, type, and slot storage index where its value stored.

**Transaction Diagnosis.** Finally, the tool passes data of *AST*, *address* and *storage* of the contract, along with all *transactions* attached with their *debug logs* into **Laser**—the diagnosing module. On each incoming transaction, this module matches it to the pre-defined attack vectors patterns, and returns whether this transaction is considered as an abnormal behaviour.

# 6   Implementation and Testing

According to the architecture introduced in Sect. 5, we successfully implemented the ABBE tool[6,7] and performed testing in our private Ethereum network. Since our implementation requires an archive node of GETH client, the large-scale experiment of ABBE in Ethereum mainnet will be carried out in future work.

To start, users have to determine the address of contract and specify the local path leading to contract sourcecode, if exist. Users are also allowed to configure the number of block where ABBE starts to perform detection. A snapshot of a sample result given by ABBE is illustrated in Fig. 5. On each input transaction,

---

[5] All releases of solcjs are listed at https://ethereum.github.io/solc-bin/bin/list.js.

[6] The private repository of ABBE is located at https://github.com/nxqbaos/abbe2. Access to this repository is granted upon requests.

[7] The ABBE tool has been invited to be presented at Hack In The Box (HITB+) Cyber Week's Conference, *Oct. 15–17, 2019*, Abu Dhabi, UAE.

**Fig. 5.** Sample result given by ABBE

if there is any abnormal behavior detected, ABBE will put out an alert. The format of output is as follows. First, the LASER yields the hash of the transaction that performs attack and its final state, which is FAILURE or SUCCESS. The next following lines represent the name of the detected attack vectors and their corresponding information. This information consists of different fields according to each type of attack vector. Generally, these fields include:

- EVMOpcode: Instruction mnemonic.
- ExecStep: The execution step counter in the debug log.
- EVMDepth: The depth number of the current call in the list of nested call. This number of depth starts from 1, equivalent to the origin call which is triggered from a normal transaction.
- ErrMsg: The cause that leads to failure of internal transaction (in Gasless-Send case); or, the cause leading to override in contract storages (in DelegateCall and UninitPointer case).

The test suite that we used for testing ABBE comprises of contracts containing vulnerabilities, or have been attacked in the past, or have been collected from [2, 22, 28]. On each attack vector, we performed multiple test and visualize the result in the confusion matrix form.

Especially, as for three attack vectors *reentrancy*, *gasless send* and *force-sending ether by suicide* in the Solidity level, the tool is able to fully detect all transactions exploiting these three vulnerabilities. The confusion matrix in Table 3 shows that there is no false detection occurring during the tests.

However, while performing test on smart contracts that contain *reentrancy* vulnerability, the tool detects that there also exist the *gasless send* attack. This is because the pattern of *gasless send* is similar to the *reentrancy* case. Recall that, a transaction related to the *reentrancy* behaviour recursively calls a specific function until gas is all consumed. When this transaction creates the call

Table 3. Testing results in Solidity level cases

|  |  | Reentrancy | | Gasless send | | Suicide to force-send | |
| --- | --- | --- | --- | --- | --- | --- | --- |
|  |  | Pos | Neg | Pos | Neg | Pos | Neg |
| Result of ABBE | Pos | **10** | 0 | **29** | 0 | **10** | 0 |
|  | Neg | 0 | **7** | 0 | **10** | 0 | **0** |

which is the most-inner internal transaction, the gas that passed into this call is insufficient to execute that function properly. Hence, we consider all *gasless send* alerts caused by *reentrancy* is valid.

Besides, for early awareness of being attacked, we also record all transactions which attempt to perform *gasless send* attack but result in failure. To achieve this, ABBE marks the transactions having the attack pattern of this case, in other words, there exists an internal transaction which got an insufficient gas stipend, although the transaction ended up in a `failed` state.

Table 4. Testing results in overflow cases

|  |  | Integer overflow | | Array overflow | |
| --- | --- | --- | --- | --- | --- |
|  |  | Pos | Neg | Pos | Neg |
| Result of ABBE | Pos | **30** | 3 | **13** | 1 |
|  | Neg | 28 | **36** | 0 | **12** |

Meanwhile, as for *integer overflow*, the result in the Table 4 shows that our ABBE tool produces positive result as it passes most of test cases. However, there are 28 test cases that lead to false negative, since the tool only defines integer overflow pattern on the field of 32-bit integer. The detection of overflow in fields whose bit-size is smaller will be supported in further work. A small number of false positive is recorded. These false positive results happen when there exists reentrancy in the transaction.

As for the *array overflow* case, the result achieved is apparently impressive since there is only 01 false positive left. In this test case, the input does create an intermediate result which is arithmetic overflowed. Recall that our algorithm detects array overflow by verifying whether the calculations of slot index that to be written are overflowed. The overflow of intermediate result, however, is equal to the index of slot that need to be written in the storage, while the calculations for identifying the slot indexes are not related to the input values.

Lastly, the results obtained when applying the heuristic to detect two attack vectors related to overriding on EVM storage is presented in Table 5. Although ABBE can recognise attacks in many testcases, our tool still fails under some tricky inputs.

**Table 5.** Testing results in heuristic-based cases

|  |  | Delegated call | | Uninitialised pointer | |
|---|---|---|---|---|---|
|  |  | Pos | Neg | Pos | Neg |
| Result of ABBE | Pos | 8 | 1 | 8 | 1 |
|  | Neg | 13 | 9 | 11 | 10 |

The false negative results are all caused by the mishandling the verification in types of value. In our proposed algorithm, the detecting pattern checks whether the actual type of the input value and the expected type of the accessing slot are mismatched. Due to this reason, if the input value and the slot have the same type, our tool cannot detect the abnormality occurred. Besides, if the slot containing data of some variables which are padded together into a form of 32 bytes, e.g. `uint16=0x6464`, `uint232=0x0`, `bool=true` sequentially, is overridden by a string, ABBE also cannot catch this illegal write access since the string has the value of `646400...0001` which matches the value-format of that slot. Generally, ABBE has a drawback in detecting attacks that exploit mismatches in types. However, this major drawback is because the checks for arithmetic instructions in EVM is not accomplished.

The only false positive is produced when an arbitrary variable is set to an extremely large value. Especially, users can set `array_name.length` to a huge value for some specific purposes. However, this situation may not happen in real contracts since `array_name.length` regularly cannot be changed manually, or altered to a huge value as in our test.

# 7  Related Work

**Taxonomy of Vulnerabilities.** Our work is guided by the previous taxonomy of Atzei et al. [2], the first classification that divides Ethereum smart contract attacks into three categories according to three levels of smart contracts. Since this work published, many new vulnerabilities have been reported and described by many personal blogs. Therefore, we append those new vulnerabilities that our tool can detect into the existed taxonomy.

**Smart Contract Security Analysis.** To the best of our knowledge, there has not existed any work investigating attacks detection in smart contracts so far. The major attacks recorded in the past few years were all discovered manually.

In efforts to feature smart contract security analyses, many security teams provide solutions to tackle this problem. The project introduced by SmartCheck [21] supports detecting vulnerabilities in the smart contracts' source code based on the defined bug patterns. Because this tool performs analysis on only Solidity level, the vulnerabilities that can be detected are independent of contracts' logic flaws. OYENTE, introduced by Luu et al. [14], is a security analysis tool that relies on both contracts' source code and bytecode to perform symbolic execution. Moreover, OYENTE aims to detect four specified vulnerabilities, including integer overflow, transaction dependency, stack-depth and reentrancy. On the other hand, our tool focuses on detecting the exploit transactions and in a wider range of vulnerabilities.

In the same vein with OYENTE, the tool MAIAN [15], MYTHRIL [17], MAN-TICORE [19] and SECURIFY [26] perform analyses for vulnerabilities in smart contracts by using symbolic execution on EVM bytecode. This approach, how-ever, produces all possible condition paths as all logic flaws that the contract execution can reach. As the size of contracts enlarges, these tools need to ver-ify a larger number of paths, the consumed-time for security analysis therefore increase. On the other hand, ABBE not only reason about EVM bytecode but it also analyses Solidity source code of the contracts since each vulnerability is expressed differently in these two levels.

Tann et al. [25] used a divergent method that applied sequence learning to detect security threats in smart contracts. By using long-short term memory neural network, this work introduced a machine learning technique that processes over smart contract bytecode. After generating the training set from over 640,000 distinct contracts which are labelled as safe or vulnerable by the MAIAN tool [15], the authors claimed their proposed model obtain a surprising result and provide improvements over symbolic analysis methods. Although ABBE currently follows the traditional approach, the idea of analysis by machine learning for detecting attacks is a viable research direction to follow.

**Formal Verification.** In addition to vulnerability detection, there have also been works on checking smart contracts against user-defined policy. F* [5] chooses a subset of EVM and Solidity to translate bytecode and source code of the smart contracts into F* respectively. This translated program is then ver-ified by the F*-based verifier against the defined-assertions of users. However, the capability of F* is limited at processing over a small subset of EVM which does not contain loop. In another work of Kalra et al. [13], the formal verification is supported by ZEUS framework. Similar to F*, ZEUS also translates both smart contracts' source code and bytecode into an intermediate representation based on LLVM, then starts the verification by using an SMT-based solver.

# 8    Conclusion

This paper expands the taxonomy of vulnerabilities in smart contracts with new types of attacks. For each vulnerability, we also propose methods to detect its attack vectors and demonstrated them in ABBE—the detecting tool. ABBE can detect seven kinds of attacks with good performance. Especially, our tool can detect all attacks which related to vulnerabilities in Solidity level and some other kinds of attack with zero false positives. Because our methodology is based on verifying all modifications on smart contract storage, not only the known attacks can be detected, but zero-day attack patterns can also be discovered.

For the intermediate future, we are working on conducting tests at a larger scale on the mainnet of Ethereum and other blockchain networks that support smart contracts written in Solidity. In order to potentially identify undefined-attacks, we also plan to apply data mining techniques based on the previous transactions in the contract's history. Further work using data classification model may allow security threats that exploit smart contract vulnerabilities can be detected in a higher efficiency.

**Acknowledgement.** During the preparation of this work, the first author was partially supported by University of Technology (HCMUT), VNU-HCM under "Student Scientific Research" Grant Number 121/HĐ-ĐHBK-KHCN&DA; and the last author was partially funded by Vietnam National University-HCMC under Grant C2019-20-14. The authors would like to thank Nguyen Van Thanh for his comments helping to improve the manuscript significantly.

# References

1. Post-Mortem Investigation (2016). https://www.kingoftheether.com/postmortem.html
2. Atzei, N., Bartoletti, M., Cimoli, T.: A survey of attacks on ethereum smart contracts (SoK). In: Maffei, M., Ryan, M. (eds.) POST 2017. LNCS, vol. 10204, pp. 164–186. Springer, Heidelberg (2017). https://doi.org/10.1007/978-3-662-54455-6_8
3. Beregszaszi, A.: EVM: overflow detection in arithmetic instructions (2016). github.com/ethereum/EIPs/issues/159
4. Beyer, S.: Storage allocation exploits in ethereum smart contracts (2018). https://medium.com/cryptronics/storage-allocation-exploits-in-ethereum-smart-contracts-16c2aa312743
5. Bhargavan, K., et al.: Formal verification of smart contracts: short paper. In: Proceedings of the 2016 ACM Workshop on Programming Languages and Analysis for Security, pp. 91–96. ACM (2016)
6. Buterin, V.: Ethereum Improvement Proposal 7 (2015). https://github.com/ethereum/EIPs/blob/master/EIPS/eip-7.md
7. Buterin, V.: Ethereum Improvement Proposal 170 (2016). https://github.com/ethereum/EIPs/blob/master/EIPS/eip-170.md
8. Buterin, V., et al.: A next-generation smart contract and decentralized application platform. White Paper (2014)
9. Buterin, V., et al.: Difference between CALL, CALLCODE and DELEGATECALL (2016). https://ethereum.stackexchange.com/questions/3667/difference-between-call-callcode-and-delegatecall
10. Consensys: Solidity Recommendations (2018). https://consensys.github.io/smart-contract-best-practices/recommendations/
11. Falkon, S.: The story of the DAO - its history and consequences (2017). https://medium.com/swlh/the-story-of-the-dao-its-history-and-consequences-71e6a8a551ee
12. Hoyte, D.: MerdeToken: it's some hot shit (2018). https://github.com/Arachnid/uscc/tree/master/submissions-2017/doughoyte
13. Kalra, S., Goel, S., Dhawan, M., Sharma, S.: Zeus: analyzing safety of smart contracts. In: NDSS (2018)
14. Luu, L., et al.: Making smart contracts smarter. In: Proceedings of the 2016 ACM SIGSAC Conference on Computer and Communications Security, pp. 254–269. ACM (2016)

15. Manticore (2018). https://github.com/trailofbits/manticore
16. McKie, S.: Solidity learning: Revert(), Assert(), and Require() in solidity, and the new REVERT Opcode in the EVM (2017). https://medium.com/blockchannel/the-use-of-revert-assert-and-require-in-solidity-and-the-new-revert-opcode-in-the-evm-1a3a7990e06e
17. Mueller, B.: Mythril - Reversing and Bug Hunting Framework for the Ethereum Blockchain
18. Nakamoto, S., et al.: Bitcoin: A Peer-to-Peer Electronic Cash System (2008)
19. Nikolić, I., et al.: Finding the greedy, prodigal, and suicidal contracts at scale. In: Proceedings of the 34th Annual Computer Security Applications Conference, pp. 653–663. ACM (2018)
20. Palladino, S.: The parity wallet hack explained - zeppelin blog (2017). https://blog.zeppelin.solutions/on-the-parity-wallet-multisig-hack-405a8c12e8f7
21. SmartDec: automatically checking smart contracts for vulnerabilities and bad practices (2018). https://tool.smartdec.net
22. SMARX: Capture the ether - the game of ethereum smart contract security (2018). https://capturetheether.com
23. SpankChain: We Got Spanked: What We Know So Far (2018). https://medium.com/spankchain/we-got-spanked-what-we-know-so-far-d5ed3a0f38fe
24. Szabo, N.: Smart Contracts. Unpublished manuscript (1994)
25. Tann, A., Han, X.J., Gupta, S.S., Ong, Y.S.: Towards safer smart contracts: a sequence learning approach to detecting vulnerabilities (2018). arXiv preprint arXiv:1811.06632
26. Tsankov, P., et al.: Securify: practical security analysis of smart contracts. In: Proceedings of the 2018 ACM SIGSAC Conference on Computer and Communications Security, pp. 67–82. ACM (2018)
27. Wood, G., et al.: Ethereum: A Secure Decentralised Generalised Transaction Ledger. Ethereum project yellow paper **151**, 1–32 (2014)
28. Zeppelin team: The Ethernaut Wargame. https://ethernaut.zeppelin.solutions

# MyWebGuard: Toward a User-Oriented Tool for Security and Privacy Protection on the Web

Panchakshari N. Hiremath[1], Jack Armentrout[1], Son Vu[2], Tu N. Nguyen[3], Quang Tran Minh[4], and Phu H. Phung[1(✉)]

[1] Intelligent Systems Security Lab, Department of Computer Science, University of Dayton, Dayton, OH, USA
{hiremathp1,armentroutj2,phu}@udayton.edu
[2] Truman State University, Kirksville, MO, USA
slv8887@truman.edu
[3] Purdue University Fort Wayne, Fort Wayne, IN, USA
nguyent@pfw.edu
[4] Ho Chi Minh City University of Technology, VNU-HCM, Ho Chi Minh City, Vietnam
quangtran@hcmut.edu.vn
https://isseclab-udayton.github.io

**Abstract.** We introduce a novel approach to implementing a browser-based tool for web users to protect their privacy. We propose to monitor the behaviors of JavaScript code within a webpage, especially operations that can read data within a browser or can send data from a browser to outside. Our monitoring mechanism is to ensure that all potential information leakage channels are detected. The detected leakage is either automatically prevented by our context-aware policies or decided by the user if needed. Our method advances the conventional same-origin policy standard of the Web by enforcing different policies for each source of the code. Although we develop the tool as a browser extension, our approach is browser-agnostic as it is based on standard JavaScript. Also, our method stands from existing proposals in the industry and literature. In particular, it does not rely on network request interception and blocking mechanisms provided by browsers, which face various technical issues.

We implement a proof-of-concept prototype and perform practical evaluations to demonstrate the effectiveness of our approach. Our experimental results evidence that the proposed method can detect and prevent data leakage channels not captured by the leading tools such as Ghostery and uBlock Origin. We show that our prototype is compatible with major browsers and popular real-world websites with promising runtime performance.

**Keywords:** Privacy · Web security · Online tracking

S. Vu—Work performed while the author was visiting the Intelligent Systems Security Lab, Department of Computer Science, University of Dayton.

# 1    Introduction

Privacy is a big challenge and risk today for Internet users [7]. This risk is mostly due to the presence of online trackers on almost all websites [17]. These trackers typically collect users' sensitive information such as personal data, browsing history, activities, and interests [33], mostly without the awareness of users [33,35]. Standard web security mechanisms such as same-origin policy [41] or Content-Security policy (CSP) [60] could not prevent these privacy risks since the trackers, either from the first- or third parties, are included by the developers [36]. Do Not Track (DNT) [61] is a mechanism to prevent tracking by sending an HTTP header indicating that a browser does not want to be tracked. Although most web browsers support DNT, there is currently no policy or mechanism about how a website has to respond upon receiving a DNT header. This technical issue of DNT leaves it a currently ineffective solution for security on the web [6].

Advanced users concerning their privacy usually adopt browser-based blocking tools for privacy protection such as ad or tracker blocker extensions [33]. While these tools are effective in blocking third-party trackers [36], there are a couple of limitations in these mechanisms. First, existing blocking browser extensions only enforce the "all-or-nothing" rule. This rule either blocks or allows a tracker or an ad network based on a URL defined in a filter list, generally identified by the tool or set by users [5]. This blocking approach creates challenges and dilemmas for users as they do not know if they should block an ad or a tracker [33]. Also, several studies show that not every user wants to block ads or trackers [9,59], and a big crowd desire advanced methods to control their footprint [1,30]. Second, the existing blocking mechanisms implemented in browser-based extensions face several technical issues outlined below.

The first technical issue is that the implementation of the blocking mechanism is browser-dependent. Extensions usually implement the blocking mechanism by intercepting all network requests from a web page and blocking it if the URL is in a filter list [13,36]. This method relies on a web API webRequest provided by major browsers [22,40], which developers have to follow the requirements of a specific browser. For example, recently, Google has just announced to replace their webRequest API by the declarativeNetRequest API together with the Manifest specification V3 [13,55]. This change will restrict the functionality of many of the current blockers on the marketplace. For example, it limits the maximum number of rules and domains that can be blocked by extensions like uBlock Origin [55]. Another technical issue is that extensions are dependent on the filter list predefined by developers. Therefore, new trackers or other third-party content are not captured or blocked by these extensions. For example, in [64], the authors demonstrated that existing extensions could not catch requests that utilize a DNS CNAME alias in order to prevent detection. Our experiments also confirm this technical issue. As demonstrated in Sect. 5.1, popular extensions such as Ghostery and uBlock Origin do not detect trackers and data leakage channels simulated in our test suite.

The limitations discussed above motivate us to develop a novel approach to protecting web users. Different from existing tools that block a particular network request, our method is to monitor the code execution in a browser. The goal of our code monitoring is to ensure that users' sensitive information cannot be leaked to the outside of a browser without the concern of users. As JavaScript is the language executed in browsers to perform all of the activities on a web page, we propose to intercept critical privacy-related JavaScript operations. In particular, we intercept JavaScript operations that can read data belonging to the user, e.g., cookies, and can send out data to the Internet. We then define and enforce context-aware policies on these operations to prevent possible privacy leakages. Our proposed method also stands from the state-of-the-art of JavaScript monitoring by tracking the origin of the code, i.e., where the code comes. From this origin tracking mechanism, we can enforce distinct policies for each origin of the code. This mechanism advances (and in contrast to) the traditional same-origin policy [41], which treats all the code, even included from an external server, within a web page as the same origin. Our main contributions in this work include:

- We introduce a novel approach to controlling the behaviors of JavaScript code within a web page to detect and prevent potential privacy leakage.
- We implement a proof-of-concept prototype as a browser extension, named `MyWebGuard`. Our `MyWebGuard` tool monitors the source of data and the sinks where the data can be sent to in order to detect potential data leakage precisely. Our mechanism is in contrast with existing blocking browser extensions that only focus on the web request interception with a static filter list.
- We perform evaluations and report practical experimental results on various aspects. Our approach is browser-agnostic, as it is compatible with major browsers. We show that our prototype implementation can detect and prevent potential data leakage while preserving the web page functionality. We also report the performance overhead of our prototype that is quite low for popular real-world websites.

We proceed as follows. In the next section, we review the background, including the landscape of browsers and their security, browser extension, and web security standards. We survey the literature and discuss related work compared with our work in Sect. 2.4. In Sect. 3, we describe our technical approach and the design of our method. We present our prototype implementation in Sect. 4. In Sect. 5, we demonstrate our evaluations and discuss the experimental results. Section 6 concludes our contributions and outlines the future work.

## 2    Background and Related Work

### 2.1    Security and Privacy in Browsers

In this subsection, we review the landscape of existing browsers and their security and privacy features. We relate these features to our work.

There are many browsers in the industry, including popular ones such as Google Chrome, Apple Safari, Mozilla Firefox, and more niche browsers such as Chromium and Brave. Almost all browsers have and implement security and privacy standards to ensure degrees of users' privacy either by default or within the browser settings. Among popular browsers, Google Chrome is considered as a leader in browser security with automatic updates and a Web Authentication API [10]. However, due to its closed-source structure and Google's incident for collecting user information, some users feel that Google has the incentive to break its stance on privacy [8]. Microsoft Edge uses sandboxing to contain browser processes, and it retains Internet Explorer's filtering of suspicious websites. However, Edge has not retained IE's tracking protection, and biannual updates can leave plenty of time for attackers to utilize unpatched exploits [38]. Mozilla Firefox offers users a wide range of security features that are comparable to Chrome. These include add-on warnings, malware protection, content blocking, and filtering of reported malicious websites. Also, thanks to its open-source, users can be confident that their browser is functioning without the inclusion of malicious code [44].

Looking at more niche browsers that advertise a greater emphasis on user privacy, Chromium retains the positives of Chrome while being open-source [10]. Privacy concerns with Chromium include the lack of automatic updates that could leave some users open to attacks, and WebRTC leaks are a concern since it cannot be disabled without third-party software [8]. Brave is a relatively new browser that focuses heavily on privacy; features include a built-in ad-blocker, chrome extension functionality, and fingerprinting blocker, to name a few. While Brave is still new and gains limited market share of browsers, its open-source structure and firm stance on privacy are gearing it up to be a strong contender in the browser landscape [8].

Although our work is to build a tool added-on in a browser, our approach can be integrated into a browser to enhance its security and privacy features for protecting web users.

## 2.2   Browser Extensions

A browser extension is an open-source software module, developed using web technology, i.e., HTML, CSS, and JavaScript, to be integrated into a browser by users. When loading a web page, a browser also loads and executes installed extensions enabled for that web page [43]. Therefore, JavaScript code in a browser extension has the same privilege as the web page, i.e., it can access and modify the data or content of the web page [43]. A typical extension contains a manifest specification in JSON format, HTML pages, and JavaScript files. A browser extension can access general web APIs, available for every web page, and a special set of JavaScript APIs provided by browsers but are not available for web pages. For example, Google Chrome and Opera browsers provide the extension API (https://developer.chrome.com/extensions), which is also supported in other major browsers such as Firefox or Microsoft Edge [43].

In this work, we develop our tool as a browser extension. In Sect. 2.4, we survey and discuss related work in browser extensions and their security.

## 2.3  Web and JavaScript Security

Our work focuses on the security and privacy of web pages within a browser. Therefore, server-side security such as SQL Injection, command injection, or denial-of-service attacks is out-of-scope of this work. In this subsection, we briefly review the web page security model and JavaScript security standards, including Same-Origin Policy and Content Security Policy.

Nowadays, almost all web pages contain JavaScript code. Statistics in [62] show that 95.2% of all websites contain JavaScript code. Among these, websites include JavaScript code from external third-party servers. These facts are evidenced in a survey of the Alexa Top 10,000 websites, which reveals that 88.45% of them include at least one third-party JavaScript library [47]. The work also exposes some contents in the trusted libraries of these sites that can be compromised. They later identify four newly discovered vulnerabilities that could be used in attacks. The work also reviews the effectiveness of proposed solutions for protecting web applications that utilize third-party content.

In principle, JavaScript code in a web page is loaded and executed by a browser within a JavaScript engine. JavaScript code can interact with users, modify the web content, and can access (read/write) data stored in a browser such as cookies. Browsers enforce the same-origin policy to ensure that JavaScript code from one origin cannot access the data belongs to other origins.

**Same-Origin Policy.** The same-origin policy (SOP) is a critical web security standard that prevents JavaScript code from one origin from accessing data of other origins [41]. An origin in the web is identified by the scheme, host, and port of a URL. The SOP does not apply for the code included in a web page but sourced from a third-party server. For example, if a web page from https://mywebguard-host.github.io (the host) includes JavaScript code from https://thirdparty.com, e.g., using

`<script src="https://thirdparty.com/script.js"></script>`,

then the script code from https://thirdparty.com/script.js is executed in the host web page and has the same origin as the host. This policy means that the external code can access data belongs to that host. This issue is a known limitation of SOP as identified in the literature, e.g., [45,48,54]. Our work addresses this drawback by tracking where the code comes from and enforce different policies for different code origin.

**Content Security Policy.** Content-Security-Policy (CSP) [60] is a web standard that functions to prevent code injection attacks such as Cross-Site Scripting (XSS). This prevention is done by allowing the creation of a whitelist of trusted content that can be rendered and executed by the browser. The CSP can be used to prevent data leakage to external domains, not in the whitelist. However, it cannot prevent potential privacy leakage to whitelisted domains, as we investigated in this work. Moreover, there has also been a surge in the attempts to study the CSP. In [63], the authors explore how challenges presented by CSP lead to a low adoption rate among the Alexa Top 1M. The results show that the inclusion of CSP lags other security headers, and CSP policies are often ineffective at preventing content injection attacks like XSS. Additionally, they also suggest an improvement in CSP that could increase its use on the web.

## 2.4   Related Work

Below, we survey the literature on topics related to our work, including JavaScript security and browser extensions. We also discuss how our work advances the state-of-the-art.

**JavaScript Security.** In the past decade, there are many research works and proposals focused on the topic of JavaScript security. In 2007, BrowserShield [52] was introduced as a JavaScript security solution by vulnerability-driven filtering dynamic HTML in web pages. The BrowserShield system rewrites web pages to secure vulnerabilities relied on embedded scripts. Caja [21,39] is a similar approach developed at Google. Google Caja allows passive data to become active content and rewrites scripts into an object-capability language to ensure that their operations are safe on a webpage. In [31], Maffeis *et al.* design language-based methods that websites use to filter untrusted JavaScript. They also propose a foundation for language-based filtering that addresses website vulnerabilities. Phung *et al.* [49] introduce a lightweight self-protecting JavaScript approach to controlling the behaviors of JavaScript code to prevent potential attacks. Meyerovich and Livshits in [37] present a new design, termed ConScript, that empowers to host webpages byways of fine-grained security policies. These policies are to constrain executed code to protect against vulnerabilities opened when untrusted JavaScript codes appear. In [48], Phung *et al.* introduce a new approach to enforcing security policies on untrusted third-party ad content, referred to as FlashJaX. Their design, FlashJaX, addresses the problem of vulnerability assessment sites that are mixed by JavaScript with Adobe ActionScript content.

There are also other JavaScript security proposals; however, they focus on advertisement networks. For example, ADSafe [12] is a safe subset of JavaScript for ads. Ad developers must follow this subset so that an ad can be included in a hosting web page; otherwise, it will be rejected. In [50], Politz *et al.* propose a lightweight and efficient technique to verify sandbox sources that utilize ADsafe to demonstrate the effectiveness of the system by securing previously unknown weakness within ADsafe rooted in sandboxing. And, Finifter *et al.* in [18] examine a vulnerability found among one-third of the Alexa Top 100, accessible via ADsafe-verified advertisements. This vulnerability is rooted in third-parties exploiting prototype objects of the hosting page. The authors propose a JavaScript subset that retains static verification while upgrading security. Furthermore, in [24], there is a development of an online advertising system, referred to as Privad, that aims to secure user privacy while still allowing advertisers to serve targeted ads. This design focuses on improving user's browser experience through increased speeds over other online advertising systems, presenting microbenchmarks and informal analysis of Privad's privacy properties. In addition to these studies, Fredrikson and Livshits in [19] present RePriv, a tracker implemented as a browser extension to collect user interests and share them with third-parties with the user's permission. This paper also shows how RePriv can collect user interests to personalize the content on various websites with high quality and keep a low overhead, as well as preserve user privacy.

Information flow-control in JavaScript to prevent potential leakages in web pages, similar to our work, has also been studied in the literature. For instance, in [11], the authors present a web system supported by inlined information flow control monitor as well as an evaluation of that monitor. This application uses "mashups" of JavaScript code that is one of the most common types of codes using on many web apps today. Hedin *et al.* [26] introduce JSFlow as a method for tracking the information flow of JavaScript on sites that utilizes third-party code, deploying it as a browser extension. Through the utilization of JSFlow, they also indicate the different main policies of sharing sensitive user information on websites.

JavaScript security is still an emerging topic in recent years. For example, in 2018, the authors in [51] provide a comprehensive survey of existing client-side web application security solutions that consider desirable features and develop a framework for specifying and enforcing security policies for JavaScript web applications, namely GUARDIA. In [45], Musch *et al.* propose a *ScriptProtect* framework that instruments third-party JavaScript code to prevent the string-to-code conversions to protect the first-party origin from potential XSS attacks.

Although the works mentioned above provide possible solutions to secure JavaScript code in web pages, they aim to be used at the development phase. In contrast, our work aims at a tool that end-users can use to protect their privacy.

**Browser Extensions.** In addition to the research works on JavaScript security, there are many studies on browser extension design problems in recent years. Although these browser extensions provide a tool for web users to protect themselves from possible attacks, their technical approaches are different from our work, as we discuss in detail below.

In [3], the authors propose a new approach to blocking malicious third-party content achieved through an analysis of inclusion sequences constructed from an in-browser vantage point and implemented with EXCISION in a modified Chromium browser. Many experiments conducted in [4] simulate how advisement and analytics companies bypass ad-block extensions and how a bug with chrome web request help to block the extension from functioning. They base on the evaluation of the bug fix in different states to indicate that some companies still use WebSocket in troubleshooting like serving advertisements, infiltrating the DOM, and fingerprinting.

In addition, Barshir *et al.* [5] develop a methodology for detecting ad exchange information flow (both client- and server-side) by leveraging retargeted ads. Also, in [2], the authors propose a new approach (referred to as ORIGINTRACER) to determining the source of content modifications done by over-privileged browser extensions or other third-party content. They indicate that this approach statistically improves the ability of users to recognize injected advertisements through the use of visual indicators while incurring a modest overhead. In [23], the authors present a framework for the verification of browser extensions to ensure they are secure and not over-privileged. Ter *et al.* in [58] also provide an approach to synthesizing abstract behavioral models from XPCOM interfaces. Their method invokes sequences of extensions obtained by the runtime interface invoking approach. This approach requires the preparatory implementation of a behavior monitoring system. It also proposes to define the vulnerable behavior sequence patterns. The design in this paper is used to guide the testing process adopted on sequence matching methods for detecting the security and reliability vulnerability of extensions.

In [14], Dhawan and Ganapathy present an in-browser system for tracking information-flow in order to analyze JavaScript-based browser extensions and identify their violations. In [65], they design `Expector`, a system for identifying chrome extensions that serve malicious ads, utilizing this system to detect extensions that inject ads or participate in malvertising. In [27], the authors propose a preliminary extension system design for protecting users' privacy from malicious extensions. Their method is also based on the idea of mandatory access control. Moreover, the authors in [57] study a comprehensive new model for extension security that aims to redress the shortcomings of existing extension mechanisms. Their proposed model works through the use of a logic-based specification language. The language describes fine-grained access control and data flow policies that govern an extension's privilege over web content. This model verifies extensions through analysis and includes a module for converting safe extensions into a form that allows for the execution of safety checks at runtime.

There are also other research studies focusing on the interaction between a browser extension and the security policy. For instance, in [25], Hausknecht *et al.* examine why browser extension's interaction with Content Security Policy is one reason for its slow adoption. They also classify three types of vulnerabilities arising from the interaction between extensions and CSP, proposing a solution, and providing a case study as a proof-of-concept. Besides, the authors in [56] explore browser extension discovery and the invasive nature of both websites and extensions. Roeshner *et al.* [53] and Mayer and Mitchell [34] investigate the web tracking. The former is with a focus on the technical implementation and functions of trackers, and the latter one is with the focusing on the policy debate over trackers. In [15], the authors explore the ability of browsers to be uniquely identified through fingerprinting. They implement a fingerprinting algorithm to estimate future success rates and discuss the privacy threats and implications posed by fingerprinting.

Likewise, in [46], the authors propose a new client-side JavaScript framework in order to check the integrity, origin, authentication, and risks of all JavaScript third-party resources, evaluating the solution through implementation. Moreover, in [36], the authors provide insight into the landscape of tracker blocker tools. Wills and Uzunoglu [64] explore the effectiveness of ad-blocking tools.

In [28], Iqbal *et al.* study a graph-based machine learning approach to blocking ads and tracker. They create a graph representation used to trace relationships between page contents (HTML structure, network requests, JavaScript behavior of the webpages) and (third-party) ads/trackers. Besides, the authors in [29] investigate a framework that manages which security mechanism is active to cut down on high overheads created by outdated security solutions.

# 3    Proposed Approach

## 3.1    Overview

The objective of our method is to monitor the JavaScript code execution and stop a JavaScript operation if it violates a given policy. To this end, we intercept JavaScript operations, including property access and method calls, to enforce policies. In our enforcement code, we track the actual caller of the operation (we termed it `code origin`) and apply a specific policy for each code origin. Listing 1 illustrates the overview of our technical approach in pseudo-code, where we implement the interception within an anonymous function. Code within an anonymous function is to ensure that any code outside of the scope cannot access our code. In the next subsection, we describe our interception method, how we track the code origin, and how we enforce policies for each code origin.

**Listing 1.** The overview of our technical approach in pseudo-code.

```
(function(){
  let reference = original;
  let code_origin = getCodeOrigin(..);
  original = wrapper(){
    if (PolicyCheck(code_origin, reference_name,arguments))
      execute(reference);
  }//the wrapping
})();
```

## 3.2    JavaScript Interception

We review the JavaScript operations and categorize them into three different types: method calls, object creation and access, and property access. For each type of operation, we propose to intercept as follows.

**Method Calls.** Method calls are functions belonging to a global object. For example, `document.getElementById(..)` is a method call, which invokes the `getElementById` function of the *document* global object. For each method call, we wrap the original reference and its aliases by capturing any available prototype inheritance chain of the reference. We leverage a prior library [32] that implements these types of wrapping for our approach. In Sect. 4, we elaborate in more details of this approach.

**Listing 2.** Simplified code of mediating the access to document.write

```
var desc= Object.getOwnPropertyDescriptor(Document.prototype,
                                        "cookie");
//assert the desc object and its prototype chain
Object.defineProperty(document, "cookie", {get: function(){
    var code_origin = getCodeOrigin(new Error().stack);
    if (originAllowed(code_origin,"cookie")) {
        setOriginSourceRead(code_origin,"cookie");
        return desc.get.call(document);
    }
    return;
  },
  set: function(val){ desc.set.call(document,val); },
  enumerable : false,
  configurable : false
});
```

**Property Access.** A property is a field of an object that can be accessed (read or write) by JavaScript code. As these properties, for example, document.cookie may contain sensitive data of users, we need to mediate the access to them. To this end, we leverage the Object.defineProperty(..) API (standardized in ECMAScript 5 and still supported in later versions [16]) to define the handler functions whenever a property is read (get) or write (set). Simplified code (for brevity) in Listing 2 illustrates this mediation process for the document.cookie property.

**Object Creation and Access.** There are several JavaScript operations that are based on object creation. For example, the "new Image(..)" operation creates a new image object (HTMLImageElement) that can be appended to a web page to display an image. In our observations and experiments, in some cases, although this object creation operation returns the same object type as an equivalent function call (for example, new Image(..) (object creation) and document.createElement("img") (method call) both return an HTMLImageElement object), wrapping the object prototype alone, e.g., HTMLImageElement.prototype, does not capture the object creation operation and therefore cannot control the property access to this newly created object. For this reason, we manually create a wrapper class for each original class and mediate the access to the wrapper class using the Proxy object, standardized in ECMAScript 6 [16] and define a specific policy each access operation. Listing 3 demonstrates an implementation example for mediating the "new Image(..)" operation.

**Listing 3.** Simplified code of mediating the access to new Image(..)

```
var imgPolicy = {
    get: function(obj, prop) { /* policies for get */},
    set: function(obj, prop, value) { /* policies for set */}
```

```
};
var OriginalImage = Image;
class ImageWrapper {
    constructor(height, width) {
        var imgObject = new OriginalImage(height,width);
        imgObject = new Proxy(imgObject,imgPolicy);
        return imgObject;
    }
}
Image = ImageWrapper;
```

### 3.3    Tracking the Source (origin) of the Code

A web page nowadays includes typically JavaScript code that can be sourced from different servers [47]. Browsers enforce the same-origin policy to ensure that JavaScript code comes from one origin (specified by the protocol, host, and port of an URL) cannot access the credentials of other origins [41]. However, the same-origin policy treats all code included in a web page as the same origin even though the code comes from an external web site [41,45,54]. Several prior works, e.g., [20,48], recognize this security issue and propose new approaches to enforcing different policies for JavaScript within a web page but is sourced from external servers. For example, FlashJax [48] provides a new JavaScript API to load and execute JavaScript under a principal and enforces principal-based policies for external JavaScript code. However, FlashJax requires web developers to use this new JavaScript API on the web page; thus, it is not applicable for a browser-based tool. In our work, we leverage the call stack of JavaScript language to trace the source of the code, i.e., from which origin (scheme, host, port) the code is included. We term this source of the code as `code origin`. We note that our code origin concept is different from the web origin term usually used in the same-origin policy [41]. To track the code origin at runtime when we want to enforce a policy, we create a new `Error` object (`new Error().stack`) to get its stack and trace the top of the stack to get the code origin (We notice that a similar approach has been introduced in [45]; however, our implementation is independent and concurrently with that work). Our experiments demonstrate that this code origin tracing method can keep track of exactly where a JavaScript operation is invoked. The usage of this approach has already been illustrated in Listing 2.

### 3.4    Context-Aware and Code Origin-Based Policies

As we can trace the origin of the code, we wish to define and enforce more precise policies that can detect and prevent possible information leakage channels. The ideal method is to encode information flow policies. However, this approach requires new language constructors with new browser implementation [26]. In this work, we propose to control the information flow at the endpoints. This method means that we monitor the operations that read from sensitive data sources or send information to the outside of a browser. When a sending operation is called, we check whether sensitive information was read. As we can keep track of the code origin, we can enforce policies that depend on the code origin. We can also consult the user and let the user decides to allow or deny a data send operation that might be suspicious.

# 4  Implementation

We realize our proposed method in a JavaScript library and deploy it into a browser extension to develop a self-protecting tool for web users. In this section, we describe our JavaScript library, the concrete policies we have implemented, and how we develop a browser extension that leverages our library.

## 4.1  JavaScript Monitoring Library

We implement our method by developing a JavaScript library to intercept Java-Script operations that might cause privacy leakage. Our library must be executed first in a web page to ensure that it can keep the original references to the intercepted operations.

We divide our interception implementation into two types: (i) data source access: operations can get sensitive data; (ii) data sink channels: operations can send data to the outside of a browser . We detail each type below.

**Data Source Access.** The data sources in a web page include the cookie, HTML local storage, browsing history, location, the values of form elements, and the web page contents [34,49]. These data can be accessed by method calls or property read. We implement each type of data source read according to the approach presented in Sect. 3.2. For each operation, we check whether the code origin is allowed to read the data. If allowed, we mark that the code origin has read the data by update the corresponding state. The code in Listing 2 (in Sect. 3.2) illustrates this interception implementation method for a property access of a data source (cookie). In Listing 4, we demonstrate the interception implementation of a data source using a method call (`localStorage.getItem(..)`). In this code, `monitorMethod` is a wrapping interface implementing the wrapping approach for method calls presented in Sect. 3. We list the common data source read operations implemented in our library in Table 1 (`document.getElement*` in the first row stand for `getElementById`, `getElementsByTagName`, `getElementsByClassName`).

**Listing 4.** Interception implementation of a method call accessing a data source

```
function localStorage_getItem_policy(args, proceed, obj) {
  var itemID = args[0];
  var code_origin = getCodeOrigin(new Error().stack);
  if (originAllowed(code_origin,"localStorage",
                    "getItem", itemID)) {
```

```
  setOriginSourceRead(code_origin,"localStorage");
  return proceed(); //execute the method call
 }
 return; //supress the method call
}
monitorMethod(localStorage, "getItem",
              localStorage_getItem_policy);
```

Table 1. List of operations that can access users' data

| Operation | Type | Data source |
|---|---|---|
| document.getElement* | Method call | Page contents |
| localStorage.getItem | Method call | Local storage |
| document.cookie | Property access | Cookies |
| window.history | Property access | Browsing history |
| navigator.geolocation.getCurrentPosition | Method call | Location |

**Data Sink Channels.** We consider the channels where data can be sent from a browser to outside. We do not consider the attack scenarios that are aware by end-users such as redirection as this is out of the scope of our work. Generally speaking, these data channels are HTTP requests sent from a browser [41]. JavaScript operations that can generate a HTTP request include assigning an URL source to an object such as Frame, IFrame, Image, Script, and Form, Ajax, and WebSocket. We note that WebSocket is not an actual HTTP request yet allows browsers to open two-way interactive communication to a server to send and receive messages asynchronously [42]. In the past, tracking companies have leverage WebSocket to circumvent the blocking mechanism in ad blockers [4]. We intercept these channels using the approach for object creation presented in Sect. 3.2. Also, we intercept method calls, for example, document.createElement(..) that create these objects and enforce the same policy as the object creation interception. We stop a data send operation if it violates a policy.

## 4.2   MyWebGuard - The Privacy Protection Tool in Browsers

In principle, our library can be deployed either at the server or client-side. However, as we aim to develop a tool for web users, we opt to implement a browser extension using our library. As discussed earlier, our method requires that the interception library run first before a web page is loaded. To this end, we put our JavaScript library code within the innerHTML property of a script object and append it to the current page. We perform experiments to confirm that our code is executed before any other code in a web page. Listing 5 depicts this inclusion method of our library.

**Listing 5.** Injection of our code in a browser extension

```
var mywebguard = document.createElement("script");
mywebguard.innerHTML = '
(function() {
  //the full JavaScript interception library here
  //...
})();';
document.documentElement.appendChild(mywebguard);
```

Implemented as a JavaScript library, our method should be able to be deployed in any browser extension. In this implementation prototype, we develop our MyWebGuard extension and evaluate it in Chromium family, including Google Chrome, Chromium, and Brave. In the future, we explore to deploy our library in other major browsers.

## 5    Evaluation

In this section, we report the evaluation of our method implemented in a browser extension. We first create a test suite that contains a web page for the first-party and a script file for the third-party. We simulate attack scenarios to evaluate the effectiveness of our method.

To evaluate our method, we installed our MyWebGuard extension in Chromium family browsers. We perform the evaluations on a Dell Inspiron 3521 machine with CPU 2127U @ 1.90 GHzx2, 8 GB memory, Ubuntu 18.04.2 LTS. We test our extension in Google Chrome (Version 76.0.3809.100 64-bit), Chromium (Version 76.0.3809.87 64-bit) and Brave (version 0.65.121) browsers.

### 5.1    Privacy Leakage Detection and Prevention

We create a test web site and develop first-party code to perform operations that we intercept. We include a third-party JavaScript code that performs similar operations. Our experiments demonstrate that potential information leakage to the first-party or third-party server is captured by our method. Figure 1 shows two test cases that leak data detected by our browser extension.

**Fig. 1.** MyWebGuard can detect and prevent potential information leakage that is ignored by Ghostery and uBlock Origin extensions

Interestingly enough, these simulated data leakage channels are not detected by leading browser extensions such as Ghostery, and uOrigin Block, demonstrated in Fig. 2. This evidence reflects and confirms our observation and motivation discussed in the introduction.

**Fig. 2.** Ghostery and uBlock Origin extensions do not detect the tracking requests on our test suite site

In an intensive mode with all alert messages turned on, MyWebGuard can detect potential leakage sent to external origins and warn the user in real-world websites. For example, Fig. 3 shows the case that our MyWebGuard extension detects a cross-origin data leakage on Youtube.

**Fig. 3.** MyWebGuard extension detects cross-origin data leakage on Youtube

### 5.2   Compatibility and Load Time Overhead

We turn on our extension with alert messages disabled in the tested browsers (Google Chrome, Chromium, and Brave) and load regular websites to test whether these sites are loaded as usual. We do not notice any issues when loading the websites with our extension. Figure 4 demonstrates that a Youtube video can play when our extension is turned on in Chromium.

We also measure if our extension slowdowns the load time of actual websites. We test this by getting the load time numbers in the Network debug in a Chromium browser for top websites in Alexa and several Vietnamese news, with and without our extension. We disable alert and debug messages and load each website ten times to get the average numbers. Figure 5 illustrates the load

**Fig. 4.** Youtube video can be played functionally with MyWebGuard extension in Chromium

time overhead of our extension over ten popular websites. As we can see from this graph, our MyWebGuard tool does not pose a great slow down in load time. The average slow down ratio is 1.33, but in some cases, the load time is even faster with our extension. For example, the slow down for https://ebay.com and https://vnexpress.net is 0.95 and 0.99, respectively. This improvement might be due to the fact that some wrapped operations can be executed faster than the original ones, as reported in the literature [48]. We note that we test https://facebook.com and https://mail.google.com in logged-in sessions because the content of these web pages are too light to test without logged-in.

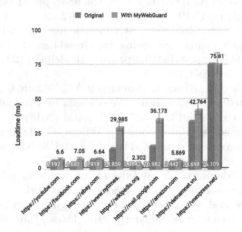

**Fig. 5.** Load time overhead of MyWebGuard in actual websites

# 6   Conclusions and Future Work

In this paper, we have presented MyWebGuard, a user-centric tool to protect the privacy of web users. MyWebGuard can enforce context-aware and code origin-based policies to prevent privacy leakage channels that cannot be captured by existing tools in the industry. The evaluations of our prototype implementation evidence that our novel enforcement method can effectively protect the privacy of web users yet pose lightweight overhead on popular real-world websites.

In the future, we plan to extend and refine the security policies as well as the enforcement mechanism to allow end-users can customize their privacy preferences. We will perform large-scale evaluations of our tool on top websites and investigate whether our tool interferes with co-existing browser extensions. We also plan to leverage machine learning to produce practical policies that protect users but do not break legitimate third-party code. Our objective is to provide a robust and mature tool that web users can use in the real-world to protect their privacy. We also want to explore the effectiveness of our approach when built-in into a browser.

**Acknowledgment.** The authors wish to thank the anonymous reviewers for their helpful comments and suggestions.

# References

1. Agarwal, L., Shrivastava, N., Jaiswal, S., Panjwani, S.: Do not embarrass: re-examining user concerns for online tracking and advertising. In: Proceedings of the Ninth Symposium on Usable Privacy and Security, SOUPS 2013, pp. 8:1–16. ACM (2013)
2. Arshad, S., Kharraz, A., Robertson, W.: Identifying extension-based ad injection via fine-grained web content provenance. In: Monrose, F., Dacier, M., Blanc, G., Garcia-Alfaro, J. (eds.) RAID 2016. LNCS, vol. 9854, pp. 415–436. Springer, Cham (2016). https://doi.org/10.1007/978-3-319-45719-2_19
3. Arshad, S., Kharraz, A., Robertson, W.: Include me out: in-browser detection of malicious third-party content inclusions. In: Grossklags, J., Preneel, B. (eds.) FC 2016. LNCS, vol. 9603, pp. 441–459. Springer, Heidelberg (2017). https://doi.org/10.1007/978-3-662-54970-4_26
4. Bashir, M.A., Arshad, S., Kirda, E., Robertson, W., Wilson, C.: How tracking companies circumvented ad blockers using Websockets. In: Proceedings of the Internet Measurement Conference 2018, pp. 471–477. ACM (2018)
5. Bashir, M.A., Arshad, S., Robertson, W., Wilson, C.: Tracing information flows between ad exchanges using retargeted ads. In: 25th USENIX Security Symposium, USENIX Security 16, pp. 481–496 (2016)
6. Batt, S.: What is "do not track" and does it protect your privacy?, August 2019 https://www.makeuseof.com/tag/not-track-actually-work/
7. Burt, A.: Privacy and cybersecurity are converging. here's why that matters for people and for companies, January 2019. https://hbr.org/2019/01/privacy-and-cybersecurity-are-converging-heres-why-that-matters-for-people-and-for-companies. Accessed 13 Aug 2019
8. Caleb: Ranked: Security and privacy for the most popular web browsers, March 2019. https://www.expressvpn.com/blog/best-browsers-for-privacy/
9. Chanchary, F., Chiasson, S.: User perceptions of sharing, advertising, and tracking. In: Proceedings of the Eleventh Symposium On Usable Privacy and Security, SOUPS 2015, pp. 53–67 (2015)
10. Chromium Blog: Improving privacy and security on the web, May 2019. https://blog.chromium.org/2019/05/improving-privacy-and-security-on-web.html
11. Chudnov, A., Naumann, D.A.: Inlined information flow monitoring for JavaScript. In: Proceedings of the 22nd ACM SIGSAC Conference on Computer and Communications Security, pp. 629–643. ACM (2015)

12. Crockford, D.: ADsafe - Making JavaScript Safe for Advertising (2007). http://www.adsafe.org. Accessed 11 Aug 2019

13. devlin@chromium.org: Manifest V3, December 2018. https://docs.google.com/document/d/1nPu6Wy4LWR66EFLeYInl3NzzhHzc-qnk4w4PX-0XMw8/edit#heading=h.xgjl2srtytjt. Accessed 14 Aug 2019

14. Dhawan, M., Ganapathy, V.: Analyzing information flow in JavaScript-based browser extensions. In: 2009 Annual Computer Security Applications Conference, pp. 382–391. IEEE (2009)

15. Eckersley, P.: How unique is your web browser? In: Atallah, M.J., Hopper, N.J. (eds.) PETS 2010. LNCS, vol. 6205, pp. 1–18. Springer, Heidelberg (2010). https://doi.org/10.1007/978-3-642-14527-8_1

16. Ecma International: ECMAScript 2015 Language Specification ECMA-262 6th Edition, June 2015. https://www.ecma-international.org/ecma-262/6.0/. Accessed 14 Aug 2019

17. Englehardt, S., Narayanan, A.: Online tracking: a 1-million-site measurement and analysis. In: Proceedings of the 2016 ACM SIGSAC conference on computer and communications security, pp. 1388–1401. ACM (2016)

18. Finifter, M., Weinberger, J., Barth, A.: Preventing capability leaks in secure JavaScript subsets. In: NDSS (2010)

19. Fredrikson, M., Livshits, B.: Repriv: re-imagining content personalization and in-browser privacy. In: 2011 IEEE Symposium on Security and Privacy, pp. 131–146. IEEE (2011)

20. Georgiev, M., Jana, S., Shmatikov, V.: Rethinking security of web-based system applications. In: Proceedings of the 24th International Conference on World Wide Web, pp. 366–376. International World Wide Web Conferences Steering Committee (2015)

21. Google Caja: Compiler for making third-party HTML, CSS, and JavaScript safe for embedding (2007). https://developers.google.com/caja/. Accessed 5 Aug 2019

22. Google Chrome: chrome. webRequest. https://developer.chrome.com/extensions/webRequest. Accessed 14 Aug 2019

23. Guha, A., Fredrikson, M., Livshits, B., Swamy, N.: Verified security for browser extensions. In: 2011 IEEE symposium on security and privacy, pp. 115–130. IEEE (2011)

24. Guha, S., Cheng, B., Francis, P.: Privad: practical privacy in online advertising. In: USENIX Conference on Networked Systems Design and Implementation, pp. 169–182 (2011)

25. Hausknecht, D., Magazinius, J., Sabelfeld, A.: May I? - Content security policy endorsement for browser extensions. In: Almgren, M., Gulisano, V., Maggi, F. (eds.) DIMVA 2015. LNCS, vol. 9148, pp. 261–281. Springer, Cham (2015). https://doi.org/10.1007/978-3-319-20550-2_14

26. Hedin, D., Bello, L., Sabelfeld, A.: Information-flow security for JavaScript and its APIs. J. Comput. Secur. 24(2), 181–234 (2016)

27. Heule, S., Rifkin, D., Russo, A., Stefan, D.: The most dangerous code in the browser. In: 15th Workshop on Hot Topics in Operating Systems (HotOS XV) (2015)

28. Iqbal, U., Snyder, P., Zhu, S., Livshits, B., Qian, Z., Shafiq, Z.: AdGraph: a graph-based approach to ad and tracker blocking. In: IEEE Symposium on Security and Privacy, May 2020

29. Katz, O., Livshits, B.: Toward an evidence-based design for reactive security policies and mechanisms. arXiv preprint arXiv:1802.08915 (2018)

30. Leon, P.G., et al.: What matters to users?: factors that affect users' willingness to share information with online advertisers. In: Proceedings of the Ninth Symposium on Usable Privacy and Security, p. 7. ACM (2013)

31. Maffeis, S., Taly, A.: Language-based isolation of untrusted Javascript. In: 2009 22nd IEEE Computer Security Foundations Symposium, pp. 77–91. IEEE (2009)

32. Magazinius, J., Phung, P.H., Sands, D.: Safe wrappers and sane policies for self protecting JavaScript. In: Proceedings of the 15th Nordic Conference in Secure IT Systems NordSec, pp. 239–255, October 2010

33. Mathur, A., Vitak, J., Narayanan, A., Chetty, M.: Characterizing the use of browser-based blocking extensions to prevent online tracking. In: Fourteenth Symposium on Usable Privacy and Security, SOUPS 2018, pp. 103–116 (2018)

34. Mayer, J.R., Mitchell, J.C.: Third-party web tracking: policy and technology. In: 2012 IEEE Symposium on Security and Privacy, pp. 413–427. IEEE (2012)

35. McDonald, A.M., Cranor, L.F.: Americans' attitudes about internet behavioral advertising practices. In: Proceedings of the 9th Annual ACM Workshop on Privacy in the Electronic Society, pp. 63–72. ACM (2010)

36. Merzdovnik, G., et al.: Block me if you can: a large-scale study of tracker-blocking tools. In: 2017 IEEE European Symposium on Security and Privacy, EuroS&P, pp. 319–333. IEEE (2017)

37. Meyerovich, L.A., Livshits, B.: ConScript: Specifying and enforcing fine-grained security policies for Javascript in the browser. In: 2010 IEEE Symposium on Security and Privacy, pp. 481–496. IEEE (2010)

38. Microsoft Edge: Security and privacy group policies (2018). https://docs.microsoft. com/en-us/microsoft-edge/deploy/group-policies/security-privacy-management-gp. Accessed 14 Aug 2019

39. Miller, M.S., Samuel, M., Laurie, B., Awad, I., Stay, M.: Safe active content in sanitized JavaScript. Tech. rep. Google Inc. (2008)

40. Mozilla: webRequest. https://developer.mozilla.org/en-US/docs/Mozilla/Add-ons/WebExtensions/API/webRequest. Accessed 14 Aug 2019

41. Mozilla Developer Network: Same-origin policy. https://developer.mozilla.org/en-US/docs/Web/Security/Same-origin_policy. Accessed 14 Aug 2019

42. Mozilla Developer Network: The WebSocket API (WebSockets), April 2019. https://developer.mozilla.org/en-US/docs/Web/API/WebSockets_API

43. Mozilla Developer Network: What are extensions? March 2019. https://developer.mozilla.org/en-US/docs/Mozilla/Add-ons/WebExtensions/What_are_WebExtensions

44. Mozilla Security Blog: Privacy archives, August 2019. https://blog.mozilla.org/security/category/privacy/. Accessed 14 Aug 2019

45. Musch, M., Steffens, M., Roth, S., Stock, B., Johns, M.: ScriptProtect: mitigating unsafe third-party javascript practices, pp. 391–402 (2019)

46. Nakhaei, K., Ansari, E., Ansari, F.: JSSignature: eliminating third-party-hosted JavaScript infection threats using digital signatures. arXiv preprint arXiv:1812.03939 (2018)

47. Nikiforakis, N., et al.: You are what you include: large-scale evaluation of remote JavaScript inclusions. In: Proceedings of the 2012 ACM Conference on Computer and Communications Security, pp. 736–747. ACM (2012)

48. Phung, P.H., Monshizadeh, M., Sridhar, M., Hamlen, K.W., Venkatakrishnan, V.: Between worlds: securing mixed JavaScript/ActionScript multi-party web content. IEEE Trans. Dependable Secure Comput. TDSC **12**(4), 443–457 (2015). https://doi.org/10.1109/TDSC.2014.2355847

49. Phung, P.H., Sands, D., Chudnov, A.: Lightweight self-protecting JavaScript. In: Proceedings of the 4th International Symposium on Information, Computer, and Communications Security (AsiaCCS), pp. 47–60, March 2009

50. Politz, J.G., Eliopoulos, S.A., Guha, A., Krishnamurthi, S.: ADsafety: type-based verification of JavaScript sandboxing. In: Proceedings of the 20th USENIX Conference on Security. SEC 2011, USENIX Association (2011)

51. Pupo, A.L.S., Nicolay, J., Boix, E.G.: GUARDIA: specification and enforcement of Javascript security policies without VM modifications. In: The 15th International Conference on Managed Languages & Runtimes, pp. 17:1–17:10. ACM (2018)

52. Reis, C., Dunagan, J., Wang, H.J., Dubrovsky, O., Esmeir, S.: BrowserShield: vulnerability-driven filtering of dynamic HTML. ACM Trans. Web (TWEB) 1(3), 11 (2007)

53. Roesner, F., Kohno, T., Wetherall, D.: Detecting and defending against third-party tracking on the web. In: Proceedings of the 9th USENIX Conference on Networked Systems Design and Implementation, p. 12. USENIX Association (2012)

54. Schwenk, J., Niemietz, M., Mainka, C.: Same-origin policy: evaluation in modern browsers. In: 26th USENIX Security Symposium (USENIX Security 17), pp. 713–727. USENIX Association, Vancouver, August 2017

55. Siddiqui, A.: Google's Manifest V3 will change how ad blocking Chrome extensions work: is it to cripple them, or is it for security? June 2019. https://www.xda-developers.com/google-chrome-manifest-v3-ad-blocker-extension-api/

56. Sjösten, A., Van Acker, S., Sabelfeld, A.: Discovering browser extensions via web accessible resources. In: Proceedings of the Seventh ACM on Conference on Data and Application Security and Privacy, pp. 329–336. ACM (2017)

57. Swamy, N., Livshits, B., Guha, A., Fredrikson, M.J.: Programming, verifying, visualizing, and deploying browser extensions with fine-grained security policies, March 2015, US Patent 8,978,106

58. Ter Louw, M., Lim, J.S., Venkatakrishnan, V.N.: Enhancing web browser security against malware extensions. J. Comput. Virol. 4(3), 179–195 (2008)

59. Ur, B., Leon, P.G., Cranor, L.F., Shay, R., Wang, Y.: Smart, useful, scary, creepy: perceptions of online behavioral advertising. In: Proceedings of the Eighth Symposium On Usable Privacy and Security, SOUPS 2012, p. 4. ACM (2012)

60. W3C: Content security policy (2018). https://www.w3.org/TR/CSP/

61. W3C: Tracking Preference Expression (DNT), January 2019. https://www.w3.org/TR/tracking-dnt/

62. W3Techs.com: Usage Statistics of JavaScript as Client-side Programming Language on Websites, August 2019. https://w3techs.com/technologies/details/cp-javascript/all/all

63. Weissbacher, M., Lauinger, T., Robertson, W.: Why is CSP failing? trends and challenges in CSP adoption. In: Stavrou, A., Bos, H., Portokalidis, G. (eds.) RAID 2014. LNCS, vol. 8688, pp. 212–233. Springer, Cham (2014). https://doi.org/10.1007/978-3-319-11379-1_11

64. Wills, C.E., Uzunoglu, D.C.: What ad blockers are (and are not) doing. In: 2016 Fourth IEEE Workshop on Hot Topics in Web Systems and Technologies (HotWeb), pp. 72–77. IEEE (2016)

65. Xing, X., et al.: Understanding malvertising through ad-injecting browser extensions. In: Proceedings of the 24th International Conference on World Wide Web, pp. 1286–1295 (2015). International World Wide Web Conferences Steering Committee

# Blockchain-Based Open Data: An Approach for Resolving Data Integrity and Transparency

Dinh-Duc Truong[1,3], Thanh Nguyen-Van[1,3], Quoc-Bao Nguyen[3],
Nguyen Huynh Huy[3], Tuan-Anh Tran[3], Nhat-Quang Le[2],
and Khuong Nguyen-An[3(✉)]

[1] R&D Department, GINAR LIMITED, Hong Kong, Hong Kong
{ductd,thanhnv}@GINAR.io
[2] R&D Department, Infinity Blockchain Labs, Ho Chi Minh City, Vietnam
quangln@blockchainlabs.asia
[3] Faculty of Computer Science and Engineering, University of Technology
(HCMUT), VNU-HCM, Ho Chi Minh City, Vietnam
{1510821,1513056,1510180,1511252,trtanh,nakhuong}@hcmut.edu.vn

**Abstract.** Smart cities bring together technology, governments, and society to enable a smart economy, smart mobility, a smart environment, smart people, smart living, and smart governance. However, they come with many technological challenges due to the lack of an efficient and secure mechanism for open data. The gap between a government and its citizens of public data prevents society from evolving. Many current proposals face serious problems of integrity and security issues. In this paper, we design and implement a mechanism for secure storing and exchanging open data leveraging Hyperledger Fabric and IPFS (InterPlanetary File System). The proposed solution relies on two of the most interesting properties of blockchain which are immutability and decentralization to bring transparency and integrity to open data while ensuring its availability. The novel idea is to enable users to check the integrity of the data and retrieve all information about data-log without the help of any third party. As a result, it improves the trust among people who need to use data in other applications, also reduces the risk of making wrong decisions due to bad data. Moreover, the implementation results show that our solution is efficient for practical uses.

**Keywords:** Open data · Integrity · Availability · Transparency · Blockchain · Hyperledger Fabric · IPFS

## 1 Introduction

The term *open data*[1] nowadays is popularized and becomes trending in many cities or nations around the world. Building a smart city or electronic government [9] requires a huge amount of data about social information and behaviors

---

[1] http://parisinnovationreview.com/articles-en/a-brief-history-of-open-data.

© Springer Nature Switzerland AG 2019
T. K. Dang et al. (Eds.): FDSE 2019, LNCS 11814, pp. 526–541, 2019.
https://doi.org/10.1007/978-3-030-35653-8_34

for research purposes. Sharing data between a federal or citizens is an efficient method that can save time and effort for data preparation. In other word, some data sets should be available to access, to use, or to be republished. The access limit is defined according to a given privileged user. For example, to solve a multidisciplinary problem, it is required to gather all necessary data and information from all relevant industries, and thus great contributions from many people and sophisticated businesses are demanding. Open data opens a possibility to share and to publish data between a government and citizens quickly, promptly and accurately, thereby motivating economic and scientific development. According to the European Data Portal statistics [4], open data in traffic has saved 629 million hours for unnecessary waiting time, reducing 5.5% of traffic accidents, generating 25000 jobs new, and save 1.7 billion Euro for the Government. Those are clear evidence that show remarkable benefits of applying open data to society.

The properties, which are selected to be principal standards of the open data portal, come from the CIA triangle [11]: *confidentiality*, *availability*, and *integrity*. Confidentiality can be understood as data restriction. Access to data would be restricted to only some users on organization by using role-based authorization. Role defines permission include READ, WRITE, MODIFY, DELETE that can be done on a particular resource, user's actions are limited by the undertaken role. However, in the context of open data, this property is not so important because the target of the portal is to publicly share data between the government and citizens. Instead, data availability must be set at top priority. It is obvious that confidentiality and integrity are meaningless if data is impossible to access to. The most common form of data availability attack is known as denial of service (DOS) attack[2], or distributed denial of service (DDOS) attack[3]. These types of attack make the user unable to access the desired resource. If the data is only stored in one place or in a centralized location, it is prone to a single point of failure[4]. A solution is to have data copied and stored in distributed places over the network. We proposed in our model IPFS as a storage solution to open data portal. IPFS is a file system that is operated over the network. Within IPFS network, data is cloned and stored in many network nodes. Therefore, if a request is sent to a corrupted node, corresponding data still be able to be responded from other nodes. IPFS also provides a node the capability to recover data loss by querying it from other nodes. Solid features of IPFS give the higher possibility of having data available at all time. Among confidentiality and availability, integrity is at higher level of exposure to be exploited. Attacks on websites or databases have been going on in recent years and inflict tremendous damage on organizations and governments. Hackers can modify or even delete data to support on their bad purposes[5]. False data, either public or private, can all cause bad consequences. For example, misinterpreting market trends

---

[2] https://us.norton.com/internetsecurity-emerging-threats-dos-attacks-explained.html.

[3] https://us.norton.com/internetsecurity-emerging-threats-what-is-a-ddos-attack-30sectech-by-norton.html.

[4] https://searchdatacenter.techtarget.com/definition/Single-point-of-failure-SPOF.

[5] https://www.itsecurityguru.org/2016/11/29/2017-year-data-integrity-breach/.

leads to wrong business decisions, causing economic damage; or modified law documents cause misunderstanding in the government's policy leading to rule violations, etc. Therefore, ensuring integrity of data will increase trust in the system. In fact, data integrity and confidentiality can mutually affect each other. As mentioned before, role based-authorization system can be used to limit access of unauthorized users. Moreover, all activities on the data are recorded in order to detect abnormal behaviors that might affect the data integrity. However, a system under protections of authorization and logging systems is still vulnerable to attacks [1]. Hacker once successfully breaks into the system can modify log files or event delete them[6].

Fortunately, blockchain technology[7] offers the capability to protect data from modifications. Reinforced by cryptography theory, blockchain's consensus guarantees that valid data of blockchain is immutable. Neither users or hackers can be able to change or delete data on blockchain which results in data integrity of the whole system.

**Our Contributions.** We first recall the definition of open data and some of its security issues. Then we propose a solution to these problems. The solution mainly focuses on dealing with data integrity and availability. In contrast to the traditional approach, in which data is stored on a centralized system, we employ the IPFS technology to distribute data over many nodes in a decentralized network. This ensures that any single corrupted node will not affect the availability of the data. Besides, thanks to the data distribution mechanism of this technology, data integrity is greatly enhanced. Moreover, we also store the checksum and the log of each dataset on the Hyperledger Fabric blockchain to help make the process of checking the integrity and history of data easier. The immutability of the blockchain guarantees that the checksum once written, cannot be changed at any time afterward. Subsequently, we also demonstrate the proposed solution through an experimental system which is comprised of a distributed file storage system, an open data portal, and a private blockchain. This demonstration has positive results in terms of fast processing time, high throughput, and the successful validation rate.

**Structure of the Paper.** The rest of this paper is structured as follows. In Sect. 2, we recall some fundamental knowledge about open data, blockchain, Hyperledger Fabric, and InterPlanetary File Storage (IPFS). In Sect. 3, we explore some of the recent related proposals and go through some of the drawbacks of each solution. The detailed architecture is given in Sect. 4. An implementation as well as the testing results can be found in Sect. 5. Finally, in Sect. 6 concludes this paper.

---

# 2   Background

## 2.1   Open Data

As defined by the Open Definition [10], *"Open data is data that can be freely used, re-used and redistributed by anyone - subject only, at most, to the requirement to attribute and share alike"*. To achieve the properties in this definition, open data should be open in both technical and legal aspects. The term technically open means that the data is available in a standard format for computer readability, or in other words, the data can be accessed and processed by computer software. The term legally open means that the data can be used without any restriction or contexts. For example, citizens can use the data sets for either commercial or non-commercial purposes.

The *Open data* is expected to bring a lot of benefits to the involved parties. We can consider the benefits of open data from the perspective of the government and the citizens. For the government, open data will help them improve their transparency and publicity since the citizens are able to get the necessary information for comparing and contrasting the results of activities among departments. The operation costs of departments will be significantly reduced, while the efficiency at work will be considerably increased. These impacts not only bring greater economic revenue but also solve some of the social problems needed to be addressed. On the citizen's side, it creates the most favorable conditions for exercising democratic rights and participating in monitoring government operation relied on access to the government data. Businesses and communities may use open data to understand potential markets better and create valuable products. For example, in the process of researching and developing artificial intelligence systems, there is always a lack of data sets to train. Once the data is set to open, the developers will be provided an abundance of data resources to train their model.

To maximize the benefits, the government should publish their data sets in the format that is "most open". Tim Berners-Lee[8] proposed a schema to evaluate the openness of the open data formats called the *five-star standard scheme* [14]. In order to obtain more stars for the data sets, it takes some cost from the data provider. However, the "more open" data will be used at scale by the users due to its convenience and effectiveness.

## 2.2   Security Analysis of Open Data

Although open data has a lot of benefits as discussed above, organizations such as the government, hospitals, etc. are reluctant to open their data. Since open data is shared publicly, it will be exploited by a large community. If the data is wrong, it will be misleading, resulting in inaccurate analysis and decision making on those data sets. The value of open data in this situation no longer exists and can cause harm. Hence, it is urgent to study security issues related to open data and proposing solutions to address those problems.

---

[8] https://www.theguardian.com/technology/2019/mar/12/tim-berners-lee-on-30-years-of-the-web-if-we-dream-a-little-we-can-get-the-web-we-want.

In terms of the law, the published open data must be ensured that there is no legal violation, no disclosure of economic secrets, personal information and especially information on infrastructure e.g. power plants, dams, transmitters, etc. to avoid the risks of attacks. For example, the attackers can not reveal personal information from a single data set but can obtain them by intermixing multiple sets of open data. This is challenging for the data providers since they have the responsibility to ensure that the above scenario does not happen before publishing the data sets.

On the other hand, from the technical aspect, open data systems need to ensure the availability and integrity of data. Currently, the government often stores their data in a centralized way. Since it produces convenience in data management and monitoring. However, this approach leads the systems to be vulnerable under deny of service attacks, distributed-deny of service attacks, unexpected altering data sets, etc. Consequently, the system can not get the trust of their user since the data integrity and availability is not ensured. Moreover, the transparency of these centralized models is not appreciated. Therefore, to enhance the transparency, data integrity and availability of the published data, the centralized modules should be eliminated by applying the distributed systems.

## 2.3   Blockchain and Hyperledger Fabric Framework

As mentioned in the previous sections, we propose a new approach to enhance the integrity of open data as well as improving transparency in the provision of city government data by using blockchain technology (See [5,13]).

A **blockchain** is an electronic ledger that stores encrypted, authenticated and shared events in the format of *transactions* in a decentralized network using consensus protocols. The potential of blockchain is created by the power of *cryptography, game theory* and *distributed networks. Cryptography* ensures the integrity of the blockchain data since the data is split into blocks that are interconnected by their hash code. Also, public key cryptography ensures the identity of participants in the network. *Game theory* acts as a consensus protocol in the distributed network.

**Hyperledger Fabric** [3] is a private blockchain developed and maintained by Linux Foundation[9] and IBM Corporation[10]. This private network is made up of *organizations*. Each *organization* consists of one or more *peers*, a *certificate authority, local state databases*, and *chaincodes. Peers* in the network will perform operations such as executing, endorsing, committing transactions or connecting with other peers. The *certificate authority* is the component that is responsible for providing and managing the identity of participants in the network. To enhance privacy and security, Hyperledger Fabric uses the concept of *channel. A channel* is a private group of participants whose all data, including transaction information, *channel* members are only visible and accessible to members inside the *channel.*

---

[9] https://www.hyperledger.org/projects/fabric.
[10] https://cloud.ibm.com/docs/services/blockchain?topic=blockchain-hyperledger-fabric.

Hyperledger Fabric provides a flexible way to configure consensus protocol as well as customize transactions to fit with specific goals. Unlike other type of blockchains which using smart contracts for handling the business logic, Hyperledger Fabric uses a chaincode instead. A chaincode includes types of participants, types of assets, access control rules, types of queries to read stored data, and especially business logic relied on transactions. To get a consensus for the entire network, Hyperledger Fabric not only uses chaincode but also uses endorsement policy and the Orderer component. The orderer plays a role in coordinating and ordering the transactions before packing them in a block so that it can be updated on the ledger.

## 2.4   InterPlanetary File System

InterPlanetary File System [8], in short IPFS, is a peer-to-peer distributed file system for storing and sharing hypermedia files over a network by synthesizing the best ideas like Distributed Hash Table[11] (DHT), BitTorrent[12], Git[13]. Because of being a peer-to-peer network, IPFS uses the DHT to coordinate and maintain metadata about the whole network. In the same vein with BitTorrent, IPFS uses the BitSwap protocol for block exchange. BitSwap operates as a persistent marketplace where node can acquire the blocks they need, regardless of what files those blocks are part of. Lastly, IPFS uses the same mechanism as Git to manage versions of data.

Due to the decentralization property of data in IPFS, this distributed file storage system can be used to improve the integrity and availability in the open data system.

# 3   Related Works

The development of smart cities and e-governments which relied on the government's open data has experimented in several countries. The US government is the pioneer for this trend since they built a protocol of open data portal in 2009 [15]. After many years put in use, this portal is able to provide a number of 229,371 data sets in various formats and related to many fields such as agriculture, ecosystems, education, energy, finance, health, natural disasters, science, and research.

There have been some data portals deployed around the world. However, the combination of open data and blockchain to increase reliability and transparency is very little. With the attempts to increase trust and transparency, the Austria government has applied the blockchain technology to the open data portal of Vienna[14] and successfully demonstrated under a project named "Data Notarization Blockchain" [16] in 2018. Once a contributor publishes a data set, a

---

[11] http://www.cs.princeton.edu/courses/archive/spr11/cos461/docs/lec22-dhts.pdf.
[12] http://people.scs.carleton.ca/mmannan/publications/bittorrent.pdf.
[13] https://git-scm.com/book/en/v2.
[14] https://digitales.wien.gv.at/site/open-data/.

checksum of it will be stored on the public blockchain network for validating the content of the data. Therefore, the citizens can independently check information via open data gateways or blockchain explorer sites without going through an intermediate third party.

In Vietnam, the government of Ho Chi Minh City has also begun to prepare the first step to implement an open data portal [6]. The portal is expected to have integration with some important databases including medical, education, invest, energy, climate, environment. However, the portal is still thin in the content due to lacking data sets.

## 4     Proposed Architecture

We construct an architecture which is comprised of 3 main components: a web based application to be the portal using NodeJS platform, a distributed file storage system IPFS for storing data, and a private blockchain network for data validation using Hyperledger Fabric. This approach is expected to improve the data integrity, data availability and enhancing the transparency of the open data system. By relying on distributed storage and cryptography, IPFS significantly improves the data availability and data integrity. Meanwhile, because of being a private blockchain network, Hyperledger Fabric enhances the data originality and authenticity. In addition, all events related to the published data are recorded and become transparent to everyone. Hence, the transparency of the open data system is increased. In particular, the data sets are stored on the IPFS network and retrieved through the use of IPFS hashes called *CID*. These *CID* are immutably recorded with metadata on the Hyperledger Fabric network.

### 4.1     Architecture Overview

Overall, our system includes three main modules, which are a Portal, a distributed file storage system IPFS and a private blockchain network Hyperledger Fabric. These modules are illustrated in the Fig. 1 below.

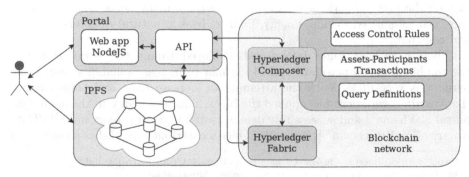

**Fig. 1.** Architecture overview

The first component in our architecture is the Portal. The Portal aims to show information gained from the blockchain network about data and handle user requests. In particular, this component is responsible for interacting with two remaining parts. The Portal receives requests from data contributors to triggers smart contracts on the blockchain network and then uploads data to the distributed file storage system if no error occurs.

Secondly, the Distributed File Storage System IPFS component is where all data sets are stored. IPFS generates a unique hash which is the address of a bundle of files containing the data set content. The hash address is used to locate and access the bundle stored on the IPFS network. This hash address will be stored on the ledger of Hyperledger Fabric blockchain to manage and access conveniently.

Finally, Hyperledger Fabric plays an important role in ensuring transparency and enhancing the data integrity. Metadata is stored in the database of all peers in the blockchain network. In order to set permission on publishing data, Hyperledger Fabric also authenticates data contributors. All activities of the contributors are recorded immutably in transactions. Besides, the transparency of our system is improved since all transactions are configured to be visible to everyone. In other words, Hyperledger Fabric enhances the data integrity better than the centralized system does. Hyperledger Fabric also provides a mechanism for the citizens to verify all data content without third parties. Obviously, Hyperledger Fabric has guaranteed a lot of transparency for the system as well as enhanced the data integrity. To achieve this idea, we use the Hyperledger Composer framework developed by IBM[15] to configure our network. Hyperledger Composer interacts with the network and defines logical components such as assets, participants, transactions, access control rules for Hyperledger Fabric network easier and more intuitive. Abstract objects are defined in the language called Modelling Language which provided by Hyperledger Composer (See Sect. 4.2).

To summarize, we introduced components and their responsibility for our model in general. In fact, the Portal implementation will be similar to most websites that allow sharing data on the Internet. IPFS is a pre-configured distributed network and has been deployed in practice. We only use it as a solution to our model. Therefore, we will not go into details on the configuration of the Portal and the IPFS but explain the Hyperledger Fabric network in Sect. 4.2. After that, in Sect. 4.3, we will describe some real-world use cases of the system.

## 4.2 Hyperledger Fabric Network

As mentioned above, the general structure of Hyperledger Fabric network is illustrated in Fig. 2 below.

---

[15] https://hyperledger.github.io/composer/latest/tutorials/tutorials.html.

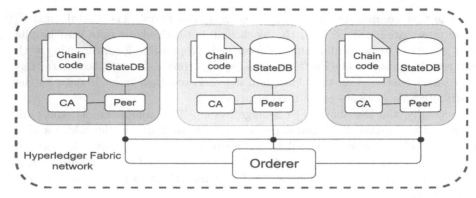

**Fig. 2.** Network architecture

In the structure of the network, organizations represent ministries that contribute data to the open data portal. On each organization, there are four modules: peer, certificate authority (CA), local state database (e.g. CouchDB) and chaincode. In the center of network topology, we have Orderer which has responsibility for ordering transactions to reach consensus. Hyperledger Fabric allows users to customize all components of the network. However, the network can be constructed following IBM guidelines [7], we only have to customize business logic through defining chaincode.

Chaincode, as mentioned in Sect. 2, typically handles business logic that is agreed by members of the network. In the context of open data, we utilize chaincode to create transactions to store metadata, user identity, and log events into the blockchain ledger and the distributed databases. More complex than smart contracts in other blockchain platforms, the chaincode not only declares types of transactions, but also defines access control rules to the network, type of participants, type of assets and custom queries. The *chaincodes* applying to each *channel* require the developers to declare an endorsement policy[16] in order to reach the consensus.

**Participants and Assets.** Note that these are two keywords of Hyperledger Fabric chaincode that represent data publishers and data sets on the open data portal. Both of them are passed into the transaction as parameters.

1. Participants are data contributors represented as DataPublisher. Each Data-Publisher will have a corresponding identity to authenticate the owner of the shared data. The implementation of DataPublisher is as follows.

```
participant DataPublisher identified by DataPublisherID {
  o String DataPublisherID
  o info PublisherInfo
}
```

2. Assets are metadata represented as Data. The following code is the implementation code of Data.

---

[16] https://hyperledger-fabric.readthedocs.io/en/release-1.2/endorsement-policies.html.

```
asset Data identified by DataID {
  o String DataID
  o metaData meta
  o String checksum
  o String cid
  --> DataPublisher publisher
}
```

The cid attribute of Data is the address which is calculated by the content of the store-in-IPFS data set, *IPFS hashes* for short. The data sets with distinct content will have distinct cid's. To get a data set, the system will only need to query the ID of the data which is much easier to access than 64 characters of cid. Another important attribute is checksum which is used for distributed checking data integrity. We will discuss in detail later in the declaration of the VerifyData() transaction.

**Transactions** are similar to smart contracts on other blockchain networks. To achieve our goal of system transparency, enhancing data integrity, we define customized transactions and use them with other built-in transactions as follows.

1. **Publishing a new data set:** This process triggers two transactions on blockchain including:
   - AddAsset() – built-in transaction. This transaction creates a new Data asset. The parameters of AddAsset() are the related information based on kind of data. To avoid tampering, some fields of metadata are provided by the publisher while other fields are provided by the server such as publisher, checksum, DataID.
   - PublishData() – user-defined transaction. The purpose of this transaction is to record the event whenever the data is published.

   ```
   transaction PublishData {
     --> DataPublisher publisher
     --> Data data
   }
   ```

2. **Modifying a data set:** This process triggers ModifyData() transaction on blockchain.

   ```
   transaction  ModifyData {
     --> Data data
     --> DataPublisher modifier
     o metaData modifiedMeta
     o String newCid
   }
   ```

   Being similar to PublishData() transaction, ModifyData() transaction also has the responsibility for recording logs of data. The newCid attribute represents a new address based on content for a new version of a data set. The citizen can retrieve the old version if needed also. Since all information is stored in an immutable way, no tampering is possible.

3. **Verifying a data set:** This process triggers the Verifydata() transaction on the blockchain. VerifyData() is called once the citizens want to check the data integrity. The checksum of the data set retrieved from IPFS will be compared with the checksum stored on the Hyperledger Fabric network.

```
transaction VerifyData {
  --> Data data
  o String checksum
}
```

Although IPFS ensures data integrity, there still exist vulnerabilities. Since each node in the Hyperledger Fabric network maintains a local database about the state of all assets, an incorrect data can be returned when the server queried to a dishonest node that alters his local database.

Hence, the citizens can retrieve the manipulated data because of wrong address. In order to improve the system reliability, the citizens can trigger VerifyData() transaction. The checksum parameter of this transaction is obtained from the data set stored on IPFS. Checking the data integrity will be performed by several nodes. Therefore, the possibility of frauding by a malicious node will be reduced.

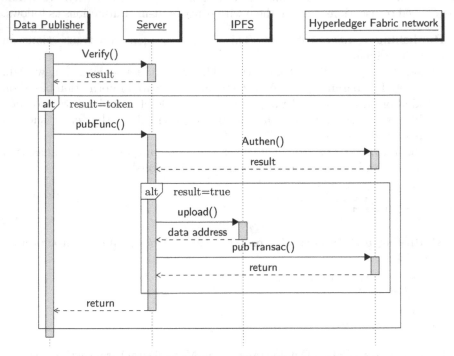

**Fig. 3.** The publishing and modifying process.

### 4.3  System Use Cases

To clarify the communication flow between components, we will describe that through some sequence diagrams in this section.

Firstly, the publishing and modifying process have the same flow in our system as illustrated in Fig. 3. The term pubFunc represents either publish or modify function on server. Similarly, the term pubTransac represents either PublishData or ModifyData transaction on the blockchain network.

The **publishing** and **modifying** process follows these steps:

- Step 1: The server verifies the publisher's account and returns an access token.
- Step 2: Data Publisher uses his token to access server and call pubData() function. After that, Server uses the stored publisher identity to trigger transactions on the Hyperledger Fabric network.
- Step 3: If no error occurs, the data set will be uploaded to the IPFS. The content-address of that data will be returned to the server.
- Step 4: The server collects all information about published data and passes into pubDataTrans transaction as parameters. Peers on Hyperledger Fabric network execute that transaction, update information to local state database and record logs on their ledger.

Secondly, we describe the downloading and verifying process in Fig. 4.

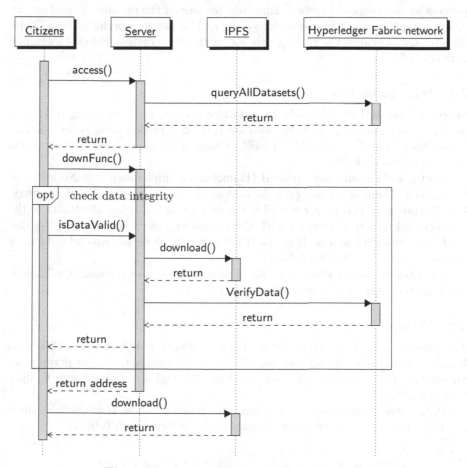

**Fig. 4.** The downloading and verifying process.

The **downloading** and **verifying** process follows these steps:

- Step 1: The citizens access to the Portal and explore data sets which are retrieved on Hyperledger Fabric network.
- Step 2: The citizens pick a desired data set and call downFunc() function to the server. The server will redirect to the address of the requested data so that users can download the requesting data.
- Step 3: The citizens can verify the data by the isDataValid() function. The server will trigger the VerifyData transaction on user-demand and return the result of verification.

# 5   Implementation and Testing

In previous sections, we described how our model be organized to achieve the integrity, availability of data in general. The model is also designed to be able to improve the transparency of the system based on the nature of the decentralized architecture. In this section, we will represent our implementation and testing process for our proposed system. However, because of the resource limitation, we can not simulate the IPFS network to evaluate this network performance. Therefore, we only perform the testing process on the Hyperledger Fabric blockchain network.

## 5.1   Implementation

**Hyperledger Fabric blockchain network** is configured according to Hyperledger project guidelines [12]. We also use tools and Docker images provided by Linux Foundation[17] and IBM[18] to create network components, connect them and run network locally.

   **Server-side open data portal (Backend)** is implemented on NodeJS and Hyperledger Composer posing out APIs in order to interact with Fabric network. One limitation of this server model is the storage of publisher identifiers in the network and uses it to interact with the network under that identifier. We also configure our server as a node in the IPFS network, so we can upload data to or download data from IPFS (Table 1).

   **Client-side open data portal (Frontend)** is a web-based application, implemented using VueJS and Webpack (Table 2).

## 5.2   Testing

The performance of the Hyperledger Fabric network is reflected by *latency* to handle transactions, *throughput, rate* of successful transactions. To perform an automatic and accurate evaluation, we have selected the Hyperledger Caliper framework[19].

   With three transaction types defined in the chain code, there will be three rounds of evaluation to measure the network's performance (Table 3).

---

[17] https://hub.docker.com/u/hyperledger/?page=2.

[18] https://hyperledger.github.io/composer/latest/installing/installing-index.html.

[19] https://github.com/hyperledger/caliper.

**Table 1.** Evaluated result of blockchain network performance number of transactions: 50, transactions rate: 100 tps

| Transaction type | Result | | Send rate (tps) | Latency (s) | | | Throughput (tps) |
|---|---|---|---|---|---|---|---|
| | Succ | Fail | | Min | Max | Avg | |
| PublishData | 50 | 0 | 96.5 | 3.96 | 8.08 | 6.40 | 5.7 |
| ModifyData | 50 | 0 | 101.8 | 4.36 | 8.96 | 6.51 | 5.5 |
| DownloadData | 50 | 0 | 101.6 | 3.93 | 8.56 | 6.36 | 5.7 |

**Table 2.** Evaluated result of blockchain network performance number of transactions: 100, transactions rate: 100 tps

| Transaction type | Result | | Send rate (tps) | Latency (s) | | | Throughput (tps) |
|---|---|---|---|---|---|---|---|
| | Succ | Fail | | Min | Max | Avg | |
| PublishData | 100 | 0 | 96.4 | 6.45 | 16.08 | 11.73 | 6.1 |
| ModifyData | 100 | 0 | 101.0 | 6.60 | 15.67 | 11.27 | 6.3 |
| DownloadData | 100 | 0 | 100.6 | 6.66 | 16.09 | 11.06 | 6.1 |

**Table 3.** Evaluated result of blockchain network performance number of transactions: 100, transactions rate: 200 tps

| Transaction type | Result | | Send rate (tps) | Latency (s) | | | Throughput (tps) |
|---|---|---|---|---|---|---|---|
| | Succ | Fail | | Min | Max | Avg | |
| PublishData | 100 | 0 | 182.5 | 6.38 | 16.18 | 11.39 | 6.1 |
| ModifyData | 100 | 0 | 174.5 | 7.04 | 16.33 | 11.81 | 6.1 |
| DownloadData | 100 | 0 | 126.6 | 7.78 | 17.89 | 13.23 | 5.5 |

Summary of results:

- 100% success rate, no faulty transactions.
- The average delay with 50 transactions and the transaction per second changes is ranged from 5 to 7 s; with 100 transaction and the transaction per second changes are in the range of 11–12 s for each test round.
- The throughput for all tests is in the range of 5–6 transactions per second.

The specification computer that runs Fabric network is 8 GB of RAM and using Intel Core i5 processor, so the evaluation results are acceptable. In fact, a real Hyperledger Fabric network has throughput over 3,000 transactions per second. We also improve network throughput to over 20,000 transactions per second (See [2]). This is an impressive performance for a decentralized network blockchain compared with other popular blockchain technologies such as Bitcoin or Ethereum.

# 6 Conclusion and Future Work

We have proposed a mechanism that allows to store, access and download open data in a secure and efficient way using the combination of the Hyperledger blockchain platform and the IPFS technology. The data is stored using the IPFS technology which offers great decentralization and thus guarantees that data can be accessed at all times which ensures availability. Besides, we make use of the Hyperledger Fabric blockchain to store the checksum and the log of each dataset to ensure that one can easily verify the history and integrity of the data. As a result, transparency is greatly enhanced. Moreover, our experimental results show that the proposed system has a great performance which can be applied to practical use cases. However, there remains a security issue in storing the private key of the publisher which we have not addressed in this paper. This limitation can be overcome using hardware security modules which we wish to have it available on the system in the near future. We also try to evaluate the performance of the distributed network in future work.

**Acknowledgment.** The authors are grateful to Prof. Dang Tran Khanh for his valuable suggestions in preparing the manuscript of this paper.

# References

1. Akanji, A.W., Elusoji, A.A., Haastrup, A.V.: A Comparative Study of Attacks on Databases and Database Security Techniques. African J. Comput. ICTs **7**(5), 1–8 (2014)
2. Gorenflo, C., Lee, S., Golab, L., Keshav, S.: FastFabric: scaling hyperledger fabric to 20,000 transactions per second (2019)
3. Androulaki, E., et al.: Hyperledger fabric: a distributed operating system for permissioned blockchains (2018). https://arxiv.org/abs/1801.10228
4. European Data Portal: Benefits of Open Data (2016). https://www.europeandataportal.eu/en/using-data/benefits-of-open-data
5. Gupta, M.: Blockchain for Dummies. Wiley, Hoboken (2018)
6. Ho Chi Minh, Vietnam: Ho Chi Minh Open data portal. https://data.hochiminhcity.gov.vn/
7. IBM: Hyperledger Fabric (2019). https://cloud.ibm.com/docs/services/blockchain?topic=blockchain-hyperledger-fabric
8. Juan Benet: IPFS - Content Addressed, Versioned, P2P File System (2018)
9. Mechant, P., Walravens, N.: E-government and smart cities: theoretical reflections and case studies. Media Commun. **6**(4), 119–122 (2018)
10. Open Knowledge Foundation: What is Open Data?. http://opendatahandbook.org/guide/en/what-is-open-data/
11. Qadir, S., Quadri, S.M.K.: Information availability: an insight into the most important attribute of information security. J. Inf. Secur. **7**(3), 185–194 (2016)
12. Baset, S.A., et al.: Blockchain Development with Hyperledger: Build Decentralized Applications with Hyperledger Fabric and Composer. Packt Publishing Ltd., Birmingham (2019)

13. Nakamoto, S.: Bitcoin: A Peer-to-Peer Electronic Cash System (2008)
14. Berners-Lee, T.: Five star open data. https://5stardata.info/en/
15. US: US Open data portal. https://catalog.data.gov/dataset
16. Vienna, Autria: Vienna Open data portal. https://digitales.wien.gv.at/site/open-data/

# Emerging Data Management Systems and Applications

# GMeta: A Novel Algorithm to Utilize Highly Connected Components for Metagenomic Binning

Hong Thanh Pham[2] , Le Van Vinh[3], Tran Van Lang[4(✉)], and Van Hoai Tran[1]

[1] Faculty of Computer Science and Engineering, Ho Chi Minh City University of
Technology, Vietnam National University Ho Chi Minh City,
Ho Chi Minh City, Vietnam
hoai@hcmut.edu.vn
[2] Information Technology Office, Hoa Sen University, Ho Chi Minh City, Vietnam
thanhphh@gmail.com, thanh.phamhong@hoasen.edu.vn
[3] Faculty of Information Technology, Ho Chi Minh City University of Technology
and Education, Ho Chi Minh City, Vietnam
vinhlv@hcmute.edu.vn
[4] Institute of Applied Mechanics and Informatics, Vietnam Academy of Science and
Technology (VAST), Hanoi, Vietnam
langtv@vast.vn

**Abstract.** Metagenomic binning refers to the means of clustering or
assigning taxonomy to metagenomic sequences or contigs. Due to the
massive abundance of organisms in metagenomic samples, the number
of nucleotide sequences skyrockets, and thus leading to the complexity of
binning algorithms. Unsupervised classification is gaining a reputation
in recent years since the lacking of the reference database required in
the reference-based methods with various state-of-the-art tools released.
By manipulating the overlapping information between reads drives to
the success of various unsupervised methods with extraordinary accuracy. These research practices on the evidence that the average proportion of common $l$-mers between genomes of different species is practically miniature when $l$ is sufficient. This paper introduces a novel algorithm for binning metagenomic sequences without requiring reference
databases by utilizing highly connected components inside a weighted
overlapping graph of reads. Experimental outcomes show that the precision is improved over other well-known binning tools for both short and
long sequences.

**Keywords:** Metagenomic binning · Highly connected components ·
Weighted overlapping graph

## 1 Introduction

Metagenomics is the study of microbial communities which contributes in
advance in many fields, e.g., biotechnology, agriculture, and environmental science. Different from traditional methods, the discipline does not need to isolate

© Springer Nature Switzerland AG 2019
T. K. Dang et al. (Eds.): FDSE 2019, LNCS 11814, pp. 545–559, 2019.
https://doi.org/10.1007/978-3-030-35653-8_35

and culture single organisms in laboratories [3]. Binning problem is one of the crucial tasks in metagenomic projects which aims to sort reads into groups of closely related organisms. Results of binning approaches can be used in other tasks of the metagenomic analysis process, such as DNA annotation, sequence assembly [12].

Initial metagenomic projects used Sanger sequencing technology to produce DNA/protein data from environmental samples. Due to its limitation in productive performance, most of the current projects are based on the next-generation sequencing (NGS) technologies, e.g., Illumina Genome Analyser, Applied Biosystems SOLID [13]. The techniques can generate massive data extremely fast with small costs. However, most of the technologies produce sequences of short length. Thus, it poses significant research challenges for the binning problem because of lacking classification information.

Binning approaches can be classified as supervised or unsupervised methods. Supervised approaches group reads based on the homology feature or genomic signatures extracted from both the reads and reference database. MEGAN [5,6] is a homology-based method which applies the lowest common ancestor (LCA) algorithm to find the best common taxon of reads. Karen [18], and LiveKaren [14] are other approaches use homology feature to classify reads. However, they compare the similarity of $k$-mers extracted from reads and reference databases instead of comparing the reads through whole sequence alignment. The homology feature used in these approaches is usually measured by alignment search tools such as BLAST [1] or BLAT [8]. On the other hand, some methods such as MetaBinG2 [10] and SeMeta [15] utilize composition features to separate reads. While MetaBinG2 only computes feature vectors of analyzed and reference reads, SeMeta performs two phases to extract both compositional and homology features to assign reads to the phylogenetic tree.

The incomplete reference database causes the limitation of most of the supervised methods for real metagenomes. Thus, unsupervised methods which do not require reference sequences received much attention of the research community. Earlier methods such as LikelyBin [9] and Scimm [7] apply Markov models of $l$-mers as the guidance for the classification process. AbundanceBin [20], and MaxBin 2.0 [19] are based on the abundance of genomes in dataset to separate reads into clusters. However, these methods can not classify reads of genomes having similar abundance levels.

Other unsupervised approaches, e.g., MetaCluster [17], BiMeta [16], utilize both compositional features and overlapping information between reads to enhance the classification quality. Both the methods apply a two-phase process in which reads are put into small groups based on the read overlapping information, and then the groups are merged into clusters using compositional vectors. Comparing with MetaCluster, BiMeta reduces noises and costs by selecting representatives of groups for merging them in the second phase. MetaProb [4] is an improvement of BiMeta in which $k$-mers count is converted into probabilistic sequence signatures for enhancement of classification quality.

In this study, an unsupervised binning method is proposed, called GMeta, which can cluster both short and long metagenomic sequences with high precision. In comparison with the similar-paradigm approaches, such as BiMeta and MetaProb, the proposed method considers deeply on the mixed status of sub-graphs to boost the clustering quality.

The next section presents a detailed explanation of the proposed method. Section 3 shows the experimental results on metagenomic datasets of short and long sequences. The conclusion is stated in the final section.

# 2    Highly Connected Components in GMeta

## 2.1    Observation on Overlapping Information Between Reads

Table 1. Overlapping information on short and long read datasets

| Dataset | Total nodes | Edges | | | Components | |
|---------|-------------|-------|-------------|---|-------|-------|
| | | Total | Inaccurate | % | Total | Mixed |
| S1 | 96,367 | 409,464 | 69 | 0.02% | 143 | 1 |
| S2 | 195,339 | 1,194,476 | 26,685 | 2.23% | 278 | 3 |
| S3 | 338,725 | 1,919,934 | 12,116 | 0.63% | 299 | 1 |
| S4 | 375,302 | 1,668,775 | 964 | 0.06% | 591 | 1 |
| R1 | 82,960 | 373,482 | 19,344 | 5.18% | 1,951 | 1 |
| R2 | 77,293 | 483,574 | 7,693 | 1.59% | 364 | 3 |
| R3 | 93,267 | 557,449 | 12,867 | 2.31% | 3,343 | 26 |
| R4 | 34,457 | 129,354 | 293 | 0.23% | 895 | 2 |
| R5 | 40,043 | 139,844 | 9 | 0.01% | 1,150 | 2 |
| R6 | 70,550 | 265,205 | 1,820 | 0.69% | 2,719 | 1 |

S1-S4: short read datasets, R1–R6: long read datasets.
Total nodes: total number of reads on each dataset.
Inaccurate edges: mismatched connections.
Total components: total number of connected components.
Mixed components: contains multiple types of species.

A weighted overlapping graph is used to represent the relationship between reads which node denotes read, whereas edge signifies the overlapping information between a pair of reads. The weight of each edge expresses the total number of common $q$-mers between two reads, e.g., the read overlapping information. $q = 30$ is commonly applied in other research, and furthermore, added parameter $m$ is used in BiMeta as a threshold to map the overlapping information to the existence of an edge. Table 1 shows the statistics of multiple short and long read datasets with $m = 5$ and $m = 45$ respectively (as explained in BiMeta).

Through data in Table 1, the average ratio of edges to nodes is approximately five to one that makes the graph denser. The graph density is managed by diversifying the parameter $m$. With the chosen value $m$, the percentage of incorrect edges - the connection between reads of two different species - is inadequate at 0.01% and 0.02% on R5 and S1 respectively. The figures increase to over two percent on S2 and R3 and jump to over five percent on R1. The statistics also reveal that the number of mixed connected components - a component that contains different types of species - is small, but its size is enormous. On R3, even the fact that there are 26 mixed connected components, but except the numerous one, the others are miniature.

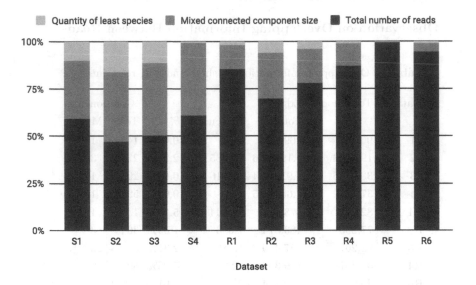

**Fig. 1.** Ratio of the least species in the mixed connected components

Based on the analyzed data in Table 1, the number of mixed connected components is tiny compared to the total. Besides, the size of these components is one of the largest one in the dataset, at 43.11% on S1 or 33.33% on R5. On average, the mixed connected component size on short read datasets is massive at over 174,500 items while it is just about 11,500 on long read datasets. One of the reasonable explanation could be because of the value of parameter $m$ practiced - which is 45 and 5 on long and short read datasets respectively - as using a more significant value of $m$ could enhance the chance of distributing reads into the proper component. Interestingly, the ratio of least species on mixed connected component over entire dataset is inadequate at 8.38% on R2, and just 0.2% on R5, the average ratio is 3%. The chart in Fig. 1 highlights that the total number of least species on the mixed connected component is short on long read datasets Rs at 3% but gets extended on short read datasets Ss at approximately 18% on average. In theoretically, the mixed ratio would be even smaller when increasing the parameter $m$ but which value is sufficient is required to examine further.

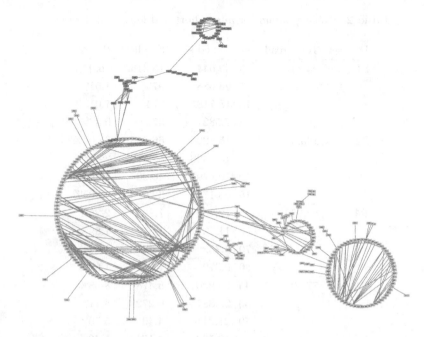

**Fig. 2.** Sub-graph of the mixed connected component on S1 dataset with $m = 35$. Red and blue nodes illustrate two difference species on the dataset (Color figure online).

The weighted overlapping graph in Fig. 2 demonstrates the association, e.g., the overlapping information between reads on S1 dataset using a threshold $m = 30$ with the red and blue nodes represent two different types of species. According to the graph, the volume of the blue-labeled species is comparatively smaller than the other one. Moreover, the internal connection - the relationship between reads of the same species - on each component is dominant while there are few connected lines between the red and blue collections. If the threshold $m$ continue increases to a sufficient number, the mixed connected component size would be lessened, and these connected components are expected to be decomposed into smaller ones.

Further to the observation analysis, the value of $m$ is diversifying to experience the transformation of the mixed connected component in term of volume and detachment. As manifested in Table 2, the degradation rate is not identical among Ss and Rs but reduces notably. The size of the mixed connected component on S1 declines significantly from 16.95% to just 1.01% when shifting $m$ from 5 to 7, while the rate only contracts by 4.26% with the equivalent parameter on S2. When $m = 15$, the amount of the least species on the mixed connected component of S1 is 370 per 96,367 reads in whole, accounted for 0.38%. It is 13.05% on S2 with the same $m$. Among Rs, the size of the mixed connected components is substantially scanty, as explained before, because of the advantage of chosen $m$. The capacity diminishes by over a quarter on R1 and indeed further on R2.

**Table 2.** Varying parameter $m$ on short and long read datasets

| Dataset | Total reads | $m$ | Mixed size | Smallest | Ratio |
|---------|------------|-----|-----------|----------|-------|
| S1 | 96,367 | 5 | 49,644 | 16,316 | 16.93% |
|    |        | 7 | 28,688 | 975 | 1.01% |
|    |        | 10 | 18,718 | 974 | 1.01% |
|    |        | 15 | 7,582 | 370 | 0.38% |
| S2 | 195,339 | 5 | 154,205 | 66,485 | 34.04% |
|    |        | 7 | 137,328 | 58,177 | 29.78% |
|    |        | 10 | 100,797 | 46,207 | 23.65% |
|    |        | 15 | 58,178 | 32,680 | 13.05% |
| R1 | 82,960 | 45 | 12,239 | 1,866 | 2.25% |
|    |        | 50 | 11,237 | 1,572 | 1.89% |
|    |        | 70 | 9,752 | 1,427 | 1.72% |
|    |        | 80 | 9,379 | 1,387 | 1.67% |
| R2 | 77,293 | 45 | 26,900 | 6,478 | 8.38% |
|    |        | 50 | 25,887 | 6,272 | 8.11% |
|    |        | 70 | 21,211 | 4,408 | 5.70% |
|    |        | 80 | 19,532 | 4,171 | 5.40% |

**Mixed size**: size of the mixed connected component.
**Smallest**: size of the least species in the mixed connected
component.
**Ratio**: ratio of the least species in the mixed connected
component.

In summary, boosting the value of threshold $m$ is helpful on the mixed graph components solely to decay them due to the vulnerable association (i.e., weak edges). It can lead to a better result in graph decomposition phase than the proposed heuristic approach used in BiMeta and MetaProb. This understanding drives to the possibility to enhance the clustering quality of the metagenomic binning algorithm by utilizing highly connected components.

## 2.2   GMeta - a Novel Three-Stage Metagenomic Binning Algorithm

Following the observation prior, a novel three-state binning algorithm named GMeta is proposed as depicted in Fig. 3. In the first stage, a weighted overlapping graph is constructed by employing the overlapping information between reads which is enhanced further to represent the strength of the edges, instead only the connectivity as in BiMeta. The next stage, the threshold $m$ is shifted from a lower value to a higher one on the mixed connected components. The feature vector is computed for each component and is provided as the input figures for the group clustering stage afterward.

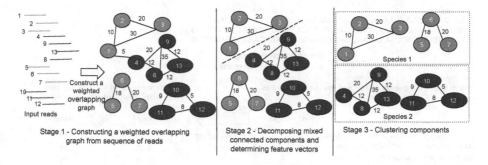

Stage 1 - Constructing a weighted overlapping graph from sequence of reads

Stage 2 - Decomposing mixed connected components and determining feature vectors

Stage 3 - Clustering components

**Fig. 3.** Three stages of GMeta. The red and blue color denote the true species of reads. The number alongside every read and in its associated graph vertex is the identification of the read, while the weight of each edge signifies the strength of association between its incident reads. (Color figure online)

## Stage 1 - Constructing a Weighted Overlapping Graph.

Let a weighted overlapping graph $G = (R, E)$, where the vertex set $R = \{r_i, i = 1, \ldots, n\}$ denotes $n$ metagenomic reads in the dataset and the edge set $E = \{(u, v) | \forall u, v \in R : u \sqcap v\}$ models the association between reads in term of overlapping information. Two reads $u, v \in R$ are called overlapping $(u \sqcap v)$ if and only if they share at least $m$ $q$-mers. Note that the operator $\sqcap$ in BiMeta is reused. The weight of each edge $w(e)$ is the overlapping level between pair of reads $e$.

The complexity to determine the overlapping between reads is high with the standard string comparison strategy. Therefore, a hash table is utilized to speed up the process of computing the overlapping information. A sliding window of dimension $q$ is applied to glide on the read to extract the hash key, and the identification of the read is extracted as the hash value. Figure 4 is an example to combine a hash table with the parameter $q$ for three reads $r_0, r_1, r_2$. On the second step, a dictionary of edges is produced, including the extent of shared $q$-mers as value and the identity of an edge as the key. Ultimately, following edge filtering, $\forall e \in E, w(e) \geq m$, a weighted overlapping graph is constructed and is used as the input data of the subsequence stage.

The approach of utilizing the overlapping graph was applied to the previous study, such as BiMeta and MetaProb, to judge the similarity between reads. A novel contribution proposed in this paper is to attach an overlapping level with edges to represent the strength of association between reads, instead of merely the connectivity between them. GMeta will partition graph $G$ on weak edges into smaller sub-graphs $G_i$ with anticipation that reads belong to the same species will be grouped in the same sub-graph.

## Stage 2 - Decomposing Mixed Connected Components and Determining Feature Vectors.

On entering the second stage, graph $G$ is considered as a collection of non-overlapping connected components $G = \bigcup_{i=1}^{l} G_l$ with $l \leq n$

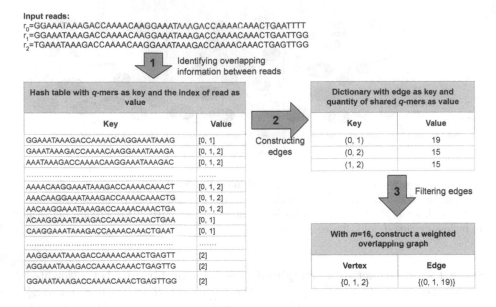

**Fig. 4.** Stage 1 - Constructing a weighted overlapping graph from sequence of reads.

where $n$ is the total number of reads, $G_i \cap G_j = \emptyset, \forall i,j \in l \wedge i \neq j$. These connected components could contain reads of different species, as observed in Sect. 2.1 and can be decomposed further. A function $f$ is used to determine if the decomposition step is required or not. The assumption is that reads on the same connected component $r_i, r_j \in R, r_i \in G_i \wedge r_j \in G_i$ are estimated as the same species. The complete algorithm is outlined in Algorithm 1.

Suppose that $w_{\min} = \min w(e) : e \in E(G_i)$ where $E(G_i)$ denotes the edge set of graph $G_i$. Then, the edges with weight equal to $w_{\min}$ are eliminated. The process is repeated for the remaining edges until the termination condition reached. The independent set $S(G_i)$ is then estimated, and following the feature vector computation $d^{G_i}$ is performed.

Because $l$-mers are composed of four kinds of nucleotides (Adenine (A), Cytosine (C), Guanine (G) and Thymine (T)), there are at most $4^l$ possibilities of $l$-mers. The normalized frequency of $l$-mer $t$ in $S(G_i)$ is calculated as follows where $h_t^{S(G_i)}$ is the frequency of $l$-mer $t$ in $S(G_i)$ and $|S(G_i)|$ is the total number of $l$-mers or the size of the independent set.

$$d_t^{S(G_i)} = \frac{h_t^{S(G_i)}}{|S(G_i)|}, t = 1, \ldots, 4^l$$

The feature vector of component $G_i$ will be $d^{G_i} = [d_1^{S(G_i)}, \ldots, d_{4^l}^{S(G_i)}]$. The value of $l$ is established as 4, and the vector dimension reduction is also applied to reduce the dimension to 136 as discussed in BiMeta. The length of $l$ has additionally experimented in the next section.

---

**Algorithm 1:** DECOMPOSE Decomposing mixed connected components and compute feature vectors

---

**Input**: Graph $G(R, E)$; maximum iteration step $maxS$
**Output**: List of connected components $G_i$ and its feature vector
$$d^{G_i}, i \in 1, \ldots, l'$$

1   $S \leftarrow \emptyset$
2   $step \leftarrow 0$
3   **repeat**
4     **foreach** $G_i \in ConnectedComponents(G)$ **do**
5       **if** $f(G_i)$ **then**
6         $S \leftarrow S \cup \{G_i\}$

7     **while** $S \neq \emptyset$ **do**
8       $H(R_H, E_H) \leftarrow S.pop()$
9       $w_{min}^{H} \leftarrow \min w(e) : e \in E_H$
10      $G \leftarrow (R, E \setminus \{e \in E_H : w(e) = w_{min}^{H}\})$
11     $step \leftarrow step + 1$
12 **until** $step < maxS$
13 **foreach** $G_i \in ConnectedComponents(G)$ **do**
14    $Compute(d^{G_i})$

---

**Stage 3 - Clustering Components.** After the decomposition step, a collection of connected components $G = \bigcup_{i=1}^{l'} G_{l'}$ with $l' \geq l$ alongside with feature vectors $d^{G_{l'}}$ are fitted to $k$-means clustering algorithm to merge the groups into $C$ clusters, where the number of clusters $C$ is explicitly provided. The $k$-means++ approach is applied to initialize the cluster seeds for the $k$-means clustering algorithm.

## 3   Experimental Result

### 3.1   Dataset

The production of GMeta is assessed on the simulated datasets generated by MetaSim [11] that is introduced on BiMeta. Four short read datasets S1, S2, S3, and S4 are experimented beside six long read datasets R1 to R6 on various trials. The number of species in the analysis is provided explicitly. The outcome is compared with some of the state-of-the-art binning algorithms, e.g., Abundance-Bin and MetaCluster, though direct correlates with BiMeta. In the parameter assessment section, three standard parameters $l$, $m$, and the maximum connected component volume are judged to understand the outgrowth.

### 3.2   Performance Measure

The production of the binning algorithm is evaluated by using three performance metrics *precision*, *recall*, and $F - measure$. The *precision* intimates the total number of the reads that have been clustered as positives are valid positives. The *recall* assessment indicates the total number of the real positives that have been detected.

Let $n$ be the number of species in the metagenomic dataset and $C$ be the number of clusters returned by the binning algorithm. Let $A_{ij}$ be the number of reads from species $j$ that is assigned to cluster $i$. The following definitions are introduced in BiMeta:

$$precision = \frac{\sum_{i=1}^{C} \max_j A_{ij}}{\sum_{i=1}^{C} \sum_{j=1}^{n} A_{ij}}$$

$$recall = \frac{\sum_{j=1}^{n} \max_i A_{ij}}{\sum_{i=1}^{C} \sum_{j=1}^{n} A_{ij} + \#unassigned\_reads}$$

The $F - measure$ is estimated to consolidate the *precision* and *recall* unitedly to produce one single number.

$$F - measure = 2 \cdot \frac{precision \cdot recall}{precision + recall}$$

### 3.3   Result on Paired-End Short Read Datasets

The first analysis is conducted on four paired-end short read datasets named S1, S2, S3, and S4. The parameter is set to 5 for $m$ and 6000 for the maximum connected component size. The result is compared among AbundanceBin, MetaCluster, BiMeta, and GMeta in term of $F - measure$. Figure 5 depicts that the performance of BiMeta and GMeta is comparable on S1 and S4. On S2, the outcome of GMeta is better than BiMeta but lower on S3. AbundanceBin drives the best result in the S2 test.

### 3.4   Outcome on Single-End Long Read Datasets

On the next experiment, the parameter is established to 45 for $m$. The result in Table 3 states that the correctness of GMeta is considerably more reliable on four out of six datasets. On R5, the result is comparable among BiMeta and GMeta and lessen on R4. The achievement of BiMeta and GMeta is more reliable than AbundanceBin in every case.

### 3.5   Parameter Assessment

**Differing $l$ Parameter.** The extent of $l$-mer is used to determine the frequency distribution, and following calculate the feature vector of each connected component. Former research [2,21] has pointed out the $l = 4$ is proficient at extracting the compositional features from DNA sequences. This $l$-mer length was also practiced on BiMeta and MetaProb.

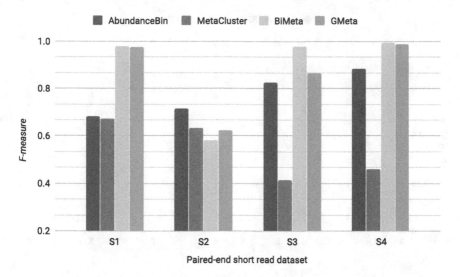

**Fig. 5.** Experimental result on paired-end short read datasets.

**Table 3.** Experimental result on single-end long read datasets, directly compared to the performance of BiMeta.

| Single-end long read dataset | Total number of reads | $F-measure$ | | |
|---|---|---|---|---|
| | | AbundanceBin | BiMeta | GMeta |
| R1 | 82,960 | 0.674 | 0.609 | **0.931** |
| R2 | 77,293 | 0.667 | 0.773 | **0.922** |
| R3 | 93,267 | 0.672 | 0.780 | **0.781** |
| R4 | 34,457 | 0.686 | **0.992** | 0.984 |
| R5 | 40,043 | 0.709 | **0.988** | **0.988** |
| R6 | 70,550 | 0.761 | 0.953 | **0.967** |
| Average | | 0.695 | 0.849 | **0.929** |

In this analysis, the value of $l$ is differing from 3 to 9 when examining both short read and long read datasets. Increasing $l$ would lead to the dimension of the feature vector boosted as the size of the vector is determined as $4^l$. The computation complexity is also raised when calculating the Euclidean distance between a component and the cluster centroid when performing $k$-means clustering procedure.

Figure 6 shows that the $F-measure$ is better when extending $l$, the peak result is archived with $l = 6$ on R2 and $l = 7$ on S1, S2, and R1. The $F-measure$ is considerably low on S2, at approximately 0.57 when $l = 4$ but then jumps to 0.75 when $l = 7$ and remains the same level after that. On S1 and R1, $F - measure$ rises steadily when $l$ shifts from 3 to 7 but then drops off when $l = 8$. The result on R2 is comparable, reduces significantly after $l = 7$.

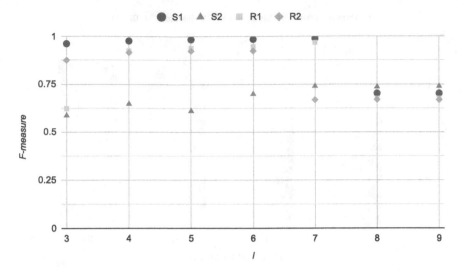

**Fig. 6.** Differing $l$ parameter in both short read and long read datasets. The $F-measure$ reaches peak performance when $l = 6$ and $l = 7$

**Alternating the Highest Connected Component Capacity.** The statistics in Tables 1 and 2 show that the total number of mixed connected components - the one that contains reads from different species - is ordinarily miniature at just 1 to 3 except in some exceptional cases. These components are considered to decompose with the expectation of separate species into its collection.

On the second stage of GMeta, the decomposition should solely be implemented on sufficient enormous components as the possibility of diverse species is noble. Figure 7 presents the $F-measure$ that is determined on S1, S2, R1, and R2 with the maximum component size varies from 100 to 7000. The conclusion indicates that the certainty wavers when the volume is tinier than 1000 nodes but advance steadily and reaches peak value when the size is surrounding 6000. The overall trend is upward on all the examined datasets.

**Shifting the Initial Overlapping Indicator $m$.** Paired-end short reads with the length of approximately 80 bp in union with single-end long reads with the length of around 700 bp are practiced throughout the tests. With short reads, the number of overlapping $q$-mers is established to $m = 5$ on various prior research, including BiMeta and MetaProb. In the next trial, the value of $m$ varies from 3 to 14 on three short read datasets S1, S2, and S3. The figures in Fig. 8 shows that the $F-measure$ is alternates slightly on S2 but continuously settles on the remaining datasets. One of the possible explanation is that the internal connectivity inside each straight connected component is robust; the weaken edges barely exist on mixed connected components so that setting $m$ higher at first does not influence incredibly the accuracy. By setting the $m$ high is additionally lessen the computation time as each component is regularly little in size when entering the decomposition stage.

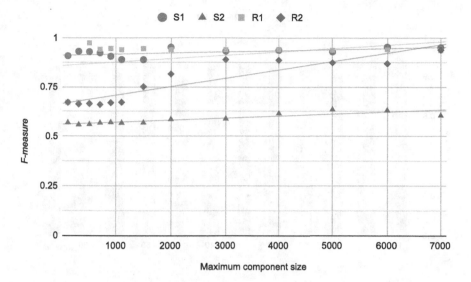

**Fig. 7.** Alternating the maximum connected component capacity. The trend is upward when the component size is sufficiently large.

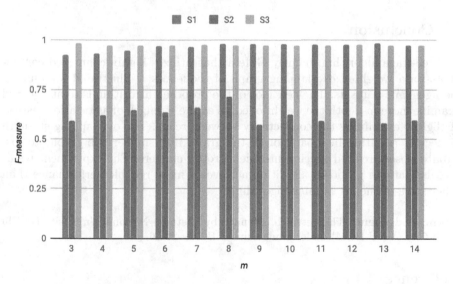

**Fig. 8.** Increasing the initial number of shared $q$-mer $m$ on short read dataset S1, S2, and S3 continuously from 3 to 14.

The column chart in Fig. 9 reflects the outcome of single-end long read datasets R1, R2, and R3 with the value $m$ changes from 10 to 65 with the step of 5. The $F - measure$ is gently up and down comparable to the patterns on the short read datasets beforehand.

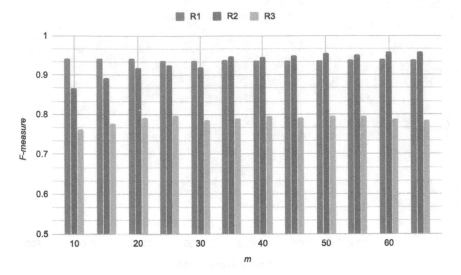

**Fig. 9.** Changing the initial number of shared $l$-mer $m$ on long read dataset R1, R2, and R3 between 10 and 65 with the step of 5.

## 4    Conclusion

A three-stage algorithm, namely GMeta that utilizes highly connected components on a weighted overlapping graph of sequences is illustrated for binning metagenomic datasets. The new idea of the proposed algorithm is to attach and examine more in-depth the weight of edges as the strength of association instead of slightly examining the connectivity between reads. The overlapping strength is elected, resulting in separation of the graph into smaller sub-graphs to distribute closely related species into their proper clusters. The experiment result reveals that the proposed algorithm achieves a more reliable performance than other state-of-the-art binning algorithms.

**Acknowledgment.** This research is funded by Vietnam National University Ho Chi Minh City (VNU-HCM) under grant number B2019-20-06.

## References

1. Altschul, S.F., Gish, W., Miller, W., Myers, E.W., Lipman, D.J.: Basic local alignment search tool. J. Mol. Biol. **215**(3), 403–410 (1990)
2. Chor, B., Horn, D., Goldman, N., Levy, Y., Massingham, T.: Genomic DNA k-mer spectra: models and modalities. Genome Biol. **10**(10), R108 (2009)
3. National Research Council: The New Science of Metagenomics: Revealing the Secrets of Our Microbial Planet. National Academies Press (2007)
4. Girotto, S., Pizzi, C., Comin, M.: MetaProb: accurate metagenomic reads binning based on probabilistic sequence signatures. Bioinformatics **32**(17), i567–i575 (2016)

5. Huson, D.H., Auch, A.F., Qi, J., Schuster, S.C.: Megan analysis of metagenomic data. Genome Res. **17**(3), 377–386 (2007)
6. Huson, D.H., et al.: Megan community edition - interactive exploration and analysis of large-scale microbiome sequencing data. PLoS Comput. Biol. **12**(6), 1–12 (2016)
7. Kelley, D.R., Salzberg, S.L.: Clustering metagenomic sequences with interpolated markov models. BMC Bioinform. **11**(1), 544 (2010)
8. Kent, W.J.: Blat-the blast-like alignment tool. Genome Res. **12**(4), 656–664 (2002)
9. Kislyuk, A., Bhatnagar, S., Dushoff, J., Weitz, J.S.: Unsupervised statistical clustering of environmental shotgun sequences. BMC Bioinform. **10**(1), 316 (2009)
10. Qiao, Y., Jia, B., Hu, Z., Sun, C., Xiang, Y., Wei, C.: Metabing2: a fast and accurate metagenomic sequence classification system for samples with many unknown organisms. Biol. Direct **13**(1), 15 (2018)
11. Richter, D.C., Ott, F., Auch, A.F., Schmid, R., Huson, D.H.: Metasim-a sequencing simulator for genomics and metagenomics. PLoS ONE **3**(10), e3373 (2008)
12. Roumpeka, D.D., Wallace, R.J., Escalettes, F., Fotheringham, I., Watson, M.: A review of bioinformatics tools for bio-prospecting from metagenomic sequence data. Front. Genet. **8**, 23 (2017)
13. Shendure, J., Ji, H.: Next-generation DNA sequencing. Nat. Biotechnol. **26**(10), 1135 (2008)
14. Tausch, S.H., et al.: Livekraken—real-time metagenomic classification of illumina data. Bioinformatics **34**(21), 3750–3752 (2018)
15. Van Le, V., Van Tran, L., Van Tran, H.: A novel semi-supervised algorithm for the taxonomic assignment of metagenomic reads. BMC Bioinform. **17**(1), 22 (2016)
16. Vinh, L.V., Lang, T.V., Binh, L.T., Hoai, T.V.: A two-phase binning algorithm using l-mer frequency on groups of non-overlapping reads. Algorithms Mol. Biol. **10**(1), 2 (2015)
17. Wang, Y., Leung, H.C., Yiu, S.M., Chin, F.Y.: Metacluster 5.0: a two-round binning approach for metagenomic data for low-abundance species in a noisy sample. Bioinformatics **28**(18), i356–i362 (2012)
18. Wood, D.E., Salzberg, S.L.: Kraken: ultrafast metagenomic sequence classification using exact alignments. Genome Biol. **15**(3), R46 (2014)
19. Wu, Y.W., Simmons, B.A., Singer, S.W.: Maxbin 2.0: an automated binning algorithm to recover genomes from multiple metagenomic datasets. Bioinformatics **32**(4), 605–607 (2015)
20. Wu, Y.W., Ye, Y.: A novel abundance-based algorithm for binning metagenomic sequences using l-tuples. J. Comput. Biol. **18**(3), 523–534 (2011)
21. Zhou, F., Olman, V., Xu, Y.: Barcodes for genomes and applications. BMC Bioinform. **9**(1), 546 (2008)

# Visualization of Medical Images Data Based on Geometric Modeling

Van Sinh Nguyen[1]([✉]), Manh Ha Tran[2], and Son Truong Le[1]

[1] School of Computer Science and Engineering, International University - Vietnam
National University of HCMC, Ho Chi Minh City, Vietnam
nvsinh@hcmiu.edu.vn
[2] Hong Bang International University, Ho Chi Minh City, Vietnam

**Abstract.** The methods for visualizing data are considered as the graphical representation of information and data. These data are first analyzed and computed depending on the criteria and purpose of users. Thereafter, they are visualized or simulated by using visual elements like charts, graphs and maps to explore, understand their characteristics and data structure. In the studies of big data analysis or data science, the methods, tools and techniques are essential and important to analyze a massive amount of information and make data-driven decisions. Which methods or solutions are best for rendering and visualizing the analyzed data? That is still a big question; even a challenge to the researchers. In this paper, we research and implement a web-based application for visualizing the medical images data based on geometric modeling. After studying the state-of-the-art in the fields of computer graphics, images processing and geometric modeling, we combine all of them to develop an application for rendering the Dicom data. The input data are slices of 2D of an object captured from CT scanner or MRI. They are processed and reconstructed for rendering its initial shape on both 2D and 3D environment. Comparing to the existing applications, our research shown the advantages of using it in practice.

**Keywords:** Medical image processing · Geometric modeling · 3D reconstruction · 3D visualization and data rendering

## 1 Introduction

Visualization of data is an important step in data analysis, data processing, data mining or simplification of data. Depending on the context of research, type of input data, structure of data and algorithms, it can be applied in many scientific researched fields such as database and data mining, computer graphics, image processing or data simulation, etc. Development of information technology and Internet brings us tools or applications that serve for data analysis efficiently. The advanced data acquisition techniques allows us producing a massive amount of different data. In the field of medical image processing [1–3], the data of

© Springer Nature Switzerland AG 2019
T. K. Dang et al. (Eds.): FDSE 2019, LNCS 11814, pp. 560–576, 2019.
https://doi.org/10.1007/978-3-030-35653-8_36

patients obtained based on CT Scanner or MRI techniques can support doctors and medical staffs in their professional works.

By checking the abnormal signals of data in the images captured from MRI and CT scanner, doctors can diagnose exactly status of patients. However, these data in the CT scanner are normally presented in 2D slices. They are difficult to understand to patients and the one who have no professional knowledge in this field. Besides, the price of CT scanner is very expensive and difficult to equip for all hospitals nowadays. In practice, there are many application softwares provided by the medical companies [4–7] that can help to solve this problems. Nevertheless, the official version for commerce has a high cost. Some of them are developed based on the desktop and therefore could not be shared with other departments in the same hospital.

In this research, we propose a method and develop a power tool for visualizing medical image data that overcome the drawbacks of traditional applications (they are built in desktop-based or integrated as modules on the CT scanner or MRI machine). The input data are Dicom images generated from the CT scanners. They are first processed and computed to build a 3D model based on many existing algorithms [9]. The set of 2D slices and 3D model of these data are then presented on a web-based application for better visualization to everyone. Comparing to the current tools, our application is running very fast and adapting the expectation of stakeholders. We intend to publish this application for free on the internet. It is considered as our contribution to the research communities and users.

The rest of the paper is structured as follows. Section 2 is related work that presents existing methods for handling 3D objects from 2D medical images. We have also studied tools, techniques and libraries for processing and reconstructing the objects from various input data. We present our proposed method in Sect. 3. Section 4 describes implementation and obtained results. The parts of discussion, evaluation and comparison are presented in Sect. 5. The last section (Sect. 6) is our conclusion.

## 2   Related Work

In this section, the state-of-the-art and existing applications in the fields of medical image processing (both in research and in practice) are studied. The tools, techniques and researched libraries in this field have also reviewed and explored for 3D modeling and visualizing medical data.

### 2.1   Characteristics of Dicom Data

Dicom (Digital Imaging and Communications in Medicine) is a medical image data set captured by using a particular device like CT scanner [10,13]. Besides, they can be also obtained from other techniques such as ultrasound (US), positron emission tomography (PET), Magnetic Resonance Imaging (MRI), endoscopy (ES), mammograms (MG), digital radiography (DR), computed radiography (CR), etc., as presented in [8]. The Dicom data are structured in a set of 2D slices. For each slice, it contains information of a part in the series of parallel slices that can be formed the shape of a 3D object scanned from patients (see Fig. 1). These 2D slices of the Dicom set are considered as input data for researches in the field of medical image processing. They includes information such as patient ID, spacing between slices, date, record, coordinated information, etc., and structured into two parts (Header and Dataset) following the PS3.10 specification (Media Storage and File Format for Media Interchange). A detail description of Dicom data has been presented in the previous work [8].

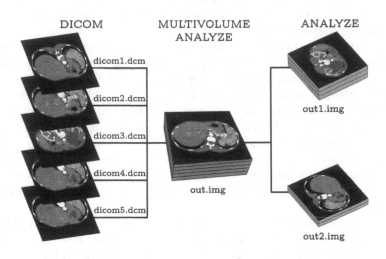

**Fig. 1.** The structure of a set of Dicom slices

## 2.2 Tools, Techniques and Libraries

In this section, we review several tools, techniques and existing libraries that can help researchers and developers to study and build a software application for medical image processing. All of these tools, techniques and libraries are open-sources and very useful for researched community in this field.

### 2.2.1 CornerstoneJS

Cornerstone is an open-source library written in JavaScript for reading and visualizing medical images on the web-based applications [14]. It can be applied and worked well to all the web browsers containing HTML5-canvas-element component. The main ambition of the Cornerstone is to motivate developers to build a medical toolkit on web platform with its separated elements. In fact, it is not considered as an entire application, it is subdivided into many components with different purposes of using such as dicomParser, cornerstoneTools, cornerstoneMath, etc. With this ideal design, developers only needs to import the necessary ones instead of loading the whole library which may contain some irrelevant components. For this reason, the web application is significantly optimized from the first stage of developing process. Comparing to other libraries in the same field, the advantaged point of Cornerstone is a collection of clear instructions and examples provided on its site [14]. Therefore, it can help developer saving time for developing process of their applications.

### 2.2.2   The Visualization Toolkit

The Visualization Toolkit (VTK) [15] is deemed as one of the most prominent libraries for creating, handling, and displaying graphical objects. It is originally implemented in C++ and has been converted into multiple programming languages like Java, Python or JavaScript. It does not depend on operating system and can run fine on different platforms like MacOS, Linux or Windows, both on the web and mobile applications. It is widely used in the field of computer graphics, geometric modeling, volume rendering, scientific visualization and specially for medical image processing. The core functions of VTK including filters, graphical renderer, data model, data interaction, 2D plots and charts, parallel processing, etc., that can help to process an object on both 2D and 3D environment. The most significant factor of using VTK is free (open-source) with a clear supported documentation. Besides, the discussion of exploring and installing this library for using are opened to the researchers and developers on its repository. In the state-of-the-art tools for 3D rendering, a suite of widgets for 3D interaction and extensive 2D plotting capability, VTK is part of Kitware's collection of supported platforms for software development. The platform is used worldwide in commercial applications, as well as in research and development.

### 2.2.3   AMI Medical Imaging

AMI Medical Imaging (AMI) [16] is a JavaScript Toolkit containing a set of JavaScript and Three.js libraries for medical image processing based on WebGL and Web3D application. Initially, the AMI toolkit is developed by a group of developers and researchers in the Fetal-Neonatal Neuroimaging Developmental Science Center at Boston Children's Hospital. Three.js is a well-known JavaScript framework for creating and rendering both 2D and 3D graphical objects on web browsers. Using Three.js, developers are supplied a set of functions that can help to visualize scientific data or medical image data, etc. The latest version is always updated monthly and the discussion of its using is regularly sharing to all the researched communities. Besides, some several open source codes for processing medical images are available uploaded on the Github. This existing libraries can accept almost the formats of medical image data like .DCM, .NRD, .STL, etc. Therefore, the combination between AMI and Three.js is a power tool to process medical image data captured from medical devices.

### 2.2.4   The X Toolkit

The X Toolkit (XTK) is an open-source JavaScript framework designed for constructing and visualizing scientific and medical data directly on the web application [17]. The main goal of XTK is to build and visualize the medical data object based on power of WebGL. The background of computation includes geometric modeling, computer graphics for web and image processing. All of these functions like 3D modeling, structure, material or texture rendering are existed in the WebGL. They are performing simple with few lines of codes. However, comparing to other tools and techniques, the XTK is not aiming to be a general purpose like Three.js or WebGL gaming engine libraries. It is totally a single and lightweight framework with wealthy examples and instructions. Because of being medical-image-processing toolkit, it has ability to read a large number of input file formats. In general, the advantages of XTK are considered as follows: (i) It can work on modern web browsers and compatible with most of web browsers and web browser engines. (ii) It does not require any adding plugins or software to install or configure the IDE. (iii) It use the GPU power to render graphical objects (see [17]).

### 2.2.5   OpenCV Library

OpenCV (Open Source Computer Vision Library) is an open-source software library which is widely knew and applied in computer vision and machine learning [19]. The OpenCV includes more than 2500 algorithms which are optimized for processing images, detecting and recognizing face, tracking moving objects, extracting object's boundary, etc. At the moment, the OpenCV has reached more than 47 thousand of users and more than 18 million in estimated amount of downloading times. It is preliminarily written in C++. However, due to its rapid growth and encouragement by users in such filed, the OpenCV has been delivered to a range of programming languages, such as Python, Java, JavaScript, etc. Besides, the essential features such as 2D and 3D toolkits, facial recognition, human-computer interaction, motion tracking, gesture recognition, etc., have been integrated in the whole library.

### 2.3   Existing Applications

In this section, several applications in the same field are reviewed. They are built very useful and designed for observing and supporting doctors in image diagnosis department of the hospitals. However, the commercial versions are expensive. Moreover, some of them are designed for desktop-based application, while the others did not enable the 3D function for visualizing the 3D objects.

### 2.3.1   RadiAnt Dicom Viewer

RadiAnt Dicom Viewer [5] is Picture-Archiving-and-Communication-System (PACS) application developed with the aim at operating and exhibiting medical images in Dicom format. RadiAnt Dicom Viewer permits user to open and view the medical objects, which are acquired from Digital Radiography, Computed Tomography, Ultrasonography, etc., directly from local storage, CD/DVD/BluRay disks, flash memory, etc. The user interface is greatly intuitive; it is no matter when we are working in window mode or full-screen mode. Furthermore, it is incredibly optimized for the outstanding performance, which means it allows multi-core and multi-processor support, up-to-date memory management system and dealing with a massive number of images at the same time and asynchronous reading. Using RadiAnt Dicom Viewer, user is offered a useful tool to do the image operations after loading the slices, such as zoom-in/out, rotation, flip, adjust color, contrast and brightness. Nevertheless, it is only available on Microsoft Windows system and requires a specific computer specification in order to be executed. Besides, RadiAnt Dicom Viewer has been not certified as an entirely medical product yet, so it cannot be used with the purpose of advanced diagnosis.

### 2.3.2   MedDream Dicom Viewer

MedDream Dicom Viewer [11] is a web-based application dealing with PACS Server with the goal of deep diagnoses, storing, visualizing and transmitting medical images, especially Dicom images. MedDream guarantees a quick and reliable way to do manipulation, interaction and profound analysis on medical data. Due to being developed on web-based platform, it can be run on various gadgets, such as computers, tablets, smartphones, etc. In fact, the images captured from medical imaging devices, like ultrasound (US), magnetic resonance (MRI), computed tomography (CT), mammography (MG), digital radiography (DR), computed radiography (CR), etc., are directly visualized on MedDream. Another crucial feature making MedDream more distinctive and more flexible is its ability to be used anywhere with the Internet connection. On the other hand, in spite of a range of significant features, MedDream is not able to ensure the accuracy of calibration data obtained from modality. Unfortunately, the measured function of MedDream stops at approximation. It means that the accuracy of the final model is close to its initial shape of the input one.

### 2.3.3   OsiriX Dicom Viewer

There is no arguing that OsiriX Dicom Viewer [12] is one of the most common Dicom viewer in the world. In fact, it is a great outcome after 15 years of conducting research and implementation in medical image processing. The main target of this software is to ship an optimal viewer for visualizing images gained from radiology machines, such as MRI, CT, Ultrasounds, etc. In addition, OsiriX is closely committed to Dicom format (*.dcm extension) with the ability to completely support Dicom standard. Also, it offers an easy method to be rapidly integrated into working environment without facing any difficulties. There is a variety of its available versions that are ready to be installed on devices running Apple's operating systems (MacOS, iOS). With the state-of-the-art post-processing techniques, OsiriX produces accurately phenomenal result of Dicom images in both 3D and 2D modes. As confirmed by OsiriX, "By adopting OsiriX you have made the right choice: it meets normal requirements, it is simple to use, it has unlimited power and the ability to evolve!". However, one drawback of using OsiriX is that it is not a free application. The price for annually using is expensive, approaching $699 per year for license version.

## 2.4    Current Researches

This section reviews several researches for building and viewing medical data objects applied in image processing, diagnostic and medical training. Sinh et al. [8] presented a research for building 3D models from 2D slices of Dicom data. The method is based on three algorithms combined between the fields of computer graphics and image processing such as marching cube [20] (based on geometric modeling); texture-based [21] and ray casting [22] are based on core techniques of computer graphics. In the next proposed method [9], they suggested a method based on geometric modeling to reconstruct the surface of 3D object from Dicom dataset. This method proved the processing time that is faster comparing existing methods. However, both these researches are developed based on the desktop application that were not along with software development tendency nowadays and uncomfortable for users in the shared database of the hospitals. Rahul et al. [23] presented their method for reconstructing 3D objects from Dicom image data based on Matlab. The 3D objects are built from a list of 2D Dicom slices based on existing functions provided by the Matlab. The application have also shown the visualization of medical data both on 2D and 3D. Nevertheless, it is developed for desktop-based, that leads to the disadvantages for multiple users in the collaborative environment.

As we knew, the researched works in the field of medical image processing are normally categorized into two kinds: image analysis and reconstructing the 3D objects from these images. The side of medical image analysis is one of the important step for finding abnormal signals or diagnosing status of patients based on their CT, MRI images [24]. Avnish et al. presented a research for building 3D model from Dicom dataset [25]. After segmentation of the 2D slices, the interested region of the object is bounded within a boundary. The marching cube algorithm [20] is then used for modeling, surface reconstructing and rendering the final models (this algorithm "marching cube" has also used in the research of Chen et al. [27]). However, marching cube algorithm is time consuming; and this drawback has been improved by the proposed method in [9].

In recent years, application of machine learning techniques has also used in image processing to reconstruct the 3D models. Ali et al. [28] presented a survey of several methods for medical image processing. By using the deep learning method in segmentation, it has proved the efficiency in time processing. This idea is deeply presented in the recent research of Ghulam et al. [29]. The research focuses on breast cancer classification by using medical imaging multi-modalities through state-of-the-art artificial deep neural network approaches. This research is considered as a valuable resource for researchers and experts in medical image classification using deep learning-based breast cancer classification through different medical imaging modalities. In fact, the application for visualizing the medical data that has been built on the websites and provided by the companies as their commercial products. Ioan et al. [30] studied many software companies all over the world where they produced the software products for viewing and handling medical images. However, the final products in practice are expensive. That is reason why for us to research and develop this application.

## 3    Proposed Method

As mentioned above, we implemented all methods for building 3D objects from Dicom dataset based on the desktop application [9]. In this research, we do the same tasks but implementing these algorithms on the web-based application. The user requirement analysis is mostly based on the tasks of doctor and medical staffs when checking the scanned images of patients. The Dicom dataset are loaded directly from any stored devices without using a database management system. We implement our method as follows: we first process input data based on digital image processing. After converting from Dicom format to 3D point clouds, we filter to remove noisy data. The 3D object is then building based on a list of algorithms. The architecture diagram of our application is illustrated as in Fig. 2: where input data are Dicom images; After loading the Dicom files, they are processed and visualized on two modes (2D and 3D). We perform four algorithms (Marching Cube; Ray Casting; Texture-Based and Sinh's Method [9]) based on a list of existing libraries (VTK [15], ITK [18], AMI [16], Three.JS, XTK [17] and OpenCV [19]) that support constructing 3D models on the web-pages.

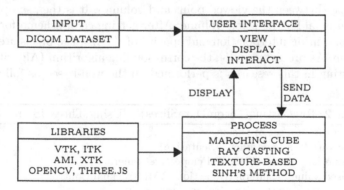

**Fig. 2.** Our proposed method

### 3.1    Marching Cube

Marching cubes is a 3D iso-surface representation technique using divide and conquer algorithm with the idea of creating a triangle mesh. Where the iso-value is used as a criterion for determining the intersection between surface and cube. It works by iterating for each cube over a uniform grid of cubes within a volume superimposed over a region of the function. As described in the previous research [8], the final triangular mesh is the union of all triangles after iterating all over cubes. The smaller making of cubes, the smaller obtaining of the triangular mesh and therefore making the approximated computation is more closely match the target function. To implement the marching cube on our web application, we build an algorithm as follows:

---

**Algorithm 1.** MarchingCube(DicomDataSlices) // Using VTK and ITK

---

 1: Load slices from a set of Dicom: itkreadImageDICOMFileSeries()
 2: Convert ITK image to VTK image: convertItkToVtkImage()
 3: Implement by calling marching cube: vtkImageMarchingCubes()
 4:     Create a cube from 8 pixels on adjacent slices
 5:     Calculate an index to find vertices on the surfaces
 6:     Use the index to look up the list of edges
 7:     Determine the intersected edges based on interpolation
 8:     Calculate vertex normals
 9: Initialize properties of the volume (iso value, color, camera)
10: Output: Call render()

---

## 3.2 Ray Casting

This method for creating 3D object from a list of 2D slices is based on the background of computer graphics. Comparing to the marching cube, it is the first direct volume rendering algorithm developed by Scott Roth in 1982 [22]. It works by casting a ray from a viewed point (eye) and go through pixels in the viewed plane (between the viewed point and volume). It is then sampled at the identified interval for the whole volume. After getting color schema for all pixels based on computing interpolation and opacity of the ray, the pixels are rendered to the screen. As presented in [8], the corresponding algorithm (Algorithm 2) for the ray casting in this research is performed on the web-based as follows:

---

**Algorithm 2.** RayCasting(DicomDataSlices) //Using Three.JS and AMI

---

 1: Load slices from a set of Dicom
 2: Initialize variables (container, orientation)
 3: Set a value for camera: THREE.PerspectiveCamera()
 4: Set a speed value for interactive action: AMI.TrackballControl()
 5: Initialize some configurations (color, mode, etc)
 6: **for** each pixel on the viewed plane **do**
 7:     **for** each primitive in the object space **do**
 8:         **if** ray intersect scene **then**
 9:             select the frontmost intersection;
10:             calculate color;
11:         **end if**
12:     **end for**
13: **end for**
14: Output: Call render()

---

Due to processing the rays based on computing their color, this method can create a 3D model that is close to its initial shape and support visualizing the shape with color. For each ray, we have to compute different color points that intersect at different samples through the volume. However, the whole processing time in this algorithm is not consuming.

## 3.3 Texture-Based

Texture-based rendering (or called texture-based mapping) is a technique approaching to the volume directly. In fact, it is considered as an essential solution in the field of computer graphics that map an image (a pattern or a texture) onto a geometrical object. Starting with a volume that formed by a set of 2D slices which are equidistantly arranged and parallel to coordinate planes. These slices from a bounding box of the object accordingly to the orthogonal direction of view. Then, each slice is mapped with a given texture and later stored into an array. At the end, color blending and opacity adjusting are compulsory computed before generating the final 3D model. The algorithm below (Algorithm 3) is performed on the web-page based on Texture-based:

---

**Algorithm 3.** TextureBased(DicomDataSlices) //Using XTK

---
 1: Load slices from a set of Dicom
 2: Initialize variables (container, orientation) for 2D mode: X.renderer2D()
 3: Initialize variables (container, orientation) for 3D mode: X.renderer3D()
 4: Initialize properties of the volume (opacity, threshold, color, etc)
 5: **for** each slice from back to front **do**
 6:     Store it on texture memory.
 7:     Create a polygon corresponding to the slice.
 8:     Assign texture coordinates to corners of the polygon.
 9:     Render and blend the polygon to the frame buffer
10: **end for**
11: Output: Call render()

---

## 3.4 Sinh's Method

The backgrounds of geometric modeling are widely used in the field of computer graphics. From the traditional researches like CAD/CAM to popular applied researches such as image processing, virtual and augmented reality in recent years. Application of geometric modeling in medical data visualization is not new. In fact, it is studied in the researched work a long time ago (i.e. [26]). However, how can we apply knowledge of geometric modeling in computer graphics combined with image processing techniques to show the best obtained results in the web browsers is still a big question to the researchers. Processing the boundary of medical images is important step to determine the shape of object. The 3D object is then reconstructed (from these list of 2D boundary) to obtain a completed 3D object [9]. In this part, we implement our method for 3D modeling from 2D Dicom slices based on geometric modeling and visualize them of the web pages. The method is based on following steps: (i) We first convert the Dicom data into point clouds data based on the intensity of pixels. (ii) The next step is extracting the boundary on each 2D slice based on [31–33], combined with idea of exterior boundary in the previous work [34]. (iii) The boundary is then refined by removing noisy points (both on interior and exterior of the boundary) and inserting new points (on the boundary) to obtain a regular one on each 2D slice. (iv) In the next step, a 3D object is reconstructed by adding z-coordinate on each 2D point based on the deep value of the 2D slice. (v) After adding functions (zoom in/out, rotate, adjust color, etc.) for handling 3D object, (vi) we show obtained results on the web page. Generally, this method is illustrated as follows (see Fig. 3): The algorithm (Algorithm 4) for building and visualizing 3D objects from a Dicom dataset is presented as follows:

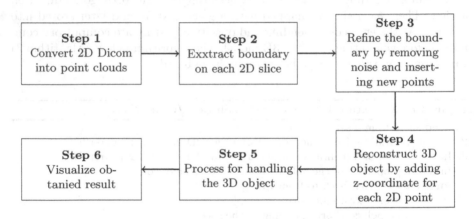

**Fig. 3.** Sinh's method on building 3D object from 2D slices

---

**Algorithm 4.** SinhMethod(DicomDataSlices) //Using ITK, OpenCV, Three.JS

---
1:  Convert Dicom data into point clouds.
2:  **for** each 2D slice **do**
3:      Get z-value of each slice: itkreadImageDICOMFileSeries()
4:      Extract exterior boundary of shape: boundaryExtraction()
5:      Remove noisy points inside and outside of the boundary.
6:      Update the boundary by inserting new points.
7:      Reconstruct 3D object by adding z-coordinate for each 2D point
8:      Add functions for handling 3D objects
9:  **end for**
10: Create a render: THREE.Scene()
11: Set a value for the camera: THREE.TrackballControls()
12: Initialize properties (point's size, point's color)
13: Output: Call render()

---

# 4    Implementation and Results

In this research, our objective is to develop a web-based application by using a list of several libraries. We combine multiple JavaScript frameworks as mentioned above to implement different rendering algorithms into our application. Following the characteristics of Dicom data scanned from the CT scanner in the hospitals, consulting from doctors and medical staffs, we construct the web interfaces of our application to adapt their work and familier to the users. In order to implement four algorithms (as mentioned above: Marching Cube, Ray Casting, Textured-Based and Sinh's Method respectively), we import existing libraries (ITK, VTK, AMI, XTK and Three.JS) and setup environment for creating and programming all functions to process input/output Dicom dataset. This application allows user interacting and controlling Dicom data objects on both 2D and 3D environment (user can test in this free host [37]). All the functions (like loading a Dicom file, viewing in the series of 2D slices, visualizing on 3D mode, rotating or zooming it, etc.) are easily to use and display by using different algorithms to compare and observe. Besides, we have created the functions to adjust the color, modify the brightness and opacity to have a better observation for users. Finally, we test our application with different Dicom datasets achieved from samples of Dicom collections (head, knee, shoulder, etc.) which can be freely downloaded from open-source sites [35] and refer from the hospital. The obtained results have been displayed as follows.

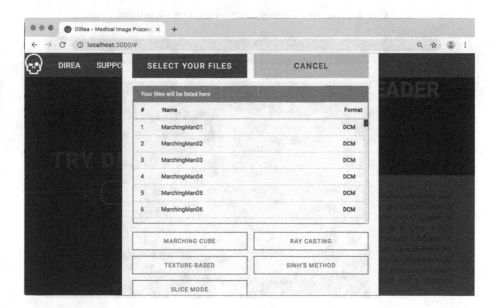

**Fig. 4.** The HomePage of our application.

After selecting a list of Dicom slices, we can choose one of the four algorithms. The different obtained results are presented in the list of figures (see Figs. 4, 5, 6, 7 and 8). The processing time depends on the different algorithms (see Table 1).

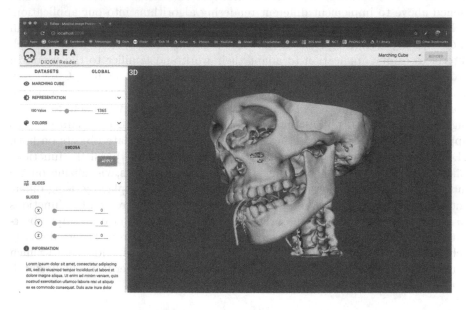

**Fig. 5.** User interface of Marching Cube algorithm

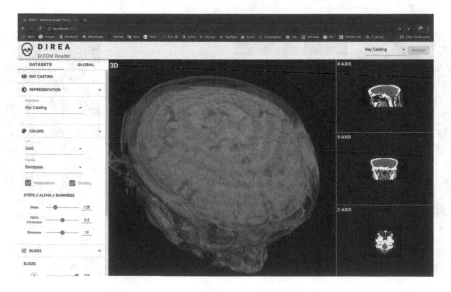

**Fig. 6.** User interface of Ray Casting algorithm

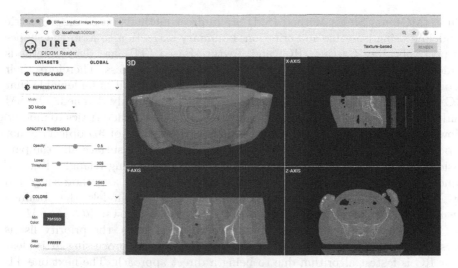

Fig. 7. User interface of Texture-Based algorithm

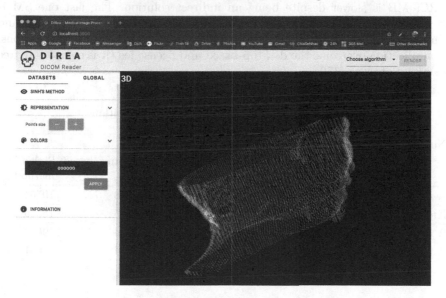

Fig. 8. User interface of Sinh's Method

## 5 Discussion and Comparison

This section discuss about the advantages, drawbacks and interactive abilities of the 4 different algorithms after reconstructing 3D models from Dicom dataset on the web application. The comparison among the algorithms such as processing time and quality of output models have also tested. The first main point focus on the way they process objects by approaching to the 3D volume. While Marching

Cube (MC) and Sinh's Method (SM) are indirect methods based on geometric modeling using iso-value and criterion, boundary extraction to form the shapes respectively. Ray Casting (RC) and Texture-Based (TB) are direct methods which do not rely on any criterion during calculating process. Therefore, their processing time is faster the MC and SM. For the quality, it is undeniable that RC creates 3D Dicom models with higher quality and highly detailed. The SM and TB algorithms obtained the 3D models with lesser characteristics to modify. However, the part inside of the 2D boundary (the surface of 3D object) is not processed in the SM. While the MC process including the surface and the part inside of the surface. In some cases, the ambiguity of making triangles leads to time consuming. However, this problem has been solved in a method suggested by Nielson et al. [36]. Comparing the quality of output models, the obtained results are distributed respectively from the best as follows: $RC \rightarrow SM \rightarrow MC \rightarrow TB$. While comparison in interactive experiences, the priority list is presented as follow: $MC \rightarrow SM \rightarrow RC \rightarrow TB$. For time processing, it is clear that RC is fastest algorithm due to being a direct approach. The next one TB is slightly slower than RC with a small approximated difference. Comparing to RC, MB is slower despite being an indirect solution. The last one SM is the slowest algorithm for visualizing the Dicom dataset due to extracting and refining on each 2D boundary. In general, comparing to the several applications, our application overcome the desktop-based and license fee (it is completely free to all kind of users [37]).

**Table 1.** Comparison between rendering algorithms

| Number of slices | Processing time (MS) | | | |
|---|---|---|---|---|
| | Marching cube | Ray casting | Texture-based | Sinh's method |
| A male head (245 slices) | 7672 | 4718 | 5068 | 10568 |
| Knees (350 slices) | 8380 | 6065 | 7145 | 15089 |
| A female head (234 slices) | 7535 | 4702 | 5534 | 9652 |
| A male pelvis (140 slices) | 6906 | 3941 | 4754 | 7081 |

## 6   Conclusion

In this paper, we have presented a web-based application for visualizing Dicom dataset in both 2D and 3D space. Users might find it highly convenient since it is feasible for our software to be used in anywhere with Internet connection. Also, we offer medical staffs different ways to handle the 3D Dicom object by providing multiple rendering algorithms. As the result, outcomes that we obtained are similar to the preliminary figures of real organs. Each rendering method has its own advantages and small limitation which can be overcome by others. Therefore, doctors and medical staffs should flexibly switch between them for obtaining most desirable result. Besides, this application is not only useful in medical diagnostic and exploration, but also in medical training and research since it is completely free of charge [37]. Evidently, we will refine algorithms for a better performance, add more measuring tools in the future work, apply the deep learning and machine learning to improve the accuracy of the final 3D models.

# References

1. Vimala, S., Bobi Nath, B.N.: A survey on medical images. Int. J. Adv. Res. Comput. Sci. Softw. Engi. **5**(10), 673–679 (2015). ISSN: 2277 128X
2. Alagendran, B., Manimurugan, S.: A survey on various medical image compression techniques. Int. J. Soft Comput. Eng. (IJSCE) **2**(1), 425–428 (2012). ISSN: 2231–2307
3. Bauer, S., Wiest, R., Nolte, L.-P., Reyes, M.: A survey of MRI-based medical image analysis for brain tumor studies. Phys. Med. Biol. **58**(13), R97–129 (2013). https://doi.org/10.1088/0031-9155/58/13/R97
4. 3D-DOCTOR: ABLE Software Corporation (2019). http://www.ablesw.com/3d-doctor/index.html
5. Medixant: PACS-DICOM viewer (2019). http://www.radiantviewer.com
6. MITK: Medical Imaging ToolKit (2019). http://www.mitk.net/
7. Santesoft: Medical Imaging Software (2019). http://www.santesoft.com/
8. Nguyen, V.S., Tran, M.H., Vu, H.M.Q.: A research on 3D model construction from 2D DICOM. In: Proceedings of International Conference on Advanced Computing and Applications (ACOMP), pp. 158–163. IEEE (2016). ISBN 978-1-5090-6143-3
9. Nguyen, V.S., Tran, M.H., Vu, H.M.Q.: An improved method for building a 3D model from 2D DICOM. In: Proceedings of International Conference on Advanced Computing and Applications (ACOMP), pp. 125–131. IEEE (2018). ISBN: 978-1-5386-9186-1
10. DICOM: Digital imaging and communications in medicine (2019). https://www.dicomstandard.org/about/
11. MedDream: MedDream Dicom Viewer (2019). www.softneta.com/products/meddream-dicom-viewer/
12. OsiriX: OsiriX Dicom Viewer (2019). https://www.osirix-viewer.com
13. LeadTools: DICOM Specification Overview: Basic DICOM File Structure (2019). https://www.leadtools.com/sdk/medical/dicom-spec1
14. MIT: Cornoerstone JS (2019). https://cornerstonejs.org
15. VTK: Visualization Toolkit (2019). https://www.vtk.org
16. AMI: AMI Medical Imaging (2019). https://medevel.com/ami-medical-imaging
17. XTK: The X Toolkit (2019). medevel.com/the-x-toolkit-webgl-medical-dicom
18. ITK: Insight Segmentation and Registration (2019). https://itk.org/
19. OpenCV: Open Computer Vision Library (2019). https://opencv.org/about/
20. William, E.L., Harvey, E.C.: Marching cubes: a high resolution 3D surface construction algorithm. J. Comput. Graph. **21**(4) (1987)
21. Levoy, M.: Display of surfaces from volume data. J. IEEE Comput. Graph. Appl. **8**(3), 29–37 (1988)
22. Scott, R.: Ray casting for modeling solids. J. Comput. Graph. Image Proces. **18**(2), 109–144 (1982)

23. Sherekar, R.M., Pawar, A.: A MATLAB image processing approach for reconstruction of DICOM images for manufacturing of customized anatomical implants by using rapid prototypingI. Am. J. Mech. Eng. Autom. **1**(5), 48–53 (2014)

24. Farzana, A., Mohamed Sathik, M.: Analysis of 2D to 3D reconstruction techniques over brain MRI. Int. J. Innovative Res. Comput. Commun. Eng. **5**(5), 9370–9376 (2017)

25. Patel, A., Mehta, K.: 3D modeling and rendering of 2D medical image. In: International Conference on Communication Systems and Network Technologies, pp. 149–152 (2012). ISBN 978-0-7695-4692-6/12

26. Hsut, J., Chelbergt, D.M., Babbst, C.F.: A geometric modeling tool for visualization of human anatomical structures. In: International Conference on Communication Systems and Network Technologies, pp. 176–183. IEEE (1994). ISBN 0-8186-5802-9

27. Chen, Y., Sun, P.: The research and practice of medical image enhancement and 3D reconstruction system. In: International Conference on Robots & Intelligent System (ICRIS), pp. 350–353 (2017). https://doi.org/10.1109/ICRIS.2017.94

28. Ali, I., Cem, D., Melike, S.: Review of MRI-based brain tumor image segmentation using deep learning methods. In: 12th International Conference on Application of Fuzzy Systems and Soft Computing, ICAFS 2016, Vienna, Austria vol. 102, pp. 317–324 (2016). Procedia Comput. Sci.

29. Ghulam, M., et al.: Deep learning-based breast cancer classification through medical imaging modalities: state of the art and research challenges. Artif. Intell. Rev. Int. Sci. Eng. J., 1–66 (2019). ISSN: 0269–2821

30. Ioan, V., Lacramioara, S.-T.: A survey of web based medical imaging application. In: 6th International Conference on Modern Power Systems, MPS2015, pp. 365–368 (2015)

31. Kattire, S.S., Shah, A.V.: Boundary detection algorithm implementation for medical images. Int. J. Eng. Res. Technol. (IJERT) **3**(12) (2014). ISSN: 2278–0181

32. Khan, A., Kashyap, R., Gupta, R.: A modified CT image boundary detection using global information and region based method. Int. J. Innovative Res. Sci. Eng. Technol. **6**(7) (2017). ISSN: 2347–6710

33. Poopathy, D., Chezian, R.M.: A survey on edge detection algorithms. Int. J. Electr. Electron. Comput. Sci. Eng. **4**(5) (2017). E-ISSN: 2348–2273

34. Nguyen, V.S., Bac, A., Daniel, M.: Boundary extraction and simplification of a surface defined by a sparse 3D volume. In: Proceeding of the Third International Symposium on Information and Communication Technology SoICT 2012, pp. 115–124. ACM (2012). ISBN: 978-1-4503-1232-5

35. The test data of DICOM are downloaded from the site: MIDAS (2016). https://placid.nlm.nih.gov/community/21

36. Nielson, G.M., Hamann, B.: The asymptotic decider: resolving the ambiguity in marching cubes. In: Proceedings of the 2nd Conference on Visualization (1991)

37. Our application: Dicom reader (2019). http://dicom-reader.herokuapp.com

# Evaluating Session-Based Recommendation Approaches on Datasets from Different Domains

Tran Khanh Dang[1(✉)], Quang Phu Nguyen[2], and Van Sinh Nguyen[2]

[1] Ho Chi Minh City University of Technology,
VNU-HCM, Ho Chi Minh City, Vietnam
khanh@hcmut.edu.vn
[2] International University, VNU-HCM, Ho Chi Minh City, Vietnam
phuguyen.ins@gmail.com, nvsinh@hcmiu.edu.vn

**Abstract.** Recommending relevant items of interest for user is the main purpose of recommendation system based on long-term user profiles. However, personal data privacy is becoming a big challenge recently. Thus, recommendation system needs to reduce the dependence on user profiles while still keeping high accuracy on recommendation. Session-based recommendation is a recent proposed approach for recommendation system to overcome the issue of user profiles dependency. The relevance of problem is quite high and has triggered interest among researchers in observing activities of users. It increased a number of proposals for session-based recommendation algorithms that aiming to make prediction of next actions. In this paper, we would like to compare the performance of such algorithms by using various datasets and evaluation metrics. The most recent deep learning approach named GRU4REC [1] and simpler methods based are included in our comparison. Six real-world datasets from three different domains are included in our experiment. Our experiments reveal that in case of numerous unpopular items dataset, GRU4REC's performance is low. However, its performance is significantly increased after applying our proposed sampling method. Therefore, our obtained results suggested that there is still room for improving deep learning session-based recommendation algorithms.

**Keywords:** Session-based recommendation · Sequential recommendation · Nearest neighbors · Recurrent neural networks · Recommendation systems

## 1 Introduction

These days recommendation system is being used more regularly in order to navigate users to their relevant sites or items which they are interested in. Recent researches show their concentration on techniques models which are established on long-term preference, identifying items which users are in need. However, personal data privacy is claiming to be strictly protected recently. Consequently, suitable recommendations need to be determined in term of information classification which is the latest interactions of users with the site or application. Recommendation approaches that based

© Springer Nature Switzerland AG 2019
T. K. Dang et al. (Eds.): FDSE 2019, LNCS 11814, pp. 577–592, 2019.
https://doi.org/10.1007/978-3-030-35653-8_37

only on the user's actions in a current session and which adapt their recommendations to the user's actions are called session-based recommendation [2].

The two most prevalent tasks of session-based recommendations are next click prediction and intent prediction. The former aims to predict the next item in the session given the previous one, while the latter desires to guess the intention of user from actual session, given the session (e.g. tile user wants to buy something, or just browses). A session is a sequence of events in close proximity, produced by the same user. If no explicit session identifier is available, it is common practice to assume the session end if the time between two consecutive events of the user is above a threshold. Many session-based algorithms only use the items of the events - similarly to most user-based collaborative filtering algorithms - but there are algorithms capable of utilizing additional information of the events (e.g. time, context) or the items (e.g. metadata).

Session-based recommendation was addressed even before the advent of deep learning. But papers on this topic were few and far between and methods did not work well in the pure session-based scenario. It is because of the complexity of the topic and classic methods being unable to deal with sequences appropriately. Therefore, in practice the real solution for this problem was the traditional item-to-item recommendation, in which items are recommended based on their similarity to or co-occurrences with the item of the user's last event while the rest of the session is ignored. While this approach works fairly well, this solution is heavily non-personalized (each user gets the same items on a given item page). It is also less accurate, since it does not consider earlier events from the session. Deep learning revitalized session-based recommendations by applying Recurrent Neural Networks (RNNs) - the de facto neural network family for dealing with sequences - for session data. With the ability of learning models from sequentially ordered data, this is a natural choice for this problem, and significant advance regarding the prediction accuracy of such algorithms were reported in the recent researches [1, 3, 4].

Though the topic has attracted lots of interest from researchers recently, there is no standardized benchmark datasets or protocols for evaluation in the community. Thus, it is such a challenge to draw conclusion which algorithmic proposals are the most effective one [5].

In order to establish a fundamental foundation for upcoming research, we would perform a comparison among various domains and datasets with a number of comparably simple as well as more sophisticated algorithms from the recent literature. The results show that modern technique which rely on the basis of deep learning models to predictions which produce more accurate outcome than other methods. However, there are still some case of datasets that the simpler method gets better accuracy. As a consequence, researchers should take into consideration these simpler methods as alternative baselines when developing new recommendation algorithms. Furthermore, our results suggest that there is substantial room for improving deep learning session-based recommendation algorithms.

The paper is organized as follows. Next, in Sect. 2, we discuss previous works and typical application areas of session-based recommendation approaches. In Sect. 3, we provide technical details about the algorithms that were compared in our work. Section 4 describes our evaluation setup and Sect. 5 are the outcomes of our experiments as well as our contributed method to improve GRU4REC's performance on some datasets.

## 2    Literature Review

The number of solutions for recommendation based on session involve certain features of sequence learning initial approaches mostly rely on identifying sequential patterns, used at recommendation time to make prediction of user's activities. For instance, the application of early methods in predicting how users navigate online [6]. Subsequently, mining techniques are also employed to recommend the next item which is often found in e-commerce and music streaming services [7]. Although it is quite easy to perform frequent pattern techniques, resulting in models which can be interpretable, the mining process can be quite demanding in term of computation. Simultaneously, it would cause lots of difficulties to come up with effective algorithm parameters, supporting threshold. Surprisingly, using frequent item sequences in certain application domains fail to produce more precise recommendation than simpler item co-occurrence patterns [7]. In the context of this work, we investigate both sequential and co-occurrence patterns in their simplest forms as baselines.

Between 2009 and 2015, neural models for recommendations were few and far between, even though deep learning in general started to gain a lot of attention even in 2012. Near the end of 2015, few papers applying deep learning for recommendations were published, signaling the beginning of the deep learning era for recommendation systems. The deep learning boom in RECSYS started in 2016 with several papers continuing the exploration of the topic. The Deep Learning for Recommendation Systems (DLRS) workshop series [1], [4] also started in that year, giving a boost to the research of the field. The trend continued in 2017, arid now having multiple deep learning recommendation system papers at top tier conferences is not rare. Since this field is very young, most of the papers were published after 2015.

RNNs has been commonly put into used in most recent research. [1] was among pioneers to gain a deep understanding of the next user action in a session for the prediction by applying Gated Recurrent Units (GRUs), a special form of RNNs. Their method called GRU4REC was afterward expanded in various ways in [4, 8]. As GRU4REC has been constantly updated since its first release, we include the latest version of the method proposed by [4] in the performance comparison reported in this paper.

## 3    Features of the Evaluated Methods

Following the aforementioned discussion, we include the four techniques which are simple heuristics method, nearest-neighbor technique, recurrent neural networks, and factorization-based method in our comparison. The main input to all methods is a training set of past user sessions. In each separated session, a set of actions which is put in sequential order such as a viewing items on an online store or media streaming site. Models obtained from the algorithms are then used to make prediction for the following events. Regarding our evaluation, a pragmatic approach is employed to identify user sessions if the datasets lack of these and use the inactive times of users to establish session borders. Detailed information for each dataset is presented later in this paper.

## 3.1  Baseline Approaches

We include the following baseline techniques in our comparison: a method that based on popularity of items (POP), popular items of the current session (S-POP), and item k nearest neighbor (Item-KNN) [9]. All baselines implement very simple prediction schemes, have a low computational complexity both for training and recommending, and only consider the very last item of a current user session to make the predictions. Furthermore, we include a prediction method based on Bayesian Personalized Ranking (BPR-MF) proposed by [10] as an alternative baseline.

**POP.** Popularity-based recommendation refers to sorting the list based on the score of the item. In spite of its power in certain domains, it is not a personalized recommendation method.

**S-POP.** This baseline recommends the most popular items of the current session. The recommendation list changes during the session as items gain more events. Ties are broken up using global popularity values. This baseline is strong in domains with high repetitiveness.

**Item-KNN.** This approach is inspired by traditional content-based filtering methods for session-based recommendations and recommends items similar to the item currently viewed. Similarity is measured based on the co-occurrence of items within sessions and calculated for each pair of products. During inference, the top k items with the highest similarity to the current item are selected for recommendation. Item-KNN is one of the most commonly used item-to-item solutions in real world systems, that provides recommendations in the "others who viewed this item also viewed these ones" setting. Despite of its simplicity it is usually a strong baseline [11].

**Bayesian Personalized Ranking (BPR-MF).** We finally include a prediction method based on BPR-MF as a baseline in our experiments. BPR-MF proposed by [10] is a learning-to-rank method designed for implicit feedback recommendation scenarios. The method is usually applied for matrix-completion problem formulations based on longer-term user-item interactions. Matrix factorization cannot be applied directly to session-based recommendations, because the new sessions do not have feature vectors precomputed. However, we can overcome this by using the average of item feature vectors of the items that had occurred in the session so far as the user feature vector. In more detail, we average the similarities of the feature vectors between a recommendable item and the items of the session so far, optimized by the following criterion:

$$\text{BPR-MF} = \sum\nolimits_{(u,i,j)\epsilon D_S} \ln \sigma(r_{u,i} - r_{u,j}) - \lambda_\Theta \|\Theta\|^2 \tag{1}$$

In the above formula, a ranking $r_{u,i}$ for user $u$ and item $i$ is approximated with the dot product of the corresponding rows in the matrices $W$ and $H$ ($r_{u,i} = \langle W_u, H_i \rangle$). The model parameters $\Theta = (W, H)$ are learned using stochastic gradient descent in multiple iterations over the dataset $D_S$, which consists of triplets of the form $(u, i, j)$. $(u, i)$ is a positive feedback pair and $(u, j)$ is a sampled negative example. $\sigma$ denotes the logistic function $\sigma(x) = 1/(1 + \exp(-x))$ and $\lambda_\Theta$ is a regularization parameter for complexity control.

The optimized criterion in Eq. (1) aims to rank the positive sample *(u, i)* higher than a non-observed sample *(u, j)*.

Generally, BPR and other methods designed for the matrix-completion problems in their original form, i.e., without considering the short-term session context, do not lead to competitive results in session-based recommendation scenarios, as reported, e.g., in [12]. Therefore, we do not consider such algorithms, e.g., traditional matrix factorization techniques, as baselines in our experiments.

## 3.2    Gated Recurrent Unit Neural Networks Model – GRU4REC

The GRU4REC algorithm [1] is a GRU based network adapted to the recommendation domain. Sessions here are represented as sequences of item IDs. Items IDs are represented by one-hot vectors. The network architecture consists of one or more GRU layers preceded by an optional embedding layer and followed by a feed-forward layer that predicts the likelihood of each item to be the next in the session (see Fig. 1).

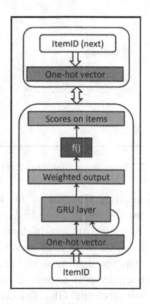

**Fig. 1.** GRU4REC schematic diagram

**Session-Parallel Mini-Batches.** Instead of using the BPTT algorithm on each session separately, GRU4REC does one step updates on mini-batches assembled from multiple sessions. Since multiple steps are computed at once (one step for each mini-batch), multiple hidden states are needed to follow each example. At the start of the training the mini-batch is composed from the items of the first events of the first M sessions (M is the mini-batch size) and the desired outputs are the items of the next events of the same sessions. After the gradient update, the mini- batch is now composed of the items of the second events of the sessions and the desired outputs are tied to the third events. This continues until one or more of the sessions has no more events. When this happens, the reciprocal hidden state is restarted to zero then the following available session is put in the place of the completed session in the mini-batch, starting from its first event (see Fig. 2). This training procedure fits data with high variance in session length well. Alternatively, the algorithm can learn from 2D mini-batches, i.e. batches of sequences, and update using the BPTT algorithm with T > 1. In this version, padding is used to fill up shorter sequences to T + 1 length. The accuracy of this methods is the same, but session-parallel mini-batching is faster.

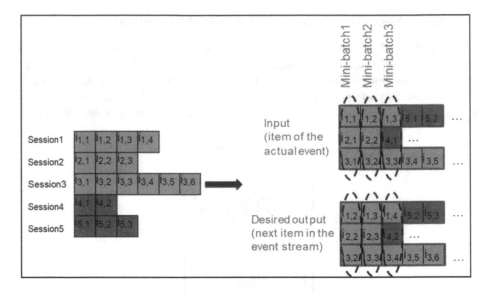

**Fig. 2.** Session parallel mini-batches

**Mini-Batch Based Output Sampling.** The size of the item catalog in a recommendation system in practice is usually in the hundreds of thousands, and it is not uncommon to see item catalogs of several millions of items. During training, GRU4REC does a prediction step in the order of the number of events in the training data. If it were to predict for all items in each step, the training would scale with the multiplication of the total items and events, which would result in poor scalability and slow training times in practical systems. To overcome this issue, GRU4REC does not predict for all items, but only for the target items and for several other items (negative samples). This significantly speeds up training process at the cost of only approximating the loss. However, this is a widespread approach for many algorithms in both recommendations and other domains. GRU4REC introduces a very efficient sampling mechanism by using the items of the desired outputs of the other mini-batch examples as the negative items for the given mini-batch example (see Fig. 3). This step can be implemented very efficiently on GPU and it doesn't require additional sampling. These two properties make this step very fast. Another advantageous property is that the sampling procedure samples negative items proportionally to their popularity. Popularity-based negative sampling is often better than uniform sampling due to (a) learning the item representations of more common items quicker; (b) capturing less of the popularity bias.

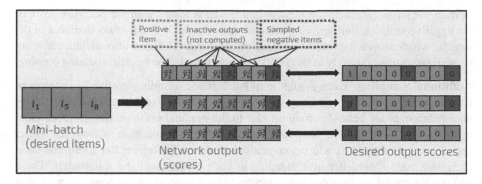

**Fig. 3.** Mini-batch based output sampling

**Ranking Loss Function.** Different loss functions were proposed for the algorithm, see the selection below. All losses are listwise ranking losses (over the target items and the negative samples) based on pointwise or pairwise scores. Currently, the BPR-max is deemed to be the best of the losses for most datasets [4].

*BPR.* The average BPR loss [10] between the target item and the negative samples. On some datasets performs better than TOP1 loss.

$$L_{bpr} = -\frac{1}{N_S} \sum_{j=1}^{N_S} \log \sigma(r_i - r_j) \qquad (2)$$

*TOP1.* A heuristic loss of two parts: the first part pushes the score of the target item above that of the negative samples; the second part regularizes the score of the negative items.

$$L_{top1} = -\frac{1}{N_S} \sum_{j=1}^{N_S} \sigma(r_i - r_j) + \sigma(r_j^2) \qquad (3)$$

*TOP1-max.* The SoftMax weighted version of the TOP1 loss. Inferior to the BPR-max loss with the following formula:

$$L_{top1-max} = \sum_{j=1}^{N_S} s_j\left(\sigma(r_i - r_j) + \lambda\sigma(r_j^2)\right) \qquad (4)$$

BPR-*max.* Introduced in 2017 by [4], BPR-max combines the benefits of pairwise losses, the SoftMax transformation and score regularization as the following formula:

$$L_{bpr-max} = -\log \sum_{j=1}^{N_S} s_j\sigma(r_i - r_j) + \lambda \sum_{j=1}^{N_S} s_j r_j^2 \qquad (5)$$

The authors concluded that the BPR and TOP1 losses are unsuitable when the score of the target item is around the score of tile top $\sim$ 10% of the negative samples. With many samples, this results in the training stopping before the desire item was put to the peak of the series. The solution is to weight the BPR losses with the SoftMax score of the negative samples, thus ignoring samples whose score is much lower than that of the targets, which solves the vanishing gradient problem. The loss also includes a score regularization term similarly to the TOP1 as it was found to be beneficial during training.

**Additional Sampling.** Even though mini-batch based sampling is efficient in terms of computations, its drawback is tying sample size to the mini-batch size. Generally, lower mini-batch sizes are better for training, due to the gradient noise serving as an efficient regularization method. On the other hand, larger sample size allows for better approximation of the loss and better gradient updates. Therefore, the additional sampling that adds shared negative samples to each example of the mini-batch. These additional samples are sampled in proportion to their support on the power of $\alpha$ ($0 \leq \alpha \leq 1$). By setting $\alpha$, sampling can be balanced between uniform and popularity-based sampling. The optimal value depends on the dataset but is usually around 0.58. Mini-batch and additional sampling together can both quickly learn good item representations for popular items in the beginning of the training and fit for long tail items at the end of the training.

## 4   Experiment

This section will describe the implement setup and provide experiment on six real-world datasets from three different domains: e-commerce; music and news, to compare the aforementioned methods in terms of to the used evaluation metrics.

### 4.1   Datasets

**YOOCHOOSE[1] Dataset.** YOOCHOOSE contain a collection of sessions from a retailer, where each session is encapsulating the click events that the user performed in the session. For some of the sessions, there are also buy events; means that the session ended with the user bought something from the web shop. Sessions of length 1 are filtered out from the training set. For testing, subsequent day's sessions are used. The data is not split in the middle of the session, each session is assigned to either the test set or the training set.

**RETAIL_ROCKET[2] Dataset.** RETAIL_ROCKET dataset was published by Retail Rocket company. It contains user's browsing activities in six months. The preprocessing way for RETAIL_ROCKET is as same as YOOCHOOSE.

**DIGINETICA[3] Dataset.** This e-commerce dataset was published in the context of CIKM Cup 2016 data challenges and contains anonymized search and browsing logs, product data, anonymized transactions, and a large data set of product images. For DIGINETICA, the preprocessing way is as same as YOOCHOOSE.

---

[1] https://2015.recsyschallenge.com/challenge.html.

[2] https://www.kaggle.com/retailrocket/ecommerce-dataset.

[3] https://cikm2016.cs.iupui.edu/cikm-cup/.

**TMALL[4] Dataset.** This e-commerce dataset was obtained from tmall.com website interaction logs for one year. For TMALL, timestamps for the events sessions were only recorded for whole day, total events from one day were considered in a session. The preprocessing way is as same as YOOCHOOSE.

**LASTFM Dataset.** This music dataset collected from last.fm music platform in 2015 [13]. For LASTFM, the last 5 days was used for testing and the 90 preceding days was used for training.

**CLEF[5] Dataset.** This news dataset is from CLEF NEWSREEL 2017 challenge. It contains user streaming actions plus article publishing events, which were collected for several publishers by PLISTA company. For Clef, only article read events is extracted, each split contains the last day for testing and the five preceding days for training.

## 4.2   GPU Optimization for GRU4REC

Adding extra negative samples will increase the computational cost on this deep learning model, but thanks to parallelization support on modern GPUs, most of this cost is mitigated while training model on GPU [14]. The training time on GPU will not be increased until the parallelization limit of the GPU is reached. Thus, the experimental codes are optimized to work on GPU. The reported results were obtained when using an Intel Core i5 4210H processor with 16 GB of DDR3-1600 memory and a Nvidia GeForce GTX 850M graphics card with 2 GB of memory and a 256 GB SSD hard drive.

## 4.3   Evaluation Metrics

While rating prediction can be considered a classical machine learning (function learning) task, the evaluation procedures and measures from this field can be applied. The probably most common approach according to the literature [15] is to measure and report recall. Instead of rating prediction, the recommendation system's mission is computing size-restricted list of recommended products for a given user. Usually, the length of the recommendation lists and correspondingly the measurement is limited to a top-10 or top-20 list of items. The quality of such a recommendation list is then numerically quantified by considering the amount and position of "relevant" items in the top-ranked lists of all users of the test set. The recall measures how many of the relevant items actually made it into the top-n list. Recall do not account for the position of the relevant items in the result set. The Recall@20 is calculated by the following equation:

$$Recall@20 = \frac{number\ of\ relevant\ items\ in\ top\ 20\ list}{total\ of\ relevant\ items} \qquad (6)$$

---

[4] https://ijcai-15.org/index.php/repeat-buyers-prediction-competition.

[5] http://clef2017.clef-initiative.eu/.

However, having a good matching proposition at position 1 is favorable over having it at a later position obviously. Researchers therefore often use measures like the Mean Reciprocal Rank (MRR) that also consider the position of the relevant elements. The reciprocal rank metric measures the position of the relevant item in the list of recommended items. This is important in cases where the order of recommendations is relevant, for example if the lower ranked items are only visible after scrolling. The experiments used the mean reciprocal rank at 20 as the second metric which is the average of the reciprocal ranks for 20 examples and calculated as:

$$MRR@20 = \frac{1}{20}\sum\nolimits_{i=1}^{20}\frac{1}{rank_i} \tag{7}$$

## 5   Results

The following section will discuss about the experimental results of six real-world datasets on three different domains: news, music and e-commerce.

### 5.1   E-Commerce Dataset

Table 1 shows the experimental results obtained from four e-commerce datasets in term of Recall and Mean Reciprocal Rank for the list length of 20 recommended items.

**Table 1.** Experimental results on e-commerce datasets.

| Dataset | YOOCHOOSE | | RETAIL_ROCKET | | DIGINETICA | | TMALL | |
|---------|-------|--------|-------|--------|-------|--------|-------|--------|
| Metric | R@20 | MRR@20 | R@20 | MRR@20 | R@20 | MRR@20 | R@20 | MRR@20 |
| POP | 0.005 | 0.001 | 0.016 | 0.003 | 0.010 | 0.003 | 0.066 | 0.038 |
| S-POP | 0.267 | 0.176 | 0.363 | **0.288** | 0.232 | 0.125 | **0.448** | **0.265** |
| Item-KNN | 0.498 | 0.201 | 0.282 | 0.122 | 0.376 | 0.118 | 0.074 | 0.025 |
| BPR-MF | 0.035 | 0.012 | 0.267 | 0.127 | 0.093 | 0.040 | 0.166 | 0.090 |
| GRU4rec | **0.718** | **0.314** | **0.541** | 0.258 | **0.477** | **0.142** | 0.230 | 0.129 |

GRU4REC is consistently outperform other methods on the first three datasets, presents competitive performance results. The lowest result is obtained from POP approaches and the BPR-MF adaptation. For TMALL case, GRU4REC's result reach only 0.230 on Recall and 0.129 on MRR. The detailed cause is not yet determined but we assume that the reason is because of the difference between this dataset and the previous three datasets. Because TMALL dataset does not have session ID attribute and the timestamps for the events were only recorded for whole day so we had to create the session ID for it.

## 5.2   Music Dataset

The music domain can be considered an alternative domain for session-based recommending approaches evaluation [14], because of its sequential order within listening sessions. Generally, music dataset obtained results pattern as same as the e-commerce datasets. Table 2 shows how GRU4REC outperform the other approaches.

Table 2.  Experimental results on music dataset.

| Dataset | LAST.FM | |
| --- | --- | --- |
| Metric | R@20 | MRR@20 |
| POP | 0.006 | 0.002 |
| S-POP | 0.187 | 0.082 |
| Item-KNN | 0.374 | 0.156 |
| BPR-MF | 0.044 | 0.011 |
| GRU4rec | **0.402** | **0.272** |

## 5.3   News Dataset

The news domain is considered particularly because it has certain distinct characteristics [16]. Firstly, fresh articles turn into feasible for recommending continually. Concurrently, articles may shortly turn into out of dated as well. Secondly, recent study denotes that a recommendation achievement might significantly depend on short-term trendiness [17]. Thus, this dataset experiment would present a measure whether the overall observations collected from previous fields established in a very specific characteristics domain like this. The experiment results presented in Table 3 confirm the trends observed for the previous datasets in general that the GRU4REC outperform the other approaches.

Table 3.  Experimental results on news dataset.

| Dataset | CLEF | |
| --- | --- | --- |
| Metric | R@20 | MRR@20 |
| POP | 0.025 | 0.025 |
| S-POP | 0.120 | 0.070 |
| Item-KNN | 0.717 | 0.260 |
| BPR-MF | 0.000 | 0.000 |
| GRU4rec | **0.902** | **0.393** |

## 5.4   Improving GRU4REC's Performance on TMALL Dataset

Due to the low performance result of GRU4REC on TMALL dataset, we did an additional analysis in order to explore whether we can improve GRU4REC's result or why this most recent model achieved low result on this dataset. The number of items on

TMALL dataset is extremely larger than the other datasets in earlier experiment, it is 1.1 million in compare with few hundred to few hundred thousand items. Due to the fact that the large number of items in TMALL dataset led to prohibitively high computational costs for the GRU4REC method. We created a deeper investigation on the number of interactions of each item and reveal that a large number of items have only few interactions. Thus, we selected a threshold to keep only the top 1% popular items from interactions for remodeling. For more detail, the items were sorted by popularity and a minimum item popularity threshold was set to keep only the items above the threshold accounted for 1% of the entire dataset. In this case, the threshold is 730 interactions. After this sampling strategy, the dataset remains only sessions of top 11k popular items. Then we extracted the last 3 days for testing purposes and trained on the preceding 27 days.

**Improved Result.** We used GRU4REC and baseline methods to evaluate the preprocessed dataset above one more time. The obtained results presented in Fig. 4 for Recall and Fig. 5 for MRR are significantly improved in compare with the previous results. Finally, we concluded that GRU4REC has weak confidence on the sparse (large number of items with few interactions) dataset and the S-POP baseline is the top performance method for this dataset.

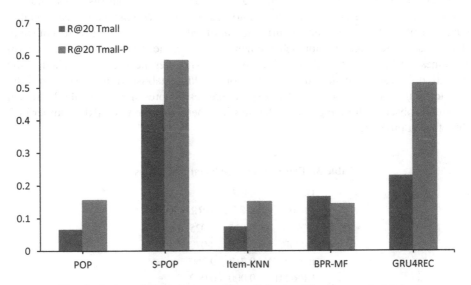

**Fig. 4.** Improved result in term of Recall for top 20 recommended items

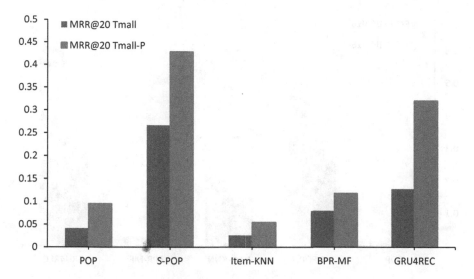

**Fig. 5.** Improved result in term of Mean Reciprocal Rank for top 20 recommended items

**Examine Discovered Method.** In order to examine the explored method on TMALL dataset, we found another dataset which has same aforementioned characteristics with TMALL named IJCAI16[6] from IJCAI-2016 Competitions which contains 2.3 million items. We apply the same proposed sampling and preprocessing method on this dataset. We trained the preprocessed dataset above with GRU4REC and baseline models to make an additional evaluation. The experimental results presented in Fig. 6 for Recall and Fig. 7 for MRR approved our discovered handling method on this kind of dataset. Our proposed method has a different impact on each model. In particular, RNN-based model's performance is the most improved. That result due to the fact that the GRU4REC mechanism itself is ranking item based on a comparison between desired item and negative item, where negative item is the popular item that user did not interact. Thus, in the case of numerous unpopular items dataset like TMALL or IJCAI16, the computational complexity of GRU4REC is increased prohibitively high. The model needs to calculate by itself to determine which are popular items among that numerous items hence its performance is drained a lot. For that reason, we propose aforementioned sampling method to solve (a) large number of items that increasing the computational complexity; (b) keeping only popular items to increase performance of ranking loss function. The obvious conclusion that we can state is our strategy improved accuracy of the deep learning model significantly. Almost datasets used in this work were experimented in a previous work of [18] and had been chosen because they are all store the information of item's interaction by session id.

---

[6] http://ijcai-16.org/.

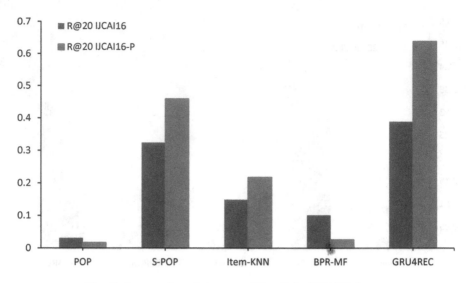

**Fig. 6.** Improved result in term of Recall for IJCAI16 dataset

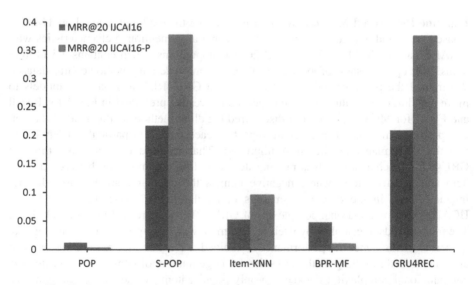

**Fig. 7.** Improved result in term of Mean Reciprocal Rank for IJCAI16 dataset

# 6  Conclusion and Future Work

## 6.1  Summary

Predicting short-term interest in an online session has triggered lots of interest in academic as well as practice. Though a wide range of algorithms measure has been proposed, benchmark datasets and baseline algorithms has not been established yet.

In this paper, we would like to make comparisons between a very recent and computationally complex algorithm for session-based recommendation with more lightweight approaches based. The experimental analysis on various domains datasets shows that in case of numerous unpopular items dataset, one simpler method is more effective than the most recent method based on recurrent neural networks when it comes to accuracy of prediction.

Generally, it is surprising that a recent and popular RNN-based algorithm is not substantially better than simpler approach on one dataset. However, this RNN-based algorithm's performance is significantly increased after applying our proposed sampling method. Our results therefore suggest that there is substantial room for improving deep learning session-based recommendation algorithms. Our main purpose in this work is to contribute better baselines to benchmark session-based algorithms in the future.

## 6.2  Future Work

Due to the prohibitively high computational costs of the experiment on TMALL and IJCAI16 datasets, our additional analysis was limited. For future work, we will create a deeper investigation on some datasets which have same characteristics with TMALL since the issue on this kind of dataset is common in real world e-commerce system. We hope that we can explore a compromise approach to overcome this issue on our next investigation. Besides, applying our proposed method to other modern application domains as similarity search in big data [19], data security [20, 21], etc. is also one of our great interest.

**Acknowledgement.** Tran Khanh Dang is supported by a project with the Department of Science and Technology, Ho Chi Minh City, Vietnam (contract with HCMUT No. 42/2019/HĐ-QPTKHCN, dated 11/7/2019).

# References

1. Hidasi, B., Karatzoglou, A., Baltrunas, L., Tikk, D.: Session-based recommendations with recurrent neural networks. In: ICLR (2016)
2. Quadrana, M., Cremonesi, P., Jannach, D.: Sequence-aware recommender systems. Comput. Surveys **54**(1), 1–36 (2018)
3. Robin, D., Hugues, B.: Collaborative filtering with recurrent neural networks. CoRR, abs/1608.07400 (2016)
4. Hidasi, B., Karatzoglou, A.: Recurrent neural networks with top-k gains for session-based recommendations. CoRR abs/1706.03847 (2017). arXiv:1706
5. Kamehkhosh, I., Jannach, D., Ludewig, M.: A comparison of frequent pattern techniques and a deep learning method for session-based recommendation. In: TempRec Workshop at ACM RecSys 2017, Como, Italy (2017)
6. Mobasher, B., Dai, H., Luo, T., Nakagawa, M.: Using sequential and non-sequential patterns in predictive web usage mining tasks. In: ICDM 2002, pp. 669–672 (2002)
7. Bonnin, G., Jannach, D.: Automated generation of music playlists: survey and experiments. Comput. Surv. **47**(2), 26:1–26:35 (2014)

8. Quadrana, M., Karatzoglou, A., Hidasi, B., Cremonesi, P.: Personalizing session-based recommendations with hierarchical recurrent neural networks. In: RecSys 2017, pp. 130–137 (2017)
9. Sarwar, B., Karypis, G., Konstan, J., Riedl, J.: Item-based collaborative filtering recommendation algorithms. In: WWW (2001)
10. Rendle, S., Freudenthaler, C., Gantner, Z., Schmidt-Thieme, L.: BPR: Bayesian personalized ranking from implicit feedback. In: 25th Conference on Uncertainty in Artificial Intelligence, UAI 2009, pp. 452–461 (2009). ISBN 978-0-9749039-5-8
11. Davidson, J., Liebald, B., Liu, J., et al.: The YouTube video recommendation system. In: ACM Conference on Recommender Systems, Recsys 2010, pp. 293–296 (2010). ISBN 978-1-60558-906-0
12. Jannach, D., Lerche, L., Jugovac, M.: Adaptation and evaluation of recommendations for short-term shopping goals. In: RecSys 2015, pp. 211–218 (2015)
13. Turrin, R., Quadrana, M., Condorelli, A., Pagano, R., Cremonesi, P.: 30Music listening and playlists dataset. In: Poster Proceedings of RecSys 2015 (2015)
14. Jannach, D., Ludewig, M.: When recurrent neural networks meet the neighborhood for session-based recommendation. In: Proceedings of RecSys 2017, Como, Italy, 27–31 August 2017, 5 p. (2017)
15. Jannach, D., Zanker, M., Ge, M., Gröning, M.: Recommender systems in computer science and information systems - a landscape of research. In: Proceedings of the 13th International Conference on E-Commerce and Web Technologies, pp. 76–87 (2012)
16. Karimi, M., Jannach, D., Jugovac, M.: News recommender systems - survey and roads ahead. Inf. Proces. Manag. (2018)
17. Ludmann, C.A.: Recommending news articles in the CLEF news recommendation evaluation lab with the data stream management system odysseus. In: Working Notes of CLEF 2017 - Conference and Labs of the Evaluation (2017)
18. Ludewig, M., Jannach, D.: Evaluation of session-based recommendation algorithms. CoRR abs/1803.09587 (2018)
19. Phan, T.N., Dang, T.K.: A lightweight indexing approach for efficient batch similarity processing with MapReduce. SN Comput. Sci. (SNCS) 1(1) (2020)
20. Dang, T.K., Pham, D.M.C., Ho, D.D.: On verifying the authenticity of e-commercial crawling data by a semi-crosschecking method. Int. J. Web Inf. Syst. (IJWIS) (2019)
21. Dang, T.K.: Ensuring correctness, completeness and freshness for outsourced tree-indexed data. Inf. Resour. Manag. J. (IRMJ) 21(1), 59–76 (2008)

# Exploiting Social Data to Enhance Web Search

Vo Hoang Phuc[1]($\boxtimes$), Vu Thanh Nguyen[2]($\boxtimes$), and Le Dinh Tuan[3]

[1] University of Information Technology, Ho Chi Minh City, Vietnam
phucvo.uit@gmail.com
[2] Van Hien University, Ho Chi Minh City, Vietnam
nguyenvt@vhu.edu.vn
[3] Long An University of Economics and Industry,
Tân An, Long An Province, Vietnam
le.tuan@daihoclongan.edu.vn

**Abstract.** With the strong growth of the internet, the search engine systems have been growing rapidly to allow web users to find relevant information with respect to their interests and needs. However, the amount of information is huge, searching information problems for users' demands still remain many challenges. Many social platforms and networks (such as Twitter, Facebook or Delicious) which allow users to tag, share and organize their favorite web pages online using social annotations easily. Moreover, these social annotations could benefit web search because of user's interesting tags and relevant information. Therefore, this paper proposed a search engine by combining following studies: (1) exploit social data from Twitter, (2) formulate query by personalized query expansion method using social annotations (SoQuES), (3) enhance the representation of documents and personalize them with social information (PerSa-DoR), (4) use the social personalized ranking function (SoPRa) to re-rank search results. Furthermore, our experiment on Twitter data showed that our method could enhance the search engine user efficiently.

**Keywords:** Social annotation · Personalized social ranking · Query expansion · Information search

## 1 Introduction

Information Retrieval (IR) is performed every day in an obvious way over the Web, typically under a search engine. However, finding relevant information remains challenging for end-users. In existing IR systems, queries are usually interpreted and processed using document indexes and/or ontologies, which are hidden for users. The resulting documents are not necessarily relevant from an end-user perspective, in spite of the ranking performed by the search engine.

To improve the classic IR process and reduce the amount of irrelevant documents, there are mainly three possible improvement tracks: (i) query reformulation, i.e. which includes expansion or reduction of the query, (ii) re-ranking of the retrieved documents (based on the user profile or context), and (iii) improvement of the IR model, i.e. the way documents and queries are represented and matched to quantify their similarities. Here, we consider the use of social information in these three tracks.

© Springer Nature Switzerland AG 2019
T. K. Dang et al. (Eds.): FDSE 2019, LNCS 11814, pp. 593–607, 2019.
https://doi.org/10.1007/978-3-030-35653-8_38

Recently, with the development of Web 2.0 technologies, there have many web platform systems enable users to tag, share and comment information and resources. Especially, it allows users to freely tag web pages with annotations. These annotations provide not only the content but also a summary, which indicate the popularity of the web page. How to take advantage of the useful information that social annotations have provided to apply the search engine to direct search results closer to users? In this paper, we combine three improvement tracks: query reformulation (using query expansion method), enhancement of document representation (personalized social document representation) and re-ranking of the retrieved documents (social personalized ranking) to build an efficient search engine.

The rest of the paper is organized as follows. Section 2 shows the related works. Section 3 we present the background. Section 4 we present Personalized Social Query Expansion method (SoQuES). Section 5 introduces the approach of Personalized Social Document Representation (PerSaDoR). Section 6 describes in detail about social personalized ranking function (SoPRa). Section 7 presents how to exploit social annotations from the Twitter system and provides some experimental results. Finally, a conclusion is presented in Sect. 8.

## 2   Related Work

### 2.1   Results Ranking

In IR, results ranking consists in the definition of a function that allows quantifying the similarities among documents and queries. We distinguish two categories for social results ranking that differ in the way they use social information. The first category uses social information by adding a social relevance to documents, while the second uses it to personalize search results.

### 2.1.1   Non-personalized Ranking

Several approaches have been proposed to improve document re-ranking using social relevance. Social relevance refers to information socially created that characterizes a document from a point of view of interest, i.e. its general interest and its popularity. Two formal models for folksonomies and ranking algorithm called *FolkRank* [1] and *SocialPageRank* [2] have been proposed. *FolkRank*, an algorithm inspired by the well-known *PageRank* method that exploits the structure of the folksonomy for assigning authority scores to elements on the network, that are subsequently used to improve the result ranking. *SocialPageRank*, an authority measure for documents that evaluates the quality of a page based on its annotations, and *SocialSimRank* which is a similarity measure for tags. In the same idea, relying on social bookmarking systems, Zhou et al. [4], has been studying and using social annotations in information retrieval and has brought positive results. He et al. [14] has proposed a new method to predict popularity of items (i.e., web pages) based on users' comments, and to incorporate this popularity into a ranking function.

### 2.1.2   Personalized Ranking

Many approaches have been proposed to improve the ranking of search results using social annotations. Noll and Meinel [12] proposed a personalized search method that exploited social annotations of users and documents, improved a Web search system during their user evaluation. Their work is rather simple while effective. Vallet et al. [8] has used users and documents profiles for personalized web search. Xu et al. [3] proposed a personalized search framework to utilize folksonomy for personalized search. Bouadjenek et al. [7] proposed a new method called *SoPRa*, the approach is similar to [3] but consider new aspect, which is the social context of the Web. Khodaei et al. [13] proposed a new relevance model called persocial relevance model utilizing three levels of social signals to improve the web search.

Almost all these approaches are in the context of folksonomies and follow the common idea that the ranking score of a document $d$ retrieved when a user $u$ submits a query $q$ is driven by (i) a term matching, which calculates the similarity between $q$ and the textual content of $d$ to generate a user unrelated ranking score; and (ii) an interest matching, which calculates the similarity between $u$ and $d$ to generate a user related ranking score. Then a merge operation is performed to generate a final ranking score based on the two previous ranking scores. A number of these algorithms are reviewed and evaluated in [11], while considering different social contexts.

## 2.2   Query Expansion

Many researchers have proposed different methods for query expansion. Yin et al. [6] expanded the search query by exploiting top web search result snippets. Collins et al. [5] combined multiple data sources (including *WordNet* and *Co-occurrence* data) using a Markov chain framework. Lin et al. [9] proposed a novel query expansion method based on social annotations which were used as the resource of expansion terms. Bouadjenek et al. [10] proposed method use social annotations in the context of folksonomies for social and personalized query expansion. Lu et al. [15] used the synonym of the synsets that had the same parts-of-speech (*POS*) with query term to extend each query terms. Each approach has partially solved the problem how to improve the effectiveness of web search.

## 2.3   Indexing and Modeling Using Social Information

Throughout the analysis of the state of the art, social information has been mainly used in two ways for modeling and enhancing documents' representations: (i) either by adding social meta-data to the content of documents, e.g., document expansion, or (ii) by personalizing the representation of documents, following the intuition that each user has his/her own vision of a given document.

### 2.3.1   Document Expansion (Non-personalized Indexing)

In [16], Nguyen proposed a framework named *SoRTESum* to combine Web document contents, sentences and users' comments from social networks to provide a viewpoint of a Web document towards a special event. *SoRTESum* obtained improvements over state of the art supervised and unsupervised baselines to generate high-quality summaries. An interesting future work is to use the obtained summaries for querying the documents.

### 2.3.2  Personalized Indexing and Modeling of Documents

In [17], Bouadjenek proposed the approach of Personalized Social Document Representation of each document per user based on his/her activities in a social tagging system. The proposed approach relied on matrix factorization to compute the *PerSaDoR* of documents that match a query.

## 3  Background

In this section, we formally define the basic concepts that we use in this paper. Social bookmarking systems are based on the techniques of social tagging. The principle is to provide the user with a mean to freely annotate resources on the Web with tags, e.g. *Delicious, YouTube, Twitter*. These annotations (also called tags) can be shared with others. This unstructured approach to classification is often referred to as a folksonomy. A folksonomy is based on the notion of bookmark defined as follows:

**Definition 1:** [Bookmark] Let $U$, $T$, $R$ be respectively the set of Users, Tags, and Resources. A bookmark is a triplet $(u, t, r)$ such as $u \in U$, $t \in T$, $r \in R$, which represents the fact that the user $u$ has annotated the resource $r$ with the tag $t$.

Then, a folksonomy is formally defined as follows:

**Definition 2:** [Folksonomy] Let $U$, $T$, $R$ be respectively the set of Users, Tags, and Resources. A folksonomy $\mathbb{F}$ $(U, T, R)$ is a subset of the Cartesian product $U \times T \times R$ such that each triple $(u, t, r) \in \mathbb{F}$ is a bookmark.

A folksonomy can be represented by a tripartite graph where each ternary edge represents a bookmark. In particular, the graph representation of the folksonomy $\mathbb{F}$ is defined as a tripartite graph $\mathcal{G}(V, E)$ where $V = U \cup T \cup R$ and $E = \{(u, t, r)|(u, t, r) \in \mathbb{F}\}$. Especially, folksonomies have provided a valuable knowledge because they may contain a good summary or relevant and interesting information of users.

**Definition 3:** [User Profile] Let U, T, R be respectively the set of Users, Tags, and Resources. A profile assigned to a user $u \in U$, is modeled as a weighted vector $\vec{p_u}$ of $m$ dimensions, where each dimension represents a tag the user employed in his/her tagging actions. More formally, $\vec{p_u} = \{w_{t1}, w_{t2}, \dots, w_{tm}\}$ such that $t_m \in T \wedge (\exists r \in R| (u, t_m, r) \in \mathbb{F})$, where $w_{tm}$ is the user term frequency, inverse user frequency (*utf-iuf*) that evaluates how important a term is to a user inside a set of users, i.e., similar to the *tf-idf* measure.

# 4 Personalized Social Query Expansion (SoQuES)

Finding relevant information becomes harder for end users because: (i) by definition, the user doesn't necessarily know what he is looking for until he finds it, and (ii) even if the user knows what he is looking for, he doesn't necessarily know how to formulate the right query.

Query expansion is a good solution to reduce the impacts of such problems. It enriches the user's initial query with additional information that could be relevant to the initial query so that the system may propose suitable results that better satisfy the user's needs. In this section, we use a query expansion method which Bouadjenek et al. proposed in [10] to formulate a query in our search engine. This method used social annotations in the context of folksonomies for social and personalized query expansion.

## 4.1 Problem Definition

The problem can be formalized as following: For a given user $u$ who issued a query $Q = \{t_1, t_2, \ldots, t_m\}$, how to provide for each $t_i \in Q$ a ranked list of its related terms $\{t_{i1}, t_{i2}, \ldots, t_{ik}\}$, such that the gap between user's expectations and system's offerings is minimized. The objective is to transform $Q$ into a new query $Q'$ such that: (i) $Q$ is necessarily included in $Q'$, (ii) the results of $Q$ are included in those of $Q'$, and (iii) the obtained results with $Q'$ should increase the accuracy of the results and doesn't decrease the user's satisfaction.

## 4.2 SoQuES Algorithm

---

**Algorithm**: Personalized Social Query Expansion (*SoQuES*)

**Require**: A social folksonomy Graph $G$; $u$: a User; $Q$: a Query;

1: $P_u[m] \leftarrow$ extract profile of $u$ from $G$
2: for all $t_i \in Q$ do
3:     $l \leftarrow$ list of neighbor of $t_i$ in tag graph $G_{tag}$
4:     for all $t_i \in l$ do
5:         $t_j.Value \leftarrow Rank_{ti}^u(t_j)$
6:     Sort $l$ w.r.t. to $t_j.Value$ and let only the top $k$ terms in $l$
7:     Make a logical $OR$ ($\vee$) between $t_i$ and all terms of $l$
8:     Update $Q'$
9: return $Q'$

---

Get user's profile $\vec{p_u}$ from $G$ (Line 1). Enrich each term $t_i$ of $Q$ with related terms (Line 2). Then, get all the neighboring tags $t_j$ of $t_i$ in tag graph $G_{tag}$ (Line 3). After that, in Line 4, we compute for each $t_j$, the ranking value that indicates its similarity with $t_i$ w.r.t. the user $u$ (Line 5). The $Rank_{ti}^u(t_j)$ is computed as follows:

$$Rank_{ti}^u(t_j) = \gamma \times Sim(t, t_i) + (1 - \gamma) \times \frac{1}{m} \sum\nolimits_{t_j \in P_u}^{m} Sim(t_i \, t_j) \times w_{tj} \qquad (1)$$

where $Sim \, (t, t_i)$ is a similarity computed between the query term $t$ and $t_i$, $m$ is the profile's length, $w_{tj}$ the weight of $t_j$ in the user profile. We use *SocialSimRank* (SSR) [2] algorithm to calculate $Sim \, (t, t_j)$.

Next, the neighborhood list has to be sorted according to the value of $Rank_{ti}^u(t_j)$ and keep only the $k$ top tags (Line 6). Finally, $t_i$ and its remaining neighbors must be linked with the OR ($\bigvee$) logical connector (Line 7) and updated in $Q'$. As an example, when user issues a query $Q = t_1 \wedge t_2 \wedge \ldots \wedge t_m$, it will be expanded to become $Q' = (t_1 \bigvee t_{11} \bigvee \ldots \bigvee t_{1l}) \wedge (t_2 \bigvee t_{21} \bigvee \ldots \bigvee t_{2k}) \wedge \ldots \wedge (t_m \bigvee t_{m1} \bigvee \ldots \bigvee t_{mr})$.

# 5   Personalized Social Document Representation (PerSaDoR)

Given a document, each user has his/her own understanding and point of view of its content. Therefore, each user employs a different vocabulary and words to describe, comment, and annotate this document. Following this, Bouadjenek et al. [17] proposed an approach in which the index model provided a Personalized Social Document Representation (*PerSaDoR*) of each document per user based on his/her activities in a social tagging system. The proposed approach relies on matrix factorization to compute the *PerSaDoR* of documents that match a query.

## 5.1   Toy Example and Approach Overview

Suppose that a user, say *Bob*, issues the query "*news on the Web*" for which a number of Web pages are retrieved. Let's consider the Web page *YouTube.com* as a document that matches this query. This Web page is associated with many bookmarks in a folksonomy as illustrated in Fig. 1. There are eight users (*Alice, Bob, Carol, Eve, Mallory, Nestor, Oscar, and Trudy*) who annotated YouTube.com using seven tags (*info, Web, video, news, blog, social, and mine*).

Our approach intends to create a representation for each of these retrieved Web pages from the perspective of *Bob* based on their associated social annotations. These representations are used in order to compute a ranking score w.r.t. the query. Since a given document representation is specific to *Bob*, it is by definition personalized and we call it from now on, a Personalized Social Document Representation (*PerSaDoR*).

For a given Web page (e.g., *YouTube.com*), the only consideration of the user's tags as his/her personalized representation will result either in: (i) ignoring this Web page if he/she didn't annotate it or (ii) assigning it an inappropriate ranking score (since the representation is only based on his/her own perspective which may be poor). Our goal is then to use other users' annotations to enrich the personalized representation of the query issuer enabling him to: (i) benefit from others' experiences and feedback, (ii) promote used/visited resources even if they are not well classified, and (iii) discover new resources. For a document that potentially matches a query, our method proceeds into three main phases in order to collect maximum useful information about this

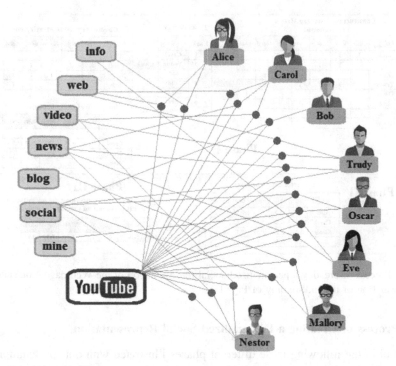

**Fig. 1.** Example of a folksonomy with eight users who annotate one resource using seven tags. The triples $(u, t, r)$ are represented as ternary-edges connecting a user, a resource and a tag.

document and its social relatives. This information is reused to create its *PerSaDoR* according to a query issuer. These phases are the following, as illustrated in Fig. 2:

1. Representing each document that matches the query terms using a Users-Tags matrix. This matrix is first sized by selecting relevant users to the query issuer, e.g., *Carol*, *Nestor*, and *Alice*. Then, each entry of the Users-Tags matrix is computed by estimating the extent to which the user would associate the tag to the considered document, e.g., *Alice* thinks that info is associated to *YouTube.com* with a weight of 0.5. This phase includes four sub-steps enumerated from 1 to 4 in Fig. 2.
2. Each row $i$ in a Users-Tags matrix of a given document translates the personal representation of the user $u_i$. This matrix is expected to be sparse, since it contains many missing values that should be inferred to build the *PerSaDoR* for the query issuer. Hence, a matrix factorization process is used to infer the *PerSaDoR* of the considered document to the query issuer based on identifying weighting patterns. This phase corresponds to step 5 in Fig. 2.

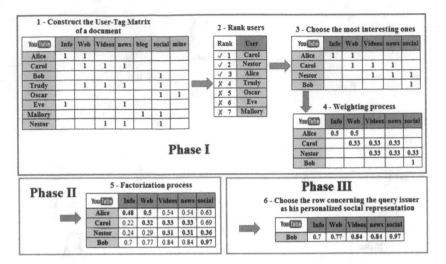

**Fig. 2.** Process of creating a personalized social representation of the Web page YouTube.com to the user Bob of the folksonomy of Fig. 1

## 5.2 Process of Creating a Personalized Social Representation

We detail in the following these different phases illustrated with our toy example.

### 5.2.1 Sizing the Users-Tags Matrix

As illustrated in Fig. 2, each Web page can be represented using an $m \times n$ Users-Tags matrix $M_{U,T}^d$ of $m$ users who annotate the Web page and the $n$ tags that they used to annotate it. Each entry $w_{ij}$ in the matrix represents the number of times the user $u_i$ used the term $t_j$ to annotate the considered Web page.

Instead of using all users' feedback to infer a *PerSaDoR* of the considered Web page to *Bob*, we propose to select only the most representative ones in order to filter out irrelevant users who may introduce noise. To do so, we use a ranking function to rank users from the most relevant to the less relevant ones, and select only the Top $k$ users as the most representative ones to both the query issuer and the considered Web page (see Step 2 of Fig. 2). The irrelevant users may: (i) have annotated a lot of documents improperly; (ii) have annotated the considered document with few terms; (iii) not be socially close to the query issuer and thus don't share the same topics of interests. The ranking score of a user $u$ according to a document $d$ and the query issuer $u_q$ is computed as follows:

$$Rank_{u_q}^d(u) = \varepsilon \times \left(1 + \log(|T_{u,d}|)\right) \times \log\left(\frac{|D|}{|D_u|}\right) + (1 - \varepsilon) \times Sim(u, u_q) \qquad (2)$$

where $Sim(u, u_q)$ denotes the similarity between a user who annotates $d$ and the query issuer. $\varepsilon$ is a weight that satisfies $0 \le \varepsilon \le 1$, which allows giving more importance to either the document proximity part or to the query issuer proximity part. Once we get a ranked list of users using Eq. (2), we select the Top $k$ to be the most representative ones to both the considered document and the query issuer. Then, we select their tags to build a new (smaller) Users-Tags matrix $M_{U,T}^d$. Finally, we add the query issuer as a new entry in the Users-Tags matrix $M_{U,T}^d$ as well as his/her tags, if any (see Step 3 of Fig. 2). Once the matrix is built, we proceed to the computation of the weights associated to each entry as detailed in the next section.

### 5.2.2    Weighting the Users-Tags Matrix

We propose to use an adaptation of the well-known $tf - idf$ measure to estimate this weight. Therefore, we define the weight $w_{ti}$ of the term $t_i$ in a document $d$ according to a user $u_i$ as the user term frequency, inverse document frequency ($utf - idf$), which is computed as follows:

$$w_{ij} = utf - idf = log\left(1 + n_{ui,tj}^d\right) \times log\left(\frac{|D_{ui}| + 1}{|D_{ui,ti}|}\right) \tag{3}$$

where $n_{ui,tj}^d$ is the number of times $u_i$ used $t_j$ to annotate d. The weights hence tend to filter out terms commonly used by a user (see Step 4 of Fig. 2).

At the end of this step, we obtain a matrix capturing the closest users (and their tags) to the query issuer, and this for each document that potentially match the query.

### 5.2.3    Matrix Factorization

Matrix factorization has proven its effectiveness in both quality and scalability to predict missing values in sparse matrices. This technique is based on the reuse of other users experience and feedback in order to predict missing values in a matrix. Concretely, to predict these missing values, the Users-Tags matrix is first factorized into two latent features matrices of users and tags. These latent features matrices are then used to make further missing values prediction. In its basic form, matrix factorization characterizes both users and tags by vectors of factors inferred from identifying weighting patterns. Therefore, the Users-Tags matrix $M_{U,T}^d$ of the Web page *YouTube.com* is factorized using $M_U^{\prime d} \times M_T^d$, where the low-dimensional matrix $M_U^d$ denotes the user latent features, and $M_T^d$ represents the low-dimensional tag latent features. Each row $i$ of the predicted matrix $M_U^{\prime d} \times M_T^d$ represents the personal representation of the $i^{th}$ user according to this Web page.

A matrix factorization seeks to approximate the Users-Tags matrix $M_{U,T}^d$ by a multiplication of l-rank factors, as follows:

$$M_{U,T}^d \approx M_U^{\prime d} \times M_T^d \tag{4}$$

where $M_U^d \in R^{l \times m}$ and $M_T^d \in R^{l \times n}$. Therefore, we can approximate the Users-Tags matrix $M_{U,T}^d$ by minimizing the sum-of- squared-errors objective function over the observed entries as follows:

$$\arg\min_{M_U^d, M_T^d} = \frac{1}{2}\sum_{i=1}^m \sum_{j=1}^n I_{ij}\left(M_{u_i,t_j}^d - M_{u_i}^{\prime d} \times M_{t_j}^d\right)^2 \tag{5}$$

where $I_{ij}$ is the indicator function that is equal to 1 if user $u_i$ used the tag $t_j$ to annotate the document $d$ and equal to 0 otherwise. In order to avoid overfitting in the learning process, two regularization terms are added to the objective function in Eq. (5) as follows:

$$\arg\min_{M_U^d, M_T^d} \mathcal{L} = \arg\min_{M_U^d, M_T^d} \frac{1}{2}\sum_{i=1}^m \sum_{j=1}^n I_{ij}\left(M_{u_i,t_j}^d - M_{u_i}^{\prime d} \times M_{t_j}^d\right)^2 + \frac{\lambda}{2}\left(\left\|M_U^d\right\|_F^2 + \left\|M_T^d\right\|_F^2\right) \tag{6}$$

where $\lambda > 0$ is a regularization weight. The optimization problem in Eq. (6) minimizes the sum-of-squared-errors between observed and predicted weightings. The gradient descent algorithm can be applied to find a local minimum in feature vectors $M_{ui}^d$ and $M_{tj}^d$, where we have:

$$\frac{\partial L}{\partial M_{ui}^d} = \sum_{j=1}^n I_{ij}\left(M_{ui}^{\prime d} \times M_{tj}^d - M_{ui,tj}^d\right)M_{tj}^d + \lambda M_{ui}^d \tag{7}$$

$$\frac{\partial L}{\partial M_{tj}^d} = \sum_{i=1}^n I_{ij}\left(M_{ui}^{\prime d} \times M_{tj}^d - M_{ui,tj}^d\right)M_{ui}^d + \lambda M_{tj}^d \tag{8}$$

Once we have computed the factorized user latent features and tag latent features matrices, we can predict missing values using $M_U^{\prime d} \times M_T^d$. Then, we consider that: The row that corresponds to the query issuer in the predicted matrix $M_U^{\prime d} \times M_T^d$ corresponds to his/her PerSaDoR for the considered document. A *PerSaDoR* is represented as a weighted vector of terms (see Step 6 of Fig. 2).

## 6 Social Personalized Ranking Function (SoPRa)

### 6.1 Problem Definition

The problem we are addressing can be formalized as follows: Let consider a folksonomy $\mathbb{F}(U, T, R)$ where a user $u \in U$ submits a query $q$ to a search engine.

We would like to re-rank the set of documents $R_q \subseteq R$ (or resources) that match $q$, such that relevant documents for u are highlighted and pushed to the top for maximizing his satisfaction and personalizing the search results. The ranking follows an ordering $\tau = [r_1 \geq r_2 \geq \ldots \geq r_k]$ in which $r_k \in R$ and the ordering relation is defined by $r_i \geq r_j \Leftrightarrow Rank(r_i, q, u) \geq Rank(r_j, q, u)$, where $Rank(r, q, u)$ is a ranking function that quantifies similarity between the query and the resource w.r.t the user [8].

## 6.2    SoPRa Function

In this section, we present about social personalized ranking function (*SoPRa*) which used for ranking results in our search engine. The approach of this function explores the social annotations for folksonomies in bookmarking systems. Following Bouadjenek et al. [7], *SoPRa* ranks the documents depending on 2 main factors: (i) a matching score between a document and a query, (ii) a social interest score of the user to documents.

On the one hand, the authors believe that the matching score between a document and a query should be based on a textual matching score and a social matching score. The textual matching score expresses the similarity between the content of document and query. The social matching score is a similarity between a social representation of document and query. This social representation is based on the annotations associated with a document. More formally, the score is computed by merging them using a linear function as follows:

$$Score(q, d) = \beta \times Cos(\vec{q}, \vec{s_d}) + (1 - \beta) \times Sim(\vec{q}, \vec{d}) \tag{9}$$

where $\vec{s_d}$ is the vector that models the social representation of the document $d$ and computed in Sect. 4, $Sim(\vec{q}, \vec{d})$ denotes the textual matching score between document $d$ and query $q$.

On the other hand, the social interest score of the user to documents is the similarity between the profile of a user and the social representation of a document. Then, we merge this interest score value to the previous ranking score computed in Eq. (9) for computing the matching score of a document to a query with respect to a user. Formally, the ranking score of a document $d$ that potentially match the query $q$ issued by a user $u$ is computed as follows:

$$Rank(d, q, u) = \alpha \times Cos(\vec{p_u}, \vec{s_d}) + (1 - \alpha) \times Score(q, d) \tag{10}$$

In summary, *SoPRa* ranks documents according to the textual matching score of documents and the query, the social matching score of documents and the query, and the social interest score of the user to documents.

## 7    Experiment

### 7.1    Exploiting Twitter Social Data

*Twitter* [18] is a microblogging social networking service where users can post and read short text based messages with up to 140 characters called tweets. According to recent social media industry figures, *Twitter* currently ranks as one of the leading social networks worldwide based on active users. As of the fourth quarter of 2018, *Twitter* had 321 million monthly active users and over 500 million tweets generate every day [19]. Registered users can read and post tweets as well as follow other users via update feed.

*Twitter* allow us to interact with its data tweets and several attributes about tweets through *Twitter APIs*. Especially, we can collect real-time tweets data through *Twitter's Streaming API*. Therefore, we exploit social data from this system to provide data for our search engine.

## 7.2   Social Annotations Dataset

For experiments and evaluation of the proposed method, we have built a module to crawl and store data from *Twitter* through *Twitter's Streaming API*. After that, we performed four data preprocessing tasks: (1) Filter non-English language tweets and removing tweets do not contain URL. (2) Extract annotations (hashtag) and web pages (URL) from tweets dataset. (3) Remove manually several annotations that are too personal or meaningless, e.g. "!picspam", "atthissummer", etc. (4) Finally, we removed all the non-English web pages using Apache Tika toolkit. Table 1 gave a description of the resulted dataset after our cleansing:

**Table 1.** Details of the Twitter dataset

| Tweets | Users | Annotation | Web pages |
|---|---|---|---|
| 3 411 172 | 404 721 | 200 354 | 813 330 |

## 7.3   Evaluation Methodology

In the community of personalized search, evaluation is not an easy task. The main idea of these experiments is based on the following assumption: For a query $q = \{t\}$ issued by $u$ with query term $t$, relevant documents are those tagged by $u$ with $t$.

We used Mean Average Precision (*MAP*) for main evaluation metric in our experience, which is a widely used evaluation metric in the IR community. More specifically, in our work, we calculated *MAP* for each user and then computed the mean of all the *MAP* values. We referred it as:

$$MMAP = \frac{\sum_{i=1}^{N_u} MAP_i}{N_u} \qquad (11)$$

where $MAP_i$ represents the MAP value of the $i^{th}$ user and $N_u$ is the number of users.

We randomly selected 1000 pairs $(u, t)$. For each pair, the user $u$ sent the query $q = \{t\}$ to the system. Then, we retrieved and ranked all the documents that matched this query using our approach. Finally, we computed the *MAP* over the 1000 queries. The random selection was carried out 10 times independently, and we reported the average results.

## 7.4   Evaluation Result

We experimented with $0 \le \alpha \le 1$ in formula (10) and fixing the $\beta$ values to 0.5 in formula (9), $\varepsilon = 0.2$ in formula (2), $\lambda = 0.02$ in formula (7) and (8). In formula (1), we

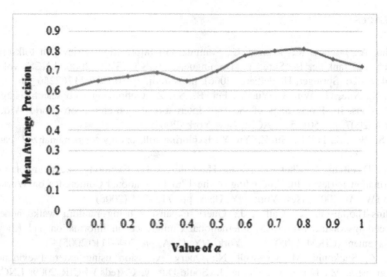

**Fig. 3.** Mean average precision by α

chose to fix $\gamma = 0.5$ and the query size was 5 per query term. Figure 3 showed the *MAP* for the difference α values, averaged over 1000 personal queries.

Finally, we noted that the better performance is obtained for $\alpha \in [0.6, 0.8]$ for our proposed method.

# 8  Conclusion

In this paper, we studied how to exploit and use of social annotations in information search. Annotations have provided not only content but also a summary, which indicated the popularity of the web page. In addition, we discussed a contribution the search engine through a combined method: a document ranking function (*SoPRa*), personalized query expansion (*SoQuES*) method, and personalized social document representation (*PerSaDoR*) which used social information to enhance web search. Our experimental results not only demonstrated the effectiveness of our search engine but also showed the benefit and potential of social annotations for a search engine. However, there were still possible improvements that we can bring. We also investigated ways to add social regularization terms to the objective function of the matrix factorization in order to model other behaviors of users. The temporal dimension of social users' behavior has not been investigated yet; this is also part of our future work to improve our proposal.

# References

1. Hotho, A., Jäschke, R., Schmitz, C., Stumme, G.: Information retrieval in folksonomies: search and ranking. In: Sure, Y., Domingue, J. (eds.) ESWC 2006. LNCS, vol. 4011, pp. 411–426. Springer, Heidelberg (2006). https://doi.org/10.1007/11762256_31
2. Bao, S., Xue, G., Wu, X., Yu, Y., Fei, B., Su, Z.: Optimizing web search using social annotations. In: Proceedings of the 16th International Conference on World Wide Web, WWW 2007, pp. 501–510. ACM, New York (2007)
3. Xu, S., Bao, S., Fei, B., Su, Z., Yu, Y.: Exploring folksonomy for personalized search. In: SIGIR (2008)
4. Zhou, D., Bian, J., Zheng, S., Zha, H., Giles, C.L.: Exploring social annotations for information retrieval. In: Proceeding of the 17th International Conference on World Wide Web (WWW 2008), New York, NY, USA, pp. 715–724 (2008)
5. Collins-Thompson, K., Callan, J.: Query expansion using random walk models. In: Proceedings of the 14th ACM International Conference on Information and Knowledge Management (CIKM 2005), New York, NY, USA, pp. 704–711 (2005)
6. Yin, Z., Shokouhi, M., Craswell, N.: Query expansion using external evidence. In: Boughanem, M., Berrut, C., Mothe, J., Soule-Dupuy, C. (eds.) ECIR 2009. LNCS, vol. 5478, pp. 362–374. Springer, Heidelberg (2009). https://doi.org/10.1007/978-3-642-00958-7_33
7. Bouadjenek, M.R., Hacid, H., Bouzeghoub, M.: SoPRa: a new social personalized ranking function for improving web search. In: Proceedings of the 36th International ACM SIGIR Conference on Research and Development in Information Retrieval, SIGIR 2013. ACM, New York (2013)
8. Vallet, D., Cantador, I., Jose, J.M.: Personalizing web search with folksonomy-based user and document profiles. In: Gurrin, C., et al. (eds.) ECIR 2010. LNCS, vol. 5993, pp. 420–431. Springer, Heidelberg (2010). https://doi.org/10.1007/978-3-642-12275-0_37
9. Lin, Y., Lin, H., Jin, S., Ye, Z.: Social annotation in query expansion: a machine learning approach. In: SIGIR 2011 (2011)
10. Bouadjenek, M.R., Hacid, H., Bouzeghoub, M., Daigremont, J.: Personalized social query expansion using social bookmarking systems. In: Proceeding of the 34th International ACM SIGIR Conference on Research and Development in Information Retrieval, SIGIR 2011, Beijing, China, 25–29 July 2011 (2011)
11. Bouadjenek, M.R., Bennamane, A., Hacid, H., Bouzeghoub, M.: Evaluation of personalized social ranking functions of information retrieval. In: Daniel, F., Dolog, P., Li, Q. (eds.) ICWE 2013. LNCS, vol. 7977, pp. 283–290. Springer, Heidelberg (2013). https://doi.org/10.1007/978-3-642-39200-9_24
12. Noll, M.G., Meinel, C.: Web search personalization via social bookmarking and tagging. In: Aberer, K., et al. (eds.) ASWC/ISWC -2007. LNCS, vol. 4825, pp. 367–380. Springer, Heidelberg (2007). https://doi.org/10.1007/978-3-540-76298-0_27
13. Khodaei, A., Sohangir, S., Shahabi, C.: Personalization of web search using social signals. In: Ulusoy, Ö., Tansel, A.U., Arkun, E. (eds.) Recommendation and Search in Social Networks. LNSN, pp. 139–163. Springer, Cham (2015). https://doi.org/10.1007/978-3-319-14379-8_8
14. He, X., Gao, M., Kan, M.-Y., Liu, Y., Sugiyama, K.: Predicting the popularity of web 2.0 items based on user comments. In: Proceedings of the 37th International ACM SIGIR Conference on Research & Development in Information Retrieval, SIGIR 2014, pp. 233–242. ACM, New York (2014)

15. Lu, M., Sun, X., Wang, S., Lo, D., Duan, Y.: Query expansion via WordNet for effective code search. In: Proceedings of IEEE 22nd International Conference on Software Analysis, Evolution, and Reengineering, pp. 545–549 (2015)
16. Nguyen, M.-T., Nguyen, M.-L.: SoRTESum: a social context framework for single-document summarization. In: Ferro, N., et al. (eds.) ECIR 2016. LNCS, vol. 9626, pp. 3–14. Springer, Cham (2016). https://doi.org/10.1007/978-3-319-30671-1_1
17. Bouadjenek, M.R., Hacid, H., Bouzeghoub, M., Vakali, A.: PerSaDoR: personalized social document representation for improving web search. Inf. Sci. **369**, 614–633 (2016)
18. Twitter. https://twitter.com
19. Twitter - Statistics & Facts, February 2019. https://www.statista.com/topics/737/twitter

# Retinal Vessels Segmentation by Improving Salient Region Combined with Sobel Operator Condition

Nguyen Thanh Binh[1(✉)], Vo Thi Hong Tuyet[1,2],
Nguyen Mong Hien[1,3], and Nguyen Thanh Thuy[4]

[1] Faculty of Computer Science and Engineering, Ho Chi Minh City University
of Technology, VNU-HCM, Ho Chi Minh City, Vietnam
{ntbinh,vthtuyet.sdh19}@hcmut.edu.vn,
[2] Faculty of Information Technology, Ho Chi Minh City Open University,
Ho Chi Minh City, Vietnam
tuyet.vth@ou.edu.vn
[3] Tra Vinh University, Tra Vinh, Vietnam
hientvu@tvu.edu.vn
[4] Faculty of Information Technology,
Ho Chi Minh City University of Education, Ho Chi Minh City, Vietnam
ntthuy889@gmail.com

**Abstract.** Medical images contribute greatly to help physicians identify abnormalities in the patient's body in today's health care. Retinal vessels are one of the effective methods for diagnosing diseases, such as: age-related macular degeneration, diabetes, hypertension, arteriosclerosis. However, manual analysis for retinal images is time-consuming and costly for ophthalmologists. In this paper, we proposed an approach for segmentation in retinal vessels by improving salient region map combined with Sobel mask. The algorithm includes two steps: superpixel detection and segmentation based on salient region map. The result of proposed method is better than the other methods.

**Keywords:** Retinal vessels · Segmentation · Sobel operator · Salient map · Salient region

## 1 Introduction

Today, demands for the automatic systems have been developing. It is evidence of this, the human will be replaced by the machines. The large systems that serve people cannot ignore the object identification system. Therefore, image segmentation has a difficult position to be replaced.

Segmentation is a process of dividing images into different regions, which accord to its characteristics like [1]: color, texture, intensity, etc. Image segmentation is often used to locate objects or regions of interest. The case is true that the region of object must be highlighted rather than background or other areas. In the past, there were many techniques such as: clustering [4], filter [7, 20], thresholding [5, 10, 11], domain combined with threshold [17, 28], deep learning [29], etc. for image segmentation.

© Springer Nature Switzerland AG 2019
T. K. Dang et al. (Eds.): FDSE 2019, LNCS 11814, pp. 608–617, 2019.
https://doi.org/10.1007/978-3-030-35653-8_39

However, their disadvantages are that time processing is very long and complex for calculating. Although the execution time of the above techniques is large, they are still used in some applications such as: content-based image retrieval, object detection, recognition tasks, automatic traffic control systems, video surveillance, and medical image segmentation and so on.

Medical images contribute greatly to help physicians identify abnormalities in the patient's body in today's health care. Retinal vessels are one of the effective methods for diagnosing diseases, such as: age-related macular degeneration, diabetes, hypertension, arteriosclerosis. However, manual analysis for retinal images is time-consuming and costly for ophthalmologists [2]. Therefore, retinal blood vessel segmentation has a consequence role in the detection to treat these diseases. Some researches have been proposed to segment the retinal blood vessels by unsupervised methods and supervised ones. Some researches solve these retinal vessels segmentation [3–12] by methods: referee and fluorescein [3], probabilistic formulation [6], classification [8], or depending on feature and ensemble learning [13], etc.

Lastly, in some cases, the contour or edge detection or active contour model (snakes) is considered as the input of segmentation method. The energy of neighbor pixels is very useful and is taken [14–16]. But the initial contour is very difficult for scientists. The seed point answers this problem. Sirshendu [18] used the seeded region growing for segmentation, but the disadvantages of this method also based on threshold. So, the above methods will be hard applied to retinal vessels of which details are very complex. The other objects segmentation methods have been proposed in the color images [19, 20]. The fuzzy logic and classification are used popularly in identification [22, 27]. However, retinal vessel segmentation is also a pressing issue [21].

We know that the object detection is not easy. The dependence on threshold, domain, contour is the prejudice with the specific object. Each object will have the different characteristics: color, shape, position, texture, etc. If we make good use of those things, we will have the clear regions. And salient map [23–25, 30, 31] is one of solutions to this. Federio [26] used saliency map for the development of salient region based on contrast filtering. Moreover, the edge detection based on salient map had been applied as input of segmentation [32]. In this method, the authors combined saliency map with texture for the edge keeping process. And, Sobel for edge detection also fits with saliency map [34]. From the positive results of saliency map, the idea for retinal vessel segmentation is developed. In this paper, we proposed an approach for segmentation in retinal vessels by improving salient region map combined with Sobel mask. The algorithm includes two steps: superpixels detection and segmentation based on salient region map. The result of proposed method is better than the other methods. The rest of this paper is organized as following: in Sect. 2, we describe saliency map. The proposed method is presented clearly in Sect. 3. The experiment results and conclusion are presented in Sects. 4 and 5 respectively.

## 2 Saliency Map

The previous approaches for retinal vessel segmentation had based on threshold or domain. However, these approaches have a lot of difficulties for object detection. The weak pixels (low-intensity) cannot be on display in the object region due to the fact that the reconciliation between super-pixels with reconstruction coefficients is very complex. To reduce these dependences, hard threshold is necessary for segmentation.

The notion of saliency in computer vision begins from the quality of each pixel. All of differences of each pixel with others are member of saliency map with an obvious method. The image characters have a wide range of information of objects, such as: texture, color, pattern, intensity, etc. The super-pixels which have high intensity or differences with others are presented in saliency map. Therefore, saliency is one of the segmentation approaches.

The existing saliency prediction methods had been divided into two groups [30]: hand-crafted and learned from the data. The first group is a computational model for saliency prediction. The results based on the feature integration theory and central surround. The disadvantage of this solution is the features limitation which are collected. The second one, learned from the data, has a lot of advantages because of calculating the distance between pixels. In addition, the useful information is applied maximum.

From the binary map (fixation map), saliency map uses Gaussian filter to create the ground truth for object in images. The solution for segmentation of saliency is different from distance between the first contrast function and the second one. Each function is done by equation:

$$SALS(I_k) = \sum F_n \times |I_k - I_n| \tag{1}$$

where $I_k$, $I_n$ is the value of pixel I in range of [0, 255]; n is the number of pixels in the frame and $F_n$ is the frequency of $I_n$ and similar calculating with color distance. The comparison has been done and subtracted of the current frame to the previous one. As a result, the new image is given by segmentation of saliency map.

As a matter of fact, the values of saliency in super-pixels are always multilevel. Therefore, the objective of salient region map (SRM) is elaborated the structure behind this issue.

The differences between saliency values depend on the increasing significantly the complexity of object's color. SRM [30] is a discrete map and this is developed from saliency map. The principles of SRM are the assigning process. The case is true that each pixel in image has a saliency level. And this is the primary key for salient region detection. In the recently, salient regions have been applied in a wide range of applications such as [27]: image retrieval, image compression, smart image resizing, etc. The saliency level is calculated by Eq. (2):

$$R(x) = \begin{cases} 0 & if\ 0 \leq S(x) < \frac{255}{K} \times 1 \\ \frac{255}{K-1} & if\ \frac{255}{K} \times 1 \leq S(x) < \frac{255}{K} \times 2 \\ \quad \vdots \\ 255 & if\ frac255K \times (K-1) \leq S(x) < \frac{255}{K} \times K \end{cases} \tag{2}$$

where, R(x) is the saliency level at pixel x in region map of image, S(x) is the saliency value at pixel x and the number of levels is K. The result of salient region map based on the ground truth in the training step.

## 3    Improving Salient Region Map for Retinal Vessel Segmentation

The problems are related eyes, being very complex and serious. Evidence of this, here they are some abnormalities of eyes such as: prolongation, bulge, cloud surrounding, etc. The information of eye is very small and detailed. The connection between superpixels is very complex. In this section, we proposed an approach for segmentation in retinal vessels based on improving salient region map and Sobel mask. The proposed method includes two periods: superpixel detection by calculating superpixels in object's region and segmentation based on salient region map combined with Sobel operator.

### 3.1    The Superpixel Pre-process and Calculation

In this section, we present the superpixel pre-process and calculation in images with three steps: choosing the object for segmentation, removing the areas which do not contain any objects and calculating the super-pixels.

Firstly, the area which contains retinal vessels is detected by a handle box in the user's graphic interface. Any pixels in this range are the vital element for retinal vessels. The benefit of this way is zoning the required area. Therefore, the information of intensity, colour and texture is also more specific. The Fig. 1 presents the process of handle box creation. Figure 1(a) contains two points by mouse, and Fig. 1(b) is the result of box which is created by two points of Fig. 1(a).

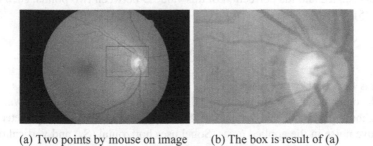

(a) Two points by mouse on image        (b) The box is result of (a)

**Fig. 1.** The process of handle box creation

Secondly, we remove the areas which do not contain any objects. With previous methods, the researchers must remove the previous frame and current frame. That is a reason why the execution time of method is very long. The proposed method only analyzes in one area instead of all parts of image. As a result, the processing time is decreased significantly. The purpose of this step is useful to compute the distance of each pixel which is calculated by Eq. (3):

$$SALS(I_k) = \sum_{i=1}^{N} |I_k - I_i| \tag{3}$$

where, $I_i$ is the value of pixel i in the range [0, 255]. $SALS(I_k)$ shows natural histogram of object.

Finally, superpixels are calculated. The value of superpixels in the area of the object in other methods is the input for central distance between the previous frame and current one. However, we use superpixels with the size which is 10 to find max of these values. Then, we continue with:

(i)  Get the region characteristics. It can be called as the read-data process.
(ii) Find the distance value of each pixel. The case is true that the centre-to-centre distance of superpixels which are calculated to forms a saliency map.

As a result, the output of this stage is the map of superpixel with fitting parameters. And, the saliency map is created by Eq. (1).

### 3.2  The Salient Region Map Based on Sobel Operator

The division of level in saliency map is the initial concept for salient region map. In each level of saliency map, distance between the average feature vector of pixel with its neighborhood is the contrast saliency value $c_{i,j}$ for pixel at position (i, j) in the retinal vessels image. And, $c_{i,j}$ is calculated by Eq. (4):

$$c_{ij} = D\left[\left(\frac{1}{N_1}\sum_{p=1}^{N_1} v_p\right), \left(\frac{1}{N_2}\sum_{p=1}^{N_2} v_q\right)\right] \tag{4}$$

where, $N_1$ and $N_2$ are the number of pixels in $R_1$ (inner region) and $R_2$ (outer region) respectively; v is the vector of feature elements corresponding to a pixel; D is the Euclidean distance and the correction of this value D between two points, such as p and q, is Eq. (5):

$$D(p, q) = \sqrt{\sum_{i=1}^{n} (q_i - p_i)^2} \tag{5}$$

where, n is the number of spaces.

On the other hand, Sobel operator [24] applies the mean of up and down, left and right neighbour pixels. The advantages of this operator not only give edge detection but also remove noise in the applied areas. Sobel uses horizontal ($S_x$) and vertical direction ($S_y$):

$$S(x) = \begin{bmatrix} -1 & -2 & -1 \\ 0 & 0 & 0 \\ 1 & 2 & 1 \end{bmatrix}$$

and

$$S(y) = \begin{bmatrix} -1 & 0 & 1 \\ -2 & 0 & 2 \\ -1 & 0 & 1 \end{bmatrix}$$

Sobel mask will be applied to the output of the previous step. The surface is created as an inevitable and uses gradient which is a vector:

$$\nabla f(x, y) = \left( \frac{\partial f}{\partial x}, \frac{\partial f}{\partial y} \right) \tag{6}$$

Sobel operator goes up the weight coefficient of central pixel. So, the direction and accurate edge are increasing. This is very necessary for superpixels of saliency map. If we only use Sobel to improve the salient region map, we will give the poor results. Retinal vessels are very complex and have a lot of details. Therefore, the size of mask, which is applied, must be adapted to superpixel's parameters. In here, we use 10 for the parameter of a superpixel. Some characteristics of retinal vessels:

(i)   The width is usually from 2 to 5 pixels and rarely than 5 pixels.
(ii)  The variety of genres: thin vessels, major vessels.
(iii) Low contrast filamentary vessels.

The next job of the proposed method solves Eq. (2) with multi-level of saliency map. The solution for showing vessels can administrate filter with hard threshold value for the best choice of vessels. In this paper, our condition is a way which uses Sobel operator as sliding window on the superpixel surface with matrix $3 \times 3$ and step for sliding is 1. The output of this step is retinal vessels segmentation.

## 4   Experiment and Results

In this section, we indicate results of the proposed method in the previous section. Experiments are developed in Matlab R2018a and carried out on computer of Intel core i5, 2.4 GHz CPU, 8 GB DDR2 memory. The retinal vessel images are color images and focus on eyes. We use DRIVE dataset [35] for this experiment. This dataset has retinal vessel images and the output of segmentation. This is an important cornerstone for the comparison between the proposed method with other approaches. The images of DRIVE dataset have true object and true size. In each image on this dataset, retinal vessels of retinal are affected by many agents, such as: membrane covered, red eyes, position and shape, etc. Figure 2 presents some images of this dataset.

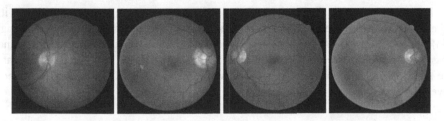

**Fig. 2.** Some images in DRIVE dataset (Color figure online)

We use the Jaccard index (JI) to evaluate the results. The JI can define by Eq. (7):

$$JI(A, B) = \frac{|A \cap B|}{|A \cup B|} \times 100 \tag{7}$$

where, A is area which is detected, B is true area. This index is within range from 0 to 100%. Jaccard index is higher is better. Now, we compare the proposed method results with the result of the salient region map method [33] and Sobel for segmentation method [34]. We test on the DRIVE dataset [35]. In the project, we only show two cases of results as Figs. 3 and 4. In each image, the JI value is also presented in each method.

Figure 3 shows the original images and the result of the proposed method with others. Figure 3(a) is the original medical image. The result of salient region map method [33] is Fig. 3(b). The result of Sobel for segmentation method [34] is Fig. 3(c) and of the proposed method is Fig. 3(d). In Fig. 3(d), the JI value is higher than the result in Fig. 3(b) and (c). Therefore, the result of the proposed method is better than the result of salient region map method [33] and Sobel for segmentation method [34].

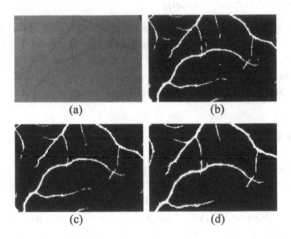

(a)     (b)

(c)     (d)

**Fig. 3.** The results of retinal vessels segmentation by proposed methods and the other methods. (a) The original medical image. (b) Retinal vessel segmentation by salient region map method [33] (JI = 81.6). (c) Retinal vessel segmentation by Sobel for segmentation method [34] (JI = 83.93). (d) Retinal vessel segmentation by the proposed method (JI = 89.38).

Figure 4 also shows the original images and the result of the proposed method with others. Figure 4(a) is the original retinal vessel image. The results of salient region map [33] method, Sobel for segmentation method [34] and the proposed method for retinal vessel segmentation are Fig. 4(b), (c) and (d). In Fig. 4(d), the JI value is higher than the result in Fig. 4(b) and (c). As a result, we can conclude that the proposed method gives better results.

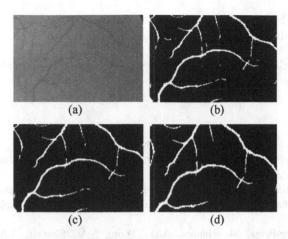

**Fig. 4.** The results of retinal vessels segmentation by proposed methods and the other methods. (a) The original medical image. (b) Retinal vessel segmentation by salient region map method [33] (JI = 82.15) (c) Retinal vessel segmentation by Sobel for segmentation method [34] (JI = 84.82) (d) Retinal vessel segmentation by the proposed method (JI = 89.97)

The average JI value of all images in this dataset is presented in Table 1.

**Table 1.** The average JI value of three methods.

| Total of retinal vessels images | The average JI value of salient region map method [33] | The average JI value of Sobel for segmentation method [34] | The average JI of the proposed method |
|---|---|---|---|
| 1350 regions from images of DRIVE dataset | 82.07 | 84.15 | 89.43 |

From Table 1, the result of the proposed method is better than the other methods. This positive result is due to the choice of conditions for Sobel operator in saliency map. The superpixels are the proper calculation for segmentation. Beyond all that is the fitting of parameter for retinal vessels. Thus, the proposed method is effective.

## 5    Conclusions

Retinal vessel segmentation is a hard task in computer vision. However, its effects are very vital for society. A lot of symptoms of diseases will be shown here. In this paper, we proposed a new method for retinal vessels segmentation based on Sobel operator and salient region map. The proposed algorithm includes two steps: superpixels detection and segmentation based on salient region map. Besides, the proposed method uses the sliding window to detect some objects. This is an improvement for the superpixel calculation based on saliency map. This idea depends on the special characteristics of retinal vessels. The results of the proposed method are better than the other recent methods by calculating the Jaccard index values.

**Acknowledgement.** This research is funded by Vietnam National University Ho Chi Minh City (VNU-HCM) under grant number B2019-20-05.

# References

1. Kaur, D., Kaur, Y.: Various image segmentation techniques: a review. Int. J. Comput. Sci. Mob. Comput. **3**(5), 809–814 (2014)
2. Staal, J., Abramoff, M.D., Niemeijer, M., Viergever, M.A., van Ginneken, B.: Ridge based vessel segmentation in color images of the retina. IEEE Trans. Med. Imaging **23**, 501–509 (2004)
3. Elena Martinez-Perez, M., Hughes, A.D., Thom, S.A., Bharath, A.A., Parker, K.H.: Segmentation of blood vessels from red-free and fluorescein retinal images. Med. Image Anal. **11**(1), 47–61 (2007)
4. Ng, H.P., Ong, S.H., Foong, K.W.C., Goh, P.S., Nowinski, W.L.: Medical image segmentation using k-means clustering and improved watershed algorithm. In: Proceedings of IEEE Southwest Symposium on Image Analysis and Interpretation, pp. 61–65 (2006)
5. Saleh Al-amri, S., Kalyankar, N.V., Khamitkar, S.D.: Image segmentation by using threshold techniques. J. Comput. **2**, 83–86 (2010)
6. Yin, Y., Adel, M., Bourenna, S.: Automatic segmentation and measurement of vasculature in retinal fundus images using probabilistic formulation. Comput. Math. Methods Med. **2013**, 1–16 (2013)
7. Li, Q., You, J., Zhang, D.: Vessel segmentation and width estimation in retinal images using multiscale production of matched filter responses. Expert Syst. Appl. **39**(9), 7600–7610 (2012)
8. Fraz, M.M., et al.: An ensemble classification-based approach applied to retinal blood vessel segmentation. IEEE Trans. Biomed. Eng. **59**(9), 2538–2548 (2012)
9. Manoj, S., Muralidharan, S.P.M., Sandeep, M.: Neural network-based classifier for retinal blood vessel segmentation. Int. J. Recent Trends Electr. Electron. Eng. **3**, 44–53 (2013)
10. Marín, D., Aquino, A., Gegundez-Arias, M.E., Bravo, J.M.: A new supervised method for blood vessel segmentation in retinal images by using gray-level and moment invariants-based features. IEEE Trans. Med. Imaging **30**(1), 146–158 (2011)
11. Evelin Sujji, G., Lakshmi, Y.V.S., Wiselin Jiji, G.: MRI brain image segmentation based on thresholding. Int. J. Adv. Comput. Res. **3**, 97–101 (2013)
12. Shan, H., Ma, J.: Curvelet-based geodesic snakes for image segmentation with multiple objects. J. Pattern Recogn. Lett. **31**, 355–360 (2010)
13. Wang, S., Yin, Y., Cao, G., Wei, B., Zheng, Y., Yang, G.: Hierarchical retinal blood vessel segmentation based on feature and ensemble learning. Neurocomputing **149**, 708–717 (2015)
14. Yuwei, W., Wang, Y., Jia, Y.: Adaptive diffusion flow active contours for image segmentation. Comput. Vis. Image Underst. **117**, 1421–1435 (2013)
15. Saadatmand-Tarzjan, M., Ghassemian, H.: Self-affine snake for medical image segmentation. Pattern Recogn. Lett. **59**, 1–10 (2015)
16. Zhang, R., Zhu, S., Zhou, Q.: A novel gradient vector flow snake model based on convex function for infrared image segmentation. Sensors **16**(10), 1–17 (2016)

17. Hamdi, M.A.: Modified algorithm marker-controlled watershed transform for image segmentation based on curvelet threshold. Can. J. Image Process. Comput. Vis. **2**(8), 88–91 (2011)

18. Hore, S., et al.: An integrated interactive technique for image segmentation using stack based seeded region growing and thresholding. Int. J. Electr. Comput. Eng. **6**(6), 2773–2780 (2016)

19. Han, J., Ngan, K.N., Li, M., Zhang, H.-J.: Unsupervised extraction of visual attention objects in color images. IEEE Trans. Circuits Syst. Video Technol. **16**(1), 141–145 (2006)

20. Permuter, H., Francos, J., Jermyn, I.: A study of Gaussian mixture models of color and texture features for image classification and segmentation. Pattern Recogn. **39**, 695–706 (2006)

21. Liu, Q., Zou, B., Chen, J., Chen, Z.: Retinal vessel segmentation from simple to difficult. In: Proceedings of MICCAI Workshop on Ophthalmic Medical Image Analysis, pp. 57–64 (2016)

22. Barkana, B.D., Saricicek, I., Yildirim, B.: Performance analysis of descriptive statistical features in retinal vessel segmentation via fuzzy logic, ANN, SVM, and classifier fusion. Knowl. Based Syst. **118**, 165–176 (2017)

23. Goferman, S., Zelnik-Manor, L., Tal, A.: Context-aware saliency detection. IEEE Trans. Pattern Anal. Mach. Intell. **34**(10), 1915–1926 (2012)

24. Jiang, H., Wang, J., Yuan, Z., Liu, T., Zheng, N.: Automatic salient object segmentation based on context and shape prior. In: Proceedings of the British Machine Vision Conference, pp. 1–12 (2011)

25. Cheng, M.-M., Warrell, J., Lin, W.-Y., Zheng, S., Vineet, V., Crook, N.: Efficient salient region detection with soft image abstraction. In: Proceedings of IEEE International Conference on Computer Vision, pp. 1529–1536 (2013)

26. Perazzi, F., Krähenbühl, P., Pritch, Y., Hornung, A.: Saliency filters: contrast based filtering for salient region detection. In: Proceedings of IEEE Conference on Computer Vision and Pattern Recognition, pp. 733–740 (2012)

27. Rezaee, K., Haddadnia, J., Tashk, A.: Optimized clinical segmentation of retinal blood vessels by using combination of adaptive filtering, fuzzy entropy and skeletonization. Appl. Soft Comput. **52**, 937–951 (2017)

28. Nageswara Reddy, P., Mohan Rao, C.P.V.N.J., Satyanarayana, Ch.: Brain MR image segmentation by modified active contours and contourlet transform. ICTACT J. Image Video Process. **8**(2), 1645–1650 (2017)

29. Roth, H.R., et al.: Deep learning and its application to medical image segmentation. Med. Imaging Technol. J. **36**(2), 1–6 (2018)

30. Achanta, R., Estrada, F., Wils, P., Süsstrunk, S.: Salient region detection and segmentation. In: Gasteratos, A., Vincze, M., Tsotsos, J.K. (eds.) ICVS 2008. LNCS, vol. 5008, pp. 66–75. Springer, Heidelberg (2008). https://doi.org/10.1007/978-3-540-79547-6_7

31. Rosin, P.L.: A simple method for detecting salient regions. Pattern Recogn. **42**(11), 2363–2371 (2009)

32. Ao, H., Yu, N.: Edge saliency map detection with texture suppression. In: Proceedings of Sixth International Conference on Image and Graphics, pp. 309–313 (2011)

33. He, S., Pugeaulty, N.: Salient region segmentation. In: Computer Vision and Pattern Recognition, pp. 1–6 (2018)

34. Yao, Y.: Image segmentation based on Sobel edge detection. In: Proceedings of 5th International Conference on Advanced Materials and Computer Science, pp. 141–144 (2016)

35. https://www.isi.uu.nl/Research/Databases/DRIVE/. Accessed 19 Apr 2019

# Energy Saving Solution for Air Conditioning Systems

Vu Thu Diep[1], Phan Duy Hung[2(✉)], and Ta Duc Tung[3]

[1] Hanoi University of Science and Technology, Hanoi, Vietnam
diep.vuthu@hust.edu.vn
[2] FPT University, Hanoi, Vietnam
hungpd2@fe.edu.vn
[3] The University of Tokyo, Tokyo, Japan
tung@akg.t.u-tokyo.ac.jp

**Abstract.** With the looming threats of environmental changes due to global warming, independence from fossil fuels together with energy saving are being prioritized. Among the electrical equipment in buildings, air conditioning has the potential to provide a lot of savings. Despite efforts in energy saving technology, the waste in air-conditioning is primarily due to the users' inattentiveness, e.g. forgetting to turn off the air-conditioning, turning it on even in cool weather, setting the temperatures too low, etc. This paper proposes a simple but effective solution to minimize this waste. A system that allows managers to remotely monitor status of devices, temperature controllers, set operating schedules or temperature thresholds, enable manual or automatic modes is developed. It also allows the export of statistical reports to improve operations.

**Keywords:** Energy saving · Air conditioner · Sensor networks · Information system

## 1 Introduction

Energy is a fundamental ingredient for all life on Earth. There is no industrial, agricultural, healthcare, domestic, or any other sort of process that doesn't require a degree of external energy. And the needs for electricity in all areas, be it office, school, home or public place is growing exponentially [1]. It is easy to recognize a refrigerator in every home, air conditioning in every office, high-voltage light bulbs in almost every street. These devices make our life better, but there are always some trade-offs. One of them is that they are consuming too much of energy. For example, a 2-way air-conditioner draws approximately 1500 W, a high-voltage lighting bulb about 1000 W to 3000 W, a television 40 W to 80 W on average. From there, it is easy to see that the cost for air-conditioning is substantial.

Energy saving has been concerned for a long time and people have many solutions. These include the search for renewable energy sources and new energy sources such as: biomass, hydropower, geothermal, wind, solar [2].

For electrical devices, many energy saving technologies have been introduced. For example, energy-efficient lightbulbs such as halogen incandescent lamps, compact

© Springer Nature Switzerland AG 2019
T. K. Dang et al. (Eds.): FDSE 2019, LNCS 11814, pp. 618–628, 2019.
https://doi.org/10.1007/978-3-030-35653-8_40

fluorescent lamps (CFLs), and light emitting diodes (LEDs) typically use about 25%–80% less energy than traditional incandescent bulbs but can last 3–25 times longer [1, 3]. The new Smart Inverter system using microcomputer control can adjust air conditioners to lower the operating costs – up to 40%, when in its high efficiency mode [4, 5].

On a larger scale, Smart Grids, electrical systems that use information and communication technologies to optimize the transmission and distribution of electricity between manufacturers and consumers, are built [6, 7]. Smart Grids are developed in all 4 stages: Smart Generation, Smart Transmission, Smart Distribution, Smart Power Consumers. Smart Grids allow the operation of the entire electrical system to be automatically optimized at all times. Also, and importantly, they will not stop at the customer's electrical meter. They can provide customers with new prices, payment options and up-to-date information. The customers can actively control their energy use, by always knowing their electricity consumption. This can also lead to significant power savings.

Another research and application segment is smart building as an energy efficiency application. The concept of Smart Building could be defined as a set of communication technologies enabling different objects, sensors and functions within a building to communicate and interact with each other, which can also be managed, controlled and automated remotely. The scope of Smart Building is very wide covering various objects within the household from windows, elevators to vehicle charging points. But energy efficiency is expected to mainly come from the two following categories: Smart lighting and Smart HVAC (Heating, Ventilation, Air Conditioning) [8–12].

The above solutions and studies have shown that there are interesting problems to study in energy saving. We conducted interviews with 10 managers, 30 staffs and 25 students of 10 buildings and 5 schools in Hanoi about using electrical equipment and obtained the following opinions:

- Managers claim that monthly electricity bills are substantial. In particular, the electricity for air conditioning accounts for about 50–70% of the total bill.
- Most managers are willing to spare a budget for power-saving solutions. However, the investment cost must be consistent with the depreciation of electrical equipment and the need to bring about significant efficiency.
- Many employees and especially students acknowledge wasteful use of air conditioners. For example, they do not turn them off even if they are the last to leave the room, they turn on the air conditioners to low temperatures even when the weather is cool, etc.

It can be seen that smart building systems, smart schools, smart offices [13, 14] are very good, but the price is too high because the system consists of many functions. In addition, they are not open or can be difficult to customize for some small and medium-sized practical needs.

This paper presents an energy saving system for buildings. The system focuses on:

- Saving power consumption from air conditioning equipment.
- The system is cheap, easy to install and expand.

- Remote monitoring and control.
- Collection of data and extraction of statistical reports.

The remainder of the paper is organized as follows. Section 2 describes the system design and implementation. Then, conclusions and perspectives are made in Sect. 3.

## 2  System Requirements

### 2.1  Architecture Overview

The system consists of three main parts: the hardware, the server and the management website (Fig. 1).

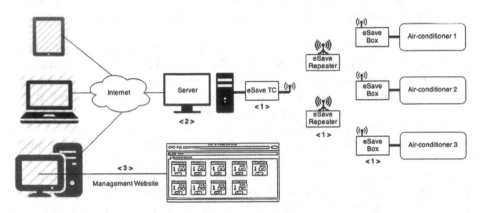

**Fig. 1.**  Architecture overview of eSave system.

### *The Hardware Consists of 3 Modules*
*eSave Box.* The first module, called the eSave Box, is attached to all air conditioners. The eSave Box receives incoming commands via radio waves and emits infrared signals that control the air conditioner as a remote control. It also measures the status of the air conditioner and responds to the system.

*The eSave TC (Transceiver).* This module is attached to the server computer. It communicates with the computer via a USB port and communicates with eSave Boxes via radio interface.

*The eSave Repeater (optional).* In case the distance between the eSave Box module and eSave TC is too large, affecting signal quality, an eSave Repeater is used to relay signals between these two modules.

### *The Server*
The server is a computer that contains a database of the system containing information such as users, air conditioners, control modules, etc. and the operating logic of the entire system. MongoDB is used as the database for the eSave system. MongoDB is a crossplatform document-oriented database system. It has many advantages, with a

dynamic schema and object-oriented structure, making it a great fit for real-time analytics and dash boarding along with ecommerce, mobile, archiving and more.

### The Management Website

The website provides interfaces for the remote monitoring of the status of all air conditioners, for management, scheduling, and report extraction by managers. The system allows the control of air conditioners according to a schedule, but it also permits manual operation, which means the user can still use the remote control, but it will be subjected to the temperature limit set according to the location or weather. The status of air conditioners, the turn-off time, user, room location will be collected and put into reports. From there, the administrator can make adjustments to operating modes and recommend users appropriately.

### 2.2   System Requirements

The system has two main types of user that are system users and administrators. The functional requirements of each user are described in Table 1.

**Table 1.**  Functional requirements.

| Type | Content |
|---|---|
| Administrator | Create/Manage schedule |
| | Manage location: Add new, Edit, Delete |
| | Manage device: Add new, Edit, Delete |
| | Manage Users: Create, Edit, Remove |
| | Manage Account: Login, Change password, Update information |
| | Control Device: Turn on/off, Adjust temperature, Set Thresholds |
| | Monitor Device: Search device, View device status, Scan active device |
| | View reports: View, Export |
| System User | Personal account management |
| | Control Device: Turn on/off, Adjust temperature |
| | Monitor Device: Search device, View device status |

## 3   System Design and Implementation

### 3.1   Network and Transmission

The system operates according to Master-Slaves architecture and transmits and receives information via radio signals. The SIM20A radio frequency communication module is used for communication between eSave Box and eSave TC with maximum distance about 1.5 km without repeaters, and more repeaters are used. The number of devices according to the datasheet can be up to more than 1000 devices, ensuring realworld usage [15].

## 3.2  Hardware Design

The designs of the eSave Box, eSave TC, eSave Repeater modules are described in Figs. 2, 3 and 4. The eSave Box device runs on the same 220 V AC source of the air conditioner, through an adapter that provides 3.3 V DC power supply to the control circuit. The STM32F100C8T6B microcontroller is selected [16]. This microcontroller is cheap, small in size and supports 2 UART ports: 1 port for communication with the SIM Module, the other port for communication with the PC (required for the eSave TC module).

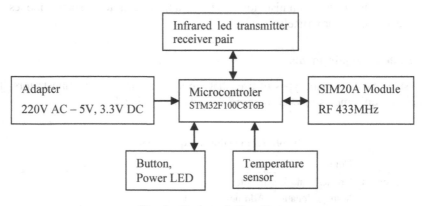

**Fig. 2.** Design of eSave Box.

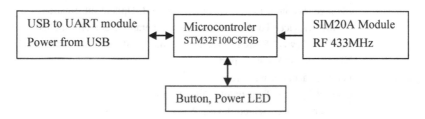

**Fig. 3.** Design of eSave TC.

**Fig. 4.** Design of eSave Repeater.

On the module there is an infrared receiver LED to learn the basic commands of air conditioners: turn on, turn off, increase temperature, reduce temperature, etc. It also has an infrared transmitter LED to be used in control mode. A red LED indicates the system's power status and microcontroller status. An LM35 temperature sensor placed directly at the air outlet of the air conditioner can determine whether the air conditioner is on or off and the current temperature [17]. For communication, a SIM20A module is used. This module operates in the 433 MHz frequency band, multi-channel with low power. It include a high speed MCU and high performance RF chip for the ideal receiving sensitivity, programmable transmitting power and data rate.

The eSave TC design is similar to the eSave Box, but it does not require the two infrared LEDs or temperature sensors. This module takes power from the computer's USB port and uses an additional conversion cable from USB to UART and vice versa.

The eSave Repeater has the simplest design. It does not use any infrared or sensor LED. The purpose of this module is only to repeat the signals to ensure the quality and to extend the distance between the eSave Box and Server.

All three modules share the same PCB, while different modules can omit some unnecessary components.

When installing the eSave Box into an air conditioner, the user can press the Button to switch it to Learning mode. Project the air conditioner's original remote controller into infrared receiver to let it learn the basic commands. The commands are obtained as a sequence of bits and will be stored in a fixed position in the EEPROM memory. After completing the commands, press the button again to go to Control mode. From then on, the eSave Box and the PC will operate under Master - Slave model, the eSave Boxes are the Slaves and the PC is the Master of the system.

### 3.3    Command Format

In the Master/Slave model, the data format for transmission and reception between Master and Slave is designed as follows:

*The Data Transfer from Master to Slave*
The data transfer from Master (eSave TC) to Slave (eSave Box) has 4 fields:

> *[Type] [Method] [ID] [CMD]*
> *[Type]*: 1 byte, indicates type of device such as air conditioner, light
> > d    air conditioner
> > c    light (for future development)
> *[Method]*: 1 byte, indicates the kind of transmission
> > D    not through transmitter
> > R    through transmitter
> *[ID]*: logical ID, between 000 - 999
> *[CMD]*: 1 byte, a character that indicates the action
> > 'A'        turn on
> > 'C'        turn fan on
> > 'E'        fan mode: High, Low, and Medium
> > 'F'        increases 1oC
> > 'G'        decrease 1oC
> > 'H'        air-conditioner mode: Heat, Cool, Cold
> > 'I'        read air-conditioner state: On/Off
> > 'K'        read fan state: On/ Off
> > 'L'        current location temperature

***The Data Transfer from Slave to Master***
The data transfer from Slave to Master has 2 fields:

> *[Method][Result]*
> *[Method]*: 1 byte, indicates the kind of transmission
>       'D'      not through transmitter
>       'R'      through transmitter
> *[Result]*: result of command

All commands are summarized in Table 2.

**Table 2.** List of commands.

| Command | Meaning | Result |
| --- | --- | --- |
| A | Turning on | [OK]/[NOT OK] |
| B | Turning off | [OK]/[NOT OK] |
| C | Turning fan on | [OK]/[NOT OK] |
| D | Turning fan off | [OK]/[NOT OK] |
| E | Choosing fan mode | [OK]/[NOT OK] |
| F | Increasing 1 Celsius | [OK]/[NOT OK] |
| G | Decreasing 1 Celsius | [OK]/[NOT OK] |
| H | Choosing air-conditioner mode | [OK]/[NOT OK] |
| I | Reading air-conditioner state | [ON]/[OFF] |
| K | Reading fan state | [ON]/[OFF] |
| L | Getting temperature | T: [temperature] |

## 3.4    Database Design

The system uses MongoDB for the database [18]. MongoDB eschews the traditional table-based relational database structure in favor of JSON-like documents with dynamic schemas (MongoDB calls the format BSON), making the integration of data in certain types of applications easier and faster. A data model for the eSave system is shown in Fig. 5.

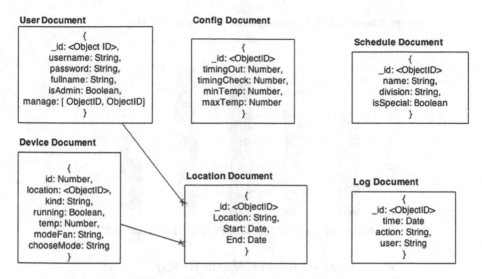

**User Document**

```
{
_id: <Object ID>,
username: String,
password: String,
fullname: String,
isAdmin: Boolean,
manage: [ ObjectID, ObjectID]
}
```

**Config Document**

```
{
_id: <ObjectID>
timingOut: Number,
timingCheck: Number,
minTemp: Number,
maxTemp: Number
}
```

**Schedule Document**

```
{
_id: <ObjectID>
name: String,
division: String,
isSpecial: Boolean
}
```

**Device Document**

```
{
id: Number,
location: <ObjectID>,
kind: String,
running: Boolean,
temp: Number,
modeFan: String,
chooseMode: String
}
```

**Location Document**

```
{
_id: <ObjectID>
Location: String,
Start: Date,
End: Date
}
```

**Log Document**

```
{
_id: <ObjectID>
time: Date,
action: String,
user: String
}
```

**Fig. 5.** Data model for eSave database.

## 3.5  Website Design

Some of the main screens of Web applications are listed below. Figure 6 shows a monitoring screen that monitors the status of all air conditioners. On each detailed window, the system users can turn on, turn off, increase or decrease the temperature. Statistics of usage time and wasted time when the user did not turn off the air conditioner according to the working schedule (when the system does not run in automatic mode) is shown in Fig. 7. The administrator's device management screen is shown in Fig. 8.

**Fig. 6.** Monitoring screen.

usage time in schedule (hours) from 1<sup>st</sup> May to 31<sup>st</sup> May

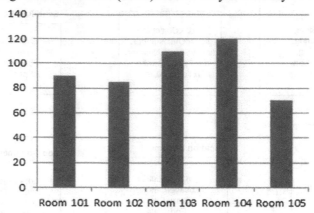

wasted time (hours) from 1<sup>st</sup> May to 31<sup>st</sup> May

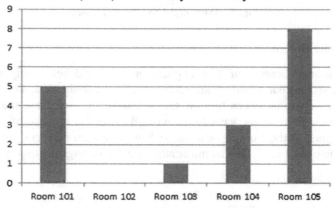

**Fig. 7.** Statistics of usage time and wasted time.

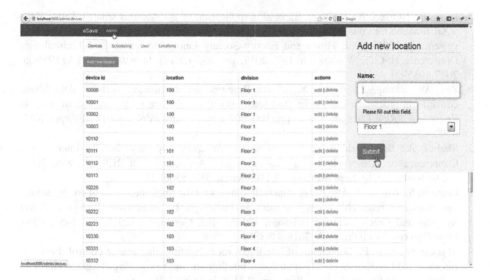

**Fig. 8.** Device management screen.

## 4 Conclusion and Perspectives

Energy saving for electrical equipment, especially for air conditioning is a practical and urgent issue. This paper has provided a centralized management, monitoring and control system for air-conditioning equipment at a low cost while still being extendable and easy to deploy. The system can be used for buildings, schools for high efficiency electrical monitor and control with low investment costs compared to integrated solutions of large technology firms, where many functions will be irrelevant where the demand for electricity savings only focuses on a few components. The system hardware can be expanded up to 1000 nodes and a distance of up to several kilometers.

This solution is also fully applicable for similar models, such as high-voltage lighting on roads or in stadiums, swimming pools, etc.

This paper is also a good reference for research directions of IoT [19, 20], Embedded Systems [21, 22], etc.

## References

1. Lopez, C.: Current challenges in energy. Front. Knowl. **2**, 257–269 (2009)
2. Pravitasari, D., Nisworo, S.: New and renewable energy: a review and perspectives. In: International Conference on Sustainable Information Engineering and Technology (SIET), Malang, 2017, pp. 284–287 (2017). https://doi.org/10.1109/siet.2017.8304149
3. Tang, Y., Chen, Q., Ju, P., et al.: Research on load characteristics of energy saving lamp and LED lamp. In: IEEE International Conference on Power System Technology (POWER-CON), Wollongong, NSW, 2016, pp. 1–5 (2016). https://doi.org/10.1109/powercon.2016. 7753932
4. Samsung: What is a Smart Inverter? https://www.samsung.com/ae/support/home-appliances/what-is-a-smart-inverter/. Accessed 20 July 2019

5. Ding, F., Nguyen, A., Walinga, S., et al.: Application of autonomous smart inverter Volt-VAR function for voltage reduction energy savings and power quality in electric distribution systems. In: 2017 IEEE Power and Energy Society Innovative Smart Grid Technologies Conference (ISGT), Washington, DC, 2017, pp. 1–5 (2017). https://doi.org/10.1109/isgt.2017.8085991

6. Zhe, W., Zhang, Z., Zhang, X., et al.: Research on distribution network data fusion considering renewable energy. In: 2nd International Conference on Power and Renewable Energy (ICPRE), Chengdu, 2017, pp. 500–504 (2017). https://doi.org/10.1109/icpre.2017.8390585

7. Shahid, A.: Smart grid integration of renewable energy systems. In: 7th International Conference on Renewable Energy Research and Applications (ICRERA), Paris, 2018, pp. 944–948 (2018). https://doi.org/10.1109/icrera.2018.8566827

8. Guzhov, S., Krolin, A.: Use of big data technologies for the implementation of energy saving measures and renewable energy sources in buildings. In: Renewable Energies, Power Systems and Green Inclusive Economy (REPSGIE), Casablanca, 2018, pp. 1–5 (2018). https://doi.org/10.1109/repsgie.2018.8488861

9. Makkar, D., Syal, P.: Simulation of intelligent room lighting illuminance control. In: IEEE International Conference on Computational Intelligence and Computing Research (ICCIC), Coimbatore, India (2017). https://doi.org/10.1109/iccic.2017.8524356

10. Jindal, A., Kumar, N., Rodrigues, J.J.P.C.: A heuristic-based smart HVAC energy management scheme for university buildings. IEEE Trans. Industr. Inf. **14**(11), 5074–5086 (2018)

11. Dezfouli, M.M.S., Yazid, M.Z.A., Zakaria, A., et al.: Application of high efficiency motors in HVAC system for energy saving purpose. In: IEEE International Conference on Innovative Research and Development (ICIRD), Bangkok, Thailand (2018). https://doi.org/10.1109/icird.2018.8376309

12. Vinogradov, K.M., Moskvichev, A.V.: Energy saving at modernization of street lighting. In: International Science and Technology Conference "EastConf", Vladivostok, Russia, 2019, pp. 1–5 (2019). https://doi.org/10.1109/eastconf.2019.8725316

13. IBM: Buildings with the power of IoT. https://www.ibm.com/internet-of-things/explore-iot/buildings. Accessed 20 July 2019

14. Samsung: Brightics IoT BMS. https://www.samsungsds.com/global/en/solutions/off/bms/building_mgmt_solution.html. Accessed 20 July 2019

15. Documents SIM20. https://at-sky.com/san-pham/2378-module-rf-sim20.html. Accessed 20 July 2019

16. Datasheet of STM32100. https://www.st.com/resource/en/datasheet/stm32f100cb.pdf. Accessed 20 July 2019

17. Datasheet of LM35. http://www.ti.com/lit/ds/symlink/lm35.pdf. Accessed 20 July 2019

18. Website of MongoDB. https://www.mongodb.com/. Accessed 20 July 2019

19. Hung, P.D., Vinh, B.T.: Vulnerabilities in IoT devices with software-defined radio. In: 4th International Conference on Computer and Communication Systems (ICCCS 2019), Singapore, 23–25 February 2019

20. Hung, P.D., Giang, T.M., Nam, L.H., et al.: Vietnamese speech command recognition using recurrent neural networks. J. Adv. Comput. Sci. Appl. (IJACSA) **10**(7), 194–200 (2019)

21. Hung, P.D., Nam, L.H., Thang, H.V.: Flexible development for embedded system software. In: 4th International Conference on Research in Intelligent and Computing in Engineering (RICE 2019), Hanoi, Vietnam (2019)

22. Linh, N.D., Hung, P.D., Diep, V.T., et al.: Risk management in projects based on open-source software. In: 8th International Conference on Software and Computer Applications, Penang, Malaysia (ICSCA 2019) (2019). https://doi.org/10.1145/3316615.3316648

# Short Papers: Security and Data Engineering

# Identifying Minimum Set of Persons that Influenced by a Promotion Campaign

Ngo Thanh Hung[1], Huynh Thanh Viet[2(✉)], Le Nhut Truong[3],
and Musab Bassam Yousef Zghoul[4]

[1] Faculty of Information Technology, Ho Chi Minh City University
of Technology (HUTECH), Ho Chi Minh City, Vietnam
nt.hung@hutech.edu.vn
[2] GRG Banking Company, Ho Chi Minh City, Vietnam
viethuynh178@gmail.com
[3] Mekong University, MKU, Vinh Long, Vietnam
lenhuttruong@mku.edu.vn
[4] College of Computing in Al-Qunfudah, Umm Al-Qura University,
Mecca, Kingdom of Saudi Arabia
mbzghool@uqu.edu.sa

**Abstract.** As it has been proved by different researches that, they just focus on finding a different sets of the $k$-key players that had shown the greatest influence such as on social media network. This is equivalent finding a set of promotion people to make the maximum influenced in promotion campaigns. However, it can't predict the outcome of the campaign in advance. In this research, we propose a new approach for a promotion campaign, that is: identifying a minimum set of players to achieve the promotion goals with "at least M people are affected by the set of players with an influence that is greater than or equal to a threshold θ". Through this approach it can be, quantify the result of the campaign first, and then find the minimum set of persons that can influenced by promotion campaign.

**Keywords:** Key player · Promotion campaign · Minimum set of influence persons

## 1 Introduction

The problem of identifying key players in social network has been studied by many researches. An approach to solve this problem is based on centrality measures [2, 9]. Another one is based on cores/peripheries structure of network [4, 7, 18]. Recently communication efficiency of a network [15] has been also used for finding key players.

Some relevant researches are aiming to find a set of key-players instead of individual key player. Domingos et al. [6] has stated the problem of influence maximization as: finding a set of nodes, whose initial adoptions of a new product or innovation that can trigger the large number of further adoptions through a social network. The authors present greedy and hill-climbing methods to solve the problem. In 2003, Kempe [14] proposed an approximation guarantees algorithm to solve the

© Springer Nature Switzerland AG 2019
T. K. Dang et al. (Eds.): FDSE 2019, LNCS 11814, pp. 631–639, 2019.
https://doi.org/10.1007/978-3-030-35653-8_41

same problem for the independent cascade model and the linear threshold model of diffusion of a new product or an innovation.

Borgatti et al. [3] proposed two problems of identifying a key-player set, referred as Key Player Problem Positive (KPP/Pos) and Key Player Problem Negative (KPP/Neg). KPP/Neg is defined as a set of those nodes whose removal would result a residual network with the lowest cohesion. KPP/Pos, on the other hand, is the set of key player that can quickly diffuse information, behaviors, or products. The authors present a new success measure for finding the set.

Tutzauer et al. [19] proposed an entropy-based measure of centrality appropriate for traffic that propagates by transfer and flows along paths. After that Ortiz-Arroyo [17] applied this measure for finding both key-player sets: KPP/Pos and KPP/Neg.

Needless to say, researches of Pedro Domingos et al. and David Kempe et al. are in another relevant stream - analyzing the diffusion in a social network, which has been actively studied. Researches in this line focus not only on maximizing the influence diffusion [6, 14, 16], but also on predicting the trend [1], on learning influence probability in diffusion process [12], on analyzing the interests diffusion [5], or on predicting adoption probabilities in social networks [8].

In [13] the researchers presented a formula for evaluating influences between any two nodes in social network, diffusion in which based on independent cascade model. The works [6, 13, 14] are motivation for this research – finding the minimum set S (set S with minimum quantity of nodes) of nodes that affects to other M persons with the influence is greater than or at least equal to a threshold $\theta$.

## 2    Evaluation of Influence to a Node by a Set of Nodes

Given a social network as a directed graph G(V, E) where V is the set of nodes and E is the set of edges in a social network. An edge $e_{ij}$ means that node $i$ can successfully affect to node $j$ with probability equal to value of $e_{ij}$ without the help of others. The influence probability of node $i$ upon node $j$ is the probability of successful diffusion of the innovation from node $i$ to node $j$ (as in [13]). In this research, the diffusion of the information in the network follows the Independent Cascade Model.

### 2.1    Formula Evaluating the Influence of a Person i on a Person j

First need remind that the formula for measuring the influence probability of node i upon node j was given in [13] as following:

$$P_{ij} = 1 - \left(1 - P_{ij}^{l1}\right)\left(1 - P_{ij}^{l2}\right)\dots\left(1 - P_{ij}^{ln}\right)$$

$$P_{ij} = 1 - \prod_{t=1..n}\left(1 - P_{ij}^{lt}\right)$$

(1)

where, $n$ – the number of different paths from i to j;

$P_{ij}^{lt} \ P_{AB}^{l_i}$ is the partial influence probability of node $i$ upon node $j$ via the path $l_i$'
separately and

$$P_{ij}^{lt} = \prod (e_r),$$

where $e_r$ is all of the edges belong to the path $l_t$ between node $i$ and node $j$.

## 2.2 Formula Determining the Influence on a Person j by a Group of Person S

Assume that there is a group S with k people. All members of this group accept an idea
and pass it to the others in the network.

Need to evaluate influence of group S to a person j.

To make the influence by a member independent from other member's, the formula
to determine the influence of a member to other people (not in group) will be changed
as following:

$$P'_{ij} = 1 - \prod_{lt=1..n} \left(1 - P_{ij}^{lt}\right),$$

where $lt$ are those paths between i (i $\epsilon$ S) and j and do not contain any other person of
the group S.

In this case, the influence of the group to a person j in the network is:

$$P_{Sj} = 1 - \left(1 - P'_{1j}\right) \cdot \left(1 - P'_{2j}\right) \ldots \left(1 - P'_{kj}\right) \tag{2}$$

## 2.3 Formula Calculating the Number of Effected People by a Group S, the Influence Values of Which More Than or Equal to a Given Threshold θ

From formula (2) this value is evaluated by formula:

$$N_S = \text{CountIf}_{j=1..n, \, j \, \text{not in} \, S} \left(P_{Sj} > = \theta\right), \tag{3}$$

# 3   Problem and Algorithm

### The Problem Statement
The problem is to identify the minimum set of members S that the total number of
affected people in the network by group S, with the affect is greater than or equal to a
threshold θ, are greater than or equal to a given M.

Input:

- Graph of social network: G (E, V),
- Influence threshold: θ,

– The number of affected nodes with the value of influence is greater than or equal to the threshold $\theta$: M.

Output:

– The set of k users, with the smallest k, that the total number of affected people by this group of k users, with the influence is greater than or equal to threshold $\theta$, are greater or equal to M.

### Algorithm Idea
The algorithm will sequentially find the combinations of members with the number of elements from small to large, starting with 1. For each combination, we will determine the total number of affected people with the influence is greater than or equal to a threshold $\theta$. If this number is greater than or equal to M, the algorithm will stop.

### Pseudocode of the Algorithm

*Step 1: k=1*
*Browsing all combinations containing one element from all the users of network, with each set S that contains a user i*
{
    $N_S = 0;$
    *Browsing all the remaining users, with each user j, j $\neq$ i*
    {
        *Calculate $P_{Sj} = P'_{ij} = P_{ij}$ by (1)*
        *If ($P_{Sj}$>=$\theta$) $N_S = N_S +1$;*
        *If ($N_S$>= M) get the solution, go to step 4.*
    }
}
*Step 2: Exclude the users that don't affect to anyone from the browsing set. Sort the rest users by the numbers of their affected users.*
*Step 3: while(k<|V|-|S|)*
{
    $k = k +1$;
    *Browsing all combinations of k users from the user set, priority to the combinations of users that affect to more users than the others, for each combination S*
    {
        $N_S=0$;
        *Browsing all remaining users j in the network, j not belong to S, for each j*
        {
            *Calculate the number of nodes K from network that doesn't belong to S and affected by any node in S*
            *If (K<M) browse the next set S*
            *If (the set of nodes, affected by each of node in set S, contain less nodes than M )*

$If\ (\ exists\ a\ node\ i \in S\!:\ P_{ij} >= \theta)$

$\qquad P_{Sj} = P_{ij}\ ;\ //no\ need\ to\ calculate\ P_{Sj}\ because\ j\ is\ certainly\ affected\ //with\ the\ affect\ is\ greater\ than\ or\ equal\ to\ the\ threshold$

$Else$

$\qquad Calculate\ P_{Sj}\ by\ (2)$

$If\ (P_{Sj} >= \theta)$

$\{$

$\qquad N_S = N_S + 1;$

$\qquad If\ (N_S >= M)\ get\ the\ solution,\ go\ to\ step\ 4.$

$\}$

$\qquad\qquad\}$

$\qquad\}$

$\}$

*Step 4: Print the solution and finish the algorithm.*

### *An Example*

Given an example of searching the minimum set of nodes from a social network (Fig. 1) with *10* nodes, that can effect minimum *M = 5* other nodes with threshold $\theta = 0.8$.

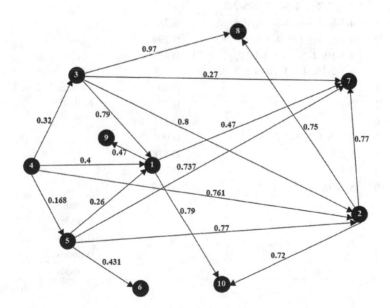

**Fig. 1.** A demo social network with 10 nodes.

The process of searching minimum set of nodes is presented in Table 1.

**Table 1.** The process of searching minimum set.

| S | j | Paths from S to j | $P_{Sj}$ | Number of affected nodes | $N_S$ |
|---|---|---|---|---|---|
| 1 | 7 | 1-7 | 0.47 | 3 nodes: 7, 9, 10 | 0 |
|  | 9 | 1-9 | 0.47 | | |
|  | 10 | 1-10 | 0.79 | | |
| 2 | 7 | 2-7 | 0.77 | 3 nodes: 7, 8, 10 | 0 |
|  | 8 | 2-8 | 0.75 | | |
|  | 10 | 2-10 | 0.72 | | |
| 3 | 1 | 3-1 | 0.79 | 6 nodes: 1, 2, 7, 8, 9, 10, | 4 |
|  | 2 | 3-2 | 0.8 | | |
|  | 7 | 3-1-7, 3-2-7, 3-7 | 0.824 | | |
|  | 8 | 3-2-8, 3-8 | 0.99 | | |
|  | 9 | 3-1-9 | 0.37 | | |
|  | 10 | 3-1-10, 3-2-10 | 0.84 | | |
| 4 | 1 | 4-1, 4-3-1, 4-5-1 | 0.57 | 9 nodes: 1, 2, 3, 5, 6, 7, 8, 9, 10 | 3 |
|  | 2 | 4-2, 3-4-2, 4-5-2 | 0.85 | | |
|  | 3 | 4-3 | 0.32 | | |
|  | 5 | 4-5 | 0.168 | | |
|  | 6 | 4-5-6 | 0.072 | | |
|  | 7 | 4-1-7, 4-2-7, 4-3-7, 4-5-7, 4-3-1-7, 4-3-2-1, 4-5-1-7, 4-5-2-7 | 0.83 | | |
|  | 8 | 4-2-8, 4-3-8, 4-3-2-8, 4-5-2-8 | 0.78 | | |
|  | 9 | 4-1-9, 4-3-1-9, 4-5-1-9 | 0.299 | | |
|  | 10 | 4-1-10, 4-2-10, 4-3-1-10, 4-3-2-10, 4-5-1-10, 4-5-2-10 | 0.823 | | |
| 5 | 1 | 5-1 | 0.26 | 7 nodes:1, 2, 6, 7, 8, 9, 10 | 1 |
|  | 2 | 5-2 | 0.77 | | |
|  | 6 | 5-6 | 0.431 | | |
|  | 7 | 5-7, 5-1-7, 5-2-7 | 0.906 | | |
|  | 8 | 5-2-8 | 0.578 | | |
|  | 9 | 5-1-9 | 0.122 | | |
|  | 10 | 5-1-10, 5-2-10 | 0.646 | | |
| 6 | | | | 0 nodes | 0 |
| 7 | | | | 0 nodes | 0 |
| 8 | | | | 0 nodes | 0 |
| 9 | | | | 0 nodes | 0 |
| 10 | | | | 0 nodes | 0 |

(continued)

**Table 1.** (*continued*)

| S | j | Paths from S to j | $P_{Sj}$ | Number of affected nodes | $N_S$ |
|---|---|---|---|---|---|
| Sorted the list of nodes for next browsing: 4, 5, 3, 1, 2 | | | | | |
| 4, 5 | 1 | 4-1, 4-3-1, 5-1 | 0.668 | 8 nodes: 1, 2, 3, 6, 7, 8, 9, 10 | 4 |
| | 2 | 4-2, 4-3-2, 5-2 | 0.959 | | |
| | 3 | 4-3 | 0.32 | | |
| | 6 | 5-6 | 0.431 | | |
| | 7 | | $P_{57} = 0.906$ | | |
| | 8 | 4-2-8, 4-3-8, 5-2-8 | 0.899 | | |
| | 9 | 4-1-9, 4-3-1-9, 5-1-9 | 0.372 | | |
| | 10 | 4-1-10, 4-2-10, 4-3-1-10, 4-3-2-10, 5-1-10, 5-2-10 | 0.929 | | |
| 4, 3 | 1 | 3-1, 4-1, 4-5-1 | 0.88 | 8 nodes: 1, 2, 5, 6, 7, 8, 9, 10 | 5 |
| | 2 | 3-2, 4-2, 4-5-2 | 0.958 | | |
| | 5 | 4-5 | 0.168 | | |
| | 6 | 4-5-6 | 0.072 | | |
| | 7 | | $P_{47} = 0.83$ | | |
| | 8 | 3-8, 3-2-8, 4-2-8, 4-5-2-8 | 0.995 | | |
| | 9 | 3-1-9, 4-1-9, 4-5-1-9 | 0.5 | | |
| | 10 | | $P_{4\_10} = 0.823$ | | |
| The algorithm ends with the min set: S = {4, 3} | | | | | |

## 4 Experiment

The program is written on Spark platform with Java language. The path's data is saved on MongoDB. The experiment is run on PC with Intel Core i5-7200U 2.5 GHz, 4 GB DDR4 memory.

The process consumes high memory, because of saving all the paths between any couple of nodes, and the implementation has not been optimized till now, so the experiment was carried out only with small graph ($\leq 10$ nodes). Execution time in this is approximately 25 s. It needs to improve the implementation of the algorithm so that the program can run with big social network that contains up to millions of nodes.

The Table 2 shows the result of minimum set searching for the above network with some various parameters. The effectiveness of the proposed algorithm is assessed by ratio of the number of combinations that is not considered by algorithm ($N_{not}$) to the number of all possible combinations ($N_{all}$). The greater this number is, the more effective algorithm is. The number of all possible combinations is calculated as below:

$$N_{all} = C_{10}^1 + C_{10}^2 + C_{10}^3 + C_{10}^4 + C_{10}^5$$
$$= 10 + 45 + 120 + 210 + 252$$
$$N_{all} = 637$$

As shown in Table 2, the algorithm has high effective.

**Table 2.** Result of searching by the proposed algorithm.

| Parameters | Number of browsed combination | $N_{not}$ | $N_{not}/N_{all}$ | Min set |
|---|---|---|---|---|
| $M = 5,\ \theta = 0.5$ | 3 | 634 | 0.99529 | {3} |
| $M = 5,\ \theta = 0.8$ | 12 | 625 | 0.98116 | {4, 3} |
| $M = 5,\ \theta = 0.9$ | 20 | 617 | 0.96860 | {4, 5, 3} |
| $M = 5,\ \theta = 0.95$ | 38 | 599 | 0.94035 | {} |

## 5 Conclusion

This study proposes a formula for calculating the influence of a person to another person as well as a group of people to another person through an independent spread network (ICM) based on probability theory. We hereby propose a new problem that is identifying the minimum set of users to create the influence to other M users, each person is affected by this group with a threshold $\theta$. This problem is very useful for identifying objects used to promote images in promotion campaigns. The proposed problem has advantages compared to the previous problems that allow to determine the basic objectives of a promotion campaign such as: the number of affected people, the degree of affect (probability of successful influence). An algorithm was also proposed but it's implementation is very expensive in computational and storage cost. The algorithm and it's implementation need to be improved so, that they can be applied to real social networks.

## References

1. Altshuler, Y., Pan, W., Pentland, A.S.: Trends prediction using social diffusion models. In: Yang, S.J., Greenberg, A.M., Endsley, M. (eds.) SBP 2012. LNCS, vol. 7227, pp. 97–104. Springer, Heidelberg (2012). https://doi.org/10.1007/978-3-642-29047-3_12
2. Bonacich, E.: A theory of ethnic antagonism: the split labor market. Am. Sociol. Rev. **37**, 547–559 (1972)
3. Borgatti, S.P.: Identifying sets of key players in a social network. Comput. Math. Organ. Theory **12**(1), 21–34 (2006)
4. Borgatti, S.P., Everett, M.G.: Models of core/periphery structures. Soc. Nctw. **21**(4), 375–395 (2000)
5. D'Agostino, G., D'Antonio, F., De Nicola, A., Tucci, S.: Interests diffusion in social networks. Physica A: Stat. Mech. Appl. **436**, 443–461 (2015)
6. Domingos, P., Richardson, M.: Mining the network value of customers. In: Proceedings of the Seventh ACM SIGKDD International Conference on Knowledge Discovery and Data Mining, pp. 57–66. ACM, August 2001
7. Everett, M.G., Borgatti, S.P.: The centrality of groups and classes. J. Math. Sociol. **23**(3), 181–201 (1999)
8. Fang, X., Hu, P.J.H., Li, Z., Tsai, W.: Predicting adoption probabilities in social networks. Inf. Syst. Res. **24**(1), 128–145 (2013)
9. Freeman, L.C.: Centrality in social networks conceptual clarification. Soc. Netw. **1**(3), 215–239 (1978)

10. Goldenberg, J., Libai, B., Muller, E.: Talk of the network: a complex systems look at the underlying process of word-of-mouth. Mark. Lett. **12**(3), 211–223 (2001)
11. Goldenberg, J., Libai, B., Muller, E.: Using complex systems analysis to advance marketing theory development: modeling heterogeneity effects on new product growth through stochastic cellular automata. Acad. Mark. Sci. Rev. **9**(3), 1–18 (2001)
12. Goyal, A., Bonchi, F., Lakshmanan, L.V.: Learning influence probabilities in social networks. In: Proceedings of the Third ACM International Conference on Web Search and Data Mining, pp. 241–250. ACM, February 2010
13. Hung, N.T., Viet, H.T.: Identifying key player using sum of influence probabilities in a social network. In: Dang, T.K., Wagner, R., Küng, J., Thoai, N., Takizawa, M., Neuhold, E. J. (eds.) FDSE 2017. LNCS, vol. 10646, pp. 444–452. Springer, Cham (2017). https://doi. org/10.1007/978-3-319-70004-5_32
14. Kempe, D., Kleinberg, J.M., Tardos, É.: Maximizing the spread of influence through a social network. Theory Comput. **11**(4), 105–147 (2015)
15. Latora, V., Marchiori, M.: How the science of complex networks can help developing strategies against terrorism. Chaos Solitons Fractals **20**(1), 69–75 (2004)
16. Lei, S., Maniu, S., Mo, L., Cheng, R., Senellart, P.: Online influence maximization. In: Proceedings of the 21th ACM SIGKDD International Conference on Knowledge Discovery and Data Mining, pp. 645–654. ACM, August 2015
17. Ortiz-Arroyo, D., Hussain, D.M.A.: An information theory approach to identify sets of key players. In: Ortiz-Arroyo, D., Larsen, H.L., Zeng, D.D., Hicks, D., Wagner, G. (eds.) EuroIsI 2008. LNCS, vol. 5376, pp. 15–26. Springer, Heidelberg (2008). https://doi.org/10.1007/ 978-3-540-89900-6_5
18. Seidman, S.B.: Network structure and minimum degree. Soc. Netw. **5**(3), 269–287 (1983)
19. Tutzauer, F.: Entropy as a measure of centrality in networks characterized by path-transfer flow. Soc. Netw. **29**(2), 249–265 (2007)

# Facial Expression Recognition on Static Images

Tan Quan Ngo and Seokhoon Yoon[✉]

Department of Electrical and Computer Engineering, University of Ulsan,
Ulsan Metropolitan City, Republic of Korea
tanquan.dn@gmail.com, seokhoonyoon@ulsan.ac.kr

**Abstract.** Facial expression recognition (FER) is currently one of the most attractive and also the most challenging topics in the computer vision and artificial fields. FER applications are ranging from medical treatment, virtual reality, to driver fatigue surveillance, and many other human-machine interaction systems. Benefit from the recent success of deep learning techniques, especially the invention of convolution neural networks (CNN), various end-to-end deep learning-based FER systems have been proposed in the past few years. However, overfitting caused by a lack of training data is still the big challenge that almost all deep FER systems have to put into a concern to achieve high-performance accuracy. In this paper, we are going to build a FER model to recognize eight commons emotions: neutral, happiness, sadness, surprise, fear, disgust, anger, and contempt on the AffectNet dataset. In order to mitigate the effect of small training data, which is prone to overfitting, we proposed a thoughtful transfer learning framework. Specifically, we fine-tuning ResNet-50 model, which is pre-trained on ImageNet dataset for object detection task, on the AffectNet dataset to recognize eight above mentioned face emotions. Experiment results demonstrate the effectiveness of our proposed FER model.

**Keywords:** Machine learning · Deep learning · Convolutional neural network · Facial expression recognition

## 1 Introduction

Facial expressions are effective channels in human communication that help us understand the intentions of others during communicating. With significant potential on both academic and commercial purposes, automatic facial expression recognition has been gaining huge attention over the last few decades. Numerous studies have been conducted to recognize seven basic emotional expressions: happiness, sadness, surprise, fear, disgust, anger, contempt, and plus neutral. There are two main categories that can be used to divide FER systems based on the feature representations: static image FER and dynamic sequence FER [7]. While static-based methods only using spatial information from a single image, the dynamic-based methods adopt spatial-temporal information from

© Springer Nature Switzerland AG 2019
T. K. Dang et al. (Eds.): FDSE 2019, LNCS 11814, pp. 640–647, 2019.
https://doi.org/10.1007/978-3-030-35653-8_42

successive frames in the input sequence. Among the two vision-based methods, the former is preferred due to the less complicated of the model that can be embedded into mobile devices for some applications.

A conventional FER model is usually composed of three main steps: face detection, feature extraction, and emotion classification. In the first step, face and some facial components (e.g. eyes, mouth, nose, and eyebrows) are detected from the input image. Next, the face and its components features are extracted from the face region. Last, one or some pre-trained facial expression classifiers (e.g. support vector machine (SVM), decision tree (DT), AdaBoost, and random forest) is employed to perform the emotion recognition task using the extracted feature from the previous step.

Almost traditional methods use handcrafted features extraction (e.g. local binary patterns (LBP) [10], a histogram of oriented gradient (HOG) [2], and scale-invariant feature transform (SIFT) [8]) to extract facial features before feeding them into the classifier. One common feature of these approaches is that they are only suitable for small-scale facial expression datasets which are created in the laboratory setting. However, in the past decade, a number of emotion recognition competitions (e.g., FER2013 held in 2013, Emotion Recognition in the Wild (EmotiW) held in 2013–2017) have collected relatively sufficient facial emotion dataset from highly challenging real-world setting. This forced the FER researches to move from laboratory-controlled to real-world scenarios. The traditional methods using handcrafted feature extractions have been described to ineffectively address a huge variance of facial factor (e.g. head poses, illumination intensity, and occlusions).

Fortunately, the recent development of deep learning in various field and especially the invention of CNN in image processing have enabled computer vision studies to use deep learning-based feature extraction to build an end-to-end, automatic system which exceeded the conventional methods by a large margin. From the resounding success of AlexNet [6] in ImageNet classification challenge in 2012, various deep CNN architectures (e.g., VGG [11], GoogleNet [12], ResNet [3]) have been proposed and achieve high accuracy in many object recognition challenges. Benefits from these powerful model architectures, deep learning techniques have increasingly been applied into FER field and achieved the state-of-art performances in almost modern facial emotion recognition competitions where challenging factors for emotion.

However, existing relatively large annotated databases of facial expressions in the wild are very limited. Training directly on these datasets is prone to overfitting. Thus, overfitting caused by the shortage of sufficient facial expression data remains a big issue that every FER systems need to focus on. A number of training methods have been proposed to mitigate the effect of the small dataset on FER system performance. Among these methods, pre-train and fine-tuning are reported to be capable to handle the overfitting issues and directly improve the overall discriminative power of FER models. For example, in [4], experiment results show that even worse face recognition (FR) models that were pre-trained on much larger FR data can achieve better performance in the FER task after fine-tuning on FER2013 dataset.

In this paper, we proposed a deep transfer learning framework to build an end-to-end deep FER model. Specifically, we fine-tuning ResNet-50 model which is pre-trained on ImageNet for object detection task on AffectNet data to recognize seven common facial expression: 1: Happiness, 2: Sadness, 3: Surprise, 4: Fear, 5: Disgust, 6: Anger, 7: Contempt, plus 0: Neutral. Initial experiment results demonstrate the effectiveness of our training framework.

## 2    Proposed Method

### 2.1    AffectNet Dataset

In this work, we aim to build a deep CNN model that recognizes facial expressions on a publicly available dataset called AffectNet [9]. The dataset contains more than one million images from the Internet obtained by querying different image search engines using more than one thousand emotion-related keywords. Especially, about 450,000 images have manually annotated labels for eights basic discrete emotions by professionals. Detail numbers of samples for each manually annotated emotion classes are shown in Table 1.

**Table 1.** The total number of manually annotated image in each emotional class

| Neutral | 75374 |
|---|---|
| Happy | 134915 |
| Sad | 25959 |
| Surprise | 14590 |
| Fear | 6878 |
| Disgust | 4303 |
| Anger | 25382 |
| Contempt | 4250 |
| None | 33588 |
| Uncertain | 12145 |
| Non-Face | 82915 |
| Total | 420299 |

### 2.2    ImageNet Dataset

ImageNet is a project and also currently one of the largest databases which include more than fourteen million images from more than 20,0000 object categories. These images have been hand-annotated by the ImageNet project to make an average of over five hundred images per each object which is pictured. Since 2010, the ImageNet project has held an annual contest called the ImageNet Large Scale Visual Recognition Challenge (ILSVRC), which is one of the largest competitions in the computer vision field.

## 2.3   Model Architecture

Convolutional neural networks have proven to be effective models for tackling a variety of FER tasks. In this paper, we adopt ResNet-50 [3] as our backbone networks architecture to perform FER task on AffectNet dataset. Resnet using residual blocks (Fig. 1) to mitigate the effect of deep CNN network on training thus improve the system performance and reduce the computational cost.

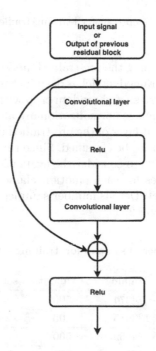

**Fig. 1.** Residual block

## 2.4   Deep Transfer Learning

As mentioned before, directly training the deep model on small scale data is prone to overfitting. To address this problem, we adopt and rectify the ResNet-50 model which is pre-trained on the large-scale object detection data ImageNet, and then fine-tuning the pre-trained model on the target dataset – AffectNet – for FER task. Figure 2 demonstrate our training framework for the two datasets.

# 3   Experiments and Results

## 3.1   Preprocessing

For the pre-trained phase, we make use of the ImageNet pre-trained ResNet-50 model which is available to download and use for other tasks. For the fine-tuning

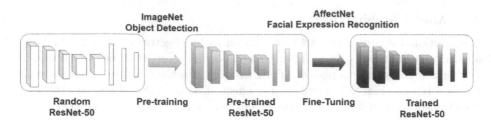

**Fig. 2.** Deep transfer learning framework.

phase, we continue to re-training the pre-trained model on the AffectNet training data. First, we use the pre-trained model as deep feature extraction. All the input images for this phase was resized and random crop with the image size $224 \times 224$; random horizontal flip and image normalization are also applied to argument the training data. The last output layer of the pre-trained model is modified to match with the number of emotions to be classified. Since the AffectNet test set has not been published yet, we decide to consider the evaluation set as the test set while randomly taking 500 images for each emotion classes from the training set to create the new validation set. Details number samples for training – validation – test set are described in Table 2.

**Table 2.** Detail number of samples for Training - Validating - Test set.

| Emotion | Training set | Validation set | Test set |
|---------|-------------|----------------|----------|
| Neutral | 74374 | 500 | 500 |
| Happy | 133915 | 500 | 500 |
| Sad | 24959 | 500 | 500 |
| Surprise | 13590 | 500 | 500 |
| Fear | 5878 | 500 | 500 |
| Disgust | 3303 | 500 | 500 |
| Anger | 24382 | 500 | 500 |
| Contempt | 3250 | 500 | 500 |
| Total | 283651 | 4000 | 4000 |

## 3.2 Evaluation Metrics

There are various evaluation metrics in the literature to measure the discriminative performance of the proposed FER model. Beside some widely used metrics for classification such as accuracy, F1-score, area under ROC curve (AUC), and area under Precision-Recall curve (AUC-PR), two measures of inter-annotator agreement Cohen's kappa [1] and Krippendorff's Alpha [5] are used in our work.

Cohen's kappa statistic measures inter-rater reliability (sometimes called inter-observer agreement). Inter-rater reliability, or precision, happens when your data raters (or collectors) give the same score to the same data item while Krippendorff-s alpha (also called Krippendorff's Coefficient) is an alternative to Cohen's Kappa for determining inter-rater reliability.

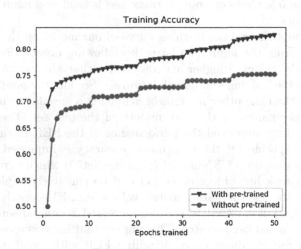

**Fig. 3.** Training accuracy of the model with/without pre-trained

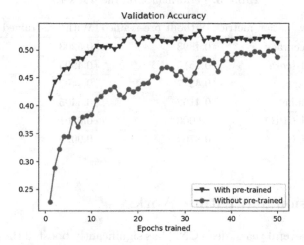

**Fig. 4.** Validation accuracy of the model with/without pre-trained

### 3.3 Experiment Results

In this section, we evaluate our training framework. We fine-tune the pre-trained model on AffectNet training data for 50 epochs. To compare the results, we also train the backbone model from scratch. The two networks are trained for 50 epochs and the parameters are updated with stochastic gradient descent (SGD) with momentum 0.9. Cross entropy softmax loss is used as a main loss function in all experiments.

Figures 3 and 4 showed the learning curve of our model on the training and validation set. From the figure, we have the following observations. First, the pre-trained model achieved higher accuracy value than the model without pre-trained on both the training set and validation set. Second, the pre-trained model takes less time than the other in term of achieving a specific accuracy. Table 3 showed the performances of the two models on the test set. The pre-training and fine-tuning have improved the performance of the FER model in all evaluation metrics. Specifically, the recognition accuracy is improved approximate 5%. This shows that deep CNN model (e.g., ResNet50) which is pre-trained on a more general task like object detection can be effectively explored in FER task. Moreover, the rest evaluation metric values (e.g., F1-score, Kappa, Alpha, AUCPR and AUC) of our method are also increased in comparison with that of the model that trained from scratch. This implies that improvement our method compromises a reliable direction on handling FER with small dataset in our future work.

**Table 3.** Performance on the test set.

| Evaluation metric | Without pre-trained | With pre-trained |
|---|---|---|
| Accuracy | 0.4893 | 0.5203 |
| F1-score | 0.4615 | 0.4905 |
| Kappa | 0.4277 | 0.4407 |
| Alpha | 0.4152 | 0.4405 |
| AUCPR | 0.6006 | 0.6301 |
| AUC | 0.8764 | 0.9026 |

## 4   Conclusion and Future Works

Over the past several years, deep CNN has significantly boosted the performance of many systems in visual classification field. Likewise, deep CNNs have increasingly been used in FER task on static images. However, the lack of relatively enough emotion training data causes overfitting issues for almost FER system. In this paper, we proposed a deep transfer learning framework to mitigate the overfitting problem, which improves the discriminative power of our FER model. Nonetheless, the recognition accuracy is still not meet our expectation. This may be caused by the high imbalance of AffectNet data where the number of sample of major classes (e.g., Happy and Sad) are much larger than that of minor classes (e.g., Contempt and Disgust). Using different models and training processes as well as apply recently successful loss functions to further boost the performance is still in our future work.

**Acknowledgment.** This research was supported by the Basic Science Research Program through the National Research Foundation of Korea (NRF) funded by the Ministry of Education (NRF2016R1D1A3B03934617) and MSIT (2019R1F1A1058147).

# References

1. Cohen, J.: A coefficient of agreement for nominal scales. Educ. Psychol. Measur. **20**(1), 37–46 (1960)
2. Dalal, N., Triggs, B.: Histograms of oriented gradients for human detection (2005)
3. He, K., Zhang, X., Ren, S., Sun, J.: Deep residual learning for image recognition. In: Proceedings of the IEEE Conference on Computer Vision and Pattern Recognition (CVPR), pp. 770–778 (2016)
4. Knyazev, B., Shvetsov, R., Efremova, N., Kuharenko, A.: Convolutional neural networks pretrained on large face recognition datasets for emotion classification from video. arXiv preprint arXiv:1711.04598 (2017)
5. Krippendorff, K.: Estimating the reliability, systematic error and random error of interval data. Educ. Psychol. Measur. **30**(1), 61–70 (1970)
6. Krizhevsky, A., Sutskever, I., Hinton, G.E.: Imagenet classification with deep convolutional neural networks. In: Advances in Neural Information Processing Systems, pp. 1097–1105 (2012)
7. Li, S., Deng, W.: Deep facial expression recognition: A survey. arXiv preprint arXiv:1804.08348 (2018)
8. Lowe, D.G., et al.: Object recognition from local scale-invariant features. In: ICCV, vol. 99, pp. 1150–1157 (1999)
9. Mollahosseini, A., Hasani, B., Mahoor, M.H.: Affectnet: a database for facial expression, valence, and arousal computing in the wild. IEEE Trans. Affect. Comput. **10**(1), 18–31 (2017)
10. Ojala, T., Pietikäinen, M., Mäenpää, T.: Multiresolution gray-scale and rotation invariant texture classification with local binary patterns. IEEE Trans. Pattern Anal. Mach. Intell. **7**, 971–987 (2002)
11. Simonyan, K., Zisserman, A.: Very deep convolutional networks for large-scale image recognition. arXiv preprint arXiv:1409.1556 (2014)
12. Szegedy, C., et al.: Going deeper with convolutions. In: Proceedings of the IEEE Conference on Computer Vision and Pattern Recognition, pp. 1–9 (2015)

# Cryptocurrencies Price Index Prediction Using Neural Networks on Bittrex Exchange

Phan Duy Hung[1(✉)] and Tran Quang Thinh[2]

[1] FPT University, Hanoi, Vietnam
hungpd2@fe.edu.vn
[2] Gosei Vietnam Join Stock Company, Hanoi, Vietnam
quangthinhtran3588@gmail.com

**Abstract.** Cryptocurrencies have become fairly popular in the market since they were first introduced in the early 2000s. Cryptocurrencies are used primarily outside existing banking and governmental institutions and are exchanged over the Internet. Cryptocurrency exchanges allow customers to trade cryptocurrencies for other assets, such as conventional fiat money, or to trade between different digital currencies. This paper proposes a method to predict fluctuations in the prices of cryptocurrencies, which are increasingly used for online transactions worldwide. A Multi-Layer Perceptron (MLP)-based Non Linear Autoregressive with Exogenous Inputs (NARX) cryptocurrencies price forecasting model using the closing past prices together with volume. The model is evaluated based on price data collected from Bittrex Exchange, a US-based famous cryptocurrency exchange. Validation tests and Prediction test indicate that the proposed model is suitable for predicting prices on collected data.

**Keywords:** Bitcoin · Bittrex Exchange · NARX · Price index prediction

## 1 Introduction

Cryptocurrency is a form of digital money that is designed to be secure and, in many cases, anonymous. The first cryptocurrency, Bitcoin, was first introduced in 2008 by Satoshi Nakamoto as a peer-to-peer electronic cash system [1, 2]. Due to its low cost of transaction, limited supply, ability to act as a store of value against volatile fiat currencies and ability to easily transfer value across state borders, the rapid success of Bitcoin in recent years has seen Bitcoin being used increasingly in commerce and recognition of digital cryptocurrencies as an emerging asset class, value transfer and exchange method, expanding its trade to over-the-market trade and derivatives market. Similar to fiat currencies and stocks, there are currently many cryptocurrencies exchanges to let people trade from fiat currencies to Bitcoin and from Bitcoin to other cryptocurrencies. One of the most popular exchanges is Bittrex. In there, people can deposit all supported currencies such as Bitcoin, Ethereum, USDT, etc. then trade among them from one to other currencies. The stock market is a complex nonlinear dynamic system [3]. Still, remarkable amounts of research have been committed to developing an efficient predictive model to assist traders in making wise investment decisions [4, 5].

© Springer Nature Switzerland AG 2019
T. K. Dang et al. (Eds.): FDSE 2019, LNCS 11814, pp. 648–655, 2019.
https://doi.org/10.1007/978-3-030-35653-8_43

Many works have tried to explore various prediction models for forecasting financial data. Some typical studies on this problem are as follows:

In [6], authors explored several machine learning models (RNN, Auto-Regressive Integrated Moving Average (ARIMA) and Long Short-Term Memory (LSTM)) to predict Bitcoin prices. The price data is sourced from the Bitcoin Price Index. As a result, non-linear deep learning methods outperform ARIMA forecast which performs poorly. In [7], a comparison between several regression models was performed for Bitcoin price prediction. The baseline, linear, SVM and ANN regression models were used to predict Bitcoin's future prices based on past data. The results indicated that the linear regression method was the most suitable for prediction. The researchers conclude that the direction of Bitcoin's price movement classification could be predicted with accuracy of approximately 55%. In [8], a four-layer multi-agent framework was proposed to predict the quarterly price movements of the DAX German Stock Exchange index over a period of eight years. The four-layer architecture called Bat Neural Network Multi Agent System (BNNMAS) consists of several autonomous decision makers called agents. The results showed that BNNMAS significantly performs accurate and reliable, so it could be considered as a suitable tool for predicting stock price specially in a long term period. Sul et al. show one way to make stock prediction by using social media sentiment [9]. 2.5 million tweets about S&P 500 firms were put through the authors own sentiment classifier and compared to the stock returns. The results showed that sentiment that disseminates through a social network quickly is anticipated to be reflected in a stock price on the same trading day, while slower spreading sentiment is more likely to be reflected on future trading days. Basing a trading strategy on these predictions are prospected to yield 11–15% annual gains.

The studies mentioned above demonstrate that neural networks gives good results. However, the results depend much and the price data of each study. In addition, the selection of neural network architecture is always required to experiment and analysis. This paper describes how data has been collected from Bittrex Exchange, how it has been corrected and formatted. And from that price data, the paper proposes a nonlinear autoregressive exogenous model (NARX) to predict price.

The remainder of the paper is organized as follows: Sect. 2 describes data collection and environment preparation. Section 3 then covers the experimentation and analyse with NARX model. Finally, Sect. 4 concludes the paper and provide some of the authors' perspectives.

## 2 Bittrex Exchange and Data Collection

Bittrex is the premier U.S. based blockchain platform, providing lightning-fast trade execution, dependable digital wallets and industry-leading security practices [10]. At the time performing the research, Bittrex has 3 main markets: Bitcoin (BTC), Ethereum (ETH) and USDT. In this work, we only focus on trading with Bitcoin and making price prediction of Bitcoin and other altcoins.

The first attempt was to collect data directly from Bittrex exchange's website. Website shows the historical candle charts within periods of time, which contains the necessary data. A tool developed by Nodejs is used to collect such data.

Each currency pair, such as BTC-EMC has historical data displayed as a list of price data. The data contains seven elements: open price (O), highest price (H), lowest price (L), close price (C), total volume of the exchange currency (in the above example, EmerCoin - EMC), the end time of the period (T) and the total volume of the base currency (in the above example, Bitcoin – BTC). As provided by Bittrex, data can be collected within periods of 1-min, 5-min, 30-min, 1-h, 1-day, 3-days, 1-week and 1 month. The 1-day period has been selected in this work because it is suitable for working time. Once finishing crawling data from Bittrex, an extra step is needed to converted data from JSON to CSV which has each row as a timestep. The final csv file is shared at Github [11].

# 3   Selection of Neural Network and Evaluation

## 3.1   Selectrion of Neural Network

Neural networks are universal approximators, they provide an analytical alternative to conventional techniques which are often limited by strict assumptions of normality, linearity, variable independence etc. [12, 13]. Because an ANN can capture many kinds of relationships it allows the user to quickly and relatively easily model phenomena which otherwise may have been very difficult or impossible to explain otherwise.

The nonlinear autoregressive network with exogenous inputs (NARX) is a recurrent dynamic network, with feedback connections enclosing several layers of the network [14]. In this paper, the NARX model used as a predictor, to predict the next value of the input signal. The output of the NARX network to be an estimate of the output of some nonlinear dynamic system that we are trying to model. The output is fed back to the input of the feedforward neural network as part of the standard NARX architecture. Because the true output is available during the training of the network, we could create a series-parallel architecture, in which the true output is used instead of feeding back the estimated output. This has two advantages: the first is that the input to the feedforward network is more accurate; the second is that the resulting network has a purely feedforward architecture, and static backpropagation can be used for training.

All of the training is done in open loop (also called series-parallel architecture), including the validation and testing steps. The typical workflow is to fully create the network in open loop, and only when it has been trained (which includes validation and testing steps) is it transformed to closed loop for multistep-ahead prediction. In order for the parallel response (iterated prediction) to be accurate, it is important that the network be trained so that the errors in the series-parallel configuration (one-step-ahead prediction) are very small. Each time a neural network is trained, can result in a different solution due to different initial weight and bias values and different divisions of data into training, validation, and test sets. As a result, different neural networks trained on the same problem can give different outputs for the same input. To ensure that a neural network of good accuracy has been found, retrain several times.

## 3.2    Implementation of NARX Model

The NARX model was realized using the MLP neural network. All programs were implemented in MATLAB version 2018a. As this MLP is used for function approximation, the hidden units use the tangent-sigmoid activation function while the output unit uses the linear activation function. We use data of LiteCoin (LTC) to train and test the network. The input signal y(t) is the close price of LTC and the independent (exogenous) input signal x(t) is the combination of base volume of LTC and price of BTC. Among allowed periods for collecting data from Bittrex: 1 min, 5 min, 30 min, 1 h, 1 day, 1 h is selected. We can get at maximum 2 months data which is equally to 1400 timesteps. The data is divided into 2 parts: the first part containing the first 1368 timesteps used to training the network, the second part containing 72 remaining latest data used to do the comparison between target and output of the network. So the problem predicted here is: Predict series y(t) given d past values of y(t) and another series x(t). The steps to make predictions are as follows:

*Step 1: Select Data*
Import 2 CSV data files which have LTC price and LTC trade volume, BTC price. Those both 2 files have 1368 timesteps (this data is shared on Github).

*Step 2: Prepare Data*
Divide the data into 3 parts: Training, Validation and Testing. The Training set takes up 70% data and is presented to the network during training. The network is adjusted according to its error. The Validation set takes 15% data is used to measure network generalization, and to halt training when generalization stops improving. The Testing set takes the remaining 15% data, has no effect on training and so provides an independent measure of network performance during and after training.

*Step 3: Select Network Architecture*
At this step, the number of hidden neurons chosen is 15 equal to the number of delay steps.

*Step 4: Select a Training Algorithm*
MATLAB supports 3 built-in algorithms: Levenberg – Marquardt, Bayesian Regularization, Scaled Conjugate Gradient. The Levenberg – Marquardt backpropagation is chosen as the one to train the network because it has shown superior performance in prediction or function approximation tasks [19]. This algorithm typically requires more memory but less time. Training automatically stops when generalization stops improving, as indicated by an increase in the Mean Square Error (MSE) of the validation samples. Mean Squared Error is the average squared difference between outputs and targets. Lower values are better. Zero means no error. Another indicator is Regression. Regression R Values measure the correlation between outputs and targets. An *R* value of 1 means a close relationship, 0 a random relationship.

### 3.3   Analysing Results

The MSE was initially high but is gradually reduced as the MLP weights were updated. At the time of 26 epochs, the results were the best, then overfitting happened. The Training network performance is described in Fig. 1.

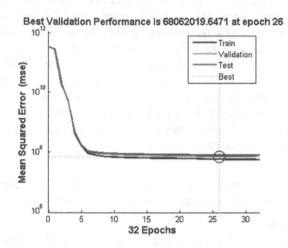

**Fig. 1.**   Training network performance.

Figure 2 shows the residuals histogram, which shows the distribution of differences between the actual output and the MLP-predicted output. An important requirement for the prediction model is that the model is random as this signals that the model has effectively captured all the dynamics of the dataset, leaving only white noise residuals. The residual distribution appears to follow the Gaussian bell-shaped curve, proving the residuals are randomly distributed. From this observation, we can interpret that the model is unbiased, valid and acceptable. Regression analysis measures how closely the target matches the desired output. Based on the observation in Fig. 3, all datasets demonstrated desirable correlation coefficients (above 0.95), indicating a good model fit. At last, the trained model is used to predict the recent price and compare it to the real data. The Fig. 4 shows a good result since the error is pretty low (0–1%) compared to the real price. Therefore, the NARX model was accepted to be a valid model for predicting Bitcoin prices.

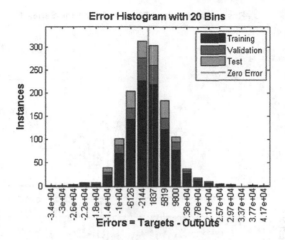

**Fig. 2.** Histogram of MLP residuals.

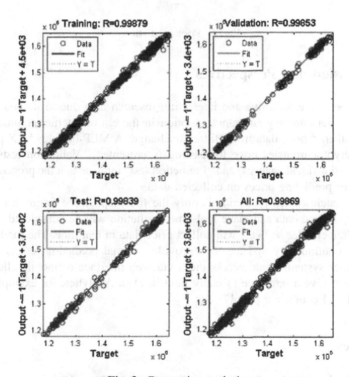

**Fig. 3.** Regression analysis.

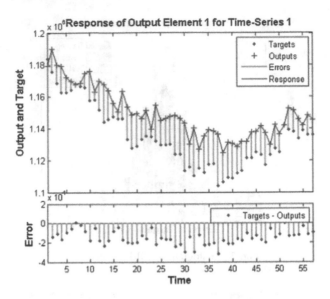

**Fig. 4.** Price prediction.

## 4 Conclusion and Perspectives

Cryptocurrencies are an active and interesting research area due to its potential as a substitute for fiat currency and rapid adoption in the era of internet commerce. This work has gathered price data from Bittrex exchange. A MLP-based NARX prediction model for cryptocurrencies price forecasting is presented. "Validation tests" (cross-correlation and residual analysis) and "Prediction test" indicate that the proposed model is suitable for predicting prices on collected data.

Crytocurrencies index prediction is only the first step. In the future, a model that could feed real-time data and make real-time prediction will be considered. Based on this research, a crawler software will collect price data in real time. The model will be learned and continuously updated then provide external prediction results as a web services. Other systems could access them via web interface or mobile clients. This paper also can give a reference to many field in Data Analytics, for example, Bioinformatics [15], Ecommerce [16, 17], etc.

## References

1. Nakamoto, S.: Bitcoin. A peer-to-peer electronic cash system (2008)
2. Reid, F., Harrigan, M.: An analysis of anonymity in the bitcoin system. In: Altshuler, Y., Elovici, Y., Cremers, A., Aharony, N., Pentland, A. (eds.) Security and Privacy in Social Networks, pp 197-223. Springer, New York (2013). https://doi.org/10.1007/978-1-4614-4139-7_10

3. Ma, W., Wang, Y., Dong, N.: Study on stock price prediction based on BP neural network. In: IEEE International Conference on Emergency Management and Management Sciences, 2010, pp. 57–60 (2010)
4. Cocianu, C.L., Grigoryan, H.: An artificial neural network for data forecasting purposes. Informatica Economica **19**(2), 34–45 (2015)
5. Sathe, S.S., Purandare, S.M., Pujari, P.D., et al.: Share market prediction using artificial neural network. Int. Educ. Res. J. **2**(3), 74–75 (2016)
6. McNally, S., Roche, J., Caton, S.: Predicting the price of Bitcoin using machine learning. In: 26th Euromicro International Conference on Parallel, Distributed and Network-based Processing (PDP), Cambridge, 2018, pp. 339–343 (2018). https://doi.org/10.1109/pdp2018. 2018.00060
7. Greaves, A., Au, B.: Using the Bitcoin transaction graph to predict the price of Bitcoin (2015)
8. Hafezi, R., Shahrabi, J., Hadavandi, E.: A bat-neural network multi-agent system (BNNMAS) for stock price prediction: case study of DAX stock price. Appl. Comput. **29**, 196–210 (2015)
9. Hong, K.S., Alan, R.D., Lingyao, I.Y.: Trading on Twitter: using social media sentiment to predict stock returns. Decis. Sci. (2016). https://doi.org/10.1111/deci.12229
10. Bittrex. https://support.bittrex.com/hc/en-us/articles/115003684411-ABOUT-US. Accessed 20 July 2019
11. Dataset. https://github.com/hungpd2/BittrexPredict. Accessed 20 July 2019
12. Zheng, X., Yang, X.: Command filter and universal approximator based backstepping control design for strict-feedback nonlinear systems with uncertainty. IEEE Trans. Autom. Control (2019). https://doi.org/10.1109/tac.2019.2929067
13. Bogoslovskii, I.A., Ermolenko, D.V., Stepanov, A.B., et al.: Implementation of universal neural network approximator on a ULP microcontroller for wavelet synthesis in electro-encephalography. In: IEEE Conference of Russian Young Researchers in Electrical and Electronic Engineering (EIConRus), Saint Petersburg and Moscow, Russia, 2019, pp. 1146–1151 (2019). https://doi.org/10.1109/eiconrus.2019.8657259
14. Zhang, W., Bai, Y.: Prediction of water consumption using NARX neural network based on grey relational analysis. In: International Conference on Sensing,Diagnostics, Prognostics, and Control (SDPC), Xi'an, China, 2018, pp. 471–475 (2018). https://doi.org/10.1109/sdpc. 2018.8664993
15. Hung, P.D., Hanh, T.D., Diep, V.T.: Breast cancer prediction using spark MLlib and ML packages. In: 5th International Conference on Bioinformatics Research and Applications (ICBRA 2018), pp. 52–59. ACM, New York (2018). https://doi.org/10.1145/3309129. 3309133
16. Tae, C.M., Hung, P.D.: Comparing ML algorithms on financial fraud detection. In: 2nd International Conference on Data Science and Information Technology (DSIT 2019), pp. 25–29. ACM, New York (2019). https://doi.org/10.1145/3352411.3352416
17. Hung, P.D., Lien, N.T.T., Ngoc, N.D.: Customer segmentation using hierarchical agglomerative clustering. In: 2nd International Conference on Information Science and Systems (ICISS 2019), pp. 33–37. ACM, New York (2019). https://doi.org/10.1145/ 3322645.3322677

# Application of Fuzzy Logic in University Suggestion System for Vietnamese High School Students

Phan Duy Hung[1(✉)] and Nguyen Cong Minh[2]

[1] FPT University, Hanoi, Vietnam
Hungpd2@fe.edu.vn
[2] Beeketing Company, Hanoi, Vietnam
mr.minh97@gmail.com

**Abstract.** Choosing which university to enter at the time of high school graduation is a life defining event for students, which will greatly affect their future career. If a student chooses a major that does not fit into his or her personality and interests, it may lead to poor results in college or work. High school students can be counseled or receive advice directly from parents and experienced people. However, not all students will be fortunate to receive accurate advice. This paper builds a system that provides complete information for high school students to choose their majors and universities based on a survey questionnaire. A fuzzy logic-based engine is used to suggest majors and appropriate schools for students.

**Keywords:** Fuzzy logic · University suggestion · Holland code · O*NET

## 1 Introduction

Education is an area of special interest in many countries as well as in Vietnam. The assessment of the current status of education in Vietnam points to a number of remaining issues, in which the followings deserve attention: the rate of students retaking the exam and courses in college is high; The percentage of graduates working in their studied majors is low [1, 2]. A number of undergraduate students did not choose their majors wisely due to several influencing factors. They may have chosen to follow the current society's trend, listen to their friends or try to obtain a college degree (in any subject) to meet family's expectation without caring about their abilities or interests.

In the current period, students get lots of advice from their predecessors, friends and even from the admissions departments of universities. Direct counseling can mislead students for the benefits of the consultant. A solution for software-based and automated knowledge-based consulting, popular for all students is a promising approach.

Survey in Vietnam shows two websites that have provided free counseling for students. "HuongNghiepViet.com" is a website where students can find lots of information about jobs and enrollments, career guidance and more [3]. "Huongnghiep-tuyensinh.com" is a similar website for users to find information about universities and

© Springer Nature Switzerland AG 2019
T. K. Dang et al. (Eds.): FDSE 2019, LNCS 11814, pp. 656–664, 2019.
https://doi.org/10.1007/978-3-030-35653-8_44

take the Holland quiz [4, 5]. Both solutions have not yet solved the important part, which is the university-major recommendation for students. They used Holland test, which can be further improved when applied to reality in this case. In addition, the website has not yet supported taking quiz on mobile devices, not yet displaying the survey results directly to participants, the information provided to students is also quite scattered, not focusing on the main content, etc.

Studying literature worldwide, we have also found some research on this issue.

The authors in [6] used fuzzy theory to propose career paths. This study proposes a system of career recommendations promoted by fuzzy logic. Using fuzzy logic helps students by making career recommendations based on career tests. Based on this method, potential careers can match the surveyer's given skills or abilities. Therefore, the system brings a better result for students when participating in the survey.

In [7], one system utilizes the multiple measurements from three-dimensional model, that is, preference, fuzzy logic, and influence. By integrating these measurements with the relative weighted set generated using Analysis Hierarchical Process decision system, a desire score of student related to each career oriented engineering stream is computed. The results of user based evaluation demonstrates that the proposed approach generates more satisfactory career based path recommendations as compared to other baseline methods.

The automatic Detection of Career Recommendation is also presented in [8]. The authors suggest a fuzzy approach and based on personality score to construct the system. A survey is conducted to test the accuracy of proposed method on 217 responses. The result shows the 74.35% candidates are satisfied with the recommended career and average rating for personality traits score was 3.58/5.

The above studies and solutions have shown that software systems that apply fuzzy logic to suggest majors and universities have brought good results. However, there is no application that applies this theory to Vietnamese students. Studies of fuzzy logic applications also always have an experimental gap of fuzzy rules and membership functions. These points can be adjusted on real data. In addition, a solution to provide complete and up-to-date information not only makes sense for students but also brings great business values. This paper presents a practical software system for students that has the following key features: The system supports Holland test for unregistered users and Fuzzy test for registered users. The paper proposes a new way to group fuzzy rules and testing membership functions. The application supports users both on the website and on mobile devices. The system is updated with information of the currently available majors and universities in Vietnam.

The remainder of the paper is organized as follows. Section 2 describes the system design. The algorithm and experiments for suggesting majors and universities is presented in Sect. 3. Finally, conclusions and perspectives are made in Sect. 4.

## 2 System Design

### 2.1 Architecture Overview

The system consists of 5 main modules: web application – front end, backend, mobile application, image storage, database (Fig. 1) and three main user groups: unregistered users (guests), registered users and system administrators.

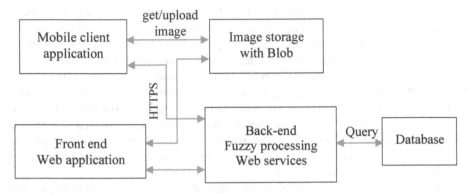

**Fig. 1.** Architecture overview.

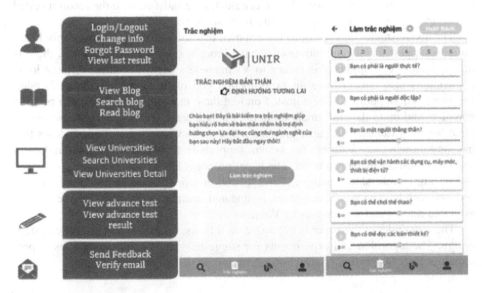

**Fig. 2.** Mobile application functions and interfaces for registered users.

Guests can only view information and take Hooland tests. Registered users can take Fuzzy tests. Users can also search information about universities on the website and receive feedback on the system. Administrators can manage the system, add, edit, delete users, questions, view statistics and reply to feedback, etc. On mobile devices, the system only supports guests and registered users but does not support administrators. Figure 2 is an example of the mobile application's functions and interfaces for registered users. Figure 3 shows the main functions and interfaces of the system administrator.

**Fig. 3.** The main functions and interfaces of the administrator.

## 3 University Recommendation

The university recommendation system is implemented by two methods and follows the steps shown in Fig. 4.

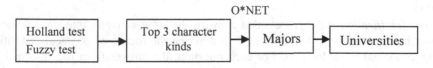

**Fig. 4.** Steps of recommendation algorithm for students about majors, universities.

## 3.1    Holland Test

John Holland's vocational/career choice theory proposes that people who choose to work in environments that are similar to their own personality type are more likely to experience success and satisfaction. Holland proposes six personality types matched with six work environments: Realistic, Investigative, Artistic, Social, Enterprising, and Conventional (also known as RIASEC) [4]. A detailed description of these personalities can be found in [9].

Holland test uses a total of 54 questions for 6 personality types (Table 1). Each question will have a choice of relevance to the user, each option will have a score and each score will be added to the total score of each personality type. The top 3 personality types will be deemed suitable for users, and used to find the most suitable career based on information from the O*NET free database, which contains hundreds of standardized and occupation specific descriptors on almost 1,000 occupations based on preferences and personality of each person [10].

**Table 1.**    Questions in the personality test.

| ID | Question | Score scale | Personality type |
|----|----------|-------------|------------------|
| Q1 | Are you practical? | 1–10 | Realistic |
| Q2 | Are you mechanically inclined? | 1–10 | Realistic |
| Q3 | Are you independent? | 1–10 | Realistic |
| Q4 | Can you solve electrical problems? | 1–10 | Realistic |
| ... | | | |
| Q54 | Like to work on electronic equipment? | 1–10 | Realistic |

## 3.2    Fuzzy Test

In binary logic we either have 1 or 0, True or False, Like or Dislike and many other forms of approval and denial. With fuzzy logic we include what is between the 1 and the 0. For example, when we ask about the height of a person, with binary logic the answer will probably be high or low. But with fuzzy logic, the answer may be high, slightly high, normal, slightly low or low. An overview of fuzzy algorithm is descripted in [11].

In this paper, the fuzzy test provides 54 questions for 6 personality types of Holland (Realistic, Investigative, Artistic, Social, Enterprising, Conventional). 9 questions for each type of personality are grouped into 3 types of questions: skills, characters and hobbies.

The *fuzzification* is the process that converts the input variables into some suitable values in the domain of discourse, and to describe the measured physical quantities using colloquial variables [11]. For each question, the answer from the student is a value between 1 and 10. This range are divided into three linguistic variables: "Weak", "Medium" and "Good". Figure 5 is an example of membership function in Question 1 (Q1). The x axis represents the universe of discourse [1, 10], whereas the y axis represents the degrees of membership in the [0, 1] interval.

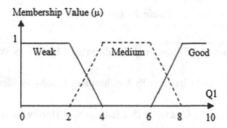

**Fig. 5.** Membership function for skill in Question 1 (Q1).

Similarly, the output for students to the each personality of career recommendation are divided into five linguistic variables which are "No", "LittleNo" "Maybe", "LittleYes" and "Yes".

***Fuzzy inference*** is a technique of formulating the mapping of fuzzy set input to an output function using the fuzzy logic. It can determine the degree to which the antecedent is satisfied for all rule. There are many types of fuzzy inference technique. This paper uses FAM as fuzzy inference because FAM will contain the knowledge from an expert that is believed to be able to react nearly any sort of control objectives [11]. The set of 27 rules is listed in Table 2.

**Table 2.** Rules.

| No | Rules |
|----|-------|
| 1 | IF Skill IS Week and Character IS Week and Hobby IS Week THEN Career IS No |
| 2 | IF Skill IS Week and Character IS Week and Hobby IS Medium THEN Career IS No |
| 3 | IF Skill IS Week and Character IS Week and Hobby IS Good THEN Career IS Maybe |
| 4 | IF Skill IS Week and Character IS Medium and Hobby IS Week THEN Career IS LitteNo |
| 5 | IF Skill IS Week and Character IS Medium and Hobby IS Medium THEN Career IS LitteNo |
| 6 | IF Skill IS Week and Character IS Medium and Hobby IS Good THEN Career IS Maybe |
| 7 | IF Skill IS Week and Character IS Good and Hobby IS Week THEN Career IS Maybe |
| 8 | IF Skill IS Week and Character IS Good and Hobby IS Medium THEN Career IS Maybe |
| 9 | IF Skill IS Week and Character IS Good and Hobby IS Good THEN Career IS LittleYes |
| 10 | IF Skill IS Medium and Character IS Week and Hobby IS Week THEN Career IS No |
| 11 | IF Skill IS Medium and Character IS Week and Hobby IS Medium THEN Career IS LitteNo |
| 12 | IF Skill IS Medium and Character IS Week and Hobby IS Good THEN Career IS Maybe |

(*continued*)

**Table 2.**  (*continued*)

| No | Rules |
|----|-------|
| 13 | IF Skill IS Medium and Character IS Medium and Hobby IS Week THEN Career IS LitteNo |
| 14 | IF Skill IS Medium and Character IS Medium and Hobby IS Medium THEN Career IS LitteNo |
| 15 | IF Skill IS Medium and Character IS Medium and Hobby IS Good THEN Career IS LittleYes |
| 16 | IF Skill IS Medium and Character IS Good and Hobby IS Week THEN Career IS Maybe |
| 17 | IF Skill IS Medium and Character IS Good and Hobby IS Medium THEN Career IS LittleYes |
| 18 | IF Skill IS Medium and Character IS Good and Hobby IS Good THEN Career IS Yes |
| 19 | IF Skill IS Good and Character IS Week and Hobby IS Week THEN Career IS Maybe |
| 20 | IF Skill IS Good and Character IS Week and Hobby IS Medium THEN Career IS Maybe |
| 21 | IF Skill IS Good and Character IS Week and Hobby IS Good THEN Career IS LittleYes |
| 22 | IF Skill IS Good and Character IS Medium and Hobby IS Week THEN Career IS Maybe |
| 23 | IF Skill IS Good and Character IS Medium and Hobby IS Medium THEN Career IS LittleYes |
| 24 | IF Skill IS Good and Character IS Medium and Hobby IS Good THEN Career IS Yes |
| 25 | IF Skill IS Good and Character IS Good and Hobby IS Week THEN Career IS LittleYes |
| 26 | IF Skill IS Good and Character IS Good and Hobby IS Medium THEN Career IS Yes |
| 27 | IF Skill IS Good and Character IS Good and Hobby IS Good THEN Career IS Yes |

Defuzzification is the last stage of fuzzy logic in which the fuzzy output variables are translated to the crisp value [11]. This study applied the center of area (COA) technique which is a central value in the universe of discourse and that is due to its complexity which may lead to a rather slow inference cycle.

From fuzzy test, the three highest scoring personalities will be notified to test participants. Each personality will be suitable for some majors and all majors will be filtered out from the database. From a database of majors in universities, the system continues to support the search for universities with appropriate major training.

### 3.3   Result Evaluation

The system is evaluated by interviewing students according to the questionnaire. For meaningful results, the study interviewed students who have completed the first year of university. Students are invited randomly from two universities in the two majors of information technology and economics. For each group of students, the interview results are divided according to their first year academic results (Good, Average, Fair and Weak). The statistics on the number of students who feel the current major is appropriate/the total number of students participating in the test is as follows (Tables 3 and 4 ):

**Table 3.** Statistics with Holland test.

|           | Good  | Average | Fair  | Weak |
|-----------|-------|---------|-------|------|
| IT        | 6/12  | 20/34   | 10/19 | 5/10 |
| Economics | 8/14  | 17/25   | 12/18 | 6/8  |

**Table 4.** Statistics with Fuzzy test.

|           | Good  | Average | Fair  | Weak |
|-----------|-------|---------|-------|------|
| IT        | 11/12 | 27/34   | 7/19  | 1/10 |
| Economics | 11/14 | 19/25   | 6/18  | 2/8  |

Obviously, among the students who have gone to college, the ratio of choosing the right major of the good/average students will be high. Conversely, the rate of choosing the right major of the fair/weak students will be low. Table 4 with the Fuzzy test has values that come closer to truth with proven students. That proves that Fuzzy test is much better than Holland test.

## 4  Conclusion and Perspectives

The article presented the university and specialized majors recommendation system for high school students. The system used fuzzy test, a method of improvement on Holland test and gave good results. The system supports both Website version and application on mobile devices with updated information.

The system is not only used to suggest and provide information to students but to software managers, university recruitment organizations as well, this system is an effective form to get more information and thereby helping students enroll more effectively. The application of fuzzy logic in information systems can also be applied to predictive problems, or used in recommendation system, etc.

## References

1. Vietnamnet news. https://english.vietnamnet.vn/fms/education/202012/what-s-behind-the-figure-of-200-000-unemployed-university-graduates-.html. Accessed 20 July 2019
2. Vietnamnet news. https://english.vietnamnet.vn/fms/education/203123/number-of-unemployed-university-graduates-in-vn-remains-high.html. Accessed 20 July 2019
3. Huongnghiepviet. https://www.huongnghiepviet.com/v3/trac-nghiem-huong-nghiep. Accessed 20 July 2019

4. Pacareerzone: Holland Code Reference. https://www.pacareerzone.org/guide/hollandcode. Accessed 20 July 2019
5. Huongnghieptuyensinh. http://huongnghieptuyensinh.com/. Accessed 20 July 2019
6. Razak, T.R., Hashim, M.A., Noor, N.M., et al.: Career path recommendation system for UiTM Perlis students using fuzzy logic. In: 5th International Conference on Intelligent and Advanced Systems (ICIAS), Kuala Lumpur, pp. 1–5 (2014). https://doi.org/10.1109/icias. 2014.6869553
7. Verma, P., Sood, S.K., Kalra, S.: Student career path recommendation in engineering stream based on three dimensional model. Comput. Appl. Eng. Educ. 25(4), 578–593 (2017)
8. Goyal, M., Krishnamurthi, R.: Automatic detection of career recommendation using fuzzy approach. J. Inf. Technol. Res. 11(4), 99–121 (2018)
9. Iofficecorp: The 6 Personality Types and How They Impact Your Career Choice. https:// www.iofficecorp.com/blog/six-personality-types-how-they-impact-your-career-choice. Accessed 20 July 2019
10. Onetcenter: About O*NET at O*NET Resource Center. https://www.onetcenter.org/ overview.html. Accessed 20 July 2019
11. Lofti, A.Z., Rafik, A.A.: Fuzzy Logic Theory and Applications. Part I (2018)

# Towards an Improvement of Complex Answer Retrieval System

Lam Ha[1] and Dang Tuan Nguyen[2(✉)]

[1] University of Information Technology, VNU-HCM,
Ho Chi Minh City, Vietnam
lamh.12@grad.uit.edu.vn
[2] Saigon University, Ho Chi Minh City, Vietnam
dangnt@sgu.edu.vn

**Abstract.** Traditional Information Retrieval (IR) systems mainly focus on answering questions about events or objects. However, there are various types of question forms that require IR systems to build complex answers from multiple data sources. Therefore, the idea of building IR systems that can create complex answers automatically, became the aim of TREC CAR 2017-2019. CAR (Complex Answer Retrieval) is one of many tracks, was hosted by TREC (The Text REtrieval Conference) where is a playground for the information retrieval community.

In this paper, we built an improved complex answer retrieval system based on the system model of Nogueira et al. [3]. Our method tries to increase the coverage of the retrieval task. Thereby, the performance of our system shows that the MAP, MRR, and NDCG evaluation scores are improved.

**Keywords:** Information retrieval · Complex answer retrieval · Retrieval algorithm

## 1 Introduction

In the traditional approaches, most Information Retrieval (IR) systems were built to retrieve data to answer queries which relate to events or objects. To answer these types of queries, the main purpose of IR systems is just to find simple pieces of data, mostly in unstructured form. However, we are facing with many kinds of queries that required comprehensive answers that are built from informative passages and are well organized. That became a challenge for modern IR systems and the goal of the TREC CAR 2017–2019. CAR (Complex Answer Retrieval) was introduced in 2017 and continue in 2019. The track focuses on developing systems which can automatically answer questions in a detailed, well-structured form, from a given corpus.

In this paper, our goal is to improve the system model of Nogueira et al. [3]. We chose Nogueira et al. [3] because their paper achieved the best result on 2017 test set in January 2019. At this time, TREC CAR only provides ranking results of 2017. By using BERT (Bidirectional Encoder Representations from Transformers) model [1] to reranking results their system improved the score significantly, but their retrieval module is not well constructed, leading to omissions when reranking results. Specifically, we aim to increase

© Springer Nature Switzerland AG 2019
T. K. Dang et al. (Eds.): FDSE 2019, LNCS 11814, pp. 665–672, 2019.
https://doi.org/10.1007/978-3-030-35653-8_45

the score of MAP, MRR and NDCG measures. To achieve this goal, we need to find a method which can build complex answers better than Nogueira et al. [3]. Our idea is to find the most related passages to each given query, as much as possible, then do reranking passages to have the right order. Our proposed method focuses on maximizing the number of retrieval passages for each given query.

# 2 Related Work

## 2.1 TREC CAR 2017: Contextualized PACRR

The TREC CAR 2017 target is to build the answer for input query by synthesizing appropriate passages from many sources. Sean MacAvaney et al. [2] submitted a system that achieved the highest scores in TREC CAR 2017. They use a variation of the Position-Aware Convolutional Recurrent Relevance Matching (PACRR) deep neural model to reranking passages. They vectorize input queries based on position or frequency of terms in heading chain. By using this statistic method, they showed improved result but their approach only focuses on query formulation ignore the context of passages.

## 2.2 TREC CAR 2018: New York University at TREC 2018 Complex Answer Retrieval Track

The aim of the TREC CAR 2018 is to complete complex answers in TREC CAR 2017 by evaluating their quality and quantity of information. Nogueira et al. [4] built a system based on reinforcement learning model by proposing the Learning to Coordinate Multiple Reinforcement Learning Agents for Diverse Query Reformulation method. In their system, each agent is trained on the different sub-dataset. These authors use an aggregator to score queries. The advantage of this model is that it can process multiple query reformulation tasks with different reformulation formulas at the same time. They proposed a new method of query reformulation by applying the reinforcement learning, but their method does not exploit the context of passages.

## 2.3 Passage Re-ranking with BERT

Nogueira et al. [3] introduced the Passage re-ranking with BERT (Bidirectional Encoder Representations from Transformers) method. These authors built a system model based on a Question-Answering pipeline that includes three modules: retrieval module, reranking module, top module.

The first component is module retrieval. This component retrieves data from a given corpus, passages that are highly similar and related to a "topic" (i.e. "a query"). This module must retrieve relevant paragraphs as much as possible. The second component is module reranking which sorts retrieval passages to form a unique coherent passage (i.e. a complex answer). This module must analyze the semantic and contextual relationship between passages. These authors used BERT to re-rank the passages. The third component is module top, which returns top 10 or 20 best passages per topic. Their method uses BERT as their reranking, BERT is a pre-training contextual representations model which obtains state-of-the-art results in early 2019. This helps Nogueira et al. [3] to get a higher result than the first team in 2017 was Sean MacAvaney et al. [2] but their retrieval module only uses the standard BM25 algorithm with no further evaluations, leading to deficiencies that we focused on improving.

# 3  Method

We mentioned in previous sections that the system of Nogueira et al. [3] lacks suitable evaluation methods for retrieval stage. This can lead to deficiencies in passage reranking stage, because the number of potentially relevant passages may be missed by the retrieval phase does not return all possible results. We proposed a retrieval system model which includes two main components. The first module called retrieval; the second module called reranking. Our retrieval module is designed to evaluate the coverage of retrieval algorithms in order to find the most suitable algorithm for a question-answering system.

## 3.1  Module Retrieval

We realized that the more passages related to a given query module retrieval can find, the more scores module reranking has. Based on this assumption, we try to increase the coverage of the retrieval module.

In the system of Nogueira et al. [3], the retrieval module only uses BM25 algorithm. However, we argue that it is possible to use a better algorithm than BM25. To examine our assumptions, we compare six algorithms: BM25, BM25 + RM3, BM25 + AX, QL, QL + RM3, QL + AX by Anserini[1] tool. These algorithms are briefly described as follows: BM25 was built based on binary independence model, RM3 was built based on probabilistic relevance model, AX randomly selects several documents from the reranking pool, QL was built based on a language model.

The algorithms will be tested based on two criteria: accuracy and coverage. We used TREC CAR 2017 dataset: benchmarkY1test (v2.0) [5]. To compare the accuracy of the six algorithms, we use the trec_eval tool which was provided by TREC CAR 2017 [9] with three evaluation measures: MAP, MRR, and NDCG. The results are given in Table 1. Best results are in bold.

**Table 1.** The accuracy of six algorithms according to MAP, MRR, NDCG measurements

| Mesaurement | BM25 | BM25 + RM3 | BM25 + AX | QL | QL + RM3 | QL + AX |
|---|---|---|---|---|---|---|
| MAP | **15.28** | 12.7 | 13.42 | 13.53 | 10.65 | 10.54 |
| MRR | **22.94** | 19.03 | 19.43 | 19.89 | 15.77 | 15.54 |
| NDCG | **27.56** | 25.08 | 26.07 | 25.37 | 22.52 | 22.42 |

---

[1] Anserini. https://github.com/castorini/anserini.

In Table 1, we found that BM25 algorithm has the best results on all three measures of accuracy. Because the trec_eval tool of the TREC CAR 2017 [9] only measures accuracy, we built an algorithm to evaluate the coverage of the six algorithms mentioned above. This algorithm will check the number of missing answers for each query. The less the missing answer is, the higher the algorithm's coverage.

The steps in Python program to evaluate the coverage are:

```
qrelDict = convertToDict("test.pages.cbor-
hierarchical.qrels") // Line 1
predictDict = convertToDict("predict.run") // Line 2
missingQueries = findDiff(qrelDict, predictDict) //
Line 3
```

Explanation:

1. The first line calls the **convertToDict** function with a parameter, called test.pages. cbor-hierarchical.qrels which contains pairs of (query-document) results, provided by TREC CAR 2017 [5].
   This function returns a dictionary called **qrelDict** which each key is a query and value is a collection of passages.
2. The second line calls the **convertToDict** function with a parameter, called predict. run which contains predictions (query-documents) returned by six chosen algorithms. This file is changed according to each algorithm.
   This function returns a dictionary called **qredictDict** which each key is a query and value is a collection of passages.
3. The third line calls **findDiff** function has two inputs, type of dictionary, named **qrelDict** and **predictDict**.
   This function returns the number of queries that have an empty passage list or missing passages, compared to test.pages.cbor-hierarchical.qrels. Lower is better.

Next, we compare the coverage of these six algorithms. The results are given in Table 2. Best results are in bold.

**Table 2.** The number of queries that are lost answers. The smaller the number of missing queries, the higher the coverage.

| Missing queries | BM25 | BM25 + RM3 | BM25 + AX | QL | QL + RM3 | QL + AX |
|---|---|---|---|---|---|---|
| benchmarkY1test | 1162 | 1169 | **1097** | 1197 | 1204 | 1166 |

In Table 2, we found the BM25 + AX has a lower number of missing queries than BM25 was 65 queries, so BM25 + AX has highest coverage. Therefore, we will use BM25 + AX for our module retrieval.

The beta parameter of BM25 algorithm is set as 0.4 by default in Anserini. This means the number of retrieval passages depends on the similarity score between the query and passage, it must be greater than a certain threshold. The Axiomatic algorithm reformulates a given query by finding expansion terms. Using BM25 with Axiomatic (BM25 + AX) increases the number of retrieval passages, moreover it only applies query expansion for query that reached the specified BM25's threshold.

## 3.2  Module Reranking

The responsibility of the module reranking is to reranking retrieved passages which returned by the module retrieval. Based on Nogueira et al. [3], we also built module reranking with BERT model. BERT is pre-trained language representation model, but its representation is contextual representations it is different from other context-free models.

## 3.3  Proposed Model Architecture

Based on Nogueira et al. [3], we propose a system architecture, called LD architecture, presented in Fig. 1.

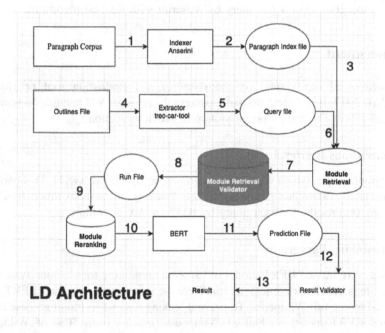

**Fig. 1.** The LD architecture model for complex answer retrieval system

In Fig. 1:

1. Paragraph corpus is indexed by Anserini.
2. The result of the first step is a paragraph index file.
3. The paragraph index file will be the input of the module retrieval
4. Tool trec-car-tool [8] of TREC CAR 2017 is used to extract the queries.
5. The result of the fourth step is a query file.
6. The query file will also be the input of the module retrieval.
7. The module retrieval validator selects the best coverage algorithm for retrieving top 1000 per query with Anserini. It also ensures queries in correct input format.
8. The result of the seventh step is a run file.
9. The run file will be the input of module reranking.
10. The pre-trained model BERT [3] is used to reranking results.
11. The result of the tenth step is a prediction file.
12. The prediction file is validated according to TREC CAR 2017's format.
13. The final result is evaluated by tool trec_eval of TREC CAR 2017 [9].

Our proposed architecture in Fig. 1, we add a special component called module retrieval validator. Its purpose is to improve the system of Nogueira et al. [3]. This component has four functions. First, it finds the algorithm has the best coverage in six algorithms (see Sect. 3.1). Second, it selects the algorithm has the best coverage. Last, it retrieves top 1000 results per query by Anserini with the best algorithm.

## 4   Experiment

We experimented our system on the data set and evaluation tool provided by TREC CAR 2017. It includes two parts: paragraphs retrieval and paragraphs reranking. Our model follows by the proposed system in previous section.

### 4.1   Paragraphs Retrieval

The paragraph corpus which we use is paragraphCorpus.v2.0.tar.xz [7]. This paragraph corpus has nearly 30 million passages. We use Anserini tool to index this corpus. Next, we get top 1000 results for each query by BM25 + AX algorithm.

### 4.2   Re-ranking Paragraphs

We used the pre-trained BERT model of [3] as the reranking tool for our system with the input file is benchmark_bm25_ax.run. Because the official pretrained BERT model was trained by the full Wikipedia. To prevent leaking data when training, these authors pre-trained BERT model on half of Wikipedia (articles from 50% of Wikipedia), named train.v2.0.tar.xz [6] which was provided by TREC CAR 2017. The paragraphs are arranged based on descending relevance with the given query.

## 4.3    Results

We compare the results of our system with the system of Nogueira et al. [3] by the trec_eval evaluation tool provided by TREC CAR 2017 [9]. The results are given in Table 3. Best results are in bold.

**Table 3.** Result of comparison our system with the system of Nogueira et al. [3] by data set called benchmarkY1-test.v2.0.tar.xz [5] and evaluate by trec_eval tool [9].

|                       | MAP   | MRR   | NDCG  |
|-----------------------|-------|-------|-------|
| Nogueira et al. [3]   | 33.56 | 47.87 | 45.13 |
| Our system            | **35.08** | **50.04** | **47.28** |

## 4.4    Discussion

Table 3 shows the scores was increased from 1.5% to 2%. It proves the effect of the improvement of module retrieval. We achieved this result by two following methods: reducing the number of missing answers and reducing the number of unanswered queries. This is the result that we drew after the process of researching and implementing the system of Nogueira et al. [3].

**Reducing the Number of Missing Answers**
We expect to get 1000 passages for each given query but the system of Nogueira et al. [3] not every query has enough 1000 passages. Moreover, we want to ensure the coverage of these queries which means the number of relevant passages in these 1000 passages. We solved this problem by using the BM25 + AX algorithm. In Table 2, this algorithm has the highest coverage and it also ensures the number of passages is always 1000 per query.

We need to note at retrieval stage we do not evaluate results based on the order in which they are returned. The reranking module will reorder passages most accurately. By increasing the number of answers and the percent of correct answers in these answers (the coverage), will help us achieve the highest possible score.

**Reducing the Number of Unanswered Queries**
We discovered 43 queries that are unanswered on the total of 2254 queries taken from test.pages.cbor-hierarchical.qrels [5]. These 43 queries contain 'enwiki:' string. This made Anserini fails to retrieve passages. Therefore, the results for these queries are empty. We solved this problem by removing 'enwiki:' and run Anserini with new queries again. Now those 43 queries contain relevant passages for input of reranking task, this will increase our final scores.

## 5    Conclusion

In this paper, we present an improvement to build a better complex answer retrieval system than the system of Nogueira et al. [3]. We implemented two methods to increase the coverage of retrieval tasks in our system model: reducing the number of missing answers and reducing the number of unanswered queries. Our improvement impacts the coverage enhancement of the retrieval task allowed our system to increase the score of MAP, MRR and NDCG measurements.

In this research, we do not focus on reranking passages task. We only tried to increase the coverage that is enough to improve the results of our system in comparison with the system of Nogueira et al. [3].

# References

1. Devlin, J., Chang, M.-W., Lee, K., Toutanova, K.: BERT: pre-training of deep bidirectional transformers for language understanding. arXiv:1810.04805v2 (2019)
2. MacAvaney, S., Yates, A., Hui, K.: Contextualized PACRR for complex answer retrieval. In: TREC CAR 2017 (2017)
3. Nogueira, R., Cho, K.: Passage Re-ranking with BERT. arXiv:1901.04085 (2019)
4. Nogueira, R., Cho, K.: New York University at TREC 2018 complex answer retrieval track. In: TREC CAR 2018 (2018)
5. benchmarkY1-test.v2.0.tar.xz. http://trec-car.cs.unh.edu/datareleases/v2.0/benchmarkY1-test.v2.0.tar.xz. Accessed 08 May 2019
6. train.v2.0.tar.xz. http://trec-car.cs.unh.edu/datareleases/v2.0/train.v2.0.tar.xz. Accessed 08 May 2019
7. paragraphCorpus.v2.0.tar.xz. http://trec-car.cs.unh.edu/datareleases/v2.0/paragraphCorpus.v2.0.tar.xz. Accessed 08 May 2019
8. trec-car-tool. https://github.com/TREMA-UNH/trec-car-tools-java. Accessed 08 May 2019
9. trec_eval. https://github.com/usnistgov/trec_eval. Accessed 08 May 2019

# Keyword-Search Interval-Query Dynamic Symmetric Searchable Encryption

Huy-Hoang Chung-Nguyen, Viet-An Pham, Dinh-Hieu Hoang,
and Minh-Triet Tran[✉]

Faculty of Information Technology, Software Engineering Lab,
University of Science, VNU-HCM, Ho Chi Minh City, Vietnam
{cnhhoang,pvan,hdhieu}@apcs.vn, tmtriet@fit.hcmus.edu.vn

**Abstract.** Searchable Symmetric Encryption (SSE) enables clients to securely store data on untrusted server while keeping the ability to search and update over the encrypted data efficiently. For practical purposes, we also need several additional properties to make our search function more versatile. In this paper, we introduce an extension type of SSE which we called Keyword-search Interval Dynamic SSE (KIDSSE). In KIDSSE we can search for encrypted files containing a keyword that occurs in a queried range. We also construct a solution for KIDSSE and show that our scheme maintains all important security properties such as forward privacy, backward privacy.

**Keywords:** Searchable Symmetric Encryption · Range query · Forward privacy · Backward privacy

## 1 Introduction

To outsource data to an untrusted server, sensitive data like messages, personal information or secret documents have to be encrypted. However, encrypted files cannot be searched through traditional means. Searchable Encryption was proposed by Song et al. [11] to solve this problem. This not only enables the client to search for any encrypted keywords but also hides the searched content from the server. Since then, SSE continuously gains attention from researchers.

However, the original SSE schemes do not allow the users to add or delete files without re-encrypting the whole database. This led to the proposal of Dynamic SSE that can add and delete files efficiently [8]. There are two important security properties that a practical Dynamic SSE scheme must have: forward privacy and backward privacy that later we will introduce in Sect. 3.

In many situations, there are additional search properties, like range query, which must be attained. Before our construction, a notable number of range query SSE schemes have been proposed [1,9]. However, these range query SSE are different from ours. Their solutions favor in creating an index for the relational database. Then in the searching step, the server only needs to return all

© Springer Nature Switzerland AG 2019
T. K. Dang et al. (Eds.): FDSE 2019, LNCS 11814, pp. 673–680, 2019.
https://doi.org/10.1007/978-3-030-35653-8_46

the files that lie within the range. In our approach, we request an additional keyword $w$ and require the untrusted server to find the appropriate files containing the keyword $w$ where its identifier is within the queried range. We believe our modification of the original range query is important in many real world applications. For example, when client wants to outsource encrypted medical data and search for a type of disease in a range of years only; or when a third party wants to check important transactions of government bank in an interval of time.

**Our Contribution.** We define a new type of SSE which we called Keyword-search Interval-query Dynamic Searchable Symmetric Encryption (KIDSSE) that searches for a keyword in a determined range. Our ideal is based on $\Sigma o\varphi o\varsigma$ from Raphael Bost et al. [2] that uses trapdoor permutation and modifies it to match our problem. For this new type of SSE, we also propose a novel solution that can achieve all the original security criteria in the newly published works [2,3,12].

## 2    Related Work

Song, Wagner and Perrig [11] introduced Searchable Encryption in 2000 where their search algorithm runtime is linear to the database size. Since then, SSE has been received a lot of attention from all over the world. Curtmola et al. [5] were the first to define security definition for SSE and proposed a scheme that achieves complexity linear to the number of returned files, which is the most optimal runtime. They also introduced some ideal allowed leakage function like the search pattern and access pattern.

Six years later, Kamara et al. [8] constructed security definition for Dynamic SSE, SSE that supports update queries like add or remove files without re-encrypting the whole database. However, Kamara construction does not achieve forward privacy. To achieve forward privacy, Raphael Bost [2] proposed a new construction that uses inverted index with trapdoor permutation. In the following year, Bost et al. [3] achieved backward privacy by using puncturable encryption. Sun et al. [12] also inherited the idea of puncturable encryption in 2018 and proposed new encryption scheme puncturable symmetric encryption (SPE) to construct backward secure SSE. However, the disadvantage of puncturable encryption is that the key-size increases drastically as deleting operations executed.

## 3    Notations and Preliminaries

Throughout this paper, we denote $n$ as the number of added files; $\mathbf{F}_n$ as the $n$-th file; $\mathbf{EF}_n$ as the encrypted version of $\mathbf{F}_n$; $m_i$ as the number of words in file $\mathbf{F}_i$; $\bot$ denotes *null* or *empty*; $\lambda$ as the security parameter. That means, unless specified explicitly, the keys used in SSE scheme are $\lambda$-bit in length.

We follow the standard definitions of symmetric encryption, pseudo random function (PRF), random oracle model and negligible function from Dan Boneh and Victor Shoup [6].

We also use Bost's definition of trapdoor permutation [2] and denote $\pi(k_s, x)$ as the trapdoor permutation with secret key $k_s$ and $x$ belongs to $\{0,1\}^\lambda$. Its inverse is $\pi^{-1}(k_p, y)$ where $k_p$ is the public key related with $k_s$ and $y$ belongs to $\{0,1\}^\lambda$. For all $x$, we have $x = \pi^{-1}(k_p, \pi(k_s, x))$.

Lastly, we follow many popular SSE works that assume the untrusted server is running in honest-but-curious environment [2,3,5,8,12].

## 3.1  Symmetric Searchable Encryption

Informally we view the problem SSE as follows. The database is an array of files $\mathbf{DB} = (f_1, f_2, ..., f_n)$ and within $f_i$ consists of multiple words $\mathbf{w} = (w_1, w_2, ..., w_m)$. These files are encrypted and stored on an untrusted server. Later when the client issues a search request on keyword $w$, the server must return all the encrypted files that contain $w$. Because the server only holds the encrypted database, he must have some algorithm in order to correctly return the appropriate files. It is noticed that the client should map the keyword $w$ into meaningless data before querying because giving the plaintext $w$ to the server would leak the meaning of the query. In this paper, we call the mapping technique as trapdoor generation.

The Dynamic Symmetric Searchable Encryption scheme is comprised of one algorithm **Setup** and two protocols **Search** and **Update**. The **Setup** algorithm is run by the client to setup keys for the scheme. The **Search** protocol consists of multiple steps between client and server when the client request for a search on some keywords. The **Update** protocol is comprised of 2 types of update: add new file and delete an existed file. Depending on which update protocol, the encrypted database on the untrusted server will be modified based on the SSE scheme.

Since this is the short version of this work, we follow Curtmola et al. [4] for the formal definition, correctness and security properties of Symmetric Searchable Encryption and do not present it here.

## 3.2  Forward Privacy

Informally, a SSE scheme achieves forward privacy if the past update queries do not leak any information about whether the newly added file contains a previously searched keyword or not. For example, the client adds a file $\mathbf{F}$ containing a keyword $w$ that has been searched before. The server should not know that $w$ exists inside the new file $\mathbf{F}$.

## 3.3  Backward Privacy

To have backward privacy in Dynamic SSE, we must prevent the adversary from gaining knowledge of deleted files from new queries. For example if there exists deleted file $\mathbf{F}$ containing a word $w$ that has never been queried, in the future when client searches on $w$, it is expected to prevent the server from knowing that $w$ was once contained inside $\mathbf{F}$.

# 4  Our Contribution

For clarity and easier to read, we first describe the definition and the security of KIDSSE, then we propose our solution in the next section.

## 4.1  Brief Description

Keyword-search Interval Dynamic SSE continues to use the model of the original Symmetric Searchable Encryption in Sect. 3.1 but modifies the **Search** protocol, **Setup** and **Update** remains the same.

In the **Search** protocol, when the client issues a search request, his first step is to choose a range $[L, R]$ where $L \leq R$, then he chooses a keyword $w$ he wants to search, finally he generates a trapdoor vector $\mathbf{T}$ that represents the keyword $w$ for the range $[L, R]$ and gives $(\mathbf{T}, L, R)$ to the server. The server when receiving $(\mathbf{T}, L, R)$ must find a list of result identifiers $\mathbf{R}_{w,L,R} = (id_1, id_2, ..., id_r)$ such that when returned to the client, for every $i$ we have $w \in \mathbf{F}_{id_i}$ and $L \leq id_i \leq R$.

## 4.2  Security

In previous SSE works [4,8], the authors defined some allowed leakage information. In this section, we also define the allowed leakage information $\mathcal{L} = (\mathcal{L}^{Stp}, \mathcal{L}^{Srch}, \mathcal{L}^{Updt})$ for KIDSSE in **Setup**, **Search**, **Update** protocols.

**Setup Leakage.** The client generates some keys and keypairs for later usage in **Search** and **Update** protocol. Because of that, the leakage of setup phase is the public keys (if there is any) that the client wants to share to the server. Formally, $\mathcal{L}^{Stp} = \mathbf{PK}$ where $\mathbf{PK}$ is a vector of public keys.

**Search Leakage.** Let us define $\mathbf{Q}$ as the search queries issued so far by the client such that the $i$-th query is $\mathbf{Q}_i = (\mathbf{T}_i, L_i, R_i)$; let $\mathbf{R}_i$ be the result of $\mathbf{Q}_i$ where its content is $\mathbf{R}_i = (id_{i,1}, id_{i,2}, ..., id_{i,r_i})$. The allowed leakage $\mathcal{L}^{Srch}$ in KIDSSE is comprised of a search pattern and access pattern.

The access pattern represents the leakage for the result values of the search queries. That is, for each query we want to leak only the existence of keyword $w$ inside the files within the interval $[L, R]$ and none elsewhere.

The search pattern represents the leakage in the query parameter from the client. For example, let there be 2 search queries $i$ and $j$ with the same keyword $w$ where $i \neq j$ and $\mathbf{Q}_i = (\mathbf{T}_i, L_i, R_i)$ and $\mathbf{Q}_j = (\mathbf{T}_j, L_j, R_j)$. The search pattern consists of multiple levels of security:

- Perfect security: when analyzing 2 different queries $i$ and $j$, it is very hard for the server to deduce $\mathbf{T}_i$ and $\mathbf{T}_j$ to be the same keyword $w$. In this setup, the client perfectly hides the search queries and can be secure against many inference attack types [7,10].
- Weak security: when analyzing 2 different queries $i$ and $j$, the server can easily deduce $\mathbf{Q}_i$ and $\mathbf{Q}_j$ as the same search keyword $w$ if and only if the queried range $[L_i, R_i]$ intersects with $[L_j, R_j]$ at some point.

**Update Leakage.** The update leakage consists of leakage of add file protocol and delete file protocol. The add file protocol leaks $n$ as the number of added files and the size of all the files even the deleted ones. The delete file protocol leaks the deleted files that was issued by the client.

# 5    Our KIDSSE Scheme

## 5.1    Scheme Outline

Our scheme consists of 7 polynomial-time algorithms (KeyGen, Enc, Dec, Trpdr, CreateIndex, SearchToken, Search).

- $(\mathbf{SK}, \mathbf{K}) \leftarrow$ KeyGen$(1^{\lambda_1}, 1^{\lambda_2})$: is a probabilistic algorithm that uses 2 security parameters $\lambda_1$ and $\lambda_2$ to generate a vector of secret keys $\mathbf{SK}$ for encryption/decryption and a vector of keypairs $\mathbf{K}$ for trapdoor generation.
- $\mathbf{EF}_n \leftarrow$ Enc$(sk, \mathbf{F}_n)$: is a probabilistic algorithm that encrypts the file $\mathbf{F}_n$.
- $\mathbf{F}_n \leftarrow$ Dec$(sk, \mathbf{EF}_n)$: is the reverse algorithm of Enc.
- $t_n \leftarrow$ Trpdr$(\mathbf{K}, n, w)$: is a deterministic algorithm that illustrates how keyword $w$ got transformed into trapdoor $t_n$ for file $\mathbf{F}_n$.
- $\mathbf{I}_n \leftarrow$ CreateIndex$(\mathbf{K}, n, \mathbf{F}_n)$: is a deterministic algorithm that illustrates the process to create encrypted index $\mathbf{I}_n$ from file $\mathbf{F}_n$. The encrypted index $\mathbf{I}_n$ will be used in search algorithm.
- $\mathbf{T} \leftarrow$ SearchToken$(\mathbf{K}, w, L, R)$: is a deterministic algorithm that is called by the client in the search protocol. $\mathbf{T}$ will be given to the server for him to run algorithm and return the correct files.
- $\mathbf{R}_{w,L,R} \leftarrow$ Search$(\mathbf{T}, \mathbf{I}_{L,...,R}, L, R)$: be a deterministic algorithm run by the server in search protocol that uses $\mathbf{T}$ to return the files in the range $[L, R]$ that contains the queried keyword.

## 5.2    Details of the Scheme in Protocols Point of View

In the following paragraphs, we describe our scheme in the perspective of 3 protocols (**Setup, Search, Update**) which uses 7 algorithms mentioned above.

**Setup Protocol.** First, the client creates $(\mathbf{SK}, \mathbf{K}) \leftarrow$ KeyGen$(1^{\lambda_1}, 1^{\lambda_2})$ where $\mathbf{SK}$ consists of 3 secret keys $sk, sk_1, sk_2$ and is generated by randomizing $\lambda_1$ bits. Formally, $sk \xleftarrow{\$} \{0,1\}^{\lambda_1}$, $sk_1 \xleftarrow{\$} \{0,1\}^{\lambda_1}$, $sk_2 \xleftarrow{\$} \{0,1\}^{\lambda_1}$. $\mathbf{K}$ consists of 2 keypairs $\mathbf{k}_1 = (k_{1,s}; k_{1,p})$ and $\mathbf{k}_2 = (k_{2,s}; k_{2,p})$ where $\mathbf{k}_{i,s}$ is the secret component and $\mathbf{k}_{i,p}$ is the public component. The keypairs are generated by creating trapdoor permutation keypairs with $\lambda_2$-bit length. Finally, the client must assure that the $ids$ of the files given to the server are incremental. Hence, $id$ starts from $-1$ and $n$ starts from 0 when no file has been added.

**Add File Protocol.** Our scheme main idea is when client needs to add a new file $\mathbf{F}_n$ to the server, not only the client gives server the encrypted file $\mathbf{EF}_n$ but client also creates an encrypted index $\mathbf{I}_n$ for that file. The server in searching protocol will use that encrypted index $\mathbf{I}_n$ to check whether a trapdoor $t$ exists inside file $\mathbf{F}_n$. After the client encrypts the file and creates the index, he increases $n$ by 1 and gives the encrypted file $\mathbf{EF}_n$ and the encrypted index $\mathbf{I}_n$ to the server.

*Encrypt File.* Because the searching step does not make use of the encrypted file $\mathbf{EF}_n$, it is trivial to encrypt the file using a symmetric encryption algorithm. Therefore, Enc and Dec algorithms in this case are: Enc : $\mathbf{EF}_n \leftarrow$ SE.enc$(sk, \mathbf{F_n})$ and Dec : $\mathbf{F}_n \leftarrow$ SE.dec$(sk, \mathbf{EF}_n)$.

*Create Index.* In this section we use a data structure called **map**. In many programming language, **map** is a data structure back-boned by red-black tree. Because of this, all of this data structure's operations in both average and worst cases, are $O(\log_2 n)$ with $n$ as the current number of elements in the data structure. Space complexity for map is $O(n)$.

First, let $\mathbf{I}_n$ be an empty map. For each word $w$ in $\mathbf{F}_n$:

1. $t_n \leftarrow$ Trpdr$(\mathbf{K}, n, w)$.
2. Check if $t_n$ exists inside $\mathbf{I}_n$. If so, repeat choosing random value for $t_n$ until $t_n$ does not exist inside $\mathbf{I}_n$. After this step, we call $t_n$ as *garbage data* if $t_n \neq$ Trpdr$(\mathbf{K}, n, w)$.
3. Mark $t_n$ as existed inside the map $\mathbf{I}_n$. In code, we usually write $\mathbf{I}_n[t_n] = True$.

*Trapdoor Generation.* Formally, we define: $t_n \leftarrow$ Trpdr$(\mathbf{K}, n, w)$ as:

1. Let $temp_{0,1} \leftarrow$ PRF$(sk_1, w)$.
2. Let $temp_{0,2} \leftarrow$ PRF$(sk_2, w)$.
3. Let $temp_{i,1} \leftarrow \pi(k_{1,s}, temp_{i-1,1})$, calculate up until reach $temp_{n,1}$.
4. Let $temp_{i,2} \leftarrow \pi(k_{2,s}, temp_{i-1,2})$, calculate up until reach $temp_{n,2}$.
5. Let $t_n \leftarrow temp_{n,1} \oplus temp_{n,2}$.

## Search Protocol

*Client-Side.* The client issues a search token $\mathbf{T}$ as: $\mathbf{T} \leftarrow$ SearchToken$(\mathbf{K}, w, L, R)$ where $\mathbf{T} = (temp_{R,1}, temp_{R,2})$ which is generated by the trapdoor generation algorithm above. Then, client gives $\mathbf{T} = (temp_{R,1}, temp_{R,2})$ to server.

*Server-Side.* With the knowledge of $k_{1,p}$ and $k_{2,p}$, the server can calculate every $temp_{i,1}$ and $temp_{i,2}$ by using the reverse trapdoor permutation: $temp_{i-1,1} \leftarrow \pi^{-1}(k_{1,p}, temp_{i,1})$ and $temp_{i-1,2} \leftarrow \pi^{-1}(k_{2,p}, temp_{i,2})$. Then for each $i$, the server can calculate $t_i$ as $t_i \leftarrow temp_{i,1} \oplus temp_{i,2}$ and checks whether $t_i$ exists inside the map $\mathbf{I}_i$.

Finally, the server returns every $\mathbf{EF}_i$ such that $L \leq i \leq R$ and $t_i$ exists inside $\mathbf{I}_i$ to the client.

*Client-Side.* When receiving the encrypted file **EF** from the server, the client recovers original file **F** by running Dec algorithm.

**Delete Protocol.** In this step, the client requests a single variable $i$ to indicate which file for the server to delete. The server will delete that data along with the encrypted index inside its database/hard drive. When the client issues a search query that hits a deleted file, because that data at that index has been deleted, the server can simply ignore and move on to the next file of the search protocol.

### 5.3  Security Analysis

**Forward Privacy.** Since our scheme only enables the server to move backward to files with smaller identifier, and all previous queries have the trapdoor identifiers smaller than the newly added file, the information about the newly added file is only leaked when the server knows the trapdoor for that very file, which is impossible. Therefore, we have proved forward privacy.

**Backward Privacy.** Because all data associated with deleted document, consisting of the encrypted document itself and its *index* map are removed after the delete protocol without a trace, it is obvious that the server cannot check whether a new keyword $w$ exists inside a deleted document or not. Hence, we achieve backward privacy in the honest-but-curious server environment. However, it is notable that without the honest-but-curious assumption, the attacker can easily clone the database without the awareness of the client. The cloned data can be used to further analyze to break the backward privacy.

**KIDSSE Search Leakage.** Although our scheme does not meet our KIDSSE requirements for the search pattern and access pattern in $\mathcal{L}^{\text{Srch}}$, the scheme however guarantees left-sided access pattern. In the search protocol, the untrusted server when receiving $\mathbf{T}_R$ can use $\pi^{-1}$ and the public keys $k_{1,p}$ and $k_{2,p}$ to get every $t_i$ where $i \leq R$. Therefore, he can even check the existence of keyword $w$ in files with identifier less than $L$. However, the client only supplies trapdoor $t_R$ at identifier $R$, which makes it impossible for the server to deduce further information in the right side of $R$. We call the access leakage in this case as left-sided access pattern and we conclude that our scheme only guarantees left-sided access pattern.

## 6  Conclusion

In this paper, we consider Keyword-search Interval-query SSE problem for the first time to improve the practicality for SSE. We also consider leakage functions and propose our scheme for this problem, which attained all the important properties of SSE: SSE security, forward secured, backward secured. Because our work does not attain security for search pattern and only achieves left-sided access pattern, this opens a new problem for future researches to discover a new scheme that achieves two-sided access pattern.

**Acknowledgement.** This research is supported by research funding from Advanced Program in Computer Science, University of Science, Vietnam National University - Ho Chi Minh City.

# References

1. Boelter, T., Poddar, R., Popa, R.A.: A secure one-roundtrip index for range queries. IACR Cryptology ePrint Archive **2016**, 568 (2016)
2. Bost, R.: οφος: forward secure searchable encryption. In: Proceedings of the 2016 ACM SIGSAC Conference on Computer and Communications Security, pp. 1143–1154. ACM (2016)
3. Bost, R., Minaud, B., Ohrimenko, O.: Forward and backward private searchable encryption from constrained cryptographic primitives. In: Proceedings of the 2017 ACM SIGSAC Conference on Computer and Communications Security, pp. 1465–1482. ACM (2017)
4. Curtmola, R., Garay, J., Kamara, S., Ostrovsky, R.: Searchable symmetric encryption: improved definitions and efficient constructions. Cryptology ePrint Archive, Report 2006/210 (2006). https://eprint.iacr.org/2006/210
5. Curtmola, R., Garay, J., Kamara, S., Ostrovsky, R.: Searchable symmetric encryption: improved definitions and efficient constructions. J. Comput. Secur. **19**(5), 895–934 (2011)
6. Dan Boneh, V.S.: A Graduate Course in Applied Cryptography (2017)
7. Grubbs, P., Sekniqi, K., Bindschaedler, V., Naveed, M., Ristenpart, T.: Leakage-abuse attacks against order-revealing encryption. In: IEEE Symposium on Security and Privacy (SP), pp. 655–672. IEEE (2017)
8. Kamara, S., Papamanthou, C., Roeder, T.: Dynamic searchable symmetric encryption. In: Proceedings of the 2012 ACM Conference on Computer and Communications Security, pp. 965–976. ACM (2012)
9. Kerschbaum, F., Tueno, A.: An efficiently searchable encrypted data structure for range queries. arXiv preprint arXiv:1709.09314 (2017)
10. Naveed, M., Kamara, S., Wright, C.V.: Inference attacks on property-preserving encrypted databases. In: Proceedings of the 22nd ACM SIGSAC Conference on Computer and Communications Security, pp. 644–655. ACM (2015)
11. Song, D.X., Wagner, D., Perrig, A.: Practical techniques for searches on encrypted data. In: Proceeding 2000 IEEE Symposium on Security and Privacy, S&P 2000, pp. 44–55. IEEE (2000)
12. Sun, S.F., et al.: Practical backward-secure searchable encryption from symmetric puncturable encryption. In: Proceedings of the 2018 ACM SIGSAC Conference on Computer and Communications Security, pp. 763–780. ACM (2018)

# The Implicit Effect of Items Rating on Recommendation System

Thi Dieu Anh Nguyen[1], Thanh Nguyen Vu[1(✉)], and Tuan Dinh Le[2]

[1] Van Hien University, Ho Chi Minh City, Vietnam
anhntdgm@gmail.com, nguyenvt@vhu.edu.vn
[2] Long An University of Economics and Industry,
Tân An, Long An Province, Vietnam
le.tuan@daihoclongan.edu.vn

**Abstract.** Currently, most of the recommendation systems use user's feedbacks to suggest an item for the user. However, the current recommendation system used only explicit rating information, which not fully evaluating the factors that directly affect the feeling of users in rating. To achieve more accurate results, this paper proposes a solution to add the implicit effect of items rating to the recommendation system based on the TrustSVD model and matrix factorization (MF) techniques. The experimental results showed our proposed solution achieve better than 18% the matrix factorization method and 15% the Multi-Relational Matrix Factorization method.

**Keywords:** Recommendation system · Collaborative filtering · Implicit effect · Matrix Factorizations · Matrix user · Trust-based recommender

## 1 Introduction

Recommendation system have been using in many application scenarios. For example, in e-commerce, the recommendation system analysis based on user interests, search keywords, product reviews to make recommendations to users. Currently, three methods, which have been widely used in a recommendation system are: content filtering, collaborative filtering, and hybrid methods.

Content filtering (CF) based on purchase history, view user information, thereby suggesting products with content similar to buyers' needs. Some popular techniques currently used for content filtering are Bag of word, TF-IDF (term frequency-inverse document frequency), Graph, Grid, TF (term frequency), VSM (Vector Space Model) [1].

Collaborative filtering is a technique that determines a user's interest in a new product based on previous products they rate, recommending similar products with consumer appreciation. The recommended system in this approach determines the similarity of the objects through adjacent measurements. Current techniques for collaborative filtering: Pearson correlation (CORR), Cosine (COS), Adjust Cosine (ACOS), Constrained Correlation (CCORR), Mean square Difference (MSD), Euclidean (EUC), SM SING (singularities) [1, 3].

Hybrid methods are a combination of content filtering and collaborative filtering, relying on the advantages of one technique to overcome the disadvantages of the other.

T. K. Dang et al. (Eds.): FDSE 2019, LNCS 11814, pp. 681–687, 2019.
https://doi.org/10.1007/978-3-030-35653-8_47

For example, collaborative filtering has a problem with cold - start, which is difficult to suggest for items that do not have a rating. This is simple for the content-based approach when the prediction for new items based on user descriptions is available and quite easy.

In 2015, Guibing Guo, Jie Zhang, Neil Yorke-Smith give a novel trust-based recommendation model TrustSVD. According to the article, We can see the importance of the implicit effect in the recommendation system. However, the TrustSVD model only analyzed the implicit effect of using social networks. This paper expands to analyze the implicit effect of rating.

The rating of the recommendation system is usually an integer value from 1..5. In the same evaluation index, the criteria for user ratings are different. For example, 1 hotel is rated 4 * as same as guest A and guest B. This rating consists: clean, service, attached utilities, location. Guest A may be more satisfied with the service in a hotel, but guest B likes the hotel's utilities. For simplicity of calculation, this information is often missed from the recommendation system.

The remainder of the paper is presented as follows: in part 2 introduces related platforms. Part 3 proposes a solution to analyze the implicit effect of rating based on the TrustSVD model. Part 4 is the empirical evaluation results and Sect. 5 is the conclusion.

## 2 Related Work

### 2.1 Trust-Base Recommender

The trust recommendation system is improved from the traditional recommendation system that adds the use of social networking information to the analysis, evaluation and recommendations for users. Based on the level of trust among users who are related to each other and this level is expressed by specific measurement values.

In the world, the development of trust recommendation systems has been studied since 2008 and has made significant progress. The first is a combination of traditional matrix and reliable neighbor model. Some methods of significant improvement such as the separation of trustees and trusted people in the user social network, or the analysis of the explicit and implicit of users in social networks [4, 7].

In this paper, the author is interested in the social network recommendation system based on collaborative filtering model. Similar to the approach of CF, the social network recommendation system also approaches two directions:

*Memory-based social recommender:* similar to the memory base method of collaborative filtering (CF), people build models that calculate the relationship between users in the system combined with social networking information for accuracy improvement. If the degree of value is greater, the relationship between the two categories is closer. According to the studies above, it has been shown that the activities of one lie will influence the decisions of the other.

*Model-based social recommender:* similar to the model base social model in traditional CFs but adds social relationships. Most of the techniques of this approach lead to the use of matrix factorization to find the potential relationship between user factors.

## 2.2   Trust-Base Methods

Many different algorithms build a recommendation system for analyzing social network data. Some typical algorithms include the SoRec model proposed by Ma et al. in 2008 [2]; RSTE model combining traditional matrix and reliable neighbors of Ma, King and Lyu [2] in 2009;

In 2010, based on the SoRec model, Jamali and Ester proposed a SocialMF model by reconfiguring reliable parameters via vector user-specific [2]; In 2011, Ma et al. continued using user-specific vector to build SoReg matrix decay model [2]; The TrustMF hybrid method proposed by Yang et al. 2013 combines the model of trust people and trusted people [2]. In 2014, Fang et al. Divided the confidence level into four sub-factors, then integrated them into the decomposition matrix [5].

In 2019, the authors Bin et al. proposed the ConRVS model to exploit the community's interests in social networks affecting users [8].

## 3   The Proposed Implicit of Items Rating

### 3.1   TrustSVD Model

In 2015, Guibing Guo, Jie Zhang, and Neil Yorke-Smith launched the TrustSVD model, an improvement based on the SVD++ model, using both explicit and implicit information of trusted users and reviews of items [1].

During the experimental observation, Guibing Guo, Jie Zhang, Neil Yorke-Smith noticed two problems:

Trust information is as sparse as ratings, which can complement each other. Based on only one factor, the accuracy of the prediction will be skewed by this component.

Users tend to be strongly associated with trust neighbors but there is almost no relationship with distant relatives (trust - alike) while both of these factors can be added to the system. Recommendations to improve the accuracy of the prediction [2].

The empty ratings of user j's items j are predicted using the following formula:

$$\hat{r}_{u,j} = b_u + b_j + \mu + q_j^T \left( p_u + |I_u|^{-\frac{1}{2}} + \sum_{i \in I_u} y_i \right) \tag{1}$$

Where:

$b_u$, $b_j$: represent the user and item biases, respectively;
$\mu$: the global average rating;
$y_i$: denotes the implicit influence of items rated by user u in the past on the ratings of unknown items in the future

Thus, user u's feature vector can be also represented by the set of items she rated, and finally modeled as: $(p_u + |I_u| - 1/2 \sum_{i \in I_u}^n y_i)$

Specifically, the implicit effect of trusted users on item ratings can be considered in the same manner as rated items, given by:

$$\hat{r}_{u,j} = b_u + b_j + \mu + q_j^T \left( p_u + |I_u|^{-\frac{1}{2}} + \sum_{i \in I_u} y_i + |T_u|^{-\frac{1}{2}} + \sum_{v \in T_u} w_v \right) \quad (2)$$

Where $w_v$ is the user-specific latent feature vector of users (trustees) trusted by user u. The objective function to minimize is then given as follows:

$$L = \frac{1}{2} \sum_u \sum_{j \in I_u} (\hat{r}_{u,j} - r_{u,j})^2 + \frac{\lambda}{2} \left( \sum_u b_u^2 + + \sum_j b_j^2 + \sum_u \|p_u\|_F^2 + \sum_j \|p_j\|_F^2 + + \sum_i \|y_i\|_F^2 + \sum_v \|w_v\|_F^2 \right) \quad (3)$$

The user-specific vectors $p_u$ by recovering the social relationships with other users. The new objective function (without the other regularization terms) is given by:

$$\mathcal{L} = \frac{1}{2} \sum_u \sum_{j \in I_u} (\hat{r}_{u,j} - r_{u,j})^2 + \frac{\lambda}{2} \sum_u \sum_{v \in T_u} (\hat{t}_{u,v} - t_{u,v})^2 \quad (4)$$

Where $\hat{t}_{u,v} = w_v^T p_u$ is the predicted trust between users u and v, and $\lambda_t$ controls the degree of trust regularization.

## 3.2    HMSVD Model Use Implicit of Items Rating

In the recommendation system, user ratings are represented by a matrix in which, elements are assigned a value from 1 to 5. Many users rated as same as for one item, but their feeling with the product is not the same. Value item rating is average after considering many factors affecting the quality of the product.

For example: A hotel received a rating of guest A and guest B of level 4, but guest A is satisfied with the hotel service, but guest B is satisfied with the utilities: Airport traveling, gym sport, swimming pool, etc.

To analyze the implicit of items rating in item reviews, we use Matrix Factorizations [7]. The technique of Matrix Factorizations to divide a large matrix into 2 matrices smaller than.

$\mathbf{R} \approx \mathbf{W.H}^T$ so that $\mathbf{R}$ is constructed as accurately as possible.

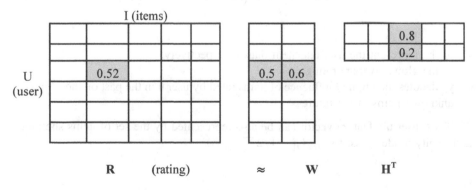

R: Matrix rating in the recommendation system

Each u column of the matrix R is a vector of k implicit elements for the user rating and each row i is a vector of k implicit elements for items i.

Call $w_{uk}$ and $h_{ik}$ the elements of the matrix W and H, then user u's rating r on item i is present by the following formula:

$$\hat{r}_{ui} = \sum_{k=1}^{K} w_{uk} h_{ik} = \left( W.H^T \right)_{u,i} \tag{5}$$

These methods evolve from the TrustSVD model, applying matrix decomposition techniques and called HMSVD. The item matrix factorization is the implicit effect matrix, where $i_k$ is index to be the rating detail of the attribute items. To add the implicit effect rating into (1) formula as H matrix, we had rating vector as bellow:

$$\hat{r}_{uj} = b_u + b_j + \mu + q_j^T \left( p_u + |I_u|^{-\frac{1}{2}} + \sum_{i \in I_u} y_i + |T_u|^{-\frac{1}{2}} + \sum_{v \in T_u} w_v + |H_u|^{-\frac{1}{2}} + \sum_{k \in H_u} v_k \right) \tag{6}$$

Where: $b_u$, $b_j$ are parameters of biases of users and products

We have the objective function of is defined as follow:

$$\mathcal{L} = \frac{1}{2} \sum_u \sum_{j \in I_u} \left( \hat{r}_{uj} - r_{uj} \right)^2 + \frac{\lambda}{2} \left( \sum_u b_u^2 + + \sum_j b_j^2 + \|I\|_F^2 + \|T\|_F^2 + \|H\|_F^2 \right) \tag{7}$$

Where **I, H** is implicit matrix users and rating, **T** is trust matrix in social users.

$\lambda$ is regularization parameter. To control computational complexity, $\lambda$ are equally assigned to all variables.

To optimize the objective function, we used:

$$\frac{\partial \mathcal{L}}{\partial b_u} = \sum_{j \in I_u} e_{u,j} + \lambda |I_u|^{-\frac{1}{2}} b_u$$

$$\frac{\partial \mathcal{L}}{\partial b_j} = \sum_{u \in U_j} e_{u,j} + \lambda |U_j|^{-\frac{1}{2}} b_j$$

$$\frac{\partial \mathcal{L}}{\partial p_u} = \sum_{j \in I_u} e_{u,j} q_j + \lambda_t \sum_{v \in T_u} e_{u,v} w_v + \left( \lambda |I_u|^{-\frac{1}{2}} + \lambda_t |T_u|^{-\frac{1}{2}} + \lambda_h |H_u|^{-\frac{1}{2}} \right) p_u$$

$$\frac{\partial \mathcal{L}}{\partial q_j} = \sum_{u \in U_j} e_{u,j} q_j \left( p_u + |I_u|^{-\frac{1}{2}} \sum_{i \in I_u} y_i + |T_u|^{-\frac{1}{2}} \sum_{v \in T_u} w_v + |H_u|^{-\frac{1}{2}} \sum_{k \in H_u} h_k \right) + \lambda |U_j|^{-\frac{1}{2}} q_j$$

Where: $e_{u,j} = \hat{r}_{u,j} - r_{u,j}$ and $e_{u,v} = \hat{t}_{u,v} - t_{u,v}$

The computational complexities of HMSVD is higher than TrustSVD model, because it adds more input data of rating items. The rating of items consists user's feeling in detail.

# 4  Experiment

## 4.1  Summary

The datasets used in our study is the Movielens [6], which was published in 1998 by the GroupLens team. This data set has 100,000 reviews made by 943 users on 1,682 movies, each user rated at least 20 movies, and the rating was assigned 1 (bad) to 5 (great) [6]. It showed below:

| Data set | Users | Items | Rating |
|---|---|---|---|
| Movielens | 943 | 1,682 | 100,000 |

Due to time constraints, data collection for a detailed rating is done manually. If apply this model in fact, we can use a form request for the user. Users will select the attributes priority that are right for themselves and feedbacks by survey table.

## 4.2  Evaluation Criteria

To evaluate the data set, it is possible to compare the error using SMSE (root mean squared error).

$$\text{SMSE} = \sqrt{\frac{\sum_{u,j}\left(\hat{r}_{u,j} - r_{u,j}\right)^2}{N}}$$

Experimental results assessed by SMSE on the dataset apply for 3 methods: Matrix Factorization (MF), Multi-Relational Matrix Factorization (MRMF) and show as table bellow:

Figure 1 showed RMSE achieved by different methods. The results shows that the HMSVD technique gives better results than other methods and suitable for improving the recommendation system. However, HMSVD is limited as the model training time is quite slow compared to other methods, because the number of parameters of input data is lager.

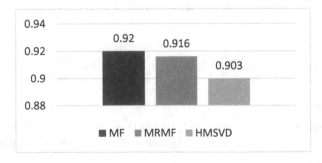

**Fig. 1.** RMSE of the compared algorithms

We use MF and MRMF compared to HMSVD because they both use Matrix Factorization technique and MF is a famous algorithm, commonly used in the recommendation system, specially in Collaborative filtering.

## 5 Conclusion

The recommendation system is getting more and more complex; users require high accuracy of recommendations. Therefore, the analysis of other aspects such as implicit, real-time, user social networks... is a more important part of improving the recommendation system.

In this paper, a matrix factorization model in combination with TrustSVD is proposed to analyze the implicit items based on their attributes, add the implicit effect of rating into recommendation system. However, compared to the use of other models, the HFSVD model takes more time in the optimization of the target function, due to more input parameters of data input. Next, I will study ways to improve the speed on the data sets training and compare other trust-base methods.

## References

1. Koren, Y.: Factorization meets the neighborhood: multifaceted collaborative filtering model. In: Proceedings of the 14th ACM SIGKDD International Conference on Knowledge Discovery and Data Mining (KDD), pp. 426–434 (2008)
2. Guo, G., Zhang, J., Yorke-Smith, N.: TrustSVD: collaborative filtering with both the explicit and implicit influence of user trust and of item ratings (2015)
3. Do, P., Nguyen, K., Vu, T.N., Dung, T.N., Le, T.D.: Integrating knowledge-based reasoning algorithms and collaborative filtering into e-learning material recommendation system. In: Dang, T.K., Wagner, R., Küng, J., Thoai, N., Takizawa, M., Neuhold, E.J. (eds.) FDSE 2017. LNCS, vol. 10646, pp. 419–432. Springer, Cham (2017). https://doi.org/10.1007/978-3-319-70004-5_30
4. He, J., Chu, W.W.: A social network-based recommender system (SNRS). In: Memon, N., Xu, J., Hicks, D., Chen, H. (eds.) Data Mining for Social Network Data. AOIS, vol. 12, pp. 47–74. Springer, Boston (2010). https://doi.org/10.1007/978-1-4419-6287-4_4
5. Fang, H., Bao, Y., Zhang, J.: Leveraging decomposed trust in probabilistic matrix factorization for effective recommendation. In: Proceedings of the 28th AAAI Conference on Artificial Intelligence (2014)
6. https://grouplens.org/datasets/movielens/
7. Badiger, M.H., Negalur, G.G.: A trust-based matrix factorization method for recommendations (2017)
8. Bin, B., et al.: A community-based collaborative filtering method for social recommender systems (2019)

# Counting People Using Images from Two Low Cost Webcams

Phan Duy Hung$^{(\boxtimes)}$

FPT University, Hanoi, Vietnam
Hungpd2@fe.edu.vn

**Abstract.** The number of people entering an exhibition, a fair or a booth, or the number of people getting on and off the bus, etc. based on time-based statistics is very meaningful for the manager. There have been many studies and solutions to implement this problem. Each solution is applied in several different situations, depending on accuracy requirements, deployment location, deployment environment, product costs. This paper proposes a solution to count people with low-cost hardware, countable for both in and out directions, and the accuracy rate of over 92%. The solution proposes using two webcams of the same type, the process of classification and processing is done on Raspberry PI.

**Keywords:** Counting people · Depth image · SVM · Object detection · Object tracking

## 1 Introduction

The problem of counting people has had the first research for a long time. Since 1999, author Kettnaker has been interested in this issue and has done this by using mutual content constraints from four cameras [1]. This is because the result of counting the number of people entering an event or location is significant for the manager. For example, with the number of people entering an exhibition, a fair or entering a booth over time can suggest changing the opening time, promotion time, or changing positions, changing items, etc. With the information of the number of passengers on each bus route or the number of passengers getting on and off at each bus stop, it is useful for the bus network planner or to find the appropriate bus stop location. If a bus has a very small average number of passengers, it may be considered that the reason is due to an unreasonable route.

There are many studies and products on the market for this problem such as mechanical counting, Wifi, counting people with 2D and 3D images. These methods can be divided into methods that participants need or don't need to carry equipment, can also be divided into methods of using or not using images.

One of the simplest device-free methods is the mechanical counting. It can be seen at the subway station control gates or control gates in the basement of apartment buildings. Each turn of the gate corresponds to one person. While Raykov et al. introduce an approach for occupancy estimation from the measurements of a single PIR sensor [2]. They test their system in more than 50 office meetings in seven different conference rooms of an office building with a data acquisition board including a PIR

© Springer Nature Switzerland AG 2019
T. K. Dang et al. (Eds.): FDSE 2019, LNCS 11814, pp. 688–695, 2019.
https://doi.org/10.1007/978-3-030-35653-8_48

sensor placed on a table positioned approximately in the middle of the room next to the wall. The height of the table varies from room to room. Their estimates deviate by $\pm 1$ individual from the ground truth for at most 14 occupants. The results do not appear to be affected by the height of the table, on which the data acquisition board was positioned, but the placement of the sensor on a particular side of the room caused occupants to conceal each other during larger meetings.

Device-based occupancy estimation comprises approaches where users are expected to carry devices to facilitate the people counting process. Through a WiFi-based passive method, the authors in [3] estimate pedestrians and locate them properly in a road traffic scenario, which can facilitate the design of intelligent systems for traffic control that take into account more actors and not only vehicle-based optimizations. The only known work on cellular-based crowd estimation is proposed in [4] by Ramachandran. The author discusses the addition of a simple hardware and software component, a crowd size analyzer, to the cellular network infrastructure which collects and analyzes information from cell tower associations to estimate the crowdedness in a given location.

Traditionally, significant efforts have been made towards providing people counting solutions based on images captured by surveillance cameras.

In [5], a people counting system based on face detection and tracking in a video is presented. In [6], the authors describe the basic scheme by setting a zenithal camera in the bus for capturing the passengers' flow bi-directionally, the captured frame is divided into many blocks and each block will be classified according to its motion vector. An image sequence analysis for counting people getting on and off of a bus in real-time is presented in [7]. Chato et al. in [8] used a single camera to count the number of people on public transport. The work proposed an algorithm to identify and count people using artificial neural networks. The counting of people to ensure no more passengers allowed on public transport to ensure safe journeys. The authors in [9] using the Kinect sensor propose a real-time algorithm for counting people from depth image sequences acquired.

Although there are many studies as above, however, each solution is suitable for several deployment situations. Always need an assessment on many factors such as cost, accuracy, location of deployment, deployment time, maintenance capability, operating costs, participants with or without technology equipment, whether or not those devices enable communication communications, etc.

This paper proposes a method with low cost criteria, simple system installation but high accuracy of up to 92%, and can be used for problems such as counting the number of people visiting booths, fairs, using public transport.

The remainder of the paper is organized as follows. Section 2 describes the data collection and processing. Then, Sect. 3 provides the algorithms and evaluation. Finally, conclusions and perspectives are made in Sect. 4.

## 2    Image Collection and Processing

### 2.1    Experimental System Design

At each gate, the system consists of two webcams of the same type Logitech C170 connected to the two USB ports of the Raspberry PI computer (Fig. 1). Data from Raspberry PI is transmitted to a computer via Ethernet. The gate allows 2 people to pass through at a maximum speed of 3 km/s, up to 6 people at the same time in the intersection of 2 webcam images.

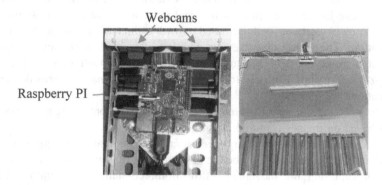

**Fig. 1.** Installation of two webcams and Raspberry PI on the gate.

From the built hardware system, data is collected and processed according to the main steps: Depth map, Background subtraction, Feature extraction, Classification, Tracking and Counting, Report and Analysis.

### 2.2    Depth Image

The depth image is a gray image whose value per pixel is proportional to the distance from the point on the object's surface to the camera. Observing a depth map we can see that closer objects will be brighter. Capture 2 images from 2 webcams of the same type placed side by side and taken at the same time. Such a two-cameras system is similar to two human eyes. The next step is to normalize the image from each webcam, then two images will be combined to calculate the depth map. The normalization process will be done once at the beginning of the system installation and consists of 2 steps: Calibration and Rectification.

*Calibration*
This step is to eliminate image distortions. Cheap cameras often use spherical lenses to save production costs. Because of such a structure, when light passes through, it will be transformed, distorting the image. Example: when the image of a square object passes through this lens and then onto the camera image plane, the edges of the square are no longer straight but become curved. People call this distortion a radial distortion (Fig. 2a). It is true that the farther away from the center the greater the deviation of the

position of the point on the image (Fig. 2b). To solve this problem, the equations to represent the relationship between the correct coordinates and deformed coordinates are used:

$$r^2 = x^2 + y^2$$

$$x_{corrected} = x(1 + k_1 r^2 + k r^4 + k_3 r^6)$$

$$y_{corrected} = y(1 + k_1 r^2 + k_2 r^4 + k_3 r^6)$$

where $k_1$, $k_2$, $k_3$ are called radial distortion parameters.

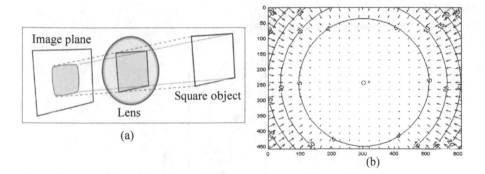

(a)

(b)

**Fig. 2.** Radial distortion.

Image calibration is the process of determining distortion parameters and is esti-mated experimentally. This work selects the chessboard image to calibrate images from webcams. Where x, y will be the coordinates of the chessboard corners on the image obtained. $x_{corrected}$ and $y_{corrected}$ are their correct coordinates. The more equations we need to find, the more accurate the parameter can be estimated.

### Rectification

The rectification process starts with the concept of epiline. Looking at Fig. 3a, X is a point in space, $X_L$ is the projection of X on the image of the left camera $P_L$, $X_R$ is the projection of X on the image of the right camera $P_R$. It is easy to see that the projection of any x point on the $O_L X$ line will be on a line $l'$. This line is called epiline of point x. So to find the projection of x on $P_R$, we just need to find it on epiline $l'$. Each point on a plane will have the corresponding epiline line on the other plane. To quickly find these epiline lines, two left and right planes are projected on the same plane, then transform two images so that the epiline lines overlap (Fig. 3b) [10].

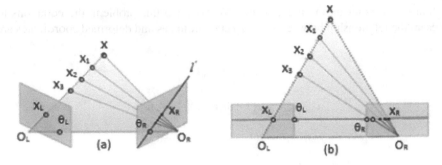

**Fig. 3.** Epiline and transformation.

*Depth Image*

Figure 4 is the normalized projection image.

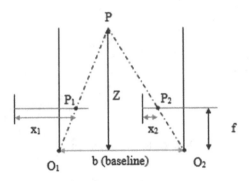

**Fig. 4.** The calculation of distance.

$O_1$ is the focus of the left camera, $O_2$ is the focus of the right camera. The line $O_1O_2$ is the baseline of length $b$. P is a point in space and projected onto two image planes at $P_1$ and $P_2$. The distance from P to baseline is Z.

Because $P_1P_2 \,//\, O_1O_2$ so $\Delta PP_1P_2 \sim \Delta PO_1O_2$, and and from there we have:

$$\frac{b}{Z} = \frac{(b+x_T) - x_R}{Z-f} \Rightarrow Z = \frac{b.f}{x_R - x_T} = \frac{b.f}{d}$$

where $x_R - x_T$ is the disparity.

### 2.3    Background Subtraction

The background image is considered a fixed part of the image so that the depth image will be subtracted from the background image. However, the resulting image is still quite noisy, so it is necessary to deal with it to find the object area on the image (foreground mask). To find this mask, the image after subtraction will cross a threshold to obtain a binary image and continue to filter out the noise. The obtained mask will be processed bitwise with the real image to find the final image.

# 3 Algorithms and Evaluations

## 3.1 People Detection

After separating the background from the image, it is necessary to find the position of the maximum values corresponding to the objects. However, the number of local maximum points is so many that the image needs to be processed by passing a blur filter, then converting the image to a scale with a smaller number of steps. The number of local maximum values will decrease on the resulting image.

## 3.2 Feature Extraction

With the depth image, the color variation is quite evident in the human image area, so the application of histogram of gradient (HOG) is quite natural to find features [11]. Each object considered is a $150 \times 150$ pixels image area around the maximum point. Split this window into cells with a cell size of $15 \times 15$ pixels. Every 4 cells is combined into one block. Blocks overlap by 50%.

In this experiment, each cell contains $15 \times 15$ pixels. We take the 225 gradient vectors and put them into a 9-bin histogram. The Histogram ranges from 0 to 180°, so there are 20° per bin. Thus, the number of components of a feature vector is equal to the number of blocks multiplied by the number of values calculated from a block and equal to: $(10 \times 10) \times (9 \times 4) = 3600$ (values).

## 3.3 Classification

The data has been recorded with a frame rate of 15 frames per second, a resolution of $320 \times 240$ pixels and a MP4 V codec. The data marked by hand consists of 370 human images of $150 \times 150$ pixels and 350 images as background images, non-human objects such as suitcases, tables, and chairs, etc.

Support vector machines (SVMs) are used for this work to classify human or non-human, and the entire machine learning process is run on Google Colab [12]. The classification report of classifier is as follows:

|  | precision | recall | f1-score |
|---|---|---|---|
| Human | 0.92 | 0.94 | 0.93 |
| Non-human | 0.93 | 0.91 | 0.92 |

## 3.4 Tracking and Counting

Tracking's purpose is to help distinguish the moving objects, where A object is and where B object is at different times. Figure 5 shows two images at times $t$ and $t + 1$.

The tracking process consists of 3 steps:

The first step is to identify the head position and then delineate the head with a circle of 40 pixels radius. In the image, at time t two objects will be called $Obj_1$ and $Obj_2$.

The next step is to identify 2 positions of 2 heads in the image at time $t + 1$.

The last step, compare the position of objects at time $t + 1$ with time $t$. The position at time $t + 1$ closest to a position at time t will determine that it is the same person at two consecutive times. The same process applies to all objects.

Image at $t$: $I\_t$         Image at $t + 1$: $I\_t + 1$

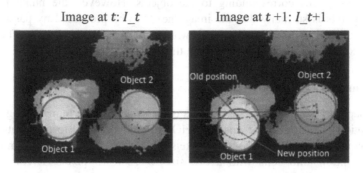

**Fig. 5.** The reduction of the number of maximum values.

The algorithm for counting people is quite simple. Use 2 lines as shown in Fig. 6 "line in" and "line out" to determine whether the person is "out" or "in". When determining a person and tracking that person from "line out" through "line in", the number of people "in" increases by 1. And vice versa, when determining a person and tracking that person from "line in" through "line out", the number of people "out" increases by 1. These data will then be sent to the computer to be saved to the database. The software allows managing multiple counters at different gates, real-time monitoring of the number of people entering and leaving each gate as well as exporting reports by hour, day, month, etc.

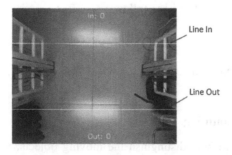

**Fig. 6.** Counting people using 2 lines.

# 4  Conclusion and Perspectives

The problem of counting people is a very interesting and there have been many studies. Managers need relative estimates of the number of people attending fairs, exhibitions, supermarkets, buses, etc. This paper proposes a solution to use images from two cheap and similar webcams. The system is installed on a Raspberry PI computer, the identification of human-non human reaches the accuracy rate of 92%. The system also tracks and counts people in both directions and supports exporting statistical reports, observing in real-time. Results can be applied in applications that need to be deployed quickly and cheaply. This work can serve as a good reference for the problem of Pattern Recognition or Object Classification, etc.

# References

1. Kettnaker, V., Zabih, R.: Counting people from multiple cameras. In: IEEE International Conference on Multimedia Computing and Systems, Florence, Italy, pp. 267–271, vol. 2 (1999). https://doi.org/10.1109/mmcs.1999.778358
2. Raykov, Y.P., Ozer, E., Dasika, G., et al.: Predicting room occupancy with a single passive infrared (PIR) sensor through behavior extraction. In: ACM International Joint Conference on Pervasive and Ubiquitous Computing, Heidelberg, Germany, pp. 1016–1027 (2016)
3. Kalikova, J., Krcal, J.: People counting by means of Wi-Fi. In: Smart City Symposium Prague (SCSP), Prague, pp. 1–3 (2017). https://doi.org/10.1109/scsp.2017.7973857
4. Ramachandran, J.: Systems, methods, and computer program products for estimating crowd sizes using information collected from mobile devices in a wireless communications network, 1 December 2011, US Patent App. 12/791,463 (2011). https://www.google.com/patents/US20110295577
5. Zhao, X., Delleandrea, E., Chen, L: A people counting system based on face detection and tracking in a video. In: Sixth IEEE International Conference on Advanced Video and Signal Based Surveillance (AVSS 2009), IEEE Computer Society, Washington, DC, USA, pp. 67–72 (2009)
6. Chen, C.H., Chang, Y.C., Chen, T.Y., et al.: people counting system for getting in/out of a bus based on video processing. In: Eighth International Conference on Intelligent Systems Design and Applications, Kaohsiung, pp. 565–569 (2008)
7. Bartolini, F., Cappellini, V., Mecocci, A.: Counting people getting in and out of a bus by real-time image-sequence processing. Image Vis. Comput. 12(1), 36–41 (1994)
8. Chato, P., Chipantasi, D.J.M., Velasco, N., et al.: Image processing and artificial neural network for counting people inside public transport. In: IEEE Third Ecuador Technical Chapters Meeting (ETCM), Cuenca, pp. 1–5 (2018)
9. Nalepa, J., Szymanek, J., Kawulok, M.: Real-time people counting from depth images. In: Kozielski, S., Mrozek, D., Kasprowski, P., Małysiak-Mrozek, B., Kostrzewa, D. (eds.) BDAS 2015. CCIS, vol. 521, pp. 387–397. Springer, Cham (2015). https://doi.org/10.1007/978-3-319-18422-7_34
10. Epiline. https://docs.opencv.org/master/da/de9/tutorial_py_epipolar_geometry.html. Accessed 20 July 2019
11. HOG. https://www.learnopencv.com/histogram-of-oriented-gradients/. Accessed 20 July 2019
12. CoLab. https://colab.research.google.com/. Accessed 20 July 2019

# Predicting the Price of Bitcoin Using Hybrid ARIMA and Machine Learning

Dinh-Thuan Nguyen[(⊠)] and Huu-Vinh Le

University of Information Technology, VNU-HCM, Ho Chi Minh City, Vietnam
thuannd@uit.edu.vn, vinhlh.10@grad.uit.edu.vn

**Abstract.** Bitcoin is one of the most popular cryptocurrencies in the world, has attracted broad interests from researchers in recent years. In this work, Autoregressive Integrate Moving Average (ARIMA) model and machine learning algorithms will be implemented to predict the closing price of Bitcoin the next day. After that, we present hybrid methods between ARIMA and machine learning to improve prediction of Bitcoin price. Experiment results showed that hybrid methods have improved accuracy of predicting through RMSE and MAPE.

**Keywords:** Bitcoin prediction · ARIMA · Machine learning · Hybrid model

## 1 Introduction

In October 2008, Bitcoin was firstly introduced by Satoshi Nakamoto in the report "Bitcoin: A Peer-to-Peer Electronic Cash System" [1]. In 2009, Nakamoto has released a software that created Bitcoin and had a large community using Bitcoin around the world so far. In recent years, Bitcoin trading has exploded into trading volume as well as the amount of money that spent on investment. They have boosted value of Bitcoin. It is estimated that the global value of Bitcoin comes to 72.1 trillion USD at the beginning of May 2019. Many investors are willing to spend large amounts of money on Bitcoin and hope to make a return. Therefore, Bitcoin price forecasting is one of the hot topics in recent years.

There are two main forecasting methods for predicting Bitcoin price. The first is that based on time series of Bitcoin price. The second is that found relationship between the price of Bitcoin and other indicators such as stock price, oil price, gold price,... In this study, we focus on method using time series. ARIMA model and machine learning algorithms such as Feedforward Neural Network (FFNN), Convolutional Neural Network (CNN), Long Short Term Memory (LSTM), Support Vector Regression (SVR) will be implemented. Then, hybrid models are proposed to improve prediction. They are that combining ARIMA model and machine learning algorithms, combining models based on fluctuation interval.

© Springer Nature Switzerland AG 2019
T. K. Dang et al. (Eds.): FDSE 2019, LNCS 11814, pp. 696–704, 2019.
https://doi.org/10.1007/978-3-030-35653-8_49

# 2   Related Works

Bitcoin price prediction can bring returns to investors. Therefore, studies in Bitcoin price prediction are done increasingly. Shah [2] presented the Bayes regression method to predict the price changes of Bitcoin in every 10 s. Based on this method, the author has come up with a simple strategy for trading Bitcoin. Then, the author has made 2872 transactions, profit achieved in 50 days about 89%.

Almeida [3] applied an artificial neural network to predict the next day's Bitcoin's trend based on the price and volume of Bitcoin transactions in the previous days. Neural network models are installed and experimented with Theano library and MATLAB tool. The experiment showed that adding Bitcoin trade Volume as input data did not result in an increased performance.

Madan [4] collected Bitcoin dataset including 25 features and selected 16 features to predict the daily price change trending of Bitcoin. Prediction accuracy is up to 98.7%. At the same time, the time series of Bitcoin price collected in every 10 s. This dataset was trained for a random forest algorithm and a linear model to predict up-down Bitcoin price movement every 10 min. The prediction accuracy is about 50–55%.

Jang [5] proposed using the Bayesian neural network to analyze the volatility of Bitcoin price. The author also selected some characteristics Blockchain information that related to the supply and demand of Bitcoin to improve prediction. The author experimented with Bayesian neural network and some other linear and non-linear methods on Bitcoin price dataset. The result of experiment indicated that the Bayesian neural network is good for forecasting and can describes the big volatility of Bitcoin price.

McNally [6] used LSTM model to forecast Bitcoin price. The experiment results showed that LSTM is better than traditional methods like ARIMA. The author also compared the performance of LSTM on CPU and GPU. It showed that GPU provided 67.7% higher performance than CPU.

Greaves [7] used Bitcoin transaction graph that consists of blockchain information to forecast up-down Bitcoin price movement. In the study of the author, neural network is better classification than baseline model, linear regression, SVM.

Yang's research [8] focused on analyzing the relationship between the number of Bitcoin transactions and its price changes. The author has built a Bitcoin trading network with complex measurements that related to profitability and price volatility. In this study, author believed that this network is reliable for predicting Bitcoin price. Ferdiansyah [9] was Bitcoin-USD trading using SVM model to detect the current day's trend. Author concluded SVM and prediction can be used to forecast current day's trend of Bitcoin on the market. In the next study, neural networks will be used to improve accuracy of predicting.

The most of current studies concentrated on predicting trend of Bitcoin by implementing individual models. We will predict Bitcoin price in the next day with time series forecasting models and propose hybrid models to combine individual models to improve prediction.

## 3  Hybrid Methodology

### 3.1  Hybrid Model Based on ARIMA and Machine Learning

Zhang [10] proposed to combine ARIMA and ANN for time series forecasting. The idea of this hybrid model is based on a combination of linear and non-linear components in time series. These two components are represented by the equation:

$$y_t = L_t + N_t$$

where $y_t$ is time series, $L_t$ is a linear component, $N_t$ is a non-linear component.

Firstly, ARIMA model is used to capture the linear component, then the residuals from the linear model will contain only the nonlinear relationship. The residuals $e_t$ at time t from the linear model is defined by:

$$e_t = y_t - \hat{L}_t$$

where $\hat{L}_t$ is the predicted value of the ARIMA model at time t.

The residuals can be modeled by using ANNs to discover nonlinear relationships. With n input nodes, the ANN model for the residuals will be:

$$e_t = f(e_{t-1}, e_{t-2}, \ldots, e_{t-n}) + \varepsilon_t$$

where f is a nonlinear function determined by the neural network and $e_t$ is the random error. Finally the combined prediction will be:

$$\hat{y}_t = \hat{L}_t + \hat{N}_t$$

where $\hat{N}_t$ represents the prediction from ANN (Fig. 1).

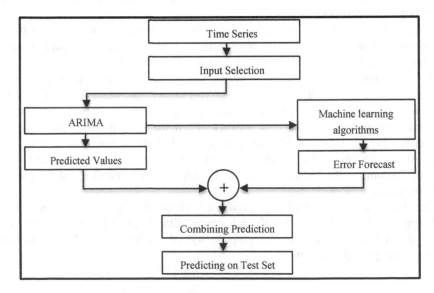

**Fig. 1.** Hybrid ARIMA and machine learning

With Zhang's proposal, combining models are expanded with ARIMA and machine learning algorithms such as FFNN, CNN, LSTM and SVR. These combining methods promise a significant improvement in prediction instead of just combining ARIMA and traditional neural network.

## 3.2  Hybrid Model Based on Fluctuation Interval

One of the biggest challenges in predicting time series is its fluctuation. There has not yet been a really effective model to forecast on highly volatile time series. In this study, we propose a hybrid model that combines to forecast based on fluctuation interval. We considered that each model will be suitable to predict on specific fluctuations interval. For example, ARIMA model has good predictability on stationarity time series, that means it is less volatility. Meanwhile, machine learning algorithms and SVR will be able to capture nonlinear component, be large fluctuations. Therefore, this combination is very promising to improve prediction (Fig. 2).

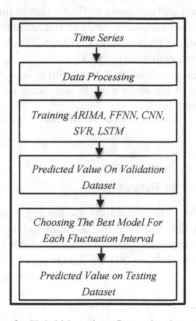

**Fig. 2.** Hybrid based on fluctuation interval

Firstly, we compute fluctuation of two consecutive time points as percentage of difference of 2 points by formula:

$$\text{fluctuation}(y_t, y_{t+1}) = \left| \frac{y_t - y_{t+1}}{y_t} \right| * 100$$

where $y_t$ is the first time point, $y_{t+1}$ is the second time point.

On the experiment dataset, determining the minimum and maximum fluctuation. And the frequency of volatility as a basis for dividing the volatility range. Of course, there are some outlier volatility with low frequency, we can ignore them and adjust the minimum and maximum volatility.

With a single series, the number of intervals can be be determined from [11]:

$$k = 1 + 3.3 \log_{10} N$$

where N is the sample size.

We can apply above formula for dividing fluctuation interval with R is range of maximum and minimum fluctuation and N is the number of time points that is computed fluctuation.

Finally, we define the best model to forecast for each interval and make prediction. The procedure of the hybrid model concludes some steps below:

---

**Step 1**. Computing fluctuation between two consecutive time points.
**Step 2**. Finding maximum and minimum of fluctuation in time series.
**Step 3**. Defining fluctuation interval of range of fluctuation.
**Step 4**. Training ARIMA, FFNN, CNN, LSTM, SVR on training dataset with defining fluctuation($y_t$) = fluctuation($y_{t-2}, y_{t-1}$)
**Step 5**. Predicting values on validation dataset with trained models.
**Step 6**. Defining a rule of choosing models and using the best model for each interval to predict on test dataset.

---

## 4 Experiment

### 4.1 Closing Price of Bitcoin Dataset

Forecasting models will be implemented on the closing price dataset of Bitcoin, is collected from October 01, 2013 to June 08, 2019, including 2070 days on CoinDesk website. Based on the closing price chart of Bitcoin, it can be seen that the price of Bitcoin has big changes, especially in 2017 and continues to have fluctuations in 2018 and 2019 (Fig. 3).

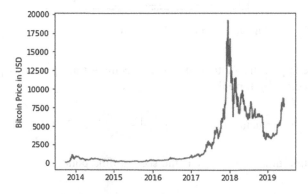

**Fig. 3.** The closing price of Bitcoin chart

## 4.2    Software Used

We used python 3.6 with Anaconda tools to manage libraries. A statistical library -
Statsmodels used to build ARIMA model. Neural network models are installed with
tensorflow library, Keras to build models quickly. Pandas library is used to process
time series data, NumPy to calculate matrices/vectors and store training, validation and
test data. Finally, the matplotlib library is used to draw illustrative charts (Fig. 4).

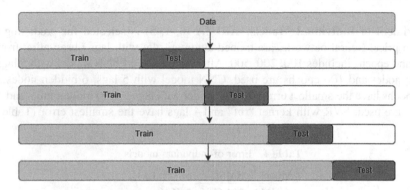

**Fig. 4.** Nested cross validation

## 4.3    Split Time Series into Training, Validation, Testing Dataset

In the experiment with individual models, the closing price of Bitoin dataset will be
divided into 2 parts: 90% of the time points used for training, 10% of the remaining
time points will be used for model testing. The experiment of hybrid ARIMA with
machine learning and regression, the dataset is divided into 3 parts: 80% of the time
points used for training, 10% used for validation, the remaining 10% used for testing.

In the experiment of hybrid based fluctuation interval, the dataset is divided into
sections to match nested cross validation. The dataset is divided into 10 equal parts.
During the first training session, 50% was used for training, the next 10% for validation, the next 10% for model testing. Just like that, until the last training session, 80%
of the training is used, 10% for validation, the remaining 10% for testing.

## 4.4    Evaluation Time Series Forecasting Models

To evaluate the forecasting quality of the models, this paper uses RMSE (Root Mean
Square Error) and MAPE (Mean Absolute Percentage Error) measurements:

$$\text{RMSE} = \sqrt{\frac{1}{n}\sum_{t=1}^{n}(y_t - \hat{y}_t)^2}$$

$$\text{MAPE} = \frac{1}{n} \sum_{t=1}^{n} \left| \frac{y_t - \hat{y}_t}{y_t} \right| * 100$$

where n is the number of time points in test dataset, $y_t$ is expected values, $\hat{y}_t$ is predicted values.

## 4.5  Predicting the Price of Bitcoin

**Experiment of Individual Models:** ARIMA (6, 1, 5) is selected for predicting the Bitcoin price. Neural networks are trained automatically with lags observation from 1 to 14 and epochs includes 100, 200, 500. After experiment, FFNN model with 5 lags, 9 hidden nodes and 100 epochs are used. CNN model with 5 lags, 6 hidden nodes and 200 epochs have the smallest error. LSTM model with lags 5, 100 hidden units and 100 epochs are used. SVR with kernel "rbf" and 4 lags have the smallest error (Table 1).

**Table 1.**  Error of individual models

| Model | RMSE | MAPE (%) |
|-------|------|----------|
| ARIMA | **214.6536** | **2.5626** |
| FFNN | 252.1017 | 3.6087 |
| CNN | 280.0976 | 4.1937 |
| SVR | 232.5739 | 2.8558 |
| LSTM | 219.3169 | 2.5852 |

With the closing price of Bitcoin, ARIMA and LSTM models have a good result with RMSE và MAPE. Meanwhile, CNN is not good for time series as expected.

**Experiment Hybrid Model based on ARIMA with Machine Learning and Regression:** Hybrid ARIMA_CNN has the best forecasting with RMSE and MAPE (Table 2).

**Table 2.**  Error of hybrid model based on ARIMA with machine learning and regression

| Hybrid model | RMSE | MAPE (%) |
|--------------|------|----------|
| ARIMA_FFNN | 213.3135 | 2.5849 |
| ARIMA_CNN | **213.0082** | **2.5563** |
| ARIMA_LSTM | 214.1901 | 2.5347 |
| ARIMA_SVR | 213.8141 | 2.6144 |

**Experiment Hybrid Model Based on fluctuation Interval:** The minimum fluctuation is 0.000679% and the maximum fluctuation is 35.849315%. Based on histogram of fluctuation, it showed that fluctuation is very little over 25% and they are outlier.

Therefore, the range of fluctuation is R = [0–25]. Applying the formula of Herbert A. Sturges [11], there are 12 fluctuation intervals, that are [0–2), [2–4), [4–6), [6–8), [8–10), [10–12), [12–14), [14–16), [16–18), [18–20), [20–22), [22–24). The fluctuation is beyond the range of R in the data set, they belong to [22–24) interval (Fig. 5).

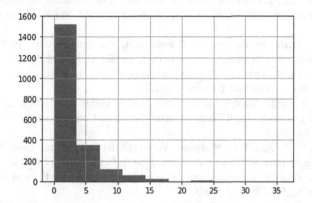

**Fig. 5.** Histogram of fluctuation in the closing price of Bitcoin

Using nested cross validation, we did experiment and choosed models corresponding to interval below: interval [0, 2): ARIMA, interval [2, 4): ARIMA, interval [4, 6): ARIMA, interval [6, 8): SVR, interval [8, 10): LSTM, interval [10, 12): CNN, interval [12, 14): ARIMA, interval [14, 16): CNN, interval [16, 18): CNN, interval [18, 20): ARIMA, interval [20, 22): LSTM, interval [22, 24): ARIMA. Prediction on test dataset, error of hybrid model is RMSE = 214.2755, MAPE = 2.5483%.

## 5  Conclusion

The time series forecasting is a difficult problem, but is very important in economics and finance. In the recently, predicting the price of Bitcoin has attracted broad interests from researchers. This work has presented hybrid methods to improve prediction of Bitcoin in the next day. The experiment showed that, the most of hybrid models are possible to improve prediction through measurements of errors such as RMSE, MAPE. The Bitcoin price often depends on investor psychology and investors' interest. In the future, Google trending or investor sentiment on social networks will be analyzed and combine with time series models to improve prediction.

## References

1. Nakamoto, S.: Bitcoin: A Peer-to-Peer Electronic Cash System (2008)
2. Shah, D., Zhang, K.: Bayesian regression and Bitcoin. arXiv preprint arXiv:1410.1231 (2014)

3. Almeida, J., Tata, S., Moser, A., Smit, V.: Bitcoin prediction using ANN. Neural Networks (2015)
4. Madan, I., Saluja, S., Zhao, A.: Automated Bitcoin trading via machine learning algorithms. Department of Computer Science, Stanford University, Stanford, CA, USA, Technical Report (2015)
5. Jang, H., Lee, J.: An empirical study on modeling and prediction of Bitcoin prices with bayesian neural networks based on blockchain information. IEEE Access **6**, 5427–5437 (2018)
6. McNally, S.: Predicting the price of Bitcoin using machine learning. Ph.D. dissertation, School of Computing, National College Ireland, Dublin, Ireland (2016)
7. Greaves, A., Au, B.: Using the Bitcoin Transaction Graph to Predict the Price of Bitcoin. Technical Notes in Standford University (2015)
8. Yang, S.Y., Kim, J.: Bitcoin market return and volatility forecasting using transaction network flow properties. In: IEEE Symposium Series on Computational Intelligence, IEEE, pp. 1778–1785 (2015)
9. Ferdiansyah, F., Negara, E.S., Widyanti, Y.: BITCOIN-USD trading using SVM to detect the current day's trend in the market. J. Inf. Syst. Inform. **1**, 70–77 (2019)
10. Zhang, G.P.: Times series forecasting using a hybrid ARIMA and neural network model. Neurocomputing **50**, 159–175 (2003)
11. Soong, T.T.: Fundamentals of Probability and Statistics for Engineers. Wiley, Hoboken (2015)

# Deep Learning Approach for Receipt Recognition

Anh Duc Le[1,2(✉)], Dung Van Pham[2], and Tuan Anh Nguyen[2]

[1] Center of Open Data in Humanities,
Research Organization of Information and Systems, Tokyo, Japan
anh@ism.ac.jp
[2] Deep Learning and Application, Ho Chi Minh City, Vietnam
dungphamvan0803@gmail.com, apollo2908@gmail.com

**Abstract.** Inspired by the recent successes of deep learning on Computer Vision and Natural Language Processing, we present a deep learning approach for recognizing scanned receipts. The recognition system has two main modules: text detection based on Connectionist Text Proposal Network and text recognition based on Attention-based Encoder-Decoder. We also proposed pre-processing to extract receipt area and OCR verification to ignore handwriting. The experiments on the dataset of the Robust Reading Challenge on Scanned Receipts OCR and Information Extraction 2019 demonstrate that the accuracies were improved by integrating the pre-processing and the OCR verification. Our recognition system achieved 71.9% of the F1 score for detection and recognition task.

**Keywords:** Receipt recognition · Connectionist Text Proposal Network · Attention-based Encoder-Decoder

## 1 Introduction

Automatically identifying and extracting key texts from scanned structured and semi-structured receipts and saving them as structured data can serve as a very first step to enable a variety of applications. For example, the knowledge of consumer behavior can be extracted from those texts through data analytics. Pipelines for automating office paper works such as in accounting or taxation can also benefit from receipt information in the form of structured data. Although there are significant improvements of OCR in many tasks such as name card recognition, license plate recognition or handwritten text recognition by the recent advance in deep learning, receipt OCR is still challenging because of its higher requirements in accuracy to be practical. Moreover, in some cases, receipts with small size and handwriting are challenging for the recognition system. Figure 1 shows two examples of receipts with a small size and handwriting. For the above reasons, manual labeling is still widely used. Therefore, fast and reliable OCR needs to be developed in order to reduce or even eliminate manual works.

For text line detection, EAST [1] and Connectionist Text Proposal Network (CTPN) [2] have been proposed for detecting text in natural images. CTPN explores rich context information of an input image, making it powerful to detect horizontal text.

© Springer Nature Switzerland AG 2019
T. K. Dang et al. (Eds.): FDSE 2019, LNCS 11814, pp. 705–712, 2019.
https://doi.org/10.1007/978-3-030-35653-8_50

For text line recognition, Convolutional Recurrent Neural Network and Attention-based Encoder-Decoder (AED) have been achieved state-of-the-art for many problems such as Scene Text Recognition [3], handwritten recognition [4–6].

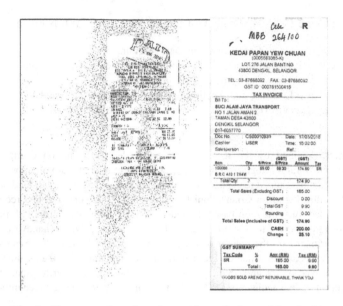

**Fig. 1.** Two examples of receipts with small size and handwriting.

In this paper, we presented a deep learning approach for text detection and recognition. We employed CTPN for text detection and AED for text recognition. Moreover, pre-processing and OCR verification were employed to extract small receipt and remove handwriting, respectively. Experimental results on the dataset from the Robust Reading Challenge on Scanned Receipts OCR and Information Extraction (SROIE 2019) demonstrate the robustness and efficiency of our system.

## 2 Methodology

Inspired by recent successes of deep learning in many tasks such as computer vision, natural language processing, we present a deep learning approach for receipt recognition. The system has two stages based on deep learning: text detection and text recognition. We employ CTPN for text detection and AED for text recognition. The structures of text detection and recognition are shown in Figs. 2 and 3.

### 2.1 Text Detection

The original CTPN detects horizontally arranged text. The CTPN structure is basically similar to Faster R-CNN, but with the addition of the LSTM layer. The network model mainly consists of three parts: feature extraction by VGG16, bidirectional LSTM, and bounding box regression, as shown in Fig. 2. The process of text detection is as follows:

(1) VGG16 extract feature from an input receipt. The size of the features is W × H × C.
(2) A sliding window on the output feature map is employed. In each row, the sequential windows connected to a Bi-directional LSTM (BLSTM).
(3) The BLSTM layer is connected to a 512D fully-connected layer. Then, the output layer predicts text/non-text scores, y-axis coordinates, and side-refinement offsets of 10.
(4) Finally, using the graph-based text line construction algorithm, the obtained one text segments are merged into a text line.

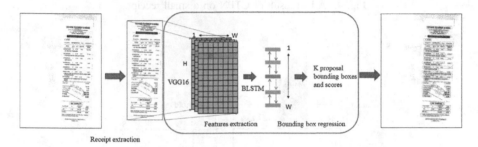

**Fig. 2.** Structure of CTPN for text detection.

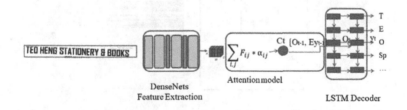

**Fig. 3.** Structure of Attention based Encoder-Decoder for text recognition.

CTPN achieved a good result for horizontal text. However, CTPN cannot detect small text line, since VGG16 reduces 16 times of input images. Figure 4 shown a result of CTPN on a small receipt. Several text lines were not detected. To overcome this problem, we have to extract the receipt area from the input image. Therefore, the scale of the image is larger. We propose a simple method by the histograms of the input image on the x-axis and y-axis. The pre-process is as follows (Fig. 5):

(1) We calculate the histogram of the input image on x-axis and y-axis.
(2) We determine the largest receipt area on each axis when the histogram is larger than a threshold. Then, we determine the receipt area.

**Fig. 4.** A bad result of CTPN on a small receipt.

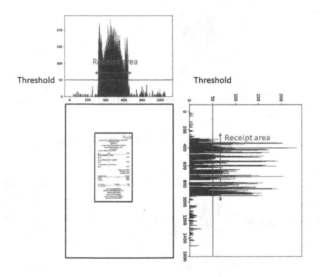

**Fig. 5.** Histograms on x-axis and y-axis of a receipt

## 2.2   Text Recognition

The AED has been successfully applied for recognizing handwritten mathematical expression [4, 5], handwritten Vietnamese [6]. In this work, we employed the previous structure of ADE for recognizing text lines. The ADE has two main modules: DenseNet for extracting features from a text image and an LSTM combined with an attention model for predicting the output text. The process for recognition of a receipt is shown in Fig. 6, and the detail of the AED is shown in Fig. 3.

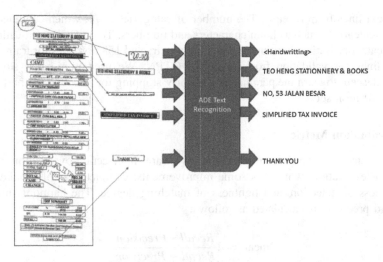

**Fig. 6.** Text recognition process.

**DenseNet Feature Extraction:** Based on our previous researches on AED, we employed DenseNet as feature extraction. DenseNet has direct connections from any preceding layers to succeeding layers, so they help the network reuse and learn features cross layers. The detailed implementation was described in [4, 6]. We employed three dense blocks of growth rate (output feature map of each convolutional layer) k = 24 and the depth (number of convolutional layers in each dense block) D = 16 to extract features.

**Attention-Based LSTM Decoder:** An LSTM decoder predicts one character at a time step. The decoder predicts the output symbol based on the embedding vector of the previous decoded symbol, the currently hidden state of the decoder, and the current context vector. The context vector is computed by the attention mechanism. The decoder is initialized by averaging the extracted features map.

**OCR Verification:** We employ OCR to verify a text line as handwriting or printing. We added a category for handwriting on the decoder. For a handwriting text line, the ADE predicts as <handwriting> symbol. If a text line is recognized as <handwriting> , we will remove this text line from the result of text line detection.

## 3 Evaluation

### 3.1 Dataset

We employ the dataset from SROIE 2019 [7] for this research. Since the testing set of SROIE has not released, we divided the training data into training, validation, and testing sets. We randomly select 80% of receipts for training, 10% of receipts for validation, and the rest for testing. As a result, we have 500 receipts for training, 63 receipts for validation, and 63 for testing. For training text detection, we fine-tune a pre-trained network [8] for 50 k iterations. For training text recognition, we extract text lines from receipts. The number of categories is 71, which contains many character categories such as Latin characters and numbers. To do OCR verification, we added a category for handwriting. We manually extracted 158 text lines for training and 23 text lines for validation from results of CTPN. We used mini-batch stochastic gradient descent to learn the parameters and early stopping for selecting the best model on the validation set.

## 3.2    Evaluation Metric

For text detection, we employed Tightness-aware Intersection-over-Union (TIoU) Metric for evaluation, which has some improvements: completeness of ground truth, compactness of detection, and tightness of matching degree. The harmonic mean of recall and precision is calculated as follows:

$$\text{Hmean} = 2\frac{Recall * Precision}{Recall + Precision}$$

$$\text{Recall} = \frac{\sum Match_{gt_i}}{Num_{gt}} \quad \text{Precision} = \frac{\sum Match_{dt_i}}{Num_{dt}}$$

where $Match_{gt_i}$ and $Match_{dt_i}$ indicate the result of the match between detection and ground truth rectangles under TIoU conditions.

For text recognition, we employed $F_1$, Precision, Recall as follows:

$$F1 = 2\frac{Recall * Precision}{Recall + Precision}$$

$$\text{Recall} = \frac{Number\ of\ correct\ words}{Number\ of\ recognized\ words} \quad \text{Precision} = \frac{Number\ of\ correct\ words}{Number\ of\ ground\ truth\ words}$$

## 3.3    Results

Table 1 shows the result of CTPN with three conditions: CTPN: employing CTPN on original images; pre-processing + CTPN: employing pre-processing to extract receipt area; pre-processing + CTPN + OCR verification: employing pre-processing and OCR verification. The CTPN with pre-processing achieved the best result on Recall and Hmean while CTPN with pre-processing and OCR verification achieved the best result on Precision. The OCR verification can remove handwriting, but in some case, it removes text. The reason is that we have a few of handwriting patterns to train the OCR.

Table 2 shows the result of AED on ground truth of bounding boxes. ADE achieved 86.1% of F1.

**Table 1.** The results of tex detection.

| Method | Recall | Precision | Hmean |
|---|---|---|---|
| CTPN | 45.2 | 72.9 | 55.8 |
| Pre-processing + CTPN | **55.9** | 75.1 | **64.1** |
| Pre-processing + CTPN + OCR verification | 53.9 | **77.5** | 63.6 |

**Table 2.** The results of the AED text recognition on ground truth bounding boxes.

| Method | Recall | Precision | F1 |
|---|---|---|---|
| Ground truth | 87.6 | 84.7 | 86.1 |

Table 3 shows the result of ADE on the detection results of CTPN. The result on bounding boxes of CTPN with pre-processing and OCR verification achieved the best result on F1 and Precision while the result on bounding boxes of CTPN with pre-processing achieved the best result on Recall.

**Table 3.** The results of text recognition.

| Method | Recall | Precision | F1 |
|---|---|---|---|
| CTPN | 60.8 | 67.4 | 63.9 |
| Pre-processing + CTPN | **72.3** | 69.5 | 70.9 |
| Pre-processing + CTPN + OCR verification | 71.3 | **72.5** | **71.9** |

Figure 7 shows an example of a good result from our system. We figured out that the system will work well if the text detection provides precise results.

In the future, we plan to do the following works to improve our system and compare with other systems that participated in SROIE 2019.

+ Analyze error of our system for further improvements of text detection and text recognition.

+ Improve OCR verification by using handwriting from IAM database.

+ Do experiments on the testing set of SROIE 2019 when the testing set released.

**Fig. 7.** Text recognition process.

## 4  Conclusion

In this paper, we have presented a deep learning based system for receipt recognition. We proposed receipt extraction and OCR verification to improve text detection. The system is able to recognize small receipt and ignore handwriting. We achieved 71.9% of F1 score for both detection and recognition task. This result is a baseline for the receipt recognition task.

## References

1. Zhou, X., et al.: EAST: an efficient and accurate scene text detector. In: CVPR 2017, pp. 5551–5560 (2017)
2. Tian, Z., Huang, W., He, T., He, P., Qiao, Y.: Detecting text in natural image with connectionist text proposal network. In: ECCV (2016)
3. Shi, B., Bai, X., Yao, C.: An end-to-end trainable neural network for image-based sequence recognition and its application to scene text recognition. PAMI 2298–2304 (2016)
4. Le, A.D., Nakagawa, M.: Training an end-to-end system for handwritten mathematical expression recognition by generated patterns. In: ICDAR 2017, pp. 1056–1061 (2017)
5. Zhang, J., Du, J., Dai, L.: Multi-scale attention with dense encoder for handwritten mathematical expression recognition. In: ICPR 2018 (2018)
6. Le, A.D., Nguyen, H.T., Nakagawa, M.: Recognizing unconstrained vietnamese handwriting by attention based encoder decoder model. In: 2018 International Conference on Advanced Computing and Applications (ACOMP), pp. 83–87 (2018)
7. ICDAR 2019 Robust Reading Challenge on Scanned Receipts OCR and Information Extraction. https://rrc.cvc.uab.es/?ch=13
8. CTPN Text Detection. https://github.com/eragonruan/text-detection-ctpn

# Efficient CNN Models for Beer Bottle
# Cap Classification Problem

Quan M. Tran[1,2](✉) ⓘ, Linh V. Nguyen[2,5] ⓘ, Tai Huynh[2,3], Hai H. Vo[2],
and Vuong T. Pham[2,4]

[1] University of Information Technology, Vietnam National University,
Ho Chi Minh City, Vietnam
15520683@gm.uit.edu.vn
[2] Kyanon Digital, Ho Chi Minh City, Vietnam
{quan.tran,linh.nguyenviet,tai.huynh,hai.vo,vuong.pham}@kyanon.digital
[3] Wecheer SA, Ho Chi Minh City, Vietnam
tai@wecheer.io
[4] Saigon University, Ho Chi Minh City, Vietnam
vuong.pham@sgu.edu.vn
[5] Industrial University of Ho Chi Minh City, Ho Chi Minh City, Vietnam
nguyenvietlinh@iuh.edu.vn

**Abstract.** In this work, we present an efficient solution to the beer bottle cap classification problem. This problem arises in the Wecheer smart opener project. Although classification problem is common in Computer Vision, there is no dedicated work for beer bottle cap dataset. We combine state-of-the-art deep learning techniques to solve the problem. Our solution outperforms the well-known commercial system that is currently used by the Wecheer project. It is also more efficient than the famous architectures such as VGG, ResNet, and DenseNet for our purposes.

**Keywords:** Beer bottle cap · Classification · Deep learning · Skipped connection · Global Average Pooling · Convolutional neural network

## 1 Introduction

Beer is one of the mostly consumed alcoholic drinks in the world [1]. It is the third most popular drink overall after water and tea [2]. There is no doubt that beer industry is immense around the world and also in Vietnam. The rise of beer consumptions and fierce competitions demand efficient data collection for analysis, business decision, etc. Human efforts so far have been the most common solution for the problem. However, manual monitoring usually lacks of precision and delays analysis speed. These problems can be solved by the IoT Smart opener system Wecheer.io [3], which automatically collects image of bottle caps and classifies them by their brands. The Wecheer.io system currently uses a well-known commercial AI platform to perform the classification. Although the

Supported by Kyanon Digital.

system worked pretty fine, we decided to seek for better solution. This work is a joint project between Kyanon Digital and Wecheer SA (the owner of Wecheer.io).

Our approach is based on deep learning, a machine learning technique that uses deep convolutional neural networks. It has recently become the dominant method for classification problem in Computer Vision. For example, Alexnet [4] won the Imagenet Large Scale Visual Recognition Challenge (ILSVRC) with a large margin in 2012. Its top-5 error rate was 15%, compared to the error rate 26% of the second winner at the same year. All the winners in later years used deep learning architectures, such as ZFnet(2013) [5], VGG (2014) [6], and ResNet (2015) [7]. It is now well-known that deep learning already outperforms human being in several Computer Vision tasks.

In this work, we employed the latest advances in deep learning to solve our problem. Our resulting model, Skipped VGG with GAP, is the combination of three ideas: VGG, DenseNet [8] (i.e., skipped connection and concatenation), and Global Average Pooling. The paper is organized as follows. In Sect. 2, we review the related works. In Sect. 3, we describe our dataset and its issues. We present the methodology for designing the models in Sect. 4. The experiment results are shown in Sect. 5.

## 2    Related Work

There was no solution in literature dedicated to beer bottle cap classification problem. We had to find our own solution for the problem. In principle, we could make use of well-known pre-trained models (such as VGG, ResNet, and DenseNet), and fine-tune them for our purposes. However, all of them did not achieve the high accuracy that we expected and came with their disadvantages. Moreover, VGG and ResNet, even with the smallest model such as VGG-16 and ResNet-50, had too many parameters (138 and 25.6 millions). DenseNet, on the other hand, had high computational cost and required a lot of memory (due to its skipped connections and concatenation). Therefore, we aimed to build a new model that is not only robust in classification but also has fewer parameters and consumes less memory. We successfully achieved all these goals (see Sect. 5).

## 3    Dataset

The dataset used for training and evaluation is collected by the Wecheer's Smart Opener devices, an overview of the dataset is given as follows.

- origin: Vietnamese beer cap,
- number of images: 7784,
- number of brands/ classes: 51,
- images shape: $(240, 320, 3)$.

To build the model, we divided the dataset into 3 sets with the ratio $2 : 1 : 1$ as *training set*, *validation set* and *test set*, respectively. Thus, the numbers of

Histogram of dataset

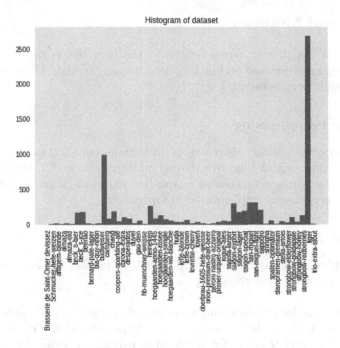

**Fig. 1.** Histogram of dataset with 51 classes

images for each set are as follows: (i) training set: 3879, (ii) validation set: 1960, (iii) test set: 1945.

As shown in Fig. 1, the dataset had some other significant issues. For instance, some pictures were too bright or too dark due to the flash uncertainty. The openers' motion also blurred many images. Stagnant drops on the camera were also a difficulty needed to be handled. Additionally, some brands belonged to the same manufacturer and had very little difference between them. All these problems (see Fig. 2) prevented machine learning models to reach high accuracy.

**Fig. 2.** Some challenges in the dataset. The first picture is too bright, the second is too dark, the third is blurred, and fourth has water drops

# 4    Proposed Methods

In this section, we present our solutions to the beer bottle cap classification problem. We mostly focused on building deep learning models. However, we also did some simple preprocessing.

## 4.1    Image Preprocessing

Our preprocessing mainly consisted of histogram equalization. Namely, we applied Contrast Limited Adaptive Histogram Equalization (CLAHE), an effective technique that has strong robust adaptation to the variation of illumination. This technique is readily implemented in Opencv [9].

## 4.2    Model Architectures

Instead of only presenting our best final model, we present several ones that we attempted to motivate the thought process.

*First Design.* The design was strongly motivated by the VGG-16 model, a popular architecture with stable training and easy implementation. Our architecture makes use of its first 9 layers for the feature extraction, since the size of our dataset and the brands needed to be classified were much smaller than the Imagenet dataset (that was used to train VGG-16). Our top model is designed to use dropout to avoid overfitting with 51 outputs using softmax activation function. The architecture is shown in Table 1.

*Second Design.* We define a **block** is the combination of two *convolutional layers* and *one max pooling layer*. Experimenting the first design, we observed that VGG-styled architecture lead to the loss of information. Namely, the low level features extracted at the beginning are pretty much flushed out when coming to the final convolutional layers. On the other hand, the lower level features also have the significant contribution on the decision of classifier. Especially for the cap bottle, simple features such as shape, color, etc are nearly enough to identify the brand. Therefore, we added **skipped connection** from output of each block to the last convolutional layer, concatenated all outputs and fetched to top model (see Table 2).

*Third Design.* We kept the second design and added skipped connection between the **blocks**. At the last block, there are 3 convolutional layers and one max pooling layer. We also apply batch normalization technique [10] for optimization. The batch normalization layer follows right after the convolutional layer. The architecture is shown in Table 3(left). This model already outperformed state-of-the-art architecture (see Table 4) in terms of accuracy. We named our network **Skipped VGG**.

We notice that dense layers for the top model used so many parameters and made the model too heavy. Therefore, **global average pooling (GAP)** layer was applied before those layers to reduce their sizes (we note that GAP was originally proposed in [11] to generate the heat map for visual attention). The idea lead to the second version of the architecture, as shown in Table 3(right). Surprisingly, this idea increased the accuracy of our model (see Sect. 5). The resulted model is named **Skipped VGG with GAP**. It outperformed all other models and had smallest number of parameters (see Table 4).

Besides, we applied automated hyper-parameters tuning using Bayesian optimization. However, the model generated by this approach did not give better performance than the third design. Because of the limitation, we did not show the results here.

## 5    Experiment Results

All proposed architectures were trained from scratch on GPU Tesla K80 for 260 epochs, with the batch size of 64. Figure 3 shows the accuracy and loss of the third model, on training data and validation data. The models quickly converged after several epochs.

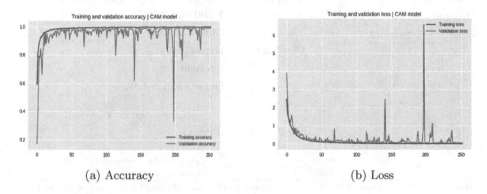

(a) Accuracy                                (b) Loss

**Fig. 3.** Training process of third model with accuracy (a) and loss (b)

### 5.1    Evaluation

We evaluated all models on the test set which had 1945 images and used the accuracy as the metric standard. Table 4 shows that the second version of third model gave the outstanding predictions with **99.33%** in accuracy. To demonstrate the significance of our work, we compare our models to others such as that of service used by the company, VGG-16, ResNet50, DenseNet121 (with 3 blocks), and DenseNet121, on the same test set. The number parameters and test accuracy for each model are shown in Table 4. More further, we also evaluated the second version of the third design using f1-score, as shown in Table 5.

**Table 1.** The first design uses 9 layers of VGG-16. Note that Conv2D contains information about the number of filters and kernel size, respectively, and Dense has number of units.

| Input (144,192,3) |
| --- |
| Conv2D (64, 3 × 3), ReLU |
| Conv2D (64, 3 × 3), ReLU |
| MaxPooling2D |
| Conv2D (128, 3 × 3), ReLU |
| Conv2D (128, 3 × 3), ReLU |
| MaxPooling2D |
| Conv2D (512, 3 × 3), ReLU |
| Conv2D (512, 3 × 3), ReLU |
| MaxPooling2D |
| Dense (512) |
| Dropout |
| Dense (51), Softmax |

**Table 2.** The second design concatenates outputs of all blocks before feeding to top model

|  | Input (144,192,3) |
| --- | --- |
| Block 1 | Conv2D (64, 3 × 3), BatchNorm, ReLU |
|  | Conv2D (64, 3 × 3), BatchNorm, ReLU |
| Block 2 | Conv2D (128, 3 × 3), BatchNorm, ReLU |
|  | Conv2D (128, 3 × 3), BatchNorm, ReLU |
| Skipped connection | Cropping2D for Block 1 |
|  | Concatenate |
| Block 3 | Conv2D (256, 3 × 3), BatchNorm, ReLU |
|  | Conv2D (256, 3 × 3), BatchNorm, ReLU |
| Skipped connection | Cropping2D for outputs of Block 1 and Block 2 |
|  | Concatenate |
| Classification | Dense (512) |
|  | Dropout |
|  | Dense (51), Softmax |

**Table 3.** The third design

|  | The first version | The second version with GAP added |
| --- | --- | --- |
|  | Input (144,192,3) | Input (144,192,3) |
| Block 1 | Conv2D (64, 3 × 3), BatchNorm, ReLU | Conv2D (64, 3 × 3), BatchNorm, ReLU |
|  | Conv2D (64, 3 × 3), BatchNorm, ReLU | Conv2D (64, 3 × 3), BatchNorm, ReLU |
| Block 2 | Conv2D (128, 3 × 3), BatchNorm, ReLU | Conv2D (128, 3 × 3), BatchNorm, ReLU |
|  | Conv2D (128, 3 × 3), BatchNorm, ReLU | Conv2D (128, 3 × 3), BatchNorm, ReLU |
| Skipped connection | Cropping2D for Block 1 | Cropping2D for Block 1 |
|  | Concatenate | Concatenate |
| Block 3 | Conv2D (256, 3 × 3), BatchNorm, ReLU | Conv2D (256, 3 × 3), BatchNorm, ReLU |
|  | Conv2D (256, 3 × 3), BatchNorm, ReLU | Conv2D (256, 3 × 3), BatchNorm, ReLU |
| Skipped connection | Cropping2D for Block 1, Block 2 | Cropping2D for Block 1, Block 2 |
|  | Concatenate | Concatenate |
| Classification | Flatten, Dense (512) | GlobalAveragePooling2D |
|  | Dense (51), BatchNorm, Softmax | Dense (51), BatchNorm, Softmax |

**Table 4.** Number of model parameters and accuracy. Note: current service accuracy: 0.9774.

| Models | Trainable params | Non-trainable | Total | Test acc. |
|---|---|---|---|---|
| 1st | 57,795,187 | 0 | 57,795,187 | 0.9512 |
| 2nd | 100,236,352 | 0 | 100,236,352 | 0.9723 |
| 3rd (v1) | 101,003,481 | 3,430 | 101,006,911 | 0.9902 |
| 3rd (v2) | 1,908,249 | 2,406 | **1,910,655** | **0.9933** |
| VGG-16 | 82,040,691 | 0 | 82,040,691 | 0.9501 |
| ResNet50 | 23,639,091 | 53,120 | 23,692,211 | 0.9820 |
| DenseNet121 (3 blocks) | 4,321,715 | 53,440 | 4,375,155 | 0.9850 |
| DenseNet 121 | 7,006,131 | 83,648 | 7,089,779 | 0.9841 |

**Table 5.** The evaluation in precision, recall, and f1-score for the second version of the third design.

| | Precision | Recall | f1-score | Support |
|---|---|---|---|---|
| Micro avg | 0.9933 | 0.9933 | 0.9933 | 1945 |
| Macro avg | 0.9896 | 0.9861 | 0.9869 | 1945 |
| Weighted avg | 0.9937 | 0.9933 | 0.9932 | 1945 |

## 5.2  Robust Classification

The experiment has shown that our model can deal with most challenges in the dataset. Figure 4 shows some hardest cases which are predicted by the model. All these images are the true predictions with the label and the probability are shown respectively. Most images had bad quality but our model could give the true prediction with high confidence.

## 5.3  Misclassified Images

There are 13 misclassified images out of 1945 predicted by the model as shown in Fig. 5. For each image, wrong labels with their confidence, true labels with the model's confidence are shown respectively.

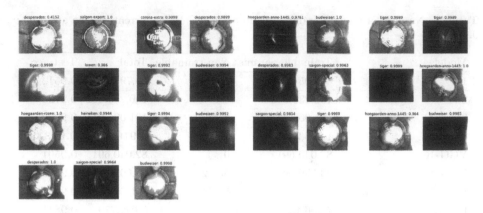

**Fig. 4.** Robust classification.

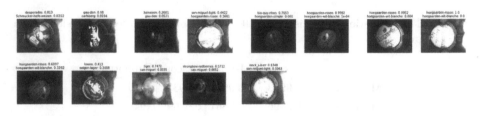

**Fig. 5.** 13 misclassified images.

## 6 Conclusion

In this paper, we presented our deep learning models for the beer bottle cap classification problem. Our final model achieved the amazing accuracy of 99.33%. Moreover, we discovered a surprising effect of GAP. We will explore this fact in future works in order to design more efficient CNNs for computer vision tasks.

**Acknowledgement.** We thank our colleagues, Hai Tran and Dac Dinh, for helpful discussions.

## References

1. Volume of World Beer Production. European Beer Guide. Accessed 17 Oct 2006
2. Nelson, M.: The Barbarian's Beverage: A History of Beer in Ancient Europe. Routledge, p. 1 (2005). ISBN 978-0-415-31121-2
3. https://www.wecheer.io/
4. Krizhevsky, A., Sutskever, I., Hinton, G.: Advances in neural information processing systems (2012)
5. Zeiler, M.D., Fergus, R.: Visualizing and Understanding Convolutional Networks. arXiv:1311.2901 (2013)
6. Zhang, X., Zou, J., He, K., et al.: Accelerating Very Deep Convolutional Networks for Classification and Detection. arXiv:1505.06798 (2015)

7. He, K., Zhang, X., Ren, S., et al.: Deep Residual Learning for Image Recognition. arXiv:1512.03385 (2015)
8. Huang, G., Liu, Z., van der Maaten, L., et al.: Densely Connected Convolutional Networks. arXiv:1608.06993 (2016)
9. https://docs.opencv.org/3.1.0/d5/daf/tutorial_py_histogram_equalization.html
10. Ioffe, S., Szegedy, C.: Batch Normalization: Accelerating Deep Network Training by Reducing Internal Covariate Shift. arXiv:1502.03167 (2015)
11. Zhou, B., Khosla, A., Lapedriza, A., et al.: Learning Deep Features for Discriminative Localization. arXiv:1512.04150 (2015)

# An Approach for Plagiarism Detection in Learning Resources

Tran Thanh Dien$^{(\boxtimes)}$, Huynh Ngoc Han, and Nguyen Thai-Nghe

Can Tho University, Can Tho City, Vietnam
{thanhdien, ntnghe}@ctu.edu.vn,
hanb1412442@student.ctu.edu.vn

**Abstract.** Plagiarism detection problem has been taken into account both individuals and organizations. This problem can be used to detect the copy of documents, e.g., publications, books, theses, and more. There are many approaches that have been proposed for plagiarism detection and they work well for English. Different countries may use different languages, thus, natural language processing (e.g. processing of acute accent, circumflex accent, etc.) as well as semantic or order of the words are still challenging. This work proposes an approach for plagiarism detection, especially for Vietnamese documents in learning/researching resources. The input data were pre-processed, extracted, vectorized and represented in term of TF-IDF. Then, Cosine similarity and word-order similarity of the documents are computed. Finally, an ensemble of these similarities is combined. Experimental results on a Vietnamese journal dataset show that the proposed approach is feasibility.

**Keywords:** Plagiarism detection · Cosine similarity · Word-order similarity

## 1 Introduction

With the rapid development of information technology, including the Internet and leaks of learning materials archives that lead to plagiarism becoming more popular [1, 2]. Due to the availability of resources and easy access on the web, plagiarism has become a serious problem for teachers, researchers and publishers [6]. According to Lewis et al. [3], plagiarism strikes at the heart of universities and academies, undermining the value of academic research. Plagiarism is to copy and paste for a text or change in some words or use synonyms or near synonyms without citing the sources [9]. In present, plagiarism can be considered cybercrime, similar to computer viruses, computer hacking, spamming and violation of copyrights [8]. The increasing proportion of plagiarism in many fields, especially higher education, has become a big problem faced by educational institutions. In the field of publishing, plagiarism is familiar to editors. It increases burden on the reviewing of researchers, decreases the quality of information of scientific literature and journals' reputations [4].

Currently, there are many tools and techniques to detect plagiarism, especially, methods based on machine learning techniques [12]. Some typical tools and services include Turnitin as a web-based tool provided by iParadigms [5, 13, 14]; iThenticate as a web-based plagiarism detection tool for any text document [15]; Quetext as a tool

© Springer Nature Switzerland AG 2019
T. K. Dang et al. (Eds.): FDSE 2019, LNCS 11814, pp. 722–730, 2019.
https://doi.org/10.1007/978-3-030-35653-8_52

using Natural Language Processing and Machine Learning to detect plagiarism[1]; Docol©c as a web-based service using capabilities like searching and ranking of Google API [15]. For example, after checking a manuscript CrossCheck of iThenticate determines how much of the submitted manuscript is similar to previously published articles that come from tens of thousands of journals, billions of web pages, and millions of other content items [4]. However, these tools and services are primarily responsive to the English language. In addition, they are relatively high costs for local journal editors. Therefore, an approach for plagiarism detection for Vietnamese documents is necessary to help the users detect plagiarism documents.

This study proposes an approach for plagiarism detection, especially for available Vietnamese learning resources such as journals, books, and theses. The input data were pre-processed, extracted, vectorized and represented in term of TF-IDF. Then, Cosine similarity and word-order similarity of the documents are computed. Finally, an ensemble of these similarities is combined.

## 2  Related Work

Using effective methods of detecting plagiarism is considered the important issue for the next generation of the web. AlSallal et al. [7] presented a new approach that used some statistical properties of the most common words, and the Latent Semantic Analysis that is applied to extract the most common words usage patterns.

Al-Shamery et al. [8] detect semantic plagiarism based on the meaning and use of synonyms and replace it instead of the original words. The study applied the a pre-processing for the words using tokenization and removing stop words, then testing by a dataset to detect semantic plagiarism through the WordNet dictionary to determine the semantic similarity based on knowledge base.

Mukherjee et al. [9] proposed a method to measure the semantic similarity between documents by mapping keywords, then find similarities between mapped words. Experimental results showed that the proposed algorithm gives significant accurate results in detecting the semantic similarity between documents.

Another approach that proposed by Vani et al. [10] built a plagiarism detection system using the effective combination of various modules. In addition, a new plagiarism score called a weighted overall similarity index was proposed, as opposed to general plagiarism scores. This approach showed that a significant improvement over the comparison baseline, and thus reflects the effectiveness of syntax-semantic-based exhaustive passage level analysis with plagiarism analysis using structural and citation information.

A technique to detect plagiarism based on semantic knowledge was also proposed [11], especially the semantic class and the thematic role. This technique analyzes and compares text based on the semantic allocation for each term in the sentence. Semantic knowledge created semantic arguments for each sentence. The weight for each argument created by semantic knowledge to study its behavior is also researched.

---

[1] http://www.quetext.com/.

Experimental results on the data set showed a significant increase, exceeding the previous plagiarism detection methods in terms of Recall and Precision scores.

In this work, we propose an approach of plagiarism detection in Vietnamese learning/researching resources such as books, theses, journals. For instance, we use a data set collected from Vietnamese articles published on Can Tho University Journal of Science. This data set was pre-processed, extracted, vectorized and represented in term of TF-IDF. Then, Cosine similarity and word-order similarity of the documents are computed. Finally, an ensemble of these similarities is combined. Details of this approach are presented in the following section.

# 3    Proposed Approach

The proposed approach is described in Algorithm 1. The input document was pre-processed, extracted, vectorized and represented in term of TF-IDF and word-order. Then, Cosine similarity and word-order similarity of the document are computed (these similarities are computed using a corpus of pre-processed documents). Finally, an ensemble of these two similarities is combined. Please note that $\alpha$ and $\beta$ are the weighted sum ($\alpha + \beta = 1$) and treated as the hyper-parameters.

```
Algorithm 1. PlagiarismDetection (InputDocument d, corpus-of-
Preprocessed-Documents D, float α, float β, float SimThreshold){
1: Convertion(d); // convert the input document (word/pdf) to text
2: WordNormalization(d) //changed to lower cases, removing blanks,..
3: WordSegmention(d) //seperate document to words
4: RemovingStopWords(d)
5: VectorizationTF-IDF(d)
6: VectorizationOrder(d) //the word-order in the sentences
7: sim ← α * CosineSimilarity(d, D) + β * OrderSimilarity(d, D)
9: Return sets of documents in D which have sim > SimThreshold
}
```

We describe the details of each step in the following.

## 3.1    Data Pre-processing (Convertion, Normalization)

In pre-processing phase, file format conversion (e.g., from .doc(x), .pdf to .txt) and word normalization were carried out. Converting format of an input article is based on Apache POI. For example, the sentence "Xử Lý Ngôn Ngữ Tự nhiên là 1 nhánh của Trí tuệ nhân tạo" is normalized to "xử lý ngôn ngữ tự nhiên là 1 nhánh của trí tuệ nhân tạo".

## 3.2    Word Segmentation

In Vietnamese, space does not segment words but separate syllables. Therefore, the segmentation phase is quite important in NLP. Currently, many tools have been successfully developed to segment Vietnamese words with relatively high accuracy. In this study, the VnTokenizer[2] segmentation tool was used. The tool was developed based on the integrated methods of maximum matching, weighted finite-state transducer and regular expression parsing, using the dataset of Vietnamese syllabary and Vietnamese vocabulary dictionary. This tool segments Vietnamese text into vocabulary units (words, names, numbers, dates, etc.) with more than 95% accuracy. For example, the sentence "xử lý ngôn ngữ tự nhiên là 1 nhánh của trí tuệ nhân tạo" is segmented into "xử_lý ngôn_ngữ tự_nhiên là 1 nhánh của trí_tuệ nhân_tạo".

### 3.3    Removing Stop Words

Stop words are the words that commonly appear in all texts of all categories in the dataset, or the words that appear only in one and several texts. It means that stop words do not make sense or do not contain information worth using. In text classification, the appearance of Vietnamese stop words such as "thì", "là", "mà", "và", "hoặc", "bởi", etc[3] not only do not help assessing the classification but also make noises and reduce the accuracy of the classification process. For example, when being removed stop words, the sentence "xử_lý ngôn_ngữ tự_nhiên là 1 nhánh của trí_tuệ nhân_tạo" becomes "xử_lý ngôn_ngữ tự_nhiên nhánh trí_tuệ nhân_tạo". In this study, after converting the article from .doc(x) to .txt format and segmenting words, the stop word dictionary was used to remove stop words.

### 3.4    Text Vectorization

There are a number of text representation models, i.e. vector space model based on the frequency weighting method, bag of words model, and graph-based model. In this study, the vector space model was applied. Since vector space model can represent an unformatted text document as simple and formulaic notation, various algorithms which had been used in data mining can be applied without any modification. Because of the advantage, lots of researches on vector space model are being actively carried out. It is a relatively simple and effective representation. In vector space model, a document is represented in an $n$-dimensional space vector, where $n$ is the size of the vocabulary of *terms* that presented in the set of documents[4].

For example, let's consider 3 documents as follows: Doc 1: *The food store*; Doc 2: *The food*; Doc 3: *The store*.

Let assume, the 3-dimensional axes (x, y and z) are called "store", "the", "food" respectively. So, documents can be represented in vector form as follows: Doc 1: [1]; Doc 2: [0, 1, 1]; Doc 3: [1, 1, 0]. The value 1 means that that word is present in the document and 0 means absent. There are many techniques to determine these "values" or "weights". In a 3-dimensional space, documents can be visualized as Fig. 1:

In the above model, each dimension corresponds to a separate *term*. If a *term* occurs in the document, its value in the vector is non-zero. There are ways of computing these

---

[2] http://vntokenizer.sourceforge.net/.

[3] https://github.com/stopwords/vietnamese-stopwords.

[4] http://trigonaminima.github.io/2016/11/vsm-to-rec-sys/.

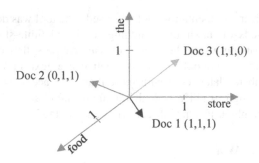

**Fig. 1.** Vector space model

values. One of the best known schemes is TF-IDF weighting. For text representation by vector space model, the input is a set of *j* documents in domain *D*, with $D = \{d_1, d_2, ... d_j\}$ and *m* terms (or words) in each document, $T = \{t_1, t_2, ... t_m\}$.

TF is used to estimate the occurrence frequency of a term in a certain document. Each document has its own length and number of terms, thus, to measure the weight of a term, the term frequency is often divided by the document length.

$$TF(t_i, d_j) = \frac{number\ of\ occurrences\ of\ term\ t_i\ in\ document\ d_j}{total\ number\ of\ terms\ in\ document\ d_j}$$

IDF is used to estimate the importance of a term in a document. While computing TF, all terms are considered equally important. However, it is known that certain terms (such as "nên", "nhưng", "như vậy", etc.) may appear a lot of times but have little importance. Thus, IDF is computed as the following:

$$IDF(t_i, D) = \log \frac{Total\ document\ in\ D}{Number\ of\ document\ containing\ word\ t_i}$$

TF-IDF is composed by TF and IDF. This common method is to calculate the TF-IDF value of a term through its importance in a document belonging to a document set.

High IF-IDF terms commonly occur in a certain document but less occur in other documents. So, it is possible to filter out common terms and retain high value terms.

$$TF - IDF(t_i, d_j, D) = TF(t_i, d_j) * IDF(t_i, D)$$

### 3.5   Computing Similarities

The words (or terms) of documents $d_1$ and $d_2$ is represented collection of terms as $T_1 = \{w_{11}, w_{12}, ..., w_{1m1}\}$ and $T_2 = \{w_{21}, w_{22}, ..., w_{2m2}\}$. After vectorizations of TF-IDF, $T_1$ and $T_2$ are represented as $V_1 = (v_{11}, v_{12}, ..., v_{1m})$, $V_2 = (v_{21}, v_{22}, ..., v_{2m})$, respectively. Then, Cosine similarity is computed using the following formula.

$$simS(T_1, T_2) = \frac{(V_1.V_2)}{|V_1|.|V_2|} = \frac{\sum_{i=1}^{m} v_{1i}.v_{2i}}{\sqrt{\sum_{i=1}^{m} v_{1i}^2}\sqrt{\sum_{i=1}^{m} v_{2i}^2}}$$

An important issue is that the word-order in the sentences could be considered. For example, two sentences "Minh yêu Loan" and "Loan yêu Minh" ("yêu" means "love" in English) have the same occurrences, but their meaning is completely different. Thus, the order of the words should be vectorized and computed. The word-order similarity in the sentences is computed as below formula:

$$simR = 1 - \frac{|R_1 - R_2|}{|R_1 + R_2|} = \frac{\sqrt{\sum_{i=1}^{m} (r_{1i} - r_{2i})^2}}{\sqrt{\sum_{i=1}^{m} (r_{1i} + r_{2i})^2}}$$

Where $R_1 = (r_{11}, r_{12}, ..., r_{1m})$ and $R_2 = (r_{21}, r_{22}, ..., r_{2m})$ are the feature vectors of the word-order. The vector of word-order represents the order of the word $w_i$ ($w_i \in T$) in $T_1$ and $T_2$.

### 3.6 Ensembling

The similarities of Cosine and word-order are combined by:
Sim = α * CosineSimilarity (d, D) + β * OrderSimilarity (d, D)
Where $\alpha$ and $\beta$ are the weighted sum ($\alpha + \beta = 1$) and treated as the hyper-parameters which we can choose by using hyper-parameter search or grid-search.

## 4  Experimental Results

The experimental dataset consists of 680 scientific articles in Vietnamese, being published in Can Tho University Journal of Science from 2016 to 2018, belonging to 10 fields/topics as described in Table 1.

**Table 1.** Distribution of articles in 10 fields

| No | Fields | # Training | # Testing | # Total |
|----|--------|-----------|-----------|---------|
| 1 | Technology | 45 | 5 | 50 |
| 2 | Environment | 54 | 6 | 60 |
| 3 | Natural sciences | 54 | 6 | 60 |
| 4 | Animal husbandry | 36 | 4 | 40 |
| 5 | Biotechnology | 27 | 3 | 30 |
| 6 | Agriculture | 90 | 10 | 100 |
| 7 | Fisheries | 135 | 15 | 150 |
| 8 | Education | 36 | 4 | 40 |
| 9 | Social sciences and humanities | 72 | 8 | 80 |
| 10 | Economics | 63 | 7 | 70 |
|  | Total | 612 | 68 | 680 |

The articles were pre-processed by converting .doc(x)/pdf to .txt files, then proceeded word segmentation. The removal of stop words was done using a stop word dictionary-based approach, there remained 4,095 words. The process of modeling each text was a weighted word vector. Therefore, the modeled dataset was the TF*IDF matrix of words with a size of 680 * 4,095 elements.

We also developed the system for plagiarism detection of Vietnamese articles as presented in Fig. 2. From this system, after selecting the source article for checking plagiarism and the given similarity threshold, the system automatically returned list of similar articles which were retrieved from the existing database.

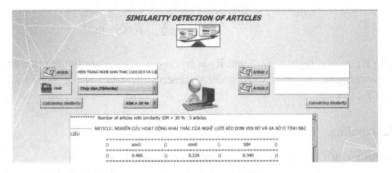

**Fig. 2.** Interface for plagiarism detection

Examples were presented in Table 2. When the user input an article for checking plagiarism (column "Article to check") with a similarity threshold ("SIM threshold"). The articles which had similarity as the given threshold were retrieved (column "Results").

**Table 2.** Experimental results of plagiarism detection for 5 articles

| No | Article to check | Results |
|---|---|---|
| *SIM threshold > 30%; Topic: Fisheries* | | |
| 1 | Hiện trạng nghề khai thác lưới kéo và lươi rê (Tàu <90 CV) ở tỉnh Kiên Giang *(The status of trawlers and gillnets (vessels of <90 CV) in Kien Giang province)* | **Result 1:** Nghiên cứu hoạt động khai thác của nghề lưới kéo đơn ven bờ và xa bờ ở tỉnh Bạc Liêu *(Study on the fishing activities of inshore and offshore single trawlers in Bac Lieu province)*; **SIM = 0.346.** **Result 2:** Nghiên cứu hoạt động khai thác của nghề lưới rê hỗn hợp ở tỉnh Trà Vinh *(Study on the status of mixed gillnet fisheries in Tra Vinh province)*; **SIM = 0.336** **Result 3:** Nghiên cứu nghề lưới rập xếp ở tỉnh Cà Mau *(Study on cage traps in Ca Mau province)*; **SIM = 0.334** |

*(continued)*

**Table 2.**  (*continued*)

| No | Article to check | Results |
|----|------------------|---------|
|    |                  | **Result 4:** Phân tích hiệu quả kỹ thuật và tài chính của nghề lưới kéo xa bờ (90 CV) ở tỉnh Bến Tre *(Performance analysis of financial and technical the offshore trawlers (90 CV) in Ben Tre Province)*; **SIM = 0.351** **Result 5:** Ứng dụng công nghệ semi biofloc trong nuôi tôm thẻ chân trắng (*Litopenaeus vannamei*) thâm canh *(Application semi biofloc technology for white leg shrimp (Litopenaeus vannamei) intensive farm)*; **SIM = 0.417** |
| *SIM threshold >40%; Topic: Natural Sciences* | | |
| 2 | Mờ hóa chuỗi thời gian dựa vào bài toán phân tích chùm *(Interpolate time series based on cluster analysis problem)* | **Result 1:** Dự báo đỉnh mặn tại các trạm đo chính của tỉnh Cà Mau bằng mô hình chuỗi thời gian mờ *(Forecasting crest of sanility at three main stations of Ca Mau province by fuzzy time series model)*; **SIM = 0.427** |
| *SIM threshold >50%; Topic remainings* | | |
| 3 | Randomly selected articles from remaining topics | Not found |

Besides developing the system for plagiarism detection of a given article to a corpus of articles, we also developed an interface for checking two given articles as presented in Table 3. We set a given threshold >30% to compare the two articles. After calculating similarity, it returned the result of 55.6%. This result showed that the proposed approach is rather appropriate to Vietnamese plagiarism detection.

**Table 3.**  Results of comparing two given articles

| No | Input article 1 | Input article 2 | SIM threshold | System result |
|----|-----------------|-----------------|---------------|---------------|
| 1 | Sinh khối rừng tràm vườn quốc gia u minh thượng, tỉnh Kiên Giang *(Biomass of Melaleuca forest at the U Minh Thuong National Part, Kien Giang Province)* | Sinh khối và khả năng hấp thụ $CO_2$ của rừng tràm khu bảo tồn thiên nhiên Lung Ngọc Hoàng *(Biomass and $CO_2$ absorption of Melaleuca forest in Lung Ngoc Hoang Natural Reserve)* | >30% | SIM = 0.556 |

# 5 Conclusions

This work proposes an approach for plagiarism detection, especially for Vietnamese documents. The input data were pre-processed, extracted, vectorized and represented in term of TF-IDF. Then, Cosine similarity and word-order similarity of the documents were computed. Finally, an ensemble of these similarities was combined. Experimental results on a Vietnamese journal dataset showed that the proposed approach was feasibility. Besides the proposed approach, we also developed the real system to help the users to detect plagiarism. This work will be continued to develop for plagiarism detection in Vietnamese theses and books.

# References

1. Born, A.: How to reduce plagiarism. J. Inf. Syst. Educ. **14**, 223–224 (2003)
2. Howard, R.: Understanding "Internet plagiarism". Comput. Compos. **24**, 3–15 (2007)
3. Lewis, B., Duchac, J., Douglas Beets, S.: An academic publisher's response to plagiarism. J. Bus. Ethics **102**, 489–506 (2011)
4. Carter, C., Blanford, C.: Plagiarism and detection. J. Mater. Sci. **51**, 7047–7048 (2016)
5. Brinkman, B.: An analysis of student privacy rights in the use of plagiarism detection systems. Sci. Eng. Ethics **19**, 1255–1266 (2012)
6. Yousuf, S., Ahmad, M., Nasrullah, S.: A review of plagiarism detection based on Lexical and Semantic Approach. In: 2013 International Conference on Emerging Trends in Communication, Control, Signal Processing and Computing Applications (C2SPCA) (2013)
7. AlSallal, M., Iqbal, R., Palade, V., Amin, S., Chang, V.: An integrated approach for intrinsic plagiarism detection. Futur. Gener. Comput. Syst. **96**, 700–712 (2019)
8. Al-Shamery, E., Gheni, H.: Plagiarism detection using semantic analysis. Indian J. Sci. Technol. **9**, 1–8 (2016). https://doi.org/10.17485/ijst/2016/v9i1/84235
9. Mukherjee, I., Kumar, B., Singh, S., Sharma, K.: Plagiarism detection based on semantic analysis. Int. J. Knowl. Learn. **12**, 242 (2018)
10. Vani, K., Gupta, D.: Integrating syntax-semantic-based text analysis with structural and citation information for scientific plagiarism detection. J. Assoc. Inf. Sci. Technol. **69**, 1330–1345 (2018)
11. Wali, W., Gargouri, B., Ben Hamadou, A.: An enhanced plagiarism detection based on syntactico-semantic knowledge. In: Abraham, A., Cherukuri, A.K., Melin, P., Gandhi, N. (eds.) ISDA 2018 2018. AISC, vol. 941, pp. 264–274. Springer, Cham (2020). https://doi.org/10.1007/978-3-030-16660-1_26
12. Chowdhury, H.A., Bhattacharyya, D.K.: Plagiarism: Taxonomy, Tools and Detection Techniques. ArXiv abs/1801.06323 (2018)
13. Ahmed, R.A.: Overview of different plagiarism detection tools. Int. J. Futur. Trends Eng. Technol. **2**, 1–3 (2015)
14. Osman, A.H., Salim, N., Binwahlan, M.S.: Plagiarism Detection Using Graph-Based Representation. ArXiv, abs/1004.4449 (2010)
15. Maurer, H.A., Kappe, F., Zaka, B.: Plagiarism - a survey. J. Univers. Comput. Sci. **12**, 1050–1084 (2006)

# Detecting Kuzushiji Characters from Historical Documents by Two-Dimensional Context Box Proposal Network

Anh Duc Le[✉]

Center for Open Data in the Humanities, Tokyo, Japan
anh@ism.ac.jp

**Abstract.** Detecting characters from historical documents is a challenging problem due to the cursive and connected characters. It is a fundamental task for recognizing historical documents. In this paper, we propose a two-dimensional context box proposal network. The network has three parts: feature extraction, two-dimensional context, and box proposal regression. For feature extraction, we employ VGG16 to extract features from an input image. Then, the extracted features are processed by two-dimensional context. We employ two Bidirectional Long Short Term Memory (BLSTM) to explore vertical and horizontal meaningful context. Finally, the bounding box is predicted from the output of the two-dimensional context. We tested our proposed system on 28 books of Kuzushiji documents. The results of the experiments show the effectiveness of our proposed two-dimensional context for character detection. Our system achieved 88.50% and 92.46% of F1 score on validation and testing sets, respectively, which outperforms the baseline system (Connectionist Text Proposal Network).

**Keywords:** Box proposal network · Two-dimensional context · Character detection · Historical document

## 1 Introduction

Japan had been using Kuzushiji or cursive writing style shortly after Chinese characters got into the country in the 8th century. The Japanese have been using three types of characters which are Kanji (Chinese character in the Japanese language), Hiragana and Katakana. Hiragana and Katakana; derived from different ways of simplifying Kanji, don't contain independent semantic meaning, but instead of carrying phonetic information (like letters in the English alphabet). Because Kuzushiji characters were written in cursive, the variation of writing styles are large and characters are written connected. Figure 1 shows an example of Kuzushiji document. Even for a human, it is difficult to read cursive scripts like Kuzushiji. While many digitized copies of manuscripts and books have been collected, only a small number of Kuzushiji experts can read and work with them. Therefore, several researchers focused on making a recognition system to read Kuzushiji document automatically.

© Springer Nature Switzerland AG 2019
T. K. Dang et al. (Eds.): FDSE 2019, LNCS 11814, pp. 731–738, 2019.
https://doi.org/10.1007/978-3-030-35653-8_53

In 2017, The Center for Open Data in the Humanities (CODH) in Japan provided Kuzushiji dataset to organize a competition, the 21st Pattern Recognition and Media Understanding (PRMU) Algorithm Contest for Kuzushiji recognition [1]. The competition focused on recognizing an isolated character or several characters on lines, which is easier than whole documents like in Fig. 1. Nguyen et al. won the competition. They developed three recognition systems based on convolutional neural network (CNN) and Bidirectional Long Short-Term Memory (BLSTM) for three tasks [2].

In our previous work, we proposed a human-inspired reading system to recognize Kuzushi characters on PRMU Algorithm Contest [3]. The recognition system based on an attention-based encoder-decoder approach to simulate human reading behavior. We achieved better accuracy than the winner of the competition.

Tarin et al. presented Kuzushi-MNIST, which contains ten classes of hiragana, Kuzushi-49, which contains 49 classes of hiragana, and Kuzishi-Kanji, which contains 3832 classes of Kanji [4]. The datasets are benchmarks to engage the machine learning community into the world of classical Japanese literature.

**Fig. 1.** An example of Kuzushi document which contains cursive and connected characters.

For text detection, An Efficient and Accurate Scene Text Detector (EAST) [5], and Connectionist Text Proposal Network (CTPN) [6] are recent methods that achieved high accuracy on text detection datasets. EAST employ multi-scale features and a simple pipeline to provide fast and accurate text detection in natural scenes. CTPN detects a text line by splitting text lines into sequences of fine-scale text proposals. A vertical anchor mechanism that jointly predicts location and text/non-text score of each text proposal was proposed to improve localization accuracy.

Although the previous works showed good performance for isolated character recognition and multiple line recognition, which are simple cases, the problem of reading and transcribing Kuzushiji documents is remaining. They have included segmentation of connected character and recognition of a large variety of character classes. In this paper, we propose a two-dimensional context box proposal network for character segmentation on a full page of Kuzushiji document. The network is based on object proposal approach [7] on object detection and bottom-up approach [6] on text detection. We integrated two-dimensional context on feature extraction, which is helpful for horizontal text like Kuzushiji documents. The effectiveness of the two-dimensional context is verified through experiments.

The following of this paper is organized as follows. Section 2 describes the overview of the two-dimensional context box proposal network. Section 3 presents the evaluation. Finally, Sect. 4 draws a conclusion of the paper.

## 2    Two-Dimensional Context Box Proposal Network

The network is inspired by Single Shot Detection [5] on object detection and Connectionist Text Proposal Network [6] on text detection. The network has three parts: features extraction, two-dimensional context, and box proposal regression. For feature extraction, we employ VGG16 to extract features from an input image. Then, the extracted features are processed by two-dimensional context. We employ two Bidirectional Long Short Term Memory (BLSTM) to explore vertical and horizontal meaningful context. Finally, the bounding box is predicted from the output of the two-dimensional context. The architecture of the network is shown in Fig. 2.

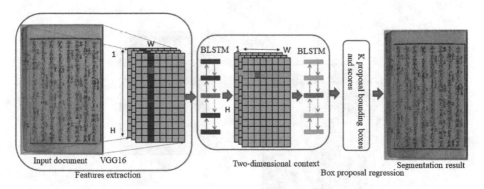

**Fig. 2.**  An example of Kuzushi document which contains cursive and connected characters.

### 2.1    Feature Extraction

Similar to CTPN and other Region Proposal Networks, we employ the very deep 16-layer vggNet (VGG16, a simple CNN) to extract features from an input image. We extract feature from the conv5 layer of the VGG16. VGG16 allows an input image of arbitrary size. The size of the extracted features is $(H \times W \times 512)$.

### 2.2    Two-Dimensional Context

For detecting horizontal text in a scene, CTPN employed a BLSTM to scan process features horizontally. As a result, CTPN extracts the horizontal context from features. We believe that context information around characters (horizontal and vertical) may also be important for box proposal decision. Our network should be able to explore both horizontal and vertical context information. They help the network to make a reliable decision. We proposed a two-dimensional context to explore vertical and horizontal context information as Fig. 1. It contains two BLSTM to scan features vertically and horizontally, respectively. We employ 128 hidden nodes for forward and backward LSTMs. The size of output features is $(H \times W \times 512)$

### 2.3    Box Proposal Regression

We split a character into a sequence of box proposals, and predict each of them separately. For box proposal regression, the network generates ten boxes for each point of the output of the two-dimensional context. As a result, the network generate $10 \times W \times H$ box proposals. Each box proposal at $(x, y)$ has a fixed width of 16 pixels (since feature extraction reduce 16 times of the input image) and x as the horizontal center. The y-center and height are varied and predicted by the network. The network also predicts a confidence score, which determines a box that contains a character. The final result is created by concatenating continuous boxes having confident score larger than 0.7. Figure 3 shows an example of the detection result. Box proposals, whose confidential score larger than 0.7, are shown as green boxes. The final result is shown as red boxes.

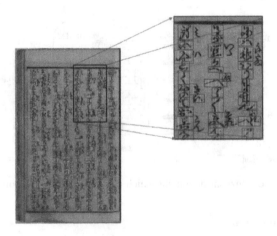

**Fig. 3.** An example of a detection result. (Color figure online)

## 3    Evaluation

### 3.1    Dataset

We employ the pre-modern Japanese dataset to train and evaluate our proposed network. The dataset was created by the National Institute of Japanese Literature (NIJL) and curated by the Center for Open Data in the Humanities (CODH). The dataset currently has 28 books. We select all images from 26 books for training, a book for

**Table 1.** Statistics of the training, validation, and testing sets.

| Dataset | # of books | # of pages | # of characters |
| --- | --- | --- | --- |
| Training | 26 | 2,633 | 521,258 |
| Validation | 1 | 500 | 79,415 |
| Testing | 1 | 466 | 83,492 |

validation, and a book for testing. The number of images and character for training, validation, testing are shown in Table 1.

## 3.2 Evaluation Metrics

In order to measure the performance of our proposed system, we use Precision, Recall, and F1 metrics, which is generally employed for evaluating character detection task. The detail of the metrics are shown in the following equations:

$$Precision = \frac{Number\ of\ correct\ detected\ characters}{Number\ of\ detected\ characters}$$

$$Recall = \frac{Number\ of\ correct\ detected\ characters}{Number\ of\ groundtruth\ characters}$$

$$F1 = 2 * \frac{Precision * Recall}{Precision + Recall}$$

For determining correct detection, if we use intersection over union (IOU), it provides a very bad evaluation. Even we use very low threshold (0.6), IOU can not determine correct detections reliable. Figure 4a shows an example of evaluation by IOU method. Red boxes are ground truth, blue boxes are correct predictions, and green boxes are incorrect predictions. We can observe that some green boxes should be correct predictions. In those case, if a predicted box covers almost a ground truth, it should be a correct prediction. We define a new condition for determining a correct detection. The confidence score (CS) of each prediction is calculated as the following:

$$CS(P) = \frac{I(P, GT_{COR}) - \sum_{box=\{GT-GT_{COR}\}} I(P, box)}{area(GT_{COR})}$$

Where $P$ is a predicted box, $I(a, b)$ is the intersection of $a$ and $b$, $GT$ is ground truth set, $GT_{COR}$ is corresponding ground truth of $P$.

We use a high threshold (0.75) for determining a correct detection. Figure 4b shows a result by using the confidence score. We observed that SC are more reliable than IOU.

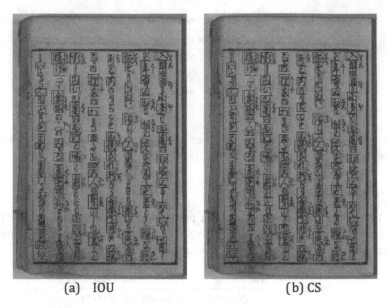

(a)  IOU                                    (b) CS

**Fig. 4.** Examples of determining correct prediction by IOU and CS. (Color figure online)

### 3.3  Training

We used stochastic gradient descent to learn the parameters. The initial learning rate was set to $10^{-5}$. The training process was stopped when the F1 score on the validation set did not improve after ten epochs.

### 3.4  Experimental Results

We employ CTPN which used on text detection as the baseline system. Two systems have the same setting as describing above, except two-dimensional context. The experiment evaluated the performance of the proposed system and baseline system on the validation and testing sets. Our proposed system achieved 88.50% and 92.46% of F1 on validation an testing sets, respectively. Our system outperforms the baseline system around 0.5%–1%. This result verified that two-dimensional context is useful and effective for character detection (Table 2).

**Table 2.** Comparison of the proposed method and baseline method (CTPN) on the validation and testing sets

| System | Validation | | | Testing | | |
|---|---|---|---|---|---|---|
| | Precision | Recall | F1 | Precision | Recall | F1 |
| Baseline system | 86.99 | 88.90 | 87.93 | 91.21 | 92.91 | 92.01 |
| Our proposed system | **87.48** | **89.55** | **88.50** | **91.61** | **93.32** | **92.46** |

Figure 5 shows two examples of good and bad detection results of our system. Red boxes are ground truth, while blue and green boxes are correct and incorrect detection, respectively. We observed that two characters are merged into one bounding box in several cases in Fig. 5(b). We can detect those case when the width is larger than two times of the height. In the future, we will focus on post-processing to revise incorrect detections.

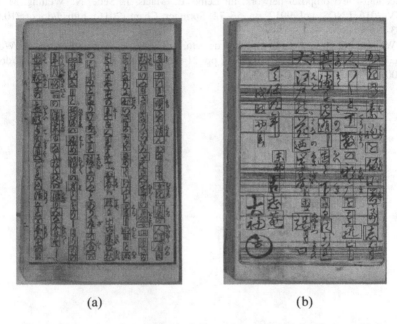

(a)                                    (b)

**Fig. 5.** Examples of good and bad detection results. (Color figure online)

## 4  Conclusion

In this paper, we have proposed the two-dimensional context box proposal network for detecting Kuzushi characters. The efficiency of the proposed system was demonstrated through experiments. We achieved 88.50% and 92.46% of F1 score on validation and testing sets, respectively. It outperforms the baseline system (Connectionist Text Proposal Network). We plan to improve the detection system by post-processing in the future.

## References

1. Kuzushi challenge. http://codh.rois.ac.jp/char-shape/
2. Nguyen, H.T., Ly, N.T., Nguyen, K.C., Nguyen, C.T., Nakagawa, M.: Attempts to recognize anomalously deformed Kana in Japanese historical documents. In: Proceedings of the 2017 Workshop on Historical Document and Processing, Kyoto, Japan, pp. 31–36, November 2017

3. Le, A.D., Clanuwat, T., Kitamoto, A.: A human-inspired recognition system for pre-modern Japanese historical documents. IEEE Access 7(1), 84163–84169

4. Clanuwat, T., Bober-Irizar, M., Kitamoto, A., Lamb, A., Yamamoto, K., Ha, D.: Deep learning for classical Japanese literature. In: NeurIPS 2018 Workshop on Machine Learning for Creativity and Design, December 2018

5. Zhou, X., et al.: EAST: an efficient and accurate scene text detector. In: CVPR (2018)

6. Tian, Z., Huang, W., He, T., He, P., Qiao, Yu.: Detecting text in natural image with connectionist text proposal network. In: Leibe, B., Matas, J., Sebe, N., Welling, M. (eds.) ECCV 2016. LNCS, vol. 9912, pp. 56–72. Springer, Cham (2016). https://doi.org/10.1007/978-3-319-46484-8_4

7. Liu, W., et al.: SSD: single shot multibox detector. In: Leibe, B., Matas, J., Sebe, N., Welling, M. (eds.) ECCV 2016. LNCS, vol. 9905, pp. 21–37. Springer, Cham (2016). https://doi.org/10.1007/978-3-319-46448-0_2

# An Empirical Study on Fabric Defect Classification Using Deep Network Models

Nguyen Thi Hong Anh[✉] and Bui Cong Giao

Faculty of Electronics and Telecomminications, Saigon University,
273 An Duong Vuong, District 5, Ho Chi Minh City, Vietnam
anhnh.vu@gmail.com

**Abstract.** Fabric defect inspection plays an essential role in the textile manufacturing process. Traditional detection is carried out using defect visualization. This method obviously is inefficient in both accuracy and inspection time. Automatic detection, which is based on image processing and machine learning, has been proven to be a suitable approach for this problem. However, due to the variety of defect kinds in a broad range of deferent fabrics, existing methods are actually proposed for typical group of fabric defects. This paper aims to investigate models of deep neural network for the general fabric classification problem. In particular, two models including VGG16 and Darknet are used to classify the defect fabric categories. The models are tested for the TILDA database to evaluate their performances.

**Keywords:** Fabric defect classification · Deep neural network · Supervised learning

## 1 Introduction

Textile fabric is manufactured with textile fibers and a widely used material in daily life. During manufacturing woven fabric, unexpected operations can form various defects on the surface. Defects can make the price of fabrics to be reduced by 45–65% [17]. It is natural with manufacturer to reduce the number of defects in the production process. To this end, a fabric defect inspection is necessary and essential task for the quality control in textile manufacturing. The traditional method usually is based on the human vision. Workers are requited to monitor for detecting potential defects, and then manually repair them. However, these defects usually are minor. Many kinds of defect are fine. It is not easy to detect by human eyes. Furthermore, human detecting will increase the working hours. Up to now, there are more than 70 defect types which have been defined in the textile industry [11]. For such s big number of defects, it thus necessary to develop an automated inspection model for not only improving fabric quality, but also reducing human costs. As mentioned in [4,11], an automated inspection system can reach an accuracy rate of higher than 90%, compared with just 75%

© Springer Nature Switzerland AG 2019
T. K. Dang et al. (Eds.): FDSE 2019, LNCS 11814, pp. 739–746, 2019.
https://doi.org/10.1007/978-3-030-35653-8_54

Fig. 1. An example of automated inspection machine.

by human. In recent years, utilizing the advantages of machine vision and image processing techniques, automated fabric defect detection has been received many attentions in researching community as well as industry. Many vision systems were developed to replace the traditionally manual methods. Figure 1 shows an example of automated inspection machines[1].

Due to variety of fabrics, there is a wide range of different characteristics. All fabrics can be categorized into 17 classifications [11]. Each of them is structured under different shapes such as rectangular, square, or hexagonal (see Fig. 2 for some common fabric structures). For more than 70 types of defects, there are a lots of categories and characteristics of defects. Figure 3 shows five defect types in a fabric category. First two images are hole-type defects in which they are classified due to the size of hole. The third one is a cut defect, the fourth is sliced hole and the last one is sliced hole with a cut. Another challenge in the fabric defect detection is data collection. It is difficult to collect a large enough

Fig. 2. Fabric samples (in the TILDA database) with different patterns.

[1] https://www.iigm.in.

number of defect samples for each type. This makes incompleteness in datasets. Consequently, though many researchers have spent much efforts to the problem (as mentioned in the next section), a method proposed for a fabric category can not be extended to another. There are various vision systems proposed for surface defect inspections in industry, for instances ceramic [1] and sheet steel [18]. For fabric defect detections, many studies were carried out. A previous common approach is based on spectral analysis. Fourier transform was widely applied to defect detection [2]. Another is Wavelet based methods [3,16,19,22]. Systematic reviews of existing methods can be found in [11] and also in [6].

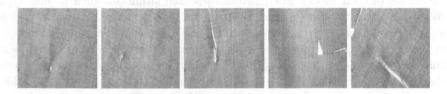

**Fig. 3.** Different defects in a fabric (in the TILDA database), from left to right: medium hole, big hole, a cut, sliced hole, and sliced hole with cut.

Deep learning techniques are increasingly taken into account in recent years. It also is proved to be an increasingly important role in computer vision and its applications. This paper aims to investigate the use of deep learning techniques for fabric defect detection. Our main purpose is to toward a general model to overcome challenges mentioned above. To this end, we apply some state-of-the-art deep learning models for variety of defect types on a number of fabric categories. The models are tested and evaluated for the TILDA database.

The rest of the paper is organized as follows. The next section quickly reviews some recent learning-based methods proposed for fabric defect detection. Section 3 describes the use of deep learning models for the problem. Experimental results are given at the end of the section. Finally, Sect. 4 gives concluding remarks.

## 2   Learning-Based Detection

Neural networks has attracted attentions for fabric defect detection, beside of vision based inspection systems in other fields. In 2000, Huang and Chen introduced a back-propagation neural network coupling with fuzzy term to classify eight different categories of fabric defect [5]. Stojanovic et al. then proposed a three layer back-propagation model to reduce the computational cost [15]. Kumar, in 2003, gave a feed-forward network model for segmentation local defects [7]. In this model, the principal components analysis (PCA) using singular value decomposition (SVD) was used to reduce the dimension of feature vectors. Also in this year, Kuo et al. developed [8,9] two other back-propagation

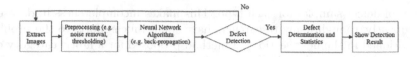

**Fig. 4.** A back-propagation model proposed by Kuo et al. in 2003 [11].

models. They applied a nonlinear regression algorithm to model a high dimensional system and also introduced a pre-processed filtering step to improve the performance of defect detection, obtained at 94.38% accuracy. Figure 4 shows an overview of their model. For more complicated situations such as hole-type defects, poor quality, and unknown size samples, some neural network models also were developed to solve [20,21]. In 2015, towards a wholly automated inspection system, Rebhi et al. presented a detection scheme which uses the local local homogeneity and neural network [12]. They compute a new homogeneity image. A discrete cosine transform (DCT) is then applied on the image to obtain different representative energy features of each DCT block. These features are finally used as inputs for training a back-propagation model.

Very recently, deep neural networks have also been investigated for fabric defect detections. Mei et al., in 2018, presented an automated model to detect and localize defects [10]. The method is developed as a multi-scale convolutional denoising autoencoder (MSCDAE) architecture. A Gaussian pyramid is used to extract defect features in different sizes for the inputs of the network. This helps to train the model with small samples. Furthermore, the model can be conducted in unsupervised way, it does not need labelled ground truth and human intervention. Thanks to the powerful of convolutional neural network (CNN), Jing et al. developed a deep CNN model for automatic fabric defect detection [6]. In the model, the fabric image is decomposed local patches and then labelled. The labelled patches are used for a pretrained deep CNN model. Finally, a inspection phase is involved to detect defects by sliding over the whole image through the trained model. Defects and their positions are classified and prompted, respectively. Figure 5 is the architecture of this model. Although, proposed deep neural network models achieved a high accuracy results, they still need image processing

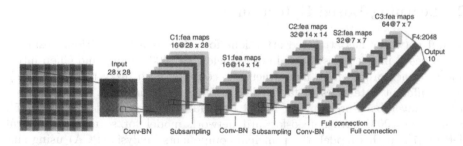

**Fig. 5.** The deep CNN model proposed by Jing et al. in 2019 [6].

tasks for the preprocessing purpose. Patches decomposition required to capture as many as possible features of defects, can make the deep CNN model to be more structurally complicated. Furthermore, as indicated in [6], a pretrained model with MNIST datasets is necessary to obtain better results.

## 3    Deep Networks for Fabric Defect Detection

In this section, we present an empirical study for fabric defect classification with two well-known CNN models, including VGG16 and Darknet tool. Experiments were conducted for the TILDA database which includes 8 categories of defects.

VGG16 was proposed by Simonyan and Zisserman [14] for large scale image classification and detection. In this model, filters of very small size of $3 \times 3$ are used in convolutional layers. These filters are to extract image features located the left, right, up, down, and center positions. The model involves also five max-pooling layers for the pooling computations. There are three fully-connected layers following the pooling ones and the soft-max one at the end. Figure 6 shows the architecture of VGG16[2]. We also perform experiments with the Darknet framework which is an open source neural network in C and Cuda [13].

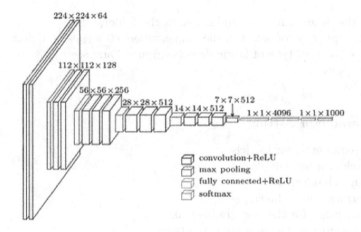

**Fig. 6.** The architecture of the VGG16 neural network.

### Dataset Organization

A folder, named `tilda_data`, is created for containing all files necessary for model training. This will contain all images of the dataset (located in folder 'r1', 'r2', and 'r3'), a file listing paths to training examples (`tilda_train.list`), a file of all paths to testing examples (`tilda_test.list`), and a file specifying a list of labels of categories (`tilda_labels.txt`). The TILDA dataset, specifically, the

---

[2] https://www.cs.toronto.edu/~frossard/post/vgg16.

**Fig. 7.** Samples of e0 with no defect

**Fig. 8.** Samples with different defects.

c1 type of this one, is used for training for all proposed convolutional networks. Each image of the dataset is renamed to this format as `order_defect_type.png`, where

- `order`: the order number of the image in the folder,
- `defect_type`: type of defect in the image, where e0 means no defect, while e1 to e7 are labels of type of fabric defects. Figure 7 and see Fig. 8 are examples of such types.

### Hyper-Parameter Setting

- Hyper-parameters for models
  - Batch size per sample: 1,
  - Image channels: 3,
  - Learning rate: 0.00001,
  - Momentum for the new gradient: 0.9.
- Hyper-parameters for data augmentation:
  - Angle: 7,
  - Hue: 0.1,
  - Saturation: 0.75,
  - Exposure: 0.75,
  - Aspect: 0.75.

Towards a general fabric defect classification, we did not label and localize the training dataset. Before the training, some fundamental image processing operators such as histogram equalization and Sobel filter, are applied to highlight defect objects. A training dataset consisting of 720 images of the TILDA database is used to train the models. Experimental results are given in Table 1.

**Table 1.** Testing results.

| Model | Top 3 accuracy | Precision | Recall |
|---|---|---|---|
| VGG16 | 68.7% | 56.7% | 60% |
| Darknet | 48.6% | 58.9% | 42.1% |

VGG16 gives higher performance than that by Darknet, since it takes advantages of the small filters (size of $3 \times 3$) in convolutional layers. This helps VGG16 to capture features with small number of samples in training datasets. However, as a consequence, the time of training is worse to that of Darknet. The results obtained are not high, but acceptable for unlabelled and unlocalized defects in the training dataset. This also indicates that a state-of-the-art deep CNN model with suitable parameters can be potential for a general fabric defect classification. This means that different defect types in numerous fabric categories can be classified with few efforts of labelling and localization.

## 4  Conclusion

This paper investigated the use of deep network models for the general fabric classification problem. In particular, two models including VGG16 and Darknet were used to classify the defect fabric categories without data labelling and localization. The models are tested for the TILDA database. Experimental results were given and discussed. Currently, the accuracies in the tests are not hight yet, since few simple preprocessing tasks applied for the training data. This will be comprehensively studied in another topic for improvement.

**Acknowledgment.** This work is funded by Saigon University, Ho Chi Minh City, Vietnam under the **grant number [CS2018-68]** (project contract No. 891/HD-QPTKHCN, dated 26/7/2018).

## References

1. Boukouvalas, C.: Color grading of randomly textured ceramic tiles using color histograms. IEEE Trans. Industr. Electron. **46**(1), 219–226 (1999)
2. Chan, C.-H., Pang, G.K.H.: Fabric defect detection by Fourier analysis. IEEE Trans. Ind. Appl. **36**(5), 1267–1276 (2000)
3. Han, Y., Shi, P.: An adaptive level-selecting wavelet transform for texture defect detection. Image Vis. Comput. **25**(8), 1239–1248 (2007)
4. Hong Kong Productivity Council. Textile Handbook 2000. The Hong Kong Cotton Spinners Association (2000)
5. Huang, C.-C., Chen, I.-C.: Neural-fuzzy classification for fabric defects. Text. Res. J. **71**(3), 220–224 (2001)
6. Jing, J.-F., Ma, H., Zhang, H.-H.: Automatic fabric defect detection using a deep convolutional neural network. Color. Technol. **135**(3), 213–223 (2019)

7. Kumar, A.: Neural network based detection of local textile defects. Pattern Recogn. **36**(7), 1645–1659 (2003)

8. Kuo, C.-F.J., Lee, C., Tsai, C.: Using a neural network to identify fabric defects in dynamic cloth inspection. Text. Res. J. **73**(3), 238–244 (2003)

9. Kuo, C.-F.J., Lee, C.: A back-propagation neural network for recognizing fabric defects. Text. Res. J. **73**(2), 147–151 (2003)

10. Mei, S., Wang, Y., Wen, G.: Automatic fabric defect detection with a multi-scale convolutional denoising autoencoder network model. Sensors **18**(4), 1064 (2018)

11. Ngan, H.Y.T., Pang, G.K.H., Yung, N.H.C.: Automated fabric defect detection - a review. Image Vis. Comput. **29**, 442–458 (2011)

12. Rebhi, A., Benmhammed, I., Abid, S., Fnaiech, F.: Fabric defect detection using local homogeneity analysis and neural network. J. Photonics **2015**, 9 (2015)

13. Redmon, J.: Darknet: Open Source Neural Networks in C, 2013–2016. http://pjreddie.com/darknet

14. Simonyan, K., Zisserman, A.: Very deep convolutional networks for large-scale image recognition. CoRR, Vol. abs/1409.1556. http://arxiv.org/abs/1409.1556

15. Stojanovic, R., Mitropulos, P., Koulamas, C., Karayiannis, Y., Koubias, S., Papadopoulos, G.: Real-time vision-based system for textile fabric inspection. Real-time Imaging **7**, 507–518 (2001)

16. Tsai, D.M., Hsiao, B.: Automatic surface inspection using wavelet reconstruction. Pattern Recogn. **34**(6), 1285–1305 (2001)

17. Vikrant, T., Gaurav, S.: Automatic fabric fault detection using morphological operations on bit plane. Int. J. Eng. Res. Technol. **2**, 856–861 (2013)

18. Wiltschi, K., Pinz, A., Lindeberg, T.: Automatic assessment scheme for steel quality inspection. Mach. Vis. Appl. **12**(3), 113–128 (2000)

19. Yang, X., Pang, G., Yung, N.: Robust fabric defect detection and classification using multiple adaptive wavelets. In: IEEE Proceedings – Vision, Image and Signal Processing, vol. 152, pp. 715–723 (2005)

20. Yin, Y., Zhang, K., Lu, W.B.: Textile flaw classification by wavelet reconstruction and BP neural network. In: Yu, W., He, H., Zhang, N. (eds.) ISNN 2009. LNCS, vol. 5552, pp. 694–701. Springer, Heidelberg (2009). https://doi.org/10.1007/978-3-642-01510-6_78

21. Zhang, Y., Lu, Z., Li, J.: Fabric defect classification using radial basis function network. Pattern Recogn. Lett. **31**(13), 2033–2042 (2010)

22. Zhi, Y.X., Pang, G.K.H., Yung, N.H.C.: Fabric defect detection using adaptive wavelet. In: Proceedings of the IEEE Interntional Conference on Acoustics, Speech, and Signal Processing, ICASSP 2001, pp. 3697–3700, May 2001

# Author Index

Anh, Nguyen Thi Hong   739
Armentrout, Jack   506
Aung, Tun Myat   371

Bennani, Mohamed Taha   15
Binh, Nguyen Thanh   608
Bruno, Emmanuel   429

Choo, Hyunseung   323, 358
Chung, Tai-Myoung   399
Chung-Nguyen, Huy-Hoang   673
Clavel, Manuel   185

Dai, H. K.   165, 239
Danciu, Vitalian   3
Dang, Quang-Vinh   411
Dang, Thien-Binh   323
Dang, Tran Khanh   45, 332, 446, 577
Dang, Tran Tri   383
Dien, Duong Lu   104
Dien, Tran Thanh   722
Diep, Vu Thu   618
Do, Thanh-Nghi   255
Draheim, Dirk   207

Eder, Johann   145

Gabillon, Alban   429
Gallier, Romane   429
Giao, Bui Cong   739

Ha, Jun Suk   399
Ha, Lam   665
Han, Huynh Ngoc   722
Hien, Nguyen Mong   608
Hiremath, Panchakshari N.   506
Hirose, Hiroo   332
Hla, Ni Ni   371
Hoang, Dinh-Hieu   673
Hoang, Nguyen Le   45
Hoang, Suong N.   132
Hung, Ngo Thanh   68, 631
Hung, Phan Duy   618, 648, 656, 688

Huu, Phat Nguyen   343
Huy, Nguyen Huynh   526
Huynh, Hiep Xuan   104
Huynh, Hieu Trung   274
Huynh, Phuoc-Hai   255
Huynh, Tai   132, 713

Kim, Jong-Myon   56
Kim, Moonseong   323, 358
Kim, Namuk   399
Kő, Andrea   33
Kovács, Tibor   33
Koyanagi, Keiichi   332
Küng, Josef   383

Lang, Tran Van   545
Le, Anh Duc   705, 731
Le, Duc-Tai   323, 358
Le, Huu-Vinh   696
Le, Nhat-Quang   526
Le, Son Truong   560
Le, Tuan Dinh   681
Le-Tien, Thuong   85, 287
Luong, Thi Ngoc Tu   56
Luong-Hoai, Thien   85

Minh, Nguyen Cong   656
Minh, Quang Tran   332, 343, 506
Mochizuki, Ryuichi   332

Ngo, Tan Quan   640
Nguyen Phuoc Bao, Hoang   185
Nguyen, Anh-Quynh   485
Nguyen, Dang Tuan   665
Nguyen, Dinh-Thuan   696
Nguyen, Dung T.   358
Nguyen, Hoang   274
Nguyen, Linh V.   132, 713
Nguyen, Phuc   85
Nguyen, Quang   68
Nguyen, Quang Phu   577
Nguyen, Quoc-Bao   485, 526
Nguyen, Thai-Nghe   117

Nguyen, Thanh Hai   117, 307
Nguyen, Thanh-Trung   68
Nguyen, Thao L. P.   446
Nguyen, Thi Dieu Anh   681
Nguyen, Tu N.   506
Nguyen, Tuan Anh   705
Nguyen, Van Sinh   560, 577
Nguyen, Van-Hoa   255, 485
Nguyen, Vu Thanh   593
Nguyen-An, Khuong   485, 526
Nguyen-Binh, Minh   85
Nguyen-Huynh, Duc   85
Nguyen-Le, Thanh   485
Nguyen-Tan, Sy   287
Nguyen-Van, Thanh   526

Pattanaik, Vishwajeet   207
Pham, Chau D. M.   446
Pham, Dung Van   705
Pham, Hong Thanh   545
Pham, Viet-An   673
Pham, Vinh   399
Pham, Vuong T.   132, 713
Pham-Thai, Hoang   85
Phan, Trong Nhan   226
Phan-Xuan, Hanh   287
Phuc, Vo Hoang   593
Phung, Phu H.   506

Seo, Eunil   399
Sharvadze, Ioane   207

Thai-Nghe, Nguyen   722
Thinh, Tran Quang   648
Thuy, Nguyen Thanh   608

Toulouse, M.   239
Toulouse, Michel   343
Trabelsi, Shaima   15
Tran, An Cong   104
Tran, Manh Ha   560
Tran, Manh-Hung   323, 358
Tran, Minh-Triet   673
Tran, Nghi Cong   104
Tran, Quan M.   713
Tran, Tuan-Anh   526
Tran, Van Hoai   545
Trang, Le Hong   45
Truong, Anh   467
Truong, Dinh-Duc   526
Truong, Le Nhut   631
Tsuchiya, Takeshi   332, 343
Tuan, Le Dinh   593
Tung, Ta Duc   618
Tuyet, Vo Thi Hong   608

Van Long, Nguyen Huu   104
Van Vo, Vi   323, 358
Viet, Huynh Thanh   631
Vinh, Le Van   545
Vo, Hai H.   713
Vu, Son   506
Vu, Thanh Nguyen   681
Vu-Minh, Tuan   85

Yahia, Sadok Ben   15
Yamada, Tetsuyasu   332
Yoon, Seokhoon   640

Zghoul, Musab Bassam Yousef   631

Printed in the United States
By Bookmasters